STUDY GUIDE

Chapters 1-9 + Combination Journal Module

College Accounting

20th EDITION

James A. Heintz, DBA, CPA

Professor of Accounting
School of Business
University of Kansas

Robert W. Parry, Jr., Ph.D.

Professor of Accounting
Kelley School of Business
Indiana University

SOUTH-WESTERN
CENGAGE Learning™

Australia • Brazil • Japan • Korea • Mexico • Singapore • Spain • United Kingdom • United States

SOUTH-WESTERN
CENGAGE Learning™

Study Guide and Working Papers for College Accounting, 20th edition Chapters 1-9 and Combination Journal Module
James A. Heintz and Robert W. Parry, Jr.

Vice President of Editorial, Business: Jack W. Calhoun

Editor-in-Chief: Rob Dewey

Executive Editor: Sharon Oblinger

Developmental Editor: Sara Wilson, CPA, CATS Publishing

Associate Marketing Manager: Laura Stopa

Marketing Coordinator: Heather Mooney

Senior Content Project Manager: Tim Bailey

Director of Media Development: Rick Lindgren

Media Editor: Bryan England

Senior Frontlist Buyer, Manufacturing: Doug Wilke

Production Service: LEAP Publishing Services, Inc.

Senior Art Director: Stacy Jenkins Shirley

Cover and Internal Designer: Grannan Graphic Design

Cover Image: Digital Vision/Juice Images

Rights Acquisition Account Manager-Image: John Hill

Photo Researcher: Megan Lessard, Pre-PressPMG

ISBN-13: 978-0-538-73705-0
ISBN-10: 0-538-73705-0

Chapters 1-9 + 10-15 Package
ISBN-13: 978-0-538-73704-3
ISBN-10: 0-538-73704-2

South-Western Cengage Learning
5191 Natorp Boulevard
Mason, OH 45040
USA

Cengage Learning products are represented in Canada by Nelson Education, Ltd.

For your course and learning solutions, visit www.cengage.com
Purchase any of our products at your local college store or at our preferred online store **www.ichapters.com**

Printed in the United States of America
1 2 3 4 5 6 7 14 13 12 11 10

Table of Contents

CHAPTER 1
INTRODUCTION TO ACCOUNTING

LEARNING OBJECTIVES

Chapter 1 is designed to introduce you to accounting—its purpose, process, and career opportunities. Businesses that keep good accounting records benefit in many ways. Users of accounting information are able to make sound decisions, which will affect the business's future. Accounting offers many career opportunities, some of which are entry level and task oriented and others that involve decision making and planning.

Objective 1. Describe the purpose of accounting.

Accounting is the process by which businesses keep track of daily transactions and determine how the business is doing. Accounting provides needed information for its many users, from owners to government agencies and others.

Objective 2. Describe the accounting process.

The accounting process contains six major steps.

Step 1 Analyzing: Looking at information available and figuring out what to do with it. This first step in the accounting process usually occurs when the business receives some type of information, such as a bill, that needs to be properly entered into the business's records. This first step also involves deciding if the piece of information should result in an accounting entry or not.

Step 2 Recording: Entering the information, manually or via a computer, into the accounting system.

Step 3 Classifying: Grouping like items together.

Step 4 Summarizing: Aggregating many similar events to provide information that is easy to understand.

Step 5 Reporting: Communicating the results, such as profit or loss, commonly using tables of numbers to tell the financial status of the business.

Step 6 Interpreting: Examining the financial statements to evaluate the financial health of the business.

Objective 3. Define GAAP and describe the process used by FASB to develop these principles.

Generally accepted accounting principles (GAAP) are the rules that businesses must follow when preparing financial statements. The Securities and Exchange Commission (SEC) has the legal power to make these rules for firms listed on one of the U.S. stock exchanges. However, the SEC has delegated this responsibility to the Financial Accounting Standards Board (FASB).

FASB takes the following steps to develop an accounting standard:

1. The issue is placed on FASB's agenda.
2. After researching an issue, FASB issues a discussion memorandum.
3. To gather additional views on the issue, the Board often holds public hearings around the country.
4. Following these hearings, the Board issues an exposure draft. This document explains the rules that FASB believes firms should follow in accounting for this event.
5. After considering feedback on the exposure draft, the Board issues a final statement of financial accounting standards (SFAS).

Objective 4. Define three types of business ownership structures.

Businesses can be classified according to who owns them and the specific way they are organized. A sole proprietorship is owned by one person who assumes all risks for the business and makes all business decisions. A partnership is owned by two or more persons who share the risks and decision making. Corporations have many owners (shareholders) whose risk is limited to their investment and who have little influence in business decisions.

Objective 5. Classify different types of businesses by activities.

Businesses also can be classified by the type of service or product they provide. A service business provides a service, a merchandising business purchases a product from another business to sell, and a manufacturing business makes a product to sell.

Objective 6. Identify career opportunities in accounting.

Accounting has varied and diverse opportunities, depending on the education and experience of the worker, the type of business, and the accounting processes used within the business.

Accounting clerks record, sort, and file accounting information. Bookkeepers supervise clerks, help with daily accounting work, and summarize information. Para-accountants provide many accounting, auditing, or tax services under the direct supervision of an accountant.

Public accountants offer services such as auditing, tax advice, and management advisory services. Under the Sarbanes-Oxley Act, however, they may not provide audit and management advisory services to the same company. Further, audit and tax services may be provided to the same company only if preapproved by the audit committee of the company.

Managerial accountants offer services to private businesses, such as designing accounting information systems, general accounting, cost accounting, budgeting, tax accounting, and internal auditing. Government and not-for-profit organizations also employ accountants.

Accounting is a professional field, which includes organizations and certifications for those who pass examinations and have relevant work experience.

REVIEW QUESTIONS

Instructions: Analyze each of the following items carefully before writing your answer in the column at the right.

	Question	Answer
LO 1	**1.** The purpose of accounting is to provide current information to users. For each user below, briefly describe what type of information is needed.	
	a. Owners (present and future)	
	b. Managers who make decisions for the business	
	c. Creditors (present and future)	
	d. Government agencies (state, local, and national)	
LO 5	**2.** A travel agency is an example of this type of business.	________________
LO 4	**3.** The ownership structure where owners share risks and decision making is called a(n) ________.	________________
LO 5	**4.** A(n) ________ business makes a product to sell.	________________
LO 5	**5.** A business that purchases a product from another business to sell to customers is called a(n) ________ business.	________________
LO 4	**6.** Under the ________ ownership structure, the owner's personal assets can be taken to pay creditors.	________________
LO 3	**7.** The Financial Accounting Standards Board develops procedures and guidelines called ________ to be followed in the accounting process.	________________

LO 3 8. The following actions are taken by FASB when developing an accounting standard. Indicate the proper sequence of events by placing a 1 through 5 in the space provided.

Step

_______ The statement of financial accounting standards (SFAS) is issued.

_______ Public hearings are held.

_______ An exposure draft is issued.

_______ The issue is placed on FASB's agenda.

_______ A discussion memorandum is issued.

LO 4 9. The owners' risk is usually limited to their initial investment in this type of ownership structure. .... ____________________

LO 6 10. Is a public accounting firm permitted to provide audit and tax services to a publicly held company? .... ____________________

LO 6 11. By meeting education and experience requirements and passing an examination, a public accountant can achieve recognition as a(n) _____. ____________________

LO 6 12. The segment of accounting practice that includes fraud detection, fraud prevention, litigation support, business valuation, expert witness services, and other investigative activities is known as ________. .... ____________________

LO 2 13. The six major steps of the accounting process are listed in the box at the right. In front of each term, write the letter that identifies the correct description provided in the column on the left.

a. The process of entering financial information about events affecting the business

b. Aggregating similar events to provide information that is easy to understand

c. The process of sorting or grouping like things together, rather than merely keeping a simple, diary-like narrative record of numerous and varied transactions

d. The process of determining the effect of various events on the business

e. The process of deciding the importance of the information in various reports

f. The process of communicating the results of operation

_______ Analyzing

_______ Recording

_______ Classifying

_______ Summarizing

_______ Reporting

_______ Interpreting

CHAPTER 2
ANALYZING TRANSACTIONS: THE ACCOUNTING EQUATION

LEARNING OBJECTIVES

Chapter 2 continues the introductory discussion of accounting—its elements, equation, and transactions. The accounting equation provides a structure for analyzing transactions. After all transactions have been analyzed, the financial statements—income statement, statement of owner's equity, and balance sheet—are prepared. Let's look at each of these learning objectives in detail.

Objective 1. Define the accounting elements.

Accounting elements are the parts that make up the accounting equation: assets, liabilities, and owner's equity. **Assets** are items *owned* by the business that will provide future benefits. **Liabilities** are debts *owed* by the business and will require a future outflow of assets. **Owner's equity** (also called net worth or capital) is the difference between assets and liabilities. **Revenues** represent the amount a business charges customers for products sold or services provided. Revenues create an inflow of assets. **Expenses** represent an outflow of assets (or increase in liabilities) as a result of the efforts made to generate revenues.

Objective 2. Construct the accounting equation.

The accounting equation shows the relationship among assets, liabilities, and owner's equity (the accounting elements).

Assets = Liabilities + Owner's Equity

When given two of the numbers for the equation above, you can calculate the missing number by adding or subtracting.

The accounting equation may be expanded to include revenues, expenses, and drawing. Although drawing is not considered a major element in the accounting equation, it is a very special type of owner's equity account. It represents the withdrawals of assets from the business by the owner.

ASSETS (Items Owned)			=	LIABILITIES (Amts. Owed)	+	OWNER'S EQUITY (Owner's Investment)				(Earnings)		
Cash	+	Delivery Equipment	=	Accounts Payable	+	Jessica Jane, Capital	−	Jessica Jane, Drawing	+	Revenues	−	Expenses

Objective 3. Analyze business transactions.

Analyzing is the first step in the accounting process. Three questions must be answered: (1) What happened? (2) Which accounts are affected, and what kind of accounts are they (asset, liability, owner's equity)? (3) How is the accounting equation affected? (Accounts will increase or decrease, but the equation always remains in balance.)

Objective 4. Show the effects of business transactions on the accounting equation.

Each transaction will affect asset, liability, owner's equity, revenue, or expense accounts. For example, when an owner invests cash in the business, the asset account called *Cash* increases, and the owner's equity account *Capital* also increases.

For each transaction, you must decide what accounts are affected and whether the accounts increase or decrease. After each transaction, the equation must still be in balance.

Objective 5. Prepare and describe the purposes of a simple income statement, statement of owner's equity, and balance sheet.

After the transactions are completed, the financial statements are prepared to show the results of those transactions. As shown below, all financial statements have a heading that indicates the name of the firm, title of the statement, and time period or date covered by the statement. The income statement reports revenues, expenses, and the net income for the period. The statement of owner's equity shows the beginning balance of the owner's capital account, plus investments and net income, less withdrawals to compute the ending capital balance. The balance sheet reports all assets, liabilities, and the owner's capital on a certain date and confirms that the accounting equation has remained in balance.

Note that net income computed on the income statement is transferred to the statement of owner's equity to compute Patty V's capital at the end of the month. Patty V's capital on December 31, 20--, is then transferred to the balance sheet to compute total liabilities and owner's equity.

Objective 6. Define the three basic phases of the accounting process.

The three basic phases of the accounting process are input, processing, and output. The inputs to the accounting process are the business transactions. These transactions are processed to recognize their effects on the assets, liabilities, owner's equity, revenues, and expenses of the business. The results of these events are then reported as outputs of the accounting process in the financial statements.

Patty V's Consulting
Income Statement
For Month Ended December 31, 20--

Revenues		
Consulting fees		$10,000.00
Expenses		
Wages expense	$5,000.00	
Rent expense	1,500.00	
Telephone expense	500.00	
Total expenses		7,000.00
Net income		$ 3,000.00

Patty V's Consulting
Statement of Owner's Equity
For Month Ended December 31, 20--

Patty V, capital, December 1, 20--		$
Investment in December		20,000.00
Total investment		$20,000.00
Net income for December	$3,000.00	
Less withdrawals for December	1,000.00	
Increase in capital		2,000.00
Patty V, capital, December 31, 20--		$22,000.00

Patty V's Consulting
Balance Sheet
December 31, 20--

Assets		Liabilities	
Cash	$ 500.00	Accounts payable	$ 6,500.00
Accounts receivable	8,000.00		
Computer equipment	20,000.00	Owner's Equity	
		Patty V, capital	22,000.00
		Total liabilities and	
Total assets	$28,500.00	owner's equity	$28,500.00

REVIEW QUESTIONS

Instructions: Analyze each of the following items carefully before writing your answer in the column at the right.

	Question	Answer
LO 2	**1.** The entire accounting process is based on one simple equation called the ________.	________
LO 1	**2.** An individual, association, or organization that engages in business activities is called a(n) ________.	________
LO 1	**3.** An item owned by a business that will provide future benefits is a(n) ________.	________
LO 1	**4.** Something owed to another business entity is a(n) ________.	________
LO 1	**5.** A(n) ________ is an unwritten promise to pay a supplier for assets purchased or a service rendered.	________
LO 2	**6.** The amount by which assets exceed the liabilities of a business is called ________.	________
LO 1	**7.** According to the ________ concept, nonbusiness assets and liabilities are not included in the business entity's records.	________
LO 2	**8.** Assets – Liabilities = ________.	________
LO 2	**9.** Assets – Owner's Equity = ________.	________
LO 2	**10.** Assets = Liabilities + ________.	________
LO 4	**11.** The outflow of assets (or increase in liabilities) as the result of efforts to produce revenue is called a(n) ________.	________
LO 4	**12.** When total revenues exceed total expenses, the difference is called ________.	________
LO 4	**13.** When expenses are greater than revenues, the difference is called ________.	________
LO 4	**14.** Any accounting period of 12 months' duration is called a(n) ________.	________
LO 4	**15.** Withdrawals, or ______, represent a reduction in owner's equity because the owner takes cash or other assets for personal use.	________
LO 5	**16.** The financial statement that reports the profitability of the business for a period of time is the ________.	________
LO 5	**17.** The financial statement that shows investments and withdrawals by the owner, as well as profit or loss generated by the business, is the ________.	________
LO 5	**18.** The financial statement that reports the assets, liabilities, and owner's equity on a specific date is the ________.	________

LO 5 19. On the balance sheet, assets are listed in order of ________, or the ease with which they can be converted to cash. .... ____________________

EXERCISES

Exercise 1 (LO 2) THE ACCOUNTING EQUATION

Using the accounting equation provided below, compute the missing amounts.

	ASSETS	=	LIABILITIES	+	OWNER'S EQUITY
(a)	____________	=	$4,000	+	$20,000
(b)	$25,000	=	$8,000	+	____________
(c)	$50,000	=	____________	+	$10,000

Exercise 2 (LO 2/4) THE EXPANDED ACCOUNTING EQUATION

Using the accounting equation provided below, compute the missing amounts.

	ASSETS (Items Owned)	=	LIABILITIES (Amts. Owed)	+	OWNER'S EQUITY (Owner's Investment)				(Earnings)		
	Cash		Accounts Payable		Capital	–	Drawing	+	Revenues	–	Expenses
(a)	_____	=	$60,000	+	$20,000	–	$10,000	+	$80,000	–	$60,000
(b)	$80,000	=	_____	+	$35,000	–	$ 5,000	+	$70,000	–	$55,000
(c)	$90,000	=	$25,000	+	_____	–	$ 2,000	+	$57,000	–	$50,000
(d)	$60,000	=	$20,000	+	$30,000	–	$ 5,000	+	_____	–	$40,000
(e)	$40,000	=	$25,000	+	$40,000	–	$ 5,000	+	$30,000	–	_____
(f)	$75,000	=	$20,000	+	$50,000	–	_____	+	$40,000	–	$25,000

Exercise 3 (LO 5) STATEMENT OF OWNER'S EQUITY

If owner's equity was $38,000 at the beginning of the period and $45,000 at the end of the period, compute the net income or loss for the period. (There were no investments or withdrawals during the period.)

Exercise 4 (LO 2) ACCOUNTING EQUATION

If Irma Elkton, a dentist, owns office equipment amounting to $3,500, laboratory equipment amounting to $10,000, and other property that is used in the business amounting to $4,620, and owes business suppliers a total of $5,000, what is the owner's equity in the business?

Exercise 5 (LO 2) ACCOUNTING EQUATION

This is an extension of Exercise 4. One year later, the amount of Dr. Elkton's business assets has increased to a total of $22,000, and the amount of business liabilities has increased to a total of $6,000. Assuming that Dr. Elkton has not made any additional investments or withdrawals, compute the following:

(a) Owner's equity at year-end $ ____________________

(b) Net income or loss for the year $ ____________________

Exercise 6 (LO 3/4) EFFECTS OF TRANSACTIONS (BALANCE SHEET ACCOUNTS)

Rich Brite has started his own business. During the first month, the following transactions occurred:

(a) Invested $15,000 cash in the business, which was used to open a bank account.
(b) Purchased office equipment for cash, $4,000.
(c) Purchased a computer on account for $9,000.
(d) Paid $2,000 on account for the computer.

Using the lines provided below, show the effect of each transaction on the basic elements of the accounting equation: assets, liabilities, and owner's equity. Compute the new amounts for each element after each transaction to satisfy yourself that the accounting equation has remained in balance.

	ASSETS	=	LIABILITIES	+	OWNER'S EQUITY
(a)	______		______		______
Bal.	______		______		______
(b)	______		______		______
	______		______		______
Bal.	______		______		______
(c)	______		______		______
Bal.	______		______		______
(d)	______		______		______
Bal.	======		======		======

Exercise 7 (LO 3/4) EFFECTS OF TRANSACTIONS (REVENUE, EXPENSE, WITHDRAWALS)

In late May, Glen Ross opened a business by investing $20,000 cash and purchasing office equipment on account for $8,000. These events were properly entered in the accounting records. In June, the following transactions took place:

(a) Received $4,000 from a client for professional services rendered.
(b) Paid $1,200 office rent for the month.
(c) Paid $200 to the power company for the month's utility bill.
(d) Withdrew $600 cash for personal use.

On the first Balance (Bal.) line provided on the following page, record the amount of assets, liabilities, and owner's equity as the result of Ross's investment and purchase of office equipment in May. Then, record the effect of transactions (a) to (d) on the expanded accounting equation: Assets = Liabilities + Owner's Equity (Capital – Drawing + Revenues – Expenses). Following transaction (d), compute the new balances for each category to satisfy yourself that the accounting equation has remained in balance.

Exercise 7 (Concluded)

	ASSETS (Items Owned)	= LIABILITIES + (Amts. Owed)	OWNER'S EQUITY (Owner's Investment)			OWNER'S EQUITY (Earnings)					
	Cash	Accounts Payable	Glen Ross, Capital	–	Glen Ross, Drawing	+	Revenues	–	Expenses	Description
Bal.										
(a)										
(b)										
(c)										
(d)										
Bal.										

Exercise 8 (LO 3/4) EFFECTS OF TRANSACTIONS (ALL ACCOUNTS)

Judith Moore started her own business. During the month of July, the following transactions occurred:

(a) Invested $10,000 cash in the business.
(b) Purchased office equipment for $5,500 on account.
(c) Received $900 cash from a client for services rendered.
(d) Purchased computer equipment for cash, $6,000.
(e) Received $1,500 cash from a client for services rendered.
(f) Paid $800 office rent for the month.
(g) Paid the telephone bill for the month, $75.
(h) Paid $100 on account, for office equipment previously purchased.
(i) Withdrew $500 for personal use.

Required:

1. Record the effect of each of the transactions listed above on the accounting equation provided in the chart on the following page. Following transaction (i), compute the new balances for the accounts to satisfy yourself that the equation has remained in balance.

Exercise 8 (Concluded)

	ASSETS (Items Owned)		= LIABILITIES + (Amts. Owed)	OWNER'S EQUITY (Owner's Investment)		OWNER'S EQUITY (Earnings)		
	Cash	+ Office Equipment	= Accounts Payable	+ J. Moore, Capital	– J. Moore, Drawing	+ Revenues	– Expenses	Description
(a)								
(b)								
(c)								
(d)								
(e)								
(f)								
(g)								
(h)								
(i)								
Bal.								

2. After recording the transactions in part (1), compute the following:

Total assets .... $ ______________________

Total liabilities .... $ ______________________

Owner's equity .... $ ______________________

Owner's equity in excess of original investment....................... $ ______________________

Total revenues.. $ ______________________

Total expenses .... $ ______________________

Net income.. $ ______________________

Exercise 9 (LO 5) PREPARATION OF AN INCOME STATEMENT

Based on the transactions reported in Exercise 8, prepare an income statement for Judith Moore Enterprises for the month ended July 31, 20--, in the form provided below.

Exercise 10 (LO 5) PREPARATION OF THE STATEMENT OF OWNER'S EQUITY

Based on the transactions reported in Exercise 8, prepare a statement of owner's equity for Judith Moore Enterprises for the month ended July 31, 20--, in the form provided below.

Exercise 11 (LO 5) PREPARATION OF A BALANCE SHEET

Based on the transactions reported in Exercise 8, prepare a balance sheet as of July 31, 20--, in the form provided below.

PROBLEMS

Problem 12 (LO 2) THE ACCOUNTING EQUATION

Dr. Abe Miller is a general practitioner. As of December 31, Miller owned the following assets related to the professional practice:

Cash	$3,300	X-ray equipment	$7,000
Office equipment	4,500	Laboratory equipment	4,000

As of that date, Miller owed business suppliers as follows:

General Office Equipment Inc.	$2,000
Young Medical Supply Company	1,500
Buck Gas Company	1,200

Required:

1. Compute the amount of assets, liabilities, and owner's equity as of December 31.

   ASSETS = LIABILITIES + OWNER'S EQUITY

   ______________ ______________ ______________

2. Assuming that during January there is an increase of $4,600 in Dr. Miller's business assets and an increase of $2,500 in business liabilities, compute the resulting accounting equation as of January 31.

   ASSETS = LIABILITIES + OWNER'S EQUITY

   ______________ ______________ ______________

3. Assuming that during February there is a decrease of $1,500 in assets and a decrease of $1,200 in liabilities, compute the resulting accounting equation as of February 28.

   ASSETS = LIABILITIES + OWNER'S EQUITY

   ______________ ______________ ______________

4. Assuming that Dr. Miller made no additional investments or withdrawals, compute the net income or loss for each month.

Problem 13 (LO 3/4) EFFECT OF TRANSACTIONS ON ACCOUNTING EQUATION

Susan Cole started her own consulting business in October 20--. During the first month, the following transactions occurred:

(a) Invested $12,000 cash in the business.
(b) Purchased office equipment for $7,500 on account.
(c) Purchased computer equipment for cash, $800.
(d) Received $700 cash from a client for services rendered.
(e) Paid $600 office rent for the month.
(f) Paid student assistant wages for the month, $150.
(g) Paid one-year insurance premium, $200.
(h) Paid $3,000 on account for the office equipment purchased in transaction (b).
(i) Withdrew cash for personal use, $100.

Problem 13 (Concluded)

Required:

1. Record the effect of each of the transactions from the previous page on the accounting equation chart provided below. Following transaction (i), compute the new amounts in the accounts.

	ASSETS			= LIABILITIES +	OWNER'S EQUITY				
	(Items Owned)			(Amts. Owed)	(Owner's Investment)		(Earnings)		
	Cash +	Office Equip. +	Prepaid Insur. =	Accounts Payable +	S. Cole, Capital –	S. Cole, Drawing +	Revenues –	Expenses	Description
(a)									
(b)									
(c)									
(d)									
(e)									
(f)									
(g)									
(h)									
(i)									
Bal.									

2. After recording the transactions, compute the following:

Total assets	$ ______
Total liabilities	$ ______
Owner's equity	$ ______
Change in owner's equity from original investment	$ ______
Total revenues	$ ______
Total expenses	$ ______
Net income (loss)	$ ______

Problem 14 (LO 5) INCOME STATEMENT

Based on the transactions in Problem 13, prepare an income statement for Susan Cole Consulting Services for the month ended October 31, 20--, in the form provided below.

Problem 15 (LO 5) STATEMENT OF OWNER'S EQUITY

Based on the transactions in Problem 13, prepare a statement of owner's equity for Susan Cole Consulting Services for the month ended October 31, 20--, in the form provided below.

Name ______________________________

Problem 16 (LO 5) BALANCE SHEET

Based on the transactions in Problem 13, prepare a balance sheet as of October 31, 20--, in the form provided below.

Problem 17 (LO 3/4/5) ANALYZE THE EFFECTS OF BUSINESS TRANSACTIONS ON THE ACCOUNTING EQUATION AND PREPARE FINANCIAL STATEMENTS

Stuart Cassady is opening a typing service. During the first month (April 20--), the following transactions occurred:

(a) Invested $10,000 in the business.
(b) Purchased office supplies for $200 cash.
(c) Purchased office supplies for $800, $400 on account and $400 in cash.
(d) Received typing fees of $300 cash.
(e) Paid the rent, $600.
(f) Withdrew $100 for personal use.
(g) Earned typing fees of $600, $200 in cash and $400 on account.
(h) Made partial payment for office supplies in transaction (c) of $200.
(i) Received $200 cash for typing fees earned on account in transaction (g).

Required:

1. Record the effect of each transaction on the accounting equation below. Following transaction (i), compute new amounts for each account.

	ASSETS			= LIABILITIES +	OWNER'S EQUITY				
	(Items Owned)			(Amts. Owed)	(Owner's Investment)		(Earnings)		
	Cash	+ Accounts Receivable.	+ Office Supplies	= Accounts Payable	+ S. Cassady, Capital	− S. Cassady, Drawing	+ Revenues	− Expenses	Description
(a)									
(b)									
(c)									
(d)									
(e)									
(f)									
(g)									
(h)									
(i)									
Bal.									

Problem 17 (Concluded)

2. Based on the transactions in part (1) of Problem 17, prepare an income statement, statement of owner's equity, and balance sheet for Stuart Cassady Typing Service.

CHAPTER 3
THE DOUBLE-ENTRY FRAMEWORK

LEARNING OBJECTIVES

Objective 1. Define the parts of a T account.

The **T account** gets its name from the fact that it resembles the letter *T*. There are three major parts of an account. The title of the account is on top. The left side of the T account is the debit side, and the right side is the credit side.

Objective 2. Foot and balance a T account.

To determine the balance of a T account, simply total the dollar amounts of the debit and credit sides. These totals are known as **footings.** The difference between the footings is called the *balance* of the account. The balance is written on the side with the larger footing.

Objective 3. Describe the effects of debits and credits on specific types of accounts.

Assets are on the left side of the accounting equation. Thus, increases are entered on the left, or debit, side; and decreases are entered on the right, or credit, side. The normal balance of an asset account is a debit.

Liabilities and owner's equity are on the right side of the equation. Thus, increases are entered on the right, or credit, side; and decreases are entered on the left, or debit, side. The normal balance of a liability and owner's capital account is a credit.

Revenues increase owner's equity. Thus, increases in revenue are recorded as credits. The normal balance of a revenue account is a credit.

Expenses decrease owner's equity. Thus, increases in expenses are recorded as debits. The normal balance of an expense account is a debit.

Withdrawals of cash and other assets by the owner for personal reasons decrease owner's equity. Thus, an increase in drawing is recorded as a debit. The normal balance of a drawing account is a debit.

The following figure should be helpful in developing your understanding of debits and credits and the accounting equation:

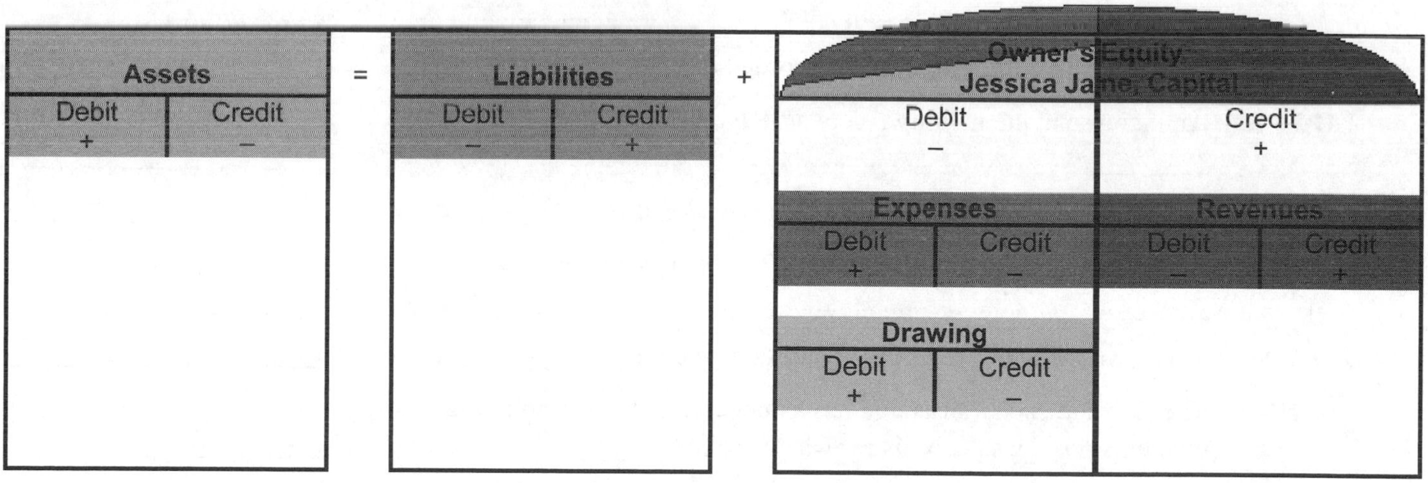

Objective 4. Use T accounts to analyze transactions.

There are three basic questions that must be answered when analyzing a transaction: (1) What happened? (2) Which accounts are affected? and (3) How is the accounting equation affected? After analyzing the transaction, in every instance, debits will equal credits.

Objective 5. Prepare a trial balance and explain its purposes and linkages with the financial statements.

There are two very important rules in double-entry accounting: (1) The sum of the debits must equal the sum of the credits. This means that at least two accounts are affected by each transaction. (2) The accounting equation must remain in balance.

A **trial balance** is a list of all accounts showing the title and balance of each account. The total debits and credits must be equal. A trial balance is not a formal statement or report. It can be used as an aid in preparing the financial statements.

REVIEW QUESTIONS

Instructions: Analyze each of the following items carefully before writing your answer in the column at the right.

		Question	**Answer**
LO 1	**1.**	A form or record used to keep track of the increases and decreases in each type of asset, liability, owner's equity, revenue, and expense is known as a(n) ________.	________
LO 1	**2.**	The left side of a T account is called the ________ side.	________
LO 1	**3.**	The right side of a T account is called the ________ side.	________
LO 2	**4.**	The process of entering totals in the debit and credit sides of a T account is referred to as ________.	________
LO 2	**5.**	The amount of the difference between the debits and credits recorded in a T account is called the ________.	________
LO 3	**6.**	An increase in the asset Cash is recorded by a(n) ________.	________
LO 3	**7.**	An increase in the liability Accounts Payable is recorded by a(n) ________.	________
LO 3	**8.**	The normal balance of a revenue account is on the ________ side.	________
LO 3	**9.**	A decrease in the liability Accounts Payable is recorded by a(n) ________.	________
LO 3	**10.**	The normal balance of a liability account is on the ________ side.	________
LO 4	**11.**	The fact that each transaction has a dual effect on the accounting elements provides the basis for what is called ________.	________
LO 5	**12.**	A list of all of the accounts showing the title and balance of each account is called the ________.	________

EXERCISES

Exercise 1 (LO 1) DEFINING PARTS OF THE T ACCOUNT

Provided below are T accounts for the six types of accounts discussed to this point. Identify the debit and credit side of each type of account by writing debit on the debit side and credit on the credit side.

Assets	Liabilities	Owner's Capital	Owner's Drawing	Expenses	Revenues

Exercise 2 (LO 3) EFFECTS OF DEBITS AND CREDITS

Indicate whether each of the following types of accounts would normally have a debit or credit balance by circling either debit or credit in the column at the right:

Type of Account	Normal Balance (Circle one)	
(a) Assets.	Debit	Credit
(b) Liabilities	Debit	Credit
(c) Owner's capital	Debit	Credit
(d) Revenues	Debit	Credit
(e) Expenses	Debit	Credit
(f) Drawing	Debit	Credit

Exercise 3 (LO 3) INCREASING AND DECREASING ACCOUNTS WITH DEBITS AND CREDITS

Provided below are T accounts representing the six types of accounts discussed. Indicate how each account would be increased and decreased by placing a (+) or (–) on the debit and credit side of each account.

Assets	Liabilities	Owner's Capital	Owner's Drawing	Expenses	Revenues

Exercise 4 (LO 4) USING T ACCOUNTS TO ANALYZE TRANSACTIONS

The following transactions were completed by Jacque Hamon, an educational consultant. Analyze each transaction and enter the amounts in the proper debit and credit positions in the T accounts at the right.

(a) Invested $3,000 cash in the business.

Cash	Jacque Hamon, Capital

(b) Received $1,000 in cash for consulting services rendered.

Cash	Professional Fees

(c) Bought office equipment from Gusse Supply Co. on account, $500.

Office Equipment	Accounts Payable

(d) Paid electric bill, $75.

Cash	Utilities Expense

Exercise 4 (Concluded)

(e) Paid Gusse Supply $200 on account.

Cash		Accounts Payable	

(f) Received $300 in cash for consulting services rendered.

Cash		Professional Fees	

(g) Borrowed $1,000 from bank by signing a note.

Cash		Notes Payable	

(h) Paid the telephone bill, $50.

Cash		Telephone Expense	

Exercise 5 (LO 4) USING T ACCOUNTS TO ANALYZE TRANSACTIONS (BALANCE SHEET ACCOUNTS)

Connie Sung has started her own typing business. During the first month, the following transactions occurred:

(a) Invested $12,000 cash in the business, and the money was deposited in a bank account.
(b) Purchased a new computer and printer on account from Stahl Electronics for $8,000.
(c) Paid the premium on a one-year insurance policy on computer equipment, $75 cash.
(d) Secured a bank loan by signing a note for $5,000.
(e) Made payment of $3,000 to Stahl Electronics on account.

Required:

Record the above transactions in the T accounts provided below.

Assets		=	Liabilities		+	Owner's Equity	
Debit +	Credit –		Debit –	Credit +		Debit –	Credit +
Cash			Accounts Payable			C. Sung, Capital	
Office Equipment			Notes Payable				
Prepaid Insurance							

Exercise 6 (LO 4) USING T ACCOUNTS TO ANALYZE TRANSACTIONS (ALL ACCOUNTS)

In late April, Frazier Baar opened a psychiatry practice by investing $9,000 cash and purchasing a couch, chair, and leather-covered note pad on account for $2,500. These events were properly entered in the accounting records. In May, Dr. Baar began seeing patients and entered into the following transactions:

(a) Received $500 for counseling services rendered.
) Paid $100 for *Psychology Today* and other magazines for patients to read in the waiting room.
(c) Paid $1,200 office rent for the month.

Required:

1. Enter the balances as of May 1 in the following accounts: Cash, Office Furnishings, Accounts Payable, and F. Baar, Capital.
2. Record the May transactions in the accounts listed below.

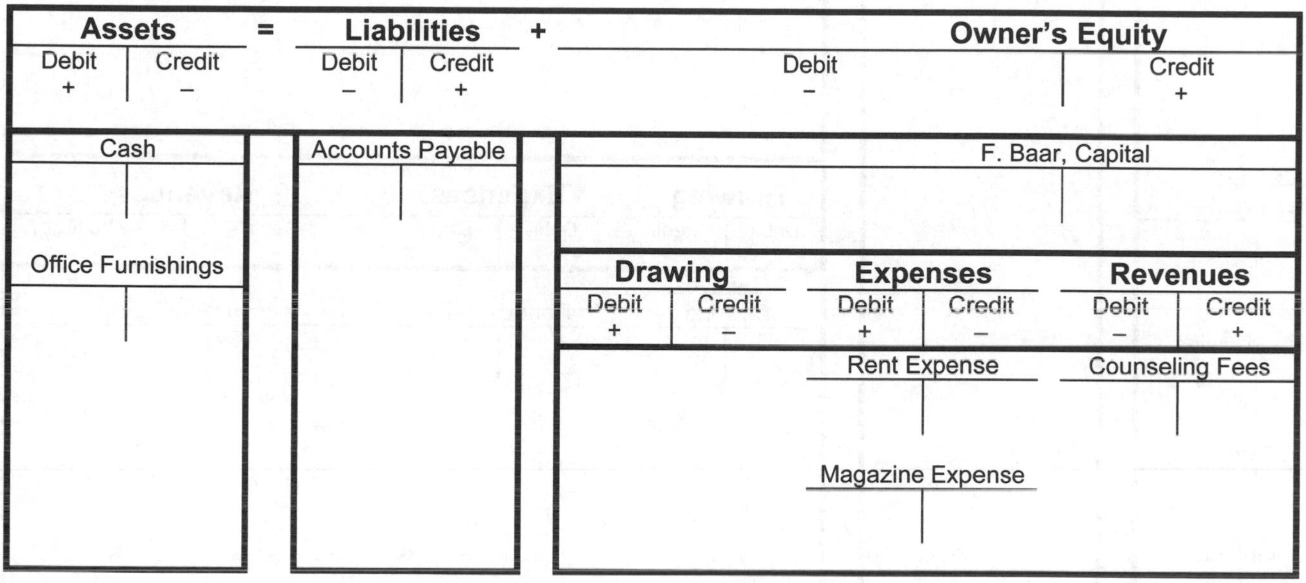

Exercise 7 (LO 2/4) USING T ACCOUNTS TO ANALYZE TRANSACTIONS, FOOTING AND BALANCING T ACCOUNTS

In January 20--, Blanca Estavez, CPA, started her own accounting practice. The following is a list of transactions for the first month:

(a) Invested $20,000 cash in the business.
(b) Purchased office supplies, $500 cash.
(c) Purchased office furniture, $6,000 cash.
(d) Purchased a computer and printer for $9,000: $5,000 cash and $4,000 on account.
(e) Paid $800 for accounting software programs.
(f) Performed accounting services and earned fees totaling $1,800: $1,200 in cash and $600 on account.
(g) Paid $700 rent for the month.
(h) Withdrew $200 for personal use.
(i) Paid $2,000 on account for the computer.

Exercise 7 (Concluded)

Required:

1. Record the transactions in the T accounts that follow.
2. After all transactions have been entered, foot and balance the T accounts.

Assets		=	Liabilities		+	Owner's Equity	
Debit +	Credit –		Debit –	Credit +		Debit –	Credit +

Assets

- Cash
- Accounts Receivable
- Office Supplies
- Office Furniture
- Computer Equipment
- Computer Software

Liabilities

- Accounts Payable

Owner's Equity

- B. Estavez, Capital

Drawing		Expenses		Revenues	
Debit +	Credit –	Debit +	Credit –	Debit –	Credit +
B. Estavez, Drawing		Rent Expense		Accounting Fees	

Exercise 8 (LO 5) PREPARE A TRIAL BALANCE

Based on the transactions recorded in Exercise 7, prepare a trial balance at the end of the first month of operations using the form provided below.

ACCOUNT	DEBIT BALANCE	CREDIT BALANCE

PROBLEMS

Problem 9 (LO 2/4/5) ANALYZING TRANSACTIONS WITH T ACCOUNTS, FOOTING AND BALANCING ACCOUNTS, AND PREPARING A TRIAL BALANCE

Jali Abdul has decided to offer his services as a promoter for local rock-n-roll bands. Following is a narrative of selected transactions completed during January, the first month of J. A. Productions' operations:

(a) Invested $10,000 in the business and opened a checking account.
(b) Purchased office furniture on account at a cost of $5,000.
(c) Purchased computer equipment for $4,500. Abdul paid $1,500 cash and promised to pay the balance over the next three months.
(d) Purchased office supplies for cash, $350.
(e) Sent letters to numerous performing groups throughout the region explaining the services available through J. A. Productions. Postage of $200 was paid in cash.
(f) Began arranging performances throughout the region after securing contracts with several groups. The telephone bill came to $300 and was paid in cash.
(g) Earned promotion revenue of $2,500: $2,000 in cash and $500 on account.
(h) Paid part-time receptionist $600.
(i) Withdrew $1,000 for personal use.
(j) Paid $2,500 on account for the office furniture.
(k) Collected $250 for promotional fees earned on account.

Problem 9 (Continued)

Required:

1. Record the transactions in the T accounts provided.
2. Foot and balance the accounts.
3. Prepare a trial balance of the accounts as of January 31, 20--, using the form provided.

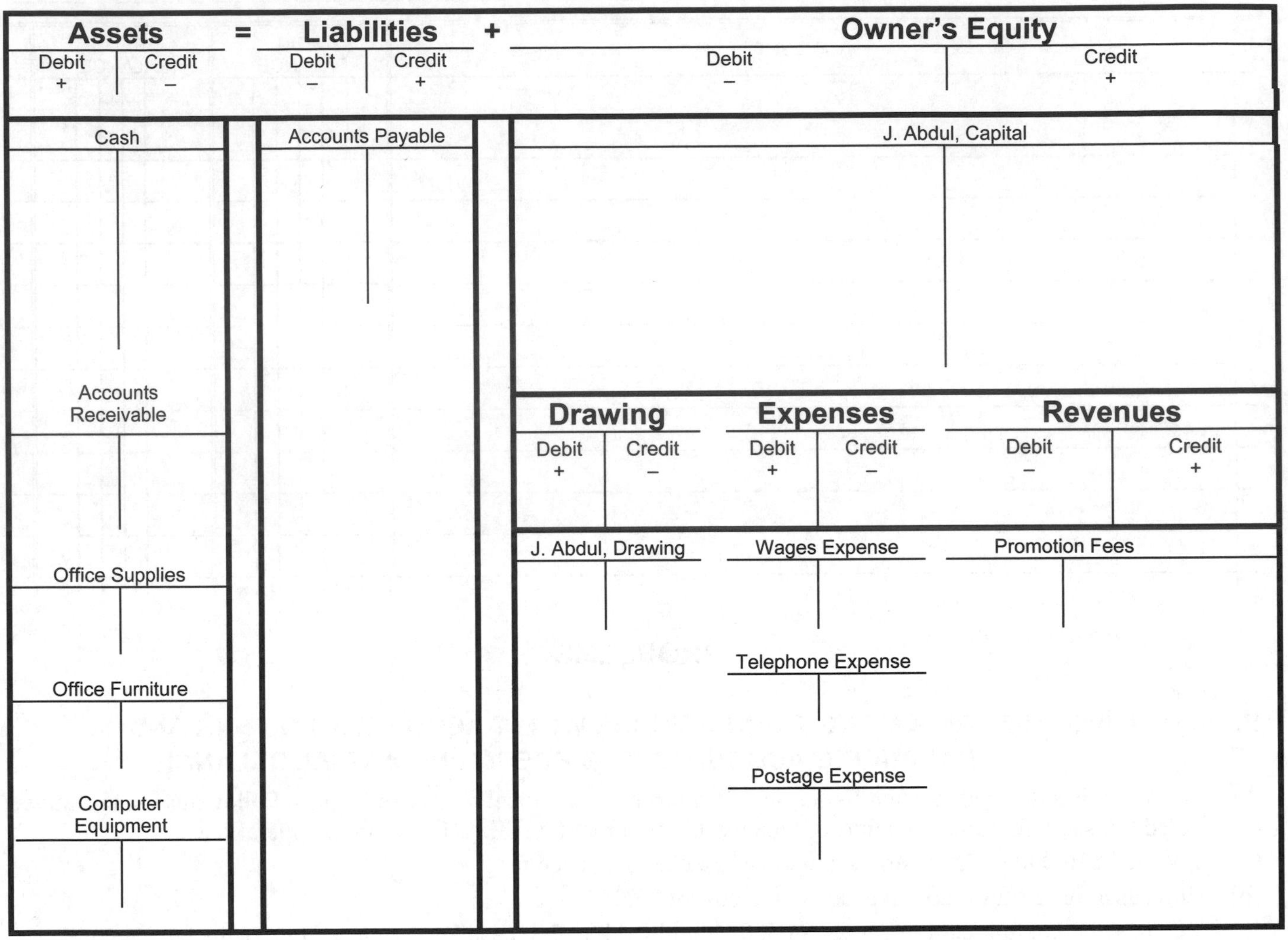

Problem 9 (Concluded)

ACCOUNT	DEBIT BALANCE	CREDIT BALANCE

Problem 10 (LO 5) REVIEW: ACCOUNTING EQUATION AND FINANCIAL STATEMENTS

Based on the transactions recorded in Problem 9, select the information needed to fill in the blank space in the following statements:

(a) Total revenue for the month ______________

(b) Total expenses for the month ______________

(c) Net income for the month ______________

(d) Abdul's original investment in the business ______________

+ Net income for the month ______________

– Owner's drawing ______________

Increase in capital ______________

= Owner's equity at the end of the month ______________

(e) End-of-month accounting equation:

Assets	=	Liabilities	+	Owner's Equity
______________		______________		______________

Problem 11 (LO 5) REVIEW: PREPARATION OF FINANCIAL STATEMENTS

Refer to the trial balance in Problem 9 and to the analysis of the change in owner's equity in Problem 10.

(a) Prepare an income statement for J. A. Productions for the month ended January 31, 20--.

(b) Prepare a statement of owner's equity for J. A. Productions for the month ended January 31, 20--.

(c) Prepare a balance sheet for J. A. Productions as of January 31, 20--.

(a)

Problem 11 (Concluded)

(b)

(c)

CHAPTER 4
JOURNALIZING AND POSTING TRANSACTIONS

LEARNING OBJECTIVES

Chapter 3 introduced the double-entry framework and illustrated the impact of debits and credits on the accounting equation and T accounts. In Chapter 4, business transactions are entered into the general journal and posted to general ledger accounts.

Objective 1. Describe the flow of data from source documents through the trial balance.

The flow of financial data from the source documents through the accounting information systems follows the steps listed below.

1. Analyze what happened by using information from source documents and the firm's chart of accounts.
2. Enter business transactions in the general journal.
3. Post entries to accounts in the general ledger.
4. Prepare a trial balance.

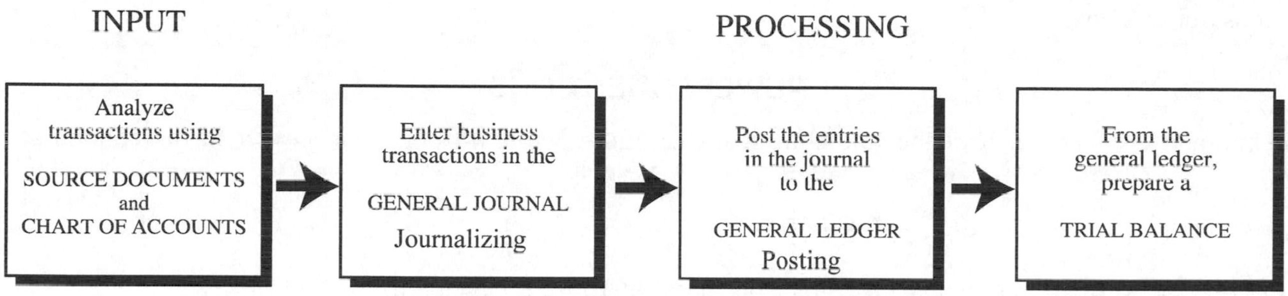

Objective 2. Describe the chart of accounts as a means of classifying financial information.

The **chart of accounts** lists in numerical order all of the accounts being used by a business. Assets are listed first (begin with "1"); liabilities are second (begin with "2"); owner's equity accounts are third (begin with "3"); revenues are fourth (begin with "4"); and expenses are last (begin with "5"). In a three-digit account numbering system, for example, Cash may be account number 101 and Accounts Receivable may be account number 122. Spacing numbers this way permits easy addition of new accounts as the business grows.

Objective 3. Describe and explain the purpose of source documents.

A **source document** provides objective information needed to record a transaction. Examples include check stubs, receipts, cash register tapes, sales invoices, and memos. Source documents are analyzed to determine which accounts should be increased or decreased.

Objective 4. Journalize transactions.

Journalizing is the process of entering information into the journal, or book of original entry. This simply means the journal is the first place a transaction is recorded. The general journal has space to enter the date of the transaction, the name of the accounts being debited and credited, the account numbers, and the amounts of the debits and credits. A brief description follows each journal entry stating the reason for the entry.

Objective 5. Post to the general ledger and prepare a trial balance.

Once the transactions are entered into the general journal, they must be **posted** to (copied to) the individual accounts, which are located in the general ledger. The accounts are in the general ledger in the chart of accounts order. That is, the assets are first, followed by liabilities, owner's equity, revenue, and expense accounts.

In this chapter, the general ledger accounts are in the form of four-column accounts. This is better than the T account because a running balance is maintained.

The **trial balance** is a listing of account balances at the end of the month—after all the transactions have been posted from the general journal to the general ledger accounts. The total of the debit balances must equal the total of the credit balances.

Objective 6. Explain how to find and correct errors.

Finding errors can be a long and frustrating process. But there are some methods to reduce the time and effort needed. The first thing to do is double check your calculations and the accuracy of the posting activities. Common errors include sliding ($230 could become $23 or $2,300), and transposing numbers ($326 could become $236). Taking the difference between the debits and credits and dividing by 9 or by 2 may help locate the error.

There are two methods of correcting errors. The **ruling method** may be used before the transaction has been posted. Under this method, you draw a line through the incorrect title or amount and write in the correct information above the ruling. The **correcting entry method** is used after an entry has been posted to the general ledger. The correcting entry increases and decreases accounts in a manner that corrects the errors made in previous transactions.

REVIEW QUESTIONS

Instructions: Analyze each of the following items carefully before writing your answer in the column at the right.

		Question	Answer
LO 2	**1.**	A list of all the accounts used by a business enterprise is called a(n) ________.	____________
LO 2	**2.**	Accounts that begin with the number "3" are ________.	____________
LO 2	**3.**	Expenses are accounts that begin with which number?	____________
LO 1/3	**4.**	A document that provides information about a business transaction is called a(n) ________.	____________
LO 4	**5.**	A document that provides a day-by-day listing of transactions of a business is called a(n) ________.	____________
LO 4	**6.**	A journal is commonly referred to as a(n) ________ because it is here that the first formal accounting record is made.	____________
LO 4	**7.**	Transactions affecting more than two accounts are called ______. .	____________
LO 4	**8.**	The act of entering transactions into a journal is called ________. .	____________
LO 4	**9.**	In a journal, debits are entered first; then credits are entered and indented ________ (how much space).	____________
LO 5	**10.**	A complete set of all accounts used by a business is known as the ________.	____________

LO 5 **11.** A(n) ________ account allows the accountant to keep a running balance. .... ____________________

LO 5 **12.** The process of copying debits and credits from the journal to the ledger accounts is called ________. .... ____________________

LO 5 **13.** Posting from the journal to the ledger is done ________ or at frequent intervals. .... ____________________

LO 5 **14.** The information in the Posting Reference columns of the journal and the ledger accounts provides a link known as a(n) ________. .... ____________________

LO 5 **15.** A(n) ________ is taken after transactions are posted to the general ledger accounts to be sure that debit and credit balances in the ledger are equal. .... ____________________

LO 6 **16.** A(n) ________ error occurs when you move a number a decimal place to the right or left. .... ____________________

LO 6 **17.** A(n) ________ error occurs when you use the right numbers but in the wrong order. .... ____________________

LO 6 **18.** Drawing a line through the incorrect amount or account title and writing correct information above it is an example of the ________ method. .... ____________________

LO 6 **19.** When an incorrect entry has been journalized and posted, a(n) _______ entry is required. .... ____________________

EXERCISES

Exercise 1 (LO 4) REVIEW: TRANSACTION ANALYSIS

Before a transaction is recorded in the journal, it should be analyzed to determine the following:

(a) What accounts are affected by the transaction.
(b) Whether each affected account is to be increased or decreased.
(c) Whether the increase or decrease is to be accomplished by a debit or credit.

In the following list of transactions for Abbott Service Co., indicate the names of the accounts to be debited and credited. Place a check mark in either the plus (+) or minus (–) column to indicate whether the account has been increased or decreased. The first transaction is entered as an illustration.

Transaction		Account	(+)	(–)
1. J. A. Abbott invested cash in a business enterprise.	Debit:	Cash	✓	
	Credit:	J. A. Abbott, Capital	✓	
2. Received cash for services provided.	Debit:			
	Credit:			

Transaction		Account	(+)	(–)
3. Paid cash for rent on the office.	Debit:			
	Credit:			
4. Purchased office equipment on account.	Debit:			
	Credit			
5. Paid cash to a creditor for a debt previously owed.	Debit:			
	Credit:			
6. Paid the telephone bill for the month.	Debit:			
	Credit:			
7. Paid supplier for office equipment purchased in transaction (4) above.	Debit:			
	Credit:			
8. Paid cash for a car for the owner's personal use.	Debit:			
	Credit:			
9. Paid temporary secretary's wages.	Debit:			
	Credit:			
10. Performed services that will be paid for later.	Debit:			
	Credit:			

Exercise 2 (LO 4) JOURNALIZING TRANSACTIONS

Susan Poe started a business, Poe's Connections. She provides resource referral services whereby she helps businesses locate vendors of specialty products and vice versa. She charges a referral fee to her clients who may be businesses or vendors. She has a part-time clerk who enters information into a database to match requests with potential users or suppliers. Her chart of accounts is as follows:

Assets
- 101 Cash
- 122 Accounts Receivable
- 182 Office Furniture

Liabilities
- 202 Accounts Payable

Owner's Equity
- 311 Susan Poe, Capital
- 312 Susan Poe, Drawing

Revenues
- 401 Referral Fees

Expenses
- 511 Wages Expense
- 521 Rent Expense

Exercise 2 (Continued)

Required:

Enter the following transactions in the two-column journal provided on the next page.

20--		
May	1	Susan invested $5,000 cash to start the business.
	5	Purchased office furniture on account, $3,000.
	9	Paid office rent for the month, $450.
	10	Received fees for referral services, $500.
	15	Made payment on account (for office furniture), $100.
	20	Earned referral fees: $125 cash and $175 on account.
	25	Paid wages to clerk for part-time work, $400.
	28	Withdrew cash for personal use, $100.
	29	Received cash for referral services previously rendered, $150.

Exercise 2 (Concluded)

GENERAL JOURNAL

PAGE 1

DATE		DESCRIPTION	POST. REF.	DEBIT	CREDIT

Exercise 3 (LO 5) POST TO THE GENERAL LEDGER

Post the transactions from Exercise 2 to the general ledger accounts provided as follows. Be sure to enter the appropriate cross-reference information in the Posting Reference columns of the general ledger accounts and the general journal.

GENERAL LEDGER

ACCOUNT: Cash ACCOUNT NO. 101

DATE	ITEM	POST. REF.	DEBIT	CREDIT	BALANCE DEBIT	BALANCE CREDIT

ACCOUNT: Accounts Receivable ACCOUNT NO. 122

DATE	ITEM	POST. REF.	DEBIT	CREDIT	BALANCE DEBIT	BALANCE CREDIT

ACCOUNT: Office Furniture ACCOUNT NO. 182

DATE	ITEM	POST. REF.	DEBIT	CREDIT	BALANCE DEBIT	BALANCE CREDIT

ACCOUNT: Accounts Payable ACCOUNT NO. 202

DATE	ITEM	POST. REF.	DEBIT	CREDIT	BALANCE DEBIT	BALANCE CREDIT

Exercise 3 (Concluded)

GENERAL LEDGER

ACCOUNT: Susan Poe, Capital ACCOUNT NO. 311

DATE		ITEM	POST. REF.	DEBIT	CREDIT	BALANCE DEBIT	BALANCE CREDIT

ACCOUNT: Susan Poe, Drawing ACCOUNT NO. 312

DATE		ITEM	POST. REF.	DEBIT	CREDIT	BALANCE DEBIT	BALANCE CREDIT

ACCOUNT: Referral Fees ACCOUNT NO. 401

DATE		ITEM	POST. REF.	DEBIT	CREDIT	BALANCE DEBIT	BALANCE CREDIT

ACCOUNT: Wages Expense ACCOUNT NO. 511

DATE		ITEM	POST. REF.	DEBIT	CREDIT	BALANCE DEBIT	BALANCE CREDIT

ACCOUNT: Rent Expense ACCOUNT NO. 521

DATE		ITEM	POST. REF.	DEBIT	CREDIT	BALANCE DEBIT	BALANCE CREDIT

Exercise 4 (LO 5) REVIEW: PREPARE A TRIAL BALANCE

After the transactions are posted in Exercise 3, prepare the trial balance.

ACCOUNT TITLE	ACCT. NO.	DEBIT BALANCE	CREDIT BALANCE

PROBLEMS

Problem 5 (LO 4/5) JOURNALIZING AND POSTING TRANSACTIONS FOLLOWED BY PREPARATION OF A TRIAL BALANCE

Della Jordan started her own business, D. J. Parties. For about $50 per hour, Della and a group of part-time associates serve as disc jockeys for parties held at the client's home. As part of the service, Della provides a lighting system, stereo equipment, CDs, and two disc jockeys working as a team for each party. A wide range of music is offered, and the client may provide additional CDs to be played. A chart of accounts is provided below.

D. J. Parties
Chart of Accounts

Assets

101	Cash
122	Accounts Receivable
181	Stereo Equipment
182	Office Furniture
183	CDs
184	Lighting Equipment
185	Van

Liabilities

202	Accounts Payable

Owner's Equity

311	Della Jordan, Capital
312	Della Jordan, Drawing

Revenue

401	Disc Jockey Fees

Expenses

511	Wages Expense
521	Rent Expense
525	Telephone Expense
538	Gas Expense

Problem 5 (Continued)

The following transactions occurred during May, the first month of operation:

20--		
May	1	Jordan invested $30,000 cash in the business. The funds were deposited in a business checking account.
	3	Purchased stereo equipment and speaker systems from Big Al's Discount Stereo for $7,000: $3,000 cash and $4,000 on account.
	4	Purchased compact discs and tapes for $2,500.
	4	Purchased lighting equipment for $2,000.
	5	Purchased office furniture on account, $500.
	7	Purchased a van to be used to haul the equipment to the clients' homes, $9,500.
	18	Earned fees for services rendered, $3,800: $800 cash and $3,000 on account.
	20	Paid part-time associates for work performed, $600.
	21	Made payment on account for stereo equipment bought on May 3, $1,500.
	25	Paid for gas for the van, $40.
	27	Paid telephone bill, $80.
	28	Received cash for services previously rendered, $1,500.
	29	Paid part-time associates, $1,100.
	30	Paid rent, $500.
	30	Made payment on account for stereo equipment bought on May 3, $1,200.
	30	Jordan made withdrawal for personal use, $1,000.

Required:

1. Enter the transactions in the two-column journal provided on pages 45–46. Use journal page 1 for transactions through May 20. Enter the remainder on page 2.
2. Post the transactions from the journal to the general ledger accounts on pages 47–50.
3. Prepare a trial balance.

Problem 5 (Continued)

1. ***[Instructor: Account numbers in Post. Ref. column are entered when completing requirement 2.]***

GENERAL JOURNAL

PAGE 1

DATE		DESCRIPTION	POST. REF.	DEBIT	CREDIT

Problem 5 (Continued)

GENERAL JOURNAL

PAGE 2

DATE		DESCRIPTION	POST. REF.	DEBIT	CREDIT

Name ______________________________

Problem 5 (Continued)

2.

GENERAL LEDGER

ACCOUNT: Cash ACCOUNT NO. 101

DATE	ITEM	POST. REF.	DEBIT	CREDIT	BALANCE DEBIT	BALANCE CREDIT

ACCOUNT: Accounts Receivable ACCOUNT NO. 122

DATE	ITEM	POST. REF.	DEBIT	CREDIT	BALANCE DEBIT	BALANCE CREDIT

ACCOUNT: Stereo Equipment ACCOUNT NO. 181

DATE	ITEM	POST. REF.	DEBIT	CREDIT	BALANCE DEBIT	BALANCE CREDIT

Problem 5 (Continued)

ACCOUNT: Office Furniture ACCOUNT NO. 182

DATE	ITEM	POST. REF.	DEBIT	CREDIT	BALANCE	
					DEBIT	CREDIT

ACCOUNT: CDs ACCOUNT NO. 183

DATE	ITEM	POST. REF.	DEBIT	CREDIT	BALANCE	
					DEBIT	CREDIT

ACCOUNT: Lighting Equipment ACCOUNT NO. 184

DATE	ITEM	POST. REF.	DEBIT	CREDIT	BALANCE	
					DEBIT	CREDIT

ACCOUNT: Van ACCOUNT NO. 185

DATE	ITEM	POST. REF.	DEBIT	CREDIT	BALANCE	
					DEBIT	CREDIT

ACCOUNT: Accounts Payable ACCOUNT NO. 202

DATE	ITEM	POST. REF.	DEBIT	CREDIT	BALANCE	
					DEBIT	CREDIT

Name ______________________________

Problem 5 (Continued)

ACCOUNT: Della Jordan, Capital — ACCOUNT NO. 311

DATE	ITEM	POST. REF.	DEBIT	CREDIT	BALANCE DEBIT	BALANCE CREDIT

ACCOUNT: Della Jordan, Drawing — ACCOUNT NO. 312

DATE	ITEM	POST. REF.	DEBIT	CREDIT	BALANCE DEBIT	BALANCE CREDIT

ACCOUNT: Disc Jockey Fees — ACCOUNT NO. 401

DATE	ITEM	POST. REF.	DEBIT	CREDIT	BALANCE DEBIT	BALANCE CREDIT

ACCOUNT: Wages Expense — ACCOUNT NO. 511

DATE	ITEM	POST. REF.	DEBIT	CREDIT	BALANCE DEBIT	BALANCE CREDIT

ACCOUNT: Rent Expense — ACCOUNT NO. 521

DATE	ITEM	POST. REF.	DEBIT	CREDIT	BALANCE DEBIT	BALANCE CREDIT

Problem 5 (Concluded)

ACCOUNT: Telephone Expense ACCOUNT NO. 525

DATE		ITEM	POST. REF.	DEBIT	CREDIT	BALANCE	
						DEBIT	CREDIT

ACCOUNT: Gas Expense ACCOUNT NO. 538

DATE		ITEM	POST. REF.	DEBIT	CREDIT	BALANCE	
						DEBIT	CREDIT

3.

ACCOUNT TITLE	ACCT. NO.	DEBIT BALANCE	CREDIT BALANCE

Problem 6 (LO 5) REVIEW: PREPARATION OF FINANCIAL STATEMENTS

From the information in Problem 5, prepare an income statement, a statement of owner's equity, and a balance sheet.

Problem 6 (Concluded)

Problem 7

1. (LO 6) CORRECTION OF ERRORS: The Ruling Method

The following journal entries were made but not posted. On January 1, $500 cash was withdrawn by the owner for personal use (R. J. Hammond) but was charged to Wages Expense. On January 2, $230 was paid on account. Make corrections using the ruling method.

GENERAL JOURNAL PAGE

	DATE		DESCRIPTION	POST. REF.	DEBIT	CREDIT	
1	20-- Jan.	1	Wages Expense		500 00		1
2			Cash			500 00	2
3			Paid R. J. Hammond				3
4							4
5		2	Accounts Payable		320 00		5
6			Cash			320 00	6
7			Payment on account				7
8							8

Problem 7 (Concluded)

2. (LO 6) CORRECTION OF ERRORS: The Correcting Entry Method

On January 10, Office Equipment was debited for $800 when the debit should have been to Office Supplies. Since the entry has been posted, show the appropriate correcting entry made in the general journal on January 15.

GENERAL JOURNAL PAGE

	DATE	DESCRIPTION	POST. REF.	DEBIT	CREDIT	
1						1
2						2
3						3
4						4
5						5
6						6
7						7
8						8

CHAPTER 5
ADJUSTING ENTRIES AND THE WORK SHEET

LEARNING OBJECTIVES

We are coming to the end of the accounting cycle, and certain things must be done at the end of the period that are not done during the regular accounting period. In Chapter 5, adjusting entries and the work sheet are presented.

Objective 1. Prepare end-of-period adjustments.

In Chapters 2 through 4, we learned how to account for business transactions—events based primarily on arm's length exchanges with other parties. During the accounting period, however, other changes occur which affect the financial condition of the business. For example, supplies are being used, equipment is wearing out, insurance is expiring, and employees may have earned wages that have not yet been paid. It is important for information reported on the financial statements to accurately reflect the results of business transactions with outside parties and other activities taking place inside the business. Therefore, adjustments must be made at the end of the accounting period to properly report assets and liabilities on the balance sheet and to comply with the matching principle. This principle requires the matching of revenues earned with expenses incurred to produce the revenues.

Objective 2. Post adjusting entries to the general ledger.

After the adjusting entries are journalized, the next step is to post them to the general ledger. The word "Adjusting" is written in the Item column in the general ledger, and each adjustment is posted to the proper general ledger account.

Objective 3. Prepare a work sheet.

The work sheet is a tool used by accountants to help organize work done at the end of the accounting period. This document is not a formal part of the accounting system. Therefore, information recorded here has no effect on the accounts or financial statements. The main purposes of the work sheet are to prepare the adjusting entries and accumulate information that will be used in the preparation of the financial statements. Five steps are taken to prepare a work sheet.

Step 1 Prepare a trial balance to ensure that the general ledger is in balance before adjusting the accounts.

Step 2 Analyze and enter the adjusting entries in the Adjustments columns of the work sheet. Every adjustment must have an equal debit and credit; and upon completion, the total debits and credits must be equal in the Adjustments columns.

Step 3 Prepare the adjusted trial balance. Every account appearing in the Trial Balance columns will be extended to the Adjusted Trial Balance columns and include any changes due to the adjusting entries. Upon completion, the total of the debits and credits in the Adjusted Trial Balance columns must be equal.

Step 4 Extend the balances in the adjusted trial balance to either the Income Statement or Balance Sheet columns. All revenue and expenses are extended to the Income Statement columns. All other accounts (assets, liabilities, owner's capital, owner's drawing) are extended to the Balance Sheet columns.

Step 5 Complete the work sheet. Initially, the totals of the Income Statement columns will not be equal. Similarly, the totals of the Balance Sheet columns will not be equal. If the Income Statement Credit column exceeds the Income Statement Debit column, the difference represents net income.

If the Income Statement Debit column exceeds the Income Statement Credit column, the difference represents net loss. The difference in the Balance Sheet columns will be exactly the same as the difference in the Income Statement columns. The amount of net income should be added to the Income Statement Debit column and the Balance Sheet Credit column for total debits to equal total credits for all four columns. If there is a net loss, this amount should be added to the Income Statement Credit column and the Balance Sheet Debit column.

Partial Work Sheet

For Net Income

	Income Statement		Balance Sheet	
	Debit	**Credit**	**Debit**	**Credit**
	2,500	3,200	6,200	5,500
Net Income	**700**			**700**
	3,200	3,200	6,200	6,200

Apart

For Net Loss

	Income Statement		Balance Sheet	
	Debit	**Credit**	**Debit**	**Credit**
	3,000	2,500	7,000	7,500
Net Loss		**500**	**500**	
	3,000	3,000	7,500	7,500

Together

Objective 4. Describe methods for finding errors on the work sheet.

The following tips may help in finding errors on the work sheet:

1. Check the addition of all columns.
2. Check the addition and subtraction required when extending to the Adjusted Trial Balance columns.
3. Make sure the adjusted account balances have been extended to the appropriate columns.
4. Make sure that the net income or net loss has been added to the appropriate columns.

Objective 5. Journalize adjusting entries from the work sheet.

Once the adjustments have been "penciled in" on the work sheet, the next step is to journalize the adjusting entries. "Adjusting Entries" is written in the Description column in the general journal, and the adjusting entries are copied from the work sheet into the general journal.

Objective 6. Explain the cash, modified cash, and accrual bases of accounting.

The *accrual basis* of accounting recognizes revenues when earned, regardless of when cash is received. Likewise, expenses are recognized when incurred, regardless of when they are actually paid. The *cash basis* is used by some small businesses and by individuals for income tax purposes. With the cash basis, no revenue or expenses are recognized until cash is actually received or paid.

The *modified cash basis* is a combination of the accrual and cash methods. Revenues and most expenses are recorded only when cash is received or paid (like the cash basis). However, when cash is paid for assets with useful lives greater than one accounting period, exceptions are made. Cash payments like these are recorded as assets, and adjustments are made each period as under the accrual basis. Figure 5-25 in the text compares these methods in different types of transactions.

REVIEW QUESTIONS

Instructions: Analyze each of the following items carefully before writing your answer in the column at the right.

Question	Answer
LO 1 1. The matching principle in accounting requires the matching of ________ and ________.	________
LO 1 2. The asset account Supplies is adjusted to the income statement account entitled ________.	________
LO 1 3. The asset account Prepaid Insurance is adjusted to the income statement account entitled ________.	________
LO 1 4. The adjustment to Wages Expense will also affect a liability account called ________.	________
LO 1 5. The period of time a plant asset is expected to help produce revenues is called its ________.	________
LO 1 6. The purpose of ________ is to spread the cost of a plant asset over its useful life.	________
LO 1 7. A plant asset's original cost less salvage value is called ________.	________
LO 1 8. A ________ has a credit balance and is deducted from the related asset account on the balance sheet.	________
LO 1 9. The depreciation adjusting entry consists of a debit to Depreciation Expense and a credit to ________.	________
LO 1 10. The difference between the original cost of a plant asset and its accumulated depreciation is called ________.	________
LO 3 11. A ________ is helpful in preparing end-of-period adjustments and financial statements.	________
LO 3 12. The first two monetary columns of a work sheet are called the ________ columns.	________
LO 3 13. To which columns of the work sheet are asset and liability accounts extended?	________
LO 3 14. To which columns of the work sheet are revenue and expense accounts extended?	________
LO 3 15. To which columns of the work sheet are the capital and drawing accounts extended?	________

LO 3 16. If the total of the Income Statement Credit column exceeds the total of the Debit column, the business has earned ________. .... ____________________

LO 6 17. In the ________ basis of accounting, revenues are recorded when earned and expenses are recorded when incurred, regardless of when cash is received or paid. .... ____________________

LO 6 18. In the ________ basis of accounting, revenues are recorded only when cash is received and expenses are recorded only when cash is paid. .... ____________________

LO 6 19. The ________ basis of accounting uses the cash basis for revenues and most expenses. .... ____________________

LO 6 20. Many small professional ________ businesses use the modified cash basis of accounting. .... ____________________

EXERCISES

Exercise 1 (LO 1) PREPARING END-OF-PERIOD ADJUSTMENTS: SUPPLIES

The beginning balance of the supplies account was $300. During the year, additional supplies costing $600 were purchased and entered as debits to the supplies account. An end-of-period inventory determined that $200 worth of supplies are still on hand.

Required:

1. Determine the balance of the supplies account just prior to making any end-of-period adjustments. ____________________
2. When preparing the balance sheet, what should be reported for Supplies at the end of the year? ____________________
3. Determine the balance of the supplies expense account just prior to making any end-of-period adjustments. ____________________
4. When preparing the income statement, what should be reported for Supplies Expense? (What was the cost of the supplies used?) ____________________
5. What adjustment must be made to the supplies and supplies expense accounts? ____________________

Exercise 2 (LO 1) PREPARING END-OF-PERIOD ADJUSTMENTS: DEPRECIATION

Office equipment with an expected life of 10 years and no salvage value was purchased on January 1 for $5,000. Assume the business has no other office equipment and straight-line depreciation is used.

Required:

1. What is the balance of the office equipment account at the end of the year? ____________________
2. What expense amount should be reported on the income statement for the use of the office equipment? ____________________
3. What book value should be reported on the balance sheet for the office equipment at the end of the first year? ____________________
4. What adjustment must be made at the end of the year to report information about the office equipment on the income statement and balance sheet? ____________________

Exercise 3 (LO 1/2) PREPARING, JOURNALIZING, AND POSTING ADJUSTING ENTRIES: SUPPLIES

The Maddie Hays modeling agency began the current period with office supplies that cost $1,225. During the period, additional supplies costing $4,545 were purchased. At the end of the accounting period, December 31, 20--, only $800 in supplies remain.

Required:

1. Enter the appropriate adjusting entry in a two-column journal.
2. Post this entry to the ledger accounts provided on the next page.

Exercise 3 (Concluded)

1. GENERAL JOURNAL PAGE 5

	DATE		DESCRIPTION	POST. REF.	DEBIT	CREDIT	
1							1
2							2
3							3
4							4

2. GENERAL LEDGER

ACCOUNT: Supplies ACCOUNT NO. 141

DATE		ITEM	POST. REF.	DEBIT	CREDIT	BALANCE DEBIT	BALANCE CREDIT
20--							
Jan.	1	Balance	✓			1 2 2 5 00	
Feb.	12		J2	4 5 4 5 00		5 7 7 0 00	

ACCOUNT: Supplies Expense ACCOUNT NO. 524

DATE		ITEM	POST. REF.	DEBIT	CREDIT	BALANCE DEBIT	BALANCE CREDIT

Exercise 4 (LO 1/2) PREPARING, JOURNALIZING, AND POSTING ADJUSTING ENTRIES: DEPRECIATION

The Billy Willis Detective Agency began the accounting period by purchasing three cars that cost a total of $75,000. The estimated useful life of these cars is only two years with no salvage value.

Required:

1. Enter the appropriate adjusting entry at the end of the first year in a two-column journal. Willis uses straight-line depreciation.
2. Post this entry to the ledger accounts provided on the next page.

Exercise 4 (Concluded)

1. **GENERAL JOURNAL** PAGE 5

	DATE		DESCRIPTION	POST. REF.	DEBIT	CREDIT	
1							1
2							2
3							3
4							4

2. **GENERAL LEDGER**

ACCOUNT: Automobiles ACCOUNT NO. 185

DATE		ITEM	POST. REF.	DEBIT	CREDIT	BALANCE DEBIT	BALANCE CREDIT
20-- Jan.	2		J1	75,000.00		75,000.00	

ACCOUNT: Accumulated Depreciation—Automobiles ACCOUNT NO. 185.1

DATE		ITEM	POST. REF.	DEBIT	CREDIT	BALANCE DEBIT	BALANCE CREDIT

ACCOUNT: Depreciation Expense—Automobiles ACCOUNT NO. 541

DATE		ITEM	POST. REF.	DEBIT	CREDIT	BALANCE DEBIT	BALANCE CREDIT

Exercise 5 (LO 1/2) PREPARING, JOURNALIZING, AND POSTING ADJUSTING ENTRIES: PREPAID INSURANCE AND WAGES PAYABLE

On June 1, the Straw Basket Herb Farm purchased a one-year liability insurance policy for $600.

As of June 30, an additional $120 was earned by the employees but not yet paid.

Required:

1. Enter the appropriate adjusting entries at the end of June in the following general journal.
2. Post the entries to the ledger accounts provided.

1. **GENERAL JOURNAL** PAGE 6

	DATE		DESCRIPTION	POST. REF.	DEBIT	CREDIT	
1							1
2							2
3							3
4							4
5							5
6							6
7							7

2. **GENERAL LEDGER**

ACCOUNT: Prepaid Insurance ACCOUNT NO. 145

DATE		ITEM	POST. REF.	DEBIT	CREDIT	BALANCE	
						DEBIT	CREDIT
20-- June	1		J2	600 00		600 00	

ACCOUNT: Wages Payable ACCOUNT NO. 219

DATE		ITEM	POST. REF.	DEBIT	CREDIT	BALANCE	
						DEBIT	CREDIT

Exercise 5 (Concluded)

ACCOUNT: Wages Expense ACCOUNT NO. 511

DATE		ITEM	POST. REF.	DEBIT	CREDIT	BALANCE DEBIT	BALANCE CREDIT
20--							
June	14		J5	500 00		500 00	
	28		J5	500 00		1000 00	

ACCOUNT: Insurance Expense ACCOUNT NO. 535

DATE		ITEM	POST. REF.	DEBIT	CREDIT	BALANCE DEBIT	BALANCE CREDIT

Exercise 6 (LO 6) CASH BASIS OF ACCOUNTING

In the space provided, indicate which account is debited and which account is credited, using the **cash basis** of accounting. If no entry is made, write "NO ENTRY."

1. Paid rent, $500.

____

____

2. Purchased typewriter (office equipment) for $300.

____

____

3. Revenue for week: $300 cash, $200 on account.

____

____

4. Purchased fax machine (office equipment) for $400, on account.

____

____

5. Made payment on fax machine, $100.

____

____

Exercise 7 (LO 6) MODIFIED CASH BASIS OF ACCOUNTING

In the space provided, indicate which account is debited and which account is credited, using the **modified cash basis** of accounting. If no entry is made, write "NO ENTRY."

1. Paid electricity bill, $50.

2. Purchased office equipment for $500, on account.

3. Revenue for week: $500 cash, $200 on account.

4. Wages earned but not paid, $500.

5. Made payment on office equipment previously purchased, $25.

Exercise 8 (LO 6) ACCRUAL BASIS OF ACCOUNTING

In the space provided, indicate which account is debited and which account is credited, using the **accrual basis** of accounting. If no entry is made, write "NO ENTRY."

1. Purchased supplies (prepaid asset), $500, on account.

2. Revenue for week: $400 cash, $250 on account.

3. Wages earned but not paid, $250.

Exercise 8 (Concluded)

4. Made payment on account, $50, for supplies previously purchased.

5. Depreciation on long-term assets, $300.

PROBLEMS

Problem 9 (LO1/3) PREPARING ADJUSTMENTS AND THE WORK SHEET

Kim Ho offers employment counseling to middle managers unemployed due to corporate downsizing. On January 1 of the current year, Ho purchased office equipment with an expected life of 12 years and no salvage value. Computer equipment with an expected life of four years and no salvage value was purchased on July 1 of the current year. Ho uses straight-line depreciation. Office supplies on hand at year-end amounted to $150. Employees earned $300 in wages that have not yet been paid. Provided are the general ledger accounts as of December 31, prior to adjustment.

Required:

1. Using the ledger accounts, complete the Trial Balance columns of the year-end work sheet provided.
2. Prepare the necessary year-end adjustments.
3. Complete the work sheet.

GENERAL LEDGER

ACCOUNT: Cash ACCOUNT NO. 101

DATE		ITEM	POST. REF.	DEBIT	CREDIT	BALANCE DEBIT	BALANCE CREDIT
20-- Dec.	1	Balance	✔			2,400.00	
	21		J20	10,800.00		13,200.00	
	27		J20		4,200.00	9,000.00	

ACCOUNT: Office Supplies ACCOUNT NO. 142

DATE		ITEM	POST. REF.	DEBIT	CREDIT	BALANCE DEBIT	BALANCE CREDIT
20-- Dec.	1	Balance	✔			200.00	
	6		J20	300.00		500.00	

Problem 9 (Continued)

ACCOUNT: Office Equipment ACCOUNT NO. 181

DATE		ITEM	POST. REF.	DEBIT	CREDIT	BALANCE DEBIT	BALANCE CREDIT
20-- Dec.	1	Balance	✔			6 0 0 0 00	

ACCOUNT: Accumulated Depreciation—Office Equipment ACCOUNT NO. 181.1

DATE		ITEM	POST. REF.	DEBIT	CREDIT	BALANCE DEBIT	BALANCE CREDIT

ACCOUNT: Computer Equipment ACCOUNT NO. 187

DATE		ITEM	POST. REF.	DEBIT	CREDIT	BALANCE DEBIT	BALANCE CREDIT
20-- Dec.	1	Balance	✔			8 0 0 0 00	

ACCOUNT: Accumulated Depreciation—Computer Equipment ACCOUNT NO. 187.1

DATE		ITEM	POST. REF.	DEBIT	CREDIT	BALANCE DEBIT	BALANCE CREDIT

ACCOUNT: Accounts Payable ACCOUNT NO. 202

DATE		ITEM	POST. REF.	DEBIT	CREDIT	BALANCE DEBIT	BALANCE CREDIT
20-- Dec.	1	Balance	✔				3 0 0 00
	6		J20		2 0 0 00		5 0 0 00
	27		J20	1 0 0 00			4 0 0 00

Problem 9 (Continued)

ACCOUNT: Wages Payable ACCOUNT NO. 219

DATE		ITEM	POST. REF.	DEBIT	CREDIT	BALANCE DEBIT	BALANCE CREDIT

ACCOUNT: Kim Ho, Capital ACCOUNT NO. 311

DATE		ITEM	POST. REF.	DEBIT	CREDIT	BALANCE DEBIT	BALANCE CREDIT
20-- Dec.	1	Balance	✔				10,200.00

ACCOUNT: Kim Ho, Drawing ACCOUNT NO. 312

DATE		ITEM	POST. REF.	DEBIT	CREDIT	BALANCE DEBIT	BALANCE CREDIT
20-- Dec.	1	Balance	✔			1,500.00	
	30		J20	1,000.00		2,500.00	

ACCOUNT: Counseling Fees ACCOUNT NO. 401

DATE		ITEM	POST. REF.	DEBIT	CREDIT	BALANCE DEBIT	BALANCE CREDIT
20-- Dec.	1	Balance	✔				22,000.00
	31		J20		10,170.00		32,170.00

Problem 9 (Continued)

ACCOUNT: Wages Expense ACCOUNT NO. 511

DATE		ITEM	POST. REF.	DEBIT	CREDIT	BALANCE DEBIT	BALANCE CREDIT
20-- Dec.	1	Balance	✔			7,000 00	
	31		J20	1,500 00		8,500 00	

ACCOUNT: Rent Expense ACCOUNT NO. 521

DATE		ITEM	POST. REF.	DEBIT	CREDIT	BALANCE DEBIT	BALANCE CREDIT
20-- Dec.	1	Balance	✔			4,400 00	
	4		J20	1,200 00		5,600 00	

ACCOUNT: Supplies Expense ACCOUNT NO. 524

DATE		ITEM	POST. REF.	DEBIT	CREDIT	BALANCE DEBIT	BALANCE CREDIT

ACCOUNT: Utilities Expense ACCOUNT NO. 533

DATE		ITEM	POST. REF.	DEBIT	CREDIT	BALANCE DEBIT	BALANCE CREDIT
20-- Dec.	1	Balance	✔			1,300 00	
	31		J20	570 00		1,870 00	

Name ______________________________

Problem 9 (Continued)

ACCOUNT: Depreciation Expense—Office Equipment ACCOUNT NO. 541

DATE		ITEM	POST. REF.	DEBIT	CREDIT	BALANCE DEBIT	BALANCE CREDIT

ACCOUNT: Depreciation Expense—Computer Equipment ACCOUNT NO. 542

DATE		ITEM	POST. REF.	DEBIT	CREDIT	BALANCE DEBIT	BALANCE CREDIT

ACCOUNT: Miscellaneous Expense ACCOUNT NO. 549

DATE		ITEM	POST. REF.	DEBIT	CREDIT	BALANCE DEBIT	BALANCE CREDIT
20— Dec.	1	Balance	✓			600 00	
	22		J20	200 00		800 00	

Problem 9 (Continued)

1., 2., and 3.

KIM HO EMPLOYMENT

WORK

FOR YEAR ENDED

	ACCOUNT TITLE	TRIAL BALANCE		ADJUSTMENTS	
		DEBIT	CREDIT	DEBIT	CREDIT
1					
2					
3					
4					
5					
6					
7					
8					
9					
10					
11					
12					
13					
14					
15					
16					
17					
18					
19					
20					
21					
22					
23					
24					
25					
26					
27					
28					
29					
30					
31					

Problem 9 (Concluded)

COUNSELING SERVICES

SHEET

DECEMBER 31, 20--

ADJUSTED TRIAL BALANCE		INCOME STATEMENT		BALANCE SHEET		
DEBIT	CREDIT	DEBIT	CREDIT	DEBIT	CREDIT	
						1
						2
						3
						4
						5
						6
						7
						8
						9
						10
						11
						12
						13
						14
						15
						16
						17
						18
						19
						20
						21
						22
						23
						24
						25
						26
						27
						28
						29
						30
						31

Problem 10 (LO 1/3) PREPARING ADJUSTMENTS AND THE WORK SHEET

The trial balance for Juan's Speedy Delivery Service as of September 30, 20--, is shown on the work sheet that follows.

Data to complete the adjustments are as follows:

(a) Supplies inventory as of September 30, $450.
(b) Insurance expired, $200.
(c) Depreciation on delivery equipment, $350.
(d) Wages earned by employees but not paid as of September 30, $215.

Required:

1. Enter the adjustments in the Adjustments columns on the work sheet.
2. Complete the work sheet.

1. and 2.

JUAN'S SPEEDY
WORK
FOR MONTH ENDED

	ACCOUNT TITLE	TRIAL BALANCE DEBIT	TRIAL BALANCE CREDIT	ADJUSTMENTS DEBIT	ADJUSTMENTS CREDIT
1	Cash	1 5 4 5 00			
2	Accounts Receivable	8 5 0 00			
3	Supplies	7 2 5 00			
4	Prepaid Insurance	1 5 0 0 00			
5	Delivery Equipment	6 3 0 0 00			
6	Accum. Depr.—Delivery Equip.				
7	Accounts Payable		9 8 0 00		
8	Wages Payable				
9	Juan Garcia, Capital		9 0 0 0 00		
10	Juan Garcia, Drawing	1 2 0 0 00			
11	Delivery Fees		5 2 4 0 00		
12	Wages Expense	1 4 7 5 00			
13	Advertising Expense	4 2 0 00			
14	Rent Expense	7 5 0 00			
15	Supplies Expense				
16	Telephone Expense	1 8 0 00			
17	Insurance Expense				
18	Repair Expense	1 9 0 00			
19	Oil and Gas Expense	8 5 00			
20	Depreciation Expense—Del. Equip.				
21		15 2 2 0 00	15 2 2 0 00		
22					
23					

Problem 10 (Concluded)

DELIVERY SERVICE

SHEET

SEPTEMBER 30, 20--

ADJUSTED TRIAL BALANCE		INCOME STATEMENT		BALANCE SHEET		
DEBIT	CREDIT	DEBIT	CREDIT	DEBIT	CREDIT	
						1
						2
						3
						4
						5
						6
						7
						8
						9
						10
						11
						12
						13
						14
						15
						16
						17
						18
						19
						20
						21
						22
						23

Problem 11 (LO 4) FINDING AND CORRECTING ERRORS ON A WORK SHEET

A work sheet for George Green's Landscaping Service follows. It should include these adjustments.

(a) Ending inventory of supplies as of July 31, $350.
(b) Insurance expired as of July 31, $225.
(c) Depreciation on tractor, $460.
(d) Wages earned but not paid as of July 31, $320.

Required:

Errors have been intentionally placed in this work sheet. Review the work sheet for addition mistakes, transpositions, and other errors and make all necessary corrections.

(*Note:* Errors are intentional.)

GREEN'S LANDSCAPING

WORK

FOR MONTH ENDED

	ACCOUNT TITLE	TRIAL BALANCE		ADJUSTMENTS	
		DEBIT	CREDIT	DEBIT	CREDIT
1	Cash	1,825.00			
2	Accounts Receivable	720.00			
3	Supplies	600.00			(a) 350.00
4	Prepaid Insurance	850.00			(b) 225.00
5	Tractor	6,550.00			(c) 460.00
6	Accum. Depr.—Tractor				
7	Accounts Payable		520.00		
8	Wages Payable				(d) 320.00
9	George Green, Capital		8,250.00		
10	George Green, Drawing	1,200.00			
11	Landscaping Fees		6,100.00		
12	Wages Expense	1,540.00		(d) 320.00	
13	Advertising Expense	250.00			
14	Rent Expense	775.00			
15	Supplies Expense			(a) 350.00	
16	Telephone Expense	140.00			
17	Utilities Expense	220.00			
18	Insurance Expense			(b) 225.00	
19	Depr. Expense—Tractor			(c) 460.00	
20	Miscellaneous Expense	200.00			
21		14,870.00	14,870.00	1,355.00	1,355.00
22	Net Income				
23					

Problem 11 (Concluded)

SERVICE

SHEET

JULY 31, 20--

ADJUSTED TRIAL BALANCE		INCOME STATEMENT		BALANCE SHEET	
DEBIT	CREDIT	DEBIT	CREDIT	DEBIT	CREDIT
1,825.00				1,825.00	
720.00				720.00	
250.00				250.00	
650.00				650.00	
6,090.00				6,090.00	
	520.00				520.00
	320.00		320.00		
	8,250.00				8,250.00
1,200.00		1,200.00			
	6,100.00		6,100.00		
1,540.00		1,540.00			1,840.00
250.00		250.00			
775.00		775.00			
350.00		350.00			
140.00		140.00			
220.00		220.00			
225.00		225.00			
460.00		460.00			
200.00		200.00			
13,355.00	15,190.00	2,417.00	6,420.00	8,347.00	8,770.00
		1,720.00			1,720.00
		4,137.00	6,420.00	8,347.00	10,490.00

Problem 12 (LO 6) CASH, MODIFIED CASH, AND ACCRUAL BASES

Mark Mosley has his own consulting business. Listed below are selected transactions from the month of April.

Apr.	1	Paid office rent, $500.
	2	Purchased office supplies, $250.
	3	Purchased office equipment on account, $1,000.
	4	Earned consulting fees: $400 cash, $150 on account.
	5	Paid telephone bill, $48.
	6	Purchased one-year insurance policy, $200.
	7	Paid $100 on account (for office equipment previously purchased).
	8	Received $150 on account from a customer (previously owed).
	9	Recorded depreciation on office equipment for month, $50.

Required:

Record the transactions in the space provided, using the following bases:

1. The cash basis.
2. The modified cash basis.
3. The accrual basis.

Problem 12 (Continued)

1. Cash Basis

GENERAL JOURNAL PAGE

	DATE		DESCRIPTION	POST. REF.	DEBIT	CREDIT	
1							1
2							2
3							3
4							4
5							5
6							6
7							7
8							8
9							9
10							10
11							11
12							12
13							13
14							14
15							15
16							16
17							17
18							18
19							19
20							20
21							21
22							22
23							23
24							24
25							25
26							26
27							27
28							28
29							29
30							30

Problem 12 (Continued)

2. Modified Cash Basis

GENERAL JOURNAL

PAGE

	DATE	DESCRIPTION	POST. REF.	DEBIT	CREDIT	
1						1
2						2
3						3
4						4
5						5
6						6
7						7
8						8
9						9
10						10
11						11
12						12
13						13
14						14
15						15
16						16
17						17
18						18
19						19
20						20
21						21
22						22
23						23
24						24
25						25
26						26
27						27
28						28
29						29
30						30

Problem 12 (Concluded)

3. Accrual Basis

GENERAL JOURNAL PAGE

	DATE		DESCRIPTION	POST. REF.	DEBIT	CREDIT	
1							1
2							2
3							3
4							4
5							5
6							6
7							7
8							8
9							9
10							10
11							11
12							12
13							13
14							14
15							15
16							16
17							17
18							18
19							19
20							20
21							21
22							22
23							23
24							24
25							25
26							26
27							27
28							28
29							29
30							30

CHAPTER 5 APPENDIX
DEPRECIATION METHODS

APPENDIX LEARNING OBJECTIVES

In Chapter 5, the straight-line method of depreciation was illustrated. In the appendix to Chapter 5, three additional methods are explained. These methods are used when a different schedule of expenses provides a more appropriate matching with the revenues generated.

Objective 1. **Prepare a depreciation schedule using the straight-line method.**
Objective 2. **Prepare a depreciation schedule using the sum-of-the-years'-digits method.**
Objective 3. **Prepare a depreciation schedule using the double-declining-balance method.**
Objective 4. **Prepare a depreciation schedule for tax purposes using the Modified Accelerated Cost Recovery System.**

Apx. Exercise 1 (LO 1) STRAIGHT-LINE DEPRECIATION

Office equipment was purchased on January 1 at a cost of $48,000. It has an estimated useful life of four years and a salvage value of $6,000. Prepare a depreciation schedule showing the depreciation expense, accumulated depreciation, and book value for each year under the straight-line method.

STRAIGHT-LINE DEPRECIATION

Apx. Exercise 2 (LO 2) SUM-OF-THE-YEARS'-DIGITS DEPRECIATION

Using the information given in Exercise 1, prepare a depreciation schedule showing the depreciation expense, accumulated depreciation, and book value for each year under the sum-of-the-years'-digits method.

SUM-OF-THE-YEARS'-DIGITS DEPRECIATION

Apx. Exercise 3 (LO 3) DOUBLE-DECLINING-BALANCE DEPRECIATION

Using the information given in Exercise 1, prepare a depreciation schedule showing the depreciation expense, accumulated depreciation, and book value for each year under the double-declining-balance method.

DOUBLE-DECLINING-BALANCE DEPRECIATION

Apx. Exercise 4 (LO 4) DEPRECIATION UNDER THE MODIFIED ACCELERATED COST RECOVERY SYSTEM

Using the information given in Exercise 1 and the rates shown in Figure 5A-4 of the text, prepare a depreciation schedule showing the depreciation expense, accumulated depreciation, and book value for each year under the Modified Accelerated Cost Recovery System. For tax purposes, assume that the office equipment has a useful life of five years. (The IRS schedule will spread depreciation over six years.) Round to the nearest dollar.

MODIFIED ACCELERATED COST RECOVERY SYSTEM

CHAPTER 6
FINANCIAL STATEMENTS AND THE CLOSING PROCESS

LEARNING OBJECTIVES

Chapter 5 introduced the work sheet and demonstrated how it is used to prepare year-end adjustments. Chapter 6 completes the discussion of the work sheet by illustrating its role in the preparation of financial statements and closing entries. The purpose of the post-closing trial balance is also explained. It is prepared after closing entries have been posted to the general ledger accounts.

Objective 1. Prepare financial statements with the aid of a work sheet.

The work sheet contains almost all the information needed to prepare the income statement, the statement of owner's equity, and the balance sheet. Numbers can be taken directly from the Income Statement columns for the income statement. The owner's capital account must be reviewed before completing the statement of owner's equity. If additional investments were made, they must be added to the beginning capital balance to compute the total investment. The net income (or net loss) is added to the total investment, and withdrawals (drawing) are subtracted, giving the ending owner's equity. The balance sheet is prepared using the ending owner's equity balance reported on the statement of owner's equity and the permanent accounts listed in the Balance Sheet columns of the work sheet.

Objective 2. Journalize and post closing entries.

After the work sheet is completed, the financial statements are prepared. Then the adjusting and closing entries are journalized and posted. All temporary accounts need zero balances to begin the new accounting period. The closing process has four journal entries:

1. to close revenue account(s) to Income Summary
2. to close expense accounts to Income Summary
3. to close Income Summary to the owner's capital account, and
4. to close Drawing to the owner's capital account.

Objective 3. Prepare a post-closing trial balance.

The **post-closing trial balance** lists all the permanent accounts that have balances to begin the new accounting period. It is prepared to prove the equality of the debit and credit balances in the general ledger accounts following the closing process. Since temporary accounts (drawing, revenues, and expenses) are closed at the end of the period, they do not appear on the post-closing trial balance.

Objective 4. List and describe the steps in the accounting cycle.

This chapter concludes the accounting cycle that began in Chapter 1. The 10 steps are as follows:

During the Accounting Period

1. Analyze source documents.
2. Journalize the transactions.
3. Post to the general ledger accounts.

End of Accounting Period

4. Prepare a trial balance.
5. Determine and prepare the needed adjustments on the work sheet.

6. Complete an end-of-period work sheet.
7. Journalize and post the adjusting entries.
8. Prepare an income statement, a statement of owner's equity, and a balance sheet.
9. Journalize and post the closing entries.
10. Prepare a post-closing trial balance.

REVIEW QUESTIONS

Instructions: Analyze each of the following items carefully before writing your answer in the column at the right.

		Question	Answer
LO 1	**1.**	The work sheet provides most of the needed information to prepare which three financial statements?	____________
LO 1	**2.**	The income statement contains which two major types of accounts?	____________
LO 1	**3.**	The statement of owner's equity adds ________ to the owner's investment and subtracts ________.	____________ ____________
LO 1	**4.**	Amounts owed that will be paid within a year are called ________.	____________
LO 1	**5.**	Expenses are listed on the income statement in the order they appear on the chart of accounts or in descending order by _______ amount.	____________
LO 1	**6.**	To find if the owner made any additional investments during the period, we must review the _______ account in the general ledger.	____________
LO 1	**7.**	When net income and additional investments are greater than withdrawals, the difference is called a(n) ________ in capital for the month.	____________
LO 1	**8.**	When the balance sheet is shown in ________ form, liabilities and owner's equity sections are placed below the assets section.	____________
LO 1	**9.**	When the balance sheet is shown in ________ form, assets are on the left and liabilities and owner's equity are on the right.	____________
LO 1	**10.**	A(n) ________ balance sheet groups similar items together such as current assets and current liabilities.	____________
LO 1	**11.**	Cash and assets that will be converted to cash or consumed within a year or the normal operating cycle are called ________ assets. ..	____________
LO 1	**12.**	The ________ is the period of time required to purchase supplies and services and convert them back into cash.	____________
LO 1	**13.**	Accounts Payable and Wages Payable are classified as ________ liabilities.	____________
LO 2	**14.**	Assets, liabilities, and the owner's capital account accumulate information across accounting periods; they are called ________ accounts.	____________

LO 2 15. Revenue, expense, and drawing accounts accumulate information for the specific period only, then they go back to ________ balances. ______________

LO 2 16. Because revenue, expense, and drawing accounts are closed each accounting period, they are called ________ accounts. .... ______________

LO 2 17. The ________ account is used to summarize the effects of revenue and expense accounts; it is then closed to the capital account. .... ______________

LO 2 18. When closing entries are posted to the general ledger, the word ________ is written in the Item column of each general ledger account affected. .... ______________

LO 3 19. The ________ trial balance only lists permanent accounts. ______________

LO 4 20. The ________ begins with analyzing source documents and ends with the post-closing trial balance. .... ______________

EXERCISES

Exercise 1 (LO 1) REVIEW: COMPUTE NET INCOME

From the information given below, compute net income. ______________

Revenue:	Delivery Fees	$4,826
Expenses:	Wages Expense	2,700
	Rent Expense	350
	Supplies Expense	55
	Insurance Expense	33
	Depreciation Expense	100

Exercise 2 (LO 1) REVIEW: COMPUTE OWNER'S EQUITY

Using the net income from Exercise 1 and the following information, compute the (a) increase to owner's equity and (b) ending owner's equity balance. Assume no additional investments were made by the owner.

(a) ______________

(b) ______________

Beginning owner's equity:	$5,680
Withdrawals by owner:	1,000

Exercise 3 (LO 2) THE CLOSING PROCESS

Based upon Exercises 1 and 2 above, list the accounts that must be closed at the end of the accounting cycle (in addition to the income summary account).

____

____

____

____

____

____

____

PROBLEMS

Problems 4–9

To complete Problems 4 through 9, use the completed work sheet for Collins Cycle Service as of April 30, 20--, below and the general ledger on pages 88-92.

COLLINS CYCLE

WORK

FOR MONTH ENDED

	ACCOUNT TITLE	TRIAL BALANCE		ADJUSTMENTS	
		DEBIT	CREDIT	DEBIT	CREDIT
1	Cash	4800 00			
2	Supplies	826 00			(a) 326 00
3	Prepaid Insurance	1300 00			(b) 200 00
4	Repair Equipment	2600 00			
5	Accum. Depr.—Repair Equip.		400 00		(c) 400 00
6	Accounts Payable		1300 00		
7	Wages Payable				(d) 100 00
8	Jean Collins, Capital		6000 00		
9	Jean Collins, Drawing	300 00			
10	Repair Fees		2839 00		
11	Wages Expense	275 00		(d) 100 00	
12	Rent Expense	400 00			
13	Supplies Expense			(a) 326 00	
14	Telephone Expense	38 00			
15	Insurance Expense			(b) 200 00	
16	Depreciation Exp.—Repair Equip.			(c) 400 00	
17		10539 00	10539 00	1026 00	1026 00
18					
19					

Problems 4–9 (Concluded)

SERVICE

SHEET

APRIL 30, 20--

ADJUSTED TRIAL BALANCE		INCOME STATEMENT		BALANCE SHEET		
DEBIT	CREDIT	DEBIT	CREDIT	DEBIT	CREDIT	
4,800.00				4,800.00		1
500.00				500.00		2
1,100.00				1,100.00		3
2,600.00				2,600.00		4
	800.00				800.00	5
	1,300.00				1,300.00	6
	100.00				100.00	7
	6,000.00				6,000.00	8
300.00				300.00		9
	2,839.00		2,839.00			10
375.00		375.00				11
400.00		400.00				12
326.00		326.00				13
38.00		38.00				14
200.00		200.00				15
400.00		400.00				16
11,039.00	11,039.00	1,739.00	2,839.00	9,300.00	8,200.00	17
		1,100.00			1,100.00	18
		2,839.00	2,839.00	9,300.00	9,300.00	19

Problem 4 REVIEW: PREPARE ADJUSTING ENTRIES

Journalize the adjusting entries and post them to the general ledger accounts. The balances shown in the general ledger accounts are *trial balance* amounts—that is, before adjusting and closing entries are entered.

GENERAL JOURNAL

PAGE 2

	DATE		DESCRIPTION	POST. REF.	DEBIT	CREDIT	
1							1
2							2
3							3
4							4
5							5
6							6
7							7
8							8
9							9
10							10
11							11
12							12
13							13
14							14

GENERAL LEDGER

ACCOUNT Cash ACCOUNT NO. 101

DATE		ITEM	POST. REF.	DEBIT	CREDIT	BALANCE	
						DEBIT	CREDIT
20-- Apr.	30	Balance	✓			4,800.00	

ACCOUNT Supplies ACCOUNT NO. 141

DATE		ITEM	POST. REF.	DEBIT	CREDIT	BALANCE	
						DEBIT	CREDIT
20-- Apr.	30	Balance	✓			826.00	

Problems 4 and 8 (Continued)

ACCOUNT Prepaid Insurance ACCOUNT NO. 145

DATE		ITEM	POST. REF.	DEBIT	CREDIT	BALANCE DEBIT	BALANCE CREDIT
20-- Apr.	30	Balance	✓			1,300.00	

ACCOUNT Repair Equipment ACCOUNT NO. 188

DATE		ITEM	POST. REF.	DEBIT	CREDIT	BALANCE DEBIT	BALANCE CREDIT
20-- Apr.	30	Balance	✓			2,600.00	

ACCOUNT Accumulated Depreciation—Repair Equipment ACCOUNT NO. 188.1

DATE		ITEM	POST. REF.	DEBIT	CREDIT	BALANCE DEBIT	BALANCE CREDIT
20-- Apr.	1	Balance	✓				400.00

ACCOUNT Accounts Payable ACCOUNT NO. 202

DATE		ITEM	POST. REF.	DEBIT	CREDIT	BALANCE DEBIT	BALANCE CREDIT
20-- Apr.	30	Balance	✓				1,300.00

Problems 4 and 8 (Continued)

ACCOUNT Wages Payable ACCOUNT NO. 219

DATE		ITEM	POST. REF.	DEBIT	CREDIT	BALANCE DEBIT	BALANCE CREDIT

ACCOUNT Jean Collins, Capital ACCOUNT NO. 311

DATE		ITEM	POST. REF.	DEBIT	CREDIT	BALANCE DEBIT	BALANCE CREDIT
20-- Apr.	1	Balance	✓				5 0 0 0 00
	15		J1		1 0 0 0 00		6 0 0 0 00

ACCOUNT Jean Collins, Drawing ACCOUNT NO. 312

DATE		ITEM	POST. REF.	DEBIT	CREDIT	BALANCE DEBIT	BALANCE CREDIT
20-- Apr.	30	Balance	✓			3 0 0 00	

ACCOUNT Income Summary ACCOUNT NO. 313

DATE		ITEM	POST. REF.	DEBIT	CREDIT	BALANCE DEBIT	BALANCE CREDIT

Problems 4 and 8 (Continued)

ACCOUNT Repair Fees ACCOUNT NO. 401

DATE		ITEM	POST. REF.	DEBIT	CREDIT	BALANCE DEBIT	BALANCE CREDIT
20-- Apr.	30	Balance	✓				2,839 00

ACCOUNT Wages Expense ACCOUNT NO. 511

DATE		ITEM	POST. REF.	DEBIT	CREDIT	BALANCE DEBIT	BALANCE CREDIT
20-- Apr.	30	Balance	✓			275 00	

ACCOUNT Rent Expense ACCOUNT NO. 521

DATE		ITEM	POST. REF.	DEBIT	CREDIT	BALANCE DEBIT	BALANCE CREDIT
20-- Apr.	30	Balance	✓			400 00	

ACCOUNT Supplies Expense ACCOUNT NO. 524

DATE		ITEM	POST. REF.	DEBIT	CREDIT	BALANCE DEBIT	BALANCE CREDIT

Problems 4 and 8 (Continued)

ACCOUNT Telephone Expense ACCOUNT NO. 525

DATE		ITEM	POST. REF.	DEBIT	CREDIT	BALANCE DEBIT	BALANCE CREDIT
20-- Apr.	30	Balance	✓			38.00	

ACCOUNT Insurance Expense ACCOUNT NO. 535

DATE		ITEM	POST. REF.	DEBIT	CREDIT	BALANCE DEBIT	BALANCE CREDIT

ACCOUNT Depreciation Expense—Repair Equipment ACCOUNT NO. 542

DATE		ITEM	POST. REF.	DEBIT	CREDIT	BALANCE DEBIT	BALANCE CREDIT

Problem 5 (LO 1) PREPARE AN INCOME STATEMENT

Prepare the income statement.

Problem 6 (LO 2) PREPARE A STATEMENT OF OWNER'S EQUITY

Prepare the statement of owner's equity. Be sure to check the capital account in the general ledger.

Problem 7 (LO 1) PREPARE A BALANCE SHEET

Prepare the balance sheet in report form.

Problem 8 (LO 2) JOURNALIZING AND POSTING CLOSING ENTRIES

Journalize the closing entries and post them to the general ledger accounts. (The general ledger accounts can be found on pages 88-92.)

GENERAL JOURNAL

PAGE 2

DATE	DESCRIPTION	POST. REF.	DEBIT	CREDIT

Problem 9 (LO 3) PREPARE A POST-CLOSING TRIAL BALANCE

Prepare the post-closing trial balance.

ACCOUNT TITLE	ACCT. NO.	DEBIT BALANCE	CREDIT BALANCE

CHAPTER 6 APPENDIX
STATEMENT OF CASH FLOWS

APPENDIX LEARNING OBJECTIVES

In Chapter 6, we reviewed in greater detail the preparation of three financial statements: the income statement, statement of owner's equity, and balance sheet. A fourth important financial statement is the statement of cash flows. The main purpose of this statement is to report the sources and uses of cash. These sources and uses are categorized into three types of business activities: operating, investing, and financing.

Objective 1. Classify business transactions as operating, investing, or financing.

Operating activities include those cash flows that are related to the revenues and expenses reported on the income statement. Examples include cash received for services performed and the payment of cash for expenses.

Investing activities are those transactions associated with buying and selling long-term assets, lending money, and collecting the principal on the related loans.

Financing activities are those cash transactions with owners and creditors. Examples include cash received from the owner to finance the operations and cash paid to the owner as withdrawals. Financing activities also include the receipt of cash from loans and the repayment of the loans.

Objective 2. Prepare a statement of cash flows by analyzing and categorizing a series of business transactions.

The main body of the statement of cash flows consists of three sections: operating, investing, and financing activities.

Name of Business Statement of Cash Flows For Period Ended Date		
Cash flows from operating activities:		
Cash received from customers		$ x x x x xx
List cash paid for various expenses	$ (x x x xx)	
Total cash paid for operations		(x x x x xx)
Net cash provided by (used for) operating activities		$ x x x xx
Cash flows from investing activities:		
List cash received from the sale of long-term assets and other investing activities	$ x x x x xx	
List cash paid for the purchase of long-term assets and other investing activities	(x x x x xx)	
Net cash provided by (used for) investing activities		x x x x xx
Cash flows from financing activities:		
List cash received from owners and creditors	$ x x x x xx	
List cash paid to owners and creditors	(x x x xx)	
Net cash provided by (used for) financing activities		x x x x xx
Net increase (decrease) in cash		$ x x x xx

Apx. Exercise 1 REVIEW: ENTERING TRANSACTIONS IN T ACCOUNTS

Sung Joon Lee opened an overseas mailing business, "Lee's Quick Sail." The following transactions occurred during August of the current year. Enter the transactions in the cash T account provided below, identifying each with its corresponding letter.

(a) Lee invested $5,000 in the business.
(b) Paid office rent, $500.
(c) Bought supplies for the month, $200.
(d) Lee made an additional investment in the business, $1,000.
(e) Bought a new scale for $1,200: $700 cash and $500 on account.
(f) Received $600 for mailing services.
(g) Paid $200 on loan [see transaction (e)].
(h) Paid electricity bill, $64.
(i) Paid gas bill, $70.
(j) Received $900 for mailing services.
(k) Paid part-time employee, $90.
(l) Lee withdrew cash for personal use, $400.

CASH

Apx. Exercise 2 REVIEW: FOOTING AND BALANCING A T ACCOUNT

Foot and balance the T account in Exercise 1. The cash balance at the end of August is _______ .

Apx. Problem 3 (LO 1) CLASSIFYING BUSINESS TRANSACTIONS AS OPERATING, INVESTING, OR FINANCING

Label each transaction in the cash T account of Exercise 1 as an operating (O), an investing (I), or a financing (F) activity.

Apx. Problem 4 (LO 2) PREPARING A STATEMENT OF CASH FLOWS BY ANALYZING BUSINESS TRANSACTIONS

Prepare a statement of cash flows based on the transactions and cash T account in Exercises 1 and 2, and Problem 3.

CHAPTER 7
ACCOUNTING FOR CASH

LEARNING OBJECTIVES

Managing cash is an essential part of every business's operations. In Chapter 7, we explore the cash account—setting up a bank account, writing checks and making deposits, preparing a bank reconciliation and the journal entries needed, operating a petty cash fund, establishing a change fund and using a cash short and over account.

Objective 1. Describe how to open and use a checking account.

Most banks have standard procedures for opening and using a **checking account.** They begin with a signature card, whereby the depositor's social security number or EIN number and signature are provided. Preparing deposit tickets, endorsing properly, and writing checks are parts of using a checking account wisely.

Objective 2. Prepare a bank reconciliation and related journal entries.

On a monthly basis, banks send **bank statements** to their checking account customers. The bank statement must be reconciled—compared to the checkbook. Adjustments are made to the ending bank balance and the checkbook balance until they are equal. Once the bank reconciliation is prepared, any changes to the book (checkbook) balance will require journal entries.

Objective 3. Establish and use a petty cash fund.

A **petty cash fund** is both convenient and cost effective. Rather than writing checks for small amounts, costing time and money, a sum of money is set aside for petty (small) cash payments during the month. Vouchers are issued for all money paid out; the petty cash fund is replenished at the end of the month (brought back up to its original amount). A journal entry is made to record all of the expenses shown in the petty cash record.

Objective 4. Establish a change fund and use the cash short and over account.

Businesses that receive cash from customers generally need to establish a change fund of currency and coins to use in handling cash sales. When many cash transactions occur, there often will be a difference between what the cash register tape says and the amount of cash actually found in the drawer. An account called Cash Short and Over is used to account for these differences. At the end of the month, if there is more cash short than over, it is an expense to the business. If there is more cash over than short, it is a revenue to the business.

REVIEW QUESTIONS

Instructions: Analyze each of the following items carefully before writing your answer in the column at the right.

		Question	Answer
LO 1	**1.**	To open a checking account, each person authorized to sign checks must fill out a(n) ________.	____________________
LO 1	**2.**	A(n) ________ lists items being deposited to a checking account.	____________________
LO 1	**3.**	Each check deposited is identified by its ________.	____________________
LO 1	**4.**	A(n) ________ consists of stamping or writing the depositor's name and other information on the back of a check.	____________________
LO 1	**5.**	A(n) ________ endorsement consists of a signature on the back of a check.	____________________
LO 1	**6.**	A(n) ________ endorsement consists of a signature together with words such as "For Deposit."..	____________________
LO 1	**7.**	Depositors using ATM machines must first key in their _______.	____________________
LO 1	**8.**	A(n) ________ is a document ordering a bank to pay cash from the depositor's account.	____________________
LO 1	**9.**	The ________ is the bank on which a check is drawn.	____________________
LO 1	**10.**	The ________ is the person being paid the cash.	____________________
LO 1	**11.**	The ________ is the depositor who orders the bank to pay the cash.	____________________
LO 1	**12.**	Space is contained to record all relevant information about a check on its ________.	____________________
LO 1	**13.**	A statement issued to the depositor once a month is called a ________.	____________________
LO 1	**14.**	Checks paid by the bank and returned to the depositor are called ________.	____________________
LO 2	**15.**	The process of bringing the bank and book balances into agreement is called preparing a(n) ________.	____________________
LO 2	**16.**	Checks issued during the period but not yet processed by the bank are called ________.	____________________
LO 2	**17.**	Deposits made but not yet recorded by the bank are called _______.	____________________
LO 2	**18.**	Bank charges for services are called ________.	____________________
LO 2	**19.**	Checks deposited but not paid because the drawer did not have enough money in the account are called ________ checks.	____________________
LO 2	**20.**	Transactions can be completed by ________ rather than by the manual process of writing checks or using cash.	____________________
LO 3	**21.**	A fund called the ________ is established to pay for small items with cash.	____________________

LO 3 **22.** A receipt called a(n) ________ is prepared for every payment from the petty cash fund. .... ______________________

LO 3 **23.** The ________ is a special multi-column record where petty cash payments are recorded. .... ______________________

LO 3 **24.** At the end of the month, the petty cash fund is ________, or brought up to its original amount. .... ______________________

LO 4 **25.** The cash short and over account is used when actual cash on hand is different from what is on the ________ tape plus the change fund. ______________________

LO 4 **26.** When actual cash on hand exceeds what is on the register tape plus the change fund, this difference is a(n) ________. .... ______________________

LO 4 **27.** When actual cash on hand is less than what is on the register tape plus the change fund, this difference is a(n) ________. .... ______________________

EXERCISES

Exercise 1 (LO1) PREPARE DEPOSIT TICKET

Using the deposit ticket shown below, enter the following information:

Date:	March 28, 20--	Checks:	33-11	$202.00
Currency:	$318.00		123-666	48.00
Coin:	33.00		2-9	211.00

PEOPLE'S BANK
Wilkes-Barre, PA 18704-1456

Date______________________ 20____

CHECKS AND OTHER ITEMS ARE RECEIVED FOR DEPOSIT SUBJECT TO THE TERMS AND CONDITIONS OF THIS FINANCIAL INSTITUTION'S ACCOUNT AGREEMENT.

____
SIGN HERE ONLY IF CASH RECEIVED FROM DEPOSIT

⑆063112094⑆ 0001632475⑈

DEPOSIT TICKET

CURRENCY		
COIN		
CHECKS		
TOTAL FROM OTHER SIDE		
SUBTOTAL		
LESS CASH RECEIVED		
NET DEPOSIT		

Exercise 2 (LO1) PREPARE CHECK AND STUB

During the month of October, you made the following payments by check. Fill in the stubs and write the checks. Use the blank checks provided on page 104. Enter $825.50 as the balance brought forward on Check No. 138, and add a deposit for $85 on October 10.

Oct.	3	Issued Check No. 138 to Emerald Lawn Care, Inc., for work done on the shrubbery around the office building, $125.00. (Miscellaneous Expense)
	8	Issued Check No. 139 to Maxwell Office Supply for stationery, $85.90. (Office Supplies)
	10	Issued Check No. 140 to Wesley's Towing for cost of towing company car to repair shop, $50.00. (Automobile Expense)

Exercise 2 (Concluded)

No. 138

DATE ______________ 20____
TO ______________________
FOR _____________________
____

ACCT. ___________________

	DOLLARS	CENTS
BAL BRO'T FOR'D		
AMT. DEPOSITED		
TOTAL		
AMT. THIS CHECK		
BAL CAR'D FOR'D		

No. 138 60-55/313

______________ 20______

PAY TO THE ORDER OF ________________________________ $ __________

____ Dollars

FOR CLASSROOM USE ONLY

PEOPLE'S BANK
Wilkes-Barre, PA 18704-1456

MEMO ____________________ BY ____________________

⑆1300555 16 3247 5⑈

No. 139

DATE ______________ 20____
TO ______________________
FOR _____________________
____

ACCT. ___________________

	DOLLARS	CENTS
BAL BRO'T FOR'D		
AMT. DEPOSITED		
TOTAL		
AMT. THIS CHECK		
BAL CAR'D FOR'D		

No. 139 60-55/313

______________ 20______

PAY TO THE ORDER OF ________________________________ $ __________

____ Dollars

FOR CLASSROOM USE ONLY

PEOPLE'S BANK
Wilkes-Barre, PA 18704-1456

MEMO ____________________ BY ____________________

⑆1300555 16 3247 5⑈

No. 140

DATE ______________ 20____
TO ______________________
FOR _____________________
____

ACCT. ___________________

	DOLLARS	CENTS
BAL BRO'T FOR'D		
AMT. DEPOSITED		
TOTAL		
AMT. THIS CHECK		
BAL CAR'D FOR'D		

No. 140 60-55/313

______________ 20______

PAY TO THE ORDER OF ________________________________ $ __________

____ Dollars

FOR CLASSROOM USE ONLY

PEOPLE'S BANK
Wilkes-Barre, PA 18704-1456

MEMO ____________________ BY ____________________

⑆1300555 16 3247 5⑈

Exercise 3 (LO2) BANK RECONCILIATION PROCEDURES

The bank reconciliation is a process of matching the checkbook balance with the bank statement balance—adding and subtracting items until the two are equal. In the exercise below, indicate which action is taken.

a. Add to checkbook balance.

b. Subtract from checkbook balance.

c. Add to bank statement balance.

d. Subtract from bank statement balance.

________ 1. Deposits in transit

________ 2. Error in checkbook whereby a check for $128 was entered into the checkbook as $182

________ 3. NSF check

________ 4. Checks outstanding (not yet processed by the bank)

________ 5. Bank service fees

________ 6. Credit memo, telling depositor that a note was collected

________ 7. Error in checkbook whereby a check for $181 was entered into the checkbook as $118

Exercise 4 (LO 2) PREPARE JOURNAL ENTRIES FOR BANK RECONCILIATION

Based on the following bank reconciliation, prepare the necessary journal entries as of January 28, 20--:

Bank statement balance, January 28		$1,896.00
Add: Deposits in transit:		
1/26	$118.00	
1/28	92.00	210.00
		$2,106.00
Deduct: Outstanding checks:		
No. 683	$ 23.00	
No. 685	6.50	
No. 687	102.50	
No. 688	13.00	
No. 689	208.00	353.00
Adjusted bank balance		$1,753.00
Book balance, January 28		$1,994.00
Add: Error on check*	$ 28.00	
Note collected**	142.00	170.00
		$2,164.00
Deduct: Unrecorded ATM withdrawal***	$ 30.00	
Service charge	11.00	
NSF check	370.00	411.00
Adjusted book balance		$1,753.00

*Accounts Payable was debited.
**Credit Notes Receivable.
***Debit Gail Bennett, Drawing.

Exercise 4 (Concluded)

GENERAL JOURNAL

PAGE

	DATE		DESCRIPTION	POST. REF.	DEBIT	CREDIT	
1							1
2							2
3							3
4							4
5							5
6							6
7							7
8							8
9							9
10							10
11							11
12							12
13							13
14							14
15							15
16							16
17							17
18							18
19							19
20							20
21							21
22							22

Exercise 5 (LO3) PETTY CASH JOURNAL ENTRIES

Based on the following petty cash information, prepare journal entries to establish the petty cash fund and to replenish the fund at the end of the month.

1. On March 1, a check is written for $100 to establish a petty cash fund.
2. During the month, the following petty cash payments are made:

Telephone Expense	$ 3.50
Automobile Expense	11.00
Postage Expense	4.50
B. Crenshaw, Drawing	35.00
Charitable Contributions Expense	25.00
Miscellaneous Expense	3.00

Exercise 5 (Concluded)

GENERAL JOURNAL PAGE 1

	DATE		DESCRIPTION	POST. REF.	DEBIT	CREDIT	
1							1
2							2
3							3
4							4
5							5
6							6
7							7
8							8
9							9
10							10
11							11
12							12

Exercise 6 (LO4) CASH SHORT AND OVER JOURNAL ENTRIES

Based on the following information, prepare weekly entries for cash receipts from service fees and cash short and over. A change fund of $100 is maintained.

Aug.	5	Cash in drawer:	$318.00	Cash register amount:	$218.00
	12		402.00		300.00
	19		388.00		292.00
	26		411.50		309.50

Exercise 6 (Concluded)

GENERAL JOURNAL

PAGE 1

	DATE		DESCRIPTION	POST. REF.	DEBIT	CREDIT	
1							1
2							2
3							3
4							4
5							5
6							6
7							7
8							8
9							9
10							10
11							11
12							12
13							13
14							14
15							15
16							16
17							17
18							18
19							19

PROBLEMS

Problem 7 (LO2) BANK RECONCILIATION AND RELATED JOURNAL ENTRIES

The following information relates to the bank account of the Mini Donut House:

Balance, March 31, per check stub		$2,923.00
Balance, March 31, per bank statement		3,199.00
March deposits not shown on bank statement	$ 302.00	
	206.00	508.00
Bank service charge shown on bank statement		14.00
Unrecorded ATM withdrawal*		60.00
NSF check shown on bank statement		153.00

Error on Check No. 144, where stub shows $132.00, but the check was made in the amount of $123.00. Accounts Payable was originally debited.

Checks outstanding, March 31, are as follows:

No. 148	$201.00
No. 151	300.00
No. 155	501.00

*Funds were withdrawn by the owner, Paolo Goes, for personal use.

Required:

1. Prepare the bank reconciliation.
2. Prepare the required journal entries.

Problem 7 (Continued)

1.

Problem 7 (Concluded)

2.

GENERAL JOURNAL

PAGE 1

DATE		DESCRIPTION	POST. REF.	DEBIT	CREDIT

Problem 8 (LO3) PETTY CASH PAYMENTS RECORD AND JOURNAL ENTRIES

On April 1, the Fitzgibbons Furniture Repair Shop established a petty cash fund of $200.00. The following cash payments were made from the petty cash fund during the first two weeks of April. The fund was replenished to the $200.00 level on April 16.

Apr.	1	Paid $5.28 for postage due on a package received. Petty Cash Voucher No. 10.
	5	Made a $25.00 contribution to the Washington Township Baseball League. Petty Cash Voucher No. 11.
	6	Reimbursed $6.25 to an employee for phone calls made from a pay telephone. Petty Cash Voucher No. 12.
	8	Paid $22.00 for office supplies. Petty Cash Voucher No. 13.
	10	Paid $32.00 for a newspaper advertisement. Petty Cash Voucher No. 14.
	12	Paid $33.00 for gas and an oil change for the company truck. Petty Cash Voucher No. 15.
	14	Paid $20.00 for postage stamps. Petty Cash Voucher No. 16.
	15	Made a $25.00 contribution to the Girl Scouts. Petty Cash Voucher No. 17.

Required:

1. Prepare the journal entry to establish the petty cash fund.
2. Enter the above payments in the petty cash payments record provided on page 113.
3. Prove the petty cash payments record.
4. Prepare the journal entry to replenish the fund on April 16.

Problem 8 (Continued)
2. and 3.

PETTY CASH PAYMENTS FOR MONTH OF 20-- PAGE 1

					DISTRIBUTION OF PAYMENTS								
	DAY	DESCRIPTION	VOU NO.	TOTAL AMOUNT	TRUCK EXPENSE	POSTAGE EXPENSE	CHARIT. CONTRIB. EXPENSE	TELE. EXPENSE	OFFICE SUPPLIES	ADVERT. EXPENSE	ACCOUNT	AMOUNT	
1													1
2													2
3													3
4													4
5													5
6													6
7													7
8													8
9													9
10													10
11													11
12													12
13													13
14													14
15													15
16													16
17													17
18													18
19													19
20													20
21													21
22													22

Problem 8 (Concluded)
1. and 4.

GENERAL JOURNAL

PAGE 1

	DATE		DESCRIPTION	POST. REF.	DEBIT	CREDIT	
1							1
2							2
3							3
4							4
5							5
6							6
7							7
8							8
9							9
10							10
11							11
12							12

Problem 9 (LO4) CASH SHORT AND OVER JOURNAL ENTRIES

Mackie's Salon deposits cash weekly. A record of cash register receipts for the month of April is shown below. A change fund of $100 is maintained.

Apr.	2	Cash in drawer:	$298.00	Cash register amount:	$196.50
	9		286.50		192.00
	16		293.50		193.50
	23		306.00		204.50
	30		301.50		203.00

Required:

Prepare weekly journal entries for cash receipts from service fees, showing cash short and over when needed.

Problem 9 (Concluded)

GENERAL JOURNAL

PAGE 1

	DATE	DESCRIPTION	POST. REF.	DEBIT	CREDIT	
1						1
2						2
3						3
4						4
5						5
6						6
7						7
8						8
9						9
10						10
11						11
12						12
13						13
14						14
15						15
16						16
17						17
18						18
19						19
20						20
21						21
22						22
23						23
24						24
25						25
26						26
27						27
28						28
29						29
30						30
31						31
32						32

CHAPTER 8
PAYROLL ACCOUNTING: EMPLOYEE EARNINGS AND DEDUCTIONS

LEARNING OBJECTIVES

Payroll accounting is an important part of any business, partly because it is such a significant expense and partly because so many laws govern its record keeping. In Chapter 8, we examine the payroll records that employers are required to keep and also those records that are maintained for administrative efficiency.

Objective 1. Distinguish between employees and independent contractors.

An **employee** is one who works under the control and direction of an employer. The employer controls how and when the job is to be done, determines working hours, and in general is responsible for all aspects of the employee's work. An **independent contractor**, on the other hand, performs a service for a fee and does not work under the control and direction of the company paying for his or her service. This is an important distinction because employers are required to maintain payroll records and file many reports for their employees but must file only one form for independent contractors.

Objective 2. Calculate employee earnings and deductions.

Three steps are required to determine how much to pay an employee for a pay period. Calculate the employee's total earnings for the pay period, determine the amounts of deductions for the same pay period, and subtract deductions from total earnings. The deductions may be required by law—for example, Social Security and Medicare taxes and federal and state income taxes—or by agreement with the employer—for example, insurance deductions and savings bond deductions.

Objective 3. Describe and prepare payroll records.

Three types of payroll records are used to accumulate required information for federal and state tax purposes: the payroll register, the payroll check with earnings statement attached, and the employee earnings record.

The **payroll register** is a multi-column form that accumulates the necessary data to prepare the journal entry. Detailed information on earnings, taxable earnings, deductions, and net pay is provided for each employee and for the employees in total.

The **payroll check** is prepared from information in the payroll register. The detachable earnings statement attached to the employee's check shows the gross earnings, total deductions, and net pay.

A separate record of each employee's earnings is called an **employee earnings record.** This information is also obtained from the payroll register. The earnings record is designed so that quarterly and annual totals can be accumulated in order for the employer to prepare several reports.

Objective 4. Account for employee earnings and deductions.

The payroll register provides all the information needed to prepare the journal entry for any pay period. The total gross earnings is debited to a wages and salaries expense account, and each deduction is credited to a current liability account. The difference between gross earnings and total deductions is called **net pay** and is credited to Cash.

Objective 5. Describe various payroll record-keeping methods.

In addition to a manual system of preparing all the necessary payroll records, payroll processing centers and electronic systems can be used to prepare the same records.

A **payroll processing center** is a business that sells payroll record-keeping services. An **electronic system** is a computer system based on a software package that performs all payroll record keeping and prepares payroll checks.

REVIEW QUESTIONS

Instructions: Analyze each of the following items carefully before writing your answer in the column at the right.

	Question	Answer
LO 1	**1.** A(n) ________ is one who works under the control and direction of an employer.	________
LO 1	**2.** A(n) ________ performs a service for a fee and does not work under the control and direction of the company paying for the service.	________
LO 2	**3.** What three steps are required to determine how much to pay an employee for a pay period?	________ ________ ________
LO 2	**4.** Compensation for managerial or administrative services, normally expressed in biweekly, monthly, or annual terms, is called ________.	________
LO 2	**5.** Compensation for skilled or unskilled labor, normally expressed in terms of hours, weeks, or units produced, is called ________.	________
LO 2	**6.** When compensation is based on time, ________ are helpful for keeping a record of the time worked by each employee.	________
LO 2	**7.** An employee's total earnings is also called ________.	________
LO 2	**8.** An employee's total earnings less all the deductions is called ______.	________
LO 2	**9.** What are the three major categories of deductions from an employee's paycheck?	________ ________ ________
LO 2	**10.** David Astin is married with two children, holds only one job, and has a spouse who is not employed. What number of withholding allowances is Astin entitled to claim, assuming that he does not anticipate large itemized deductions?	________

LO 2 11. Upon employment, each employee is required to furnish the employer a Form ________ that details, among other things, the number of withholding allowances and marital status. .... ______________________

LO 2 12. Name the four factors that determine the amount to be withheld from an employee's gross pay each pay period. .... ______________________

____

____

____

LO 3 13. A form used to assemble the data required at the end of each payroll period is called a(n) ________. .... ______________________

LO 3 14. A method of payment in which the employee's net pay is placed directly in the employee's bank account is called a(n) ________. ..... ______________________

LO 3 15. A separate, detailed record of each employee's earnings is called a(n) ________ . ... ______________________

LO 5 16. Name two approaches in addition to a manual system used to accumulate and record payroll information. .... ______________________

____

EXERCISES

Exercise 1 (LO 2) COMPUTING OVERTIME PAY RATE

Lu-yin Cheng receives a regular salary of $2,500 a month and is entitled to overtime pay at the rate of 1½ times the regular hourly rate for any time worked in excess of 40 hours per week. Compute Cheng's overtime hourly rate.

Exercise 2 (LO 2) COMPUTING GROSS PAY

Roger Watkins earns a regular hourly rate of $12.50 and receives time and a half for any time worked over 8 hours per weekday. Roger earns double time for hours worked on Saturday or Sunday. During the past week, Roger worked 8 hours each day Monday through Wednesday, 5 hours on Thursday, 12 hours on Friday, and 6 hours on Saturday. Compute Watkins's gross pay.

Exercise 3 (LO 2) COMPUTING NET PAY

Bill Burry is married, has three children, and claims five withholding allowances for federal income tax purposes. Burry's gross pay for the week was $683.00. Using the federal income tax withholding tables provided in Figure 8-4 of the text and the information provided below, compute Burry's net pay for the week.

(a) Social Security tax rate is 6.2% (Burry's prior earnings equaled $23,455.00).
(b) Medicare tax rate is 1.45%.
(c) State income tax is 2% of gross earnings.
(d) City income tax is 1% of gross earnings.
(e) Contribution to pension plan is $25.00.
(f) Health insurance deduction is $8.50.

Exercise 4 (LO 4) JOURNALIZING PAYROLL TRANSACTIONS

Using the information provided in Exercise 3, enter the payment of Bill Burry's wages in a general journal. Assume a pay period ending on July 31, 20--.

GENERAL JOURNAL

PAGE 1

	DATE		DESCRIPTION	POST. REF.	DEBIT	CREDIT	
1							1
2							2
3							3
4							4
5							5
6							6
7							7
8							8
9							9
10							10

Exercise 5 (LO 3, 4) PAYROLL JOURNAL ENTRIES

The following data were taken from the payroll register of United Processors as of May 14, 20--.

Regular earnings	$6,516.00
Overtime earnings	710.00
Total earnings	______
Deductions:	
Federal income tax	______
Social Security tax	448.01
Medicare tax	104.78
Pension plan	134.00
Health insurance	260.00
United Way	190.00
Net pay	$5,394.21

Required:

1. Determine the missing amounts.
2. Prepare the journal entry for the payroll, crediting Cash for the net pay.

1.

____

____

____

____

Exercise 5 (Concluded)

2.

GENERAL JOURNAL

PAGE

	DATE		DESCRIPTION	POST. REF.	DEBIT	CREDIT	
1							1
2							2
3							3
4							4
5							5
6							6
7							7
8							8
9							9
10							10
11							11
12							12

PROBLEMS

Problem 6 (LO 2, 3, 4) PAYROLL REGISTER AND PAYROLL JOURNAL ENTRIES

Earl Wilson operates a business known as Wilson Enterprises. Listed below are the name, number of allowances claimed, marital status, total hours worked, and hourly rate of each employee. All hours worked in excess of 40 a week are paid for at the rate of time and a half.

The employer uses a weekly federal income tax withholding table. A portion of this weekly table is provided in Chapter 8 of your textbook. Social Security tax is withheld at the rate of 6.2%, Medicare tax is withheld at the rate of 1.45%, state income tax is withheld at the rate of 3.5%, and city earnings tax is withheld at the rate of 1%. O'Connor, Perez, Scalia, and Stephens each have $15.00 withheld this payday for group life insurance. Each employee, except Marshall, has $5.00 withheld for health insurance. All of the employees use payroll deduction to the credit union for varying amounts as listed below. Bertucci, Perez, and White each have $18.25 withheld this payday under a savings bond purchase plan.

Wilson Enterprises follows the practice of drawing a single check for the net amount of the payroll and depositing the check in a special payroll account at the bank. Individual paychecks are then drawn for the amount due each employee. The checks issued this payday were numbered consecutively beginning with Check No. 531.

Wilson Enterprises
Payroll Information for the Week Ended January 15, 20--

Name	Allow-ances	Marital Status	Total Hours Worked	Regular Hourly Rate	Credit Union Deposit	Cumul. Earnings thru 1/8
Bertucci, Harry	3	M	45	$12.00	$114.00	$525.00
Brennan, Joyce	4	M	50	10.00	110.00	480.00
Marshall, Teddy	3	M	43	11.00	97.90	500.00
O'Connor, Sandra	2	S	48	11.00	114.40	625.00
Perez, Lucy	3	M	43	13.00	115.70	730.00
Rehnquist, Willie	5	M	40	17.00	136.00	850.00
Scalia, Tonya	2	S	38	9.00	68.40	425.00
Stephens, J. P.	4	M	47	11.00	111.10	635.00
White, Bryan	1	S	60	10.00	140.00	615.00

Required:

1. Prepare a payroll register for Wilson Enterprises for the pay period ended January 15, 20--. Use the form provided on pages 124–125. (In the Taxable Earnings/Unemployment Compensation column, enter the same amounts as in the Social Security column.)
2. Assuming that the wages for the week ended January 15 were paid on January 17, enter the payment in the general journal provided on page 125.

Problem 6 (Continued)
1.

PAYROLL REGISTER

	NAME	EMP. NO.	NO. ALLOW.	MARIT. STATUS	EARNINGS				TAXABLE EARNINGS	
					REGULAR	OVERTIME	TOTAL	CUMULATIVE TOTAL	UNEMPLOY. COMP.	SOCIAL SECURITY
1										
2										
3										
4										
5										
6										
7										
8										
9										
10										
11										
12										
13										
14										

Name ______________________________

Problem 6 (Continued)

FOR PERIOD ENDED 20--

FEDERAL INC. TAX	SOC. SEC. TAX	MEDICARE TAX	STATE INC. TAX	CITY EARN. TAX	LIFE INS.	HEALTH INS.	CREDIT UNION	OTHER	TOTAL	NET PAY	CK. NO.	
												1
												2
												3
												4
												5
												6
												7
												8
												9
												10
												11
												12
												13
												14

2.

GENERAL JOURNAL

PAGE 1

	DATE	DESCRIPTION	POST. REF.	DEBIT	CREDIT	
1						1
2						2
3						3
4						4
5						5
6						6
7						7
8						8
9						9
10						10
11						11
12						12
13						13

Problem 7 (LO 3) EMPLOYEE EARNINGS RECORD

The current employee earnings record for Joyce Brennan is provided below and on page 127. Using the information provided in Problem 6, update Brennan's earnings record to reflect the January 15 payroll. Although this information should have been entered earlier, complete the required information at the bottom of the earnings record. The necessary information is provided below.

Name:	Joyce W. Brennan
Address:	422 Long Plain Rd. Leverett, MA 01054
Employee No.:	2
Gender:	Female
Department:	Sanitation
Occupation:	Janitor
S.S. No.:	336-56-7534
Marital Status:	Married
Allowances:	4
Pay Rate:	$10.00 per hour
Birth Date:	7/6/69
Date Employed:	6/22/--

EMPLOYEE EARNINGS RECORD

20 -- PERIOD ENDED	EARNINGS: REGULAR	OVERTIME	TOTAL	CUMULATIVE TOTAL	TAXABLE EARNINGS: UNEMPLOY. COMP.	SOCIAL SECURITY	DEDUCTIONS: FEDERAL INCOME TAX	SOCIAL SECURITY TAX
Jan. 1	200 00		200 00	200 00	200 00	200 00	0 00	12 40
8	280 00		280 00	480 00	280 00	280 00	0 00	17 36

GENDER	DEPARTMENT	OCCUPATION	SOCIAL SECURITY NO.	MARITAL STATUS	ALLOW-ANCES
M F					

Problem 7 (Concluded)

FOR PERIOD ENDED 20--

DEDUCTIONS																				
MEDICARE TAX		STATE INCOME TAX		CITY EARNINGS TAX		LIFE INSUR.		HEALTH INSUR.		CREDIT UNION		OTHER			TOTAL		NET PAY		CK. NO.
2	90	7	00	2	00			5	00	40	00				69	30	130	70	321
4	06	9	80	2	80			5	00	56	00				95	02	184	98	422

PAY RATE	DATE OF BIRTH	DATE HIRED	NAME/ADDRESS	EMP. NO.

CHAPTER 9
PAYROLL ACCOUNTING:
EMPLOYER TAXES AND REPORTS

LEARNING OBJECTIVES

Chapter 8 discussed taxes levied on the employee and withheld by the employer. None of these taxes was an expense of the employer. In Chapter 9, we examine several taxes that represent an additional payroll expense imposed directly on the employer.

Objective 1. Describe and calculate employer payroll taxes.

Most employers are subject to a matching portion of the Social Security and Medicare taxes and to federal and state unemployment taxes. The employer's **Social Security and Medicare taxes** are levied on employers at the same rates and on the same bases as the employee Social Security and Medicare taxes. The **FUTA** tax is levied only on employers. The purpose of this tax is to raise funds to administer the federal/state unemployment compensation program. The **SUTA** tax is also levied only on employers. The purpose of this tax is to raise funds to pay unemployment benefits.

The Social Security, FUTA, and SUTA taxes are calculated from the accumulated amounts found in the Taxable Earnings columns in the payroll register. The Medicare tax is calculated from the Earnings—Total column.

Objective 2. Account for employer payroll taxes expense.

To journalize employer payroll taxes, debit the total of the employer Social Security, Medicare, FUTA, and SUTA taxes to a single account entitled Payroll Taxes Expense. The liabilities for the Social Security, Medicare, FUTA, and SUTA taxes payable normally are credited to separate accounts. The general format of this entry appears below.

Payroll Taxes Expense	xx	
Social Security Tax Payable		xx
Medicare Tax Payable		xx
FUTA Tax Payable		xx
SUTA Tax Payable		xx

Objective 3. Describe employer reporting and payment responsibilities.

Employer payroll reporting and payment responsibilities fall in six areas.

1. Federal income tax withholding and Social Security and Medicare taxes
2. FUTA taxes
3. SUTA taxes
4. Employee Wage and Tax Statement (Form W-2)
5. Summary of employee wages and taxes (Form W-3)
6. Employment eligibility notification (Form I-9)

The due date for federal income tax withholding and Social Security and Medicare taxes varies, depending on the amount of these taxes. Deposits are made using EFTPS or Form 8109. In addition, a Form 941 must be completed each quarter and filed with the IRS.

The federal unemployment taxes must be computed on a quarterly basis. In addition, Form 940 must be filed with the IRS by the beginning of the second week of February.

Deposit rules and forms for state unemployment taxes vary among the states. Deposits usually are required on a quarterly basis.

Employers must furnish each employee with a Wage and Tax Statement (Form W-2) by January 31 of each year. Information needed to complete this form is contained in the employee earnings records. The employer also must file Form W-3 with the Social Security Administration by the last day of February. This form summarizes the employee earnings and tax information from Forms W-2.

The purpose of Form I-9 is to document that each employee is authorized to work in the United States. It must be completed by the employee and employer and retained by the employer.

Objective 4. Describe and account for workers' compensation insurance.

Workers' compensation insurance provides insurance for employees who suffer a job-related illness or injury. The cost of the insurance depends on the number of employees, the riskiness of the job, and the company's accident history. The employer usually pays the premium at the beginning of the year, based on the estimated annual payroll, and makes an adjustment at the end of the year when the actual annual payroll is known.

REVIEW QUESTIONS

Instructions: Analyze each of the following items carefully before writing your answer in the column at the right.

	Question	Answer
LO 1	**1.** Name the four payroll taxes paid by the employer.	________________ ________________ ________________ ________________
LO 1	**2.** The textbook uses a Social Security tax rate of 6.2% applied to maximum employee earnings of ________.	________________
LO 1	**3.** The ________ is a key source of information for computing employer payroll taxes.	________________
LO 1	**4.** Individuals who own and run their own business are considered ____.	________________
LO 1	**5.** The law requires persons earning net self-employment income of $400 or more to pay a(n) ________.	________________
LO 1	**6.** The textbook uses a FUTA tax rate of 0.8% applied to maximum employee earnings of ________.	________________
LO 2	**7.** When journalizing the employer's payroll taxes, debit the total of the employer Social Security, Medicare, FUTA, and SUTA taxes to a single account entitled ________.	________________
LO 3	**8.** Name the three taxes that are associated with Form 941.	________________ ________________ ________________
LO 3	**9.** In addition to making quarterly deposits, employers are required to file an annual report of federal unemployment tax on Form ________.	________________
LO 3	**10.** By January 31 of each year, employers must furnish each employee with a(n) ________.	________________

LO 3 11. ________ documents that an employee is authorized to work in the United States. .... ______________________

LO 4 12. ________ provides insurance for employees who suffer a job-related illness or injury. .... ______________________

EXERCISES

Exercise 1 (LO 1) CALCULATION OF EMPLOYER PAYROLL TAXES

Sylvania Bookstore pays a SUTA tax of 5.4% and a FUTA tax of 0.8%. The total taxable wages for unemployment compensation on a certain payday amount to $16,800. Compute the unemployment taxes payable to the state and federal government.

Exercise 2 (LO 2) CALCULATION OF PAYROLL TAXES AND PREPARATION OF JOURNAL ENTRIES

The Totals line from Wong Drug Store's payroll register for the week ended December 31, 20--, is shown on pages 132 and 133.

Payroll taxes are imposed as follows:

Social Security tax	6.2%
Medicare tax	1.45%
FUTA tax	0.8%
SUTA tax	5.4%

Required:

1. Prepare the journal entry for payment of this payroll on December 31, 20--.
2. Prepare the journal entry for the employer's payroll taxes for the period ended December 31, 20--.

Exercise 2 (Continued)

PAYROLL REGISTER

	NAME	EMPL. NO.	NO. ALLOW.	MARIT. STATUS	EARNINGS				TAXABLE EARNINGS	
					REGULAR	OVERTIME	TOTAL	CUMULATIVE TOTAL	UNEMPLOY. COMP.	SOCIAL SECURITY
1	Totals				4,200 00	500 00	4,700 00	203,700 00	300 00	3,600 00
2										
3										
4										
5										
6										
7										
8										
9										
10										

1. and 2.

GENERAL JOURNAL

PAGE 1

	DATE		DESCRIPTION	POST. REF.	DEBIT	CREDIT	
1							1
2							2
3							3
4							4
5							5
6							6
7							7
8							8
9							9
10							10
11							11
12							12
13							13
14							14
15							15
16							16

Exercise 2 (Concluded)

FOR PERIOD ENDED December 31, 20--

DEDUCTIONS									
FEDERAL INC. TAX	SOC. SEC. TAX	MEDICARE TAX	HEALTH INS.	CREDIT UNION	OTHER	TOTAL	NET PAY	CK. NO.	
420 00	223 20	68 15	80 00	200 00		991 35	3,708 65		1
									2
									3
									4
									5
									6
									7
									8
									9
									10

Exercise 3 (LO1/2) TOTAL COST OF AN EMPLOYEE

Compute the total annual cost to an employer of employing a person whose gross salary is $45,000. (Assume a 5.4% state unemployment tax rate and a FUTA tax rate of 0.8%, both on the first $7,000 of earnings, an employer's Social Security tax rate of 6.2% on the first $106,800 of earnings and a Medicare tax rate of 1.45% on gross earnings.)

Exercise 4 (LO 3) JOURNAL ENTRIES FOR PAYMENT OF PAYROLL TAXES

The general ledger of GNU Co. includes the following accounts and balances related to payroll as of October 15 of the current year:

Social Security Tax Payable	$12,400
Medicare Tax Payable	2,900
FUTA Tax Payable	640
SUTA Tax Payable	4,320
Employee Income Tax Payable	7,780

Required:

Journalize the payment of the employee income taxes and Social Security and Medicare taxes on October 15, 20--, and the deposit of the FUTA and SUTA taxes on October 31, 20--.

GENERAL JOURNAL

PAGE

	DATE	DESCRIPTION	POST. REF.	DEBIT	CREDIT	
1						1
2						2
3						3
4						4
5						5
6						6
7						7
8						8
9						9
10						10
11						11
12						12
13						13
14						14

Exercise 5 (LO 4) WORKERS' COMPENSATION INSURANCE AND ADJUSTMENT

Curtis Company paid a premium of $360 for workers' compensation insurance based on the estimated payroll as of the beginning of the year. Based on actual payroll as of the end of the year, the actual premium is $397. Prepare the adjusting entry to reflect the underpayment of the insurance premium.

GENERAL JOURNAL PAGE 1

	DATE		DESCRIPTION	POST. REF.	DEBIT	CREDIT	
1							1
2							2
3							3
4							4
5							5

PROBLEMS

Problem 6 (LO 1/2) CALCULATING PAYROLL TAXES EXPENSE AND PREPARING JOURNAL ENTRY

A partial payroll register for the pay period ended August 31, 20--, is provided on the following page for the Astroscope Company.

Required:

1. Compute the total earnings subject to federal and state unemployment taxes and the Social Security tax by completing the Taxable Earnings columns of the payroll register.
2. Assume the company is in a state with an unemployment tax rate of 5.4% and a FUTA tax rate of 0.8%, both on the first $7,000 of earnings. The Social Security tax rate is 6.2% on the first $106,800 of earnings, and the Medicare tax rate is 1.45% on gross earnings. Compute the state and federal unemployment taxes and the Social Security and Medicare taxes on the lines provided on page 136.
3. Prepare the entry for the employer's payroll taxes in the general journal provided on page 137.

Problem 6 (Continued)

1.

PAYROLL REGISTER

	NAME	NO. ALLOW.	MARIT. STATUS	EARNINGS REGULAR	EARNINGS OVERTIME	EARNINGS TOTAL	EARNINGS CUMULATIVE TOTAL	TAXABLE EARNINGS UNEMPLOY. COMP.	TAXABLE EARNINGS SOCIAL SECURITY
1	Coolie, Betty					350 00	7,150 00		
2	Covar, Mike					200 00	6,800 00		
3	Hagen, Frank					375 00	6,200 00		
4	Gutierrez, Bob					1,540 00	47,300 00		
5	Moten, Alice					1,500 00	50,500 00		
6	Rice, Darlene					3,300 00	109,700 00		
7									

2.

Problem 6 (Concluded)

3.

GENERAL JOURNAL PAGE 1

	DATE		DESCRIPTION	POST. REF.	DEBIT	CREDIT	
1							1
2							2
3							3
4							4
5							5
6							6
7							7
8							8
9							9

Problem 7 (LO 2/3) JOURNALIZING AND POSTING PAYROLL ENTRIES

Rock Creek Company has five employees. All are paid on a monthly basis. The fiscal year of the business is March 1 to February 28. Payroll taxes are imposed as follows:

Social Security tax to be withheld from employees' wages and imposed on the employer, 6.2% each on the first $106,800 of earnings.

Medicare tax to be withheld from employees' wages and imposed on the employer, 1.45% each on gross earnings.

SUTA tax imposed on the employer, 5.4% on the first $7,000 of earnings.

FUTA tax imposed on the employer, 0.8% on the first $7,000 of earnings.

The accounts kept by Rock Creek Company include the following:

Account Number	Title	Balance on March 1
101	Cash	$62,500.00
211	Employee Income Tax Payable	3,375.00
212	Social Security Tax Payable	4,740.00
213	Medicare Tax Payable	1,110.00
218	Savings Bond Deductions Payable	1,200.00
221	FUTA Tax Payable	525.00
222	SUTA Tax Payable	2,670.00
511	Wages and Salaries Expense	0.00
530	Payroll Taxes Expense	0.00

Problem 7 (Continued)

Following is a narrative of selected transactions relating to payrolls and payroll taxes that occurred during the months of March and April:

Mar.	15	Paid $9,225.00 covering the following February taxes:		
		Employee income tax withheld		$3,375.00
		Social Security tax		4,740.00
		Medicare tax		1,110.00
		Total		$9,225.00
	31	March payroll:		
		Total wages and salaries expense		$39,000.00
		Less amounts withheld:		
		Employee income tax	$3,690.00	
		Social Security tax	2,418.00	
		Medicare tax	565.50	
		Savings bond deductions payable	1,200.00	7,873.50
		Net amount paid		$31,126.50
	31	Purchased savings bonds for employees, $2,400.00		
	31	Data for completing employer's payroll taxes expense for March:		
		Social Security taxable wages		$39,000.00
		Unemployment taxable wages		12,000.00
Apr.	15	Paid $9,657.00 covering the following March taxes:		
		Employee income tax payable		$ 3,690.00
		Social Security tax		4,836.00
		Medicare tax		1,131.00
	30	Paid SUTA tax for the quarter, $3,318.00		
	30	Paid FUTA tax, $621.00		

Required:

1. Using a general journal, journalize the preceding transactions.
2. Open T accounts for the payroll expense and liabilities. Enter the beginning balances and post the transactions recorded in the journal.

Name ____________________

Problem 7 (Continued)

1.

GENERAL JOURNAL

PAGE

	DATE		DESCRIPTION	POST. REF.	DEBIT	CREDIT	
1							1
2							2
3							3
4							4
5							5
6							6
7							7
8							8
9							9
10							10
11							11
12							12
13							13
14							14
15							15
16							16
17							17
18							18
19							19
20							20
21							21
22							22
23							23
24							24
25							25
26							26
27							27
28							28
29							29
30							30

Problem 7 (Continued)

GENERAL JOURNAL

PAGE

	DATE		DESCRIPTION	POST. REF.	DEBIT	CREDIT	
1							1
2							2
3							3
4							4
5							5
6							6
7							7
8							8
9							9
10							10
11							11
12							12
13							13
14							14

2.

Cash 101

Employee Income Tax Payable 211

Social Security Tax Payable 212

Medicare Tax Payable 213

Problem 7 (Concluded)

Savings Bond Deductions Payable 218

FUTA Tax Payable 221

SUTA Tax Payable 222

Wages and Salaries Expense 511

Payroll Taxes Expense 530

Problem 8 (LO 4) WORKERS' COMPENSATION INSURANCE AND ADJUSTMENT

Jackson Manufacturing estimated its total payroll for the coming year to be $630,000. The workers' compensation insurance premium rate is 0.35%.

Required:

1. Calculate the estimated workers' compensation insurance premium and prepare the journal entry for the payment as of January 2, 20--.
2. Assume Jackson Manufacturing's actual payroll for the year is $658,000. Calculate the total insurance premium owed. Prepare a journal entry as of December 31, 20--, to record the adjustment for the underpayment. The actual payment of the additional insurance premium will take place in January of the next year.
3. Assume, instead, that Jackson Manufacturing's actual payroll for the year is $607,000. Prepare a journal entry as of December 31, 20--, for the total amount that should be refunded. The refund will not be received until the next year.

1., 2., and 3.

GENERAL JOURNAL PAGE 1

	DATE		DESCRIPTION	POST. REF.	DEBIT	CREDIT	
1							1
2							2
3							3
4							4
5							5
6							6
7							7
8							8
9							9
10							10
11							11
12							12
13							13
14							14

MODULE
ACCOUNTING FOR A PROFESSIONAL SERVICE BUSINESS: THE COMBINATION JOURNAL

LEARNING OBJECTIVES

The cash, modified cash, and accrual bases of accounting are illustrated in Chapter 5. In this module, we review the differences between the modified cash and accrual bases of accounting, and we use the modified cash basis of accounting throughout the module. The combination journal is used for journalizing all transactions for a professional service business. Posting from a combination journal to the general ledger is illustrated. As introduced previously, the work sheet and financial statements are also prepared following the transactions.

Objective 1. Explain the differences between the modified cash and accrual bases of accounting.

The accrual basis of accounting recognizes revenues when earned, regardless of when cash is received. Likewise, expenses are recognized when incurred, regardless of when cash is paid.

The modified cash basis is essentially the same as the accrual basis of accounting, except receivables are not recognized for revenues and payables are not used for operating expenses. Thus, three types of events are accounted for differently as shown below.

DIFFERENCES BETWEEN MODIFIED CASH AND ACCRUAL BASES OF ACCOUNTING

Event	Accrual Basis	Modified Cash Basis
Expenses Bills for services received, but not yet paid.	Expense Accounts Payable	No entry. (Record when paid.)
Wages earned by employees, but not yet paid.	Wages Expense Wages Payable	No entry. (Record when paid.)
Revenues Services provided on account.	Accounts Receivable Professional Fees	No entry. (Record when cash is received.)

Objective 2. Describe special records for a professional service business using the modified cash basis.

The modified cash basis is often used by small professional service businesses such as accounting, law, dentistry, medicine, and engineering. Since, under the modified cash basis, no adjusting entries are made for accrued wages expense and revenues from services performed on account are not recorded until cash is received, other records must be maintained. Two records commonly used are an appointment record and a client or patient ledger record.

Objective 3. Describe and use a combination journal to record transactions of a professional service business.

The combination journal saves time, space, and energy in recording transactions (in comparison to the general journal). It also reduces the possibility of error since totals, rather than numerous individual entries, are posted.

This is done by providing special columns for accounts frequently used. For example, the debits and credits to the cash account are posted only once—at the end of the month. Infrequently used accounts are entered in the General Debit column or the General Credit column. The Description column of a combination journal is used to enter the account titles for the General Debit and General Credit columns; to identify specific creditors when assets are purchased, or payments made, on account; to identify amounts forwarded; and to identify adjusting, closing, and reversing entries.

At the end of the accounting period, the sum of the debit columns should be compared with the sum of the credit columns to verify that they are equal. This is called proving the combination journal.

Objective 4. Post from the combination journal to the general ledger.

Accounts that have been debited or credited in the general columns are posted individually from the combination journal. "CJ" and the page number are entered into the Posting Reference column of the general ledger account. Because individual items are posted, the totals of these columns are not posted, and check marks in parentheses are placed under the column totals.

Special columns are totaled and posted at the end of the accounting period. The account number is written in parentheses under the special column to show that the total has been posted.

The **cash balance** can be computed at any time during the month. The beginning balance (of the cash account) is added to the Cash debits (to date); the Cash credits (to date) are subtracted.

Objective 5. Prepare a work sheet, financial statements, and adjusting and closing entries for a professional service business.

When the combination journal has been posted to the general ledger, the end-of-period work sheet and financial statements are prepared in the same way as described in Chapters 5 and 6. By using the Description and General Debit and General Credit columns, adjusting and closing entries are made in the combination journal in the same manner demonstrated for the general journal in Chapter 6.

REVIEW QUESTIONS

Instructions: Analyze each of the following items carefully before writing your answer in the column at the right.

		Question	Answer
LO 1	**1.**	In the ________ basis of accounting, revenues are recorded when earned and expenses are recorded when incurred, regardless of when cash is received or paid.	________________
LO 1	**2.**	The ________ basis of accounting uses the cash basis for revenues and most expenses.	________________
LO 1	**3.**	Many small professional ________ businesses use the modified cash basis of accounting.	________________
LO 3	**4.**	Time and space are saved when a journal contains ________ columns for cash debits and cash credits, rather than posting each transaction separately.	________________
LO 3	**5.**	When accounts are used infrequently, the ________ column and the ________ column are used for individual postings.	________________ ________________
LO 3	**6.**	A journal with special columns and general columns is called a(n) ________ journal.	________________

LO 3 **7.** The ________ column of a combination journal is used to enter the account titles for the General Debit and General Credit columns; to identify specific creditors when assets are purchased, or payments made, on account; to identify amounts forwarded; and to identify adjusting, closing, and reversing entries. .... ______________________

LO 3 **8.** At the end of the month, all columns of the combination journal are ________, and the sums of the debit columns are compared with the sums of the credit columns. .... ______________________

LO 3 **9.** Totaling and ruling the columns and comparing totals is the process of ________ the combination journal. .... ______________________

LO 4 **10.** When posting from the combination journal, the letters "________" are used. .... ______________________

LO 4 **11.** The cash balance at any time during the month is found by adding ________ to the beginning balance and subtracting ________ to date. ______________________

____

EXERCISES

Exercise 1 (LO 1) MODIFIED CASH BASIS OF ACCOUNTING

In the space provided, indicate which account is debited and which account is credited, using the **modified cash basis** of accounting. If no entry is made, write "No Entry."

1. Paid electricity bill, $50.

2. Purchased office equipment for $500, on account.

3. Revenue for week: $500 cash, $200 on account.

4. Wages earned but not paid, $500.

5. Made payment on office equipment previously purchased, $25.

Exercise 2 (LO 1) ACCRUAL BASIS OF ACCOUNTING

In the space provided, indicate which account is debited and which account is credited, using the **accrual basis** of accounting. If no entry is made, write "No Entry."

1. Purchased supplies (prepaid asset), $500, on account.

2. Revenue for week: $400 cash, $250 on account.

3. Wages earned but not paid, $250.

Exercise 2 (Concluded)

4. Made payment on account, $50, for supplies previously purchased.

____

____

5. Depreciation on long-term assets, $300.

____

____

Exercise 3 (LO 3) SPECIAL COLUMNS FOR A COMBINATION JOURNAL

Ray Elkton is opening a delivery service. He owns a used van and will use it for deliveries. He has a part-time worker who is paid once a week. He receives delivery fees every three or four days and runs ads in the newspaper daily. Recommend to him which accounts should have **special columns** in a combination journal and give him three reasons why he should use a combination journal instead of a general journal.

Special Columns: ____

____

Reasons:

1. ____
2. ____
3. ____

PROBLEMS

Problem 4 (LO 1) MODIFIED CASH AND ACCRUAL BASES

Mark Mosley has his own consulting business. Listed below are selected transactions from the month of April.

Apr.	1	Paid office rent, $500.
	2	Purchased office supplies, $250.
	3	Purchased office equipment on account, $1,000.
	4	Earned consulting fees: $400 cash, $150 on account.
	5	Paid telephone bill, $48.
	6	Purchased one-year insurance policy, $200.
	7	Paid $100 on account (for office equipment previously purchased).
	8	Received $150 on account from a customer (previously owed).
	9	Depreciation on office equipment for month, $50.

Required:
Record the transactions in the space provided, using:

1. the modified cash basis
2. the accrual basis

To save space, don't enter the descriptions for each entry.

Problem 4 (Continued)

1. Modified Cash Basis

GENERAL JOURNAL

PAGE

	DATE		DESCRIPTION	POST. REF.	DEBIT	CREDIT	
1							1
2							2
3							3
4							4
5							5
6							6
7							7
8							8
9							9
10							10
11							11
12							12
13							13
14							14
15							15
16							16
17							17
18							18
19							19
20							20
21							21
22							22
23							23
24							24
25							25
26							26
27							27
28							28
29							29
30							30

Name ____________________ **Module** SG M-7

Problem 4 (Concluded)

2. Accrual Basis

GENERAL JOURNAL

PAGE

	DATE		DESCRIPTION	POST. REF.	DEBIT	CREDIT	
1							1
2							2
3							3
4							4
5							5
6							6
7							7
8							8
9							9
10							10
11							11
12							12
13							13
14							14
15							15
16							16
17							17
18							18
19							19
20							20
21							21
22							22
23							23
24							24
25							25
26							26
27							27
28							28
29							29
30							30

Problem 5 (LO 3) JOURNAL ENTRIES USING A COMBINATION JOURNAL

Marilyn Davis is the owner of Davis Interior Designing that offers advice to clients wishing to decorate their homes. Listed below are representative transactions for the month of February.

Feb.	1	Issued a check for $500 to Pedro Rodriguez for the February office rent.
	3	Received $300 for services rendered to Linda Johnson.
	5	Issued a check for $800 to Maxwell's Office Supply to purchase office equipment.
	10	Invested $5,000 additional cash in the business.
	28	Issued a check for $400 to Homer Utilities in payment of electric and water bill.
	28	Issued a check for $200 to Buck's Furniture for payment on office furniture previously purchased.

Required:

1. Davis uses the **modified cash basis** of accounting. Enter the above transactions in the combination journal shown below and on page M-9.
2. Total and prove the combination journal.

1. and 2.

COMBINATION

	DATE		CASH DEBIT	CASH CREDIT	DESCRIPTION	POST. REF.	
1							1
2							2
3							3
4							4
5							5
6							6
7							7
8							8
9							9
10							10
11							11
12							12
13							13
14							14

Name ______________________________

Problem 5 (LO 3) (Concluded)

Proving the Combination Journal:

JOURNAL

PAGE

	GENERAL DEBIT	GENERAL CREDIT	CLIENT FEES CREDIT	RENT EXPENSE DEBIT	UTILITIES EXPENSE DEBIT	
1						1
2						2
3						3
4						4
5						5
6						6
7						7
8						8
9						9
10						10
11						11
12						12
13						13
14						14

Problem 6 (LO3/4/5) JOURNALIZING AND POSTING TRANSACTIONS AND PREPARING A TRIAL BALANCE

Jolene Knight operates a cartographer's map service, Knight Maps. During the month of May, she entered the following transactions:

May	1	Issued a check for $400 to purchase new surveying equipment.
	3	Received a check for $900 from Diane Branam for surveying her property. Earned $1,500 on account from Troy Laakman.
	4	Issued a check for $600 to CFC Rental to pay May office rent.
	6	Purchased office supplies from Bynum Office Supply on account, $250.
	10	Received a check for $3,500 from B. Sims, a real estate developer, for surveying a new subdivision.
	12	Issued a check for $300 to Oscar Miller, a part-time secretary.
	15	Issued a check for $85 to Winona's Service Station for gas and oil for the business truck.
	16	Issued a check for $200 to Bynum Office Supply in payment on account.
	18	Issued a check for $150 to George Wilson, a part-time employee.
	20	Issued a check for $200 to Winona's Service Station for work done on a company truck.
	22	Issued a check for $100 to the American Cancer Society.
	25	Received a check for $1,500 from Troy Laakman for surveying work previously performed.
	30	Issued a check for $500 as a personal withdrawal from the business.
	31	Issued a check for $300 to Oscar Miller, a part-time secretary.

Required:

1. Using the **modified cash basis** of accounting, enter the above transactions in the combination journal provided on pages M-12–M-13.
2. Prove the combination journal.
3. Post the entries from the combination journal to the ledger accounts provided on pages M-13–M16.
4. Prepare a trial balance for Knight Maps as of May 31, 20--, to confirm accuracy of the debits and credits.

This page left intentionally blank.

Problem 6 (Continued)

1.

COMBINATION

	DATE		CASH DEBIT	CASH CREDIT	DESCRIPTION	POST. REF.	
1							1
2							2
3							3
4							4
5							5
6							6
7							7
8							8
9							9
10							10
11							11
12							12
13							13
14							14
15							15
16							16
17							17
18							18
19							19
20							20

2. Proving the Combination Journal:

Name ______________________________ **Module** SG M-13

Problem 6 (Continued)

JOURNAL PAGE 15

	GENERAL DEBIT	GENERAL CREDIT	CLIENT FEES CREDIT	WAGES EXPENSE DEBIT	TRUCK EXPENSE DEBIT	
1						1
2						2
3						3
4						4
5						5
6						6
7						7
8						8
9						9
10						10
11						11
12						12
13						13
14						14
15						15
16						16
17						17
18						18
19						19
20						20

3.

GENERAL LEDGER

ACCOUNT Cash ACCOUNT NO. 101

DATE		ITEM	POST. REF.	DEBIT	CREDIT	BALANCE DEBIT	BALANCE CREDIT
20-- May	1	Balance	✓			12,000 00	

Problem 6 (Continued)

ACCOUNT Office Supplies ACCOUNT NO. 142

DATE		ITEM	POST. REF.	DEBIT	CREDIT	BALANCE DEBIT	BALANCE CREDIT
20-- May	1	Balance	✓			1 0 0 00	

ACCOUNT Surveying Equipment ACCOUNT NO. 181

DATE		ITEM	POST. REF.	DEBIT	CREDIT	BALANCE DEBIT	BALANCE CREDIT
20-- May	1	Balance	✓			13 0 0 0 00	

ACCOUNT Accumulated Depreciation—Surveying Equipment ACCOUNT NO. 181.1

DATE		ITEM	POST. REF.	DEBIT	CREDIT	BALANCE DEBIT	BALANCE CREDIT

ACCOUNT Truck ACCOUNT NO. 185

DATE		ITEM	POST. REF.	DEBIT	CREDIT	BALANCE DEBIT	BALANCE CREDIT
20-- May	1	Balance	✓			12 0 0 0 00	

ACCOUNT Accumulated Depreciation—Truck ACCOUNT NO. 185.1

DATE		ITEM	POST. REF.	DEBIT	CREDIT	BALANCE DEBIT	BALANCE CREDIT

ACCOUNT Notes Payable ACCOUNT NO. 201

DATE		ITEM	POST. REF.	DEBIT	CREDIT	BALANCE DEBIT	BALANCE CREDIT
20-- May	1	Balance	✓				10 0 0 0 00

Problem 6 (Continued)

ACCOUNT Accounts Payable ACCOUNT NO. 202

DATE		ITEM	POST. REF.	DEBIT	CREDIT	BALANCE DEBIT	BALANCE CREDIT
20-- May	1	Balance	✓				2 0 0 00

ACCOUNT Jolene Knight, Capital ACCOUNT NO. 311

DATE		ITEM	POST. REF.	DEBIT	CREDIT	BALANCE DEBIT	BALANCE CREDIT
20 May	1	Balance	✓				12 7 0 0 00

ACCOUNT Jolene Knight, Drawing ACCOUNT NO. 312

DATE		ITEM	POST. REF.	DEBIT	CREDIT	BALANCE DEBIT	BALANCE CREDIT
20-- May	1	Balance	✓			1 0 0 0 00	

ACCOUNT Client Fees ACCOUNT NO. 401

DATE		ITEM	POST. REF.	DEBIT	CREDIT	BALANCE DEBIT	BALANCE CREDIT
20-- May	1	Balance	✓				12 0 0 0 00

ACCOUNT Wages Expense ACCOUNT NO. 511

DATE		ITEM	POST. REF.	DEBIT	CREDIT	BALANCE DEBIT	BALANCE CREDIT
20-- May	1	Balance	✓			4 0 0 0 00	

Problem 6 (Continued)

ACCOUNT Rent Expense ACCOUNT NO. 521

DATE		ITEM	POST. REF.	DEBIT	CREDIT	BALANCE DEBIT	BALANCE CREDIT
20-- May	1	Balance	✓			2,400.00	

ACCOUNT Truck Expense ACCOUNT NO. 526

DATE		ITEM	POST. REF.	DEBIT	CREDIT	BALANCE DEBIT	BALANCE CREDIT
20-- May	1	Balance	✓			800.00	

ACCOUNT Charitable Contributions Expense ACCOUNT NO. 534

DATE		ITEM	POST. REF.	DEBIT	CREDIT	BALANCE DEBIT	BALANCE CREDIT
20-- May	1	Balance	✓			400.00	

ACCOUNT Depreciation Expense—Surveying Equipment ACCOUNT NO. 541

DATE		ITEM	POST. REF.	DEBIT	CREDIT	BALANCE DEBIT	BALANCE CREDIT

ACCOUNT Depreciation Expense—Truck ACCOUNT NO. 542

DATE		ITEM	POST. REF.	DEBIT	CREDIT	BALANCE DEBIT	BALANCE CREDIT

Problem 6 (Concluded)

4.

____

____

____

ACCOUNT	ACCT. NO.	DEBIT BALANCE	CREDIT BALANCE

Problem 7 (LO 5) PREPARING A WORK SHEET, FINANCIAL STATEMENTS, ADJUSTING AND CLOSING ENTRIES

The work sheet for Charlotte Cruz, a financial planner, is shown on pages M-18–M-19. The Trial Balance columns have been completed. There were no additional investments by the owner. Adjustments are as follows:

(a) Prepaid insurance expired, $200.
(b) Unused office supplies on hand, $228.
(c) Depreciation expense—office equipment, $125.

Required:

1. Complete the work sheet.
2. Record the adjusting entries in the combination journal on pages M-22–M-23.
3. Prepare the income statement, statement of owner's equity, and balance sheet.
4. Record the closing entries in the combination journal on pages M-22–M-23.

Problem 7 (Continued)

1.

CRUZ FINANCIAL

WORK

FOR MONTH

	Account Title	Trial Balance Debit	Trial Balance Credit	Adjustments Debit	Adjustments Credit
1	Cash	3,082.00			
2	Office Supplies	628.00			
3	Prepaid Insurance	350.00			
4	Office Equipment	1,800.00			
5	Accum. Depr.—Office Equipment		250.00		
6	Accounts Payable		900.00		
7	Charlotte Cruz, Capital		3,000.00		
8	Charlotte Cruz, Drawing	100.00			
9	Planning Fees		3,026.00		
10	Wages Expense	800.00			
11	Rent Expense	300.00			
12	Office Supplies Expense				
13	Telephone Expense	52.00			
14	Electricity Expense	38.00			
15	Insurance Expense				
16	Depreciation Exp.—Office Equip.				
17	Miscellaneous Expense	26.00			
18		7,176.00	7,176.00		
19	Net Income				
20					
21					
22					
23					
24					
25					
26					
27					
28					
29					
30					
31					

Name ______________________________ **Module** SG M-19

Problem 7 (Continued)

PLANNING

SHEET

ENDED DECEMBER 31, 20--

ADJUSTED TRIAL BALANCE		INCOME STATEMENT		BALANCE SHEET		
DEBIT	CREDIT	DEBIT	CREDIT	DEBIT	CREDIT	
						1
						2
						3
						4
						5
						6
						7
						8
						9
						10
						11
						12
						13
						14
						15
						16
						17
						18
						19
						20
						21
						22
						23
						24
						25
						26
						27
						28
						29
						30
						31

Problem 7 (Continued)

3.

Problem 7 (Continued)

Problem 7 (Continued)

2. and 4.

COMBINATION

	DATE		CASH DEBIT	CASH CREDIT	DESCRIPTION	POST. REF.	
1							1
2							2
3							3
4							4
5							5
6							6
7							7
8							8
9							9
10							10
11							11
12							12
13							13
14							14
15							15
16							16
17							17
18							18
19							19
20							20
21							21
22							22
23							23
24							24
25							25
26							26
27							27
28							28

Name ______________________________ **Module** SG M-23

Problem 7 (Concluded)

JOURNAL

PAGE

	GENERAL		PLANNING FEES CREDIT	WAGES EXPENSE DEBIT	MISC. EXPENSE DEBIT	
	DEBIT	CREDIT				
1						1
2						2
3						3
4						4
5						5
6						6
7						7
8						8
9						9
10						10
11						11
12						12
13						13
14						14
15						15
16						16
17						17
18						18
19						19
20						20
21						21
22						22
23						23
24						24
25						25
26						26
27						27
28						28

Contents

Hewlett-Packard, Baker and Hughes, Verizon—*Applying your skills*

Chapter 12

Quicken—*Overview of compounding of money*

Kiplinger Magazine—*Magic of compounding*

Dow Jones—*Applying your skills*

Chapter 13

FedEx—*401k plans*

Dunkin' Donuts—*Power of compounding*

FSP Associates—*Applying your skills*

Chapter 14

U.S. Govt.—*Credit card overhaul bill*

Toyota, Ford—*Seven year car loans*

MasterCard—*Calculation of finance charges*

TrueCredit.com—*Applying your skills*

Chapter 15

Moody's Economy.com—*Home bailouts*

Credit Suisse, First American CoreLogic, HUD—*Home foreclosures*

Freddie Mac—*Mortgage rates*

Bankrate.com—*Closing costs*

Federal Reserve—*Mortgage refinancing*

Fannie Mae, Freddie Mac—*Applying your skills*

Chapter 16

Hershey—*Profit report*

Financial Executives International—*Sarbanes-Oxley Costs*

Kraft Foods—*International profit*

Nestlé, Unilever, Pepsi, Kraft, General Mills—*Sales and operating profit margin*

Bernard Madoff Investment Securities, Citigroup—*Applying your skills*

Chapter 17

General Motors, Honda, Toyota—*Residual values*

Avantair.com—*Bonus depreciation*

Dell—*Applying your skills*

Chapter 18

Sears Holdings Inc.—*Buy online and pickup at store in car*

Warner Bros.—*Controlling overhead*

Toyota—*Applying your skills*

Chapter 19

U.S. Commerce Dept.—*Controlling inventory*

Procter & Gamble—*Tax exempt*

Hertz Global Holdings—*Applying your skills*

Chapter 20

Travelers, State Farm Mutual Insurance—*Cutting back on insurance*

Safeco Corp., Nationwide Mutual, American Family, State Farm—*Auto insurance*

State Farm Mutual Insurance, Traveler's—*Low mileage discounts for auto insurance*

Insurance Research Council—*Applying your skills*

Chapter 21

Barrons—*The Dow Jones average*

Liz Claiborne—*Intro into stocks*

General Electric—*Reading stock quotes*

IBM, Alcoa, Merck, Pfizer—*Dividends*

Putnam Investments—*Mutual funds*

Macy's—*Applying your skills*

Chapter 22

Nickelodeon—*Revenues per household*

International Energy Agency—*Pie charts*

Toyota—*Applying your skills*

Academic Experts, Contributors

Eric Ball
Ellen Benowitz
Tom Bilyeu
Sylvia Brown
Richard Bruce
Lisa Bryde
Charles Bunn, Jr.
Linda Cress
Patrick Cunningham
Stanley Dabrowski
Dorothy Dean
Michael Discello
Jacqueline Donovan
Mary Frey
Joe Hanson
Jennifer Herrera
Jeff Hong
Deanna Knight
Amy McAnally
Jeffrey Rabish
Stan Rickert
Lawrence Roman
Tim Samolis
Ellen Sawyer
Gabrielle Serrano
Jeneen Smith Sims
Margene Sunderland
Leslie Thompson
Judith Toland
Patricia Tyunaitis
Peter VanderWeyst

Special thanks to Sharon Meyer for all the help she provided in the revision of the text.

Company/*Applications*

Chapter 1

Dunkin'Donuts—*Problem solving*
Coca-Cola Co—*Reading, writing and rounding numbers*
Salary.com—*Rounding numbers*
Tootsie Roll Industries—*Dissecting word problems and rounding*
Flexcar/Zipcar—*Adding and subtracting whole numbers*
Starbucks—*Rounding all the way*
Hershey —*Subtraction of whole numbers*
United Airlines—*Multiplying and dividing whole numbers*
Disney, InGrid, Alarm.com, AT&T—*Applying your skills*

Chapter 2

Apple—*Fractions*
M&M's Mars—*Fractions and multiplication*
Google—*Adding and subtracting fractions*
Albertsons—*Dissecting word problems with fractions*
M&M's Mars—*Multiplying and dividing fractions*
IRS, Canyons Grand Summit, Four Seasons, Ritz Carlton, Stowe Mountain Lodge, Whiteface Lodge, Gap—*Applying your skills*

Chapter 3

Starbucks—*International currency*
American Airlines, Lufthansa—*Subtracting decimals*
Toyota—*Shortcuts for multiples of 10*
Gap, H&R Block, McDonald's, Roto-Rooter—*Applying your skills*

Chapter 4

Bank of America—*Overdraft fees*
Comerica Inc—*New social security debit cards*
Wells Fargo, Citigroup, Regions, Financial, Sun Trust, Key Corp, Fifth Third PNC Financial, U.S. Bancorp, BB&T, Capital One—*Stress test by government*
HSBC Holdings, First National of Nebraska, ING Group—*Online banking*
Bank of America, Apple, Wells Fargo, JPMorgan Chase, Banc Plus—*Applying your skills*

Chapter 5

Google—*Formulas*
McDonald's—*International sales*
Marvel Entertainment, Scholastic Inc—*Solving for the unknown*
Webmath.com—*Applying your skills*

Chapter 6

Chrysler Corp., Toyota—*Concept of percents*
Motorola, Coca-Cola, PepsiCo, Red Bull—*Concept of percents*
IRS—*Reading percents*
Apple—*Converting percents to decimal*
M&M's Mars—*Base, rate, and portion*
National Energy Assistance Directors Association—*Percent Increase and decrease*
National Association of Realtors—*Applying your skills*

Chapter 7

BillQ Plus, Rudder.com—*Insight into discounts*
Shopstyle.com, Glimpse.com, Anheuser-Busch—*Trade discounts*
McGraw-Hill Publishers—*Trade discount*
DHL, UPS, FedEx—*Freight terms*
Desa LLC,—*Freight costs*
Walmart, Folcroft, Enterprise, Target, Sears Holdings—*Applying your skills*

Chapter 8

Zara, Gap—*International retailing*
Gap—*Markup on cost and selling price*
Macy's, JCPenney, Lord & Taylor—*Applying your skills*

Chapter 9

Walt Disney Co.—*Layoffs*
Walmart—*Payroll settlement*
Yum Brands, McDonald's—*Labor laws*
Goodyear Tire & Rubber Co.—*Pay scales*
IRS—*Circular E tables*
FedEx, Janus Capital Group Inc.—*Applying your skills*

Chapter 10

Quiznos, Cold Stone Creamery, Curves, Domino's Pizza—*Intro to bad loans*
Citigroup, Wachovia, Bank of America, JPMorgan Chase—*Simple interest*
Cash and More, SIM Corp., Citigroup—*Applying your skills*

Chapter 11

JPMorgan Chase—*Short sales for financial troubled borrowers*
Goodyear—*Credit lines*
U.S. Treasury—*Buying treasuries*
Talbots, Bank of America, HSBC Holdings—*Credit lines*

FEATURES

Features students have told me have helped them the most.

Blueprint Aid Boxes

For the first eight chapters (not in Chapter 4), blueprint aid boxes are available to help you map out a plan to solve a word problem. I know that often the hardest thing to do in solving word problems is where to start. Use the blueprint as a model to get started.

Business Math Handbook

This reference guide contains all the tables found in the text. It makes homework, exams, etc. easier to deal with than flipping back and forth through the text.

Chapter Organizer

At the end of each chapter is a quick reference guide called the Chapter Organizer. Key points, formulas, and examples are provided. A list of vocabulary terms is also included, as well as Check Figures for Extra Practice Quizzes. All have page references. (A complete glossary is found at the end of the text.) Think of the chapter organizer as your set of notes and use it as a reference when doing homework problems, and to review before exams.

DVD-ROM

The DVD packaged with the text includes practice quizzes, links to Web sites listed in the Business Math Internet Resource Guide, the Excel® templates, PowerPoint, videocases, and tutorial videos—which cover all the Learning Unit Practice Quizzes and Summary Practice Tests.

The Business Math Web site

Visit the site at www.mhhe.com/slater10e and find the Internet Resource Guide with hot links, tutorials, practice quizzes, Excel® workbook and templates, and other study materials useful for the course.

Video Cases

There are seven video cases applying business math concepts to real companies such as American President Lines, FedEx, Noodles & Company, Washburn Guitars, Honda, Buycostume.com, and Federal Signal Corporation. These are included on the student DVD. Some background case information and assignment problems incorporating information on the companies are included at the end of Chapters 6, 7, 8, 9, 14, 16, and 21.

Compounding/Present Value Overlays

A set of color overlays are inserted in Chapter 13. These color graphics are intended to demonstrate for students the concepts of present value and future value and, even more important, the basic relationship between the two.

Business Math Scrapbook

At the end of each chapter you will find clippings from *The Wall Street Journal* and various other publications. These articles will give you a chance to use the theory provided in the chapter to apply to the real world. It allows you to put your math skills to work.

Group Activity: Personal Finance, a Kiplinger Approach

In each chapter you can debate a business math issue based on a *Kiplinger's Personal Finance* magazine article that is presented. This is great for critical thinking, as well as improving your writing skills.

Spreadsheet Templates

Excel® templates are available for selected end-of-chapter problems. You can run these templates as is or enter your own data. The templates also include an interest table feature that enables you to input any percentage rate and any terms. The program will then generate table values for you.

Cumulative Reviews

At the end of Chapters 3, 8, and 13 are word problems that test your retention of business math concepts and procedures. Check figures for *all* cumulative review problems are in Appendix C.

Vocabulary

On each chapter opener is a Vocabulary Preview covering the key terms in the chapter. The Chapter Organizer includes page references to the terms. There's also a glossary at the end of the text.

ROADMAP TO SUCCESS — **How to use this book and the Total Slater Learning System.**

Step 1: **Each chapter broken down into Learning Units. You should read one learning unit at a time.**

How do I know if I understand it?

- Try the practice quiz. All the worked out solutions are provided. If you still have questions, watch the author on your DVD (comes with your text) and work each problem out.
- Need more practice? Try the extra practice quiz provided. Worked-out solutions are in Appendix B.
- Go on to next Learning Unit in chapter.

Step 2: **Review the "Chapter Organizer" at the end of the chapter.**

How do I know if I understand it?

- Cover over the second or third column and see if you can explain the key points or the examples.

Step 3: **Do assigned problems at the end of the chapter (or Appendix A). These may include discussion questions, drill, word problems, challenge problems, video cases, as well as projects from the Business Math Scrapbook and Kiplinger's magazine.**

Can I check my homework?

- Appendix C has check figures for all the odd-numbered problems.

Step 4: **Take the Summary Practice Test.**

Can I check my progress?

- Appendix C has check figures for all problems.

What do I do if I do not match check figures?

- Review the video tutorial on the student DVD the author works out each problem.

To aid you in studying the book, I have developed the following color code.

Blue: Movement, cancellations, steps to solve, arrows, blueprints

Gold: Formulas and steps

Green: Tables and forms

Red: Key items we are solving for

If you have difficulty with any text examples, pay special attention to the red and the blue. These will help remind you what you are looking for as well as what the procedures are.

Dedication

To Shelley,
my best friend
—Love, PaPa Jeff

The McGraw·Hill Companies

McGraw-Hill Irwin

PRACTICAL BUSINESS MATH PROCEDURES
Published by McGraw-Hill/Irwin, a business unit of The McGraw-Hill Companies, Inc., 1221 Avenue of the Americas, New York, NY, 10020.

Some ancillaries, including electronic and print components, may not be available to customers outside the United States.

This book is printed on acid-free paper.

1 2 3 4 5 6 7 8 9 0 DOW/DOW 10 9 8 7 6 5 4 3 2 1 0

ISBN 978-0-07-337753-7 (student edition)
MHID 0-07-337753-8 (student edition)
ISBN 978-0-07-732784-2 (teacher's edition)
MHID 0-07-732784-5 (teacher's edition)

Vice president and editor-in-chief: *Brent Gordon*
Editorial director: *Stewart Mattson*
Executive editor: *Richard T. Hercher, Jr.*
Director of development: *Ann Torbert*
Managing development editor: *Gail Korosa*
Vice president and director of marketing: *Robin J. Zwettler*
Marketing director: *Sankha Basu*
Vice president of editing, design and production: *Sesha Bolisetty*
Lead project manager: *Pat Frederickson*
Lead production supervisor: *Michael R. McCormick*
Interior designer: *JoAnne Schopler*
Senior photo research coordinator: *Jeremy Cheshareck*
Photo research: *Teri Stratford*
Media project manager: *Jennifer Lohn*
Cover design: *Joanne Schopler*
Interior design: *Joanne Schopler*
Typeface: *10/12 Times Roman*
Compositor: *Aptara®, Inc.*
Printer: *R. R. Donnelley*

Library of Congress Cataloging-in-Publication Data

Slater, Jeffrey, 1947-
Practical business math procedures / Jeffrey Slater. — 10th ed.
p. cm.
Includes index.
ISBN-13: 978-0-07-337753-7 (student edition : alk. paper)
ISBN-10: 0-07-337753-8 (student edition : alk. paper)
ISBN-13: 978-0-07-732784-2 (teacher's edition : alk. paper)
ISBN-10: 0-07-732784-5 (teacher's edition : alk. paper)
1. Business mathematics—Problems, exercises, etc. I. Title.
HF5694.S57 2011
650.01′513—dc22

2009050020

www.mhhe.com

Practical Business Math Procedures

Tenth Edition

JEFFREY SLATER
North Shore Community College
Danvers, Massachusetts

SHARON MEYER
Pikes Peak Community College
Contributor

McGraw-Hill Irwin

Practical Business Math Procedures

WORKING PAPERS

Chapters 1-9 + Combination Journal Module

College Accounting

20th EDITION

James A. Heintz, DBA, CPA

Professor of Accounting
School of Business
University of Kansas

Robert W. Parry, Jr., Ph.D.

Professor of Accounting
Kelley School of Business
Indiana University

SOUTH-WESTERN
CENGAGE Learning™

Australia • Brazil • Japan • Korea • Mexico • Singapore • Spain • United Kingdom • United States

SOUTH-WESTERN
CENGAGE Learning

Study Guide and Working Papers for College Accounting, 20th edition Chapters 1-9 and Combination Journal Module
James A. Heintz and Robert W. Parry, Jr.

Vice President of Editorial, Business: Jack W. Calhoun

Editor-in-Chief: Rob Dewey

Executive Editor: Sharon Oblinger

Developmental Editor: Sara Wilson, CPA, CATS Publishing

Associate Marketing Manager: Laura Stopa

Marketing Coordinator: Heather Mooney

Senior Content Project Manager: Tim Bailey

Director of Media Development: Rick Lindgren

Media Editor: Bryan England

Senior Frontlist Buyer, Manufacturing: Doug Wilke

Production Service: LEAP Publishing Services, Inc.

Senior Art Director: Stacy Jenkins Shirley

Cover and Internal Designer: Grannan Graphic Design

Cover Image: Digital Vision/Juice Images

Rights Acquisition Account Manager-Image: John Hill

Photo Researcher: Megan Lessard, Pre-PressPMG

ISBN-13: 978-0-538-73705-0
ISBN-10: 0-538-73705-0

Chapters 1-9 + 10-15 Package
ISBN-13: 978-0-538-73704-3
ISBN-10: 0-538-73704-2

South-Western Cengage Learning
5191 Natorp Boulevard
Mason, OH 45040
USA

Cengage Learning products are represented in Canada by Nelson Education, Ltd.

For your course and learning solutions, visit www.cengage.com
Purchase any of our products at your local college store or at our preferred online store **www.ichapters.com**

Printed in the United States of America
1 2 3 4 5 6 7 14 13 12 11 10

Table of Contents

Exercise 2-1B

Account	Classification
Cash	
Accounts Payable	
Supplies	
Bill Jones, Drawing	
Prepaid Insurance	
Accounts Receivable	
Bill Jones, Capital	

Exercise 2-2B

Assets	=	Liabilities	+	Owner's Equity
	=	$20,000	+	$5,000
$30,000	=	$15,000	+	
$20,000	=		+	$10,000

Exercise 2-3B

	Assets	=	Liabilities	+	Owner's Equity
(a)					
Bal.					
(b)					
Bal.					
(c)					
Bal.					
(d)					
Bal.					

Exercise 2-4B

				Owner's Equity								
	Assets	=	Liabilities	+	Capital	–	Drawing	+	Revenues	–	Expenses	Description
Bal. from E 2-3B												
(d)												
(e)												
(f)												
(g)												
(h)												
(i)												
(j)												
(k)												
Bal.												

Name ______________________

Exercise 2-5B

Account	Classification	Financial Statement
Cash		
Rent Expense		
Accounts Payable		
Service Fees		
Supplies		
Wages Expense		
Amanda Wong, Drawing		
Amanda Wong, Capital		
Prepaid Insurance		
Accounts Receivable		

Exercise 2-6B

Exercise 2-7B

Problem 2-8B

	Assets	=	Liabilities	+	Owner's Equity
1.					
2.					
3.					

Problem 2-9B: See page WP-13

Problem 2-10B

Problem 2-9B

	Assets				= Liabilities	+	Owner's Equity			
	(Items Owned)				(Amts. Owed)		(Owner's Investment)		(Earnings)	
	Cash	+ Accounts Receivable	+ Office Supplies	+ Prepaid Insurance	= Accounts Payable	+ D. Segal, Capital	– D. Segal, Drawing	+ Revenues	– Expenses	Description
(a)										
(b)										
(c)										
(d)										
(e)										
(f)										
(g)										
Bal.										

Problem 2-11B

Problem 2-12B

Exercises 3-5A and 3-6A

Assets		=	Liabilities		+	Owner's Equity	
Dr. +	Cr. –		Dr. –	Cr. +		Dr. –	Cr. +

Drawing		Expenses		Revenues	
Dr. +	Cr. –	Dr. +	Cr. –	Dr. –	Cr. +

Exercise 3-7A

Assets		=	Liabilities		+	Owner's Equity	
Dr. +	Cr. –		Dr. –	Cr. +		Dr. –	Cr. +

Drawing		Expenses		Revenues	
Dr. +	Cr. –	Dr. +	Cr. –	Dr. –	Cr. +

Name ______________________________

Exercise 3-8A

ACCOUNT	DEBIT BALANCE	CREDIT BALANCE

Exercise 3-9A

ACCOUNT	DEBIT BALANCE	CREDIT BALANCE

Exercise 3-10A

Name ______________________________

Exercise 3-4B

	Account	Debit or Credit
1.	Cash	____________
2.	Rent Expense	____________
3.	Notes Payable	____________
4.	Owner's Drawing	____________
5.	Accounts Receivable	____________
6.	Owner's Capital	____________
7.	Tools	____________

Exercises 3-5B and 3-6B: See page WP-32

Exercises 3-5B and 3-6B

Assets		=	Liabilities		+	Owner's Equity	
Dr. +	Cr. –		Dr. –	Cr. +		Dr. –	Cr. +

Drawing		Expenses		Revenues	
Dr. +	Cr. –	Dr. +	Cr. –	Dr. –	Cr. +

Exercise 3-7B

Assets = Liabilities + Owner's Equity

Assets		Liabilities		Owner's Equity	
Dr. +	Cr. –	Dr. –	Cr. +	Dr. –	Cr. +

Drawing		Expenses		Revenues	
Dr. +	Cr. –	Dr. +	Cr. –	Dr. –	Cr. +

Exercise 3-8B

ACCOUNT	DEBIT BALANCE	CREDIT BALANCE

Name ______________________

Exercise 3-9B

ACCOUNT	DEBIT BALANCE	CREDIT BALANCE

Exercise 3-10B

Exercise 3-11B

Exercise 3-12B

Name ______________________

Problem 3-13B

1. and 2.

Assets		=	Liabilities		+	Owner's Equity	
Dr. +	Cr. –		Dr. –	Cr. +		Dr. –	Cr. +

Drawing		Expenses		Revenues	
Dr. +	Cr. –	Dr. +	Cr. –	Dr. –	Cr. +

Problem 3-13B (Concluded)

3.

ACCOUNT	DEBIT BALANCE	CREDIT BALANCE

Name ______________________

Problem 3-14B

1.

a. Total revenue for the month .... ______

b. Total expenses for the month.. ______

c. Net income for the month.. ______

2.

a. Sue Jantz's original investment in the business.......... ______

+ Net income for the month.. ______

– Owner's drawing... ______

Increase in capital .... ______

= Ending owner's equity .... ______

b. End-of-month accounting equation:

Assets	=	Liabilities	+	Owner's Equity
______		______		______

Problem 3-15B

1.

Problem 3-15B (Concluded)

2.

3.

Exercise 4-1A

1.	________	Check stubs or check register	a. A good or service has been sold.
2.	________	Purchase invoice from suppliers (vendors)	b. Cash has been received by the business.
3.	________	Sales tickets or invoices to customers	c. Cash has been paid by the business.
4.	________	Receipts or cash register tapes	d. Goods or services have been purchased by the business.

Exercise 4-2A

Transaction	Debit	Credit
1. Invested cash in the business, $5,000.	________	________
2. Paid office rent, $500.	________	________
3. Purchased office supplies on account, $300.	________	________
4. Received cash for services rendered (fees), $400.	________	________
5. Paid cash on account, $50.	________	________
6. Rendered services on account, $300.	________	________
7. Received cash for an amount owed by a customer, $100.	________	________

Exercise 4-3A

Exercise 4-3A (Concluded)

Total Debits:

Total Credits:

Exercise 4-4A

GENERAL JOURNAL

PAGE 1

	DATE	DESCRIPTION	POST. REF.	DEBIT	CREDIT	
1						1
2						2
3						3
4						4
5						5
6						6
7						7
8						8
9						9
10						10
11						11
12						12
13						13
14						14
15						15
16						16
17						17
18						18
19						19
20						20
21						21
22						22
23						23
24						24

Exercise 4-4A (Concluded)

GENERAL JOURNAL

PAGE 2

	DATE		DESCRIPTION	POST. REF.	DEBIT	CREDIT	
1							1
2							2
3							3
4							4
5							5
6							6
7							7
8							8
9							9
10							10
11							11
12							12
13							13
14							14
15							15
16							16
17							17
18							18
19							19
20							20
21							21
22							22
23							23
24							24
25							25
26							26
27							27
28							28
29							29
30							30
31							31
32							32
33							33
34							34
35							35
36							36

Exercise 4-5A

GENERAL LEDGER

ACCOUNT ACCOUNT NO.

DATE	ITEM	POST. REF.	DEBIT	CREDIT	BALANCE DEBIT	BALANCE CREDIT

ACCOUNT ACCOUNT NO.

DATE	ITEM	POST. REF.	DEBIT	CREDIT	BALANCE DEBIT	BALANCE CREDIT

ACCOUNT ACCOUNT NO.

DATE	ITEM	POST. REF.	DEBIT	CREDIT	BALANCE DEBIT	BALANCE CREDIT

Name ____________________

Exercise 4-5A (Continued)

ACCOUNT ____________________ ACCOUNT NO. ______

DATE	ITEM	POST. REF.	DEBIT	CREDIT	BALANCE DEBIT	BALANCE CREDIT

ACCOUNT ____________________ ACCOUNT NO. ______

DATE	ITEM	POST. REF.	DEBIT	CREDIT	BALANCE DEBIT	BALANCE CREDIT

ACCOUNT ____________________ ACCOUNT NO. ______

DATE	ITEM	POST. REF.	DEBIT	CREDIT	BALANCE DEBIT	BALANCE CREDIT

ACCOUNT ____________________ ACCOUNT NO. ______

DATE	ITEM	POST. REF.	DEBIT	CREDIT	BALANCE DEBIT	BALANCE CREDIT

Exercise 4-5A (Continued)

ACCOUNT ACCOUNT NO.

DATE	ITEM	POST. REF.	DEBIT	CREDIT	BALANCE DEBIT	BALANCE CREDIT

ACCOUNT ACCOUNT NO.

DATE	ITEM	POST. REF.	DEBIT	CREDIT	BALANCE DEBIT	BALANCE CREDIT

ACCOUNT ACCOUNT NO.

DATE	ITEM	POST. REF.	DEBIT	CREDIT	BALANCE DEBIT	BALANCE CREDIT

ACCOUNT ACCOUNT NO.

DATE	ITEM	POST. REF.	DEBIT	CREDIT	BALANCE DEBIT	BALANCE CREDIT

ACCOUNT ACCOUNT NO.

DATE	ITEM	POST. REF.	DEBIT	CREDIT	BALANCE DEBIT	BALANCE CREDIT

Name ______________________

Exercise 4-5A (Concluded)

ACCOUNT TITLE	ACCT. NO.	DEBIT BALANCE	CREDIT BALANCE

Exercise 4-6A

Exercise 4-6A (Concluded)

Name ______________________

Exercise 4-7A

Exercise 4-7A (Concluded)

Exercise 4-8A

GENERAL JOURNAL

PAGE

DATE		DESCRIPTION	POST. REF.	DEBIT	CREDIT
May	17	Office Equipment		400 00	
		Cash			400 00
		Purchased copy paper			
	23	Cash	101	1000 00	
		Service Fees	401		1000 00
		Received cash for services previously earned			

Name ______________________

Exercise 4-2B

Transaction	Debit	Credit
1. Invested cash in the business, $1,000.		
2. Performed services on account, $200.		
3. Purchased office equipment on account, $500.		
4. Received cash on account for services previously rendered, $200.		
5. Made a payment on account, $100.		

Exercise 4-3B

Total Debits:	Total Credits:

Exercise 4-4B

GENERAL JOURNAL

PAGE 1

	DATE	DESCRIPTION	POST. REF.	DEBIT	CREDIT	
1						1
2						2
3						3
4						4
5						5
6						6
7						7
8						8
9						9
10						10
11						11
12						12
13						13
14						14
15						15
16						16
17						17
18						18
19						19
20						20
21						21
22						22
23						23
24						24
25						25
26						26
27						27
28						28
29						29
30						30
31						31
32						32
33						33
34						34
35						35
36						36

Exercise 4-4B (Concluded)

GENERAL JOURNAL

PAGE 2

DATE		DESCRIPTION	POST. REF.	DEBIT	CREDIT

Exercise 4-5B

GENERAL LEDGER

ACCOUNT ACCOUNT NO.

DATE	ITEM	POST. REF.	DEBIT	CREDIT	BALANCE DEBIT	BALANCE CREDIT

ACCOUNT ACCOUNT NO.

DATE	ITEM	POST. REF.	DEBIT	CREDIT	BALANCE DEBIT	BALANCE CREDIT

ACCOUNT ACCOUNT NO.

DATE	ITEM	POST. REF.	DEBIT	CREDIT	BALANCE DEBIT	BALANCE CREDIT

Exercise 4-5B (Continued)

ACCOUNT ACCOUNT NO.

DATE		ITEM	POST. REF.	DEBIT	CREDIT	BALANCE DEBIT	BALANCE CREDIT

ACCOUNT ACCOUNT NO.

DATE		ITEM	POST. REF.	DEBIT	CREDIT	BALANCE DEBIT	BALANCE CREDIT

ACCOUNT ACCOUNT NO.

DATE		ITEM	POST. REF.	DEBIT	CREDIT	BALANCE DEBIT	BALANCE CREDIT

ACCOUNT ACCOUNT NO.

DATE		ITEM	POST. REF.	DEBIT	CREDIT	BALANCE DEBIT	BALANCE CREDIT

Exercise 4-5B (Continued)

ACCOUNT ACCOUNT NO.

DATE	ITEM	POST. REF.	DEBIT	CREDIT	BALANCE	
					DEBIT	CREDIT

ACCOUNT ACCOUNT NO.

DATE	ITEM	POST. REF.	DEBIT	CREDIT	BALANCE	
					DEBIT	CREDIT

ACCOUNT ACCOUNT NO.

DATE	ITEM	POST. REF.	DEBIT	CREDIT	BALANCE	
					DEBIT	CREDIT

ACCOUNT ACCOUNT NO.

DATE	ITEM	POST. REF.	DEBIT	CREDIT	BALANCE	
					DEBIT	CREDIT

ACCOUNT ACCOUNT NO.

DATE	ITEM	POST. REF.	DEBIT	CREDIT	BALANCE	
					DEBIT	CREDIT

Exercise 4-5B (Concluded)

ACCOUNT TITLE	ACCT. NO.	DEBIT BALANCE	CREDIT BALANCE

Exercise 4-6B

Exercise 4-6B (Concluded)

Exercise 4-7B

Exercise 4-7B (Concluded)

Exercise 4-8B

GENERAL JOURNAL

PAGE

DATE		DESCRIPTION	POST. REF.	DEBIT	CREDIT
Apr.	6	Office Supplies		530 00	
		Cash			530 00
		Purchased office equipment			
	21	Cash	101	300 00	
		Service Fees	401		300 00
		Revenue earned from services			
		previously rendered			

Problem 4-9B

2. (For parts 1. and 3., see page WP-88.)

GENERAL JOURNAL

PAGE 1

	DATE	DESCRIPTION	POST. REF.	DEBIT	CREDIT	
1						1
2						2
3						3
4						4
5						5
6						6
7						7
8						8
9						9
10						10
11						11
12						12
13						13
14						14
15						15
16						16
17						17
18						18
19						19
20						20
21						21
22						22
23						23
24						24
25						25
26						26
27						27
28						28
29						29
30						30
31						31
32						32
33						33
34						34
35						35
36						36

Problem 4-9B (Continued)

GENERAL JOURNAL

PAGE 2

	DATE	DESCRIPTION	POST. REF.	DEBIT	CREDIT	
1						1
2						2
3						3
4						4
5						5
6						6
7						7
8						8
9						9
10						10
11						11
12						12
13						13
14						14
15						15
16						16
17						17
18						18
19						19
20						20
21						21
22						22
23						23
24						24
25						25
26						26
27						27
28						28
29						29
30						30
31						31
32						32
33						33
34						34
35						35
36						36

Problem 4-9B (Continued)

GENERAL JOURNAL

PAGE 3

	DATE		DESCRIPTION	POST. REF.	DEBIT	CREDIT	
1							1
2							2
3							3
4							4
5							5
6							6
7							7
8							8
9							9
10							10
11							11
12							12
13							13
14							14
15							15
16							16
17							17
18							18
19							19
20							20
21							21
22							22
23							23
24							24
25							25
26							26
27							27
28							28
29							29
30							30
31							31
32							32
33							33
34							34
35							35
36							36

Problem 4-9B (Continued)

1. and 3.

GENERAL LEDGER

ACCOUNT Cash ACCOUNT NO. 101

DATE	ITEM	POST. REF.	DEBIT	CREDIT	BALANCE	
					DEBIT	CREDIT

ACCOUNT Accounts Receivable ACCOUNT NO. 122

DATE	ITEM	POST. REF.	DEBIT	CREDIT	BALANCE	
					DEBIT	CREDIT

Problem 4-9B (Continued)

ACCOUNT Office Supplies ACCOUNT NO. 142

DATE	ITEM	POST. REF.	DEBIT	CREDIT	BALANCE	
					DEBIT	CREDIT

ACCOUNT Office Equipment ACCOUNT NO. 181

DATE	ITEM	POST. REF.	DEBIT	CREDIT	BALANCE	
					DEBIT	CREDIT

ACCOUNT Accounts Payable ACCOUNT NO. 202

DATE	ITEM	POST. REF.	DEBIT	CREDIT	BALANCE	
					DEBIT	CREDIT

ACCOUNT Benito Mendez, Capital ACCOUNT NO. 311

DATE	ITEM	POST. REF.	DEBIT	CREDIT	BALANCE	
					DEBIT	CREDIT

Problem 4-9B (Continued)

ACCOUNT Benito Mendez, Drawing — ACCOUNT NO. 312

DATE	ITEM	POST. REF.	DEBIT	CREDIT	BALANCE DEBIT	BALANCE CREDIT

ACCOUNT Appraisal Fees — ACCOUNT NO. 401

DATE	ITEM	POST. REF.	DEBIT	CREDIT	BALANCE DEBIT	BALANCE CREDIT

ACCOUNT Wages Expense — ACCOUNT NO. 511

DATE	ITEM	POST. REF.	DEBIT	CREDIT	BALANCE DEBIT	BALANCE CREDIT

ACCOUNT Advertising Expense — ACCOUNT NO. 512

DATE	ITEM	POST. REF.	DEBIT	CREDIT	BALANCE DEBIT	BALANCE CREDIT

Problem 4-9B (Continued)

ACCOUNT Rent Expense ACCOUNT NO. 521

DATE	ITEM	POST. REF.	DEBIT	CREDIT	BALANCE DEBIT	BALANCE CREDIT

ACCOUNT Telephone Expense ACCOUNT NO. 525

DATE	ITEM	POST. REF.	DEBIT	CREDIT	BALANCE DEBIT	BALANCE CREDIT

ACCOUNT Transportation Expense ACCOUNT NO 526

DATE	ITEM	POST. REF.	DEBIT	CREDIT	BALANCE DEBIT	BALANCE CREDIT

ACCOUNT Electricity Expense ACCOUNT NO. 533

DATE	ITEM	POST. REF.	DEBIT	CREDIT	BALANCE DEBIT	BALANCE CREDIT

ACCOUNT Miscellaneous Expense ACCOUNT NO. 549

DATE	ITEM	POST. REF.	DEBIT	CREDIT	BALANCE DEBIT	BALANCE CREDIT

Problem 4-9B (Continued)

4.

ACCOUNT TITLE	ACCT. NO.	DEBIT BALANCE	CREDIT BALANCE

Problem 4-9B (Continued)

5.

Problem 4-9B (Concluded)

Name ______________________________

Problem 4-10B

2. (For 1. and 3., see page WP-98.)

GENERAL JOURNAL

PAGE 7

	DATE		DESCRIPTION	POST. REF.	DEBIT	CREDIT	
1							1
2							2
3							3
4							4
5							5
6							6
7							7
8							8
9							9
10							10
11							11
12							12
13							13
14							14
15							15
16							16
17							17
18							18
19							19
20							20
21							21
22							22
23							23
24							24
25							25
26							26
27							27
28							28
29							29
30							30
31							31
32							32
33							33
34							34

Problem 4-10B (Continued)

GENERAL JOURNAL PAGE 8

DATE	DESCRIPTION	POST. REF.	DEBIT	CREDIT

Problem 4-10B (Continued)

GENERAL JOURNAL

PAGE 9

	DATE	DESCRIPTION	POST. REF.	DEBIT	CREDIT	
1						1
2						2
3						3
4						4
5						5
6						6
7						7
8						8
9						9
10						10
11						11
12						12
13						13
14						14
15						15
16						16
17						17
18						18
19						19
20						20
21						21
22						22
23						23
24						24
25						25
26						26
27						27
28						28
29						29
30						30
31						31
32						32
33						33
34						34
35						35
36						36

Problem 4-10B (Continued)

1. and 3.

GENERAL LEDGER

ACCOUNT Cash ACCOUNT NO. 101

DATE	ITEM	POST. REF.	DEBIT	CREDIT	BALANCE	
					DEBIT	CREDIT

ACCOUNT Accounts Receivable ACCOUNT NO. 122

DATE	ITEM	POST. REF.	DEBIT	CREDIT	BALANCE	
					DEBIT	CREDIT

Problem 4-10B (Continued)

ACCOUNT Tailoring Supplies ACCOUNT NO. 141

DATE	ITEM	POST. REF.	DEBIT	CREDIT	BALANCE DEBIT	BALANCE CREDIT

ACCOUNT Tailoring Equipment ACCOUNT NO. 183

DATE	ITEM	POST. REF.	DEBIT	CREDIT	BALANCE DEBIT	BALANCE CREDIT

ACCOUNT Accounts Payable ACCOUNT NO. 202

DATE	ITEM	POST. REF.	DEBIT	CREDIT	BALANCE DEBIT	BALANCE CREDIT

ACCOUNT Ann Taylor, Capital ACCOUNT NO. 311

DATE	ITEM	POST. REF.	DEBIT	CREDIT	BALANCE DEBIT	BALANCE CREDIT

Problem 4-10B (Continued)

ACCOUNT Ann Taylor, Drawing ACCOUNT NO. 312

DATE	ITEM	POST. REF.	DEBIT	CREDIT	BALANCE DEBIT	BALANCE CREDIT

ACCOUNT Tailoring Fees ACCOUNT NO. 401

DATE	ITEM	POST. REF.	DEBIT	CREDIT	BALANCE DEBIT	BALANCE CREDIT

ACCOUNT Wages Expense ACCOUNT NO. 511

DATE	ITEM	POST. REF.	DEBIT	CREDIT	BALANCE DEBIT	BALANCE CREDIT

ACCOUNT Advertising Expense ACCOUNT NO. 512

DATE	ITEM	POST. REF.	DEBIT	CREDIT	BALANCE DEBIT	BALANCE CREDIT

Problem 4-10B (Continued)

ACCOUNT Rent Expense ACCOUNT NO. 521

DATE	ITEM	POST. REF.	DEBIT	CREDIT	BALANCE DEBIT	BALANCE CREDIT

ACCOUNT Telephone Expense ACCOUNT NO. 525

DATE	ITEM	POST. REF.	DEBIT	CREDIT	BALANCE DEBIT	BALANCE CREDIT

ACCOUNT Electricity Expense ACCOUNT NO. 533

DATE	ITEM	POST. REF.	DEBIT	CREDIT	BALANCE DEBIT	BALANCE CREDIT

ACCOUNT Miscellaneous Expense ACCOUNT NO. 549

DATE	ITEM	POST. REF.	DEBIT	CREDIT	BALANCE DEBIT	BALANCE CREDIT

Problem 4-10B (Concluded)

4.

ACCOUNT TITLE	ACCT. NO.	DEBIT BALANCE	CREDIT BALANCE

Name ______________________________

Exercise 5-1A

(Balance Sheet) Supplies	(Income Statement) Supplies Expense

GENERAL JOURNAL PAGE

	DATE		DESCRIPTION	POST. REF.	DEBIT	CREDIT	
1							1
2							2
3							3
4							4
5							5
6							6

Exercise 5-2A

(Balance Sheet) Prepaid Insurance	(Income Statement) Insurance Expense

GENERAL JOURNAL PAGE

	DATE		DESCRIPTION	POST. REF.	DEBIT	CREDIT	
1							1
2							2
3							3
4							4
5							5
6							6

Exercise 5-3A

(Income Statement) Wages Expense		(Balance Sheet) Wages Payable	

GENERAL JOURNAL PAGE

	DATE	DESCRIPTION	POST. REF.	DEBIT	CREDIT	
1						1
2						2
3						3
4						4

Exercise 5-4A

(Income Statement) Depr. Expense—Delivery Equipment		(Balance Sheet) Accum. Depr.—Delivery Equipment	

GENERAL JOURNAL PAGE

	DATE	DESCRIPTION	POST. REF.	DEBIT	CREDIT	
1						1
2						2
3						3
4						4

Exercise 5-5A

Exercise 5-6A

1.

(Balance Sheet)
Supplies

TB	460		
		Adj.	______
Bal.	______		

(Income Statement)
Supplies Expense

Adj.	______		

2.

(Balance Sheet)
Supplies

TB	545		
		Adj.	______
Bal.	______		

(Income Statement)
Supplies Expense

Adj.	______		

Exercise 5-7A

1.

(Balance Sheet)
Prepaid Insurance

TB	1,300		
		Adj.	______
Bal.	______		

(Income Statement)
Insurance Expense

Adj.	______		

2.

(Balance Sheet)
Prepaid Insurance

TB	860		
		Adj.	______
Bal.	______		

(Income Statement)
Insurance Expense

Adj.	______		

Exercise 5-8A

GENERAL JOURNAL

PAGE 9

	DATE		DESCRIPTION	POST. REF.	DEBIT	CREDIT	
1			Adjusting Entries				1
2	20-- Dec.	31	Supplies Expense		85 00		2
3			Supplies			85 00	3
4							4
5		31	Wages Expense		220 00		5
6			Wages Payable			220 00	6
7							7
8							8
9							9
10							10
11							11
12							12
13							13
14							14
15							15
16							16
17							17
18							18

Exercise 5-8A (Concluded)

GENERAL LEDGER

ACCOUNT Supplies ACCOUNT NO. 141

DATE		ITEM	POST. REF.	DEBIT	CREDIT	BALANCE DEBIT	BALANCE CREDIT
20-- Dec.	1	Balance	✓			150 00	
	15		J8	50 00		200 00	

ACCOUNT Wages Payable ACCOUNT NO. 219

DATE		ITEM	POST. REF.	DEBIT	CREDIT	BALANCE DEBIT	BALANCE CREDIT

ACCOUNT Wages Expense ACCOUNT NO. 511

DATE		ITEM	POST. REF.	DEBIT	CREDIT	BALANCE DEBIT	BALANCE CREDIT
20-- Dec.	1	Balance	✓			900 00	
	15		J8	300 00		1200 00	

ACCOUNT Supplies Expense ACCOUNT NO. 523

DATE		ITEM	POST. REF.	DEBIT	CREDIT	BALANCE DEBIT	BALANCE CREDIT

Exercise 5-9A

Jim Jacobs' Furniture Repair
Work Sheet (Partial)
For Year Ended December 31, 20--

	ACCOUNT TITLE	TRIAL BALANCE		ADJUSTMENTS		ADJUSTED TRIAL BALANCE		
		DEBIT	CREDIT	DEBIT	CREDIT	DEBIT	CREDIT	
1	Cash	1 0 0 00				1 0 0 00		1
2	Supplies	8 5 0 00				2 0 0 00		2
3	Prepaid Insurance	9 0 0 00				3 0 0 00		3
4	Delivery Equipment	3 6 0 0 00				3 6 0 0 00		4
5	Accum. Depr.—Delivery Equip.		6 0 0 00				8 0 0 00	5
6	Wages Payable						1 0 0 00	6
7	Jim Jacobs, Capital		4 0 0 0 00				4 0 0 0 00	7
8	Repair Fees		1 6 5 0 00				1 6 5 0 00	8
9	Wages Expense	6 0 0 00				7 0 0 00		9
10	Advertising Expense	2 0 0 00				2 0 0 00		10
11	Supplies Expense					6 5 0 00		11
12	Insurance Expense					6 0 0 00		12
13	Depr. Exp.—Delivery Equip.					2 0 0 00		13
14		6 2 5 0 00	6 2 5 0 00			6 5 5 0 00	6 5 5 0 00	14
15								15
16								16
17								17
18								18
19								19
20								20
21								21
22								22
23								23
24								24
25								25

Exercise 5-10A

GENERAL JOURNAL

PAGE

	DATE		DESCRIPTION	POST. REF.	DEBIT	CREDIT	
1							1
2							2
3							3
4							4
5							5
6							6
7							7
8							8
9							9
10							10
11							11
12							12
13							13
14							14
15							15

Exercise 5-11A

	Income Statement		Balance Sheet	
	Debit	**Credit**	**Debit**	**Credit**
Cash				
Accounts Receivable				
Supplies				
Prepaid Insurance				
Delivery Equipment				
Accum. Depr.—Delivery Equip.				
Accounts Payable				
Wages Payable				
Owner, Capital				
Owner, Drawing				
Delivery Fees				
Wages Expense				
Rent Expense				

Exercise 5-11A (Concluded)

	Income Statement		Balance Sheet	
	Debit	**Credit**	**Debit**	**Credit**
Supplies Expense				
Insurance Expense				
Depr. Exp.—Delivery Equip.				

Exercise 5-12A

	Income Statement		Balance Sheet	
	Debit	**Credit**	**Debit**	**Credit**
Net Income				
Net Loss				

Name ____________________

Exercise 5-13A

	Cash Basis	Modified Cash Basis	Accrual Basis
1. Purchase supplies on account.			
2. Make payment on asset previously purchased.			
3. Purchase supplies for cash.			
4. Purchase insurance for cash.			
5. Pay cash for wages.			
6. Pay cash for telephone expense.			
7. Pay cash for new equipment.			
8. Wages earned but not paid.			
9. Prepaid item purchased, partly used.			
10. Depreciation on long-term assets.			

Problem 5-14A

Mason's Delivery

Work

For Month Ended

	ACCOUNT TITLE	TRIAL BALANCE		ADJUSTMENTS	
		DEBIT	CREDIT	DEBIT	CREDIT
1	Cash	1,600.00			
2	Accounts Receivable	940.00			
3	Supplies	635.00			
4	Prepaid Insurance	1,200.00			
5	Delivery Equipment	6,400.00			
6	Accum. Depr.—Delivery Equip.				
7	Accounts Payable		1,220.00		
8	Wages Payable				
9	Jill Mason, Capital		8,000.00		
10	Jill Mason, Drawing	1,400.00			
11	Delivery Fees		6,200.00		
12	Wages Expense	1,500.00			
13	Advertising Expense	460.00			
14	Rent Expense	800.00			
15	Supplies Expense				
16	Telephone Expense	165.00			
17	Insurance Expense				
18	Repair Expense	230.00			
19	Oil and Gas Expense	90.00			
20	Depr. Exp.—Delivery Equip.				
21		15,420.00	15,420.00		
22					
23					
24					
25					
26					
27					
28					
29					
30					
31					
32					
33					

Problem 5-14A (Concluded)

Service

Sheet

September 30, 20--

ADJUSTED TRIAL BALANCE		INCOME STATEMENT		BALANCE SHEET		
DEBIT	CREDIT	DEBIT	CREDIT	DEBIT	CREDIT	
						1
						2
						3
						4
						5
						6
						7
						8
						9
						10
						11
						12
						13
						14
						15
						16
						17
						18
						19
						20
						21
						22
						23
						24
						25
						26
						27
						28
						29
						30
						31
						32
						33

Problem 5-15A

Campus Delivery

Work

For Month Ended

	ACCOUNT TITLE	TRIAL BALANCE DEBIT	TRIAL BALANCE CREDIT	ADJUSTMENTS DEBIT	ADJUSTMENTS CREDIT
1	Cash	980 00			
2	Accounts Receivable	590 00			
3	Supplies	575 00			
4	Prepaid Insurance	1300 00			
5	Van	5800 00			
6	Accumulated Depreciation—Van				
7	Accounts Payable		960 00		
8	Wages Payable				
9	Jason Armstrong, Capital		10000 00		
10	Jason Armstrong, Drawing	600 00			
11	Delivery Fees		2600 00		
12	Wages Expense	1800 00			
13	Advertising Expense	380 00			
14	Rent Expense	900 00			
15	Supplies Expense				
16	Telephone Expense	220 00			
17	Insurance Expense				
18	Repair Expense	315 00			
19	Oil and Gas Expense	100 00			
20	Depreciation Expense—Van				
21		13560 00	13560 00		
22					
23					
24					
25					
26					
27					
28					
29					
30					
31					
32					
33					

Problem 5-15A (Concluded)

Service

Sheet

November 30, 20--

ADJUSTED TRIAL BALANCE		INCOME STATEMENT		BALANCE SHEET		
DEBIT	CREDIT	DEBIT	CREDIT	DEBIT	CREDIT	
						1
						2
						3
						4
						5
						6
						7
						8
						9
						10
						11
						12
						13
						14
						15
						16
						17
						18
						19
						20
						21
						22
						23
						24
						25
						26
						27
						28
						29
						30
						31
						32
						33

Problem 5-16A

1. **GENERAL JOURNAL** PAGE 5

	DATE	DESCRIPTION	POST. REF.	DEBIT	CREDIT	
1						1
2						2
3						3
4						4
5						5
6						6
7						7
8						8
9						9
10						10
11						11
12						12
13						13
14						14
15						15
16						16
17						17
18						18
19						19
20						20
21						21
22						22
23						23
24						24
25						25
26						26
27						27
28						28
29						29
30						30
31						31
32						32
33						33
34						34
35						35
36						36

Problem 5-16A (Continued)

2. **GENERAL LEDGER**

ACCOUNT Supplies ACCOUNT NO. 141

DATE		ITEM	POST. REF.	DEBIT	CREDIT	BALANCE DEBIT	BALANCE CREDIT
20-- Nov.	1		J1	475.00		475.00	
	15		J4	100.00		575.00	

ACCOUNT Prepaid Insurance ACCOUNT NO. 145

DATE		ITEM	POST. REF.	DEBIT	CREDIT	BALANCE DEBIT	BALANCE CREDIT
20-- Nov.	1		J1	1,300.00		1,300.00	

ACCOUNT Accumulated Depreciation—Van ACCOUNT NO. 185.1

DATE		ITEM	POST. REF.	DEBIT	CREDIT	BALANCE DEBIT	BALANCE CREDIT

ACCOUNT Wages Payable ACCOUNT NO. 219

DATE		ITEM	POST. REF.	DEBIT	CREDIT	BALANCE DEBIT	BALANCE CREDIT

Problem 5-16A (Concluded)

GENERAL LEDGER

ACCOUNT Wages Expense ACCOUNT NO. 511

DATE		ITEM	POST. REF.	DEBIT	CREDIT	BALANCE DEBIT	BALANCE CREDIT
20-- Nov.	15		J3	900 00		900 00	
	26		J4	900 00		1,800 00	

ACCOUNT Supplies Expense ACCOUNT NO. 523

DATE		ITEM	POST. REF.	DEBIT	CREDIT	BALANCE DEBIT	BALANCE CREDIT

ACCOUNT Insurance Expense ACCOUNT NO. 535

DATE		ITEM	POST. REF.	DEBIT	CREDIT	BALANCE DEBIT	BALANCE CREDIT

ACCOUNT Depreciation Expense—Van ACCOUNT NO. 541

DATE		ITEM	POST. REF.	DEBIT	CREDIT	BALANCE DEBIT	BALANCE CREDIT

Problem 5-17A: See pages 130 and 131

Exercise 5-1B

(Balance Sheet) Supplies	(Income Statement) Supplies Expense

GENERAL JOURNAL

PAGE

	DATE	DESCRIPTION	POST. REF.	DEBIT	CREDIT	
1						1
2						2
3						3
4						4
5						5
6						6

Exercise 5-2B

(Balance Sheet) Prepaid Insurance	(Income Statement) Insurance Expense

GENERAL JOURNAL

PAGE

	DATE	DESCRIPTION	POST. REF.	DEBIT	CREDIT	
1						1
2						2
3						3
4						4
5						5
6						6

Problem 5-17A

Joyce Lee's

Work

For Month Ended

	ACCOUNT TITLE	TRIAL BALANCE DEBIT	TRIAL BALANCE CREDIT	ADJUSTMENTS DEBIT	ADJUSTMENTS CREDIT
1	Cash	1,725 00			
2	Accounts Receivable	960 00			
3	Supplies	525 00			
4	Prepaid Insurance	930 00			
5	Office Equipment	5,450 00			
6	Accum. Depr.—Office Equipment				
7	Accounts Payable		480 00		
8	Wages Payable				
9	Joyce Lee, Capital		7,500 00		
10	Joyce Lee, Drawing	1,125 00			
11	Professional Fees		5,700 00		
12	Wages Expense	1,420 00			
13	Advertising Expense	350 00			
14	Rent Expense	700 00			
15	Supplies Expense				
16	Telephone Expense	130 00			
17	Utilities Expense	190 00			
18	Insurance Expense				
19	Depr. Expense—Office Equipment				
20	Miscellaneous Expense	175 00			
21		13,680 00	13,680 00		
22					
23					
24					
25					
26					
27					
28					
29					
30					
31					

Problem 5-17A (Concluded)

Tax Service

Sheet

March 31, 20--

ADJUSTED TRIAL BALANCE		INCOME STATEMENT		BALANCE SHEET		
DEBIT	CREDIT	DEBIT	CREDIT	DEBIT	CREDIT	
						1
						2
						3
						4
						5
						6
						7
						8
						9
						10
						11
						12
						13
						14
						15
						16
						17
						18
						19
						20
						21
						22
						23
						24
						25
						26
						27
						28
						29
						30
						31

Exercise 5-3B

(Income Statement)
Wages Expense

(Balance Sheet)
Wages Payable

GENERAL JOURNAL PAGE

	DATE	DESCRIPTION	POST. REF.	DEBIT	CREDIT	
1						1
2						2
3						3
4						4

Exercise 5-4B

(Income Statement)
Depr. Expense—Delivery Equipment

(Balance Sheet)
Accum. Depr.—Delivery Equipment

GENERAL JOURNAL PAGE

	DATE	DESCRIPTION	POST. REF.	DEBIT	CREDIT	
1						1
2						2
3						3
4						4

Exercise 5-5B

Exercise 5-6B

1.

(Balance Sheet)
Supplies

TB	540		
		Adj.	______
Bal.	______		

(Income Statement)
Supplies Expense

Adj.	______		

2.

(Balance Sheet)
Supplies

TB	330		
		Adj.	______
Bal.	______		

(Income Statement)
Supplies Expense

Adj.	______		

Exercise 5-7B

1.

(Balance Sheet)
Prepaid Insurance

TB	960		
		Adj.	______
Bal.	______		

(Income Statement)
Insurance Expense

Adj.	______		

2.

(Balance Sheet)
Prepaid Insurance

TB	1,135		
		Adj.	______
Bal.	______		

(Income Statement)
Insurance Expense

Adj.	______		

Exercise 5-8B

GENERAL JOURNAL

PAGE 7

	DATE		DESCRIPTION	POST. REF.	DEBIT	CREDIT	
1			Adjusting Entries				1
2	20-- July	31	Insurance Expense		320 00		2
3			Prepaid Insurance			320 00	3
4							4
5		31	Depreciation Expense—Cleaning Equipment		145 00		5
6			Accumulated Depreciation—Cleaning Equipment			145 00	6
7							7
8							8
9							9
10							10
11							11
12							12
13							13
14							14
15							15
16							16

Exercise 5-8B (Concluded)

GENERAL LEDGER

ACCOUNT Prepaid Insurance ACCOUNT NO. 145

DATE		ITEM	POST. REF.	DEBIT	CREDIT	BALANCE DEBIT	BALANCE CREDIT
20-- July	1	Balance	✓			3 2 0 00	
	15		J6	6 4 0 00		9 6 0 00	

ACCOUNT Accumulated Depreciation—Cleaning Equipment ACCOUNT NO. 183.1

DATE		ITEM	POST. REF.	DEBIT	CREDIT	BALANCE DEBIT	BALANCE CREDIT
20-- July	1	Balance	✓				8 7 0 00

ACCOUNT Insurance Expense ACCOUNT NO. 535

DATE		ITEM	POST. REF.	DEBIT	CREDIT	BALANCE DEBIT	BALANCE CREDIT

ACCOUNT Depreciation Expense—Cleaning Equipment ACCOUNT NO. 541

DATE		ITEM	POST. REF.	DEBIT	CREDIT	BALANCE DEBIT	BALANCE CREDIT

Exercise 5-9B

Jasmine Kah's Auto Detailing
Work Sheet (Partial)
For Month Ended June 30, 20--

	ACCOUNT TITLE	TRIAL BALANCE		ADJUSTMENTS		ADJUSTED TRIAL BALANCE		
		DEBIT	CREDIT	DEBIT	CREDIT	DEBIT	CREDIT	
1	Cash	150 00				150 00		1
2	Supplies	520 00				90 00		2
3	Prepaid Insurance	750 00				200 00		3
4	Cleaning Equipment	5400 00				5400 00		4
5	Accum. Depr.—Cleaning Equip.		850 00				1150 00	5
6	Wages Payable						250 00	6
7	Jasmine Kah, Capital		4600 00				4600 00	7
8	Detailing Fees		2220 00				2220 00	8
9	Wages Expense	700 00				950 00		9
10	Advertising Expense	150 00				150 00		10
11	Supplies Expense					430 00		11
12	Insurance Expense					550 00		12
13	Depr. Exp.—Cleaning Equip.					300 00		13
14		7670 00	7670 00			8220 00	8220 00	14
15								15
16								16
17								17
18								18
19								19
20								20
21								21
22								22
23								23
24								24
25								25

Name ______________________________

Exercise 5-10B

GENERAL JOURNAL

PAGE

	DATE		DESCRIPTION	POST. REF.	DEBIT	CREDIT	
1							1
2							2
3							3
4							4
5							5
6							6
7							7
8							8
9							9
10							10
11							11
12							12
13							13
14							14
15							15

Exercise 5-11B

	Income Statement		Balance Sheet	
	Debit	**Credit**	**Debit**	**Credit**
Cash				
Accounts Receivable				
Supplies				
Prepaid Insurance				
Automobile				
Accum. Depr.—Automobile				
Accounts Payable				
Wages Payable				
Owner, Capital				
Owner, Drawing				
Service Fees				
Wages Expense				
Supplies Expense				

Exercise 5-11B (Concluded)

	Income Statement		Balance Sheet	
	Debit	Credit	Debit	Credit
Utilities Expense				
Insurance Expense				
Depr. Exp.—Automobile				

Exercise 5-12B

	Income Statement		Balance Sheet	
	Debit	Credit	Debit	Credit
Net Income				
Net Loss				

Name ______________________________

Exercise 5-13B

	Cash Basis	Modified Cash Basis	Accrual Basis
1. Office Equipment Cash Purchased equipment for cash			
2. Office Equipment Accounts Payable Purchased equipment on account			
3. Cash Revenue Cash receipts for week			
4. Accounts Receivable Revenue Services performed on account			
5. Prepaid Insurance Cash Purchased prepaid asset			
6. Supplies Accounts Payable Purchased prepaid asset			
7. Telephone Expense Cash Paid telephone bill			
8. Wages Expense Cash Paid wages for month			
9. Accounts Payable Cash Made payment on account			
10. Supplies Expense Supplies			

Exercise 5-13B (Concluded)

	Cash Basis	Modified Cash Basis	Accrual Basis
11. Wages Expense Wages Payable			
12. Depreciation Expense—Office Equipment Accum. Depr.—Office Equipment			

Problem 5-16B (Continued)

2. **GENERAL LEDGER**

ACCOUNT Supplies ACCOUNT NO. 141

DATE		ITEM	POST. REF.	DEBIT	CREDIT	BALANCE DEBIT	BALANCE CREDIT
20-- Oct.	2		J1	625.00		625.00	

ACCOUNT Prepaid Insurance ACCOUNT NO. 145

DATE		ITEM	POST. REF.	DEBIT	CREDIT	BALANCE DEBIT	BALANCE CREDIT
20-- Oct.	3		J1	950.00		950.00	

ACCOUNT Accumulated Depreciation—Automobile ACCOUNT NO. 185.1

DATE		ITEM	POST. REF.	DEBIT	CREDIT	BALANCE DEBIT	BALANCE CREDIT

Problem 5-16B (Continued)

ACCOUNT Wages Payable ACCOUNT NO. 219

DATE		ITEM	POST. REF.	DEBIT	CREDIT	BALANCE DEBIT	BALANCE CREDIT

ACCOUNT Wages Expense ACCOUNT NO. 511

DATE		ITEM	POST. REF.	DEBIT	CREDIT	BALANCE DEBIT	BALANCE CREDIT
20-- Oct.	15		J2	700 00		700 00	
	26		J2	860 00		1560 00	

ACCOUNT Supplies Expense ACCOUNT NO. 523

DATE		ITEM	POST. REF.	DEBIT	CREDIT	BALANCE DEBIT	BALANCE CREDIT

Name ______________________________

Problem 5-16B (Concluded)

ACCOUNT Insurance Expense ACCOUNT NO. 535

DATE	ITEM	POST. REF.	DEBIT	CREDIT	BALANCE DEBIT	BALANCE CREDIT

ACCOUNT Depreciation Expense—Automobile ACCOUNT NO. 541

DATE	ITEM	POST. REF.	DEBIT	CREDIT	BALANCE DEBIT	BALANCE CREDIT

Problem 5-17B

Dick Ady's

Work

For Month Ended

	ACCOUNT TITLE	TRIAL BALANCE DEBIT	TRIAL BALANCE CREDIT	ADJUSTMENTS DEBIT	ADJUSTMENTS CREDIT
1	Cash	1 3 6 5 00			
2	Accounts Receivable	8 4 5 00			
3	Supplies	6 2 0 00			
4	Prepaid Insurance	1 1 5 0 00			
5	Office Equipment	6 4 0 0 00			
6	Accum. Depr.—Office Equipment				
7	Accounts Payable		7 3 5 00		
8	Wages Payable				
9	Dick Ady, Capital		7 8 0 0 00		
10	Dick Ady, Drawing	1 2 0 0 00			
11	Professional Fees		6 3 5 0 00		
12	Wages Expense	1 4 9 5 00			
13	Advertising Expense	3 8 0 00			
14	Rent Expense	8 5 0 00			
15	Supplies Expense				
16	Telephone Expense	2 0 5 00			
17	Utilities Expense	2 8 5 00			
18	Insurance Expense				
19	Depr. Expense—Office Equipment				
20	Miscellaneous Expense	9 0 00			
21		14 8 8 5 00	14 8 8 5 00		
22					
23					
24					
25					
26					
27					
28					
29					
30					
31					
32					

Name ______________________________

Challenge Problem

See pages 156–157 for work sheet for Challenge Problem.

Challenge Problem

1.

Diane Kiefner's Wilderness

Work

For Summer

	ACCOUNT TITLE	TRIAL BALANCE DEBIT	TRIAL BALANCE CREDIT	ADJUSTMENTS DEBIT	ADJUSTMENTS CREDIT
1	Cash	11,500.00			
2					
3					
4					
5	Diane Kiefner, Capital		15,000.00		
6	Tour Revenue		10,000.00		
7	Advertising Supplies Expense	1,000.00			
8	Food Expense	2,000.00			
9	Equipment Rental Expense	3,000.00			
10	Travel Expense	4,000.00			
11	Kayak Expense	3,500.00			
12					
13		25,000.00	25,000.00		
14					
15					
16					
17					
18					
19					

Name ______________________

Challenge Problem (Concluded)

Kayaking Tours

Sheet

Ended 20--

ADJUSTED TRIAL BALANCE		INCOME STATEMENT		BALANCE SHEET		
DEBIT	CREDIT	DEBIT	CREDIT	DEBIT	CREDIT	
						1
						2
						3
						4
						5
						6
						7
						8
						9
						10
						11
						12
						13
						14
						15
						16
						17
						18
						19

2.

APPENDIX: DEPRECIATION METHODS

Exercise 5Apx-1A

Straight-Line Depreciation

Year	Depreciable Cost	×	Rate	=	Depreciation Expense	Accumulated Depreciation End of Year	Book Value End of Year

Exercise 5Apx-2A

Sum-of-the-Years'-Digits

Year	Depreciable Cost	×	Rate	=	Depreciation Expense	Accumulated Depreciation End of Year	Book Value End of Year

Exercise 5Apx-3A

Double-Declining-Balance Method

Year	Book Value Beginning of Year	×	Rate	=	Depreciation Expense	Accumulated Depreciation End of Year	Book Value End of Year

Name ______________________________

Exercise 5Apx-4A

Modified Accelerated Cost Recovery System

Year	Cost	×	Rate	=	Depreciation Expense	Accumulated Depreciation End of Year	Book Value End of Year

Exercise 5Apx-1B

Straight-Line Depreciation

Year	Depreciable Cost	×	Rate	=	Depreciation Expense	Accumulated Depreciation End of Year	Book Value End of Year

Exercise 5Apx-2B

Sum-of-the-Years'-Digits

Year	Depreciable Cost	×	Rate	=	Depreciation Expense	Accumulated Depreciation End of Year	Book Value End of Year

Exercise 5Apx-3B

Double-Declining-Balance Method

Year	Book Value Beginning of Year	×	Rate	=	Depreciation Expense	Accumulated Depreciation End of Year	Book Value End of Year

Exercise 5Apx-4B

Modified Accelerated Cost Recovery System

Year	Cost	×	Rate	=	Depreciation Expense	Accumulated Depreciation End of Year	Book Value End of Year

Exercise 6-1A

Exercise 6-2A

Exercise 6-3A

Exercise 6-4A

GENERAL JOURNAL

PAGE 1

	DATE		DESCRIPTION	POST. REF.	DEBIT	CREDIT	
1							1
2							2
3							3
4							4
5							5
6							6
7							7
8							8
9							9
10							10
11							11
12							12
13							13
14							14
15							15
16							16
17							17
18							18
19							19
20							20
21							21
22							22
23							23

Exercise 6-4A (Concluded)

Name ______________________________

Exercise 6-5A

GENERAL JOURNAL

PAGE

	DATE		DESCRIPTION	POST. REF.	DEBIT	CREDIT	
1							1
2							2
3							3
4							4
5							5
6							6
7							7
8							8
9							9
10							10
11							11
12							12
13							13
14							14
15							15
16							16
17							17
18							18
19							19
20							20
21							21
22							22
23							23
24							24
25							25
26							26
27							27
28							28
29							29
30							30
31							31
32							32
33							33
34							34
35							35
36							36

Exercise 6-5A (Concluded)

Cash 101

Debit		Credit	
Bal.	500		

Accounts Receivable 122

Debit		Credit	
Bal.	1,500		

Wages Payable 219

Debit		Credit	
		Bal.	400

Chris Williams, Capital 311

Debit		Credit	
		Bal.	9,000

Chris Williams, Drawing 312

Debit		Credit	
Bal.	1,000		

Income Summary 313

Debit		Credit	

Golf Instruction Fees 401

Debit		Credit	
		Bal.	4,000

Wages Expense 511

Debit		Credit	
Bal.	800		

Advertising Expense 512

Debit		Credit	
Bal.	200		

Travel Expense 515

Debit		Credit	
Bal.	600		

Supplies Expense 524

Debit		Credit	
Bal.	500		

Insurance Expense 535

Debit		Credit	
Bal.	100		

Postage Expense 536

Debit		Credit	
Bal.	50		

Gas and Oil Expense 538

Debit		Credit	
Bal.	150		

Miscellaneous Expense 549

Debit		Credit	
Bal.	80		

Name ______________________________

Exercise 6-6A

GENERAL JOURNAL

PAGE

	DATE	DESCRIPTION	POST. REF.	DEBIT	CREDIT	
1						1
2						2
3						3
4						4
5						5
6						6
7						7
8						8
9						9
10						10
11						11
12						12
13						13
14						14
15						15
16						16
17						17
18						18
19						19
20						20
21						21
22						22
23						23
24						24
25						25
26						26
27						27
28						28
29						29
30						30
31						31
32						32
33						33
34						34
35						35
36						36

Exercise 6-6A (Concluded)

Accum. Depr.—Delivery Equip. 185.1

		Bal.	100

Wages Payable 219

		Bal.	200

Saburo Goto, Capital 311

		Bal.	4,000

Saburo Goto, Drawing 312

Bal.	800		

Income Summary 313

Delivery Fees 401

		Bal.	2,200

Wages Expense 511

Bal.	1,800		

Advertising Expense 512

Bal.	80		

Rent Expense 521

Bal.	500		

Supplies Expense 523

Bal.	120		

Telephone Expense 525

Bal.	58		

Electricity Expense 533

Bal.	44		

Insurance Expense 535

Bal.	30		

Gas and Oil Expense 538

Bal.	38		

Depr. Exp.—Delivery Equip. 541

Bal.	100		

Miscellaneous Expense 549

Bal.	33		

Problem 6-7A

1.

2.

Problem 6-7A (Concluded)

3.

Problem 6-9A (Continued)

2.

GENERAL JOURNAL

PAGE 11

	DATE	DESCRIPTION	POST. REF.	DEBIT	CREDIT	
1						1
2						2
3						3
4						4
5						5
6						6
7						7
8						8
9						9
10						10
11						11
12						12
13						13
14						14
15						15
16						16
17						17
18						18
19						19
20						20
21						21
22						22
23						23

1. and 2.

GENERAL LEDGER

ACCOUNT Cash ACCOUNT NO. 101

DATE		ITEM	POST. REF.	DEBIT	CREDIT	BALANCE DEBIT	BALANCE CREDIT
20-- Jan.	31	Balance	✓			3 0 8 0 00	

Problem 6-9A (Continued)

ACCOUNT Accounts Receivable ACCOUNT NO. 122

DATE		ITEM	POST. REF.	DEBIT	CREDIT	BALANCE DEBIT	BALANCE CREDIT
20-- Jan.	31	Balance	✓			1,200.00	

ACCOUNT Supplies ACCOUNT NO. 141

DATE		ITEM	POST. REF.	DEBIT	CREDIT	BALANCE DEBIT	BALANCE CREDIT
20-- Jan.	31	Balance	✓			800.00	

ACCOUNT Prepaid Insurance ACCOUNT NO. 145

DATE		ITEM	POST. REF.	DEBIT	CREDIT	BALANCE DEBIT	BALANCE CREDIT
20-- Jan.	31	Balance	✓			900.00	

ACCOUNT Delivery Equipment ACCOUNT NO. 185

DATE		ITEM	POST. REF.	DEBIT	CREDIT	BALANCE DEBIT	BALANCE CREDIT
20-- Jan.	31	Balance	✓			3,000.00	

ACCOUNT Accumulated Depreciation—Delivery Equipment ACCOUNT NO. 185.1

DATE		ITEM	POST. REF.	DEBIT	CREDIT	BALANCE DEBIT	BALANCE CREDIT

Problem 6-9A (Continued)

ACCOUNT Accounts Payable ACCOUNT NO. 202

DATE		ITEM	POST. REF.	DEBIT	CREDIT	BALANCE DEBIT	BALANCE CREDIT
20-- Jan.	31	Balance	✓				1,100 00

ACCOUNT Wages Payable ACCOUNT NO. 219

DATE		ITEM	POST. REF.	DEBIT	CREDIT	BALANCE DEBIT	BALANCE CREDIT

ACCOUNT Monte Eli, Capital ACCOUNT NO. 311

DATE		ITEM	POST. REF.	DEBIT	CREDIT	BALANCE DEBIT	BALANCE CREDIT
20-- Jan.	31	Balance	✓				7,000 00

ACCOUNT Monte Eli, Drawing ACCOUNT NO. 312

DATE		ITEM	POST. REF.	DEBIT	CREDIT	BALANCE DEBIT	BALANCE CREDIT
20-- Jan.	31	Balance	✓			1,000 00	

ACCOUNT Income Summary ACCOUNT NO. 313

DATE		ITEM	POST. REF.	DEBIT	CREDIT	BALANCE DEBIT	BALANCE CREDIT

Problem 6-9A (Continued)

ACCOUNT Repair Fees ACCOUNT NO. 401

DATE		ITEM	POST. REF.	DEBIT	CREDIT	BALANCE DEBIT	BALANCE CREDIT
20-- Jan.	31	Balance	✓				4,230.00

ACCOUNT Wages Expense ACCOUNT NO. 511

DATE		ITEM	POST. REF.	DEBIT	CREDIT	BALANCE DEBIT	BALANCE CREDIT
20-- Jan.	31	Balance	✓			1,650.00	

ACCOUNT Advertising Expense ACCOUNT NO. 512

DATE		ITEM	POST. REF.	DEBIT	CREDIT	BALANCE DEBIT	BALANCE CREDIT
20-- Jan.	31	Balance	✓			170.00	

ACCOUNT Rent Expense ACCOUNT NO. 521

DATE		ITEM	POST. REF.	DEBIT	CREDIT	BALANCE DEBIT	BALANCE CREDIT
20-- Jan.	31	Balance	✓			420.00	

ACCOUNT Supplies Expense ACCOUNT NO. 523

DATE		ITEM	POST. REF.	DEBIT	CREDIT	BALANCE DEBIT	BALANCE CREDIT

Problem 6-9A (Continued)

ACCOUNT Telephone Expense ACCOUNT NO. 525

DATE		ITEM	POST. REF.	DEBIT	CREDIT	BALANCE DEBIT	BALANCE CREDIT
20-- Jan.	31	Balance	✓			49 00	

ACCOUNT Insurance Expense ACCOUNT NO. 535

DATE		ITEM	POST. REF.	DEBIT	CREDIT	BALANCE DEBIT	BALANCE CREDIT

ACCOUNT Gas and Oil Expense ACCOUNT NO. 538

DATE		ITEM	POST. REF.	DEBIT	CREDIT	BALANCE DEBIT	BALANCE CREDIT
20-- Jan.	31	Balance	✓			33 00	

ACCOUNT Depreciation Expense—Delivery Equipment ACCOUNT NO. 541

DATE		ITEM	POST. REF.	DEBIT	CREDIT	BALANCE DEBIT	BALANCE CREDIT

ACCOUNT Miscellaneous Expense ACCOUNT NO. 549

DATE		ITEM	POST. REF.	DEBIT	CREDIT	BALANCE DEBIT	BALANCE CREDIT
20-- Jan.	31	Balance	✓			28 00	

Problem 6-9A (Concluded)

3.

ACCOUNT TITLE	ACCT. NO.	DEBIT BALANCE	CREDIT BALANCE

Name ______________________________

Exercise 6-1B

Exercise 6-2B

Exercise 6-3B

Name ______________________________

Exercise 6-4B

GENERAL JOURNAL

PAGE 1

	DATE		DESCRIPTION	POST. REF.	DEBIT	CREDIT	
1							1
2							2
3							3
4							4
5							5
6							6
7							7
8							8
9							9
10							10
11							11
12							12
13							13
14							14
15							15
16							16
17							17
18							18
19							19
20							20
21							21
22							22
23							23

Exercise 6-4B (Concluded)

Name ______________________________

Exercise 6-5B

GENERAL JOURNAL

PAGE

	DATE		DESCRIPTION	POST. REF.	DEBIT	CREDIT	
1							1
2							2
3							3
4							4
5							5
6							6
7							7
8							8
9							9
10							10
11							11
12							12
13							13
14							14
15							15
16							16
17							17
18							18
19							19
20							20
21							21
22							22
23							23
24							24
25							25
26							26
27							27
28							28
29							29
30							30
31							31
32							32
33							33
34							34
35							35
36							36

Exercise 6-5B (Concluded)

Cash — 101

Debit		Credit	
Bal.	600		

Accounts Receivable — 122

Debit		Credit	
Bal.	1,800		

Wages Payable — 219

Debit		Credit	
		Bal.	500

Mark Thrasher, Capital — 311

Debit		Credit	
		Bal.	8,000

Mark Thrasher, Drawing — 312

Debit		Credit	
Bal.	800		

Income Summary — 313

Debit		Credit	

Lawn Service Fees — 401

Debit		Credit	
		Bal.	5,000

Wages Expense — 511

Debit		Credit	
Bal.	400		

Advertising Expense — 512

Debit		Credit	
Bal.	600		

Travel Expense — 515

Debit		Credit	
Bal.	100		

Supplies Expense — 524

Debit		Credit	
Bal.	900		

Insurance Expense — 535

Debit		Credit	
Bal.	300		

Postage Expense — 536

Debit		Credit	
Bal.	40		

Gas and Oil Expense — 538

Debit		Credit	
Bal.	700		

Miscellaneous Expense — 549

Debit		Credit	
Bal.	200		

Problem 6-7B

1.

2.

Problem 6-7B (Concluded)

3.

Problem 6-8B

Problem 6-9B

1.

GENERAL JOURNAL

PAGE 10

	DATE		DESCRIPTION	POST. REF.	DEBIT	CREDIT	
1							1
2							2
3							3
4							4
5							5
6							6
7							7
8							8
9							9
10							10
11							11
12							12
13							13
14							14
15							15
16							16
17							17
18							18

Problem 6-9B (Continued)

2.

GENERAL JOURNAL

PAGE 11

	DATE		DESCRIPTION	POST. REF.	DEBIT	CREDIT	
1							1
2							2
3							3
4							4
5							5
6							6
7							7
8							8
9							9
10							10
11							11
12							12
13							13
14							14
15							15
16							16
17							17
18							18
19							19
20							20
21							21
22							22
23							23

1. and 2.

GENERAL LEDGER

ACCOUNT Cash ACCOUNT NO. 101

DATE		ITEM	POST. REF.	DEBIT	CREDIT	BALANCE	
						DEBIT	CREDIT
20-- June	30	Balance	✓			5,285.00	

Problem 6-9B (Continued)

ACCOUNT Accounts Receivable ACCOUNT NO. 122

DATE		ITEM	POST. REF.	DEBIT	CREDIT	BALANCE DEBIT	BALANCE CREDIT
20-- June	30	Balance	✓			1 0 7 5 00	

ACCOUNT Supplies ACCOUNT NO. 141

DATE		ITEM	POST. REF.	DEBIT	CREDIT	BALANCE DEBIT	BALANCE CREDIT
20-- June	30	Balance	✓			7 5 0 00	

ACCOUNT Prepaid Insurance ACCOUNT NO. 145

DATE		ITEM	POST. REF.	DEBIT	CREDIT	BALANCE DEBIT	BALANCE CREDIT
20-- June	30	Balance	✓			5 0 0 00	

ACCOUNT Office Equipment ACCOUNT NO. 181

DATE		ITEM	POST. REF.	DEBIT	CREDIT	BALANCE DEBIT	BALANCE CREDIT
20-- June	30	Balance	✓			2 2 0 0 00	

ACCOUNT Accumulated Depreciation—Office Equipment ACCOUNT NO. 181.1

DATE		ITEM	POST. REF.	DEBIT	CREDIT	BALANCE DEBIT	BALANCE CREDIT

Problem 6-9B (Continued)

ACCOUNT Accounts Payable — ACCOUNT NO. 202

DATE		ITEM	POST. REF.	DEBIT	CREDIT	BALANCE DEBIT	BALANCE CREDIT
20-- June	30	Balance	✓				1,500 00

ACCOUNT Wages Payable — ACCOUNT NO. 219

DATE		ITEM	POST. REF.	DEBIT	CREDIT	BALANCE DEBIT	BALANCE CREDIT

ACCOUNT Juanita Alvarez, Capital — ACCOUNT NO. 311

DATE		ITEM	POST. REF.	DEBIT	CREDIT	BALANCE DEBIT	BALANCE CREDIT
20-- June	30	Balance	✓				7,000 00

ACCOUNT Juanita Alvarez, Drawing — ACCOUNT NO. 312

DATE		ITEM	POST. REF.	DEBIT	CREDIT	BALANCE DEBIT	BALANCE CREDIT
20-- June	30	Balance	✓			800 00	

ACCOUNT Income Summary — ACCOUNT NO. 313

DATE		ITEM	POST. REF.	DEBIT	CREDIT	BALANCE DEBIT	BALANCE CREDIT

Problem 6-9B (Continued)

ACCOUNT Consulting Fees ACCOUNT NO. 401

DATE		ITEM	POST. REF.	DEBIT	CREDIT	BALANCE DEBIT	BALANCE CREDIT
20-- June	30	Balance	✓				4,204.00

ACCOUNT Wages Expense ACCOUNT NO. 511

DATE		ITEM	POST. REF.	DEBIT	CREDIT	BALANCE DEBIT	BALANCE CREDIT
20-- June	30	Balance	✓			1,400.00	

ACCOUNT Advertising Expense ACCOUNT NO. 512

DATE		ITEM	POST. REF.	DEBIT	CREDIT	BALANCE DEBIT	BALANCE CREDIT
20-- June	30	Balance	✓			60.00	

ACCOUNT Rent Expense ACCOUNT NO. 521

DATE		ITEM	POST. REF.	DEBIT	CREDIT	BALANCE DEBIT	BALANCE CREDIT
20-- June	30	Balance	✓			500.00	

ACCOUNT Supplies Expense ACCOUNT NO. 523

DATE		ITEM	POST. REF.	DEBIT	CREDIT	BALANCE DEBIT	BALANCE CREDIT

Problem 6-9B (Continued)

ACCOUNT Telephone Expense ACCOUNT NO. 525

DATE		ITEM	POST. REF.	DEBIT	CREDIT	BALANCE DEBIT	BALANCE CREDIT
20-- June	30	Balance	✓			46 00	

ACCOUNT Electricity Expense ACCOUNT NO. 533

DATE		ITEM	POST. REF.	DEBIT	CREDIT	BALANCE DEBIT	BALANCE CREDIT
20-- June	30	Balance	✓			39 00	

ACCOUNT Insurance Expense ACCOUNT NO. 535

DATE		ITEM	POST. REF.	DEBIT	CREDIT	BALANCE DEBIT	BALANCE CREDIT

ACCOUNT Gas and Oil Expense ACCOUNT NO. 538

DATE		ITEM	POST. REF.	DEBIT	CREDIT	BALANCE DEBIT	BALANCE CREDIT
20-- June	30	Balance	✓			28 00	

ACCOUNT Depreciation Expense—Office Equipment ACCOUNT NO. 541

DATE		ITEM	POST. REF.	DEBIT	CREDIT	BALANCE DEBIT	BALANCE CREDIT

Challenge Problem

Challenge Problem (Concluded)

Name ______________________________

Exercise 6Apx-1A

a. ____________________ g. ____________________
b. ____________________ h. ____________________
c. ____________________ i. ____________________
d. ____________________ j. ____________________
e. ____________________ k. ____________________
f. ____________________

Problem 6Apx-2A

Exercise 6Apx-1B

a. ____________________ g. ____________________

b. ____________________ h. ____________________

c. ____________________ i. ____________________

d. ____________________ j. ____________________

e. ____________________ k. ____________________

f. ____________________

Problem 6Apx-2B

Name ______________________

Comprehensive Problem 1: The Accounting Cycle

1.

GENERAL JOURNAL

PAGE 1

	DATE	DESCRIPTION	POST. REF.	DEBIT	CREDIT	
1						1
2						2
3						3
4						4
5						5
6						6
7						7
8						8
9						9
10						10
11						11
12						12
13						13
14						14
15						15
16						16
17						17
18						18
19						19
20						20
21						21
22						22
23						23
24						24
25						25
26						26
27						27
28						28
29						29
30						30
31						31
32						32
33						33
34						34

Comprehensive Problem 1 (Continued)

GENERAL JOURNAL

PAGE 2

	DATE	DESCRIPTION	POST. REF.	DEBIT	CREDIT	
1						1
2						2
3						3
4						4
5						5
6						6
7						7
8						8
9						9
10						10
11						11
12						12
13						13
14						14
15						15
16						16
17						17
18						18
19						19
20						20
21						21
22						22
23						23
24						24
25						25
26						26
27						27
28						28
29						29
30						30
31						31
32						32
33						33
34						34
35						35

Comprehensive Problem 1 (Continued)

GENERAL JOURNAL

PAGE 3

	DATE	DESCRIPTION	POST. REF.	DEBIT	CREDIT	
1						1
2						2
3						3
4						4
5						5
6						6
7						7
8						8
9						9
10						10
11						11
12						12
13						13
14						14
15						15
16						16
17						17
18						18
19						19
20						20
21						21
22						22
23						23
24						24
25						25
26						26
27						27
28						28
29						29
30						30
31						31
32						32
33						33
34						34
35						35

Comprehensive Problem 1 (Continued)

GENERAL JOURNAL

PAGE 4

	DATE	DESCRIPTION	POST. REF.	DEBIT	CREDIT	
1						1
2						2
3						3
4						4
5						5
6						6
7						7
8						8
9						9
10						10
11						11

2., 6., and 11.

GENERAL LEDGER

ACCOUNT Cash ACCOUNT NO. 101

DATE	ITEM	POST. REF.	DEBIT	CREDIT	BALANCE	
					DEBIT	CREDIT

Comprehensive Problem 1 (Continued)

ACCOUNT Office Supplies ACCOUNT NO. 142

DATE	ITEM	POST. REF.	DEBIT	CREDIT	BALANCE	
					DEBIT	CREDIT

ACCOUNT Food Supplies ACCOUNT NO. 144

DATE	ITEM	POST. REF.	DEBIT	CREDIT	BALANCE	
					DEBIT	CREDIT

ACCOUNT Prepaid Insurance ACCOUNT NO. 145

DATE	ITEM	POST. REF.	DEBIT	CREDIT	BALANCE	
					DEBIT	CREDIT

ACCOUNT Fishing Boats ACCOUNT NO. 181

DATE	ITEM	POST. REF.	DEBIT	CREDIT	BALANCE	
					DEBIT	CREDIT

Comprehensive Problem 1 (Continued)

ACCOUNT Accumulated Depreciation—Fishing Boats ACCOUNT NO. 181.1

DATE	ITEM	POST. REF.	DEBIT	CREDIT	BALANCE	
					DEBIT	CREDIT

ACCOUNT Accounts Payable ACCOUNT NO. 202

DATE	ITEM	POST. REF.	DEBIT	CREDIT	BALANCE	
					DEBIT	CREDIT

ACCOUNT Wages Payable ACCOUNT NO. 219

DATE	ITEM	POST. REF.	DEBIT	CREDIT	BALANCE	
					DEBIT	CREDIT

ACCOUNT Bob Night, Capital ACCOUNT NO. 311

DATE	ITEM	POST. REF.	DEBIT	CREDIT	BALANCE	
					DEBIT	CREDIT

Comprehensive Problem 1 (Continued)

ACCOUNTM Bob Night, Drawing ACCOUNT NO. 312

DATE	ITEM	POST. REF.	DEBIT	CREDIT	BALANCE	
					DEBIT	CREDIT

ACCOUNT Income Summary ACCOUNT NO. 313

DATE	ITEM	POST. REF.	DEBIT	CREDIT	BALANCE	
					DEBIT	CREDIT

ACCOUNT Registration Fees ACCOUNT NO. 401

DATE	ITEM	POST. REF.	DEBIT	CREDIT	BALANCE	
					DEBIT	CREDIT

Comprehensive Problem 1 (Continued)

ACCOUNT Wages Expense ACCOUNT NO. 511

DATE	ITEM	POST. REF.	DEBIT	CREDIT	BALANCE DEBIT	BALANCE CREDIT

ACCOUNT Rent Expense ACCOUNT NO. 521

DATE	ITEM	POST. REF.	DEBIT	CREDIT	BALANCE DEBIT	BALANCE CREDIT

ACCOUNT Office Supplies Expense ACCOUNT NO. 523

DATE	ITEM	POST. REF.	DEBIT	CREDIT	BALANCE DEBIT	BALANCE CREDIT

ACCOUNT Food Supplies Expense ACCOUNT NO. 524

DATE	ITEM	POST. REF.	DEBIT	CREDIT	BALANCE DEBIT	BALANCE CREDIT

Comprehensive Problem 1 (Continued)

ACCOUNT Telephone Expense ACCOUNT NO. 525

DATE	ITEM	POST. REF.	DEBIT	CREDIT	BALANCE DEBIT	BALANCE CREDIT

ACCOUNT Utilities Expense ACCOUNT NO. 533

DATE	ITEM	POST. REF.	DEBIT	CREDIT	BALANCE DEBIT	BALANCE CREDIT

ACCOUNT Insurance Expense ACCOUNT NO. 535

DATE	ITEM	POST. REF.	DEBIT	CREDIT	BALANCE DEBIT	BALANCE CREDIT

ACCOUNT Postage Expense ACCOUNT NO. 536

DATE	ITEM	POST. REF.	DEBIT	CREDIT	BALANCE DEBIT	BALANCE CREDIT

ACCOUNT Depreciation Expense—Fishing Boats ACCOUNT NO. 542

DATE	ITEM	POST. REF.	DEBIT	CREDIT	BALANCE DEBIT	BALANCE CREDIT

Comprehensive Problem 1 (Continued)

3. and 4.

	ACCOUNT TITLE	TRIAL BALANCE		ADJUSTMENTS	
		DEBIT	CREDIT	DEBIT	CREDIT
1					
2					
3					
4					
5					
6					
7					
8					
9					
10					
11					
12					
13					
14					
15					
16					
17					
18					
19					
20					
21					
22					
23					
24					
25					
26					
27					
28					
29					
30					
31					

Comprehensive Problem 1 (Continued)

ADJUSTED TRIAL BALANCE		INCOME STATEMENT		BALANCE SHEET		
DEBIT	CREDIT	DEBIT	CREDIT	DEBIT	CREDIT	
						1
						2
						3
						4
						5
						6
						7
						8
						9
						10
						11
						12
						13
						14
						15
						16
						17
						18
						19
						20
						21
						22
						23
						24
						25
						26
						27
						28
						29
						30
						31

Comprehensive Problem 1 (Continued)

7.

8.

Comprehensive Problem 1 (Continued)

9.

Comprehensive Problem 1 (Continued)

5. and 10.

GENERAL JOURNAL

PAGE 5

	DATE	DESCRIPTION	POST. REF.	DEBIT	CREDIT	
1						1
2						2
3						3
4						4
5						5
6						6
7						7
8						8
9						9
10						10
11						11
12						12
13						13
14						14
15						15
16						16
17						17
18						18
19						19
20						20
21						21
22						22
23						23
24						24
25						25
26						26
27						27
28						28
29						29
30						30
31						31
32						32
33						33
34						34
35						35

Name ______________________

Comprehensive Problem 1 (Concluded)

GENERAL JOURNAL

PAGE 6

	DATE		DESCRIPTION	POST. REF.	DEBIT	CREDIT	
1							1
2							2
3							3
4							4
5							5
6							6
7							7
8							8
9							9

12.

ACCOUNT	ACCT. NO.	DEBIT BALANCE	CREDIT BALANCE

Comprehensive Problem 1, Period 2: The Accounting Cycle

1.

GENERAL JOURNAL

PAGE 5

	DATE	DESCRIPTION	POST. REF.	DEBIT	CREDIT	
1						1
2						2
3						3
4						4
5						5
6						6
7						7
8						8
9						9
10						10
11						11
12						12
13						13
14						14
15						15
16						16
17						17
18						18
19						19
20						20
21						21
22						22
23						23
24						24
25						25
26						26
27						27
28						28
29						29
30						30
31						31
32						32
33						33
34						34
35						35

Comprehensive Problem 1, Period 2 (Continued)

GENERAL JOURNAL

PAGE 6

	DATE	DESCRIPTION	POST. REF.	DEBIT	CREDIT	
1						1
2						2
3						3
4						4
5						5
6						6
7						7
8						8
9						9
10						10
11						11
12						12
13						13
14						14
15						15
16						16
17						17
18						18
19						19
20						20
21						21
22						22
23						23
24						24
25						25
26						26
27						27
28						28
29						29
30						30
31						31
32						32
33						33
34						34
35						35
36						36
37						37
38						38
39						39
40						40
41						41
42						42

Name ______________________________

Comprehensive Problem 1, Period 2 (Continued)

GENERAL JOURNAL

PAGE 7

	DATE	DESCRIPTION	POST. REF.	DEBIT	CREDIT	
1						1
2						2
3						3
4						4
5						5
6						6
7						7
8						8
9						9
10						10
11						11
12						12
13						13
14						14
15						15
16						16
17						17
18						18
19						19
20						20
21						21
22						22
23						23
24						24
25						25
26						26
27						27
28						28
29						29
30						30
31						31
32						32
33						33
34						34

Comprehensive Problem 1, Period 2 (Continued)

2., 6., and 11.

GENERAL LEDGER

ACCOUNT Cash ACCOUNT NO. 101

DATE		ITEM	POST. REF.	DEBIT	CREDIT	BALANCE DEBIT	BALANCE CREDIT
20-- Apr.	30	Balance	✓			130,650.00	

ACCOUNT Accounts Receivable ACCOUNT NO. 122

DATE		ITEM	POST. REF.	DEBIT	CREDIT	BALANCE DEBIT	BALANCE CREDIT

Comprehensive Problem 1, Period 2 (Continued)

ACCOUNT Office Supplies — ACCOUNT NO. 142

DATE		ITEM	POST. REF.	DEBIT	CREDIT	BALANCE DEBIT	BALANCE CREDIT
20-- Apr.	30	Balance	✓			100 00	

ACCOUNT Food Supplies — ACCOUNT NO. 144

DATE		ITEM	POST. REF.	DEBIT	CREDIT	BALANCE DEBIT	BALANCE CREDIT
20-- Apr.	30	Balance	✓			8000 00	

ACCOUNT Prepaid Insurance — ACCOUNT NO. 145

DATE		ITEM	POST. REF.	DEBIT	CREDIT	BALANCE DEBIT	BALANCE CREDIT
20-- Apr.	30	Balance	✓			7500 00	

ACCOUNT Prepaid Subscriptions — ACCOUNT NO. 146

DATE		ITEM	POST. REF.	DEBIT	CREDIT	BALANCE DEBIT	BALANCE CREDIT

Comprehensive Problem 1, Period 2 (Continued)

ACCOUNT Land ACCOUNT NO. 161

DATE	ITEM	POST. REF.	DEBIT	CREDIT	BALANCE DEBIT	BALANCE CREDIT

ACCOUNT Buildings ACCOUNT NO. 171

DATE	ITEM	POST. REF.	DEBIT	CREDIT	BALANCE DEBIT	BALANCE CREDIT

ACCOUNT Accumulated Depreciation—Buildings ACCOUNT NO. 171.1

DATE	ITEM	POST. REF.	DEBIT	CREDIT	BALANCE DEBIT	BALANCE CREDIT

ACCOUNT Fishing Boats ACCOUNT NO. 181

DATE	ITEM	POST. REF.	DEBIT	CREDIT	BALANCE DEBIT	BALANCE CREDIT
20-- Apr. 30	Balance	✓			60 0 0 0 00	

Comprehensive Problem 1, Period 2 (Continued)

ACCOUNT Accumulated Depreciation—Fishing Boats ACCOUNT NO. 181.1

DATE		ITEM	POST. REF.	DEBIT	CREDIT	BALANCE DEBIT	BALANCE CREDIT
20-- Apr.	30	Balance	✓				1,000.00

ACCOUNT Surround Sound System ACCOUNT NO. 182

DATE		ITEM	POST. REF.	DEBIT	CREDIT	BALANCE DEBIT	BALANCE CREDIT

ACCOUNT Accumulated Depreciation—Surround Sound System ACCOUNT NO. 182.1

DATE		ITEM	POST. REF.	DEBIT	CREDIT	BALANCE DEBIT	BALANCE CREDIT

ACCOUNT Big Screen TV ACCOUNT NO. 183

DATE		ITEM	POST. REF.	DEBIT	CREDIT	BALANCE DEBIT	BALANCE CREDIT

ACCOUNT Accumulated Depreciation—Big Screen TV ACCOUNT NO. 183.1

DATE		ITEM	POST. REF.	DEBIT	CREDIT	BALANCE DEBIT	BALANCE CREDIT

Comprehensive Problem 1, Period 2 (Continued)

ACCOUNT Accounts Payable ACCOUNT NO. 202

DATE		ITEM	POST. REF.	DEBIT	CREDIT	BALANCE DEBIT	BALANCE CREDIT
20-- Apr.	30	Balance	✓				66 5 0 0 00

ACCOUNT Wages Payable ACCOUNT NO. 219

DATE		ITEM	POST. REF.	DEBIT	CREDIT	BALANCE DEBIT	BALANCE CREDIT
20-- Apr.	30	Balance	✓				5 0 0 00

ACCOUNT Bob Night, Capital ACCOUNT NO. 311

DATE		ITEM	POST. REF.	DEBIT	CREDIT	BALANCE DEBIT	BALANCE CREDIT
20-- Apr.	30	Balance	✓				138 2 5 0 00

ACCOUNT Bob Night, Drawing ACCOUNT NO. 312

DATE		ITEM	POST. REF.	DEBIT	CREDIT	BALANCE DEBIT	BALANCE CREDIT

Comprehensive Problem 1, Period 2 (Continued)

ACCOUNT Income Summary ACCOUNT NO. 313

DATE	ITEM	POST. REF.	DEBIT	CREDIT	BALANCE DEBIT	BALANCE CREDIT

ACCOUNT Registration Fees ACCOUNT NO. 401

DATE	ITEM	POST. REF.	DEBIT	CREDIT	BALANCE DEBIT	BALANCE CREDIT

ACCOUNT Vending Commission Revenue ACCOUNT NO. 404

DATE	ITEM	POST. REF.	DEBIT	CREDIT	BALANCE DEBIT	BALANCE CREDIT

ACCOUNT Wages Expense ACCOUNT NO. 511

DATE	ITEM	POST. REF.	DEBIT	CREDIT	BALANCE DEBIT	BALANCE CREDIT

Comprehensive Problem 1, Period 2 (Continued)

ACCOUNT Advertising Expense ACCOUNT NO. 512

DATE	ITEM	POST. REF.	DEBIT	CREDIT	BALANCE DEBIT	BALANCE CREDIT

ACCOUNT Rent Expense ACCOUNT NO. 521

DATE	ITEM	POST. REF.	DEBIT	CREDIT	BALANCE DEBIT	BALANCE CREDIT

ACCOUNT Office Supplies Expense ACCOUNT NO. 523

DATE	ITEM	POST. REF.	DEBIT	CREDIT	BALANCE DEBIT	BALANCE CREDIT

ACCOUNT Food Supplies Expense ACCOUNT NO. 524

DATE	ITEM	POST. REF.	DEBIT	CREDIT	BALANCE DEBIT	BALANCE CREDIT

Comprehensive Problem 1, Period 2 (Continued)

ACCOUNT Telephone Expense ACCOUNT NO. 525

DATE	ITEM	POST. REF.	DEBIT	CREDIT	BALANCE DEBIT	BALANCE CREDIT

ACCOUNT Utilities Expense ACCOUNT NO. 533

DATE	ITEM	POST. REF.	DEBIT	CREDIT	BALANCE DEBIT	BALANCE CREDIT

ACCOUNT Insurance Expense ACCOUNT NO. 535

DATE	ITEM	POST. REF.	DEBIT	CREDIT	BALANCE DEBIT	BALANCE CREDIT

ACCOUNT Postage Expense ACCOUNT NO. 536

DATE	ITEM	POST. REF.	DEBIT	CREDIT	BALANCE DEBIT	BALANCE CREDIT

Comprehensive Problem 1, Period 2 (Continued)

ACCOUNT Repair Expense ACCOUNT NO. 537

DATE	ITEM	POST. REF.	DEBIT	CREDIT	BALANCE DEBIT	BALANCE CREDIT

ACCOUNT Depreciation Expense—Buildings ACCOUNT NO. 540

DATE	ITEM	POST. REF.	DEBIT	CREDIT	BALANCE DEBIT	BALANCE CREDIT

ACCOUNT Depreciation Expense—Surround Sound System ACCOUNT NO. 541

DATE	ITEM	POST. REF.	DEBIT	CREDIT	BALANCE DEBIT	BALANCE CREDIT

ACCOUNT Depreciation Expense—Fishing Boats ACCOUNT NO. 542

DATE	ITEM	POST. REF.	DEBIT	CREDIT	BALANCE DEBIT	BALANCE CREDIT

Comprehensive Problem 1, Period 2 (Continued)

ACCOUNT Depreciation Expense—Big Screen TV ACCOUNT NO. 543

DATE	ITEM	POST. REF.	DEBIT	CREDIT	BALANCE	
					DEBIT	CREDIT

ACCOUNT Satellite Programming Expense ACCOUNT NO. 546

DATE	ITEM	POST. REF.	DEBIT	CREDIT	BALANCE	
					DEBIT	CREDIT

ACCOUNT Subscriptions Expense ACCOUNT NO. 548

DATE	ITEM	POST. REF.	DEBIT	CREDIT	BALANCE	
					DEBIT	CREDIT

Comprehensive Problem 1, Period 2 (Continued)

3. and 4.

	ACCOUNT TITLE	TRIAL BALANCE		ADJUSTMENTS	
		DEBIT	CREDIT	DEBIT	CREDIT
1					
2					
3					
4					
5					
6					
7					
8					
9					
10					
11					
12					
13					
14					
15					
16					
17					
18					
19					
20					
21					
22					
23					
24					
25					
26					
27					
28					
29					
30					
31					
32					
33					
34					
35					
36					
37					
38					
39					
40					

Comprehensive Problem 1, Period 2 (Continued)

ADJUSTED TRIAL BALANCE		INCOME STATEMENT		BALANCE SHEET		
DEBIT	CREDIT	DEBIT	CREDIT	DEBIT	CREDIT	
						1
						2
						3
						4
						5
						6
						7
						8
						9
						10
						11
						12
						13
						14
						15
						16
						17
						18
						19
						20
						21
						22
						23
						24
						25
						26
						27
						28
						29
						30
						31
						32
						33
						34
						35
						36
						37
						38
						39
						40

Comprehensive Problem 1, Period 2 (Continued)

5.

GENERAL JOURNAL

PAGE 8

	DATE	DESCRIPTION	POST. REF.	DEBIT	CREDIT	
1						1
2						2
3						3
4						4
5						5
6						6
7						7
8						8
9						9
10						10
11						11
12						12
13						13
14						14
15						15
16						16
17						17
18						18
19						19
20						20
21						21
22						22
23						23
24						24
25						25
26						26
27						27
28						28
29						29
30						30
31						31
32						32
33						33
34						34
35						35

Comprehensive Problem 1, Period 2 (Continued)

7.

8.

Comprehensive Problem 1, Period 2 (Continued)

9.

omprehensive Problem 1, Period 2 (Continued)

).

GENERAL JOURNAL

PAGE 9

DATE		DESCRIPTION	POST. REF.	DEBIT	CREDIT	
						1
						2
						3
						4
						5
						6
						7
						8
						9
						10
						11
						12
						13
						14
						15
						16
						17
						18
						19
						20
						21
						22
						23
						24
						25
						26
						27
						28
						29
						30
						31
						32
						33
						34
						35

Comprehensive Problem 1, Period 2 (Concluded)

12.

ACCOUNT TITLE	ACCT. NO.	DEBIT BALANCE	CREDIT BALANCE

me ______________________

ercise 7-1A

______________ 5. ______________

______________ 6. ______________

______________ 7. ______________

____

ercise 7-2A

DEPOSIT TICKET 63-1209/631

WIZARD BANK
3711 Buena Vista Dr.
Orlando, FL 32811-1314

Date ______________ 20____

CHECKS AND OTHER ITEMS ARE RECEIVED FOR DEPOSIT SUBJECT TO THE TERMS AND CONDITIONS OF THIS FINANCIAL INSTITUTION'S ACCOUNT AGREEMENT.

____
SIGN HERE ONLY IF CASH RECEIVED FROM DEPOSIT

CURRENCY			
COIN			
CHECKS			
TOTAL FROM OTHER SIDE			
SUBTOTAL			
LESS CASH RECEIVED			
NET DEPOSIT			

⑆063112094⑆ 0001632475⑈

ercise 7-3A

No. 1

DATE ______________ 20____
TO ______________
FOR ______________
____
ACCT. ______________

	DOLLARS	CENTS
BAL BRO'T FOR'D		
AMT. DEPOSITED		
TOTAL		
AMT. THIS CHECK		
BAL CAR'D FOR'D		

No. 1 63-1209/631

______________ 20____

PAY TO THE ORDER OF ______________ $ ______

______________ Dollars

WIZARD BANK
3711 Buena Vista Dr.
Orlando, FL 32811-1314

FOR CLASSROOM USE ONLY

MEMO ______________ BY ______________

⑆063112094⑆ 0001632475⑈

Exercise 7-4A

	Ending Bank Balance	Ending Checkbook Balance
1.		
2.		
3.		
4.		
5.		
6.		
7.		

Exercise 7-5A

GENERAL JOURNAL

PAGE

	DATE		DESCRIPTION	POST. REF.	DEBIT	CREDIT
1						
2						
3						
4						
5						
6						
7						
8						
9						
10						
11						
12						
13						
14						
15						
16						
17						
18						
19						
20						
21						

ame ______________________________

xercise 7-6A

GENERAL JOURNAL

PAGE

DATE		DESCRIPTION	POST. REF.	DEBIT	CREDIT	
						1
						2
						3
						4
						5
						6
						7
						8
						9
						10
						11
						12
						13
						14
						15
						16
						17
						18
						19
						20
						21
						22
						23
						24
						25
						26
						27
						28
						29
						30
						31
						32
						33
						34
						35
						36

Exercise 7-7A

GENERAL JOURNAL

PAGE

	DATE	DESCRIPTION	POST. REF.	DEBIT	CREDIT
1					
2					
3					
4					
5					
6					
7					
8					
9					
10					
11					
12					
13					
14					
15					
16					
17					
18					
19					
20					
21					
22					
23					
24					
25					
26					
27					
28					
29					
30					
31					
32					
33					
34					
35					
36					

ame ____________________

xercise 7-4B

Ending Bank Balance	Ending Checkbook Balance

xercise 7-5B

GENERAL JOURNAL

PAGE

DATE		DESCRIPTION	POST. REF.	DEBIT	CREDIT	
						1
						2
						3
						4
						5
						6
						7
						8
						9
						10
						11
						12
						13
						14
						15
						16
						17
						18
						19
						20
						21

Exercise 7-6B

GENERAL JOURNAL

PAGE

	DATE		DESCRIPTION	POST. REF.	DEBIT	CREDIT
1						
2						
3						
4						
5						
6						
7						
8						
9						
10						
11						
12						
13						
14						
15						
16						
17						
18						
19						
20						
21						
22						
23						
24						
25						
26						
27						
28						
29						
30						
31						
32						
33						
34						
35						
36						

ame ______________________________

xercise 7-7B

GENERAL JOURNAL

PAGE

DATE		DESCRIPTION	POST. REF.	DEBIT	CREDIT	
						1
						2
						3
						4
						5
						6
						7
						8
						9
						10
						11
						12
						13
						14
						15
						16
						17
						18
						19
						20
						21
						22
						23
						24
						25
						26
						27
						28
						29
						30
						31
						32
						33
						34
						35
						36

Problem 7-8B

1.

ame ______________________

roblem 7-8B (Concluded)

GENERAL JOURNAL

PAGE

DATE		DESCRIPTION	POST. REF.	DEBIT	CREDIT	
						1
						2
						3
						4
						5
						6
						7
						8
						9
						10
						11
						12
						13
						14
						15

Problem 7-9B

1.

Tori's Health Center
Bank Reconciliation
April 30, 20--

Bank statement Balance, April 30		3,275.60
Add Deposit in transit		1,592.00
		4,867.60
Deduct outstanding checks		
No. 481	215.00	
No. 493	71.00	
No. 494	24.30	
No. 397	38.60	348.90
Adjusted Bank Balance		4,518.70
Book Balance, April 30		4,690.30
Add interest		28.00
Add error in check No. 422		54.00
		4,772.30
Deduct - unrecorded ATM withdrawal	200.00	
NSF check	29.10	
Bank service charge	24.50	253.60
		4,518.70

ame Kyle Kaper

roblem 7-9B (Concluded)

GENERAL JOURNAL

PAGE

DATE		DESCRIPTION	POST. REF.	DEBIT	CREDIT	
April 20--	30					1
						2
						3
						4
						5
						6
						7
						8
						9
						10
						11
						12
						13
						14
						15
						16
						17
						18
						19

Problem 7-10B

1. and 3.

GENERAL JOURNAL

PAGE

	DATE		DESCRIPTION	POST. REF.	DEBIT	CREDIT
1						
2						
3						
4						
5						
6						
7						
8						
9						
10						
11						
12						
13						

Name

Problem 7-10B (Concluded)

2. and 3.

PETTY CASH PAYMENTS FOR MONTH OF 20-- PAGE

					DISTRIBUTION OF PAYMENTS								
	DAY	DESCRIPTION	VOU. NO.	TOTAL AMOUNT	OFFICE SUPPLIES	POSTAGE EXPENSE	CHARIT. CONTRIB. EXPENSE	TELEPHONE EXPENSE	TRAVEL & ENTER. EXPENSE	MISC. EXPENSE	ACCOUNT	AMOUNT	
1													1
2													2
3													3
4													4
5													5
6													6
7													7
8													8
9													9
10													10
11													11
12													12
13													13
14													14
15													15
16													16
17													17
18													18
19													19
20													20
21													21
22													22

Problem 7-11B

1.

GENERAL JOURNAL

PAGE 8

	DATE		DESCRIPTION	POST. REF.	DEBIT	CREDIT
1						
2						
3						
4						
5						
6						
7						
8						
9						
10						
11						
12						
13						
14						
15						
16						
17						
18						
19						
20						
21						
22						
23						

2.

ACCOUNT ACCOUNT NO.

DATE		ITEM	POST. REF.	DEBIT	CREDIT	BALANCE	
						DEBIT	CREDIT

3. The balance represents:

Name ____________________

Challenge Problem (Concluded)

. Lawrence Bank

GENERAL JOURNAL

PAGE

DATE	DESCRIPTION	POST. REF.	DEBIT	CREDIT	
					1
					2
					3
					4
					5
					6
					7
					8
					9
					10
					11
					12
					13
					14
					15
					16
					17
					18
					19
					20
					21
					22
					23
					24
					25
					26
					27
					28
					29

APPENDIX: Internal Controls

Exercise 7Apx-1A

1. ____

   ____

2. ____

   ____

3. ____

   ____

4. ____

   ____

5. ____

   ____

Exercise 7Apx-2A

1. _____
2. _____
3. _____
4. _____
5. _____

Exercise 7Apx-3A

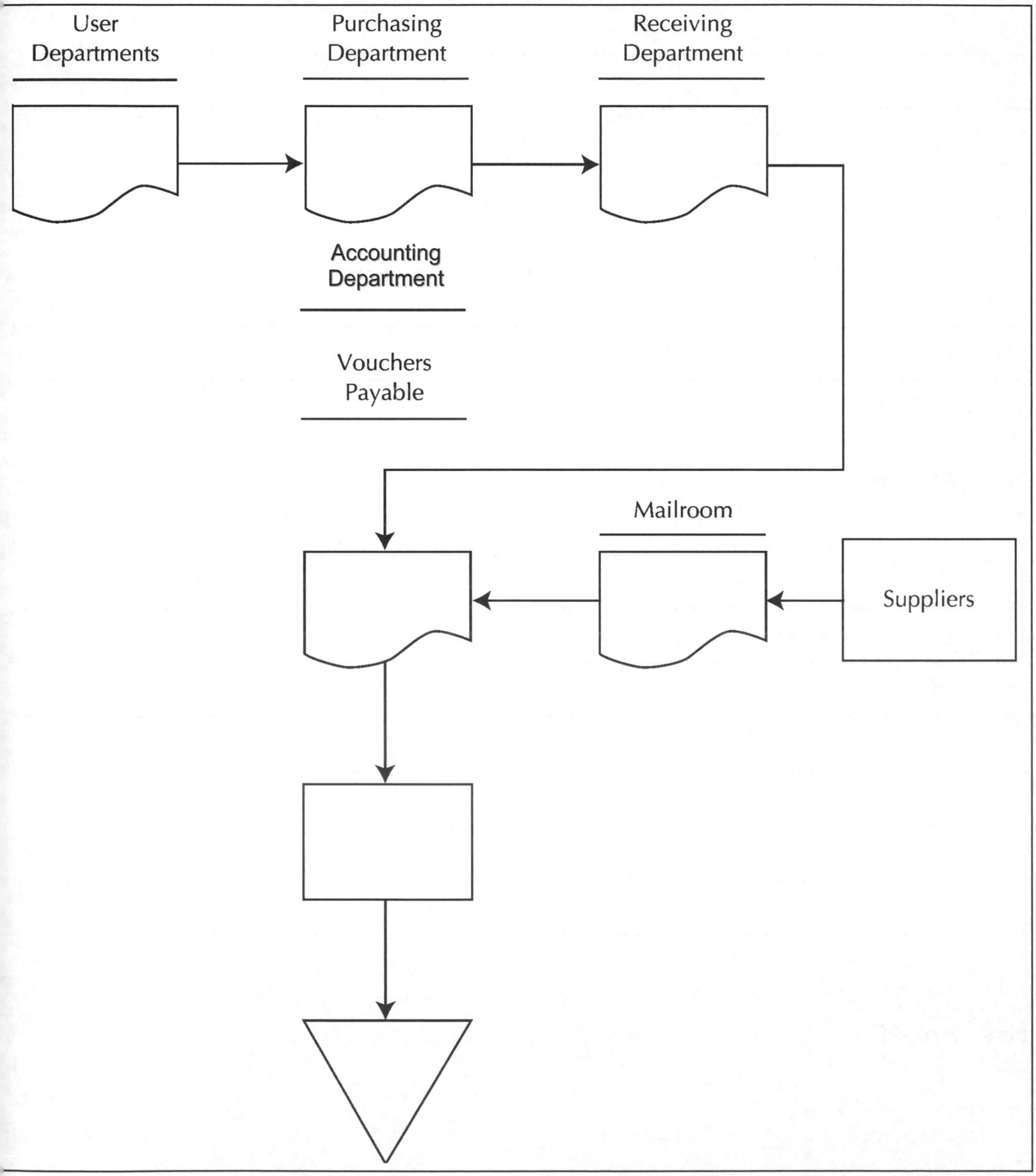

Problem 7Apx-4A

1. ______

2. ______

3. ______

4. ______

Exercise 7Apx-1B

1. ______

2. ______

3. ______

4. ______

Exercise 7Apx-2B

1. ____

2. ____

3. ____

4. ____

Exercise 7Apx-3B

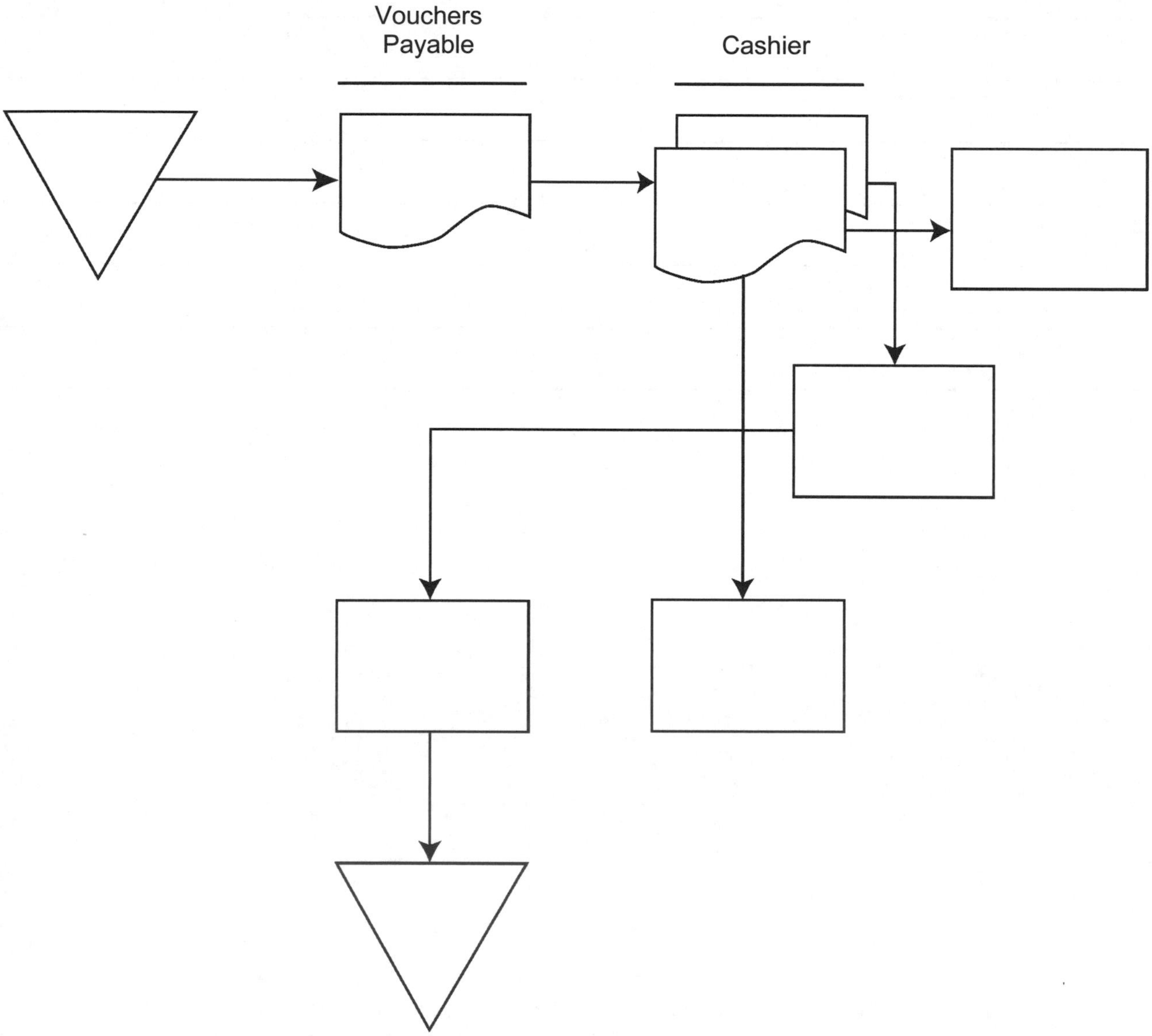

Problem 7Apx-4B

1.

2.

3.

4.

Problem 8-9A (Concluded)

OR PERIOD ENDED 20--

DEDUCTIONS										
FEDERAL INCOME TAX	SOCIAL SECURITY TAX	MEDICARE TAX	CITY TAX	HEALTH INSUR.	OTHER		TOTAL	NET PAY	CK. NO.	
										1
										2
										3
										4
										5
										6
										7
										8
										9
										10
										11
										12
										13
										14

2.

GENERAL JOURNAL

PAGE

	DATE	DESCRIPTION	POST. REF.	DEBIT	CREDIT	
1						1
2						2
3						3
4						4
5						5
6						6
7						7
8						8
9						9
10						10
11						11
12						12
13						13
14						14

Problem 8-10A

EMPLOYEE EARNINGS RECORD

20 -- PERIOD ENDED	EARNINGS				TAXABLE EARNINGS		DEDUCTIONS	
	REGULAR	OVERTIME	TOTAL	CUMULATIVE TOTAL	UNEMPLOY. COMP.	SOCIAL SECURITY	FEDERAL INCOME TAX	SOCIAL SECURITY TAX

GENDER	DEPARTMENT	OCCUPATION	SOCIAL SECURITY NO.	MARITAL STATUS	ALLOW-ANCES
M / F					

Name ______________________________

Problem 8-10A (Concluded)

FOR PERIOD ENDED 20--

DEDUCTIONS						
MEDICARE TAX	CITY TAX	HEALTH INSURANCE	OTHER	TOTAL	CK. NO.	AMOUNT

PAY RATE	DATE OF BIRTH	DATE HIRED	NAME/ADDRESS	EMP. NO.

Exercise 8-1B

a. __________ regular hours × $12.00 per hour __________

b. __________ overtime hours × $18.00 per hour __________

c. Total gross wages __________

d. Federal income tax withholding (from tax tables in Figure 8-4) __________

e. Social Security withholding at 6.2% __________

f. Medicare withholding at 1.45% __________

g. Total withholding __________

h. Net pay __________

Exercise 8-2B

Exercise 8-3B

Exercise 8-4B

	Marital Status	Total Weekly Earnings	Number of Allowances	Amount of Withholding
a.	M	$546.00	4	__________
b.	M	390.00	3	__________
c.	S	461.39	2	__________
d.	M	522.88	2	__________
e.	S	612.00	0	__________

ame Kyle Kaper

hallenge Problem

GENERAL JOURNAL

PAGE

DATE		DESCRIPTION	POST. REF.	DEBIT	CREDIT	
						1
						2
						3
						4
						5
						6
						7
						8
						9
						10

Problem 9-8A

GENERAL JOURNAL

PAGE

DATE		DESCRIPTION	POST. REF.	DEBIT	CREDIT	
						1
						2
						3
						4
						5
						6
						7
						8
						9
						10
						11
						12
						13
						14
						15
						16
						17
						18
						19
						20
						21
						22
						23
						24
						25
						26
						27
						28
						29
						30
						31
						32
						33
						34
						35
						36

Problem 9-8A (Continued)

GENERAL JOURNAL

PAGE

	DATE	DESCRIPTION	POST. REF.	DEBIT	CREDIT	
1						1
2						2
3						3
4						4
5						5
6						6
7						7
8						8
9						9
10						10
11						11
12						12
13						13
14						14
15						15
16						16
17						17
18						18
19						19
20						20
21						21
22						22
23						23
24						24
25						25
26						26
27						27
28						28
29						29
30						30
31						31
32						32
33						33
34						34
35						35

Exercise 9-3B (Concluded)

GENERAL JOURNAL

PAGE

DATE		DESCRIPTION	POST. REF.	DEBIT	CREDIT	
						1
						2
						3
						4
						5
						6
						7

Exercise 9-4B: See page WP-302.

Exercise 9-5B

GENERAL JOURNAL

PAGE

	DATE		DESCRIPTION	POST. REF.	DEBIT	CREDIT	
1							1
2							2
3							3
4							4
5							5
6							6
7							7
8							8
9							9
10							10
11							11
12							12
13							13
14							14

Exercise 9-4B

Exercise 9-6B

1.

GENERAL JOURNAL

PAGE

	DATE	DESCRIPTION	POST. REF.	DEBIT	CREDIT	
1						1
2						2
3						3
4						4
5						5

2.

GENERAL JOURNAL

PAGE

	DATE	DESCRIPTION	POST. REF.	DEBIT	CREDIT	
1						1
2						2
3						3
4						4
5						5

ame ______________________________

roblem 9-7B

.

		Taxable Earnings	
Name	**Current Earnings**	**Unemploy. Comp.**	**Social Security**
ckers, Alice			
onley, Dorothy			
avis, James			
awrence, Kevin			
awlings, Judy			
anaka, Sumio			
adillo, Raynette			
Total			

.

GENERAL JOURNAL

PAGE

	DATE		DESCRIPTION	POST. REF.	DEBIT	CREDIT	
1							1
2							2
3							3
4							4
5							5
6							6
7							7
8							8
9							9
0							10
1							11
2							12

Problem 9-8B

1.

GENERAL JOURNAL

PAGE

DATE		DESCRIPTION	POST. REF.	DEBIT	CREDIT

ame ______________________

roblem 9-8B (Continued)

GENERAL JOURNAL

PAGE

DATE		DESCRIPTION	POST. REF.	DEBIT	CREDIT	
						1
						2
						3
						4
						5
						6
						7
						8
						9
						10
						11
						12
						13
						14
						15
						16
						17
						18
						19
						20
						21
						22
						23
						24
						25
						26
						27
						28
						29
						30
						31
						32
						33
						34
						35

Problem 9-8B (Concluded)

2.

Cash 101

Employee Income Tax Payable 211

Social Security Tax Payable 212

Medicare Tax Payable 213

Savings Bond Deductions Payable 218

FUTA Tax Payable 221

SUTA Tax Payable 222

Wages and Salaries Expense 511

Payroll Taxes Expense 530

Mastery Problem

1., 2., and 3.

GENERAL JOURNAL

PAGE

	DATE	DESCRIPTION	POST. REF.	DEBIT	CREDIT	
1						1
2						2
3						3
4						4
5						5
6						6
7						7
8						8
9						9
10						10
11						11
12						12
13						13
14						14
15						15
16						16
17						17
18						18
19						19
20						20
21						21
22						22
23						23
24						24
25						25
26						26
27						27
28						28
29						29
30						30
31						31
32						32
33						33
34						34
35						35

Mastery Problem (Concluded)

GENERAL JOURNAL

PAGE

	DATE		DESCRIPTION	POST. REF.	DEBIT	CREDIT	
1							1
2							2
3							3
4							4
5							5
6							6
7							7
8							8
9							9
10							10
11							11
12							12
13							13
14							14
15							15
16							16
17							17
18							18
19							19
20							20
21							21
22							22
23							23
24							24
25							25
26							26
27							27
28							28
29							29
30							30
31							31
32							32
33							33
34							34
35							35

This page left intentionally blank.

Exercise M-1A

COMBINATION JOURNAL

	DATE	CASH DEBIT	CASH CREDIT	DESCRIPTION	POST. REF.	
1						1
2						2
3						3
4						4
5						5
6						6
7						7
8						8
9						9
10						10
11						11
12						12
13						13
14						14
15						15
16						16
17						17
18						18
19						19
20						20
21						21
22						22
23						23
24						24
25						25
26						26
27						27
28						28
29						29
30						30
31						31
32						32
33						33
34						34

Exercise M-1A (Concluded)

PAGE 1

	GENERAL				
	DEBIT	CREDIT			
1					1
2					2
3					3
4					4
5					5
6					6
7					7
8					8
9					9
10					10
11					11
12					12
13					13
14					14
15					15
16					16
17					17
18					18
19					19
20					20
21					21
22					22
23					23
24					24
25					25
26					26
27					27
28					28
29					29
30					30
31					31
32					32
33					33
34					34

Exercise M-2A

COMBINATION JOURNAL

	DATE	CASH		DESCRIPTION	POST. REF.	
		DEBIT	CREDIT			
1						1
2						2
3						3
4						4
5						5
6						6
7						7
8						8
9						9
10						10
11						11
12						12
13						13
14						14
15						15
16						16
17						17
18						18
19						19
20						20
21						21
22						22
23						23
24						24
25						25
26						26
27						27
28						28

Proving the Combination Journal:

Exercise M-2A (Concluded)

PAGE 1

	GENERAL				
	DEBIT	CREDIT			
1					1
2					2
3					3
4					4
5					5
6					6
7					7
8					8
9					9
10					10
11					11
12					12
13					13
14					14
15					15
16					16
17					17
18					18
19					19
20					20
21					21
22					22
23					23
24					24
25					25
26					26
27					27
28					28

Problem M-3A

1. and 4.

COMBINATION JOURNAL

	DATE		CASH DEBIT	CASH CREDIT	DESCRIPTION	POST. REF.	
1							1
2							2
3							3
4							4
5							5
6							6
7							7
8							8
9							9
10							10
11							11
12							12
13							13
14							14
15							15
16							16
17							17
18							18
19							19
20							20
21							21
22							22
23							23
24							24
25							25
26							26
27							27
28							28
29							29
30							30
31							31
32							32
33							33
34							34

Name ______________________________

Problem M-3A (Continued)

PAGE 1

	GENERAL					
	DEBIT	CREDIT				
1						1
2						2
3						3
4						4
5						5
6						6
7						7
8						8
9						9
10						10
11						11
12						12
13						13
14						14
15						15
16						16
17						17
18						18
19						19
20						20
21						21
22						22
23						23
24						24
25						25
26						26
27						27
28						28
29						29
30						30
31						31
32						32
33						33
34						34

Problem M-3A (Continued)

2. Cash balance, January 12:

3. Proving the Combination Journal:

5.

ACCOUNT	ACCT. NO.	DEBIT BALANCE	CREDIT BALANCE

Problem M-3A (Continued)

4.

PARTIAL GENERAL LEDGER

ACCOUNT Cash ACCOUNT NO. 101

DATE	ITEM	POST. REF.	DEBIT	CREDIT	BALANCE DEBIT	BALANCE CREDIT

ACCOUNT Office Supplies ACCOUNT NO. 142

DATE	ITEM	POST. REF.	DEBIT	CREDIT	BALANCE DEBIT	BALANCE CREDIT

ACCOUNT Office Equipment ACCOUNT NO. 181

DATE	ITEM	POST. REF.	DEBIT	CREDIT	BALANCE DEBIT	BALANCE CREDIT

ACCOUNT Accounts Payable ACCOUNT NO. 202

DATE	ITEM	POST. REF.	DEBIT	CREDIT	BALANCE DEBIT	BALANCE CREDIT

Problem M-3A (Continued)

ACCOUNT Angela McWharton, Capital ACCOUNT NO. 311

DATE	ITEM	POST. REF.	DEBIT	CREDIT	BALANCE DEBIT	BALANCE CREDIT

ACCOUNT Angela McWharton, Drawing ACCOUNT NO. 312

DATE	ITEM	POST. REF.	DEBIT	CREDIT	BALANCE DEBIT	BALANCE CREDIT

ACCOUNT Income Summary ACCOUNT NO. 313

DATE	ITEM	POST. REF.	DEBIT	CREDIT	BALANCE DEBIT	BALANCE CREDIT

ACCOUNT Nursing Care Fees ACCOUNT NO. 401

DATE	ITEM	POST. REF.	DEBIT	CREDIT	BALANCE DEBIT	BALANCE CREDIT

ACCOUNT Wages Expense ACCOUNT NO. 511

DATE	ITEM	POST. REF.	DEBIT	CREDIT	BALANCE DEBIT	BALANCE CREDIT

Problem M-3A (Continued)

ACCOUNT Advertising Expense ACCOUNT NO. 512

DATE	ITEM	POST. REF.	DEBIT	CREDIT	BALANCE	
					DEBIT	CREDIT

ACCOUNT Rent Expense ACCOUNT NO. 521

DATE	ITEM	POST. REF.	DEBIT	CREDIT	BALANCE	
					DEBIT	CREDIT

ACCOUNT Telephone Expense ACCOUNT NO. 525

DATE	ITEM	POST. REF.	DEBIT	CREDIT	BALANCE	
					DEBIT	CREDIT

ACCOUNT Transportation Expense ACCOUNT NO. 526

DATE	ITEM	POST. REF.	DEBIT	CREDIT	BALANCE	
					DEBIT	CREDIT

ACCOUNT Electricity Expense ACCOUNT NO. 533

DATE	ITEM	POST. REF.	DEBIT	CREDIT	BALANCE	
					DEBIT	CREDIT

Problem M-3A (Concluded)

ACCOUNT Miscellaneous Expense ACCOUNT NO. 549

DATE	ITEM	POST. REF.	DEBIT	CREDIT	BALANCE	
					DEBIT	CREDIT

This page left intentionally blank.

Problem M-4A

1. and 4.

COMBINATION JOURNAL

	DATE	CASH DEBIT	CASH CREDIT	DESCRIPTION	POST. REF.	
1						1
2						2
3						3
4						4
5						5
6						6
7						7
8						8
9						9
10						10
11						11
12						12
13						13
14						14
15						15
16						16
17						17
18						18
19						19
20						20
21						21
22						22
23						23
24						24
25						25
26						26
27						27
28						28
29						29
30						30
31						31
32						32
33						33
34						34

Problem M-4A (Continued)

PAGE 5

GENERAL				
DEBIT	CREDIT			

Problem M-4A (Continued)

2. Cash balance, November 12:

3. Proving the Combination Journal:

4., 6., and 8.

GENERAL LEDGER

ACCOUNT Cash ACCOUNT NO. 101

DATE	ITEM	POST. REF.	DEBIT	CREDIT	BALANCE	
					DEBIT	CREDIT

ACCOUNT Tailoring Supplies ACCOUNT NO. 141

DATE	ITEM	POST. REF.	DEBIT	CREDIT	BALANCE	
					DEBIT	CREDIT

Problem M-4A (Continued)

ACCOUNT Office Supplies — ACCOUNT NO. 142

DATE	ITEM	POST. REF.	DEBIT	CREDIT	BALANCE DEBIT	BALANCE CREDIT

ACCOUNT Prepaid Insurance — ACCOUNT NO. 145

DATE	ITEM	POST. REF.	DEBIT	CREDIT	BALANCE DEBIT	BALANCE CREDIT

ACCOUNT Tailoring Equipment — ACCOUNT NO. 188

DATE	ITEM	POST. REF.	DEBIT	CREDIT	BALANCE DEBIT	BALANCE CREDIT

ACCOUNT Accumulated Depreciation—Tailoring Equipment — ACCOUNT NO. 188.1

DATE	ITEM	POST. REF.	DEBIT	CREDIT	BALANCE DEBIT	BALANCE CREDIT

Problem M-4A (Continued)

ACCOUNT Accounts Payable ACCOUNT NO. 202

DATE	ITEM	POST. REF.	DEBIT	CREDIT	BALANCE	
					DEBIT	CREDIT

ACCOUNT Sue Reyton, Capital ACCOUNT NO. 311

DATE	ITEM	POST. REF.	DEBIT	CREDIT	BALANCE	
					DEBIT	CREDIT

ACCOUNT Sue Reyton, Drawing ACCOUNT NO. 312

DATE	ITEM	POST. REF.	DEBIT	CREDIT	BALANCE	
					DEBIT	CREDIT

ACCOUNT Income Summary ACCOUNT NO. 313

DATE	ITEM	POST. REF.	DEBIT	CREDIT	BALANCE	
					DEBIT	CREDIT

Problem M-4A (Continued)

ACCOUNT Tailoring Fees ACCOUNT NO. 401

DATE	ITEM	POST. REF.	DEBIT	CREDIT	BALANCE DEBIT	BALANCE CREDIT

ACCOUNT Wages Expense ACCOUNT NO. 511

DATE	ITEM	POST. REF.	DEBIT	CREDIT	BALANCE DEBIT	BALANCE CREDIT

ACCOUNT Advertising Expense ACCOUNT NO. 512

DATE	ITEM	POST. REF.	DEBIT	CREDIT	BALANCE DEBIT	BALANCE CREDIT

ACCOUNT Rent Expense ACCOUNT NO. 521

DATE	ITEM	POST. REF.	DEBIT	CREDIT	BALANCE DEBIT	BALANCE CREDIT

Problem M-4A (Continued)

ACCOUNT Office Supplies Expense ACCOUNT NO. 523

DATE	ITEM	POST. REF.	DEBIT	CREDIT	BALANCE DEBIT	BALANCE CREDIT

ACCOUNT Tailoring Supplies Expense ACCOUNT NO. 524

DATE	ITEM	POST. REF.	DEBIT	CREDIT	BALANCE DEBIT	BALANCE CREDIT

ACCOUNT Telephone Expense ACCOUNT NO. 525

DATE	ITEM	POST. REF.	DEBIT	CREDIT	BALANCE DEBIT	BALANCE CREDIT

ACCOUNT Electricity Expense ACCOUNT NO. 533

DATE	ITEM	POST. REF.	DEBIT	CREDIT	BALANCE DEBIT	BALANCE CREDIT

roblem M-4A (Continued)

CCOUNT Insurance Expense ACCOUNT NO. 535

DATE	ITEM	POST. REF.	DEBIT	CREDIT	BALANCE	
					DEBIT	CREDIT

CCOUNT Depreciation Expense—Tailoring Equipment ACCOUNT NO. 542

DATE	ITEM	POST. REF.	DEBIT	CREDIT	BALANCE	
					DEBIT	CREDIT

CCOUNT Miscellaneous Expense ACCOUNT NO. 549

DATE	ITEM	POST. REF.	DEBIT	CREDIT	BALANCE	
					DEBIT	CREDIT

Problem M-4A (Continued)

5.

	ACCOUNT TITLE	TRIAL BALANCE		ADJUSTMENTS	
		DEBIT	CREDIT	DEBIT	CREDIT
1					
2					
3					
4					
5					
6					
7					
8					
9					
10					
11					
12					
13					
14					
15					
16					
17					
18					
19					
20					
21					
22					
23					
24					
25					
26					
27					
28					
29					
30					
31					
32					

roblem M-4A (Continued)

ADJUSTED TRIAL BALANCE		INCOME STATEMENT		BALANCE SHEET		
DEBIT	CREDIT	DEBIT	CREDIT	DEBIT	CREDIT	
						1
						2
						3
						4
						5
						6
						7
						8
						9
						10
						11
						12
						13
						14
						15
						16
						17
						18
						19
						20
						21
						22
						23
						24
						25
						26
						27
						28
						29
						30
						31
						32

Problem M-4A (Continued)

7.

Name ________________________

Problem M-4A (Continued)

Problem M-4A (Continued)

6. and 8.

COMBINATION JOURNAL

	DATE	CASH		DESCRIPTION	POST. REF.	
		DEBIT	CREDIT			
1						1
2						2
3						3
4						4
5						5
6						6
7						7
8						8
9						9
10						10
11						11
12						12
13						13
14						14
15						15
16						16
17						17
18						18
19						19
20						20
21						21
22						22
23						23
24						24
25						25
26						26
27						27
28						28
29						29
30						30
31						31
32						32
33						33
34						34

Problem M-4A (Concluded)

PAGE 6

	GENERAL					
	DEBIT	CREDIT				
1						1
2						2
3						3
4						4
5						5
6						6
7						7
8						8
9						9
10						10
11						11
12						12
13						13
14						14
15						15
16						16
17						17
18						18
19						19
20						20
21						21
22						22
23						23
24						24
25						25
26						26
27						27
28						28
29						29
30						30
31						31
32						32
33						33
34						34

Exercise M-1B

COMBINATION JOURNAL

	DATE	CASH DEBIT	CASH CREDIT	DESCRIPTION	POST. REF.	
1						1
2						2
3						3
4						4
5						5
6						6
7						7
8						8
9						9
10						10
11						11
12						12
13						13
14						14
15						15
16						16
17						17
18						18
19						19
20						20
21						21
22						22
23						23
24						24
25						25
26						26
27						27
28						28
29						29
30						30
31						31
32						32
33						33
34						34

Name ______________________________

Exercise M-1B (Concluded)

PAGE 1

	GENERAL				
	DEBIT	CREDIT			
1					1
2					2
3					3
4					4
5					5
6					6
7					7
8					8
9					9
10					10
11					11
12					12
13					13
14					14
15					15
16					16
17					17
18					18
19					19
20					20
21					21
22					22
23					23
24					24
25					25
26					26
27					27
28					28
29					29
30					30
31					31
32					32
33					33
34					34

Exercise M-2B

COMBINATION JOURNAL

	DATE	CASH DEBIT	CASH CREDIT	DESCRIPTION	POST. REF.	
1						1
2						2
3						3
4						4
5						5
6						6
7						7
8						8
9						9
10						10
11						11
12						12
13						13
14						14
15						15
16						16
17						17
18						18
19						19
20						20
21						21
22						22
23						23
24						24
25						25
26						26
27						27
28						28

Proving the Combination Journal:

Name ____________________

Exercise M-2B (Concluded)

PAGE 1

	GENERAL				
	DEBIT	CREDIT			
1					1
2					2
3					3
4					4
5					5
6					6
7					7
8					8
9					9
10					10
11					11
12					12
13					13
14					14
15					15
16					16
17					17
18					18
19					19
20					20
21					21
22					22
23					23
24					24
25					25
26					26
27					27
28					28

Problem M-3B

1. and 4.

COMBINATION JOURNAL

	DATE	CASH		DESCRIPTION	POST. REF.	
		DEBIT	CREDIT			
1						1
2						2
3						3
4						4
5						5
6						6
7						7
8						8
9						9
10						10
11						11
12						12
13						13
14						14
15						15
16						16
17						17
18						18
19						19
20						20
21						21
22						22
23						23
24						24
25						25
26						26
27						27
28						28
29						29
30						30
31						31
32						32
33						33
34						34

Name ______________________________

Problem M-3B (Continued)

PAGE 1

	GENERAL						
	DEBIT	CREDIT					
1							1
2							2
3							3
4							4
5							5
6							6
7							7
8							8
9							9
10							10
11							11
12							12
13							13
14							14
15							15
16							16
17							17
18							18
19							19
20							20
21							21
22							22
23							23
24							24
25							25
26							26
27							27
28							28
29							29
30							30
31							31
32							32
33							33
34							34

Problem M-3B (Continued)

2. Cash balance, July 14:

3. Proving the Combination Journal:

5.

ACCOUNT	ACCT. NO.	DEBIT BALANCE	CREDIT BALANCE

Problem M-3B (Continued)

4.

GENERAL LEDGER

ACCOUNT Cash ACCOUNT NO. 101

DATE		ITEM	POST. REF.	DEBIT	CREDIT	BALANCE	
						DEBIT	CREDIT

ACCOUNT Office Supplies ACCOUNT NO. 142

DATE		ITEM	POST. REF.	DEBIT	CREDIT	BALANCE	
						DEBIT	CREDIT

ACCOUNT Skiing Equipment ACCOUNT NO. 183

DATE		ITEM	POST. REF.	DEBIT	CREDIT	BALANCE	
						DEBIT	CREDIT

ACCOUNT Accounts Payable ACCOUNT NO. 202

DATE		ITEM	POST. REF.	DEBIT	CREDIT	BALANCE	
						DEBIT	CREDIT

Problem M-3B (Continued)

ACCOUNT J. B. Hoyt, Capital ACCOUNT NO. 311

DATE	ITEM	POST. REF.	DEBIT	CREDIT	BALANCE DEBIT	BALANCE CREDIT

ACCOUNT J. B. Hoyt, Drawing ACCOUNT NO. 312

DATE	ITEM	POST. REF.	DEBIT	CREDIT	BALANCE DEBIT	BALANCE CREDIT

ACCOUNT Income Summary ACCOUNT NO. 313

DATE	ITEM	POST. REF.	DEBIT	CREDIT	BALANCE DEBIT	BALANCE CREDIT

ACCOUNT Training Fees ACCOUNT NO. 401

DATE	ITEM	POST. REF.	DEBIT	CREDIT	BALANCE DEBIT	BALANCE CREDIT

ACCOUNT Wages Expense ACCOUNT NO. 511

DATE	ITEM	POST. REF.	DEBIT	CREDIT	BALANCE DEBIT	BALANCE CREDIT

Name ______________________________

Problem M-3B (Continued)

ACCOUNT Rent Expense ACCOUNT NO. 521

DATE	ITEM	POST. REF.	DEBIT	CREDIT	BALANCE	
					DEBIT	CREDIT

ACCOUNT Telephone Expense ACCOUNT NO. 525

DATE	ITEM	POST. REF.	DEBIT	CREDIT	BALANCE	
					DEBIT	CREDIT

ACCOUNT Transportation Expense ACCOUNT NO. 526

DATE	ITEM	POST. REF.	DEBIT	CREDIT	BALANCE	
					DEBIT	CREDIT

ACCOUNT Electricity Expense ACCOUNT NO. 533

DATE	ITEM	POST. REF.	DEBIT	CREDIT	BALANCE	
					DEBIT	CREDIT

ACCOUNT Repair Expense ACCOUNT NO. 537

DATE	ITEM	POST. REF.	DEBIT	CREDIT	BALANCE	
					DEBIT	CREDIT

Problem M-3B (Concluded)

ACCOUNT Miscellaneous Expense ACCOUNT NO. 549

DATE	ITEM	POST. REF.	DEBIT	CREDIT	BALANCE	
					DEBIT	CREDIT

Name ______________________________

This page left intentionally blank.

Problem M-4B

1. and 4.

COMBINATION JOURNAL

	DATE	CASH		DESCRIPTION	POST. REF.	
		DEBIT	CREDIT			
1						1
2						2
3						3
4						4
5						5
6						6
7						7
8						8
9						9
10						10
11						11
12						12
13						13
14						14
15						15
16						16
17						17
18						18
19						19
20						20
21						21
22						22
23						23
24						24
25						25
26						26
27						27
28						28
29						29
30						30
31						31
32						32
33						33
34						34

Problem M-4B (Continued)

PAGE 5

	GENERAL					
	DEBIT	CREDIT				
1						1
2						2
3						3
4						4
5						5
6						6
7						7
8						8
9						9
10						10
11						11
12						12
13						13
14						14
15						15
16						16
17						17
18						18
19						19
20						20
21						21
22						22
23						23
24						24
25						25
26						26
27						27
28						28
29						29
30						30
31						31
32						32
33						33
34						34

Problem M-4B (Continued)

2. Cash balance, June 12:

3. Proving the Combination Journal:

4., 6., and 8.

GENERAL LEDGER

ACCOUNT Cash ACCOUNT NO. 101

DATE		ITEM	POST. REF.	DEBIT	CREDIT	BALANCE DEBIT	BALANCE CREDIT

ACCOUNT Lawn Care Supplies ACCOUNT NO. 141

DATE		ITEM	POST. REF.	DEBIT	CREDIT	BALANCE DEBIT	BALANCE CREDIT

Problem M-4B (Continued)

ACCOUNT Office Supplies ACCOUNT NO. 142

DATE	ITEM	POST. REF.	DEBIT	CREDIT	BALANCE	
					DEBIT	CREDIT

ACCOUNT Prepaid Insurance ACCOUNT NO. 145

DATE	ITEM	POST. REF.	DEBIT	CREDIT	BALANCE	
					DEBIT	CREDIT

ACCOUNT Lawn Care Equipment ACCOUNT NO. 189

DATE	ITEM	POST. REF.	DEBIT	CREDIT	BALANCE	
					DEBIT	CREDIT

ACCOUNT Accumulated Depreciation—Lawn Care Equipment ACCOUNT NO. 189.1

DATE	ITEM	POST. REF.	DEBIT	CREDIT	BALANCE	
					DEBIT	CREDIT

Problem M-4B (Continued)

ACCOUNT Accounts Payable ACCOUNT NO. 202

DATE		ITEM	POST. REF.	DEBIT	CREDIT	BALANCE	
						DEBIT	CREDIT

ACCOUNT Molly Claussen, Capital ACCOUNT NO. 311

DATE		ITEM	POST. REF.	DEBIT	CREDIT	BALANCE	
						DEBIT	CREDIT

ACCOUNT Molly Claussen, Drawing ACCOUNT NO. 312

DATE		ITEM	POST. REF.	DEBIT	CREDIT	BALANCE	
						DEBIT	CREDIT

ACCOUNT Income Summary ACCOUNT NO. 313

DATE		ITEM	POST. REF.	DEBIT	CREDIT	BALANCE	
						DEBIT	CREDIT

Problem M-4B (Continued)

ACCOUNT Lawn Care Fees ACCOUNT NO. 401

DATE	ITEM	POST. REF.	DEBIT	CREDIT	BALANCE DEBIT	BALANCE CREDIT

ACCOUNT Wages Expense ACCOUNT NO. 511

DATE	ITEM	POST. REF.	DEBIT	CREDIT	BALANCE DEBIT	BALANCE CREDIT

ACCOUNT Rent Expense ACCOUNT NO. 521

DATE	ITEM	POST. REF.	DEBIT	CREDIT	BALANCE DEBIT	BALANCE CREDIT

ACCOUNT Office Supplies Expense ACCOUNT NO. 523

DATE	ITEM	POST. REF.	DEBIT	CREDIT	BALANCE DEBIT	BALANCE CREDIT

Problem M-4B (Continued)

ACCOUNT Lawn Care Supplies Expense ACCOUNT NO. 524

DATE	ITEM	POST. REF.	DEBIT	CREDIT	BALANCE DEBIT	BALANCE CREDIT

ACCOUNT Telephone Expense ACCOUNT NO. 525

DATE	ITEM	POST. REF.	DEBIT	CREDIT	BALANCE DEBIT	BALANCE CREDIT

ACCOUNT Electricity Expense ACCOUNT NO. 533

DATE	ITEM	POST. REF.	DEBIT	CREDIT	BALANCE DEBIT	BALANCE CREDIT

ACCOUNT Insurance Expense ACCOUNT NO. 535

DATE	ITEM	POST. REF.	DEBIT	CREDIT	BALANCE DEBIT	BALANCE CREDIT

Problem M-4B (Continued)

ACCOUNT Repair Expense ACCOUNT NO. 537

DATE	ITEM	POST. REF.	DEBIT	CREDIT	BALANCE	
					DEBIT	CREDIT

ACCOUNT Gas and Oil Expense ACCOUNT NO. 538

DATE	ITEM	POST. REF.	DEBIT	CREDIT	BALANCE	
					DEBIT	CREDIT

ACCOUNT Depreciation Expense—Lawn Care Equipment ACCOUNT NO. 542

DATE	ITEM	POST. REF.	DEBIT	CREDIT	BALANCE	
					DEBIT	CREDIT

Problem M-4B (Continued)

5.

	ACCOUNT TITLE	TRIAL BALANCE		ADJUSTMENTS	
		DEBIT	CREDIT	DEBIT	CREDIT
1					
2					
3					
4					
5					
6					
7					
8					
9					
10					
11					
12					
13					
14					
15					
16					
17					
18					
19					
20					
21					
22					
23					
24					
25					
26					
27					
28					
29					
30					
31					
32					

Name ______________________________

Problem M-4B (Continued)

ADJUSTED TRIAL BALANCE		INCOME STATEMENT		BALANCE SHEET		
DEBIT	CREDIT	DEBIT	CREDIT	DEBIT	CREDIT	
						1
						2
						3
						4
						5
						6
						7
						8
						9
						10
						11
						12
						13
						14
						15
						16
						17
						18
						19
						20
						21
						22
						23
						24
						25
						26
						27
						28
						29
						30
						31
						32

Problem M-4B (Continued)

7.

Name ______________________________

Problem M-4B (Continued)

Problem M-4B (Continued)

6. and 8.

COMBINATION JOURNAL

	DATE	CASH		DESCRIPTION	POST. REF.	
		DEBIT	CREDIT			
1						1
2						2
3						3
4						4
5						5
6						6
7						7
8						8
9						9
10						10
11						11
12						12
13						13
14						14
15						15
16						16
17						17
18						18
19						19
20						20
21						21
22						22
23						23
24						24
25						25
26						26
27						27
28						28
29						29
30						30
31						31
32						32
33						33
34						34

Problem M-4B (Concluded)

PAGE 6

	GENERAL					
	DEBIT	CREDIT				
1						1
2						2
3						3
4						4
5						5
6						6
7						7
8						8
9						9
10						10
11						11
12						12
13						13
14						14
15						15
16						16
17						17
18						18
19						19
20						20
21						21
22						22
23						23
24						24
25						25
26						26
27						27
28						28
29						29
30						30
31						31
32						32
33						33
34						34

Mastery Problem

1.

COMBINATION JOURNAL

	DATE		CASH		DESCRIPTION	POST. REF.	
			DEBIT	CREDIT			
1							1
2							2
3							3
4							4
5							5
6							6
7							7
8							8
9							9
10							10
11							11
12							12
13							13
14							14
15							15
16							16
17							17
18							18
19							19
20							20
21							21
22							22
23							23
24							24
25							25
26							26
27							27
28							28
29							29
30							30
31							31
32							32
33							33
34							34

Mastery Problem (Continued)

PAGE 1

	GENERAL					
	DEBIT	CREDIT				
1						1
2						2
3						3
4						4
5						5
6						6
7						7
8						8
9						9
10						10
11						11
12						12
13						13
14						14
15						15
16						16
17						17
18						18
19						19
20						20
21						21
22						22
23						23
24						24
25						25
26						26
27						27
28						28
29						29
30						30
31						31
32						32
33						33
34						34

Mastery Problem (Continued)

2. Proving the Combination Journal:

3.

GENERAL LEDGER

ACCOUNT Cash ACCOUNT NO. 101

DATE	ITEM	POST. REF.	DEBIT	CREDIT	BALANCE	
					DEBIT	CREDIT

ACCOUNT Office Supplies ACCOUNT NO. 142

DATE	ITEM	POST. REF.	DEBIT	CREDIT	BALANCE	
					DEBIT	CREDIT

Mastery Problem (Continued)

ACCOUNT Food Supplies ACCOUNT NO. 144

DATE	ITEM	POST. REF.	DEBIT	CREDIT	BALANCE DEBIT	BALANCE CREDIT

ACCOUNT Tennis Facilities ACCOUNT NO. 184

DATE	ITEM	POST. REF.	DEBIT	CREDIT	BALANCE DEBIT	BALANCE CREDIT

ACCOUNT Accumulated Depreciation—Tennis Facilities ACCOUNT NO. 184.1

DATE	ITEM	POST. REF.	DEBIT	CREDIT	BALANCE DEBIT	BALANCE CREDIT

ACCOUNT Exercise Equipment ACCOUNT NO. 186

DATE	ITEM	POST. REF.	DEBIT	CREDIT	BALANCE DEBIT	BALANCE CREDIT

Mastery Problem (Continued)

ACCOUNT Accumulated Depreciation—Exercise Equipment ACCOUNT NO. 186.1

DATE	ITEM	POST. REF.	DEBIT	CREDIT	BALANCE DEBIT	BALANCE CREDIT

ACCOUNT Accounts Payable ACCOUNT NO. 202

DATE	ITEM	POST. REF.	DEBIT	CREDIT	BALANCE DEBIT	BALANCE CREDIT

ACCOUNT John McRoe, Capital ACCOUNT NO. 311

DATE	ITEM	POST. REF.	DEBIT	CREDIT	BALANCE DEBIT	BALANCE CREDIT

ACCOUNT John McRoe, Drawing ACCOUNT NO. 312

DATE	ITEM	POST. REF.	DEBIT	CREDIT	BALANCE DEBIT	BALANCE CREDIT

Mastery Problem (Continued)

ACCOUNT Income Summary ACCOUNT NO. 313

DATE	ITEM	POST. REF.	DEBIT	CREDIT	BALANCE DEBIT	BALANCE CREDIT

ACCOUNT Registration Fees ACCOUNT NO. 401

DATE	ITEM	POST. REF.	DEBIT	CREDIT	BALANCE DEBIT	BALANCE CREDIT

ACCOUNT Wages Expense ACCOUNT NO. 511

DATE	ITEM	POST. REF.	DEBIT	CREDIT	BALANCE DEBIT	BALANCE CREDIT

ACCOUNT Rent Expense ACCOUNT NO. 521

DATE	ITEM	POST. REF.	DEBIT	CREDIT	BALANCE DEBIT	BALANCE CREDIT

ACCOUNT Office Supplies Expense ACCOUNT NO. 523

DATE	ITEM	POST. REF.	DEBIT	CREDIT	BALANCE DEBIT	BALANCE CREDIT

Mastery Problem (Continued)

ACCOUNT Food Supplies Expense ACCOUNT NO. 524

DATE	ITEM	POST. REF.	DEBIT	CREDIT	BALANCE	
					DEBIT	CREDIT

ACCOUNT Telephone Expense ACCOUNT NO. 525

DATE	ITEM	POST. REF.	DEBIT	CREDIT	BALANCE	
					DEBIT	CREDIT

ACCOUNT Utilities Expense ACCOUNT NO. 533

DATE	ITEM	POST. REF.	DEBIT	CREDIT	BALANCE	
					DEBIT	CREDIT

ACCOUNT Insurance Expense ACCOUNT NO. 535

DATE	ITEM	POST. REF.	DEBIT	CREDIT	BALANCE	
					DEBIT	CREDIT

ACCOUNT Postage Expense ACCOUNT NO. 536

DATE	ITEM	POST. REF.	DEBIT	CREDIT	BALANCE	
					DEBIT	CREDIT

Mastery Problem (Continued)

ACCOUNT Depreciation Expense—Tennis Facilities ACCOUNT NO. 541

DATE	ITEM	POST. REF.	DEBIT	CREDIT	BALANCE	
					DEBIT	CREDIT

ACCOUNT Depreciation Expense—Exercise Equipment ACCOUNT NO. 542

DATE	ITEM	POST. REF.	DEBIT	CREDIT	BALANCE	
					DEBIT	CREDIT

Mastery Problem (Concluded)

4.

ACCOUNT	ACCT. NO.	DEBIT BALANCE	CREDIT BALANCE

Name ______________________________

Challenge Problem

Resler Financial Consulting

Income Statements

For Month Ended June 20--

	Modified Cash Basis		Accrual Basis	

END PAGE OF
WORKING PAPERS

END PAGE OF
STUDY GUIDE

Practical Business Math Procedures

chapter 1

WHOLE NUMBERS: HOW TO DISSECT AND SOLVE WORD PROBLEMS

Hillary Price, Rymes with Orange, © 2008

Doing the Math to Find the Good Jobs

Mathematicians Land Top Spot in New Ranking of Best and Worst Occupations in the U.S.

Making a Living

BEST
1) Mathematician
2) Actuary
3) Statistician
4) Biologist
5) Software Engineer
6) Computer Systems Analyst
7) Historian
8) Sociologist
9) Industrial Designer
10) Accountant

WORST
1) Lumberjack
2) Dairy Farmer
3) Taxi Driver
4) Seaman
5) Emergency Medical Technician
6) Roofer
7) Garbage Collector
8) Welder
9) Roustabout (Oil worker)
10) Ironworker

Scott Brundage

Wall Street Journal © 2009

Photodisc/Punchstock

LEARNING UNIT OBJECTIVES

LU 1–1: Reading, Writing, and Rounding Whole Numbers

1. Use place values to read and write numeric and verbal whole numbers *(p. 4)*.
2. Round whole numbers to the indicated position *(p. 6)*.
3. Use blueprint aid for dissecting and solving a word problem *(p. 8)*.

LU 1–2: Adding and Subtracting Whole Numbers

1. Add whole numbers; check and estimate addition computations *(p. 10)*.
2. Subtract whole numbers; check and estimate subtraction computations *(p. 11)*.

LU 1–3: Multiplying and Dividing Whole Numbers

1. Multiply whole numbers; check and estimate multiplication computations *(p. 14)*.
2. Divide whole numbers; check and estimate division computations *(p. 16)*.

VOCABULARY PREVIEW

Here are the key terms in this chapter. When you finish the chapter, if you feel you know the term, place a checkmark within the parentheses following the term. If you are not certain of the definition, look it up and write the page number where it can be found in the text. The chapter organizer includes page references to the terms. There is also a complete glossary at the end of the text.

addends . ( ) decimal point . ( ) decimal system . ( ) difference . ( ) dividend . ( ) divisor . ( ) minuend . ( ) multiplicand . ( ) multiplier . ( ) partial products . ( ) partial quotient . ( ) product . ( ) quotient . ( ) remainder . ( ) rounding all the way . ( ) subtrahend . ( ) sum . ( ) whole number . ( )

GLOBAL

People of all ages make personal business decisions based on the answers to number questions. Numbers also determine most of the business decisions of companies. For example, click on your computer, go to the Web site of a company such as Dunkin' Donuts and note the importance of numbers in the company's business decision-making process.

The following *Wall Street Journal* clipping "Dunkin' Donuts Targets Shanghai" announces plans to expand into China:

Oilai Shen/Bloomberg News/Landov

Dunkin' Donuts Targets Shanghai

Dunkin' Donuts plans to open in Shanghai this spring as part of a push into China.

The coffee-and-bakery chain, **Dunkin' Brands** Inc. unit, says it plans to open fewer than 10 locations in the Shanghai area this year, with an additional 10 in the area, and possibly other Chinese cities, in 2009. Dunkin' Donuts first opened a handful of stores in China during the 1990s, but closed them.

In the U.S., Dunkin' has expanded in recent years on the success of its coffee drinks while emphasizing its convenience as a no-frills coffee destination. In China, its locations will have more seating, and they are expected to sell more food than beverages, said Will Kussell, president and chief brand officer for Dunkin' Donuts Worldwide.

China has become an increasingly important market for U.S.-based coffee chains because of its rapidly growing middle class and affinity for Western brands. **Starbucks** Corp. has said it wants to make China its largest market outside the U.S. Dunkin' started its push into the region last year by opening a store in Taiwan, where it now has 10 locations.

In Shanghai, Dunkin' plans to build its drinks around coffee while offering a variety of teas.

Wall Street Journal © 2008

Companies often follow a general problem-solving procedure to arrive at a change in company policy. Using Dunkin' Donuts as an example, the following steps illustrate this procedure:

Step 1. State the problem(s).	Increase market share and profitability.
Step 2. Decide on the best methods to solve the problem(s).	Expand operations in China.
Step 3. Does the solution make sense?	Adapt to Chinese eating habits—more food than beverages.
Step 4. Evaluate the results.	Dunkin' Donuts will evaluate new plan.

Your study of numbers begins with a review of basic computation skills that focuses on speed and accuracy. You may think, "But I can use my calculator." Even if your instructor allows you to use a calculator, you still must know the basic computation skills. You need these skills to know what to calculate, how to interpret your calculations, how to make estimates to recognize errors you made in using your calculator, and how to make calculations when you do not have a calculator.

The United States' numbering system is the **decimal system** or *base 10 system.* Your calculator gives the 10 single-digit numbers of the decimal system—0, 1, 2, 3, 4, 5, 6, 7, 8, and 9. The center of the decimal system is the **decimal point.** When you have a number with a decimal point, the numbers to the left of the decimal point are **whole numbers** and the numbers to the right of the decimal point are decimal numbers (discussed in Chapter 3). When you have a number *without* a decimal, the number is a whole number and the decimal is assumed to be after the number.

This chapter discusses reading, writing, and rounding whole numbers; adding and subtracting whole numbers; and multiplying and dividing whole numbers.

Learning Unit 1–1: Reading, Writing, and Rounding Whole Numbers

LO 1

Coca-Cola over the years has acquired many companies. In 2008 Coke acquired a Chinese maker of juices for 2 billion, 300 million dollars. Numerically we can write this as 2,300,000,000. In 2009 Chinese regulaters blocked the acquisition.

Now let's begin our study of whole numbers.

Reading and Writing Numeric and Verbal Whole Numbers

GLOBAL

The decimal system is a *place-value system* based on the powers of 10. Any whole number can be written with the 10 digits of the decimal system because the position, or placement, of the digits in a number gives the value of the digits.

ImagineChina/AP Images

To determine the value of each digit in a number, we use a place-value chart (Figure 1.1) that divides numbers into named groups of three digits, with each group separated by a comma. To separate a number into groups, you begin with the last digit in the number and insert commas every three digits, moving from right to left. This divides the number into the named groups (units, thousands, millions, billions, trillions) shown in the place-value chart. Within each group, you have a ones, tens, and hundreds place. Keep in mind that the leftmost group may have fewer than three digits.

In Figure 1.1, the numeric number 1,605,743,891,412 illustrates place values. When you study the place-value chart, you can see that the value of each place in the chart is 10 times the value of the place to the right. We can illustrate this by analyzing the last four digits in the number 1,605,743,891,412:

$$1{,}412 = (1 \times 1{,}000) + (4 \times 100) + (1 \times 10) + (2 \times 1)$$

So we can also say, for example, that in the number 745, the "7" means seven hundred (700); in the number 75, the "7" means 7 tens (70).

To read and write a numeric number in verbal form, you begin at the left and read each group of three digits as if it were alone, adding the group name at the end (except the last units group and groups of all zeros). Using the place-value chart in Figure 1.1, the number 1,605,743,891,412 is read as one trillion, six hundred five billion, seven hundred forty-three million, eight hundred ninety-one thousand, four hundred twelve. You do not read zeros. They fill vacant spaces as placeholders so that you can correctly state the number values. Also,

FIGURE 1.1

Whole number place-value chart

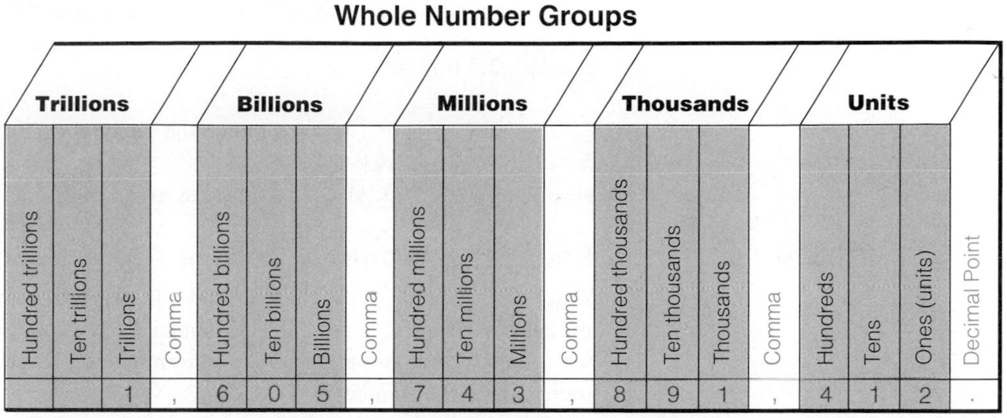

the numbers twenty-one to ninety-nine must have a hyphen. And most important, when you read or write whole numbers in verbal form, do not use the word *and*. In the decimal system, *and* indicates the decimal, which we discuss in Chapter 3.

By reversing this process of changing a numeric number to a verbal number, you can use the place-value chart to change a verbal number to a numeric number. Remember that you must keep track of the place value of each digit. The place values of the digits in a number determine its total value.

Before we look at how to round whole numbers, we should look at how to convert a number indicating parts of a whole number to a whole number. We will use the following *Wall Street Journal* clip "Coke Sets China Deal" as an example.

GLOBAL

Coke Sets China Deal

BY BETSY MCKAY

Coca-Cola Co. said it plans to acquire a Chinese maker of juices and nectars for $2.3 billion, the second-largest acquisition in the Atlanta company's history.

The planned acquisition of **China Huiyuan Juice Group** Ltd. also represents a major investment by a foreign company in China.

Coke has been steadily acquiring companies around the world in recent years that make juice, water and other noncarbonated drinks, to broaden its portfolio and beat back competitors.

Coke's largest acquisition is its $4.1 billion purchase in 2007 of Energy Brands Inc., the Whitestone, N.Y., maker of Vitaminwater.

Huiyuan is "highly complementary to the Coca-Cola China business," Coke's chief executive officer, Muhtar Kent, said in a statement.

Huiyuan said the deal would help it develop its brand. "The business combination of Coca-Cola and Huiyuan creates a win-win partnership that combines Coca-Cola's expertise as a global beverage company with Huiyuan's knowledge and understanding of the China beverage market," company Chairman Zhu Xinli said in a statement.

Coke said the purchase of Huiyuan requires approval from Chinese regulators, who have blocked some recent foreign acquisitions.

The $2,300,000,000 Coca-Cola plans to pay for a Chinese maker of juices could be written as $2.3 billion. This amount is two billion plus three hundred million of an additional billion. The following steps explain how to convert these decimal numbers into a regular whole number:

CONVERTING PARTS OF A MILLION, BILLION, TRILLION, ETC., TO A REGULAR WHOLE NUMBER

Step 1. Drop the decimal point and insert a comma.

Step 2. Add zeros so the leftmost digit ends in the word name of the amount you want to convert. Be sure to add commas as needed.

EXAMPLE Convert 2.3 billion to a regular whole number.

Step 1. 2.3 billion
↓
2,3 — Change the decimal point to a comma.
↓↓↓↓↓↓↓↓↓

Step 2. 2,300,000,000 — Add zeros and commas so the whole number indicates billion.

LO 2

Rounding Whole Numbers

Many of the whole numbers you read and hear are rounded numbers. Government statistics are usually rounded numbers. The financial reports of companies also use rounded numbers. All rounded numbers are *approximate* numbers. The more rounding you do, the more you approximate the number.

Rounded whole numbers are used for many reasons. With rounded whole numbers you can quickly estimate arithmetic results, check actual computations, report numbers that change quickly such as population numbers, and make numbers easier to read and remember.

Numbers can be rounded to any identified digit place value, including the first digit of a number (rounding all the way). To round whole numbers, use the following three steps:

ROUNDING WHOLE NUMBERS

Step 1. Identify the place value of the digit you want to round.

Step 2. If the digit to the right of the identified digit in Step 1 is 5 or more, increase the identified digit by 1 (round up). If the digit to the right is less than 5, do not change the identified digit.

Step 3. Change all digits to the right of the rounded identified digit to zeros.

EXAMPLE 1 Round 9,362 to the nearest hundred.

Step 1. 9,362 — The digit 3 is in the hundreds place value.

Step 2. → The digit to the right of 3 is 5 or more (6). Thus, 3, the identified digit in Step 1, is now rounded to 4. You change the identified digit only if the digit to the right is 5 or more.

9,462
↓↓

Step 3. 9,400 — Change digits 6 and 2 to zeros, since these digits are to the right of 4, the rounded number.

By rounding 9,362 to the nearest hundred, you can see that 9,362 is closer to 9,400 than to 9,300.

Next, we show you how to round to the nearest thousand.

EXAMPLE 2 Round 67,951 to the nearest thousand.

Step 1. 67,951 — The digit 7 is in the thousands place value.

Step 2. → Digit to the right of 7 is 5 or more (9). Thus, 7, the identified digit in Step 1, is now rounded to 8.

68,951
↓↓↓

Step 3. 68,000 — Change digits 9, 5, and 1 to zeros, since these digits are to the right of 8, the rounded number.

By rounding 67,951 to the nearest thousand, you can see that 67,951 is closer to 68,000 than to 67,000.

Now let's look at **rounding all the way.** To round a number all the way, you round to the first digit of the number (the leftmost digit) and have only one nonzero digit remaining in the number.

EXAMPLE 3 Round 7,843 all the way.

Step 1. 7,843 Identified leftmost digit is 7.

Step 2. → Digit to the right of 7 is greater than 5, so 7 becomes 8.

8,843

Step 3. 8,000 Change all other digits to zeros.

Rounding 7,843 all the way gives 8,000.

Remember that rounding a digit to a specific place value depends on the degree of accuracy you want in your estimate. For example, In the *Wall Street Journal* clip "A Mother's Pay? $117,000" rounds all the way to $100,000 because the digit to the right of 1 (leftmost digit) is less than 5. The $100,000 is $17,000 less than the original $117,000. You would be more accurate if you rounded $117,000 to the ten thousand place value of 1 identified digit, which is $120,000.

Before concluding this unit, let's look at how to dissect and solve a word problem.

Ariel Skelley/Getty Images

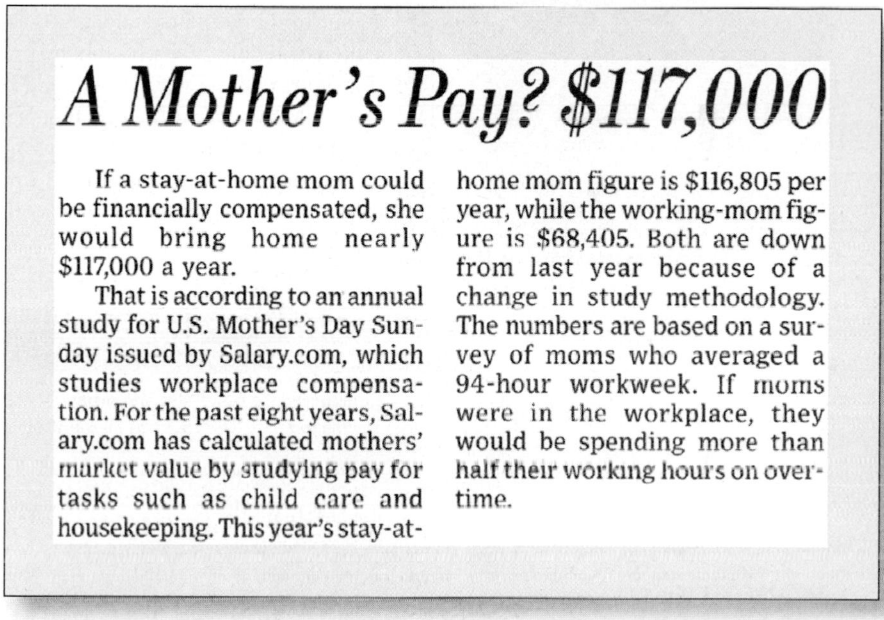

A Mother's Pay? $117,000

If a stay-at-home mom could be financially compensated, she would bring home nearly $117,000 a year.

That is according to an annual study for U.S. Mother's Day Sunday issued by Salary.com, which studies workplace compensation. For the past eight years, Salary.com has calculated mothers' market value by studying pay for tasks such as child care and housekeeping. This year's stay-at-home mom figure is $116,805 per year, while the working-mom figure is $68,405. Both are down from last year because of a change in study methodology. The numbers are based on a survey of moms who averaged a 94-hour workweek. If moms were in the workplace, they would be spending more than half their working hours on overtime.

Wall Street Journal © 2008

How to Dissect and Solve a Word Problem

As a student, your author found solving word problems difficult. Not knowing where to begin after reading the word problem caused the difficulty. Today, students still struggle with word problems as they try to decide where to begin.

Solving word problems involves *organization* and *persistence*. Recall how persistent you were when you learned to ride a two-wheel bike. Do you remember the feeling of success you experienced when you rode the bike without help? Apply this persistence to word problems. Do not be discouraged. Each person learns at a different speed. Your goal must be to FINISH THE RACE and experience the success of solving word problems with ease.

To be organized in solving word problems, you need a plan of action that tells you where to begin—a blueprint aid. Like a builder, you will refer to this blueprint aid constantly until you know the procedure. The blueprint aid for dissecting and solving a word problem follows on page 8. Note that the blueprint aid serves an important function—**it decreases your math anxiety.**

Blueprint Aid for Dissecting and Solving a Word Problem

The facts	Solving for?	Steps to take	Key points

LO 3

David Young Wolff/Photoedit

Now let's study this blueprint aid. The first two columns require that you *read* the word problem slowly. Think of the third column as the basic information you must know or calculate before solving the word problem. Often this column contains formulas that provide the foundation for the step-by-step problem solution. The last column reinforces the key points you should remember.

It's time now to try your skill at using the blueprint aid for dissecting and solving a word problem.

The Word Problem On the 100th anniversary of Tootsie Roll Industries, the company reported sharply increased sales and profits. Sales reached one hundred ninety-four million dollars and a record profit of twenty-two million, five hundred fifty-six thousand dollars. The company president requested that you round the sales and profit figures all the way.

Study the following blueprint aid and note how we filled in the columns with the information in the word problem. You will find the organization of the blueprint aid most helpful. Be persistent! You *can* dissect and solve word problems! When you are finished with the word problem, make sure the answer seems reasonable.

The facts	Solving for?	Steps to take	Key points
Sales: One hundred ninety-four million dollars. *Profit:* Twenty-two million, five hundred fifty-six thousand dollars.	Sales and profit rounded all the way.	Express each verbal form in numeric form. Identify leftmost digit in each number.	Rounding all the way means only the left-most digit will remain. All other digits become zeros.

MONEY TIPS

Rounding numbers is a useful tool when you need to add or subtract numbers quickly. Consider grocery shopping with a $50 limit. Rounding the price of your purchases as you shop lets you keep a running total without having to take time to add each item individually. This also helps curtail the desire to buy items not on your list.

Steps to solving problem

1. Convert verbal to numeric.
   One hundred ninety-four million dollars ⟶ $194,000,000
   Twenty-two million, five hundred fifty-six thousand dollars ⟶ $ 22,556,000
2. Identify leftmost digit of each number.
   $194,000,000 $22,556,000
3. Round.
   $200,000,000 $20,000,000

Note that in the final answer, $200,000,000 and $20,000,000 have only one nonzero digit.

Remember that you cannot round numbers expressed in verbal form. You must convert these numbers to numeric form.

Now you should see the importance of the information in the third column of the blueprint aid. When you complete your blueprint aids for word problems, do not be concerned if the order of the information in your boxes does not follow the order given in the text boxes. Often you can dissect a word problem in more than one way.

Your first Practice Quiz follows. Be sure to study the paragraph that introduces the Practice Quiz.

LU 1–1 PRACTICE QUIZ

Complete this **Practice Quiz** to see how you are doing.

At the end of each learning unit, you can check your progress with a Practice Quiz. If you had difficulty understanding the unit, the Practice Quiz will help identify your area of weakness. Work the problems on scrap paper. Check your answers with the worked-out solutions that follow the quiz. Ask your instructor about specific assignments and the videos available on your DVD for each chapter Practice Quiz.

1. Write in verbal form:
   a. 7,948 **b.** 48,775 **c.** 814,410,335,414
2. Round the following numbers as indicated:

Nearest ten	Nearest hundred	Nearest thousand	Rounded all the way
a. 92	**b.** 745	**c.** 8,341	**d.** 4,752

3. Kellogg's reported its sales as five million, one hundred eighty-one thousand dollars. The company earned a profit of five hundred two thousand dollars. What would the sales and profit be if each number were rounded all the way? (*Hint:* You might want to draw the blueprint aid since we show it in the solution.)

DVD *Solutions with Step-by-Step Help on DVD*

✓ Solutions

1. **a.** Seven thousand, nine hundred forty eight
   b. Forty-eight thousand, seven hundred seventy-five
   c. Eight hundred fourteen billion, four hundred ten million, three hundred thirty-five thousand, four hundred fourteen
2. **a.** 90 **b.** 700 **c.** 8,000 **d.** 5,000
3. Kellogg's sales and profit:

The facts	Solving for?	Steps to take	Key points
Sales: Five million, one hundred eighty-one thousand dollars. *Profit:* Five hundred two thousand dollars.	Sales and profit rounded all the way.	Express each verbal form in numeric form. Identify leftmost digit in each number.	Rounding all the way means only the left-most digit will remain. All other digits become zeros.

Steps to solving problem

1. Convert verbal to numeric.
   Five million, one hundred eighty-one thousand ——→ $5,181,000
   Five hundred two thousand ——→ $ 502,000
2. Identify leftmost digit of each number.
   $5,181,000 $502,000
3. Round.
   ↓ ↓
   $5,000,000 $500,000

LU 1–1a EXTRA PRACTICE QUIZ WITH WORKED-OUT SOLUTIONS

Need more practice? Try this **Extra Practice Quiz** (check figures in Chapter Organizer, p. 20). Worked-out Solutions can be found in Appendix B at end of text.

1. Write in verbal form:
   a. 8,682 **b.** 56,295 **c.** 732,310,444,888
2. Round the following numbers as indicated:

Nearest ten	Nearest hundred	Nearest thousand	Rounded all the way
a. 43	**b.** 654	**c.** 7,328	**d.** 5,980

3. Kellogg's reported its sales as three million, two hundred ninety-one thousand dollars. The company earned a profit of four hundred five thousand dollars. What would the sales and profit be if each number were rounded all the way?

Learning Unit 1–2: Adding and Subtracting Whole Numbers

LO 1

Did you know the cost of car-sharing services varies in different locations? The following *Wall Street Journal* "Flexcar Gain Traction" identifies the cost of car-sharing for Flexcar and Zipcar programs. For example, note the difference in daily costs between Flexcar at Johns Hopkins University and Zipcar at the University of North Carolina.

Flexcar	$60
Zipcar	55
	$ 5

Flexcar Gain Traction

Cars on Campus

Schools around the country are partnering with car-sharing services. Here are a few of the programs:

School	Program	Car Types Available	Cost	Comment
Johns Hopkins University	Flexcar	Honda Civic hybrid, Toyota Prius hybrid	$35 annual fee; rates from $6/hour, $60/day	Flexcar is offering a $35 credit toward usage fees.
University of Michigan	Zipcar	Ford Escape SUV, Mazda 3, Toyota Matrix	$30 annual fee; rates from $8/hour, $60/day	Not enough cars for such a spread-out school. Just two each for Central Campus, North Campus and the medical center.
University of North Carolina	Zipcar	Honda Civic, Ford Escape, Mazda 3.	$20 annual fee; rates from $5/hour, $55/day	The prices at UNC are among the lowest at any school.
Wellesley College	Zipcar	Toyota Matrix, Mazda 3, Scion xB.	$25 annual fee; rates from $8/hour, $60/day	The Scion, which isn't available at Wellesley in the summer, offers van-style cargo room.

This unit teaches you how to manually add and subtract whole numbers. When you least expect it, you will catch yourself automatically using this skill.

Addition of Whole Numbers

To add whole numbers, you unite two or more numbers called **addends** to make one number called a **sum,** *total,* or *amount.* The numbers are arranged in a column according to their place values—units above units, tens above tens, and so on. Then, you add the columns of numbers from top to bottom. To check the result, you re-add the columns from bottom to top. This procedure is illustrated in the steps that follow.

ADDING WHOLE NUMBERS

Step 1. Align the numbers to be added in columns according to their place values, beginning with the units place at the right and moving to the left (Figure 1.1).

Step 2. Add the units column. Write the sum below the column. If the sum is more than 9, write the units digit and carry the tens digit.

Step 3. Moving to the left, repeat Step 2 until all place values are added.

EXAMPLE

Adding top bottom ↓	2 11 1,362 5,913 8,924 +6,594 **22,793**	↑ Checking bottom to to top	**Alternate check** Add each column as a separate total and then combine. The end result is the same.

1,362
5,913
8,924
+ 6,594
13
18
2 6
20
22,793

How to Quickly Estimate Addition by Rounding All the Way

In Learning Unit 1–1, you learned that rounding whole numbers all the way gives quick arithmetic estimates. Using the following *Wall Street Journal* clipping "Bean Count" note how you can round each number all the way and the total will not be rounded all the way. Remember that rounding all the way does not replace actual computations, but it is helpful in making quick commonsense decisions.

GLOBAL

Wall Street Journal © 2008

Rounded all the way

→ $ 600	← Rounding all the way means each number has only one nonzero digit.
100	
100	
70	
70	
40	
40	
20	
10	*Note:* The final answer could have more than one nonzero digit since the total is not rounded all the way.
9	
4	
3	
3	
+ 2	
$1,071	

LO 2

Subtraction of Whole Numbers

Subtraction is the opposite of addition. Addition unites numbers; subtraction takes one number away from another number. In subtraction, the top (largest) number is the **minuend.** The number you subtract from the minuend is the **subtrahend,** which gives you the **difference** between the minuend and the subtrahend. The steps for subtracting whole numbers follow.

SUBTRACTING WHOLE NUMBERS

Step 1. Align the minuend and subtrahend according to their place values.

Step 2. Begin the subtraction with the units digits. Write the difference below the column. If the units digit in the minuend is smaller than the units digit in the subtrahend, borrow 1 from the tens digit in the minuend. One tens digit is 10 units.

Step 3. Moving to the left, repeat Step 2 until all place values in the subtrahend are subtracted.

EXAMPLE The following *Wall Street Journal* clipping on page 12 "Powering That Fancy TV" illustrates the subtraction of whole numbers:

Wall Street Journal © 2007

What is the difference in yearly cost between powering a 60" plasma television and a refrigerator? As shown below you can use subtraction to arrive at the $70 difference.

$$\begin{array}{rl} \overset{13}{\not{1}\not{3}0} & \leftarrow \text{Minuend (larger number)} \\ -\ \underline{60} & \leftarrow \text{Subtrahend} \\ 70 & \leftarrow \text{Difference} \end{array}$$

Check $70
+ 60
$130

Teri Stratford

In subtraction, borrowing from the column at the left is often necessary. Remember that 1 ten = 10 units, 1 hundred = 10 tens, and 1 thousand = 10 hundreds.

In the above example, the 0 in the subtrahend of the rightmost column (ones or units column) can be subtracted from the 0 in the minuend to give a difference of 0. This means we do not have to borrow from the tens column at the left. However, in the tens column, we cannot subtract 6 in the subtrahend from 3 in the minuend, so we move left and borrow 1 from the hundreds column. Since 1 hundred = 10 tens, we have 10 + 3, or 13 tens in the minuend. Now we can subtract 6 tens in the subtrahend from 13 tens in the minuend to give us 7 tens in the difference.

Checking subtraction requires adding the difference ($70) to the subtrahend ($60) to arrive at the minuend ($130).

How to Dissect and Solve a Word Problem

Accurate subtraction is important in many business operations. In Chapter 4 we discuss the importance of keeping accurate subtraction in your checkbook balance. Now let's check your progress by dissecting and solving a word problem.

The Word Problem Hershey's produced 25 million Kisses in one day. The same day, the company shipped 4 million to Japan, 3 million to France, and 6 million throughout the United States. At the end of that day, what is the company's total inventory of Kisses? What is the inventory balance if you round the number all the way?

The facts	Solving for?	Steps to take	Key points
Produced: 25 million. *Shipped:* Japan, 4 million; France, 3 million; United States, 6 million.	Total Kisses left in inventory. Inventory balance rounded all the way.	Total Kisses produced − Total Kisses shipped = Total Kisses left in inventory.	Minuend − Subtrahend = Difference. Rounding all the way means rounding to last digit on the left.

Steps to solving problem

1. Calculate the total Kisses shipped.

$$\begin{array}{r} 4{,}000{,}000 \\ 3{,}000{,}000 \\ +\ 6{,}000{,}000 \\ \hline 13{,}000{,}000 \end{array}$$

2. Calculate the total Kisses left in inventory.

$$\begin{array}{r} 25{,}000{,}000 \\ -\ 13{,}000{,}000 \\ \hline 12{,}000{,}000 \end{array}$$

3. Rounding all the way.

Identified digit is 1. Digit to right of 1 is 2, which is less than 5. *Answer:* 10,000,000.

The Practice Quiz that follows will tell you how you are progressing in your study of Chapter 1.

$ MONEY TIPS

Calculating personal income tax is easy when you know the process. First total your income, then subtract adjustments to income to get adjusted gross income. From adjusted gross income, subtract either standard or itemized deductions, and finally subtract the exemption allowance. That will equal your taxable income. You want to keep that number as low as possible. Any time you add a dependent (such as a child) for tax purposes, the amount you can deduct for exemptions increases.

LU 1–2 PRACTICE QUIZ

Complete this **Practice Quiz** to see how you are doing.

1. Add by totaling each separate column:

   8,974
   6,439
   + 6,941

2. Estimate by rounding all the way (do not round the total of estimate) and then do the actual computation:

   4,241
   8,794
   + 3,872

3. Subtract and check your answer:

   9,876
   − 4,967

4. Jackson Manufacturing Company projected its year 2011 furniture sales at $900,000. During 2011, Jackson earned $510,000 in sales from major clients and $369,100 in sales from the remainder of its clients. What is the amount by which Jackson over- or underestimated its sales? Use the blueprint aid, since the answer will show the completed blueprint aid.

Solutions with Step-by-Step Help on DVD

✓ Solutions

1.

14
14
2 2
20
22,354

2.

Estimate	Actual
4,000	4,241
9,000	8,794
+ 4,000	+ 3,872
17,000	16,907

3.

	Check
8 18 6 16	
9,876	4,909
− 4,967	+ 4,967
4,909	9,876

4. Jackson Manufacturing Company over- or underestimated sales:

The facts	Solving for?	Steps to take	Key points
Projected 2011 sales: $900,000. *Major clients:* $510,000. *Other clients:* $369,100.	How much were sales over- or underestimated?	Total projected sales − Total actual sales = Over- or underestimated sales.	Projected sales (minuend) − Actual sales (subtrahend) = Difference.

Steps to solving problem

1. Calculate total actual sales.

   $510,000
   + 369,100
   $879,100

2. Calculate overestimated or underestimated sales.

   $900,000
   − 879,100
   $ 20,900 (overestimated)

LU 1–2a EXTRA PRACTICE QUIZ WITH WORKED-OUT SOLUTIONS

Need more practice? Try this **Extra Practice Quiz** (check figures in Chapter Organizer, p. 20). Worked-out Solutions can be found in Appendix B at end of text.

1. Add by totaling each separate column:

   9,853
   7,394
   +8,843

2. Estimate by rounding all the way (do not round the total of estimate) and then do the actual computation:

   3,482
   6,981
   +5,490

3. Subtract and check your answer:

   9,787
   −5,968

4. Jackson Manufacturing Company projected its year 2011 furniture sales at $878,000. During 2011, Jackson earned $492,900 in sales from major clients and $342,000 in sales from the remainder of its clients. What is the amount by which Jackson over- or underestimated its sales?

Learning Unit 1–3: Multiplying and Dividing Whole Numbers

LO 1

The *Wall Street Journal* clip "United to Charge Some Fliers $25 per Extra Checked Bag" shows a new charge facing passengers. If you fly on United and have 6 extra bags to check it would cost you an additional $150:

$25 × 6 bags = $150

If you divide $150 by $25 per bag you get 6 bags.

> *United to Charge Some Fliers $25 per Extra Checked Bag; Others Consider Similar Move*
>
> By Susan Carey
>
> Bucking convention, United Airlines plans to charge passengers buying its cheapest, nonrefundable tickets for domestic and Canadian flights $25 to check a second piece of luggage—unless the travelers have elite status in its Mileage Plus frequent-flier program.
>
> Until this change, all United passengers could check two 50-pound suitcases free of charge, the in-

Wall Street Journal © 2008

This unit will sharpen your skills in two important arithmetic operations—multiplication and division. These two operations frequently result in knowledgeable business decisions.

Multiplication of Whole Numbers—Shortcut to Addition

From calculating your cost of checking extra baggage you know that multiplication is a *shortcut to addition:*

$25 × 6 = $150   or $25 + $25 + $25 + $25 + $25 + $25 = $150

Before learning the steps used to multiply whole numbers with two or more digits, you must learn some multiplication terminology.

Note in the following example that the top number (number we want to multiply) is the **multiplicand.** The bottom number (number doing the multiplying) is the **multiplier.** The final number (answer) is the **product.** The numbers between the multiplier and the product are **partial products.** Also note how we positioned the partial product 2090. This number is the result of multiplying 418 by 50 (the 5 is in the tens position). On each line in the partial products, we placed the first digit directly below the digit we used in the multiplication process.

EXAMPLE

	418	← Top number (multiplicand)		
Partial	× 52	← Bottom number (multiplier)		
products	836		2 × 418 =	836
	20 90		50 × 418 =	+ 20,900
	21,736	← Product answer →		21,736

We can now give the following steps for multiplying whole numbers with two or more digits:

MULTIPLYING WHOLE NUMBERS WITH TWO OR MORE DIGITS

Step 1. Align the multiplicand (top number) and multiplier (bottom number) at the right. Usually, you should make the smaller number the multiplier.

Step 2. Begin by multiplying the right digit of the multiplier with the right digit of the multiplicand. Keep multiplying as you move left through the multiplicand. Your first partial product aligns at the right with the multiplicand and multiplier.

Step 3. Move left through the multiplier and continue multiplying the multiplicand. Your partial product right digit or first digit is placed directly below the digit in the multiplier that you used to multiply.

Step 4. Continue Steps 2 and 3 until you have completed your multiplication process. Then add the partial products to get the final product.

Checking and Estimating Multiplication

We can check the multiplication process by reversing the multiplicand and multiplier and then multiplying. Let's first estimate 52 × 418 by rounding all the way.

EXAMPLE

```
   50 ←    52
×  400 ← × 418
 20,000    416
           52
         20 8
         21,736
```

By estimating before actually working the problem, we know our answer should be about 20,000. When we multiply 52 by 418, we get the same answer as when we multiply 418 × 52—and the answer is about 20,000. Remember, if we had not rounded all the way, our estimate would have been closer. If we had used a calculator, the rounded estimate would have helped us check the calculator's answer. Our commonsense estimate tells us our answer is near 20,000—not 200,000.

Before you study the division of whole numbers, you should know (1) the multiplication shortcut with numbers ending in zeros and (2) how to multiply a whole number by a power of 10.

MULTIPLICATION SHORTCUT WITH NUMBERS ENDING IN ZEROS

Step 1. When zeros are at the end of the multiplicand or the multiplier, or both, disregard the zeros and multiply.

Step 2. Count the number of zeros in the multiplicand and multiplier.

Step 3. Attach the number of zeros counted in Step 2 to your answer.

EXAMPLE

```
 65,000        65        3 zeros
×   420     ×  42      + 1 zero
             1 30        4 zeros
            26 0
            27,300,000
```

No need to multiply rows of zeros

```
   65,000
×     420
   00 000
  1 300 00
 26 000 0
 27,300,000
```

MULTIPLYING A WHOLE NUMBER BY A POWER OF 10

Step 1. Count the number of zeros in the power of 10 (a whole number that begins with 1 and ends in one or more zeros such as 10, 100, 1,000, and so on).

Step 2. Attach that number of zeros to the right side of the other whole number to obtain the answer. Insert comma(s) as needed every three digits, moving from right to left.

EXAMPLE

99 × 10 = 990 = **990** ← Add 1 zero
99 × 100 = 9,900 = **9,900** ← Add 2 zeros
99 × 1,000 = 99,000 = **99,000** ← Add 3 zeros

When a zero is in the center of the multiplier, you can do the following:

EXAMPLE

```
    658
×   403
  1 974
263 2□
265,174
```

```
  3 × 658 =     1,974
400 × 658 = + 263,200
              265,174
```

Division of Whole Numbers

LO 2

Division is the reverse of multiplication and a time-saving shortcut related to subtraction. For example, in the introduction of this learning unit you determined you would pay \$150 extra to check 6 additional bags. You can also multiply \$25 × 6 to get \$150. Since division is the reverse of multiplication you can say that \$150 ÷ 6 = \$25.

Universal Press Syndicate © 2008

Division can be indicated by the common symbols ÷ and $\overline{)\ \ }$, or by the bar — in a fraction and the forward slant / between two numbers, which means the first number is divided by the second number. Division asks how many times one number **(divisor)** is contained in another number **(dividend).** The answer, or result, is the **quotient.** When the divisor (number used to divide) doesn't divide evenly into the dividend (number we are dividing), the result is a **partial quotient,** with the leftover amount the **remainder** (expressed as fractions in later chapters). The following example illustrates *even division* (this is also an example of *long division* because the divisor has more than one digit).

EXAMPLE

```
                  18  ← Quotient
Divisor ──→ 15)270  ← Dividend
               15
               ───
               120
               120
               ───
```

This example divides 15 into 27 once with 12 remaining. The 0 in the dividend is brought down to 12. Dividing 120 by 15 equals 8 with no remainder; that is, even division. The following example illustrates *uneven division with a remainder* (this is also an example of *short division* because the divisor has only one digit).

EXAMPLE

```
  24 R1 ← Remainder
7)169
  14
  ──
   29        Check
   28          (7   ×   24)   +   1   =  169
   ──
    1        Divisor × Quotient + Remainder = Dividend
```

Note how doing the check gives you assurance that your calculation is correct. When the divisor has one digit (short division) as in this example, you can often calculate the division mentally as illustrated in the following examples:

EXAMPLES

```
  108       16 R6
8)864     7)118
```

Next, let's look at the value of estimating division.

Estimating Division

Before actually working a division problem, estimate the quotient by rounding. This estimate helps check the answer. The example that follows is rounded all the way. After you make an estimate, work the problem and check your answer by multiplication.

EXAMPLE

	Estimate	Check
36 R111	50	138
$138\overline{)5{,}079}$	$100\overline{)5{,}000}$	× 36
4 14		828
939		4 14
828		4,968
111		+ 111 ← Add remainder
		5,079

Now let's turn our attention to division shortcuts with zeros.

Division Shortcuts with Zeros

The steps that follow show a shortcut that you can use when you divide numbers with zeros.

DIVISION SHORTCUT WITH NUMBERS ENDING IN ZEROS

Step 1. When the dividend and divisor have ending zeros, count the number of ending zeros in the divisor.

Step 2. Drop the same number of zeros in the dividend as in the divisor, counting from right to left.

Note the following examples of division shortcut with numbers ending in zeros. Since two of the symbols used for division are ÷ and $\overline{)}$, our first examples show the zero shortcut method with the ÷ symbol.

EXAMPLES

One ending zero

Drop 1 zero in dividend

Dividend	Divisor			
95,000 ÷	10	→ 95,00~~0~~ =	9,500	
95,000 ÷	100	→ 95,0~~00~~ =	950	Drop 2 zeros
95,000 ÷	1,000	→ 95,~~000~~ =	95	Drop 3 zeros

In a long division problem with the $\overline{)}$ symbol, you again count the number of ending zeros in the divisor. Then drop the same number of ending zeros in the dividend and divide as usual.

EXAMPLE $6{,}5\underline{00}\overline{)88{,}0\underline{00}}$ ← Drop 2 zeros

$65\overline{)880}$

13 R35
$65\overline{)880}$
65
230
195
35

You are now ready to practice what you learned by dissecting and solving a word problem.

How to Dissect and Solve a Word Problem

The blueprint aid on page 18 will be your guide to dissecting and solving the following word problem.

The Word Problem Dunkin' Donuts sells to four different companies a total of $3,500 worth of doughnuts per week. What is the total annual sales to these companies? What is the yearly sales per company? (Assume each company buys the same amount.) Check your answer to show how multiplication and division are related.

MONEY TIPS

Calculating an approximate annual salary is easy when given the hourly rate. Simply double the rate and add three zeros. To determine an approximate hourly rate based on an annual salary, do the reverse. This can help out in an interview when discussing wages and salaries.

The facts	Solving for?	Steps to take	Key points
Sales per week: $3,500. *Companies:* 4.	Total annual sales to all four companies. Yearly sales per company.	Sales per week × Weeks in year (52) = Total annual sales. Total annual sales ÷ Total companies = Yearly sales per company.	Division is the reverse of multiplication.

Steps to solving problem

1. Calculate total annual sales. $3,500 × 52 weeks = **$182,000**
2. Calculate yearly sales per company, $182,000 ÷ 4 = **$45,500**

Check

$45,500 × 4 = $182,000

It's time again to check your progress with a Practice Quiz.

LU 1–3 PRACTICE QUIZ

Complete this **Practice Quiz** to see how you are doing.

1. Estimate the actual problem by rounding all the way, work the actual problem, and check:

   Actual **Estimate** **Check**
   3,894
   × 18

2. Multiply by shortcut method:
   77,000
   × 1,800
3. Multiply by shortcut method:
   95 × 10,000
4. Divide by rounding all the way, complete the actual calculation, and check, showing remainder as a whole number.
   26)5,325
5. Divide by shortcut method:
   4,000)96,000
6. Assume General Motors produces 960 Chevrolets each workday (Monday through Friday). If the cost to produce each car is $6,500, what is General Motors' total cost for the year? Check your answer.

Solutions with Step-by-Step Help on DVD

✓ Solutions

1. **Estimate**
   4,000
   × 20
   80,000

   Actual
   3,894
   × 18
   31 152
   38 94
   70,092

   Check
   8 × 3,894 = 31,152
   10 × 3,894 = + 38,940
   70,092

2. 77 × 18 = 1,386 + 5 zeros = **138,600,000**
3. 95 + 4 zeros = **950,000**
4. **Rounding**
   166 R20
   30)5,000
   3 0
   2 00
   1 80
   200
   180
   20

   Actual
   204 R21
   26)5,325
   5 2
   125
   104
   21

   Check
   26 × 204 = 5,304
   + 21
   5,325

5. Drop 3 zeros = $4\overline{)96}$ with quotient 24

6. General Motors' total cost per year:

The facts	Solving for?	Steps to take	Key points
Cars produced each workday: 960. *Workweek:* 5 days. *Cost per car:* $6,500.	Total cost per year.	Cars produced per week × 52 = Total cars produced per year. Total cars produced per year × Total cost per car = Total cost per year.	Whenever possible, use multiplication and division shortcuts with zeros. Multiplication can be checked by division.

Steps to solving problem

1. Calculate total cars produced per week. — 5 × 960 = 4,800 cars produced per week
2. Calculate total cars produced per year. — 4,800 cars × 52 weeks = 249,600 total cars produced per year
3. Calculate total cost per year. — 249,600 cars × $6,500 = $1,622,400,000 (multiply 2,496 × 65 and add zeros)

Check

$1,622,400,000 ÷ 249,600 = $6,500 (drop 2 zeros before dividing)

LU 1–3a EXTRA PRACTICE QUIZ WITH WORKED-OUT SOLUTIONS

Need more practice? Try this **Extra Practice Quiz** (check figures in Chapter Organizer, p. 20). Worked-out Solutions can be found in Appendix B at end of text.

1. Estimate the actual problem by rounding all the way, work the actual problem, and check:

   Actual **Estimate** **Check**

   4,938
   × 19

2. Multiply by shortcut method:

   86,000
   × 1,900

3. Multiply by shortcut method:

   86 × 10,000

4. Divide by rounding all the way, complete the actual calculation, and check, showing remainder as a whole number.

   $26\overline{)6,394}$

5. Divide by the shortcut method:

   $3,000\overline{)99,000}$

6. Assume General Motors produces 850 Chevrolets each workday (Monday through Friday). If the cost to produce each car is $7,000, what is General Motors's total cost for the year? Check your answer.

CHAPTER ORGANIZER AND REFERENCE GUIDE

Topic	Key point, procedure, formula	Example(s) to illustrate situation
Reading and writing numeric and verbal whole numbers, p. 4	Placement of digits in a number gives the value of the digits (Figure 1.1). Commas separate every three digits, moving from right to left. Begin at left to read and write number in verbal form. Do not read zeros or use *and*. Hyphenate numbers twenty-one to ninety-nine. Reverse procedure to change verbal number to numeric.	462 → Four hundred sixty-two 6,741 → Six thousand, seven hundred forty-one
Rounding whole numbers, p. 6	**1.** Identify place value of the digit to be rounded. **2.** If digit to the right is 5 or more, round up; if less than 5, do not change. **3.** Change all digits to the right of rounded identified digit to zeros.	643 to nearest ten 4 in tens place value. 3 is not 5 or more Thus, 643 rounds to 640.
Rounding all the way, p. 7	Round to first digit of number. One nonzero digit remains. In estimating, you round each number of the problem to one nonzero digit. The final answer is not rounded.	468,451 → 500,000 The 5 is the only nonzero digit remaining.
Adding whole numbers, p. 10	**1.** Align numbers at the right. **2.** Add units column. If sum more than 9, carry tens digit. **3.** Moving left, repeat Step 2 until all place values are added. Add from top to bottom. Check by adding bottom to top or adding each column separately and combining.	$\begin{array}{r} \scriptstyle 1 \\ 65 \\ +\ 47 \\ \hline 112 \end{array}$ $\begin{array}{r} 12 \\ +10 \\ \hline 112 \end{array}$ Checking sum of each digit
Subtracting whole numbers, p. 11	**1.** Align minuend and subtrahend at the right. **2.** Subtract units digits. If necessary, borrow 1 from tens digit in minuend. **3.** Moving left, repeat Step 2 until all place values are subtracted. Minuend less subtrahend equals difference.	**Check** $\begin{array}{r} \scriptstyle 5\ 18 \\ 685 \\ -492 \\ \hline 193 \end{array}$ $\begin{array}{r} 193 \\ +492 \\ \hline 685 \end{array}$
Multiplying whole numbers, p. 14	**1.** Align multiplicand and multiplier at the right. **2.** Begin at the right and keep multiplying as you move to the left. First partial product aligns at the right with multiplicand and multiplier. **3.** Move left through multiplier and continue multiplying multiplicand. Partial product right digit or first digit is placed directly below digit in multiplier. **4.** Continue Steps 2 and 3 until multiplication is complete. Add partial products to get final product. **Shortcuts:** (a) When multiplicand or multiplier, or both, end in zeros, disregard zeros and multiply; attach same number of zeros to answer. If zero in center of multiplier, no need to show row of zeros. (b) If multiplying by power of 10, attach same number of zeros to whole number multiplied.	$\begin{array}{r} 223 \\ \times\ 32 \\ \hline 446 \\ 6\ 69 \\ \hline 7,136 \end{array}$ a. $\begin{array}{r} 48,000 \\ \times\ 40 \\ \hline \end{array}$ $\begin{array}{r} 48 \\ 4 \\ \hline 1,920,000 \end{array}$ ← 4 zeros (3 zeros + 1 zero) $\begin{array}{r} 524 \\ \times\ 206 \\ \hline 3\ 144 \\ 104\ 8 \\ \hline 107,944 \end{array}$ b. 14 × 10 = 140 (attach 1 zero) 14 × 1,000 = 14,000 (attach 3 zeros)

(continues)

CHAPTER ORGANIZER AND REFERENCE GUIDE

Topic	Key point, procedure, formula		Example(s) to illustrate situation
Dividing whole numbers, p. 16	1. When divisor is divided into the dividend, the remainder is less than divisor. 2. Drop zeros from dividend right to left by number of zeros found in the divisor. Even division has no remainder; uneven division has a remainder; divisor with one digit is short division; and divisor with more than one digit is long division.		1. 5 R6 14)76 70 6 2. 5,000 ÷ 100 = 50 ÷ 1 = 50 5,000 ÷ 1,000 = 5 ÷ 1 = 5
KEY TERMS	addends, *p. 10* decimal point, *p. 4* decimal system, p. 4 difference, *p. 11* dividend, *p. 16* divisor, *p. 16*	minuend, *p. 11* multiplicand, *p. 14* multiplier, *p. 14* partial products, *p. 14* partial quotient, *p. 16* product, *p. 14*	quotient, *p. 16* remainder, *p. 16* rounding all the way, *p. 7* subtrahend, *p. 11* sum, *p. 10* whole number, *p. 4*
CHECK FIGURE FOR EXTRA PRACTICE QUIZZES WITH PAGE REFERENCES. (WORKED-OUT SOLUTIONS IN APPENDIX B.)	LU 1–1a (p. 9) 1. A. Eight thousand, six hundred eighty-two; B. Fifty-six thousand, two hundred ninety-five; C. Seven hundred thirty-two billion, three hundred ten million, four hundred forty-four thousand, eight hundred eighty-eight 2. A. 40; B. 700; C. 7,000; D. 6,000 3. 3,000,000; 400,000	LU 1–2a (p. 13) 1. 26,090 2. 15,000; 15,953 3. 3,819 4. 43,100 (over)	LU 1–3a (p. 19) 1. 100,000; 93,822 2. 163,400,000 3. 860,000 4. 245 R24 5. 33 6. $1,547,000,000

Critical Thinking Discussion Questions

1. List the four steps of the decision-making process. Do you think all companies should be required to follow these steps? Give an example.
2. Explain the three steps used to round whole numbers. Pick a whole number and explain why it should not be rounded.
3. How do you check subtraction? If you were to attend a movie, explain how you might use the subtraction check method.
4. Explain how you can check multiplication. If you visit a local supermarket, how could you show multiplication as a shortcut to addition?
5. Explain how division is the reverse of multiplication. Using the supermarket example, explain how division is a timesaving shortcut related to subtraction.

Classroom Notes

END-OF-CHAPTER PROBLEMS

connect plus+ www.mhhe.com/slater10e

Check figures for odd-numbered problems in Appendix C

Name ______________________ Date ________

DRILL PROBLEMS

Add the following:

1–1. 99 + 15

1–2. 790 + 755

1–3. 88 + 88

1–4. 88 + 75

1–5. 6,251 + 7,329

1–6. 59,481 + 51,411 + 70,821

1–7. 78,159 + 15,850 + 19,681

Subtract the following:

1–8. 68 − 19

1–9. 80 − 42

1–10. 287 − 199

1–11. 9,000 − 5,400

1–12. 9,800 − 8,900

1–13. 1,622 − 548

Multiply the following:

1–14. 75 × 8

1–15. 510 × 61

1–16. 800 × 200

1–17. 677 × 503

1–18. 309 × 850

1–19. 450 × 280

Divide the following by short division:

1–20. $6\overline{)1,200}$

1–21. $9\overline{)810}$

1–22. $4\overline{)164}$

Divide the following by long division. Show work and remainder.

1–23. $6\overline{)520}$

1–24. $62\overline{)8,915}$

Add the following without rearranging:

1–25. 87 + 325

1–26. 1,055 + 88

1–27. 666 + 950

1–28. 1,011 + 17

1–29. Add the following and check by totaling each column individually without carrying numbers:

Check

$$\begin{array}{r} 8{,}539 \\ 6{,}842 \\ +\ 9{,}495 \\ \hline \end{array}$$

Estimate the following by rounding all the way and then do actual addition:

1–30. **Actual** **Estimate**

$$\begin{array}{r} 7{,}700 \\ 9{,}286 \\ +\ 3{,}900 \\ \hline \end{array}$$

1–31. **Actual** **Estimate**

$$\begin{array}{r} 6{,}980 \\ 3{,}190 \\ +\ 7{,}819 \\ \hline \end{array}$$

Subtract the following without rearranging:

1–32. 190 − 66

1–33. 950 − 870

1–34. Subtract the following and check answer:

$$\begin{array}{r} 591{,}001 \\ -\ 375{,}956 \\ \hline \end{array}$$

Multiply the following horizontally:

1–35. 17 × 8

1–36. 84 × 8

1–37. 27 × 8

1–38. 17 × 6

Divide the following and check by multiplication:

1–39. $45\overline{)876}$ **Check**

1–40. $46\overline{)1{,}950}$ **Check**

Complete the following:

1–41.

$$\begin{array}{r} 9{,}200 \\ -\ 1{,}510 \\ \hline \\ -\ \ 700 \\ \hline \end{array}$$

1–42.

$$\begin{array}{r} 3{,}000{,}000 \\ -\ \ 769{,}459 \\ \hline \\ -\ \ \ 68{,}541 \\ \hline \end{array}$$

1–43. Estimate the following problem by rounding all the way and then do the actual multiplication:

Actual **Estimate**

$$\begin{array}{r} 870 \\ \times\ 81 \\ \hline \end{array}$$

Divide the following by the shortcut method:

1–44. $1{,}000\overline{)950{,}000}$

1–45. $100\overline{)70{,}000}$

In order to receive 10 bonus points for your class, you will need to stop by the Library, and wish or sing Happy 60th Birthday to Betsy Morgan.

Betsy is our Librarian and her birthday is on Thursday, September 8th.

You need to return this certificate signed by Betsy indicating that you have completed your Happy Birthday assignment. Betsy may not working Thursday, so you will need to have this completed no later than Thursday, September 15th to receive your points. It is ok to share any fun comments about Betsy turning 60….

Only other requirement is that this is done quietly…. This is a Library!

Signed: ______________________________

Betsy Morgan

Student Name: Kyle Kaper

Bill Furr's Course Name and Course #: Business Math

1–46. Estimate actual problem by rounding all the way and do actual division:

Actual	Estimate
$695\overline{)8{,}950}$	

WORD PROBLEMS

1–47. Home Heating Service, Inc., out of Colorado Springs is offering a special on winter maintenance advertised in the Gazette Telegraph for household furnaces for the fall of 2009. The offer is buy one service for $95 or two services (this year and next year) for $150. What is the per service cost if the two-year service is purchased?

1–48. An education can be the key to higher earnings. In a U.S. Census Bureau study, high school graduates earned $30,400 per year. Associate's degree graduates averaged $38,200 per year. Bachelor's degree graduates averaged $52,200 per year. Assuming a 50-year work-life, calculate the lifetime earnings for a high school graduate, associate's degree graduate, and bachelor's degree graduate. What's the lifetime income difference between a high school and associate's agree? What about the lifetime difference between a high school and bachelor's degree?

1–49. Assume season-ticket prices in the lower bowl for the Buffalo Bills will rise from $480 for a 10-game package to $600. Fans sitting in the best seats in the upper deck will pay an increase from $440 to $540. Don Manning plans to purchase 2 season tickets for either lower bowl or upper deck. **(a)** How much more will 2 tickets cost for lower bowl? **(b)** How much more will 2 tickets cost for upper deck? **(c)** What will be his total cost for a 10-game package for lower bowl? **(d)** What will be his total cost for a 10-game package for upper deck?

1–50. Some ticket prices for *Grease* on Broadway were $50, $75, $100, and $150. For a family of four, estimate the cost of the $75 tickets by rounding all the way and then do the actual multiplication:

1–51. Walt Disney World Resort and United Vacations got together to create a special deal. The air-inclusive package features accommodations for three nights at Disney's All-Star Resort, hotel taxes, and a four-day unlimited Magic Pass. Prices are $609 per person traveling from Washington, DC, and $764 per person traveling from Los Angeles. **(a)** What would be the cost for a family of four leaving from Washington, DC? **(b)** What would be the cost for a family of four leaving from Los Angeles? **(c)** How much more will it cost the family from Los Angeles?

1–52. NTB Tires bought 910 tires from its manufacturer for $36 per tire. What is the total cost of NTB's purchase? If the store can sell all the tires at $65 each, what will be the store's gross profit, or the difference between its sales and costs (Sales − Costs = Gross profit)?

1–53. What was the total average number of visits for these Internet Web sites?

Web site	Average daily unique visitors
1. Orbitz.com	1,527,000
2. Mypoints.com	1,356,000
3. Americangreetings.com	745,000
4. Bizrate.com	503,000
5. Half.com	397,000

1–54. Lee Wong bought 5,000 shares of GE stock. She held the stock for 6 months. Then Lee sold 190 shares on Monday, 450 shares on Tuesday and again on Thursday, and 900 shares on Friday. How many shares does Lee still own? The average share of the stock Lee owns is worth $48 per share. What is the total value of Lee's stock?

1–55. A report from the Center for Science in the Public Interest—a consumer group based in Washington, DC—released a study listing calories of various ice cream treats sold by six of the largest ice cream companies. The worst treat tested by the group was 1,270 total calories. People need roughly 2,200 to 2,500 calories per day. Using a daily average, how many additional calories should a person consume after eating the ice cream?

1–56. At Rose State College, Alison Wells received the following grades in her online accounting class: 90, 65, 85, 80, 75, and 90. Alison's instructor, Professor Clark, said he would drop the lowest grade. What is Alison's average?

1–57. Lee Wills, professor of business, has 18 students in Accounting I, 26 in Accounting II, 22 in Introduction to Computers, 23 in Business Law, and 29 in Introduction to Business. What is the total number of students in Professor Wills's classes? If 12 students withdraw, how many total students will Professor Wills have?

1–58. Ron Alf, owner of Alf's Moving Company, bought a new truck. On Ron's first trip, he drove 1,200 miles and used 80 gallons of gas. How many miles per gallon did Ron get from his new truck? On Ron's second trip, he drove 840 miles and used 60 gallons. What is the difference in miles per gallon between Ron's first trip and his second trip?

1–59. If Office Depot reduced its $450 Kodak digital camera by $59, what is the new selling price of the digital camera? If Office Depot sold 1,400 cameras at the new price, what were the store's digital camera dollar sales?

1–60. Assume Barnes and Noble.com has 289 business math texts in inventory. During one month, the online bookstore ordered and received 1,855 texts; it also sold 1,222 on the Web. What is the bookstore's inventory at the end of the month? If each text costs $59, what is the end-of-month inventory cost?

1–61. Assume Cabot Company produced 2,115,000 cans of paint in August. Cabot sold 2,011,000 of these cans. If each can cost $18, what were Cabot's ending inventory of paint cans and its total ending inventory cost?

1–62. A local community college has 20 faculty members in the business department, 40 in psychology, 26 in English, and 140 in all other departments. What is the total number of faculty at this college? If each faculty member advises 25 students, how many students attend the local college?

1–63. Hometown Buffet had 90 customers on Sunday, 70 on Monday, 65 on Tuesday, and a total of 310 on Wednesday to Saturday. How many customers did Hometown Buffet serve during the week? If each customer spends $9, what were the total sales for the week?

If Hometown Buffet had the same sales each week, what were the sales for the year?

1–64. A local travel agency projected its year 2009 sales at $880,000. During 2009, the agency earned $482,900 sales from its major clients and $116,500 sales from the remainder of its clients. How much did the agency overestimate its sales?

1–65. Ryan Seary works at US Airways and earned $71,000 last year before tax deductions. From Ryan's total earnings, his company subtracted $1,388 for federal income taxes, $4,402 for Social Security, and $1,030 for Medicare taxes. What was Ryan's actual, or net, pay for the year?

1–66. Assume Macy's received the following invoice amounts from some of its local suppliers. How much does the company owe?

	Per item
22 paintings	$210
39 rockers	75
40 desk lamps	65
120 coffee tables	155

1–67. Roger Company produces beach balls and operates three shifts. Roger produces 5,000 balls per shift on shifts 1 and 2. On shift 3, the company can produce 6 times as many balls as on shift 1. Assume a 5-day workweek. How many beach balls does Roger produce per week and per year?

1–68. Assume 6,000 children go to Disneyland today. How much additional revenue will Disneyland receive if it raises the cost of admission from $31 to $41 and lowers the age limit for adults from 12 years old to 10 years old?

1–69. Moe Brink has a $900 balance in his checkbook. During the week, Moe wrote the following checks: rent, $350; telephone, $44; food, $160; and entertaining, $60. Moe also made a $1,200 deposit. What is Moe's new checkbook balance?

1–70. A local Sports Authority store, an athletic sports shop, bought and sold the following merchandise:

	Cost	Selling price
Tennis rackets	$ 2,900	$ 3,999
Tennis balls	70	210
Bowling balls	1,050	2,950
Sneakers	+ 8,105	+ 14,888

What was the total cost of the merchandise bought by Sports Authority? If the shop sold all its merchandise, what were the sales and the resulting gross profit (Sales − Costs = Gross profit)?

1–71. Rich Engel, the bookkeeper for Engel's Real Estate, and his manager are concerned about the company's telephone bills. Last year the company's average monthly phone bill was $32. Rich's manager asked him for an average of this year's phone bills. Rich's records show the following:

January	$ 34	July	$ 28
February	60	August	23
March	20	September	29
April	25	October	25
May	30	November	22
June	59	December	41

What is the average of this year's phone bills? Did Rich and his manager have a justifiable concern?

1–72. On Monday, a local True Value Hardware sold 15 paint brushes at $3 each, 6 wrenches at $5 each, 7 bags of grass seed at $3 each, 4 lawn mowers at $119 each, and 28 cans of paint at $8 each. What were True Value's total dollar sales on Monday?

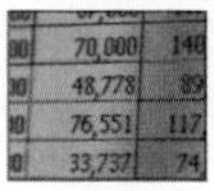

1–73. While redecorating, Lee Owens went to Carpet World and bought 150 square yards of commercial carpet. The total cost of the carpet was $6,000. How much did Lee pay per square yard?

1–74. Washington Construction built 12 ranch houses for $115,000 each. From the sale of these houses, Washington received $1,980,000. How much gross profit (Sales − Costs = Gross profit) did Washington make on the houses?

The four partners of Washington Construction split all profits equally. How much will each partner receive?

CHALLENGE PROBLEMS

1–75. Douglas and Mallori Rouse have the following monthly budget items: mortgage, $1,252; car payment, $458; food, $325; insurance, $112; cable, $75; cell phones, $80; utilities, $295; credit card payment, $50; cash donations, $100; gym fee, $25; car and home maintenance, $250; gasoline, $200; and savings, $500. Douglas earns $2,800 and Mallori earns $1,000 per month. Mallori wants to quit her job and go back to school. Can they afford for her to do this? Explain using math calculations.

1–76. Paula Sanchez is trying to determine her 2011 finances. Paula's actual 2010 finances were as follows:

Income:		Assets:		
Gross income	$69,000	Checking account	$ 1,950	
Interest income	450	Savings account	8,950	
Total	$69,450	Automobile	1,800	
Expenses:		Personal property	14,000	
Living	$24,500	Total	$26,700	
Insurance premium	350	Liabilities:		
Taxes	14,800	Note to bank	4,500	
Medical	585	Net worth	$22,200	($26,700 − $4,500)
Investment	4,000			
Total	$44,235			

Net worth = Assets − Liabilities
(own) (owe)

Paula believes her gross income will double in 2011 but her interest income will decrease $150. She plans to reduce her 2011 living expenses by one-half. Paula's insurance company wrote a letter announcing that her insurance premiums would triple in 2011. Her accountant estimates her taxes will decrease $250 and her medical costs will increase $410. Paula also hopes to cut her investments expenses by one-fourth. Paula's accountant projects that her savings and checking accounts will each double in value. On January 2, 2011, Paula sold her automobile and began to use public transportation. Paula forecasts that her personal property will decrease by one-seventh. She has sent her bank a $375 check to reduce her bank note. Could you give Paula an updated list of her 2011 finances? If you round all the way each 2010 and 2011 asset and liability, what will be the difference in Paula's net worth?

DVD SUMMARY PRACTICE TEST

1. Translate the following verbal forms to numbers and add. *(p. 4)*

   a. Four thousand, eight hundred thirty-nine

   b. Seven million, twelve

   c. Twelve thousand, three hundred ninety-two

2. Express the following number in verbal form. *(p. 4)*

   9,622,364

3. Round the following numbers. *(p. 6)*

Nearest ten	**Nearest hundred**	**Nearest thousand**	**Round all the way**
a. 68	**b.** 888	**c.** 8,325	**d.** 14,821

4. Estimate the following actual problem by rounding all the way, work the actual problem, and check by adding each column of digits separately. *(pp. 7, 10)*

Actual	**Estimate**	**Check**
1,886		
9,411		
+ 6,395		

5. Estimate the following actual problem by rounding all the way and then do the actual multiplication. *(pp. 7, 14)*

Actual	**Estimate**
8,843	
× 906	

6. Multiply the following by the shortcut method. *(p. 15)*

829,412 × 1,000

7. Divide the following and check the answer by multiplication. *(p. 14)*

Check

$39\overline{)14{,}800}$

8. Divide the following by the shortcut method. *(p. 17)*

6,000 ÷ 60

9. Ling Wong bought a $299 iPod that was reduced to $205. Ling gave the clerk 3 $100 bills. What change will Ling receive? *(p. 11)*

10. Sam Song plans to buy a $16,000 Ford Focus with an interest charge of $4,000. Sam figures he can afford a monthly payment of $400. If Sam must pay 40 equal monthly payments, can he afford the Ford Focus? *(pp. 10, 14)*

11. Lester Hal has the oil tank at his business filled 20 times per year. The tank has a capacity of 200 gallons. Assume **(a)** the price of oil fuel is $3 per gallon and **(b)** the tank is completely empty each time Lester has it filled. What is Lester's average monthly oil bill? Complete the following blueprint aid for dissecting and solving the word problem. *(pp. 10, 14, 16)*

The facts	Solving for?	Steps to take	Key points

Steps to solving problem

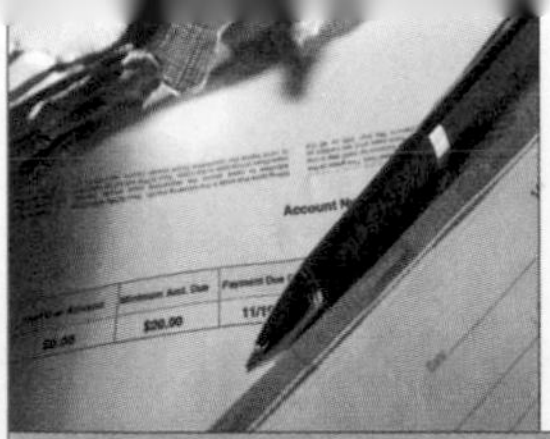

Personal Finance

A KIPLINGER APPROACH

An Early Look at Retirement

At 43, Steve Gurney spent a week in a retirement community and was surprised by what he found. AS TOLD TO MARY BETH FRANKLIN

WHY DID YOU MAKE THE MOVE? During my 20 years publishing the *Guide to Retirement Living SourceBook* (www.retirement-living.com), I've visited more than 500 communities. But I felt I didn't understand what it was like to be a resident. I wanted to experience moving into a retirement home so I could help my readers prepare themselves and make more-informed choices.

WERE THERE ANY SURPRISES? Lots of them. As I walked through my house deciding what I would take into a one-bedroom apartment and what I would leave behind, I realized how my memories were tied to my belongings. I felt a bit of the loss that elders must feel when they have to cull a lifetime of possessions.

WHAT ABOUT COSTS? It really hit home that my monthly rent, including dining and housekeeping services, would be more than the mortgage payment on my four-bedroom house. At the retirement community I moved into, rates range from $2,700 to $4,000 a month for independent living and up to $6,300 a month for assisted living.

WHAT WAS THE HARDEST PART? Adjusting to a new environment. Just like being the new kid at school, it was a bit unnerving at first to decide where to sit at dinner. Some of the residents who volunteer to help newcomers transition invited me to join them in the dining room.

WHAT WAS THE BEST PART? The people. Many of them have lived fascinating lives, and I'd often get an interesting nugget of information or a history lesson from someone who actually experienced an event.

HOW HAS THE EXPERIENCE CHANGED YOU? I learned to slow down. One day I went with a group to visit a museum and I did something I had never done before: I read every single word at the exhibit. Although it seems as though the sky is falling these days, an exhibit on the Civil War reminded me that our country has overcome much worse challenges. It helped put today's bad news in perspective.

WHAT'S NEXT? I hope to repeat the project in other types of communities, including a nursing home and an Alzheimer's facility. ■

■ WHEN GURNEY FELT LIKE THE NEW KID ON THE BLOCK, RESIDENTS OF PAUL SPRING RETIREMENT COMMUNITY, IN ALEXANDRIA, VA., MADE HIM WELCOME.

From *Kiplinger's Personal Finance*, p. 80.

BUSINESS MATH ISSUE

Rates at resident communities for assisted living make retirement impossible.

1. List the key points of the article and information to support your position.
2. Write a group defense of your position using math calculations to support your view.

Slater's Business Math Scrapbook

Applying Your Skills

PROJECT A

Write each attendance number numerically and calculate total attendance.

Misadventure?

Attendance at Disney theme parks in 2006:

Park	Attendance (in millions)
Magic Kingdom (Florida)	16.64
Disneyland (California)	14.73
Tokyo Disneyland	12.90
Tokyo Disney Sea	12.10
Disneyland Paris	10.60
Epcot (Florida)	10.46
Disney-MGM Studios (Florida)	9.10
Animal Kingdom (Florida)	8.91
California Adventure	**5.95**
Hong Kong Disneyland	5.20
Walt Disney Studios Paris	2.20

Source: TEA/ERA Theme Park Attendance Report

AP

The 'Tower of Terror' ride at Disney's California Adventure.

PROJECT B

Assuming you set up a home safety system for 12 months, what would be the difference in cost between InGrid and iControl?

Home, Safe Home

A comparison of basic features offered by wireless home-security systems, in which homeowners can arm/disarm the sensors via the Internet and receive alerts through email and text messaging.

	Installation	Features	Cost
InGrid	Do-it-yourself installation.	Integrated smoke/fire sensors; weather forecasts and severe-weather alerts.	$299 hardware cost plus $30 in monthly fees*
iControl	Professional installation in most cases, though some security dealers sell do-it-yourself versions.	Video monitoring; smoke-detection sensors; Can also activate lights, change or schedule thermostat settings to save energy.	$100 hardware cost plus $15 monthly fees
Alarm.com	Professional installation in most cases.	Video monitoring; temperature, water, motion sensors; uses cellular technology, so no broadband connection is needed.	$200 hardware cost plus $20 to $30 in monthly fees
AT&T	Do-it-yourself installation.	Temperature and water sensors; sends live video to Internet-connected PC or AT&T mobile device.	$200 hardware cost plus $10 in monthly fees*

* With a one-year commitment

Internet Projects: See text Web site (www.mhhe.com/slater10e) and The Business Math Internet Resource Guide.

chapter

2 FRACTIONS

Tuesday, June 9, 2009 **B1**

Apple's Philip Schiller took the stage Monday to unveil the iPhone 3G S.

To Sustain iPhone, Apple Halves Price

By Yukari Iwatani Kane

Apple Inc. halved the price of its entry-level iPhone to $99 and rolled out a next-generation model, looking to sustain the momentum for its popular smart phone amid the recession and fresh competition.

Apple also announced several new lower-priced notebook computers at its annual conference for software developers, which kicked off Monday. Chief Executive Steve Jobs, who went on medical leave in January, didn't make an appearance.

Sankei/Getty Images

LEARNING UNIT OBJECTIVES

LU 2–1: Types of Fractions and Conversion Procedures

1. Recognize the three types of fractions *(pp. 36–37)*.
2. Convert improper fractions to whole or mixed numbers and mixed numbers to improper fractions *(pp. 37–38)*.
3. Convert fractions to lowest and highest terms *(pp. 38–39)*.

LU 2–2: Adding and Subtracting Fractions

1. Add like and unlike fractions *(pp. 41–42)*.
2. Find the least common denominator by inspection and prime numbers *(pp. 42–43)*.
3. Subtract like and unlike fractions *(p. 44)*.
4. Add and subtract mixed numbers with the same or different denominators *(pp. 44–46)*.

LU 2–3: Multiplying and Dividing Fractions

1. Multiply and divide proper fractions and mixed numbers *(pp. 47–48)*.
2. Use the cancellation method in the multiplication and division of fractions *(pp. 48–49)*.

VOCABULARY PREVIEW

Here are the key terms in this chapter. When you finish the chapter, if you feel you know the term, place a checkmark within the parentheses following the term. If you are not certain of the definition, look it up and write the page number where it can be found in the text. The chapter organizer includes page references to the terms. There is also a complete glossary at the end of the text.

Cancellation . ( ) Common denominator . ( ) Denominator . ( ) Equivalent . ( ) Fraction . ( ) Greatest common divisor . ( ) Higher terms . ( ) Improper fraction . ( ) Least common denominator (LCD) . ( ) Like fractions . ( ) Lowest terms . ( ) Mixed numbers . ( ) Numerator . ( ) Prime numbers . ( ) Proper fractions . ( ) Reciprocal . ( ) Unlike fractions . ( )

Paid Leave: Workers Like It, But Some Businesses May Not

BY SARA SCHAEFER MUÑOZ

New Jersey's Senate recently passed legislation that would give employees the right to take paid leave to care for a newborn or a sick relative. Those taking the leave would be eligible for two-thirds of their salary—up to $524 a week—for six weeks. It would be financed by payroll deductions, costing every worker around $33 a year.

"I would be happy to pay for [this], even though I will probably not be using the benefits it provides. I think overall it is a benefit to society."

The following *Wall Street Journal* clipping "Paid Leave: Workers Like It, But Some Businesses May Not" illustrates the use of a fraction. From the clipping you learn that two-thirds ($\frac{2}{3}$) of an employee's salary would be paid when taking leave to care for a newborn or sick relative.

Now let's look at Milk Chocolate M&M's® candies as another example of using fractions.

As you know, M&M's® candies come in different colors. Do you know how many of each color are in a bag of M&M's®? If you go to the M&M's website, you learn that a typical bag of M&M's® contains approximately 17 brown, 11 yellow, 11 red, and 5 each of orange, blue, and green M&M's®.[1]

[1]Off 1 due to rounding.

The 1.69-ounce bag of M&M's® shown here contains 55 M&M's®. In this bag, you will find the following colors:

18 yellow	9 blue	6 brown
10 red	7 orange	5 green

55 pieces in the bag

The number of yellow candies in a bag might suggest that yellow is the favorite color of many people. Since this is a business math text, however, let's look at the 55 M&M's® in terms of fractional arithmetic.

Of the 55 M&M's® in the 1.69-ounce bag, 5 of these M&M's® are green, so we can say that 5 parts of 55 represent green candies. We could also say that 1 out of 11 M&M's® is green. Are you confused?

For many people, fractions are difficult. If you are one of these people, this chapter is for you. First you will review the types of fractions and the fraction conversion procedures. Then you will gain a clear understanding of the addition, subtraction, multiplication, and division of fractions.

Learning Unit 2–1: Types of Fractions and Conversion Procedures

LO 1

GLOBAL

This chapter explains the parts of whole numbers called **fractions.** With fractions you can divide any object or unit—a whole—into a definite number of equal parts. For example, the bag of 55 M&M's® shown at the beginning of this chapter contains 6 brown candies. If you eat only the brown M&M's®, you have eaten 6 parts of 55, or 6 parts of the whole bag of M&M's®. We can express this in the following fraction:

Hewlett-Packard to Lay Off 24,600

Nearly Half in U.S.; Firm Restructures After Buying EDS

By Justin Scheck And Ben Charny

Hewlett-Packard Co. said it will cut 24,600 jobs as part of its plan to integrate tech-services giant Electronic Data Systems Corp., providing the first details of how extensive its restructuring of the combined company will be.

The cuts are intended to combined work force. Before the $13.25 billion acquisition of EDS, which was finalized last month, H-P had 178,000 employees and EDS had 142,000.

The staff cuts will be spread across both companies, H-P said, with nearly half coming in the U.S. The company added that it "expects to replace roughly half of these positions over the next three years to create a global work force."

Wall Street Journal © 2008

$\frac{6}{55}$

6 is the **numerator,** or top of the fraction. The numerator describes the number of equal parts of the whole bag that you ate.

55 is the **denominator,** or bottom of the fraction. The denominator gives the total number of equal parts in the bag of M&M's®.

Before reviewing the arithmetic operations of fractions, you must recognize the three types of fractions described in this unit. You must also know how to convert fractions to a workable form.

Types of Fractions

When you read the *Wall Street Journal* clipping "Hewlett-Packard to Lay Off 24,600" you see that Hewlett-Packard is planning to make one-half ($\frac{1}{2}$) of the job cuts in the United States. The fraction $\frac{1}{2}$ is a proper fraction.

PROPER FRACTIONS

A **proper fraction** has a value less than 1; its numerator is smaller than its denominator.

EXAMPLES $\frac{1}{4}, \frac{1}{2}, \frac{1}{10}, \frac{1}{12}, \frac{1}{3}, \frac{4}{7}, \frac{9}{10}, \frac{12}{13}, \frac{18}{55}$

Boston Globe © 2009

IMPROPER FRACTIONS

An **improper fraction** has a value equal to or greater than 1; its numerator is equal to or greater than its denominator.

EXAMPLES $\frac{14}{14}, \frac{7}{6}, \frac{15}{14}, \frac{22}{19}$

MIXED NUMBERS

A **mixed number** is the sum of a whole number greater than zero and a proper fraction.

EXAMPLES $5\frac{1}{6}, 5\frac{9}{10}, 8\frac{7}{8}, 33\frac{5}{6}, 139\frac{9}{11}$

Conversion Procedures

In Chapter 1 we worked with two of the division symbols (÷ and $\overline{)\ \ }$). The horizontal line (or the diagonal) that separates the numerator and the denominator of a fraction also indicates division. The numerator, like the dividend, is the number we are dividing into. The denominator, like the divisor, is the number we use to divide. Then, referring to the 6 brown M&M's® in the bag of 55 M&M's® ($\frac{6}{55}$) shown at the beginning of this unit, we can say that we are dividing 55 into 6, or 6 is divided by 55. Also, in the fraction $\frac{3}{4}$, we can say that we are dividing 4 into 3, or 3 is divided by 4.

Working with the smaller numbers of simple fractions such as $\frac{3}{4}$ is easier, so we often convert fractions to their simplest terms. In this unit we show how to convert improper fractions to whole or mixed numbers, mixed numbers to improper fractions, and fractions to lowest and highest terms.

Converting Improper Fractions to Whole or Mixed Numbers

Business situations often make it necessary to change an improper fraction to a whole number or mixed number. You can use the following steps to make this conversion:

LO 2

CONVERTING IMPROPER FRACTIONS TO WHOLE OR MIXED NUMBERS

Step 1. Divide the numerator of the improper fraction by the denominator.

Step 2. **a.** If you have no remainder, the quotient is a whole number.

b. If you have a remainder, the whole number part of the mixed number is the quotient. The remainder is placed over the old denominator as the proper fraction of the mixed number.

EXAMPLES

$$\frac{15}{15} = 1 \qquad \frac{16}{5} = 3\frac{1}{5} \qquad \begin{array}{r} 3\text{ R1} \\ 5\overline{)16} \\ \underline{15} \\ 1 \end{array}$$

Converting Mixed Numbers to Improper Fractions

By reversing the procedure of converting improper fractions to mixed numbers, we can change mixed numbers to improper fractions.

CONVERTING MIXED NUMBERS TO IMPROPER FRACTIONS

Step 1. Multiply the denominator of the fraction by the whole number.

Step 2. Add the product from Step 1 to the numerator of the old fraction.

Step 3. Place the total from Step 2 over the denominator of the old fraction to get the improper fraction.

EXAMPLE $6\frac{1}{8} = \frac{(8 \times 6) + 1}{8} = \frac{49}{8}$ ← Note that the denominator stays the same.

Converting (Reducing) Fractions to Lowest Terms

When solving fraction problems, you always reduce the fractions to their lowest terms. This reduction does not change the value of the fraction. For example, in the bag of M&M's®, 5 out of 55 were green. The fraction for this is $\frac{5}{55}$. If you divide the top and bottom of the fraction by 5, you have reduced the fraction to $\frac{1}{11}$ without changing its value. Remember, we said in the chapter introduction that 1 out of 11 M&M's® in the bag of 55 M&M's® represents green candies. Now you know why this is true.

To reduce a fraction to its lowest terms, begin by inspecting the fraction, looking for the largest whole number that will divide into both the numerator and the denominator without leaving a remainder. This whole number is the **greatest common divisor,** which cannot be zero. When you find this largest whole number, you have reached the point where the fraction is reduced to its **lowest terms.** At this point, no number (except 1) can divide evenly into both parts of the fraction.

LO 3

REDUCING FRACTIONS TO LOWEST TERMS BY INSPECTION

Step 1. By inspection, find the largest whole number (greatest common divisor) that will divide evenly into the numerator and denominator (does not change the fraction value).

Step 2. Now you have reduced the fraction to its lowest terms, since no number (except 1) can divide evenly into the numerator and denominator.

EXAMPLE $\frac{24}{30} = \frac{24 \div 6}{30 \div 6} = \frac{4}{5}$

Using inspection, you can see that the number 6 in the above example is the greatest common divisor. When you have large numbers, the greatest common divisor is not so obvious. For large numbers, you can use the following step approach to find the greatest common divisor:

STEP APPROACH FOR FINDING GREATEST COMMON DIVISOR

Step 1. Divide the smaller number (numerator) of the fraction into the larger number (denominator).

Step 2. Divide the remainder of Step 1 into the divisor of Step 1.

Step 3. Divide the remainder of Step 2 into the divisor of Step 2. Continue this division process until the remainder is a 0, which means the last divisor is the greatest common divisor.

EXAMPLE $\frac{24}{30}$

Step 1

$$\begin{array}{r} 1 \\ 24\overline{)30} \\ \underline{24} \\ 6 \end{array}$$

Step 2

$$\begin{array}{r} 4 \\ 6\overline{)24} \\ \underline{24} \\ 0 \end{array}$$

$$\frac{24 \div 6}{30 \div 6} = \frac{4}{5}$$

Reducing a fraction by inspection is to some extent a trial-and-error method. Sometimes you are not sure what number you should divide into the top (numerator) and bottom (denominator) of the fraction. The following reference table on divisibility tests will be helpful. Note that to reduce a fraction to lowest terms might result in more than one division.

Will divide evenly into number if	2	3	4	5	6	10
	Last digit is 0, 2, 4, 6, 8.	Sum of the digits is divisible by 3.	Last two digits can be divided by 4.	Last digit is 0 or 5.	The number is even and 3 will divide into the sum of the digits.	The last digit is 0.
Examples	$\frac{12}{14} = \frac{6}{7}$	$\frac{36}{69} = \frac{12}{23}$ $3 + 6 = 9 \div 3 = 3$ $6 + 9 = 15 \div 3 = 5$	$\frac{140}{160} = \frac{1(40)}{1(60)}$ $= \frac{35}{40} = \frac{7}{8}$	$\frac{15}{20} = \frac{3}{4}$	$\frac{12}{18} = \frac{2}{3}$	$\frac{90}{100} = \frac{9}{10}$

Converting (Raising) Fractions to Higher Terms

Later, when you add and subtract fractions, you will see that sometimes fractions must be raised to **higher terms.** Recall that when you reduced fractions to their lowest terms, you looked for the largest whole number (greatest common divisor) that would divide evenly into both the numerator and the denominator. When you raise fractions to higher terms, you do the opposite and multiply the numerator and the denominator by the same whole number. For example, if you want to raise the fraction $\frac{1}{4}$, you can multiply the numerator and denominator by 2.

EXAMPLE $\frac{1}{4} \times \frac{2}{2} = \frac{2}{8}$

The fractions $\frac{1}{4}$ and $\frac{2}{8}$ are **equivalent** in value. By converting $\frac{1}{4}$ to $\frac{2}{8}$, you only divided it into more parts.

Let's suppose that you have eaten $\frac{4}{7}$ of a pizza. You decide that instead of expressing the amount you have eaten in 7ths, you want to express it in 28ths. How would you do this?

To find the new numerator when you know the new denominator (28), use the steps that follow.

RAISING FRACTIONS TO HIGHER TERMS WHEN DENOMINATOR IS KNOWN

Step 1. Divide the *new* denominator by the *old* denominator to get the common number that raises the fraction to higher terms.

Step 2. Multiply the common number from Step 1 by the old numerator and place it as the new numerator over the new denominator.

$ MONEY TIPS

Do you want to save $\frac{1}{5}$ or so of your income? Cancel your cable; get rid of a second vehicle; eat, drink coffee, and entertain at home; wear out your clothing; rent out a room; and cancel your cell phone (use a prepaid phone plan instead).

EXAMPLE $\frac{4}{7} = \frac{?}{28}$

Step 1. Divide 28 by 7 = 4.

Step 2. Multiply 4 by the numerator 4 = 16.

Result:

$$\frac{4}{7} = \frac{16}{28} \quad \left(\textit{Note}: \text{This is the same as multiplying } \frac{4}{7} \times \frac{4}{4}.\right)$$

Note that the $\frac{4}{7}$ and $\frac{16}{28}$ are equivalent in value, yet they are different fractions.

Now try the following Practice Quiz to check your understanding of this unit.

LU 2–1 PRACTICE QUIZ

Complete this **Practice Quiz** to see how you are doing.

1. Identify the type of fraction—proper, improper, or mixed:

   a. $\frac{4}{5}$ **b.** $\frac{6}{5}$ **c.** $19\frac{1}{5}$ **d.** $\frac{20}{20}$

2. Convert to a mixed number:

   $\frac{160}{9}$

3. Convert the mixed number to an improper fraction:

   $9\frac{5}{8}$

4. Find the greatest common divisor by the step approach and reduce to lowest terms:

   a. $\frac{24}{40}$ **b.** $\frac{91}{156}$

5. Convert to higher terms:

   a. $\frac{14}{20} = \frac{\quad}{200}$ **b.** $\frac{8}{10} = \frac{\quad}{60}$

Solutions with Step-by-Step Help on DVD

✓ Solutions

1. **a.** Proper
   b. Improper
   c. Mixed
   d. Improper

2. $9\overline{)160}$ = $17\frac{7}{9}$; 160 − 9 = 70 (bring down); 70 − 63 = 7

3. $\frac{(9 \times 8) + 5}{8} = \frac{77}{8}$

4. **a.** $24\overline{)40}$ = 1, remainder 16 → $16\overline{)24}$ = 1, remainder 8 → $8\overline{)16}$ = 2, remainder 0

   8 is greatest common divisor.

   $\frac{24 \div 8}{40 \div 8} = \frac{3}{5}$

   b. $91\overline{)156}$ = 1, remainder 65 → $65\overline{)91}$ = 1, remainder 26 → $26\overline{)65}$ = 2, remainder 13 → $13\overline{)26}$ = 2, remainder 0

   13 is greatest common divisor.

   $\frac{91 \div 13}{156 \div 13} = \frac{7}{12}$

5. **a.** $20\overline{)200}$ = 10 $10 \times 14 = 140$ $\frac{14}{20} = \frac{140}{200}$

   b. $10\overline{)60}$ = 6 $6 \times 8 = 48$ $\frac{8}{10} = \frac{48}{60}$

LU 2–1a EXTRA PRACTICE QUIZ WITH WORKED-OUT SOLUTIONS

Need more practice? Try this **Extra Practice Quiz** (check figures in Chapter Organizer, p. 53). Worked-out Solutions can be found in Appendix B at end of text.

1. Identify the type of fraction—proper, improper, or mixed:

   a. $\frac{2}{5}$ **b.** $\frac{7}{6}$ **c.** $18\frac{1}{3}$ **d.** $\frac{40}{40}$

2. Convert to a mixed number (do not reduce):

   $\frac{155}{7}$

3. Convert the mixed number to an improper fraction:

   $8\frac{7}{9}$

4. Find the greatest common divisor by the step approach and reduce to lowest terms:

   a. $\frac{42}{70}$ b. $\frac{96}{182}$

5. Convert to higher terms:

   a. $\frac{16}{30} = \frac{\quad}{300}$ b. $\frac{9}{20} = \frac{\quad}{60}$

Learning Unit 2–2: Adding and Subtracting Fractions

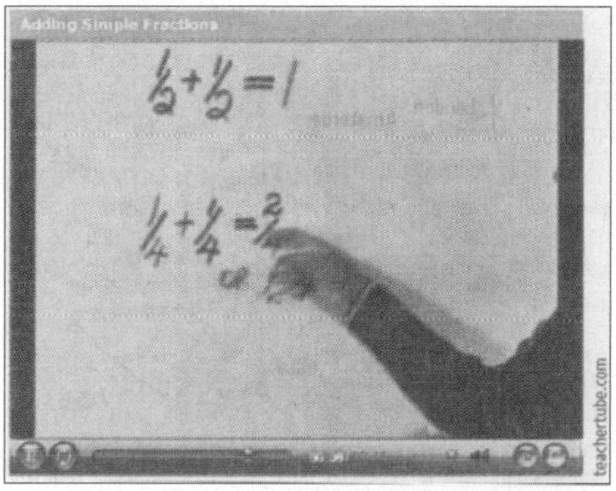

Wall Street Journal © 2005

The *Wall Street Journal* clipping shows how more teachers are using online video-sharing sites that are modeled after Google Inc.'s YouTube. Note in clip how a fraction lesson is shown on TeacherTube. Note these fractions can be added because the fractions have the same denominator. These are called *like fractions.*

In this unit you learn how to add and subtract fractions with the same denominators **(like fractions)** and fractions with different denominators **(unlike fractions).** We have also included how to add and subtract mixed numbers.

Addition of Fractions

LO 1

When you add two or more quantities, they must have the same name or be of the same denomination. You cannot add 6 quarts and 3 pints unless you change the denomination of one or both quantities. You must either make the quarts into pints or the pints into quarts. The same principle also applies to fractions. That is, to add two or more fractions, they must have a **common denominator.**

Adding Like Fractions

In our video-sharing clipping at the beginning of this unit we stated that because the fractions had the same denominator, or a common denominator, they were *like fractions.* Adding like fractions is similar to adding whole numbers.

ADDING LIKE FRACTIONS

Step 1. Add the numerators and place the total over the original denominator.

Step 2. If the total of your numerators is the same as your original denominator, convert your answer to a whole number; if the total is larger than your original denominator, convert your answer to a mixed number.

EXAMPLE $\frac{1}{7} + \frac{4}{7} = \frac{5}{7}$

The denominator, 7, shows the number of pieces into which some whole was divided. The two numerators, 1 and 4, tell how many of the pieces you have. So if you add 1 and 4, you get 5, or $\frac{5}{7}$.

Adding Unlike Fractions

Since you cannot add *unlike fractions* because their denominators are not the same, you must change the unlike fractions to *like fractions*—fractions with the same denominators. To do this, find a denominator that is common to all the fractions you want to add. Then look for the **least common denominator (LCD).**[2] The LCD is the smallest nonzero whole

[2]Often referred to as the *lowest common denominator.*

number into which all denominators will divide evenly. You can find the LCD by inspection or with prime numbers.

Finding the Least Common Denominator (LCD) by Inspection The example that follows shows you how to use inspection to find an LCD (this will make all the denominators the same).

EXAMPLE $\frac{3}{7} + \frac{5}{21}$

Inspection of these two fractions shows that the smallest number into which denominators 7 and 21 divide evenly is 21. Thus, 21 is the LCD.

You may know that 21 is the LCD of $\frac{3}{7} + \frac{5}{21}$, but you cannot add these two fractions until you change the denominator of $\frac{3}{7}$ to 21. You do this by building (raising) the equivalent of $\frac{3}{7}$, as explained in Learning Unit 2–1. You can use the following steps to find the LCD by inspection:

Step 1. Divide the new denominator (21) by the old denominator (7): $21 \div 7 = 3$.

Step 2. Multiply the 3 in Step 1 by the old numerator (3): $3 \times 3 = 9$. The new numerator is 9.

Result:

$$\frac{3}{7} = \frac{9}{21}$$

Now that the denominators are the same, you add the numerators.

$$\frac{9}{21} + \frac{5}{21} = \frac{14}{21} = \frac{2}{3}$$

Note that $\frac{14}{21}$ is reduced to its lowest terms $\frac{2}{3}$. Always reduce your answer to its lowest terms.

You are now ready for the following general steps for adding proper fractions with different denominators. These steps also apply to the following discussion on finding LCD by prime numbers.

LO 2

ADDING UNLIKE FRACTIONS

Step 1. Find the LCD.

Step 2. Change each fraction to a like fraction with the LCD.

Step 3. Add the numerators and place the total over the LCD.

Step 4. If necessary, reduce the answer to lowest terms.

As of 9/4/06
9,808,358 is the number of digits in the largest known prime number.

Finding the Least Common Denominator (LCD) by Prime Numbers When you cannot determine the LCD by inspection, you can use the prime number method. First you must understand prime numbers.

PRIME NUMBERS

A **prime number** is a whole number greater than 1 that is only divisible by itself and 1. The number 1 is not a prime number.

EXAMPLES 2, 3, 5, 7, 11, 13, 17, 19, 23, 29, 31, 37, 41, 43

Note that the number 4 is not a prime number. Not only can you divide 4 by 1 and by 4, but you can also divide 4 by 2. A whole number that is greater than 1 and is only divisible by itself and 1 has become a source of interest to some people.

EXAMPLE $\frac{1}{3} + \frac{1}{8} + \frac{1}{9} + \frac{1}{12}$

Step 1. Copy the denominators and arrange them in a separate row.

3 8 9 12

Step 2. Divide the denominators in Step 1 by prime numbers. Start with the smallest number that will divide into at least two of the denominators. Bring down any number that is not divisible. Keep in mind that the lowest prime number is 2.

$$\begin{array}{r|rrrr} 2 & 3 & 8 & 9 & 12 \\ \hline & 3 & 4 & 9 & 6 \end{array}$$

Note: The 3 and 9 were brought down, since they were not divisible by 2.

Step 3. Continue Step 2 until no prime number will divide evenly into at least two numbers.

Note: The 3 is used, since 2 can no longer divide evenly into at least two numbers.

$$\begin{array}{r|rrrr} 2 & 3 & 8 & 9 & 12 \\ \hline 2 & 3 & 4 & 9 & 6 \\ \hline 3 & 3 & 2 & 9 & 3 \\ \hline & 1 & 2 & 3 & 1 \end{array}$$

Step 4. To find the LCD, multiply all the numbers in the divisors (2, 2, 3) and in the last row (1, 2, 3, 1).

$$\boxed{2 \times 2 \times 3} \times \boxed{1 \times 2 \times 3 \times 1} = 72 \text{ (LCD)}$$

Divisors × Last row

Step 5. Raise each fraction so that each denominator will be 72 and then add fractions.

$$\frac{1}{3} = \frac{?}{72} \qquad 72 \div 3 = 24 \qquad 24 \times 1 = 24$$

$$\frac{24}{72} + \frac{9}{72} + \frac{8}{72} + \frac{6}{72} = \frac{47}{72}$$

$$\frac{1}{8} = \frac{?}{72} \qquad 72 \div 8 = 9 \qquad 9 \times 1 = 9$$

The above five steps used for finding LCD with prime numbers are summarized as follows:

FINDING LCD FOR TWO OR MORE FRACTIONS

Step 1. Copy the denominators and arrange them in a separate row.

Step 2. Divide the denominators by the smallest prime number that will divide evenly into at least two numbers.

Step 3. Continue until no prime number divides evenly into at least two numbers.

Step 4. Multiply all the numbers in divisors and last row to find the LCD.

Step 5. Raise all fractions so each has a common denominator and then complete the computation.

Adding Mixed Numbers

The following steps will show you how to add mixed numbers:

ADDING MIXED NUMBERS

Step 1. Add the fractions (remember that fractions need common denominators, as in the previous section).

Step 2. Add the whole numbers.

Step 3. Combine the totals of Steps 1 and 2. Be sure you do not have an improper fraction in your final answer. Convert the improper fraction to a whole or mixed number. Add the whole numbers resulting from the improper fraction conversion to the total whole numbers of Step 2. If necessary, reduce the answer to lowest terms.

Using prime numbers to find LCD of example

$$\begin{array}{r|rrr} 2 & 20 & 5 & 4 \\ 2 & 10 & 5 & 2 \\ 5 & 5 & 5 & 1 \\ \hline & 1 & 1 & 1 \end{array}$$

$2 \times 2 \times 5 = 20$ LCD

EXAMPLE

$$\begin{array}{rrl} 4\frac{7}{20} & 4\frac{7}{20} & \\ 6\frac{3}{5} & 6\frac{12}{20} & \\ +\,7\frac{1}{4} & +\,7\frac{5}{20} & \\ \hline \text{Step 1} \rightarrow & \frac{24}{20} = & 1\frac{4}{20} \\ \text{Step 2} & & +\,17 \\ \text{Step 3} & = & 18\frac{4}{20} = 18\frac{1}{5} \end{array}$$

$\frac{3}{5} = \frac{?}{20}$

$20 \div 5 = 4$

$\times\ 3$

12

Subtraction of Fractions

The subtraction of fractions is similar to the addition of fractions. This section explains how to subtract like and unlike fractions and how to subtract mixed numbers.

Subtracting Like Fractions

To subtract like fractions, use the steps that follow.

LO 3

SUBTRACTING LIKE FRACTIONS

Step 1. Subtract the numerators and place the answer over the common denominator.

Step 2. If necessary, reduce the answer to lowest terms.

EXAMPLE $\frac{9}{10} - \frac{1}{10} = \frac{8 \div 2}{10 \div 2} = \frac{4}{5}$

↑ Step 1 ↑ Step 2

Subtracting Unlike Fractions

Now let's learn the steps for subtracting unlike fractions.

SUBTRACTING UNLIKE FRACTIONS

Step 1. Find the LCD.

Step 2. Raise the fraction to its equivalent value.

Step 3. Subtract the numerators and place the answer over the LCD.

Step 4. If necessary, reduce the answer to lowest terms.

EXAMPLE

$$\begin{array}{rr} \frac{5}{8} & \frac{40}{64} \\ -\,\frac{2}{64} & -\,\frac{2}{64} \\ \hline & \frac{38}{64} = \frac{19}{32} \end{array}$$

By inspection, we see that LCD is 64.
Thus $64 \div 8 = 8 \times 5 = 40$.

Subtracting Mixed Numbers

When you subtract whole numbers, sometimes borrowing is not necessary. At other times, you must borrow. The same is true of subtracting mixed numbers.

LO 4

SUBTRACTING MIXED NUMBERS

When Borrowing Is Not Necessary

Step 1. Subtract fractions, making sure to find the LCD.

Step 2. Subtract whole numbers.

Step 3. Reduce the fraction(s) to lowest terms.

When Borrowing Is Necessary

Step 1. Make sure the fractions have the LCD.

Step 2. Borrow from the whole number of the minuend (top number).

Step 3. Subtract the whole numbers and fractions.

Step 4. Reduce the fraction(s) to lowest terms.

EXAMPLE Where borrowing is not necessary: Find LCD of 2 and 8. LCD is 8.

$$\begin{array}{r} 6\frac{1}{2} \\ -\ \frac{3}{8} \\ \hline \end{array} \qquad \begin{array}{r} 6\frac{4}{8} \\ -\ \frac{3}{8} \\ \hline 6\frac{1}{8} \end{array}$$

EXAMPLE Where borrowing is necessary:

$$\begin{array}{r} 3\frac{1}{2} = \\ -\ 1\frac{3}{4} = \\ \hline \end{array} \quad \begin{array}{r} 3\frac{2}{4} = \\ -\ 1\frac{3}{4} = \\ \hline \end{array} \quad \begin{array}{r} 2\frac{6}{4} \\ 1\frac{3}{4} \\ \hline 1\frac{3}{4} \end{array} \left(\frac{4}{4} + \frac{2}{4}\right)$$

LCD is 4.

$\frac{48}{40} - \frac{25}{40} \quad \frac{23}{40}$

Since $\frac{3}{4}$ is larger than $\frac{2}{4}$, we must borrow 1 from the 3. This is the same as borrowing $\frac{4}{4}$. A fraction with the same numerator and denominator represents a whole. When we add $\frac{4}{4} + \frac{2}{4}$, we get $\frac{6}{4}$. Note how we subtracted the whole number and fractions, being sure to reduce the final answer if necessary.

Rick Bowmer/AP Images

How to Dissect and Solve a Word Problem

Let's now look at how to dissect and solve a word problem involving fractions.

The Word Problem The Albertsons grocery store has $550\frac{1}{4}$ total square feet of floor space. Albertsons' meat department occupies $115\frac{1}{2}$ square feet, and its deli department occupies $145\frac{7}{8}$ square feet. If the remainder of the floor space is for groceries, what square footage remains for groceries?

The facts	Solving for?	Steps to take	Key points
Total square footage: $550\frac{1}{4}$ sq. ft. *Meat department:* $115\frac{1}{2}$ sq. ft. *Deli department:* $145\frac{7}{8}$ sq. ft.	Total square footage for groceries.	Total floor space − Total meat and deli floor space = Total grocery floor space.	Denominators must be the same before adding or subtracting fractions. $\frac{8}{8} = 1$ Never leave improper fraction as final answer.

MONEY TIPS

Remember the advice "Always pay yourself first." When deciding whether or not to buy more clothes, another cup of "joe," or another lunch out, remember that the money you spend could be making you money instead. Calculate the total amount of money you spend in a month on those things in your life that you merely want but do not need. Divide that total by 30 days and see what you could be saving daily.

Steps to solving problem

1. Calculate total square footage of the meat and deli departments.

$$\begin{array}{lrr} \text{Meat:} & 115\frac{1}{2} = & 115\frac{4}{8} \\ \text{Deli:} & +\ 145\frac{7}{8} = & +\ 145\frac{7}{8} \\ \hline & & 260\frac{11}{8} = 261\frac{3}{8} \text{ sq. ft.} \end{array}$$

2. Calculate total grocery square footage.

$$\begin{array}{r} 550\frac{1}{4} = \\ -\ 261\frac{3}{8} = \\ \hline \end{array} \quad \begin{array}{r} 550\frac{2}{8} = \\ -\ 261\frac{3}{8} = \\ \hline \end{array} \quad \begin{array}{r} 549\frac{10}{8} \\ -\ 261\frac{3}{8} \\ \hline 288\frac{7}{8} \text{ sq. ft.} \end{array} \left(\frac{2}{8} + \frac{8}{8}\right)$$

Check

$$\begin{array}{r} 261\frac{3}{8} \\ +\ 288\frac{7}{8} \\ \hline 549\frac{10}{8} = 550\frac{2}{8} = 550\frac{1}{4} \text{ sq. ft.} \end{array}$$

Note how the above blueprint aid helped to gather the facts and identify what we were looking for. To find the total square footage for groceries, we first had to sum the areas for meat and deli. Then we could subtract these areas from the total square footage. Also note that in Step 1 above, we didn't leave the answer as an improper fraction. In Step 2, we borrowed from the 550 so that we could complete the subtraction.

It's your turn to check your progress with a Practice Quiz.

LU 2–2 PRACTICE QUIZ

Complete this **Practice Quiz** to see how you are doing.

1. Find LCD by the division of prime numbers:
   12, 9, 6, 4
2. Add and reduce to lowest terms if needed:
   a. $\frac{3}{40} + \frac{2}{5}$ **b.** $2\frac{3}{4} + 6\frac{1}{20}$
3. Subtract and reduce to lowest terms if needed:
   a. $\frac{6}{7} - \frac{1}{4}$ **b.** $8\frac{1}{4} - 3\frac{9}{28}$ **c.** $4 - 1\frac{3}{4}$
4. Computerland has $600\frac{1}{4}$ total square feet of floor space. Three departments occupy this floor space: hardware, $201\frac{1}{8}$ square feet; software, $242\frac{1}{4}$ square feet; and customer service, __________ square feet. What is the total square footage of the customer service area? You might want to try a blueprint aid, since the solution will show a completed blueprint aid.

✓ Solutions

Solutions with Step-by-Step Help on DVD

1.

$$\begin{array}{r|rrrr} 2 & 12 & 9 & 6 & 4 \\ 2 & 6 & 9 & 3 & 2 \\ 3 & 3 & 9 & 3 & 1 \\ & 1 & 3 & 1 & 1 \end{array}$$

$\text{LCD} = 2 \times 2 \times 3 \times 1 \times 3 \times 1 \times 1 = \boxed{36}$

2. a. $\frac{3}{40} + \frac{2}{5} = \frac{3}{40} + \frac{16}{40} = \boxed{\frac{19}{40}}$ $\left(\frac{2}{5} = \frac{?}{40} \quad 40 \div 5 = 8 \times 2 = 16\right)$

b.

$$\begin{array}{r} 2\frac{3}{4} \\ +\,6\frac{1}{20} \\ \hline \end{array} \qquad \begin{array}{r} 2\frac{15}{20} \\ +\,6\frac{1}{20} \\ \hline 8\frac{16}{20} \end{array} = \boxed{8\frac{4}{5}}$$

$\frac{3}{4} = \frac{?}{20}$ $\quad 20 \div 4 = 5 \times 3 = 15$

3. a.

$$\begin{array}{rcr} \frac{6}{7} & = & \frac{24}{28} \\ -\frac{1}{4} & = & -\frac{7}{28} \\ \hline & & \boxed{\frac{17}{28}} \end{array}$$

b.

$$\begin{array}{rcrcr} 8\frac{1}{4} & = & 8\frac{7}{28} & = & 7\frac{35}{28} \\ -\,3\frac{9}{28} & = & -\,3\frac{9}{28} & = & -\,3\frac{9}{28} \\ \hline & & & & 4\frac{26}{28} \end{array} = \boxed{4\frac{13}{14}}$$

$\left(\frac{28}{28} + \frac{7}{28}\right)$

c.

$$\begin{array}{r} 3\frac{4}{4} \\ -\,1\frac{3}{4} \\ \hline \boxed{2\frac{1}{4}} \end{array}$$

Note how we showed the 4 as $3\frac{4}{4}$.

4. Computerland's total square footage for customer service:

The facts	Solving for?	Steps to take	Key points
Total square footage: $660\frac{1}{4}$ sq. ft. *Hardware:* $201\frac{1}{8}$ sq. ft. *Software:* $242\frac{1}{4}$ sq. ft.	Total square footage for customer service.	Total floor space − Total hardware and software floor space = Total customer service floor space.	Denominators must be the same before adding or subtracting fractions.

Steps to solving problem

1. Calculate the total square footage of hardware and software.

$$201\frac{1}{8} = \quad 201\frac{1}{8} \text{ (hardware)}$$
$$+\ 242\frac{1}{4} = \ +\ 242\frac{2}{8} \text{ (software)}$$
$$443\frac{3}{8}$$

2. Calculate the total square footage for customer service.

$$660\frac{1}{4} = 660\frac{2}{8} = 659\frac{10}{8} \text{ (total square footage)}$$
$$-\ 443\frac{3}{8} = -\ 443\frac{3}{8} = -\ 443\frac{3}{8} \text{ (hardware plus software)}$$
$$216\frac{7}{8} \text{ sq. ft. (customer service)}$$

LU 2–2a EXTRA PRACTICE QUIZ WITH WORKED-OUT SOLUTIONS

Need more practice? Try this **Extra Practice Quiz** (check figures in Chapter Organizer, p. 53). Worked-out Solutions can be found in Appendix B at end of text.

1. Find the LCD by the division of prime numbers: 10, 15, 9, 4
2. Add and reduce to lowest terms if needed:
   a. $\frac{2}{25} + \frac{3}{5}$ **b.** $3\frac{3}{8} + 6\frac{1}{32}$
3. Subtract and reduce to lowest terms if needed:
   a. $\frac{5}{6} - \frac{1}{3}$ **b.** $9\frac{1}{8} - 3\frac{7}{32}$ **c.** $6 - 1\frac{2}{5}$
4. Computerland has $985\frac{1}{4}$ total square feet of floor space. Three departments occupy this floor space: hardware, $209\frac{1}{8}$ square feet; software, $382\frac{1}{4}$ square feet; and customer service, ____________ square feet. What is the total square footage of the customer service area?

Learning Unit 2–3: Multiplying and Dividing Fractions

LO 1

The following recipe for Coconutty "M&M's"® Brownies makes 16 brownies. What would you need if you wanted to triple the recipe and make 48 brownies?

Coconutty "M&M's"® Brownies

6 squares (1 ounce each) semi-sweet chocolate
½ cup (1 stick) butter
¾ cup granulated sugar
2 large eggs
1 tablespoon vegetable oil
1 teaspoon vanilla extract
1¼ cups all-purpose flour
3 tablespoons unsweetened cocoa powder
1 teaspoon baking powder
½ teaspoon salt
1½ cups "M&M's"® Chocolate Mini Baking Bits, divided
Coconut Topping (recipe follows)

Preheat oven to 350°F. Grease 8 × 8 × 2-inch pan; set aside. In small saucepan combine chocolate, butter, and sugar over low heat; stir constantly until smooth. Remove from heat; let cool. In bowl beat eggs, oil, and vanilla; stir in chocolate mixture until blended. Stir in flour, cocoa powder, baking powder, and salt. Stir in 1 cup "M&M's"® Chocolate Mini Baking Bits. Spread batter in prepared pan. Bake 35 to 40 minutes or until toothpick inserted in center comes out clean. Cool. Prepare a coconut topping. Spread over brownies; sprinkle with $\frac{1}{2}$ cup "M&M's"® Chocolate Mini Baking Bits.

In this unit you learn how to multiply and divide fractions.

Multiplication of Fractions

Multiplying fractions is easier than adding and subtracting fractions because you do not have to find a common denominator. This section explains the multiplication of proper fractions and the multiplication of mixed numbers.

MULTIPLYING PROPER FRACTIONS[3]

Step 1. Multiply the numerators and the denominators.

Step 2. Reduce the answer to lowest terms or use the cancellation method.

First let's look at an example that results in an answer that we do not have to reduce.

EXAMPLE $\frac{1}{7} \times \frac{5}{8} = \boxed{\frac{5}{56}}$

In the next example, note how we reduce the answer to lowest terms.

EXAMPLE $\frac{5}{1} \times \frac{1}{6} \times \frac{4}{7} = \frac{20}{42} = \boxed{\frac{10}{21}}$ Keep in mind $\frac{5}{1}$ is equal to 5.

We can reduce $\frac{20}{42}$ by the step approach as follows:

$$20\overline{)42} = 2 \text{ remainder } 2 \quad (42 - 40 = 2) \qquad 2\overline{)20} = 10 \text{ remainder } 0 \quad (20 - 20 = 0)$$

$$\frac{20 \div 2}{42 \div 2} = \boxed{\frac{10}{21}}$$

We could also have found the greatest common divisor by inspection.

As an alternative to reducing fractions to lowest terms, we can use the **cancellation** technique. Let's work the previous example using this technique.

LO 2

EXAMPLE $\frac{5}{1} \times \frac{1}{\cancel{6}_{3}} \times \frac{\cancel{4}^{2}}{7} = \boxed{\frac{10}{21}}$ 2 divides evenly into 4 twice and into 6 three times.

Note that when we cancel numbers, we are reducing the answer before multiplying. We know that multiplying or dividing both numerator and denominator by the same number gives an equivalent fraction. So we can divide both numerator and denominator by any number that divides them both evenly. It doesn't matter which we divide first. Note that this division reduces $\frac{10}{21}$ to its lowest terms.

Multiplying Mixed Numbers

The following steps explain how to multiply mixed numbers:

MULTIPLYING MIXED NUMBERS

Step 1. Convert the mixed numbers to improper fractions.

Step 2. Multiply the numerators and denominators.

Step 3. Reduce the answer to lowest terms or use the cancellation method.

EXAMPLE $2\frac{1}{3} \times 1\frac{1}{2} = \frac{7}{\cancel{3}_{1}} \times \frac{\cancel{3}^{1}}{2} = \frac{7}{2} = \boxed{3\frac{1}{2}}$

Step 1 Step 2 Step 3

[3]You would follow the same procedure to multiply improper fractions.

Division of Fractions

When you studied whole numbers in Chapter 1, you saw how multiplication can be checked by division. The multiplication of fractions can also be checked by division, as you will see in this section on dividing proper fractions and mixed numbers.

Dividing Proper Fractions

The division of proper fractions introduces a new term—the **reciprocal.** To use reciprocals, we must first recognize which fraction in the problem is the divisor—the fraction that we divide by. Let's assume the problem we are to solve is $\frac{1}{8} \div \frac{2}{3}$. We read this problem as "$\frac{1}{8}$ divided by $\frac{2}{3}$." The divisor is the fraction after the division sign (or the second fraction). The steps that follow show how the divisor becomes a reciprocal.

DIVIDING PROPER FRACTIONS

Step 1. Invert (turn upside down) the divisor (the second fraction). The inverted number is the *reciprocal.*

Step 2. Multiply the fractions.

Step 3. Reduce the answer to lowest terms or use the cancellation method.

Do you know why the inverted fraction number is a reciprocal? Reciprocals are two numbers that when multiplied give a product of 1. For example, 2 (which is the same as $\frac{2}{1}$) and $\frac{1}{2}$ are reciprocals because multiplying them gives 1.

EXAMPLE $\frac{1}{8} \div \frac{2}{3} \qquad \frac{1}{8} \times \frac{3}{2} = \frac{3}{16}$

Dividing Mixed Numbers

Now you are ready to divide mixed numbers by using improper fractions.

DIVIDING MIXED NUMBERS

Step 1. Convert all mixed numbers to improper fractions.

Step 2. Invert the divisor (take its reciprocal) and multiply. If your final answer is an improper fraction, reduce it to lowest terms. You can do this by finding the greatest common divisor or by using the cancellation technique.

EXAMPLE $8\frac{3}{4} \div 2\frac{5}{6}$

Step 1. $\frac{35}{4} \div \frac{17}{6}$

Step 2. $\frac{35}{\not{4}_{2}} \times \frac{\not{6}^{3}}{17} = \frac{105}{34} = 3\frac{3}{34}$ Here we used the cancellation technique.

How to Dissect and Solve a Word Problem

The Word Problem Jamie Slater ordered $5\frac{1}{2}$ cords of oak. The cost of each cord is \$150. He also ordered $2\frac{1}{4}$ cords of maple at \$120 per cord. Jamie's neighbor, Al, said that he would share the wood and pay him $\frac{1}{5}$ of the total cost. How much did Jamie receive from Al?

Note how we filled in the blueprint aid columns. We first had to find the total cost of all the wood before we could find Al's share—$\frac{1}{5}$ of the total cost.

$ MONEY TIPS

An easy way to remember how to divide fractions is copy dot flip. Copy the first fraction, change the division sign to a multiplication sign, and invert the second fraction and solve. This can really help out when taking advanced placement tests like the GMAT or MCAT.

The facts	Solving for?	Steps to take	Key points
Cords ordered: $5\frac{1}{2}$ at \$150 per cord; $2\frac{1}{4}$ at \$120 per cord. *Al's cost share:* $\frac{1}{5}$ the total cost.	What will Al pay Jamie?	Total cost of wood × $\frac{1}{5}$ = Al's cost.	Convert mixed numbers to improper fractions when multiplying. Cancellation is an alternative to reducing fractions.

Steps to solving problem

1. Calculate the cost of oak. $5\frac{1}{2} \times \$150 = \frac{11}{2} \times \$150 = \$825$ (cancellation: $\frac{11}{\cancel{2}_1} \times \cancel{\$150}^{\$75}$)

2. Calculate the cost of maple. $2\frac{1}{4} \times \$120 = \frac{9}{4} \times \$120 = +270$ (cancellation: $\frac{9}{\cancel{4}_1} \times \cancel{\$120}^{\$30}$)

   \$1,095 (total cost of wood)

3. What Al pays. $\frac{1}{5} \times \$1,095 = \$219$ (cancellation: $\frac{1}{\cancel{5}_1} \times \cancel{\$1,095}^{\$219}$)

You should now be ready to test your knowledge of the final unit in the chapter.

LU 2–3 PRACTICE QUIZ

Complete this **Practice Quiz** to see how you are doing.

1. Multiply (use cancellation technique):

   a. $\frac{4}{8} \times \frac{4}{6}$ b. $35 \times \frac{4}{7}$

2. Multiply (do not use canceling; reduce by finding the greatest common divisor):

   $\frac{14}{15} \times \frac{7}{10}$

3. Complete the following. Reduce to lowest terms as needed.

   a. $\frac{1}{9} \div \frac{5}{6}$ b. $\frac{51}{5} \div \frac{5}{9}$

4. Jill Estes bought a mobile home that was $8\frac{1}{8}$ times as expensive as the home her brother bought. Jill's brother paid \$16,000 for his mobile home. What is the cost of Jill's new home?

Solutions with Step-by-Step Help on DVD

✓ Solutions

1. a. $\frac{\cancel{4}^{\cancel{2}^{1}}}{\cancel{8}_{\cancel{2}_{1}}} \times \frac{\cancel{4}^{1}}{\cancel{6}_{3}} = \frac{1}{3}$ b. $\cancel{35}^{5} \times \frac{4}{\cancel{7}_{1}} = 20$

2. $\frac{14}{15} \times \frac{7}{10} = \frac{98 \div 2}{150 \div 2} = \frac{49}{75}$

   $150 \div 98 = 1$ R 52 → $98 \div 52 = 1$ R 46 → $52 \div 46 = 1$ R 6 → $46 \div 6 = 7$ R 4 → $6 \div 4 = 1$ R 2 → $4 \div 2 = 2$ R 0

3. a. $\frac{1}{9} \times \frac{6}{5} = \frac{6 \div 3}{45 \div 3} = \frac{2}{15}$ b. $\frac{51}{5} \times \frac{9}{5} = \frac{459}{25} = 18\frac{9}{25}$

4. Total cost of Jill's new home:

The facts	Solving for?	Steps to take	Key points
Jill's mobile home: $8\frac{1}{8}$ as expensive as her brother's. *Brother paid:* \$16,000.	Total cost of Jill's new home.	$8\frac{1}{8}$ × Total cost of Jill's brother's mobile home = Total cost of Jill's new home.	Canceling is an alternative to reducing.

Steps to solving problem

1. Convert $8\frac{1}{8}$ to a mixed number. $\frac{65}{8}$
2. Calculate the total cost of Jill's home. $\frac{65}{\cancel{8}_1} \times \cancel{\$16,000}^{\$2,000} = \$130,000$

LU 2–3a EXTRA PRACTICE QUIZ WITH WORKED-OUT SOLUTIONS

Need more practice? Try this **Extra Practice Quiz** (check figures in Chapter Organizer, p. 53). Worked-out Solutions can be found in Appendix B at end of text.

1. Multiply (use cancellation technique):
   a. $\frac{6}{8} \times \frac{3}{6}$ **b.** $42 \times \frac{1}{7}$
2. Multiply (do not use canceling; reduce by finding the greatest common divisor):
   $\frac{13}{117} \times \frac{9}{5}$
3. Complete the following. Reduce to lowest terms as needed.
   a. $\frac{1}{8} \div \frac{4}{5}$ **b.** $\frac{61}{6} \div \frac{6}{7}$
4. Jill Estes bought a mobile home that was $10\frac{1}{8}$ times as expensive as the home her brother brought. Jill's brother paid $10,000 for his mobile home. What is the cost of Jill's new home?

CHAPTER ORGANIZER AND REFERENCE GUIDE

Topic	Key point, procedure, formula	Example(s) to illustrate situation
Types of fractions, p. 36	*Proper:* Value less than 1; numerator smaller than denominator. *Improper:* Value equal to or greater than 1; numerator equal to or greater than denominator. *Mixed:* Sum of whole number greater than zero and a proper fraction.	$\frac{3}{5}, \frac{7}{9}, \frac{8}{15}$ $\frac{14}{14}, \frac{19}{18}$ $6\frac{3}{8}, 9\frac{8}{9}$
Fraction conversions, p. 37	*Improper to whole or mixed:* Divide numerator by denominator; place remainder over *old* denominator. *Mixed to improper:* $\frac{\text{Whole number} \times \text{Denominator} + \text{Numerator}}{\text{Old denominator}}$	$\frac{17}{4} = 4\frac{1}{4}$ $4\frac{1}{8} = \frac{32+1}{8} = \frac{33}{8}$
Reducing fractions to lowest terms, p. 38	1. Divide numerator and denominator by largest possible divisor (does not change fraction value). 2. When reduced to lowest terms, no number (except 1) will divide evenly into both numerator and denominator.	$\frac{18 \div 2}{46 \div 2} = \frac{9}{23}$
Step approach for finding greatest common denominator, p. 39	1. Divide smaller number of fraction into larger number. 2. Divide remainder into divisor of Step 1. Continue this process until no remainder results. 3. The last divisor used is the greatest common divisor.	$\frac{15}{65}$ → $15\overline{)65}$ = 4, 60, remainder 5 → $5\overline{)15}$ = 3, 15, 0 5 is greatest common divisor.
Raising fractions to higher terms, p. 39	Multiply numerator and denominator by same number. Does not change fraction value.	$\frac{15}{41} = \frac{?}{410}$ $410 \div 41 = 10 \times 15 = 150$

(continues)

CHAPTER ORGANIZER AND REFERENCE GUIDE

Topic	Key point, procedure, formula	Example(s) to illustrate situation
Adding and subtracting like and unlike fractions, p. 41	When denominators are the same (like fractions), add (or subtract) numerators, place total over original denominator, and reduce to lowest terms. When denominators are different (unlike fractions), change them to like fractions by finding LCD using inspection or prime numbers. Then add (or subtract) the numerators, place total over LCD, and reduce to lowest terms.	$\frac{4}{9}+\frac{1}{9}=\frac{5}{9}$ $\frac{4}{9}-\frac{1}{9}=\frac{3}{9}=\frac{1}{3}$ $\frac{4}{5}+\frac{2}{7}=\frac{28}{35}+\frac{10}{35}=\frac{38}{35}=1\frac{3}{35}$
Prime numbers, p. 42	Whole numbers larger than 1 that are only divisible by itself and 1.	2, 3, 5, 7, 11
LCD by prime numbers, p. 42	1. Copy denominators and arrange them in a separate row. 2. Divide denominators by smallest prime number that will divide evenly into at least two numbers. 3. Continue until no prime number divides evenly into at least two numbers. 4. Multiply all the numbers in the divisors and last row to find LCD. 5. Raise fractions so each has a common denominator and complete computation.	$\frac{1}{3}+\frac{1}{6}+\frac{1}{8}+\frac{1}{12}+\frac{1}{9}$ 2 / 3 6 8 12 9 2 / 3 3 4 6 9 3 / 3 3 2 3 9 1 1 2 1 3 $2\times2\times3\times1\times1\times2\times1\times3=72$
Adding mixed numbers, p. 43	1. Add fractions. 2. Add whole numbers. 3. Combine totals of Steps 1 and 2. If denominators are different, a common denominator must be found. Answer cannot be left as improper fraction.	$1\frac{4}{7}+1\frac{3}{7}$ Step 1: $\frac{4}{7}+\frac{3}{7}=\frac{7}{7}$ Step 2: $1+1=2$ Step 3: $2\frac{7}{7}=3$
Subtracting mixed numbers, p. 44	1. Subtract fractions. 2. If necessary, borrow from whole numbers. 3. Subtract whole numbers and fractions if borrowing was necessary. 4. Reduce fractions to lowest terms. If denominators are different, a common denominator must be found.	$12\frac{2}{5}-7\frac{3}{5}$ $11\frac{7}{5}-7\frac{3}{5}$ $=4\frac{4}{5}$ Due to borrowing $\frac{5}{5}$ from number 12 $\frac{5}{5}+\frac{2}{5}=\frac{7}{5}$ The whole number is now 11.
Multiplying proper fractions, p. 48	1. Multiply numerators and denominators. 2. Reduce answer to lowest terms or use cancellation method.	$\frac{4}{\cancel{7}_{1}}\times\frac{\cancel{7}^{1}}{9}=\frac{4}{9}$
Multiplying mixed numbers, p. 48	1. Convert mixed numbers to improper fractions. 2. Multiply numerators and denominators. 3. Reduce answer to lowest terms or use cancellation method.	$1\frac{1}{8}\times2\frac{5}{8}$ $\frac{9}{8}\times\frac{21}{8}=\frac{189}{64}=2\frac{61}{64}$
Dividing proper fractions, p. 49	1. Invert divisor. 2. Multiply. 3. Reduce answer to lowest terms or use cancellation method.	$\frac{1}{4}\div\frac{1}{8}=\frac{1}{\cancel{4}_{1}}\times\frac{\cancel{8}^{2}}{1}=2$

(continues)

CHAPTER ORGANIZER AND REFERENCE GUIDE

Topic	Key point, procedure, formula	Example(s) to illustrate situation
Dividing mixed numbers p. 49	1. Convert mixed numbers to improper fractions. 2. Invert divisor and multiply. If final answer is an improper fraction, reduce to lowest terms by finding greatest common divisor or using the cancellation method.	$1\frac{1}{2} \div 1\frac{5}{8} = \frac{3}{2} \div \frac{13}{8}$ $= \frac{3}{\not{2}_{1}} \times \frac{\not{8}^{4}}{13}$ $= \frac{12}{13}$

KEY TERMS	Cancellation, *p. 48* Common denominator, *p. 41* Denominator, *p. 36* Equivalent, *p. 39* Fraction, *p. 36* Greatest common divisor, *p. 38*	Higher terms, *p. 39* Improper fraction, *p. 37* Least common denominator (LCD), *p. 41* Like fractions, *p. 41* Lowest terms, *p. 38* Mixed numbers, *p. 37*	Numerator, *p. 36* Prime numbers, *p. 42* Proper fractions, *p. 37* Reciprocal, *p. 49* Unlike fractions, *p. 41*
CHECK FIGURE FOR EXTRA PRACTICE QUIZZES WITH PAGE REFERENCES. (WORKED-OUT SOLUTIONS IN APPENDIX B.)	LU 2–1a (p. 40) 1. a. P b. I c. M d. I 2. $22\frac{1}{7}$ 3. $\frac{79}{9}$ 4. a. 14; $\frac{3}{5}$ b. 2; $\frac{48}{91}$ 5. a. 160; b. 27	LU 2–2a (p. 47) 1. 180 2. a. $\frac{17}{25}$ b. $9\frac{13}{32}$ 3. a. $\frac{1}{2}$ b. $5\frac{29}{32}$ c. $4\frac{3}{5}$ 4. $393\frac{7}{8}$ ft.	LU 2–3a (p. 51) 1. a. $\frac{3}{8}$ b. 6 2. 117; $\frac{1}{5}$ 3. a. $\frac{5}{32}$ b. $11\frac{31}{36}$ 4. $101,250

Critical Thinking Discussion Questions

1. What are the steps to convert improper fractions to whole or mixed numbers? Give an example of how you could use this conversion procedure when you eat at Pizza Hut.
2. What are the steps to convert mixed numbers to improper fractions? Show how you could use this conversion procedure when you order doughnuts at Dunkin' Donuts.
3. What is the greatest common divisor? How could you use the greatest common divisor to write an advertisement showing that 35 out of 60 people prefer MCI to AT&T?
4. Explain the step approach for finding the greatest common divisor. How could you use the MCI–AT&T example in question 3 to illustrate the step approach?
5. Explain the steps of adding or subtracting unlike fractions. Using a ruler, measure the heights of two different size cans of food and show how to calculate the difference in height.
6. What is a prime number? Using the two cans in question 5, show how you could use prime numbers to calculate the LCD.
7. Explain the steps for multiplying proper fractions and mixed numbers. Assume you went to Staples (a stationery superstore). Give an example showing the multiplying of proper fractions and mixed numbers.

Classroom Notes

END-OF-CHAPTER PROBLEMS

Connect plus+ www.mhhe.com/slater10e

Check figures for odd-numbered problems in Appendix C

Name ______________________ Date ________

DRILL PROBLEMS

Identify the following types of fractions:

2–1. $11\frac{1}{7}$ **2–2.** $\frac{12}{11}$ **2–3.** $\frac{3}{7}$

Convert the following to mixed numbers:

2–4. $\frac{89}{9} =$ **2–5.** $\frac{921}{15} =$

Convert the following to improper fractions:

2–6. $8\frac{7}{8}$ **2–7.** $19\frac{2}{3}$

Reduce the following to the lowest terms. Show how to calculate the greatest common divisor by the step approach.

2–8. $\frac{16}{38}$ **2–9.** $\frac{44}{52}$

Convert the following to higher terms:

2–10. $\frac{9}{10} = \frac{}{70}$

Determine the LCD of the following (a) by inspection and (b) by division of prime numbers:

2–11. $\frac{3}{4}, \frac{7}{12}, \frac{5}{6}, \frac{1}{5}$ **Check**

Inspection

2–12. $\frac{5}{6}, \frac{7}{18}, \frac{5}{9}, \frac{2}{72}$ **Check**

Inspection

2–13. $\frac{1}{4}, \frac{3}{32}, \frac{5}{48}, \frac{1}{8}$ **Check**

Inspection

Add the following and reduce to lowest terms:

2–14. $\frac{3}{9} + \frac{3}{9}$ **2–15.** $\frac{3}{7} + \frac{4}{21}$

2–16. $6\frac{1}{8} + 4\frac{3}{8}$ **2–17.** $6\frac{3}{8} + 9\frac{1}{24}$

2–18. $9\frac{9}{10} + 6\frac{7}{10}$

Subtract the following and reduce to lowest terms:

2–19. $\frac{11}{12} - \frac{1}{12}$

2–20. $14\frac{3}{8} - 10\frac{5}{8}$

2–21. $12\frac{1}{9} - 4\frac{2}{3}$

Multiply the following and reduce to lowest terms. Do not use the cancellation technique for these problems.

2–22. $17 \times \frac{4}{2}$

2–23. $\frac{5}{6} \times \frac{3}{8}$

2–24. $8\frac{7}{8} \times 64$

Multiply the following. Use the cancellation technique.

2–25. $\frac{4}{10} \times \frac{30}{60} \times \frac{6}{10}$

2–26. $3\frac{3}{4} \times \frac{8}{9} \times 4\frac{9}{12}$

Divide the following and reduce to lowest terms. Use the cancellation technique as needed.

2–27. $\frac{12}{9} \div 4$

2–28. $18 \div \frac{1}{5}$

2–29. $4\frac{2}{3} \div 12$

2–30. $3\frac{5}{6} \div 3\frac{1}{2}$

WORD PROBLEMS

2–31. Michael Wittry has been investing in his Roth IRA retirement account for 20 years. Two years ago, his account was worth $215,658. After losing $\frac{1}{3}$ of its original value, it then gained $\frac{1}{2}$ of its new value back, what is the current value of his Roth IRA?

2–32. Delta pays Pete Rose $180 per day to work in the maintenance department at the airport. Pete became ill on Monday and went home after $\frac{1}{6}$ of a day. What did he earn on Monday? Assume no work, no pay.

2–33. Britney Summers visited Curves and lost $2\frac{1}{4}$ pounds in week 1, $1\frac{3}{4}$ pounds in week 2, and $\frac{5}{8}$ pound in week 3. What is the total weight loss for Britney?

2–34. Joy Wigens, who works at Putnam Investments, received a check for $1,600. She deposited $\frac{1}{4}$ of the check in her Citibank account. How much money does Joy have left after the deposit?

2–35. Lee Jenkins worked the following hours as a manager for a local Pizza Hut: $14\frac{1}{4}$, $5\frac{1}{4}$, $8\frac{1}{2}$, and $7\frac{1}{4}$. How many total hours did Lee work?

2–36. Lester bought a piece of property in Vail, Colorado. The sides of the land measure $115\frac{1}{2}$ feet, $66\frac{1}{4}$ feet, $106\frac{1}{8}$ feet, and $110\frac{1}{4}$ feet. Lester wants to know the perimeter (sum of all sides) of his property. Can you calculate the perimeter for Lester?

2–37. Tiffani Lind got her new weekly course schedule from Roxbury Community College in Boston. Following are her classes and their length: Business Math-$2\frac{1}{2}$ hours, Introduction to Business-$1\frac{1}{2}$ hours, Microeconomics-$1\frac{1}{2}$ hours, Spanish-$2\frac{1}{4}$ hours, Marketing-$1\frac{1}{4}$ hours and Business Statistics-$1\frac{3}{4}$ hours long. How long will she be in class each week?

2–38. From Lowes, Pete Wong ordered $\frac{6}{7}$ of a ton of crushed rock to make a patio. If Pete used only $\frac{3}{4}$ of the rock, how much crushed rock remains unused?

2–39. At a local Wal-Mart store, a Coke dispenser held $19\frac{1}{4}$ gallons of soda. During working hours, $12\frac{3}{4}$ gallons were dispensed. How many gallons of Coke remain?

2–40. Bernie Falls bought a home from Century 21 in Houston, Texas, that is $9\frac{1}{2}$ times as expensive as the home his parents bought. Bernie's parents paid $30,000 for their home. What is the cost of Bernie's new home?

2–41. A local garden center charges $250 per cord of wood. If Logan Grace orders $3\frac{1}{2}$ cords, what will the total cost be?

2–42. A local Target store bought 90 pizzas at Pizza Hut for their holiday party. Each guest ate $\frac{1}{6}$ of a pizza and there was no pizza left over. How many guests did Learning.com have for the party?

2–43. Marc, Steven, and Daniel entered into a Subway sandwich shop partnership. Marc owns $\frac{1}{9}$ of the shop and Steven owns $\frac{1}{4}$. What part does Daniel own?

2–44. Lionel Sullivan works for Burger King. He is paid time and one-half for Sundays. If Lionel works on Sunday for 6 hours at a regular pay of $8 per hour, what does he earn on Sunday?

2–45. Hertz pays Al Davis, an employee, $125 per day. Al decides to donate $\frac{1}{5}$ of a day's pay to his church. How much will Al donate?

2–46. A trip to the White Mountains of New Hampshire from Boston will take you $2\frac{3}{4}$ hours. Assume you have traveled $\frac{1}{11}$ of the way. How much longer will the trip take?

2–47. Andy, who loves to cook, makes apple cobbler for his family. The recipe (serves 6) calls for $1\frac{1}{2}$ pounds of apples, $3\frac{1}{4}$ cups of flour, $\frac{1}{4}$ cup of margarine, $2\frac{3}{8}$ cups of sugar, and 2 teaspoons of cinnamon. Since guests are coming, Andy wants to make a cobbler that will serve 15 (or increase the recipe $2\frac{1}{2}$ times). How much of each ingredient should Andy use?

2–48. Mobil allocates $1{,}692\frac{3}{4}$ gallons of gas per month to Jerry's Service Station. The first week, Jerry sold $275\frac{1}{2}$ gallons; second week, $280\frac{1}{4}$ gallons; and third week, $189\frac{1}{8}$ gallons. If Jerry sells $582\frac{1}{2}$ gallons in the fourth week, how close is Jerry to selling his allocation?

2–49. A marketing class at North Shore Community College conducted a viewer preference survey. The survey showed that $\frac{5}{6}$ of the people surveyed preferred Apple's iPhone over the Blackberry. Assume 2,400 responded to the survey. How many favored using a Blackberry?

2–50. The price of a used Toyota LandCruiser has increased to $1\frac{1}{4}$ times its earlier price. If the original price of the LandCruiser was $30,000, what is the new price?

2–51. Tempco Corporation has a machine that produces $12\frac{1}{2}$ baseball gloves each hour. In the last 2 days, the machine has run for a total of 22 hours. How many baseball gloves has Tempco produced?

2–52. Alicia, an employee of Dunkin' Donuts, receives $23\frac{1}{4}$ days per year of vacation time. So far this year she has taken $3\frac{1}{8}$ days in January, $5\frac{1}{2}$ days in May, $6\frac{1}{4}$ days in July, and $4\frac{1}{4}$ days in September. How many more days of vacation does Alicia have left?

2–53. A Hamilton multitouch watch was originally priced at $600. At a closing of the Alpha Omega Jewelry Shop, the watch is being reduced by $\frac{1}{4}$. What is the new selling price?

2–54. Shelly Van Doren hired a contractor to refinish her kitchen. The contractor said the job would take $49\frac{1}{2}$ hours. To date, the contractor has worked the following hours:

Monday	$4\frac{1}{4}$
Tuesday	$9\frac{1}{8}$
Wednesday	$4\frac{1}{4}$
Thursday	$3\frac{1}{2}$
Friday	$10\frac{5}{8}$

How much longer should the job take to be completed?

ADDITIONAL SET OF WORD PROBLEMS

2–55. An issue of *Taunton's Fine Woodworking* included plans for a hall stand. The total height of the stand is $81\frac{1}{2}$ inches. If the base is $36\frac{5}{16}$ inches, how tall is the upper portion of the stand?

2–56. Albertsons grocery planned a big sale on apples and received 750 crates from the wholesale market. Albertsons will bag these apples in plastic. Each plastic bag holds $\frac{1}{9}$ of a crate. If Albertsons has no loss to perishables, how many bags of apples can be prepared?

2–57. Frank Puleo bought 6,625 acres of land in ski country. He plans to subdivide the land into parcels of $13\frac{1}{4}$ acres each. Each parcel will sell for $125,000. How many parcels of land will Frank develop? If Frank sells all the parcels, what will be his total sales?

If Frank sells $\frac{3}{5}$ of the parcels in the first year, what will be his total sales for the year?

2–58. A local Papa Gino's conducted a food survey. The survey showed that $\frac{1}{9}$ of the people surveyed preferred eating pasta to hamburger. If 5,400 responded to the survey, how many actually favored hamburger?

2–59. Tamara, Jose, and Milton entered into a partnership that sells men's clothing on the Web. Tamara owns $\frac{3}{8}$ of the company, and Jose owns $\frac{1}{4}$. What part does Milton own?

2–60. *Quilters Newsletter Magazine* gave instructions on making a quilt. The quilt required $4\frac{1}{2}$ yards of white-on-white print, 2 yards blue check, $\frac{1}{2}$ yard blue-and-white stripe, $2\frac{3}{4}$ yards blue scraps, $\frac{3}{4}$ yard yellow scraps, and $4\frac{7}{8}$ yards lining. How many total yards are needed?

2–61. A trailer carrying supplies for a Krispy Kreme from Virginia to New York will take $3\frac{1}{4}$ hours. If the truck traveled $\frac{1}{5}$ of the way, how much longer will the trip take?

2–62. Land Rover has increased the price of a FreeLander by $\frac{1}{5}$ from the original price. The original price of the FreeLander was \$30,000. What is the new price?

CHALLENGE PROBLEMS

2–63 A recipe calls for $2\frac{1}{2}$ cups flour, 1 cup sugar, $1\frac{1}{2}$ cups butter, 4 eggs, 1 teaspoon baking soda, $\frac{1}{2}$ teaspoon salt, and $1\frac{1}{2}$ teaspoon vanilla. If you need to cut the recipe in half, how much of each will you need?

2–64. Jack MacLean has entered into a real estate development partnership with Bill Lyons and June Reese. Bill owns $\frac{1}{4}$ of the partnership, while June has a $\frac{1}{5}$ interest. The partners will divide all profits on the basis of their fractional ownership.

The partnership bought 900 acres of land and plans to subdivide each lot into $2\frac{1}{4}$ acres. Homes in the area have been selling for \$240,000. By time of completion, Jack estimates the price of each home will increase by $\frac{1}{3}$ of the current value. The partners sent a survey to 12,000 potential customers to see whether they should heat the homes with oil or gas. One-fourth of the customers responded by indicating a 5-to-1 preference for oil. From the results of the survey, Jack now plans to install a 270-gallon oil tank at each home. He estimates that each home will need 5 fills per year. Current price of home heating fuel is \$1 per gallon. The partnership estimates its profit per home will be $\frac{1}{8}$ the selling price of each home.

From the above, please calculate the following:

a. Number of homes to be built.

b. Selling price of each home.

c. Number of people responding to survey.

d. Number of people desiring oil.

e. Average monthly cost to run oil heat per house.

f. Amount of profit Jack will receive from the sale of homes.

DVD SUMMARY PRACTICE TEST

Identify the following types of fractions. *(p. 36)*

1. $5\frac{1}{8}$

2. $\frac{2}{7}$

3. $\frac{20}{19}$

4. Convert the following to a mixed number. *(p. 37)*

$\frac{163}{9}$

5. Convert the following to an improper fraction. *(p. 37)*

$8\frac{1}{8}$

6. Calculate the greatest common divisor of the following by the step approach and reduce to lowest terms. *(p. 39)*

$$\frac{63}{90}$$

7. Convert the following to higher terms. *(p. 39)*

$$\frac{16}{94} = \frac{?}{376}$$

8. Find the LCD of the following by using prime numbers. Show your work. *(p. 41)*

$$\frac{1}{8} + \frac{1}{3} + \frac{1}{2} + \frac{1}{12}$$

9. Subtract the following. *(p. 44)*

$$\begin{array}{r} 15\frac{4}{5} \\ -8\frac{19}{20} \\ \hline \end{array}$$

Complete the following using the cancellation technique. *(p. 48)*

10. $\frac{3}{4} \times \frac{2}{4} \times \frac{6}{9}$

11. $7\frac{1}{9} \times \frac{6}{7}$

12. $\frac{3}{7} \div 6$

13. A trip to Washington from Boston will take you $5\frac{3}{4}$ hours. If you have traveled $\frac{1}{3}$ of the way, how much longer will the trip take? *(p. 48)*

14. Quiznos produces 640 rolls per hour. If the oven runs $12\frac{1}{4}$ hours, how many rolls will the machine produce? *(p. 49)*

15. A taste-testing survey of Zing Farms showed that $\frac{2}{3}$ of the people surveyed preferred the taste of veggie burgers to regular burgers. If 90,000 people were in the survey, how many favored veggie burgers? How many chose regular burgers? *(p. 48)*

16. Jim Janes, an employee of Enterprise Co., worked $9\frac{1}{4}$ hours on Monday, $4\frac{1}{2}$ hours on Tuesday, $9\frac{1}{4}$ hours on Wednesday, $7\frac{1}{2}$ hours on Thursday, and 9 hours on Friday. How many total hours did Jim work during the week? *(p. 41)*

17. JCPenney offered a $\frac{1}{3}$ rebate on its $39 hair dryer. Joan bought a JCPenney hair dryer. What did Joan pay after the rebate? *(p. 48)*

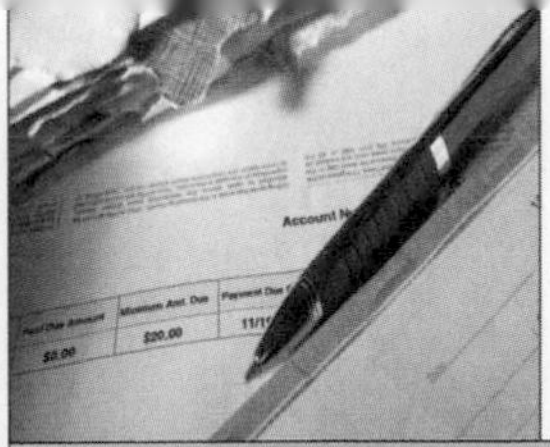

Personal Finance

A KIPLINGER APPROACH

MAJOR MARKDOWNS

THESE HOMES ARE PRICED TO SELL.

NAPA VALLEY, CAL.
3 BR, 2.5 BA, in gated community
LAST SOLD FOR: $1,071,200
CURRENT PRICE: $654,900

LAKEVILLE, MINN.
4 BR, 3.5 BA, on nearly an acre
LAST SOLD FOR: $473,989
CURRENT PRICE: $335,500

HALLANDALE, FLA.
3 BR, 3 BA, oceanfront condo
LAST SOLD FOR: $1,002,800
CURRENT PRICE: $785,000

HUNTINGTON, N.Y.
5 BR, 3 BA, heated pool
LAST SOLD FOR: $1,450,000
CURRENT PRICE: $1,039,000

THIS ARTICLE WAS WRITTEN BY **JESSICA ANDERSON, THOMAS M. ANDERSON, JANE BENNETT CLARK, LAURA COHN, PATRICIA MERTZ ESSWEIN, MARY BETH FRANKLIN, CANDICE LEE JONES, JEFFREY R. KOSNETT, DAVID LANDIS, ELIZABETH ODY, STACY RAPACON** AND **ANDREW TANZER**.

DEL POSTO

DEALS ON FANCY MEALS

RITZY RESTAURANTS ARE DRUMMING UP BUSINESS WITH SPECIAL PROMOTIONS AND *PRIX FIXE* MENUS.

And you thought *you* were having a bad year. High wholesale prices and newly cost-conscious consumers have created "the most challenging environment for the restaurant industry in several decades," says Hudson Riehle, of the National Restaurant Association. Even high-end restaurants, including those operated by big-name chefs such as Mario Batali, have responded to weak sales by offering diners reduced prices, *prix fixe* meals, nightly specials, free appetizers or desserts, and small plates at (relatively) low cost. Restaurateurs who try to hold out for *le prix scandaleux* do so at their peril, says Riehle. "With the competition so intense, consumers are quick to vote with their feet."

What constitutes a bargain at a ritzy restaurant? At Batali's Del Posto, in New York City, that would be the tasting menu, recently reduced from $175 to $125 for a seven-item assortment that includes gourmet ingredients such as foie gras and truffles. The *prix fixe* lunch goes for a mere $32.

But it's not just pricey Manhattan eateries that are dishing out savings. Splash!, a seafood restaurant in Tampa, draws bottom feeders with such weeknight "stimulus" specials as the shrimp jambalaya for $5 (plus the price of a beverage)—about one-fifth the price of the seafood risotto from the regular menu. Ruth's Chris Steakhouse, where the average dinner tab runs $74, recently introduced a *prix fixe* meal that includes an appetizer, a side, a 16-ounce strip steak and dessert for $40.

WINE AT A PALATABLE PRICE

FORGET FRANCE AND CALIFORNIA. THINK RED, WHITE AND BUBBLY FROM SPAIN AND ARGENTINA.

Argentina is the fastest-growing exporter of wine to the U.S. market. It's not hard to see why: The country is producing impressive wines at reasonable prices. Wines made with Malbec grapes—lesser blending grapes from Bordeaux that have flourished in Argentina's soil since they were transplanted there in the 19th century—are particularly hot. One elegant example is **Bodega Luigi Bosca Malbec Reserva Lujan de Cuyo 2006** ($15 to $18), an inky red wine with raspberry and tobacco notes.

Tucked away in the northwest corner of Spain, Galicia is bottling some stunning white wines at affordable prices. The region's Albarino grape produces crisp, dry, aromatic wines that pair perfectly with shellfish and other seafood and make a refreshing summer aperitif. You can find many fine examples of Albarino wines in the $10-to-$20 price range. One is **Nessa Albarino Rias Baixas 2007** ($13 to $15), a fragrant wine with citrus and mineral overtones and enough acidity to cut through that fish oil.

Champagne, the effervescent wine of northern France, has been priced out of sight due to sturdy global demand and tight supply. The French government simply will not expand the region's tightly delineated boundaries. But you can do very well at a fraction of the price with a sparkling wine from Spain, such as **Mont Marcal Brut Reserva Cava 2005 (or 2006)**, which costs about $15. Mont Marcal is made mostly from indigenous Spanish grapes you've never heard of, but it is a delicate, refined potion.

From Kiplinger's *Personal Finance*, August 2009, p. 62.

BUSINESS MATH ISSUE

Lowering food prices by 4/5 means a business will always turn a profit.

1. List the key points of the article and information to support your position.
2. Write a group defense of your position using math calculations to support your view.

Slater's Business Math Scrapbook

Applying Your Skills

PROJECT A

At Whiteface Lodge what is the selling cost of a whole unit?

PROJECT B

Convert these tax facts to fractions.

TAX FACTS

Odds that your individual tax return was audited by the IRS in 2008, by income level.

Under $200,000	1 in 100
Between $200,000 and $1 million	1 in 37
Over $1 million	1 in 18

Source: WSJ calculations based on IRS data

A Piece of the Mountain

More mountain resorts are offering fractional ownerships alongside standard hotel fare. Prices are for a standard double-occupancy room in the summer, except where indicated.

NAME / LOCATION / PRICE	COMMENTS
The Canyons Grand Summit Park City, Utah / $194	365-room hotel has both fractional and whole-ownership units, offered as hotel rooms when not being used by owners. Open in summer, but some restaurants close in off-season. Quarter shares in studios from $60K.
Four Seasons Jackson Hole Teton Village, Wyo. / $525	This 124-unit hotel operates fully in summer. The 12 Residence Club units start from $185K.
Ritz-Carlton Bachelor Gulch Avon, Colo. / $375	Resort, with 180 rooms and 54 fractional. units, offers patrons the chance to borrow Bachelor, the hotel's yellow Labrador. Fractionals start at $220K. One restaurant is closed until November.
Stowe Mountain Lodge Stowe, Vt. / $435 (at fall opening)	New 139-room hotel won't be ready until late November at the earliest; the 34 additional fractional suites, with 1/8 shares starting at $349K, won't be available for rental.
Whiteface Lodge Lake Placid, N.Y. / $490	All 94 units are sold as fractionals, starting at $120K for a 1/12 share. Owners can make units available for rental through the hotel.

—Ben Casselman

PROJECT C

Assume Gap had 120,000 customers ordering online today. How many customers can it expect to sell across its brand lines?

Gap Links 4 Web Sites to Spur Sales

BY JENNIFER SARANOW

In an effort to get shoppers to use all four of its Web sites, **Gap** Inc. is allowing them to move more easily between the sites, fill one virtual shopping bag and pay one shipping fee.

Until now, shoppers had to visit the company's Gap, Banana Republic, Old Navy and Piperlime sites separately to make purchases.

By integrating the sites, the San Francisco-based company hopes to encourage shoppers to purchase products from more than one of its brands. Gap says about a third of its online orders are placed by customers who shopped at more than one of its Web sites in the past year.

"We are creating an extremely compelling advantage for our customers to stay within our family and shop multiple sites," said Toby Lenk, president of Gap Inc. Direct. "In one sense, it's one big Web site now, whereas before it was four completely separate Web sites." Gap announced the feature in emails sent to customers early Tuesday morning.

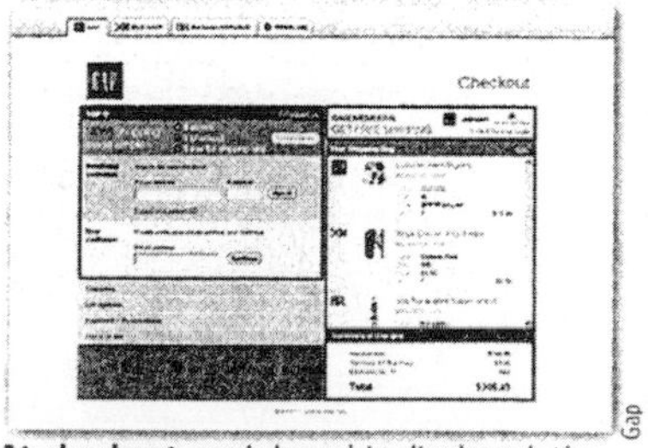

Gap

At checkout, each brand is displayed; the items will be shipped together.

Internet Projects: See text Web site (www.mhhe.com/slater10e) and The Business Math Internet Resource Guide.

chapter

3 DECIMALS

ARBITRAGE

The Price of a 'Grande' Coffee Frappuccino at Starbucks

CITY	CURRENCY	US$
Tokyo	¥440	$3.72
Hong Kong	HK$31	3.96
New York	$4.25	4.25
London	£2.60	5.23
Frankfurt	€4.40	5.99
Vienna	€4.40	5.99
Paris	€4.50	6.12

Note: Prices, including taxes, as provided by retailers in each city, averaged and converted to the nearest U.S. dollar

Wall Street Journal © 2007

Wall Street Journal © 2009

Pornchai Kittiwongsakul/AFP/Getty Image

LEARNING UNIT OBJECTIVES

LU 3–1: Rounding Decimals; Fraction and Decimal Conversions

1. Explain the place values of whole numbers and decimals; round decimals *(pp. 66, 67).*
2. Convert decimal fractions to decimals, proper fractions to decimals, mixed numbers to decimals, and pure and mixed decimals to decimal fractions *(pp. 68–70).*

LU 3–2: Adding, Subtracting, Multiplying, and Dividing Decimals

1. Add, subtract, multiply, and divide decimals *(pp. 71–73).*
2. Complete decimal applications in foreign currency *(pp. 73–74).*
3. Multiply and divide decimals by shortcut methods *(pp. 74–75).*

VOCABULARY PREVIEW

Here are the key terms in this chapter. When you finish the chapter, if you feel you know the term, place a checkmark within the parentheses following the term. If you are not certain of the definition, look it up and write the page number where it can be found in the text. The chapter organizer includes page references to the terms. There is also a complete glossary at the end of the text.

Decimal . ( ) Decimal fraction . ( ) Decimal point . ( ) Mixed decimal . ( ) Pure decimal . ( ) Repeating decimal . ( ) Rounding decimals . ( )

Oh, the Fees You'll Pay . . .

Here are two sample air tickets with taxes, fees and surcharges broken out.

	Boston-San Diego on American	Chicago-Frankfurt on Lufthansa
Base fare	$593.49	$1,191.00
U.S. federal tax	58.51	30.80
Security fees	10.00	12.67
Airport charges	18.00	36.68
Fuel surcharge	NA	200.00
Customs, immigration and agriculture inspection fees	NA	17.50
Total taxes and fees	86.51	297.65
Total ticket cost	680.00	1,488.65

Source: the airlines. NA=not applicable

Are you looking to vacation in San Diego or Frankfurt? As you can see from the *Wall Street Journal* clip "Oh, the Fees You'll Pay" airplane ticket prices do vary. The difference in cost between the American and Lufthansa routes is $808.65.

Lufthansa:	$1,488.65
American:	− 680.00
	$ 808.65

TABLE 3.1

Analyzing a bag of M&M's®

Sharon Hoogstraten

Color*	Fraction	Decimal
Yellow	$\frac{18}{55}$	.33
Red	$\frac{10}{55}$	.18
Blue	$\frac{9}{55}$	.16
Orange	$\frac{7}{55}$	.13
Brown	$\frac{6}{55}$	.11
Green	$\frac{5}{55}$	.09
Total	$\frac{55}{55} = 1$	1.00

*The color ratios currently given are a sample used for educational purposes. They do not represent the manufacturer's color ratios.

LO 1

Chapter 2 introduced the 1.69-ounce bag of M&M's® shown in Table 3.1. In Table 3.1, the six colors in the 1.69-ounce bag of M&M's® are given in fractions and their values expressed in decimal equivalents that are rounded to the nearest hundredths.

This chapter is divided into two learning units. The first unit discusses rounding decimals, converting fractions to decimals, and converting decimals to fractions. The second unit shows you how to add, subtract, multiply, and divide decimals, along with some shortcuts for multiplying and dividing decimals. Added to this unit is a global application of decimals dealing with foreign exchange rates. One of the most common uses of decimals occurs when we spend dollars and cents, which is a *decimal number.*

A **decimal** is a decimal number with digits to the right of a *decimal point,* indicating that decimals, like fractions, are parts of a whole that are less than one. Thus, we can interchange the terms *decimals* and *decimal numbers.* Remembering this will avoid confusion between the terms *decimal, decimal number,* and *decimal point.*

Learning Unit 3–1: Rounding Decimals; Fraction and Decimal Conversions

Remember to read the decimal point as *and.*

In Chapter 1 we stated that the **decimal point** is the center of the decimal numbering system. So far we have studied the whole numbers to the left of the decimal point and the parts of whole numbers called fractions. We also learned that the position of the digits in a whole number gives the place values of the digits (Figure 1.1, p. 5). Now we will study the position (place values) of the digits to the right of the decimal point (Figure 3.1, p. 67). Note that the words to the right of the decimal point end in *ths.*

You should understand why the decimal point is the center of the decimal system. If you move a digit to the left of the decimal point by place (ones, tens, and so on), *you increase its value 10 times for each place (power of 10).* If you move a digit to the right of the decimal point by place (tenths, hundredths, and so on), *you decrease its value 10 times for each place.*

EXAMPLES

$.06 → The 6 is in the hundred*ths* place value.

1.527 → The 5 is in the ten*ths* place value.

2.8394 → The 4 is in the ten thousand*ths* place value.

.33 → The thirty-three hundred*ths* represents the yellow M&M's® in our M&M's® bag of 55 M&M's®.

1.69 oz. → The one ounce and sixty-nine hundred*ths* of another ounce is the weight of our bag of M&M's®.

FIGURE 3.1

Decimal place-value chart

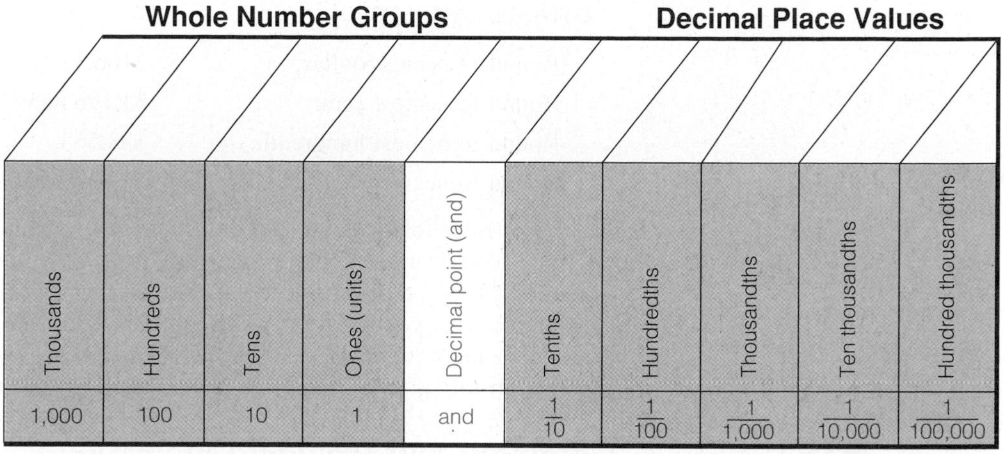

Do you recall from Chapter 1 how you used a place-value chart to read or write whole numbers in verbal form? To read or write decimal numbers, you read or write the decimal number as if it were a whole number. Then you use the name of the decimal place of the last digit as given in Figure 3.1. For example, you would read or write the decimal .0796 as seven hundred ninety-six ten thousandths (the last digit, 6, is in the ten thousandths place).

To read a decimal with four or fewer whole numbers, you can also refer to Figure 3.1. For larger whole numbers, refer to the whole-number place-value chart in Chapter 1 (Figure 1.1, p. 5). For example, from Figure 3.1 you would read the number 126.2864 as one hundred twenty-six and two thousand eight hundred sixty-four ten thousandths. Remember that the *and* is the decimal point.

Now let's round decimals. Rounding decimals is similar to the rounding of whole numbers that you learned in Chapter 1.

Rounding Decimals

From Table 3.1, you know that the 1.69-ounce bag of M&M's® introduced in Chapter 2 contained $\frac{18}{55}$, or .33, yellow M&M's®. The .33 was rounded to the nearest hundredth. **Rounding decimals** involves the following steps:

ROUNDING DECIMALS TO A SPECIFIED PLACE VALUE

Step 1. Identify the place value of the digit you want to round.

Step 2. If the digit to the right of the identified digit in Step 1 is 5 or more, increase the identified digit by 1. If the digit to the right is less than 5, do not change the identified digit.

Step 3. Drop all digits to the right of the identified digit.

Let's practice rounding by using the $\frac{18}{55}$ yellow M&M's® that we rounded to .33 in Table 3.1. Before we rounded $\frac{18}{55}$ to .33, the number we rounded was .32727. This is an example of a **repeating decimal** since the 27 repeats itself.

EXAMPLE Round .3272727 to nearest hundredth.

Step 1. .3272727 — The identified digit is 2, which is in the hundredths place (two places to the right of the decimal point).

Step 2. → The digit to the right of 2 is more than 5 (7). Thus, 2, the identified digit in Step 1, is changed to 3.

.3372727

Step 3. .33 — Drop all other digits to right of the identified digit 3.

We could also round the .3272727 M&M's® to the nearest tenth or thousandth as follows:

Tenth	or	Thousandth
.3272727 → .3		.3272727 → .327

OTHER EXAMPLES

Round to nearest dollar:	\$166.39	→	\$166
Round to nearest cent:	\$1,196.885	→	\$1,196.89
Round to nearest hundredth:	\$38.563	→	\$38.56
Round to nearest thousandth:	\$1,432.9981	→	\$1,432.998

The rules for rounding can differ with the situation in which rounding is used. For example, have you ever bought one item from a supermarket produce department that was marked "3 for \$1" and noticed what the cashier charged you? One item marked "3 for \$1" would not cost you $33\frac{1}{3}$ cents rounded to 33 cents. You will pay 34 cents. Many retail stores round to the next cent even if the digit following the identified digit is less than $\frac{1}{2}$ of a penny. In this text we round on the concept of 5 or more.

LO 2

Fraction and Decimal Conversions

In business operations we must frequently convert fractions to decimal numbers and decimal numbers to fractions. This section begins by discussing three types of fraction-to-decimal conversions. Then we discuss converting pure and mixed decimals to decimal fractions.

Converting Decimal Fractions to Decimals

From Figure 3.1 you can see that a **decimal fraction** (expressed in the digits to the right of the decimal point) is a fraction with a denominator that has a power of 10, such as $\frac{1}{10}$, $\frac{17}{100}$, and $\frac{23}{1{,}000}$. To convert a decimal fraction to a decimal, follow these steps:

CONVERTING DECIMAL FRACTIONS TO DECIMALS

Step 1. Count the number of zeros in the denominator.

Step 2. Place the numerator of the decimal fraction to the right of the decimal point the same number of places as you have zeros in the denominator. (The number of zeros in the denominator gives the number of digits your decimal has to the right of the decimal point.) Do not go over the total number of denominator zeros.

Now let's change $\frac{3}{10}$ and its higher multiples of 10 to decimals.

EXAMPLES

Verbal form	Decimal fraction	Decimal[1]	Number of decimal places to right of decimal point
a. Three tenths	$\frac{3}{10}$	.3	1
b. Three hundredths	$\frac{3}{100}$	.03	2
c. Three thousandths	$\frac{3}{1{,}000}$	.003	3
d. Three ten thousandths	$\frac{3}{10{,}000}$	.0003	4

Note how we show the different values of the decimal fractions above in decimals. The zeros after the decimal point and before the number 3 indicate these values. If you add zeros after the number 3, you do not change the value. Thus, the numbers .3, .30, and .300 have the same value. So 3 tenths of a pizza, 30 hundredths of a pizza, and 300 thousandths of a pizza are the same total amount of pizza. The first pizza is sliced into 10 pieces. The second pizza is sliced into 100 pieces. The third pizza is sliced into 1,000 pieces. Also, we don't need to place a zero to the left of the decimal point.

[1]From .3 to .0003, the values get smaller and smaller, but if you go from .3 to .3000, the values remain the same.

Converting Proper Fractions to Decimals

Recall from Chapter 2 that proper fractions are fractions with a value less than 1. That is, the numerator of the fraction is smaller than its denominator. How can we convert these proper fractions to decimals? Since proper fractions are a form of division, it is possible to convert proper fractions to decimals by carrying out the division.

CONVERTING PROPER FRACTIONS TO DECIMALS

Step 1. Divide the numerator of the fraction by its denominator. (If necessary, add a decimal point and zeros to the number in the numerator.)

Step 2. Round as necessary.

EXAMPLES

$$\frac{3}{4} = 4\overline{)3.00}\ \ (\text{quotient } .75) \qquad \begin{array}{r} 2\,8 \\ \hline 20 \\ 20 \\ \hline \end{array}$$

$$\frac{3}{8} = 8\overline{)3.000}\ \ (\text{quotient } .375) \qquad \begin{array}{r} 2\,4 \\ \hline 60 \\ 56 \\ \hline 40 \\ 40 \\ \hline \end{array}$$

$$\frac{1}{3} = 3\overline{)1.000}\ \ (\text{quotient } .33\bar{3}) \qquad \begin{array}{r} 9 \\ \hline 10 \\ 9 \\ \hline 10 \\ 9 \\ \hline 1 \end{array}$$

Note that in the last example $\frac{1}{3}$, the 3 in the quotient keeps repeating itself (never ends). The short bar over the last 3 means that the number endlessly repeats.

Converting Mixed Numbers to Decimals

A mixed number, you will recall from Chapter 2, is the sum of a whole number greater than zero and a proper fraction. To convert mixed numbers to decimals, use the following steps:

CONVERTING MIXED NUMBERS TO DECIMALS

Step 1. Convert the fractional part of the mixed number to a decimal (as illustrated in the previous section).

Step 2. Add the converted fractional part to the whole number.

EXAMPLE

$8\frac{2}{5}$ = **(Step 1)** $5\overline{)2.0}$ (quotient .4; $2\,0$) **(Step 2)** = $\begin{array}{r} 8.00 \\ +\ .40 \\ \hline 8.40 \end{array}$

Now that we have converted fractions to decimals, let's convert decimals to fractions.

Converting Pure and Mixed Decimals to Decimal Fractions

A **pure decimal** has no whole number(s) to the left of the decimal point (.43, .458, and so on). A **mixed decimal** is a combination of a whole number and a decimal. An example of a mixed decimal follows.

EXAMPLE 737.592 = Seven hundred thirty-seven and five hundred ninety-two thousandths

Note the following conversion steps for converting pure and mixed decimals to decimal fractions:

CONVERTING PURE AND MIXED DECIMALS TO DECIMAL FRACTIONS

Step 1. Place the digits to the right of the decimal point in the numerator of the fraction. Omit the decimal point. (For a decimal fraction with a fractional part, see examples **c** and **d** below.)

Step 2. Put a 1 in the denominator of the fraction.

Step 3. Count the number of digits to the right of the decimal point. Add the same number of zeros to the denominator of the fraction. For mixed decimals, add the fraction to the whole number.

If desired, you can reduce the fractions in Step 3.

MONEY TIPS

It is always useful to know that $\frac{1}{8} = .125$, $\frac{3}{8} = .375$, $\frac{5}{8} = .625$, and $\frac{7}{8} = .875$ by memory. These commonly used fractions are as useful to know as are $\frac{1}{4}$, $\frac{1}{2}$, and $\frac{3}{4}$, which most of us know. These are especially handy when dealing with your personal finance.

EXAMPLES	Step 1	Step 2	Places	Step 3
a. .3	$\frac{3}{}$	$\frac{3}{1}$	1	$\frac{3}{10}$
b. .24	$\frac{24}{}$	$\frac{24}{1}$	2	$\frac{24}{100}$
c. $.24\frac{1}{2}$	$\frac{245}{}$	$\frac{245}{1}$	3	$\frac{245}{1{,}000}$

Before completing Step 1 in example **c,** we must remove the fractional part, convert it to a decimal ($\frac{1}{2} = .5$), and multiply it by .01 ($.5 \times .01 = .005$). We use .01 because the 4 of .24 is in the hundredths place. Then we add $.005 + .24 = .245$ (three places to right of the decimal) and complete Steps 1, 2, and 3.

	Step 1	Step 2	Places	Step 3
d. $.07\frac{1}{4}$	$\frac{725}{}$	$\frac{725}{1}$	4	$\frac{725}{10{,}000}$

In example **d,** be sure to convert $\frac{1}{4}$ to .25 and multiply by .01. This gives .0025. Then add .0025 to .07, which is .0725 (four places), and complete Steps 1, 2, and 3.

	Step 1	Step 2	Places	Step 3
e. 17.45	$\frac{45}{}$	$\frac{45}{1}$	2	$\frac{45}{100} = 17\frac{45}{100}$

Example **e** is a mixed decimal. Since we substitute *and* for the decimal point, we read this mixed decimal as seventeen and forty-five hundredths. Note that after we converted the .45 of the mixed decimals to a fraction, we added it to the whole number 17.

The Practice Quiz that follows will help you check your understanding of this unit.

LU 3–1 PRACTICE QUIZ

Complete this **Practice Quiz** to see how you are doing.

Write the following as a decimal number.

1. Four hundred eight thousandths

Name the place position of the identified digit:

2. 6.8241 (arrow under 8) **3.** 9.3942 (arrow under 4)

Round each decimal to place indicated:

	Tenth	Thousandth
4. .62768	**a.**	**b.**
5. .68341	**a.**	**b.**

Convert the following to decimals:

6. $\frac{9}{10{,}000}$ **7.** $\frac{14}{100{,}000}$

Convert the following to decimal fractions (do not reduce):

8. .819 **9.** 16.93 **10.** $.05\frac{1}{4}$

Convert the following fractions to decimals and round answer to nearest hundredth:

11. $\frac{1}{6}$ **12.** $\frac{3}{8}$ **13.** $12\frac{1}{8}$

Solutions with Step-by-Step Help on DVD

✓ Solutions

1. .408 (3 places to right of decimal)
2. Hundredths
3. Thousandths
4. a. .6 (identified digit 6—digit to right less than 5)
   b. .628 (identified digit 7—digit to right greater than 5)
5. a. .7 (identified digit 6—digit to right greater than 5)
   b. .683 (identified digit 3—digit to right less than 5)
6. .0009 (4 places)
7. .00014 (5 places)
8. $\frac{819}{1,000}$ $\left(\frac{819}{1 + 3 \text{ zeros}}\right)$
9. $16\frac{93}{100}$
10. $\frac{525}{10,000}$ $\left(\frac{525}{1 + 4 \text{ zeros}}\ \frac{1}{4} \times .01 = .0025 + .05 = .0525\right)$
11. .16666 = .17
12. .375 = .38
13. 12.125 = 12.13

LU 3–1a EXTRA PRACTICE QUIZ WITH WORKED-OUT SOLUTIONS

Need more practice? Try this **Extra Practice Quiz** (check figures in Chapter Organizer, p. 78). Worked-out Solutions can be found in Appendix B at end of text.

Write the following as a decimal number:

1. Three hundred nine thousandths

Name the place position of the identified digit:

2. 7.9324 (↑ under 9)
3. 8.3682 (↑ under 2)

Round each decimal to place indicated:

	Tenth	Thousandth
4. .84361	a.	b.
5. .87938	a.	b.

Convert the following to decimals:

6. $\frac{8}{10,000}$
7. $\frac{16}{100,000}$

Convert the following to decimal fractions (do not reduce):

8. .938
9. 17.95
10. $.03\frac{1}{4}$

Convert the following fractions to decimals and round answer to nearest hundredth:

11. $\frac{1}{8}$
12. $\frac{4}{7}$
13. $13\frac{1}{9}$

Learning Unit 3–2: Adding, Subtracting, Multiplying, and Dividing Decimals

Would you like to save almost $2,000 per year? The *Wall Street Journal* clip "Some Workers Downsize Lunch" (p. 72) shows by brown-bagging you can save $5.45 each day. The following calculation shows that over one year savings could be $1,989.25.

Lunch from deli:	$10.69
Homemade lunch:	5.24
	$5.45 × 365 = $1,989.25

This learning unit shows you how to add, subtract, multiply, and divide decimals. You also make calculations involving decimals, including decimals used in foreign currency.

Addition and Subtraction of Decimals

Since you know how to add and subtract whole numbers, to add and subtract decimal numbers you have only to learn about the placement of the decimals. The following steps on page 72 will help you:

ADDING AND SUBTRACTING DECIMALS

Step 1. Vertically write the numbers so that the decimal points align. You can place additional zeros to the right of the decimal point if needed without changing the value of the number.

Step 2. Add or subtract the digits starting with the right column and moving to the left.

Step 3. Align the decimal point in the answer with the above decimal points.

"Misplace one decimal point . . ."

EXAMPLES Add 4 + 7.3 + 36.139 + .0007 + 8.22.

Whole number to the right of the last digit is assumed to have a decimal. → 4.0000

Extra zeros have been added to make calculation easier. → 7.3000

$$\begin{array}{r} 4.0000 \\ 7.3000 \\ 36.1390 \\ .0007 \\ \underline{8.2200} \\ \boxed{55.6597} \end{array}$$

Subtract 45.3 − 15.273.

$$\begin{array}{r} {\scriptstyle 2\,9\,10} \\ 45.\cancel{3}\cancel{0}\cancel{0} \\ \underline{-\ 15.273} \\ \boxed{30.027} \end{array}$$

Subtract 7 − 6.9.

$$\begin{array}{r} {\scriptstyle 6\ \ 10} \\ \cancel{7}.\cancel{0} \\ \underline{-\ 6.9} \\ \boxed{.1} \end{array}$$

Multiplication of Decimals

The multiplication of decimal numbers is similar to the multiplication of whole numbers except for the additional step of placing the decimal in the answer (product). The steps that follow on page 73 simplify this procedure.

MULTIPLYING DECIMALS

Step 1. Multiply the numbers as whole numbers ignoring the decimal points.

Step 2. Count and total the number of decimal places in the multiplier and multiplicand.

Step 3. Starting at the right in the product, count to the left the number of decimal places totaled in Step 2. Place the decimal point so that the product has the same number of decimal places as totaled in Step 2. If the total number of places is greater than the places in the product, insert zeros in front of the product.

EXAMPLES

```
           8.52  (2 decimal places)          2.36  (2 places)
Step 1 → × 6.7   (1 decimal place) ← Step 2  × .016  (3 places)
          5 964                              1416
         51 12                               236
Step 3 → 57.084                             .03776  Need to add zero
```

Division of Decimals

If the divisor in your decimal division problem is a whole number, first place the decimal point in the quotient directly above the decimal point in the dividend. Then divide as usual. If the divisor has a decimal point, complete the steps that follow.

DIVIDING DECIMALS

Step 1. Make the divisor a whole number by moving the decimal point to the right.

Step 2. Move the decimal point in the dividend to the right the same number of places that you moved the decimal point in the divisor (Step 1). If there are not enough places, add zeros to the right of the dividend.

Step 3. Place the decimal point in the quotient above the new decimal point in the dividend. Divide as usual.

EXAMPLE

```
                        Step 3
                  ↓
              1 3.12
Step 1 → 2.5)32.8.00 ← Step 2
             25
              7 8
              7 5
                3 0
                2 5
                  50
                  50
```

Stop a moment and study the above example. Note that the quotient does not change when we multiply the divisor and the dividend by the same number. This is why we can move the decimal point in division problems and always divide by a whole number.

LO 2 GLOBAL

Decimal Applications in Foreign Currency

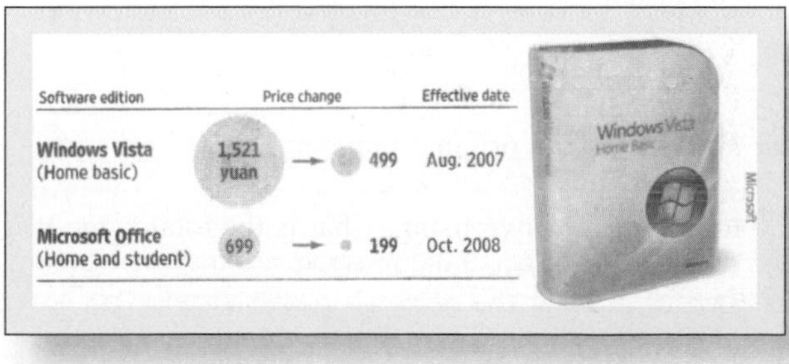

Wall Street Journal © 2008

EXAMPLE

The *Wall Street Journal* clip shows in China the price of Microsoft Office was reduced to 199 yuan from an original price of 699 yuan. Using the currencies table (p. 74) lets us see what the original as well as sales price is in U.S. dollars. In the table 1 yuan equals \$.1463. To find the original selling price you multiply the number of yuan (699) times \$.1463.

$$699 \text{ yuan} \times \$.1463 = \$102.26$$

GLOBAL

Currencies

U.S.-dollar foreign-exchange rates in late New York trading

Country/currency	Wed in US$	Wed per US$	US$ vs, YTD chg (%)
Americas			
Argentina peso*	.3100	3.2258	2.4
Brazil real	.4196	2.3832	33.9
Canada dollar	.7969	1.2549	26.3
1-mos forward	.7972	1.2544	26.3
3-mos forward	.7988	1.2519	26.1
6-mos forward	.7997	1.2505	25.9
Chile peso	.001556	642.67	29.0
Colombia peso	.0004230	2364.07	17.1
Ecuador US dollar	1	1	unch
Mexico peso*	.0721	13.8773	27.2
Peru new sol	.3229	3.097	3.3
Uruguay peso†	.04380	22.83	5.9
Venezuela b. fuerte	.465701	2.1473	0.1
Asia-Pacific			
Australian dollar	.6685	1.4959	31.1
China yuan	.1463	6.8348	−6.4
Hong Kong dollar	.1290	7.7527	−0.6
India rupee	.02028	49.310	25.1
Indonesia rupiah	.0001010	9901	5.4
Japan yen	.010235	97.70	−12.3
1-mos forward	.010259	97.48	−12.2
3-mos forward	.010314	96.96	−12.1
6-mos forward	.010362	96.51	−11.8
Malaysia ringgit§	.2820	3.5461	7.2
New Zealand dollar	.5838	1.7129	31.3
Pakistan rupee	.01235	80.972	31.3
Philippines peso	.0206	48.662	18.0
Singapore dollar	.6667	1.4999	4.1
South Korea won	.0007339	1362.58	45.6
Taiwan dollar	.03034	32.960	1.6
Thailand baht	.02897	34.519	14.9
Vietnam dong	.00005940	16834	5.0

Country/currency	Wed in US$	Wed per US$	US$ vs, YTD chg (%)
Europe			
Czech Rep. koruna**	.04905	20.387	12.2
Denmark krone	.1721	5.8106	13.8
Euro area euro	1.2830	.7794	13.8
Hungary forint	.004555	219.54	26.7
Norway krone	.1378	7.2569	33.6
Poland zloty	.3377	2.9612	20.0
Russia ruble‡	.03709	26.961	9.7
Slovak Rep koruna	.04210	23.753	3.2
Sweden krona	.1275	7.8431	21.3
Switzerland franc	.8592	1.1639	2.7
1-mos forward	.8601	1.1627	2.8
3-mos forward	.8614	1.1609	3.0
6-mos forward	.8621	1.1600	3.3
Turkey lira**	.5902	1.6942	45.1
UK pound	1.6241	.6157	22.3
1-mos forward	1.6215	.6167	22.4
3-mos forward	1.6181	.6180	22.5
6-mos forward	1.6115	.6205	22.6
Middle East/Africa			
Bahrain dinar	2.6522	.3770	0.3
Eqypt pound*	.1791	5.5832	0.9
Israel shekel	.2581	3.8745	0.5
Jordan dinar	1.4129	.7078	−0.1
Kuwait dinar	3.7122	.2694	−1.5
Lebanon pound	.0006662	1501.05	−0.7
Saudi Arabia riyal	.2665	3.7523	unch
South Africa rand	.0851	11.7509	71.7
UAE dirham	.2723	3.6724	unch
SDR††	1.4932	.6697	5.7

Wall Street Journal © 2008

The original selling price in U.S. dollars is \$102.26. To find the new selling price in U.S. dollars, you multiply the number of yuan 199 times \$.1463. The new selling price in U.S. dollars is \$29.11.

199 × \$.1463 = \$29.11

To check you could multiply the new price \$29.11 in U.S. dollars times the table factor 6.8348.

\$29.11 × 6.8348 = 198.96 yuan
each \$1 equals 6.8348 yuan

Multiplication and Division Shortcuts for Decimals

LO 3

The shortcut steps that follow show how to solve multiplication and division problems quickly involving multiples of 10 (10, 100, 1,000, 10,000, etc.).

SHORTCUTS FOR MULTIPLES OF 10

Multiplication

Step 1. Count the zeros in the multiplier.

Step 2. Move the decimal point in the multiplicand the same number of places to the right as you have zeros in the multiplier.

Division

Step 1. Count the zeros in the divisor.

Step 2. Move the decimal point in the dividend the same number of places to the left as you have zeros in the divisor.

Zumawirewestphotostwo/Newscom

In multiplication, the answers are *larger* than the original number.

EXAMPLE If Toyota spends \$60,000 for magazine advertising, what is the total value if it spends this same amount for 10 years? What would be the total cost?

\$60,000 × 10 = \$600,000 (1 place to the right)

OTHER EXAMPLES 6.89 × 10 = 68.9 (1 place to the right)

6.89 × 100 = 689. (2 places to the right)

6.89 × 1,000 = 6,890. (3 places to the right)

In division, the answers are *smaller* than the original number.

EXAMPLES 6.89 ÷ 10 = .689 (1 place to the left)

6.89 ÷ 100 = .0689 (2 places to the left)

6.89 ÷ 1,000 = .00689 (3 places to the left)

6.89 ÷ 10,000 = .000689 (4 places to the left)

Next, let's dissect and solve a word problem.

How to Dissect and Solve a Word Problem

The Word Problem May O'Mally went to Sears to buy wall-to-wall carpet. She needs 101.3 square yards for downstairs, 16.3 square yards for the upstairs bedrooms, and 6.2 square yards for the halls. The carpet cost $14.55 per square yard. The padding cost $3.25 per square yard. Sears quoted an installation charge of $6.25 per square yard. What was May O'Mally's total cost?

By completing the following blueprint aid, we will slowly dissect this word problem. Note that before solving the problem, we gather the facts, identify what we are solving for, and list the steps that must be completed before finding the final answer, along with any key points we should remember. Let's go to it!

MONEY TIPS

Calculate your gas mileage based on gas from different gas stations. Record the mileage you have after filling the tank. Keep track of the mileage up through your next filling. Divide the miles recorded by the number of gallons purchased. This will tell you your gas mileage. Compare your results from different gas stations taking into account city or highway driving as well. You may be surprised that certain gas stations have gas that lasts longer.

The facts	Solving for?	Steps to take	Key points
Carpet needed: 101.3 sq. yd.; 16.3 sq. yd.; 6.2 sq. yd. *Costs:* Carpet, $14.55 per sq. yd.; padding, $3.25 per sq. yd.; installation, $6.25 per sq. yd.	Total cost of carpet	Total square yards × Cost per square yard = Total cost.	Align decimals. Round answer to nearest cent.

Steps to solving problem

1. Calculate the total number of square yards.

```
101.3
 16.3
  6.2
123.8 square yards
```

2. Calculate the total cost per square yard.

```
$14.55
  3.25
  6.25
$24.05
```

3. Calculate the total cost of carpet.

123.8 × $24.05 = $2,977.39

It's time to check your progress.

LU 3–2 PRACTICE QUIZ

Complete this **Practice Quiz** to see how you are doing.

1. Rearrange vertically and add: 14, .642, 9.34, 15.87321
2. Rearrange and subtract: 28.1549 − .885
3. Multiply and round the answer to the nearest tenth: 28.53 × 17.4
4. Divide and round to the nearest hundredth: 2,182 ÷ 2.83

Complete by the shortcut method:

5. 14.28 × 100
6. 9,680 ÷ 1,000
7. 9,812 ÷ 10,000

(cont. p. 76)

8. Could you help Mel decide which product is the "better buy"?
Dog food A: \$9.01 for 64 ounces **Dog food B:** \$7.95 for 50 ounces
Round to the nearest cent as needed.

9. At Avis Rent-A-Car, the cost per day to rent a medium-size car is \$39.99 plus 29 cents per mile. What will it cost to rent this car for 2 days if you drive 602.3 miles? Since the solution shows a completed blueprint, you might use a blueprint also.

10. A trip to Mexico cost 6,000 pesos. What would this be in U.S. dollars? Check your answer.

Solutions with Step-by-Step Help on DVD

✓ Solutions

1.
14.00000
.64200
9.34000
15.87321
39.85521

2.
7 101414
28.1549
−.8850
27.2699

3.
28.53
× 17.4
11 412
199 71
285 3
496.422 = **496.4**

4.
771.024 = 771.02
2.83)218200.000
1981
2010
1981
290
283
7 00
5 66
1 340
1 132

5. 14.28 = **1,428**   **6.** 9.680 = **9.680**   **7.** .9812 = **.9812**

8. **A:** \$9.01 ÷ 64 = **\$.14**   **B:** \$7.95 ÷ 50 = **\$.16**   **Buy A.**

9. Avis Rent-A-Car total rental charge:

The facts	Solving for?	Steps to take	Key points
Cost per day, \$39.99. 29 cents per mile. Drove 602.3 miles. 2-day rental.	Total rental charge.	Total cost for 2 days' rental + Total cost of driving = Total rental charge.	In multiplication, count the number of decimal places. Starting from right to left in the product, insert decimal in appropriate place. Round to nearest cent.

Steps to solving problem

1. Calculate total costs for 2 days' rental. \$39.99 × 2 = \$79.98
2. Calculate the total cost of driving. \$.29 × 602.3 = \$174.667 = \$174.67
3. Calculate the total rental charge.
   \$ 79.98
   + 174.67
   \$254.65

10. 6,000 × \$.0721 = **\$432.60**
Check \$432.60 × 13.8773 = 6003.3 pesos due to rounding

LU 3–2a EXTRA PRACTICE QUIZ WITH WORKED-OUT SOLUTIONS

Need more practice? Try this **Extra Practice Quiz** (check figures in Chapter Organizer, p. 78). Worked-out Solutions can be found in Appendix B at end of text.

1. Rearrange vertically and add:
16, .831, 9.85, 17.8321

2. Rearrange and subtract:
29.5832 − .998

3. Multiply and round the answer to the nearest tenth:
29.64 × 18.2

4. Divide and round to the nearest hundredth:
 3,824 ÷ 4.94

Complete by the shortcut method:

5. 17.48 × 100 6. 8,432 ÷ 1,000 7. 9,643 ÷ 10,000
8. Could you help Mel decide which product is the "better buy"?
 Dog food A: $8.88 for 64 ounces **Dog food B:** $7.25 for 50 ounces

Round to the nearest cent as needed:

9. At Avis Rent-A-Car, the cost per day to rent a medium-size car is $29.99 plus 22 cents per mile. What will it cost to rent this car for 2 days if you drive 709.8 miles?
10. A trip to Mexico costs 7,000 pesos. What would this be in U.S. dollars? Check your answer.

CHAPTER ORGANIZER AND REFERENCE GUIDE

Topic	Key point, procedure, formula	Example(s) to illustrate situation
Identifying place value, p. 67	$10, 1, \frac{1}{10}, \frac{1}{100}, \frac{1}{1,000}$, etc.	.439 in thousandths place value
Rounding decimals, p. 67	1. Identify place value of digit you want to round. 2. If digit to right of identified digit in Step 1 is 5 or more, increase identified digit by 1; if less than 5, do not change identified digit. 3. Drop all digits to right of identified digit.	.875 rounded to nearest tenth = .9 Identified digit (arrow pointing to 8)
Converting decimal fractions to decimals, p. 68	1. Decimal fraction has a denominator with multiples of 10. Count number of zeros in denominator. 2. Zeros show how many places are in the decimal.	$\frac{8}{1,000} = .008$ $\frac{6}{10,000} = .0006$
Converting proper fractions to decimals, p. 69	1. Divide numerator of fraction by its denominator. 2. Round as necessary.	$\frac{1}{3}$ (to nearest tenth) = .3
Converting mixed numbers to decimals, p. 69	1. Convert fractional part of the mixed number to a decimal. 2. Add converted fractional part to whole number.	$6\frac{1}{4}$ $\frac{1}{4} = .25 + 6 = 6.25$
Converting pure and mixed decimals to decimal fractions, p. 69	1. Place digits to right of decimal point in numerator of fraction. 2. Put 1 in denominator. 3. Add zeros to denominator, depending on decimal places of original number. For mixed decimals, add fraction to whole number.	.984 (3 places) 1. $\frac{984}{}$ 2. $\frac{984}{1}$ 3. $\frac{984}{1,000}$
Adding and subtracting decimals, p. 71	1. Vertically write and align numbers on decimal points. 2. Add or subtract digits, starting with right column and moving to the left. 3. Align decimal point in answer with above decimal points.	Add 1.3 + 2 + .4 1.3 2.0 .4 3.7 Subtract 5 − 3.9 4 10 ~~5~~.~~0~~ −3.9 1.1

(continues)

CHAPTER ORGANIZER AND REFERENCE GUIDE

Topic	Key point, procedure, formula	Example(s) to illustrate situation
Multiplying decimals, p. 72	1. Multiply numbers, ignoring decimal points. 2. Count and total number of decimal places in multiplier and multiplicand. 3. Starting at right in the product, count to the left the number of decimal places totaled in Step 2. Insert decimal point. If number of places greater than space in answer, add zeros.	2.48 (2 places) × .018 (3 places) 1 984 2 48 .04464
Dividing a decimal by a whole number, p. 73	1. Place decimal point in quotient directly above the decimal point in dividend. 2. Divide as usual.	1.1 42)46.2 42 42 42
Dividing if the divisor is a decimal, p. 73	1. Make divisor a whole number by moving decimal point to the right. 2. Move decimal point in dividend to the right the same number of places as in Step 1. 3. Place decimal point in quotient above decimal point in dividend. Divide as usual.	14.2 2.9)41.39 29 123 116 79 58 21
Shortcuts on multiplication and division of decimals, p. 74	When multiplying by 10, 100, 1,000, and so on, move decimal point in multiplicand the same number of places to the right as you have zeros in multiplier. For division, move decimal point to the left.	4.85 × 100 = 485 4.85 ÷ 100 = .0485

KEY TERMS	Decimal, *p. 66* Decimal fraction, *p. 68* Decimal point, *p. 66*	Mixed decimal, *p. 69* Pure decimal, *p. 69* Repeating decimal, *p. 67*	Rounding decimals, *p. 67*

CHECK FIGURES FOR EXTRA PRACTICE QUIZZES WITH PAGE REFERENCES. (WORKED-OUT SOLUTIONS IN APPENDIX B.)	LU 3–1a (p. 71)		LU 3–2a (p. 76)	
	1. .309	8. $\frac{938}{1,000}$	1. 44.5131	6. 8.432
	2. Hundredths	9. $17\frac{95}{100}$	2. 28.5852	7. .9643
	3. Ten-thousandths	10. $\frac{325}{10,000}$	3. 539.4	8. Buy A $.14
	4. A. .8 B. .844	11. .13	4. 774.09	9. $216.14
	5. A. .9 B. .879	12. .57	5. 1,748	10. $504.70
	6. .0008	13. 13.11		
	7. .00016			

Note: For how to dissect and solve a word problem, see page 75.

Critical Thinking Discussion Questions

1. What are the steps for rounding decimals? Federal income tax forms allow the taxpayer to round each amount to the nearest dollar. Do you agree with this?
2. Explain how to convert fractions to decimals. If 1 out of 20 people buys a Land Rover, how could you write an advertisement in decimals?
3. Explain why .07, .70, and .700 are not equal. Assume you take a family trip to Disney World that covers 500 miles. Show that $\frac{8}{10}$ of the trip, or .8 of the trip, represents 400 miles.
4. Explain the steps in the addition or subtraction of decimals. Visit a car dealership and find the difference between two sticker prices. Be sure to check each sticker price for accuracy. Should you always pay the sticker price?

END-OF-CHAPTER PROBLEMS

connect plus+ www.mhhe.com/slater10e

Check figures for odd-numbered problems in Appendix C Name ______________________ Date ________

DRILL PROBLEMS

Identify the place value for the following:

3–1. 9.4391 (arrow under 4) **3–2.** 293.9438 (arrow under 4)

Round the following as indicated:

	Tenth	Hundredth	Thousandth
3–3. .8466			
3–4. 6.8629			
3–5. 5.8312			
3–6. 6.8415			
3–7. 6.5555			
3–8. 75.9913			

Round the following to the nearest cent:

3–9. $4,822.775 **3–10.** $4,892.046

Convert the following types of decimal fractions to decimals (round to nearest hundredth as needed):

3–11. $\frac{6}{100}$ **3–12.** $\frac{4}{10}$ **3–13.** $\frac{61}{1,000}$ **3–14.** $\frac{610}{1,000}$

3–15. $\frac{82}{100}$ **3–16.** $\frac{979}{1,000}$ **3–17.** $16\frac{61}{100}$

Convert the following decimals to fractions. Do not reduce to lowest terms.

3–18. .7 **3–19.** .71 **3–20.** .009 **3–21.** .0125

3–22. .609 **3–23.** .825 **3–24.** .9999 **3–25.** .7065

Convert the following to mixed numbers. Do not reduce to the lowest terms.

3–26. 9.2 **3–27.** 28.48 **3–28.** 6.025

Write the decimal equivalent of the following:

3–29. Four thousandths **3–30.** Three hundred three and two hundredths

3–31. Eighty-five ten thousandths **3–32.** Seven hundred seventy-five thousandths

Rearrange the following and add:

3–33. .115, 10.8318, 4.7, 802.4811 **3–34.** .005, 2,002.181, 795.41, 14.0, .184

Rearrange the following and subtract:

3–35. 9.2 − 5.8 **3–36.** 7 − 2.0815 **3–37.** 3.4 − 1.08

Estimate by rounding all the way and multiply the following (do not round final answer):

3–38. 6.24×3.9 **3–39.** $.413 \times 3.07$

Estimate **Estimate**

3–40. 675×1.92 **3–41.** $4.9 \times .825$

Estimate **Estimate**

Divide the following and round to the nearest hundredth:

3–42. .8931 ÷ 3

3–43. 29.432 ÷ .0012

3–44. .0065 ÷ .07

3–45. 7,742.1 ÷ 48

3–46. 8.95 ÷ 1.18

3–47. 2,600 ÷ .381

Convert the following to decimals and round to the nearest hundredth:

3–48. $\frac{1}{8}$

3–49. $\frac{1}{25}$

3–50. $\frac{5}{6}$

3–51. $\frac{5}{8}$

Complete these multiplications and divisions by the shortcut method (do not do any written calculations):

3–52. 96.7 ÷ 10

3–53. 258.5 ÷ 100

3–54. 8.51 × 1,000

3–55. .86 ÷ 100

3–56. 9.015 × 100

3–57. 48.6 × 10

3–58. 750 × 10

3–59. 3,950 ÷ 1,000

3–60. 8.45 ÷ 10

3–61. 7.9132 × 1,000

WORD PROBLEMS

As needed, round answers to the nearest cent.

3–62. A Ford Flex costs $24,000. What would it cost in London? Check your answer.

3–63. Ken Griffey Jr. got 7 hits out of 12 at bats. What was his batting average to the nearest thousandths place?

3–64. The August 17, 2009, *San Francisco Chronicle* reported on the rapid growth of Facebook.com. Facebook is becoming a social superpower with 120 million registered members who log in at least once daily. They share 1 billion photos and 10 million videos each month. What is the average number of photos and videos that each active member posts? Round to the nearest ten thousandth.

3–65. At the Party Store, Joan Lee purchased 21.50 yards of ribbon. Each yard costs 91 cents. What was the total cost of the ribbon? Round to the nearest cent.

3–66. Douglas Noel went to Home Depot and bought 4 doors at $42.99 each and 6 bags of fertilizer at $8.99 per bag. What was the total cost to Douglas? If Douglas had $300 in his pocket, what does he have left to spend?

3–67. The stock of Intel has a high of $30.25 today. It closed at $28.85. How much did the stock drop from its high?

3–68. Pete is traveling by car to a computer convention in San Diego. His company will reimburse him $.48 per mile. If Pete travels 210.5 miles, how much will Pete receive from his company?

3–69. Mark Ogara rented a truck from Avis Rent-A-Car for the weekend (2 days). The base rental price was $29.95 per day plus $14\frac{1}{2}$ cents per mile. Mark drove 410.85 miles. How much does Mark owe?

3–70. Nursing home costs are on the rise as consumeraffairs.com reports in their quarterly newsletter. The average cost is around $192 a day with an average length of stay of 2.5 years. Calculate the cost of the average nursing home stay.

3–71. Bob Ross bought a Blackberry on the Web for $89.99. He saw the same Blackberry in the mall for $118.99. How much did Bob save by buying on the Web?

3–72. Russell is preparing the daily bank deposit for his coffee shop. Before the deposit, the coffee shop had a checking account balance of $3,185.66. The deposit contains the following checks:

No. 1	$ 99.50	No. 3	$8.75
No. 2	110.35	No. 4	6.83

Russell included $820.55 in currency with the deposit. What is the coffee shop's new balance, assuming Russell writes no new checks?

3–73. Assume US Airways Express is offering a $190 round-trip fare for Chattanooga, Tennessee–New York for those who buy tickets in the next couple of weeks. Ticket prices had been running between $230 and $330 round-trip. Mark VanLoh, Airport Authority president, said the new fare is lower than the $219 ticket price offered by Southwest Airlines. How much would a family of four save using US Airways versus Southwest Airlines?

3–74. Randi went to Lowe's to buy wall-to-wall carpeting. She needs 110.8 square yards for downstairs, 31.8 square yards for the halls, and 161.9 square yards for the bedrooms upstairs. Randi chose a shag carpet that costs $14.99 per square yard. She ordered foam padding at $3.10 per square yard. The carpet installers quoted Randi a labor charge of $3.75 per square yard. What will the total job cost Randi?

3–75. Paul Rey bought 4 new Dunlop tires at Goodyear for $95.99 per tire. Goodyear charged $3.05 per tire for mounting, $2.95 per tire for valve stems, and $3.80 per tire for balancing. If Paul paid no sales tax, what was his total cost for the 4 tires?

3–76. Shelly is shopping for laundry detergent, mustard, and canned tuna. She is trying to decide which of two products is the better buy. Using the following information, can you help Shelly?

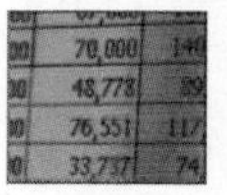

Laundry detergent A	**Mustard A**	**Canned tuna A**
$2.00 for 37 ounces	$.88 for 6 ounces	$1.09 for 6 ounces
Laundry detergent B	**Mustard B**	**Canned tuna B**
$2.37 for 38 ounces	$1.61 for $12\frac{1}{2}$ ounces	$1.29 for $8\frac{3}{4}$ ounces

3–77. Roger bought season tickets for weekend games to professional basketball games. The cost was $945.60. The season package included 36 home games. What is the average price of the tickets per game? Round to the nearest cent. Marcelo, Roger's friend, offered to buy 4 of the tickets from Roger. What is the total amount Roger should receive?

3–78. A nurse was to give each of her patients a 1.32-unit dosage of a prescribed drug. The total remaining units of the drug at the hospital pharmacy were 53.12. The nurse has 38 patients. Will there be enough dosages for all her patients?

3–79. Audrey Long went to Japan and bought an animation cel of Mickey Mouse. The price was 25,000 yen. What is the price in U.S. dollars? Check your answer.

ADDITIONAL SET OF WORD PROBLEMS

3–80. On Monday, the stock of Google closed at $488.40. At the end of trading on Tuesday, Google closed at $492.80. How much did the price of stock increase from Monday to Tuesday?

3–81. Tie Yang bought season tickets to the Boston Pops for $698.55. The season package included 38 performances. What is the average price of the tickets per performance? Round to nearest cent. Sam, Tie's friend, offered to buy 4 of the tickets from Tie. What is the total amount Tie should receive?

3–82. Morris Katz bought 4 new tires at Goodyear for $95.49 per tire. Goodyear also charged Morris $2.50 per tire for mounting, $2.40 per tire for valve stems, and $3.95 per tire for balancing. Assume no tax. What was Morris's total cost for the 4 tires?

3–83. The *Denver Post* reported that Xcel Energy is revising customer charges for monthly residential electric bills and gas bills. Electric bills will increase $3.32. Gas bills will decrease $1.74 a month. **(a)** What is the resulting new monthly increase for the entire bill? **(b)** If Xcel serves 2,350 homes, how much additional revenue would Xcel receive each month?

3–84. Steven is traveling to a auto show by car. His company will reimburse him $.29 per mile. If Steven travels 890.5 miles, how much will he receive from his company?

3–85. Gracie went to Home Depot to buy wall-to-wall carpeting for her house. She needs 104.8 square yards for downstairs, 17.4 square yards for halls, and 165.8 square yards for the upstairs bedrooms. Gracie chose a shag carpet that costs $13.95 per square yard. She ordered foam padding at $2.75 per square yard. The installers quoted Gracie a labor cost of $5.75 per square yard in installation. What will the total job cost Gracie?

CHALLENGE PROBLEMS

3–86. The DeQuarto family is planning a 14-day trip to Colorado. Debbie, Mike, and their three kids, Courtney, Alexis, and Andres, will be going. They want to compare costs between driving and flying. They found a flight for $210 round-trip per person. The airport is 15 miles from their home and charges $10 per night in parking. If they drove, they would be traveling 900 miles one way. Gas is $2.92 and their vehicle gets 24 miles a gallon. They would need to stay in a hotel two nights each way. The estimated hotel cost is $110 a night. Because they have to eat whether they drive or fly, they are not concerned with those costs. Do you recommend they fly or drive?

3–87. Jill and Frank decided to take a long weekend in New York. City Hotel has a special getaway weekend for $79.95. The price is per person per night, based on double occupancy. The hotel has a minimum two-night stay. For this price, Jill and Frank will receive $50 credit toward their dinners at City's Skylight Restaurant. Also included in the package is a $3.99 credit per person toward breakfast for two each morning.

Since Jill and Frank do not own a car, they plan to rent a car. The car rental agency charges $19.95 a day with an additional charge of $.22 a mile and $1.19 per gallon of gas used. The gas tank holds 24 gallons.

From the following facts, calculate the total expenses of Jill and Frank (round all answers to nearest hundredth or cent as appropriate). Assume no taxes.

Car rental (2 days):		Dinner cost at Skylight	$182.12
Beginning odometer reading	4,820	Breakfast for two:	
Ending odometer reading	4,940	Morning No. 1	24.17
Beginning gas tank: $\frac{3}{4}$ full.		Morning No. 2	26.88
Gas tank on return: $\frac{1}{7}$ full.			
Tank holds 24 gallons.			

DVD SUMMARY PRACTICE TEST

1. Add the following by translating the verbal form to the decimal equivalent. *(pp. 67, 71)*

Three hundred thirty-eight and seven hundred five thousandths
Nineteen and fifty-nine hundredths
Five and four thousandths
Seventy-five hundredths
Four hundred three and eight tenths

Convert the following decimal fractions to decimals. *(p. 68)*

2. $\frac{7}{10}$ **3.** $\frac{7}{100}$ **4.** $\frac{7}{1{,}000}$

Convert the following to proper fractions or mixed numbers. Do not reduce to the lowest terms. *(p. 69)*

5. .9 **6.** 6.97 **7.** .685

Convert the following fractions to decimals (or mixed decimals) and round to the nearest hundredth as needed. *(p. 69)*

8. $\frac{2}{7}$ **9.** $\frac{1}{8}$ **10.** $4\frac{4}{7}$ **11.** $\frac{1}{13}$

12. Rearrange the following decimals and add. *(p. 71)*

5.93, 11.862, 284.0382, 88.44

13. Subtract the following and round to the nearest tenth. *(p. 72)*

13.111 − 3.872

14. Multiply the following and round to the nearest hundredth. *(p. 73)*

7.4821 × 15.861

15. Divide the following and round to the nearest hundredth. *(p. 73)*

203,942 ÷ 5.88

Complete the following by the shortcut method. *(p. 74)*

16. 62.94 × 1,000

17. 8,322,249.821 × 100

18. The average pay of employees is $795.88 per week. Lee earns $820.44 per week. How much is Lee's pay over the average? *(p. 72)*

19. Lowes reimburses Ron $.49 per mile. Ron submitted a travel log for a total of 1,910.81 miles. How much will Lowes reimburse Ron? Round to the nearest cent. *(p. 73)*

20. Lee Chin bought 2 new car tires from Michelin for $182.11 per tire. Michelin also charged Lee $3.99 per tire for mounting, $2.50 per tire for valve stems, and $4.10 per tire for balancing. What is Lee's final bill? *(pp. 71, 73)*

21. Could you help Judy decide which of the following products is cheaper per ounce? *(p. 73)*

Canned fruit A	**Canned fruit B**
$.37 for 3 ounces	$.58 for $3\frac{3}{4}$ ounces

22. Paula Smith bought an iPod for 350 euros. What is this price in U.S. dollars? *(p. 73)*

23. Google stock traded at a high of $438.22 and closed at $410.12. How much did the stock fall from its high? *(p. 72)*

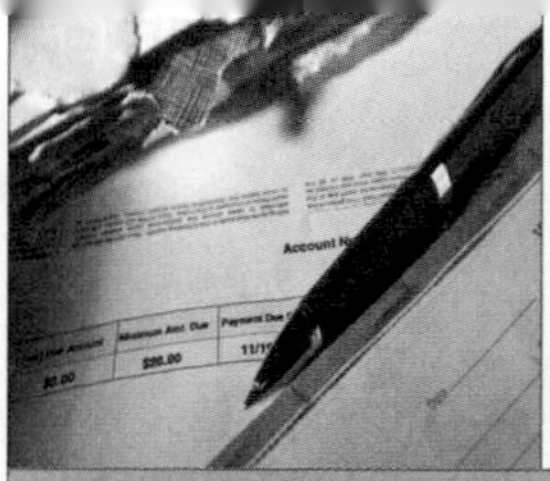

Personal Finance

A KIPLINGER APPROACH

NATURAL GAS GLUT

PROFIT FROM THE SURPLUS WITH AN ETF.

Natural gas doesn't get much respect. In early June, domestic gas traded at $3.74 per million cubic feet, near its six-year low. Meanwhile, traders had pushed the price of oil to $69 a barrel, up from its recent low of $33 in December. In terms of the two carbon-based commodities' energy-equivalent prices, oil is now some three times costlier than gas. In an age of environmental awareness, that doesn't make sense: Gas is cleaner; it has a future as a fuel for buses, cars and trucks; and it's popular in heavy industry and for power generation. Right now, there's a glut of gas in storage, but energy surpluses have a habit of vanishing quickly. The easiest way to bet on the price of gas is exchange-traded **UNITED STATES NATURAL GAS** fund **(UNG)**, which tracks changes in the price of gas by buying futures contracts. Note, however, that the fund is set up as a limited partnership, so you may face tax hassles.

PENNY-PINCHING BROKERS

WE PICK FIRMS FOR TWO KINDS OF INVESTORS.

BEST FOR TRADERS: JUST2TRADE

If low-cost trades are what you're after, look no further than Just2Trade (www.just2trade.com). It charges just $2.50 for stock, exchange-traded-fund and mutual fund transactions on trades of any size. But don't expect many frills or access to outside research—this broker is bare-bones.

You can open an account with $2,500, and you won't pay account-maintenance or inactivity fees. The site courts market-savvy types, so it requires that new customers have at least two years' experience using another online broker.

BEST FOR AVERAGE INVESTORS: FIDELITY

Fidelity (www.fidelity.com) boasts reasonable commissions and no maintenance fees, plus a world of user-friendly extras. Stock commissions range from $8 per trade to $19.95 per transaction for up to 1,000 shares, depending on your account's size and how often you trade. You can invest in 1,400 funds without paying sales or transaction fees, although you'll get hit with a stiff $75 commission for straying from this list. But you also get access to stock research from 18 different firms and useful asset-allocation and retirement-planning tools.

COUPON QUEEN

SAVING MONEY WITH SCISSORS IS A PASSION, NOT A PAIN.

You may begin your weekend by perusing the newspaper and savoring a cup of coffee. Sara Moothart starts her Saturday by scouring the advertising circulars for the week's best deals and clipping coupons.

Moothart, 31, of Baltimore, began "couponing" as a way to stretch her graduate-student budget. She buys groceries for herself and a roommate, and the value of the coupons alone saves her almost $40 a month. She reckons that she has saved triple that amount by leveraging the coupons against store markdowns.

Each week, Moothart reviews the offerings of three local grocery stores as well as Target. She creates a list for each store, taking note of relevant coupons, and sorts her collection in an accordion organizer labeled by section of the store. She also visits CouponMom.com to find more discounts and links to other Web sites. Moothart uses coupons to buy only what she will use—for example, she and her roommate eat fresh foods, so she skips the ubiquitous coupons for processed products. She buys items in large quantities only if she can freeze them or if they're nonperishable and she'll use them quickly.

The savings, which Moothart records in a notebook, have fired her passion for more couponing. And she's been thinking about putting aside the money she saves for something special—say, airfare to visit her family on the West Coast or a weekend getaway.

TOP TIPS

Plan your shopping list around sale items.

Look for stores that double or triple a coupon's value.

If "buy one, get one free" means you pay half price for each item, use two coupons.

From Kiplinger's Personal Finance, August 2009, p. 65.

BUSINESS MATH ISSUE

Natural gas will never replace gasoline in automobiles.

1. List the key points of the article and information to support your position.
2. Write a group defense of your position using math calculations to support your view.

PROJECT A

Assuming you drove the Toyota Prius 15,000 miles this year, what would be your total gas cost assuming 48 miles per gallon?

Slater's Business Math Scrapbook

Applying Your Skills

Comparing Costs of Hybrid Cars

A look at 2008 hybrid models, which generally cost more than their gas-powered counterparts. An analysis shows the amount of time it would take a buyer to break even—where fuel savings offset the premium paid for a hybrid model. Estimates are based on a car driven 15,000 miles annually, with gas that costs $4.01 a gallon.

2008 model	Final net price**	Hybrid premium***	MPG (city/hwy)	Annual gas savings	Years to break even
Toyota Prius	$22,939	$3,708	48/45	$1,073	3.5
Nissan Altima*	22,666	1,879	35/33	499	3.8
GMC Yukon*	47,653	5,680	21/22	1,170	4.9
Toyota Camry	25,732	3,046	33/34	562	5.4
Mercury Mariner*	24,946	4,324	34/30	784	5.5
Ford Escape*	24,051	4,622	34/30	784	5.9
Honda Civic*	21,082	3,601	40/45	587	6.1

2008 model	Final net price**	Hybrid premium***	MPG (city/hwy)	Annual gas savings	Years to break even
Saturn Vue*	$24,445	$4,570	27/32	$661	6.9
Lexus RX400H	39,923	5,069	26/24	731	6.9
Chevy Malibu*	22,931	1,867	24/32	171	10.9
Chevy Tahoe*	46,862	11,058	21/22	800	13.8
Toyota Highlander	40,921	10,805	27/25	603	17.9
Saturn Aura*	22,990	5,295	24/32	171	31
Lexus LS600H	102,423	18,858	20/22	192	98.5

*Vehicles with available tax credit; **Final net price is average national figure; ***Amount the car exceeds the cost of a comparable gas-powered model.

Source: Edmunds.com

Consumer Purchases

	2005	2006	2007
Single-Family Home Median resale price	$219,600[1]	$221,900[1]	$217,600[2]
Toyota Camry Manufacturer's suggested retail price for the LE manual transmission	$19,545	$19,725	$20,025
Unleaded Gasoline Average national price per gallon for all grades of unleaded gasoline combined, including taxes	$2.32	$2.60	$2.82
Pair of Jeans Gap's Easy Fit, stonewashed, starting price	$39.50	$39.50	$44.50
Internet Service Average monthly subscription cost for broadband cable service from Comcast, standard tier	$42.95	$42.95	$42.95
Tax Preparation Average cost of federal, state and local tax return preparation by H&R Block	$146.75[1]	$155.20[1]	$165.06
Hospital Stay Average cost of one day in a semiprivate room, including ancillary services except private physician's fee (Cleveland)	$4,848	$5,261	$5,504
McDonald's Big Mac Average price for company-owned restaurants. Prices vary at independently owned franchised locations	$2.43[1]	$2.57[1]	$2.76[2]

PROJECT B

If you bought 25 movie tickets in 2007. How much more expensive were they than they were in 2005?

	2005	2006	2007
Clearing Clogged Sink Roto-Rooter sewer and drain service, residential nat'l avera	$212.00	$230.55[1]	$243.46[3]
Movie Ticket Average price for all tickets sold at all prices at all times	$6.41	$6.55	$6.82[4]
Airline Ticket Domestic round-trip, based on a 2,000-mile trip, excluding aviation taxes	$246	$260[1]	$258[3]
Birth Average hospital cost for mother and child, excluding private physician's fee (Cleveland)	$7,907	$8,162	$9,873
A Year in College In-state, including room and board and fees, undergraduate student at Penn State	$17,799	$19,014	$20,024
Funeral National average, excluding cemetery costs	$6,734[1]	$6,951[1]	$7,170

[1]Revised [2]Preliminary [3]Through October [4]Through September

Sources: National Association of Realtors; Lundberg Survey; National Association of Theatre Owners; Air Transport Association of America; Federated Funeral Directors of America; Medical Mutual of Ohio

Internet Projects: See text Web site (www.mhhe.com/slater10e) and The Business Math Internet Resource Guide.

CUMULATIVE REVIEW

A Word Problem Approach—Chapters 1, 2, 3

1. The top rate at the Waldorf Towers Hotel in New York is $390. The top rate at the Ritz Carlton in Boston is $345. If John spends 9 days at the hotel, how much can he save if he stays at the Ritz? *(p. 10)*

2. Robert Half Placement Agency was rated best by 4 to 1 in an independent national survey. If 250,000 responded to the survey, how many rated Robert Half the best? *(p. 47)*

3. Of the 63.2 million people who watch professional football, only $\frac{1}{5}$ watch the commercials. How many viewers do not watch the commercials? *(p. 47)*

4. AT&T advertised a 10-minute call for $2.27. MCI WorldCom's rate was $2.02. Assuming Bill Splat makes forty 10-minute calls, how much could he save by using MCI WorldCom? *(p. 14)*

5. A square foot of rental space in New York City, Boston, and Rhode Island costs as follows: New York City, $6.25; Boston, $5.75; and Rhode Island, $3.75. If Compaq Computer wants to rent 112,500 square feet of space, what will Compaq save by renting in Rhode Island rather than Boston? *(p. 14)*

6. American Airlines has a frequent-flier program. Coupon brokers who buy and sell these awards pay between 1 and $1\frac{1}{2}$ cents for each mile earned. Fred Dietrich earned a 50,000-mile award (worth two free tickets to any city). If Fred decided to sell his award to a coupon broker, approximately how much would he receive? *(p. 71)*

7. Lillie Wong bought 4 new Firestone tires at $82.99 each. Firestone also charged $2.80 per tire for mounting, $1.95 per tire for valves, and $3.15 per tire for balancing. Lillie turned her 4 old tires in to Firestone, which charged $1.50 per tire to dispose of them. What was Lillie's final bill? *(p. 72)*

8. Tootsie Roll Industries bought Charms Company for $65 million. Some analysts believe that in 4 years the purchase price could rise to 3 times as much. If the analysts are right, how much did Tootsie Roll save by purchasing Charms immediately? *(p. 10)*

9. Today the average business traveler will spend $47.73 a day on food. The breakdown is dinner, $22.26; lunch, $10.73; breakfast, $6.53; tips, $6.23; and tax, $1.98. If Clarence Donato, an executive for Honeywell, spends only .33 of the average, what is Clarence's total cost for food for the day? If Clarence wanted to spend $\frac{1}{3}$ more than the average on the next day, what would be his total cost on the second day? Round to the nearest cent. *(p. 71)*

Be sure you use the fractional equivalent in calculating $.3\overline{3}$.

chapter

4 BANKING

Bank Suspends Overdraft Fee Increase

By Jane J. Kim

Bank of America Corp. is suspending a previously announced rise in its overdraft fees. Earlier this month, the bank sent notices to customers, announcing pricing changes scheduled to go into effect June 5 that would have raised the overdraft fee to $39 from $35 per item. On Monday, citing the "increase in unemployment," the bank said it was suspending that increase and keeping the fee at $35, according to spokesman Jim Pierpoint.

The bank is also introducing a program for customers who have lost their jobs, where it will waive monthly account-maintenance fees for three months, and will refund or waive insufficient funds and overdraft fees for some customers on a case-by-case basis.

Among the other changes to take effect in June: Customers will be hit with another $35 fee if their account is overdrawn for more than five days. Meanwhile, the bank is raising monthly maintenance fees on certain checking accounts, as well as the balance requirements needed to avoid fees.

The changes represent the second time this year that Bank of America has tinkered with its overdraft program.

LEARNING UNIT OBJECTIVES

LU 4–1: The Checking Account

1. Define and state the purpose of signature cards, checks, deposit slips, check stubs, check registers, and endorsements *(pp. 90–93).*
2. Correctly prepare deposit slips and write checks *(pp. 90–93).*

LU 4–2: Bank Statement and Reconciliation Process; Trends in Online Banking

1. Explain trends in the banking industry *(pp. 93–94).*
2. Define and state the purpose of the bank statement *(pp. 94–95).*
3. Complete a check register and a bank reconciliation *(pp. 95–98).*
4. Explain the trends in online banking pro and con *(p. 99).*

VOCABULARY PREVIEW

Here are the key terms in this chapter. When you finish the chapter, if you feel you know the term, place a checkmark within the parentheses following the term. If you are not certain of the definition, look it up and write the page number where it can be found in the text. The chapter organizer includes page references to the terms. There is also a complete glossary at the end of the text.

Automatic teller machine (ATM) . ( ) Bank reconciliation . ( ) Bank statement . ( ) Blank endorsement . ( ) Check . ( ) Check register . ( ) Check stub . ( ) Credit memo (CM) . ( ) Debit card . ( ) Debit memo (DM) . ( ) Deposit slip . ( ) Deposits in transit . ( ) Draft . ( ) Drawee . ( ) Drawer . ( ) Electronic funds transfer (EFT) . ( ) Endorse . ( ) Full endorsement . ( ) Nonsufficient funds (NSF) . ( ) Outstanding checks . ( ) Overdrafts . ( ) Payee . ( ) Restrictive endorsement . ( ) Signature card . ( )

Social Security Administration/AP Images

New Social-Security Debit Cards

WASHINGTON—As part of a program that could save taxpayers millions, the Treasury Department Tuesday will start offering prepaid debit cards to Social Security recipients in 10 states.

The card, to be issued by Dallas-based **Comerica** Inc., will be available to recipients of Social Security or Supplemental Security Income checks who live in Alabama, Arkansas, Florida, Georgia, Louisiana, Mississippi, North Carolina, Oklahoma, South Carolina and Texas. The Treasury plans to launch the program nationwide this summer.

The program enables recipients without bank accounts to get their monthly benefit payments electronically.

Wall Street Journal © 2008

Many people getting Social Security may be able to get their monthly payments even if they do not have a bank account. The *Wall Street Journal* clip "New Social-Security Debit Cards" states the Treasury Department will offer prepaid debit cards.

An important fixture in today's banking is the **automatic teller machine (ATM).** The ability to get instant cash is a convenience many bank customers enjoy.

The effect of using an ATM card is the same as using a **debit card**—both transactions result in money being immediately deducted from your checking account balance. As a result, debit cards have been called enhanced ATM cards or *check cards*. Often banks charge fees for these card transactions. The frequent complaints of bank customers have made many banks offer their ATMs as a free service, especially if customers use an ATM in the same network as their bank. Some banks charge fees for using another bank's ATM.

Remember that the use of debit cards involves planning. As *check cards,* you must be aware of your bank balance every time you use a debit card. Also, if you use a credit card instead of a debit card, you can only be held responsible for $50 of illegal charges; and during the time the credit card company investigates the illegal charges, they are removed from your account. However, with a debit card, this legal limit only applies if you report your card lost or stolen within two business days.

This chapter begins with a discussion of the checking account. You will follow Molly Kate as she opens a checking account for Gracie's Natural Superstore and performs her banking transactions. Pay special attention to the procedure used by Gracie's to reconcile its checking account and bank statement. This information will help you reconcile your checkbook records with the bank's record of your account. The chapter concludes by discussing how the trends in online banking may affect your banking procedures.

Learning Unit 4–1: The Checking Account

LO 1

A **check** or **draft** is a written order instructing a bank, credit union, or savings and loan institution to pay a designated amount of your money on deposit to a person or an organization. Checking accounts are offered to individuals and businesses. Note that the business checking account usually receives more services than the personal checking account but may come with additional fees.

Most small businesses depend on a checking account for efficient record keeping. In this learning unit you will follow the checking account procedures of a newly organized small business. You can use many of these procedures in your personal check writing. You will also learn about e-checks—a new trend.

Opening the Checking Account

Molly Kate, treasurer of Gracie's Natural Superstore, went to Ipswich Bank to open a business checking account. The bank manager gave Molly a **signature card.** The signature card contained space for the company's name and address, references, type of account, and the signature(s) of the person(s) authorized to sign checks. If necessary, the bank will use the signature card to verify that Molly signed the checks. Some companies authorize more than one person to sign checks or require more than one signature on a check.

Molly then lists on a **deposit slip** (or deposit ticket) the checks and/or cash she is depositing in her company's business account. The bank gave Molly a temporary checkbook to use until the company's printed checks arrived. Molly also will receive *preprinted* checking account deposit slips like the one shown in Figure 4.1 below. Since the deposit slips are in duplicate, Molly can keep a record of her deposit. Note that the increased use of making deposits at ATM machines has made it more convenient for people to make their deposits.

LO 2

Writing business checks is similar to writing personal checks. Before writing any checks, however, you must understand the structure of a check and know how to write a check. Carefully study Figure 4.2 (p. 91). Note that the verbal amount written in the check should match the figure amount. If these two amounts are different, by law the bank uses the verbal amount. Also, note the bank imprint on the bottom right section of the check. When processing the check, the bank imprints the check's amount. This makes it easy to detect bank errors.

FIGURE 4.1 Deposit slip

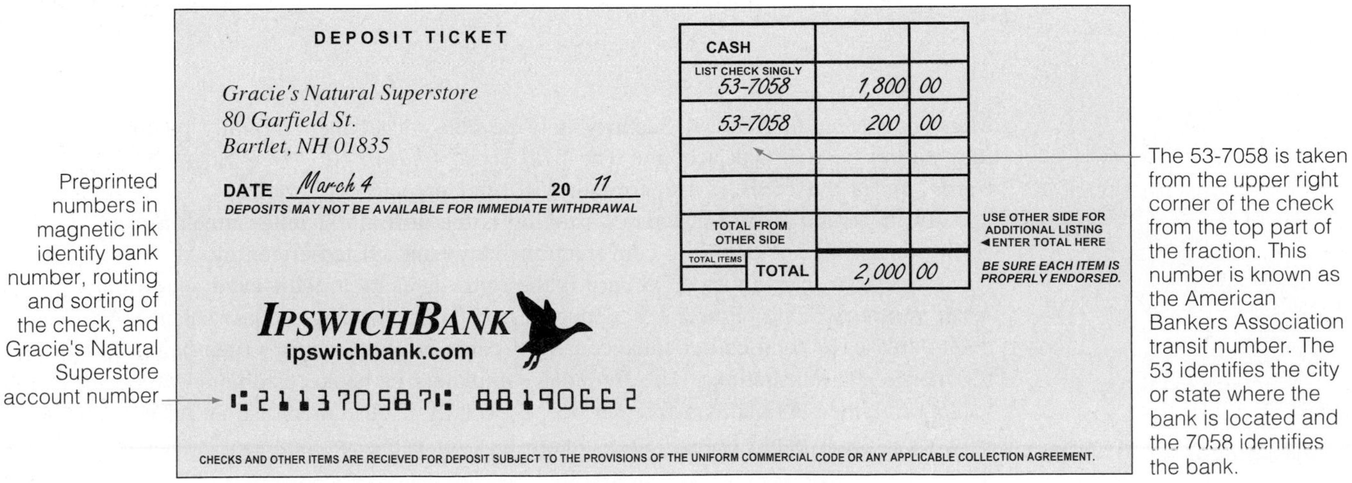
DEPOSIT TICKET

Gracie's Natural Superstore
80 Garfield St.
Bartlet, NH 01835

DATE *March 4* 20 *11*

DEPOSITS MAY NOT BE AVAILABLE FOR IMMEDIATE WITHDRAWAL

CASH		
LIST CHECK SINGLY 53-7058	1,800	00
53-7058	200	00
TOTAL FROM OTHER SIDE		
TOTAL ITEMS / TOTAL	2,000	00

USE OTHER SIDE FOR ADDITIONAL LISTING ◄ENTER TOTAL HERE

BE SURE EACH ITEM IS PROPERLY ENDORSED.

IPSWICHBANK
ipswichbank.com

⑆211370587⑆ 88190662

CHECKS AND OTHER ITEMS ARE RECIEVED FOR DEPOSIT SUBJECT TO THE PROVISIONS OF THE UNIFORM COMMERCIAL CODE OR ANY APPLICABLE COLLECTION AGREEMENT.

FIGURE 4.2 The structure of a check

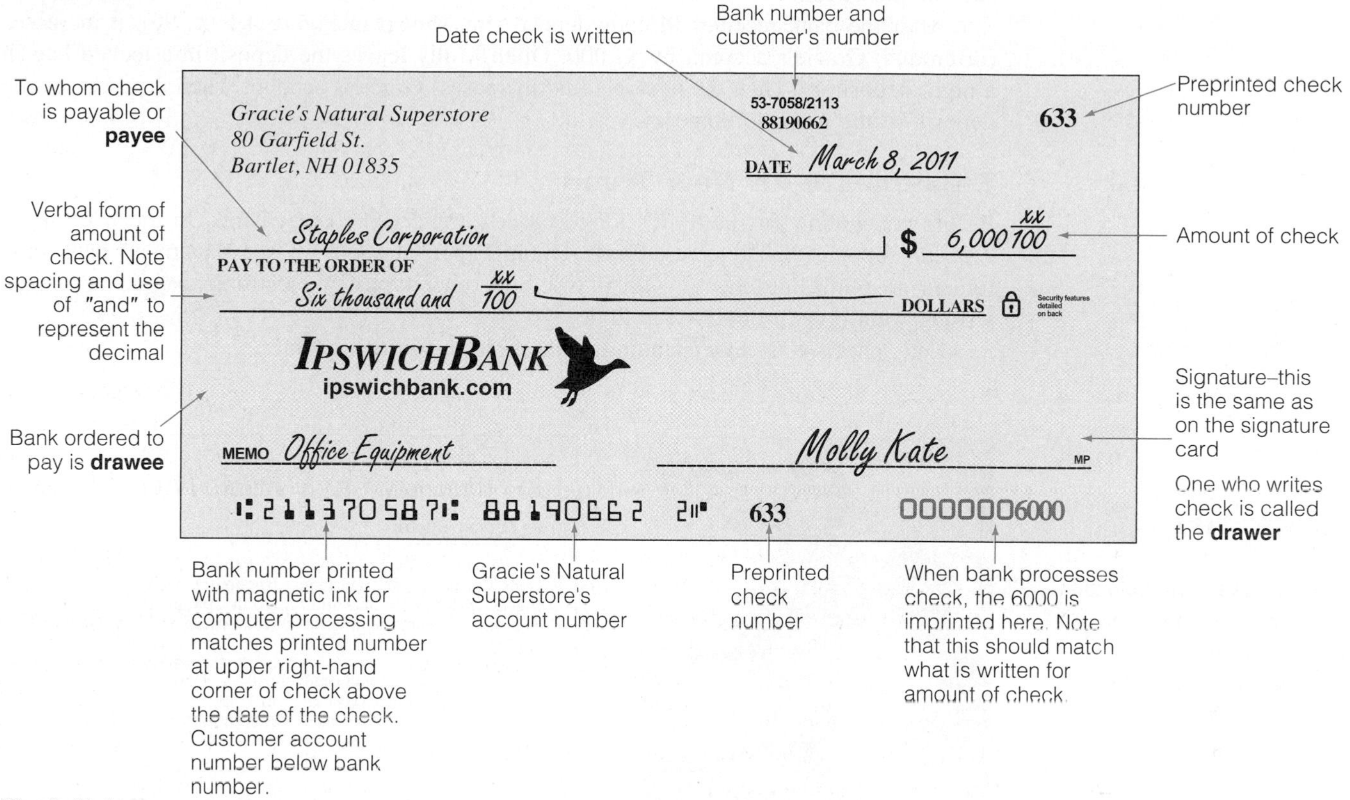

Check Stub
It should be completed before the check is written.

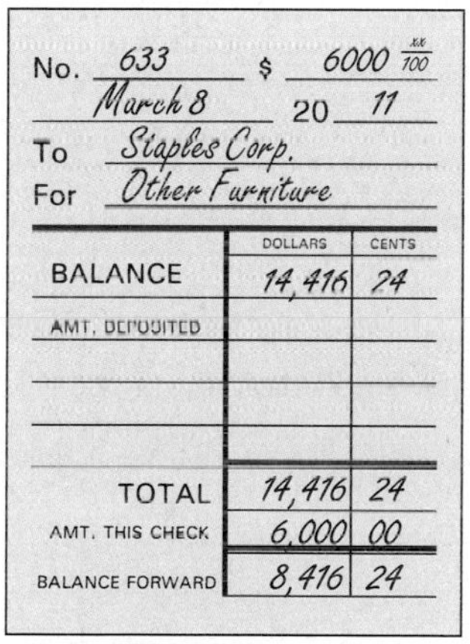

Using the Checking Account

Once the check is written, the writer must keep a record of the check. Knowing the amount of your written checks and the amount in the bank should help you avoid writing a bad check. Business checkbooks usually include attached **check stubs** to keep track of written checks. The sample check stub in the margin shows the information that the check writer will want to record. Some companies use a **check register** to keep their check records instead of check stubs. Figure 4.6 (p. 96) shows a check register with a ✓ column that is often used in balancing the checkbook with the bank statement (Learning Unit 4–2).

Gracie's Natural Superstore has had a busy week, and Molly must deposit its checks in the company's checking account. However, before she can do this, Molly must **endorse,** or sign, the back left side of the checks. Figure 4.3 below explains the three types of check endorsements: **blank endorsement, full endorsement,** and **restrictive endorsement.** These endorsements transfer Gracie's ownership to the bank, which

FIGURE 4.3

Types of common endorsements

A. Blank Endorsement

Gracie's Natural Superstore
88190662

The company stamp or a signature alone on the back left side of a check legally makes the check payable to anyone holding the check. It can be *further* endorsed. This is not a safe type of endorsement.

B. Full Endorsement

Pay to the order of
Ipswich Bank
Gracie's Natural Superstore
88190662

Safer type of endorsement since Gracie's Natural Superstore indicates the name of the company or person to whom the check is to be payable to. Only the person or company named in the endorsement can transfer the check to someone else.

C. Restrictive Endorsement

Pay to the order of
Ipswich Bank
For deposit only
Gracie's Natural Superstore
88190662

Safest endorsement for businesses. Gracie's stamps the back of the check so that this check must be deposited in the firm's bank account. This limits any further negotiation of the check.

collects the money from the person or company issuing the check. Federal Reserve regulation limits all endorsements to the top $1\frac{1}{2}$ inches of the trailing edge on the back left side of the check.

After the bank receives Molly's deposit slip, shown in Figure 4.1 (p. 90), it increases (or credits) Gracie's account by $2,000. Often Molly leaves the deposit in a locked bag in a night depository. Then the bank credits (increases) Gracie's account when it processes the deposit on the next working day.

E-Payments—A New Trend

Before concluding this unit, let's look at a new trend using e-payments. In the *Wall Street Journal* clipping "E-Payments, Cards Trump Paper Checks" we see that many bank customers are replacing checks with plastic and other types of electronic payments. Check writing went down from 2003 to 2006.

Let's check your understanding of the first unit in this chapter.

$ MONEY TIPS

Apply for overdraft protection on each of your checking or draft accounts. Because mistakes happen, it is best to be prepared. This can also help during cash flow problems if you ever need it.

Flying colors Ltd./Getty Images

E-Payments, Cards Trump Paper Checks

By Sudeep Reddy

Bye-bye, checks, hello, debit cards. Consumers are replacing checks with plastic and other electronic payments at an accelerating pace, a new Federal Reserve study says.

Electronic payments—including credit and debit cards—accounted for more than two-thirds of the 93.3 billion noncash transactions in the U.S. last year.

Debit cards are now the most frequently used type of electronic payment, surpassing credit cards, the Fed said. Consumers made about 25.3 billion debit transactions—about $1 trillion worth—compared with 21.7 billion credit-card purchases valued at $2.1 trillion.

Wall Street Journal © 2007

LU 4–1 PRACTICE QUIZ

Complete this **Practice Quiz** to see how you are doing.

Complete the following check and check stub for Long Company. Note the $9,500.60 balance brought forward on check stub No. 113. You must make a $690.60 deposit on May 3. Sign the check for Roland Small.

Date	Check no.	Amount	Payable to	For
June 5, 2011	113	$83.76	Angel Corporation	Rent

No. *113* $ ______

______ 20 ______

To ______

For ______

	DOLLARS	CENTS
BALANCE	*9,500*	*60*
AMT. DEPOSITED		
TOTAL		
AMT. THIS CHECK		
BALANCE FORWARD		

Long Company
22 Aster Rd.
Salem, MA 01970

No. 113

______ 20 ______ 5-13/110

PAY TO THE ORDER OF ______ $ ______

______ DOLLARS

IPSWICHBANK
ipswichbank.com

MEMO ______

⑆011000138⑆ 14 0380 113

Solution with Step-by-Step Help on DVD

✓ **Solution**

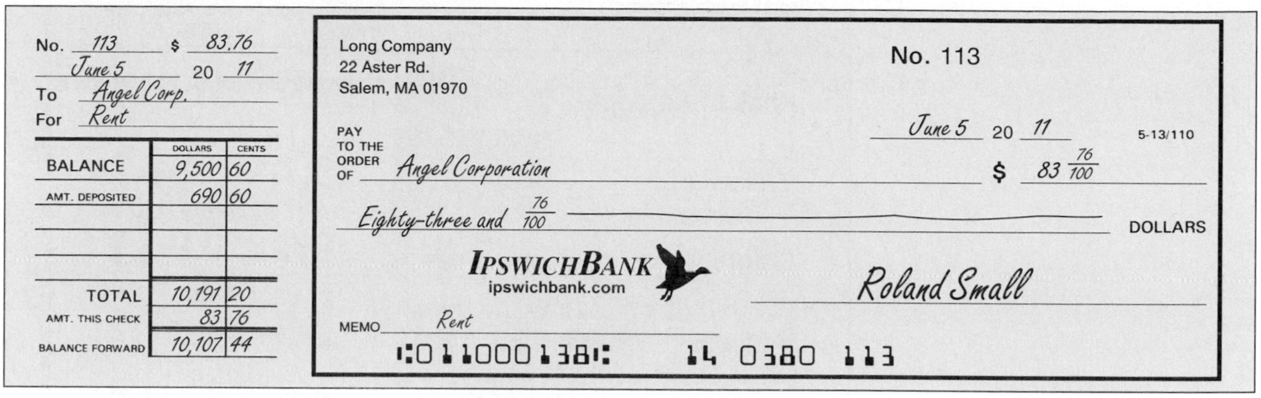

LU 4–1a EXTRA PRACTICE QUIZ WITH WORKED-OUT SOLUTIONS

Need more practice? Try this **Extra Practice Quiz** (check figures in Chapter Organizer, p. 101). Worked-out Solutions can be found in Appendix B at end of text.

Complete the following check and stub for Long Company. Note the $10,800.80 balance brought forward on check stub No. 113. You must make an $812.88 deposit on May 3. Sign the check for Roland Small.

Date	Check No.	Amount	Payable to	For
July 8, 2011	113	$79.88	Lowe Corp	Advertising

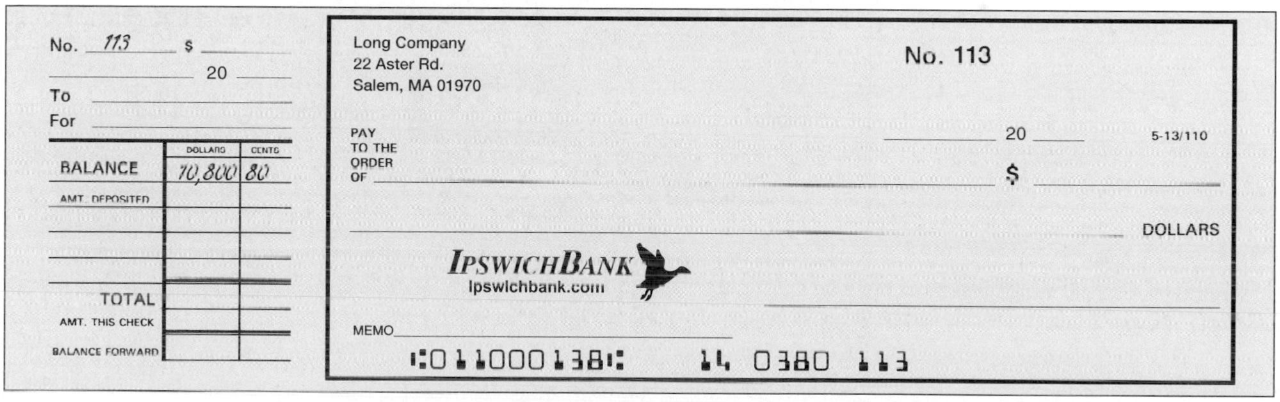

Learning Unit 4–2: Bank Statement and Reconciliation Process; Trends in Online Banking

Trends in Banking Industry[1]

Since 2008 trends in banking have been changing rapidly. The government has been involved in many bailout packages due to the financial crises. Some banks have had to close or merge. The following *Wall Street Journal* clip on stress test for banks shows the results of stress tests that evaluate how big banks are doing and if they need more capital. Take a moment to look at the stress test scorecard on top of page 94.

The rest of this learning unit is divided into two sections: (1) bank statement and reconciliation process, and (2) trends in online banking. The bank statement discussion will teach you why it was important for Gracie's Natural Superstore to reconcile its checkbook balance with the balance reported on its bank balance. Note that you can also use this reconciliation process in reconciling your personal checking account and avoiding the expensive error of an overdrawn account.

[1]Check my Web site for the latest updates on banking bailouts and government intervention. www.mhhe.com/slater10e.

Stress Test Scorecard
How key banks fared

	Capital needed in billions	Worst-case loss estimates in billions
Bank of America	$33.9	$136.6
Wells Fargo	13.7	86.1
Citigroup	5.5	104.7
Regions Financial	2.5	9.2
SunTrust	2.2	11.8
KeyCorp	1.8	6.7
Fifth Third	1.1	9.1
PNC Financial	0.6	18.8
U.S. Bancorp	NONE	15.7
J.P. Morgan Chase	NONE	97.4
BB&T	NONE	8.7
Capital One	NONE	13.4

LO 2

Bank Statement and Reconciliation Process

Each month, Ipswich Bank sends Gracie's Natural Superstore a **bank statement** (Figure 4.4, p. 95). We are interested in the following:

1. Beginning bank balance.
2. Total of all the account increases. Each time the bank increases the account amount, it *credits* the account.
3. Total of all account decreases. Each time the bank decreases the account amount, it *debits* the account.
4. Final ending balance.

Due to differences in timing, the bank balance on the bank statement frequently does not match the customer's checkbook balance. Also, the bank statement can show transactions that have not been entered in the customer's checkbook. Figure 4.5, p. 95, tells you what to look for when comparing a checkbook balance with a bank balance.

Gracie's Natural Superstore is planning to offer to its employees the option of depositing their checks directly into each employee's checking account. This is accomplished through the **electronic funds transfer (EFT)**—a computerized operation that electronically transfers funds among parties without the use of paper checks. Gracie's, who sublets space in the store, receives rental payments by EFT. Gracie's also has the bank pay the store's health insurance premiums by EFT.

FIGURE 4.4

Bank statement

Ipswich Bank
1 Pleasant St.
Bartlett, NH 01835

Account Statement

Gracie's Natural Superstore
80 Garfield St.
Bartlett, NH 01835

Checking Account: 881900662

Checking Account Summary as of 3/31/11

Beginning Balance	Total Deposits	Total Withdrawals	Service Charge	Ending Balance
$13,112.24	$8,705.28	$9,926.00	$28.50	$11,863.02

Checking Accounts Transactions

Deposits	Date	Amount
Deposit	3/05	2,000.00
Deposit	3/05	224.00
Deposit	3/09	389.20
EFT leasing: Bakery dept.	3/18	1,808.06
EFT leasing: Meat dept.	3/27	4,228.00
Interest	3/31	56.02

Charges	Date	Amount
Service charge: Check printing	3/31	28.50
EFT: Health insurance	3/21	722.00
NSF	3/21	104.00

Checks

Number	Date	Amount
301	3/07	200.00
633	3/13	6,000.00
634	3/13	300.00
635	3/11	200.00
636	3/18	200.00
637	3/31	2,200.00

Daily Balance

Date	Balance	Date	Balance
2/28	13,112.24	3/18	10,529.50
3/05	15,232.24	3/21	9,807.50
3/07	14,832.24	3/28	14,035.50
3/09	15,221.44	3/31	11,863.02
3/11	15,021.44		
3/13	8,721.44		

FIGURE 4.5

Reconciling checkbook with bank statement

Checkbook balance		Bank balance
+ EFT (electronic funds transfer)	− NSF check	+ Deposits in transit
+ Interest earned	− Online fees	− Outstanding checks
+ Notes collected	− Automatic payments*	± Bank errors
+ Direct deposits	− Overdrafts†	
− ATM withdrawals	− Service charges	
− Automatic withdrawals	− Stop payments‡	
	± Book errors§	

*Preauthorized payments for utility bills, mortgage payments, insurance, etc.

†**Overdrafts** occur when the customer has no overdraft protection and a check bounces back to the company or person who received the check because the customer has written a check without enough money in the bank to pay for it.

‡A stop payment is issued when the writer of the check does not want the receiver to cash the check.

§If a $60 check is recorded at $50, the checkbook balance must be decreased by $10.

To reconcile the difference between the amount on the bank statement and in the checkbook, the customer should complete a **bank reconciliation.** Today, many companies and home computer owners are using software such as Quicken and QuickBooks to complete their bank reconciliation. However, you should understand the following steps for manually reconciling a bank statement.

RECONCILING A BANK STATEMENT

Step 1. Identify the outstanding checks (checks written but not yet processed by the bank). You can use the ✓ column in the check register (Figure 4.6) to check the canceled checks listed in the bank statement against the checks you wrote in the check register. The unchecked checks are the outstanding checks.

Step 2. Identify the deposits in transit (deposits made but not yet processed by the bank), using the same method in Step 1.

Step 3. Analyze the bank statement for transactions not recorded in the check stubs or check registers (like EFT).

Step 4. Check for recording errors in checks written, in deposits made, or in subtraction and addition.

Step 5. Compare the adjusted balances of the checkbook and the bank statement. If the balances are not the same, repeat Steps 1–4.

Molly uses a check register (Figure 4.6) to keep a record of Gracie's checks and deposits. By looking at Gracie's check register, you can see how to complete Steps 1 and 2 above. The explanation that follows for the first four bank statement reconciliation steps will help you understand the procedure.

FIGURE 4.6

Gracie's Natural Superstore check register

RECORD ALL CHARGES OR CREDITS THAT AFFECT YOUR ACCOUNT

NUMBER	DATE 2007	DESCRIPTION OF TRANSACTION	PAYMENT/DEBIT (−)	√	FEE (IF ANY) (−)	DEPOSIT/CREDIT (+)	BALANCE
							$ 12,912 24
	3/04	Deposit				$ 2,000 00	+ 2,000 00 14,912 24
	3/04	Deposit				224 00	+ 224 00 15,136 24
633	3/08	Staples Company	6,000 00	✓			− 6,000 00 9,136 24
634	3/09	Health Foods Inc.	1,020 00	✓			− 1,020 00 8,116 24
	3/09	Deposit				389 20	+ 389 20 8,505 44
635	3/10	Liberty Insurance	200 00	✓			− 200 00 8,305 44
636	3/18	Ryan Press	200 00	✓			− 200 00 8,105 44
637	3/29	Logan Advertising	2,200 00	✓			− 2,200 00 5,905 44
	3/30	Deposit				3,383 26	+ 3,383 26 9,288 70
638	3/31	Sears Roebuck	572 00				− 572 00 8,716 70
639	3/31	Flynn Company	638 94				− 638 94 8,077 76
640	3/31	Lynn's Farm	166 00				− 166 00 7,911 76
641	3/31	Ron's Wholesale	406 28				− 406 28 7,505 48
642	3/31	Grocery Natural, Inc.	917 06				− 917 06 $6,588 42

REMEMBER TO RECORD AUTOMATIC PAYMENTS/DEPOSITS ON DATE AUTHORIZED.

Step 1. Identify Outstanding Checks

Outstanding checks are checks that Gracie's Natural Superstore has written but Ipswich Bank has not yet recorded for payment when it sends out the bank statement. Gracie's treasurer identifies the following checks written on 3/31 as outstanding:

No. 638	$572.00
No. 639	638.94
No. 640	166.00
No. 641	406.28
No. 642	917.06

Step 2. Identify Deposits in Transit

Deposits in transit are deposits that did not reach Ipswich Bank by the time the bank prepared the bank statement. The March 30 deposit of $3,383.26 did not reach Ipswich Bank by the bank statement date. You can see this by comparing the company's bank statement with its check register.

Step 3. Analyze Bank Statement for Transactions Not Recorded in Check Stubs or Check Register

The bank statement of Gracie's Natural Superstore (Figure 4.4, p. 95) begins with the deposits, or increases, made to Gracie's bank account. Increases to accounts are known as credits. These are the result of a **credit memo (CM).** Gracie's received the following increases or credits in March:

1. *EFT leasing:* $1,808.06 and $4,228.00. — Each month the bakery and meat departments pay for space they lease in the store.
2. *Interest credited:* $56.02. — Gracie's has a checking account that pays interest; the account has earned $56.02.

When Gracie's has charges against her bank account, the bank decreases, or debits, Gracie's account for these charges. Banks usually inform customers of a debit transaction by a **debit memo (DM).** The following items will result in debits to Gracie's account:

1. *Service charge:* $28.50 — The bank charged $28.50 for printing Gracie's checks.
2. *EFT payment:* $722. — The bank made a health insurance payment for Gracie's.
3. *NSF check:* $104. — One of Gracie's customers wrote Gracie's a check for $104. Gracie's deposited the check, but the check bounced for **nonsufficient funds (NSF).** Thus, Gracie's has $104 less than it figured.

Step 4. Check for Recording Errors

The treasurer of Gracie's Natural Superstore, Molly Kate, recorded check No. 634 for the wrong amount—$1,020 (see the check register). The bank statement showed that check No. 634 cleared for $300. To reconcile Gracie's checkbook balance with the bank balance, Gracie's must add $720 to its checkbook balance. Neglecting to record a deposit also results in an error in the company's checkbook balance. As you can see, reconciling the bank's balance with a checkbook balance is a necessary part of business and personal finance.

Step 5. Completing the Bank Reconciliation

Now we can complete the bank reconciliation on the back side of the bank statement as shown in Figure 4.7 (p. 98). This form is usually on the back of a bank statement. If necessary, however, the person reconciling the bank statement can construct a bank reconciliation form similar to Figure 4.8 (p. 98).

FIGURE 4.7

Reconciliation process

CHECKS OUTSTANDING
(NOT YET CHARGED TO ACCOUNT)

NUMBER OR DATE	DOLLARS	CENTS
638	$572	00
639	638	94
640	166	00
641	406	28
642	917	06
TOTAL	$2,700	28

CHECKING ACCOUNT RECONCILEMENT

Enter the new balance shown on the other side of this statement	$ 11,863.02
ADD	
Deposits not shown	3,383.26
ADD	
Advances and Transfers to Checking not shown.	
SUBTOTAL	15,246.28
DEDUCT	
Checks outstanding	2,700.28
SUBTOTAL	12,546.00
DEDUCT	
Transfers from Checking not shown	
This amount should agree with the balance in your checkbook register.	$ 12,546.00

Checkbook balance		$6,588.42
+ EFT leasing	$6,036.06	
+ Interest	56.02	
+ Checkbook error	720.00	6,812.08
– Service charge	$ 28.50	
– EFT: health insurance	722.00	
– NSF	104.00	854.50
Ending checkbook balance		$12,546.00

FIGURE 4.8

Bank reconciliation

GRACIE'S NATURAL SUPERSTORE
Bank Reconciliation as of March 31, 2011

Checkbook balance			Bank balance		
Gracie's checkbook balance		$6,588.42	Bank balance		$11,863.02
Add:			Add:		
EFT leasing: Bakery dept.	$1,808.06		Deposit in transit, 3/30		3,383.26
					$15,246.28
EFT leasing: Meat dept.	4,228.00				
Interest	56.02				
Error: Overstated check No. 634	720.00	$ 6,812.08			
		$13,400.50			
Deduct:			Deduct:		
Service charge	$ 28.50		Outstanding checks:		
NSF check	104.00		No. 638	$572.00	
EFT health insurance payment	722.00	854.50	No. 639	638.94	
			No. 640	166.00	
			No. 641	406.28	
			No. 642	917.06	2,700.28
Reconciled balance		$12,546.00	Reconciled balance		$12,546.00

LO 3

Trends in Online Banking: Pro and Con[2]

Did you know that banking online is quite safe? The *Wall Street Journal* clip "The Holdup at Online Banks" states that out of $41.7 trillion, about $969 million was lost in fraud. Note in this clip the pros and cons of online banking are discussed. With more and more people banking online, read this article carefully.

FAMILY MONEY

The Holdup at Online Banks

At a time of uncertainty in nearly every market, I'm a big fan of online savings accounts, many of which are paying 3% to 4% interest right now. But they have a frustrating quirk: Transferring money between a savings account at one bank and a checking account at another easily takes two days—and sometimes as many as four.

This delay has become more apparent and more irritating during the continuing financial crisis, as consumers seek two basics: safety and yield. (Yields on these savings accounts have tended to be higher than those on money-market accounts.)

By Karen Blumenthal

Online accounts, like all bank accounts, are protected by the Federal Deposit Insurance Corp. up to $250,000 per account holder. Offerings from **HSBC Holdings** PLC's HSBC Direct, **Emigrant Bank**'s EmigrantDirect and **First National of Nebraska** Inc.'s FNBO Direct typically have low minimum-balance requirements. They can be good places for holding your cash reserves or earning interest on money set aside for tax payments or tuition, especially since interest-bearing checking accounts and traditional bank savings accounts typically pay well below 1% interest.

But in a remarkably interconnected, instantaneous world, where a debit-card purchase shows up in our bank accounts right away, it's equally remarkable that online transfers can be so slow.

Here's the hitch: Funds transferred between two different banks or a bank and a brokerage firm aren't really sent "online" in the way we have come to expect. Instead, these large transfers move in steps. Banks have slowed down the process further to reduce the chance of fraud, even though such fraud is fairly rare. (Years ago, Congress forced banks to speed up the clearing of checks and the availability of deposits, but it hasn't addressed electronic payments.)

You may have seen this when you tried to move money to or from a brokerage account. I ran into it most recently when I went to my ING Direct savings account first thing on a Monday morning to transfer money for a new car to my Bank of America checking account. While it showed up as "pending" on Wednesday, it wasn't mine to spend until Thursday.

What happens during that time? ING sends transactions in batches during the day to an automated clearinghouse, which sorts them and moves them to the receiving bank in a matter of two to four hours, according to Arkadi Kuhlmann, chief executive officer of ING Direct USA, a unit of **ING Groep** NV, and Elliott C. McEntee, chief executive of Nacha, the Electronic Payments Association, a not-for-profit group that oversees the automated clearinghouses.

In many cases, the receiving bank gets the transfer the same day. Under rules established by Nacha, money that moves on Monday should be available by the end of Tuesday. If the transfer slips to early Tuesday morning, the money should be available first thing Wednesday morning.

But the money isn't always available that quickly. **Bank of America** Corp. says such transfers typically take two to three days. EmigrantDirect says on its Web site that transfers take two to four days, while HSBC Direct says customers should expect transfers to take up to three days. The industry calls this a "three-day good funds model," says David Goeden, an HSBC executive vice president in personal financial services. That is, the bank wants to make sure our funds are good before it lets us have them.

MONEY TIPS

It is critical to balance your checkbook regularly, but not less than monthly. You may be amazed at the errors you find. A bounced check can really cost you in bank charges and fees. Be aware that bounced checks may even show up on consumer reports ordered by potential employers for up to seven years, creating a potential problem during the job search.

[2]Be sure to read about mobile banking in Business Math Scrapbook.

LU 4–2 PRACTICE QUIZ

Complete the **Practice Quiz** to see how you are doing.

Rosa Garcia received her February 3, 2011, bank statement showing a balance of $212.80. Rosa's checkbook has a balance of $929.15. The bank statement showed that Rosa had an ATM fee of $12.00 and a deposited check returned fee of $20.00. Rosa earned interest of $1.05. She had three outstanding checks: No. 300, $18.20; No. 302, $38.40; and No. 303, $68.12. A deposit for $810.12 was not on her bank statement. Prepare Rosa Garcia's bank reconciliation.

Solution with Step-by-Step Help on DVD

✓ Solution

ROSA GARCIA
Bank Reconciliation as of February 3, 2011

Checkbook balance			Bank balance		
Rosa's checkbook balance		$929.15	Bank balance		$ 212.80
Add:			Add:		
Interest		1.05	Deposit in transit		810.12
		$930.20			$1,022.92
Deduct:			Deduct:		
Deposited check returned fee	$20.00		Outstanding checks:		
			No. 300	$18.20	
ATM	12.00	32.00	No. 302	38.40	
			No. 303	68.12	124.72
Reconciled balance		$898.20	Reconciled balance		$ 898.20

LU 4–2a EXTRA PRACTICE QUIZ WITH WORKED-OUT SOLUTIONS

Need more practice? Try this **Extra Practice Quiz** (check figures in Chapter Organizer, p. 101). Worked-out Solutions can be found in Appendix B at end of text.

Earl Miller received his March 8, 2011, bank statement, which had a $300.10 balance. Earl's checkbook has a $1,200.10 balance. The bank statement showed a $15.00 ATM fee and a $30.00 deposited check returned fee. Earl earned $24.06 interest. He had three outstanding checks: No. 300, $22.88; No. 302, $15.90; and No. 303, $282.66. A deposit for $1,200.50 was not on his bank statement. Prepare Earl's bank reconciliation.

CHAPTER ORGANIZER AND REFERENCE GUIDE

Topic	Key point, procedure, formula	Example(s) to illustrate situation
Types of endorsements, p. 91	*Blank:* Not safe; can be further endorsed.	Jones Co. 21-333-9
	Full: Only person or company named in endorsement can transfer check to someone else.	Pay to the order of Regan Bank Jones Co. 21-333-9
	Restrictive: Check must be deposited. Limits any further negotiation of the check.	Pay to the order of Regan Bank. For deposit only. Jones Co. 21-333-9
Bank reconciliation, p. 95	**Checkbook balance** + EFT (electronic funds transfer) + Interest earned + Notes collected + Direct deposits − ATM withdrawals − NSF check − Online fees − Automatic withdrawals − Overdrafts − Service charges − Stop payments ± Book errors* CM—adds to balance DM—deducts from balance **Bank balance** + Deposits in transit − Outstanding checks ± Bank errors *If a $60 check is recorded as $50, we must decrease checkbook balance by $10.	**Checkbook balance** Balance $800 − NSF 40 $760 − Service charge 4 $756 **Bank balance** Balance $ 632 + Deposits in transit 416 $1,048 − Outstanding checks 292 $ 756

KEY TERMS	Automatic teller machine (ATM), *p. 89* Bank reconciliation, *p. 95* Bank statement, *p. 94* Blank endorsement, *p. 91* Check, *p. 90* Check register, *p. 91* Credit stub, *p. 91* Credit memo (CM), *p. 97* Debit card, *p. 89*	Debit memo (DM), *p. 97* Deposit slip, *p. 90* Deposits in transit, *p. 97* Draft, *p. 90* Drawee, *p. 91* Drawer, *p. 91* Electronic funds transfer (EFT), *p. 94* Endorse, *p. 91* Full endorsement, *p. 91*	Nonsufficient funds (NSF), *p. 97* Outstanding checks, *p. 97* Overdrafts, *p. 95* Payee, *p. 91* Restrictive endorsement, *p. 91* Signature card, *p. 90*

CHECK FIGURES FOR EXTRA PRACTICE QUIZZES WITH PAGE REFERENCES. (WORKED-OUT SOLUTIONS IN APPENDIX B.)	LU 4–1a (p. 93) Ending Balance Forward $11,533.80	LU 4–2a (p. 102) Reconciled Balance $1,179.16

Critical Thinking Discussion Questions

1. Explain the structure of a check. The trend in bank statements is not to return the canceled checks. Do you think this is fair?
2. List the three types of endorsements. Endorsements are limited to the top $1\frac{1}{2}$ inches of the trailing edge on the back left side of your check. Why do you think the Federal Reserve made this regulation?
3. List the steps in reconciling a bank statement. Today, many banks charge a monthly fee for certain types of checking accounts. Do you think all checking accounts should be free? Please explain.
4. What are some of the trends in online banking? Will we become a cashless society in which all transactions are made with some type of credit card?
5. What do you think of the government's intervention in trying to bail out banks? Should banks be allowed to fail?

END-OF-CHAPTER PROBLEMS

connect plus+ www.mhhe.com/slater10e

Check figures for odd-numbered problems in Appendix C

Name ____________________ Date ________

DRILL PROBLEMS

4–1. Fill out the check register that follows with this information:

2010			
July 7	Check No. 482	AOL	$143.50
15	Check No. 483	Staples	66.10
19	Deposit		800.00
20	Check No. 484	Sprint	451.88
24	Check No. 485	Krispy Kreme	319.24
29	Deposit		400.30

RECORD ALL CHARGES OR CREDITS THAT AFFECT YOUR ACCOUNT

NUMBER	DATE 2009	DESCRIPTION OF TRANSACTION	PAYMENT/DEBIT (−)	√	FEE (IF ANY) (−)	DEPOSIT/CREDIT (+)	BALANCE
							$ 4,500 75
			$		$	$	

4–2. November 1, 2010, Payroll.com, an Internet company, has a $10,481.88 checkbook balance. Record the following transactions for Payroll.com by completing the two checks and check stubs provided. Sign the checks Garth Scholten, controller.

a. November 8, 2010, deposited $688.10

b. November 8, check No. 190 payable to Staples for office supplies—$766.88

c. November 15, check No. 191 payable to Best Buy for computer equipment—$3,815.99.

No. ________ $ ________
________ 20 ____
To ________
For ________

	DOLLARS	CENTS
BALANCE		
AMT. DEPOSITED		
TOTAL		
AMT. THIS CHECK		
BALANCE FORWARD		

PAYROLL.COM
1 LEDGER RD.
ST. PAUL, MN 55113

No. 190

________ 20 ____ 5-13/110

PAY TO THE ORDER OF ________________ $ ________

________________ DOLLARS

IPSWICHBANK
ipswichbank.com

____

MEMO ________

⑆011000138⑆ 25 11103 190

No. ________ $ ________
________ 20 ____
To ________
For ________

	DOLLARS	CENTS
BALANCE		
AMT. DEPOSITED		
TOTAL		
AMT. THIS CHECK		
BALANCE FORWARD		

PAYROLL.COM
1 LEDGER RD.
ST. PAUL, MN 55113

No. 191

________ 20 ____ 5-13/110

PAY TO THE ORDER OF ________________ $ ________

________________ DOLLARS

IPSWICHBANK
ipswichbank.com

____

MEMO ________

⑆011000138⑆ 25 11103 191

4–3. Using the check register in Problem 4–1 and the following bank statement, prepare a bank reconciliation for Lee.com.

BANK STATEMENT			
Date	**Checks**	**Deposits**	**Balance**
7/1 balance			$4,500.75
7/18	$143.50		4,357.25
7/19		$ 800.00	5,157.25
7/26	319.24		4,838.81
7/30	15.00 SC		4,823.01

WORD PROBLEMS

4–4. According to Bankrate's 2008 Checking Study (a survey of leading banks), ATM surcharges, bounced check fees, monthly service charges, and minimal balances are all increasing. To help reverse this trend, Hometown Bank offers a free checking account for up to 5 checks written a month. After five checks, they charge a fee of $.25 per check. Best Bank offers a checking account with a charge of $.10 per check. Sammy Smith typically writes 15 checks per month. Which bank should he go to for the lowest cost?

4–5. The U.S. Chamber of Commerce provides a free monthly bank reconciliation template at business.uschamber.com/tools/bankre_m.asp. Annie Moats just received her bank statement notice online. She wants to reconcile her checking account with her bank statement and has chosen to reconcile her accounts manually. Her checkbook shows a balance of $698. Her bank statement reflects a balance of $1,348. Checks outstanding are No. 2146, $25; No. 2148, $58; No. 2152, $198; and No. 2153, $464. Deposits in transit are $100 and $50. There is a $15 service charge and $5 ATM charge in addition to notes collected of $50 and $25. Reconcile Annie's balances.

4–6. A local bank began charging $2.50 each month for returning canceled checks. The bank also has an $8.00 "maintenance" fee if a checking account slips below $750. Donna Sands likes to have copies of her canceled checks for preparing her income tax. She has received her bank statement with a balance of $535.85. Donna received $2.68 in interest and has been charged for the canceled checks and the maintenance fee. The following checks were outstanding: No. 94, $121.16; No. 96, $106.30; No. 98, $210.12; and No. 99, $64.84. A deposit of $765.69 was not recorded on Donna's bank statement. Her checkbook shows a balance of $806.94. Prepare Donna's bank reconciliation.

4–7. Ben Luna received his bank statement with a $27.04 fee for a bounced-check (NSF). He has an $815.75 monthly mortgage payment paid through his bank. There was also a $3.00 teller fee and a check printing fee of $3.50. His ATM card fee was $6.40. There was also a $530.50 deposit in transit. The bank shows a balance of $119.17. The bank paid Ben $1.23 in interest. Ben's checkbook shows a balance of $1,395.28. Check No. 234 for $80.30 and check No. 235 for $28.55 were outstanding. Prepare Ben's bank reconciliation.

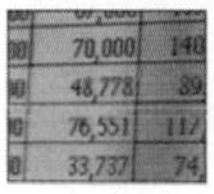

4–8. Kameron Gibson's bank statement showed a balance of $717.72. Kameron's checkbook had a balance of $209.50. Check No. 104 for $110.07 and check No. 105 for $15.55 were outstanding. A $620.50 deposit was not on the statement. He has his payroll check electronically deposited to his checking account—the payroll check was for $1,025.10. There was also a $4 teller fee and an $18 service charge. Prepare Kameron Gibson's bank reconciliation.

4–9. Banks are finding more ways to charge fees, such as a $25 overdraft fee. Sue McVickers has an account in Fayetteville; she has received her bank statement with this $25 charge. Also, she was charged a $6.50 service fee; however, the good news is she earned $5.15 interest. Her bank statement's balance was $315.65, but it did not show the $1,215.15 deposit she had made. Sue's checkbook balance shows $604.30. The following checks have not cleared: No. 250, $603.15; No. 253, $218.90; and No. 254, $130.80. Prepare Sue's bank reconciliation.

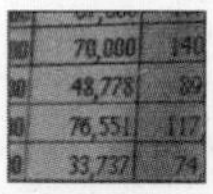

4–10. Carol Stokke receives her April 6 bank statement showing a balance of $859.75; her checkbook balance is $954.25. The bank statement shows an ATM charge of $25.00, NSF fee of $27.00, earned interest of $2.75, and Carol's $630.15 refund check, which was processed by the IRS and deposited to her account. Carol has two checks that have not cleared—No. 115 for $521.15 and No. 116 for $205.50. There is also a deposit in transit for $1,402.05. Prepare Carol's bank reconciliation.

4–11. Lowell Bank reported the following checking account fees: $2 to see a real-live teller, $20 to process a bounced check, and $1 to $3 if you need an original check to prove you paid a bill or made a charitable contribution. This past month you had to transact business through a teller 6 times—a total $12 cost to you. Your bank statement shows a $305.33 balance; your checkbook shows a $1,009.76 balance. You received $1.10 in interest. An $801.15 deposit was not recorded on your statement. The following checks were outstanding: No. 413, $28.30; No. 414, $18.60; and No. 418, $60.72. Prepare your bank reconciliation.

CHALLENGE PROBLEMS

4–12. Sue Walker has a part-time job as a bookkeeper. She's been working on reconciling the bank statement with the business checking account. The business checking account reflects a balance of $9,871. The bank statement reflects $2,792. Sue made an EFT of $1,500 from the savings account. Notes collected of $250 and $500 along with a service fee of $25 were recorded on the bank statement. The business checking account earned $28 in interest. Outstanding checks were: No. 4598, $500; No. 5000, $24; No. 5001, $87; and No. 5005, $675. Deposits in transit were for $8,500 and $1,103. Sue had to make a stop payment on check No. 5006 for $175. The $175 had already been added back into the checkbook balance. The bank charges $25 for each stop payment. Sue noticed a recording error on check No. 5002. The check had correctly cleared the bank last month for $1,100 but was recorded in the checkbook at $110. Help her reconcile the accounts.

4–13. Melissa Jackson, bookkeeper for Kinko Company, cannot prepare a bank reconciliation. From the following facts, can you help her complete the June 30, 2009, reconciliation? The bank statement showed a $2,955.82 balance. Melissa's checkbook showed a $3,301.82 balance.

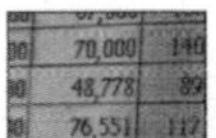

Melissa placed a $510.19 deposit in the bank's night depository on June 30. The deposit did not appear on the bank statement. The bank included two DMs and one CM with the returned checks: $690.65 DM for NSF check, $8.50 DM for service charges, and $400.00 CM (less $10 collection fee) for collecting a $400.00 non-interest-bearing note. Check No. 811 for $110.94 and check No. 912 for $82.50, both written and recorded on June 28, were not with the returned checks. The bookkeeper had correctly written check No. 884, $1,000, for a new cash register, but she recorded the check as $1,069. The May bank reconciliation showed check No. 748 for $210.90 and check No. 710 for $195.80 outstanding on April 30. The June bank statement included check No. 710 but not check No. 748.

DVD SUMMARY PRACTICE TEST

Do you need help? DVD has Step-by-Step worked-out solutions

1. Walgreens has a $12,925.55 beginning checkbook balance. Record the following transactions in the check stubs provided. *(p. 92)*

a. November 4, 2010, check No. 180 payable to Ace Medical Corporation, $1,700.88 for drugs.

b. $5,250 deposit—November 24.

c. November 24, 2010, check No. 181 payable to John's Wholesale, $825.55 merchandise.

No. ________ $ ________
________ 20 ____
To ________
For ________

	DOLLARS	CENTS
BALANCE		
AMT. DEPOSITED		
TOTAL		
AMT. THIS CHECK		
BALANCE FORWARD		

No. ________ $ ________
________ 20 ____
To ________
For ________

	DOLLARS	CENTS
BALANCE		
AMT. DEPOSITED		
TOTAL		
AMT. THIS CHECK		
BALANCE FORWARD		

2. On April 1, 2010, Lester Company received a bank statement that showed a $8,950 balance. Lester showed an $8,000 checking account balance. The bank did not return check No. 115 for $750 or check No. 118 for $370. A $900 deposit made on March 31 was in transit. The bank charged Lester $20 for printing and $250 for NSF checks. The bank also collected a $1,400 note for Lester. Lester forgot to record a $400 withdrawal at the ATM. Prepare a bank reconciliation. *(p. 95)*

3. Felix Babic banks at Role Federal Bank. Today he received his March 31, 2010, bank statement showing a $762.80 balance. Felix's checkbook shows a balance of $799.80. The following checks have not cleared the bank: No. 140, $130.55; No. 149, $66.80; and No. 161, $102.90. Felix made a $820.15 deposit that is not shown on the bank statement. He has his $617.30 monthly mortgage payment paid through the bank. His $1,100.20 IRS refund check was mailed to his bank. Prepare Felix Babic's bank reconciliation. *(p. 95)*

4. On June 30, 2010, Wally Company's bank statement showed a $7,500.10 bank balance. Wally has a beginning checkbook balance of $9,800.00. The bank statement also showed that it collected a $1,200.50 note for the company. A $4,500.10 June 30 deposit was in transit. Check No. 119 for $650.20 and check No. 130 for $381.50 are outstanding. Wally's bank charges $.40 cents per check. This month, 80 checks were processed. Prepare a reconciled statement. *(p. 95)*

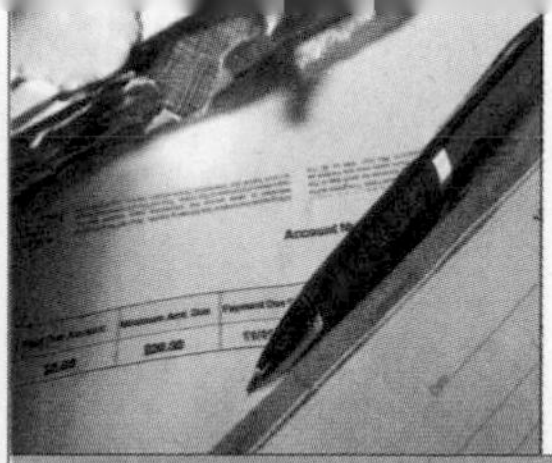

Personal Finance

A KIPLINGER APPROACH

WHEN TIMOTHY STITT OF LEEPER, PA., FIRST HEARD ABOUT A NEW CHECKING ACCOUNT at a small western Pennsylvania bank, he was intrigued. The "preferred account" from S&T Bank would give him free ATM transactions and a debit card with cash-back rewards. That appealed to Stitt because he frequently uses his debit card to purchase equipment for his landscaping business. So he signed up for an account.

"It was something I couldn't pass up," says Stitt. "It was a no-brainer."

The icing on the cake was the personal service: The bank's account executives took the time to answer all of his questions. And they helped him refinance his mortgage, to a 15-year fixed-rate loan at 5.5%.

Community banks, credit unions and online banks are luring refugees from the big money-center banks by offering lower fees, better rates on savings and a level of personal service that may remind you of George Bailey's building and loan. And just in case that's not enough, they're offering freebies to sweeten the deal—the 21st-century version of the free toaster.

For example, when you set up an account today, you may get a cash-back debit card or a free iPod. KeyBank hands over a Garmin GPS device. BBVA Compass, of Birmingham, Ala., gives you the chance to win a Mini Cooper. If you refer a friend to Chevy Chase Bank, which serves the Washington, D.C., area, you'll be rewarded with a three-day getaway (not including airfare) to St. Thomas, Las Vegas, Orlando or another vacation spot. "This is a great time for consumers," says Jon Paul, president of Value Added Finance Resources, a consulting firm. "Banks are very hungry for your deposits."

Big banks want your money, too, but they're turning customers off with higher fees and tighter lending—not to mention stress tests and troubled assets. They continue to raise fees, even as the grab for business intensifies and consumers are more cost-conscious.

Bank of America recently raised the monthly maintenance fees on some of its checking accounts; for example, fees for MyAccess Checking went from $5.95 a month to $8.95 a month. Wachovia, now a Wells Fargo company, boosted its transfer fee to cover checking-account overdrafts from $5 to $10 on some accounts. Charges for using credit cards overseas are also on the rise.

Bank customers are ready for a change. A survey by Aite Group found that just 2% of consumers have a high degree of trust in banks. And satisfaction with the major banks—such as Bank of America, Citigroup and JPMorgan Chase—has either leveled off or dropped, as measured by the American Customer Satisfaction Index and TowerGroup. "Banks are just not where they need to be," says Kathleen Khirallah, of TowerGroup.

FIND A BETTER DEAL

Community banks appeal to customers like Stitt because they have close ties to local residents and tend to offer more personal assistance than the big money-center banks. "Community banks are in the relationship-building business," says Karen Tyson, senior vice-president of the Independent Community Bankers of America. They tend to have fewer—and lower—fees than the major banks. And they generally offer lower rates on loans and higher yields on savings.

Likewise, credit unions are focused on their members. According to a study by the Credit Union National Association, credit unions charge an average of $25 for overdrafts; banks charge an average of $30. Similarly, banks sock you with a $35 fee if you're late paying your credit-card bill, but credit unions charge $20. Interest payments on a $25,000, 60-month car loan from a credit union would be $184 a year less than they would be if you got the loan from a bank, according to an analysis by Datatrac. Over five years, that would save you nearly $1,000. And average closing costs on a mortgage are lower at a credit union: $2,280, versus $2,309 at banks.

Online banks are another good option, particularly if you want to avoid ATM fees. If you need to use a brick-and-mortar bank's ATM, many online banks will reimburse you for any fees it charges. For example, UFBDirect.com reimburses its free-checking-account customers up to $4.50 a month for ATM charges from other banks. If you open a checking account at Charles Schwab (www.schwab.com), you'll get a refund of all ATM fees.

BUSINESS MATH ISSUE

The government should allow large banks to fail.

1. List the key points of the article and information to support your position.
2. Write a group defense of your position using math calculations to support your view.

Slater's Business Math Scrapbook

Applying Your Skills

PROJECT A

Would you do mobile banking. What are the pros and cons?

Branching Out: Mobile Banking Finds New Users

Improved Technology Helps Attract Younger Customers, Even as Balances Dwindle

By Ben Worthen

You may not want to learn how much smaller your bank account has gotten. But banks are making it easier than ever for consumers to access account information on their mobile devices.

Big banks are offering new services or improving existing ones that allow people to access their accounts while on the go. In January, **Bank of America** Corp. launched an updated software application that allows consumers to check their balances and pay bills through **Apple** Inc.'s iPhone. **Wells Fargo** & Co. has begun promoting a service that lets business clients approve wire transfers through their cellphones. And mobile banking is at the center of a major new ad campaign from Chase, a division of **J.P. Morgan Chase** & Co, which is offering a service that lets customers check their balances and get other information via text messages.

Smaller banks are beginning to invest in mobile services as well. BankPlus, a subsidiary of **BancPlus** Corp. with 65 offices throughout Mississippi, unveiled a service last year that lets customers transfer funds and view their transaction history from their mobile phones. "We wanted to offer a service that the big boys offered," says Ike Aslam, vice president of information services at BankPlus, who adds that around 4,000 customers have signed up for the service.

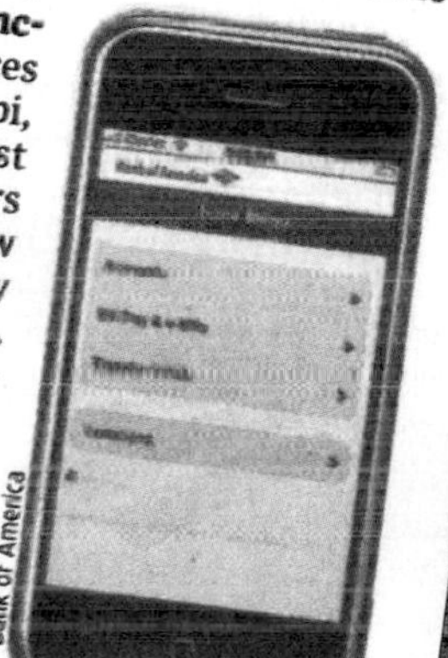

Bank of America

Bank of America customers can check balances and pay bills on an Apple iPhone.

Overall, the number of people in the U.S. that use mobile-banking services grew to 3.1 million in 2008 from 400,000 in 2007, and that number is expected to hit seven million this year, according to ABI Research, a technology-research firm based in New York. At the same time, the number of U.S. banks that offer mobile banking is expected to jump to 614 this year—about 4% of all banks in the country—from 245 in 2008, according to Aite Group, a Boston-based financial-services research firm.

The services are making banking more convenient for customers and small businesses. Customers can use their phones to check how much money they have in their accounts before making a purchase, or pay a bill while waiting to board a plane. Small-business owners can approve payments without having to turn on their computers. In most cases, banks are offering these services free.

Internet Projects: See text Web site (www.mhhe.com/slater10e) and The Business Math Internet Resource Guide.

chapter 5

SOLVING FOR THE UNKNOWN: A HOW-TO APPROACH FOR SOLVING EQUATIONS

Marcio Jose Sanchez/AP Images

Google Searches for Staffing Answers

By Scott Morrison

Concerned a brain drain could hurt its long-term ability to compete, **Google** Inc. is tackling the problem with its typical tool: an algorithm.

The Internet search giant recently began crunching data from employee reviews and promotion and pay histories in a mathematical formula Google says can identify which of its 20,000 employees are most likely to quit.

Google officials are reluctant to share details of the formula, which is still being tested. The inputs include information from surveys and peer reviews, and Google says the algorithm already has identified employees who felt underused, a key complaint among those who contemplate leaving.

LEARNING UNIT OBJECTIVES

LU 5–1: Solving Equations for the Unknown

1. Explain the basic procedures used to solve equations for the unknown *(pp. 114–116)*.
2. List the five rules and the mechanical steps used to solve for the unknown in seven situations; know how to check the answers *(pp. 116–118)*.

LU 5–2: Solving Word Problems for the Unknown

1. List the steps for solving word problems *(p. 120)*.
2. Complete blueprint aids to solve word problems; check the solutions *(pp. 121–122)*.

VOCABULARY PREVIEW

Here are the key terms in this chapter. When you finish the chapter, if you feel you know the term, place a checkmark within the parentheses following the term. If you are not certain of the definition, look it up and write the page number where it can be found in the text. The chapter organizer includes page references to the terms. There is also a complete glossary at the end of the text.

Constants . ( ) Equation . ( ) Expression . ( ) Formula . ( ) Knowns . ( ) Unknown . ( ) Variables . ( )

Do you eat at McDonald's. Have you ever thought which country can boast it has the most business per location? Of the 118 countries in which McDonald's does business, Russia serves 850,000 dinners annually per location. This is more than twice the store traffic of other markets. We could calculate volume in other markets as follows:

$$\frac{1}{2} \times 850{,}000 = 425{,}000$$

GLOBAL

Martin Thomas Photography/Alamy

As Burgers Boom in Russia, McDonald's Touts Discipline

To Maximize Potential, Chain Rations Growth; Trimming Wait Lines

By Janet Adamy

MOSCOW—At lunch time on a recent day here, Khamzat Khasbulatov sat in the world's second-busiest McDonald's and watched as dozens of people lined up at its 26 cash registers.

"I have too many customers," said Mr. Khasbulatov, chief executive of McDonald's Russia, as workers scrambled to assemble Big Macs and stuff french fries into red cartons.

Of the 118 countries where McDonald's Corp. does business, none can boast more activity than Russia. On average, each location serves about 850,000 diners annually—more than twice the store traffic in McDonald's other markets.

That has presented the world's largest restaurant chain with an unusual dilemma. Russia, with its burgeoning middle-class and consumer appetites for all things American, is a jewel in the McDonald's system. But the company is being prudent about expansion here—due partly to Russia's famous bureaucracy and partly to the chain's own philosophical shift.

Khamzat Khasbulatov

Aggressive growth plans at McDonald's backfired badly in the past. During the 1990s, the company was fixated on adding restaurants throughout the chain—as many as 2,500 stores a year. But by 2000, the condition of its existing locations, as well as the appeal of certain menu items, deteriorated. Two years later, the company's flawed expansion strategy was hammering its profits and stock price.

Wall Street Journal © 2007

Learning Unit 5–1 explains how to solve for unknowns in equations. In Learning Unit 5–2 you learn how to solve for unknowns in word problems. When you complete these learning units, you will not have to memorize as many formulas to solve business and personal math applications. Also, with the increasing use of computer software, a basic working knowledge of solving for the unknown has become necessary.

Learning Unit 5–1: Solving Equations for the Unknown

LO 1

The Rose Smith letter below is based on a true story. Note how Rose states that the blueprint aids, the lesson on repetition, and the chapter organizers were important factors in the successful completion of her business math course.

Rose Smith
15 Locust Street
Lynn, MA 01915

Flowers.net
Decorating Service

Dear Professor Slater,

Thank you for helping me get through your Business Math class. When I first started, my math anxiety level was real high. I felt I had no head for numbers. When you told us we would be covering the chapter on solving equations, I'll never forget how I started to shake. I started to panic. I felt I could never solve a word problem. I thought I was having an algebra attack.

Now that it's over (90 on the chapter on unknowns), I'd like to tell you what worked for me so you might pass this on to other students. It was your blueprint aids. Drawing boxes helped me to think things out. They were a tool that helped me more clearly understand how to dissect each word problem. They didn't solve the problem for me, but gave me the direction I needed. Repetition was the key to my success. At first I got them all wrong but after the third time, things started to click. I felt more confident. Your chapter organizers at the end of the chapter were great. Thanks for your patience – your repetition breeds success – now students are asking me to help them solve a word problem. Can you believe it!

Best,

Rose

Rose Smith

Many of you are familiar with the terms *variables* and *constants*. If you are planning to prepare for your retirement by saving only what you can afford each year, your saving is a *variable;* if you plan to save the same amount each year, your saving is a *constant*. Now you can also say that you cannot buy clothes by size because of the many variables involved. This unit explains the importance of mathematical variables and constants when solving equations.

Basic Equation-Solving Procedures

When you go to a shopping mall does your purchase(s) depend upon price, who you are shopping with, time of year, or just impulse buying?

From the *Wall Street Journal* heading "Less Shopping = Fewer Malls" may mean you will have fewer new malls in which to shop due to the economy. But no explanation is given as to how the equation has changed. The definition of an equation which follows may suggest to you what is meant by the equation.

Less Shopping = Fewer Malls

Construction of New Centers Slows Along With Economy; 'We're Not Going to Build'

Do you know the difference between a mathematical expression, equation, and formula? A mathematical **expression** is a meaningful combination of numbers and letters called *terms*. Operational signs (such as + or −) within the expression connect the terms to show a relationship between them. For example, $6 + 2$ or $6A - 4A$ are mathematical expressions. An **equation** is a mathematical statement with an equal sign showing that a mathematical expression on the left equals the mathematical expression on the right. An equation has an equal sign; an expression does not have an equal sign. A **formula** is an equation that expresses in symbols a general fact, rule, or principle. Formulas are shortcuts for expressing a word concept. For example, in Chapter 10 you will learn that the formula for simple interest is Interest (I) = Principal (P) × Rate (R) × Time (T). This means that when you see $I = P \times R \times T$, you recognize the simple interest formula. Now let's study basic equations.

As a mathematical statement of equality, equations show that two numbers or groups of numbers are equal. For example, $6 + 4 = 10$ shows the equality of an equation. Equations also use letters as symbols that represent one or more numbers. These symbols, usually a letter of the alphabet, are **variables** that stand for a number. We can use a variable even though we may not know what it represents. For example, $A + 2 = 6$. The variable A represents the number or **unknown** (4 in this example) for which we are solving. We distinguish variables from numbers, which have a fixed value. Numbers such as 3 or −7 are **constants** or **knowns,** whereas A and $3A$ (this means 3 times the variable A) are variables. So we can now say that variables and constants are *terms of mathematical expressions*.

Usually in solving for the unknown, we place variable(s) on the left side of the equation and constants on the right. The following rules for variables and constants are important.

VARIABLES AND CONSTANTS RULES

1. If no number is in front of a letter, it is a 1: $B = 1B$; $C = 1C$.
2. If no sign is in front of a letter or number, it is a +: $C = +C$; $4 = +4$.

You should be aware that in solving equations, the meaning of the symbols +, −, ×, and ÷ has not changed. However, some variations occur. For example, you can also write $A \times B$ (A times B) as $A \cdot B$, $A(B)$, or AB. Also, A divided by B is the same as A/B. Remember that to solve an equation, you must find a number that can replace the unknown in the equation and make it a true statement. Now let's take a moment to look at how we can change verbal statements into variables.

Assume Dick Hersh, an employee of Nike, is 50 years old. Let's assign Dick Hersh's changing age to the symbol A. The symbol A is a variable.

Verbal statement	Variable A (age)
Dick's age 8 years ago	$A - 8$
Dick's age 8 years from today	$A + 8$
Four times Dick's age	$4A$
One-fifth Dick's age	$A/5$

FIGURE 5.1

Equality in equations

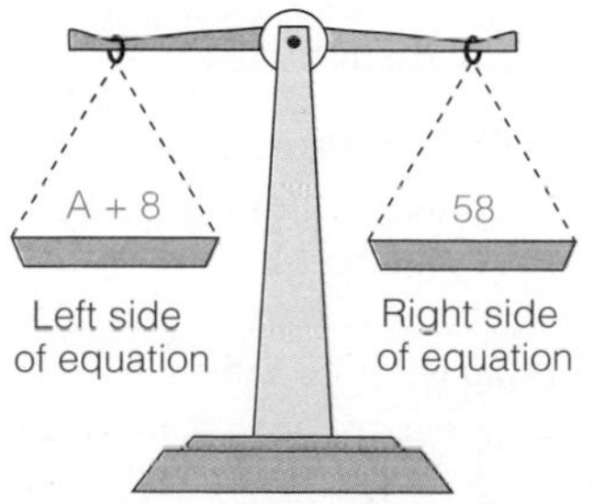

Dick's age in 8 years will equal 58.

To visualize how equations work, think of the old-fashioned balancing scale shown in Figure 5.1. The pole of the scale is the equals sign. The two sides of the equation are the two pans of the scale. In the left pan or left side of the equation, we have $A + 8$; in the right pan or right side of the equation, we have 58. To solve for the unknown (Dick's present age), we isolate or place the unknown (variable) on the left side and the numbers on the right. We will do this soon. For now, remember that to keep an equation (or scale) in balance, we must perform mathematical operations (addition, subtraction, multiplication, and division) to *both* sides of the equation.

SOLVING FOR THE UNKNOWN RULE

Whatever you do to one side of an equation, you must do to the other side.

How to Solve for Unknowns in Equations

This section presents seven drill situations and the rules that will guide you in solving for unknowns in these situations. We begin with two basic rules—the opposite process rule and the equation equality rule.

OPPOSITE PROCESS RULE

If an equation indicates a process such as addition, subtraction, multiplication, or division, solve for the unknown or variable by using the opposite process. For example, if the equation process is addition, solve for the unknown by using subtraction.

EQUATION EQUALITY RULE

You can add the same quantity or number to both sides of the equation and subtract the same quantity or number from both sides of the equation without affecting the equality of the equation. You can also divide or multiply both sides of the equation by the same quantity or number *(except zero)* without affecting the equality of the equation.

To check your answer(s), substitute your answer(s) for the letter(s) in the equation. The sum of the left side should equal the sum of the right side.

LO 2

Drill Situation 1: Subtracting Same Number from Both Sides of Equation

Example	Mechanical steps	Explanation
$A + 8 = 58$ Dick's age A plus 8 equals 58.	$A + 8 = 58$ $\underline{-8 \quad -8}$ $A = \boxed{50}$	8 is subtracted from *both* sides of equation to isolate variable A on the left. **Check** $50 + 8 = 58$ $58 = 58$

Note: Since the equation process used *addition,* we use the opposite process rule and solve for variable A with *subtraction.* We also use the equation equality rule when we subtract the same quantity from both sides of the equation.

Drill Situation 2: Adding Same Number to Both Sides of Equation

Example	Mechanical steps	Explanation
$B - 50 = 80$ Some number B less 50 equals 80.	$B - 50 = 80$ $\underline{+50 \quad +50}$ $B = \boxed{130}$	50 is added to *both* sides to isolate variable B on the left. **Check** $130 - 50 = 80$ $80 = 80$

Note: Since the equation process used *subtraction,* we use the opposite process rule and solve for variable B with *addition.* We also use the equation equality rule when we add the same quantity to both sides of the equation.

Drill Situation 3: Dividing Both Sides of Equation by Same Number

Example	Mechanical steps	Explanation
$7G = 35$ Some number G times 7 equals 35.	$7G = 35$ $\frac{\not{7}G}{\not{7}} = \frac{35}{7}$ $G = \boxed{5}$	By dividing both sides by 7, G equals 5. **Check** $7(5) = 35$ $35 = 35$

Note: Since the equation process used *multiplication,* we use the opposite process rule and solve for variable G with *division.* We also use the equation equality rule when we divide both sides of the equation by the same quantity.

Drill Situation 4: Multiplying Both Sides of Equation by Same Number

Example	Mechanical steps	Explanation
$\frac{V}{5} = 70$	$\frac{V}{5} = 70$	By multiplying both sides by 5, V is equal to 350.
Some number V divided by 5 equals 70.	$5\left(\frac{V}{5}\right) = 70(5)$ $V = 350$	**Check** $\frac{350}{5} = 70$ $70 = 70$

Note: Since the equation process used *division,* we use the opposite process rule and solve for variable V with *multiplication.* We also use the equation equality rule when we multiply both sides of the equation by the same quantity.

Drill Situation 5: Equation That Uses Subtraction and Multiplication to Solve for Unknown

MULTIPLE PROCESSES RULE

When solving for an unknown that involves more than one process, do the addition and subtraction before the multiplication and division.

Example	Mechanical steps	Explanation
$\frac{H}{4} + 2 = 5$	$\frac{H}{4} + 2 = 5$	1. Move constant to right side by subtracting 2 from both sides.
When we divide unknown H by 4 and add the result to 2, the answer is 5.	$\frac{H}{4} + 2 = 5$ $-2 \quad -2$ $\frac{H}{4} = 3$	2. To isolate H, which is divided by 4, we do the opposite process and multiply 4 times *both* sides of the equation.
	$4\left(\frac{H}{4}\right) = 4(3)$ $H = 12$	**Check** $\frac{12}{4} + 2 = 5$ $3 + 2 = 5$ $5 = 5$

Drill Situation 6: Using Parentheses in Solving for Unknown

PARENTHESES RULE

When equations contain parentheses (which indicate grouping together), you solve for the unknown by first multiplying each item inside the parentheses by the number or letter just outside the parentheses. Then you continue to solve for the unknown with the opposite process used in the equation. Do the additions and subtractions first; then the multiplications and divisions.

Example

$5(P - 4) = 20$

The unknown P less 4, multiplied by 5 equals 20.

Mechanical steps

$$\begin{aligned} 5(P - 4) &= 20 \\ 5P - 20 &= 20 \\ +20 &\quad +20 \\ \frac{\cancel{5}P}{\cancel{5}} &= \frac{40}{5} \\ P &= \boxed{8} \end{aligned}$$

Explanation

1. Parentheses tell us that everything inside parentheses is multiplied by 5. Multiply 5 by P and 5 by -4.
2. Add 20 to both sides to isolate $5P$ on left.
3. To remove 5 in front of P, divide both sides by 5 to result in P equals 8.

Check

$$\begin{aligned} 5(8 - 4) &= 20 \\ 5(4) &= 20 \\ 20 &= 20 \end{aligned}$$

MONEY TIPS

Don't forget the basics of solving for the unknown: whatever you do to one side, do to the other; combine like terms; and do the correct order of operations—PEMDAS (please excuse my dear aunt sally: parenthesis, exponents, multiplication, division, addition, subtraction). You never know when you will need to use this information to solve everyday problems such as adjusting a pattern or ordering landscaping materials.

Drill Situation 7: Combining Like Unknowns

LIKE UNKNOWNS RULE

To solve equations with like unkowns, you first combine the unknowns and then solve with the opposite process used in the equation.

Example

$4A + A = 20$

Mechanical steps

$$\begin{aligned} 4A + A &= 20 \\ \frac{\cancel{5}A}{\cancel{5}} &= \frac{20}{5} \\ \boxed{A} &= 4 \end{aligned}$$

Explanation

To solve this equation: $4A + 1A = 5A$. Thus, $5A = 20$. To solve for A, divide both sides by 5, leaving A equals 4.

Before you go to Learning Unit 5–2, let's check your understanding of this unit.

LU 5–1 PRACTICE QUIZ

Complete this **Practice Quiz** to see how you are doing.

1. Write equations for the following (use the letter Q as the variable). Do not solve for the unknown.
   - **a.** Nine less than one-half a number is fourteen.
   - **b.** Eight times the sum of a number and thirty-one is fifty.
   - **c.** Ten decreased by twice a number is two.
   - **d.** Eight times a number less two equals twenty-one.
   - **e.** The sum of four times a number and two is fifteen.
   - **f.** If twice a number is decreased by eight, the difference is four.
2. Solve the following:
   - **a.** $B + 24 = 60$
   - **b.** $D + 3D = 240$
   - **c.** $12B = 144$
   - **d.** $\frac{B}{6} = 50$
   - **e.** $\frac{B}{4} + 4 = 16$
   - **f.** $3(B - 8) = 18$

Solutions with Step-by-Step Help on DVD

✓ Solutions

1. **a.** $\frac{1}{2}Q - 9 = 14$ **b.** $8(Q + 31) = 50$ **c.** $10 - 2Q = 2$
   d. $8Q - 2 = 21$ **e.** $4Q + 2 = 15$ **f.** $2Q - 8 = 4$
2. **a.** $$\begin{aligned} B + 24 &= -60 \\ -24 &\quad -24 \\ B &= \boxed{36} \end{aligned}$$
   b. $$\frac{\cancel{4}D}{\cancel{4}} = \frac{240}{4} \qquad D = \boxed{60}$$
   c. $$\frac{\cancel{12}B}{\cancel{12}} = \frac{144}{12} \qquad B = \boxed{12}$$

d.
$$\not{6}\left(\frac{B}{\not{6}}\right) = 50(6)$$
$$B = \boxed{300}$$

e.
$$\frac{B}{4} + 4 = 16$$
$$\underline{-4} \quad \underline{-4}$$
$$\frac{B}{4} = 12$$
$$\not{4}\left(\frac{B}{\not{4}}\right) = 12(4)$$
$$B = \boxed{48}$$

f.
$$3(B - 8) = 18$$
$$3B - 24 = 18$$
$$\underline{+24} \quad \underline{+24}$$
$$\frac{\not{3}B}{\not{3}} = \frac{42}{3}$$
$$B = \boxed{14}$$

LU 5–1a EXTRA PRACTICE QUIZ WITH WORKED-OUT SOLUTIONS

Need more practice? Try this **Extra Practice Quiz** (check figures in Chapter Organizer, p. 126). Worked-out Solutions can be found in Appendix B at end of text.

1. Write equations for the following (use the letter Q as the variable). Do not solve for the unknown.
   - **a.** Eight less than one-half a number is sixteen.
   - **b.** Twelve times the sum of a number and forty-one is 1,200.
   - **c.** Seven decreased by twice a number is one.
   - **d.** Four times a number less two equals twenty-four.
   - **e.** The sum of three times a number and three is nineteen.
   - **f.** If twice a number is decreased by six, the difference is five.
2. Solve the following:
   - **a.** $B + 14 = 70$ **b.** $D + 4D = 250$ **c.** $11B = 121$
   - **d.** $\frac{B}{8} = 90$ **e.** $\frac{B}{2} + 2 = 16$ **f.** $3(B - 6) = 18$

Learning Unit 5–2: Solving Word Problems for the Unknown

LO 1

When you buy a candy bar such as a Snickers, you should turn the candy bar over and carefully read the ingredients and calories contained on the back of the candy bar wrapper. For example, on the back of the Snickers wrapper you will read that there are "170 calories per piece." You could misread this to mean that the entire Snickers bar has 170 calories. However, look closer and you will see that the Snickers bar is divided into three pieces, so if you eat the entire bar, instead of consuming 170 calories, you will consume 510 calories. Making errors like this could result in a weight gain that you cannot explain.

$$\frac{1}{3}S = 170 \text{ calories}$$
$$\not{3}\left(\frac{1}{\not{3}}S\right) = 170 \times 3$$
$$S = \boxed{510} \text{ calories per bar}$$

In this unit, we use blueprint aids in six different situations to help you solve for unknowns. Be patient and *persistent.* Remember that the more problems you work, the easier the process becomes. Do not panic! Repetition is the key. Study the five steps that follow. They will help you solve for unknowns in word problems.

SOLVING WORD PROBLEMS FOR UNKNOWNS

Step 1. Carefully read the entire problem. You may have to read it several times.

Step 2. Ask yourself: "What is the problem looking for?"

Step 3. When you are sure what the problem is asking, let a variable represent the unknown. If the problem has more than one unknown, represent the second unknown in terms of the same variable. For example, if the problem has two unknowns, *Y* is one unknown. The second unknown is 4*Y*—4 times the first unknown.

Step 4. Visualize the relationship between unknowns and variables. Then set up an equation to solve for unknown(s).

Step 5. Check your result to see if it is accurate.

Word Problem Situation 1: Number Problems From the *Wall Street Journal* clipping "Why Dora the Explorer Can't Come to Your Kid's Birthday Party" you can see the price of costumes could be affected. If we assume the price of a Dora costume has dropped in price \$40 to \$150, what was the price of the original Dora costume?

Why Dora the Explorer Can't Come To Your Kid's Birthday Party

* * *

The Issue Is Trademark Infringement; Invite SpongeBob, Get SquishyGuy

By Katherine Rosman

In planning birthday parties for their children, parents are facing stumbling blocks that include trademark infringement.

For children's parties, many companies around the country provide costumed characters popular with kids—characters like Dora the Explorer, Bob the Builder and Hannah Montana. In recent years, corporations that own the rights to some of the more popular characters, companies that include Marvel Entertainment Inc., Scholastic Inc., and HIT Entertainment, have sent cease-and-desist letters, threatened lawsuits and in some cases received settlements from companies that market unauthorized character impersonators.

The threats rattle the costume industry. Some companies hire lawyers to advise them on how to stay out of trouble and remain in business. Others are now commissioning costumes that only slightly resemble characters owned by media companies. They have names like "Big Red Tickle Monster," instead of Elmo, and "Explorer Girl with Backpack," rather than Dora.

Dora the Explorer

Nickelodeon/Everett Collection

Wall Street Journal © 2008

Blueprint aid

LO 2

Unknown(s)	Variable(s)	Relationship*
Original Dora rental price	*D*	*D* − \$40 = New price

*This column will help you visualize the equation before setting up the actual equation.

Mechanical steps

$$\begin{aligned} D - 40 &= \$150 \\ +40 &\quad +40 \\ D &= \$190 \end{aligned}$$

Explanation

The original price less $40 = $150. Note that we added $40 to both sides to isolate D on the left. Remember, $1D = D$.

Check

$\$190 - 40 = \$150$

$\$150 = \$150$

Word Problem Situation 2: Finding the Whole When Part Is Known A local Burger King budgets $\frac{1}{8}$ of its monthly profits on salaries. Salaries for the month were $12,000. What were Burger King's monthly profits?

Blueprint aid

Unknown(s)	Variable(s)	Relationship
Monthly profits	P	$\frac{1}{8}P$ Salaries = $12,000

Mechanical steps

$$\frac{1}{8}P = \$12{,}000$$

$$8\left(\frac{P}{8}\right) = \$12{,}000(8)$$

$$P = \$96{,}000$$

Explanation

$\frac{1}{8}P$ represents Burger King's monthly salaries. Since the equation used division, we solve for P by multiplying both sides by 8.

Check

$\frac{1}{8}(\$96{,}000) = \$12{,}000$

$\$12{,}000 = \$12{,}000$

Word Problem Situation 3: Difference Problems ICM Company sold 4 times as many computers as Ring Company. The difference in their sales is 27. How many computers of each company were sold?

Blueprint aid

Unknown(s)	Variable(s)	Relationship
ICM	$4C$	$4C$
Ring	C	$-C$
		27

Note: If problem has two unknowns, assign the variable to smaller item or one who sells less. Then assign the other unknown using the same variable. *Use the same letter.*

Mechanical steps

$$4C - C = 27$$

$$\frac{3C}{3} = \frac{27}{3}$$

$$C = 9$$

Ring = 9 computers

ICM = 4(9)

= 36 computers

Explanation

The variables replace the names ICM and Ring. We assigned Ring the variable C, since it sold fewer computers. We assigned ICM $4C$, since it sold 4 times as many computers.

Check

36 computers
−9
27 computers

Word Problem Situation 4: Calculating Unit Sales Together Barry Sullivan and Mitch Ryan sold a total of 300 homes for Regis Realty. Barry sold 9 times as many homes as Mitch. How many did each sell?

Blueprint aid

Unknown(s)	Variable(s)	Relationship
Homes sold:		
B. Sullivan	$9H$	$9H$
M. Ryan	H*	$+H$
		300 homes

*Assign H to Ryan since he sold less.

Mechanical steps

$$9H + H = 300$$

$$\frac{10H}{10} = \frac{300}{10}$$

$$H = 30$$

Ryan: 30 homes

Sullivan: 9(30) = 270 homes

Explanation

We assigned Mitch H, since he sold fewer homes. We assigned Barry $9H$, since he sold 9 times as many homes. Together Barry and Mitch sold 300 homes.

Check

$30 + 270 = 300$

Word Problem Situation 5: Calculating Unit and Dollar Sales (Cost per Unit) When Total Units Are Not Given Andy sold watches (\$9) and alarm clocks (\$5) at a flea market. Total sales were \$287. People bought 4 times as many watches as alarm clocks. How many of each did Andy sell? What were the total dollar sales of each?

Blueprint aid

Unknown(s)	Variable(s)	Price	Relationship
Unit sales:			
Watches	4C	\$9	36C
Clocks	C	5	+ 5C
			\$287 total sales

Mechanical steps

$$36C + 5C = 287$$
$$\frac{41C}{41} = \frac{287}{41}$$
$$C = 7$$

7 clocks

4(7) = 28 watches

Explanation

Number of watches times \$9 sales price plus number of alarm clocks times \$5 equals \$287 total sales.

Check

7(\$5) + 28(\$9) = \$287
\$35 + \$252 = \$287
\$287 = \$287

Word Problem Situation 6: Calculating Unit and Dollar Sales (Cost per Unit) When Total Units Are Given Andy sold watches (\$9) and alarm clocks (\$5) at a flea market. Total sales for 35 watches and alarm clocks were \$287. How many of each did Andy sell? What were the total dollar sales of each?

Blueprint aid

Unknown(s)	Variable(s)	Price	Relationship
Unit sales:			
Watches	W*	\$9	9W
Clocks	35 − W	5	+ 5(35 − W)
			\$287 total sales

*The more expensive item is assigned to the variable first only for this situation to make the mechanical steps easier to complete.

Mechanical steps

$$9W + 5(35 - W) = 287$$
$$9W + 175 - 5W = 287$$
$$4W + 175 = 287$$
$$-175 \quad -175$$
$$\frac{4W}{4} = \frac{112}{4}$$
$$W = 28$$

Watches = 28

Clocks = 35 − 28 = 7

Explanation

Number of watches (W) times price per watch plus number of alarm clocks times price per alarm clock equals \$287. Total units given was 35.

Check

28(\$9) + 7(\$5) = \$287
\$252 + \$35 = \$287
\$287 = \$287

MONEY TIPS

Solving for the unknown or using algebra can be a great help with decision making. You can use algebra to help you create an annual budget or to plan the meal for your next party. Whether you drive a car and need to calculate distance or need to reduce a recipe in half, you are solving for the unknown. We use math everyday without even realizing it. So, polish up those math skills and start using math to simplify your life.

Why did we use 35 − *W*? Assume we had 35 pizzas (some cheese, others meatball). If I said that I ate all the meatball pizzas (5), how many cheese pizzas are left? Thirty? Right, you subtract 5 from 35. Think of 35 − *W* as meaning one number.

Note in Word Problem Situations 5 and 6 that the situation is the same. In Word Problem Situation 5, we were not given total units sold (but we were told which sold better). In Word Problem Situation 6, we were given total units sold, but we did not know which sold better.

Now try these six types of word problems in the Practice Quiz. Be sure to complete blueprint aids and the mechanical steps for solving the unknown(s).

LU 5–2 PRACTICE QUIZ

Complete this **Practice Quiz** to see how you are doing.

Situations

1. An L. L. Bean sweater was reduced \$30. The sale price was \$90. What was the original price?
2. Kelly Doyle budgets $\frac{1}{8}$ of her yearly salary for entertainment. Kelly's total entertainment bill for the year is \$6,500. What is Kelly's yearly salary?
3. Micro Knowledge sells 5 times as many computers as Morse Electronics. The difference in sales between the two stores is 20 computers. How many computers did each store sell?
4. Susie and Cara sell stoves at Elliott's Appliances. Together they sold 180 stoves in January. Susie sold 5 times as many stoves as Cara. How many stoves did each sell?

5. Pasquale's Pizza sells meatball pizzas ($6) and cheese pizzas ($5). In March, Pasquale's total sales were $1,600. People bought 2 times as many cheese pizzas as meatball pizzas. How many of each did Pasquale sell? What were the total dollar sales of each?

6. Pasquale's Pizza sells meatball pizzas ($6) and cheese pizzas ($5). In March, Pasquale's sold 300 pizzas for $1,600. How many of each did Pasquale's sell? What was the dollar sales price of each?

Solutions with Step-by-Step Help on DVD

✓ Solutions

1.

Unknown(s)	Variable(s)	Relationship
Original price	P*	$P - \$30 =$ Sale price Sale price $= \$90$

*P = Original price.

Mechanical steps

$$\begin{aligned} P - \$30 &= \$90 \\ +30 &\quad +30 \\ P &= \$120 \end{aligned}$$

2.

Unknown(s)	Variable(s)	Relationship
Yearly salary	S*	$\frac{1}{8}S$ Entertainment $= \$6{,}500$

*S = Salary.

Mechanical steps

$$\frac{1}{8}S = \$6{,}500$$

$$8\left(\frac{S}{8}\right) = \$6{,}500(8)$$

$$S = \$52{,}000$$

3.

Unknown(s)	Variable(s)	Relationship
Micro Morse	$5C$* C	$5C$ $-C$ 20 computers

*C = Computers.

Mechanical steps

$$5C - C = 20$$

$$\frac{4C}{4} = \frac{20}{4}$$

$$C = 5 \text{ (Morse)}$$

$$5C = 25 \text{ (Micro)}$$

4.

Unknown(s)	Variable(s)	Relationship
Stoves sold:		
Susie Cara	$5S$* S	$5S$ $+S$ 180 stoves

*S = Stoves.

Mechanical steps

$$5S + S = 20$$

$$\frac{6S}{6} = \frac{180}{6}$$

$$S = 30 \text{ (Cara)}$$

$$5S = 150 \text{ (Susie)}$$

5.

Unknown(s)	Variable(s)	Price	Relationship
Meatball Cheese	M $2M$	$6 5	$6M$ $+10M$ $1,600 total sales

Mechanical steps

$$6M + 10M = 1{,}600$$

$$\frac{16M}{16} = \frac{1{,}600}{16}$$

$$M = 100 \text{ (meatball)}$$

$$2M = 200 \text{ (cheese)}$$

Check

$$(100 \times \$6) + (200 \times \$5) = \$1{,}600$$
$$\$600 + \$1{,}000 = \$1{,}600$$
$$\$1{,}600 = \$1{,}600$$

6.

Unknown(s)	Variable(s)	Price	Relationship
Unit sales:			
Meatball Cheese	M* $300 - M$	$6 5	$6M$ $+5(300 - M)$ $1,600 total sales

*We assign the variable to the most expensive to make the mechanical steps easier to complete.

Mechanical steps

$$\begin{aligned} 6M + 5(300 - M) &= 1{,}600 \\ 6M + 1{,}500 - 5M &= 1{,}600 \\ M + 1{,}500 &= 1{,}600 \\ -1{,}500 &\quad -1{,}500 \\ M &= 100 \end{aligned}$$

Meatball = 100

Cheese = 300 − 100 = 200

Check

$$100(\$6) + 200(\$5) = \$600 + \$1{,}000$$
$$= \$1{,}600$$

LU 5–2a EXTRA PRACTICE QUIZ WITH WORKED-OUT SOLUTIONS

Need more practice? Try this **Extra Practice Quiz** (check figures in Chapter Organizer, p. 126). Worked-out Solutions can be found in Appendix B at end of text.

Situations

1. An L. L. Bean sweater was reduced $50. The sale price was $140. What was the original price?
2. Kelly Doyle budgets $\frac{1}{7}$ of her yearly salary for entertainment. Kelly's total entertainment bill for the year is $7,000. What is Kelly's yearly salary?
3. Micro Knowledge sells 8 times as many computers as Morse Electronics. The difference in sales between the two stores is 49 computers. How many computers did each store sell?
4. Susie and Cara sell stoves at Elliott's Appliances. Together they sold 360 stoves in January. Susie sold 2 times as many stoves as Cara. How many stoves did each sell?
5. Pasquale's Pizza sells meatball pizzas ($7) and cheese pizzas ($6). In March, Pasquale's total sales were $1,800. People bought 3 times as many cheese pizzas as meatball pizzas. How many of each did Pasquale sell? What were the total dollar sales of each?
6. Pasquale's Pizza sells meatball pizzas ($7) and cheese pizzas ($6). In March, Pasquale sold 288 pizzas for $1,800. What was the dollar sales price of each?

CHAPTER ORGANIZER AND REFERENCE GUIDE

Solving for unknowns from basic equations	Mechanical steps to solve unknowns	Key point(s)
Situation 1: Subtracting same number from both sides of equation, p. 116	$D + 10 = 12$ $\underline{-10 \quad -10}$ $D = \boxed{2}$	Subtract 10 from both sides of equation to isolate variable *D* on the left. Since equation used addition, we solve by using opposite process—subtraction.
Situation 2: Adding same number to both sides of equation, p. 116	$L - 24 = 40$ $\underline{+24 \quad +24}$ $L = \boxed{64}$	Add 24 to both sides to isolate unknown *L* on left. We solve by using opposite process of subtraction—addition.
Situation 3: Dividing both sides of equation by same number, p. 116	$6B = 24$ $\frac{\cancel{6}B}{\cancel{6}} = \frac{24}{\cancel{6}}$ $B = \boxed{4}$	To isolate *B* by itself on the left, divide both sides of the equation by 6. Thus, the 6 on the left cancels—leaving *B* equal to 4. Since equation used multiplication, we solve unknown by using opposite process—division.
Situation 4: Multiplying both sides of equation by same number, p. 117	$\frac{R}{3} = 15$ $\cancel{3}\left(\frac{R}{\cancel{3}}\right) = 15(3)$ $R = \boxed{45}$	To remove denominator, multiply both sides of the equation by 3—the 3 on the left side cancels, leaving *R* equal to 45. Since equation used division, we solve unknown by using opposite process—multiplication.
Situation 5: Equation that uses subtraction and multiplication to solve for unknown, p. 117	$\frac{B}{3} + 6 = 13$ $\underline{-6 \quad -6}$ $\frac{B}{3} = 7$ $\cancel{3}\left(\frac{B}{\cancel{3}}\right) = 7(3)$ $B = \boxed{21}$	1. Move constant 6 to right side by subtracting 6 from both sides. 2. Isolate *B* by itself on left by multiplying both sides by 3.

(continues)

CHAPTER ORGANIZER AND REFERENCE GUIDE

<table>
<tr><th>Solving for unknowns from basic equations</th><th>Mechanical steps to solve unknowns</th><th>Key point(s)</th></tr>
<tr><td>Situation 6: Using parentheses in solving for unknown, pp. 117–118</td><td>$6(A - 5) = 12$
$6A - 30 = 12$
$\quad + 30 \quad + 30$
$\frac{\cancel{6}A}{\cancel{6}} = \frac{42}{6}$
$A = 7$</td><td>Parentheses indicate multiplication. Multiply 6 times A and 6 times -5. Result is $6A - 30$ on left side of the equation. Now add 30 to both sides to isolate $6A$ on left. To remove 6 in front of A, divide both sides by 6, to result in A equal to 7. Note that when deleting parentheses, we did not have to multiply the right side.</td></tr>
<tr><td>Situation 7: Combining like unknowns, p. 118</td><td>$6A + 2A = 64$
$\frac{\cancel{8}A}{\cancel{8}} = \frac{64}{8}$
$A = 8$</td><td>$6A + 2A$ combine to $8A$. To solve for A, we divide both sides by 8.</td></tr>
<tr><th>Solving for unknowns from word problems</th><th>Blueprint aid</th><th>Mechanical steps to solve unknown with check</th></tr>
<tr><td>Situation 1: Number problems, p. 120
U.S. Air reduced its airfare to California by $60. The sale price was $95. What was the original price?</td><td><table><tr><th>Unknown(s)</th><th>Variable(s)</th><th>Relationship</th></tr><tr><td>Original price</td><td>P</td><td>P − $60 = Sale price
Sale price = $95</td></tr></table></td><td>$P - \$60 = \$\,95$
$\quad + 60 \quad + 60$
$P = \$155$
Check
$\$155 - \$60 = \$95$
$\$95 = \$95$</td></tr>
<tr><td>Situation 2: Finding the whole when part is known, p. 121
K. McCarthy spends ⅛ of her budget for school. What is the total budget if school costs $5,000?</td><td><table><tr><th>Unknown(s)</th><th>Variable(s)</th><th>Relationship</th></tr><tr><td>Total budget</td><td>B</td><td>$\frac{1}{8}B$
School = $5,000</td></tr></table></td><td>$\frac{1}{8}B = \$5{,}000$
$\cancel{8}\left(\frac{B}{\cancel{8}}\right) = \$5{,}000(8)$
$B = \$10{,}000$
Check
$\frac{1}{8}(\$40{,}000) = \$5{,}000$
$\$5{,}000 = \$5{,}000$</td></tr>
<tr><td>Situation 3: Difference problems, p. 121
Moe sold 8 times as many suitcases as Bill. The difference in their sales is 280 suitcases. How many suitcases did each sell?</td><td><table><tr><th>Unknown(s)</th><th>Variable(s)</th><th>Relationship</th></tr><tr><td>Suitcases sold:
Moe
Bill</td><td>
$8S$
S</td><td>
$8S$
$-S$
280 suitcases</td></tr></table></td><td>$8S - S = 280$ (Bill)
$\frac{7S}{7} = \frac{280}{7}$
$S = 40$ (Bill)
$8(40) = 320$ (Moe)
Check
$320 - 40 = 280$
$280 = 280$</td></tr>
<tr><td>Situation 4: Calculating unit sales, p. 121
Moe sold 8 times as many suitcases as Bill. Together they sold a total of 360. How many did each sell?</td><td><table><tr><th>Unknown(s)</th><th>Variable(s)</th><th>Relationship</th></tr><tr><td>Suitcases sold:
Moe
Bill</td><td>
$8S$
S</td><td>
$8S$
$+S$
360 suitcases</td></tr></table></td><td>$8S + S = 280$
$\frac{\cancel{9}S}{\cancel{9}} = \frac{360}{9}$
$S = 40$ (Bill)
$8(40) = 320$ (Moe)
Check
$320 + 40 = 360$
$360 = 360$</td></tr>
</table>

(continues)

CHAPTER ORGANIZER AND REFERENCE GUIDE

Solving for unknowns from word problems	Blueprint aid	Mechanical steps to solve unknown with check

Situation 5: Calculating unit and dollar sales (cost per unit) when *total units not given,* p. 122

Blue Furniture Company ordered sleepers ($300) and nonsleepers ($200) that cost $8,000. Blue expects sleepers to outsell nonsleepers 2 to 1. How many units of each were ordered? What were dollar costs of each?

Blueprint aid:

Unknown(s)	Variable(s)	Price	Relationship
Sleepers	$2N$	$300	$600N$
Nonsleepers	N	200	$+200N$
			$8,000 total cost

Mechanical steps to solve unknown with check:

$$600N + 200N = 8{,}000$$

$$\frac{\cancel{800}N}{\cancel{800}} = \frac{8{,}000}{800}$$

$$N = 10 \text{ (nonsleepers)}$$

$$2N = 20 \text{ (sleepers)}$$

Check

$$10 \times \$200 = \$2{,}000$$

$$20 \times \$300 = 6{,}000$$

$$= \$8{,}000$$

Situation 6: Calculating unit and dollar sales (cost per unit) when *total units given,* p. 122

Blue Furniture Company ordered 30 sofas (sleepers and nonsleepers) that cost $8,000. The wholesale unit cost was $300 for the sleepers and $200 for the nonsleepers. How many units of each were ordered? What were dollar costs of each?

Blueprint aid:

Unknown(s)	Variable(s)	Price	Relationship
Unit costs			
Sleepers	S	$300	$300S$
Nonsleepers	$30 - S$	200	$+200(30 - S)$
			$ 8,000 total cost

Note: When the total units are given, the higher-priced item (sleepers) is assigned to the variable first. This makes the mechanical steps easier to complete.

Mechanical steps to solve unknown with check:

$$300S + 200(30 - S) = 8{,}000$$

$$300S + 6{,}000 - 200S = 8{,}000$$

$$100S + 6{,}000 = 8{,}000$$

$$-6{,}000 \qquad -6{,}000$$

$$\frac{\cancel{100}S}{\cancel{100}} = \frac{2{,}000}{100}$$

$$S = 20$$

$$\text{Nonsleepers} = 30 - 20$$

$$= 10$$

Check

$$20(\$300) + 10(\$200) = \$8{,}000$$

$$\$6{,}000 + \$2{,}000 = \$8{,}000$$

$$\$8{,}000 = \$8{,}000$$

KEY TERMS

Constants, p. 115
Equation, p. 114
Expression, p. 114
Formula, p. 115
Knowns, p. 115
Unknown, p. 115
Variables, p. 115

CHECK FIGURES FOR EXTRA PRACTICE QUIZZES WITH PAGE REFERENCES. (WORKED-OUT SOLUTIONS IN APPENDIX B.)

LU 5–1a (p. 119)

1. A. $Q/2 - 8 = 16$ B. $12(Q + 41) = 1{,}200$
   C. $7 - 2Q = 1$ D. $4Q - 2 = 24$
   E. $3Q + 3 = 19$ F. $2Q - 6 = 5$
2. A. 56 B. 50 C. 11
   D. 720 E. 496 F. 12

LU 5–2a (p. 124)

1. $P = \$190$
2. $S = \$49{,}000$
3. Morse 7; Micro 56
4. Cara 120; Susie 240
5. Meatball 72; cheese 216; Meatball = $504; cheese = $1,296
6. Meatball $504; cheese $1,296

Critical Thinking Discussion Questions

1. Explain the difference between a variable and a constant. What would you consider your monthly car payment—a variable or a constant?
2. How does the opposite process rule help solve for the variable in an equation? If a Mercedes costs 3 times as much as a Saab, how could the opposite process rule be used? The selling price of the Mercedes is $60,000.
3. What is the difference between Word Problem Situations 5 and 6 in Learning Unit 5–2? Show why the more expensive item in Word Problem Situation 6 is assigned to the variable first.

END-OF-CHAPTER PROBLEMS

Connect plus+ www.mhhe.com/slater10e

Check figures for odd-numbered problems in Appendix C

Name ______________________________ Date ________

DRILL PROBLEMS (First of Three Sets)

Solve the unknown from the following equations:

5–1. $E - 20 = 110$

5–2. $B + 110 = 400$

5–3. $Q + 100 = 400$

5–4. $Q - 60 = 850$

5–5. $5Y = 75$

5–6. $\frac{P}{6} = 92$

5–7. $8Y = 96$

5–8. $\frac{N}{16} = 5$

5–9. $4(P - 9) = 64$

5–10. $3(P - 3) = 27$

WORD PROBLEMS (First of Three Sets)

5–11. Kathy and Jeanne are elementary school teachers. Jeanne works for Marquez Charter School in Pacific Palisades, California, where class size reduction is a goal for 2009. Kathy works for a noncharter school where funds do not allow for class size reduction policies. Kathy's fifth-grade class has 1.5 times as many students as Jeanne's. If there are a total of 60 students, how many students does Jeanne's class have? How many students does Kathy's class have?

5–12. In 1955 an antique car that originally cost $3,668 is valued today at $62,125 if in excellent condition, which is $1\frac{3}{4}$ times as much as a car in very nice condition—if you can find an owner willing to part with one for any price. What would be the value of the car in very nice condition?

5–13. Joe Sullivan and Hugh Kee sell cars for a Ford dealer. Over the past year, they sold 300 cars. Joe sells 5 times as many cars as Hugh. How many cars did each sell?

5–14. Nanda Yueh and Lane Zuriff sell homes for ERA Realty. Over the past 6 months they sold 120 homes. Nanda sold 3 times as many homes as Lane. How many homes did each sell?

5–15. Dots sells T-shirts ($2) and shorts ($4). In April, total sales were $600. People bought 4 times as many T-shirts as shorts. How many T-shirts and shorts did Dots sell? Check your answer.

5–16. Dots sells 250 T-shirts ($2) and shorts ($4). In April, total sales were $600. How many T-shirts and shorts did Dots sell? Check your answer. *Hint:* Let S = Shorts.

DRILL PROBLEMS (Second of Three Sets)

5–17. $7B = 490$

5–18. $7(A - 5) = 63$

5–19. $\frac{N}{9} = 7$

5–20. $18(C - 3) = 162$

5–21. $9Y - 10 = 53$

5–22. $7B + 5 = 26$

WORD PROBLEMS (Second of Three Sets)

5–23. On a flight from Boston to San Diego, American reduced its Internet price by $190.00. The sale price was $420.99. What was the original price?

5–24. Jill, an employee at Old Navy, budgets $\frac{1}{5}$ of her yearly salary for clothing. Jill's total clothing bill for the year is $8,000. What is her yearly salary?

5–25. Bill's Roast Beef sells 5 times as many sandwiches as Pete's Deli. The difference between their sales is 360 sandwiches. How many sandwiches did each sell?

5–26. The count of discouraged unemployed workers rose to 503,000, $2\frac{1}{2}$ times as many as in the previous year. How many discouraged unemployed workers were there in the previous year?

5–27. A local Computer City sells batteries ($3) and small boxes of pens ($5). In August, total sales were $960. Customers bought 5 times as many batteries as boxes of pens. How many of each did Computer City sell? Check your answer.

5–28. Staples sells boxes of pens ($10) and rubber bands ($4). Leona ordered a total of 24 cartons for $210. How many boxes of each did Leona order? Check your answer. *Hint:* Let P = Pens.

DRILL PROBLEMS (Third of Three Sets)

5–29. $A + 90 - 15 = 210$

5–30. $5Y + 15(Y + 1) = 35$

5–31. $3M + 20 = 2M + 80$

5–32. $20(C - 50) = 19{,}000$

WORD PROBLEMS (Third of Three Sets)

5–33. In 2008, FDNY, New York City Fire Department, had 221 fire houses with 11,275 full-time uniformed firefighters. During 2008, they responded to a total of 473,335 incidents. The top five engine companies responded to an average of 5,254 calls. Engine 75 had a total of 18 calls in one 24-hour shift. They responded to five times as many medical emergencies as they did structural fires. How many structural fires did they respond to in that 24-hour shift?

5–34. At General Electric, shift 1 produced 4 times as much as shift 2. General Electric's total production for July was 5,500 jet engines. What was the output for each shift?

5–35. Ivy Corporation gave 84 people a bonus. If Ivy had given 2 more people bonuses, Ivy would have rewarded $\frac{2}{3}$ of the workforce. How large is Ivy's workforce?

5–36. Jim Murray and Phyllis Lowe received a total of $50,000 from a deceased relative's estate. They decided to put $10,000 in a trust for their nephew and divide the remainder. Phyllis received $\frac{3}{4}$ of the remainder; Jim received $\frac{1}{4}$. How much did Jim and Phyllis receive?

5–37. The first shift of GME Corporation produced $1\frac{1}{2}$ times as many lanterns as the second shift. GME produced 5,600 lanterns in November. How many lanterns did GME produce on each shift?

5–38. Wal-Mart sells thermometers ($2) and hot-water bottles ($6). In December, Wal-Mart's total sales were $1,200. Customers bought 7 times as many thermometers as hot-water bottles. How many of each did Wal-Mart sell? Check your answer.

5–39. Ace Hardware sells boxes of wrenches ($100) and hammers ($300). Howard ordered 40 boxes of wrenches and hammers for $8,400. How many boxes of each are in the order? Check your answer.

CHALLENGE PROBLEMS

5–40. Kent Christy is organizing a fundraiser for the pool he manages. He bought ice-cream cones ($.75) and ice-cream sandwiches ($1.00) to sell. His total bill was $225. **(a)** If he ordered twice the number of ice-cream cones than ice-cream sandwiches, how many of each did he buy? **(b)** What did he spend for ice-cream cones? **(c)** What did he spend for ice-cream sandwiches?

5–41. Bessy has 6 times as much money as Bob, but when each earns $6, Bessy will have 3 times as much money as Bob. How much does each have before and after earning the $6?

DVD SUMMARY PRACTICE TEST

1. Delta reduced its round-trip ticket price from Portland to Boston by $140. The sale price was $401.90. What was the original price? *(p. 120)*

2. David Role is an employee of Google. He budgets $\frac{1}{7}$ of his salary for clothing. If Dave's total clothing for the year is $12,000, what is his yearly salary? *(p. 121)*

3. A local Best Buy sells 8 times as many iPods as Sears. The difference between their sales is 490 iPods. How many iPods did each sell? *(p. 121)*

4. Working at Staples, Jill Reese and Abby Lee sold a total of 1,200 calculators. Jill sold 5 times as many calculators as Abby. How many did each sell? *(p. 121)*

5. Target sells sets of pots ($30) and dishes ($20) at the local store. On the July 4 weekend, Target's total sales were $2,600. People bought 6 times as many pots as dishes. How many of each did Target sell? Check your answer. *(p. 122)*

6. A local Dominos sold a total of 1,600 small pizzas ($9) and pasta dinners ($13) during the Super Bowl. How many of each did Dominos sell if total sales were $15,600? Check your answer. *(p. 122)*

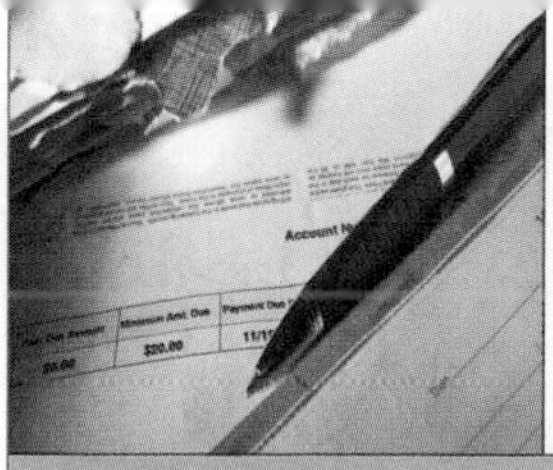

Personal Finance

A KIPLINGER APPROACH

one-fourth of the local workforce.

But UVA provides Charlottesville with more than employment. The faculty's research, especially in biotechnology, often results in private spinoff companies, such as former professor Martin Chapman's Indoor Biotechnologies, which develops allergen-detecting products. And UVA produces fine employees, too. Graduates "provide good intellectual talent," says Michael Latsko, chief talent officer for SNL Financial, a global financial-research firm headquartered in Charlottesville.

The city is a two-hour drive from Washington, D.C., and three hours from the Norfolk naval base. This proximity helped it draw in the U.S. Army National Ground Intelligence Center, which employs 750 people in a variety of fields, including engineering and foreign affairs. Next year the center will add 800 to 1,600 jobs.

Big, stable employers plus the UVA student body add up to paying customers for the small businesses that give Charlottesville its spunk. An eclectic mix of more than 150 shops, galleries and restaurants line the historic downtown pedestrian mall.

For example, one-year-old Siips Wine and Champagne Bar has already become a hot spot with its ballroom-dancing and tango nights. Just a block away, Sharon Nichols opened her Dog and Horse Lovers Boutique a year earlier. She chose Charlottesville for her dream store because it's a "vibrant city surrounded by horse country."

STACY RAPACON

Behind the Numbers

THE MAKING OF THE TOP 10

Below are some key numbers we used to choose our Best Cities for 2009. But they're only a fraction of the factors we considered. Our process is based on the work of Kevin Stolarick, of the Martin Prosperity Institute, a think tank that studies economic prosperity. Stolarick came up with a formula that identifies cities with stable employment, even in tough times. "We found cities that are independent of the national trends—places that may slow down but still keep adding jobs," Stolarick says.

Based on the formula, we looked for places with a professional, high-quality workforce that will help generate new jobs and businesses once the recession ends.

Stolarick also included in the formula a measurement of the "creative class," which comes from his work with Richard Florida, academic director of the Martin Institute and author of *The Rise of the Creative Class*. Creative-class workers—scientists, engineers, educators, writers, artists, entertainers and others—inject both economic and cultural vitality into a city and help make it a vibrant place to live.

We whittled the list of candidates to ten cities based on the numbers and our preliminary reporting. Then we traveled to most of the cities to interview business and community leaders. Our rankings factor in both the data and the results of our travels.

Metro area*	Population	Unemployment rate	Income growth†	Cost of living index#	Median household income‡	Percentage of workforce in creative class
Huntsville, Ala.	395,645	6.8%	12.5%	83.1	$50,647	40%
Albuquerque, N.M.	845,913	6.3	7.5	88.5	45,325	30
Washington, D.C.	5,358,130	5.9	13.0	102.1	83,200	44
Charlottesville, Va.	194,391	5.7	9.4	96.4	53,398	38
Athens, Ga.	189,264	6.8	15.6	88.9	40,774	32
Olympia, Wash.	245,181	8.3	8.6	112.4	57,773	35
Austin, Tex.	1,652,602	6.2	7.6	87.1	56,746	36
Madison, Wis.	561,505	6.4	8.0	86.6	59,709	35
Flagstaff, Ariz.	128,558	6.6	15.0	100.2	49,633	28
Raleigh, N.C.	1,088,765	8.6	2.4	86.7	58,111	36

*Represents the metropolitan statistical area. †Reflects household-income growth from 2004 to 2008. #National average equals 100. ‡As of 2007.
SOURCES: Bureau of Labor Statistics, City-Data.com, Martin Prosperity Institute, U.S. Census Bureau.

5 ATHENS
SOUTHERN COMFORT

It's nicknamed the Classic City for both its name and its neoclassical architecture, but Athens, Ga., is anything but old-fashioned. Although Southern charm clings to streets lined with Greek Revival mansions and Victorian-era storefronts, the air is charged with change.

The University of Georgia, for which Athens was created as a home, is in large part responsible for that energy. Athens has 110,000 residents, almost a third of whom are students. The university is the city's largest employer.

Though the economy in much of the state is in crisis—half of Georgia's counties are reporting unemployment of 10% or higher, and the rate has jumped to 9.1% in Atlanta—the unemployment rate in Athens is 6.8%.

In addition to the university, Athens boasts a hub of regional medical services and has an unexpected manufacturing base. Athens Regional Medical Center, St. Mary's Health Care System and Landmark Hospital, a long-term acute-care facility, provide health care and jobs not only for the community but also for nearby counties. International manufacturing companies, such as Carrier and DuPont, have operations in Athens.

Hospitality is another driver of the economy, and the only sector to have shown employment growth in 2009. Tourism and conventions add to the pot, but the big show is football season, when the Bulldogs come out to play.

The city offers an impressively eclectic variety of entertainment. As the birthplace of the B-52s, R.E.M. and Widespread Panic, Athens serves up music from rock and blues to alt-country. Boutiques and restaurants keep the downtown streets buzzing. Loft space and apartments sit above the hum, adding life after the last note of the night fades away. **JESSICA ANDERSON**

From *Kiplinger's Personal Finance*, July 2009, p. 73.

BUSINESS MATH ISSUE

The formula used in the study is based on wrong assumptions.

1. List the key points of the article and information to support your position.
2. Write a group defense of your position using math calculations to support your view.

PROJECT A

Is the online homework help worth the cost? Answer yes or no and support your answer.

Slater's Business Math Scrapbook

Applying Your Skills

Finding Online Homework Help for Kids

We Seek an Answer To a Pizza Problem; Ignored by Dr. Math

By Peggy Edersheim Kalb

Christoph Hitz

CRANKY CONSUMER

With school in full swing, many kids are shouldering hours of nightly homework. When students are stumped, they can turn to their (sometimes clueless) parents or head to a flurry of online homework help sites.

We looked around for sites appropriate for our sixth-grade tester. And we wanted help solving this geometry problem: what is a better buy? A square pizza measuring 8 inches by 8 inches that costs $10 or a round pizza with a 9-inch diameter that also costs $10?

Our first site was thebeehive.org. Created by the not-for-profit One Economy Corp. as a tool to help low-income families, the site offers easy access to information on a wide range of topics. By clicking on "school" on the home page (none of the other topics looked at all relevant), we got right to homework help. The section is divided into elementary-, middle- and high-school help.

Our answer was just a few clicks away. "Math" in the high-school section took us to Webmath.com, which offered a coherent explanation of how to do the problem along with a "circle calculator" on which to do the arithmetic. We went to "geometry problem solver," then to "geometry-circles," and there was the formula; we plugged in the information we find an online calculator—but it has a wealth of formulas, as well as answers to commonly asked questions (ours included). The "Frequently Asked Questions" list included everything from "What years are leap years?" "How do I find the day of the week for any date?" "How do I find a calendar for any year?" to "What is a prime number?" To those questions, the site offers explanations along with sample problems and their solutions.

For less common questions, the site offers "Ask Dr. Math," where new questions are fielded. We did try asking Dr. Math the pizza math question, but we weren't surprised that we never heard back—the site warns that if the answer is among the most commonly asked questions, and an applicable answer is already available, Dr. Math probably won't respond. We also tried a logic problem but didn't hear back on that one either. Turns out, Dr. Math is manned by volunteers who love math; if there is a volunteer who finds your problem interesting, or feels with everything from how to calculate your age in dog years, to an "airport calculator," which calculates distances and bearing between U.S. airports, are some very useful tools, including one that helped us calculate the area of our circular pizza. Our one complaint? We found the multicolored shapes and numbers which jump around on the already-busy Web page a little distracting, but our tester liked them.

Getting our math question answered by a "live" person at sites that offer personalized tutoring, however, was more complicated. At Any-timetutor.com, we never did figure out how to take advantage of the "one free math session" offered on the home page, even though we tried a few times. (There was no response to our email requests for the free session either). We gave up and forked over our credit-card number. The cost: $1 per email question to be answered in up to 12 hours, $2 for an answer in up to four hours, $2.25 for one hour and $2.50 for live help was offline the first time we checked. Eventually, we were able to IM with the "Live Support" person who explained the system, and we emailed our question late in the afternoon. Our question was answered at 4:37 the next morning; the solution was written out but it wasn't explained in a way that really helped our tester.

Next up was VistaTutor.com, a Bangladesh-based tutoring site. The company, started by entrepreneur K. Ganesh, provides a team of tutors in 31 subjects, 24 hours a day. The price averages $100 per month for unlimited tutoring, with an introductory month at $50. But we were offered one month for $25 in an email the company sent us the day after our free trial.

Still, signing up for the free trial wasn't smooth sailing. We got a hard sell from the "academic coordinator": he tried to persuade us to sign up for the service before we tried it, offering us a discount—that was already on the Web site—if we signed up immediately. When we said we wanted him to solve our math problem first, he tried solving it and got it wrong. Finally, he passed us to a tutor. (John Stuppy, president of TutorVista, regretted that had happened, but pointed out that the "academic coordinators" are sales people, not tutors, and that he was probably just trying to fill in at a busy time.)

Internet Projects: See text Web site (www.mhhe.com/slater10e) and The Business Math Internet Resource Guide.

Classroom Notes

chapter

6 PERCENTS AND THEIR APPLICATIONS

Wall Street Journal © 2009

Jeff Haynes/AFP/Getty Images

LEARNING UNIT OBJECTIVES

LU 6–1: Conversions

1. Convert decimals to percents (including rounding percents), percents to decimals, and fractions to percents *(pp. 138–141)*.
2. Convert percents to fractions *(p. 141)*.

LU 6–2: Application of Percents—Portion Formula

1. List and define the key elements of the portion formula *(p. 143)*.
2. Solve for one unknown of the portion formula when the other two key elements are given *(pp. 143–147)*.
3. Calculate the rate of percent increases and decreases *(pp. 147–149)*.

VOCABULARY PREVIEW

Here are the key terms in this chapter. When you finish the chapter, if you feel you know the term, place a checkmark within the parentheses following the term. If you are not certain of the definition, look it up and write the page number where it can be found in the text. The chapter organizer includes page references to the terms. There is also a complete glossary at the end of the text.

Base . ( ) Percent decrease . ( ) Percent increase . ( ) Percents . ( ) Portion . ( ) Rate . ( )

Did you know that 70% of Internet users in China are thirty years of age or younger? This fact is from the *Wall Street Journal* clipping "Youthful Target." Note in the *Wall Street Journal* clipping how percents are used to express various decreases and increases between two or more numbers, or to determine a decrease or increase. Note in the *Wall Street Journal* clip "Popped Bubbles" Coca-Cola has 42.7% market share.

GLOBAL

To understand percents, you should first understand the conversion relationship between decimals, percents, and fractions as explained in Learning Unit 6–1. Then, in Learning Unit 6–2, you will be ready to apply percents to personal and business events.

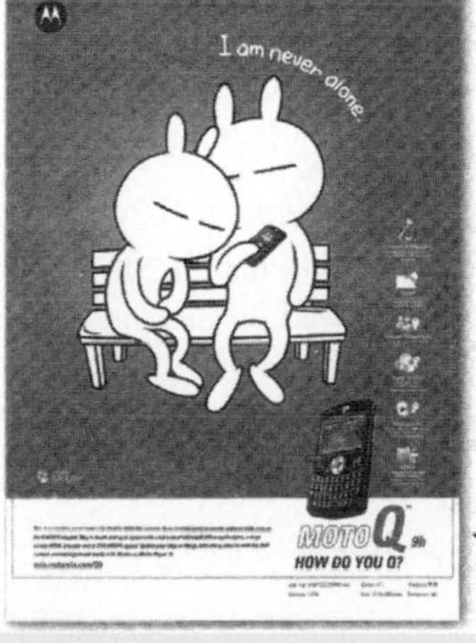

Youthful Target

More than 70% of Internet users in China are 30 years old or younger. Internet users, by age:

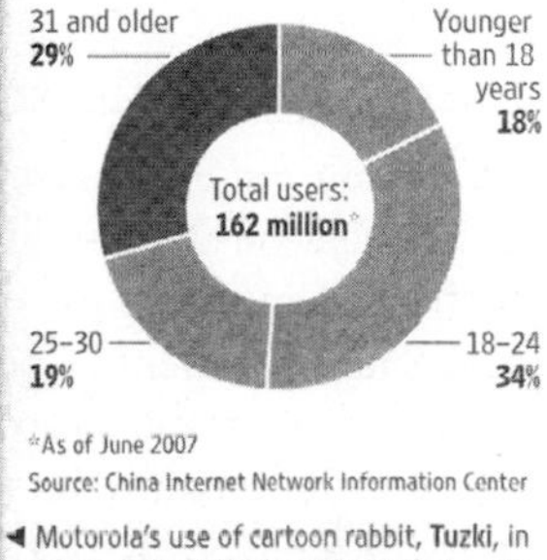

*As of June 2007

Source: China Internet Network Information Center

◀ Motorola's use of cartoon rabbit, Tuzki, in ads underlines the importance that youth culture plays in China's tech sector.

Wall Street Journal © 2007

Popped Bubbles

Major soda companies hold the larges carbonated drinks, but some smaller

Company	Market share in 2008	
1. Coca-Cola	42.7%	
2. PepsiCo	30.8	
3. Dr Pepper Snapple	15.3	
4. Cott	4.7	-6
5. National Beverage	2.6	
6. Hansen Natural	0.8	
7. Red Bull	0.7	
8. Big Red	0.4	
9. Rockstar	0.4	
10. Private label and other	1.6	

Source: Beverage Digest

Wall Street Journal © 2008

Learning Unit 6–1: Conversions

LO 1

When we described parts of a whole in previous chapters, we used fractions and decimals. Percents also describe parts of a whole. The word *percent* means per 100. The percent symbol (%) indicates hundredths (division by 100). **Percents** are the result of expressing numbers as part of 100.

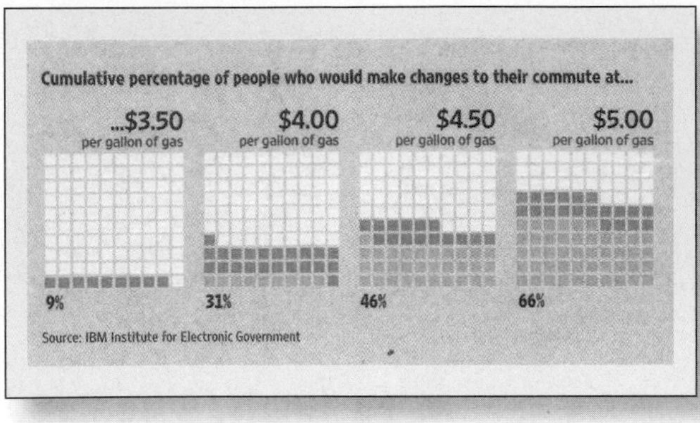

Wall Street Journal © 2008

Percents can provide some revealing information. The *Wall Street Journal* clipping "Cumulative Percentage of People Who Would Make Changes to Their Commute at . . ." shows that if gas were to reach \$5.00 per gallon, 66% would change their daily commuting routine.

Let's return to the M&M's® example from earlier chapters. In Table 6.1, we use our bag of 55 M&M's® to show how fractions, decimals, and percents can refer to the same parts of a whole. For example, the bag of 55 M&M's® contains 18 yellow M&M's®. As you can see in Table 6.1, the 18 candies in the bag of 55 can be expressed as a fraction ($\frac{18}{55}$), decimal (.33), and percent (32.73%). If you visit the M&M's® website, you will see that the standard is 11 yellow M&M's®. The clipping (in margin) "What Colors Come in Your Bag?" shows an M&M's® Milk Chocolate Candies Color Chart.

In this unit we discuss converting decimals to percents (including rounding percents), percents to decimals, fractions to percents, and percents to fractions. You will see when you study converting fractions to percents why you should first learn how to convert decimals to percents.

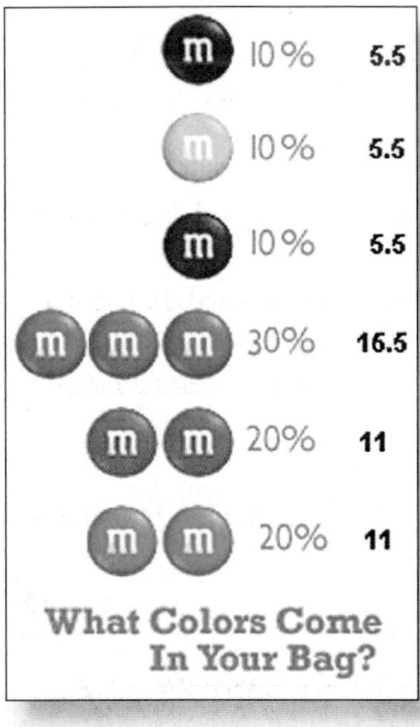

Information adapted from http://us.mms.com/us/about/products/milkchocolate/

TABLE 6.1 Analyzing a bag of M&M's®

Color	Fraction	Decimal (hundredth)	Percent (hundredth)
Yellow	$\frac{18}{55}$	.33	32.73%
Red	$\frac{10}{55}$	.18	18.18
Blue	$\frac{9}{55}$	.16	16.36
Orange	$\frac{7}{55}$	.13	12.73
Brown	$\frac{6}{55}$	.11	10.91
Green	$\frac{5}{55}$	.09	9.09
Total	$\frac{55}{55} = 1$	1.00	100.00%

Converting Decimals to Percents

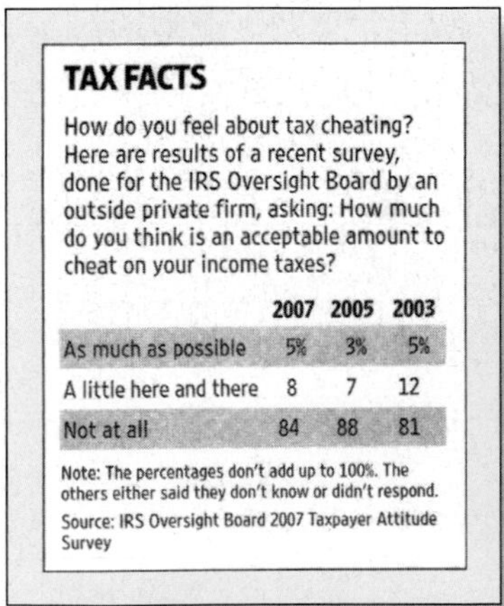

TAX FACTS

How do you feel about tax cheating? Here are results of a recent survey, done for the IRS Oversight Board by an outside private firm, asking: How much do you think is an acceptable amount to cheat on your income taxes?

	2007	2005	2003
As much as possible	5%	3%	5%
A little here and there	8	7	12
Not at all	84	88	81

Note: The percentages don't add up to 100%. The others either said they don't know or didn't respond.

Source: IRS Oversight Board 2007 Taxpayer Attitude Survey

Wall Street Journal © 2008

The *Wall Street Journal* clip "Tax Facts" shows that in 2007 the payers thought that it would be all right to cheat on the amount they owed on income tax. In 2007, 5% thought it was all right to cheat as much as possible. If the clipping had stated the 5% as a decimal (.05), could you give its equivalent in percent? The decimal .05 in decimal fraction is $\frac{5}{100}$. As you know, percents are the result of expressing numbers as part of 100, so $5\% = \frac{5}{100}$. You can now conclude that $.05 = \frac{5}{100} = 5\%$.

The steps for converting decimals to percents are as follows:

CONVERTING DECIMALS TO PERCENTS

Step 1. Move the decimal point two places to the right. You are multiplying by 100. If necessary, add zeros. This rule is also used for whole numbers and mixed decimals.

Step 2. Add a percent symbol at the end of the number.

EXAMPLES

.66 = .66. = **66%**	.8 = .80. = **80%** (Add 1 zero to make two places.)	8 = 8.00. = **800%** (Add 2 zeros to make two places.)
.425 = .42.5 = **42.5%**	.007 = .00.7 = **.7%**	2.51 = 2.51. = **251%**

Caution: One percent means 1 out of every 100. Since .7% is less than 1%, it means $\frac{7}{10}$ of 1%—a very small amount. Less than 1% is less than .01. To show a number less than 1%, you must use more than two decimal places and add 2 zeros. Example: .7% = .007.

Rounding Percents

When necessary, percents should be rounded. Rounding percents is similar to rounding whole numbers. Use the following steps to round percents:

ROUNDING PERCENTS

Step 1. When you convert from a fraction or decimal, be sure your answer is in percent before rounding.

Step 2. Identify the specific digit. If the digit to the right of the identified digit is 5 or greater, round up the identified digit.

Step 3. Delete digits to right of the identified digit.

For example, Table 6.1 (p. 138) shows that the 18 yellow M&M's® rounded to the nearest hundredth percent is 32.73% of the bag of 55 M&M's®. Let's look at how we arrived at this figure.

When using a calculator, you press [18] [÷] [55] [%]. This allows you to go right to percent, avoiding the decimal step.

Step 1. $\frac{18}{55}$ = .3272727 = 32.72727% Note that the number is in percent! Identify the hundredth percent digit.

Step 2. 32.73727% Digit to the right of the identified digit is greater than 5, so the identified digit is increased by 1.

Step 3. **32.73%** Delete digits to the right of the identified digit.

Converting Percents to Decimals

Note in the following *Wall Street Journal* clip "Still a Small Bite" that Apple Computer has only a .4% share of the personal-computer market in China.

GLOBAL

Associated Press

Apple employees answer questions from customers following the opening of the company's first store in China.

Still a Small Bite

Apple has a tiny share of China's personal-computer market—0.4% as of first quarter of 2008—but hopes to increase it by opening stores. Here's a look at the rest.

In the paragraph and steps that follow, you will learn how to convert percents to decimals. The example below the steps using 5% comes from the clipping "Tax Facts" (p. 138). As previously indicated, the example using .4% comes from the clipping "Still a Small Bite."

To convert percents to decimals, you reverse the process used to convert decimals to percents. In our earlier discussion on converting decimals to percents (p. 138), we asked if the 5% in the "Tax Facts" clipping had been in decimals and not percent, could you convert the decimals to the 5%? Once again, the definition of percent states that $5\% = \frac{5}{100}$. The fraction $\frac{5}{100}$ can be written in decimal form as .05. You can conclude that $5\% = \frac{5}{100} = .05$. Now you can see this procedure in the following conversion steps:

CONVERTING PERCENTS TO DECIMALS

Step 1. Drop the percent symbol.

Step 2. Move the decimal point two places to the left. You are dividing by 100. If necessary, add zeros.

EXAMPLES

Note that when a percent is less than 1%, the decimal conversion has at least two leading zeros before the number .004.

.4% = .00.4 = **.004**   (Add 2 zeros to make two places.)

2% = .02. = **.02**   (Add 1 zero to make two places.)

66% = .66. = **.66**

54.5% = .54.5 = **.545**

824.4% = 8.24.4 = **8.244**

Now we must explain how to change fractional percents such as $\frac{1}{5}\%$ to a decimal. Remember that fractional percents are values less than 1%. For example, $\frac{1}{5}\%$ is $\frac{1}{5}$ of 1%. Fractional percents can appear singly or in combination with whole numbers. To convert them to decimals, use the following steps:

CONVERTING FRACTIONAL PERCENTS TO DECIMALS

Step 1. Convert a single fractional percent to its decimal equivalent by dividing the numerator by the denominator. If necessary, round the answer.

Step 2. If a fractional percent is combined with a whole number (mixed fractional percent), convert the fractional percent first. Then combine the whole number and the fractional percent.

Step 3. Drop the percent symbol; move the decimal point two places to the left (this divides the number by 100).

EXAMPLES

$\frac{1}{5}\%$ = .20% = .00.20 = **.0020**

$\frac{1}{4}\%$ = .25% = .00.25 = **.0025**

$7\frac{3}{4}\%$ = 7.75% = .07.75 = **.0775**

$6\frac{1}{2}\%$ = 6.5% = .06.5 = **.065**

Think of $7\frac{3}{4}\%$ as

7% =	.07
$+\frac{3}{4}\%$ =	+ .0075
$7\frac{3}{4}\%$ =	.0775

Converting Fractions to Percents

When fractions have denominators of 100, the numerator becomes the percent. Other fractions must be first converted to decimals; then the decimals are converted to percents.

CONVERTING FRACTIONS TO PERCENTS

Step 1. Divide the numerator by the denominator to convert the fraction to a decimal.

Step 2. Move the decimal point two places to the right; add the percent symbol.

EXAMPLES

$\frac{3}{4} = .75 = .75. = 75\%$ $\quad \frac{1}{5} = .20 = .20. = 20\%$ $\quad \frac{1}{20} = .05 = .05. = 5\%$

LO 2

Converting Percents to Fractions

Using the definition of percent, you can write any percent as a fraction whose denominator is 100. Thus, when we convert a percent to a fraction, we drop the percent symbol and write the number over 100, which is the same as multiplying the number by $\frac{1}{100}$. This method of multiplying by $\frac{1}{100}$ is also used for fractional percents.

CONVERTING A WHOLE PERCENT (OR A FRACTIONAL PERCENT) TO A FRACTION

Step 1. Drop the percent symbol.

Step 2. Multiply the number by $\frac{1}{100}$.

Step 3. Reduce to lowest terms.

EXAMPLES

$76\% = 76 \times \frac{1}{100} = \frac{76}{100} = \frac{19}{25}$ $\quad \frac{1}{8}\% = \frac{1}{8} \times \frac{1}{100} = \frac{1}{800}$

$156\% = 156 \times \frac{1}{100} = \frac{156}{100} = 1\frac{56}{100} = 1\frac{14}{25}$

Sometimes a percent contains a whole number and a fraction such as $12\frac{1}{2}\%$ or 22.5%. Extra steps are needed to write a mixed or decimal percent as a simplified fraction.

MONEY TIPS

Nearly half, 47%, of adult Americans have no life-insurance coverage. Even though this is an unpleasant topic to think about, consider the impact on the loved ones you leave behind if they have to come up with funeral costs for you while they are going through the grieving process.

CONVERTING A MIXED OR DECIMAL PERCENT TO A FRACTION

Step 1. Drop the percent symbol.

Step 2. Change the mixed percent to an improper fraction.

Step 3. Multiply the number by $\frac{1}{100}$.

Step 4. Reduce to lowest terms.

Note: If you have a mixed or decimal percent, change the decimal portion to fractional equivalent and continue with Steps 1 to 4.

EXAMPLES $12\frac{1}{2}\% = \frac{25}{2} \times \frac{1}{100} = \frac{25}{200} = \frac{1}{8}$

$12.5\% = 12\frac{1}{2}\% = \frac{25}{2} \times \frac{1}{100} = \frac{25}{200} = \frac{1}{8}$

$22.5\% = 22\frac{1}{2}\% = \frac{45}{2} \times \frac{1}{100} = \frac{45}{200} = \frac{9}{40}$

It's time to check your understanding of Learning Unit 6–1.

LU 6–1 PRACTICE QUIZ

Complete this **Practice Quiz** to see how you are doing.

Convert to percents (round to the nearest tenth percent as needed):

1. .6666 ______ **2.** .832 ______

3. .004 ______ **4.** 8.94444 ______

Convert to decimals (remember, decimals representing less than 1% will have at least 2 leading zeros before the number):

5. $\frac{1}{4}\%$ ______ **6.** $6\frac{3}{4}\%$ ______

7. 87% ______ **8.** 810.9% ______

Convert to percents (round to the nearest hundredth percent):

9. $\frac{1}{7}$ ______ **10.** $\frac{2}{9}$ ______

Convert to fractions (remember, if it is a mixed number, first convert to an improper fraction):

11. 19% ______ **12.** $71\frac{1}{2}\%$ ______ **13.** 130% ______

14. $\frac{1}{2}\%$ ______ **15.** 19.9% ______

Solutions with Step-by-Step Help on DVD

✓ Solutions

1. .66.66 = **66.7%**

2. .83.2 = **83.2%**

3. .00.4 = **.4%**

4. 8.94.444 = **894.4%**

5. $\frac{1}{4}\% = .25\% =$ **.0025**

6. $6\frac{3}{4}\% = 6.75\% =$ **.0675**

7. 87% = .87. = **.87**

8. 810.9% = 8.10.9 = **8.109**

9. $\frac{1}{7} = .14.285 =$ **14.29%**

10. $\frac{2}{9} = .22.2\bar{2} =$ **22.22%**

11. $19\% = 19 \times \frac{1}{100} = \boxed{\frac{19}{100}}$

12. $71\frac{1}{2}\% = \frac{143}{2} \times \frac{1}{100} = \boxed{\frac{143}{200}}$

13. $130\% = 130 \times \frac{1}{100} = \frac{130}{100} = 1\frac{30}{100} = \boxed{1\frac{3}{10}}$

14. $\frac{1}{2}\% = \frac{1}{2} \times \frac{1}{100} = \boxed{\frac{1}{200}}$

15. $19\frac{9}{10}\% = \frac{199}{10} \times \frac{1}{100} = \boxed{\frac{199}{1{,}000}}$

LU 6–1a EXTRA PRACTICE QUIZ WITH WORKED-OUT SOLUTIONS

Need more practice? Try this **Extra Practice Quiz** (check figures in Chapter Organizer, p. 155). Worked-out Solutions can be found in Appendix B at end of text.

Convert to percents (round to the nearest tenth percent as needed):

1. .4444 **2.** .782

3. .006 **4.** 7.93333

Convert to decimals (remember, decimals representing less than 1% will have at least 2 leading zeros before the number):

5. $\frac{1}{5}\%$ **6.** $7\frac{4}{5}\%$

7. 92% **8.** 765.8%

Convert to percents (round to the nearest hundredth percent):

9. $\frac{1}{3}$ **10.** $\frac{3}{7}$

Convert to fractions (remember, if it is a mixed number, first convert to an improper fraction):

11. 17% **12.** $82\frac{1}{4}\%$ **13.** 150%

14. $\frac{1}{4}\%$ **15.** 17.8%

Learning Unit 6–2: Application of Percents—Portion Formula

LO 1

The bag of M&M's® we have been studying contains Milk Chocolate M&M's®. M&M/Mars also makes Peanut M&M's® and some other types of M&M's®. To study the application of percents to problems involving M&M's®, we make two key assumptions:

1. Total sales of Milk Chocolate M&M's®, Peanut M&M's®, and other M&M's® chocolate candies are $400,000.
2. Eighty percent of M&M's® sales are Milk Chocolate M&M's®. This leaves the Peanut and other M&M's® chocolate candies with 20% of sales (100% − 80%).

80% M&M's® Milk Chocolate M&M's®	+	20% M&M's® Peanut and other chocolate candies	=	100% Total sales ($400,000)

Before we begin, you must understand the meaning of three terms—*base, rate,* and *portion.* These terms are the key elements in solving percent problems.

- **Base (*B*).** The **base** is the beginning whole quantity or value (100%) with which you will compare some other quantity or value. Often the problems give the base after the word *of.* For example, the whole (total) sales of M&M's®—Milk Chocolate M&M's, Peanut, and other M&M's® chocolate candies—are $400,000.
- **Rate (*R*).** The **rate** is a percent, decimal, or fraction that indicates the part of the base that you must calculate. The percent symbol often helps you identify the rate. For example, Milk Chocolate M&M's® currently account for 80% of sales. So the rate is 80%. Remember that 80% is also $\frac{4}{5}$, or .80.
- **Portion (*P*).** The **portion** is the amount or part that results from the base multiplied by the rate. For example, total sales of M&M's® are $400,000 (base); $400,000 times .80 (rate) equals $320,000 (portion), or the sales of Milk Chocolate M&M's®. *A key point to remember is that portion is a number and not a percent. In fact, the portion can be larger than the base if the rate is greater than 100%.*

Solving Percents with the Portion Formula

LO 2

In problems involving portion, base, and rate, we give two of these elements. You must find the third element. Remember the following key formula:

Portion (*P*) = Base (*B*) × Rate (*R*)

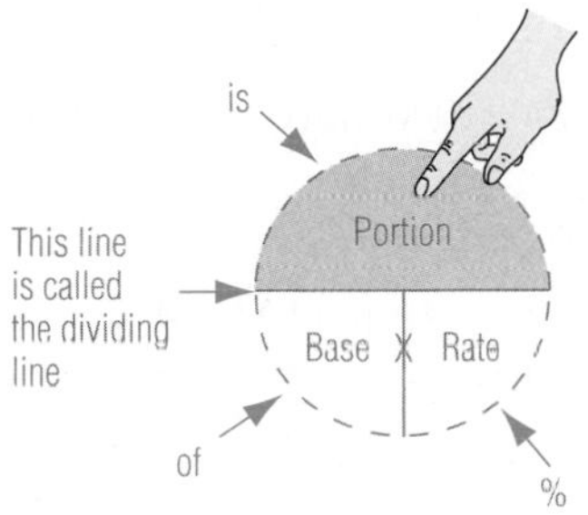

To help you solve for the portion, base, and rate, this unit shows pie charts. The shaded area in each pie chart indicates the element that you must solve for. For example, since we shaded *portion* in the pie chart at the left, you must solve for portion. To use the pie charts, put your finger on the shaded area (in this case portion). The formula that remains tells you what to do. So in the pie chart at the left, you solve the problem by multiplying base by the rate. Note the circle around the pie chart is broken since we want to emphasize that portion can be larger than base if rate is greater than 100%. The horizontal line in the pie chart is called the dividing line, and we will use it when we solve for base or rate.

The following example summarizes the concept of base, rate, and portion. Assume that you received a small bonus check of $100. This is a gross amount—your company did not withhold any taxes. You will have to pay 20% in taxes.

Base: 100%—whole. Usually given after the word *of*—but not always.	Rate: Usually expressed as a percent but could also be a decimal or fraction.	Portion: A number—not a percent and not the whole.
$100 bonus check	20% taxes	$20 taxes

First decide what you are looking for. You want to know how much you must pay in taxes—the portion. How do you get the portion? From the portion formula Portion (*P*) = Base (*B*) × Rate (*R*), you know that you must multiply the base ($100) by the rate (20%). When you do this, you get $100 × .20 = $20. So you must pay $20 in taxes.

Let's try our first word problem by taking a closer look at the M&M's® example to see how we arrived at the $320,000 sales of Milk Chocolate M&M's® given earlier. We will be using blueprint aids to help dissect and solve each word problem.

Solving for Portion

The Word Problem Sales of Milk Chocolate M&M's® are 80% of the total M&M's® sales. Total M&M's® sales are $400,000. What are the sales of Milk Chocolate M&M's®?

The facts	Solving for?	Steps to take	Key points
Milk Chocolate M&M's® sales: 80%. *Total M&M's® sales:* $400,000.	Sales of Milk Chocolate M&M's®.	Identify key elements. *Base:* $400,000. *Rate:* .80. *Portion:* ? Portion = Base × Rate.	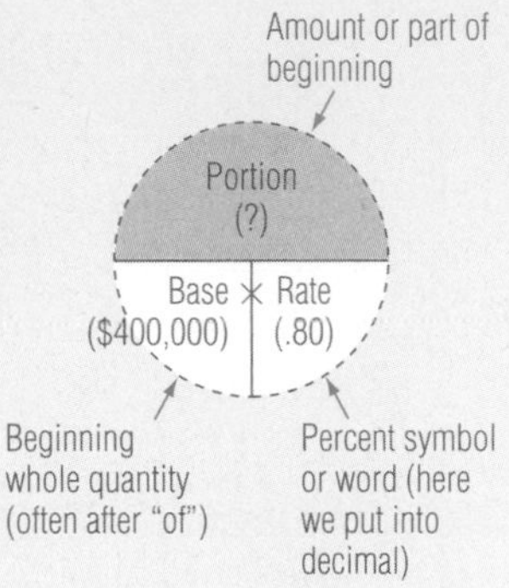 Portion and rate must relate to same piece of base.

Steps to solving problem

1. Set up the formula. Portion = Base × Rate
2. Calculate portion (sales of Milk Chocolate M&M's®). P = $400,000 × .80
   P = $320,000

In the first column of the blueprint aid, we gather the facts. In the second column, we state that we are looking for sales of Milk Chocolate M&M's®. In the third column, we identify each key element and the formula needed to solve the problem. Review the pie chart in the fourth column. Note that the portion and rate must relate to the same piece of the base. In this word problem, we can see from the solution below the blueprint aid that sales of Milk Chocolate M&M's® are $320,000. The $320,000 does indeed represent 80% of the base. Note here that the portion ($320,000) is less than the base of $400,000 since the rate is less than 100%.

Now let's work another word problem that solves for the portion.

The Word Problem Sales of Milk Chocolate M&M's® are 80% of the total M&M's® sales. Total M&M's® sales are $400,000. What are the sales of Peanut and other M&M's® chocolate candies?

The facts	Solving for?	Steps to take	Key points
Milk Chocolate M&M's® sales: 80%. *Total M&M's® sales:* $400,000.	Sales of Peanut and other M&M's® chocolate candies.	Identify key elements. *Base:* $400,000. *Rate:* .20 (100% − 80%). *Portion:* ? Portion = Base × Rate.	If 80% of sales are Milk Chocolate M&M's, then 20% are Peanut and other M&M's® chocolate candies. 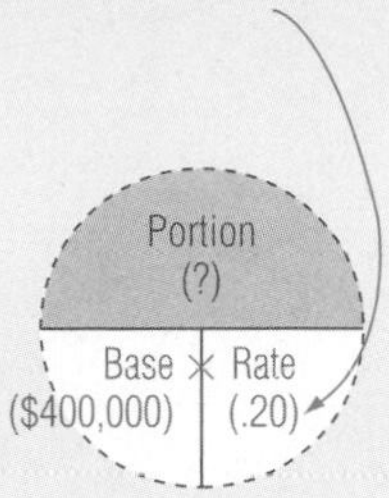 Portion and rate must relate to same piece of base.

Steps to solving problem

1. Set up the formula.	Portion = Base × Rate
2. Calculate portion (sale of Peanut and other M&M's® chocolate candies).	$P = \$400{,}000 \times .20$ $P = \$80{,}000$

In the previous blueprint aid, note that we must use a rate that agrees with the portion so the portion and rate refer to the same piece of the base. Thus, if 80% of sales are Milk Chocolate M&M's®, 20% must be Peanut and other M&M's® chocolate candies (100% − 80% = 20%). So we use a rate of .20.

In Step 2, we multiplied $400,000 × .20 to get a portion of $80,000. This portion represents the part of the sales that were *not* Milk Chocolate M&M's®. Note that the rate of .20 and the portion of $80,000 relate to the same piece of the base—$80,000 is 20% of $400,000. Also note that the portion ($80,000) is less than the base ($400,000) since the rate is less than 100%.

Take a moment to review the two blueprint aids in this section. Be sure you understand why the rate in the first blueprint aid was 80% and the rate in the second blueprint aid was 20%.

Solving for Rate

The Word Problem Sales of Milk Chocolate M&M's® are $320,000. Total M&M's® sales are $400,000. What is the percent of Milk Chocolate M&M's® sales compared to total M&M's® sales?

The facts	Solving for?	Steps to take	Key points
Milk Chocolate M&M's® sales: $320,000. *Total M&M's® sales:* $400,000.	Percent of Milk Chocolate M&M's® sales to total M&M's® sales.	Identify key elements. *Base:* $400,000. *Rate:* ? *Portion:* $320,000 $\text{Rate} = \frac{\text{Portion}}{\text{Base}}$	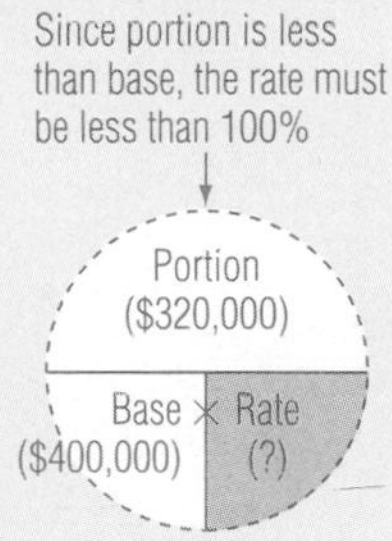 Portion and rate must relate to the same piece of base.

Steps to solving problem

1. Set up the formula.	$\text{Rate} = \frac{\text{Portion}}{\text{Base}}$
2. Calculate rate (percent of Milk Chocolate M&M's® sales).	$R = \frac{\$320{,}000}{\$400{,}000}$ $R = 80\%$

Note that in this word problem, the rate of 80% and the portion of \$320,000 refer to the same piece of the base.

The Word Problem Sales of Milk Chocolate M&M's® are \$320,000. Total sales of Milk Chocolate M&M's, Peanut, and other M&M's® chocolate candies are \$400,000. What percent of Peanut and other M&M's® chocolate candies are sold compared to total M&M's® sales?

The facts	Solving for?	Steps to take	Key points
Milk Chocolate M&M's® sales: \$320,000. *Total M&M's® sales:* \$400,000.	Percent of Peanut and other M&M's® chocolate candies sales compared to total M&M's® sales.	Identify key elements. *Base:* \$400,000. *Rate:* ? *Portion:* \$80,000 (\$400,000 − \$320,000). Rate = $\frac{\text{Portion}}{\text{Base}}$	Represents sales of Peanut and other M&M's® chocolate candies 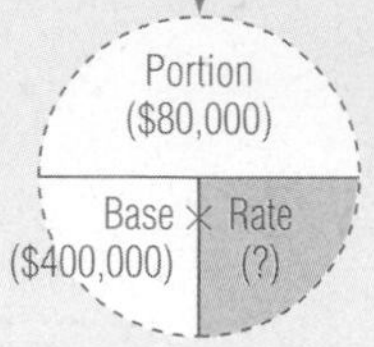 When portion becomes \$80,000, the portion and rate now relate to same piece of base.

Steps to solving problem

1. Set up the formula. $\text{Rate} = \frac{\text{Portion}}{\text{Base}}$

2. Calculate rate. $R = \frac{\$80{,}000}{\$400{,}000}$ (\$400,000 − \$320,000)

$R = 20\%$

The word problem asks for the rate of candy sales that are *not* Milk Chocolate M&M's. Thus, \$400,000 of total candy sales less sales of Milk Chocolate M&M's® (\$320,000) allows us to arrive at sales of Peanut and other M&M's® chocolate candies (\$80,000). The \$80,000 portion represents 20% of total candy sales. The \$80,000 portion and 20% rate refer to the same piece of the \$400,000 base. Compare this blueprint aid with the blueprint aid for the previous word problem. Ask yourself why in the previous word problem the rate was 80% and in this word problem the rate is 20%. In both word problems, the portion was less than the base since the rate was less than 100%.

Now we go on to calculate the base. Remember to read the word problem carefully so that you match the rate and portion to the same piece of the base.

Solving for Base

The Word Problem Sales of Peanut and other M&M's® chocolate candies are 20% of total M&M's® sales. Sales of Milk Chocolate M&M's® are \$320,000. What are the total sales of all M&M's®?

The facts	Solving for?	Steps to take	Key points
Peanut and other M&M's® chocolate candies sales: 20%. *Milk Chocolate M&M's® sales:* \$320,000.	Total M&M's® sales.	Identify key elements. *Base:* ? *Rate:* .80 (100% − 20%) *Portion:* \$320,000 Base = $\frac{\text{Portion}}{\text{Rate}}$	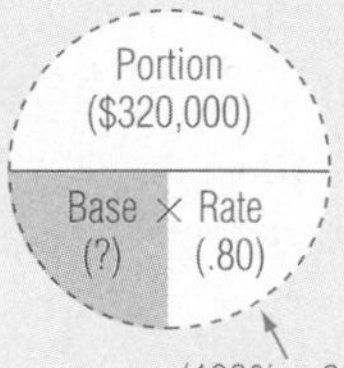 (100% – 20%) Portion (\$320,000) and rate (.80) do relate to the same piece of base.

Steps to solving problem

1. Set up the formula. $\text{Base} = \dfrac{\text{Portion}}{\text{Rate}}$

2. Calculate the base. $B = \dfrac{\$320{,}000}{.80}$ ← $320,000 is 80% of base

$B = \$400{,}000$

Note that we could not use 20% for the rate. The $320,000 of Milk Chocolate M&M's® represents 80% (100% − 20%) of the total sales of M&M's®. We use 80% so that the portion and rate refer to same piece of the base. Remember that the portion ($320,000) is less than the base ($400,000) since the rate is less than 100%.

LO 3

Calculating Percent Increases and Decreases

The following *Wall Street Journal* clipping, "Winter Could Test Energy Math," states that heating oil could face increases of between 50% and 100%. Using this clipping, let's look at how to calculate percent increases and decreases.

Winter Could Test Energy Math

Rising Heat Costs May Be Last Straw For Family Budgets

BY REBECCA SMITH

The next blow from high energy prices could come in the dead of winter.

Utilities and industry analysts estimate that it will cost families 30% to 50% more to heat their homes with natural gas this winter. Families who use heating oil could face increases of between 50% and 100%.

Expecting Pain at Other Pumps

The National Energy Assistance Directors' Association estimates that the cost to heat a home with heating oil might rise by nearly 48% between 2005 and 2009*

Average cost to heat a home

Wall Street Journal © 2008

Rate of Percent Increase

Assume: Home heating oil increases from $3.00 to $4.50 per gallon.

$$\text{Rate} = \frac{\text{Portion}}{\text{Base}} \quad \begin{array}{l}\leftarrow \text{Difference between old and new oil price} \\ \leftarrow \text{Old oil price}\end{array}$$

$$R = \frac{\$1.50\,(\$4.50 - \$3.00)}{\$3.00}$$

$$R = 50\%$$

Let's prove the 50% with a pie chart.

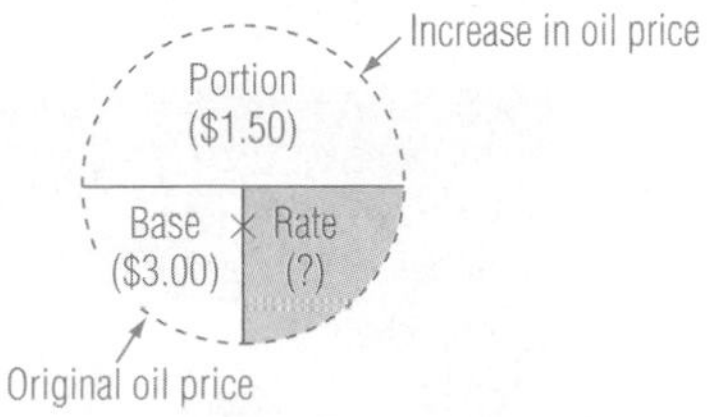

The formula for calculating oil's **percent increase** is as follows:

Percent increase

$$\text{Percent of increase } (R) \ (50\%) = \frac{\text{Amount of increase } (P) \ (\$1.50)}{\text{Original oil price } (B) \ (\$3.00)}$$

Now let's look at how to calculate the math for a decrease in oil prices from \$3.00 to \$2.70.

Rate of Percent Decrease

Assume: Home heating oil per gallon drops from \$3.00 per gallon to \$2.70 per gallon.

$$\text{Rate} = \frac{\text{Portion}}{\text{Base}} \quad \begin{matrix} \leftarrow \text{Difference between old and new oil price} \\ \leftarrow \text{Old oil price amount} \end{matrix}$$

$$R = \frac{\$.30\,(\$3.00 - \$2.70)}{\$3.00}$$

$$R = 10\%$$

Let's prove the 10% with a pie chart.

The formula for calculating oil **percent decrease** is as follows:

Percent decrease

$$\text{Percent of decrease } (R) \ (10\%) = \frac{\text{Amount of decrease } (P) \ (\$.30)}{\text{Original oil price } (B) \ (\$3.00)}$$

In conclusion, the following steps can be used to calculate percent increases and decreases:

CALCULATING PERCENT INCREASES AND DECREASES

Step 1. Find the difference between amounts (such as oil costs).

Step 2. Divide Step 1 by the original amount (the base): $R = P \div B$. Be sure to express your answer in percent.

Before concluding this chapter, we will show how to calculate a percent increase and decrease using M&M's® (Figure 6.1).

FIGURE 6.1

Bag of 18.40-ounce M&M's®

Additional Examples Using M&M's

The Word Problem Sheila Leary went to her local supermarket and bought the bag of M&M's® shown in Figure 6.1 (p. 148). The bag gave its weight as 18.40 ounces, which was 15% more than a regular 1-pound bag of M&M's®. Sheila, who is a careful shopper, wanted to check and see if she was actually getting a 15% increase. Let's help Sheila dissect and solve this problem.

The facts	Solving for?	Steps to take	Key points
New bag of M&M's®: 18.40 oz. 15% increase in weight. *Original bag of M&M's®:* 16 oz. (1 lb.)	Checking percent increase of 15%.	Identify key elements. *Base:* 16 oz. *Rate:* ? *Portion:* 2.40 oz. (18.40 oz. − 16.00 = 2.40 oz.) $\text{Rate} = \frac{\text{Portion}}{\text{Base}}$	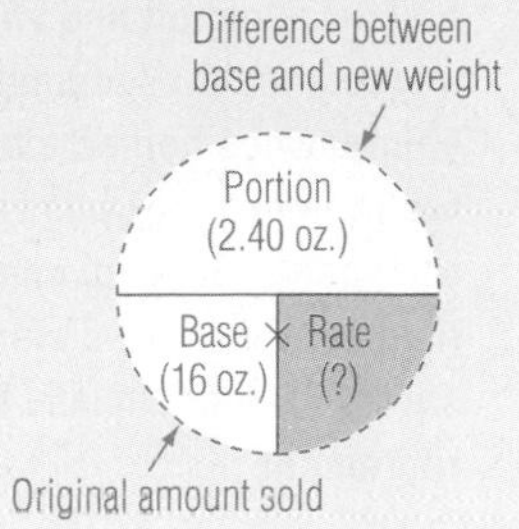

Steps to solving problem

1. Set up the formula. $\text{Rate} = \frac{\text{Portion}}{\text{Base}}$

2. Calculate the rate. $R = \frac{2.40 \text{ oz.}}{16.00 \text{ oz.}}$ ← Difference between base and new weight. ← Old weight equals 100%.

$R = 15\%$ increase

The new weight of the bag of M&M's® is really 115% of the old weight:

$$\begin{array}{rcl} 16.00 \text{ oz.} & = & 100\% \\ +\ 2.40 & = & +\ 15 \\ \hline 18.40 \text{ oz.} & = & 115\% = 1.15 \end{array}$$

We can check this by looking at the following pie chart:

Portion = Base × Rate

18.40 oz. = 16 oz. × 1.15

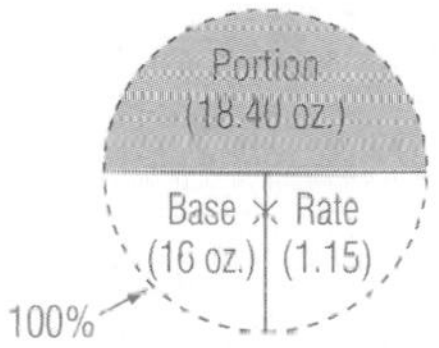

Why is the portion greater than the base? Remember that the portion can be larger than the base only if the rate is greater than 100%. Note how the portion and rate relate to the same piece of the base—18.40 oz. is 115% of the base (16 oz.).

Let's see what could happen if M&M/Mars has an increase in its price of sugar. This is an additional example to reinforce the concept of percent decrease.

The Word Problem The increase in the price of sugar caused the M&M/Mars company to decrease the weight of each 1-pound bag of M&M's® to 12 ounces. What is the rate of percent decrease?

The facts	Solving for?	Steps to take	Key points
16-oz. bag of M&M's®: reduced to 12 oz.	Rate of percent decrease.	Identify key elements. *Base:* 16 oz. *Rate:* ? *Portion:* 4 oz. (16 oz. − 12 oz.) $\text{Rate} = \frac{\text{Portion}}{\text{Base}}$	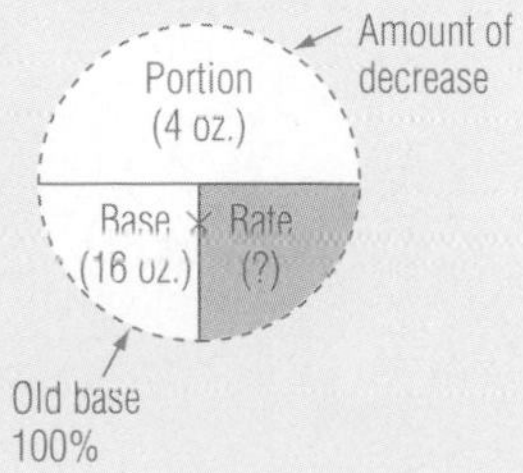

MONEY TIPS

When planning for retirement, a rule of thumb is that you will need 70% of your preretirement pay to live comfortably. This number assumes your house is paid off and you are in good health. Automating your savings can be a huge factor in helping you reach your goals. So, begin planning early in life and start saving for a financially sound retirement.

Steps to solving problem

1. Set up the formula. $\text{Rate} = \frac{\text{Portion}}{\text{Base}}$
2. Calculate the rate. $R = \frac{4 \text{ oz.}}{16.00 \text{ oz.}}$

$R = 25\%$ decrease

The new weight of the bag of M&M's® is 75% of the old weight:

$$\begin{array}{rcr} 16 \text{ oz.} & = & 100\% \\ -\ 4 & & -\ 25 \\ \hline 12 \text{ oz.} & = & 75\% \end{array}$$

We can check this by looking at the following pie chart:

Portion = Base × Rate

12 oz. = 16 oz. × .75

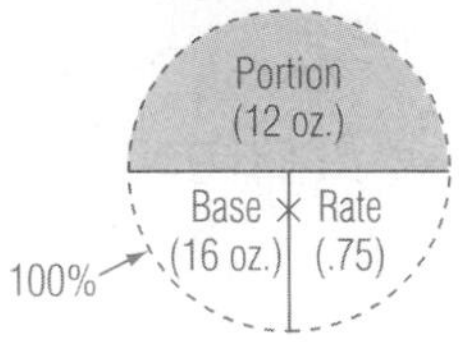

Note that the portion is smaller than the base because the rate is less than 100%. Also note how the portion and rate relate to the same piece of the base—12 ounces is 75% of the base (16 oz.).

After your study of Learning Unit 6–2, you should be ready for the Practice Quiz.

LU 6–2 PRACTICE QUIZ

Complete this **Practice Quiz** to see how you are doing.

Solve for portion:

1. 38% of 900.
2. 60% of $9,000.

Solve for rate (round to nearest tenth percent as needed):

3. 430 is ______% of 5,000.
4. 200 is ______% of 700.

Solve for base (round to the nearest tenth as needed):

5. 55 is 40% of ______.
6. 900 is $4\frac{1}{2}$% of ______.

Solve the following (blueprint aids are shown in the solution; you might want to try some on scrap paper):

7. Five out of 25 students in Professor Ford's class received an A grade. What percent of the class *did not* receive the A grade?
8. Abby Biernet has yet to receive 60% of her lobster order. Abby received 80 lobsters to date. What was her original order?
9. Assume in 2009, Dunkin' Donuts Company had $300,000 in doughnut sales. In 2010, sales were up 40%. What are Dunkin' Donuts sales for 2010?
10. The price of an Apple computer dropped from $1,600 to $1,200. What was the percent decrease?
11. In 1982, a ticket to the Boston Celtics cost $14. In 2010, a ticket cost $50. What is the percent increase to the nearest hundredth percent?

DVD *Solutions with Step-by-Step Help on DVD*

✓ Solutions

1. $342 = 900 \times .38$
   $(P) = (B) \times (R)$
2. $\$5{,}400 = \$9{,}000 \times .60$
   $(P) = (B) \times (R)$
3. $\frac{(P)430}{(B)5{,}000} = .086 = 8.6\%\ (R)$
4. $\frac{(P)200}{(B)700} = .2857 = 28.6\%\ (R)$
5. $\frac{(P)55}{(R).40} = 137.5\ (B)$
6. $\frac{(P)900}{(R).045} = 20{,}000\ (B)$

7. Percent of Professor Ford's class that did not receive an A grade:

The facts	Solving for?	Steps to take	Key points
5 As. 25 in class.	Percent that did not receive A.	Identify key elements. *Base:* 25 *Rate:* ? *Portion:* 20 (25 − 5). $\text{Rate} = \frac{\text{Portion}}{\text{Base}}$	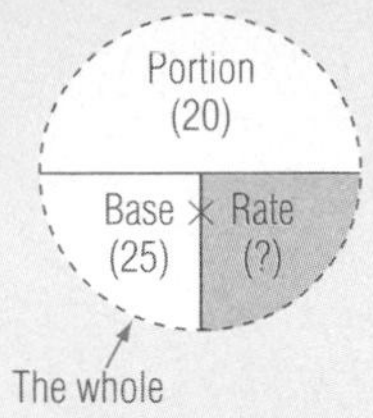 Portion and rate must relate to same piece of base.

Steps to solving problem

1. Set up the formula. $\text{Rate} = \frac{\text{Portion}}{\text{Base}}$
2. Calculate the base rate. $R = \frac{20}{25}$

$R = 80\%$

8. Abby Biernet's original order:

The facts	Solving for?	Steps to take	Key points
60% of the order not in. 80 lobsters received.	Total order of lobsters.	Identify key elements. *Base:* ? *Rate:* .40 (100% − 60%) *Portion:* 80. $\text{Base} = \frac{\text{Portion}}{\text{Rate}}$	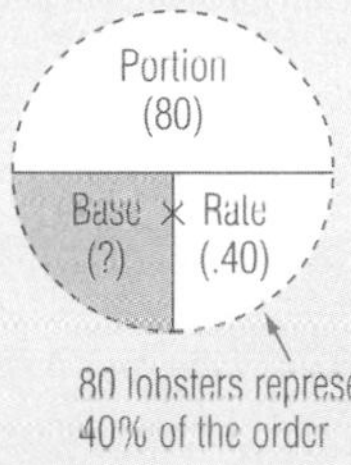 Portion and rate must relate to same piece of base.

Steps to solving problem

1. Set up the formula. $\text{Base} = \frac{\text{Portion}}{\text{Rate}}$
2. Calculate the base rate. $B = \frac{80}{.40}$ ← 80 lobsters is 40% of base.

$B = 200$ lobsters

9. Dunkin' Donuts Company sales for 2010:

The facts	Solving for?	Steps to take	Key points
2009: $300,000 sales. *2010:* Sales up 40% from 2009.	Sales for 2010.	Identify key elements. *Base:* $300,000. *Rate:* 1.40. Old year 100% New year +40 140% *Portion:* ? Portion = Base × Rate.	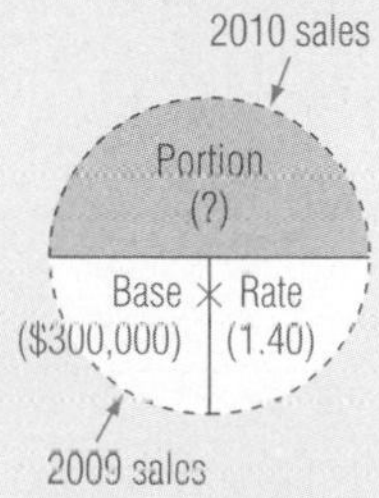 When rate is greater than 100%, portion will be larger than base.

Steps to solving problem

1. Set up the formula. Portion = Base × Rate
2. Calculate the portion. $P = \$300{,}000 \times 1.40$

$P = \$420{,}000$

10. Percent decrease in Apple computer price:

The facts	Solving for?	Steps to take	Key points
Apple computer was $1,600; now, $1,200.	Percent decrease in price.	Identify key elements. *Base:* $1,600. *Rate:* ? *Portion:* $400 ($1,600 − $1,200). $\text{Rate} = \frac{\text{Portion}}{\text{Base}}$	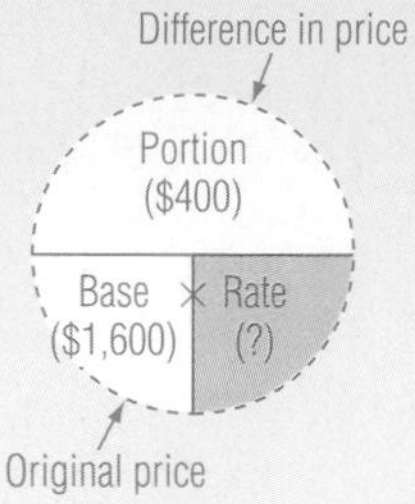

Steps to solving problem

1. Set up the formula. $\text{Rate} = \frac{\text{Portion}}{\text{Base}}$
2. Calculate the rate. $R = \frac{\$400}{\$1{,}600}$

$R = 25\%$

11. Percent increase in Boston Celtics ticket:

Pat Greenhouse/Boston Globe/Landov

The facts	Solving for?	Steps to take	Key points
$14 ticket (old). $50 ticket (new).	Percent increase in price.	Identify key elements. *Base:* $14 *Rate:* ? *Portion:* $36 ($50 − $14) $\text{Rate} = \frac{\text{Portion}}{\text{Base}}$	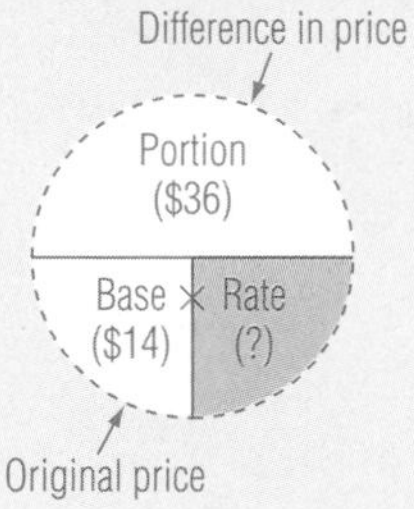 When portion is greater than base, rate will be greater than 100%.

Steps to solving problem

1. Set up the formula. $\text{Rate} = \frac{\text{Portion}}{\text{Base}}$
2. Calculate the rate. $R = \frac{\$36}{\$14}$

$R = 2.5714 = 257.14\%$

LU 6–2a EXTRA PRACTICE QUIZ WITH WORKED-OUT SOLUTIONS

Need more practice? Try this **Extra Practice Quiz** (check figures in Chapter Organizer, p. 155). Worked-out Solutions can be found in Appendix B at end of text.

Solve for portion:

1. 42% of 1,200 **2.** 7% of $8,000

Solve for rate (round to nearest tenth percent as needed):

3. 510 is ______% of 6,000. **4.** 400 is ______% of 900.

Solve for base (round to the nearest tenth as needed):

5. 30 is 60% of ______. **6.** 1,200 is $3\frac{1}{2}$% of ______.

7. Ten out of 25 students in Professor Ford's class received an A grade. What percent of the class did not receive the A grade?

8. Abby Biernet has yet to receive 70% of her lobster order. Abby received 90 lobsters to date. What was her original order?

9. A local Dunkin' Donuts Company had $400,000 in doughnut sales in 2009. In 2010, sales were up 35%. What are Dunkin' Donuts sales for 2010?

10. The price of an Apple computer dropped from $1,800 to $1,000. What was the percent decrease? (Round to the nearest hundredth percent.)

11. In 1982, a ticket to the Boston Celtics cost $14. In 2010, a ticket cost $75. What is the percent increase to the nearest hundredth percent?

CHAPTER ORGANIZER AND REFERENCE GUIDE

Topic	Key point, procedure, formula	Example(s) to illustrate situation
Converting decimals to percents, pp. 138–139	1. Move decimal point two places to right. If necessary, add zeros. This rule is also used for whole numbers and mixed decimals. 2. Add a percent symbol at end of number.	.81 = .81. = 81% .008 = .00.8 = .8% 4.15 = 4.15. = 415%
Rounding percents, p. 139	1. Answer must be in percent before rounding. 2. Identify specific digit. If digit to right is 5 or greater, round up. 3. Delete digits to right of identified digit.	Round to the nearest hundredth percent. $\frac{3}{7}$ = .4285714 = 42.85714% = 42.86%
Converting percents to decimals, pp. 139–140	1. Drop percent symbol. 2. Move decimal point two places to left. If necessary, add zeros. For fractional percents: 1. Convert to decimal by dividing numerator by denominator. If necessary, round answer. 2. If a mixed fractional percent, convert fractional percent first. Then combine whole number and fractional percent. 3. Drop percent symbol, move decimal point two places to left.	.89% = .0089 95% = .95 195% = 1.95 $8\frac{3}{4}$% = 8.75% = .0875 $\frac{1}{4}$% = .25% = .0025 $\frac{1}{5}$% = .20% = .0020
Converting fractions to percents, p. 141	1. Divide numerator by denominator. 2. Move decimal point two places to right; add percent symbol.	$\frac{4}{5}$ = .80 = 80%

(continues)

CHAPTER ORGANIZER AND REFERENCE GUIDE

Topic	Key point, procedure, formula	Example(s) to illustrate situation
Converting percents to fractions, p. 141	Whole percent (or fractional percent) to a fraction: **1.** Drop percent symbol. **2.** Multiply number by $\frac{1}{100}$. **3.** Reduce to lowest terms. Mixed or decimal percent to a fraction: **1.** Drop percent symbol. **2.** Change mixed percent to an improper fraction. **3.** Multiply number by $\frac{1}{100}$. **4.** Reduce to lowest terms. If you have a mixed or decimal percent, change decimal portion to fractional equivalent and continue with Steps 1 to 4.	$64\% \rightarrow 64 \times \frac{1}{100} = \frac{64}{100} = \frac{16}{25}$ $\frac{1}{4}\% \rightarrow \frac{1}{4} \times \frac{1}{100} = \frac{1}{400}$ $119\% \rightarrow 119 \times \frac{1}{100} = \frac{119}{100} = 1\frac{19}{100}$ $16\frac{1}{4}\% \rightarrow \frac{65}{4} \times \frac{1}{100} = \frac{65}{400} = \frac{13}{80}$ $16.25\% \rightarrow 16\frac{1}{4}\% = \frac{65}{4} \times \frac{1}{100}$ $= \frac{65}{400} = \frac{13}{80}$
Solving for portion, pp. 144–145	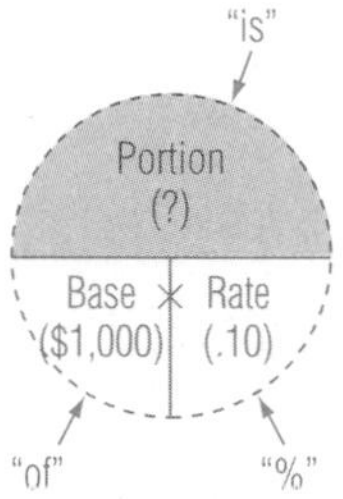	10% of Mel's paycheck of $1,000 goes for food. What portion is deducted for food? $100 = $1,000 × .10 *Note:* If question was what amount does not go for food, the portion would have been: $900 = $1,000 × .90 (100% 10% = 90%
Solving for rate, pp. 145–146	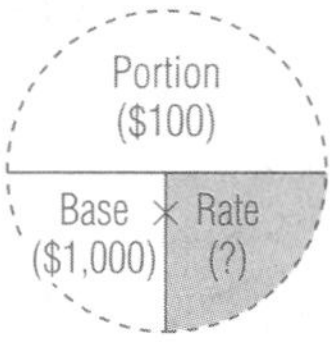	Assume Mel spends $100 for food from his $1,000 paycheck. What percent of his paycheck is spent on food? $\frac{\$100}{\$1,000} = .10 = 10\%$ *Note:* Portion is less than base since rate is less than 100%.
Solving for base, pp. 146–147	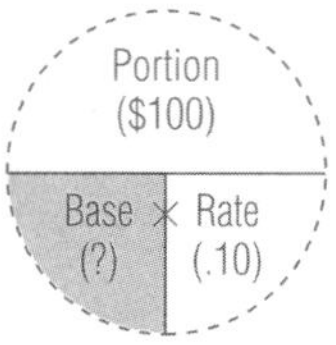	Assume Mel spends $100 for food, which is 10% of his paycheck. What is Mel's total paycheck? $\frac{\$100}{.10} = \$1,000$
Calculating percent increases and decreases, pp. 147–149	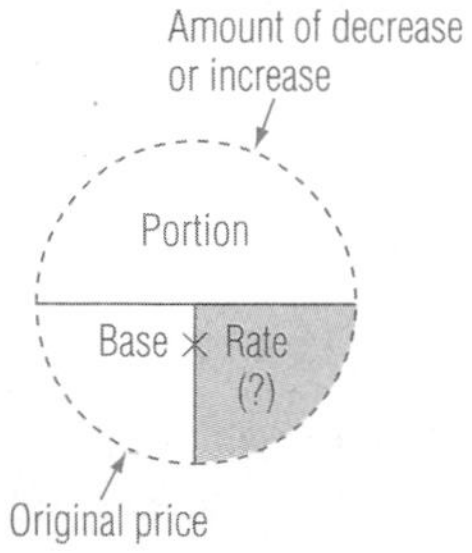	Stereo, $2,000 original price. Stereo, $2,500 new price. $\frac{\$500}{\$2,000} = .25 = 25\%$ increase **Check** $2,000 × 1.25 = $2,500 *Note:* Portion is greater than base since rate is greater than 100%. 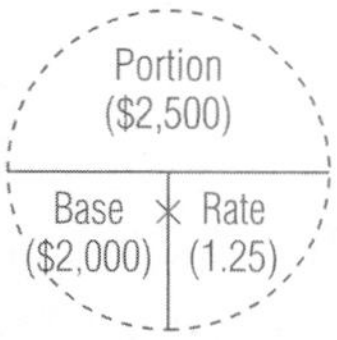
KEY TERMS	Base, *p. 143* Percent increase, *p. 148* Percent decrease, *p. 148* Percents, *p. 138*	Portion, *p. 143* Rate, *p. 143*

(continues)

CHAPTER ORGANIZER AND REFERENCE GUIDE

Topic	Key point, procedure, formula	Example(s) to illustrate situation
CHECK FIGURES FOR EXTRA PRACTICE QUIZZES WITH PAGE REFERENCES. (WORKED-OUT SOLUTIONS IN APPENDIX B.)	LU 6–1a (p. 142) **1.** 44.4% **2.** 78.2% **3.** .6% **4.** 793.3% **5.** .0020 **6.** .0780 **7.** .92 **8.** 7.658 **9.** 33.33% **10.** 42.86% **11.** $\frac{17}{100}$ **12.** $\frac{329}{400}$ **13.** $1\frac{1}{2}$ **14.** $\frac{1}{400}$ **15.** $\frac{89}{500}$	LU 6–2a (p. 153) **1.** 504 **2.** 560 **3.** 8.5% **4.** 44.4% **5.** 50 **6.** 34,285.7 **7.** 60% **8.** 300 **9.** $540,000 **10.** 44.44% **11.** 435.71%

Note: For how to dissect and solve a word problem, see page 144.

Critical Thinking Discussion Questions

1. In converting from a percent to a decimal, when will you have at least 2 leading zeros before the whole number? Explain this concept, assuming you have 100 bills of $1.
2. Explain the steps in rounding percents. Count the number of students who are sitting in the back half of the room as a percent of the total class. Round your answer to the nearest hundredth percent. Could you have rounded to the nearest whole percent without changing the accuracy of the answer?
3. Define portion, rate, and base. Create an example using Walt Disney World to show when the portion could be larger than the base. Why must the rate be greater than 100% for this to happen?
4. How do we solve for portion, rate, and base? Create an example using IBM computer sales to show that the portion and rate do relate to the same piece of the base.
5. Explain how to calculate percent decreases or increases. Many years ago, comic books cost 10 cents a copy. Visit a bookshop or newsstand. Select a new comic book and explain the price increase in percent compared to the 10-cent comic. How important is the rounding process in your final answer?

Classroom Notes

END-OF-CHAPTER PROBLEMS

connect plus+ www.mhhe.com/slater10e

6

Check figures for odd-numbered problems in Appendix C

Name ______________________ Date ________

DRILL PROBLEMS

Convert the following decimals to percents:

6–1. .66 **6–2.** .943 **6–3.** .8

6–4. 8.00 **6–5.** 3.561 **6–6.** 6.006

Convert the following percents to decimals:

6–7. 9% **6–8.** 16% **6–9.** $64\frac{3}{10}\%$

6–10. 75.9% **6–11.** 119% **6–12.** 89%

Convert the following fractions to percents (round to the nearest tenth percent as needed):

6–13. $\frac{1}{12}$ **6–14.** $\frac{1}{400}$

6–15. $\frac{7}{8}$ **6–16.** $\frac{11}{12}$

Convert the following to fractions and reduce to the lowest terms:

6–17. 4% **6–18.** $18\frac{1}{2}\%$

6–19. $31\frac{2}{3}\%$ **6–20.** $61\frac{1}{2}\%$

6–21. 6.75% **6–22.** 182%

Solve for the portion (round to the nearest hundredth as needed):

6–23. 7% of 150 **6–24.** 125% of 4,320 **6–25.** 25% of 410

6–26. 119% of 128.9 **6–27.** 17.4% of 900 **6–28.** 11.2% of 85

6–29. $12\frac{1}{2}\%$ of 919 **6–30.** 45% of 300

6–31. 18% of 90 **6–32.** 30% of 2,000

Solve for the base (round to the nearest hundredth as needed):

6–33. 170 is 120% of ________ **6–34.** 36 is .75% of ________

6–35. 50 is .5% of ________ **6–36.** 10,800 is 90% of ________

6–37. 800 is $4\frac{1}{2}\%$ of ________

Solve for rate (round to the nearest tenth percent as needed):

6–38. ________ of 80 is 50 **6–39.** ________ of 85 is 92

6–40. ________ of 250 is 65 **6–41.** 110 is ________ of 100

6–42. .09 is ________ of 2.25 **6–43.** 16 is ________ of 4

Solve the following problems. Be sure to show your work. Round to the nearest hundredth or hundredth percent as needed:

6–44. What is 180% of 310?

6–45. 66% of 90 is what?

6–46. 40% of what number is 20?

6–47. 770 is 70% of what number?

6–48. 4 is what percent of 90?

6–49. What percent of 150 is 60?

Complete the following table:

	Product	Selling price 2008	Selling price 2009	Amount of decrease or increase	Percent change (to nearest hundredth percent as needed)
6–50.	Hamilton watch	$650	$500		
6–51.	College textbook	$100	$120		

WORD PROBLEMS (First of Four Sets)

6–52. At a local Dunkin' Donuts, a survey showed that out of 1,200 customers eating lunch, 240 ordered coffee with their meal. What percent of customers ordered coffee?

6–53. What percent of customers in Problem 6–52 did not order coffee?

6–54. In August 2008, gas was selling for $4.07 a gallon. The price of a gallon of regular unleaded dropped to $3.52 on September 11, 2008. What was the percent decrease? Round to the nearest hundredth percent.

6–55. Wally Chin, the owner of an ExxonMobil station, bought a used Ford pickup truck, paying $2,000 as a down payment. He still owes 80% of the selling price. What was the selling price of the truck?

6–56. Maria Fay bought 4 Dunlop tires at a local Goodyear store. The salesperson told her that her mileage would increase by 8%. Before this purchase, Maria was getting 24 mpg. What should her mileage be with the new tires to the nearest hundredth?

6–57. Jeff Rowe went to Best Buy and bought a Canon digital camera. The purchase price was $400. Jeff made a down payment of 40%. How much was Jeff's down payment?

6–58. Assume that in the year 2010, 800,000 people attended the Christmas Eve celebration at Walt Disney World. If in 2011, attendance for the Christmas Eve celebration is expected to increase by 35%. What is the total number of people expected at Walt Disney World for this event?

6–59. Pete Smith found in his attic a Woody Woodpecker watch in its original box. It had a price tag on it for $4.50. The watch was made in 1949. Pete brought the watch to an antiques dealer and sold it for $35. What was the percent of increase in price? Round to the nearest hundredth percent.

6–60. Christie's Auction sold a painting for $24,500. It charges all buyers a 15% premium of the final bid price. How much did the bidder pay Christie's?

WORD PROBLEMS (Second of Four Sets)

6–61. Out of 9,000 college students surveyed, 540 responded that they do not eat breakfast. What percent of the students do not eat breakfast?

6–62. What percent of college students in Problem 6–61 eat breakfast?

6–63. Alice Hall made a $3,000 down payment on a new Ford Explorer wagon. She still owes 90% of the selling price. What was the selling price of the wagon?

6–64. Rainfall for January in Fiji averages 12″ according to *World Travel Guide*. This year it rained 5% less. How many inches (to the nearest tenth) did it rain this year?

6–65. Jim and Alice Lange, employees at Walmart, have put themselves on a strict budget. Their goal at year's end is to buy a boat for $15,000 in cash. Their budget includes the following:

40% food and lodging   20% entertainment   10% educational

Jim earns $1,900 per month and Alice earns $2,400 per month. After one year, will Alice and Jim have enough cash to buy the boat?

6–66. The price of a Fossil watch dropped from $49.95 to $30.00. What was the percent decrease in price? Round to the nearest hundredth percent.

6–67. The Museum of Science in Boston estimated that 64% of all visitors came from within the state. On Saturday, 2,500 people attended the museum. How many attended the museum from out of state?

6–68. Staples pays George Nagovsky an annual salary of $36,000. Today, George's boss informs him that he will receive a $4,600 raise. What percent of George's old salary is the $4,600 raise? Round to the nearest tenth percent.

6–69. In 2010, a local Dairy Queen had $550,000 in sales. In 2011, Dairy Queen's sales were up 35%. What were Dairy Queen's sales in 2011?

6–70. Blue Valley College has 600 female students. This is 60% of the total student body. How many students attend Blue Valley College?

6–71. Dr. Grossman was reviewing his total accounts receivable. This month, credit customers paid $44,000, which represented 20% of all receivables (what customers owe) due. What was Dr. Grossman's total accounts receivable?

6–72. Massachusetts has a 5% sales tax. Timothy bought a Toro lawn mower and paid $20 sales tax. What was the cost of the lawn mower before the tax?

6–73. The price of an antique doll increased from $600 to $800. What was the percent of increase? Round to the nearest tenth percent.

6–74. A local Borders bookstore ordered 80 marketing books but received 60 books. What percent of the order was missing?

WORD PROBLEMS (Third of Four Sets)

6–75. At a Christie's auction, the auctioneer estimated that 40% of the audience was from within the state. Eight hundred people attended the auction. How many out-of-state people attended?

6–76. Due to increased mailing costs, the new rate will cost publishers $50 million; this is 12.5% more than they paid the previous year. How much did it cost publishers last year? Round to the nearest hundreds.

6–77. In 2011, Jim Goodman, an employee at Walgreens, earned \$45,900, an increase of 17.5% over the previous year. What were Jim's earnings in 2010? Round to the nearest cent.

6–78. If the number of mortgage applications declined by 7% to 1,625,415, what had been the previous year's number of applications?

6–79. In 2011, the price of a business math text rose to \$150. This is 8% more than the 2010 price. What was the old selling price? Round to the nearest cent.

6–80. Web Consultants, Inc., pays Alice Rose an annual salary of \$48,000. Today, Alice's boss informs her that she will receive a \$6,400 raise. What percent of Alice's old salary is the \$6,400 raise? Round to the nearest tenth percent.

6–81. Earl Miller, a lawyer, charges Lee's Plumbing, his client, 25% of what he can collect for Lee from customers whose accounts are past due. The attorney also charges, in addition to the 25%, a flat fee of \$50 per customer. This month, Earl collected \$7,000 from 3 of Lee's past-due customers. What is the total fee due to Earl?

6–82. A local Petco ordered 100 dog calendars but received 60. What percent of the order was missing?

6–83. Blockbuster Video uses MasterCard. MasterCard charges $2\frac{1}{2}\%$ on net deposits (credit slips less returns). Blockbuster made a net deposit of $4,100 for charge sales. How much did MasterCard charge Blockbuster?

6–84. In 2010, Internet Access had $800,000 in sales. In 2011, Internet Access sales were up 45%. What are the sales for 2011?

WORD PROBLEMS (Fourth of Four Sets)

6–85. Saab Corporation raised the base price of its popular 900 series by $1,200 to $33,500. What was the percent increase? Round to the nearest tenth percent.

6–86. The sales tax rate is 8%. If Jim bought a new Buick and paid a sales tax of $1,920, what was the cost of the Buick before the tax?

6–87. Puthina Unge bought a new Compaq computer system on sale for $1,800. It was advertised as 30% off the regular price. What was the original price of the computer? Round to the nearest dollar.

6–88. John O'Sullivan has just completed his first year in business. His records show that he spent the following in advertising:

Newspaper	$600	Radio	$650	Yellow Pages	$700	Local flyers	$400

What percent of John's advertising was spent on the Yellow Pages? Round to the nearest hundredth percent.

6–89. Jay Miller sold his ski house at Attitash Mountain in New Hampshire for \$35,000. This sale represented a loss of 15% off the original price. What was the original price Jay paid for the ski house? Round your answer to the nearest dollar.

6–90. Out of 4,000 colleges surveyed, 60% reported that SAT scores were not used as a high consideration in viewing their applications. How many schools view the SAT as important in screening applicants?

6–91. If refinishing your basement at a cost of \$45,404 would add \$18,270 to the resale value of your home, what percent of your cost is recouped? Round to the nearest percent.

6–92. A major airline laid off 4,000 pilots and flight attendants. If this was a 12.5% reduction in the workforce, what was the size of the workforce after the layoffs?

6–93. Assume 450,000 people line up on the streets to see the Macy's Thanksgiving Parade in 2010. If attendance is expected to increase 30%, what will be the number of people lined up on the street to see the 2011 parade?

CHALLENGE PROBLEMS

6–94. Kyle Drummond works as an auto mechanic. He just finished a job taking 3.25 hours of labor at \$60 per hour. The parts he used totaled \$55. If there is a 120% markup on parts, what was the customer charged?

6–95. A local Dunkin' Donuts shop reported that its sales have increased exactly 22% per year for the last 2 years. This year's sales were \$82,500. What were Dunkin' Donuts sales 2 years ago? Round each year's sales to the nearest dollar.

SUMMARY PRACTICE TEST

Convert the following decimals to percents. *(p. 139)*

1. .921 **2.** .4 **3.** 15.88 **4.** 8.00

Convert the following percents to decimals. *(p. 140)*

5. 42% **6.** 7.98% **7.** 400% **8.** $\frac{1}{4}\%$

Convert the following fractions to percents. Round to the nearest tenth percent. *(p. 141)*

9. $\frac{1}{6}$ **10.** $\frac{1}{3}$

Convert the following percents to fractions and reduce to the lowest terms as needed. *(p. 141)*

11. $19\frac{3}{8}\%$ **12.** 6.2%

Solve the following problems for portion, base, or rate:

13. An Arby's franchise has a net income before taxes of $900,000. The company's treasurer estimates that 40% of the company's net income will go to federal and state taxes. How much will the Arby's franchise have left? *(p. 144)*

14. Domino's projects a year-end net income of $699,000. The net income represents 30% of its annual sales. What are Domino's projected annual sales? *(p. 146)*

15. Target ordered 400 iPods. When Target received the order, 100 iPods were missing. What percent of the order did Target receive? *(p. 145)*

16. Matthew Song, an employee at Putnam Investments, receives an annual salary of $120,000. Today his boss informed him that he would receive a $3,200 raise. What percent of his old salary is the $3,200 raise? Round to the nearest hundredth percent. *(p. 145)*

17. The price of a Delta airline ticket from Los Angeles to Boston increased to \$440. This is a 15% increase. What was the old fare? Round to the nearest cent. *(p. 146)*

18. Scupper Grace earns a gross pay of \$900 per week at Office Depot. Scupper's payroll deductions are 29%. What is Scupper's take-home pay? *(p. 144)*

19. Mia Wong is reviewing the total accounts receivable of Wong's department store. Credit customers paid \$90,000 this month. This represents 60% of all receivables due. What is Mia's total accounts receivable? *(p. 146)*

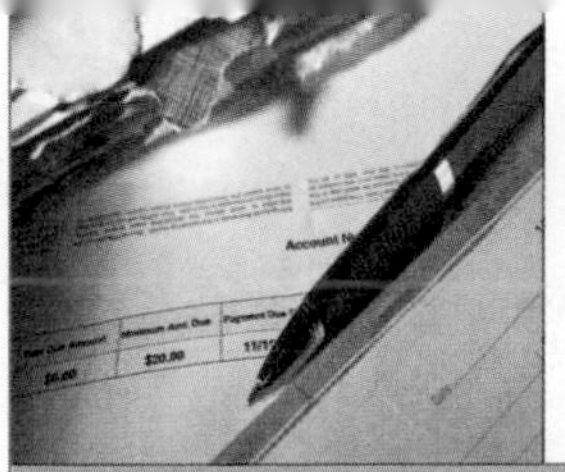

LOWDOWN

What You Need to Know About Your Credit Score

It's the key to many of life's major purchases.

BY JESSICA ANDERSON

1. LEARN THE COMBINATION. The three-digit number that is your credit score predicts how likely you are to repay a loan, based on information in your credit report. The two major criteria, which account for up to two-thirds of your score, are your payment history and your outstanding debt. You should pay at least the minimum amount due each month—on time. The amount of debt relative to your credit limit is your credit utilization; it's best to keep it below 25%. How long you've had credit counts, too, and authorized-user accounts can help you build credit even if you're not the one paying the bills. (FICO reversed an earlier decision to drop authorized-user accounts.) Among other factors affecting your score are the number of inquiries on your account and your mix of credit.

2. ALL CREDIT SCORES ARE NOT CREATED EQUAL. The FICO score, which ranges from 300 to 850, is the only one you need to know. It's the basis for at least 75% of mortgage decisions, and 90% of the largest banks rely on it. The credit-monitoring bureaus have created others, such as the VantageScore, but few lenders use them.

3. ONE SCORE, THREE VERSIONS. You actually have three FICO scores, one with each of the major credit bureaus: Equifax, Experian and TransUnion. Lenders often contract exclusively with one bureau, which in turn will give them a price break when they buy scores. Ask your lender which bureau it uses—you could get a leg up. Mortgage lenders are the exception: They obtain all three scores and have to resolve the differences among them. The crudest method, says Craig Watts, public affairs director for FICO, is for a lender to kick out the top and bottom scores and consider only the middle number.

4. HOW TO GET A TWOFER. The cheapest way to get your FICO score is to order one along with your request for a free annual credit report from Equifax (go to www.annualcreditreport.com); it'll cost you $8. Your FICO score and credit report from Equifax and TransUnion are available at myFICO.com, but you'll pay $15.95 each. Of the three bureaus, Equifax is the only one that will sell you a credit report and FICO score from its main Web site ($15.95). For TransUnion FICO scores, go to www.transunioncs.com ($14.95). As of mid February, Experian had stopped selling FICO credit scores to consumers.

5. GARBAGE IN, GARBAGE OUT. The credit bureaus are obligated to report correctly only what lenders report to them. So if an error affecting your score originates with your lender, complaining to the credit bureau probably won't help and could be a waste of time—the bureaus typically have 30 to 45 days to respond to a complaint. If you think a mistake has been made, contact your lender immediately. And keep an eye on your credit report. An annual checkup using your free credit report should suffice, unless you're shopping for a large loan.

6. YOU CAN SCORE *TOO* HIGH. A score of 820 to 830 could make you seem unprofitable, says John Ulzheimer, president of consumer education at Credit.com. "Culprits" are usually at least in their forties, with long credit histories and little or no outstanding debt. You won't be turned down, but you may not receive new offers. "The sweet spot is 750 to 800," says Ulzheimer. ■

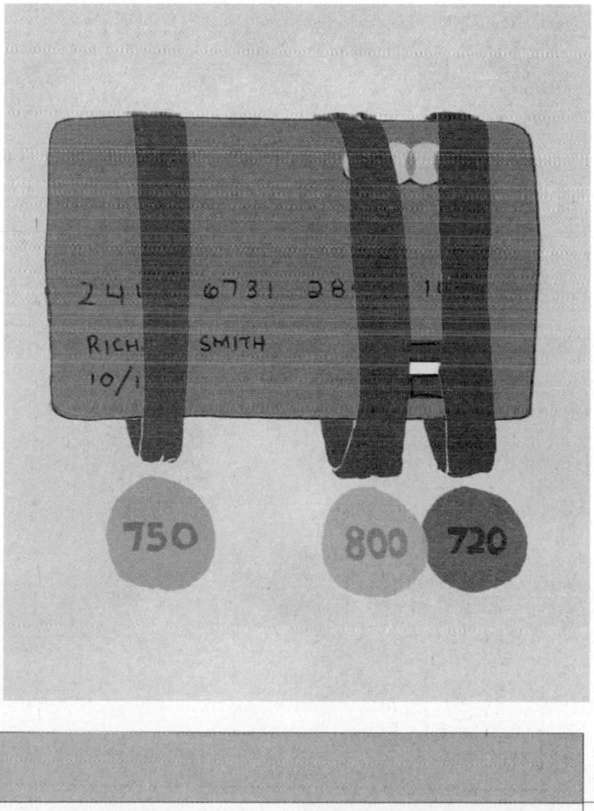

From Kiplinger's Personal Finance, August 2009, p. 69

BUSINESS MATH ISSUE

FICO scores should be used less by banks in loan decisions.

1. List the key points of the article and information to support your position.
2. Write a group defense of your position using math calculations to support your view.

Slater's Business Math Scrapbook

Applying Your Skills

PROJECT A

Calculate the actual cost of a bathroom remodel that was not recovered. Prove your answer.

Payback Time

Selected remodeling projects with average estimated percentage of costs recovered when home is sold.

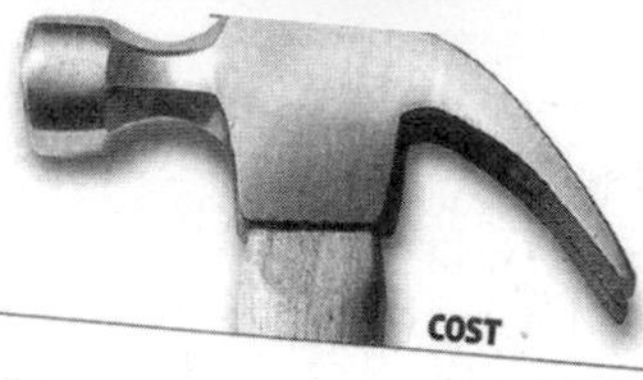

PROJECT	COST	AMOUNT RECOUPED
Deck addition (wood) Build a 16-by-20-foot deck, including a built-in bench, planter, stairs and rail system	$10,347	85.4%
Siding replacement Replace 1,250 square feet with new vinyl siding, including trim	$9,910	83.2%
Minor kitchen remodel Includes new laminated countertops and fronts for 30 linear feet of cabinetry, oven, cooktop, sink and faucet, flooring	$21,185	83%
Window replacement – wood Replace 10 3-by-5-foot double-hung windows with new insulated windows	$11,384	81.2%
Bathroom remodel Includes new tub and tiling, solid-surface counter and sink, recessed medicine cabinet, vinyl wallpaper	$15,789	78.3%
Basement remodel Includes a 5-by-8-foot bathroom and a wet bar with under-counter refrigerator	$59,435	75.1%
Two-story addition A 24-by-16-foot wing including family room with prefabricated fireplace and a bedroom with full bath	$139,297	73.9%
Master suite addition A 24-by-16-foot bedroom with walk-in closet and bathroom with shower and raised whirlpool tub	$98,863	69%
Sunroom addition Build a 200-square-foot room with 10 large skylights, casement windows with movable shades and quarry tile floor	$69,817	59.1%
Home office remodel Convert a 12-by-12-foot room with custom cabinetry including 20 linear feet of laminated desktop, computer workstation, wall storage and rewiring for computer, telephone and other electronics	$27,193	57%

Source: Remodeling 2007 Cost vs. Value Report. Cost data from HomeTech Information Systems; includes labor. Recoup values are based on a 2007 survey of 2,700 members of the National Association of Realtors. Data for 60 cities can be downloaded free from www.costvsvalue.com

PROJECT B

Calculate the percent change of stores for each chain as of 12/31/08. Round to nearest hundredth percent.

Slicing Away

Two of the three big pizza chains lost U.S. outlets last year; in contrast, burger giant McDonald's grew

Chain	Stores as of 12/31/08	Stores as of 12/31/07
Pizza Hut	6,103	6,144
Domino's	5,086*	5,155
Papa John's	2,792	2,760
McDonald's	13,918	13,862

*Nine-month figures as of Sept. 30, 2008

Sources: company reports

Internet Projects: See text Web site (www.mhhe.com/slater10e) and The Business Math Internet Resource Guide.

Video Case

American President Lines

American President Lines (APL) has automated its terminal so the average turnaround time for a trucker picking up a 40-foot container is only 17 minutes.

APL uses an automated wireless system to track containers parked across its recently remodeled 160-acre facility in Seattle.

The fast turnaround time gives customers who operate under the just-in-time mode the opportunity to make more trips. Independent truck drivers also benefit.

The international freight industry is plagued by red tape and inefficiency. APL has used its website to help clients like Excel Corporation, the country's second-largest beef packer and processor, speed up its billing time. Excel now wants to ask online for a place on a ship and for a call from APL when room will be available.

The shipping market is enormous, estimated anywhere from $100 billion to $1 trillion. Imports in the United States alone totaled 10 million containers, while exports totaled 6.5 million containers, together carrying $375 billion worth of goods. One of the most difficult transactions is to source goods from overseas and have them delivered with minimal paperwork all the way through to the end customer. Shipping lines must provide real-time information on the location of ships and goods.

Most significant are attempts to automate shipping transactions online. The industry's administrative inefficiencies, which account for 4% to 10% of international trade costs, are targeted. Industry insiders peg error rates on documents even higher, at 25% to 30%. It's no secret that start-ups must overcome the reluctance of hidebound shipping lines, which have deep-seated emotional fears of dot-coms coming between them and their customers.

In conclusion, American President Lines needs to get on board by staying online, or it might go down with the ship.

PROBLEM 1

The $170 billion in international trade volume per year given in the video is expected to increase by 50% in 5 years and expected to double over the next 25 years. **(a)** What is the expected total dollar amount in 5 years? **(b)** What is the expected total dollar amount in 25 years?

PROBLEM 2

The video stated that thousands of containers arrive each day. Each 40-foot container will hold, for example, 16,500 boxes of running shoes, 132,000 videotapes, or 25,000 blouses. At an average retail price of $49.50 for a pair of running shoes, $14.95 for a videotape, and $26.40 for a blouse, what would be the total retail value of the goods in these three containers (assume different goods in each container)?

PROBLEM 3

APL spent $600 million to build a 230-acre shipping terminal in California. The terminal can handle 4 wide-body container ships. Each ship can hold 4,800 20-foot containers, or 2,400 40-foot containers. **(a)** What was the cost per acre to build the facility? **(b)** How many 20-foot containers can the terminal handle at one time? **(c)** How many 40-foot containers can the terminal handle at one time?

PROBLEM 4

According to *Shanghai Daily*, the recent decline in China's export container prices (which fell by 1.4%) has not taken its toll on the general interest in this sector. China's foreign trade grew by 35%, reaching $387.1 billion. APL reported that it would increase its services from Asia to Europe to take advantage of China's growth in exports. What was the dollar amount of China's foreign trade last year?

PROBLEM 5

APL has expanded its domestic fleet to 5,100 53-foot containers; it is expanding its global fleet to 253,000 containers. The 5,100 containers represent what percent of APL's total fleet? Round to the nearest hundredth percent.

PROBLEM 6

The cost of owning a shipping vessel is very high. Operating costs for large vessels can run between $75,000 and $80,000 per day. Using an average cost per day, what would be the operating costs for one week?

PROBLEM 7

The Port of Los Angeles financed new terminal construction through operating revenues and bonds. They will collect about $30 million a year in rent from APL, who signed a 30-year lease on the property. What is APL's monthly payment?

PROBLEM 8

According to port officials, APL expanded cargo-handling capabilities at the Los Angeles facility that are expected to generate 10,500 jobs, with $335 million in wages and annual industry sales of $1 billion. What would be the average wage received? Round to the nearest dollar.

PROBLEM 9

APL has disclosed that it ordered over 34,000 containers from a Chinese container manufacturer. With 253,000 containers in its possession, what will be the percent increase in containers owned by APL? Round to the nearest hundredth percent.

chapter 7

DISCOUNTS: TRADE AND CASH

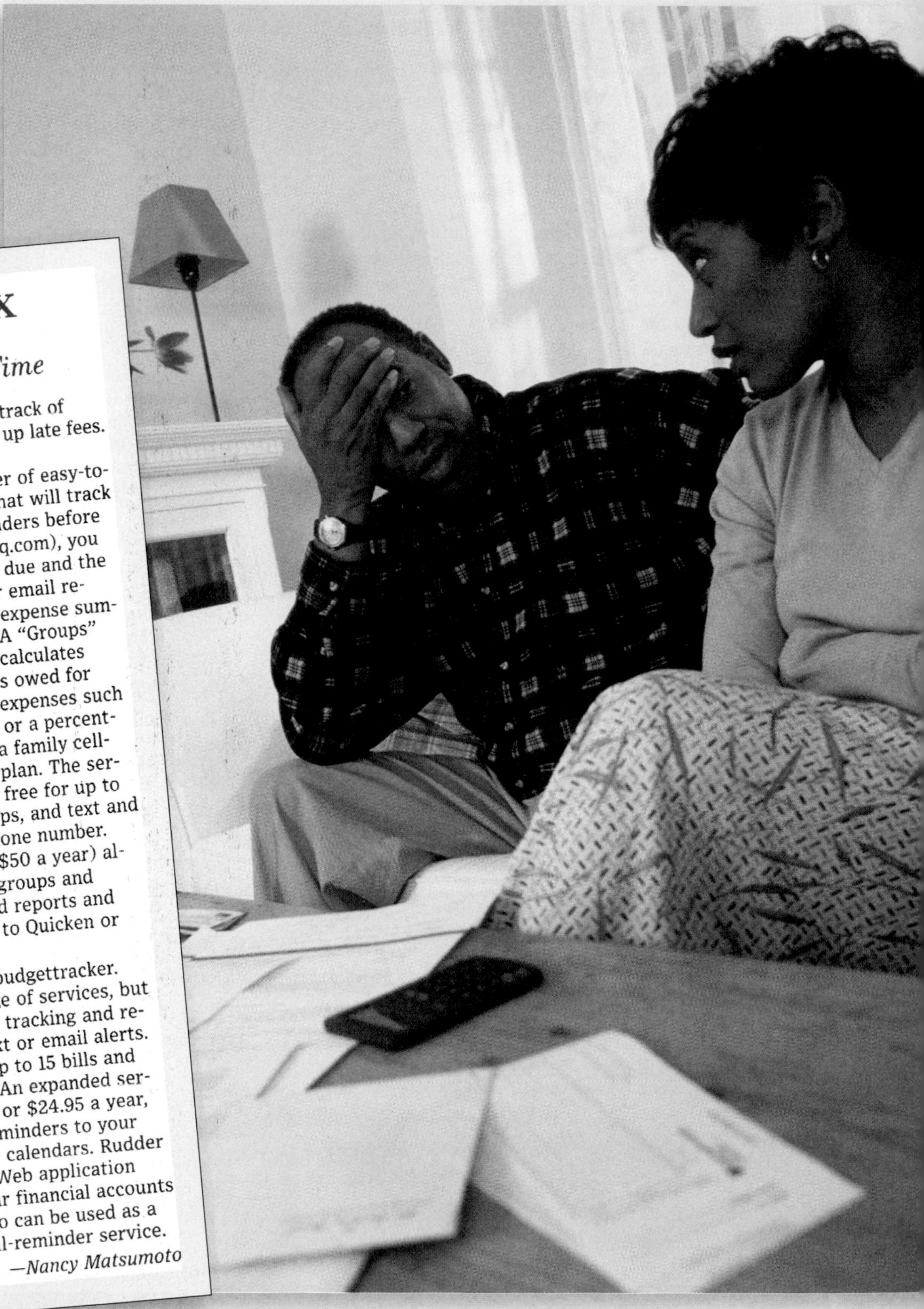

Quick Fix

Paying Bills On Time

■ Problem: You've been losing track of when bills are due and racking up late fees.

■ Solution: There are a number of easy-to-use Web-based applications that will track your bills and send you reminders before they are due. At BillQ (mybillq.com), you enter your bills and amounts due and the site will send you text and/or email reminders, as well as monthly expense summaries. A "Groups" feature calculates amounts owed for shared expenses such as rent or a percentage of a family cellphone plan. The service is free for up to 10 bill schedules, five groups, and text and email reminders to one phone number. BillQ Plus ($5 a month or $50 a year) allows for more schedules, groups and email addresses, expanded reports and the ability to export data to Quicken or Money.

Budget Tracker Inc. (budgettracker.com) offers a broad range of services, but its most popular is a bill tracking and reminder feature using text or email alerts. The service is free for up to 15 bills and 50 calendar reminders. An expanded service, for $2.95 a month or $24.95 a year, allows you to export reminders to your Outlook, iCal or Google calendars. Rudder (rudder.com) is a free Web application that aggregates all your financial accounts in one place, but it also can be used as a bill-manager and email-reminder service.

—Nancy Matsumoto

Buccina Studios/Getty Images

LEARNING UNIT OBJECTIVES

LU 7–1: Trade Discounts—Single and Chain (Includes Discussion of Freight)

1. Calculate single trade discounts with formulas and complements *(pp. 172–173).*
2. Explain the freight terms *FOB shipping point* and *FOB destination (pp. 173–175).*
3. Find list price when net price and trade discount rate are known *(p. 176).*
4. Calculate chain discounts with the net price equivalent rate and single equivalent discount rate *(pp. 176–178).*

LU 7–2: Cash Discounts, Credit Terms, and Partial Payments

1. List and explain typical discount periods and credit periods that a business may offer *(pp. 180–185).*
2. Calculate outstanding balance for partial payments *(p. 187).*

VOCABULARY PREVIEW

Here are key terms in this chapter. After completing the chapter, if you know the term, place a checkmark in the parenthesis. If you don't know the term, look it up and put the page number where it can be found.

Cash discount . ( ) Chain discounts . ( ) Complement . ( ) Credit period . ( ) Discount period . ( ) Due dates . ( ) End of credit period . ( ) End of month (EOM) . ( ) FOB destination . ( ) FOB shipping point . ( ) Freight terms . ( ) Invoice . ( ) List price . ( ) Net price . ( ) Net price equivalent rate . ( ) Ordinary dating . ( ) Receipt of goods (ROG) . ( ) Series discounts . ( ) Single equivalent discount rate . ( ) Single trade discount . ( ) Terms of the sale . ( ) Trade discount . ( ) Trade discount amount . ( ) Trade discount rate . ( )

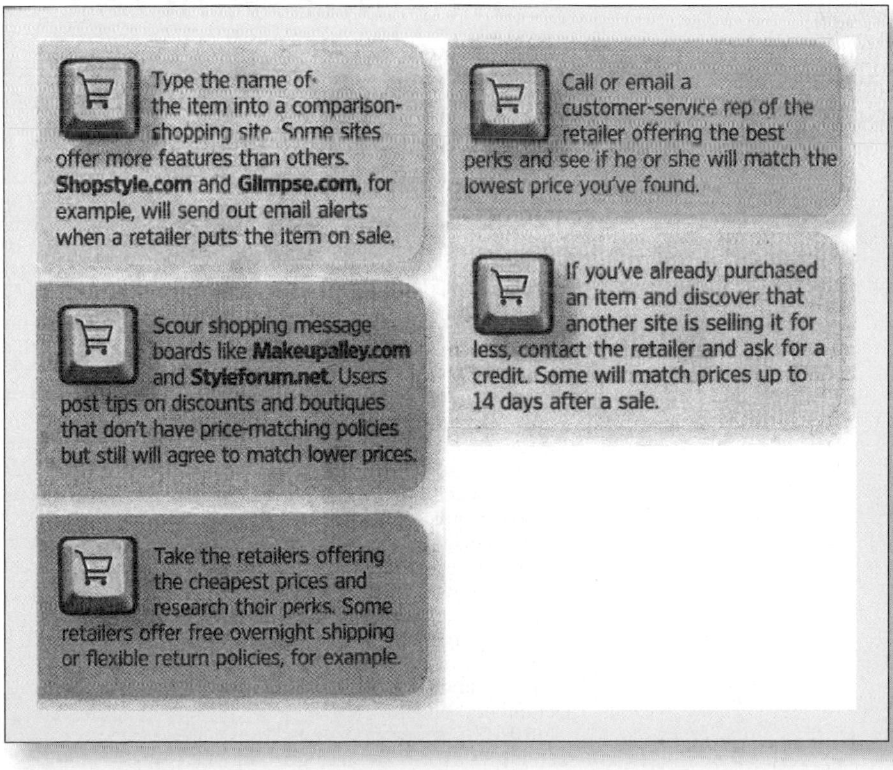

Wall Street Journal © 2007

Have you ever tried to negotiate bargains with online clothing retailers? The above *Wall Street Journal* clipping shows a variety of strategies customers can use to get the best price online.

This chapter discusses two types of discounts taken by retailers—trade and cash. A **trade discount** is a reduction off the original selling price (list price) of an item and is not related to early payment. A **cash discount** is the result of an early payment based on the terms of the sale.

Learning Unit 7–1: Trade Discounts—Single and Chain (Includes Discussion of Freight)

The merchandise sold by retailers is bought from manufacturers like Anheuser-Busch and wholesalers who sell only to retailers and not to customers. These manufacturers and wholesalers offer retailer discounts so retailers can resell the merchandise at a profit. The following *Wall Street Journal* clip about Anheuser-Busch shows what incentives Anheuser gives to promote its products. The discounts are off the manufacturers' and wholesalers' **list price** (suggested retail price), and the amount of discount that retailers receive off the list price is the **trade discount amount.**

The McGraw-Hill Companies, Inc./Lars A. Niki, photographer

When you make a purchase, the retailer (seller) gives you a purchase **invoice.** Invoices are important business documents that help sellers keep track of sales transactions and buyers keep track of purchase transactions. North Shore Community College Bookstore is a retail seller of textbooks to students. The bookstore usually purchases its textbooks directly from publishers. Figure 7.1 (p. 173) shows a textbook invoice from McGraw-Hill/Irwin Publishing Company to the North Shore Community College Bookstore. Note that the trade discount

LO 1

Anheuser Eases Its Policy On What Sellers Can Carry

By David Kesmodel

Anheuser-Busch Cos., acknowledging shifts in beer preferences by U.S. consumers, is relaxing a policy that deters many of its distributors from carrying rival brands.

Anheuser, the largest U.S. brewer by sales, said it would let certain distributors hawk a small percentage of competing products and still pay those distributors financial incentives for carrying Anheuser's brews.

Distributors that continue to sell only Budweiser and other products made by the St. Louis beer company would receive a higher incentive.

The move changes a policy that has been in place for about a decade. Called "100% Share of Mind," the campaign provided incentives, including a payment of two cents per case of beer, if distributors jettisoned competing products.

But in recent years, as sales of Anheuser's mass-market brews have cooled and competing small-batch craft beers and imports have driven the industry's growth, the brewer has come under pressure from distributors to change its policy.

The brewer's decision was necessary to address concerns from distributors, who face increasing financial challenges, said Mark Swartzberg, an analyst with Stifel Nicolaus.

"We are bringing more flexibility," said Dave Peacock, Anheuser's vice president of marketing. "The [industry] environment is certainly different."

Distributors that have been unable to begin selling Anheuser-affiliated products, such as imports Stella Artois and Bass Ale, will be allowed to sell certain competing beers, but those beers can't account for more than 3% of the distributor's total volume.

Such distributors would receive incentives of at least one cent per case of beer. Distributors only carrying Anheuser products would receive at least two cents a case.

FIGURE 7.1

Bookstore invoice showing a trade discount

Invoice No.: 5582

McGraw-Hill/Irwin Publishing Co.
1333 Burr Ridge Parkway
Burr Ridge, Illinois 60527

Date: July 8, 2010
Ship: Two-day UPS
Terms: 2/10, n/30

Sold to: North Shore Community College Bookstore
1 Ferncroft Road
Danvers, MA 01923

Description	Unit list price	Total amount
50 Financial Management—Block/Hirt	$95.66	$4,783.00
10 Introduction to Business—Nichols	89.50	895.00
	Total List Price	$5,678.00
	Less: Trade Discount 25%	−1,419.50
	Net Price	$4,258.50
	Plus: Prepaid Shipping Charge	125.00
	Total Invoice Amount	$4,383.50

amount is given in percent. This is the **trade discount rate,** which is a percent off the list price that retailers can deduct. The following formula for calculating a trade discount amount gives the numbers from the Figure 7.1 invoice in parentheses:

TRADE DISCOUNT AMOUNT FORMULA

Trade discount amount = List price × Trade discount rate
($1,419.50) ($5,678.00) (25%)

The price that the retailer (bookstore) pays the manufacturer (publisher) or wholesaler is the **net price.** The following formula for calculating the net price gives the numbers from the Figure 7.1 invoice in parentheses:

NET PRICE FORMULA

Net price = List price − Trade discount amount
($4,258.50) ($5,678.00) ($1,419.50)

Frequently, manufacturers and wholesalers issue catalogs to retailers containing list prices of the seller's merchandise and the available trade discounts. To reduce printing costs when prices change, these sellers usually update the catalogs with new *discount sheets.* The discount sheet also gives the seller the flexibility of offering different trade discounts to different classes of retailers. For example, some retailers buy in quantity and service the products. They may receive a larger discount than the retailer who wants the manufacturer to service the products. Sellers may also give discounts to meet a competitor's price, to attract new retailers, and to reward the retailers who buy product-line products. Sometimes the ability of the retailer to negotiate with the seller determines the trade discount amount.

Retailers cannot take trade discounts on freight, returned goods, sales tax, and so on. Trade discounts may be single discounts or a chain of discounts. Before we discuss single trade discounts, let's study freight terms.

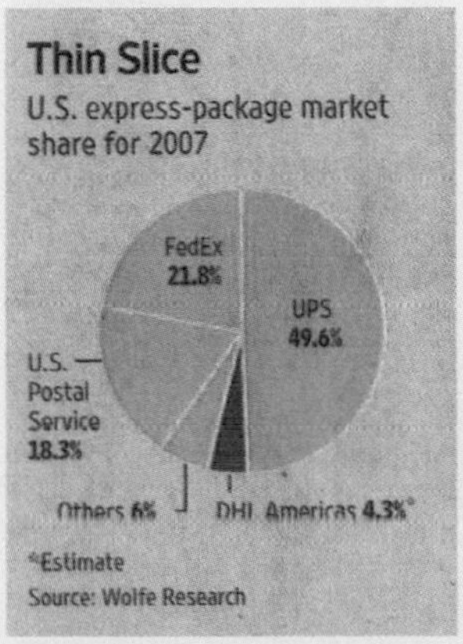

Wall Street Journal © 2008

Freight Terms

If you think in 2007 Federal Express had the largest market share you would be wrong. The *Wall Street Journal* clip "Thin Slice" at left in margin shows the leader is UPS with 49.6% of the express package market.

The most common **freight terms** are *FOB shipping point* and *FOB destination.* These terms determine how the freight will be paid. The key words in the terms are *shipping point* and *destination.*

Frances Roberts/Alamy

FOB shipping point means free on board at shipping point; that is, the buyer pays the freight cost of getting the goods to the place of business.

For example, assume that IBM in San Diego bought goods from Argo Suppliers in Boston. Argo ships the goods FOB Boston by plane. IBM takes title to the goods when the aircraft in Boston receives the goods, so IBM pays the freight from Boston to San Diego. Frequently, the seller (Argo) prepays the freight and adds the amount to the buyer's (IBM) invoice. When paying the invoice, the buyer takes the cash discount off the net price and adds the freight cost. FOB shipping point can be illustrated as follows:

FOB shipping point (Boston)

Boston — **Argo Suppliers** (IBM takes title here) → Buyer pays the freight → San Diego — **IBM** (Buyer pays the freight costs)

LO 2

FOB destination means the seller pays the freight cost until it reaches the buyer's place of business. If Argo ships its goods to IBM FOB destination or FOB San Diego, the title to the goods remains with Argo. Then it is Argo's responsibility to pay the freight from Boston to IBM's place of business in San Diego. FOB destination can be illustrated as follows:

FOB destination (San Diego)

Boston — **Argo Suppliers** (Has title) → Seller pays the freight → **IBM** (Get title on arrival of goods)

The following *Wall Street Journal* clipping "Stung by Soaring Transport Costs, Factories Bring Jobs Home Again" reveals how the costs of shipping have risen.

GLOBAL

OIL SHOCKER

Stung by Soaring Transport Costs, Factories Bring Jobs Home Again

BY TIMOTHY AEPPEL

The rising cost of shipping everything from industrial-pump parts to lawn-mower batteries to living-room sofas is forcing some manufacturers to bring production back to North America and freeze plans to send even more work overseas.

"My cost of getting a shipping container here from China just keeps going up—and I don't see any end in sight," says Claude Hayes, president of the retail heating division at DESA LLC. He says that cost has jumped about 15%, to about $5,300, since January and is set to increase again next month to $5,600.

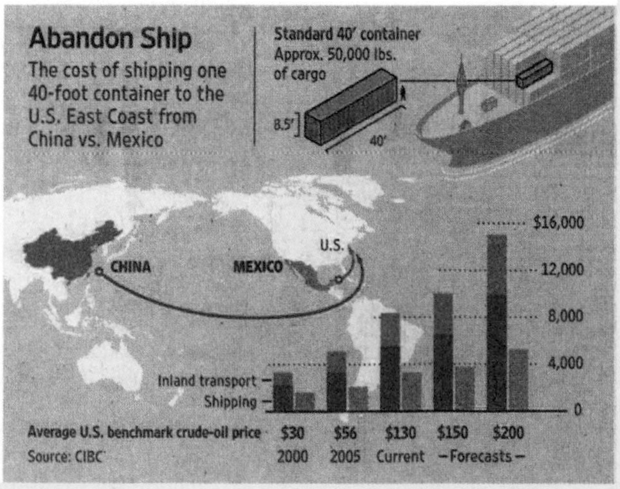

Now you are ready for the discussion on single trade discounts.

Single Trade Discount

In the introduction to this unit, we showed how to use the trade discount amount formula and the net price formula to calculate the McGraw-Hill/Irwin Publishing Company textbook sale to the North Shore Community College Bookstore. Since McGraw-Hill/Irwin gave the bookstore only one trade discount, it is a **single trade discount.** In the following word problem, we use the formulas to solve another example of a single trade discount. Again, we will use a blueprint aid to help dissect and solve the word problem.

The Word Problem The list price of a Macintosh computer is $2,700. The manufacturer offers dealers a 40% trade discount. What are the trade discount amount and the net price?

The facts	Solving for?	Steps to take	Key points
List price: $2,700. *Trade discount rate:* 40%.	Trade discount amount. Net price.	Trade discount amount = List price × Trade discount rate. Net price = List price − Trade discount amount.	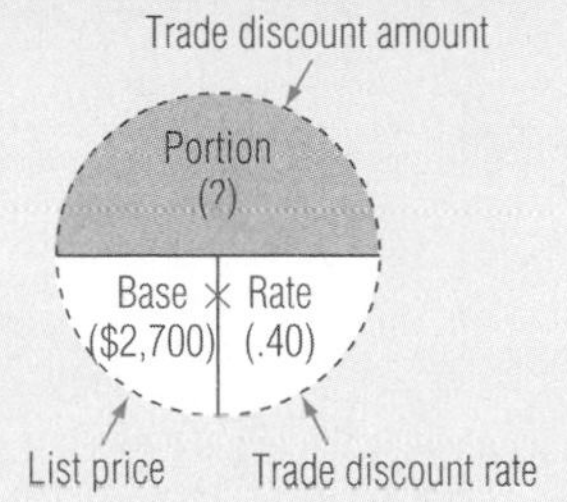

Steps to solving problem

1. Calculate the trade discount amount. $2,700 × .40 = $1,080
2. Calculate the net price. $2,700 − $1,080 = **$1,620**

Now let's learn how to check the dealers' net price of $1,620 with an alternate procedure using a complement.

How to Calculate the Net Price Using Complement of Trade Discount Rate

The **complement** of a trade discount rate is the difference between the discount rate and 100%. The following steps show you how to use the complement of a trade discount rate:

CALCULATING NET PRICE USING COMPLEMENT OF TRADE DISCOUNT RATE
Step 1. To find the complement, subtract the single discount rate from 100%.
Step 2. Multiply the list price times the complement (from step 1).

Think of a complement of any given percent (decimal) as the result of subtracting the percent from 100%.

Step 1. 100%
− 40 ← Trade discount rate
60% or .60

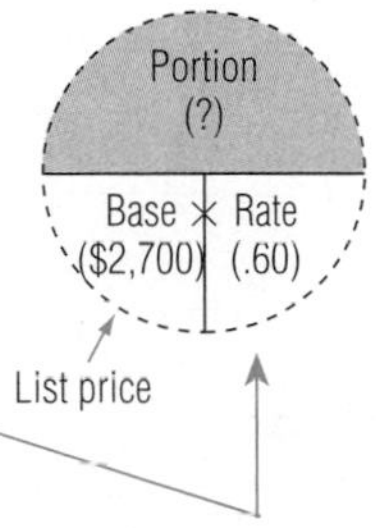

The complement means that we are spending 60 cents per dollar because we save 40 cents per dollar. Since we planned to spend $2,700, we multiply .60 by $2,700 to get a net price of $1,620.

Step 2. **$1,620** = $2,700 × .60

Note how the portion ($1,620) and rate (.60) relate to the same piece of the base ($2,700). The portion ($1,620) is smaller than the base, since the rate is less than 100%.

Be aware that some people prefer to use the trade discount amount formula and the net price formula to find the net price. Other people prefer to use the complement of the trade discount rate to find the net price. The result is always the same.

Finding List Price When You Know Net Price and Trade Discount Rate

LO 3

The following formula has many useful applications:

CALCULATING LIST PRICE WHEN NET PRICE AND TRADE DISCOUNT RATE ARE KNOWN

$$\text{List price} = \frac{\text{Net price}}{\text{Complement of trade discount rate}}$$

Next, let's see how to dissect and solve a word problem calculating list price.

The Word Problem A Macintosh computer has a $1,620 net price and a 40% trade discount. What is its list price?

The facts	Solving for?	Steps to take	Key points
Net price: $1,620. *Trade discount rate:* 40%.	List price.	$\text{List price} = \frac{\text{Net price}}{\text{Complement of trade discount rate}}$	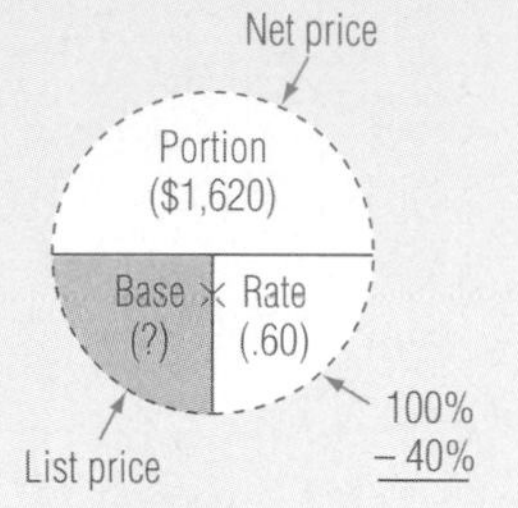

Steps to solving problem

1. Calculate the complement of the trade discount. $100\% - 40 = 60\% = .60$

2. Calculate the list price. $\frac{\$1,620}{.60} = \$2,700$

Note that the portion ($1,620) and rate (.60) relate to the same piece of the base.

Let's return to the McGraw-Hill/Irwin invoice in Figure 7.1 (p. 173) and calculate the list price using the formula for finding list price when net price and trade discount rate are known. The net price of the textbooks is $4,258.50. The complement of the trade discount rate is 100% − 25% = 75% = .75. Dividing the net price $4,258.50 by the complement .75 equals $5,678.00, the list price shown in the McGraw-Hill/Irwin invoice. We can show this as follows:

$$\frac{\$4,258.50}{.75} = \$5,678.00, \text{ the list price}$$

Chain Discounts

LO 4

Frequently, manufacturers want greater flexibility in setting trade discounts for different classes of customers, seasonal trends, promotional activities, and so on. To gain this flexibility, some sellers give **chain** or **series discounts**—trade discounts in a series of two or more successive discounts.

Sellers list chain discounts as a group, for example, 20/15/10. Let's look at how Mick Company arrives at the net price of office equipment with a 20/15/10 chain discount.

EXAMPLE The list price of the office equipment is $15,000. The chain discount is 20/15/10. The long way to calculate the net price is as follows:

Step 1	Step 2	Step 3	Step 4
$15,000	$15,000	$12,000	$10,200
× .20	− 3,000	− 1,800	− 1,020
$ 3,000	$12,000	$10,200	$ 9,180 net price
	× .15	× .10	
	$ 1,800	$ 1,020	

Never add the 20/15/10 together

Note how we multiply the percent (in decimal) times the new balance after we subtract the previous trade discount amount. For example, in Step 3, we change the last discount, 10%, to decimal form and multiply times $10,200. Remember that each percent is multiplied by a successively *smaller* base. You could write the 20/15/10 discount rate in any order and still arrive at the same net price. Thus, you would get the $9,180 net price if the discount were 10/15/20 or 15/20/10. However, sellers usually give the larger discounts first. *Never try to shorten this step process by adding the discounts.* Your net price will be incorrect because, when done properly, each percent is calculated on a different base.

Net Price Equivalent Rate

In the example above, you could also find the $9,180 net price with the **net price equivalent rate**—a shortcut method. Let's see how to use this rate to calculate net price.

CALCULATING NET PRICE USING NET PRICE EQUIVALENT RATE

Step 1. Subtract each chain discount rate from 100% (find the complement) and convert each percent to a decimal.

Step 2. Multiply the decimals. Do not round off decimals, since this number is the net price equivalent rate.

Step 3. Multiply the list price times the net price equivalent rate (Step 2).

The following word problem with its blueprint aid illustrates how to use the net price equivalent rate method.

The Word Problem The list price of office equipment is $15,000. The chain discount is 20/15/10. What is the net price?

The facts	Solving for?	Steps to take	Key points
List price: $15,000. *Chain discount:* 20/15/10	Net price.	Net price equivalent rate. Net price = List price × Net price equivalent rate.	Do not round net price equivalent rate.

Steps to solving problem

1. Calculate the complement of each rate and convert each percent to a decimal.

100%	100%	100%
− 20	− 15	− 10
80%	85%	90%
↓	↓	↓
.8	.85	.9

2. Calculate the net price equivalent rate. (Do not round.) .8 × .85 × .9 = .612 — Net price equivalent rate. For each $1, you are spending about 61 cents.

3. Calculate the net price (actual cost to buyer). $15,000 × .612 = **$9,180**

Next we see how to calculate the trade discount amount with a simpler method.

In the previous word problem, we could calculate the trade discount amount as follows:

$15,000 ← List price
− 9,180 ← Net price
$ 5,820 ← Trade discount amount

Single Equivalent Discount Rate

You can use another method to find the trade discount by using the **single equivalent discount rate.**

CALCULATING TRADE DISCOUNT AMOUNT USING SINGLE EQUIVALENT DISCOUNT RATE
Step 1. Subtract the net price equivalent rate from 1. This is the single equivalent discount rate.
Step 2. Multiply the list price times the single equivalent discount rate. This is the trade discount amount.

> **MONEY TIPS**
>
> The average household has almost $8,000 in credit card debt and millions pay late fees. Take advantage of a 12-month 0% interest balance transfer to help you begin paying off the debt. This trade discount is a great way to help you get your finances on the right track.

Let's now do the calculations.

Step 1. 1.000 ← If you are using a calculator, just press 1.
− .612
.388 ← This is the single equivalent discount rate.

Step 2. $15,000 × .388 = **$5,820** → This is the trade discount amount.

Remember that when we use the net price equivalent rate, the buyer of the office equipment pays $.612 on each $1 of list price. Now with the single equivalent discount rate, we can say that the buyer saves $.388 on each $1 of list price. The .388 is the single equivalent discount rate for the 20/15/10 chain discount. Note how we use the .388 single equivalent discount rate as if it were the only discount.

It's time to try the Practice Quiz.

LU 7–1 PRACTICE QUIZ

Complete this **Practice Quiz** to see how you are doing.[1]

1. The list price of a dining room set with a 40% trade discount is $12,000. What are the trade discount amount and net price (use complement method for net price)?
2. The net price of a video system with a 30% trade discount is $1,400. What is the list price?
3. Lamps Outlet bought a shipment of lamps from a wholesaler. The total list price was $12,000 with a 5/10/25 chain discount. Calculate the net price and trade discount amount. (Use the net price equivalent rate and single equivalent discount rate in your calculation.)

Solutions with Step-by-Step Help on DVD

✓ Solutions

1. Dining room set trade discount amount and net price:

The facts	Solving for?	Steps to take	Key points
List price: $12,000. *Trade discount rate:* 40%.	Trade discount amount. Net price.	Trade discount amount = List price × Trade discount rate. Net price = List price × Complement of trade discount rate.	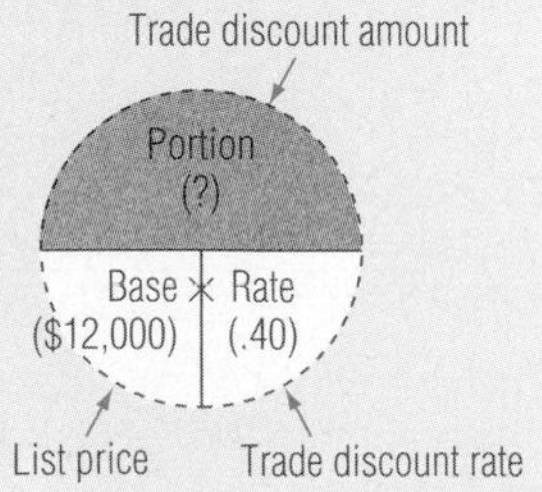

[1]For all three problems we will show blueprint aids. You might want to draw them on scrap paper.

Steps to solving problem

1. Calculate the trade discount. $12,000 × .40 = **$4,800** Trade discount amount
2. Calculate the net price. $12,000 × .60 = **$7,200** (100% − 40% = 60%)

2. Video system list price:

The facts	Solving for?	Steps to take	Key points
Net price: $1,400. *Trade discount rate:* 30%.	List price.	List price = $\frac{\text{Net price}}{\text{Complement of trade discount}}$	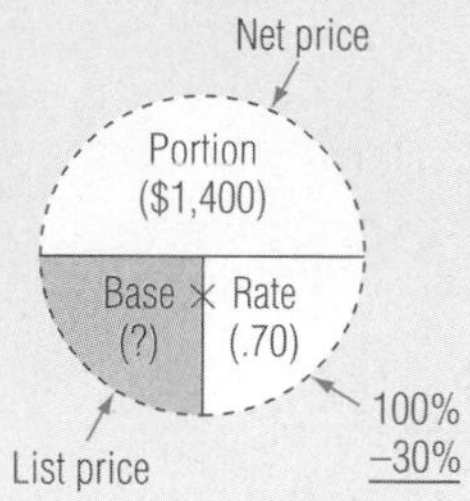

Steps to solving problem

1. Calculate the complement of trade discount.

$$100\% - 30 = 70\% = .70$$

2. Calculate the list price.

$$\frac{\$1{,}400}{.70} = \$2{,}000$$

3. Lamps Outlet's net price and trade discount amount:

The facts	Solving for?	Steps to take	Key points
List price: $12,000. *Chain discount:* 5/10/25.	Net price. Trade discount amount.	Net price = List price × Net price equivalent rate. Trade discount amount = List price × Single equivalent discount rate.	Do not round off net price equivalent rate or single equivalent discount rate.

Steps to solving problem

1. Calculate the complement of each chain discount.

$$100\% - 5 = 95\% \qquad 100\% - 10 = 90\% \qquad 100\% - 25 = 75\%$$

2. Calculate the net price equivalent rate.

$$.95 \times .90 \times .75 = .64125$$

3. Calculate the net price. $12,000 × .64125 = **$7,695**

4. Calculate the single equivalent discount rate.

$$1.00000 - .64125 = .35875$$

5. Calculate the trade discount amount. $12,000 × .35875 = **$4,305**

LU 7–1a EXTRA PRACTICE QUIZ WITH WORKED-OUT SOLUTIONS

Need more practice? Try this **Extra Practice Quiz** (check figures in Chapter Organizer, p. 191). Worked-out Solutions can be found in Appendix B at end of text.

1. The list price of a dining room set with a 30% trade discount is $16,000. What are the trade discount amount and net price (use complement method for net price)?
2. The net price of a video system with a 20% trade discount is $400. What is the list price?
3. Lamps Outlet bought a shipment of lamps from a wholesaler. The total list price was $14,000 with a 4/8/20 chain discount. Calculate the net price and trade discount amount. (Use the net price equivalent rate and single equivalent discount rate in your calculation.)

Learning Unit 7–2: Cash Discounts, Credit Terms, and Partial Payments

LO 1

To introduce this learning unit, we will use the New Hampshire Propane Company invoice that follows. The invoice shows that if you pay your bill early, you will receive a 19-cent discount. Every penny counts.

Sean Clayton/The Image Works

New Hampshire Propane Company

Date	Description	Qty.	Price	Total
	Previous Balance			**$0.00**
06/24/10	PROPANE	3.60	$3.40	$12.24

Invoice No. 004433L

Invoice Date 6/26/10

Totals this invoice: **$12.24**

AMOUNT DUE: **$12.24**

Prompt Pay Discount: $0.19

Net Amount Due if RECEIVED by 07/10/10: **$12.05**

Due Date 7/26/10

Now let's study cash discounts.

Cash Discounts

In the New Hampshire Propane Company invoice, we receive a cash discount of 19 cents. This amount is determined by the **terms of the sale,** which can include the credit period, cash discount, discount period, and freight terms.

Buyers can often benefit from buying on credit. The time period that sellers give buyers to pay their invoices is the **credit period.** Frequently, buyers can sell the goods bought during this credit period. Then, at the end of the credit period, buyers can pay sellers with the funds from the sales of the goods. When buyers can do this, they can use the consumer's money to pay the invoice instead of their money.

A cash discount is for prompt payment. A trade discount is not.

Sellers can also offer a cash discount, or reduction from the invoice price, if buyers pay the invoice within a specified time. This time period is the **discount period,** which is part of the total credit period. Sellers offer this cash discount because they can use the dollars to better advantage sooner than later. Buyers who are not short of cash like cash discounts because the goods will cost them less and, as a result, provide an opportunity for larger profits.

Trade discounts should be taken before cash discounts.

Remember that buyers do not take cash discounts on freight, returned goods, sales tax, and trade discounts. Buyers take cash discounts on the *net price* of the invoice. Before we discuss how to calculate cash discounts, let's look at some aids that will help you calculate credit **due dates** and **end of credit periods.**

Aids in Calculating Credit Due Dates

Sellers usually give credit for 30, 60, or 90 days. Not all months of the year have 30 days. So you must count the credit days from the date of the invoice. The trick is to remember the number of days in each month. You can choose one of the following three options to help you do this.

Years divisible by 4 are leap years. Leap years occur in 2012 and 2016.

Option 1: Days-in-a-Month Rule You may already know this rule. Remember that every 4 years is a leap year.

Thirty days has September, April, June, and November; all the rest have 31 except February has 28, and 29 in leap years.

Option 2: Knuckle Months Some people like to use the knuckles on their hands to remember which months have 30 or 31 days. Note in the following diagram that each knuckle represents a month with 31 days. The short months are in between the knuckles.

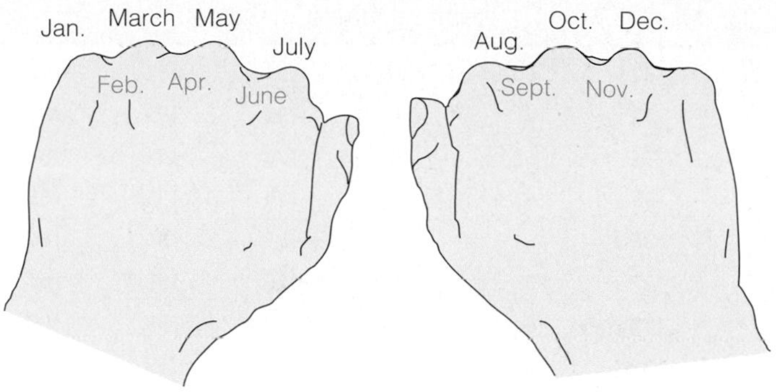

31 days: Jan., March, May, July, Aug., Oct., Dec.

Option 3: Days-in-a-Year Calendar The days-in-a-year calendar (excluding leap year) is another tool to help you calculate dates for discount and credit periods (Table 7.1, p. 182). For example, let's use Table 7.1 to calculate 90 days from August 12.

EXAMPLE By Table 7.1: August 12 — 224 days
+ 90
314 days

Search for day 314 in Table 7.1. You will find that day 314 is November 10. In this example, we stayed within the same year. Now let's try an example in which we overlap from year to year.

EXAMPLE What date is 80 days after December 5?

Table 7.1 shows that December 5 is 339 days from the beginning of the year. Subtracting 339 from 365 (the end of the year) tells us that we have used up 26 days by the end of the year. This leaves 54 days in the new year. Go back in the table and start with the beginning of the year and search for 54 (80 − 26) days. The 54th day is February 23.

By table

365 days in year
− 339 days until December 5
26 days used in year

80 days from December 5
− 26 days used in year
54 days in new year or February 23

Without use of table

December 31
− December 5
26
+ 31 days in January
57
+ 23 due date (February 23)
80 total days

When you know how to calculate credit due dates, you can understand the common business terms sellers offer buyers involving discounts and credit periods. Remember that discount and credit terms vary from one seller to another.

Common Credit Terms Offered by Sellers

The common credit terms sellers offer buyers include *ordinary dating, receipt of goods (ROG),* and *end of month (EOM).* In this section we examine these credit terms. To determine the due dates, we used the exact days-in-a-year calendar (Table 7.1, p. 182).

Ordinary Dating

Today, businesses frequently use the **ordinary dating** method. It gives the buyer a cash discount period that begins with the invoice date. The credit terms of two common ordinary dating methods are 2/10, n/30 and 2/10, 1/15, n/30.

2/10, n/30 Ordinary Dating Method The 2/10, n/30 is read as "two ten, net thirty." Buyers can take a 2% cash discount off the gross amount of the invoice if they pay the bill within 10 days from the invoice date. If buyers miss the discount period, the net amount—without a

TABLE 7.1 Exact days-in-a-year calendar (excluding leap year)*

Day of month	31 Jan.	28 Feb.	31 Mar.	30 Apr.	31 May	30 June	31 July	31 Aug.	30 Sept.	31 Oct.	30 Nov.	31 Dec.
1	1	32	60	91	121	152	182	213	244	274	305	335
2	2	33	61	92	122	153	183	214	245	275	306	336
3	3	34	62	93	123	154	184	215	246	276	307	337
4	4	35	63	94	124	155	185	216	247	277	308	338
5	5	36	64	95	125	156	186	217	248	278	309	339
6	6	37	65	96	126	157	187	218	249	279	310	340
7	7	38	66	97	127	158	188	219	250	280	311	341
8	8	39	67	98	128	159	189	220	251	281	312	342
9	9	40	68	99	129	160	190	221	252	282	313	343
10	10	41	69	100	130	161	191	222	253	283	314	344
11	11	42	70	101	131	162	192	223	254	284	315	345
12	12	43	71	102	132	163	193	224	255	285	316	346
13	13	44	72	103	133	164	194	225	256	286	317	347
14	14	45	73	104	134	165	195	226	257	287	318	348
15	15	46	74	105	135	166	196	227	258	288	319	349
16	16	47	75	106	136	167	197	228	259	289	320	350
17	17	48	76	107	137	168	198	229	260	290	321	351
18	18	49	77	108	138	169	199	230	261	291	322	352
19	19	50	78	109	139	170	200	231	262	292	323	353
20	20	51	79	110	140	171	201	232	263	293	324	354
21	21	52	80	111	141	172	202	233	264	294	325	355
22	22	53	81	112	142	173	203	234	265	295	326	356
23	23	54	82	113	143	174	204	235	266	296	327	357
24	24	55	83	114	144	175	205	236	267	297	328	358
25	25	56	84	115	145	176	206	237	268	298	329	359
26	26	57	85	116	146	177	207	238	269	299	330	360
27	27	58	86	117	147	178	208	239	270	300	331	361
28	28	59	87	118	148	179	209	240	271	301	332	362
29	29	—	88	119	149	180	210	241	272	302	333	363
30	30	—	89	120	150	181	211	242	273	303	334	364
31	31	—	90	—	151	—	212	243	—	304	—	365

*Often referred to as a Julian calendar.

discount—is due between day 11 and day 30. *Freight, returned goods, sales tax, and trade discounts must be subtracted from the gross before calculating a cash discount.*

EXAMPLE $400 invoice dated July 5: terms 2/10, n/30; no freight; paid on July 11.

Step 1. Calculate end of 2% discount period:

July 5 date of invoice
+ 10 days
July 15 end of 2% discount period

Step 2. Calculate end of credit period:

July 5 by Table 7.1 → 186 days
+ 30
216 days

Search in Table 7.1 for 216 → August 4 → end of credit period

Step 3. Calculate payment on July 11:

$.02 \times \$400 = \$8$ cash discount

$\$400 - \$8 = \$392$ paid

> *Note:* A 2% cash discount means that you save 2 cents on the dollar and pay 98 cents on the dollar. Thus, $\$.98 \times \$400 = \$392.$

The following time line illustrates the 2/10, n/30 ordinary dating method beginning and ending dates of the above example:

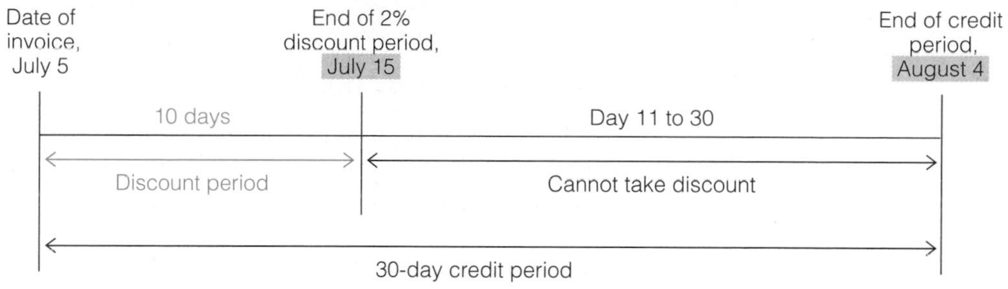

2/10, 1/15, n/30 Ordinary Dating Method The 2/10, 1/15, n/30 is read "two ten, one fifteen, net thirty." The seller will give buyers a 2% (2 cents on the dollar) cash discount if they pay within 10 days of the invoice date. If buyers pay between day 11 and day 15 from the date of the invoice, they can save 1 cent on the dollar. If buyers do not pay on day 15, the net or full amount is due 30 days from the invoice date.

EXAMPLE $600 invoice dated May 8; $100 of freight included in invoice price; paid on May 22. Terms 2/10, 1/15, n/30.

Step 1. Calculate the end of the 2% discount period:

May 8 date of invoice
+ 10 days
May 18 end of 2% discount period

Step 2. Calculate end of 1% discount period:

May 18 end of 2% discount period
+ 5 days
May 23 end of 1% discount period

Step 3. Calculate end of credit period:

May 8 by Table 7.1 → 128 days
+ 30
158 days

Search in Table 7.1 for 158 → June 7 → end of credit period

Step 4. Calculate payment on May 22 (14 days after date of invoice):

$600 invoice
− 100 freight
$500
× .01
$5.00

$\$500 - \$5.00 + \$100 \text{ freight} = \$595$

> A 1% discount means we pay $.99 on the dollar or $\$500 \times \$.99 = \$495 + \$100 \text{ freight} = \$595.$
>
> *Note:* Freight is added back since no cash discount is taken on freight.

The following time line illustrates the 2/10, 1/15, n/30 ordinary dating method beginning and ending dates of the above example:

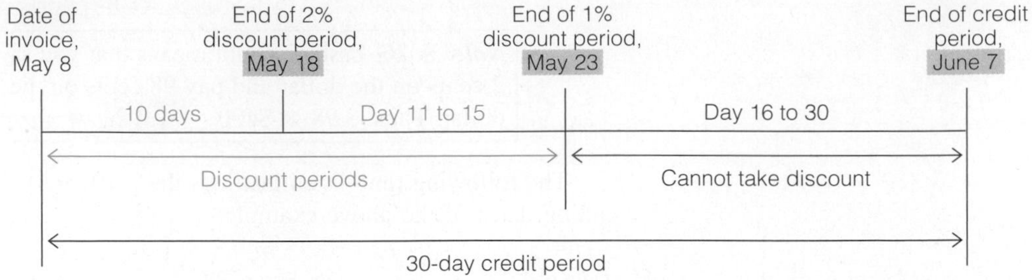

Receipt of Goods (ROG)

3/10, n/30 ROG With the **receipt of goods (ROG),** the cash discount period begins when buyer receives goods, *not* the invoice date. Industry often uses the ROG terms when buyers cannot expect delivery until a long time after they place the order. Buyers can take a 3% discount within 10 days *after* receipt of goods. Full amount is due between day 11 and day 30 if cash discount period is missed.

EXAMPLE $900 invoice dated May 9; no freight or returned goods; the goods were received on July 8; terms 3/10, n/30 ROG; payment made on July 20.

Step 1. Calculate the end of the 3% discount period:

July 8 date goods arrive
+ 10 days
July 18 end of 3% discount period

Step 2. Calculate the end of the credit period:

July 8 by Table 7.1 →
189 days
+ 30
219 days

Search in Table 7.1 for 219 → August 7 → end of credit period

Step 3. Calculate payment on July 20:

Missed discount period and paid net or full amount of $900.

The following time line illustrates 3/10, n/30 ROG beginning and ending dates of the above example:

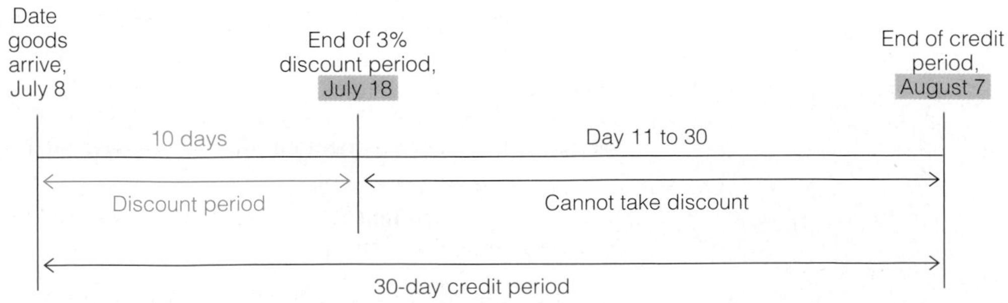

The McGraw-Hill Companies, Inc./Christopher Kerrigan, photographer

End of Month (EOM)[2]

In this section we look at terms involving **end of the month (EOM).** If an invoice is dated the *25th or earlier* of a month, we follow one set of rules. If an invoice is dated after the 25th of the month, a new set of rules is followed. Let's look at each situation.

Invoice Dated 25th or Earlier in Month, 1/10 EOM If sellers date an invoice on the 25th or earlier in the month, buyers can take the cash discount if they pay the invoice by the first 10 days of the month following the sale (next month). If buyers miss the discount period, the full amount is due within 20 days after the end of the discount period.

EXAMPLE $600 invoice dated July 6; no freight or returns; terms 1/10 EOM; paid on August 8.

Step 1. Calculate the end of the 1% discount period:

August 10 ← First 10 days of month following sale.

Step 2. Calculate the end of the credit period:

August 10
+ 20 days
August 30 → Credit period is 20 days after discount period.

Step 3. Calculate payment on August 8:

$.99 \times \$600 = \$594$

The following time line illustrates the beginning and ending dates of the EOM invoice of the previous example:

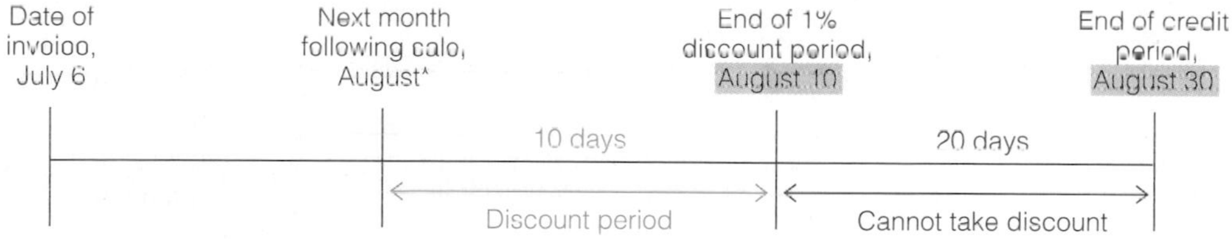

*Even though the discount period begins with the next month following the sale, if buyers wish, they can pay before the discount period (date of invoice until the discount period).

Invoice Dated after 25th of Month, 2/10 EOM When sellers sell goods *after* the 25th of the month, buyers gain an additional month. The cash discount period ends on the 10th day of the second month that follows the sale. Why? This occurs because the seller guarantees the 15 days' credit of the buyer. If a buyer bought goods on August 29, September 10 would be only 12 days. So the buyer gets the extra month.

EXAMPLE $800 invoice dated April 29; no freight or returned goods; terms 2/10 EOM; payment made on June 18.

Step 1. Calculate the end of the 2% discount period:

June 10 ← First 10 days of second month following sale

(cont. on next page)

[2]Sometimes the Latin term *proximo* is used. Other variations of EOM exist, but the key point is that the seller guarantees the buyer 15 days' credit. We assume a 30-day month.

Step 2. Calculate the end of the credit period:

June 10
+ 20 days
June 30 — Credit period is 20 days after discount period.

Step 3. Calculate the payment on June 18:

No discount; **$800 paid.**

The following time line illustrates the beginning and ending dates of the EOM invoice of the above example:

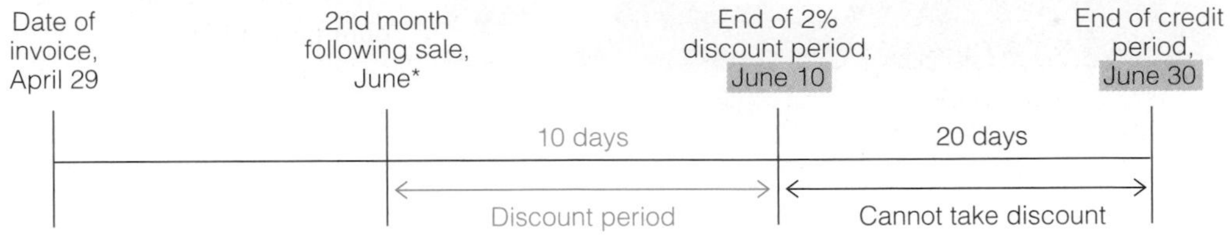

*Even though the discount period begins with the second month following the sale, if buyers wish, they can pay before the discount date (date of invoice until the discount period)

War on Product Returns

Bringing It Back

Consumers bring back to the store between 11% and 20% of all the electronic goods they purchase, with the highest return rates for wireless phones, GPS units, MP3 players, and wireless networking gear. Here are the chief reasons:

Reason	Percentage of returns	Comment
"No Trouble Found"	68%	A large portion of these returns are because consumers didn't understand the product, not that it didn't work.
"Buyer's Remorse"	27%	These products are often returned within 48 hours of purchase for reasons such as it was too expensive or that the spouse didn't like it.
Defective	5%	The rate of defective products has declined over time as the technology in consumer electronics has gotten better.

Have you ever wondered why customers return some purchases? The following *Wall Street Journal* article, "War on Product Returns: Bringing It Back," says that 68% of electronic products returns are not because the product doesn't work but because the customer doesn't understand how to use the product.

Solving a Word Problem with Trade and Cash Discount

Now that we have studied trade and cash discounts, let's look at a combination that involves both a trade and a cash discount.

The Word Problem Hardy Company sent Regan Corporation an invoice for office equipment with a $10,000 list price. Hardy dated the invoice July 29 with terms of 2/10 EOM (end of month). Regan receives a 30% trade discount and paid the invoice on September 6. Since terms were FOB destination, Regan paid no freight charge. What was the cost of office equipment for Regan?

The facts	Solving for?	Steps to take	Key points
List price: $10,000. *Trade discount rate:* 30%. *Terms:* 2/10 EOM. *Invoice date:* 7/29. *Date paid:* 9/6.	Cost of office equipment.	Net price = List price × Complement of trade discount rate. After 25th of month for EOM. Discount period is 1st 10 days of second month that follows sale.	Trade discounts are deducted before cash discounts are taken. Cash discounts are not taken on freight or returns.

Steps to solving problem

1. Calculate the net price. $10,000 × .70 = $7,000 ← 100% − 30% (trade discount)

2. Calculate the discount period. Sale: 7/29 Month 1: Aug. Month 2: Sept 10 → Paid on Sept. 6—is entitled to 2% off.

LO 2

3. Calculate the cost of office equipment. $7,000 × .98 = **$6,860** ← 100% − 2%. If you save 2 cents on a dollar, you are spending 98 cents.

Partial Payments

Often buyers cannot pay the entire invoice before the end of the discount period. To calculate partial payments and outstanding balance, use the following steps:

CALCULATING PARTIAL PAYMENTS AND OUTSTANDING BALANCE

Step 1. Calculate the complement of a discount rate.

Step 2. Divide partial payments by the complement of a discount rate (Step 1). This gives the amount credited.

Step 3. Subtract Step 2 from the total owed. This is the outstanding balance.

MONEY TIPS

A great credit score can do wonders for credit terms offered to you. Make certain to regularly check your credit report; you are entitled to a free one annually. To help build credit: establish a checking and savings account, pay your bills on time, be aware of how much of your available credit you use (30% of your credit limit is the maximum), apply for credit while you're a college student (apply for a secured credit card if you can't get a regular one), get a store credit card, get an installment loan, and use revolving accounts regularly but lightly.

EXAMPLE Molly McGrady owed $400. Molly's terms were 2/10, n/30. Within 10 days, Molly sent a check for $80. The actual credit the buyer gave Molly is as follows:

Step 1. 100% − 2% = 98% → .98

Step 2. $\frac{\$80}{.98} = \$81.63$ $\frac{\$80}{1 - .02}$ ← Discount rate

Step 3. $400.00
− 81.63 partial payment—although sent in $80
$318.37 outstanding balance

Note: We do not multiply .02 × $80 because the seller did not base the original discount on $80. When Molly makes a payment within the 10-day discount period, 98 cents pays each $1 she owes. Before buyers take discounts on partial payments, they must have permission from the seller. Not all states allow partial payments.

You have completed another unit. Let's check your progress.

LU 7–2 PRACTICE QUIZ

Complete this **Practice Quiz** to see how you are doing.

Complete the following table:

	Date of invoice	Date goods received	Terms	Last day* of discount period	End of credit period
1.	July 6		2/10, n/30		
2.	February 19	June 9	3/10, n/30 ROG		
3.	May 9		4/10, 1/30, n/60		
4.	May 12		2/10 EOM		
5.	May 29		2/10 EOM		

*If more than one discount, assume date of last discount.

6. Metro Corporation sent Vasko Corporation an invoice for equipment with an $8,000 list price. Metro dated the invoice May 26. Terms were 2/10 EOM. Vasko receives a 20% trade discount and paid the invoice on July 3. What was the cost of equipment for Vasko? (A blueprint aid will be in the solution to help dissect this problem.)
7. Complete amount to be credited and balance outstanding:

   Amount of invoice: $600
   Terms: 2/10, 1/15, n/30
   Date of invoice: September 30
   Paid October 3: $400

Solutions with Step-by-Step Help on DVD

✓ Solutions

1. End of discount period: July 6 + 10 days = **July 16**
   End of credit period: By Table 7.1, July 6 = 187 days
   + 30 days
   217 → search → **Aug. 5**
2. End of discount period: June 9 + 10 days = **June 19**
   End of credit period: By Table 7.1, June 9 = 160 days
   + 30 days
   190 → search → **July 9**
3. End of discount period: By Table 7.1, May 9 = 129 days
   + 30 days
   159 → search → **June 8**
   End of credit period: By Table 7.1, May 9 = 129 days
   + 60 days
   189 → search → **July 8**
4. End of discount period: **June 10**
   End of credit period: June 10 + 20 = **June 30**
5. End of discount period: **July 10**
   End of credit period: July 10 + 20 = **July 30**
6. Vasko Corporation's cost of equipment:

The facts	Solving for?	Steps to take	Key points
List price: $8,000. *Trade discount rate:* 20%. *Terms:* 2/10 EOM. *Invoice date:* 5/26. *Date paid:* 7/3.	Cost of equipment.	Net price = List price × Complement of trade discount rate. *EOM before 25th:* Discount period is 1st 10 days of month that follows sale.	Trade discounts are deducted before cash discounts are taken. Cash discounts are not taken on freight or returns.

Steps to solving problem

1. Calculate the net price. $8,000 × .80 = $6,400 (100% − 20%)
2. Calculate the discount period. Until July 10
3. Calculate the cost of office equipment. $6,400 × .98 = **$6,272** (100% − 2%)

7. $\frac{\$400}{.98}$ = $408.16, amount credited.
   $600 − $408.16 = **$191.84,** balance outstanding.

LU 7–2a EXTRA PRACTICE QUIZ WITH WORKED-OUT SOLUTIONS

Need more practice? Try this **Extra Practice Quiz** (check figures in Chapter Organizer, p. 191). Worked-out Solutions can be found in Appendix B at end of text.

Complete the following table:

	Date of invoice	Date goods received	Terms	Last day of discount period*	End of credit period
1.	July 8		2/10, n/30		
2.	February 24	June 12	3/10, n/30 ROG		
3.	May 12		4/10, 1/30, n/60		
4.	April 14		2/10 EOM		
5.	April 27		2/10 EOM		

*If more than one discount, assume date of last discount.

6. Metro Corporation sent Vasko Corporation an invoice for equipment with a $9,000 list price. Metro dated the invoice June 29. Terms were 2/10 EOM. Vasko receives a 30% trade discount and paid the discount on August 9. What was the cost of equipment for Vasko?

7. Complete amount to be credited and balance outstanding:

Amount of invoice: $700
Terms: 2/10, 1/15, n/30
Date of invoice: September 28
Paid October 3: $600

CHAPTER ORGANIZER AND REFERENCE GUIDE

Topic	Key point, procedure, formula	Example(s) to illustrate situation
Trade discount amount, p. 173	Trade discount amount = List price × Trade discount rate	$600 list price 30% trade discount rate Trade discount amount = $600 × .30 = **$180**
Calculating net price, p. 173	Net price = List price − Trade discount amount or List price × Complement of trade discount price	$600 list price 30% trade discount rate Net price = $600 × .70 = **$420** 1.00 − .30 .70
Freight, p. 174	FOB shipping point—buyer pays freight. FOB destination—seller pays freight.	Moose Company of New York sells equipment to Agee Company of Oregon. Terms of shipping are FOB New York. Agee pays cost of freight since terms are FOB shipping point.
Calculating list price when net price and trade discount rate are known, p. 176	List price = $\frac{\text{Net price}}{\text{Complement of trade discount rate}}$	40% trade discount rate Net price, $120 $\frac{\$120}{.60}$ = **$200** list price (1.00 − .40)

(continues)

CHAPTER ORGANIZER AND REFERENCE GUIDE

Topic	Key point, procedure, formula	Example(s) to illustrate situation
Chain discounts, p. 176	Successively lower base.	5/10 on a $100 list item $ 100 $ 95 × .05 × .10 $ 5.00 $9.50 (running balance) $95.00 − 9.50 **$85.50** net price
Net price equivalent rate, p. 177	Actual cost to buyer = List price × Net price equivalent rate Take complement of each chain discount and multiply—do not round. Trade discount amount = List price − Actual cost to buyer	Given: 5/10 on $1,000 list price Take complement: .95 × .90 = .855 (net price equivalent) $1,000 × .855 = **$855** (actual cost or net price) $1,000 − 855 **$ 145** trade discount amount
Single equivalent discount rate, p. 178	Trade discount amount = List price × 1 − Net price equivalent rate	See preceding example for facts: 1 − .855 = .145 .145 × $1,000 = **$145**
Cash discounts, p. 180	Cash discounts, due to prompt payment, are not taken on freight, returns, etc.	Gross $1,000 (includes freight) Freight $25 Terms, 2/10, n/30 Returns $25 Purchased: Sept. 9; paid Sept. 15 Cash discount = $950 × .02 = **$19**
Calculating due dates, p. 180	*Option 1:* Thirty days has September, April, June, and November; all the rest have 31 except February has 28, and 29 in leap years. *Option 2:* Knuckles—31-day month; in between knuckles are short months. *Option 3:* Days-in-a-year table.	Invoice $500 on March 5; terms 2/10, n/30 March 5 + 10 *End of discount period:* → **March 15** *End of credit period by Table 7.1:* March 5 = 64 days + 30 → 94 days Search in Table 7.1 → **April 4**
Common terms of sale **a. Ordinary dating, p. 181**	Discount period begins from date of invoice. Credit period ends 20 days from the end of the discount period unless otherwise stipulated; example, 2/10, n/60—the credit period ends 50 days from end of discount period.	Invoice $600 (freight of $100 included in price) dated March 8; payment on March 16; 3/10, n/30. March 8 + 10 *End of discount period:* → **March 18** *End of credit period by Table 7.1:* March 8 = 67 days + 30 → 97 days Search in Table 7.1 → **April 7** *If paid on March 16:* .97 × $500 = $485 + 100 freight **$585**

(continues)

CHAPTER ORGANIZER AND REFERENCE GUIDE

Topic	Key point, procedure, formula	Example(s) to illustrate situation
b. Receipt of goods (ROG), p. 184	Discount period begins when goods are received. Credit period ends 20 days from end of discount period.	4/10, n/30, ROG. $600 invoice; no freight; dated August 5; goods received October 2, payment made October 20. October 2 + 10 *End of discount period:* → **October 12** *End of credit period by Table 7.1:* October 2 = 275 + 30 → 305 ↓ Search in Table 7.1 **November 1** *Payment on October 20:* No discount, pay **$600**
c. End of month (EOM), p. 185	On or before 25th of the month, discount period is 10 days after month following sale. After 25th of the month, an additional month is gained.	$1,000 invoice dated May 12; no freight or returns; terms 2/10 EOM. *End of discount period* → **June 10** *End of credit period* → **June 30**
Partial payments, p. 187	$\text{Amount credited} = \frac{\text{Partial payment}}{1 - \text{Discount rate}}$	$200 invoice, terms 2/10, n/30, dated March 2, paid $100 on March 5. $\frac{\$100}{1 - .02} = \frac{\$100}{.98} = \$102.04$
KEY TERMS	Cash discount, *p. 172* Chain discounts, *p. 176* Complement, *p. 175* Credit period, *p. 180* Discount period, *p. 180* Due dates, *p. 180* End of credit period, *p. 180* End of month (EOM), *p. 185* FOB destination, *p. 174* FOB shipping point, *p. 174* Freight terms, *p. 173* Invoice, *p. 172* List price, *p. 172* Net price, *p. 173* Net price equivalent rate, *p. 177* Ordinary dating, *p. 181* Receipt of goods (ROG), *p. 184*	Series discounts, *p. 176* Single equivalent discount rate, *p. 178* Single trade discount, *p. 175* Terms of the sale, *p. 180* Trade discount, *p. 172* Trade discount amount, *p. 172* Trade discount rate, *p. 173*
CHECK FIGURES FOR EXTRA PRACTICE QUIZZES WITH PAGE REFERENCES. (WORKED-OUT SOLUTIONS IN APPENDIX B)	LU 7–1a (p. 179) **1.** $4,800 TD; $11,200 NP **2.** $500 **3.** $9,891.84 NP; TD $4,108.16	LU 7–2a (p. 189) **1.** July 18; Aug. 7 **2.** June 22; July 12 **3.** June 11; July 11 **4.** May 10; May 30 **5.** June 10; June 30 **6.** $6,174 **7.** a) $612.24 b) $87.76

Critical Thinking Discussion Questions

1. What is the net price? June Long bought a jacket from a catalog company. She took her trade discount off the original price plus freight. What is wrong with June's approach? Who would benefit from June's approach—the buyer or the seller?
2. How do you calculate the list price when the net price and trade discount rate are known? A publisher tells the bookstore its net price of a book along with a suggested trade discount of 20%. The bookstore uses a 25% discount rate. Is this ethical when textbook prices are rising?
3. If Jordan Furniture ships furniture FOB shipping point, what does that mean? Does this mean you get a cash discount?
4. What are the steps to calculate the net price equivalent rate? Why is the net price equivalent rate *not* rounded?

(cont. on next page)

5. What are the steps to calculate the single equivalent discount rate? Is this rate off the list or net price? Explain why this calculation of a single equivalent discount rate may not always be needed.
6. What is the difference between a discount and credit period? Are all cash discounts taken before trade discounts? Agree or disagree? Why?
7. Explain the following credit terms of sale:
   a. 2/10, n/30.
   b. 3/10, n/30 ROG.
   c. 1/10 EOM (on or before 25th of month).
   d. 1/10 EOM (after 25th of month).
8. Explain how to calculate a partial payment. Whom does a partial payment favor—the buyer or the seller?

END-OF-CHAPTER PROBLEMS

connect plus+ www.mhhe.com/slater10e

Check figures for odd-numbered problems in Appendix C   Name ____________________   Date ________

DRILL PROBLEMS

For all problems, round your final answer to the nearest cent. Do not round net price equivalent rates or single equivalent discount rates.

Complete the following:

	Item	List price	Chain discount	Net price equivalent rate (in decimals)	Single equivalent discount rate (in decimals)	Trade discount	Net price
7–1.	Verizon Blackberry	$299	4/1				
7–2.	Panasonic DVD player	$199	8/4/3				
7–3.	IBM scanner	$269	7/3/1				

Complete the following:

	Item	List price	Chain discount	Net price	Trade discount
7–4.	Trotter treadmill	$3,000	9/4		
7–5.	Maytag dishwasher	$450	8/5/6		
7–6.	Hewlett-Packard scanner	$320	3/5/9		
7–7.	Land Rover roofrack	$1,850	12/9/6		

7–8. Which of the following companies, A or B, gives a higher discount? Use the single equivalent discount rate to make your choice (convert your equivalent rate to the nearest hundredth percent).

Company A
8/10/15/3

Company B
10/6/16/5

Complete the following:

	Invoice	Dates when goods received	Terms	Last day* of discount period	Final day bill is due (end of credit period)
7–9.	June 18		1/10, n/30		
7–10.	Nov. 27		2/10 EOM		
7–11.	May 15	June 5	3/10, n/30, ROG		
7–12.	April 10		2/10, 1/30, n/60		
7–13.	June 12		3/10 EOM		
7–14.	Jan. 10	Feb. 3 (no leap year)	4/10, n/30, ROG		

*If more than one discount, assume date of last discount.

Complete the following by calculating the cash discount and net amount paid:

	Gross amount of invoice (freight charge already included)	Freight charge	Date of invoice	Terms of invoice	Date of payment	Cash discount	Net amount paid
7–15.	$7,000	$100	4/8	2/10, n/60	4/15		
7–16.	$600	None	8/1	3/10, 2/15, n/30	8/13		
7–17.	$200	None	11/13	1/10 EOM	12/3		
7–18.	$500	$100	11/29	1/10 EOM	1/4		

Complete the following:

	Amount of invoice	Terms	Invoice date	Actual partial payment made	Date of partial payment	Amount of payment to be credited	Balance outstanding
7–19.	$700	2/10, n/60	5/6	$400	5/15		
7–20.	$600	4/10, n/60	7/5	$400	7/14		

WORD PROBLEMS (Round to Nearest Cent as Needed)

7–21. The list price of an orange dial Luminox watch is $650. Katz Jewelers receives a trade discount of 30%. Find the trade discount amount and the net price.

7–22. A model NASCAR race car lists for $79.99 with a trade discount of 40%. What is the net price of the car?

7–23. Lucky you! You went to couponcabin.com and found a 20% off coupon to your significant other's favorite store. Armed with that coupon, you went to the store only to find a storewide sale offering 10% off everything in the store. In addition, your credit card has a special offer that allows you to save 10% if you use your credit card for all purchases that day. Using your credit card, what will you pay before tax for the $155 gift you found? Use the single equivalent discount to calculate how much you save and then calculate your final price.

7–24. Levin Furniture buys a living room set with a $4,000 list price and a 55% trade discount. Freight (FOB shipping point) of $50 is not part of the list price. What is the delivered price (including freight) of the living room set, assuming a cash discount of 2/10, n/30, ROG? The invoice had an April 8 date. Levin received the goods on April 19 and paid the invoice on April 25.

7–25. A manufacturer of skateboards offered a 5/2/1 chain discount to many customers. Bob's Sporting Goods ordered 20 skateboards for a total $625 list price. What was the net price of the skateboards? What was the trade discount amount?

7–26. Home Depot wants to buy a new line of fertilizers. Manufacturer A offers a 21/13 chain discount. Manufacturer B offers a 26/8 chain discount. Both manufacturers have the same list price. What manufacturer should Home Depot buy from?

7–27. Maplewood Supply received a $5,250 invoice dated 4/15/06. The $5,250 included $250 freight. Terms were 4/10, 3/30, n/60. **(a)** If Maplewood pays the invoice on April 27, what will it pay? **(b)** If Maplewood pays the invoice on May 21, what will it pay?

7–28. A local Sports Authority ordered 50 pairs of tennis shoes from Nike Corporation. The shoes were priced at $85 for each pair with the following terms: 4/10, 2/30, n/60. The invoice was dated October 15. Sports Authority sent in a payment on October 28. What should have been the amount of the check?

7–29. Macy of New York sold LeeCo. of Chicago office equipment with a $6,000 list price. Sale terms were 3/10, n/30 FOB New York. Macy agreed to prepay the $30 freight. LeeCo. pays the invoice within the discount period. What does LeeCo. pay Macy?

7–30. Royal Furniture bought a sofa for $800. The sofa had a $1,400 list price. What was the trade discount rate Royal received? Round to the nearest hundredth percent.

7–31. Amazon.com paid a $6,000 net price for textbooks. The publisher offered a 30% trade discount. What was the publisher's list price? Round to the nearest cent.

7–32. Bally Manufacturing sent Intel Corporation an invoice for machinery with a $14,000 list price. Bally dated the invoice July 23 with 2/10 EOM terms. Intel receives a 40% trade discount. Intel pays the invoice on August 5. What does Intel pay Bally?

7–33. On August 1, Intel Corporation (Problem 7–32) returns $100 of the machinery due to defects. What does Intel pay Bally on August 5? Round to nearest cent.

7–34. Stacy's Dress Shop received a $1,050 invoice dated July 8 with 2/10, 1/15, n/60 terms. On July 22, Stacy's sent a $242 partial payment. What credit should Stacy's receive? What is Stacy's outstanding balance?

7–35. On March 11, Jangles Corporation received a $20,000 invoice dated March 8. Cash discount terms were 4/10, n/30. On March 15, Jangles sent an $8,000 partial payment. What credit should Jangles receive? What is Jangles' outstanding balance?

ADDITIONAL SET OF WORD PROBLEMS

7–36. MONEY Magazine published an article titled "Take the bite out of dental costs." This article recommends a few tips for saving money at the dentist: 1. get a dentist who is part of your insurance plan, 2. join a non-insurance related discount club, 3. choose your treatment wisely—there is more than one way to treat a dental problem, 4. be flexible—if the treatment is not urgent, consider waiting until next year so you can make a financial plan, 5. Negotiate—politely, and 6. brush up—take care of your teeth by brushing and flossing twice daily. If you negotiated successfully with your dentist on the cost of a treatment and she is willing to provide you 3/15, n/30 terms, what amount will be credited to your balance if you make a partial payment of $150 within the discount period?

7–37. Borders.com paid a $79.99 net price for each calculus textbook. The publisher offered a 20% trade discount. What was the publisher's list price?

7–38. HomeOffice.com buys a computer from Compaq Corporation. The computer has a $1,200 list price with a 30% trade discount. What is the trade discount amount? What is the net price of the computer? Freight charges are FOB destination.

7–39. Vail Ski Shop received a $1,201 invoice dated July 8 with 2/10, 1/15, n/60 terms. On July 22, Vail sent a $485 partial payment. What credit should Vail receive? What is Vail's outstanding balance?

7–40. True Value received an invoice dated 4/15/02. The invoice had a $5,500 balance that included $300 freight. Terms were 4/10, 3/30, n/60. True Value pays the invoice on April 29. What amount does True Value pay?

7–41. Baker's Financial Planners purchased seven new computers for $850 each. It received a 15% discount because it purchased more than five and an additional 6% discount because it took immediate delivery. Terms of payment were 2/10, n/30. Baker's pays the bill within the cash discount period. How much should the check be? Round to the nearest cent.

7–42. On May 14, Talbots of Boston sold Forrest of Los Angeles $7,000 of fine clothes. Terms were 2/10 EOM FOB Boston. Talbots agreed to prepay the $80 freight. If Forrest pays the invoice on June 8, what will Forrest pay? If Forrest pays on June 20, what will Forrest pay?

7–43. Sam's Ski Boards.com offers 5/4/1 chain discounts to many of its customers. The Ski Hut ordered 20 ski boards with a total list price of $1,200. What is the net price of the ski boards? What was the trade discount amount? Round to the nearest cent.

7–44. Majestic Manufacturing sold Jordans Furniture a living room set for an $8,500 list price with 35% trade discount. The $100 freight (FOB shipping point) was not part of the list price. Terms were 3/10, n/30 ROG. The invoice date was May 30. Jordans received the goods on July 18 and paid the invoice on July 20. What was the final price (include cost of freight) of the living room set?

7–45. Boeing Truck Company received an invoice showing 8 tires at $110 each, 12 tires at $160 each, and 15 tires at $180 each. Shipping terms are FOB shipping point. Freight is $400; trade discount is 10/5; and a cash discount of 2/10, n/30 is offered. Assuming Boeing paid within the discount period, what did Boeing pay?

7–46. Verizon offers to sell cellular phones listing for $99.99 with a chain discount of 15/10/5. Cellular Company offers to sell its cellular phones that list at $102.99 with a chain discount of 25/5. If Irene is to buy 6 phones, how much could she save if she buys from the lower-priced company?

7–47. Bryant Manufacture sells its furniture to wholesalers and retailers. It offers to wholesalers a chain discount of 15/10/5 and to retailers a chain discount of 15/10. If a sofa lists for $500, how much would the wholesaler and retailer pay?

CHALLENGE PROBLEMS

7–48. The nonprofit dog adoption organization, Wags are Us, is purchasing dog food from their local pet store for $335. Because the organization is a nonprofit, the store is offering Wags are Us a trade discount of 35% at 5/15 EOM. If Wags are Us purchases the dog food on June 28, when is the end of its discount period and credit period? What will *Wags are Us* owe if the organization pays before the end of the discount period?

7–49. On March 30, Century Television received an invoice dated March 28 from ACME Manufacturing for 50 televisions at a cost of $125 each. Century received a 10/4/2 chain discount. Shipping terms were FOB shipping point. ACME prepaid the $70 freight. Terms were 2/10 EOM. When Century received the goods, 3 sets were defective. Century returned these sets to ACME. On April 8, Century sent a $150 partial payment. Century will pay the balance on May 6. What is Century's final payment on May 6? Assume no taxes.

DVD SUMMARY PRACTICE TEST (Round to the Nearest Cent as Needed)

Complete the following: *(pp. 173, 176)*

	Item	List price	Single trade discount	Net price
1.	Apple iPod	$350	5%	
2.	Palm Pilot		10%	$190

Calculate the net price and trade discount (use net price equivalent rate and single equivalent discount rate) for the following: *(pp. 176–178)*

	Item	List price	Chain discount	Net price	Trade discount
3.	Sony HD flat-screen TV	$899	5/4		

4. From the following, what is the last date for each discount period and credit period? *(p. 180)*

	Date of invoice	Terms	End of discount period	End of credit period
a.	Nov. 4	2/10, n/30		
b.	Oct. 3, 2009	3/10, n/30 ROG (Goods received March 10, 2010)		
c.	May 2	2/10 EOM		
d.	Nov. 28	2/10 EOM		

5. Best Buy buys an iPod from a wholesaler with a $300 list price and a 5% trade discount. What is the trade discount amount? What is the net price of the iPod? *(p. 173)*

6. Jordan's of Boston sold Lee Company of New York computer equipment with a $7,000 list price. Sale terms were 4/10, n/30 FOB Boston. Jordan's agreed to prepay the $400 freight. Lee pays the invoice within the discount period. What does Lee pay Jordan's? *(pp. 173, 180)*

7. Julie Ring wants to buy a new line of Tonka trucks for her shop. Manufacturer A offers a 14/8 chain discount. Manufacturer B offers a 15/7 chain discount. Both manufacturers have the same list price. Which manufacturer should Julie buy from? *(p. 177)*

8. Office.com received a $8,000 invoice dated April 10. Terms were 2/10, 1/15, n/60. On April 14, Office.com sent an $1,900 partial payment. What credit should Office.com receive? What is Office.com's outstanding balance? Round to the nearest cent. *(p. 187)*

9. Logan Company received from Furniture.com an invoice dated September 29. Terms were 1/10 EOM. List price on the invoice was $8,000 (freight not included). Logan receives a 8/7 chain discount. Freight charges are Logan's responsibility, but Furniture.com agreed to prepay the $300 freight. Logan pays the invoice on November 7. What does Logan Company pay Furniture.com? *(pp. 177, 185)*

Personal Finance

A KIPLINGER APPROACH

WAL-MART'S PROGRAM HAS SPURRED COMPETITORS TO MEET ITS ROCK-BOTTOM PRICES.

SAVE BIG ON PRESCRIPTIONS

Do your drugs cost too much? Find out how to get well for less. BY JESSICA L. ANDERSON

WHEN ORDERING YOUR prescriptions, it helps to think jeans. You could buy a designer pair for, say, $200. But if the fit is right, $50 Gap jeans would do just as well and cost a lot less.

Likewise, if you're a savvy shopper, you'll compare drug prices and choose the medication that fits you best and costs the least. Nobody but you will know the difference.

Go generic. Switching to generic drugs could save you up to 80% per prescription. Thanks to a tidal wave of brand-name drugs losing patent protection—among them popular medications such as cholesterol-reducing Zocor, antihypertensive Toprol-XL and antidepressant Zoloft—more generics are available than ever before, and chances are your medication is among them. Kristin Begley, of benefits consultant Hewitt Associates, says that $60 billion worth of brand-name drugs are coming off patent in the next three years.

If your medication hasn't gone generic yet, you're not out of luck. Ask your doctor if there is a similar generic drug in the same therapeutic class. The most common conditions—high cholesterol, depression, allergies and diabetes—all have generics available, says Ron Fontanetta, a principal at benefits-consulting firm Towers Perrin. "It's the single best way to save money."

Because generics cost less on the retail side, employers typically offer better coverage for them, too. Company plans that still use co-payments commonly charge $10, $20 or $40 for prescriptions, with generics the least expensive, preferred brands (on the plan's approved, or formulary, list) in the middle and nonpreferred brands the most expensive. By switching from a nonpreferred brand to a generic, you could save $30 in a snap.

The push for transparency in health-care costs has led many employers to switch from co-pays to co-insurance, meaning that the insurer pays a percentage of a drug's cost—typically 80%—and you pick up the rest. Lipitor, a widely used cholesterol reducer, costs $82 for a 30-day supply at Drugstore.com, so you'd pay $16.40. But for a similar generic drug that costs $28, you'd pay just $5.60, saving you an additional 66%.

Some companies up the ante by adding extra incentives to make the switch, such as offering tiered co-insurance rates—say, 80% for generic drugs but just 50% for brand-name medicines. Reducing the co-insurance on Lipitor from 80% to 50% makes using a generic drug even more attractive. Begley says she is starting to see "coupon" programs in which companies foot the whole bill for a few months after an employee makes the switch.

If you still need an incentive, here it is: generic drugs for $4. Wal-Mart and its warehouse retailer, Sam's Club, started the ball rolling in 2006, offering 30-day supplies of some drugs for just $4. The program has expanded to more than 360 medications. Rival Target has a $4-drug program that includes 315 medications; Walgreens offers 90-day supplies of some 300 generics for $12.99.

Costco jumped on the $4 bandwagon early on, but it dropped that approach and switched to a program of 100 pills for $10 because of lost revenue. One regional grocery chain, Giant Eagle, now offers 400 generic drugs for $4. Meijer, another regional chain, offers seven common antibiotics free. Missing in action? Big names CVS and Rite Aid.

Meds by mail. More than half the money spent on drugs today goes toward treating chronic conditions,

From Kiplinger's Personal Finance, May 2008, p. 71.

BUSINESS MATH ISSUE

Generic drugs should never be bought online.

1. List the key points of the article and information to support your position.
2. Write a group defense of your position using math calculations to support your view.

PROJECT A

Do you agree with minimum pricing? Define your position.

Slater's Business Math Scrapbook

Applying Your Skills

State Law Targets 'Minimum Pricing'

By Joseph Pereira

In a move that could lead to lower prices for consumers across the country, Maryland has passed a law that prohibits manufacturers from requiring retailers to charge minimum prices for their goods.

The law, which takes effect Oct. 1, takes aim at agreements that many manufacturers have been forcing on retailers, requiring them to charge minimum prices on certain products. The practice has surged since a controversial 2007 U.S. Supreme Court ruling that no longer makes such agreements automatically illegal under federal antitrust law.

Under the new state law, retailers doing business in Maryland—as well as state officials—can sue manufacturers that impose minimum-pricing agreements. The law also covers transactions in which consumers in Maryland buy goods on the Internet, even when the retailer is based out of state. That could potentially affect manufacturers throughout the country.

Minimum-pricing agreements keep retail profit margins higher, which in turn keeps retailers from pressuring manufacturers to lower the wholesale prices they pay for those goods. Suppliers also think that eliminating pricing competition can help retailers spend more money promoting their products to consumers. But certain retailers—particularly online ones—that attract customers because of low prices say the agreements stifle competition and gouge consumers.

Maryland's legislation is one of a series of recent initiatives aimed at circumventing the Supreme Court decision. A congressional subcommittee is scheduled to hold a hearing today in which several opponents of minimum-pricing agreements are expected to testify, including **eBay** Inc. and Federal Trade Commissioner Pamela Jones Harbour.

Hearings are expected next month in the U.S. Senate on a bill called the Discount Pricing Consumer Protection Act. Introduced by Sen. Herb Kohl (D., Wis.), it is aimed at circumventing the Supreme Court's ruling and making minimum-pricing agreements between manufacturers and retailers illegal under federal law once again.

In a 5-4 decision, a majority of Supreme Court justices said such agreements, which previously had been illegal, must be reviewed on a case-by-case basis—a leniency that legal experts say has emboldened manufacturers over the past two years to require retailers to enter into the agreements.

"Today there are an estimated 5,000 companies that have implemented minimum-pricing policies, much of it happening in the wake of the Supreme Court decision," said Christopher S. Finnerty, a Boston attorney who advises manufacturers on pricing issues.

Maryland stores can now sue manufacturers that impose minimum-pricing agreements.

Charles Shafer, a University of Baltimore law professor and president of the Maryland Consumer Rights Coalition, said: "The Supreme Court has basically abandoned the consumer, and now the states and the federal government are finding they have to step into the breach."

One company with a minimum-pricing policy is **Kolcraft Enterprises** Inc., a Chicago-based supplier of bassinets and strollers sold by **Wal-Mart Stores** Inc. According to a copy of a pricing agreement obtained by The Wall Street Journal, Kolcraft requires retailers to charge a minimum price of $159.99 for its Contours Classique 3-in-1 Bassinet. Wal-Mart's price is $169.88. The price dictated by Kolcraft for its Options Tandem Stroller is $219.99; Wal-Mart charges $219.98.

The agreement states that the policy is intended, among other things, "to protect all Kolcraft and Kolcraft-licensed brands from diminution." Kolcraft also sells products under the Sealy and Jeep brands. Eileen Lysaught, Kolcraft's general counsel and vice-president of operations, declined to comment, as did Wal-Mart.

The Maryland bill won the support of the Maryland Retailers Association, whose members include Wal-Mart, **Target** Corp. and **Sears Holdings** Corp. Wal-Mart did not take a position on the Maryland bill. But Rhoda M. Washington, Wal-Mart's regional senior manager for state and local government relations, says, "Wal-Mart customers expect competitive, reasonable prices, and the Maryland legislature is seeking to ensure that we can deliver on that promise." Target and Sears declined to comment.

The association's president, Tom Saquella, said high-end retailers initially expressed reservations about the bill, while mass merchandisers favored it. But eventually "we got a majority" supporting it, he said. "Basically our merchants don't want manufacturers telling us what we can sell our merchandise at."

Maryland already has an antitrust law that bans price fixing. But because Maryland is one of a number of states where federal-court interpretations take precedent over state law, the Supreme Court's ruling essentially nullified state law. By creating a new law that explicitly bans all minimum-pricing agreements between manufacturers and retailers, state legal experts say, Maryland is now able to preempt the high-court ruling. Legal experts say more than 30 other states that filed briefs with the Supreme Court could join Maryland in enacting such a law.

"We're making it clear to the judges in this state that Maryland was not adopting

Please turn to page D6

Internet Projects: See text Web site (www.mhhe.com/slater10e) and The Business Math Internet Resource Guide.

Video Case

FEDEX LOGISTICS

FedEx is well-known for its small package delivery business, which successfully transports millions of small packages worldwide daily. FedEx is also the number 1 provider of expedited freight shipments transporting 3,500 to 5,000 express skid shipments a night. The planning and coordination required to ship this volume of large or heavy shipments is a challenge for the logistics side of the freight business.

In order to qualify as freight, a package must weigh at least 151 pounds. It must be palletized, stackable, forklift-friendly, and shrink-wrapped or banded for stability. The uniform cargo footprint can be no larger than 16 square feet and no taller than 70 inches with a maximum weight for a standard freight package of 2,200 pounds. These requirements are necessary to meet the specific center of gravity and weight-limit qualifications required by each aircraft.

FedEx's cutting-edge tracking technology and logistic capabilities allow them to guarantee pickup and subsequent delivery times within a three- to four-hour time span. This core attribute paved the way for FedEx Custom Critical—the fastest, 24/7, door-to-door, same-day delivery of urgent freight, valuable items and hazardous goods service available. Utilizing a service fleet of ground-expedited transportation vehicles equipped with satellite monitoring systems as well as an array of air options provides the quick turnaround time demanded. In most cases packages are picked up within 90 minutes from the customer's call and delivered within 15 minutes of the scheduled delivery time.

FedEx continues to strive to meet and beat customer expectations through its array of package and freight delivery systems. With a history that officially began operations on April 17, 1973, with 14 small aircraft, FedEx has come a long way . . . baby.

PROBLEM 1

The video discusses the requirements of a package to qualify as freight. A package must weigh at least 151 pounds. It must be palletized, stackable, forklift-friendly and shrink-wrapped or banded for stability. The uniform cargo footprint can be no larger than 16 square feet and no taller than 70 inches with a maximum weight for a standard freight package of 2,200 pounds. If you are shipping 6,751 pounds of stackable 8 foot square items with a value of $33,150, does your shipment qualify as freight? If so, how many freight packages would you need? Calculate the actual pounds for each freight package.

PROBLEM 2

The video discusses the logistics involved in some of FedEx's service offerings. FedEx ships FOB destination because the seller pays the freight. If there is damage to a domestic freight shipment, FedEx will provide up to $50 per pound insurance on new items or $0.50 per pound on used items up to $100,000. Is the shipment of new items discussed in problem 1 fully covered? Will you need to buy additional coverage? Why or why not?

PROBLEM 3

In the December 9, 2008, *New York Times* article, "FedEx Lowers 2009 Earnings Forecast," FedEx said it expected to earn an average of $4.13 a share for the fiscal year ending in May, down from its original estimate of an average of $5.00 a share. Analysts were predicting that the company would earn $5.15 a share, according to Thomson Reuters. What percent reduction is the company's new estimate from the original estimate in earnings per share? What percent reduction in earnings per share is there between the original estimate and the analysts' predictions? Round to the nearest tenth percent.

PROBLEM 4

The *Wall Street Journal* reported on September 19, 2008, that FedEx Corp., in response to a 22% decline in net income for its first fiscal quarter, "will raise prices in January, cut capital spending, park aircraft, freeze most hiring and trim employees' hours." FedEx announced on March 2, 2009, an average increase of 6.9% for U.S. services to help offset a reduction in business effective immediately. If a FedEx First Overnight package costs $67.41 for a 1 pound package to ship today, what did it cost to ship before the increase? Round to the nearest cent.

PROBLEM 5

On January 5, 2009, UPS posted their new rates. UPS ground rates have increased an average of 5.9%. Air and international services have increased an average of 4.9%. UPS Next Day Air costs $42.81 for a 1 pound package. This reflects an increase of 4.9%. What was the cost to ship this package before the air increase? Round to the nearest cent. Comparing against data in problem 4, what is the difference in price between UPS and FedEx to ship a 1 pound package overnight? Would you choose FedEx or UPS to ship your package? Why?

PROBLEM 6

Despite an historical "no layoff" policy, FedEx laid off 900 employees in the early part of 2009 as reported the February 9, 2009, *Memphis Business Journal*. If FedEx (FDX), headquartered in Memphis, Tennessee, has 233,457 U.S. employees, what percent were laid off in February? Round to the nearest tenth percent.

chapter

8 MARKUPS AND MARKDOWNS: PERISHABLES AND BREAKEVEN ANALYSIS

Bloomberg News

Shopping Around

Cash-strapped shoppers are continuing to crowd cheap-and-chic Zara stores, like this one in Madrid, owned by Inditex, a Spanish fashion retailer. Inditex is now challenging Gap's rank as the world's biggest specialty clothing vendor by revenue.

	Inditex	Gap
Annual sales	$14.1 billion	$14.5 billion
Number of stores	4,264	3,100
Number of countries	73	6
Biggest brand	Zara	Gap
Number of other brands	6	3
Based in	Arteixo, Spain	San Francisco
First store opened	1975	1969
First foreign store	1989 Oporto, Portugal	1987 London

Source: the companies

Aly Song/Reuters/Landov

LEARNING UNIT OBJECTIVES

LU 8–1: Markups[1] Based on Cost (100%)

1. Calculate dollar markup and percent markup on cost *(p. 205)*.
2. Calculate selling price when you know the cost and percent markup on cost *(p. 206)*.
3. Calculate cost when dollar markup and percent markup on cost are known *(p. 207)*.
4. Calculate cost when you know the selling price and percent markup on cost *(p. 207)*.

LU 8–2: Markups Based on Selling Price (100%)

1. Calculate dollar markup and percent markup on selling price *(p. 210)*.
2. Calculate selling price when dollar markup and percent markup on selling price are known *(p. 210)*.
3. Calculate selling price when cost and percent markup on selling price are known *(p. 211)*.
4. Calculate cost when selling price and percent markup on selling price are known *(p. 212)*.
5. Convert from percent markup on cost to percent markup on selling price and vice versa *(p. 212)*.

LU 8–3: Markdowns and Perishables

1. Calculate markdowns; compare markdowns and markups *(p. 215)*.
2. Price perishable items to cover spoilage loss *(pp. 215–216)*.

LU 8–4: Breakeven Analysis

1. Calculate contribution margin *(p. 219)*.
2. Calculate breakeven point *(p. 219)*.

VOCABULARY PREVIEW

Here are key terms in this chapter. After completing the chapter, if you know the term, place a checkmark in the parenthesis. If you don't know the term, look it up and put the page number where it can be found.

Breakeven point . ( ) Contribution margin . ( ) Cost . ( ) Dollar markdown . ( ) Dollar markup . ( ) Fixed cost . ( ) Gross profit . ( ) Margin . ( ) Markdowns . ( ) Markup . ( ) Net profit (net income) . ( ) Operating expenses (overhead) . ( ) Percent markup on cost . ( ) Percent markup on selling price . ( ) Perishables . ( ) Selling price . ( ) Variable cost . ( )

Are you one of the many shoppers who shop at the Gap? If you read the *Wall Street Journal* clip, "Gap to Merge Brands Into Single Stores," (p. 204) you will see that your shopping experience will change. Gap plans to have kids, baby, maternity body, and adult merchandise in one store. They also plan to cut inventory and cost by this new strategy.

Before we study the two pricing methods available to Gap (percent markup on cost and percent markup on selling price), we must know the following terms:

- **Selling price.** The price retailers charge consumers. The total selling price of all the goods sold by a retailer (like Gap) represents the retailer's total sales.
- **Cost.** The price retailers pay to a manufacturer or supplier to bring the goods into the store.
- **Markup, margin, or gross profit.** These three terms refer to the difference between the cost of bringing the goods into the store and the selling price of the goods.

[1]Some texts use the term *markon* (selling price minus cost).

Paul Sakuma/AP Photo

Gap to Merge Brands Into Single Stores

Gap Inc. plans to close a handful of small stand-alone GapBody, GapKids and babyGap stores to test a strategy of consolidating Gap brand offerings in its namesake stores and reducing its square footage.

"It's been clear to us by doing the numbers and talking to customers in our stores, having kids, baby, maternity, body, and adult in the same box makes sense," Chief Executive Glenn Murphy said at a conference hosted by Piper Jaffray Cos. in New York.

The consolidation was one example Mr. Murphy used to illustrate the San Francisco-based apparel retailer's new real-estate strategy, which involves figuring out which of its 3,100 stores to reposition, relocate, remodel and "right size."

For the retail strategy in general, he said, "we probably won't see much of a benefit in 2008, but in 2009 going forward..."

By combining a 10,000-square-foot Gap adult and body store with a 5,000-square-foot kids-only store, Gap could save $225,000 a year in rent alone, he said.

The "sweetspot" for Gap stores is 6,000 to 10,000 square feet and for Old Navy, 14,000 to 16,000 square feet, he said.

Gap has been struggling with sluggish sales across all its brands and has been trying to boost earnings by cutting inventory and costs.

- **Operating expenses or overhead.** The regular expenses of doing business such as wages, rent, utilities, insurance, and advertising.
- **Net profit or net incomes.** The profit remaining after subtracting the cost of bringing the goods into the store and the operating expenses from the sale of the goods (including any returns or adjustments). In Learning Unit 8–4 we will take a closer look at the point at which costs and expenses are covered. This is called the *breakeven* point.

From these definitions, we can conclude that *markup* represents the amount that retailers must add to the cost of the goods to cover their operating expenses and make a profit.[2]

Let's assume Gap plans to sell hooded fleece jackets for $23 that cost them $18.

Basic selling price formula

Selling price (S)	=	Cost (C)	+	Markup (M)
↑		↑		↑
$23	=	$18 (price paid to bring fleece jackets into store)	+	$5 (amount in dollars to cover operating expenses and make a profit)

In the Gap example, the markup is a dollar amount, or a **dollar markup.** Markup is also expressed in percent. When expressing markup in percent, retailers can choose a percent based on *cost* (Learning Unit 8–1) or a percent based on *selling price* (Learning Unit 8–2).

When you go out to dinner at a salad bar, you might be amazed to discover how much certain foods are marked up. For example, at one restaurant, potatoes are marked up 62.5% and shrimp are marked up 75%. Now let's look at how to calculate markup percents.

Learning Unit 8–1: Markups Based on Cost (100%)

In Chapter 6 you were introduced to the portion formula, which we used to solve percent problems. We also used the portion formula in Chapter 7 to solve problems involving trade and cash discounts. In this unit you will see how we use the basic selling price formula and the portion formula to solve percent markup situations based on cost. We will be using blueprint aids to show how to dissect and solve all word problems in this chapter.

[2]In this chapter, we concentrate on the markup of retailers. Manufacturers and suppliers also use markup to determine selling price.

Many manufacturers mark up goods on cost because manufacturers can get cost information more easily than sales information. Since retailers have the choice of using percent markup on cost or selling price, in this unit we assume Gap has chosen percent markup on cost. In Learning Unit 8–2 we show how Gap would determine markup if it decided to use percent markup on selling price.

Businesses that use **percent markup on cost** recognize that cost is 100%. This 100% represents the base of the portion formula. All situations in this unit use cost as 100%.

To calculate percent markup on cost, we will use the hooded fleece jacket sold by Gap and begin with the basic selling price formula given in the chapter introduction. When we know the dollar markup, we can use the portion formula to find the percent markup on cost.

Markup expressed in dollars:

Selling price ($23) = Cost ($18) + Markup ($5)

Markup expressed as a percent markup on cost:

Cost	100.00%	→ Cost is 100%—the base. Dollar markup is the portion, and percent markup on cost is the rate.
+ Markup	+ 27.78	
= Selling price	127.78%	

In Situation 1 (below) we show why Gap has a 27.78% markup based on cost by presenting the hooded fleece jacket as a word problem. We solve the problem with the blueprint aid used in earlier chapters. In the second column, however, you will see footnotes after two numbers. These refer to the steps we use below the blueprint aid to solve the problem. Throughout the chapter, the numbers that we are solving for are in red. Remember that cost is the base for this unit.

LO 1

Situation 1: Calculating Dollar Markup and Percent Markup on Cost

Dollar markup is calculated with the basic selling price formula $S = C + M$. When you know the cost and selling price of goods, reverse the formula to $M = S - C$. Subtract the cost from the selling price, and you have the dollar markup.

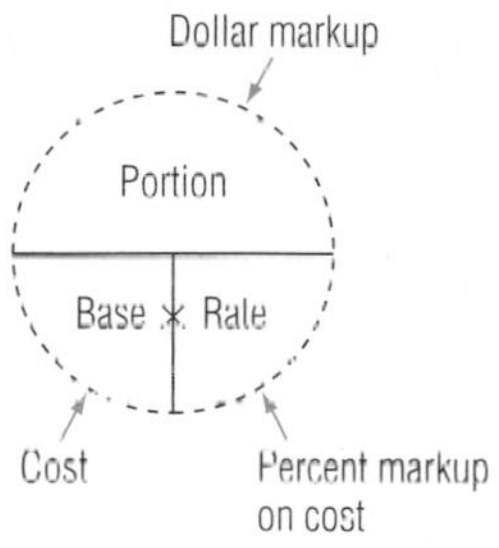

The percent markup on cost is calculated with the portion formula. For Situation 1 the *portion* (P) is the dollar markup, which you know from the selling price formula. In this unit the *rate* (R) is always the percent markup on cost and the *base* (B) is always the cost (100%). To find the percent markup on cost (R), use the portion formula $R = \frac{P}{B}$ and divide the dollar markup (P) by the cost (B). Convert your answer to a percent and round if necessary.

Now we will look at the Gap example to see how to calculate the 27.78% markup on cost.

The Word Problem The Gap pays $18 for a hooded fleece jacket, which the store plans to sell for $23. What is Gap's dollar markup? What is the percent markup on cost (round to the nearest hundredth percent)?

The facts	Solving for?	Steps to take	Key points
Hooded fleece jacket cost: $18. *Hooded fleece jacket selling price:* $23.	% $ C 100.00% $18 + M 27.78[2] 5[1] = S 127.78% $23 [1]Dollar markup. [2]Percent markup on cost.	Dollar markup = Selling price − Cost. Percent markup on cost = $\frac{\text{Dollar markup}}{\text{Cost}}$	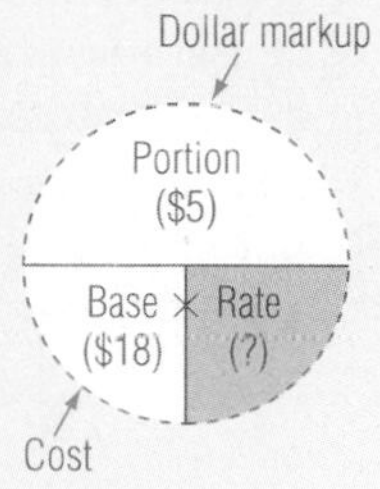

Steps to solving problem

1. Calculate the dollar markup.

Dollar markup = Selling price − Cost

$5 = $23 − $18

2. Calculate the percent markup on cost.

$$\text{Percent markup on cost} = \frac{\text{Dollar markup}}{\text{Cost}}$$

$$= \frac{\$5}{\$18} = 27.78\%$$

To check the percent markup on cost, you can use the basic selling price formula $S = C + M$. Convert the percent markup on cost found with the portion formula to a decimal and multiply it by the cost. This gives the dollar markup. Then add the cost and the dollar markup to get the selling price of the goods.

You could also check the cost (B) by dividing the dollar markup (P) by the percent markup on cost (R).

Check

Selling price = Cost + Markup   or $\text{Cost } (B) = \dfrac{\text{Dollar markup } (P)}{\text{Percent markup on cost } (R)}$

$\$23 = \$18 + .2778(\$18)$ $= \dfrac{\$5}{.2778} = \$18$

$\$23 = \$18 + \$5$

$\$23 = \$23$

Parentheses mean that you multiply the percent markup on cost in decimal by the cost.

LO 2

Situation 2: Calculating Selling Price When You Know Cost and Percent Markup on Cost

When you know the cost and the percent markup on cost, you calculate the selling price with the basic selling formula $S = C + M$. Remember that when goods are marked up on cost, the cost is the base (100%). So you can say that the selling price is the cost plus the markup in dollars (percent markup on cost times cost).

Now let's look at Mel's Furniture where we calculate Mel's dollar markup and selling price.

The Word Problem Mel's Furniture bought a lamp that cost $100. To make Mel's desired profit, he needs a 65% markup on cost. What is Mel's dollar markup? What is his selling price?

The facts	Solving for?	Steps to take	Key points
Lamp cost: $100. *Markup on cost:* 65%.	% / $ C: 100% / $100 + M: 65 / 65[1] = S: 165% / $165[2] [1]Dollar markup. [2]Selling price.	Dollar markup: $S = C + M$. or $S = \text{Cost} \times \left(1 + \begin{matrix}\text{Percent}\\\text{markup}\\\text{on cost}\end{matrix}\right)$	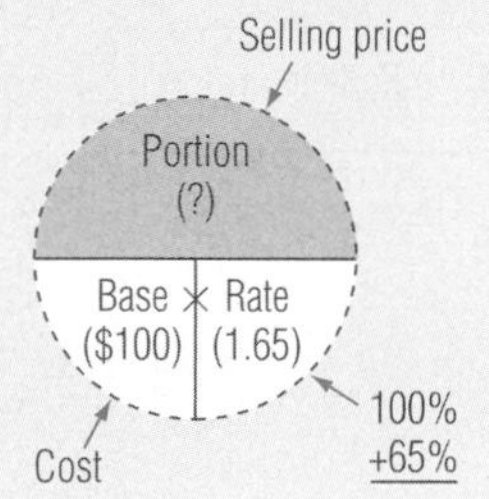

Steps to solving problem

1. Calculate the dollar markup. $S = C + M$

   $S = \$100 + .65(\$100)$ ← Parentheses mean you multiply the percent markup in decimal by the cost.

   $S = \$100 + \$65$ ← Dollar markup

2. Calculate the selling price. $S = \$165$

You can check the selling price with the formula $P = B \times R$. You are solving for the portion (P)—the selling price. Rate (R) represents the 100% cost plus the 65% markup on cost. Since in this unit the markup is on cost, the base is the cost. Convert 165% to a decimal and multiply the cost by 1.65 to get the selling price of $165.

Check

Selling price (P) = Cost (B) × (1 + Percent markup on cost) (R) $= \$100 \times 1.65 = \$165$

LO 3

Situation 3: Calculating Cost When You Know Selling Price and Percent Markup on Cost

When you know the selling price and the percent markup on cost, you calculate the cost with the basic selling formula $S = C + M$. Since goods are marked up on cost, the percent markup on cost is added to the cost.

Let's see how this is done in the following Jill Sport example.

The Word Problem Jill Sport, owner of Sports, Inc., sells tennis rackets for $50. To make her desired profit, Jill needs a 40% markup on cost. What do the tennis rackets cost Jill? What is the dollar markup?

The facts	Solving for?	Steps to take	Key points
Selling price: $50. *Markup on cost:* 40%.	% | \$ C 100% | \$35.71[1] $+ M$ 40 | 14.29[2] $= S$ 140% | \$50.00 [1]Cost. [2]Dollar markup.	$S = C + M.$ or $\text{Cost} = \dfrac{\text{Selling price}}{1 + \text{Percent markup on cost}}$ $M = S - C.$	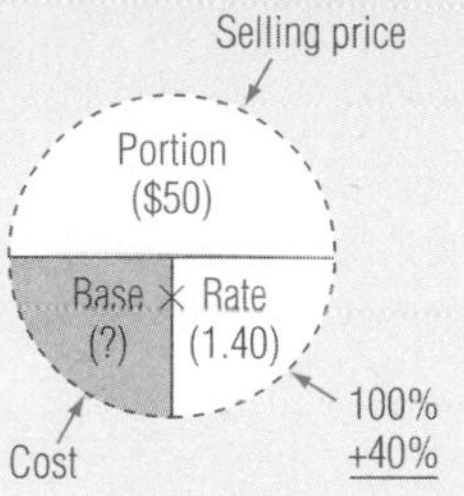

LO 4

Steps to solving problem

1. Calculate the cost.

$$S = C + M$$

$$\$50.00 = C + .40C$$ ← This means 40% times cost. C is the same as $1C$. Adding $.40C$ to $1C$ gives the percent markup on cost of $1.40C$ in decimal.

$$\frac{\$50.00}{1.40} = \frac{1.40C}{1.40}$$

$$\$35.71 = C$$

2. Calculate the dollar markup.

$$M = S - C$$

$$M = \$50.00 - \$35.71$$

$$M = \$14.29$$

$ MONEY TIPS

Before purchasing a high-ticket item, make certain to research brand quality and costs. The variability in both tends to be quite high and you want to get the most for your money.

You can check your cost answer with the portion formula $B = \frac{P}{R}$. Portion (P) is the selling price. Rate (R) represents the 100% cost plus the 40% markup on cost. Convert the percents to decimals and divide the portion by the rate to find the base, or cost.

Check

$$\text{Cost } (B) = \frac{\text{Selling price } (P)}{1 + \text{Percent markup on cost } (R)} = \frac{\$50.00}{1.40} = \$35.71$$

Now try the following Practice Quiz to check your understanding of this unit.

LU 8–1 PRACTICE QUIZ

Complete this **Practice Quiz** to see how you are doing.

Solve the following situations (markups based on cost):

1. Irene Westing bought a desk for $400 from an office supply house. She plans to sell the desk for $600. What is Irene's dollar markup? What is her percent markup on cost? Check your answer.
2. Suki Komar bought dolls for her toy store that cost $12 each. To make her desired profit, Suki must mark up each doll 35% on cost. What is the dollar markup? What is the selling price of each doll? Check your answer.

3. Jay Lyman sells calculators. His competitor sells a new calculator line for $14 each. Jay needs a 40% markup on cost to make his desired profit, and he must meet price competition. At what cost can Jay afford to bring these calculators into the store? What is the dollar markup? Check your answer.

Solutions with Step-by-Step Help on DVD

✓ Solutions

1. Irene's dollar markup and percent markup on cost:

The facts	Solving for?	Steps to take	Key points
Desk cost: $400. *Desk selling price:* $600.	% | $ *C* 100% | $400 + *M* 50[2] | 200[1] = *S* 150% | $600 [1]Dollar markup. [2]Percent markup on cost.	Dollar markup = Selling price − Cost. Percent markup on cost = Dollar markup / Cost	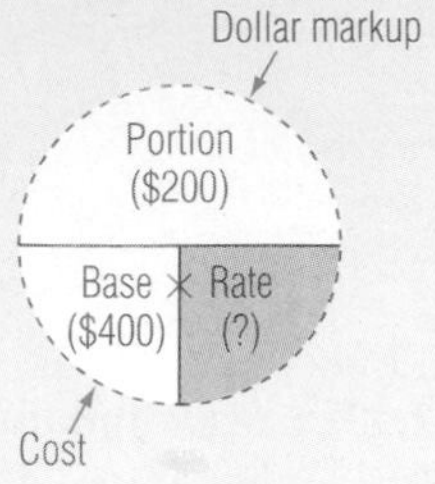

Steps to solving problem

1. Calculate the dollar markup. Dollar markup = Selling price − Cost

$$\$200 = \$600 - \$400$$

2. Calculate the percent markup on cost.

$$\text{Percent markup on cost} = \frac{\text{Dollar markup}}{\text{Cost}}$$

$$= \frac{\$200}{\$400} = 50\%$$

Check

$$\text{Selling price} = \text{Cost} + \text{Markup}$$
$$\$600 = \$400 + .50(\$400)$$
$$\$600 = \$400 + \$200$$
$$\$600 = \$600$$

or

$$\text{Cost }(B) = \frac{\text{Dollar markup }(P)}{\text{Percent markup on cost }(R)}$$

$$= \frac{\$200}{.50} = \$400$$

2. Dollar markup and selling price of doll:

The facts	Solving for?	Steps to take	Key points
Doll cost: $12 each. *Markup on cost:* 35%.	% | $ *C* 100% | $12.00 + *M* 35 | 4.20[1] = *S* 135% | $16.20[2] [1]Dollar markup. [2]Selling price.	Dollar markup: *S* = *C* + *M*. or $S = \text{Cost} \times \left(1 + \text{Percent markup on cost}\right)$	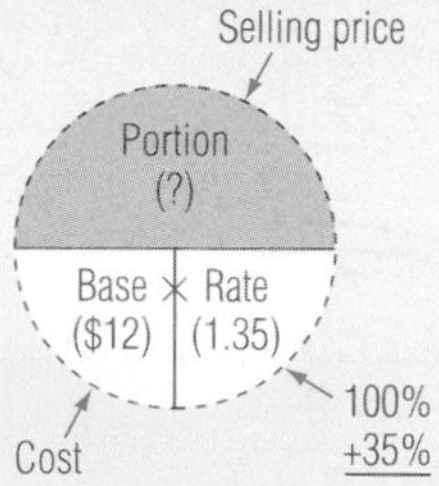

Steps to solving problem

1. Calculate the dollar markup.

$$S = C + M$$
$$S = \$12.00 + .35(\$12.00)$$
$$S = \$12.00 + \$4.20 \leftarrow \text{Dollar markup}$$

2. Calculate the selling price.

$$S = \$16.20$$

Check

$$\underset{(P)}{\text{Selling price}} = \underset{(B)}{\text{Cost}} \times (1 + \underset{(R)}{\text{Percent markup on cost}}) = \$12.00 \times 1.35 = \$16.20$$

3. Cost and dollar markup:

The facts	Solving for?	Steps to take	Key points
Selling price: $14. *Markup on cost:* 40%.	% | $ C 100% | $10[1] + M 40 | 4[2] = S 140% | $14 [1]Cost. [2]Dollar markup.	$S = C + M.$ or $\text{Cost} = \dfrac{\text{Selling price}}{\text{Percent } 1 + \text{markup on cost}}$ $M = S - C.$	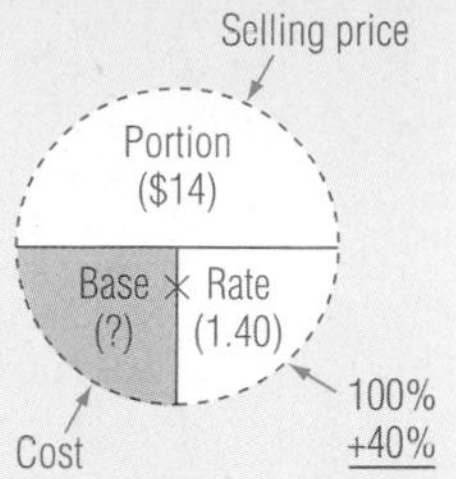

Steps to solving problem

1. Calculate the cost.

$$S = C + M$$
$$\$14 = C + .40C$$
$$\frac{\$14}{1.40} = \frac{\cancel{1.40}C}{\cancel{1.40}}$$
$$\$10 = C$$

2. Calculate the dollar markup.

$$M = S - C$$
$$M = \$14 - \$10$$
$$M = \$4$$

Check

$$\text{Cost } (B) = \frac{\text{Selling price } (P)}{1 + \text{Percent markup on cost } (R)} = \frac{\$14}{1.40} = \$10$$

LU 8–1a EXTRA PRACTICE QUIZ WITH WORKED-OUT SOLUTIONS

Need more practice? Try this **Extra Practice Quiz** (check figures in Chapter Organizer, p. 221). Worked-out Solutions can be found in Appendix B at end of text.

Solve the following situations (markups based on cost):

1. Irene Westing bought a desk for $800 from an office supply house. She plans to sell the desk for $1,200. What is Irene's dollar markup? What is her percent markup on cost? Check your answer.
2. Suki Komar bought dolls for her toy store that cost $14 each. To make her desired profit, Suki must mark up each doll 38% on cost. What is the dollar markup? What is the selling price of each doll? Check your answer.
3. Jay Lyman sells calculators. His competitor sells a new calculator line for $16 each. Jay needs a 42% markup on cost to make his desired profit, and he must meet price competition. At what cost can Jay afford to bring these calculators into the store? What is the dollar markup? Check your answer.

Learning Unit 8–2: Markups Based on Selling Price (100%)

Tony Anderson/Getty Images

Many retailers mark up their goods on the selling price since sales information is easier to get than cost information. These retailers use retail prices in their inventory and report their expenses as a percent of sales.

Businesses that mark up their goods on selling price recognize that selling price is 100%. We begin this unit by assuming Gap has decided to use percent markup based on selling price. We repeat Gap's selling price formula expressed in dollars.

Markup expressed in dollars:

Selling price ($23) = Cost ($18) + Markup ($5)

Markup expressed as **percent markup on selling price:**

Cost	78.26%
+ Markup	+ 21.74
= Selling price	100.00%

Selling price is 100%—the base. Dollar markup is the portion, and percent markup on selling price is the rate.

In Situation 1 (below) we show why Gap has a 21.74% markup based on selling price. In the last unit, markups were on *cost*. In this unit, markups are on *selling price*.

LO 1

Situation 1: Calculating Dollar Markup and Percent Markup on Selling Price

The dollar markup is calculated with the selling price formula used in Situation 1, Learning Unit 8–1: $M = S - C$. To find the percent markup on selling price, use the portion formula $R = \frac{P}{B}$, where rate (the percent markup on selling price) is found by dividing the portion (dollar markup) by the base (selling price). Note that when solving for percent markup on cost in Situation 1, Learning Unit 8–1, you divided the dollar markup by the cost.

The Word Problem The cost to Gap for a hooded fleece jacket is $18; the store then plans to sell them for $23. What is Gap's dollar markup? What is its percent markup on selling price? (Round to the nearest hundredth percent.)

The facts	Solving for?	Steps to take	Key points
Hooded fleece jacket cost: $18. *Hooded fleece jacket price:* $23.	| | % | $ | | *C* | 78.26% | $18 | | + *M* | 21.74%[2] | 5[1] | | = *S* | 100.00% | $23 | [1]Dollar markup. [2]Percent markup on selling price.	Dollar markup = Selling price − Cost. Percent markup on selling price = $\frac{\text{Dollar markup}}{\text{Selling price}}$	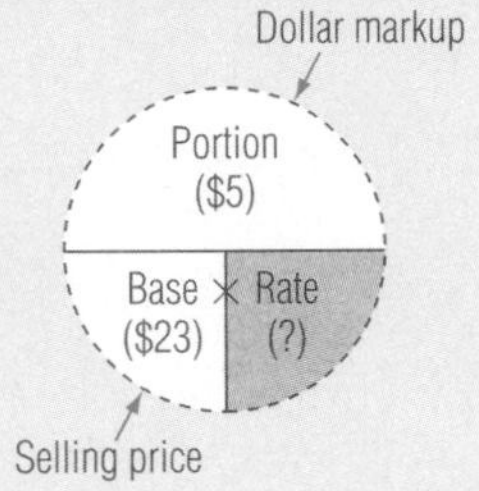

Steps to solving problem

1. Calculate the dollar markup.

   Dollar markup = Selling price − Cost

   $5 = $23 − $18

2. Calculate the percent markup on selling price.

   $$\text{Percent markup on selling price} = \frac{\text{Dollar markup}}{\text{Selling price}}$$

   $$= \frac{\$5}{\$23} = \mathbf{21.74\%}$$

You can check the percent markup on selling price with the basic selling price formula $S = C + M$. You can also use the portion formula by dividing the dollar markup (P) by the percent markup on selling price (R).

Check

Selling price = Cost + Markup

$23 = $18 + .2174($23)

$23 = $18 + $5

$23 = $23

or

$$\text{Selling price } (B) = \frac{\text{Dollar markup } (P)}{\text{Percent markup on selling price } (R)}$$

$$= \frac{\$5}{.2174} = \$23$$

Parentheses mean you multiply the percent markup on selling price in decimal by the selling price.

LO 2

Situation 2: Calculating Selling Price When You Know Cost and Percent Markup on Selling Price

When you know the cost and percent markup on selling price, you calculate the selling price with the basic selling formula $S = C + M$. Remember that when goods are marked up on selling price, the selling price is the base (100%). Since you do not know the selling price, the percent markup is based on the unknown selling price. To find the dollar markup after you find the selling price, use the selling price formula $M = S - C$.

The Word Problem Mel's Furniture bought a lamp that cost \$100. To make Mel's desired profit, he needs a 65% markup on selling price. What are Mel's selling price and his dollar markup?

The facts	Solving for?	Steps to take	Key points
Lamp cost: \$100. *Markup on selling price:* 65%.	% / \$ C 35% \$100.00 + M 65 185.71[2] = S 100% \$285.71[1] [1]Selling price. [2]Dollar markup.	$S = C + M$. or $S = \dfrac{\text{Cost}}{1 - \text{Percent markup on selling price}}$	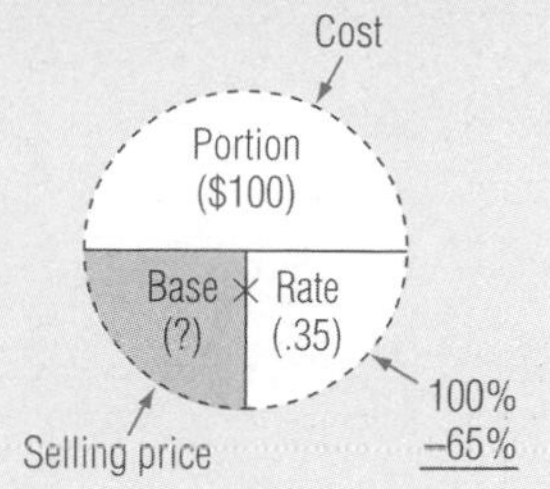

Steps to solving problem

1. Calculate the selling price.

$$S = C + M$$
$$S = \$100.00 + .65S$$
$$-.65S \qquad -.65S$$
$$\frac{.35S}{.35} = \frac{\$100.00}{.35}$$
$$S = \$285.71$$

(1.00S − .65S = .35S)

Do not multiply the .65 times \$100.00. The 65% is based on selling price not cost.

2. Calculate the dollar markup.

$$M = S - C$$
$$\$185.71 = \$285.71 - \$100.00$$

You can check your selling price with the portion formula $B = \frac{P}{R}$. To find the selling price (B), divide the cost (P) by the rate (100% − percent markup on selling price).

Check

$$\text{Selling price } (B) = \frac{\text{Cost } (P)}{1 - \text{Percent markup on selling price } (R)}$$

$$= \frac{\$100.00}{1 - .65} = \frac{\$100.00}{.35} = \$285.71$$

LO 3

Situation 3: Calculating Cost When You Know Selling Price and Percent Markup on Selling Price

When you know the selling price and the percent markup on selling price, you calculate the cost with the basic formula $S = C + M$. To find the dollar markup, multiply the markup percent by the selling price. When you have the dollar markup, subtract it from the selling price to get the cost.

The Word Problem Jill Sport, owner of Sports, Inc., sells tennis rackets for \$50. To make her desired profit, Jill needs a 40% markup on the selling price. What is the dollar markup? What do the tennis rackets cost Jill?

The facts	Solving for?	Steps to take	Key points
Selling price: \$50. *Markup on selling price:* 40%.	% / \$ C 60% \$30[2] + M 40 20[1] = S 100% \$50 [1]Dollar markup. [2]Cost.	$S = C + M$. or Cost = Selling price × (1 − Percent markup on selling price)	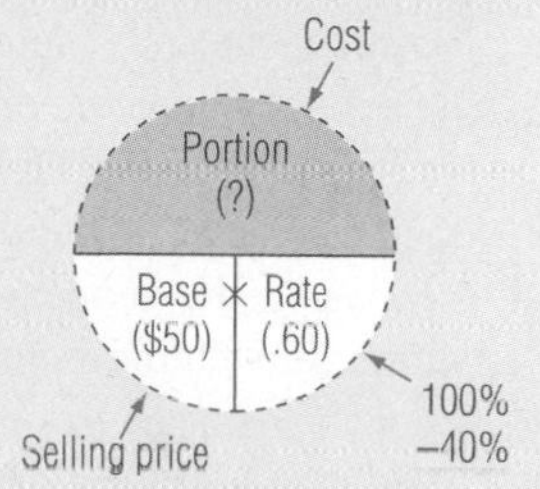

Steps to solving problem

1. Calculate the dollar markup.

$$S = C + M$$
$$\$50 = C + .40(\$50)$$

2. Calculate the cost.

$$\$50 = C + \$20 \leftarrow \text{Dollar markup}$$
$$-20 \qquad -20$$
$$\$30 = C$$

To check your cost, use the portion formula Cost (P) = Selling price (B) × (100% selling price − Percent markup on selling price) (R).

LO 4

Check

$$\text{Cost } (P) = \text{Selling price } (B) \times \left(1 - \text{Percent markup on selling price } (R)\right) = \$50 \times .60 = \$30$$

(1.00 − .40)

In Table 8.1, we compare percent markup on cost with percent markup on retail (selling price). This table is a summary of the answers we calculated from the word problems in Learning Units 8–1 and 8–2. The word problems in the units were the same except in Learning Unit 8–1, we assumed markups were on cost, while in Learning Unit 8–2, markups were on selling price. Note that in Situation 1, the dollar markup is the same $5, but the percent markup is different.

Let's now look at how to convert from percent markup on cost to percent markup on selling price and vice versa. We will use Situation 1 from Table 8.1.

LO 5

Formula for Converting Percent Markup on Cost to Percent Markup on Selling Price

To convert percent markup on cost to percent markup on selling price:

$$\frac{\text{Percent markup on cost}}{1 + \text{Percent markup on cost}}$$

$$\frac{.2778}{1 + .2778} = 21.74\%$$

TABLE 8.1

Comparison of markup on cost versus markup on selling price

Markup based on cost—Learning Unit 8–1	Markup based on selling price—Learning Unit 8–2
Situation 1: Calculating dollar amount of markup and percent markup on cost. Hooded fleece jacket cost, $18. Hooded fleece jacket selling price, $23. $M = S - C$ $M = \$23 - \$18 = \$5$ markup (p. 205) $M \div C = \$5 \div \$18 = 27.78\%$	*Situation 1: Calculating dollar amount of markup and percent markup on selling price.* Hooded fleece jacket cost, $18. Hooded fleece jacket selling price, $23. $M = S - C$ $M = \$23 - \$18 = \$5$ markup (p. 210) $M \div S = \$5 \div \$23 = 21.74\%$
Situation 2: Calculating selling price on cost. Lamp cost, $100. 65% markup on cost $S = C \times (1 + \text{Percent markup on cost})$ $S = \$100 \times 1.65 = \$165$ (p. 206) (100% + 65% = 165% = 1.65)	*Situation 2: Calculating selling price on selling price.* Lamp cost, $100. 65% markup on selling price $S = C \div (1 - \text{Percent markup on selling price})$ $S = \$100.00 \div .35$ (100% − 65% = 35% = .35) $S = \$285.71$ (p. 210)
Situation 3: Calculating cost on cost. Tennis racket selling price, $50. 40% markup on cost $C = S \div (1 + \text{Percent markup on cost})$ $C = \$50.00 \div 1.40$ (100% + 40% = 140% = 1.40) $C = \$35.71$ (p. 207)	*Situation 3: Calculating cost on selling price.* Tennis racket selling price, $50. 40% markup on selling price $C = S \times (1 - \text{Percent markup on selling price})$ $C = \$50 \times .60 = \$30$ (p. 211) (100% − 40% = 60% = .60)

$ MONEY TIPS

Use coupons and rebates to help reduce the price of items you are purchasing. Check the newspaper for coupons and sign up for in-house offers. The Internet is full of coupon and discount offers. Before buying online or in person, do an Internet search for the retail outlet in which you are shopping. You may find an offer you can't refuse.

Formula for Converting Percent Markup on Selling Price to Percent Markup on Cost

To convert percent markup on selling price to percent markup on cost:

$$\frac{\text{Percent markup on selling price}}{1 - \text{Percent markup on selling price}}$$

$$\frac{.2174}{1 - .2174} = 27.78\%$$

Key point: A 21.74% markup on selling price or a 27.78% markup on cost results in same dollar markup of $5.

Now let's test your knowledge of Learning Unit 8–2.

LU 8–2 PRACTICE QUIZ

Complete this **Practice Quiz** to see how you are doing.

Solve the following situations (markups based on selling price). Note numbers 1, 2, and 3 are parallel problems to those in Practice Quiz 8–1.

1. Irene Westing bought a desk for $400 from an office supply house. She plans to sell the desk for $600. What is Irene's dollar markup? What is her percent markup on selling price (round to the nearest tenth percent)? Check your answer. Selling price will be slightly off due to rounding.
2. Suki Komar bought dolls for her toy store that cost $12 each. To make her desired profit, Suki must mark up each doll 35% on the selling price. What is the selling price of each doll? What is the dollar markup? Check your answer.
3. Jay Lyman sells calculators. His competitor sells a new calculator line for $14 each. Jay needs a 40% markup on the selling price to make his desired profit, and he must meet price competition. What is Jay's dollar markup? At what cost can Jay afford to bring these calculators into the store? Check your answer.
4. Dan Flow sells wrenches for $10 that cost $6. What is Dan's percent markup at cost? Round to the nearest tenth percent. What is Dan's percent markup on selling price? Check your answer.

Solutions with Step-by-Step Help on DVD

✓ Solutions

1. Irene's dollar markup and percent markup on selling price:

The facts	Solving for?	Steps to take	Key points
Desk cost: $400. *Desk selling price:* $600.	% $ C 66.7% $400 + M 33.3[2] 200[1] = S 100% $600 [1]Dollar markup. [2]Percent markup on selling price.	Dollar markup = Selling price − Cost Percent markup on selling price = Dollar markup / Selling price	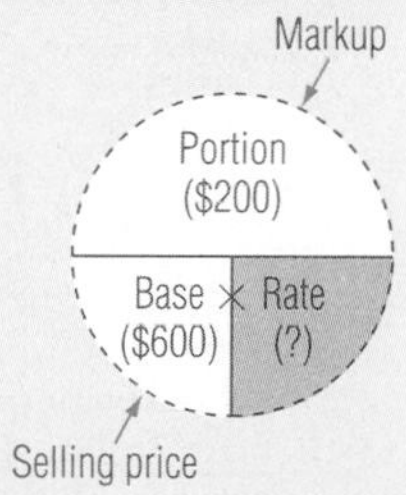

Steps to solving problem

1. Calculate the dollar markup.

Dollar markup = Selling price − Cost

$200 = $600 − $400

2. Calculate the percent markup on selling price.

$$\text{Percent markup on selling price} = \frac{\text{Dollar markup}}{\text{Selling price}}$$

$$= \frac{\$200}{\$600} = 33.3\%$$

Check

$$\text{Selling price} = \text{Cost} + \text{Markup} \quad \textbf{or} \quad \text{Selling price } (B) = \frac{\text{Dollar markup } (P)}{\text{Percent markup on selling price } (R)}$$

$$\$600 = \$400 + .333(\$600)$$

$$\$600 = \$400 + \$199.80 \qquad = \frac{\$200}{.333} = \$600.60^*$$

$$\$600 = \$599.80^* \qquad \text{(not exactly \$600 due to rounding)}$$

*Off due to rounding.

2. Selling price of doll and dollar markup:

The facts	Solving for?	Steps to take	Key points
Doll cost: $12 each. *Markup on selling price:* 35%.	% / \$ *C* 65% / \$12.00 + *M* 35 / 6.46[2] = *S* 100% / \$18.46[1] [1]Selling price. [2]Dollar markup.	$S = C + M$ or $S = \dfrac{\text{Cost}}{1 - \text{Percent markup on selling price}}$	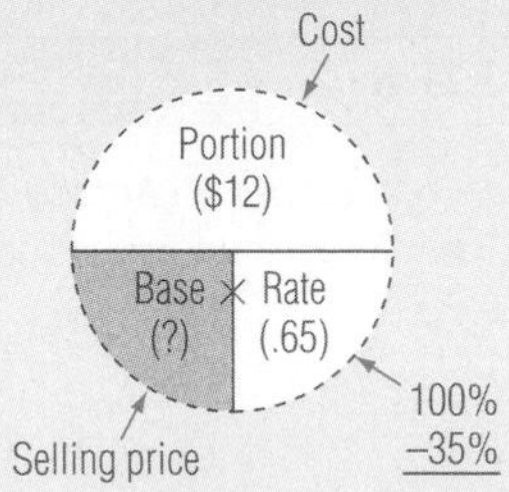

Steps to solving problem

1. Calculate the selling price.

$$S = C + M$$
$$S = \$12.00 + .35S$$
$$-.35S \qquad -.35S$$
$$\frac{.65S}{.65} = \frac{\$12.00}{.65}$$
$$S = \boxed{\$18.46}$$

2. Calculate the dollar markup.

$$M = S - C$$
$$\boxed{\$6.46} = \$18.46 - \$12.00$$

Check

$$\text{Selling price } (B) = \frac{\text{Cost } (P)}{1 - \text{Percent markup on selling price } (R)} = \frac{\$12.00}{.65} = \boxed{\$18.46}$$

3. Dollar markup and cost:

The facts	Solving for?	Steps to take	Key points
Selling price: $14. *Markup on selling price:* 40%.	% / \$ *C* 60% / \$ 8.40[2] + *M* 40 / 5.60[1] = *S* 100% / \$14.00 [1]Dollar markup. [2]Cost.	$S = C + M$ or Cost = Selling price × (1 − Percent markup on selling price)	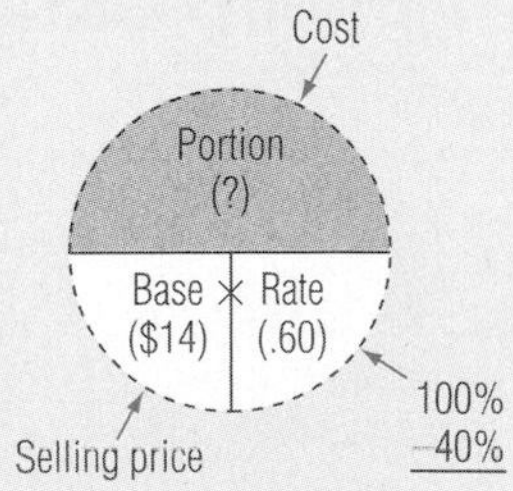

Steps to solving problem

1. Calculate the dollar markup.

$$S = C + M$$
$$\$14.00 = C + .40(\$14.00)$$

2. Calculate the cost.

$$\$14.00 = C + \boxed{\$5.60} \leftarrow \text{Dollar markup}$$
$$-5.60 \qquad -5.60$$
$$\boxed{\$8.40} = C$$

Check

$$\underset{(P)}{\text{Cost}} = \underset{(B)}{\text{Selling price}} \times \underset{(R)}{(1 - \text{Percent markup on selling price})} = \$14.00 \times .60 = \boxed{\$8.40}$$

(.60 = 1.00 − .40)

4. $\text{Cost} = \dfrac{\$4}{\$6} = \boxed{66.7\%}$ $\qquad \dfrac{.40}{1 - .40} = \dfrac{.40}{.60} = \dfrac{2}{3} = 66.7\%$

$\text{Selling price} = \dfrac{\$4}{\$10} = \boxed{40\%}$ $\qquad \dfrac{.667}{1 + .667} = \dfrac{.667}{1.667} = 40\%$ (due to rounding)

LU 8–2a EXTRA PRACTICE QUIZ WITH WORKED-OUT SOLUTIONS

Need more practice? Try this **Extra Practice Quiz** (check figures in Chapter Organizer, p. 221). Worked-out Solutions can be found in Appendix B at end of text.

Solve the following situations (markups based on selling price).

1. Irene Westing bought a desk for $800 from an office supply house. She plans to sell the desk for $1,200. What is Irene's dollar markup? What is her percent markup on selling price (round to the nearest tenth percent)? Check your answer. Selling price will be slightly off due to rounding.
2. Suki Komar bought dolls for her toy store that cost $14 each. To make her desired profit, Suki must mark up each doll 38% on selling price. What is the selling price of each doll? What is the dollar markup? Check your answer.
3. Jay Lyman sells calculators. His competitor sells a new calculator line for $16 each. Jay needs a 42% markup on the selling price to make his desired profit, and he must meet price competition. What is Jay's dollar markup? At what cost can Jay afford to bring these calculators into the store? Check your answer.
4. Dan Flow sells wrenches for $12 that cost $7. What is Dan's percent markup at cost? Round to the nearest tenth percent. What is Dan's percent markup on selling price? Check your answer.

Learning Unit 8–3: Markdowns and Perishables

© Blend Images/Alamy

Have you ever wondered how your local retail store determines a typical markdown on clothing? The following *Wall Street Journal* clipping "Sale Rack Shuffle" explains the typical markdown money arrangement between a clothing vendor and a retailer. Evidently, the retailer does not always take the entire financial loss when a piece of clothing is marked down until it sells.

Sale Rack Shuffle

How a typical markdown-money arrangement between a clothing vendor and a retailer works:

1. Vendor makes dress at cost of **$50**
2. Sells to retailer at wholesale price of **$80**
3. Retailer marks up dress to **$200**
4. Dress gets marked down after 8 to 12 weeks (starting at 25% off) **$150**
5. The dress gets marked down again until it sells; the retailer and the vendor negotiate how to share the cost of the markdown.

Wall Street Journal © 2005

This learning unit focuses your attention on how to calculate markdowns. Then you will learn how a business prices perishable items that may spoil before customers buy them.

LO 1

Markdowns

Markdowns are reductions from the original selling price caused by seasonal changes, special promotions, style changes, and so on. We calculate the markdown percent as follows:

$$\text{Markdown percent} = \frac{\text{Dollar markdown}}{\text{Selling price (original)}}$$

Let's look at the following Kmart example:

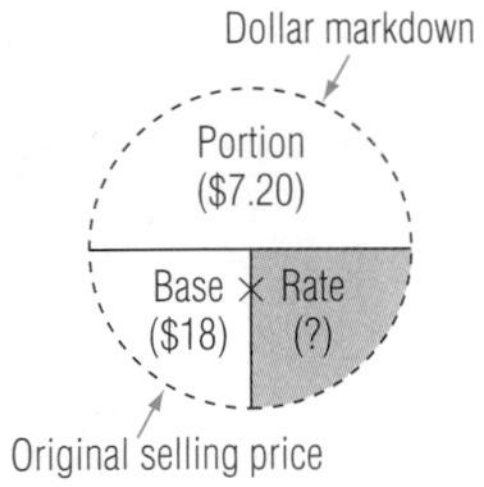

EXAMPLE Kmart marked down an $18 video to $10.80. Calculate the **dollar markdown** and the markdown percent.

$$\begin{array}{rl} \$18.00 & \text{Original selling price} \\ -\ 10.80 & \text{Sale price} \\ \hline \$\ 7.20 & \text{Markdown} \end{array} \longrightarrow \frac{\text{Dollar markdown, } \$7.20}{\text{Selling price (original), } \$18.00} = 40\%$$

Calculating a Series of Markdowns and Markups

Often the final selling price is the result of a series of markdowns (and possibly a markup in between markdowns). We calculate additional markdowns on the previous selling price. Note in the following example how we calculate markdown on selling price after we add a markup.

EXAMPLE Jones Department Store paid its supplier $400 for a TV. On January 10, Jones marked the TV up 60% on selling price. As a special promotion, Jones marked the TV down 30% on February 8 and another 20% on February 28. No one purchased the TV, so Jones marked it up 10% on March 11. What was the selling price of the TV on March 11?

$$\begin{array}{rcll} \text{January 10: Selling price} & = & \text{Cost} & +\ \text{Markup} \\ S & = & \$400 & +\ .60S \\ -\ .60S & & & -\ .60S \\ \hline \frac{.40S}{.40} & = & \frac{\$400}{.40} & \\ S & = & \$1{,}000 & \end{array}$$

Check $$S = \frac{\text{Cost}}{1 - \text{Percent markup on selling price}}$$

$$S = \frac{\$400}{1 - .60} = \frac{\$400}{.40} = \$1{,}000$$

February 8 markdown:
$$\begin{array}{r} 100\% \\ -\ 30 \\ \hline 70\% \end{array} \rightarrow .70 \times \$1{,}000 = \$700 \text{ selling price}$$

February 28 additional markdown:
$$\begin{array}{r} 100\% \\ -\ 20 \\ \hline 80\% \end{array} \rightarrow .80 \times \$700 = \$560$$

March 11 additional markup:
$$\begin{array}{r} 100\% \\ +\ 10 \\ \hline 110\% \end{array} \rightarrow 1.10 \times \$560 = \$616$$

LO 2

Pricing Perishable Items

The following formula can be used to determine the price of goods that have a short shelf life such as fruit, flowers, and pastry. (We limit this discussion to obviously **perishable** items.)

$$\text{Selling price of perishables} = \frac{\text{Total dollar sales}}{\text{Number of units produced} - \text{Spoilage}}$$

The Word Problem Audrey's Bake Shop baked 20 dozen bagels. Audrey expects 10% of the bagels to become stale and not salable. The bagels cost Audrey $1.20 per dozen. Audrey wants a 60% markup on cost. What should Audrey charge for each dozen bagels so she will make her profit? Round to the nearest cent.

The facts	Solving for?	Steps to take	Key points
Bagels cost: $1.20 per dozen. *Not salable:* 10%. *Baked:* 20 dozen. *Markup on cost:* 60%.	Price of a dozen bagels.	Total cost. Total dollar markup. Total selling price. Bagel loss. $TS = TC + TM$.	Markup is based on cost.

$ MONEY TIPS

Buying in bulk can be a great cost savings, but make certain to compare the unit bulk price to the nonbulk price to make certain it is cheaper. In addition, determine the shelf life of what you are buying. Can you use it before it spoils?

Steps to solving problem

1. Calculate the total cost. $TC = 20 \text{ dozen} \times \$1.20 = \$24.00$
2. Calculate the total dollar markup. $TS = TC + TM$

$TS = \$24.00 + .60(\$24.00)$

$TS = \$24.00 + \$14.40$ ← Total dollar markup

3. Calculate the total selling price. $TS = \$38.40$ ← Total selling price
4. Calculate the bagel loss. $20 \text{ dozen} \times .10 = 2 \text{ dozen}$
5. Calculate the selling price for a dozen bagels. $\frac{\$38.10}{18} = \$2.13$ per dozen ($20 - 2 = 18$)

It's time to try the Practice Quiz.

LU 8–3 PRACTICE QUIZ

Complete this **Practice Quiz** to see how you are doing.

1. Sunshine Music Shop bought a stereo for $600 and marked it up 40% on selling price. To promote customer interest, Sunshine marked the stereo down 10% for one week. Since business was slow, Sunshine marked the stereo down an additional 5%. After a week, Sunshine marked the stereo up 2%. What is the new selling price of the stereo to the nearest cent? What is the markdown percent based on the original selling price to the nearest hundredth percent?
2. Alvin Rose owns a fruit and vegetable stand. He knows that he cannot sell all his produce at full price. Some of his produce will be markdowns, and he will throw out some produce. Alvin must put a high enough price on the produce to cover markdowns and rotted produce and still make his desired profit. Alvin bought 300 pounds of tomatoes at 14 cents per pound. He expects a 5% spoilage and marks up tomatoes 60% on cost. What price per pound should Alvin charge for the tomatoes?

Solutions with Step-by-Step Help on DVD

✓ Solutions

1.
$$S = C + M$$
$$S = \$600 + .40S$$
$$-.40S \qquad -.40S$$
$$\frac{.60S}{.60} = \frac{\$600}{.60}$$
$$S = \$1,000$$

Check

$$S = \frac{\text{Cost}}{1 - \text{Percent markup on selling price}}$$
$$S = \frac{\$600}{1 - .40} = \frac{\$600}{.60} = \$1,000$$

First markdown: $.90 \times \$1,000 = \$900$ selling price

Second markdown: $.95 \times \$900 = \$855$ selling price

Markup: $1.02 \times \$855 = \$872.10$ final selling price

$$\$1,000 - \$872.10 = \frac{\$127.90}{\$1,000} = 12.79\%$$

2. Price of tomatoes per pound.

The facts	Solving for?	Steps to take	Key points
300 lb. tomatoes at \$.14 per pound. *Spoilage:* 5%. *Markup on cost:* 60%.	Price of tomatoes per pound.	Total cost. Total dollar markup. Total selling price. Spoilage amount. $TS = TC + TM$.	Markup is based on cost.

Steps to solving problem

1. Calculate the total cost. $TC = 300 \text{ lb.} \times \$.14 = \$42.00$

2. Calculate the total dollar markup.

$TS = TC + TM$

$TS = \$42.00 + .60(\$42.00)$

$TS = \$42.00 + \$25.20$ ← Total dollar markup

3. Calculate the total selling price. $TS = \$67.20$ ← Total selling price

4. Calculate the tomato loss. 300 pounds × .05 = 15 pounds spoilage

5. Calculate the selling price per pound of tomatoes. $\frac{\$67.20}{285} = \$.24$ per pound (rounded to nearest hundredth)

(300 − 15)

LU 8–3a EXTRA PRACTICE QUIZ WITH WORKED-OUT SOLUTIONS

Need more practice? Try this **Extra Practice Quiz** (check figures in Chapter Organizer, p. 221). Worked-out Solutions can be found in Appendix B at end of text.

1. Sunshine Music Shop bought a stereo for \$800 and marked it up 30% on selling price. To promote customer interest, Sunshine marked the stereo down 10% for one week. Since business was slow, Sunshine marked the stereo down an additional 5%. After a week, Sunshine marked the stereo up 2%. What is the new selling price of the stereo to the nearest cent? What is the markdown percent based on the original selling price to the nearest hundredth percent?

2. Alvin Rose owns a fruit and vegetable stand. He knows that he cannot sell all his produce at full price. Some of his produce will be markdowns, and he will throw out some produce. Alvin must put a high enough price on the produce to cover markdowns and rotted produce and still make his desired profit. Alvin bought 500 pounds of tomatoes at 16 cents per pound. He expects a 10% spoilage and marks up tomatoes 55% on cost. What price per pound should Alvin charge for the tomatoes?

Learning Unit 8–4: Breakeven Analysis

So far in this chapter, cost is the price retailers pay to a manufacturer or supplier to bring the goods into the store. In this unit, we view costs from the perspective of manufacturers or suppliers who produce goods to sell in units, such as pens, calculators, lamps, and so on. These manufacturers or suppliers deal with two costs—fixed costs (*FC*) and variable costs (*FC*).

To understand how the owners of manufacturers or suppliers that produce goods per unit operate their businesses, we must understand fixed costs (*FC*), variable costs (*VC*), contribution margin (*CM*), and breakeven point (*BE*). Carefully study the following definitions of these terms:

- **Fixed costs (*FC*).** Costs that *do not change* with increases or decreases in sales; they include payments for insurance, a business license, rent, a lease, utilities, labor, and so on.
- **Variable costs (*VC*).** Costs that *do change* in response to changes in the volume of sales; they include payments for material, some labor, and so on.
- **Selling price (*S*).** In this unit we focus on manufacturers and suppliers who produce goods to sell in units.

- **Contribution margin (*CM*).** The difference between selling price (*S*) and variable costs (*VC*). This difference goes *first* to pay off total fixed costs (*FC*); when they are covered, *profits* (*or losses*) start to accumulate.
- **Breakeven point (*BE*).** The point at which the seller has covered all expenses and costs of a unit and has not made any profit or suffered any loss. Every unit sold after the breakeven point (*BE*) will bring some profit or cause a loss.

Learning Unit 8–4 is divided into two sections: calculating a contribution margin (*CM*) and calculating a breakeven point (*BE*). You will learn the importance of these two concepts and the formulas that you can use to calculate them. Study the example given for each concept to help you understand why the success of business owners depends on knowing how to use these two concepts.

LO 1

Calculating a Contribution Margin (*CM*)

Before we calculate the breakeven point, we must first calculate the contribution margin. The formula is as follows:

$$\text{Contribution margin } (CM) = \text{Selling price } (S) - \text{Variable cost } (VC)$$

EXAMPLE Assume Jones Company produces pens that have a selling price (*S*) of \$2.00 and a variable cost (*VC*) of \$.80. We calculate the contribution margin (*CM*) as follows:

$$\text{Contribution margin } (CM) = \$2.00\ (S) - \$.80\ (VC)$$
$$CM = \$1.20$$

This means that for each pen sold, \$1.20 goes to cover fixed costs (*FC*) and results in a profit. It makes sense to cover fixed costs (*FC*) first because the nature of a *FC* is that it does not change with increases or decreases in sales.

Now we are ready to see how Jones Company will reach a breakeven point (*BE*).

LO 2

MONEY TIPS

Being financially healthy helps reduce stress, which benefits your personal health. While working on the health of your finances, don't forget to work on your personal health as well. Exercise, eat right, maintain an appropriate weight, reduce the intake of drugs and alcohol, and stop complaining and gossiping. There is no better way to break even!

Calculating a Breakeven Point (*BE*)

Sellers like Jones Company can calculate their profit or loss by using a concept called the **breakeven point (*BE*).** This important point results after sellers have paid all their expenses and costs. Study the following formula and the example:

$$\text{Breakeven point } (BE) = \frac{\text{Fixed costs } (FC)}{\text{Contribution margin } (CM)}$$

EXAMPLE Jones Company produces pens. The company has a fixed cost (*FC*) of \$60,000. Each pen sells for \$2.00 with a variable cost (*VC*) of \$.80 per pen.

Fixed cost (*FC*)	\$60,000
Selling price (*S*) per pen	\$2.00
Variable cost (*VC*) per pen	\$.80

$$\text{Breakeven point } (BE) = \frac{\$60{,}000\ (FC)}{\$2.00\ (S) - \$.80\ (VC)} = \frac{\$60{,}000\ (FC)}{\$1.20\ (CM)} = 50{,}000 \text{ units (pens)}$$

At 50,000 units (pens), Jones Company is just covering its costs. Each unit after 50,000 brings in a profit of \$1.20 (*CM*).

It is time to try the Practice Quiz.

LU 8–4 PRACTICE QUIZ

Complete this **Practice Quiz** to see how you are doing.

Blue Company produces holiday gift boxes. Given the following, calculate (1) the contribution margin (*CM*) and (2) the breakeven point (*BE*) for Blue Company.

Fixed cost (*FC*)	\$45,000
Selling price (*S*) per gift box	\$20
Variable cost (*VC*) per gift box	\$8

Solutions with Step-by-Step Help on DVD

✓ Solutions

1. Contribution margin (*CM*) = \$20 (*S*) − \$8 (*VC*) = **\$12**
2. Breakeven point (*BE*) = $\frac{\$45{,}000\ (FC)}{\$20\ (S) - \$8\ (VC)} = \frac{\$45{,}000\ (FC)}{\$12\ (CM)}$ = **3,750 units (gift boxes)**

LU 8–4a EXTRA PRACTICE QUIZ WITH WORKED-OUT SOLUTIONS

Need more practice? Try this **Extra Practice Quiz** (check figures in Chapter Organizer, p. 221). Worked-out Solutions can be found in Appendix B at end of text.

Angel Company produces car radios. Given the following, calculate (1) the contribution margin (*CM*) and (2) the breakeven point (*BE*) for Angel Company.

Fixed cost (*FC*)	\$96,000
Selling price (*S*) per radio	\$240
Variable cost (*VC*) per radio	\$80

CHAPTER ORGANIZER AND REFERENCE GUIDE

Topic	Key point, procedure, formula	Example(s) to illustrate situation
Markups based on cost: Cost is 100% (base), p. 204	Selling price (*S*) = Cost (*C*) + Markup (*M*)	**\$400** = \$300 + \$100 *S* = *C* + *M*
Percent markup on cost, p. 205	$\frac{\text{Dollar markup (portion)}}{\text{Cost (base)}} = \text{Percent markup on cost (rate)}$	$\frac{\$100}{\$300} = \frac{1}{3} = 33\frac{1}{3}\%$
Cost, p. 206	$C = \frac{\text{Dollar markup}}{\text{Percent markup on cost}}$	$\frac{\$100}{.33}$ = \$303 Off slightly due to rounding
Calculating selling price, p. 206	*S* = *C* + *M* **Check** *S* = Cost × (1 + Percent markup on cost)	Cost, \$6; percent markup on cost, 20% *S* = \$6 + .20(\$6) *S* = \$6 + \$1.20 *S* = **\$7.20** **Check** → \$6 × 1.20 = \$7.20
Calculating cost, p. 207	*S* = *C* + *M* **Check** $\text{Cost} = \frac{\text{Selling price}}{1 + \text{Percent markup on cost}}$	*S* = \$100; *M* = 70% of cost *S* = *C* + *M* \$100 = *C* + .70*C* \$100 = 1.7*C* $\frac{\$100}{1.7} = C$ **\$58.82** = *C* (Remember, *C* = 1.00*C*) **Check** → $\frac{\$100}{1 + .70}$ = \$58.82
Markups based on selling price: selling price is 100% (Base), p. 209	Dollar markup = Selling price − Cost	*M* = *S* − *C* **\$600** = \$1,000 − \$400
Percent markup on selling price, p. 210	$\frac{\text{Dollar markup (portion)}}{\text{Selling price (base)}} = \text{Percent markup selling price (rate)}$	$\frac{\$600}{\$1{,}000}$ = **60%**
Selling price, p. 210	$S = \frac{\text{Dollar markup}}{\text{Percent markup on selling price}}$	$\frac{\$600}{.60}$ = **\$1,000**
Calculating selling price, p. 211	*S* = *C* + *M* **Check** $\text{Selling price} = \frac{\text{Cost}}{1 - \text{Percent markup on selling price}}$	Cost, \$400; percent markup on *S*, 60% *S* = *C* + *M* *S* = \$400 + .60*S* *S* − .60*S* = \$400 + .60*S* − .60*S* $\frac{.40S}{.40} = \frac{\$400}{.40}$ **S = \$1,000** **Check** → $\frac{\$400}{1 - .60} = \frac{\$400}{.40}$ = \$1,000

(continues)

CHAPTER ORGANIZER AND REFERENCE GUIDE

Topic	Key point, procedure, formula	Example(s) to illustrate situation
Calculating cost, p. 211	$S = C + M$ **Check** $\text{Cost} = \text{Selling price} \times \left(1 - \text{Percent markup on selling price}\right)$	$\$1{,}000 = C + 60\%(\$1{,}000)$ $\$1{,}000 = C + \$600$ $\$400 = C$ **Check** ⟶ $\$1{,}000 \times (1 - .60)$ $\$1{,}000 \times .40 = \$400$
Conversion of markup percent, p. 213	Percent markup on cost to Percent markup on selling price $\frac{\text{Percent markup on cost}}{1 + \text{Percent markup on cost}}$ Percent markup on selling price to Percent markup on cost $\frac{\text{Percent markup on selling price}}{1 - \text{Percent markup on selling price}}$	*Round to nearest percent:* 54% markup on cost ⟶ 35% markup on selling price $\frac{.54}{1 + .54} = \frac{.54}{1.54} = 35\%$ 35% markup on selling price ⟶ 54% markup on cost $\frac{.35}{1 - .35} = \frac{.35}{.65} = 54\%$
Markdowns, p. 216	$\text{Markdown percent} = \frac{\text{Dollar markdown}}{\text{Selling price (original)}}$	\$40 selling price 10% markdown $\$40 \times .10 = \$4$ markdown $\frac{\$4}{\$40} = 10\%$
Pricing perishables, p. 217	**1.** Calculate total cost and total selling price. **2.** Calculate selling price per unit by dividing total sales in Step 1 by units expected to be sold after taking perishables into account.	50 pastries cost 20 cents each; 10 will spoil before being sold. Markup is 60% on cost. **1.** $TC = 50 \times \$.20 = \$10$ $TS = TC + TM$ $TS = \$10 + .60(\$10)$ $TS = \$10 + \$6$ $TS = \$16$ **2.** $\frac{\$16}{40 \text{ pastries}} = \$.40$ per pastry
Breakeven point (*BE*), p. 219	$BE = \frac{\text{Fixed cost } (FC)}{\text{Contribution margin } (CM)}$ (Selling price, S − Variable cost, (VC))	Fixed cost (FC) \$60,000 Selling price (S) \$90 Variable cost (VC) \$30 $BE = \frac{\$60{,}000}{\$90 - \$30} = \frac{\$60{,}000}{\$60} = 1{,}000$ units

KEY TERMS

Breakeven point, *p. 219*
Contribution margin, *p. 219*
Cost, *p. 203*
Dollar markdown, *p. 216*
Dollar markup, *p. 204*
Fixed cost, *p. 218*
Gross profit, *p. 203*
Margin, *p. 203*
Markdowns, *p. 216*
Markup, *p. 203*
Net profit (net income), *p. 204*
Operating expenses (overhead), *p. 204*
Percent markup on cost, *p. 205*
Percent markup on selling price, *p. 209*
Perishables, *p. 216*
Selling price, *p. 203, 218*
Variable cost, *p. 218*

CHECK FIGURES FOR EXTRA PRACTICE QUIZZES WITH PAGE REFERENCES. (WORKED-OUT SOLUTIONS IN APPENDIX B)	LU 8–1a (p. 209)	LU 8–2a (p. 215)	LU 8–3a (p. 218)	LU 8–4a (p. 220)
	1. \$400; 50% **2.** \$5.32; \$19.32 **3.** \$11.27; \$4.73	**1.** \$400; 33.3% **2.** \$22.58; \$8.58 **3.** \$6.72; \$9.28 **4.** 71.4%; 41.7%	**1.** \$996.69; 12.79% **2.** .28	**1.** \$160; 600

Critical Thinking Discussion Questions

1. Assuming markups are based on cost, explain how the portion formula could be used to calculate cost, selling price, dollar markup, and percent markup on cost. Pick a company and explain why it would mark goods up on cost rather than on selling price.
2. Assuming markups are based on selling price, explain how the portion formula could be used to calculate cost, selling price, dollar markup, and percent markup on selling price. Pick a company and explain why it would mark up goods on selling price rather than on cost.
3. What is the formula to convert percent markup on selling price to percent markup on cost? How could you explain that a 40% markup on selling price, which is a 66.7% markup on cost, would result in the same dollar markup?
4. Explain how to calculate markdowns. Do you think stores should run one-day-only markdown sales? Would it be better to offer the best price "all the time"?
5. Explain the five steps in calculating a selling price for perishable items. Recall a situation where you saw a store that did *not* follow the five steps. How did it sell its items?
6. Explain how Walmart uses breakeven analysis. Give an example.

END-OF-CHAPTER PROBLEMS

Check figures for odd-numbered problems in Appendix C

Name ______________________ Date ________

DRILL PROBLEMS

Assume markups in Problems 8–1 to 8–6 are based on cost. Find the dollar markup and selling price for the following problems. Round answers to the nearest cent.

	Item	Cost	Markup percent	Dollar markup	Selling price
8–1.	HP Paulson Laptop	$700	30%		
8–2.	Hamilton khaki multi-touch watch	$400	40%		

Solve for cost (round to the nearest cent):

8–3. Selling price of office furniture at Staples, $6,000

Percent markup on cost, 40%

Actual cost?

8–4. Selling price of lumber at Home Depot, $4,000

Percent markup on cost, 30%

Actual cost?

Complete the following:

	Cost	Selling price	Dollar markup	Percent markup on cost*
8–5.	$15.10	$22.00	?	?
8–6.	?	?	$4.70	102.17%

*Round to the nearest hundredth percent.

Assume markups in Problems 8–7 to 8–12 are based on selling price. Find the dollar markup and cost (round answers to the nearest cent):

	Item	Selling price	Markup percent	Dollar markup	Cost
8–7.	Sony LCD TV	$1,000	45%		
8–8.	IBM scanner	$80	30%		

Solve for the selling price (round to the nearest cent):

8–9. Selling price of a complete set of pots and pans at Walmart?
40% markup on selling price
Cost, actual, $66.50

8–10. Selling price of a dining room set at Macy's?
55% markup on selling price
Cost, actual, $800

Complete the following:

	Cost	Selling price	Dollar markup	Percent markup on selling price (round to nearest tenth percent)
8–11.	$14.80	$49.00	?	?
8–12.	?	?	$4	20%

By conversion of the markup formula, solve the following (round to the nearest whole percent as needed):

	Percent markup on cost	Percent markup on selling price
8–13.	12.4%	?
8–14.	?	13%

Complete the following:

8–15. Calculate the final selling price to the nearest cent and markdown percent to the nearest hundredth percent:

Original selling price	First markdown	Second markdown	Markup	Final markdown
$5,000	20%	10%	12%	5%

	Item	Total quantity bought	Unit cost	Total cost	Percent markup on cost	Total selling price	Percent that will spoil	Selling price per brownie
8–16.	Brownies	20	$.79	?	60%	?	10%	?

Complete the following:

	Breakeven point	Fixed cost	Contribution margin	Selling price per unit	Variable cost per unit
8–17.		$65,000		$5.00	$1.00
8–18.		$90,000		$9.00	$4.00

WORD PROBLEMS

8–19. Sam Slater bought an old Walter Lantz Woody Woodpecker oil painting for $12,000. He plans to resell it on eBay for $15,000. What are the dollar markup and percent markup on cost? Check the cost figure.

8–20. Chin Yov, store manager for Best Buy, does not know how to price a GE freezer that cost the store $600. Chin knows his boss wants a 45% markup on cost. Help Chin price the freezer.

8–21. Cecil Green sells golf hats. He knows that most people will not pay more than $20 for a golf hat. Cecil needs a 40% markup on cost. What should Cecil pay for his golf hats? Round to the nearest cent.

8–22. Macy's was selling Calvin Klein jean shirts that were originally priced at $58.00 for $8.70. **(a)** What was the amount of the markdown? **(b)** Based on the selling price, what is the percent markdown?

8–23. Brownsville, Texas, boasts being the southernmost international seaport and the largest city in the lower Rio Grande Valley. Ben Supple, an importer in Brownsville, has just received a shipment of Peruvian opals that he is pricing for sale. He paid $150 for the shipment. If he wants a 75% markup, calculate the selling price based on selling price. Then calculate the selling price based on cost.

8–24. "Approximately 57% of Americans drink coffee every day, between three and four cups on average. In fact, coffee is the second most valuable commodity in the world, after petroleum, and the largest food import in the United States," says Erin Joyce from Financial Edge Investopedia. Seattle, Washington, was the birthplace of the coffee shop era providing a cup of "joe" along with a relaxing atmosphere ripe for the gathering of friends. This atmosphere is not without cost. The latest calculations for brewing a cup of drip coffee showed cost per cup to be $.42. Purchasing a cup of drip coffee from a coffee shop costs $1.50. What is the percent markup based on cost to the nearest hundredth percent for purchasing a cup of brewed coffee?

8–25. Misu Sheet, owner of the Bedspread Shop, knows his customers will pay no more than $120 for a comforter. Misu wants a 30% markup on selling price. What is the most that Misu can pay for a comforter?

8–26. Assume Misu Sheet (Problem 8–25) wants a 30% markup on cost instead of on selling price. What is Misu's cost? Round to the nearest cent.

8–27. Misu Sheet (Problem 8–25) wants to advertise the comforter as "percent markup on cost." What is the equivalent rate of percent markup on cost compared to the 30% markup on selling price? Check your answer. Is this a wise marketing decision? Round to the nearest hundredth percent.

8–28. DeWitt Company sells a kitchen set for $475. To promote July 4, DeWitt ran the following advertisement:

> Beginning each hour up to 4 hours we will mark down the kitchen set 10%. At the end of each hour, we will mark up the set 1%.

Assume Ingrid Swenson buys the set 1 hour 50 minutes into the sale. What will Ingrid pay? Round each calculation to the nearest cent. What is the markdown percent? Round to the nearest hundredth percent.

8–29. Angie's Bake Shop makes birthday chocolate chip cookies that cost $2 each. Angie expects that 10% of the cookies will crack and be discarded. Angie wants a 60% markup on cost and produces 100 cookies. What should Angie price each cookie? Round to the nearest cent.

8–30. Assume that Angie (Problem 8–29) can sell the cracked cookies for $1.10 each. What should Angie price each cookie?

8–31. Jane Corporation produces model toy cars. Each sells for $29.99. Its variable cost per unit is $14.25. What is the breakeven point for Jane Corporation assuming it has a fixed cost of $314,800?

ADDITIONAL SET OF WORD PROBLEMS

8–32. PFS Fitness bought a treadmill for $700. PFS has a 70% markup on selling price. What is the selling price of the treadmill (to the nearest dollar)?

8–33. Sachi Wong, store manager for Hawk Appliance, does not know how to price a GE dishwasher that cost the store $399. Sachi knows her boss wants a 40% markup on cost. Can you help Sachi price the dishwasher?

8–34. Working off an 18% margin, with markups based on cost, the Food Co-op Club boasts that they have 5,000 members and a 200% increase in sales. The markup is 36% based on cost. What would be their percent markup if selling price were the base? Round to the nearest hundredth percent.

8–35. At a local Bed and Bath Superstore, the manager, Jill Roe, knows her customers will pay no more than $300 for a bedspread. Jill wants a 35% markup on selling price. What is the most that Jill can pay for a bedspread?

8–36. Jim Abbott purchased a $60,000 RV with a 40 percent markup on selling price. **(a)** What was the amount of the dealer's markup? **(b)** What was the dealer's original cost?

8–37. Best Buy sells a handheld personal planner for $199.99. Best Buy marked up the personal planner 35% on the selling price. What is the cost of the handheld personal planner?

8–38. Arley's Bakery makes fat-free cookies that cost $1.50 each. Arley expects 15% of the cookies to fall apart and be discarded. Arley wants a 45% markup on cost and produces 200 cookies. What should Arley price each cookie? Round to the nearest cent.

8–39. Assume that Arley (Problem 8–38) can sell the broken cookies for $1.40 each. What should Arley price each cookie?

8–40. An Apple Computer Center sells computers for $1,258.60. Assuming the computers cost $10,788 per dozen, find for each computer the **(a)** dollar markup, **(b)** percent markup on cost, and **(c)** percent markup on selling price (nearest hundredth percent).

Prove **(b)** and **(c)** of the above problem using the equivalent formulas.

8–41. Pete Corporation produces bags of peanuts. Its fixed cost is $17,280. Each bag sells for $2.99 with a unit cost of $1.55. What is Pete's breakeven point?

CHALLENGE PROBLEMS

8–42. Sonja Tanner is going to Nepal on a buying trip. She wants to purchase purses, scarves, and hats to import into the United States. Her customers do not want to pay more than $35 for a purse, $25 for a scarf, and $50 for a hat. Because Sonja would like to keep a markup based on cost of 150%, what is the most she can pay for **(a)** a purse, **(b)** a scarf, and **(c)** a hat?

8–43. On July 8, 2009, Leon's Kitchen Hut bought a set of pots with a $120 list price from Lambert Manufacturing. Leon's receives a 25% trade discount. Terms of the sale were 2/10, n/30. On July 14, Leon's sent a check to Lambert for the pots. Leon's expenses are 20% of the selling price. Leon's must also make a profit of 15% of the selling price. A competitor marked down the same set of pots 30%. Assume Leon's reduces its selling price by 30%.

a. What is the sale price at Kitchen Hut?

b. What was the operating profit or loss?

DVD SUMMARY PRACTICE TEST

1. Sunset Co. marks up merchandise 40% on cost. A DVD player costs Sunset $90. What is Sunset's selling price? Round to the nearest cent. *(p. 206)*

2. JCPenney sells jeans for $49.50 that cost $38.00. What is the percent markup on cost? Round to the nearest hundredth percent. Check the cost. *(p. 208)*

3. Best Buy sells a flat-screen high-definition TV for $700. Best Buy marks up the TV 45% on cost. What is the cost and dollar markup of the TV? *(p. 206)*

4. Sports Authority marks up New Balance sneakers $30 and sells them for $109. Markup is on cost. What are the cost and percent markup to the nearest hundredth percent? *(p. 205)*

5. The Shoe Outlet bought boots for $60 and marks up the boots 55% on the selling price. What is the selling price of the boots? Round to the nearest cent. *(p. 211)*

6. Office Max sells a desk for $450 and marks up the desk 35% on the selling price. What did the desk cost Office Max? Round to the nearest cent. *(p. 211)*

7. Zales sells diamonds for $1,100 that cost $800. What is Zales's percent markup on selling price? Round to the nearest hundredth percent. Check the selling price. *(p. 211)*

8. Earl Miller, a customer of J. Crew, will pay $400 for a new jacket. J. Crew has a 60% markup on selling price. What is the most that J. Crew can pay for this jacket? *(p. 211)*

9. Home Liquidators mark up its merchandise 35% on cost. What is the company's equivalent markup on selling price? Round to the nearest tenth percent. *(p. 213)*

10. The Muffin Shop makes no-fat blueberry muffins that cost $.70 each. The Muffin Shop knows that 15% of the muffins will spoil. If The Muffin Shop wants 40% markup on cost and produces 800 muffins, what should The Muffin Shop price each muffin? Round to the nearest cent. *(p. 217)*

11. Angel Corporation produces calculators selling for $25.99. Its unit cost is $18.95. Assuming a fixed cost of $80,960, what is the breakeven point in units? *(p. 218)*

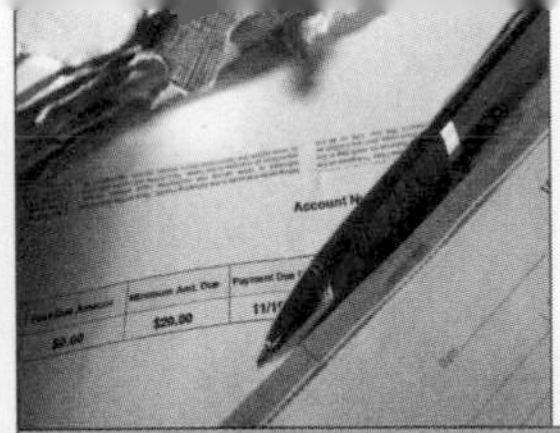

Personal Finance

A KIPLINGER APPROACH

Wear it once and request a REFUND?

MONEY & ETHICS
by Knight Kiplinger

I have a friend who habitually buys expensive clothes, wears them once to a fancy party, then reattaches all the tags and returns them to the store, as if unused, for a refund. What do you think about this?

As I see it, anyone who "buys" products with the intention of using them and then returning them is stealing that one-time use from the store. Sadly, I hear from friends in retail that this practice is quite common—and not confined to apparel. It has led many stores to accept returns only for store credit, not a refund. So who gets hurt in the end? All the other customers.

My sisters and I are shareholders in a closely held firm founded by our late father and now run by our brother. We suspect that he is charging some personal living expenses (such as nonprofessional travel and entertainment) to the business, which diminishes its profitability and our dividends. What should we do?

If true, it is not only unethical but illegal, and it could get your business into trouble with the IRS. Ask your brother about it, raising your concerns in a courteous way that presumes nothing. If you are not satisfied, exercise your shareholder right to examine the books and commission a professional audit.

Have a money-and-ethics question you'd like answered in this column? Write editor in chief Knight Kiplinger at ethics@kiplinger.com.

WHAT'S THE DEAL? | These loans help homeowners turn their equity into cash.

More seniors tap their homes for INCOME

MORE OLDER Americans wanting to take advantage of the rise in home prices over the past decade without having to move are considering a reverse mortgage to tap their equity. About 150,000 homeowners will apply for one this year—twice last year's number, reports the National Reverse Mortgage Lenders Association.

With a reverse mortgage, you receive tax-free cash instead of making payments. Your debt increases rather than decreases, but you do not have to repay it until you move. If you die, your estate settles up. Payout options include a line of credit or fixed monthly payments for life or a specific period. You must be 62 to qualify.

The most common type is the federally insured home-equity conversion mortgage, which is subject to the Federal Housing Administration's loan limits ($362,790 for high-cost urban areas, $200,160 elsewhere), but you will get only a percentage of that. The exact amount depends on your locale, your age, your equity in your home and the interest rate.

For now, high up-front fees make reverse mortgages useful mainly for people who plan to stay in their homes for more than a few years and have few other assets.

STOCK TO WATCH

Perfect DIVIDEND stream

For low-risk income and nice growth, try a pipeline. **Magellan Midstream Partners, LP**, one of the largest operators in the U.S., with 8,500 miles of conduits for gasoline and other refined fuels, has a perfect record. Since the partnership went public in 2001, Magellan (don't confuse it with the fund) has raised dividends every quarter. Today's rate of 63 cents gives you a yield of 6%-plus. The shares have risen steadily.

IN THE PIPELINE

Magellan Midstream Partners, LP
SYMBOL: MMP
PRICE: $40
DISTRIBUTIONS PER SHARE:
2006: $2.34
2007: $1.25
Data to August 20.

SITTING PRETTY: Americans who are age 62 and older hold a total of $4.3 trillion of equity in their homes.

From Kiplinger's, October 2007, p. 20.

BUSINESS MATH ISSUE

Retail stores should always charge customers a fee for returned goods

1. List the key points of the article and information to support your position.
2. Write a group defense of your position using math calculations to support your view.

Slater's Business Math Scrapbook

Applying Your Skills

PROJECT A

Based on the economic downturn of 2009 and 2010, have Macy's strategies worked?

Check it out on the Web and report back.

Macy's to Bring FAO Schwarz Into Its Stores

By Vanessa O'Connell

IN AN EFFORT to attract more shoppers, **Macy's** Inc. is expected to announce Friday plans to open FAO Schwarz toy boutiques in all 685 Macy's stores that carry children's clothing.

As many as 275 of Macy's 812 locations, including those in downtown Minneapolis, Union Square in San Francisco and Dadeland Mall in Miami, will get the toy boutiques by fall, in time for the holiday shopping season. The rest will open in 2009 and 2010.

Under the deal, FAO Schwarz will lease the floor space and pay Macy's an undisclosed percentage of sales as rent.

The venture is part of a broader trend in which big retailers are teaming up with specialty merchants to create stores within stores. With foot traffic down at many malls, department stores and other big chains are scrambling to give shoppers more reasons to step inside. For their smaller partners, such deals provide a chance to reach new customers with less financial risk than opening independent outlets.

J.C. Penney Co. is trying to attract younger shoppers with upscale Sephora cosmetic and fragrance shops in its stores. Over the past two years, it has installed them in 72 J.C. Penney locations and is working with Sephora—a unit of Paris-based **LVMH Moët Hennessy Louis Vuitton** SA—to roll them out in more than 300 of its 1,074 stores by 2010. Penney staffs the in-store shops and owns the Sephora merchandise.

Lord & Taylor, a unit of **NRDC Equity Partners**, plans to open Fortunoff jewelry-and-watch boutiques in all 47 of its stores in February. NRDC, a big retail developer, acquired the 21-store Fortunoff chain in March.

Along with its potential advantages, however, the strategy poses the risk of tarnishing the specialty retailer's more-exclusive brand. Penney says that is why it doesn't cut prices in its Sephora shops, even when it offers discounts elsewhere in its stores.

At FAO Schwarz, "We spent a lot of time thinking about the risk" before concluding that the Macy's rollout would broaden the store's image and help counter the perception that all of its toys are expensive, said Chief Executive Edward Schmults. "At a time of economic weakness, to be able to roll out this many stores at one time is just tremendous," he added. "Macy's is where Mom is shopping."

Macy's Inc.

Macy's opened an **FAO Schwarz boutique** in Chicago as a test in November.

Macy's Chief Executive Terry J. Lundgren said the deal "will drive store traffic, particularly to our children's departments," which traditionally have had lower sales per square foot than other departments.

In a test over the past seven months, a 5,300-square-foot FAO Schwarz boutique at Macy's cavernous State Street store in Chicago produced a "ripple effect" of higher sales in children's apparel and accessories, he said.

For FAO Schwarz, the arrangement is a way to raise its profile. At its peak in the late 1990s, the fabled toy retailer had 40 stores. But after running into financial trouble, it closed 18 stores in 2002 and sold the rest to Right Start Co., which filed for bankruptcy protection in 2003 and closed the remaining FAO Schwarz stores.

In 2004, hedge fund **D.E. Shaw** & Co. bought and reopened FAO Schwarz's flagship Fifth Avenue store in New York and a second location at Caesar's Palace in Las Vegas, as well as the retailer's catalog and Internet-sales businesses. D.E. Shaw is currently seeking to expand the 145-year-old brand.

The FAO Schwarz deal is part of a push by Cincinnati-based Macy's to differentiate its stores from the competition. It recently struck agreements with celebrities and well-known designers, including Martha Stewart, Donald Trump and Tommy Hilfiger, for exclusive merchandise.

Macy's has struggled to integrate the 400 department stores it acquired in its 2005 purchase of May Department Stores. Earlier this week, it reported a $59 million loss for the first quarter ended May 3, because of restructuring costs and a decline in sales. Sales in the period fell 2.9% to $5.75 billion.

Macy's plans to play up the FAO Schwarz connection in its fourth-quarter marketing campaign, according to Peter Sachse, its chief marketing officer. The chain hasn't had a year-round toy department in its stores for many years, according to spokesman Jim Sluzewski.

The new boutiques will include FAO Schwarz's private-label toys as well as independent brands such as Alex crafts and Lionel trains. FAO Schwarz toys will eventually be sold on the Macy's Web site, but Mr. Lundgren said there wasn't a timetable for online sales.

—Rachel Dodes contributed to this article

Internet Projects: See text Web site (www.mhhe.com/slater10e) and The Business Math Internet Resource Guide.

Video Case

DVD

Noodles & Company

Noodles & Company is a rapidly expanding restaurant in the "quick-casual" dining world. Close attention to detail through effective and efficient operations management is the core attribute that enables Noodles & Company to provide hot, fresh food in a timely manner. With time a scarce resource for many, Noodles & Company has found a way to satisfy the time-hungry niche market by providing high-quality food quickly.

Management spends much time analyzing business processes and functions to ensure customers receive a premium food experience. Noodles & Company plans the customers' experience from the moment they enter the restaurant to the moment they leave. Operations goals require each customer to have his or her meal within five minutes of placing an order.

Once the order is taken through the guest interaction point of purchase (30 seconds), the order is sent to the kitchen technologically. Through the division of tasks, every function of the kitchen is made as efficient as possible. The line is set up with previously portioned meats and vegetables that flow in the same flow process each dish requires. Stations have a "job aid" providing the appropriate weight and ingredients for each dish. The preheated pan is critical to throughput and operational efficiency. With the help of 30,000 BTU burners, each dish gets through the sauté line in 3.5 minutes. An additional 30 seconds is used at the garnish station and the meal is served to the customer within 5 minutes.

Just-in-time inventory maintains that only what is needed is prepared. First-in first-out (FIFO) inventory method ensures the freshest ingredients. Food preparation is conducted throughout the day to ensure freshness. Focusing on every element from entry to exit allows Noodles & Company to deliver on the company's promise of quick, fresh, customized food served in a no-tip welcoming setting.

PROBLEM 1

The video discusses the extensive planning required to meet the operational goals for serving high-quality foods quickly. The goal of 5 minutes from order-taking to serving each meal is critical to maintaining Noodles & Company's promise to the customer of high-quality food served quickly. If a meal needs to be remade due to a processing error, what percent increase is this additional 3.5 minutes?

PROBLEM 2

In a June 17, 2009, press release, Noodles & Company says it was named one of the top three restaurants in America by a national magazine for the second time in six months. *Parents* magazine placed Noodles & Company third on its top 10 list of Best Fast-Casual Family Restaurants. In 2004, Noodles & Company decided to offer franchises for a $35,000 up-front fee and 5% of their annual revenue. Units average more than $1 million in annual sales. As a franchisee, how much revenue must be submitted to Noodles & Company with annual sales of $989,675?

PROBLEM 3

A May 20, 2009, Noodles & Company press release mentions there are more than 205 locations in 18 states. If they expect to grow by 17% in 2009, what is the expected number of restaurants they plan to open? Round to the nearest whole number.

PROBLEM 4

The Noodles & Company location in Parker, Colorado, sells its Pad Thai for $4.25 for a small, $5.25 for a regular with an additional $2.00 for protein for either size. If Noodles & Company is making a 300% markup based on the cost on their food, what is the cost for a small size Pad Thai with protein? Round to the nearest cent.

PROBLEM 5

As noted in the video, Noodles & Company has a no-tip policy. This helps to streamline operations while keeping the focus of employees on their tasks at hand. In problem 4 above, what would you save on a meal of a large Pad Thai with protein if you typically tip 20%? How much would you save if you brought your family of four with each meal averaging $6.50?

PROBLEM 6

In problem 4 above, the markup based on cost was 300%. What is the corresponding markup based on selling price?

PROBLEM 7

If a regular Pad Thai with protein costs $11.50 in Annapolis, Maryland, how much more are you paying in Maryland than in Parker, CO (see problem 4)? What percent is this difference? Round to the nearest percent.

CUMULATIVE REVIEW

A Word Problem Approach—Chapters 6, 7, 8

1. Assume Kellogg's produced 715,000 boxes of Corn Flakes this year. This was 110% of the annual production last year. What was last year's annual production? *(p. 147)*

2. A new Sony camcorder has a list price of $420. The trade discount is 10/20 with terms of 2/10, n/30. If a retailer pays the invoice within the discount period, what is the amount the retailer must pay? *(p. 177)*

3. JCPenney sells loafers with a markup of $40. If the markup is 30% on cost, what did the loafers cost JCPenney? Round to the nearest dollar. *(p. 206)*

4. Aster Computers received from Ring Manufacturers an invoice dated August 28 with terms 2/10 EOM. The list price of the invoice is $3,000 (freight not included). Ring offers Aster a 9/8/2 trade chain discount. Terms of freight are FOB shipping point, but Ring prepays the $150 freight. Assume Aster pays the invoice on October 9. How much will Ring receive? *(p. 173)*

5. Runners World marks up its Nike jogging shoes 25% on selling price. The Nike shoe sells for $65. How much did the store pay for them? *(p. 211)*

6. Ivan Rone sells antique sleds. He knows that the most he can get for a sled is $350. Ivan needs a 35% markup on cost. Since Ivan is going to an antiques show, he wants to know the maximum he can offer a dealer for an antique sled. *(p. 208)*

7. Bonnie's Bakery bakes 60 loaves of bread for $1.10 each. Bonnie's estimates that 10% of the bread will spoil. Assume a 60% markup on cost. What is the selling price of each loaf? If Bonnie's can sell the old bread for one-half the cost, what is the selling price of each loaf? *(p. 218)*

chapter

9 PAYROLL

Disney Plans To Reduce Staff At Theme Parks

By Peter Sanders

Walt Disney Co. said Wednesday it will restructure its domestic theme-park operations, including an unspecified number of layoffs, amid languishing attendance and sharply reduced operating income.

The announcement came less than two weeks after a deadline to accept voluntary buyouts that the company offered to about 600 executives in its Parks and Resorts division. Disney officials declined to say how many executives took a voluntary buyout, but said the number was "satisfactory."

Wall Street Journal © 2009

Gene Duncan/AP Photo

LEARNING UNIT OBJECTIVES

LU 9–1: Calculating Various Types of Employees' Gross Pay

1. Define, compare, and contrast weekly, biweekly, semimonthly, and monthly pay periods *(p. 236)*.
2. Calculate gross pay with overtime on the basis of time *(p. 237)*.
3. Calculate gross pay for piecework, differential pay schedule, straight commission with draw, variable commission scale, and salary plus commission *(pp. 237–239)*.

LU 9–2: Computing Payroll Deductions for Employees' Pay; Employers' Responsibilities

1. Prepare and explain the parts of a payroll register *(pp. 240–243)*.
2. Explain and calculate federal and state unemployment taxes *(p. 243)*.

VOCABULARY PREVIEW

Here are key terms in this chapter. After completing the chapter, if you know the term, place a checkmark in the parenthesis. If you don't know the term, look it up and put the page number where it can be found.

Biweekly . ( ) Deductions . ( ) Differential pay schedule . ( ) Draw . ( ) Employee's Withholding Allowance Certificate (W-4) . ( ) Fair Labor Standards Act . ( ) Federal income tax withholding (FIT) . ( ) Federal Insurance Contribution Act (FICA) . ( ) Federal Unemployment Tax Act (FUTA) . ( ) Gross pay . ( ) Medicare . ( ) Monthly . ( ) Net pay . ( ) Overrides . ( ) Overtime . ( ) Payroll register . ( ) Percentage method . ( ) Semimonthly . ( ) Social Security . ( ) State income tax (SIT) . ( ) State Unemployment Tax Act (SUTA) . ( ) Straight commission . ( ) Variable commission scale . ( ) W-4 . ( ) Weekly . ( )

Wal-Mart to Pay Millions in Fees

Associated Press

Wal-Mart Stores Inc. has been ordered to pay $36.4 million in fees and expenses to attorneys representing Pennsylvania employees who won a class-action award for working off the clock.

The award, including fees and interest, now totals $187.6 million. The suit involved 187,000 current and former employees who worked at Wal-Mart and Sam's Club from March 1998 through May 2006.

A Philadelphia jury last year rejected Wal-Mart's claim that some people chose to work through breaks or that a few minutes of extra work was insignificant.

The plaintiffs initially won a $78.5 million class-action award for lost wages. Most of the group qualified for a share of an additional $62.3 million in damages under a state law invoked when a company withholds pay without cause for more than 30 days.

Wall Street Journal © 2007

Jason Janik/Bloomberg News/Landov

The *Wall Street Journal* clipping "Wal-Mart to Pay Millions in Fees" shows how the company was penalized for not paying employees who worked through breaks or who put in a few minutes of extra work off the clock.

This chapter discusses (1) the type of pay people work for, (2) how employers calculate paychecks and deductions, and (3) what employers must report and pay in taxes.

Learning Unit 9–1: Calculating Various Types of Employees' Gross Pay

LO 1

Logan Company manufactures dolls of all shapes and sizes. These dolls are sold worldwide. We study Logan Company in this unit because of the variety of methods Logan uses to pay its employees.

Companies usually pay employees **weekly, biweekly, semimonthly,** or **monthly.** How often employers pay employees can affect how employees manage their money. Some employees prefer a weekly paycheck that spreads the inflow of money. Employees who have monthly bills may find the twice-a-month or monthly paycheck more convenient. All employees would like more money to manage.

Let's assume you earn $50,000 per year. The following table shows what you would earn each pay period. Remember that 13 weeks equals one quarter. Four quarters or 52 weeks equals a year.

Salary paid	Period (based on a year)	Earnings for period (dollars)
Weekly	52 times (once a week)	$ 961.54 ($50,000 ÷ 52)
Biweekly	26 times (every two weeks)	$1,923.08 ($50,000 ÷ 26)
Semimonthly	24 times (twice a month)	$2,083.33 ($50,000 ÷ 24)
Monthly	12 times (once a month)	$4,166.67 ($50,000 ÷ 12)

Now let's look at some pay schedule situations and examples of how Logan Company calculates its payroll for employees of different pay status.

LO 2

Situation 1: Hourly Rate of Pay; Calculation of Overtime

The **Fair Labor Standards Act** sets minimum wage standards and overtime regulations for employees of companies covered by this federal law. The law provides that employees working for an hourly rate receive time-and-a-half pay for hours worked in excess of their regular 40-hour week. The current hourly minimum wage is $7.25 effective summer of 2009. Many managerial people, however, are exempt from the time-and-a-half pay for all hours in excess of a 40-hour week.

In addition to many managerial people being exempt from time-and-a-half pay for more than 40 hours, other workers may also be exempt. Note in the *Wall Street Journal* clipping "Golden Arches in China," McDonald's is raising wages in China amid tightening labor laws by China's government-backed union.

GLOBAL

BEIJING—**McDonald's** Corp. is raising wages and adopting new uniforms, stepping up efforts to burnish its image as an employer in China amid tightening labor laws and scrutiny by China's government-backed trade union.

McDonald's said it will raise wages for its restaurant crews 12% to 56% above China's minimum-wage guidelines as of Sept. 1, a move that will affect about 45,000 full-time and part-time workers, including students. Full-time workers in the large southern city of Guangzhou, for example, will see their monthly wages rise 21% to 1,072 yuan ($142).

The change will average out to a 30% pay rise for all McDonald's frontline staff, said Jeffrey Schwartz, chief executive for China for McDonald's, based in Oak Brook, Ill.

Wages at McDonald's and its fast-food rival **Yum Brands** Inc., which runs the KFC and Pizza Hut chains, have been under increased scrutiny in China after the powerful All-China Federation of Trade Unions in April accused the fast-food giants of violating labor laws by underpaying part-time workers in Guangzhou.

Local authorities later absolved the companies of wrongdoing, but McDonald's, KFC and Pizza Hut received negative publicity in local media reports that focused especially on the issue of part-time workers, who weren't covered under the city's legal minimum wage of 7.50 yuan an hour.

Mr. Schwartz said the Guangzhou incident "expedited" the company's pay-rise program, which he said had been in the planning process for a year. While the negative publicity didn't appear to affect sales, Mr. Schwartz said, "for me as an employer, I didn't want to be portrayed that way, because we're not that way."

Yum Brands, of Louisville, Ky., didn't respond yesterday to requests for comment.

While the American fast-food giants have been under particular scrutiny because of their size and high-profile brands, wage pressures in China in general have risen lately amid a sharp increase in the price of basic necessities.

Golden Arches in China

815 restaurants currently, with plans for 100 new restaurants a year

50,000 crew workers employed

1990, first restaurant opens in Shenzhen

2% of company's global revenue generated in China

Olympic sponsor

80,000 to 120,000 new uniforms will be issued this year

Runs 46 food-processing plants

Source: the company

Bloomberg News/Landov

Now we return to our Logan Company example. Logan Company is calculating the weekly pay of Ramon Valdez who works in its manufacturing division. For the first 40 hours Ramon works, Logan calculates his **gross pay** (earnings before **deductions**) as follows:

Gross pay = Hours employee worked × Rate per hour

Ramon works more than 40 hours in a week. For every hour over his 40 hours, Ramon must be paid an **overtime** pay of at least 1.5 times his regular pay rate. The following formula is used to determine Ramon's overtime:

Hourly overtime pay rate = Regular hourly pay rate × 1.5

Logan Company must include Ramon's overtime pay with his regular pay. To determine Ramon's gross pay, Logan uses the following formula:

Gross pay = Earnings for 40 hours + Earnings at time-and-a-half rate (1.5)

We are now ready to calculate Ramon's gross pay from the following data:

EXAMPLE

Employee	M	T	W	Th	F	S	Total hours	Rate per hour
Ramon Valdez	13	$8\frac{1}{2}$	10	8	$11\frac{1}{4}$	$10\frac{3}{4}$	$61\frac{1}{2}$	$9

$61\frac{1}{2}$ total hours
-40 regular hours
$21\frac{1}{2}$ hours overtime[1]   Time-and-a-half pay: $\$9 \times 1.5 = \$13.50$

$$\text{Gross pay} = (40 \text{ hours} \times \$9) + (21\tfrac{1}{2} \text{ hours} \times \$13.50)$$
$$= \$360 + \$290.25$$
$$= \$650.25$$

Note that the $13.50 overtime rate came out even. However, throughout the text, *if an overtime rate is greater than two decimal places, do not round it. Round only the final answer. This gives greater accuracy.*

LO 3

Situation 2: Straight Piece Rate Pay

Some companies, especially manufacturers, pay workers according to how much they produce. Logan Company pays Ryan Foss for the number of dolls he produces in a week. This gives Ryan an incentive to make more money by producing more dolls. Ryan receives $.96 per doll, less any defective units. The following formula determines Ryan's gross pay:

Gross pay = Number of units produced × Rate per unit

Companies may also pay a guaranteed hourly wage and use a piece rate as a bonus. However, Logan uses straight piece rate as wages for some of its employees. The *Wall Street Journal* article "Pay Scales Divide Factory" (p. 238) show the trend that has companies such as Goodyear Tire not providing all employees with the same pay packages.

[1]Some companies pay overtime for time over 8 hours in one day; Logan Company pays overtime for time over 40 hours per week

Pay Scales Divide Factory

Issue Gets Touchy As More Firms Use Two-Tier System

BY TIMOTHY AEPPEL

GADSDEN, Ala.—Few things better illustrate the diminished fortunes of the American factory worker than the emergence of "$13 workers" at **Goodyear Tire & Rubber** Co.

Jobs at the U.S.'s largest tire maker by revenue used to be coveted mainly because everyone from janitors to skilled machine operators could expect to eventually earn more than $20 an hour, with lush benefits.

That rich compensation is now slipping away. New workers hired under Goodyear's latest labor agreement earn just $13 an hour with fewer benefits for the first three years and many will likely never achieve the lofty pay packages of the past.

EXAMPLE During the last week of April, Ryan Foss produced 900 dolls. Using the above formula, Logan Company paid Ryan $864.

$$\text{Gross pay} = 900 \text{ dolls} \times \$.96$$
$$= \$864$$

Situation 3: Differential Pay Schedule

Some of Logan's employees can earn more than the $.96 straight piece rate for every doll they produce. Logan Company has set up a **differential pay schedule** for these employees. The company determines the rate these employees make by the amount of units the employees produce at different levels of production.

EXAMPLE Logan Company pays Abby Rogers on the basis of the following schedule:

	Units produced	Amount per unit
First 50 →	1–50	$ .50
Next 100 →	51–150	.62
Next 50 →	151–200	.75
	Over 200	1.25

Last week Abby produced 300 dolls. What is Abby's gross pay?

Logan calculated Abby's gross pay as follows:

$$(50 \times \$.50) + (100 \times \$.62) + (50 \times \$.75) + (100 \times \$1.25)$$
$$\$25 \quad + \quad \$62 \quad + \quad \$37.50 \quad + \quad \$125 \quad = \$249.50$$

Now we will study some of the other types of employee commission payment plans.

Situation 4: Straight Commission with Draw

Companies frequently use **straight commission** to determine the pay of salespersons. This commission is usually a certain percentage of the amount the salesperson sells. An example of one group of companies ceasing to pay commissions is the rental-car companies.

Companies such as Logan Company allow some of its salespersons to draw against their commission at the beginning of each month. A **draw** is an advance on the salesperson's commission. Logan subtracts this advance later from the employee's commission earned based on sales. When the commission does not equal the draw, the salesperson owes Logan the difference between the draw and the commission.

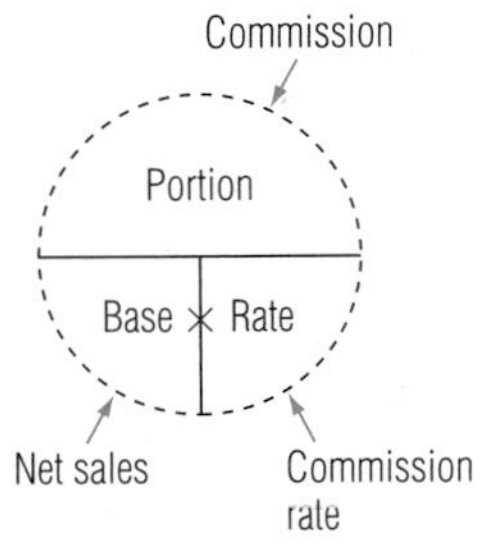

EXAMPLE Logan Company pays Jackie Okamoto a straight commission of 15% on her net sales (net sales are total sales less sales returns). In May, Jackie had net sales of $56,000. Logan gave Jackie a $600 draw in May. What is Jackie's gross pay?

Logan calculated Jackie's commission minus her draw as follows:

$$\$56{,}000 \times .15 = \$8{,}400$$
$$-\ 600$$
$$\$7{,}800$$

Logan Company pays some people in the sales department on a variable commission scale. Let's look at this, assuming the employee had no draw.

Situation 5: Variable Commission Scale

A company with a **variable commission scale** uses different commission rates for different levels of net sales.

EXAMPLE Last month, Jane Ring's net sales were $160,000. What is Jane's gross pay based on the following schedule?

Up to $35,000	4%
Excess of $35,000 to $45,000	6%
Over $45,000	8%

Gross pay = ($35,000 × .04) + ($10,000 × .06) + ($115,000 × .08)
= $1,400 + $600 + $9,200
= $11,200

Situation 6: Salary Plus Commission

Logan Company pays Joe Roy a $3,000 monthly salary plus a 4% commission for sales over $20,000. Last month Joe's net sales were $50,000. Logan calculated Joe's gross monthly pay as follows:

Gross pay = Salary + (Commission × Sales over $20,000)
= $3,000 + (.04 × $30,000)
= $3,000 + $1,200
= $4,200

$ MONEY TIPS

Check the details of your pay stub each paycheck. You may be amazed at how many mistakes you find.

Before you take the Practice Quiz, you should know that many managers today receive **overrides.** These managers receive a commission based on the net sales of the people they supervise.

LU 9–1 PRACTICE QUIZ

Complete this **Practice Quiz** to see how you are doing.

1. Jill Foster worked 52 hours in one week for Delta Airlines. Jill earns $10 per hour. What is Jill's gross pay, assuming overtime is at time-and-a-half?
2. Matt Long had $180,000 in sales for the month. Matt's commission rate is 9%, and he had a $3,500 draw. What was Matt's end-of-month commission?
3. Bob Meyers receives a $1,000 monthly salary. He also receives a variable commission on net sales based on the following schedule (commission doesn't begin until Bob earns $8,000 in net sales):

$8,000–$12,000	1%	Excess of $20,000 to $40,000	5%
Excess of $12,000 to $20,000	3%	More than $40,000	8%

Assume Bob earns $40,000 net sales for the month. What is his gross pay?

Solutions with Step-by-Step Help on DVD

✓ Solutions

1. 40 hours × $10.00 = $400.00
   12 hours × $15.00 = 180.00 ($10.00 × 1.5 = $15.00)
   $580.00
2. $180,000 × .09 = $16,200
   − 3,500
   $12,700
3. Gross pay = $1,000 + ($4,000 × .01) + ($8,000 × .03) + ($20,000 × .05)
   = $1,000 + $40 + $240 + $1,000
   = $2,280

LU 9–1a EXTRA PRACTICE QUIZ WITH WORKED-OUT SOLUTIONS

Need more practice? Try this **Extra Practice Quiz** (check figures in Chapter Organizer, p. 246). Worked-out Solutions can be found in Appendix B at end of text.

1. Jill Foster worked 54 hours in one week for Delta Airlines. Jill earns $12 per hour. What is Jill's gross pay, assuming overtime is at time-and-a-half?
2. Matt Long had $210,000 in sales for the month. Matt's commission rate is 8%, and he had a $4,000 draw. What was Matt's end-of-month commission?

3. Bob Myers receives a $1,200 monthly salary. He also receives a variable commission on net sales based on the following schedule (commission doesn't begin until Bob earns $9,000 in net sales).

$9,000 to $12,000	1%	Excess of $20,000 to $40,000	5%
Excess of $12,000 to $20,000	3%	More than $40,000	8%

Assume Bob earns $60,000 net sales for the month. What is his gross pay?

Learning Unit 9–2: Computing Payroll Deductions for Employees' Pay; Employers' Responsibilities

Did you know that Walmart is the largest employer in twenty-one states? Can you imagine the accounting involved to pay all these employees?

This unit begins by dissecting a paycheck. Then we give you an insight into the tax responsibilities of employers.

LO 1

Computing Payroll Deductions for Employees

Companies often record employee payroll information in a multicolumn form called a **payroll register.** The increased use of computers in business has made computerized registers a timesaver for many companies.

Glo Company uses a multicolumn payroll register. Below is Glo's partial payroll register showing the payroll information for Alice Rey during week 47. Let's check each column to see if Alice's take-home pay of $1,573.81 is correct. Note how the circled letters in the register correspond to the explanations that follow.

GLO COMPANY
Payroll Register
Week #47

Employee name	Allow. & marital status	Cum. earn.	Sal. per week	Earnings: Reg.	Earnings: Ovt.	Earnings: Gross	Cum. earn.	FICA Taxable Earnings: S.S.	FICA Taxable Earnings: Med.	Deductions: FICA S.S.	Deductions: FICA Med.	Deductions: FIT	Deductions: SIT	Deductions: Health ins.	Net pay
Rey, Alice	M-2	105,750	2,250	2,250	—	2,250	108,000	1,050	2,250	65.10	32.63	343.46	135	100	1,573.81
	(A)	(B)	(C)		(D)		(E)	(F)	(G)	(H)	(I)	(J)	(K)	(L)	(M)

Payroll Register Explanations
(A)—Allowance and marital status
(B), (C), (D)—Cumulative earnings before payroll, salaries, earnings
(E)—Cumulative earnings after payroll

When Alice was hired, she completed the **W-4 (Employee's Withholding Allowance Certificate)** form shown in Figure 9.1 stating that she is married and claims an allowance (exemption) of 2. Glo Company will need this information to calculate the federal income tax (J).

FIGURE 9.1

Employee's W-4 form

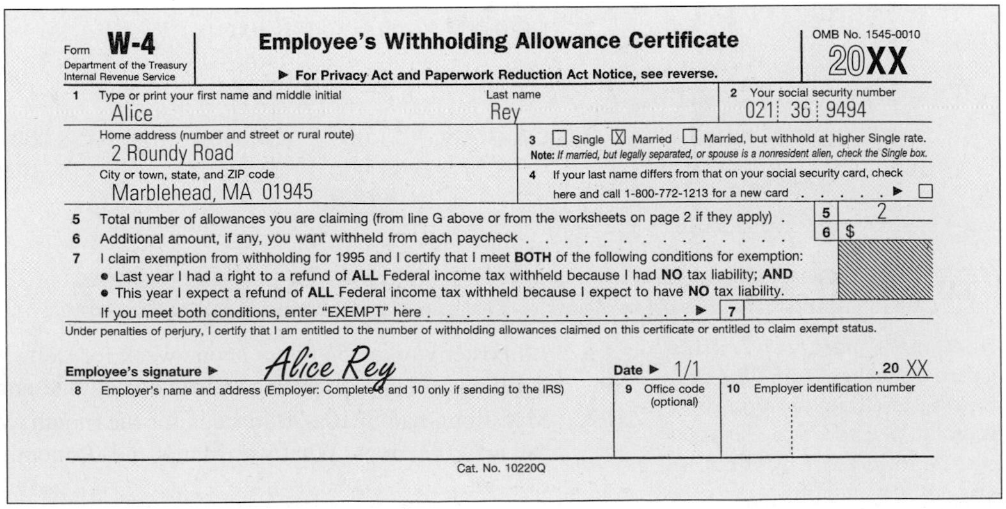
Form **W-4** Department of the Treasury Internal Revenue Service
Employee's Withholding Allowance Certificate
▶ **For Privacy Act and Paperwork Reduction Act Notice, see reverse.**
OMB No. 1545-0010 **20XX**

1 Type or print your first name and middle initial: Alice — Last name: Rey — 2 Your social security number: 021 36 9494
Home address (number and street or rural route): 2 Roundy Road — 3 ☐ Single ☒ Married ☐ Married, but withhold at higher Single rate. Note: If married, but legally separated, or spouse is a nonresident alien, check the Single box.
City or town, state, and ZIP code: Marblehead, MA 01945 — 4 If your last name differs from that on your social security card, check here and call 1-800-772-1213 for a new card ▶ ☐
5 Total number of allowances you are claiming (from line G above or from the worksheets on page 2 if they apply) . 5 — 2
6 Additional amount, if any, you want withheld from each paycheck . 6 — $
7 I claim exemption from withholding for 1995 and I certify that I meet **BOTH** of the following conditions for exemption:
• Last year I had a right to a refund of **ALL** Federal income tax withheld because I had **NO** tax liability; **AND**
• This year I expect a refund of **ALL** Federal income tax withheld because I expect to have **NO** tax liability.
If you meet both conditions, enter "EXEMPT" here ▶ 7
Under penalties of perjury, I certify that I am entitled to the number of withholding allowances claimed on this certificate or entitled to claim exempt status.
Employee's signature ▶ Alice Rey — **Date** ▶ 1/1, 20 XX
8 Employer's name and address (Employer: Complete 8 and 10 only if sending to the IRS) — 9 Office code (optional) — 10 Employer identification number
Cat. No. 10220Q

Before this pay period, Alice has earned $105,750 (47 weeks × $2,250 salary per week). Since Alice receives no overtime, her $2,250 salary per week represents her gross pay (pay before any deductions).

After this pay period, Alice has earned $108,000 ($105,750 + $2,250).

The **Federal Insurance Contribution Act (FICA)** funds the **Social Security** program. The program includes Old Age and Disability, Medicare, Survivor Benefits, and so on. The FICA tax requires separate reporting for Social Security and **Medicare.** We will use the following rates for Glo Company:

	Rate	Base
Social Security	6.20%	$106,800
Medicare	1.45	No base

These rates mean that Alice Rey will pay Social Security taxes on the first $106,800 she earns this year. After earning $106,800, Alice's wages will be exempt from Social Security. Note that Alice will be paying Medicare taxes on all wages since Medicare has no base cutoff.

Ⓕ,Ⓖ—Taxable earnings for Social Security and Medicare

To help keep Glo's record straight, the *taxable earnings column only shows what wages will be taxed. This amount is not the tax.* For example, in week 47, only $1,050 of Alice's salary will be taxable for Social Security.

$106,800 Social Security base
− 105,750 Ⓑ
$ 1,050

Ⓗ—Social Security

To calculate Alice's Social Security tax, we multiply $1,050 Ⓕ by 6.2%:

$1,050 × .062 = **$65.10**

Ⓘ—Medicare

Since Medicare has no base, Alice's entire weekly salary is taxed 1.45%, which is multiplied by $2,250.

$2,250 × .0145 = **$32.63**

Ⓙ—FIT

Using the W-4 form Alice completed, Glo deducts **federal income tax withholding (FIT).** The more allowances an employee claims, the less money Glo deducts from the employee's paycheck. Glo uses the percentage method to calculate FIT.[2]

The Percentage Method[3]

Today, since many companies do not want to store the tax tables, they use computers for their payroll. These companies use the **percentage method.** For this method we use Table 9.1 and Table 9.2 on page 242 from Circular E to calculate Alice's FIT.

Step 1. In Table 9.1, locate the weekly withholding for one allowance. Multiply this number by 2.

$70.19 × 2 = $140.38

Step 2. Subtract $140.38 in Step 1 from Alice's total pay.

$2,250.00
− 140.38
$2,109.62

Step 3. In Table 9.2, locate the married person's weekly pay table. The $2,109.62 falls between $1,455 and $2,785. The tax is $179.80 plus 25% of the excess over $1,455.00.

$2,109.62
− 1,455.00
$ 654.62

Tax $179.80 + .25 ($654.62)

$179.80 + $163.66 = **$343.46**

[2]The *Business Math Handbook* has a sample of the wage bracket method.

[3]An alternative method is called the wage bracket method that is shown in the *Business Math Handbook*.

TABLE 9.1

Percentage method income tax withholding table

Payroll Period	One Withholding Allowance
Weekly	$ 70.19
Biweekly	140.38
Semimonthly	152.08
Monthly	304.17
Quarterly	912.50
Semiannually	1,825.00
Annually	3,650.00
Daily or miscellaneous (each day of the payroll period)	14.04

TABLE 9.2 Percentage method income tax withholding taxes

TABLE 1—WEEKLY Payroll Period

(a) SINGLE person (including head of household)—

If the amount of wages (after subtracting withholding allowances) is: Not over $51 — The amount of income tax to withhold is: $0

Over—	But not over—	The amount of income tax to withhold is:	of excess over—
$51	—$200	10%	—$51
$200	—$681	$14.90 plus 15%	—$200
$681	—$1,621	$87.05 plus 25%	—$681
$1,621	—$3,338	$322.05 plus 28%	—$1,621
$3,338	—$7,212	$802.81 plus 33%	—$3,338
$7,212		$2,081.23 plus 35%	—$7,212

(b) MARRIED person—

If the amount of wages (after subtracting withholding allowances) is: Not over $154 — The amount of income tax to withhold is: $0

Over—	But not over—	The amount of income tax to withhold is:	of excess over—
$154	—$461	10%	—$154
$461	—$1,455	$30.70 plus 15%	—$461
$1,455	—$2,785	$179.80 plus 25%	—$1,455
$2,785	—$4,165	$512.30 plus 28%	—$2,785
$4,165	—$7,321	$898.70 plus 33%	—$4,165
$7,321		$1,940.18 plus 35%	—$7,321

TABLE 2—BIWEEKLY Payroll Period

(a) SINGLE person (including head of household)—

If the amount of wages (after subtracting withholding allowances) is: Not over $102 — The amount of income tax to withhold is: $0

Over—	But not over—	The amount of income tax to withhold is:	of excess over—
$102	—$400	10%	—$102
$400	—$1,362	$29.80 plus 15%	—$400
$1,362	—$3,242	$174.10 plus 25%	—$1,362
$3,242	—$6,677	$644.10 plus 28%	—$3,242
$6,677	—$14,423	$1,605.90 plus 33%	—$6,677
$14,423		$4,162.08 plus 35%	—$14,423

(b) MARRIED person—

If the amount of wages (after subtracting withholding allowances) is: Not over $308 — The amount of income tax to withhold is: $0

Over—	But not over—	The amount of income tax to withhold is:	of excess over—
$308	—$921	10%	—$308
$921	—$2,910	$61.30 plus 15%	—$921
$2,910	—$5,569	$359.65 plus 25%	—$2,910
$5,569	—$8,331	$1,024.40 plus 28%	—$5,569
$8,331	—$14,642	$1,797.76 plus 33%	—$8,331
$14,642		$3,880.39 plus 35%	—$14,642

TABLE 3—SEMIMONTHLY Payroll Period

(a) SINGLE person (including head of household)—

If the amount of wages (after subtracting withholding allowances) is: Not over $110 — The amount of income tax to withhold is: $0

Over—	But not over—	The amount of income tax to withhold is:	of excess over—
$110	—$433	10%	—$110
$433	—$1,475	$32.30 plus 15%	—$433
$1,475	—$3,513	$188.60 plus 25%	—$1,475
$3,513	—$7,233	$698.10 plus 28%	—$3,513
$7,233	—$15,625	$1,739.70 plus 33%	—$7,233
$15,625		$4,509.06 plus 35%	—$15,625

(b) MARRIED person—

If the amount of wages (after subtracting withholding allowances) is: Not over $333 — The amount of income tax to withhold is: $0

Over—	But not over—	The amount of income tax to withhold is:	of excess over—
$333	—$998	10%	—$333
$998	—$3,152	$66.50 plus 15%	—$998
$3,152	—$6,033	$389.60 plus 25%	—$3,152
$6,033	—$9,025	$1,109.85 plus 28%	—$6,033
$9,025	—$15,863	$1,947.61 plus 33%	—$9,025
$15,863		$4,204.15 plus 35%	—$15,863

TABLE 4—MONTHLY Payroll Period

(a) SINGLE person (including head of household)—

If the amount of wages (after subtracting withholding allowances) is: Not over $221 — The amount of income tax to withhold is: $0

Over—	But not over—	The amount of income tax to withhold is:	of excess over—
$221	—$867	10%	—$221
$867	—$2,950	$64.60 plus 15%	—$867
$2,950	—$7,025	$377.05 plus 25%	—$2,950
$7,025	—$14,467	$1,395.80 plus 28%	—$7,025
$14,467	—$31,250	$3,479.56 plus 33%	—$14,467
$31,250		$9,017.95 plus 35%	—$31,250

(b) MARRIED person—

If the amount of wages (after subtracting withholding allowances) is: Not over $667 — The amount of income tax to withhold is: $0

Over—	But not over—	The amount of income tax to withhold is:	of excess over—
$667	—$1,996	10%	—$667
$1,996	—$6,304	$132.90 plus 15%	—$1,996
$6,304	—$12,067	$779.10 plus 25%	—$6,304
$12,067	—$18,050	$2,219.85 plus 28%	—$12,067
$18,050	—$31,725	$3,895.09 plus 33%	—$18,050
$31,725		$8,407.84 plus 35%	—$31,725

Ⓚ—SIT

We assume a 6% **state income tax (SIT).**

$2,250 × .06 = $135.00

Ⓛ—Health insurance

Ⓜ—Net pay

Alice contributes $100 per week for health insurance.
Alice's **net pay** is her gross pay less all deductions.

	$2,250.00	gross
−	65.10	Social Security
−	32.63	Medicare
−	343.46	FIT
−	135.00	SIT
−	100.00	health insurance
=	$1,573.81	net pay

Employers' Responsibilities

In the first section of this unit, we saw that Alice contributed to Social Security and Medicare. Glo Company has the legal responsibility to match her contributions. Besides matching Social Security and Medicare, Glo must pay two important taxes that employees do not have to pay—federal and state unemployment taxes.

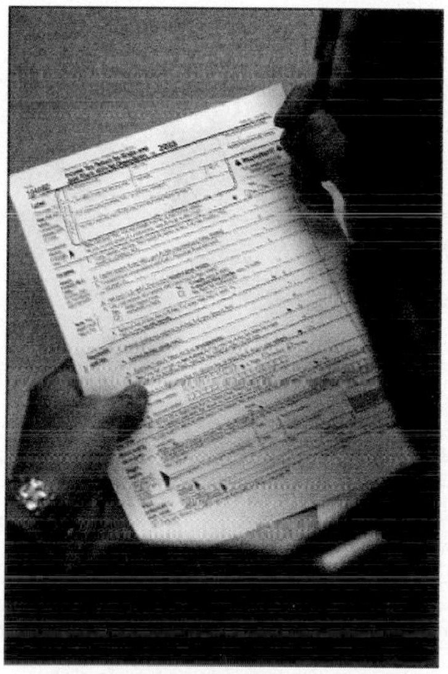

RF/Corbis

Federal Unemployment Tax Act (FUTA)

The federal government participates in a joint federal-state unemployment program to help unemployed workers. At this writing, employers pay the government a 6.2% **FUTA** tax on the first $7,000 paid to employees as wages during the calendar year. Any wages in excess of $7,000 per worker are exempt wages and are not taxed for FUTA. If the total cumulative amount the employer owes the government is less than $100, the employer can pay the liability yearly (end of January in the following calendar year). If the tax is greater than $100, the employer must pay it within a month after the quarter ends.

Companies involved in a state unemployment tax fund can usually take a 5.4% credit against their FUTA tax. *In reality, then, companies are paying .8% (.008) to the federal unemployment program.* In all our calculations, FUTA is .008.

LO 2

EXAMPLE Assume a company had total wages of $19,000 in a calendar year. No employee earned more than $7,000 during the calendar year. The FUTA tax is .8% (6.2% minus the company's 5.4% credit for state unemployment tax). How much does the company pay in FUTA tax?

The company calculates its FUTA tax as follows:

	6.2%	FUTA tax
−	5.4%	credit for SUTA tax
=	.8%	tax for FUTA

.008 × $19,000 = $152 FUTA tax due to federal government

$ MONEY TIPS

You should know your tax liability throughout the year and adjust the number of exemptions you claim based on this information. The goal for tax time is to be within +/− $100. That way you are not giving a free loan to the government and you have use of your money throughout the year.

State Unemployment Tax Act (SUTA)

The current **SUTA** tax in many states is 5.4% on the first $7,000 the employer pays an employee. Some states offer a merit rating system that results in a lower SUTA rate for companies with a stable employment period. The federal government still allows 5.4% credit on FUTA tax to companies entitled to the lower SUTA rate. Usually states also charge companies with a poor employment record a higher SUTA rate. However, these companies cannot take any more than the 5.4% credit against the 6.2% federal unemployment rate.

EXAMPLE Assume a company has total wages of $20,000 and $4,000 of the wages are exempt from SUTA. What are the company's SUTA and FUTA taxes if the company's SUTA rate is 5.8% due to a poor employment record?

The exempt wages (over $7,000 earnings per worker) are not taxed for SUTA or FUTA. So the company owes the following SUTA and FUTA taxes:

$20,000
− 4,000 (exempt wages)
$16,000 × .058 = $928 SUTA

Federal FUTA tax would then be:
$16,000 × .008 = $128

You can check your progress with the following Practice Quiz.

LU 9–2 PRACTICE QUIZ

Complete this **Practice Quiz** to see how you are doing.

1. Calculate Social Security taxes, Medicare taxes, and FIT for Joy Royce. Joy's company pays her a monthly salary of \$9,500. She is single and claims 1 deduction. Before this payroll, Joy's cumulative earnings were \$103,300. (Social Security maximum is 6.2% on \$106,800, and Medicare is 1.45%.) Calculate FIT by the percentage method.
2. Jim Brewer, owner of Arrow Company, has three employees who earn \$300, \$700, and \$900 a week. Assume a state SUTA rate of 5.1%. What will Jim pay for state and federal unemployment taxes for the first quarter?

Solutions with Step-by-Step Help on DVD

✓ Solutions

1. **Social Security**

\$106,800
− 103,300
\$ 3,500 × .062 = **\$217.00**

Medicare

\$9,500 × .0145 = \$137.75

FIT

Percentage method: \$304.17 × 1 =

\$9,500.00
− 304.17 (Table 9.1)
\$9,195.83

\$7,025 to \$14,467 → \$1,395.80 plus 28% of excess over \$7,025 (Table 9.2)

\$9,195.83
− 7,025.00
\$2,170.83 × .28 = \$ 607.83
+ 1,395.80
\$2,003.63

2. 13 weeks × \$300 = \$ 3,900
13 weeks × \$700 = 9,100 (\$9,100 − \$7,000) → \$2,100
13 weeks × \$900 = 11,700 (\$11,700 − \$7,000) → 4,700
\$24,700 — \$6,800 Exempt wages (not taxed for FUTA or SUTA)

\$24,700 − \$6,800 = \$17,900 taxable wages
SUTA = .051 × \$17,900 = **\$912.90**
FUTA = .008 × \$17,900 = **\$143.20**

Note: FUTA remains at .008 whether SUTA rate is higher or lower than standard.

LU 9–2a EXTRA PRACTICE QUIZ WITH WORKED-OUT SOLUTIONS

Need more practice? Try this **Extra Practice Quiz** (check figures in Chapter Organizer, p. 246). Worked-out Solutions can be found in Appendix B at end of text.

1. Calculate Social Security taxes, Medicare taxes, and FIT for Joy Royce. Joy's company pays her a monthly salary of \$10,000. She is single and claims 1 deduction. Before this payroll, Joy's cumulative earnings were \$106,300. (Social Security maximum is 6.2% on \$106,800, and Medicare is 1.45%.) Calculate FIT by the percentage method.
2. Jim Brewer, owner of Arrow Company, has three employees who earn \$200, \$800, and \$950 a week. Assume a state SUTA rate of 5.1%. What will Jim pay for state and federal unemployment taxes for the first quarter?

CHAPTER ORGANIZER AND REFERENCE GUIDE

<table>
<tr><th>Topic</th><th>Key point, procedure, formula</th><th>Example(s) to illustrate situation</th></tr>
<tr><td>Gross pay, p. 237</td><td>$\text{Hours employee worked} \times \text{Rate per hour}$</td><td>$6.50 per hour at 36 hours
Gross pay = 36 × $6.50 = $234</td></tr>
<tr><td>Overtime, p. 237</td><td>$\text{Gross earnings (pay)} = \text{Regular pay} + \text{Earnings at overtime rate } (1\frac{1}{2})$</td><td>$6 per hour; 42 hours
Gross pay = (40 × $6) + (2 × $9)
= $240 + $18 = $258</td></tr>
<tr><td>Straight piece rate, p. 237</td><td>$\text{Gross pay} = \text{Number of units produced} \times \text{Rate per unit}$</td><td>1,185 units; rate per unit, $.89
Gross pay = 1,185 × $.89
= $1,054.65</td></tr>
<tr><td>Differential pay schedule, p. 238</td><td>Rate on each item is related to the number of items produced.</td><td>1–500 at $.84; 501–1,000 at $.96;
900 units produced.
Gross pay = (500 × $.84) + (400 × $.96)
= $420 + $384 = $804</td></tr>
<tr><td>Straight commission, p. 238</td><td>Total sales × Commission rate
Any draw would be subtracted from earnings.</td><td>$155,000 sales; 6% commission
$155,000 × .06 = $9,300</td></tr>
<tr><td>Variable commission scale, p. 238</td><td>Sales at different levels pay different rates of commission.</td><td>Up to $5,000, 5%; $5,001 to $10,000, 8%; over $10,000, 10%
Sold: $6,500
Solution: ($5,000 × .05) + ($1,500 × .08)
= $250 + $120 = $370</td></tr>
<tr><td>Salary plus commission, p. 239</td><td>$\text{Regular wages (fixed)} + \text{Commissions earned}$</td><td>Base $400 per week + 2% on sales over $14,000
Actual sales: $16,000
$400 (base) + (.02 × $2,000) = $440</td></tr>
<tr><td>Payroll register, p. 240</td><td>Multicolumn form to record payroll.
Married and paid weekly. (Table 9.2)
Claims 1 allowance.
FICA rates from chapter.</td><td><table>
<tr><th rowspan="3">Earnings
Gross</th><th colspan="3">Deductions</th><th rowspan="3">Net pay</th></tr>
<tr><th colspan="2">FICA</th><th></th></tr>
<tr><th>S.S.</th><th>Med.</th><th>FIT</th></tr>
<tr><td>1,100</td><td>68.20</td><td>15.95</td><td>116.02</td><td>899.83</td></tr>
</table></td></tr>
<tr><td>FICA, p. 241
Social Security Medicare</td><td>6.2% on $106,800 (S.S.)
1.45% (Med.)</td><td>If John earns $107,000, what did he contribute for the year to Social Security and Medicare?
S.S.: $107,000 × .062 = $6,634.00
Med.: $106,800 × .0145 = $1,548.60</td></tr>
<tr><td>FIT calculation (percentage method), p. 241</td><td>Facts:
Al Doe: Married
Claims: 2
Paid weekly: $1,600</td><td>$1,600.00
− 140.38 ($70.19 × 2) Table 9.1
$1,459.62
By Table 9.2
$1,459.62
− 1,455.00
$ 4.62
$179.80 + .25($4.62)
$179.80 + $1.16 = $180.96</td></tr>
<tr><td>State and federal unemployment, p. 243</td><td>Employer pays these taxes. Rates are 6.2% on $7,000 for federal and 5.4% for state on $7,000. 6.2% − 5.4% = .8% federal rate after credit. If state unemployment rate is higher than 5.4%, no additional credit is taken. If state unemployment rate is less than 5.4%, the full 5.4% credit can be taken for federal unemployment.</td><td>Cumulative pay before payroll, $6,400; this week's pay, $800. What are state and federal unemployment taxes for employer, assuming a 5.2% state unemployment rate?
State → .052 × $600 = $31.20
Federal → .008 × $600 = $4.80
($6,400 + $600 = $7,000 maximum)</td></tr>
</table>

(continues)

CHAPTER ORGANIZER AND REFERENCE GUIDE

Topic	Key point, procedure, formula	Example(s) to illustrate situation
KEY TERMS	Biweekly, *p. 236* Deductions, *p. 237* Differential pay schedule, *p. 238* Draw, *p. 238* Employee's Withholding Allowance Certificate (W-4), *p. 240* Fair Labor Standards Act, *p. 236* Federal income tax withholding (FIT), *p. 241* Federal Insurance Contribution Act (FICA), *p. 241* Federal Unemployment Tax Act (FUTA), *p. 243* Gross pay, *p. 237* Medicare, *p. 241* Monthly, *p. 236* Net pay, *p. 243* Overrides, *p. 239* Overtime, *p. 237* Payroll register, *p. 240* Percentage method, *p. 241*	Semimonthly, *p. 241* Social Security, *p. 241* State income tax (SIT), *p. 243* State Unemployment Tax Act (SUTA), *p. 243* Straight commission, *p. 238* Variable commission scale, *p. 238* W-4, *p. 240* Weekly, *p. 236*
CHECK FIGURES FOR EXTRA PRACTICE QUIZZES WITH PAGE REFERENCES. (WORKED-OUT SOLUTIONS IN APPENDIX B.)	LU 9–1a (p. 239) **1.** $732 **2.** $12,800 **3.** $4,070	LU 9–2a (p. 244) **1.** $31; 145; $2,143.63 **2.** $846.60; $132.80

Critical Thinking Discussion Questions

1. Explain the difference between biweekly and semimonthly. Explain what problems may develop if a retail store hires someone on straight commission to sell cosmetics.
2. Explain what each column of a payroll register records (p. 240) and how each number is calculated. Social Security tax is based on a specific rate and base; Medicare tax is based on a rate but no base. Do you think this is fair to all taxpayers?
3. What taxes are the responsibility of the employer? How can an employer benefit from a merit-rating system for state unemployment?

END-OF-CHAPTER PROBLEMS

connect plus+ www.mhhe.com/slater10e

Check figures for odd-numbered problems in Appendix C

Name ________________________ Date ________

DRILL PROBLEMS

Complete the following table:

	Employee	M	T	W	Th	F	Hours	Rate per hour	Gross pay
9–1.	Tom Bradey	10	7	8	7	6		$7.39	
9–2.	Kristina Shaw	5	9	10	8	8		$8.10	

Complete the following table (assume the overtime for each employee is a time-and-a-half rate after 40 hours):

	Employee	M	T	W	Th	F	Sa	Total regular hours	Total overtime hours	Regular rate	Overtime rate	Gross earnings
9–3.	Bluc	12	9	9	9	9	3			$8.00		
9–4.	Tagney	14	8	9	9	5	1			$7.60		

Calculate gross earnings:

	Worker	Number of units produced	Rate per unit	Gross earnings
9–5.	Lang	480	$3.50	
9–6.	Swan	846	$ .58	

Calculate the gross earnings for each apple picker based on the following differential pay scale:

1–1,000: $.03 each 1,001–1,600: $.05 each Over 1,600: $.07 each

	Apple picker	Number of apples picked	Gross earnings
9–7.	Ryan	1,600	
9–8.	Rice	1,925	

	Employee	Total sales	Commission rate	Draw	End-of-month commission received
9–9.	Reese	$300,000	7%	$8,000	

Ron Company has the following commission schedule:

Commission rate	Sales
2%	Up to $80,000
3.5%	Excess of $80,000 to $100,000
4%	More than $100,000

Calculate the gross earnings of Ron Company's two employees:

	Employee	Total sales	Gross earnings
9–10.	Bill Moore	\$ 70,000	
9–11.	Ron Ear	\$155,000	

Complete the following table, given that A Publishing Company pays its salespeople a weekly salary plus a 2% commission on all net sales over \$5,000 (no commission on returned goods):

	Employee	Gross sales	Return	Net sales	Given quota	Commission sales	Commission rates	Total commission	Regular wage	Total wage
9–12.	Ring	\$ 8,000	\$ 25		\$5,000		2%		\$250	
9–13.	Porter	\$12,000	\$100		\$5,000		2%		\$250	

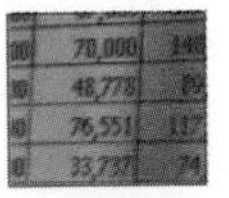

Calculate the Social Security and Medicare deductions for the following employees (assume a tax rate of 6.2% on \$106,800 for Social Security and 1.45% for Medicare):

	Employee	Cumulative earnings before this pay period	Pay amount this period	Social Security	Medicare
9–14.	Lee	\$105,800	\$2,000		
9–15.	Chin	\$99,300	\$8,000		
9–16.	Davis	\$600,000	\$4,000		

Complete the following payroll register. Calculate FIT by the percentage method for this weekly period; Social Security and Medicare are the same rates as in the previous problems. No one will reach the maximum for FICA.

	Employee	Marital status	Allowances claimed	Gross pay	FIT	FICA S.S.	FICA Med.	Net pay
9–17.	Jim Day	M	2	\$1,400				
9–18.	Ursula Lang	M	4	\$1,900				

9–19. Given the following, calculate the state (assume 5.3%) and federal unemployment taxes that the employer must pay for each of the first two quarters. The federal unemployment tax is .8% on the first $7,000.

PAYROLL SUMMARY		
	Quarter 1	Quarter 2
Bill Adams	$4,000	$ 8,000
Rich Haines	8,000	14,000
Alice Smooth	3,200	3,800

WORD PROBLEMS

9–20. Cycling through Pittsburgh, Pennsylvania, to look at its industrial heritage is an event open to the public. This intriguing ride is laced with the economic challenges that steel mills in Pittsburgh and other areas in the United States have faced resulting in company reductions and shutdowns. Situations similar to the following example are not uncommon. Full-time employees (40 hours per week) at the local steel mill were used to earning up to 10 hours of overtime in a two-week time period. They would typically work five overtime hours Monday through Friday and five overtime hours on the weekend. Many got used to the extra pay and began living beyond the means of their regular pay. Then overtime was cut. The average laborer's pay is $25 an hour. They earned 1.5 times their regular hourly pay for overtime Monday through Friday and 2 times their regular hourly pay on weekends and holidays. Calculate what their typical pay was before overtime was cut. Then calculate what percent pay they lost when overtime was cut. Round to the nearest tenth of a percent.

9–21. Rhonda Brennan found her first job after graduating from college through the classifieds of the *Miami Herald.* She was delighted when the offer came through at $18.50 per hour. She completed her W-4 stating that she is married with a child and claims an allowance of 3. Her company will pay her biweekly for 80 hours. Calculate her take-home pay for her first check.

9–22. The Social Security Administration increased the taxable wage base from $102,000 to $106,800. The 6.2% tax rate is unchanged. Joe Burns earned over $100,000 each of the past two years. **(a)** What is the percent increase in the base? Round to the nearest hundredth percent. **(b)** What is Joe's increase in Social Security tax for the new year?

9–23. Dennis Toby is a salesclerk at Northwest Department Store. Dennis receives $8 per hour plus a commission of 3% on all sales. Assume Dennis works 30 hours and has sales of $1,900. What is his gross pay?

9–24. Diane Palter, single, works 37 hours per week at $8.00 an hour. How much is taken out for federal income tax with one withholding exemption?

9–25. Robin Hartman earns $600 per week plus 3% of sales over $6,500. Robin's sales are $14,000. How much does Robin earn?

9–26. Pat Maninen earns a gross salary of $2,100 each week. What are Pat's first week's deductions for Social Security and Medicare? Will any of Pat's wages be exempt from Social Security and Medicare for the calendar year? Assume a rate of 6.2% on $106,800 for Social Security and 1.45% for Medicare.

9–27. Richard Gaziano is a manager for Health Care, Inc. Health Care deducts Social Security, Medicare, and FIT (by percentage method) from his earnings. Assume the same Social Security and Medicare rates as in Problem 9–26. Before this payroll, Richard is $1,000 below the maximum level for Social Security earnings. Richard is married, is paid weekly, and claims 2 exemptions. What is Richard's net pay for the week if he earns $1,300?

9–28. Len Mast earned $2,200 for the last two weeks. He is married, is paid biweekly, and claims 3 exemptions. What is Len's income tax? Use the percentage method.

9–29. Westway Company pays Suzie Chan $2,200 per week. By the end of week 50, how much did Westway deduct for Suzie's

Social Security and Medicare for the year? Assume Social Security is 6.2% on $106,800 and 1.45% for Medicare. What state and federal unemployment taxes does Westway pay on Suzie's yearly salary? The state unemployment rate is 5.1%. FUTA is .8%.

9–30. Morris Leste, owner of Carlson Company, has three employees who earn $400, $500, and $700 per week. What are the total state and federal unemployment taxes that Morris owes for the first 11 weeks of the year and for week 30? Assume a state rate of 5.6% and a federal rate of .8%.

CHALLENGE PROBLEMS

9–31. The Victorville, California, *Daily Press* stated that the San Bernardino County Fair hires about 150 people during fair time. Their wages range from \$6.75 to \$8.00. California has a state income tax of 9%. Sandy Denny earns \$8.00 per hour; George Barney earns \$6.75 per hour. They both worked 35 hours this week. Both are married; however, Sandy claims 2 exemptions and George claims 1 exemption. Assume a rate of 6.2% on \$106,800 for Social Security and 1.45% for Medicare. **(a)** What is Sandy's net pay after FIT, Social Security tax, state income tax, and Medicare have been taken out? **(b)** What is George's net pay after the same deductions? **(c)** How much more is Sandy's net pay versus George's net pay? Round to the nearest cent.

9–32. Bill Rose is a salesperson for Boxes, Inc. He believes his \$1,460.47 monthly paycheck is in error. Bill earns a \$1,400 salary per month plus a 9.5% commission on sales over \$1,500. Last month, Bill had \$8,250 in sales. Bill believes his traveling expenses are 16% of his weekly gross earnings before commissions. Monthly deductions include Social Security, \$126.56; Medicare, \$29.60; FIT, \$189.50; union dues, \$25.00; and health insurance, \$16.99. Calculate the following: **(a)** Bill's monthly take-home pay, and indicate the amount his check was under- or overstated, and **(b)** Bill's weekly traveling expenses. Round your final answer to the nearest dollar.

DVD SUMMARY PRACTICE TEST

1. Calculate Sam's gross pay (he is entitled to time-and-a-half). *(p. 237)*

M	T	W	Th	F	Total hours	Rate per hour	Gross pay
$9\frac{1}{4}$	$9\frac{1}{4}$	$10\frac{1}{2}$	$8\frac{1}{2}$	$11\frac{1}{2}$		\$8.00	

2. Mia Kaminsky sells shoes for Macy's. Macy's pays Mia \$12 per hour plus a 5% commission on all sales. Assume Mia works 37 hours for the week and has \$7,000 in sales. What is Mia's gross pay? *(p. 238)*

3. Lee Company pays its employees on a graduated commission scale: 6% on the first $40,000 sales, 7% on sales from $40,001 to $80,000, and 13% on sales of more than $80,000. May West, an employee of Lee, has $230,000 in sales. What commission did May earn? *(p. 238)*

4. Matty Kim, an accountant for Vernitron, earned $99,300 from January to June. In July, Matty earned $20,000. Assume a tax rate of 6.2% for Social Security on $106,800 and 1.45% on Medicare. How much are the July taxes for Social Security and Medicare? *(p. 241)*

5. Grace Kelley earns $2,000 per week. She is married and claims 2 exemptions. What is Grace's income tax? Use the percentage method. *(p. 241)*

6. Jean Michaud pays his two employees $900 and $1,200 per week. Assume a state unemployment tax rate of 5.7% and a federal unemployment tax rate of .8%. What state and federal unemployment taxes will Jean pay at the end of quarter 1 and quarter 2? *(p. 243)*

Personal Finance

A KIPLINGER APPROACH

» **MONEY** // INSURANCE / ASK KIM

THIS COBRA SAVES LIVES

If you lose your job, you won't lose your health insurance. BY KIMBERLY LANKFORD

CAN YOU Translate, please?

WHAT IS COBRA?
The Consolidated Omnibus Budget Reconciliation Act is a federal law passed in 1986. It requires companies with 20 or more employees to continue offering health insurance at group rates to former employees and their family members after they're no longer eligible for the group—because of job loss or divorce, for example. Some states have similar rules for companies with fewer than 20 employees.

WHO QUALIFIES?
Former employees, spouses, former spouses and dependent children are eligible, regardless of their health. There are exceptions: You cannot get COBRA if your employer no longer offers health insurance to current employees. You're also out of luck if the company goes out of business. Federal employees are covered by a law similar to COBRA.

HOW LONG DOES IT LAST?
COBRA provides up to 18 months of coverage from the time you leave your job or drop to part-time status. The coverage lasts up to 36 months after you no longer qualify as a dependent on an employee's policy. That includes, for example, a child who reaches the cutoff age for coverage or a former spouse who gets a divorce from the employee.

HOW MUCH DOES IT COST?
Probably more than you expect. You have to pay the employee's and the employer's share of the premium—or an average of $12,680 for families this year—plus up to 2% in administrative costs. But legislation Congress passed earlier this year provides a 65% COBRA subsidy for up to nine months for people who lose their job between September 1, 2008, and December 31, 2009.

WHO SHOULD TAKE IT?
You can't be rejected or charged more under COBRA because of your health, so it's a good deal for people with medical conditions who might otherwise have a tough time finding affordable insurance. But if you're healthy and live in a state with a competitive health-insurance market (which includes most states other than New York and New Jersey), you may find a better deal on your own. You can search for individual policies at Ehealthinsurance.com. ■

BUSINESS MATH ISSUE

Even with government subsidies COBRA is still too expensive.

1. List the key points of the article and information to support your position.
2. Write a group defense of your position using math calculations to support your view.

Slater's Business Math Scrapbook

Applying Your Skills

PROJECT A

Do you believe COBRA is the answer for laid-off workers? Agree or disagree.

PROJECT B

Do you agree with the IRS ruling?

Stimulus Makes Cobra Coverage A Better Bet

Subsidy for Laid-Off Workers Eliminates Barrier That Kept Many Out of the Program

By M.P. McQueen

Congress has just given a big assist to millions of jobless Americans facing a tough decision: Do they reach into their wallet to continue health insurance coverage with their old employer or not?

As part of the economic-stimulus package signed into law this week, the federal government will provide a nine-month subsidy covering 65% of the Cobra premium for people who qualify. Eligible workers who originally opted not to take Cobra but who now want the subsidized version have 60 days after they receive notice from their employers to sign up, says Richard G. Schwartz, a benefits lawyer in New York.

Fewer than one in 10 eligible workers recently opted for continuing insurance coverage in 2007 under Cobra, the federal law that allows many workers to continue group health insurance when they leave a job. The big reason: Cobra is expensive. Under the law, workers must pay the entire premium—plus a 2% administrative fee—even though employers typically picked up the lion's share of the cost. The average cost of Cobra coverage for a family is $13,000 a year—big money for someone who is unemployed.

The new legislation might help people like Chuck Fleming, 41 years old, of Aurora, Colo. His job in the legal department of Janus Capital Group Inc., a Denver-based financial-services company,

Uncoiling Cobra

The stimulus package makes it easier to afford extended health coverage after losing a job:

- The law provides a federal subsidy for 65% of the premium for nine months for workers who qualify.
- The subsidy applies to workers who lose their jobs between Sept. 1, 2008, and Dec. 31, 2009.
- Workers who may have pre-existing conditions must maintain coverage to protect insurability.

IRS Deals FedEx a Setback On Classification of Workers

By Corey Dade

The Internal Revenue Service has determined that the roughly 13,000 independent contractors for **FedEx** Corp.'s U.S. ground-delivery business in 2002 were, in fact, employees and assessed the company $319 million in back taxes and fines, according to a filing by the company with the Securities and Exchange Commission.

FedEx also said the IRS currently is investigating the status of contractors hired by the company between 2004 and 2006, raising the prospect of additional penalties. FedEx couldn't immediately say how many contractors were engaged in that span, but the work force currently stands at about 15,000.

The decision is the most significant blow to an embattled model whose low operating costs have been critical to the rapid growth of the FedEx Ground unit, in which the contractors are hired as drivers.

Separately, the SEC filing said FedEx received a grand jury subpoena from the Department of Justice for documents as part of a probe into possible price-fixing among air-freight forwarders. (Please see related article on Page A6A.)

The Memphis, Tenn., company, which posted $35.2 billion in revenue last year, has seen revenue from its ground-delivery business grow by a quarterly average of about 10% over the past five years. In that time, package volume in the unit has exploded 86%. On each delivery, FedEx Ground earns 23 cents more than heavily unionized rival United Parcel Service Inc.

FedEx says it will appeal the decision to the IRS in a process that could move to the federal courts and take years to resolve. FedEx wouldn't have to pay the penalty until its final challenge is denied.

Scores of current and former drivers and organized labor, which has targeted FedEx as ripe for unionization, have alleged that FedEx controls virtually every aspect of contractors' work, from the wearing of uniforms to delivery routes, and that they should be reclassified as employees and given benefits.

Internet Projects: See text Web site (www.mhhe.com/slater10e) and The Business Math Internet Resource Guide.

Video Case

WASHBURN GUITARS

Washburn International, founded in 1883, makes 80 models of instruments, both custom and for the mass market. Washburn is a privately held company with over 100 employees and annual sales of $48 million. This compares to its annual sales of $300,000 when Rudy Schlacher took over in 1976. When he acquired the company, about 250 guitars were produced per month; now 15,000 are produced each month.

The Washburn tradition of craftsmanship and innovation has withstood the tests of economics, brand competition, and fashion. Since its birth in Chicago, the name Washburn has been branded into the world's finest stringed instruments. To maintain quality, Washburn must have an excellent pool of qualified employees who are passionate about craftsmanship.

Washburn consolidated its four divisions in an expansive new 130,000 square foot plant in Mundelein, Illinois. The catalyst for consolidating operations in Mundelein was a chronic labor shortage in Elkhart and Chicago. The Mundelein plant was the ideal home for all Washburn operations because it had the necessary space, was cost effective, and gave Washburn access to a labor pool.

To grow profitably, Washburn must also sell its other products. To keep Washburn's 16 domestic salespeople tuned in to the full line, the company offers an override incentive. It is essential that to produce quality guitars, Washburn must keep recruiting dedicated, well-qualified, and team-oriented employees and provide them with profitable incentives.

PROBLEM 1

$120,000 was paid to 16 of Washburn's salespeople in override commissions. **(a)** What was the average amount paid to each salesperson? **(b)** What amount of the average sales commission will go toward the salesperson's Social Security tax? **(c)** What amount will go toward Medicare?

PROBLEM 2

Washburn is seeking a Sales and Marketing Coordinator with a bachelor's degree or equivalent experience, knowledgeable in Microsoft Office. This position pays $25,000 to $35,000, depending on experience. Assume a person is paid weekly and earns $32,500. Using the percentage method, what would be the taxes withheld for a married person who claims 3 exemptions?

PROBLEM 3

Guitarists hoping for a little country music magic in their playing can now buy an instrument carved out of oak pews from the former home of the Grand Ole Opry. Only 243 of the Ryman Limited Edition Acoustic Guitars are being made, each costing $6,250. Among the first customers were singers Vince Gill, Amy Grant, and Loretta Lynn, Ms. Lynn purchased two guitars. What would be the total revenue received by Washburn if all the guitars are sold?

PROBLEM 4

Under Washburn's old pay system, phone reps received a commission of 1.5% only on instruments they sold. Now the phone reps are paid an extra .75% commission on field sales made in their territory; the outside salespeople still get a commission up to 8%, freeing them to focus on introducing new products and holding in-store clinics. Assume sales were $65,500: **(a)** How much would phone reps receive? **(b)** How much would the outside salespeople receive?

PROBLEM 5

Washburn introduced the Limited Edition EA27 Gregg Allman Signature Series Festival guitar—only 500 guitars were produced with a selling price of $1,449.90. If Washburn's markup is 35% on selling price, what was Washburn's total cost for the 500 guitars?

PROBLEM 6

Retailers purchased $511 million worth of guitars from manufacturers—some 861,300 guitars—according to a study done by the National Association of Music Merchants. **(a)** What would be the average selling price of a guitar? **(b)** Based on the average selling price, if manufacturer's markup on cost is 40%, what would be the average cost?

PROBLEM 7

A Model NV 300 acoustic-electric guitar is being sold for a list price of $1,899.90, with a cash discount of 3/10, n/30. Sales tax is 7% and shipping is $30.40. How much is the final price if the cash discount period was met?

PROBLEM 8

A Model M3SWE mandolin has a list price of $1,299.90, with a chain discount of 5/3/2. **(a)** What would be the trade discount amount? **(b)** What would be the net price?

PROBLEM 9

A purchase was made of 2 Model J282DL six-string acoustic guitars at $799.90 each, with cases priced at $159.90, and 3 Model EA10 festival series acoustic-electric guitars at $729.90, with cases listed at $149.90. If sales tax is 6%, what is the total cost?

PROBLEM 10

Production of guitars has increased by what percent since Rudy Schlacher took over Washburn?

chapter

10 SIMPLE INTEREST

William West/AFP/Getty Images

Left Unpaid

Highest default rates over the past eight years for franchises with 50 or more SBA-backed loans

Franchise	Number of loans 2001–08	8-year default rate
Mr. Goodcents	55	55%
Philly Connection	63	51
Cottman Transmission	165	49
All Tune & Lube	81	47
Cornwell Quality Tools	55	42

Fiscal 2008* loan defaults at franchises with 50 or more SBA-backed loans

Franchise	Total loans 2001–08	Number of defaulted loans in '08
Quiznos	1,963	108
Cold Stone Creamery	763	75
Subway	2,148	42
Curves for Women	362	24
Planet Beach	230	22
Aamco Transmission	169	15

Franchise	Total loans 2001–08	Number of defaulted loans in '08
CiCi's Pizza	155	13
Carvel Ice Cream	78	12
Domino's Pizza	242	11
Dream Dinners	61	11
Taco Del Mar	71	11

Source: U.S. Small Business Administration

*Year ended Sept. 30

Wall Street Journal © 2008

LEARNING UNIT OBJECTIVES

LU 10–1: Calculation of Simple Interest and Maturity Value

1. Calculate simple interest and maturity value for months and years *(p. 258).*
2. Calculate simple interest and maturity value by **(a)** exact interest and **(b)** ordinary interest *(pp. 259–260).*

LU 10–2: Finding Unknown in Simple Interest Formula

1. Using the interest formula, calculate the unknown when the other two (principal, rate, or time) are given *(pp. 260–262).*

LU 10–3: U.S. Rule—Making Partial Note Payments before Due Date

1. List the steps to complete the U.S. Rule *(pp. 262–263).*
2. Complete the proper interest credits under the U.S. Rule *(p. 263).*

VOCABULARY PREVIEW

Here are key terms in this chapter. After completing the chapter, if you know the term, place a checkmark in the parenthesis. If you don't know the term, look it up and put the page number where it can be found.

Adjusted balance . ( ) Banker's Rule . ( ) Exact interest . ( ) Interest . ( ) Maturity value . ( ) Ordinary interest . ( ) Principal . ( ) Simple interest . ( ) Simple interest formula . ( ) Time . ( ) U.S. Rule . ( )

As Big Banks Converge, Depositors Find Deals At Smaller Institutions

BY JANE J. KIM AND JOSEPH DE AVILA

AS THE BIG BANKS get bigger, it may be time for savers to shop around.

Citigroup Inc.'s decision this week to gobble up most of ailing **Wachovia** Corp. is the latest in a string of blockbuster acquisitions that have transformed the banking landscape. A huge chunk of consumer deposits are now consolidated in three banking behemoths—Citigroup, **Bank of America** Corp. and **J.P. Morgan Chase** & Co.—not known for wooing consumers with high interest rates and low fees.

"Good news for people who hide their money under mattresses."

In today's economy, choosing a bank is not an easy choice. In the *Wall Street Journal* clip, "As Big Banks Converge, Depositors Find Deals at Smaller Institutions," the article indicates big bank mergers may mean better interest rates at smaller banks. You need to shop around.

In this chapter, you will study simple interest. The principles discussed apply whether you are paying interest or receiving interest. Let's begin by learning how to calculate simple interest.

Learning Unit 10–1: Calculation of Simple Interest and Maturity Value

LO 1

Jan Carley, a young attorney, rented an office in a professional building. Since Jan recently graduated from law school, she was short of cash. To purchase office furniture for her new office, Jan went to her bank and borrowed $30,000 for 6 months at an 8% annual interest rate.

The original amount Jan borrowed ($30,000) is the **principal** (face value) of the loan. Jan's price for using the $30,000 is the interest rate (8%) the bank charges on a yearly basis. Since Jan is borrowing the $30,000 for 6 months, Jan's loan will have a **maturity value** of $31,200—the principal plus the interest on the loan. Thus, Jan's price for using the furniture before she can pay for it is $1,200 interest, which is a percent of the principal for a specific time period. To make this calculation, we use the following formula:

Maturity value (*MV*) = Principal (*P*) + Interest (*I*)

$$\$31{,}200 = \$30{,}000 + \$1{,}200$$

Jan's furniture purchase introduces **simple interest**—the cost of a loan, usually for 1 year or less. Simple interest is only on the original principal or amount borrowed. Let's examine how the bank calculated Jan's $1,200 interest.

Simple Interest Formula

To calculate simple interest, we use the following **simple interest formula:**

Simple interest (*I*) = Principal (*P*) × Rate (*R*) × Time (*T*)

In this formula, rate is expressed as a decimal, fraction, or percent; and time is expressed in years or a fraction of a year.

EXAMPLE Jan Carley borrowed $30,000 for office furniture. The loan was for 6 months at an annual interest rate of 8%. What are Jan's interest and maturity value?

Using the simple interest formula, the bank determined Jan's interest as follows:

In your calculator, multiply $30,000 times .08 times 6. Divide your answer by 12. You could also use the % key—multiply $30,000 times 8% times 6 and then divide your answer by 12.

Step 1. Calculate the interest.

$$I = \underset{(P)}{\$30{,}000} \times \underset{(R)}{.08} \times \underset{(T)}{\frac{6}{12}} = \$1{,}200$$

Step 2. Calculate the maturity value.

$$MV = \underset{(P)}{\$30{,}000} + \underset{(I)}{\$1{,}200} = \$31{,}200$$

Now let's use the same example and assume Jan borrowed $30,000 for 1 year. The bank would calculate Jan's interest and maturity value as follows:

Step 1. Calculate the interest.

$$I = \underset{(P)}{\$30{,}000} \times \underset{(R)}{.08} \times \underset{(T)}{1 \text{ year}} = \$2{,}400$$

Step 2. Calculate the maturity value.

$$MV = \underset{(P)}{\$30{,}000} + \underset{(I)}{\$2{,}400} = \$32{,}400$$

Let's use the same example again and assume Jan borrowed $30,000 for 18 months. Then Jan's interest and maturity value would be calculated as follows:

Step 1. Calculate the interest.

$$I = \underset{(P)}{\$30{,}000} \times \underset{(R)}{.08} \times \underset{(T)}{\frac{18^{1}}{12}} = \$3{,}600$$

[1]This is the same as 1.5 years.

Step 2. Calculate the maturity value. $MV = \$30{,}000 + \$3{,}600$
$\qquad (P) \qquad (I)$
$= \$33{,}600$

Next we'll turn our attention to two common methods we can use to calculate simple interest when a loan specifies its beginning and ending dates.

LO 2

Two Methods for Calculating Simple Interest and Maturity Value

Method 1: Exact Interest (365 Days) The Federal Reserve banks and the federal government use the **exact interest** method. The *exact interest* is calculated by using a 365-day year. For **time,** we count the exact number of days in the month that the borrower has the loan. The day the loan is made is not counted, but the day the money is returned is counted as a full day. This method calculates interest by using the following fraction to represent time in the formula:

$$\text{Time} = \frac{\text{Exact number of days}}{365}$$ ← Exact interest

From the *Business Math Handbook*

July 6	187th day
March 4	− 63rd day
	124 days (exact time of loan)
March	31
	− 4
	27
April	30
May	31
June	30
July	+ 6
	124 days

For this calculation, we use the exact days-in-a-year calendar from the *Business Math Handbook*. You learned how to use this calendar in Chapter 7, p. 182.

EXAMPLE On March 4, Peg Carry borrowed \$40,000 at 8% interest. Interest and principal are due on July 6. What is the interest cost and the maturity value?

Step 1. Calculate the interest. $I = P \times R \times T$

$= \$40{,}000 \times .08 \times \frac{124}{365}$

$= \$1{,}087.12$ (rounded to nearest cent)

Step 2. Calculate the maturity value. $MV = P + I$

$= \$40{,}000 + \$1{,}087.12$

$= \$41{,}087.12$

Method 2: Ordinary Interest (360 Days) In the **ordinary interest** method, time in the formula $I = P \times R \times T$ is equal to the following:

$$\text{Time} = \frac{\text{Exact number of days}}{360}$$ ← Ordinary Interest

Since banks commonly use the ordinary interest method, it is known as the **Banker's Rule.** Banks charge a slightly higher rate of interest because they use 360 days instead of 365 in the denominator. By using 360 instead of 365, the calculation is supposedly simplified. Consumer groups, however, are questioning why banks can use 360 days, since this benefits the bank and not the customer. The use of computers and calculators no longer makes the simplified calculation necessary. For example, after a court case in Oregon, banks began calculating interest on 365 days except in mortgages.

Now let's replay the Peg Carry example we used to illustrate Method 1 to see the difference in bank interest when we use Method 2.

MONEY TIPS

Calculating the amount of interest you will pay on a loan may be a deterrent to making a purchase. Understand the terms of your loan before signing any contracts. Calculate the total out-of-pocket costs and make certain this is less than the value of what you are buying or you may be making a poor purchasing decision.

EXAMPLE On March 4, Peg Carry borrowed \$40,000 at 8% interest. Interest and principal are due on July 6. What are the interest cost and the maturity value?

Step 1. Calculate the interest. $I = \$40{,}000 \times .08 \times \frac{124}{360}$

$= \$1{,}102.22$

(continued on next page)

Step 2. Calculate the maturity value.

$$MV = P + I$$
$$= \$40{,}000 + \$1{,}102.22$$
$$= \$41{,}102.22$$

Note: By using Method 2, the bank increases its interest by $15.10.

$$\begin{array}{rl} \$1{,}102.22 & \leftarrow \text{Method 2} \\ -\ 1{,}087.12 & \\ \hline \$\quad 15.10 & \leftarrow \text{Method 1} \end{array}$$

Now you should be ready for your first Practice Quiz in this chapter.

LU 10–1 PRACTICE QUIZ

Complete this **Practice Quiz** to see how you are doing.

Calculate simple interest (round to the nearest cent):

1. $14,000 at 4% for 9 months
2. $25,000 at 7% for 5 years
3. $40,000 at $10\frac{1}{2}$% for 19 months
4. On May 4, Dawn Kristal borrowed $15,000 at 8%. Dawn must pay the principal and interest on August 10. What are Dawn's simple interest and maturity value if you use the exact interest method?
5. What are Dawn Kristal's (Problem 4) simple interest and maturity value if you use the ordinary interest method?

DVD *Solutions with Step-by-Step Help on DVD*

✓ Solutions

1. $\$14{,}000 \times .04 \times \frac{9}{12} = \$420$
2. $\$25{,}000 \times .07 \times 5 = \$8{,}750$
3. $\$40{,}000 \times .105 \times \frac{19}{12} = \$6{,}650$
4. August 10 → 222
   May 4 → − 124
   98

   $\$15{,}000 \times .08 \times \frac{98}{365} = \$322.19$

   $MV = \$15{,}000 + \$322.19 = \$15{,}322.19$
5. $\$15{,}000 \times .08 \times \frac{98}{360} = \$326.67$

   $MV = \$15{,}000 + \$326.67 = \$15{,}326.67$

LU 10–1a EXTRA PRACTICE QUIZ WITH WORKED-OUT SOLUTIONS

Need more practice? Try this **Extra Practice Quiz** (check figures in Chapter Organizer, p. 265). Worked-out Solutions can be found in Appendix B at end of text.

Calculate simple interest (round to the nearest cent):

1. $16,000 at 3% for 8 months
2. $15,000 at 6% for 6 years
3. $50,000 at 7% for 18 months
4. On May 6, Dawn Kristal borrowed $20,000 at 7%. Dawn must pay the principal and interest on August 14. What are Dawn's simple interest and maturity value if you use the exact interest method?
5. What are Dawn Kristal's (Problem 4) simple interest and maturity value if you use the ordinary interest method?

Learning Unit 10–2: Finding Unknown in Simple Interest Formula

LO 1

This unit begins with the formula used to calculate the principal of a loan. Then it explains how to find the *principal, rate,* and *time* of a simple interest loan. In all the calculations, we use 360 days and round only final answers.

Finding the Principal

EXAMPLE Tim Jarvis paid the bank $19.48 interest at 9.5% for 90 days. How much did Tim borrow using the ordinary interest method?

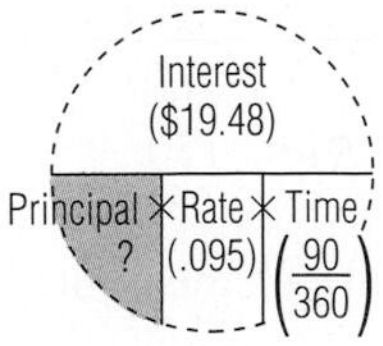

The following formula is used to calculate the principal of a loan:

$$\text{Principal} = \frac{\text{Interest}}{\text{Rate} \times \text{Time}}$$

Note how we illustrated this in the margin. The shaded area is what we are solving for. When solving for principal, rate, or time, you are dividing. Interest will be in the numerator, and the denominator will be the other two elements multiplied by each other.

Step 1. Set up the formula. $P = \dfrac{\$19.48}{.095 \times \dfrac{90}{360}}$

Step 2. When using a calculator, press .095 × 90 ÷ 360 M+.

Step 2. Multiply the denominator. .095 times 90 divided by 360 (do not round)

$P = \dfrac{\$19.48}{.02375}$

Step 3. When using a calculator, press 19.48 ÷ MR =.

Step 3. Divide the numerator by the result of Step 2. $P = \$820.21$

Step 4. Check your answer. $\$19.48 = \$820.21 \times .095 \times \dfrac{90}{360}$

$(I) \quad (P) \quad (R) \quad (T)$

Finding the Rate

EXAMPLE Tim Jarvis borrowed $820.21 from a bank. Tim's interest is $19.48 for 90 days. What rate of interest did Tim pay using the ordinary interest method?

The following formula is used to calculate the rate of interest:

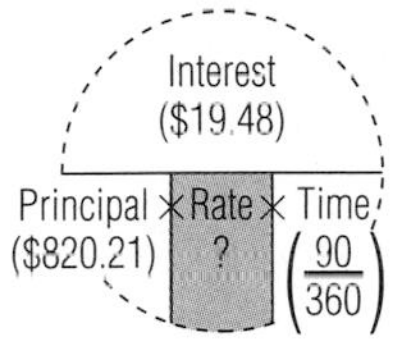

$$\text{Rate} = \frac{\text{Interest}}{\text{Principal} \times \text{Time}}$$

Step 1. Set up the formula. $R = \dfrac{\$19.48}{\$820.21 \times \dfrac{90}{360}}$

Step 2. Multiply the denominator. Do not round the answer. $R = \dfrac{\$19.48}{\$205.0525}$

Step 3. Divide the numerator by the result of Step 2. $R = 9.5\%$

Step 4. Check your answer. $\$19.48 = \$820.21 \times .095 \times \dfrac{90}{360}$

$(I) \quad (P) \quad (R) \quad (T)$

Step 2. When using a calculator, press 820.21 × .095 M+.

Step 3. When using a calculator, press 19.48 ÷ MR =.

Finding the Time

EXAMPLE Tim Jarvis borrowed $820.21 from a bank. Tim's interest is $19.48 at 9.5%. How much time does Tim have to repay the loan using the ordinary interest method?

The following formula is used to calculate time:

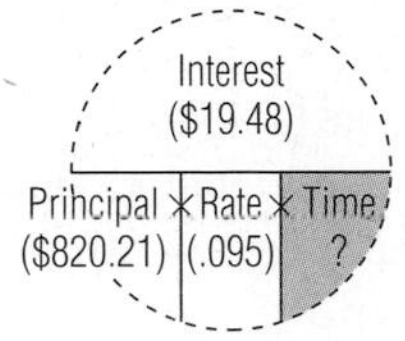

$$\text{Time (in years)} = \frac{\text{Interest}}{\text{Principal} \times \text{Rate}}$$

Step 1. Set up the formula. $T = \dfrac{\$19.48}{\$820.21 \times .095}$

Step 2. Multiply the denominator. Do not round the answer. $T = \dfrac{\$19.48}{\$77.91995}$

Step 3. Divide the numerator by the result of Step 2. $T = .25$ years

Step 4. Convert years to days (assume 360 days). $.25 \times 360 = 90$ days

MONEY TIPS

Be wary of using payday loans. A payday loan is a small, short-term *loan* that is intended to cover a borrower's expenses until his or her next payday. These services tend to keep you upside-down with your cash flow due to high interest rate charges encouraging repeat use.

(continued on next page)

Step 5. Check your answer.

$$\underset{(I)}{\$19.48} = \underset{(P)}{\$820.21} \times \underset{(R)}{.095} \times \underset{(T)}{\frac{90}{360}}$$

Before we go on to Learning Unit 10–3, let's check your understanding of this unit.

LU 10–2 PRACTICE QUIZ

Complete this **Practice Quiz** to see how you are doing.

Complete the following (assume 360 days):

	Principal	Interest rate	Time (days)	Simple interest
1.	?	5%	90 days	$8,000
2.	$7,000	?	220 days	350
3.	$1,000	8%	?	300

Solutions with Step-by-Step Help on DVD

✓ Solutions

1. $\dfrac{\$8{,}000}{.05 \times \frac{90}{360}} = \dfrac{\$8{,}000}{.0125} = \boxed{\$640{,}000}$ $\quad P = \dfrac{I}{R \times T}$

2. $\dfrac{\$350}{\$7{,}000 \times \frac{220}{360}} = \dfrac{\$350}{\$4{,}277.7777} = \boxed{8.18\%}$ $\quad R = \dfrac{I}{P \times T}$

(do not round) → $4,277.7777

3. $\dfrac{\$300}{\$1{,}000 \times .08} = \dfrac{\$300}{\$80} = 3.75 \times 360 = \boxed{1{,}350 \text{ days}}$ $\quad T = \dfrac{I}{P \times R}$

LU 10–2a EXTRA PRACTICE QUIZ WITH WORKED-OUT SOLUTIONS

Need more practice? Try this **Extra Practice Quiz** (check figures in Chapter Organizer, p. 265). Worked-out Solutions can be found in Appendix B at end of text.

Complete the following (assume 360 days):

	Principal	Interest rate	Time (days)	Simple interest
1.	?	4%	90 days	$9,000
2.	$6,000	?	180 days	280
3.	$900	6%	?	190

Learning Unit 10–3: U.S. Rule—Making Partial Note Payments before Due Date

Often a person may want to pay off a debt in more than one payment before the maturity date. The **U.S. Rule** allows the borrower to receive proper interest credits. This rule states that any partial loan payment first covers any interest that has built up. The remainder of the partial payment reduces the loan principal. Courts or legal proceedings generally use the U.S. Rule. The Supreme Court originated the U.S. Rule in the case of *Story* v. *Livingston.*

LO 1

EXAMPLE Joe Mill owes $5,000 on an 11%, 90-day note. On day 50, Joe pays $600 on the note. On day 80, Joe makes an $800 additional payment. Assume a 360-day year. What is Joe's adjusted balance after day 50 and after day 80? What is the ending balance due?

To calculate $600 payment on day 50:

Step 1. Calculate interest on principal from date of loan to date of first principal payment. Round to nearest cent.

$$I = P \times R \times T$$

$$I = \$5{,}000 \times .11 \times \frac{50}{360}$$

$$I = \$76.39$$

Milos Jokic/Shutterstock

Step 2. Apply partial payment to interest due. Subtract remainder of payment from principal. This is the **adjusted balance** (principal).

$600.00 payment
− 76.39 interest
$523.61

$5,000.00 pri
− 523.61
$4,476.39 adjusted balance—principal

To calculate $800 payment on day 80:

Step 3. Calculate interest on adjusted balance that starts from previous payment date and goes to new payment date. Then apply Step 2.

Compute interest on $4,476.39 for 30 days (80 − 50)

$$I = \$4{,}476.39 \times .11 \times \frac{30}{360}$$

$$I = \$41.03$$

$800.00 payment
− 41.03 interest
$758.97

$4,476.39
− 758.97
$3,717.42 adjusted balance

$ MONEY TIPS

Make a partial payment only if the interest rate on the loan you are paying on is greater than the interest rate on your other loans or the rate you can earn on investing your money. Always use your money where it does the most for you.

Step 4. At maturity, calculate interest from last partial payment. *Add* this interest to adjusted balance.

Ten days are left on note since last payment.

$$I = \$3{,}717.42 \times .11 \times \frac{10}{360}$$

$$I = \$11.36$$

Balance owed = **$3,728.78** $\begin{pmatrix} \$3{,}717.42 \\ + \quad 11.36 \end{pmatrix}$

Note that when Joe makes two partial payments, Joe's total interest is $128.78 ($76.39 + $41.03 + $11.36). If Joe had repaid the entire loan after 90 days, his interest payment would have been $137.50—a total savings of $8.72.

Let's check your understanding of the last unit in this chapter.

LU 10–3 PRACTICE QUIZ

Complete this **Practice Quiz** to see how you are doing.

Polly Flin borrowed $5,000 for 60 days at 8%. On day 10, Polly made a $600 partial payment. On day 40, Polly made a $1,900 partial payment. What is Polly's ending balance due under the U.S. Rule (assume a 360-day year)?

DVD *Solutions with Step-by-Step Help on DVD*

✓ Solutions

$$\$5{,}000 \times .08 \times \frac{10}{360} = \$11.11$$

$600.00
− 11.11
$588.89

$5,000.00
− 588.89
$4,411.11

$$\$4{,}411.11 \times .08 \times \frac{30}{360} = \$29.41$$

$1,900.00
− 29.41
$1,870.59

$4,411.11
− 1,870.59
$2,540.52

$$\$2{,}540.52 \times .08 \times \frac{20}{360} = \$11.29$$

$ 11.29
+ 2,450.52
$2,551.81

...ncipal

...ICE QUIZ WITH WORKED-OUT SOLUTIONS

Polly Flin borrowed \$4,000 for 60 days at 4%. On day 15, Polly made a \$700 partial payment. On day 40, Polly made a \$2,000 partial payment. What is Polly's ending balance due under the U.S. Rule (assume a 360-day year)?

CHAPTER ORGANIZER AND REFERENCE GUIDE

Topic	Key point, procedure, formula	Example(s) to illustrate situation
Simple interest for months, p. 258	Interest = Principal × Rate × Time (I) (P) (R) (T)	\$2,000 at 9% for 17 months $I = \$2,000 \times .09 \times \frac{17}{12}$ $I =$ **\$255**
Exact interest, p. 259	$T = \frac{\text{Exact number of days}}{365}$ $I = P \times R \times T$	\$1,000 at 10% from January 5 to February 20 $I = \$1,000 \times .10 \times \frac{46}{365}$ Feb. 20: 51 days Jan. 5: − 5 46 days $I =$ **\$12.60**
Ordinary interest (Bankers Rule), p. 259	$T = \frac{\text{Exact number of days}}{360}$ $I = P \times R \times T$ Higher interest costs	$I = \$1,000 \times .10 \times \frac{46}{360}$ (51 − 5) $I =$ **\$12.78**
Finding unknown in simple interest formula (use 360 days), p. 260	$I = P \times R \times T$	Use this example for illustrations of simple interest formula parts: \$1,000 loan at 9%, 60 days $I = \$1,000 \times .09 \times \frac{60}{360} =$ **\$15**
Finding the principal, p. 261	$P = \frac{I}{R \times T}$ 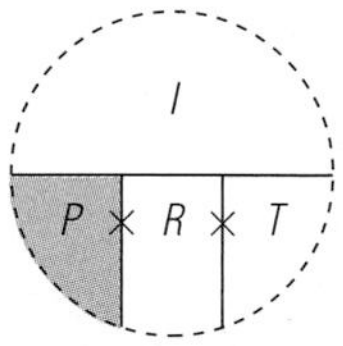	$P = \frac{\$15}{.09 \times \frac{60}{360}} = \frac{\$15}{.015} =$ **\$1,000**
Finding the rate, p. 261	$R = \frac{I}{P \times T}$ 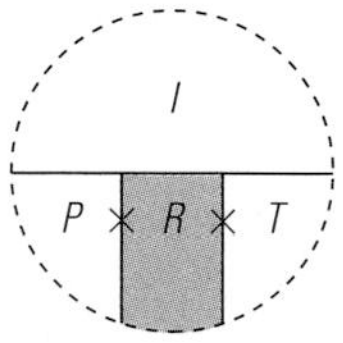	$R = \frac{\$15}{\$1,000 \times \frac{60}{360}} = \frac{\$15}{166.66666} = .09$ = **9%** *Note:* We did not round the denominator.
Finding the time, p. 261	$T = \frac{I}{P \times R}$ (in years) 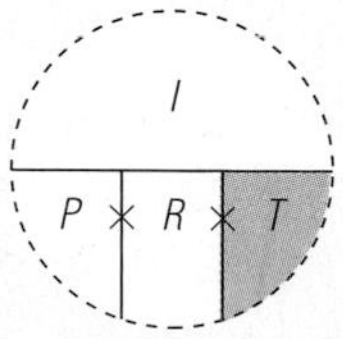 Multiply answer by 360 days to convert answer to days for ordinary interest.	$T = \frac{\$15}{\$1,000 \times .09} = \frac{\$15}{\$90} = .1666666$ $.1666666 \times 360 = 59.99 =$ **60 days**

(continues)

CHAPTER ORGANIZER AND REFERENCE GUIDE

Topic	Key point, procedure, formula	Example(s) to illustrate situation
U.S. Rule (use 360 days), p. 262	Calculate interest on principal from date of loan to date of first partial payment. Calculate adjusted balance by subtracting from principal the partial payment less interest cost. The process continues for future partial payments with the adjusted balance used to calculate cost of interest from last payment to present payment. Balance owed equals last adjusted balance plus interest cost from last partial payment to final due date.	12%, 120 days, $2,000 *Partial payments:* On day 40; $250 On day 60; $200 *First payment:* $I = \$2{,}000 \times .12 \times \frac{40}{360}$ $I = \$26.67$ $250.00 payment − 26.67 interest $223.33 $2,000.00 principal − 223.33 $1,776.67 adjusted balance *Second payment:* $I = \$1{,}776.67 \times .12 \times \frac{20}{360}$ $I = \$11.84$ $200.00 payment − 11.84 interest $188.16 $1,776.67 − 188.16 $1,588.51 adjusted balance *60 days left:* $\$1{,}588.51 \times .12 \times \frac{60}{360} = \$31.77$ $\$1{,}588.51 + \$31.77 =$ $1,620.28 balance due Total interest = $26.67 11.84 + 31.77 $70.28

KEY TERMS			
	Adjusted balance, *p. 263* Banker's Rule, *p. 259* Exact interest, *p. 259* Interest, *p. 258*	Maturity value, *p. 258* Ordinary interest, *p. 259* Principal, *p. 258* Simple interest, *p. 258*	Simple interest formula, *p. 258* Time, *p. 259* U.S. Rule, *p. 262*

CHECK FIGURES FOR EXTRA PRACTICE QUIZZES WITH PAGE REFERENCES. (WORKED-OUT SOLUTIONS IN APPENDIX B.)	LU 10–1a (p. 260)	LU 10–2a (p. 262)	LU 10–3a (p. 264)
	1. $320 **2.** $5,400 **3.** $5,250 **4.** $20,383.56; Interest = $383.56 **5.** $20,388.89; Interest = $388.89	**1.** $900,000 **2.** 9.33% **3.** 1,267 days	$1,318.78

Critical Thinking Discussion Questions

1. What is the difference between exact interest and ordinary interest? With the increase of computers in banking, do you think that the ordinary interest method is a dinosaur in business today?
2. Explain how to use the portion formula to solve the unknowns in the simple interest formula. Why would rounding the answer of the denominator result in an inaccurate final answer?
3. Explain the U.S. Rule. Why in the last step of the U.S. Rule is the interest added, not subtracted?
4. Do you believe the government bailout of banks is in the best interest of the country? Defend your position.

Classroom Notes

END-OF-CHAPTER PROBLEMS

connect plus+ www.mhhe.com/slater10e

Check figures for odd-numbered problems in Appendix C.

Name ____________________ Date ________

DRILL PROBLEMS

Calculate the simple interest and maturity value for the following problems. Round to the nearest cent as needed.

	Principal	Interest rate	Time	Simple interest	Maturity value
10–1.	\$18,000	$4\frac{1}{2}$%	18 mo.		
10–2.	\$21,000	5%	$1\frac{3}{4}$ yr.		
10–3.	\$18,000	$7\frac{1}{4}$%	9 mo.		

Complete the following, using ordinary interest:

	Principal	Interest rate	Date borrowed	Date repaid	Exact time	Interest	Maturity value
10–4.	\$1,000	8%	Mar. 8	June 9			
10–5.	\$585	9%	June 5	Dec. 15			
10–6.	\$1,200	12%	July 7	Jan. 10			

Complete the following, using exact interest:

	Principal	Interest rate	Date borrowed	Date repaid	Exact time	Interest	Maturity value
10–7.	\$1,000	8%	Mar. 8	June 9			
10–8.	\$585	9%	June 5	Dec. 15			
10–9.	\$1,200	12%	July 7	Jan. 10			

Solve for the missing item in the following (round to the nearest hundredth as needed):

	Principal	Interest rate	Time (months or years)	Simple interest
10–10.	\$400	5%	?	\$100
10–11.	?	7%	$1\frac{1}{2}$ years	\$200
10–12.	\$5,000	?	6 months	\$300

10–13. Use the U.S. Rule to solve for total interest costs, balances, and final payments (use ordinary interest).

Given Principal: \$10,000, 8%, 240 days
Partial payments: On 100th day, \$4,000
On 180th day, \$2,000

WORD PROBLEMS

10–14. The main concept to investing is diversify your investments. The old saying of "don't put all of your eggs in one basket" exemplifies this concept. Kerry Stutsman has saved \$500 and is wondering how to invest it. She was researching different investment options and found a June 2009 article called "What You Need to Know About CD's" in *Kiplinger's Personal Finance* magazine. She currently is investing in real estate through her home as well as contributing to the 401k she has at work and is thinking about investing in CD's as well. She has the \$500 in a savings account earning .45% interest. She is considering buying a 1-year certificate of deposit (CD) that pays 3.25% interest. What will be the annual difference in her interest earnings between the savings account and the CD?

10–15. Leslie Hart borrowed \$15,000 to pay for her child's education at Riverside Community College. Leslie must repay the loan at the end of 9 months in one payment with $5\frac{1}{2}$% interest. How much interest must Leslie pay? What is the maturity value?

10–16. On September 12, Jody Jansen went to Sunshine Bank to borrow \$2,300 at 9% interest. Jody plans to repay the loan on January 27. Assume the loan is on ordinary interest. What interest will Jody owe on January 27? What is the total amount Jody must repay at maturity?

10–17. Kelly O'Brien met Jody Jansen (Problem 10–16) at Sunshine Bank and suggested she consider the loan on exact interest. Recalculate the loan for Jody under this assumption. How much would she save in interest?

10–18. May 3, 2010, Leven Corp. negotiated a short-term loan of \$685,000. The loan is due October 1, 2010, and carries a 6.86% interest rate. Use ordinary interest to calculate the interest. What is the total amount Leven would pay on the maturity date?

10–19. Gordon Rosel went to his bank to find out how long it will take for \$1,200 to amount to \$1,650 at 8% simple interest. Please solve Gordon's problem. Round time in years to the nearest tenth.

10–20. Bill Moore is buying a used Winnebago. His April monthly interest at 12% was \$125. What was Bill's principal balance at the beginning of April? Use 360 days.

10–21. On April 5, 2010, Janeen Camoct took out an $8\frac{1}{2}$% loan for \$20,000. The loan is due March 9, 2011. Use ordinary interest to calculate the interest. What total amount will Janeen pay on March 9, 2011?

10–22. Sabrina Bowers took out the same loan as Janeen (Problem 10–21). Sabrina's terms, however, are exact interest. What is Sabrina's difference in interest? What will she pay on March 9, 2011?

10–23. Max Wholesaler borrowed $2,000 on a 10%, 120-day note. After 45 days, Max paid $700 on the note. Thirty days later, Max paid an additional $630. What is the final balance due? Use the U.S. Rule to determine the total interest and ending balance due. Use ordinary interest.

ADDITIONAL SET OF WORD PROBLEMS

10–24. Lane French had a bad credit rating and went to a local cash center. He took out a $100 loan payable in two **weeks** at $115. What is the percent of interest paid on this loan? Do not round denominator before dividing.

10–25. Availability of state and federal disaster loans was the featured article in *The Enterprise Ledger* (AL) on March 14, 2007. Alabama Deputy Treasurer Anthony Leigh said the state program allows the state treasurer to place state funds in Alabama banks at 2 percent below the market interest rate. The bank then agrees to lend the funds to individuals or businesses for 2 percent below the normal charge, to help Alabama victims of disaster to secure emergency short-term loans. Laura Harden qualifies for an emergency loan. She will need $3,500 for 5 months and the local bank has an interest rate of $4\frac{3}{4}$ percent. **(a)** What would have been the maturity value of a non-emergency loan? **(b)** What will be the maturity value of the emergency loan? Round to the nearest cent.

10–26. On September 14, Jennifer Rick went to Park Bank to borrow $2,500 at $11\frac{3}{4}\%$ interest. Jennifer plans to repay the loan on January 27. Assume the loan is on ordinary interest. What interest will Jennifer owe on January 27? What is the total amount Jennifer must repay at maturity?

10–27. Steven Linden met Jennifer Rick (Problem 10–26) at Park Bank and suggested she consider the loan on exact interest. Recalculate the loan for Jennifer under this assumption.

10–28. Lance Lopes went to his bank to find out how long it will take for $1,000 to amount to $1,700 at 12% simple interest. Can you solve Lance's problem? Round time in years to the nearest tenth.

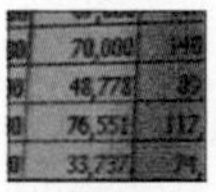

10–29. Margie Pagano is buying a car. Her June monthly interest at $12\frac{1}{2}$% was $195. What was Margie's principal balance at the beginning of June? Use 360 days. Do not round the denominator before dividing.

10–30. Shawn Bixby borrowed $17,000 on a 120-day, 12% note. After 65 days, Shawn paid $2,000 on the note. On day 89, Shawn paid an additional $4,000. What is the final balance due? Determine total interest and ending balance due by the U.S. Rule. Use ordinary interest.

10–31. Carol Miller went to Europe and forgot to pay her $740 mortgage payment on her New Hampshire ski house. For her 59 days overdue on her payment, the bank charged her a penalty of $15. What was the rate of interest charged by the bank? Round to the nearest hundredth percent (assume 360 days).

10–32. Abe Wolf bought a new kitchen set at Sears. Abe paid off the loan after 60 days with an interest charge of $9. If Sears charges 10% interest, what did Abe pay for the kitchen set (assume 360 days)?

10–33. Joy Kirby made a $300 loan to Robinson Landscaping at 11%. Robinson paid back the loan with interest of $6.60. How long in days was the loan outstanding (assume 360 days)? Check your answer.

10–34. Molly Ellen, bookkeeper for Keystone Company, forgot to send in the payroll taxes due on April 15. She sent the payment November 8. The IRS sent her a penalty charge of 8% simple interest on the unpaid taxes of $4,100. Calculate the penalty. (Remember that the government uses exact interest.)

10–35. Oakwood Plowing Company purchased two new plows for the upcoming winter. In 200 days, Oakwood must make a single payment of $23,200 to pay for the plows. As of today, Oakwood has $22,500. If Oakwood puts the money in a bank today, what rate of interest will it need to pay off the plows in 200 days (assume 360 days)?

CHALLENGE PROBLEMS

10–36. You have the opportunity to purchase a used car in great condition for $14,500. A $2,000 down payment is required to receive 6% interest for 6 years. The car you currently own is in perfect working condition but you would like a change. Your spouse recommends using the $2,000 to remodel a bathroom in your home. The remodel is estimated to bring the value of your home up by $5,000. Determine the interest you will pay on the loan for the car. Considering the opportunity cost (value of the next best alternative forgone as the result of making a decision) for the $2,000, what should you do with the money?

10–37. Janet Foster bought a computer and printer at Computerland. The printer had a $600 list price with a $100 trade discount and 2/10, n/30 terms. The computer had a $1,600 list price with a 25% trade discount but no cash discount. On the computer, Computerland offered Janet the choice of (1) paying $50 per month for 17 months with the 18th payment paying the remainder of the balance or (2) paying 8% interest for 18 months in equal payments.

a. Assume Janet could borrow the money for the printer at 8% to take advantage of the cash discount. How much would Janet save (assume 360 days)?

b. On the computer, what is the difference in the final payment between choices 1 and 2?

DVD SUMMARY PRACTICE TEST

1. Lorna Hall's real estate tax of $2,010.88 was due on December 14, 2009. Lorna lost her job and could not pay her tax bill until February 27, 2010. The penalty for late payment is $6\frac{1}{2}\%$ ordinary interest. *(p. 259)*

a. What is the penalty Lorna must pay?

b. What is the total amount Lorna must pay on February 27?

2. Ann Hopkins borrowed $60,000 for her child's education. She must repay the loan at the end of 8 years in one payment with $5\frac{1}{2}\%$ interest. What is the maturity value Ann must repay? *(p. 258)*

3. On May 6, Jim Ryan borrowed $14,000 from Lane Bank at $7\frac{1}{2}\%$ interest. Jim plans to repay the loan on March 11. Assume the loan is on ordinary interest. How much will Jim repay on March 11? *(p. 259)*

4. Gail Ross met Jim Ryan (Problem 3) at Lane Bank. After talking with Jim, Gail decided she would like to consider the same loan on exact interest. Can you recalculate the loan for Gail under this assumption? *(p. 259)*

5. Claire Russell is buying a car. Her November monthly interest was \$210 at $7\frac{3}{4}\%$ interest. What is Claire's principal balance (to the nearest dollar) at the beginning of November? Use 360 days. Do not round the denominator in your calculation. *(p. 261)*

6. Comet Lee borrowed \$16,000 on a 6%, 90-day note. After 20 days, Comet paid \$2,000 on the note. On day 50, Comet paid \$4,000 on the note. What are the total interest and ending balance due by the U.S. Rule? Use ordinary interest. *(p. 262)*

Personal Finance

A KIPLINGER APPROACH

Scams Exploit Hard Times

Prime targets are the unemployed and homeowners behind on their mortgages.

BY LAURA COHN

WHEN NANCY DIX RECEIVED A letter promising to help her prevent foreclosure on her home in Ansted, W.Va., she jumped at the chance. The letter, from an organization called Mortgage Rescue, said all she had to do to save her home was send the company a check for $921. So she did. Then she didn't hear anything—and got suspicious. The 67-year-old widow called the state attorney general's office, which referred her to Mountain State Justice, a nonprofit legal service. Turns out Mortgage Rescue was operating a scam, says Bren Pomponio, Dix's lawyer at Mountain State.

Fortunately, Dix hadn't signed over her deed when she sent the check—an additional layer of some similar scams. She never got her money back, but the legal service worked with her lender to keep her in her home. "Before you start sending money, talk to an attorney or a consumer group, or you'll be in the same mess I was in," Dix says.

Over the past five years, the FBI's mortgage-fraud caseload has jumped by nearly 400%, to more than 2,100. The general rule still applies: If it sounds too good to be true, it is. If, for example, you receive a call from a firm that guarantees to stop a foreclosure but asks you not to contact your lender, it's a scam: Your lender is the only route to modifying your mortgage or preventing foreclosure. If you're having trouble making your payments, find a housing counselor approved by the U.S. Department of Housing and Urban Development at www.hud.gov.

Easy money. The sagging economy has inspired a number of schemes to watch for, from work-at-home ploys to tax and stimulus frauds (see "Ask Kim," May). Shady operators take advantage of economic hard times, says Edward Johnson, president of the Better Business Bureau of Metro Washington and Eastern Pennsylvania. "If you don't have a job and are having trouble keeping up with your mortgage, you will let your guard down."

If you're looking for quick cash, be on the alert for job-related scams, such as an ad that promises you can earn money at home by stuffing envelopes—it's likely to be a pyramid scheme. You pay a fee upfront, and to make money you place ads and wait for people to respond and pay *you* a fee. Before you participate, ask the company to spell out, in writing, exactly what the job entails and whether you'll be on salary or commission. Also run the company's name by the BBB (www.bbb.org) and call the firm to make sure it's soliciting workers.

Another sneaky ploy involves bogus mystery-shopping firms that promise to pay shoppers to check out local stores. Scam operators may send out a letter with the company logo of an actual mystery-shopping service plus BBB certification, along with a check for several thousand dollars. The letter tells recipients to deposit the check, evaluate a money-wiring service, and then wire part of the money back to the firm to test the service—often within seven days. The check bounces after you've wired the money back.

Now that credit is harder to get, the Federal Deposit Insurance Corp. has reported a jump in "advance-fee loan" scams. Someone calls you and says that if you simply pay a fee of $500 or $1,000 upfront, you'll be guaranteed a loan. But you never get the money.

Finally, watch out for "phishing" scams. You get a phony e-mail from a trusted institution that asks for your Social Security number or other information that could be used to tap into your financial accounts (see "Lowdown," on page 79). One prevalent scheme is an e-mail promising you a tax refund from the IRS—except the IRS never e-mails taxpayers. Phony Bank of America and Citibank messages are also common. ■

■ EARN MONEY AT HOME BY STUFFING ENVELOPES? IT COULD BE A PYRAMID SCHEME.

BUSINESS MATH ISSUE

You should never take out a loan online.

1. List the key points of the article and information to support your position.
2. Write a group defense of your position using math calculations to support your view.

Slater's Business Math Scrapbook

Applying Your Skills

PROJECT A

Check-cashing shops should be outlawed. Agree or disagree and support your answer.

Alternative Way to Pay Utility Bills Draws Fire

Use of Check-Cashing Shops, Critics Say, Exposes Customers To Lure of High-Interest Loans

By Rebecca Smith

AP

Retired high-school math teacher Cynthia Elgar often pays her bills online, but when she got a disconnection notice from her Phoenix electric utility, Arizona Public Service, she realized a payment had gone awry somehow. In the past, she would have scooted over to a nearby utility office to make the late payment.

But the utility has shut down most of its neighborhood offices and relies on a network of retail stores and check-cashing facilities to receive in-person payments. APS directed Ms. Elgar to a Cash & More storefront in Phoenix. There, she waited along with fellow customers engaged in transactions such as cashing checks and getting short-term, high-interest "payday loans"—a business that consumer advocates say often preys on low-income people in dire financial straits.

"Why APS needs to use this sort of place to accept payments, I don't know," she says.

It is an experience that is increasingly common for utility customers. Across the U.S., utilities have shut down scores of customer-service centers in recent years and turned to retail outlets to take payments, in order to save money. Many of these locations are check-cashing centers, which cater to mainly low-income customers who don't use traditional banks, providing services such as loans and wire transfers on a fee basis.

The trend has sparked criticism from utility customers, regulators and consumer advocates. Customers say they miss the local centers where they were able to get personal service, such as arranging special payment plans. And some are simply uncomfortable going to check-cashing facilities.

But perhaps of greatest concern is that check-cashing facilities may be using utilities to build foot traffic, so they can steer consumers into expensive and addictive loan products that can carry annual interest rates in excess of 400%. At least one operator of check-cashing centers says that a number of customers who come in to pay utility bills also wind up taking out a payday loan, which is a short-term loan tied to the borrower's next paycheck.

Wall Street Journal © 2007

Student Loans: Default Rates Are Soaring

As Job Market Tightens, Graduates Are Squeezed; The 'Forbearance' Option

By Anne Marie Chaker

Defaults on student loans are skyrocketing amid a weak job market for graduates and steadily rising tuition costs.

According to new numbers from the U.S. Department of Education, default rates for federally guaranteed student loans are expected to reach 6.9% for fiscal year 2007. That's up from 4.6% two years earlier and would be the highest rate since 1998.

The situation is mirrored in the smaller private student-loan market. In 2008, **SLM** Corp. also known as Sallie Mae, wrote off 3.4% of its private loans that were already considered troubled, according to its latest annual report—more than double the figure in 2006. Student Loan Corp., a unit of **Citigroup** Inc., wrote off 2.3% of those loans in 2008, compared with 1.5% a year earlier.

"The volume of people in trouble is definitely increasing," says Deanne Loonin, a staff attorney at the Boston-based National Consumer Law Center who counsels low-income consumers on student loans and other debt issues.

Lenders say they are hearing more pleas for help as the unemployment rate worsens and debt levels soar among graduates.

Sarah Kostecki, a 24-year-old sales associate in New York, graduated last year from DePaul University with a major in international studies and $87,000 in debt, translating to monthly payments of $685, the vast majority of which are private loans.

Getting Relief

Here are some options for student borrowers who find themselves in trouble:

- **Forbearance.** This allows borrowers to put payments on hold, though they are on the hook for the interest that accrues.
- **Interest-only payments.** Borrowers can defer other payments until a later date.
- **Increase the borrowing period.** Allows borrowers to lower their monthly payments.

Wall Street Journal © 2009

PROJECT B

Go to the Web and find the latest student default rates.

Internet Projects: **See text Web site (www.mhhe.com/slater10e) and The Business Math Internet Resource Guide.**

chapter 11 PROMISSORY NOTES, SIMPLE DISCOUNT NOTES, AND THE DISCOUNT PROCESS

Ethan Miller/Getty Images

A Short Sale May Not Mean You're Home Free

By Ruth Simon

Financially troubled borrowers may think that foreclosure or a short sale of their home means their mortgage woes are over.

Not necessarily.

Some homeowners are finding that when they sell their homes for less than the outstanding mortgages—a so-called short sale—their mortgage companies are going after them for some or all of the difference. Mortgage companies are also sometimes taking legal action to recover unpaid amounts after a foreclosure is completed.

In a growing number of cases, holders of mortgages or home-equity loans are requiring borrowers in short sales to sign a promissory note, which is a written promise to pay back a loan or debt. Real-estate agents and attorneys say they have seen an increase in requests for promissory notes as mortgage companies look to short sales as an alternative to foreclosure.

In many states, lenders have always had the right to pursue former homeowners for unpaid mortgage debt. Yet until recently, most borrowers who ran into trouble were able to refinance or sell their homes and pay off their loans. Now, falling home prices are widening the gap between home values and mortgage balances, and the number of homeowners who can't make their mortgage payments is rising as the economy has weakened. More than 3.8 million homes will be lost in 2009 and 2010 because borrowers can't make their mortgage payments, according to forecasts from Moody's Economy.com.

Wall Street Journal © 2009

LEARNING UNIT OBJECTIVES

LU 11–1: Structure of Promissory Notes; the Simple Discount Note

1. Differentiate between interest-bearing and noninterest-bearing notes *(pp. 278–279).*
2. Calculate bank discount and proceeds for simple discount notes *(p. 279).*
3. Calculate and compare the interest, maturity value, proceeds, and effective rate of a simple interest note with a simple discount note *(p. 279).*
4. Explain and calculate the effective rate for a Treasury bill *(p. 280).*

LU 11–2: Discounting an Interest-Bearing Note before Maturity

1. Calculate the maturity value, bank discount, and proceeds of discounting an interest-bearing note before maturity *(p. 281).*
2. Identify and complete the four steps of the discounting process *(p. 281).*

VOCABULARY PREVIEW

Here are key terms in this chapter. After completing the chapter, if you know the term, place a checkmark in the parenthesis. If you don't know the term, look it up and put the page number where it can be found.

Bank discount . ( ) Bank discount rate . ( ) Contingent liability . ( ) Discounting a note . ( ) Discount period . ( ) Effective rate . ( ) Face value . ( ) Interest-bearing note . ( ) Maker . ( ) Maturity date . ( ) Maturity value (MV) . ( ) Noninterest-bearing note . ( ) Payee . ( ) Proceeds . ( ) Promissory note . ( ) Simple discount note . ( ) Treasury bill . ( )

Goodyear to Tap Credit Due to Money-Fund Woes

BY JOHN KELL

Goodyear Tire & Rubber Co. will draw $600 million from its credit lines because of an inability to access some U.S. cash investments, more than half of which are held in a troubled money-market fund.

The company also said finalization of a trust to handle current and future retirees' health benefits is at hand, allowing Goodyear to remove $1.2 billion in liabilities from its balance sheet.

Goodyear said it will use the $600 million to support seasonal needs and enhance cash liquidity. The amount covers $360 million locked in the Reserve Primary Fund, the money-market mutual fund that "broke the buck" last week. Its net asset value dipped to 97 cents a share last week as a result of **Lehman Brothers Holdings** Inc.'s bankruptcy filing, marking the first time since 1994 that a money-market fund broke the buck.

Redemptions from the fund have been suspended, prompting Goodyear to make the credit-line drawdown. The company added that its other U.S. cash investments remain accessible.

Goodyear has faced continuing pressure, driven by the slumping U.S. economy that is causing customers to delay or skip new-car purchases and auto makers to subsequently ratchet back production. Goodyear's stock has been in a free fall, falling about 45% in the past four months amid concerns over raw-material prices and slowing car production.

Wall Street Journal © 2008

Eric Glenn/Alamy

The *Wall Street Journal* clip "Goodyear to Tap Credit Due to Money-Fund Woes" shows the financial crises facing Goodyear. Goodyear will have to draw $600 million from its credit line.

This chapter begins with a discussion of the structure of promissory notes and simple discount notes. We also look at the application of discounting with Treasury bills. The chapter concludes with an explanation of how to calculate the discounting of promissory notes.

Learning Unit 11–1: Structure of Promissory Notes; the Simple Discount Note

Although businesses frequently sign promissory notes, customers also sign promissory notes. For example, some student loans may require the signing of promissory notes. Appliance stores often ask customers to sign a promissory note when they buy large appliances on credit. In this unit, promissory notes usually involve interest payments.

LO 1

Structure of Promissory Notes

To borrow money, you must find a lender (a bank or a company selling goods on credit). You must also be willing to pay for the use of the money. In Chapter 10 you learned that interest is the cost of borrowing money for periods of time.

Money lenders usually require that borrowers sign a **promissory note.** (See chapter opener regarding promissory notes and real estate.) This note states that the borrower will repay a certain sum at a fixed time in the future. The note often includes the charge for the use of the money, or the rate of interest. Figure 11.1 shows a sample promissory note with its terms identified and defined. Take a moment to look at each term.

In this section you will learn the difference between interest-bearing notes and noninterest-bearing notes.

Interest-Bearing versus Noninterest-Bearing Notes

A promissory note can be interest bearing or noninterest bearing. To be **interest bearing,** the note must state the rate of interest. Since the promissory note in Figure 11.1 states that its interest is 9%, it is an interest-bearing note. When the note matures, Regal Corporation "will pay back the original amount (**face value**) borrowed plus interest. The simple interest formula (also known as the interest formula) and the maturity value formula from Chapter 10 are used for this transaction."

$$\text{Interest} = \text{Face value (principal)} \times \text{Rate} \times \text{Time}$$
$$\text{Maturity value} = \text{Face value (principal)} + \text{Interest}$$

FIGURE 11.1

Interest-bearing promissory note

$10,000 a. LAWTON, OKLAHOMA October 2, 2010 c.
Sixty days b. AFTER DATE we PROMISE TO PAY TO
THE ORDER OF G.J. Equipment Company d.
Ten thousand and 00/100------------------DOLLARS.
PAYABLE AT Able National Bank
VALUE RECEIVED WITH INTEREST AT 9% e. REGAL CORPORATION f.
NO. 114 DUE December 1, 2010 g. J.M. Moore TREASURER

a. **Face value:** Amount of money borrowed—$10,000. The face value is also the principal of the note.
b. **Term:** Length of time that the money is borrowed—60 days.
c. **Date:** The date that the note is issued—October 2, 2010.
d. **Payee:** The company extending the credit—G.J. Equipment Company.
e. **Rate:** The annual rate for the cost of borrowing the money—9%.
f. **Maker:** The company issuing the note and borrowing the money—Regal Corporation.
g. **Maturity date:** The date the principal and interest rate are due—December 1, 2010.

If you sign a **noninterest-bearing** promissory note for $10,000, you pay back $10,000 at maturity. The maturity value of a noninterest-bearing note is the same as its face value. Usually, noninterest-bearing notes occur for short time periods under special conditions. For example, money borrowed from a relative could be secured by a noninterest-bearing promissory note.

LO 2

Simple Discount Note

The total amount due at the end of the loan, or the **maturity value (*MV*),** is the sum of the face value (principal) and interest. Some banks deduct the loan interest in advance. When banks do this, the note is a **simple discount note.**

In the simple discount note, the **bank discount** is the interest that banks deduct in advance and the **bank discount rate** is the percent of interest. The amount that the borrower receives after the bank deducts its discount from the loan's maturity value is the note's **proceeds.** Sometimes we refer to simple discount notes as noninterest-bearing notes. Remember, however, that borrowers *do* pay interest on these notes.

In the example that follows, Pete Runnels has the choice of a note with a simple interest rate (Chapter 10) or a note with a simple discount rate (Chapter 11). Table 11.1 provides a summary of the calculations made in the example and gives the key points that you should remember. Now let's study the example, and then you can review Table 11.1.

EXAMPLE Pete Runnels has a choice of two different notes that both have a face value (principal) of $14,000 for 60 days. One note has a simple interest rate of 8%, while the other note has a simple discount rate of 8%. For each type of note, calculate **(a)** interest owed, **(b)** maturity value, **(c)** proceeds, and **(d)** effective rate.

LO 3

Simple interest note—Chapter 10	Simple discount note—Chapter 11
Interest **a.** I = Face value (principal) $\times R \times T$ $I = \$14{,}000 \times .08 \times \frac{60}{360}$ $I = \$186.67$	**Interest** **a.** I = Face value (principal) $\times R \times T$ $I = \$14{,}000 \times .08 \times \frac{60}{360}$ $I = \$186.67$
Maturity value **b.** MV = Face value + Interest $MV = \$14{,}000 + \$186.67$ $MV = \$14{,}186.67$	**Maturity value** **b.** MV = Face value $MV = \$14{,}000$
Proceeds **c.** Proceeds = Face value = $14,000	**Proceeds** **c.** Proceeds = MV − Bank discount = $14,000 − $186.67 = $13,813.33
Effective rate **d.** $\text{Rate} = \frac{\text{Interest}}{\text{Proceeds} \times \text{Time}}$ $= \frac{\$186.67}{\$14{,}000 \times \frac{60}{360}}$ = 8%	**Effective rate** **d.** $\text{Rate} = \frac{\text{Interest}}{\text{Proceeds} \times \text{Time}}$ $= \frac{\$186.67}{\$13{,}813.33 \times \frac{60}{360}}$ = 8.11%

TABLE 11.1

Comparison of simple interest note and simple discount note (Calculations from the Pete Runnels example)

Simple interest note (Chapter 10)	Simple discount note (Chapter 11)
1. A promissory note for a loan with a term of usually less than 1 year. *Example:* 60 days.	**1.** A promissory note for a loan with a term of usually less than 1 year. *Example:* 60 days.
2. Paid back by one payment at maturity. Face value equals actual amount (or principal) of loan (this is not maturity value).	**2.** Paid back by one payment at maturity. Face value equals maturity value (what will be repaid).
3. Interest computed on face value or what is actually borrowed. *Example:* $186.67.	**3.** Interest computed on maturity value or what will be repaid and not on actual amount borrowed. *Example:* $186.67.
4. Maturity value = Face value + Interest. *Example:* $14,186.67.	**4.** Maturity value = Face value. *Example:* $14,000.
5. Borrower receives the face value. *Example:* $14,000.	**5.** Borrower receives proceeds = Face value − Bank discount. *Example:* $13,813.33.
6. Effective rate (true rate is same as rate stated on note). *Example:* 8%.	**6.** Effective rate is higher since interest was deducted in advance. *Example:* 8.11%.
7. Used frequently instead of the simple discount note. *Example:* 8%.	**7.** Not used as much now because in 1969 congressional legislation required that the true rate of interest be revealed. Still used where legislation does not apply, such as personal loans.

Note that the interest of $186.67 is the same for the simple interest note and the simple discount note. The maturity value of the simple discount note is the same as the face value. In the simple discount note, interest is deducted in advance, so the proceeds are less than the face value. Note that the **effective rate** for a simple discount note is higher than the stated rate, since the bank calculated the rate on the face of the note and not on what Pete received.

LO 4

Application of Discounting—Treasury Bills

Full Slate of Treasury Sales

WASHINGTON—The Treasury announced plans to sell $135 billion next week in short-term securities.

Details of the offerings (all with minimum denominations of $100):

■ In the usual weekly sale on Monday, the Treasury plans to sell $29 billion in 13-week bills and $28 billion in 26-week bills.

The issue date of the reopened bills is Jan. 29, 2009. They mature April. 30, 2009, and July 30, 2009, respectively. The Cusip number for the 13-week bills is 912795L66 and for the 26-week bills is 912795Q95.

Noncompetitive tenders for the bills must be received by 11 a.m. Eastern time Monday, and competitive tenders by 11:30 a.m.

■ The Treasury will sell $8 billion in 20-year Treasury inflation-protected securities Monday.

The issue date of the so-called TIPS is Jan. 30, 2009. The securities mature Jan. 15, 2029. The Cusip number is 912810PZ5.

Noncompetitive tenders for the notes must be received by noon Monday, and competitive tenders by 1 p.m.

■ The Treasury plans to sell $40 billion in two-year notes Tuesday, in addition to the usual four-week bill auction (to be announced on Monday).

The issue date is Feb. 2, 2009. The notes mature Jan. 31, 2011. The Cusip number is 912828JY7.

Noncompetitive tenders for the notes must be received by noon Tuesday, and competitive tenders by 1 p.m.

■ The Treasury sell $30 billion in five-year notes Thursday.

The issue date is Feb. 2, 2009. The notes mature Jan. 31, 2014. The Cusip number is 912828JZ4.

Noncompetitive tenders for the notes must be received by noon Thursday, and competitive tenders by 1 p.m.

When the government needs money, it sells Treasury bills. A **Treasury bill** is a loan to the federal government for 28 days (4 weeks), 91 days (13 weeks), or 1 year. Note that the *Wall Street Journal* clipping "Full Slate of Treasury Sales" announces a new sale.

Treasury bills can be bought over the phone or on the government Web site. The purchase price (or proceeds) of a Treasury bill is the value of the Treasury bill less the discount. For example, if you buy a $10,000, 13-week Treasury bill at 8%, you pay $9,800 since you have not yet earned your interest ($\$10{,}000 \times .08 \times \frac{13}{52} = \$200$). At maturity—13 weeks—the government pays you $10,000. You calculate your effective yield (8.16% rounded to the nearest hundredth percent) as follows:

$ MONEY TIPS

Be wary of anything you sign your name to. Make certain to read and understand everything, including the small print, before you sign.

$$(\$10{,}000 - \$200) \longrightarrow \frac{\$200}{\$9{,}800 \times \frac{13}{52}} = \boxed{8.16\%} \text{ effective rate}$$

Now it's time to try the Practice Quiz and check your progress.

LU 11–1 PRACTICE QUIZ

Complete this **Practice Quiz** to see how you are doing.

1. Warren Ford borrowed $12,000 on a noninterest-bearing, simple discount, $9\frac{1}{2}$%, 60-day note. Assume ordinary interest. What are **(a)** the maturity value, **(b)** the bank's discount, **(c)** Warren's proceeds, and **(d)** the effective rate to the nearest hundredth percent?
2. Jane Long buys a $10,000, 13-week Treasury bill at 6%. What is her effective rate? Round to the nearest hundredth percent.

DVD Solutions with Step-by-Step Help on DVD

✓ Solutions

1. **a.** Maturity value = Face value = $12,000

   b. Bank discount = *MV* × Bank discount rate × Time

   $$= \$12{,}000 \times .095 \times \frac{60}{360}$$

   $$= \$190$$

   c. Proceeds = *MV* − Bank discount
   = $12,000 − $190
   = $11,810

   d. $$\text{Effective rate} = \frac{\text{Interest}}{\text{Proceeds} \times \text{Time}} = \frac{\$190}{\$11{,}810 \times \frac{60}{360}} = \$9.65\%$$

2. $$\$10{,}000 \times .06 \times \frac{13}{52} = \$150 \text{ interest} \qquad \frac{\$150}{\$9{,}850 \times \frac{13}{52}} = 6.09\%$$

LU 11–1a EXTRA PRACTICE QUIZ WITH WORKED-OUT SOLUTIONS

Need more practice? Try this **Extra Practice Quiz** (check figures in Chapter Organizer, p. 284). Worked-out Solutions can be found in Appendix B at end of text.

1. Warren Ford borrowed $14,000 on a noninterest-bearing, simple discount, $4\frac{1}{2}$%, 60-day note. Assume ordinary interest. What are **(a)** the maturity value, **(b)** the bank's discount, **(c)** Warren's proceeds, and **(d)** the effective rate to the nearest hundredth percent?
2. Jane Long buys a $10,000 13-week Treasury bill at 4%. What is her effective rate? Round to the nearest hundredth percent.

Learning Unit 11–2: Discounting an Interest-Bearing Note before Maturity

Manufacturers frequently deliver merchandise to retail companies and do not request payment for several months. For example, Roger Company manufactures outdoor furniture that it delivers to Sears in March. Payment for the furniture is not due until September. Roger will have its money tied up in this furniture until September. So Roger requests that Sears sign promissory notes.

LO 1

If Roger Company needs cash sooner than September, what can it do? Roger Company can take one of its promissory notes to the bank, assuming the company that signed the note is reliable. The bank will buy the note from Roger. Now Roger has discounted the note and has cash instead of waiting until September when Sears would have paid Roger.

Remember that when Roger Company discounts the promissory note to the bank, the company agrees to pay the note at maturity if the maker of the promissory note fails to pay the bank. The potential liability that may or may not result from discounting a note is called a **contingent liability.**

Think of **discounting a note** as a three-party arrangement. Roger Company realizes that the bank will charge for this service. The bank's charge is a **bank discount.** The actual amount Roger receives is the **proceeds** of the note. The four steps below and the formulas in the example that follows will help you understand this discounting process.

DISCOUNTING A NOTE

Step 1. Calculate the interest and maturity value.

Step 2. Calculate the discount period (time the bank holds note).

Step 3. Calculate the bank discount.

Step 4. Calculate the proceeds.

EXAMPLE Roger Company sold the following promissory note to the bank:

Date of note	Face value of note	Length of note	Interest rate	Bank discount rate	Date of discount
March 8	$2,000	185 days	10%	9%	August 9

What are Roger's (1) interest and maturity value (MV)? What are the (2) discount period and (3) bank discount? (4) What are the proceeds?

1. *Calculate Roger's interest and maturity value (MV):*

MV = Face value (principal) + Interest

$$\text{Interest} = \$2{,}000 \times .10 \times \frac{185}{360} \quad \text{Exact number of days over 360}$$

$$= \$102.78$$

$$MV = \$2{,}000 + \$102.78$$

$$= \$2{,}102.78$$

2. *Calculate **discount period:***

Determine the number of days that the bank will have to wait for the note to come due (discount period).

August 9	221 days	
March 8	− 67	
	154 days passed before note is discounted	
	185 days	
	− 154	
	31 days bank waits for note to come due	

Calculating days without table:

March	31
	− 8
	23
April	30
May	31
June	30
July	31
August	9
	154

185 days—length of note
−154 days Roger held note
31 days bank waits

(continued on next page)

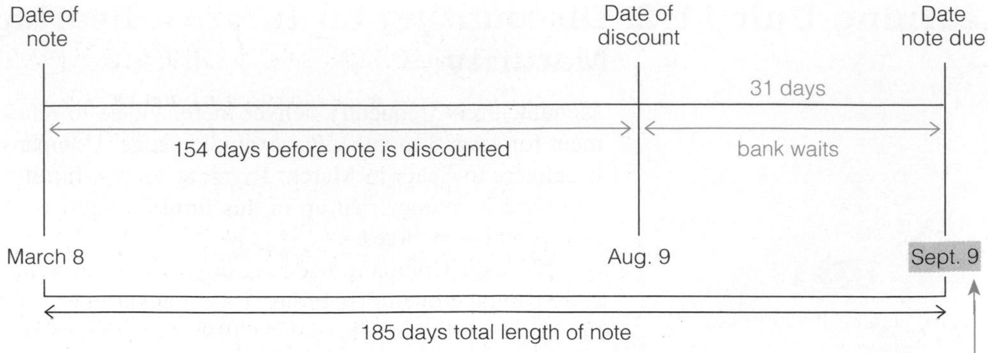

By table: March 8 = 67 days
+ 185
252 search in table

3. *Calculate bank discount (bank charge):*

$$\$2{,}102.78 \times .09 \times \frac{31}{360} = \$16.30$$

$$\text{Bank discount} = MV \times \text{Bank discount rate} \times \frac{\text{Number of days bank waits for note to come due}}{360}$$

4. *Calculate proceeds:*

	\$2,102.78
−	16.30
	\$2,086.48

Step 1

Proceeds = *MV* − Bank discount (charge)

Step 3

If Roger had waited until September 9, it would have received \$2,102.78. Now, on August 9, Roger received \$2,000 plus \$86.48 interest.

MONEY TIPS

Should you lend money to family and friends? Lending money or co-signing on a loan will affect your relationship even if the loan doesn't sour. Always have a written agreement. Consider making it a gift rather than a loan to help preserve the relationship. Up to \$12,000 can be given as a gift with no tax consequences on either side.

Now let's assume Roger Company received a noninterest-bearing note. Then we follow the four steps for discounting a note except the maturity value is the amount of the loan. No interest accumulates on a noninterest-bearing note. Today, many banks use simple interest instead of discounting. Also, instead of discounting notes, many companies set up *lines of credit* so that additional financing is immediately available.

The *Wall Street Journal* clipping "Talbots Loses Credit Lines at 2 Banks" on page 283 shows how the financial banking crises in the fall of 2008 resulted in two banks canceling Talbots line of credit.

The Practice Quiz that follows will test your understanding of this unit.

LU 11–2 PRACTICE QUIZ

Complete this **Practice Quiz** to see how you are doing.

Date of note	Face value (principal) of note	Length of note	Interest rate	Bank discount rate	Date of discount
April 8	\$35,000	160 days	11%	9%	June 8

From the above, calculate **(a)** interest and maturity value, **(b)** discount period, **(c)** bank discount, and **(d)** proceeds. Assume ordinary interest.

Talbots Loses Credit Lines at 2 Bank

Shares of Women's-Clothing Chain Plummet 29% on Nev
New Financing Won't Be Easy or Cheap, Some Analysts

BY DAVID GAFFEN

Ladies and gentlemen, the credit crunch is contained—to the economy.

More evidence of the banking sector's unwillingness to lend erupted at **Talbots** Inc., the women's-clothing chain. Talbots shares dropped 29% Wednesday after the company disclosed in a regulatory filing late Tuesday that two banks had canceled lines of credit.

Bank of America Corp. shut down a $130 million line, while **HSBC Holdings** PLC dumped its $135 million line of credit. The latter is being shaved down every month until it runs out in August.

To some, this doesn't matter. Lazard Capital Market the development is more of a "perception problem" than a reflection of a real liquidity crunch at the chain. They wrote that Talbots plans to rein in its inventory—letters of credit are generally used to stock the shelves—and that even if it doesn't secure a replacement for the lost credit lines, Talbots should generate enough cash during the first half to purchase more stuff to sell.

Others are more concerned. Analysts at D.A. Davidson & Co. downgraded the shares, estimating Talbots' remaining borrowing facilities at around $125 million. Talbots will have to pay $35 million in yearly debt interest and $28 million for its dividend, they note. The retailer had $35.9 million in cash on hand at the end of February.

Oppenheimer & Co. analysts estimate Talbots available credit at about $78 million. "Clearly, Talbots will need to find a new form of financing. But with two major banks walking away it won't be easy, and financing will not be cheap," they write. "In our view, Talbots' best-case scenario is that it will find other LOCs, but at a much higher cost."

Read the continuously updated look inside the markets, free online at **wsj.com/marketbeat**

Are banks willing to put their money to work at **Talbots**?

Solutions with Step-by-Step Help on DVD

✓ Solutions

a. $I = \$35{,}000 \times .11 \times \frac{160}{360} = \boxed{\$1{,}711.11}$

$MV = \$35{,}000 + \$1{,}711.11 = \boxed{\$36{,}711.11}$

b. Discount period $= 160 - 61 = \boxed{99 \text{ days.}}$

April	30
	− 8
	22
May	+ 31
	53
June	+ 8
	61

Or by table:

June 8	159
April 8	− 98
	61

c. Bank discount $= \$36{,}711.11 \times .09 \times \frac{99}{360} = \boxed{\$908.60}$

d. Proceeds $= \$36{,}711.11 - \$908.60 = \boxed{\$35{,}802.51}$

LU 11–2a EXTRA PRACTICE QUIZ WITH WORKED-OUT SOLUTIONS

Need more practice? Try this **Extra Practice Quiz** (check figures in Chapter Organizer, p. 284). Worked-out Solutions can be found in Appendix B at end of text.

From the information below, calculate **(a)** interest and maturity value, **(b)** discount period, **(c)** bank discount, and **(d)** proceeds. Assume ordinary interest.

Date of note	Face value (principal) of note	Length of note	Interest rate	Bank discount rate	Date of discount
April 10	$40,000	170 days	5%	2%	June 10

CHAPTER ORGANIZER AND REFERENCE GUIDE

Topic	Key point, procedure, formula	Example(s) to illustrate situation
Simple discount note, p. 278	Bank discount (interest) = MV × Bank discount rate × Time Interest based on amount paid back and not what received.	$\$6{,}000 \times .09 \times \frac{60}{360} = \$90$ Borrower receives $5,910 (the proceeds) and pays back $6,000 at maturity after 60 days. A Treasury bill is a good example of a simple discount note.
Effective rate, p. 280	$\frac{\text{Interest}}{\text{Proceeds} \times \text{Time}}$ ↑ What borrower receives (Face value − Discount)	*Example:* $10,000 note, discount rate 12% for 60 days. $I = \$10{,}000 \times .12 \times \frac{60}{360} = \$200$ Effective rate: $\frac{\$200}{\$9{,}800 \times \frac{60}{360}} = \frac{\$200}{\$1{,}633.3333} = 12.24\%$ ↑ Amount borrower received
Discounting an interest-bearing note, p. 281	**1.** Calculate interest and maturity value. I = Face value × Rate × Time MV = Face value + Interest **2.** Calculate number of days bank will wait for note to come due (discount period). **3.** Calculate bank discount (bank charge). $MV \times$ Bank discount rate $\times \frac{\text{Number of days bank waits}}{360}$ **4.** Calculate proceeds. MV − Bank discount (charge)	*Example:* $1,000 note, 6%, 60-day, dated November 1 and discounted on December 1 at 8%. **1.** $I = \$1{,}000 \times .06 \times \frac{60}{360} = \$10$ $MV = \$1{,}000 + \$10 = \$1{,}010$ **2.** 30 days **3.** $\$1{,}010 \times .08 \times \frac{30}{360} = \$6.73$ **4.** $\$1{,}010 - \$6.73 = \$1{,}003.27$

KEY TERMS			
	Bank discount, *pp. 278, 281* Bank discount rate, *p. 278* Contingent liability, *p. 281* Discounting a note, *p. 281* Discount period, *p. 281* Effective rate, *p. 280*	Face value, *p. 278* Interest-bearing note, *p. 278* Maker, *p. 278* Maturity date, *p. 278* Maturity value (*MV*), *p. 278* Noninterest-bearing note, *p. 278*	Payee, *p. 278* Proceeds, *pp. 279, 281* Promissory note, *p. 278* Simple discount note, *p. 278* Treasury bill, *p. 280*

CHECK FIGURES FOR EXTRA PRACTICE QUIZZES WITH PAGE REFERENCES. (WORKED-OUT SOLUTIONS IN APPENDIX B.)	LU 11–1a (p. 280)	LU 11–2a (p. 283)
	1. A. $14,000 B. $105 C. $13,895 D. 4.53% **2.** 4.04%	**1.** A. Int. = $944.44; $40,944.44 B. 109 days C. $247.94 D. $40,696.50

Critical Thinking Discussion Questions

1. What are the differences between a simple interest note and a simple discount note? Which type of note would have a higher effective rate of interest? Why?
2. What are the four steps of the discounting process? Could the proceeds of a discounted note be less than the face value of the note?
3. What is a line of credit? What could be a disadvantage of having a large credit line?
4. Discuss the impact of the financial crises of 2009 on small business borrowing.

END-OF-CHAPTER PROBLEMS

Check figures for odd-numbered problems in Appendix C   Name ____________________   Date ________

DRILL PROBLEMS

Complete the following table for these simple discount notes. Use the ordinary interest method.

	Amount due at maturity	Discount rate	Time	Bank discount	Proceeds
11–1.	$14,000	$3\frac{3}{4}$%	280 days		
11–2.	$20,000	$6\frac{1}{4}$%	180 days		

Calculate the discount period for the bank to wait to receive its money:

	Date of note	Length of note	Date note discounted	Discount period
11–3.	April 12	45 days	May 2	
11–4.	March 7	120 days	June 8	

Solve for maturity value, discount period, bank discount, and proceeds (assume for Problems 11–5 and 11–6 a bank discount rate of 9%).

	Face value (principal)	Rate of interest	Length of note	Maturity value	Date of note	Date note discounted	Discount period	Bank discount	Proceeds
11–5.	$50,000	11%	95 days		June 10	July 18			
11–6.	$25,000	9%	60 days		June 8	July 10			

11–7. Calculate the effective rate of interest (to the nearest hundredth percent) of the following Treasury bill.
Given: $10,000 Treasury bill, 4% for 13 weeks.

WORD PROBLEMS

Use ordinary interest as needed.

11–8. Megan Green is interested in taking out a personal loan for $1,500. However, last year an identity theft scam left her with poor credit. Since then she has learned about the perils of identity theft from personal experience as well as from a variety of sources, including the August 18, 2009, article "Avoiding the Identity Theft Underworld" on www.forbes.com. Because of the resulting poor credit score due to the identity theft and the fact that she is providing no collateral, the bank is going to charge her a fee of 2% of her loan amount as well as take out the interest upfront. The bank is offering her 15% APR for six months. Calculate the effective interest rate.

11–9. Bill Blank signed an $8,000 note at Citizen's Bank. Citizen's charges a $6\frac{1}{2}$% discount rate. If the loan is for 300 days, find **(a)** the proceeds and **(b)** the effective rate charged by the bank (to the nearest tenth percent).

11–10. On January 18, 2007, *BusinessWeek* reported yields on Treasury bills. Bruce Martin purchased a $10,000 13-week Treasury bill at $9,881.25. **(a)** What was the amount of interest? **(b)** What was the effective rate of interest? Round to the nearest hundredth percent.

11–11. On September 5, Sheffield Company discounted at Sunshine Bank a $9,000 (maturity value), 120-day note dated June 5. Sunshine's discount rate was 9%. What proceeds did Sheffield Company receive?

11–12. The Treasury Department auctioned $21 billion in three-month bills in denominations of ten thousand dollars at a discount rate of 4.965%. What would be the effective rate of interest? Round your answer to the nearest hundredth percent.

11–13. Annika Scholten bought a $10,000, 13-week Treasury bill at 5%. What is her effective rate? Round to the nearest hundredth percent.

11–14. Ron Prentice bought goods from Shelly Katz. On May 8, Shelly gave Ron a time extension on his bill by accepting a $3,000, 8%, 180-day note. On August 16, Shelly discounted the note at Roseville Bank at 9%. What proceeds does Shelly Katz receive?

11–15. Rex Corporation accepted a \$5,000, 8%, 120-day note dated August 8 from Regis Company in settlement of a past bill. On October 11, Rex discounted the note at Park Bank at 9%. What are the note's maturity value, discount period, and bank discount? What proceeds does Rex receive?

11–16. On May 12, Scott Rinse accepted an \$8,000, 12%, 90-day note for a time extension of a bill for goods bought by Ron Prentice. On June 12, Scott discounted the note at Able Bank at 10%. What proceeds does Scott receive?

11–17. Hafers, an electrical supply company, sold \$4,800 of equipment to Jim Coates Wiring, Inc. Coates signed a promissory note May 12 with 4.5% interest. The due date was August 10. Short of funds, Hafers contacted Charter One Bank on July 20; the bank agreed to take over the note at a 6.2% discount. What proceeds will Hafers receive?

CHALLENGE PROBLEMS

11–18. On March 30, Wade Thompson accepted a nine-month \$32,250 promissory note at 7% interest from one of his clients to pay for some carpentry work he had completed. On April 27, he sold the note to Hammond Bank at 9.5% interest. What were his proceeds?

11–19. Tina Mier must pay a \$2,000 furniture bill. A finance company will loan Tina \$2,000 for 8 months at a 9% discount rate. The finance company told Tina that if she wants to receive exactly \$2,000, she must borrow more than \$2,000. The finance company gave Tina the following formula:

$$\text{What to ask for} = \frac{\text{Amount in cash to be received}}{1 - (\text{Discount} \times \text{Time of loan})}$$

Calculate Tina's loan request and the effective rate of interest to nearest hundredth percent.

SUMMARY PRACTICE TEST

1. On December 12, Lowell Corporation accepted a \$160,000, 120-day, noninterest-bearing note from Able.com. What is the maturity value of the note? *(p. 278)*

2. The face value of a simple discount note is \$17,000. The discount is 4% for 160 days. Calculate the following. *(p. 278)*

   a. Amount of interest charged for each note.

   b. Amount borrower would receive.

   c. Amount payee would receive at maturity.

   d. Effective rate (to the nearest tenth percent).

3. On July 14, Gracie Paul accepted a \$60,000, 6%, 160-day note from Mike Lang. On November 12, Gracie discounted the note at Lend Bank at 7%. What proceeds did Gracie receive? *(p. 281)*

4. Lee.com accepted a \$70,000, $6\frac{3}{4}$%, 120-day note on July 26. Lee discounts the note on October 28 at LB Bank at 6%. What proceeds did Lee receive? *(p. 281)*

5. The owner of Lease.com signed a \$60,000 note at Reese Bank. Reese charges a $7\frac{1}{4}$% discount rate. If the loan is for 210 days, find **(a)** the proceeds and **(b)** the effective rate charged by the bank (to the nearest tenth percent). *(p. 282)*

6. Sam Slater buys a \$10,000, 13-week Treasury bill at $5\frac{1}{2}$%. What is the effective rate? Round to the nearest hundredth percent. *(p. 280)*

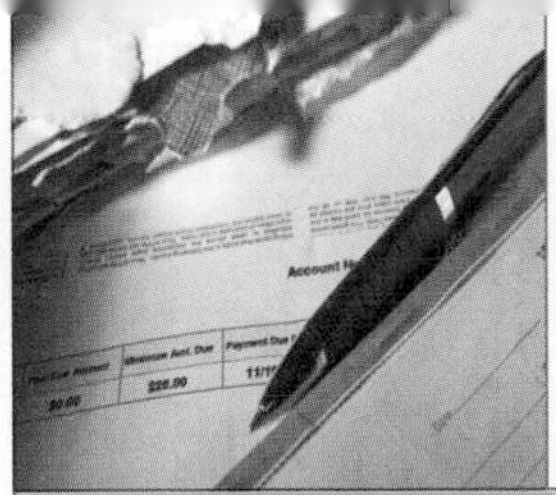

Personal Finance

A KIPLINGER APPROACH

CASH IN HAND
JEFFREY R. KOSNETT

Good Mortgage Bonds

When you lend money to Uncle Sam, you know he'll pay you back. However, the government must plug huge holes in its budget through massive borrowing, and that will inevitably undermine the value of its long-term Treasury bonds. So you face an unpleasant choice: Buy Treasuries, which yield little and could depreciate significantly in the future, or aim for more yield now by taking your money to some of the edgier neighborhoods of the bond market, such as junk bonds and emerging-markets bonds.

But most of us just want a safe investment that pays more than the 3.3% that ten-year Treasuries pay now, or the 3.1% you get from the average five-year CD. Those yields are so paltry you might as well feed an online savings account paying less than 2% while you wait for the economy to recover and interest rates to rise.

The Ginnie alternative. There is, however, an often-overlooked option that is safe and pays more than Treasuries. I'm referring to Ginnie Maes, or mortgage securities guaranteed by the Government National Mortgage Association.

Before you think I've lost my marbles recommending investing in home loans less than a year after mortgage derivatives nearly incinerated the nation's financial system, let me explain. The Ginnie Mae brand is different. Ginnie Mae isn't a company whose executives' overarching goal is to boost the share price; it is an agency within the U.S. Department of Housing and Urban Development that simply stamps Uncle Sam's full faith and credit on pools of conservative, privately issued home loans. Ginnie doesn't mess with exotic mortgages. It mostly guarantees securities that are insured by the likes of the Department of Veterans Affairs and the Federal Housing Administration.

During the financial meltdown, Ginnie Mae securities stood tall. From September 10 through May 8, Vanguard GNMA (symbol VFIIX), the largest mortgage mutual fund, returned 5.1%, three percentage points better than the Barclays Capital U.S. Aggregate Bond index, which tracks the broad bond market. BlackRock GNMA (BGPAX), Fidelity Ginnie Mae (FGMNX) and Payden GNMA (PYGNX) did even better. American Century Ginnie Mae (BGNMX) virtually equaled Vanguard. Dreyfus GNMA (GPGAX), which can put up to 20% of its assets in credit-card receivables and mortgage securities that aren't guaranteed, lagged. But even it gained 4% in those eight months.

GNMA funds got some help from the red tape and scarcity of credit that's made it hard for homeowners to refinance mortgages. Refis, which replace higher paying loans with lower-paying ones, are a headache for investors in mortgage pools. Because of refis, Treasury bonds usually do better than Ginnies when interest rates fall.

"Ginnie Maes are an overlooked option that are safe and pay more than Treasuries."

But Ginnies typically outpace Treasuries when rates go up. Although rising rates will erode some principal, they also make it more likely that older, higher-paying mortgages will remain in the mortgage securities that you or your fund owns. And because Ginnies yield more than Treasuries, their prices will probably fall less when rates rise.

You need $25,000 to buy a single Ginnie. Throw in the complexity of mortgage securities, and this is one area of the bond market in which it often makes more sense to invest in funds rather than individual issues. Besides, funds normally hold some older, higher-rate pools, which can serve as a buffer when yields rise.

I asked a broker for some current quotes on individual GNMA securities. Although the yield spread between Ginnies and Treasuries has narrowed of late, mortgages still pay more. A GNMA pool issued in April was priced to yield about 3.9% on the assumption that half of the loans would be turned over in six and a half years. That's a scant return if you have to worry about heavy defaults. But it's not bad considering Ginnie has Uncle Sam's full faith and credit at her back. ■

JEFF KOSNETT IS A SENIOR EDITOR AT *KIPLINGER'S PERSONAL FINANCE*.

From *Kiplinger's Personal Finance*, July 2009, p. 45.

BUSINESS MATH ISSUE

Treasuries are the best investment when you are in a poor economy.

1. List the key points of the article and information to support your position.
2. Write a group defense of your position using math calculations to support your view.

Slater's Business Math Scrapbook

Applying Your Skills

PROJECT A

Do you agree with bank actions regarding credit lines?

Banks Get Tougher on Credit Line Provisions

By Serena Ng

Banks are shortening the terms on lines of credit that have long been used by companies to avoid cash crunches—a sign that while lending is reviving, businesses are facing new hurdles to obtaining credit.

These revolving lines of credit typically ran for three or five years and let companies borrow at low interest rates, in part because they were rarely drawn upon before the credit crunch. Companies could use the money if they were cut off from other sources of cash such as the commercial-paper market.

Now, lenders are cutting the length of many commitments to less than a year. They are charging higher fees for the lines of credit, known as revolvers. And instead of promising an interest rate determined mainly by the company's credit rating, banks will now charge more if the cost of insuring the company's debt against default is higher.

The trend, unfolding for months, mirrors what's going on in the rest of the credit markets: Lending is occurring again following last year's freeze. But many borrowers are facing tougher terms. As the economy slows, companies are more likely to need extra cash to keep their businesses running. At the same time, rising loan defaults are making banks more cautious. Even the strongest companies must pay more for revolving credit lines, regardless of their plans to use them.

Companies including Hewlett-Packard Co., Baker Hughes Inc. and Verizon Communications Inc. recently obtained new revolvers with such terms, according to Thomson Reuters Loan Pricing Corp.

Internet Projects: See text Web site (www.mhhe.com/slater10e) and The Business Math Internet Resource Guide.

Classroom Notes

chapter

12 COMPOUND INTEREST AND PRESENT VALUE

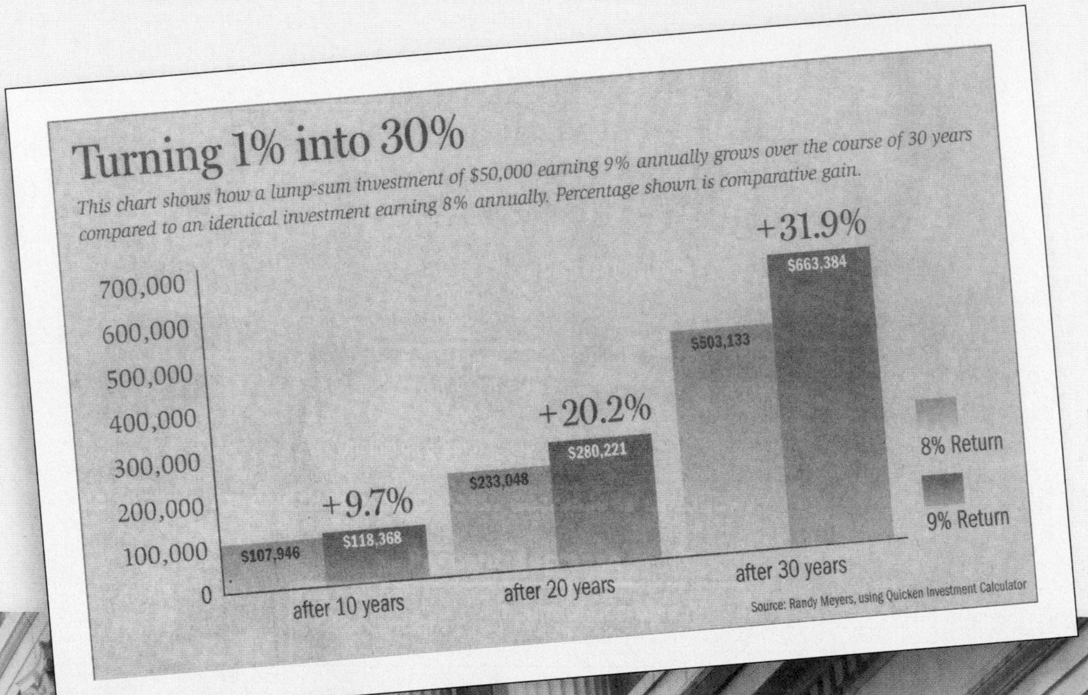

Wall Street Journal © 2007

Royalty-Free/Corbis

LEARNING UNIT OBJECTIVES

Note: A complete set of plastic overlays showing the concepts of compound interest and present value is found in Chapter 13.

LU 12–1: Compound Interest (Future Value)—The Big Picture

1. Compare simple interest with compound interest *(pp. 293–294).*
2. Calculate the compound amount and interest manually and by table lookup *(pp. 295–298).*
3. Explain and compute the effective rate (APY) *(p. 298).*

LU 12–2: Present Value—The Big Picture

1. Compare present value (PV) with compound interest (FV) *(p. 300).*
2. Compute present value by table lookup *(pp. 301–303).*
3. Check the present value answer by compounding *(p. 303).*

VOCABULARY PREVIEW

Here are key terms in this chapter. After completing the chapter, if you know the term, place a checkmark in the parenthesis. If you don't know the term, look it up and put the page number where it can be found.

Annual percentage yield (APY) . ( ) Compound amount . ( ) Compounded annually . ( ) Compounded daily . ( ) Compounded monthly . ( ) Compounded quarterly . ( ) Compounded semiannually . ( ) Compounding . ( ) Compound interest . ( ) Effective rate . ( ) Future value (FV) . ( ) Nominal rate . ( ) Number of periods . ( ) Present value (PV) . ( ) Rate for each period . ( )

KipTip

THE MAGIC OF COMPOUNDING

IF YOU START AT AGE 22, SAVE $100 A MONTH AND EARN AN 8% RETURN UNTIL YOU'RE 65, YOU'LL HAVE

$450,478

IF YOU START AT AGE 32, SAVE $100 A MONTH AND EARN AN 8% RETURN UNTIL YOU'RE 65, YOU'LL HAVE

$194,654

So when should you start saving for retirement? The *Kiplinger* clip "The Magic of Compounding" shows that if you wait 10 years (Age 22 to Age 32) to invest $100 a month at 8% you can lose $255,824 ($450,478 − $194,654).

In this chapter we look at the power of compounding—interest paid on earned interest. Let's begin by studying Learning Unit 12–1, which shows you how to calculate compound interest.

Learning Unit 12–1: Compound Interest (Future Value)—The Big Picture

So far we have discussed only simple interest, which is interest on the principal alone. Simple interest is either paid at the end of the loan period or deducted in advance. From the chapter introduction, you know that interest can also be compounded.

Compounding involves the calculation of interest periodically over the life of the loan (or investment). After each calculation, the interest is added to the principal. Future calculations are on the adjusted principal (old principal plus interest). **Compound interest,** then, is the interest on the principal plus the interest of prior periods. **Future value (FV),** or the **compound amount,** is the final amount of the loan or investment at the end of the last period. In the beginning of this unit, do not be concerned with how to calculate compounding but try to understand the meaning of compounding.

FIGURE 12.1

Future value of $1 at 8% for four periods

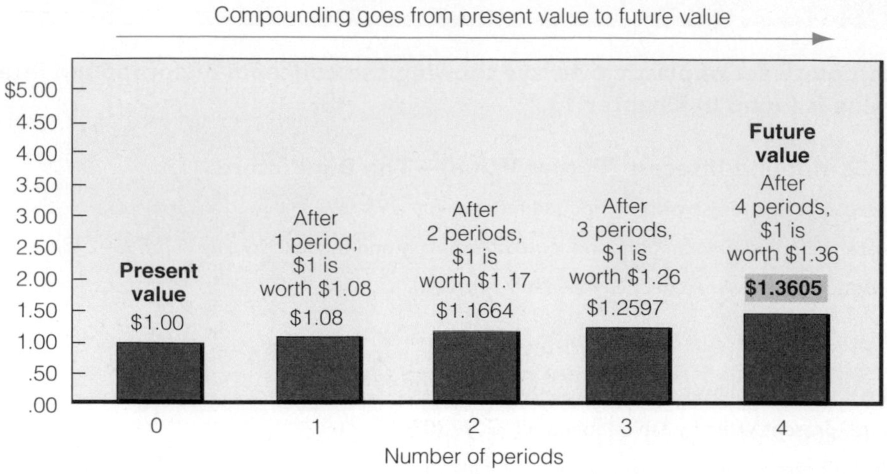

Check out the plastic overlays that appear within Chapter 13 to review these concepts.

Figure 12.1 shows how $1 will grow if it is calculated for 4 years at 8% annually. This means that the interest is calculated on the balance once a year. In Figure 12.1, we start with $1, which is the **present value (PV).** After year 1, the dollar with interest is worth $1.08. At the end of year 2, the dollar is worth $1.17. By the end of year 4, the dollar is worth $1.36. Note how we start with the present and look to see what the dollar will be worth in the future. *Compounding goes from present value to future value.*

Before you learn how to calculate compound interest and compare it to simple interest, you must understand the terms that follow. These terms are also used in Chapter 13.

- **Compounded annually:** Interest calculated on the balance once a year.
- **Compounded semiannually:** Interest calculated on the balance every 6 months or every $\frac{1}{2}$ year.
- **Compounded quarterly:** Interest calculated on the balance every 3 months or every $\frac{1}{4}$ year.
- **Compounded monthly:** Interest calculated on the balance each month.
- **Compounded daily:** Interest calculated on the balance each day.
- **Number of periods:**[1] Number of years multiplied by the number of times the interest is compounded per year. For example, if you compound $1 for 4 years at 8% annually, semiannually, or quarterly, the following periods will result:

  Annually: 4 years × 1 = 4 periods
  Semiannually: 4 years × 2 = 8 periods
  Quarterly: 4 years × 4 = 16 periods

- **Rate for each period:**[2] Annual interest rate divided by the number of times the interest is compounded per year. Compounding changes the interest rate for annual, semiannual, and quarterly periods as follows:

  Annually: 8% ÷ 1 = 8%
  Semiannually: 8% ÷ 2 = 4%
  Quarterly: 8% ÷ 4 = 2%

  Note that both the number of periods (4) and the rate (8%) for the annual example did not change. You will see later that rate and periods (not years) will always change unless interest is compounded yearly.

Now you are ready to learn the difference between simple interest and compound interest.

LO 1

Simple versus Compound Interest

Did you know that money invested at 6% will double in 12 years? The following *Wall Street Journal* clipping "Confused by Investing?" shows how to calculate the number of years it takes for your investment to double.

[1]Periods are often expressed with the letter *N* for number of periods.

[2]Rate is often expressed with the letter *i* for interest.

Confused by Investing?

If there's something about your investment portfolio that doesn't seem to add up, maybe you should check your math.

Lots of folks are perplexed by the mathematics of investing, so I thought a refresher course might help. Here's a look at some key concepts:

■ **10 Plus 10 is 21**

Imagine you invest $100, which earns 10% this year and 10% next. How much have you made? If you answered 21%, go to the head of the class.

Here's how the math works. This year's 10% gain turns your $100 into $110. Next year, you also earn 10%, but you start the year with $110. Result? You earn $11, boosting your wealth to $121.

Thus, your portfolio has earned a *cumulative* 21% return over two years, but the *annualized* return is just 10%. The fact that 21% is more than double 10% can be attributed to the effect of investment compounding, the way that you earn money each year not only on your original investment, but also on earnings from prior years that you've reinvested.

■ **The Rule of 72**

To get a feel for compounding, try the rule of 72. What's that? If you divide a particular annual return into 72, you'll find out how many years it will take to double your money. Thus, at 10% a year, an investment will double in value in a tad over seven years.

The following three situations of Bill Smith will clarify the difference between simple interest and compound interest.

Situation 1: Calculating Simple Interest and Maturity Value

EXAMPLE Bill Smith deposited $80 in a savings account for 4 years at an annual interest rate of 8%. What is Bill's simple interest?

To calculate simple interest, we use the following simple interest formula:

$$\text{Interest } (I) = \text{Principal } (P) \times \text{Rate } (R) \times \text{Time } (T)$$

$$\$25.60 = \$80 \times .08 \times 4$$

In 4 years Bill receives a total of $105.60 ($80.00 + $25.60)—principal plus simple interest.

Now let's look at the interest Bill would earn if the bank compounded Bill's interest on his savings.

Situation 2: Calculating Compound Amount and Interest without Tables[3]

You can use the following steps to calculate the compound amount and the interest manually:

CALCULATING COMPOUND AMOUNT AND INTEREST MANUALLY

Step 1. Calculate the simple interest and add it to the principal. Use this total to figure next year's interest.

Step 2. Repeat for the total number of periods.

Step 3. Compound amount − Principal = Compound interest.

EXAMPLE Bill Smith deposited $80 in a savings account for 4 years at an annual compounded rate of 8%. What are Bill's compound amount and interest?

The following shows how the compounded rate affects Bill's interest:

	Year 1	Year 2	Year 3	Year 4
	$80.00	$86.40	$ 93.31	$100.77
	× .08	× .08	× .08	× .08
Interest	$ 6.40	$ 6.91	$ 7.46	$ 8.06
Beginning balance	+ 80.00	+ 86.40	+ 93.31	+ 100.77
Amount at year-end	$86.40	$93.31	$100.77	$108.83

[3]For simplicity of presentation, round each calculation to nearest cent before continuing the compounding process. The compound amount will be off by 1 cent.

Note that the beginning year 2 interest is the result of the interest of year 1 added to the principal. At the end of each interest period, we add on the period's interest. This interest becomes part of the principal we use for the calculation of the next period's interest. We can determine Bill's compound interest as follows:[4]

Compound amount	$108.83	
Principal	− 80.00	*Note:* In Situation 1 the interest was $25.60.
Compound interest	$ 28.83	

We could have used the following simplified process to calculate the compound amount and interest:

Year 1	Year 2	Year 3	Year 4
$80.00	$86.40	$ 93.31	$100.77
× 1.08	× 1.08	× 1.08	× 1.08
$86.40	$93.31	$100.77	$108.83[5] ← Future value

When using this simplification, you do not have to add the new interest to the previous balance. Remember that compounding results in higher interest than simple interest. Compounding is the *sum* of principal and interest multiplied by the interest rate we use to calculate interest for the next period. So, 1.08 above is 108%, with 100% as the base and 8% as the interest.

LO 2

Situation 3: Calculating Compound Amount by Table Lookup

To calculate the compound amount with a future value table, use the following steps:

CALCULATING COMPOUND AMOUNT BY TABLE LOOKUP

Step 1. Find the periods: Years multiplied by number of times interest is compounded in 1 year.

Step 2. Find the rate: Annual rate divided by number of times interest is compounded in 1 year.

Step 3. Go down the Period column of the table to the number of periods desired; look across the row to find the rate. At the intersection of the two columns is the table factor for the compound amount of $1.

Step 4. Multiply the table factor by the amount of the loan. This gives the compound amount.

In Situation 2, Bill deposited $80 into a savings account for 4 years at an interest rate of 8% compounded annually. Bill heard that he could calculate the compound amount and interest by using tables. In Situation 3, Bill learns how to do this. Again, Bill wants to know the value of $80 in 4 years at 8%. He begins by using Table 12.1 (p. 297).

Looking at Table 12.1, Bill goes down the Period column to period 4, then across the row to the 8% column. At the intersection, Bill sees the number 1.3605. The marginal notes show how Bill arrived at the periods and rate. The 1.3605 table number means that $1 compounded at this rate will increase in value in 4 years to about $1.36. Do you recognize the $1.36? Figure 12.1 showed how $1 grew to $1.36. Since Bill wants to know the value of $80, he multiplies the dollar amount by the table factor as follows:

Four Periods
No. of times compounded in 1 year × No. of years
1 × 4

$80.00 × 1.3605 = $108.84

Principal × Table factor = Compound amount (future value)

8% Rate
$8\% \text{ rate} = \frac{8\%}{1}$ → Annual rate / → No. of times compounded in 1 year

Figure 12.2 (p. 297) illustrates this compounding procedure. We can say that compounding is a future value (FV) since we are looking into the future. Thus,

$108.84 − $80.00 = $28.84 interest for 4 years at 8% compounded annually on $80.00

Now let's look at two examples that illustrate compounding more than once a year.

[4]The formula for compounding is $A = P(1 + i)^N$, where *A* equals compound amount, *P* equals the principal, *i* equals interest per period, and *N* equals number of periods. The calculator sequence would be as follows for Bill Smith: 1 [+] .08 [y^x] 4 × 80 [=] 108.84. A Financial Calculator Guide booklet is available that shows how to operate HP 10BII and TI BA II Plus.

[5]Off 1 cent due to rounding.

TABLE 12.1 Future value of $1 at compound interest

Period	1%	$1\frac{1}{2}$%	2%	3%	4%	5%	6%	7%	8%	9%	10%
1	1.0100	1.0150	1.0200	1.0300	1.0400	1.0500	1.0600	1.0700	1.0800	1.0900	1.1000
2	1.0201	1.0302	1.0404	1.0609	1.0816	1.1025	1.1236	1.1449	1.1664	1.1881	1.2100
3	1.0303	1.0457	1.0612	1.0927	1.1249	1.1576	1.1910	1.2250	1.2597	1.2950	1.3310
4	1.0406	1.0614	1.0824	1.1255	1.1699	1.2155	1.2625	1.3108	1.3605	1.4116	1.4641
5	1.0510	1.0773	1.1041	1.1593	1.2167	1.2763	1.3382	1.4026	1.4693	1.5386	1.6105
6	1.0615	1.0934	1.1262	1.1941	1.2653	1.3401	1.4185	1.5007	1.5869	1.6771	1.7716
7	1.0721	1.1098	1.1487	1.2299	1.3159	1.4071	1.5036	1.6058	1.7138	1.8280	1.9487
8	1.0829	1.1265	1.1717	1.2668	1.3686	1.4775	1.5938	1.7182	1.8509	1.9926	2.1436
9	1.0937	1.1434	1.1951	1.3048	1.4233	1.5513	1.6895	1.8385	1.9990	2.1719	2.3579
10	1.1046	1.1605	1.2190	1.3439	1.4802	1.6289	1.7908	1.9672	2.1589	2.3674	2.5937
11	1.1157	1.1780	1.2434	1.3842	1.5395	1.7103	1.8983	2.1049	2.3316	2.5804	2.8531
12	1.1268	1.1960	1.2682	1.4258	1.6010	1.7959	2.0122	2.2522	2.5182	2.8127	3.1384
13	1.1381	1.2135	1.2936	1.4685	1.6651	1.8856	2.1329	2.4098	2.7196	3.0658	3.4523
14	1.1495	1.2318	1.3195	1.5126	1.7317	1.9799	2.2609	2.5785	2.9372	3.3417	3.7975
15	1.1610	1.2502	1.3459	1.5580	1.8009	2.0789	2.3966	2.7590	3.1722	3.6425	4.1772
16	1.1726	1.2690	1.3728	1.6047	1.8730	2.1829	2.5404	2.9522	3.4259	3.9703	4.5950
17	1.1843	1.2880	1.4002	1.6528	1.9479	2.2920	2.6928	3.1588	3.7000	4.3276	5.0545
18	1.1961	1.3073	1.4282	1.7024	2.0258	2.4066	2.8543	3.3799	3.9960	4.7171	5.5599
19	1.2081	1.3270	1.4568	1.7535	2.1068	2.5270	3.0256	3.6165	4.3157	5.1417	6.1159
20	1.2202	1.3469	1.4859	1.8061	2.1911	2.6533	3.2071	3.8697	4.6610	5.6044	6.7275
21	1.2324	1.3671	1.5157	1.8603	2.2788	2.7860	3.3996	4.1406	5.0338	6.1088	7.4002
22	1.2447	1.3876	1.5460	1.9161	2.3699	2.9253	3.6035	4.4304	5.4365	6.6586	8.1403
23	1.2572	1.4084	1.5769	1.9736	2.4647	3.0715	3.8197	4.7405	5.8715	7.2579	8.9543
24	1.2697	1.4295	1.6084	2.0328	2.5633	3.2251	4.0489	5.0724	6.3412	7.9111	9.8497
25	1.2824	1.4510	1.6406	2.0938	2.6658	3.3864	4.2919	5.4274	6.8485	8.6231	10.8347
26	1.2953	1.4727	1.6734	2.1566	2.7725	3.5557	4.5494	5.8074	7.3964	9.3992	11.9182
27	1.3082	1.4948	1.7069	2.2213	2.8834	3.7335	4.8223	6.2139	7.9881	10.2451	13.1100
28	1.3213	1.5172	1.7410	2.2879	2.9987	3.9201	5.1117	6.6488	8.6271	11.1672	14.4210
29	1.3345	1.5400	1.7758	2.3566	3.1187	4.1161	5.4184	7.1143	9.3173	12.1722	15.8631
30	1.3478	1.5631	1.8114	2.4273	3.2434	4.3219	5.7435	7.6123	10.0627	13.2677	17.4494

Note: For more detailed tables, see your reference booklet, the *Business Math Handbook*.

EXAMPLE Find the interest on $6,000 at 10% compounded semiannually for 5 years. We calculate the interest as follows:

Periods = 2 × 5 years = 10

Rate = 10% ÷ 2 = 5%

10 periods, 5%, in Table 12.1 = 1.6289 (table factor)

$6,000 × 1.6289 = $9,773.40
− 6,000.00
$3,773.40 interest

FIGURE 12.2

Compounding (FV)

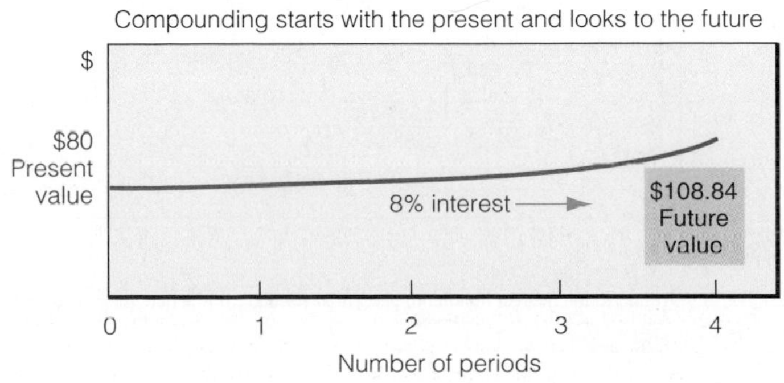

EXAMPLE Pam Donahue deposits $8,000 in her savings account that pays 6% interest compounded quarterly. What will be the balance of her account at the end of 5 years?

Periods = 4×5 years = 20

Rate = $6\% \div 4 = 1\frac{1}{2}\%$

20 periods, $1\frac{1}{2}\%$, in Table 12.1 = 1.3469 (table factor)

$8,000 × 1.3469 = **$10,775.20**

Next, let's look at bank rates and how they affect interest.

Bank Rates—Nominal versus Effective Rates (Annual Percentage Yield, or APY)

Banks often advertise their annual (nominal) interest rates and *not* their true or effective rate (annual percentage yield, or APY). This has made it difficult for investors and depositors to determine the actual rates of interest they were receiving. The Truth in Savings law forced savings institutions to reveal their actual rate of interest. The APY is defined in the Truth in Savings law as the percentage rate expressing the total amount of interest that would be received on a $100 deposit based on the annual rate and frequency of compounding for a 365-day period. As you can see from the advertisement on the left, banks now refer to the effective rate of interest as the annual percentage yield.

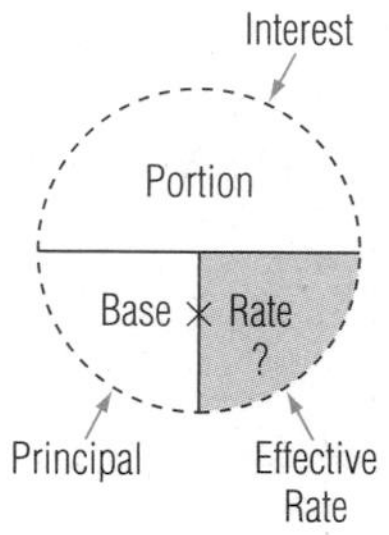

LO 3

Let's study the rates of two banks to see which bank has the better return for the investor. Blue Bank pays 8% interest compounded quarterly on $8,000. Sun Bank offers 8% interest compounded semiannually on $8,000. The 8% rate is the **nominal rate,** or stated rate, on which the bank calculates the interest. To calculate the **effective rate (annual percentage yield, or APY),** however, we can use the following formula:

Effective rate (APY)[6] = $\dfrac{\text{Interest for 1 year}}{\text{Principal}}$

Now let's calculate the effective rate (APY) for Blue Bank and Sun Bank.

Note the effective rates (APY) can be seen from Table 12.1 for $1:
1.0824 ← 4 periods, 2%
1.0816 ← 2 periods, 4%

Blue, 8% compounded quarterly	Sun, 8% compounded semiannually
Periods = 4 (4 × 1)	Periods = 2 (2 × 1)
Percent = $\frac{8\%}{4}$ = 2%	Percent = $\frac{8\%}{2}$ = 4%
Principal = $8,000	Principal = $8,000
Table 12.1 lookup: 4 periods, 2%	Table 12.1 lookup: 2 periods, 4%
1.0824	1.0816
× $8,000	× $8,000
$8,659.20	$8,652.80
Less principal − 8,000.00	− 8,000.00
$ 659.20	$ 652.80
Effective rate (APY) = $\frac{\$659.20}{\$8,000}$ = .0824	$\frac{\$652.80}{\$8,000}$ = .0816
= **8.24%**	= **8.16%**

[6]Round to the nearest hundredth percent as needed. In practice, the rate is often rounded to the nearest thousandth.

FIGURE 12.3

Nominal and effective rates (APY) of interest compared

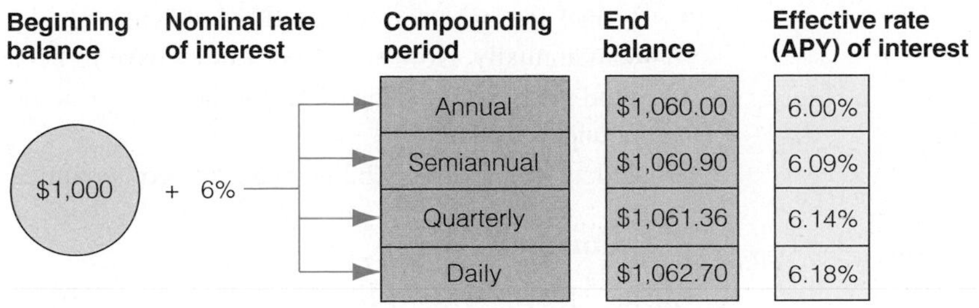

$ MONEY TIPS

The younger you are when you begin saving for retirement, the fewer dollars you will need to invest due to the magnifying affect of compound interest. Begin saving for retirement ***now*** whatever your age is.

Figure 12.3 illustrates a comparison of nominal and effective rates (APY) of interest. This comparison should make you question any advertisement of interest rates before depositing your money.

Before concluding this unit, we briefly discuss compounding interest daily.

Compounding Interest Daily

Although many banks add interest to each account quarterly, some banks pay interest that is **compounded daily,** and other banks use *continuous compounding*. Remember that continuous compounding sounds great, but in fact, it yields only a fraction of a percent more interest over a year than daily compounding. Today, computers perform these calculations.

Table 12.2 is a partial table showing what $1 will grow to in the future by daily compounded interest, 360-day basis. For example, we can calculate interest compounded daily on $900 at 6% per year for 25 years as follows:

$900 × 4.4811 = $4,032.99 daily compounding

TABLE 12.2 Interest on a $1 deposit compounded daily—360-day basis

Number of years	6.00%	6.50%	7.00%	7.50%	8.00%	8.50%	9.00%	9.50%	10.00%
1	1.0618	1.0672	1.0725	1.0779	1.0833	1.0887	1.0942	1.0996	1.1052
2	1.1275	1.1388	1.1503	1.1618	1.1735	1.1853	1.1972	1.2092	1.2214
3	1.1972	1.2153	1.2337	1.2523	1.2712	1.2904	1.3099	1.3297	1.3498
4	1.2712	1.2969	1.3231	1.3498	1.3771	1.4049	1.4333	1.4622	1.4917
5	1.3498	1.3840	1.4190	1.4549	1.4917	1.5295	1.5682	1.6079	1.6486
6	1.4333	1.4769	1.5219	1.5682	1.6160	1.6652	1.7159	1.7681	1.8220
7	1.5219	1.5761	1.6322	1.6904	1.7506	1.8129	1.8775	1.9443	2.0136
8	1.6160	1.6819	1.7506	1.8220	1.8963	1.9737	2.0543	2.1381	2.2253
9	1.7159	1.7949	1.8775	1.9639	2.0543	2.1488	2.2477	2.3511	2.4593
10	1.8220	1.9154	2.0136	2.1168	2.2253	2.3394	2.4593	2.5854	2.7179
15	2.4594	2.6509	2.8574	3.0799	3.3197	3.5782	3.8568	4.1571	4.4808
20	3.3198	3.6689	4.0546	4.4810	4.9522	5.4728	6.0482	6.6842	7.3870
25	4.4811	5.0777	5.7536	6.5195	7.3874	8.3708	9.4851	10.7477	12.1782
30	6.0487	7.0275	8.1645	9.4855	11.0202	12.8032	14.8747	17.2813	20.0772

Now it's time to check your progress with the following Practice Quiz.

LU 12–1 PRACTICE QUIZ

Complete this **Practice Quiz** to see how you are doing.

1. Complete the following without a table (round each calculation to the nearest cent as needed):

Principal	Time	Rate of compound interest	Compounded	Number of periods to be compounded	Total amount	Total interest
$200	1 year	8%	Quarterly	**a.**	**b.**	**c.**

2. Solve the previous problem by using compound value (FV) in Table 12.1.

(continued on next page)

3. Lionel Rodgers deposits $6,000 in Victory Bank, which pays 3% interest compounded semiannually. How much will Lionel have in his account at the end of 8 years?
4. Find the effective rate (APY) for the year: principal, $7,000; interest rate, 12%; and compounded quarterly.
5. Calculate by Table 12.2 what $1,500 compounded daily for 5 years will grow to at 7%.

Solutions with Step-by-Step Help on DVD

✓ Solutions

1. **a.** 4 (4 × 1) **b.** $216.48 **c.** $16.48 ($216.48 − $200)
   $200 × 1.02 = $204 × 1.02 = $208.08 × 1.02 = $212.24 × 1.02 = $216.48
2. $200 × 1.0824 = $216.48 (4 periods, 2%)
3. 16 periods, $1\frac{1}{2}$%, $6,000 × 1.2690 = $7,614
4. 4 periods, 3%,
   $7,000 × 1.1255 = $7,878.50 − 7,000.00 = $ 878.50
   $$\frac{\$878.50}{\$7{,}000.00} = 12.55\%$$
5. $1,500 × 1.4190 = $2,128.50

Check out the plastic overlays that appear within Chapter 13 to review these concepts.

LU 12–1a EXTRA PRACTICE QUIZ WITH WORKED-OUT SOLUTIONS

Need more practice? Try this **Extra Practice Quiz** (check figures in Chapter Organizer, p. 305). Worked-out Solutions can be found in Appendix B at end of text.

1. Complete the following without a table (round each calculation to the nearest cent as needed):

Principal	Time	Rate of compound interest	Compounded	Number of periods to be compounded	Total amount	Total interest
$500	1 year	8%	Quarterly	a.	b.	c.

2. Solve the previous problem by using compound value (FV). See Table 12.1.
3. Lionel Rodgers deposits $7,000 in Victory Bank, which pays 4% interest compounded semiannually. How much will Lionel have in his account at the end of 8 years?
4. Find the effective rate (APY) for the year: principal, $8,000; interest rate, 6%; and compounded quarterly. Round to the nearest hundredth percent.
5. Calculate by Table 12.2 what $1,800 compounded daily for 5 years will grow to at 6%.

Learning Unit 12–2: Present Value—The Big Picture

Figure 12.1 (p. 294) in Learning Unit 12–1 showed how by compounding, the *future value* of $1 became $1.36. This learning unit discusses *present value.* Before we look at specific calculations involving present value, let's look at the concept of present value.

Figure 12.4 shows that if we invested 74 cents today, compounding would cause the 74 cents to grow to $1 in the future. For example, let's assume you ask this question: "If I need $1 in 4 years in the future, how much must I put in the bank *today* (assume an 8% annual interest)?" To answer this question, you must know the present value of that $1 today.

FIGURE 12.4

Present value of $1 at 8% for four periods

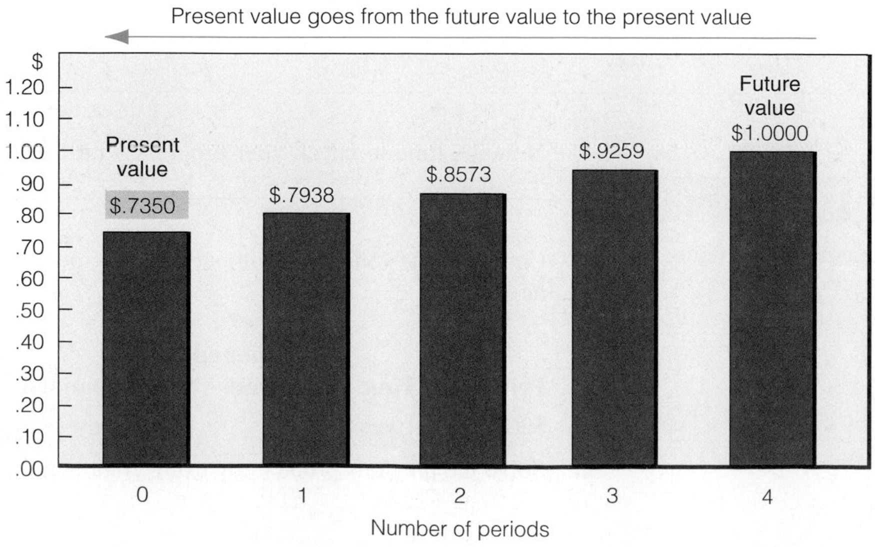

RF/Corbis

From Figure 12.4, you can see that the present value of \$1 is .7350. Remember that the \$1 is only worth 74 cents if you wait 4 periods to receive it. This is one reason why so many athletes get such big contracts—much of the money is paid in later years when it is not worth as much.

Relationship of Compounding (FV) to Present Value (PV)—The Bill Smith Example Continued

LO 1

In Learning Unit 12–1, our consideration of compounding started in the *present* (\$80) and looked to find the *future* amount of \$108.84. Present value (PV) starts with the *future* and tries to calculate its worth in the *present* (\$80). For example, in Figure 12.5, we assume Bill Smith knew that in 4 years he wanted to buy a bike that cost \$108.84 (future). Bill's bank pays 8% interest compounded annually. How much money must Bill put in the bank *today* (present) to have \$108.84 in 4 years? To work from the future to the present, we can use a present value (PV) table. In the next section you will learn how to use this table.

FIGURE 12.5

Present value

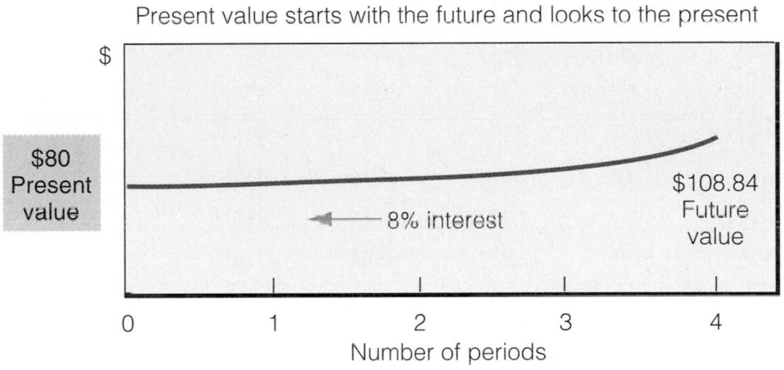

How to Use a Present Value (PV) Table[7]

To calculate present value with a present value table, use the following steps:

LO 2

CALCULATING PRESENT VALUE BY TABLE LOOKUP

Step 1. Find the periods: Years multiplied by number of times interest is compounded in 1 year.

Step 2. Find the rate: Annual rate divided by numbers of times interest is compounded in 1 year.

Step 3. Go down the Period column of the table to the number of periods desired; look across the row to find the rate. At the intersection of the two columns is the table factor for the compound value of \$1.

Step 4. Multiply the table factor times the future value. This gives the present value.

Periods

4 × 1 = 4

No. of years — No. of times compounded in 1 year

Table 12.3 (p. 302) is a present value (PV) table that tells you what \$1 is worth today at different interest rates. To continue our Bill Smith example, go down the Period column in Table 12.3 to 4. Then go across to the 8% column. At 8% for 4 periods, we see a table factor of .7350. This means that \$1 in the future is worth approximately 74 cents today. If Bill invested 74 cents today at 8% for 4 periods, Bill would have \$1.

Since Bill knows the bike will cost \$108.84 in the future, he completes the following calculation:

\$108.84 × .7350 = **\$80.00**

This means that \$108.84 in today's dollars is worth \$80.00. Now let's check this.

[7]The formula for present value is $PV = \frac{A}{(1+i)^N}$, where A equals future amount (compound amount), N equals number of compounding periods, and i equals interest rate per compounding period. The calculator sequence for Bill Smith would be as follows: 1 [+] .08 [y^x] 4 [=] [M+] 108.84 [÷] [MR] [=] 80.03.

TABLE 12.3 Present value of $1 at end period

Period	1%	$1\frac{1}{2}$%	2%	3%	4%	5%	6%	7%	8%	9%	10%
1	.9901	.9852	.9804	.9709	.9615	.9524	.9434	.9346	.9259	.9174	.9091
2	.9803	.9707	.9612	.9426	.9246	.9070	.8900	.8734	.8573	.8417	.8264
3	.9706	.9563	.9423	.9151	.8890	.8638	.8396	.8163	.7938	.7722	.7513
4	.9610	.9422	.9238	.8885	.8548	.8227	.7921	.7629	.7350	.7084	.6830
5	.9515	.9283	.9057	.8626	.8219	.7835	.7473	.7130	.6806	.6499	.6209
6	.9420	.9145	.8880	.8375	.7903	.7462	.7050	.6663	.6302	.5963	.5645
7	.9327	.9010	.8706	.8131	.7599	.7107	.6651	.6227	.5835	.5470	.5132
8	.9235	.8877	.8535	.7894	.7307	.6768	.6274	.5820	.5403	.5019	.4665
9	.9143	.8746	.8368	.7664	.7026	.6446	.5919	.5439	.5002	.4604	.4241
10	.9053	.8617	.8203	.7441	.6756	.6139	.5584	.5083	.4632	.4224	.3855
11	.8963	.8489	.8043	.7224	.6496	.5847	.5268	.4751	.4289	.3875	.3505
12	.8874	.8364	.7885	.7014	.6246	.5568	.4970	.4440	.3971	.3555	.3186
13	.8787	.8240	.7730	.6810	.6006	.5303	.4688	.4150	.3677	.3262	.2897
14	.8700	.8119	.7579	.6611	.5775	.5051	.4423	.3878	.3405	.2992	.2633
15	.8613	.7999	.7430	.6419	.5553	.4810	.4173	.3624	.3152	.2745	.2394
16	.8528	.7880	.7284	.6232	.5339	.4581	.3936	.3387	.2919	.2519	.2176
17	.8444	.7764	.7142	.6050	.5134	.4363	.3714	.3166	.2703	.2311	.1978
18	.8360	.7649	.7002	.5874	.4936	.4155	.3503	.2959	.2502	.2120	.1799
19	.8277	.7536	.6864	.5703	.4746	.3957	.3305	.2765	.2317	.1945	.1635
20	.8195	.7425	.6730	.5537	.4564	.3769	.3118	.2584	.2145	.1784	.1486
21	.8114	.7315	.6598	.5375	.4388	.3589	.2942	.2415	.1987	.1637	.1351
22	.8034	.7207	.6468	.5219	.4220	.3418	.2775	.2257	.1839	.1502	.1228
23	.7954	.7100	.6342	.5067	.4057	.3256	.2618	.2109	.1703	.1378	.1117
24	.7876	.6995	.6217	.4919	.3901	.3101	.2470	.1971	.1577	.1264	.1015
25	.7798	.6892	.6095	.4776	.3751	.2953	.2330	.1842	.1460	.1160	.0923
26	.7720	.6790	.5976	.4637	.3607	.2812	.2198	.1722	.1352	.1064	.0839
27	.7644	.6690	.5859	.4502	.3468	.2678	.2074	.1609	.1252	.0976	.0763
28	.7568	.6591	.5744	.4371	.3335	.2551	.1956	.1504	.1159	.0895	.0693
29	.7493	.6494	.5631	.4243	.3207	.2429	.1846	.1406	.1073	.0822	.0630
30	.7419	.6398	.5521	.4120	.3083	.2314	.1741	.1314	.0994	.0754	.0573
35	.7059	.5939	.5000	.3554	.2534	.1813	.1301	.0937	.0676	.0490	.0356
40	.6717	.5513	.4529	.3066	.2083	.1420	.0972	.0668	.0460	.0318	.0221

Note: For more detailed tables, see your booklet, the *Business Math Handbook.*

Comparing Compound Interest (FV) Table 12.1 with Present Value (PV) Table 12.3

We know from our calculations that Bill needs to invest $80 for 4 years at 8% compound interest annually to buy his bike. We can check this by going back to Table 12.1 and comparing it with Table 12.3. Let's do this now.

LO 3

Compound value Table 12.1					Present value Table 12.3				
Table 12.1		Present value		Future value	Table 12.3		Future value		Present value
1.3605	×	$80.00	=	$108.84	.7350	×	$108.84	=	$80.00
(4 per., 8%)					(4 per., 8%)				
We know the present dollar amount and find what the dollar amount is worth in the future.					We know the future dollar amount and find what the dollar amount is worth in the present.				

FIGURE 12.6

Present value

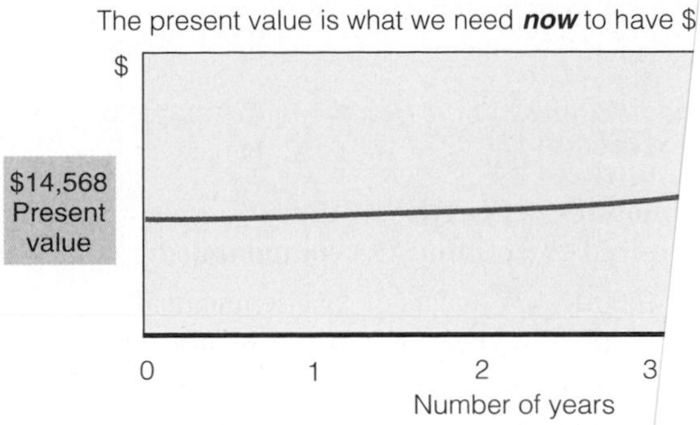

Note that the table factor for compounding is over 1 (1.3605) and the table factor for present value is less than 1 (.7350). The compound value table starts with the present and goes to the future. The present value table starts with the future and goes to the present.

Let's look at another example before trying the Practice Quiz.

$ MONEY TIPS

It is critical to control your debt and make good spending decisions. Because the money you make is finite, you only have one chance to use it wisely. Choosing housing that meets your needs, transportation that fits your budget, investments that meet your retirement goals, insurance that reduces your risk, and taxes that are wisely managed will help prepare you for spending the American average of 20 years in retirement.

EXAMPLE Rene Weaver needs $20,000 for college in 4 years. She can earn 8% compounded quarterly at her bank. How much must Rene deposit at the beginning of the year to have $20,000 in 4 years?

Remember that in this example the bank compounds the interest *quarterly*. Let's first determine the period and rate on a quarterly basis:

$$\text{Periods} = 4 \times 4 \text{ years} = 16 \text{ periods} \qquad \text{Rate} = \frac{8\%}{4} = 2\%$$

Now we go to Table 12.3 and find 16 under the Period column. We then move across to the 2% column and find the .7284 table factor.

$$\$20{,}000 \times .7284 = \$14{,}568$$

(future value) (present value)

We illustrate this in Figure 12.6.

We can check the $14,568 present value by using the compound value Table 12.1:

16 periods, 2% column = 1.3728 × $14,568 = $19,998.95[8]

Let's test your understanding of this unit with the Practice Quiz.

LU 12–2 PRACTICE QUIZ

Complete this **Practice Quiz** to see how you are doing.

Use the present value Table 12.3 to complete:

	Future amount desired	Length of time	Rate compounded	Table period	Rate used	PV factor	PV amount
1.	$ 7,000	6 years	6% semiannually	_____	_____	_____	_____
2.	$15,000	20 years	10% annually	_____	_____	_____	_____

3. Bill Blum needs $20,000 6 years from today to attend V.P.R. Tech. How much must Bill put in the bank today (12% quarterly) to reach his goal?

4. Bob Fry wants to buy his grandson a Ford Taurus in 4 years. The cost of a car will be $24,000. Assuming a bank rate of 8% compounded quarterly, how much must Bob put in the bank today?

DVD *Solutions with Step-by-Step Help on DVD*

✓ Solutions

1. 12 periods (6 years × 2) 3% (6% ÷ 2) .7014 $4,909.80 ($7,000 × .7014)

2. 20 periods (20 years × 1) 10% (10% ÷ 1) .1486 $2,229.00 ($15,000 × .1486)

3. $6 \text{ years} \times 4 = 24 \text{ periods} \quad \frac{12\%}{4} = 3\% \quad .4919 \times \$20{,}000 = \$9{,}838$

4. $4 \times 4 \text{ years} = 16 \text{ periods} \quad \frac{8\%}{4} = 2\% \quad .7284 \times \$24{,}000 = \$17{,}481.60$

[8] Not quite $20,000 due to rounding of table factors.

PRACTICE QUIZ WITH WORKED-OUT SOLUTIONS

e? Try this uiz (check pter Organizer, ked-out Solutions und in Appendix B of text.

Use the *Business Math Handbook* to complete:

	Future amount desired	Length of time	Rate compounded	Table period	Rate used	PV factor	PV amount
1.	$ 9,000	7 years	5% semiannually	_____	_____	_____	_____
2.	$20,000	20 years	4% annually	_____	_____	_____	_____

3. Bill Blum needs $40,000 6 years from today to attend V.P.R. Tech. How much must Bill put in the bank today (8% quarterly) to reach his goal?

4. Bob Fry wants to buy his grandson a Ford Taurus in 4 years. The cost of a car will be $28,000. Assuming a bank rate of 4% compounded quarterly, how much must Bob put in the bank today?

CHAPTER ORGANIZER AND REFERENCE GUIDE

Topic	Key point, procedure, formula	Example(s) to illustrate situation
Calculating compound amount without tables (future value),* p. 293	Determine new amount by multiplying rate times new balance (that includes interest added on). Start in present and look to future. Compound interest = Compound amount − Principal PV —Compounding→ FV	$100 in savings account, compounded annually for 2 years at 8%: $100 × 1.08 = $108 $108 × 1.08 = **$116.64** (future value)
Calculating compound amount (future value) by table lookup, p. 296	$\text{Periods} = \frac{\text{Number of times compounded}}{\text{per year}} \times \text{Years of loan}$ $\text{Rate} = \frac{\text{Annual rate}}{\text{Number of times compounded per year}}$ Multiply table factor (intersection of period and rate) times amount of principal.	*Example:* $2,000 @ 12% 5 years compounded quarterly: Periods = 4 × 5 years = 20 $\text{Rate} = \frac{12\%}{4} = 3\%$ 20 periods, 3% = 1.8061 (table factor) $2,000 × 1.8061 = **$3,612.20** (future value)
Effective rate (APY), p. 298	$\text{Effective rate (APY)} = \frac{\text{Interest for 1 year}}{\text{Principal}}$ or Rate can be seen in Table 12.1 factor.	$1,000 at 10% compounded semiannually for 1 year. By Table 12.1: 2 periods, 5% 1.1025 means at end of year investor has earned 110.25% of original principal. Thus the interest is 10.25%. $1,000 × 1.1025 = $1,102.50 − 1,000.00 $ 102.50 $\frac{\$102.50}{\$1,000} =$ **10.25%** effective rate (APY)
Calculating present value (PV) with table lookup†, p. 301	Start with future and calculate worth in the present. Periods and rate computed like in compound interest. PV ←Present value— FV Find periods and rate. Multiply table factor (intersection of period and rate) times amount of loan.	*Example:* Want $3,612.20 after 5 years with rate of 12% compounded quarterly: Periods = 4 × 5 = 20; % = 3% By Table 12.3: 20 periods, 3% = .5537 $3,612.20 × .5537 = **$2,000.08** Invested today will yield desired amount in future

*$A = P(1 + i)^N$.

†$\frac{A}{(1 + i)^N}$ if table not used.

(continues)

CHAPTER ORGANIZER AND REFERENCE GUIDE

Topic	Key point, procedure, formula	Example(s) to illustrate situation
KEY TERMS	Annual percentage yield (APY), *p. 298* Compound amount, *p. 293* Compounded annually, *p. 294* Compounded daily, *pp. 294, 299* Compounded monthly, *p. 294* Compounded quarterly, *p. 294* Compounded semiannually, *p. 294* Compounding, *p. 293* Compound interest, *p. 293* Effective rate, *p. 298*	Future value (FV), *p. 293* Nominal rate, *p. 298* Number of periods, *p. 294* Present value (PV), *p. 294* Rate for each period, *p. 294*
CHECK FIGURES FOR EXTRA PRACTICE QUIZZES WITH PAGE REFERENCES. (WORKED-OUT SOLUTIONS IN APPENDIX B.)	LU 12–1a (p. 300) **1.** 4 periods; Int. = \$41.22; \$541.21 **2.** \$541.21 **3.** \$9,609.60 **4.** 6.14% **5.** \$2,429.64	LU 12–2a (p. 304) **1.** \$6,369.30 **2.** \$9,128 **3.** \$24,868 **4.** \$23,878.40

Critical Thinking Discussion Questions

1. Explain how periods and rates are calculated in compounding problems. Compare simple interest to compound interest.
2. What are the steps to calculate the compound amount by table? Why is the compound table factor greater than \$1?
3. What is the effective rate (APY)? Why can the effective rate be seen directly from the table factor?
4. Explain the difference between compounding and present value. Why is the present value table factor less than \$1?

Classroom Notes

END-OF-CHAPTER PROBLEMS

connect plus+ www.mhhe.com/slater10e

Check figures for odd-numbered problems in Appendix C.

Name ______________________________ Date __________

DRILL PROBLEMS

Complete the following without using Table 12.1 (round to the nearest cent for each calculation) and then check by Table 12.1 (check will be off due to rounding).

	Principal	Time (years)	Rate of compound interest	Compounded	Periods	Rate	Total amount	Total interest
12–1.	$1,600	2	6%	Semiannually				

Complete the following using compound future value Table 12.1:

	Time	Principal	Rate	Compounded	Amount	Interest
12–2.	12 years	$15,000	$3\frac{1}{2}$%	Annually		
12–3.	6 months	$10,000	8%	Quarterly		
12–4.	3 years	$2,000	12%	Semiannually		

Calculate the effective rate (APY) of interest for 1 year.

12–5. Principal: $15,500
Interest rate: 12%
Compounded quarterly
Effective rate (APY):

12–6. Using Table 12.2, calculate what $700 would grow to at $6\frac{1}{2}$% per year compounded daily for 7 years.

Complete the following using present value of Table 12.3 or *Business Math Handbook* Table.

	Amount desired at end of period	Length of time	Rate	Compounded	On PV Table 12.3: Period used	On PV Table 12.3: Rate used	PV factor used	PV of amount desired at end of period
12–7.	$6,000	8 years	3%	Semiannually				
12–8.	$8,900	4 years	6%	Monthly				
12–9.	$17,600	7 years	12%	Quarterly				

12–10. $20,000 20 years 8% Annually

12–11. Check your answer in Problem 12–9 by the compound value Table 12.1. The answer will be off due to rounding.

WORD PROBLEMS

12–12. Greg Lawrence anticipates he will need approximately $218,000 in 15 years to cover his 3-year-old daughter's college bills for a 4-year degree. How much would he have to invest today, at an interest rate of 8 percent compounded semiannually?

12–13. Lynn Ally, owner of a local Subway shop, loaned $40,000 to Pete Hall to help him open a Subway franchise. Pete plans to repay Lynn at the end of 8 years with 6% interest compounded semiannually. How much will Lynn receive at the end of 8 years?

12–14. Molly Hamilton deposited $50,000 at Bank of America at 8% interest compounded quarterly. What is the effective rate (APY) to the nearest hundredth percent?

12–15. Melvin Indecision has difficulty deciding whether to put his savings in Mystic Bank or Four Rivers Bank. Mystic offers 10% interest compounded semiannually. Four Rivers offers 8% interest compounded quarterly. Melvin has $10,000 to invest. He expects to withdraw the money at the end of 4 years. Which bank gives Melvin the better deal? Check your answer.

12–16. Lee Holmes deposited $15,000 in a new savings account at 9% interest compounded semiannually. At the beginning of year 4, Lee deposits an additional $40,000 at 9% interest compounded semiannually. At the end of 6 years, what is the balance in Lee's account?

12–17. Lee Wills loaned Audrey Chin $16,000 to open Snip Its Hair Salon. After 6 years, Audrey will repay Lee with 8% interest compounded quarterly. How much will Lee receive at the end of 6 years?

12–18. Morningstar.com is a useful personal and business investment site with in-depth detail on personal financial planning. After reading a March 19, 2009, article, "Preparing a Portfolio for Retirement," Arlene Supple, 47 years old, is evaluating her retirement portfolio. She paid her house off in anticipation of an early retirement. In addition, she has invested wisely in her company's 401k, a Roth IRA, municipal bonds, and certificates of deposit. She has amassed $287,000 in her diversified portfolio. Today, she has the opportunity to deposit her money at 4.0% compounded quarterly. If she retires at 54 years old, how much will her investment be worth?

12–19. John Roe, an employee of the Gap, loans $3,000 to another employee at the store. He will be repaid at the end of 4 years with interest at 6% compounded quarterly. How much will John be repaid?

12–20. In the aftermath of the mortgage crisis, Kyle and Mary Ellis from Las Vegas, NV, are considering remodeling their home. They originally wanted to sell their home and move to another area, but news from the *Las Vegas Sun* continues to show a decline in real estate values. Their plan now is to improve their home's curb appeal as well as update the interior. They estimate the cost will be $65,000. How much must they invest today at 6% interest compounded quarterly in order to have the money they need to remodel in 10 years?

12–21. Security National Bank is quoting 1-year certificates of deposit with an interest rate of 5% compounded semiannually. Joe Saver purchased a $5,000 CD. What is the CD's effective rate (APY) to the nearest hundredth percent? Use tables in the *Business Math Handbook.*

12–22. Jim Ryan, an owner of a Burger King restaurant, assumes that his restaurant will need a new roof in 7 years. He estimates the roof will cost him $9,000 at that time. What amount should Jim invest today at 6% compounded quarterly to be able to pay for the roof? Check your answer.

12–23. Tony Ring wants to attend Northeast College. He will need $60,000 4 years from today. Assume Tony's bank pays 12% interest compounded semiannually. What must Tony deposit today so he will have $60,000 in 4 years?

12–24. Could you check your answer (to the nearest dollar) in Problem 12–23 by using the compound value Table 12.1? The answer will be slightly off due to rounding.

12–25. Pete Air wants to buy a used Jeep in 5 years. He estimates the Jeep will cost $15,000. Assume Pete invests $10,000 now at 12% interest compounded semiannually. Will Pete have enough money to buy his Jeep at the end of 5 years?

12–26. Lance Jackson deposited $5,000 at Basil Bank at 9% interest compounded daily. What is Lance's investment at the end of 4 years?

12–27. Paul Havlik promised his grandson Jamie that he would give him $6,000 8 years from today for graduating from high school. Assume money is worth 6% interest compounded semiannually. What is the present value of this $6,000?

12–28. Earl Ezekiel wants to retire in San Diego when he is 65 years old. Earl is now 50. He believes he will need $300,000 to retire comfortably. To date, Earl has set aside no retirement money. Assume Earl gets 6% interest compounded semiannually. How much must Earl invest today to meet his $300,000 goal?

12–29. Jackie Rich would like to buy a $19,000 Toyota hybrid car in 4 years. Jackie wants to put the money aside now. Jackie's bank offers 8% interest compounded semiannually. How much must Jackie invest today?

12–30. John Smith saw the following advertisement. Could you show him how $88.77 was calculated?

9-Month CD **6.05%** *Annual* Percentage Yield*

*As of January 31, 200X, and subject to change. Interest on the 9-month CD is credited on the maturity date and is not compounded. For example, a $2,000, 9-month CD on deposit for an interest rate of 6.00% (6.05% APY) will earn $88.77 at maturity. Withdrawals prior to maturity require the consent of the bank and are subject to a substantial penalty. There is $500 minimum deposit for IRA, SEP IRA, and Keogh CDs (except for 9-month CD for which the minimum deposit is $1,000). There is $1,000 minimum deposit for all personal CDs (except for 9-month CD for which the minimum deposit is $2,000). Offer not valid on jumbo CDs.

CHALLENGE PROBLEMS

12–31. Linda Roy received a $200,000 inheritance after taxes from her parents. She invested it at 4% interest compounded quarterly for 3 years. A year later, she sold one of her rental properties for $210,000 and invested that money at 3% compounded semi-annually for 2 years. Both of the investments have matured. She is hoping to have at least $500,000 in 7 years compounded annually at 2% interest so she can move to Hawaii. Will she meet her goal?

12–32. You are the financial planner for Johnson Controls. Assume last year's profits were $700,000. The board of directors decided to forgo dividends to stockholders and retire high-interest outstanding bonds that were issued 5 years ago at a face value of $1,250,000. You have been asked to invest the profits in a bank. The board must know how much money you will need from the profits earned to retire the bonds in 10 years. Bank A pays 6% compounded quarterly, and Bank B pays $6\frac{1}{2}$% compounded annually. Which bank would you recommend, and how much of the company's profit should be placed in the bank? If you recommended that the remaining money not be distributed to stockholders but be placed in Bank B, how much would the remaining money be worth in 10 years? Use tables in the *Business Math Handbook.** Round final answer to nearest dollar.

*Check glossary for unfamiliar terms.

DVD SUMMARY PRACTICE TEST

1. Lorna Ray, owner of a Starbucks franchise, loaned $40,000 to Lee Reese to help him open a new flower shop online. Lee plans to repay Lorna at the end of 5 years with 4% interest compounded semiannually. How much will Lorna receive at the end of 5 years? *(p. 295)*

2. Joe Beary wants to attend Riverside College. Eight years from today he will need $50,000. If Joe's bank pays 6% interest compounded semiannually, what must Joe deposit today to have $50,000 in 8 years? *(p. 301)*

3. Shelley Katz deposited $30,000 in a savings account at 5% interest compounded semiannually. At the beginning of year 4, Shelley deposits an additional $80,000 at 5% interest compounded semiannually. At the end of 6 years, what is the balance in Shelley's account? *(p. 295)*

4. Earl Miller, owner of a Papa Gino's franchise, wants to buy a new delivery truck in 6 years. He estimates the truck will cost $30,000. If Earl invests $20,000 now at 5% interest compounded semiannually, will Earl have enough money to buy his delivery truck at the end of 6 years? *(pp. 295, 301)*

5. Minnie Rose deposited $16,000 in Street Bank at 6% interest compounded quarterly. What was the effective rate (APY)? Round to the nearest hundredth percent. *(p. 298)*

6. Lou Ling, owner of Lou's Lube, estimates that he will need $70,000 for new equipment in 7 years. Lou decided to put aside money today so it will be available in 7 years. Reel Bank offers Lou 6% interest compounded quarterly. How much must Lou invest to have $70,000 in 7 years? *(p. 301)*

7. Bernie Long wants to retire to California when she is 60 years of age. Bernie is now 40. She believes that she will need $900,000 to retire comfortably. To date, Bernie has set aside no retirement money. If Bernie gets 8% compounded semiannually, how much must Bernie invest today to meet her $900,000 goal? *(p. 301)*

8. Jim Jones deposited $19,000 in a savings account at 7% interest compounded daily. At the end of 6 years, what is the balance in Jim's account? *(p. 294)*

34803
114803

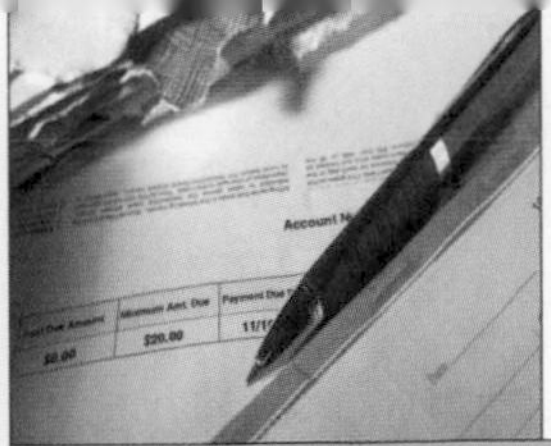

Personal Finance

A KIPLINGER APPROACH

KipTip

How to Find a Better Bank

SMALL BANKS, CREDIT UNIONS AND ONLINE banks are hungry for your business, so they're beating big banks on fees and rates.

Community bank. Go to the Web site of the Independent Community Bankers of America (www.icba.org) and click on "community bank locator."

Credit union. Click on "locate a credit union" at the Credit Union National Association's site (www.creditunion.coop). You may be eligible to join one where you work or live, or because a family member belongs. Some credit unions have other entrees to membership. For example, you can become a member of the Pentagon Federal Credit Union if you join the National Military Family Association for a one-time $20 membership fee.

Online bank. Start at Bankrate.com, which lists the latest interest rates and offers. Click on the "compare rates" tab to find banks with above-average yields. If you find a deal at an online bank that you're not familiar with, make sure the institution is covered by FDIC insurance. Run the bank's name through the agency's Bank Find database (www2.fdic.gov/idasp/main_bankfind.asp).

the accompanying debit card.

Capital One, the credit-card issuer, has been expanding into banking and is offering incentives to attract customers. Recently, you could sign up to earn double rewards on checking accounts. Ira J. Furman, a 65-year-old lawyer in Freeport, N.Y., was already a customer of Capital One. But after receiving a call from the bank, he signed up for a rewards checking account, and he registered his wife, Carole, who will be eligible for a total of 5,000 points for opening a new account and using the bank for direct deposit. In addition, Capital One customers earn rewards for using their debit card, for paying bills online and for making withdrawals. "The rewards-program incentive is, for me, the cherry on top," Furman says.

Savings accounts. If you're looking for a safe parking place for your cash, certificates of deposit are a better deal than money-market funds or Treasury securities. You can earn 2% on a six-month CD at Corus Bank in Illinois (www.corusbank.com) with a $10,000 deposit, or 1.93% at Nexity Bank in Alabama (www.nexity.com) with only a $1,000 deposit. If you commit your funds for a year, you can earn 2.49% at Ally Bank (www.ally.com) with no minimum deposit. Credit unions offer rates on a $10,000, one-year CD that are 0.7 point higher, on average, than bank rates, according to Datatrac.

Loans. Community banks, such as Liberty Bank, compete with credit unions for auto-loan business, so their rates are similar. "Larger institutions charge higher rates because they are not competing for this business," says Dale Blachford, of Liberty Bank.

At banks, car-loan interest rates average 7.04% for 60 months and 7.31% for 36 months, according to Bankrate.com. Liberty charges customers with good credit 5.95% for loans of all lengths. Jim MacPhee, chief executive of Kalamazoo County State Bank, in Michigan, says that at a community bank your credit score isn't the only criterion: "We look the customer in the eye. We try to analyze their credit situation so we understand what they can afford."

Some credit unions offer even lower rates on auto loans. Pentagon Federal Credit Union charges 3.99% for loans from 12 to 60 months. Georgia's Own Credit Union offers loans as low as 5.2% for 60 months. It will also lower your rate by 0.5 point if you buy a hybrid car, and promises members $100 if it can't lower their monthly payments when it refinances their car loan. ■

From *Kiplinger's Personal Finance*, August 2009, p. 46.

BUSINESS MATH ISSUE

Credit unions are always a better choice for CD's than large banks.

1. List the key points of the article and information to support your position.
2. Write a group defense of your position using math calculations to support your view.

Slater's Business Math Scrapbook

Applying Your Skills

PROJECT A

Go to the Web and find out the latest rates for 6-month, 1-year, and 5-year CDs along with the current rates for markets.

GETTING GOING

If You Don't Know Your Math, You'll End Up Taking a Bath

By Jonathan Clements

Maybe we're just lousy at math.

The official savings rate remains stubbornly close to zero, mortgage and consumer debt leapt 7.4% in the 12 months through September, and the Pew Research Center recently reported that half of Americans rate their personal finances as fair or poor.

It's tempting to blame all this on financial recklessness. But consider another culprit: Our feeble math skills. Here's a look at where we go wrong—and how we can do better.

■ Losing interest. In a recent study, marketing professors Eric Eisenstein and Stephen Hoch found that most folks underestimated how much savings would grow and how much debt would end up costing.

The problem: People think in terms of simple interest, not compound interest. For instance, if our investments clock 8% a year for 10 years, we don't earn 80%, as many people assume. Rather, we would notch a cumulative 116%. Remember, we earn returns not only on our original investment, but also on the investment gains earned in earlier years. Similarly, with credit-card debt, we pay interest both on our original purchases and on any monthly interest charges we didn't pay off in full.

"People use simple interest because they don't know to use anything else," says Prof. Eisenstein, of Cornell University's Johnson Graduate School of Management. "The higher the interest rate and the longer the time horizon, the worse the error." He argues that this basic math mistake helps explain why people delay saving for retirement and why they postpone paying off credit-card debt.

■ Guessing wrong. It isn't just credit cards that trip us up. We also don't appreciate how much interest we're paying on loans that promise "low monthly payments," according to new research by Dartmouth College economics professors Victor Stango and Jonathan Zinman.

The two authors analyzed data from the Federal Reserve's 1983 Survey of Consumer Finances. For that survey, consumers were asked how much they would expect to repay in total, assuming 12 monthly payments, if they took out a $1,000 one-year loan to buy furniture.

In response, folks gave answers such as $1,200, which means the effective interest rate was 35%. Yet, when consumers were asked what interest rate was implied, 98% underestimated the rate.

The fewer the number of monthly payments, the more we're likely to underestimate the interest rate charged. Why? When we do our mental calculation, we overlook the fact that, with each monthly payment, we're reducing the loan balance. With a short-term loan, these principal repayments are a big chunk of each monthly payment.

"We know these are hard problems," says Prof. Stango, of Dartmouth's Tuck School of Business. "It isn't surprising that people get the answers wrong. What's really surprising is that people are almost always wrong in the sa[me direction. They] underestimate t[he] ... and they underestimate the costs of borrowing."

■ Getting better. What can we do to avoid these mistakes? Try three strategies:

■ If you're considering a loan with "low monthly payments," ask the lender what the finance charge is as an annual percentage rate. That will tell you whether the monthly payments are truly low.

"People are scared to ask the tough questions," Prof. Stango says. "They're worried about not getting approved for the loan. They don't want to seem naive."

■ To get a handle on the costs of borrowing and the benefits of saving, try playing around with some online financial calculators. You can find a great collection of calculators at www.dinkytown.com.

■ As you toy with whether to spend or save, keep in mind the rule of 72. If you divide 72 by the rate of return you expect to earn, that will tell you how long it takes to double your money.

Think you can earn 7% a year? Divide that into 72, and you will learn that doubling your money takes 10.2 years. The implication: If you saved $1,000, rather than spending it, you would have roughly $2,000 after 10 years, $4,000 after 20 years—and an impressive $8,000 after 30 years.

WSJ.com

ONLINE TODAY: Jonathan Clements answers a question about investing 100% in stocks, at **WSJ.com/Video.**

PROJECT B

List the key points of this article.
Do you disagree with any of these points?

Internet Projects: See text Web site (www.mhhe.com/slater10e) and The Business Math Internet Resource Guide.

chapter

13 ANNUITIES AND SINKING FUNDS

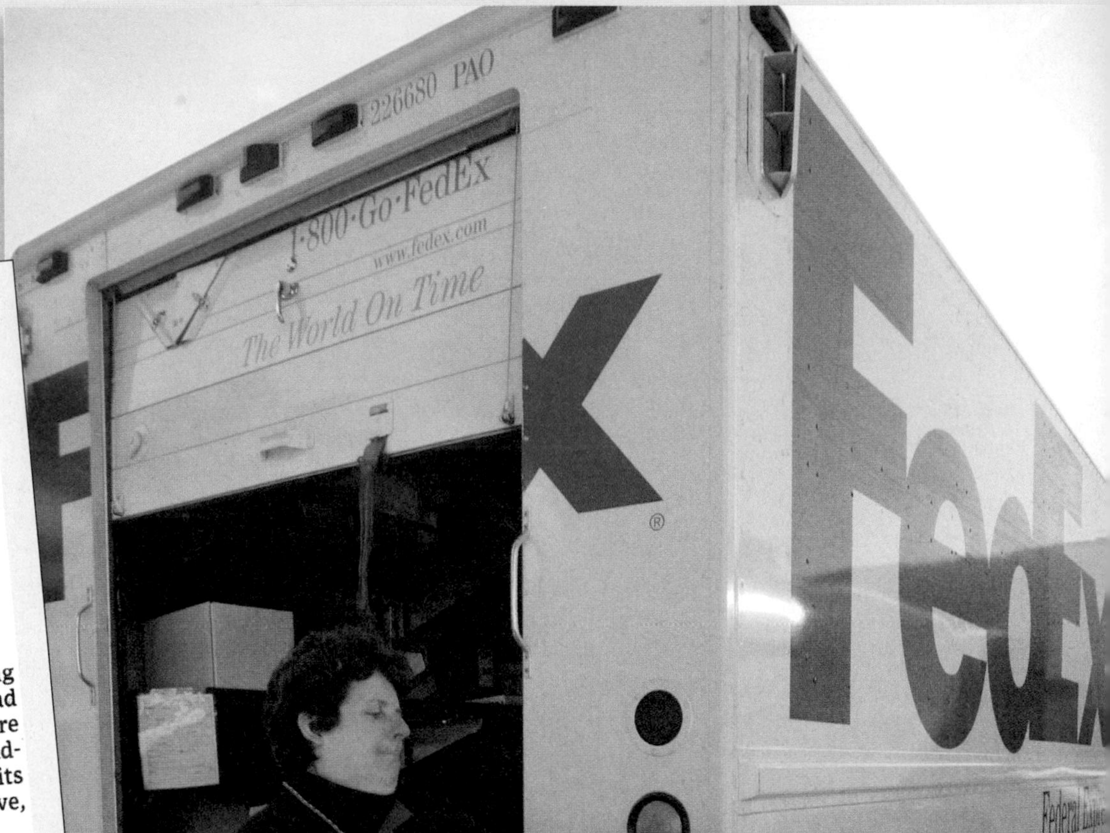

FedEx Joins Other Firms Cutting Pay, Retirement

By Corey Dade And Cari Tuna

FedEx Corp., struggling against intense economic head winds, slashed the pay of more than 35,000 employees, including a 20% base pay cut for its chairman and chief executive, Frederick W. Smith.

The delivery company also said Thursday it will stop contributing to employee retirement plans for at least a year.

FedEx joined a growing list of companies announcing across-the-board pay and benefit cuts or freezes for salaried employees. Compensation experts say salary reductions, as opposed to layoffs, are unusual because executives worry that lower pay for the same work could demoralize employees.

Hoping to shed at least $1 billion in annual costs, Mr. Smith, who founded FedEx 35 years ago, said pay for senior executives and nonunion salaried employees in the U.S. will be cut 5% to 10% as of Jan. 1. The freeze in retirement contributions will affect more than 140,000 workers who participate in the company's 401(k) plan, according to FedEx.

Wall Street Journal © 2008

Paul Sakuma/AP Photo

LEARNING UNIT OBJECTIVES

***Note:* A complete set of plastic overlays showing the concept of annuities is found at the end of the chapter.**

LU 13–1: Annuities: Ordinary Annuity and Annuity Due (Find Future Value)

1. Differentiate between contingent annuities and annuities certain *(p. 317)*.
2. Calculate the future value of an ordinary annuity and an annuity due manually and by table lookup *(pp. 317–321)*.

LU 13–2: Present Value of an Ordinary Annuity (Find Present Value)

1. Calculate the present value of an ordinary annuity by table lookup and manually check the calculation *(pp. 322–324)*.
2. Compare the calculation of the present value of one lump sum versus the present value of an ordinary annuity *(p. 324)*.

LU 13–3: Sinking Funds (Find Periodic Payments)

1. Calculate the payment made at the end of each period by table lookup *(pp. 325–326)*.
2. Check table lookup by using ordinary annuity table *(p. 326)*.

VOCABULARY PREVIEW

Here are key terms in this chapter. After completing the chapter, if you know the term, place a checkmark in the parenthesis. If you don't know the term, look it up and put the page number where it can be found.

Annuities certain . ( ) Annuity . ( ) Annuity due . ( ) Contingent annuities . ( ) Future value of an annuity . ( ) Ordinary annuity . ( ) Payment periods . ( ) Present value of an ordinary annuity . ( ) Sinking fund . ( ) Term of the annuity . ( )

INVESTING YOUR SAVINGS
Assuming the price of coffee remains the same, we added up what you would save if you gave up coffee over 30 years and what you would save if you made coffee at home instead of buying it.

We then invested the savings. We compounded each amount weekly at annual rates: 0 percent, which means you did nothing with the money; at 6 percent, which is an average expected rate of return on a stock portfolio, and at 10 percent, an aggressive expected rate of return.

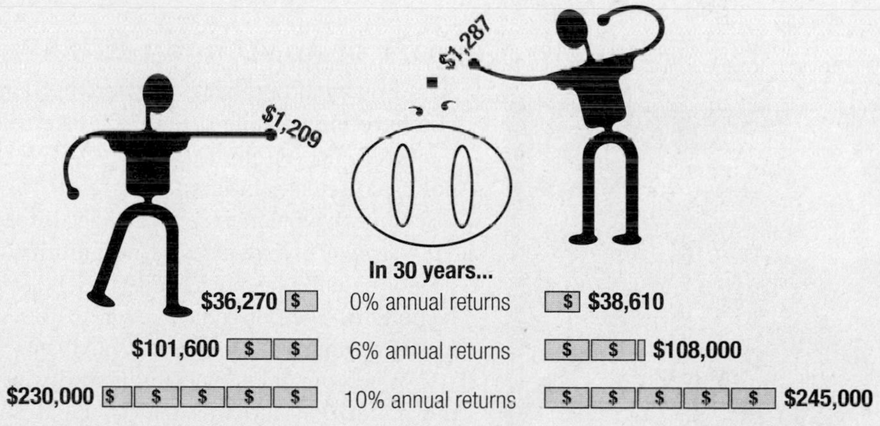

Boston Sunday Globe © 2004

Would you like to save $1,287? A *Boston Globe* article entitled "Cost of Living: A Cup a Day" states at the beginning of the clipping that each month the *Globe* runs a feature on an everyday expense to see how much it costs an average person. Since many people are coffee drinkers, the Globe assumed that a person drank 3 cups a day of Dunkin' Donuts

Tim Boyle/Getty Images

coffee at the cost of $1.65 a cup. For a five-day week, the person would spend $1,287 annually (52 weeks). If the person brewed the coffee at home, the cost of the beans per cup would be $0.10 a cup with an annual expense of $78, saving $1,209 over the Dunkin' Donuts coffee. If a person gave up drinking coffee, the person would save $1,287.

The clipping continued with the discussion on "Investing Your Savings" shown on p. 315. Note how much you would have in 30 years if you invested your money in 0%, 6%, and 10% annual returns. Using the magic of compounding, if you saved $1,287 a year, your money could grow to a quarter of a million dollars.

This chapter shows how to compute compound interest that results from a *stream* of payments, or an annuity. Chapter 12 showed how to calculate compound interest on a lump-sum payment deposited at the beginning of a particular time. Knowing how to calculate interest compounding on a lump sum will make the calculation of interest compounding on annuities easier to understand.

We begin the chapter by explaining the difference between calculating the future value of an ordinary annuity and an annuity due. Then you learn how to find the present value of an ordinary annuity. The chapter ends with a discussion of sinking funds.

Learning Unit 13–1: Annuities: Ordinary Annuity and Annuity Due (Find Future Value)

Many parents of small children are concerned about being able to afford to pay for their children's college educations. Some parents deposit a lump sum in a financial institution when the child is in diapers. The interest on this sum is compounded until the child is 18, when the parents withdraw the money for college expenses. Parents could also fund their children's educations with annuities by depositing a series of payments for a certain time. The concept of annuities is the first topic in this learning unit.

Concept of an Annuity—The Big Picture

Sharon Hoogstraten

All of us would probably like to win $1 million in a state lottery. What happens when you have the winning ticket? You take it to the lottery headquarters. When you turn in the ticket, do you immediately receive a check for $1 million? No. Lottery payoffs are not usually made in lump sums.

Lottery winners receive a series of payments over a period of time—usually years. This *stream* of payments is an **annuity.** By paying the winners an annuity, lotteries do not actually spend $1 million. The lottery deposits a sum of money in a financial institution. The continual growth of this sum through compound interest provides the lottery winner with a series of payments.

When we calculated the maturity value of a lump-sum payment in Chapter 12, the maturity value was the principal and its interest. Now we are looking not at lump-sum payments but at a series of payments (usually of equal amounts over regular **payment periods**) plus the interest that accumulates. So the **future value of an annuity** is the future *dollar amount* of a series of payments plus interest.[1] The **term of the annuity** is the time from the beginning of the first payment period to the end of the last payment period.

[1]The term *amount of an annuity* has the same meaning as *future value of an annuity*.

FIGURE 13.1

Future value of an annuity of $1 at 8%

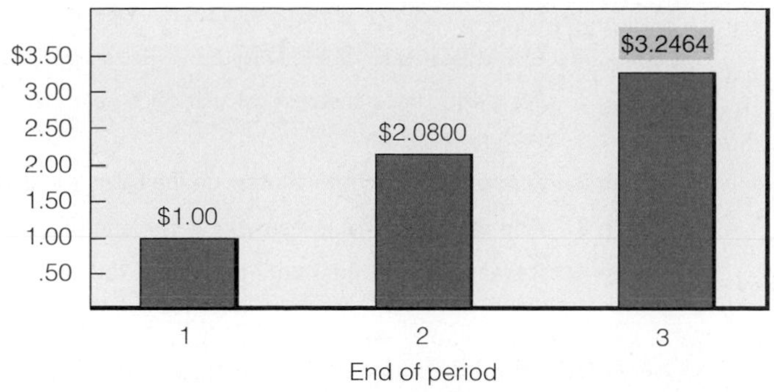

The concept of the future value of an annuity is illustrated in Figure 13.1. Do not be concerned about the calculations (we will do them soon). Let's first focus on the big picture of annuities. In Figure 13.1 we see the following:

At end of period 1:	The $1 is still worth $1 because it was invested at the *end* of the period.
At end of period 2:	An additional $1 is invested. The $2.00 is now worth $2.08. Note the $1 from period 1 earns interest but not the $1 invested at the end of period 2.
At end of period 3:	An additional $1 is invested. The $3.00 is now worth $3.25. Remember that the last dollar invested earns no interest.

Before learning how to calculate annuities, you should understand the two classifications of annuities.

How Annuities Are Classified

Annuities have many uses in addition to lottery payoffs. Some of these uses are insurance companies' pension installments, Social Security payments, home mortgages, businesses paying off notes, bond interest, and savings for a vacation trip or college education.

LO 1

Annuities are classified into two major groups: contingent annuities and annuities certain. **Contingent annuities** have no fixed number of payments but depend on an uncertain event (e.g., life insurance payments that cease when the insured dies). **Annuities certain** have a specific stated number of payments (e.g., mortgage payments on a home). Based on the time of the payment, we can divide each of these two major annuity groups into the following:

1. **Ordinary annuity**—regular deposits (payments) made at the *end* of the period. Periods could be months, quarters, years, and so on. An ordinary annuity could be salaries, stock dividends, and so on.
2. **Annuity due**—regular deposits (payments) made at the *beginning* of the period, such as rent or life insurance premiums.

The remainder of this unit shows you how to calculate and check ordinary annuities and annuities due. Remember that you are calculating the *dollar amount* of the annuity at the end of the annuity term or at the end of the last period.

Ordinary Annuities: Money Invested at End of Period (Find Future Value)

Before we explain how to use a table that simplifies calculating ordinary annuities, let's first determine how to calculate the future value of an ordinary annuity manually.

LO 2

Calculating Future Value of Ordinary Annuities Manually

Remember that an ordinary annuity invests money at the *end* of each year (period). After we calculate ordinary annuities manually, you will see that the total value of the investment comes from the *stream* of yearly investments and the buildup of interest on the current balance.

Check out the plastic overlays that appear in Chapter 13, p. 337A, to review these concepts.

CALCULATING FUTURE VALUE OF AN ORDINARY ANNUITY MANUALLY

Step 1. For period 1, no interest calculation is necessary, since money is invested at the end of the period.

Step 2. For period 2, calculate interest on the balance and add the interest to the previous balance.

Step 3. Add the additional investment at the end of period 2 to the new balance.

Step 4. Repeat Steps 2 and 3 until the end of the desired period is reached.

EXAMPLE Find the value of an investment after 3 years for a $3,000 ordinary annuity at 8%. We calculate this manually as follows:

Step 1. →	End of year 1:	$3,000.00	→ No interest, since this is put in at end of year 1. (Remember, payment is made at end of period.)
	Year 2:	$3,000.00	→ Value of investment before investment at end of year 2.
Step 2. →		+ 240.00	→ Interest (.08 × $3,000) for year 2.
		$3,240.00	→ Value of investment at end of year 2 before second investment.
Step 3. →	End of year 2:	+ 3,000.00	→ Second investment at end of year 2.
	Year 3:	$6,240.00	→ Investment balance going into year 3.
		+ 499.20	→ Interest for year 3 (.08 × $6,240).
Step 4. →		$6,739.20	→ Value before investment at end of year 3.
→		+ 3,000.00	→ Investment at end of year 3.
	End of year 3:	$9,739.20	→ Total value of investment after investment at end of year 3.

Note: We totally invested $9,000 over three different periods. It is now worth $9,739.20

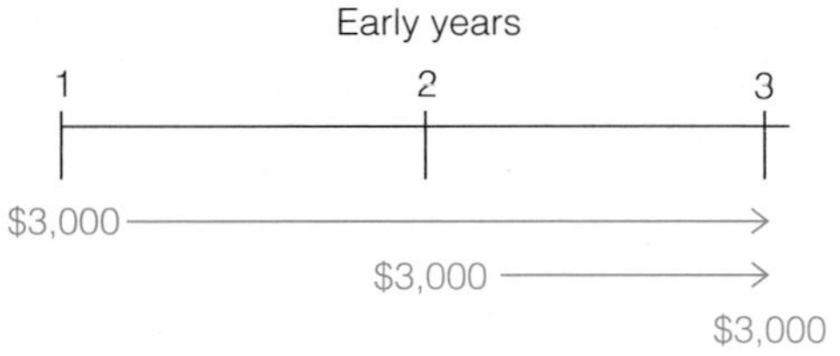

When you deposit $3,000 at the end of each year at an annual rate of 8%, the total value of the annuity is $9,739.20. What we called *maturity value* in compounding is now called the *future value of the annuity.* Remember that Interest = Principal × Rate × Time, with the principal changing because of the interest payments and the additional deposits. We can make this calculation easier by using Table 13.1 (p. 319).

Calculating Future Value of Ordinary Annuities by Table Lookup

Use the following steps to calculate the future value of an ordinary annuity by table lookup.[2]

CALCULATING FUTURE VALUE OF AN ORDINARY ANNUITY BY TABLE LOOKUP

Step 1. Calculate the number of periods and rate per period.

Step 2. Look up the periods and rate in an ordinary annuity table. The intersection gives the table factor for the future value of $1.

Step 3. Multiply the payment each period by the table factor. This gives the future value of the annuity.

$$\text{Future value of ordinary annuity} = \text{Annuity payment each period} \times \text{Ordinary annuity table factor}$$

[2]The formula for an ordinary annuity is $A = Pmt \times \left[\frac{(1+i)^n - 1}{i}\right]$ where A equals future value of an ordinary annuity, Pmt equals annuity payment, i equals interest, and n equals number of periods. The calculator sequence for this example is: 1 [+] .08 = [y^x] 3 [−] 1 [÷] .08 [×] 3,000 [=] 9,739.20. A *Financial Calculator Guide* booklet is available that shows how to operate HP 10BII and TI BA II Plus.

TABLE 13.1 Ordinary annuity table: Compound sum of an annuity of $1

Period	2%	3%	4%	5%	6%	7%	8%	9%	10%	11%	12%	13%
1	1.0000	1.0000	1.0000	1.0000	1.0000	1.0000	1.0000	1.0000	1.0000	1.0000	1.0000	1.0000
2	2.0200	2.0300	2.0400	2.0500	2.0600	2.0700	2.0800	2.0900	2.1000	2.1100	2.1200	2.1300
3	3.0604	3.0909	3.1216	3.1525	3.1836	3.2149	3.2464	3.2781	3.3100	3.3421	3.3744	3.4069
4	4.1216	4.1836	4.2465	4.3101	4.3746	4.4399	4.5061	4.5731	4.6410	4.7097	4.7793	4.8498
5	5.2040	5.3091	5.4163	5.5256	5.6371	5.7507	5.8666	5.9847	6.1051	6.2278	6.3528	6.4803
6	6.3081	6.4684	6.6330	6.8019	6.9753	7.1533	7.3359	7.5233	7.7156	7.9129	8.1152	8.3227
7	7.4343	7.6625	7.8983	8.1420	8.3938	8.6540	8.9228	9.2004	9.4872	9.7833	10.0890	10.4047
8	8.5829	8.8923	9.2142	9.5491	9.8975	10.2598	10.6366	11.0285	11.4359	11.8594	12.2997	12.7573
9	9.7546	10.1591	10.5828	11.0265	11.4913	11.9780	12.4876	13.0210	13.5795	14.1640	14.7757	15.4157
10	10.9497	11.4639	12.0061	12.5779	13.1808	13.8164	14.4866	15.1929	15.9374	16.7220	17.5487	18.4197
11	12.1687	12.8078	13.4863	14.2068	14.9716	15.7836	16.6455	17.5603	18.5312	19.5614	20.6546	21.8143
12	13.4120	14.1920	15.0258	15.9171	16.8699	17.8884	18.9771	20.1407	21.3843	22.7132	24.1331	25.6502
13	14.6803	15.6178	16.6268	17.7129	18.8821	20.1406	21.4953	22.9534	24.5227	26.2116	28.0291	29.9847
14	15.9739	17.0863	18.2919	19.5986	21.0150	22.5505	24.2149	26.0192	27.9750	30.0949	32.3926	34.8827
15	17.2934	18.5989	20.0236	21.5785	23.2759	25.1290	27.1521	29.3609	31.7725	34.4054	37.2797	40.4174
16	18.6392	20.1569	21.8245	23.6574	25.6725	27.8880	30.3243	33.0034	35.9497	39.1899	42.7533	46.6717
17	20.0120	21.7616	23.6975	25.8403	28.2128	30.8402	33.7503	36.9737	40.5447	44.5008	48.8837	53.7390
18	21.4122	23.4144	25.6454	28.1323	30.9056	33.9990	37.4503	41.3014	45.5992	50.3959	55.7497	61.7251
19	22.8405	25.1169	27.6712	30.5389	33.7599	37.3789	41.4463	46.0185	51.1591	56.9395	63.4397	70.7494
20	24.2973	26.8704	29.7781	33.0659	36.7855	40.9954	45.7620	51.1602	57.2750	64.2028	72.0524	80.9468
25	32.0302	36.4593	41.6459	47.7270	54.8644	63.2489	73.1060	84.7010	98.3471	114.4133	133.3338	155.6194
30	40.5679	47.5754	56.0849	66.4386	79.0580	94.4606	113.2833	136.3077	164.4941	199.0209	241.3327	293.1989
40	60.4017	75.4012	95.0254	120.7993	154.7616	199.6346	259.0569	337.8831	442.5928	581.8260	767.0913	1013.7030
50	84.5790	112.7968	152.6669	209.3470	290.3351	406.5277	573.7711	815.0853	1163.9090	1668.7710	2400.0180	3459.5010

Note: This is only a sampling of tables available. The *Business Math Handbook* shows tables from $\frac{1}{2}$% to 15%.

EXAMPLE Find the value of an investment after 3 years for a $3,000 ordinary annuity at 8% (see below).

Step 1. Periods = 3 years × 1 = 3 Rate = $\frac{8\%}{\text{Annually}}$ = 8%

Step 2. Go to Table 13.1, an ordinary annuity table. Look for 3 under the Period column. Go across to 8%. At the intersection is the table factor, 3.2464. (This was the example we showed in Figure 13.1.)

Step 3. Multiply $3,000 × 3.2464 = $9,739.20 (the same figure we calculated manually).

Annuities Due: Money Invested at Beginning of Period (Find Future Value)

In this section we look at what the difference in the total investment would be for an annuity due. As in the previous section, we will first make the calculation manually and then use the table lookup.

Calculating Future Value of Annuities Due Manually

Use the steps that follow to calculate the future value of an annuity due manually.

CALCULATING FUTURE VALUE OF AN ANNUITY DUE MANUALLY

Step 1. Calculate the interest on the balance for the period and add it to the previous balance.

Step 2. Add additional investment at the *beginning* of the period to the new balance.

Step 3. Repeat Steps 1 and 2 until the end of the desired period is reached.

Remember that in an annuity due, we deposit the money at the *beginning* of the year and gain more interest. Common sense should tell us that the *annuity due* will give a higher final value. We will use the same example that we used before.

EXAMPLE Find the value of an investment after 3 years for a \$3,000 annuity due at 8%.

We calculate this manually as follows:

	Beginning year 1:	\$3,000.00	→ First investment (will earn interest for 3 years).
Step 1. →		+ 240.00	→ Interest (.08 × \$3,000).
		\$3,240.00	→ Value of investment at end of year 1.
Step 2. →	Year 2:	+ 3,000.00	→ Second investment (will earn interest for 2 years).
		\$6,240.00	
Step 3. →		+ 499.20	→ Interest for year 2 (.08 × \$6,240).
		\$6,739.20	→ Value of investment at end of year 2.
→	Year 3:	+ 3,000.00	
		\$9,739.20	→ Third investment (will earn interest for 1 year).
		+ 779.14	→ Interest (.08 × \$9,739.20).
	End of year 3:	\$10,518.34	→ At the end of year 3, final value.

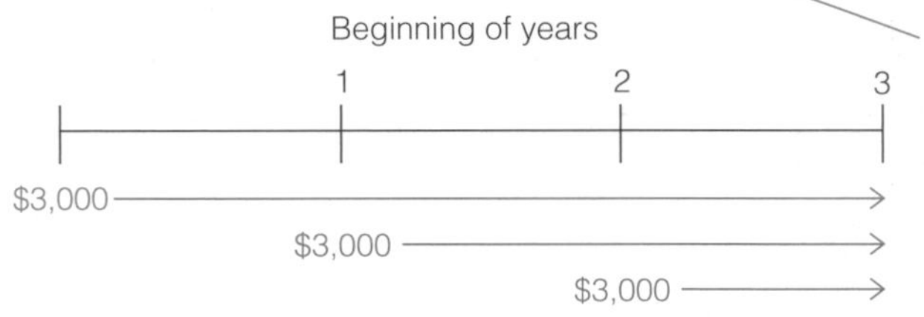

Note: Our total investment of \$9,000 is worth \$10,518.34. For an ordinary annuity, our total investment was only worth \$9,739.20.

Calculating Future Value of Annuities Due by Table Lookup

To calculate the future value of an annuity due with a table lookup, use the steps that follow.

CALCULATING FUTURE VALUE OF AN ANNUITY DUE BY TABLE LOOKUP[3]

Step 1. Calculate the number of periods and the rate per period. Add one extra period.

Step 2. Look up in an ordinary annuity table the periods and rate. The intersection gives the table *factor* for future value of \$1.

Step 3. Multiply payment each period by the table factor.

Step 4. Subtract 1 payment from Step 3.

$$\text{Future value of an annuity due} = \left(\begin{array}{c}\text{Annuity} \\ \text{payment} \\ \text{each period}\end{array} \times \begin{array}{c}\text{Ordinary}^* \\ \text{annuity} \\ \text{table factor}\end{array}\right) - 1 \text{ Payment}$$

*Add 1 period.

Let's check the \$10,518.34 by table lookup.

Step 1. Periods = 3 years × 1 = 3 + 1 extra = 4

Rate $= \frac{8\%}{\text{Annually}} = 8\%$

Step 2. Table factor, 4.5061

Step 3. \$3,000 × 4.5061 = \$13,518.30

Step 4. − 3,000.00 ← Be sure to subtract 1 payment.

= \$10,518.30 (off 4 cents due to rounding)

[3]The formula for an annuity due is $A = Pmt \times \frac{(1+i)^n - 1}{i} \times (1 + i)$, where *A* equals future value of annuity due, *Pmt* equals annuity payment, *i* equals interest, and *n* equals number of periods. This formula is the same as that in footnote 2 except we multiply the future value of annuity by 1 + *i* since payments are made at the beginning of the period. The calculator sequence for this example is: 1 [+] .08 [=] [×] 9,739.20 [=] 10,518.34.

Note that the annuity due shows an ending value of $10,518.30, while the ending value of ordinary annuity was $9,739.20. We had a higher ending value with the annuity due because the investment took place at the beginning of each period.

Annuity payments do not have to be made yearly. They could be made semiannually, monthly, quarterly, and so on. Let's look at one more example with a different number of periods and rate.

Different Number of Periods and Rates

By using a different number of periods and rates, we will contrast an ordinary annuity with an annuity due in the following example:

MONEY TIPS

Consider setting up annuities for a child's college fund. The small monthly payment can add up to a large contribution to his or her education.

EXAMPLE Using Table 13.1 (p. 319), find the value of a $3,000 investment after 3 years made quarterly at 8%.

In the annuity due calculation, be sure to add one period and subtract one payment from the total value.

	Ordinary annuity	Annuity due	
Step 1.	Periods = 3 years × 4 = 12	Periods = 3 years × 4 = 12	**Step 1**
	Rate = 8% ÷ 4 = 2%	Rate = 8% ÷ 4 = 2%	
Step 2.	Table 13.1:	Table 13.1:	**Step 2**
	12 periods, 2% = 13.4120	13 periods, 2% = 14.6803	
Step 3.	$3,000 × 13.4120 = $40,236	$3,000 × 14.6803 = $44,040.90	**Step 3**
		− 3,000.00	**Step 4**
		$41,040.90	

Again, note that with annuity due, the total value is greater since you invest the money at the beginning of each period.

Now check your progress with the Practice Quiz.

LU 13–1 PRACTICE QUIZ

Complete this Practice Quiz to see how you are doing.

1. Using Table 13.1, **(a)** find the value of an investment after 4 years on an ordinary annuity of $4,000 made semiannually at 10%; and **(b)** recalculate, assuming an annuity due.
2. Wally Beaver won a lottery and will receive a check for $4,000 at the beginning of each 6 months for the next 5 years. If Wally deposits each check into an account that pays 6%, how much will he have at the end of the 5 years?

Solutions with Step-by-Step Help on DVD

✓ Solutions

1. a. Step 1. Periods = 4 years × 2 = 8
10% ÷ 2 = 5%
Step 2. Factor = 9.5491
Step 3. $4,000 × 9.5491
= $38,196.40

b. **Step 1** Periods = 4 years × 2
= 8 + 1 − 9
10% ÷ 2 = 5%
Step 2 Factor = 11.0265
Step 3 $4,000 × 11.0265 = $44,106
Step 4 − 1 payment − 4,000
$40,106

2. Step 1. 5 years × 2 = 10
+ 1
11 periods

$\frac{6\%}{2} = 3\%$

Step 2. Table factor, 12.8078
Step 3. $4,000 × 12.8078 = $51,231.20
Step 4. 4,000.00
$47,231.20

LU 13–1a EXTRA PRACTICE QUIZ WITH WORKED-OUT SOLUTIONS

Need more practice? Try this **Extra Practice Quiz** (check figures in Chapter Organizer, p. 327). Worked-out Solutions can be found in Appendix B at end of text.

1. Using Table 13.1, **(a)** find the value of an investment after 4 years on an ordinary annuity of $5,000 made semiannually at 4%; and **(b)** recalculate, assuming an annuity due.
2. Wally Beaver won a lottery and will receive a check for $2,500 at the beginning of each 6 months for the next 6 years. If Wally deposits each check into an account that pays 6%, how much will he have at the end of the 6 years?

Learning Unit 13–2: Present Value of an Ordinary Annuity (Find Present Value)[4]

This unit begins by presenting the concept of present value of an ordinary annuity. Then you will learn how to use a table to calculate the present value of an ordinary annuity.

LO 1

Concept of Present Value of an Ordinary Annuity—The Big Picture

Let's assume that we want to know how much money we need to invest *today* to receive a stream of payments for a given number of years in the future. This is called the **present value of an ordinary annuity.**

In Figure 13.2 you can see that if you wanted to withdraw $1 at the end of one period, you would have to invest 93 cents *today.* If at the end of each period for three periods, you wanted to withdraw $1, you would have to put $2.58 in the bank *today* at 8% interest. (Note that we go from the future back to the present.)

FIGURE 13.2

Present value of an annuity of $1 at 8%

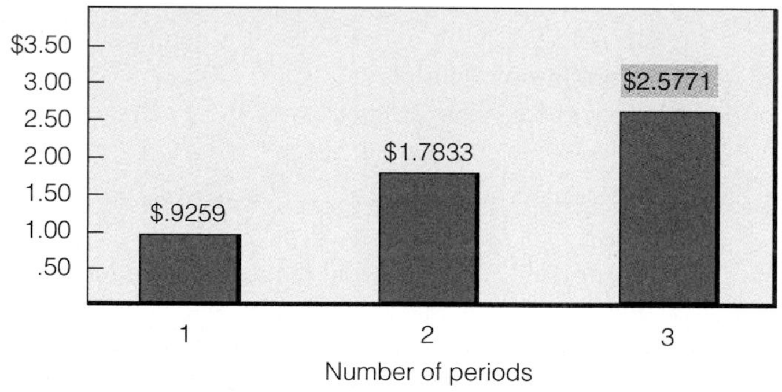

Now let's look at how we could use tables to calculate the present value of annuities and then check our answer.

Calculating Present Value of an Ordinary Annuity by Table Lookup

Use the steps to calculate by table lookup the present value of an ordinary annuity.[5]

CALCULATING PRESENT VALUE OF AN ORDINARY ANNUITY BY TABLE LOOKUP

Step 1. Calculate the number of periods and rate per period.

Step 2. Look up the periods and rate in the present value of an annuity table. The intersection gives the table factor for the present value of $1.

Step 3. Multiply the withdrawal for each period by the table factor. This gives the present value of an ordinary annuity.

$$\text{Present value of ordinary annuity payment} = \text{Annuity payment} \times \text{Present value of ordinary annuity table}$$

[4]For simplicity we omit a discussion of present value of annuity due that would require subtracting a period and adding a 1.

[5]The formula for the present value of an ordinary annuity is $P = Pmt \times \frac{1 - 1 \div (1 + i)^n}{i}$, where P equals present value of annuity, Pmt equals annuity payment, i equals interest, and n equals number of periods. The calculator sequence would be as follows for the John Fitch example: 1 [+] .08 [y^x] 3 [+−] [=] [M+] 1 [−] [MR] [÷] .08 [×] 8,000 [=] 21,000.

TABLE 13.2 Present value of an annuity of $1

Period	2%	3%	4%	5%	6%	7%	8%	9%	10%	11%	12%	13%
1	0.9804	0.9709	0.9615	0.9524	0.9434	0.9346	0.9259	0.9174	0.9091	0.9009	0.8929	0.8850
2	1.9416	1.9135	1.8861	1.8594	1.8334	1.8080	1.7833	1.7591	1.7355	1.7125	1.6901	1.6681
3	2.8839	2.8286	2.7751	2.7232	2.6730	2.6243	2.5771	2.5313	2.4869	2.4437	2.4018	2.3612
4	3.8077	3.7171	3.6299	3.5459	3.4651	3.3872	3.3121	3.2397	3.1699	3.1024	3.0373	2.9745
5	4.7134	4.5797	4.4518	4.3295	4.2124	4.1002	3.9927	3.8897	3.7908	3.6959	3.6048	3.5172
6	5.6014	5.4172	5.2421	5.0757	4.9173	4.7665	4.6229	4.4859	4.3553	4.2305	4.1114	3.9975
7	6.4720	6.2303	6.0021	5.7864	5.5824	5.3893	5.2064	5.0330	4.8684	4.7122	4.5638	4.4226
8	7.3255	7.0197	6.7327	6.4632	6.2098	5.9713	5.7466	5.5348	5.3349	5.1461	4.9676	4.7988
9	8.1622	7.7861	7.4353	7.1078	6.8017	6.5152	6.2469	5.9952	5.7590	5.5370	5.3282	5.1317
10	8.9826	8.5302	8.1109	7.7217	7.3601	7.0236	6.7101	6.4177	6.1446	5.8892	5.6502	5.4262
11	9.7868	9.2526	8.7605	8.3064	7.8869	7.4987	7.1390	6.8052	6.4951	6.2065	5.9377	5.6869
12	10.5753	9.9540	9.3851	8.8632	8.3838	7.9427	7.5361	7.1607	6.8137	6.4924	6.1944	5.9176
13	11.3483	10.6350	9.9856	9.3936	8.8527	8.3576	7.9038	7.4869	7.1034	6.7499	6.4235	6.1218
14	12.1062	11.2961	10.5631	9.8986	9.2950	8.7455	8.2442	7.7862	7.3667	6.9819	6.6282	6.3025
15	12.8492	11.9379	11.1184	10.3796	9.7122	9.1079	8.5595	8.0607	7.6061	7.1909	6.8109	6.4624
16	13.5777	12.5611	11.6523	10.8378	10.1059	9.4466	8.8514	8.3126	7.8237	7.3792	6.9740	6.6039
17	14.2918	13.1661	12.1657	11.2741	10.4773	9.7632	9.1216	8.5436	8.0216	7.5488	7.1196	6.7291
18	14.9920	13.7535	12.6593	11.6896	10.8276	10.0591	9.3719	8.7556	8.2014	7.7016	7.2497	6.8399
19	15.6784	14.3238	13.1339	12.0853	11.1581	10.3356	9.6036	8.9501	8.3649	7.8393	7.3658	6.9380
20	16.3514	14.8775	13.5903	12.4622	11.4699	10.5940	9.8181	9.1285	8.5136	7.9633	7.4694	7.0248
25	19.5234	17.4131	15.6221	14.0939	12.7834	11.6536	10.6748	9.8226	9.0770	8.4217	7.8431	7.3300
30	22.3964	19.6004	17.2920	15.3724	13.7648	12.4090	11.2578	10.2737	9.4269	8.6938	8.0552	7.4957
40	27.3554	23.1148	19.7928	17.1591	15.0463	13.3317	11.9246	10.7574	9.7790	8.9511	8.2438	7.6344
50	31.4236	25.7298	21.4822	18.2559	15.7619	13.8007	12.2335	10.9617	9.9148	9.0417	8.3045	7.6752

EXAMPLE John Fitch wants to receive an $8,000 annuity in 3 years. Interest on the annuity is 8% annually. John will make withdrawals at the end of each year. How much must John invest today to receive a stream of payments for 3 years? Use Table 13.2. Remember that interest could be earned semiannually, quarterly, and so on, as shown in the previous unit.

Step 1. 3 years × 1 = 3 periods $\frac{8\%}{\text{Annually}} = 8\%$

Step 2. Table factor, 2.5771 (we saw this in Figure 13.2)

Step 3. $8,000 × 2.5771 = **$20,616.80**

If John wants to withdraw $8,000 at the end of each period for 3 years, he will have to deposit $20,616.80 in the bank *today.*

	$20,616.80	
+	1,649.34	→ Interest at end of year 1 (.08 × $20,616.80)
	$22,266.14	
−	8,000.00	→ First payment to John
	$14,266.14	
+	1,141.29	→ Interest at end of year 2 (.08 × $14,266.14)
	$15,407.43	
−	8,000.00	→ Second payment to John
	$ 7,407.43	
+	592.59	→ Interest at end of year 3 (.08 × $7,407.43)
	$ 8,000.02	
−	8,000.00	→ After end of year 3 John receives his last $8,000
	.02[6]	

[6]Off due to rounding.

Before we leave this unit, let's work out two examples that show the relationship of Chapter 13 to Chapter 12. Use the tables in your *Business Math Handbook*.

LO 2

Lump Sum versus Annuities

EXAMPLE John Sands made deposits of $200 semiannually to Floor Bank, which pays 8% interest compounded semiannually. After 5 years, John makes no more deposits. What will be the balance in the account 6 years after the last deposit?

Step 1. Calculate amount of annuity: (Table 13.1)

10 periods, 4% $200 × 12.0061 = $2,401.22

Step 2. Calculate how much the final value of the annuity will grow by the compound interest table. (Table 12.1)

12 periods, 4% $2,401.22 × 1.6010 = **$3,844.35**

$ MONEY TIPS

Note how much interest is saved when paying more principal than is required. Paying one extra house payment per year can save you thousands in interest cost while significantly reducing the length of the mortgage.

For John, the stream of payments grows to $2,401.22. Then this *lump sum* grows for 6 years to $3,844.35. Now let's look at a present value example.

EXAMPLE Mel Rich decided to retire in 8 years to New Mexico. What amount should Mel invest today so he will be able to withdraw $40,000 at the end of each year for 25 years *after* he retires? Assume Mel can invest money at 5% interest (compounded annually).

Step 1. Calculate the present value of the annuity: (Table 13.2)

25 periods, 5% $40,000 × 14.0939 = $563,756

Step 2. Find the present value of $563,756 since Mel will not retire for 8 years: (Table 12.3)

8 periods, 5% (PV table) $563,756 × .6768 = **$381,550.06**

If Mel deposits $381,550 in year 1, it will grow to $563,756 after 8 years.

It's time to try the Practice Quiz and check your understanding of this unit.

LU 13–2 PRACTICE QUIZ

Complete this **Practice Quiz** to see how you are doing.

1. What must you invest today to receive an $18,000 annuity for 5 years semiannually at a 10% annual rate? All withdrawals will be made at the end of each period.
2. Rase High School wants to set up a scholarship fund to provide five $2,000 scholarships for the next 10 years. If money can be invested at an annual rate of 9%, how much should the scholarship committee invest today?
3. Joe Wood decided to retire in 5 years in Arizona. What amount should Joe invest today so he can withdraw $60,000 at the end of each year for 30 years after he retires? Assume Joe can invest money at 6% compounded annually.

DVD *Solutions with Step-by-Step Help on DVD*

(Use tables in *Business Math Handbook*)

✓ Solutions

1. **Step 1.** Periods = 5 years × 2 = 10; Rate = 10% ÷ 2 = 5%
   Step 2. Factor, 7.7217
   Step 3. $18,000 × 7.7217 = **$138,990.60**
2. **Step 1.** Periods = 10; Rate = 9%
   Step 2. Factor, 6.4177
   Step 3. $10,000 × 6.4177 = **$64,177**
3. **Step 1.** Calculate present value of annuity: 30 periods, 6%.
   $60,000 × 13.7648 = $825,888
   Step 2. Find present value of $825,888 for 5 years: 5 periods, 6%.
   $825,888 × .7473 = **$617,186.10**

LU 13–2a EXTRA PRACTICE QUIZ WITH WORKED-OUT SOLUTIONS

Need more practice? Try this **Extra Practice Quiz** (check figures in Chapter Organizer, p. 327). Worked-out Solutions can be found in Appendix B at end of text.

1. What must you invest today to receive a $20,000 annuity for 5 years semiannually at a 5% annual rate? All withdrawals will be made at the end of each period.
2. Rase High School wants to set up a scholarship fund to provide five $3,000 scholarships for the next 10 years. If money can be invested at an annual rate of 4%, how much should the scholarship committee invest today?
3. Joe Wood decided to retire in 5 years in Arizona. What amount should Joe invest today so he can withdraw $80,000 at the end of each year for 30 years after he retires? Assume Joe can invest money at 3% compounded annually.

Learning Unit 13–3: Sinking Funds (Find Periodic Payments)

LO 1

A **sinking fund** is a financial arrangement that sets aside regular periodic payments of a particular amount of money. Compound interest accumulates on these payments to a specific sum at a predetermined future date. Corporations use sinking funds to discharge bonded indebtedness, to replace worn-out equipment, to purchase plant expansion, and so on.

A sinking fund is a different type of an annuity. In a sinking fund, you determine the amount of periodic payments you need to achieve a given financial goal. In the annuity, you know the amount of each payment and must determine its future value. Let's work with the following formula:

Sinking fund payment = Future value × Sinking fund table factor[7]

EXAMPLE To retire a bond issue, Moore Company needs $60,000 in 18 years from today. The interest rate is 10% compounded annually. What payment must Moore make at the end of each year? Use Table 13.3.

TABLE 13.3

Sinking fund table based on $1

Period	2%	3%	4%	5%	6%	8%	10%
1	1.0000	1.0000	1.0000	1.0000	1.0000	1.0000	1.0000
2	0.4951	0.4926	0.4902	0.4878	0.4854	0.4808	0.4762
3	0.3268	0.3235	0.3203	0.3172	0.3141	0.3080	0.3021
4	0.2426	0.2390	0.2355	0.2320	0.2286	0.2219	0.2155
5	0.1922	0.1884	0.1846	0.1810	0.1774	0.1705	0.1638
6	0.1585	0.1546	0.1508	0.1470	0.1434	0.1363	0.1296
7	0.1345	0.1305	0.1266	0.1228	0.1191	0.1121	0.1054
8	0.1165	0.1125	0.1085	0.1047	0.1010	0.0940	0.0874
9	0.1025	0.0984	0.0945	0.0907	0.0870	0.0801	0.0736
10	0.0913	0.0872	0.0833	0.0795	0.0759	0.0690	0.0627
11	0.0822	0.0781	0.0741	0.0704	0.0668	0.0601	0.0540
12	0.0746	0.0705	0.0666	0.0628	0.0593	0.0527	0.0468
13	0.0681	0.0640	0.0601	0.0565	0.0530	0.0465	0.0408
14	0.0626	0.0585	0.0547	0.0510	0.0476	0.0413	0.0357
15	0.0578	0.0538	0.0499	0.0463	0.0430	0.0368	0.0315
16	0.0537	0.0496	0.0458	0.0423	0.0390	0.0330	0.0278
17	0.0500	0.0460	0.0422	0.0387	0.0354	0.0296	0.0247
18	0.0467	0.0427	0.0390	0.0355	0.0324	0.0267	0.0219
19	0.0438	0.0398	0.0361	0.0327	0.0296	0.0241	0.0195
20	0.0412	0.0372	0.0336	0.0302	0.0272	0.0219	0.0175
24	0.0329	0.0290	0.0256	0.0225	0.0197	0.0150	0.0113
28	0.0270	0.0233	0.0200	0.0171	0.0146	0.0105	0.0075
32	0.0226	0.0190	0.0159	0.0133	0.0110	0.0075	0.0050
36	0.0192	0.0158	0.0129	0.0104	0.0084	0.0053	0.0033
40	0.0166	0.0133	0.0105	0.0083	0.0065	0.0039	0.0023

LO 2

$ MONEY TIPS

In the personal finance world, using sinking funds to help save for large, infrequent expenses can be a huge stress reliever. Try saving for high-ticket expenses such as insurance or vacations by putting money into a sinking fund you create. By the time the money is needed, you will already have saved it, thereby reducing stress while simultaneously creating a healthy financial situation.

[7]Sinking fund table is the reciprocal of the ordinary annuity table.

We begin by looking down the Period column in Table 13.3 until we come to 18. Then we go across until we reach the 10% column. The table factor is .0219.

Now we multiply $60,000 by the factor as follows:

$60,000 × .0219 = **$1,314**

This states that if Moore Company pays $1,314 at the end of each period for 18 years, then $60,000 will be available to pay off the bond issue at maturity.

We can check this by using Table 13.1 on p. 319 (the ordinary annuity table):

$1,314 × 45.5992 = $59,917.35[8]

It's time to try the following Practice Quiz.

LU 13–3 PRACTICE QUIZ

Complete this **Practice Quiz** to see how you are doing.

Today, Arrow Company issued bonds that will mature to a value of $90,000 in 10 years. Arrow's controller is planning to set up a sinking fund. Interest rates are 12% compounded semiannually. What will Arrow Company have to set aside to meet its obligation in 10 years? Check your answer. Your answer will be off due to the rounding of Table 13.3.

DVD *Solution with Step-by-Step Help on DVD*

✓ Solution

10 years × 2 = 20 periods $\qquad \frac{12\%}{2} = 6\% \qquad$ $90,000 × .0272 = **$2,448**

Check $2,448 × 36.7855 = $90,050.90

LU 13–3a EXTRA PRACTICE QUIZ WITH WORKED-OUT SOLUTIONS

Need more practice? Try this **Extra Practice Quiz** (check figures in Chapter Organizer, p. 327). Worked-out Solutions can be found in Appendix B at end of text.

Today Arrow Company issued bonds that will mature to a value of $120,000 in 20 years. Arrow's controller is planning to set up a sinking fund. Interest rates are 6% compounded semiannually. What will Arrow Company have to set aside to meet its obligation in 10 years? Check your answer. Your answer will be off due to rounding of Table 13.3.

[8]Off due to rounding.

CHAPTER ORGANIZER AND REFERENCE GUIDE

Topic	Key point, procedure, formula	Example(s) to illustrate situation
Ordinary annuities (find future value), p. 317–319	Invest money at end of each period. Find future value at maturity. Answers question of how much money accumulates. Future value of ordinary annuity = Annuity payment each period × Ordinary annuity table factor $FV = PMT\left[\frac{(1+i)^n - 1}{i}\right]$	Use Table 13.1: 2 years, $4,000 ordinary annuity at 8% annually. Value = $4,000 × 2.0800 = **$8,320** (2 periods, 8%) $FV = 4{,}000\left[\frac{(1+.08)^2 - 1}{.08}\right] = \$8{,}320$

(continues)

CHAPTER ORGANIZER AND REFERENCE GUIDE

Topic	Key point, procedure, formula	Example(s) to illustrate situation
Annuities due (find future value), p. 319–321	Invest money at beginning of each period. Find future value at maturity. Should be higher than ordinary annuity since it is invested at beginning of each period. Use Table 13.1, but add one period and subtract one payment from answer. Future value of an annuity due = (Annuity payment each period × Ordinary* annuity table factor) − 1 Payment *Add 1 period. $FV_{due} = PMT\left[\frac{(1+i)^n - 1}{i}\right](1+i)$	*Example:* Same example as above but invest money at beginning of period. $4,000 × 3.2464 = $12,985.60 − 4,000.00 **$ 8,985.60** (3 periods, 8%) $FV_{due} = 4{,}000\left(\frac{(1+.08)^2 - 1}{.08}\right)(1+.08)$ = $8,985.60
Present value of an ordinary annuity (find present value), p. 322–324	Calculate number of periods and rate per period. Use Table 13.2 to find table factor for present value of $1. Multiply withdrawal for each period by table factor to get present value of an ordinary annuity. Present value of an ordinary annuity payment = Annuity payment × Present value of ordinary annuity table $PV = PMT\left[\frac{1-(1+i)^{-n}}{i}\right]$	*Example:* Receive $10,000 for 5 years. Interest is 10% compounded annually. Table 13.2: 5 periods, 10% 3.7908 × $10,000 What you put in today = **$37,908** $PV = 10{,}000\left[\frac{1-(1+.1)^{-5}}{.1}\right] = \$37{,}907.88$
Sinking funds (find periodic payment), p. 325	Paying a particular amount of money for a set number of periodic payments to accumulate a specific sum. We know the future and must calculate the periodic payments needed. Answer can be proved by ordinary annuity table. Sinking fund payment = Future value × Sinking fund table factor	*Example:* $200,000 bond to retire 15 years from now. Interest is 6% compounded annually. By Table 13.3: $200,000 × .0430 = **$8,600** Check by Table 13.1: $8,600 × 23.2759 = $200,172.74

KEY TERMS	Annuities certain, *p. 317* Annuity, *p. 316* Annuity due, *p. 317* Contingent annuities, *p. 317*	Future value of an annuity, *p. 316* Ordinary annuity, *p. 317* Payment periods, *p. 316*	Present value of an ordinary annuity, *p. 322* Sinking fund, *p. 325* Term of the annuity, *p. 316*

CHECK FIGURES FOR EXTRA PRACTICE QUIZZES WITH PAGE REFERENCES. (WORKED-OUT SOLUTIONS IN APPENDIX A.)	LU 13–1a (p. 322) **1.** a. $42,914.50 b. $43,773 **2.** $36,544.50	LU 13–2a (p. 325) **1.** $175,042 **2.** $121,663.50 **3.** $1,352,584.40	LU 13–3a (p. 326) $1,596

Critical Thinking Discussion Questions

1. What is the difference between an ordinary annuity and an annuity due? If you were to save money in an annuity, which would you choose and why?
2. Explain how you would calculate ordinary annuities and annuities due by table lookup. Create an example to explain the meaning of a table factor from an ordinary annuity.
3. What is a present value of an ordinary annuity? Create an example showing how one of your relatives might plan for retirement by using the present value of an ordinary annuity. Would you ever have to use lump-sum payments in your calculation from Chapter 12?
4. What is a sinking fund? Why could an ordinary annuity table be used to check the sinking fund payment?
5. With the tight economy, more businesses such as FedEx are cutting back on matching the retirement contributions of its employees (see chapter opener). Do you think this is ethical?

END-OF-CHAPTER PROBLEMS

connect plus+ www.mhhe.com/slater10e

Check figures for odd-numbered problems in Appendix C.

Name ________________ Date ________

DRILL PROBLEMS

Complete the ordinary annuities for the following using tables in the *Business Math Handbook:*

	Amount of payment	Payment payable	Years	Interest rate	Value of annuity
13–1.	$15,000	Quarterly	8	6%	
13–2.	$7,000	Semiannually	8	7%	

Redo Problem 13–1 as an annuity due:

13–3.

Calculate the value of the following annuity due without a table. Check your results by Table 13.1 or the *Business Math Handbook* (they will be slightly off due to rounding):

	Amount of payment	Payment payable	Years	Interest rate
13–4.	$2,000	Annually	3	6%

Complete the following using Table 13.2 or the *Business Math Handbook* for the present value of an ordinary annuity.

	Amount of annuity expected	Payment	Time	Interest rate	Present value (amount needed now to invest to receive annuity)
13–5.	$900	Annually	4 years	6%	
13–6.	$15,000	Quarterly	4 years	8%	

13–7. Check Problem 13–5 without the use of Table 13.2.

Using the sinking fund Table 13.3 or the *Business Math Handbook,* complete the following:

	Required amount	Frequency of payment	Length of time	Interest rate	Payment amount end of each period
13–8.	$25,000	Quarterly	6 years	8%	
13–9.	$15,000	Annually	8 years	8%	

13–10. Check the answer in Problem 13–9 by Table 13.1.

WORD PROBLEMS (Use Tables in the *Business Math Handbook*)

13–11. John Regan, an employee at Home Depot, made deposits of $800 at the end of each year for 4 years. Interest is 4% compounded annually. What is the value of Regan's annuity at the end of 4 years?

13–12. Ed Long promised to pay his son $400 semiannually for 12 years. Assume Ed can invest his money at 6% in an ordinary annuity. How much must Ed invest today to pay his son $400 semiannually for 12 years?

13–13. "The most powerful force in the universe is compound interest," according to an article in the *Morningstar Column* dated February 13, 2007. Patricia Wiseman is 30 years old and she invests $2,000 in an annuity, earning 5% compound annual return at the beginning of each period, for 18 years. What is the cash value of this annuity due at the end of 18 years?

13–14. *RaisingMaine* magazine's August 5, 2009, "Home GREEN Home" article about going green discusses ways to improve a home's energy efficiency while keeping conservation in mind. From an efficient floor plan, to a house plan maximizing sunlight, triple-pane glass windows, radiant floor heating, and the use of recycled materials, the goal is to reduce the amount of fossil fuels consumed. Jim and Sonja Tanner were inspired by the article and are beginning the planning process for updating their home to reduce its environmental footprint. They received an initial quote of $23,500. What payment must they make at the end of each quarter at 8% compounded quarterly for five years to reach their goal of $23,500?

13–15. The average American has $99 lying about. Stick $99 in an ordinary annuity account each year for 10 years at 5% interest and watch it grow. What is the cash value of this annuity at the end of year 10? Round to the nearest dollar.

13–16. Patricia and Joe Payne are divorced. The divorce settlement stipulated that Joe pay $525 a month for their daughter Suzanne until she turns 18 in 4 years. How much must Joe set aside today to meet the settlement? Interest is 6% a year.

13–17. Josef Company borrowed money that must be repaid in 20 years. The company wants to make sure the loan will be repaid at the end of year 20. So it invests $12,500 at the end of each year at 12% interest compounded annually. What was the amount of the original loan?

13–18. Jane Frost wants to receive yearly payments of $15,000 for 10 years. How much must she deposit at her bank today at 11% interest compounded annually?

13–19. Toby Martin invests $2,000 at the end of each year for 10 years in an ordinary annuity at 11% interest compounded annually. What is the final value of Toby's investment at the end of year 10?

13–20. Alice Longtree has decided to invest $400 quarterly for 4 years in an ordinary annuity at 8%. As her financial adviser, calculate for Alice the total cash value of the annuity at the end of year 4.

13–21. At the beginning of each period for 10 years, Merl Agnes invests $500 semiannually at 6%. What is the cash value of this annuity due at the end of year 10?

13–22. Jeff Associates borrowed $30,000. The company plans to set up a sinking fund that will repay the loan at the end of 8 years. Assume a 12% interest rate compounded semiannually. What must Jeff pay into the fund each period of time? Check your answer by Table 13.1.

13–23. On Joe Martin's graduation from college, Joe's uncle promised him a gift of $12,000 in cash or $900 every quarter for the next 4 years after graduation. If money could be invested at 8% compounded quarterly, which offer is better for Joe?

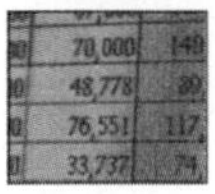

13–24. You are earning an average of $46,500 and will retire in 10 years. If you put 20% of your gross average income in an ordinary annuity compounded at 7% annually, what will be the value of the annuity when you retire?

13–25. A local Dunkin' Donuts franchise must buy a new piece of equipment in 5 years that will cost $88,000. The company is setting up a sinking fund to finance the purchase. What will the quarterly deposit be if the fund earns 8% interest?

13–26. Mike Macaro is selling a piece of land. Two offers are on the table. Morton Company offered a $40,000 down payment and $35,000 a year for the next 5 years. Flynn Company offered $25,000 down and $38,000 a year for the next 5 years. If money can be invested at 8% compounded annually, which offer is better for Mike?

13–27. Al Vincent has decided to retire to Arizona in 10 years. What amount should Al invest today so that he will be able to withdraw $28,000 at the end of each year for 15 years *after* he retires? Assume he can invest the money at 8% interest compounded annually.

13–28. Victor French made deposits of $5,000 at the end of each quarter to Book Bank, which pays 8% interest compounded quarterly. After 3 years, Victor made no more deposits. What will be the balance in the account 2 years after the last deposit?

13–29. Janet Woo decided to retire to Florida in 6 years. What amount should Janet invest today so she can withdraw $50,000 at the end of each year for 20 years after she retires? Assume Janet can invest money at 6% compounded annually.

CHALLENGE PROBLEMS

13–30. Ameila Jones would like to set up a sinking fund to pay for a $5,600 surprise anniversary vacation for her mother and father in five years. How much does she need to set aside at the end of each six months at 6% compounded semiannually in order to reach her goal?

13–31. Ajax Corporation has hired Brad O'Brien as its new president. Terms included the company's agreeing to pay retirement benefits of $18,000 at the end of each semiannual period for 10 years. This will begin in 3,285 days. If the money can be invested at 8% compounded semiannually, what must the company deposit today to fulfill its obligation to Brad?

DVD SUMMARY PRACTICE TEST (Use Tables in the *Business Math Handbook*)

1. Lin Lowe plans to deposit $1,800 at the end of every 6 months for the next 15 years at 8% interest compounded semiannually. What is the value of Lin's annuity at the end of 15 years? *(p. 317)*

2. On Abby Ellen's graduation from law school, Abby's uncle, Bull Brady, promised her a gift of $24,000 or $2,400 every quarter for the next 4 years after graduating from law school. If the money could be invested at 6% compounded quarterly, which offer should Abby choose? *(p. 319)*

3. Sanka Blunck wants to receive $8,000 each year for 20 years. How much must Sanka invest today at 4% interest compounded annually? *(p. 324)*

4. In 9 years, Rollo Company will have to repay a $100,000 loan. Assume a 6% interest rate compounded quarterly. How much must Rollo Company pay each period to have $100,000 at the end of 9 years? *(p. 317)*

5. Lance Industries borrowed $130,000. The company plans to set up a sinking fund that will repay the loan at the end of 18 years. Assume a 6% interest rate compounded semiannually. What amount must Lance Industries pay into the fund each period? Check your answer by Table 13.1 *(p. 325)*

6. Joe Jan wants to receive $22,000 each year for the next 22 years. Assume a 6% interest rate compounded annually. How much must Joe invest today? *(p. 322)*

7. Twice a year for 15 years, Warren Ford invested $1,700 compounded semiannually at 6% interest. What is the value of this annuity due? *(p. 319)*

8. Scupper Molly invested $1,800 semiannually for 23 years at 8% interest compounded semiannually. What is the value of this annuity due? *(p. 319)*

9. Nelson Collins decided to retire to Canada in 10 years. What amount should Nelson deposit so that he will be able to withdraw $80,000 at the end of each year for 25 years after he retires? Assume Nelson can invest money at 7% interest compounded annually. *(p. 322)*

10. Bob Bryan made deposits of $10,000 at the end of each quarter to Lion Bank, which pays 8% interest compounded quarterly. After 9 years, Bob made no more deposits. What will be the account's balance 4 years after the last deposit? *(p. 317)*

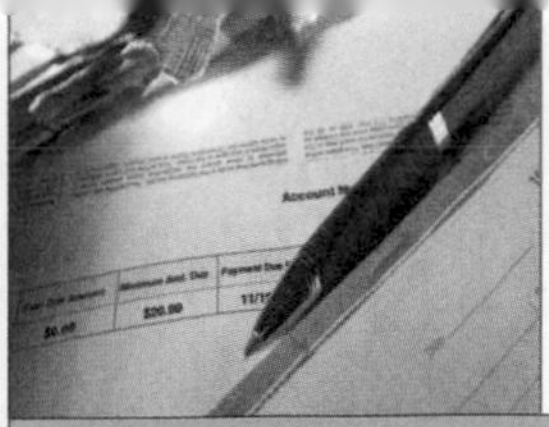

Personal Finance

A KIPLINGER APPROACH

BUILDING YOUR OWN RETIREMENT PLAN

MIMIC THE TAX ADVANTAGES OF A 401(k). BY STACY RAPACON

OUR READER

WHO: MACDEM TEKLEMARIAM, 33
WHERE: GALLATIN, TENN.
QUESTION: HIS EMPLOYER DOESN'T OFFER A 401(k). WHAT ARE HIS OPTIONS?

FOR ABOUT HALF HIS LIFE, Macdem has worked hard and saved plenty; he's already socked away more than $160,000 in retirement and investment accounts. But the printing company where he's general manager isn't much help. It doesn't offer a 401(k) nor any other pretax benefit plan. "I'm saving all this money, but I'm getting taxed," says Macdem. "It's a little bit frustrating."

Considering that 401(k) accounts are the country's primary retirement vehicle, Macdem's situation is more than frustrating—it's surprising. "I don't know why a company would not want to offer a 401(k)," says Craig Mont, a certified public accountant in Fair Lawn, N.J. "The plans are relatively inexpensive to administer, and if you want to keep good employees, you're going to have to offer something."

If your company is like Macdem's, lobby for a retirement plan. Greg Plechner, a principal of Modera Wealth Management, in Old Tappan, N.J., advises that you speak to the human-resources director and rally other employees. Plechner estimates that it would cost a small company just $2,000 a year to operate a no-frills 401(k).

Open an IRA. Meanwhile, Macdem is diligently trying to compensate. He plans to continue squirreling away 20% of his pay, or about $15,000 a year. Can he more or less replicate a 401(k) and its current and deferred tax breaks?

Yes, he can. For starters, he can fund a traditional IRA. Because Macdem is not covered by an employer's retirement plan, he can deduct his contributions, which grow tax-deferred inside the IRA. The rub: The contribution limit for 2009 is $5,000, far less than the $16,500 limit for a 401(k). But it's a start.

Another possibility is to open a health savings account. Macdem is single, so he can deduct up to $3,000 in HSA contributions if he also signs up for a high-deductible health-insurance plan. An HSA balance grows tax-deferred, and withdrawals for qualified medical expenses are tax-free. If you don't get sick, you can roll over the balance from year to year. As a result, an HSA acts as a kind of supplemental IRA.

Minimize taxes. That means Macdem could save $8,000 tax-free this year, almost half of a 401(k)'s limit. Plus, he can structure the rest of his annual savings to trim the tax bite. Plechner recommends exchange-traded funds, municipal bonds and index funds, all of which generally result in little or no tax liability. "As long as you create an efficient investment portfolio, you can make it tax-deferred for the most part," he says. And when Macdem withdraws his money, profits will be taxed as capital gains—unlike withdrawals from a 401(k) or a deductible IRA, which count as ordinary income.

Some advisers would suggest that Macdem open a Roth IRA, which would shield him from substantial taxes in retirement. But he earns a good salary and has few deductions, so the tax savings from a deductible IRA are important to him now. It would be terrific if he could deduct $5,000 and also have a Roth, but no dice. You can mix and match IRAs, but you can't exceed the total annual limit. ■

From Kiplinger's Personal Finance, July 2009, p. 18.

BUSINESS MATH ISSUE

All employers should by law be required to offer retirement for its employees.

1. List the key points of the article and information to support your position.
2. Write a group defense of your position using math calculations to support your view.

PROJECT A

List five key points of the article. Do you agree with them?

Slater's Business Math Scrapbook

Applying Your Skills

FAMILY MONEY | *By Karen Blumenthal*

Mom and Dad, You're Broke

Dave Klug

There are few more unpleasant topics for adult children and their aging parents than talking about money. But after the financial devastation of the past year, you have more reasons than ever to have that conversation.

After all, the same forces that have walloped your 401(k) may also have wreaked havoc on your parents' retirement savings—and they probably don't have years to sit tight and hope for a recovery. While you're trying to figure out how much longer you may have to work, they may need to rethink everything from their daily budget to their estate planning, and they may need your help to do so.

"We've all planned for greater money in the future. No one has planned for less money," says Gary Altman, a Rockville, Md., lawyer who specializes in estates.

Starting the conversation may be the hardest part, especially if your parents are extremely private about their financial affairs, embarrassed about their losses or simply suspicious of your motives. Sharing your own experience may give you an opening line, financial planners and lawyers suggest. "My 401(k) is half of what it was," you might say. "Have your savings been affected as well?"

Once the door is open, here are some questions to ask:

■ **"How are you doing financially?"** Falling stock prices, lower interest rates and reduced dividends at many stalwart companies may also have sliced retirees' monthly income, requiring them to sharply cut spending or consider new ways to get income out of their assets.

Elderly parents may need your help revising their budgets, or they may need to rework their investment mix. Others may need to explore ways to tap their home equity. If that isn't your strong suit, you may want to help them find a financial adviser.

Craig C. Reaves, a Kansas City, Mo., lawyer and president of the National Academy of Elder Law Attorneys, says his clients, who generally have total assets of $1 million to $2 million, are worrying about outliving their money and are cutting back on gifts to their children and grandchildren—another topic worthy of discussion.

If your parents are 70½ and older, however, there is a bright spot: They don't have to take their required minimum distribution from their individual retirement accounts this year unless they need it. That means their funds have some time to recover and they can avoid paying income tax on a required distribution.

■ **"Will you be able to afford a nursing home?"** Those in their 50s, 60s and even 70s who have seen their total net worth decline should revisit whether they want to buy long-term-care insurance to cover the possibility of nursing-home care, which now averages more than $75,000 a year.

W. Thomas Curtis of financial-planning firm FSP & Associates in Gaithersburg, Md., says many of his clients expect to pay nursing-home costs out of their savings. But one of them has seen his investments fall by 40%. Now in his 70s, he also has a heart murmur that would disqualify him for most insurance. Luckily, as a federal government retiree, he can sign up for the insurance during open-enrollment season without a medical exam.

Long-term-care policies are expensive, and they don't make sense for everyone. If your parent feels like it's a good idea, advisers recommend lining it up in your later 50s or in your 60s, before any serious medical problems develop. They suggest looking for a policy with a highly rated insurer that adjusts for inflation and covers in-home and assisted living as well as nursing homes.

■ **"Is there a salesperson trying to sell you something?"** Adult children should ask their parents that question. If the answer is yes, encourage them to talk with you or an adviser before they buy anything.

Among the possibilities: telemarketing scammers promising sweepstakes and lottery winnings in return for initial payments, and slick salesmen selling seniors products or services they don't need. Senior citizens particularly need to beware of investments that may sound good—offering regular income or guaranteed returns—but that may be inappropriate for retirees.

Many annuities, for instance, come with steep expenses and "surrender" fees, which prevent the holder from withdrawing their money for several years without a huge penalty, making the funds inaccessible in an emergency.

■ **"Should you update your will?"** Talking about an estate can be particularly touchy—especially if a parent thinks you're trying to get your hands on it. But it's worth asking if financial losses change the way a parent wants the estate handled. A commitment in a will to donate, say, $100,000 to a charity may leave less than intended for others because the estate's value has fallen so much.

When reviewing a will, make sure that documents spelling out who can make financial and medical decisions are up-to-date.

Email: familymoney@wsj.com

Internet Projects: See text Web site (www.mhhe.com/slater10e) and The Business Math Internet Resource Guide.

CUMULATIVE REVIEW

A Word Problem Approach—Chapters 10, 11, 12, 13

1. Amy O'Mally graduated from high school. Her uncle promised her as a gift a check for $2,000 or $275 every quarter for 2 years. If money could be invested at 6% compounded quarterly, which offer is better for Amy? (Use the tables in the *Business Math Handbook.*) *(p. 322)*

2. Alan Angel made deposits of $400 semiannually to Sag Bank, which pays 10% interest compounded semiannually. After 4 years, Alan made no more deposits. What will be the balance in the account 3 years after the last deposit? (Use the tables in the *Business Math Handbook.*) *(pp. 317, 297)*

3. Roger Disney decides to retire to Florida in 12 years. What amount should Roger invest today so that he will be able to withdraw $30,000 at the end of each year for 20 years *after* he retires? Assume he can invest money at 8% interest compounded annually. (Use tables in the *Business Math Handbook.*) *(p. 322)*

4. On September 15, Arthur Westering borrowed $3,000 from Vermont Bank at $10\frac{1}{2}$% interest. Arthur plans to repay the loan on January 25. Assume the loan is based on exact interest. How much will Arthur totally repay? *(p. 259)*

5. Sue Cooper borrowed $6,000 on an $11\frac{3}{4}$%, 120-day note. Sue paid $300 toward the note on day 50. On day 90, Sue paid an additional $200. Using the U.S. Rule, Sue's adjusted balance after her first payment is the following. *(p. 262)*

6. On November 18, Northwest Company discounted an $18,000, 12%, 120-day note dated September 8. Assume a 10% discount rate. What will be the proceeds? Use ordinary interest. *(p. 260)*

7. Alice Reed deposits $16,500 into Rye Bank, which pays 10% interest compounded semiannually. Using the appropriate table, what will Alice have in her account at the end of 6 years? *(p. 297)*

8. Peter Regan needs $90,000 5 years from today to retire in Arizona. Peter's bank pays 10% interest compounded semiannually. What will Peter have to put in the bank today to have $90,000 in 5 years? *(p. 302)*

Special Supplement

Time-Value Relationship Using Plastic Overlays
Contents

One Lump Sum (Single Amount)

Annuity (Stream of Payments)

Turn transparency over to see relationship of compounding to present value.

EXHIBIT 13.1 Compound (future value) of $.68 at 10% for 4 periods

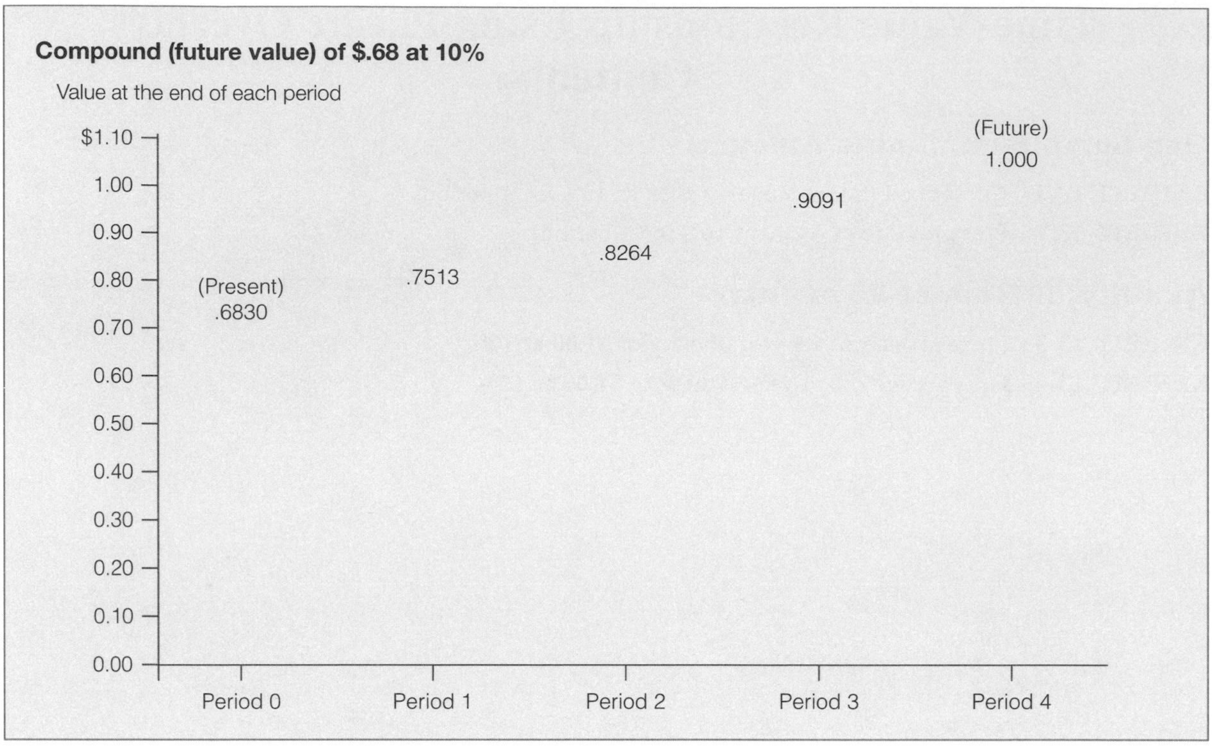

68¢ today will grow to $1.00 in the future.

What Exhibit 13.1 Means

If you take $.68 to a bank that pays 10% after 4 periods you will be able to get $1.00. The $.68 is the present value, and the $1.00 is the compound value or future value. Keep in mind that the $.68 is a one lump-sum investment.

EXHIBIT 13.2 Present value of $1.00 at 10% for 4 periods

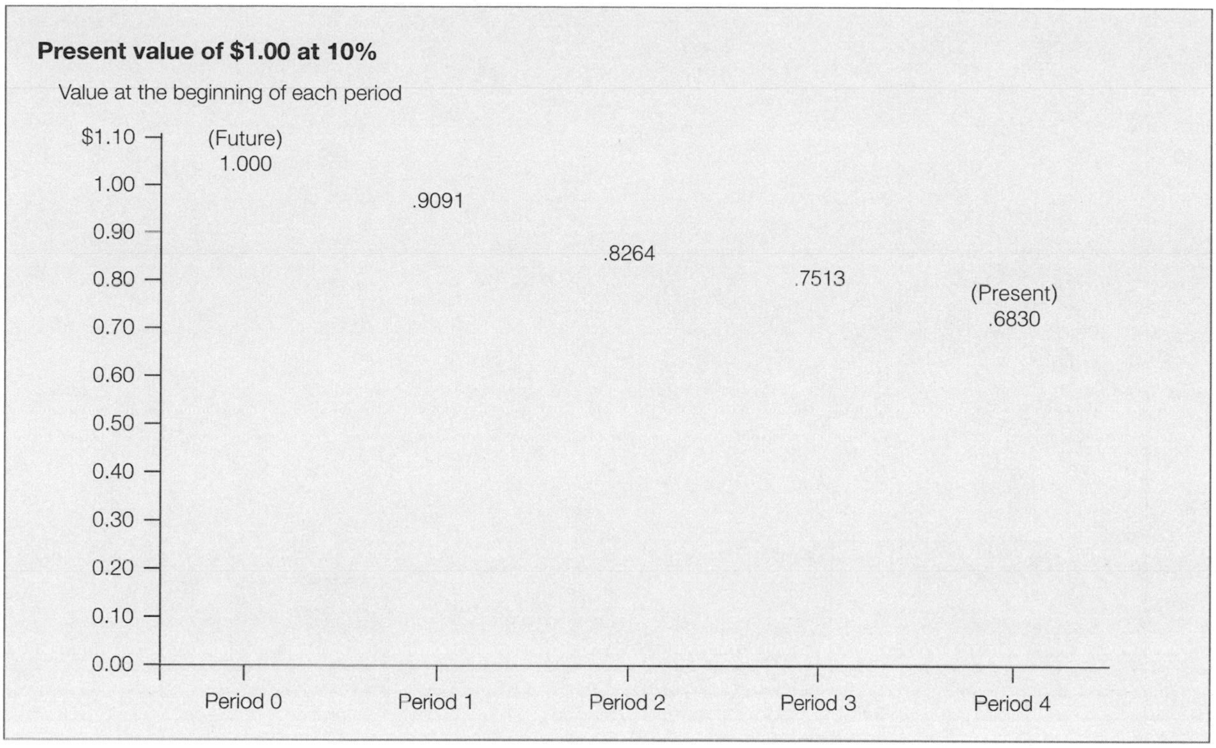

If I need $1 in four periods, I need to invest $0.68 today.

What Exhibit 13.2 Means

If you want to receive $1.00 at the end of 4 periods at a bank paying 10%, you will have to deposit $.68 in the bank today. The longer you have to wait for your money, the less it is worth. The $1.00 is the compound or future amount, and the $.68 is the present value of a dollar that you will not receive for 4 periods.

EXHIBIT 13.3 Present value of a 4-year annuity of $1.00 at 10%

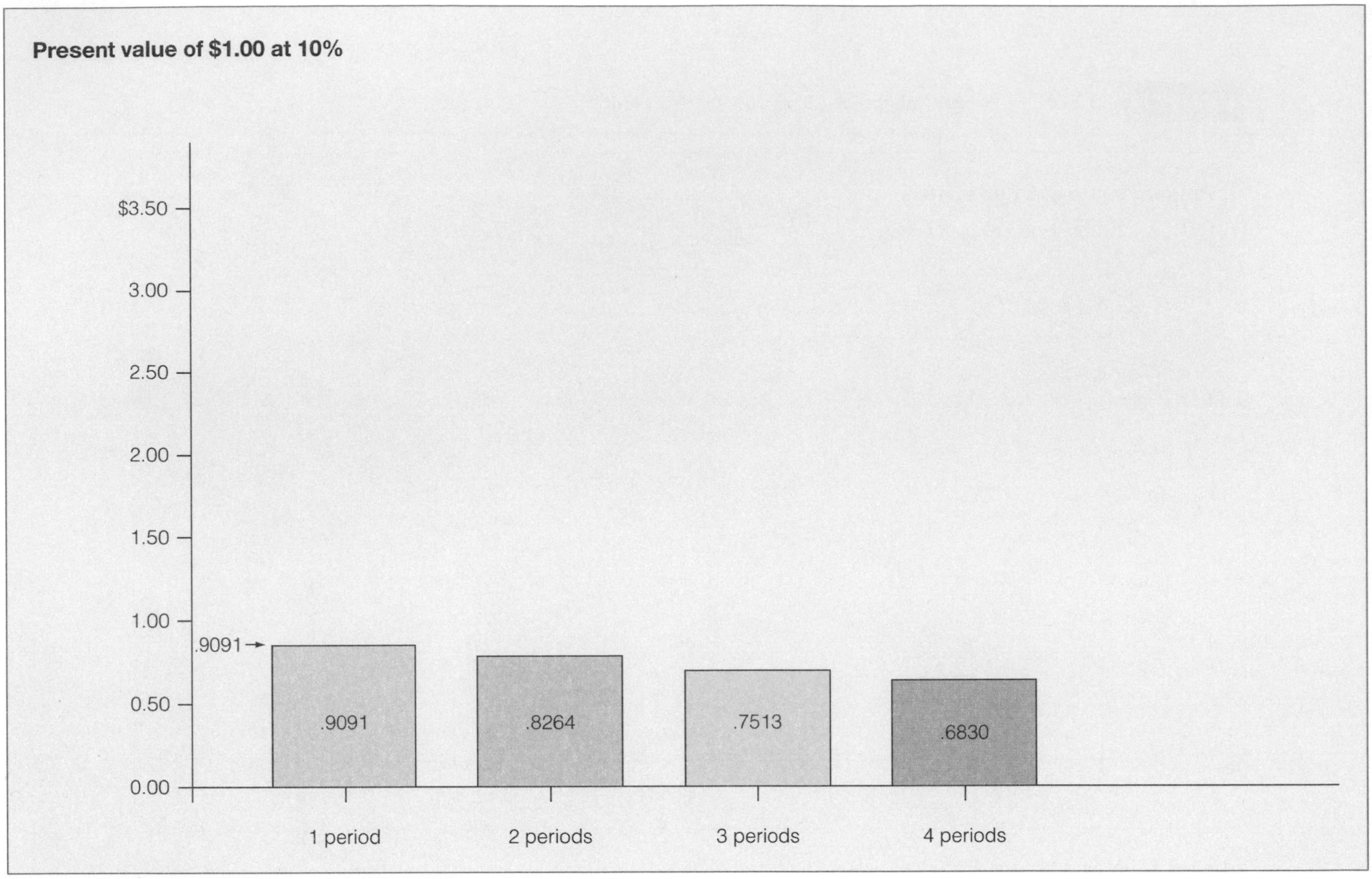

EXHIBIT 13.4 Future value of a 4-year annuity of $1.00 at 10%

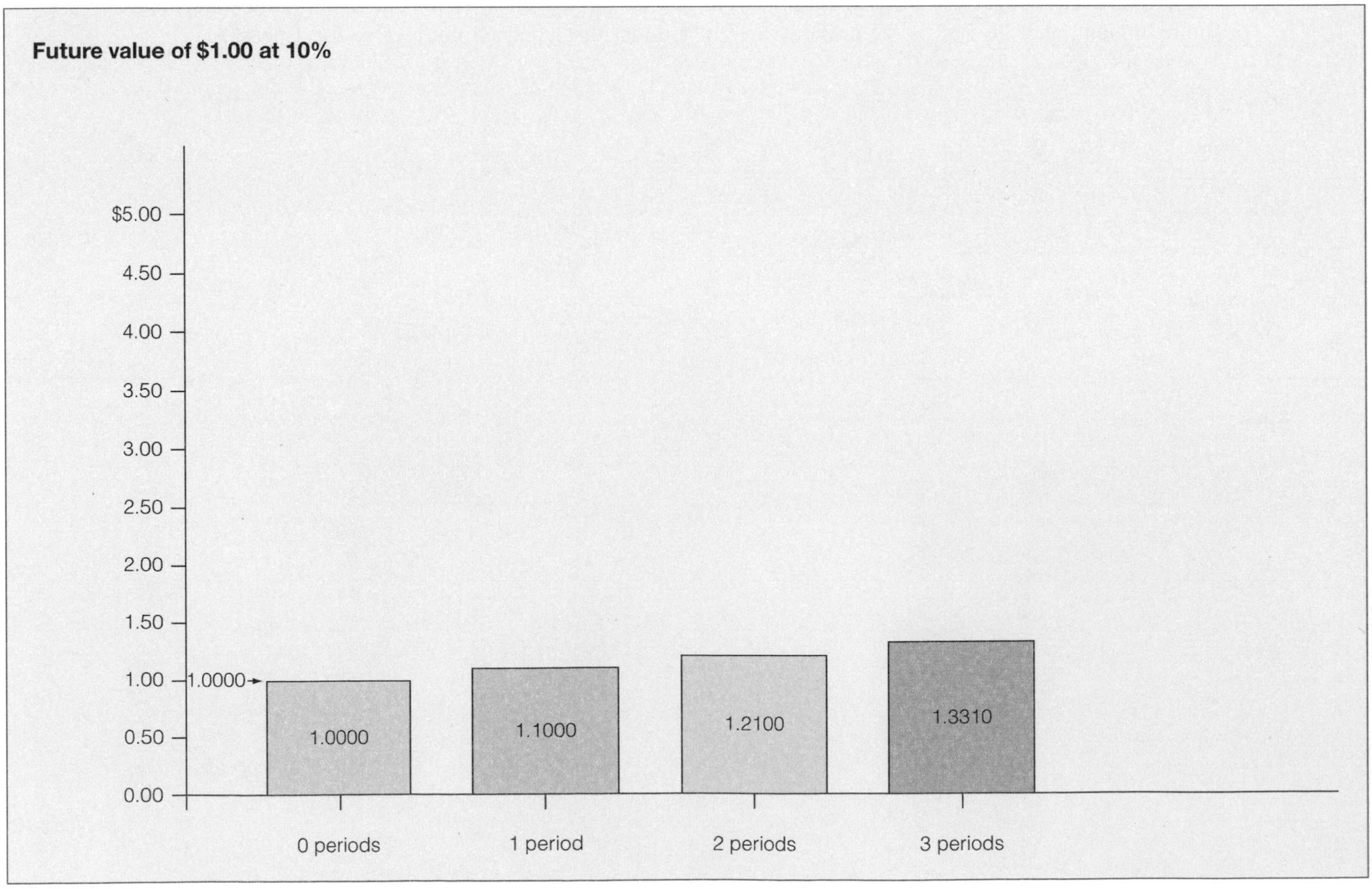

What Exhibit 13.3 Means*

BLUE BOX (Top box)

Blue shows how to receive $1.00 after 1 period. You must put in $.91 today.

PURPLE BOX (2nd box from top)

Purple shows how to receive $1.00 after 2 periods. You must put in $.83 today to get $1.00 for 2 periods. You must put in the bank today $1.74 ($.91 + $.83) to take out $1.00 for 2 periods.

YELLOW BOX (3rd box from top)

Yellow shows how to receive $1.00 after 3 periods. You must put in $.75 today to get $1.00 for 3 periods. You also must put in the bank today $2.49 ($.91 + $.83 + $.75) to take out $1.00 for 3 periods.

GREEN BOX (4th box from top)

Green shows how to receive $1.00 after 4 periods. You must put in $.68 today to get $1.00 for 4 periods. You also must put in the bank today $3.17 ($.91 + $.83 + $.75 + $.68) to take out $1.00 for 4 periods.

What Exhibit 13.4 Means*

BLUE BOX (Top box)

Blue shows $1.00 invested at the end of each period. The $1.00 has no time to earn interest.

PURPLE BOX (2nd box from top)

Purple shows the value of $1.00 after the end of 2nd period. The $1.00 is now worth $1.10 due to compounding for 1 period.

YELLOW BOX (3rd box from top)

Yellow shows the value of $1.00 after the end of 3rd period. The $1.00 is now worth $1.21 due to the compounding for 2 periods.

GREEN BOX (4th box from top)

Green shows that the value of $1.00 after the end of 4 periods is $1.33 due to compounding for 3 periods. If you put $1.00 in the bank at 10% for 4 years, the $4.00 grows to $4.64.

*From table in Handbook for 10%.

Periods	Amount of annuity	Present value of an annuity
1	1. 1.0000	. 9091
2	2. 2.1000	1. 7355
3	3. 3100	2. 4869
4	4. 6410	3. 1699

Classroom Notes

chapter

14 INSTALLMENT BUYING, RULE OF 78, AND REVOLVING CHARGE CREDIT CARDS

Credit-Card Fees Curbed

Senate Approves Sweeping Restrictions, House Passage Seen; Limiting Interest Hikes

By Sudeep Reddy

Sweeping new restrictions on credit-card companies would ban extra fees and fluctuating rates and arm tens of millions of consumers with more information on their debts.

Starting in February 2010, a Senate bill passed Tuesday would ban practices such as charging consumers to pay by phone and sudden surges in interest rates. Payments above the minimum due would be applied to balances with the highest interest rates. Information once relegated to tiny print must be made clearer, and consumers will soon be told how long it would take to pay off a balance if they pay only the minimum due.

The credit-card overhaul is set to become the first major legislative change to financial regulation outside housing since the emergency bank bailout enacted last fall, and it's not the last expected this year. Tuesday's 90-5 vote followed pressure from the White House on card issuers to improve fairness and transparency for the three-fourths of U.S. households that use credit cards. The measure is likely to pass the House in the coming days, and President Barack Obama is expected to sign it into law next week.

For consumers, the legislation aims to change habits— perhaps leading them to make fewer big-ticket purchases with credit cards—by clarifying the cost of using card debt. Several provisions in the legislation are geared toward forcing consumers to recognize how much they're paying in interest. Card issuers would also have to provide information on consumer-counseling and debt-management services.

The Fine Print

The law would require new information to be added to credit-card statements (examples in red)

PAYMENT SUMMARY	
NEW BALANCE:	$1,000
MINIMUM PAYMENT:	$35
PAYMENT DUE DATE: (would require 21-day notification)	03/22/10
MONTHS BEFORE BILL IS PAID OFF IF ONLY MIN. PAYMENTS MADE:	49
INTEREST PAID OVER TIME IF ONLY MIN. PAYMENTS ARE MADE:	$667

Note: Figures are rough estimates

LEARNING UNIT OBJECTIVES

LU 14–1: Cost of Installment Buying

1. Calculate the amount financed, finance charge, and deferred payment *(p. 340)*.
2. Calculate the estimated APR by table lookup *(p. 341)*.
3. Calculate the monthly payment by formula and by table lookup *(p. 343)*.

LU 14–2: Paying Off Installment Loans before Due Date

1. Calculate the rebate and payoff for Rule of 78 *(p. 346)*.

LU 14–3: Revolving Charge Credit Cards

1. Calculate the finance charges on revolving charge credit card accounts *(p. 349)*.

VOCABULARY PREVIEW

Here are key terms in this chapter. After completing the chapter, if you know the term, place a checkmark in the parenthesis. If you don't know the term, look it up and put the page number where it can be found.

Amortization . ( ) Amount financed . ( ) Annual percentage rate (APR) . ( ) Average daily balance . ( ) Cash advance . ( ) Daily balance . ( ) Deferred payment price . ( ) Down payment . ( ) Fair Credit and Charge Card Disclosure Act of 1988 . ( ) Finance charge . ( ) Installment loan . ( ) Loan amortization table . ( ) Open-end credit . ( ) Outstanding balance . ( ) Rebate . ( ) Rebate fraction . ( ) Revolving charge account . ( ) Rule of 78 . ( ) Truth in Lending Act . ( )

Toyota Opens Loans to Seven Years

By John D. Stoll
And Norihiko Shirouzu

Toyota Motor Corp. has begun offering customers 84-month loans on new cars in an effort to help dealers ride out the most severe downturn in the U.S. auto industry in the past decade.

The seven-year loans are unusually long. Just a few years ago, 72-month auto loans were rare.

The move reflects the lengths to which auto makers are going to pump up sales without resorting to the hefty cash rebates that they have relied on in the past. Over time, big cash discounts eat into profits and tarnish an auto maker's image. Most are now trying to curtail the practice. **Chrysler** recently began offering navigation systems and other interior upgrades at no additional costs to tempt buyers.

George Borst, chief executive of Toyota Financial Services, said at a financial-services conference in San Francisco that the company started offering seven-year car loans in late summer. These loans, which carry slightly higher rates than 72-month deals, have risen to represent 4% of all cars Toyota Financial Services lends money on.

A Toyota Financial spokesman said there were too many variables to say what rates are charged on the loans. But rates quoted by Toyota dealers ranged from 6.9% to 7.59% for 84-month loans, compared with 5.85% to 6.84% for 72-month financing.

Mr. Borst said he sees the loans growing to represent 5% of business. He said Toyota's in-house lender, known as a "captive finance arm," started making the loans after realizing it was losing business to other noncaptive lenders offering loans with longer terms.

Toyota Financial Services originates loans for about three-quarters of the cars financed in the U.S. at Toyota dealers, or about 50% of total sales for the auto maker, a spokeswoman said. She said the seven-year loans are given only to customers with top credit.

GMAC Financial Services, the largest auto lender in the world, offers 84-month loans but says they make up a tiny portion of its business. **Ford Motor** Co.'s credit arm did some pilot programs related to 84-month loans, but isn't aggressively offering them. "We don't like these loans," Ford Motor Credit Chief Executive Michael Bannister said on the sidelines of the conference.

If you are thinking of financing a car, the *Wall Street Journal* clipping, "Toyota Opens Loans to Seven Years," may be of interest to you. Owing to the financial crises of 2008 auto sales have tumbled. In response, Toyota is offering an 84-month loan on new autos. Prior to this, the longest car loan offered was 72 months. This chapter discusses the cost of buying products in installments (closed-end credit) and revolving credit card (open-end credit).

Learning Unit 14–1: Cost of Installment Buying

LO 1

Installment buying, a form of *closed-end credit,* can add a substantial amount to the cost of big-ticket purchases. To illustrate this, we follow the procedure of buying a pickup truck, including the amount financed, finance charge, and deferred payment price. Then we study the effect of the Truth in Lending Act.

Amount Financed, Finance Charge, and Deferred Payment

This advertisement for the sale of a pickup truck appeared in a local paper. As you can see from this advertisement, after customers make a **down payment,** they can buy the truck with an **installment loan.** This loan is paid off with a series of equal periodic payments. These payments include both interest and principal. The payment process is called **amortization.** In the promissory notes of earlier chapters, the loan was paid off in one ending payment. Now let's look at the calculations involved in buying a pickup truck.

Car Culture/Getty Images

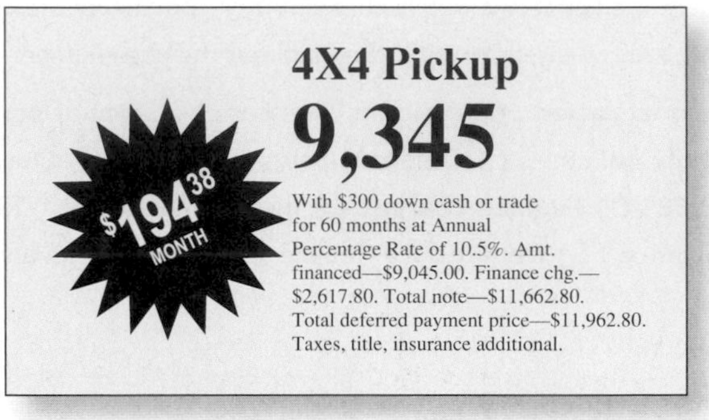

Checking Calculations in Pickup Advertisement

Calculating Amount Financed The **amount financed** is what you actually borrow. To calculate this amount, use the following formula:

Amount financed	=	Cash price	−	Down payment
↑		↑		↑
$9,045	=	$9,345	−	$300

Calculating Finance Charge The words **finance charge** in the advertisement represent the **interest** charge. The interest charge resulting in the finance charge includes the cost of credit reports, mandatory bank fees, and so on. You can use the following formula to calculate the total interest on the loan:

Total finance charge (interest charge)	=	Total of all monthly payments	−	Amount financed
↑		↑		↑
$2,617.80	=	$11,662.80 ($194.38 × 60 months)	−	$9,045

Calculating Deferred Payment Price The **deferred payment price** represents the total of all monthly payments plus the down payment. The following formula is used to calculate the deferred payment price:

$$\text{Deferred payment price} = \text{Total of all monthly payments} + \text{Down payment}$$

$$\$11{,}962.80 = \$11{,}662.80\ (\$194.38 \times 60) + \$300$$

Truth in Lending: APR Defined and Calculated

In 1969, the Federal Reserve Board established the **Truth in Lending Act** (Regulation Z). The law doesn't regulate interest charges; its purpose is to make the consumer aware of the true cost of credit.

The Truth in Lending Act requires that creditors provide certain basic information about the actual cost of buying on credit. Before buyers sign a credit agreement, creditors must inform them in writing of the amount of the finance charge and the **annual percentage rate (APR).** The APR represents the true or effective annual interest creditors charge. This is helpful to buyers who repay loans over different periods of time (1 month, 48 months, and so on).

To illustrate how the APR affects the interest rate, assume you borrow $100 for 1 year and pay a finance charge of $9. Your interest rate would be 9% if you waited until the end of the year to pay back the loan. Now let's say you pay off the loan and the finance charge in 12 monthly payments. Each month that you make a payment, you are losing some of the value or use of that money. So the true or effective APR is actually greater than 9%.

The APR can be calculated by formula or by tables. We will use the table method since it is more exact.

LO 2

Calculating APR Rate by Table 14.1 (p. 342)

Note the following steps for using a table to calculate APR:

CALCULATING APR BY TABLE

Step 1. Divide the finance charge by amount financed and multiply by $100 to get the table lookup factor.

Step 2. Go to APR Table 14.1. At the left side of the table are listed the number of payments that will be made.

Step 3. When you find the number of payments you are looking for, move to the right and look for the two numbers closest to the table lookup number. This will indicate the APR.

Now let's determine the APR for the pickup truck advertisement given earlier in the chapter.

As stated in Step 1, we begin by dividing the finance charge by the amount financed and multiply by $100:

$$\frac{\text{Finance charge}}{\text{Amount financed}} \times \$100 = \text{Table 14.1 lookup number}$$

$$\frac{\$2{,}617.80}{\$9{,}045.00} \times \$100 = \$28.94$$

We multiply by $100, since the table is based on $100 of financing.

TABLE 14.1 Annual percentage rate table per $100

NUMBER OF PAYMENTS	ANNUAL PERCENTAGE RATE															
	10.00%	10.25%	10.50%	10.75%	11.00%	11.25%	11.50%	11.75%	12.00%	12.25%	12.50%	12.75%	13.00%	13.25%	13.50%	13.75%
	(FINANCE CHARGE PER $100 OF AMOUNT FINANCED)															
1	0.83	0.85	0.87	0.90	0.92	0.94	0.96	0.98	1.00	1.02	1.04	1.06	1.08	1.10	1.12	1.15
2	1.25	1.28	1.31	1.35	1.38	1.41	1.44	1.47	1.50	1.53	1.57	1.60	1.63	1.66	1.69	1.72
3	1.67	1.71	1.76	1.80	1.84	1.88	1.92	1.96	2.01	2.05	2.09	2.13	2.17	2.22	2.26	2.30
4	2.09	2.14	2.20	2.25	2.30	2.35	2.41	2.46	2.51	2.57	2.62	2.67	2.72	2.78	2.83	2.88
5	2.51	2.58	2.64	2.70	2.77	2.83	2.89	2.96	3.02	3.08	3.15	3.21	3.27	3.34	3.40	3.46
6	2.94	3.01	3.08	3.16	3.23	3.31	3.38	3.45	3.53	3.60	3.68	3.75	3.83	3.90	3.97	4.05
7	3.36	3.45	3.53	3.62	3.70	3.78	3.87	3.95	4.04	4.12	4.21	4.29	4.38	4.47	4.55	4.64
8	3.79	3.88	3.98	4.07	4.17	4.26	4.36	4.46	4.55	4.65	4.74	4.84	4.94	5.03	5.13	5.22
9	4.21	4.32	4.43	4.53	4.64	4.75	4.85	4.96	5.07	5.17	5.28	5.39	5.49	5.60	5.71	5.82
10	4.64	4.76	4.88	4.99	5.11	5.23	5.35	5.46	5.58	5.70	5.82	5.94	6.05	6.17	6.29	6.41
11	5.07	5.20	5.33	5.45	5.58	5.71	5.84	5.97	6.10	6.23	6.36	6.49	6.62	6.75	6.88	7.01
12	5.50	5.64	5.78	5.92	6.06	6.20	6.34	6.48	6.62	6.76	6.90	7.04	7.18	7.32	7.46	7.60
13	5.93	6.08	6.23	6.38	6.53	6.68	6.84	6.99	7.14	7.29	7.44	7.59	7.75	7.90	8.05	8.20
14	6.36	6.52	6.69	6.85	7.01	7.17	7.34	7.50	7.66	7.82	7.99	8.15	8.31	8.48	8.64	8.81
15	6.80	6.97	7.14	7.32	7.49	7.66	7.84	8.01	8.19	8.36	8.53	8.71	8.88	9.06	9.23	9.41
16	7.23	7.41	7.60	7.78	7.97	8.15	8.34	8.53	8.71	8.90	9.08	9.27	9.46	9.64	9.83	10.02
17	7.67	7.86	8.06	8.25	8.45	8.65	8.84	9.04	9.24	9.44	9.63	9.83	10.03	10.23	10.43	10.63
18	8.10	8.31	8.52	8.73	8.93	9.14	9.35	9.56	9.77	9.98	10.19	10.40	10.61	10.82	11.03	11.24
19	8.54	8.76	8.98	9.20	9.42	9.64	9.86	10.08	10.30	10.52	10.74	10.96	11.18	11.41	11.63	11.85
20	8.98	9.21	9.44	9.67	9.90	10.13	10.37	10.60	10.83	11.06	11.30	11.53	11.76	12.00	12.23	12.46
21	9.42	9.66	9.90	10.15	10.39	10.63	10.88	11.12	11.36	11.61	11.85	12.10	12.34	12.59	12.84	13.08
22	9.86	10.12	10.37	10.62	10.88	11.13	11.39	11.64	11.90	12.16	12.41	12.67	12.93	13.19	13.44	13.70
23	10.30	10.57	10.84	11.10	11.37	11.63	11.90	12.17	12.44	12.71	12.97	13.24	13.51	13.78	14.05	14.32
24	10.75	11.02	11.30	11.58	11.86	12.14	12.42	12.70	12.98	13.26	13.54	13.82	14.10	14.38	14.66	14.95
25	11.19	11.48	11.77	12.06	12.35	12.64	12.93	13.22	13.52	13.81	14.10	14.40	14.69	14.98	15.28	15.57
26	11.64	11.94	12.24	12.54	12.85	13.15	13.45	13.75	14.06	14.36	14.67	14.97	15.28	15.59	15.89	16.20
27	12.09	12.40	12.71	13.03	13.34	13.66	13.97	14.29	14.60	14.92	15.24	15.56	15.87	16.19	16.51	16.83
28	12.53	12.86	13.18	13.51	13.84	14.16	14.49	14.82	15.15	15.48	15.81	16.14	16.47	16.80	17.13	17.46
29	12.98	13.32	13.66	14.00	14.33	14.67	15.01	15.35	15.70	16.04	16.38	16.72	17.07	17.41	17.75	18.10
30	13.43	13.78	14.13	14.48	14.83	15.19	15.54	15.89	16.24	16.60	16.95	17.31	17.66	18.02	18.38	18.74
31	13.89	14.25	14.61	14.97	15.33	15.70	16.06	16.43	16.79	17.16	17.53	17.90	18.27	18.63	19.00	19.38
32	14.34	14.71	15.09	15.46	15.84	16.21	16.59	16.97	17.35	17.73	18.11	18.49	18.87	19.25	19.63	20.02
33	14.79	15.18	15.57	15.95	16.34	16.73	17.12	17.51	17.90	18.29	18.69	19.08	19.47	19.87	20.26	20.66
34	15.25	15.65	16.05	16.44	16.85	17.25	17.65	18.05	18.46	18.86	19.27	19.67	20.08	20.49	20.90	21.31
35	15.70	16.11	16.53	16.94	17.35	17.77	18.18	18.60	19.01	19.43	19.85	20.27	20.69	21.11	21.53	21.95
36	16.16	16.58	17.01	17.43	17.86	18.29	18.71	19.14	19.57	20.00	20.43	20.87	21.30	21.73	22.17	22.60
37	16.62	17.06	17.49	17.93	18.37	18.81	19.25	19.69	20.13	20.58	21.02	21.46	21.91	22.36	22.81	23.25
38	17.08	17.53	17.98	18.43	18.88	19.33	19.78	20.24	20.69	21.15	21.61	22.07	22.52	22.99	23.45	23.91
39	17.54	18.00	18.46	18.93	19.39	19.86	20.32	20.79	21.26	21.73	22.20	22.67	23.14	23.61	24.09	24.56
40	18.00	18.48	18.95	19.43	19.90	20.38	20.86	21.34	21.82	22.30	22.79	23.27	23.76	24.25	24.73	25.22
41	18.47	18.95	19.44	19.93	20.42	20.91	21.40	21.89	22.39	22.88	23.38	23.88	24.38	24.88	25.38	25.88
42	18.93	19.43	19.93	20.43	20.93	21.44	21.94	22.45	22.96	23.47	23.98	24.49	25.00	25.51	26.03	26.55
43	19.40	19.91	20.42	20.94	21.45	21.97	22.49	23.01	23.53	24.05	24.57	25.10	25.62	26.15	26.68	27.21
44	19.86	20.39	20.91	21.44	21.97	22.50	23.03	23.57	24.10	24.64	25.17	25.71	26.25	26.79	27.33	27.88
45	20.33	20.87	21.41	21.95	22.49	23.03	23.58	24.12	24.67	25.22	25.77	26.32	26.88	27.43	27.99	28.55
46	20.80	21.35	21.90	22.46	23.01	23.57	24.13	24.69	25.25	25.81	26.37	26.94	27.51	28.08	28.65	29.22
47	21.27	21.83	22.40	22.97	23.53	24.10	24.68	25.25	25.82	26.40	26.98	27.56	28.14	28.72	29.31	29.89
48	21.74	22.32	22.90	23.48	24.06	24.64	25.23	25.81	26.40	26.99	27.58	28.18	28.77	29.37	29.97	30.57
49	22.21	22.80	23.39	23.99	24.58	25.18	25.78	26.38	26.98	27.59	28.19	28.80	29.41	30.02	30.63	31.24
50	22.69	23.29	23.89	24.50	25.11	25.72	26.33	26.95	27.56	28.18	28.80	29.42	30.04	30.67	31.29	31.92
51	23.16	23.78	24.40	25.02	25.64	26.26	26.89	27.52	28.15	28.78	29.41	30.05	30.68	31.32	31.96	32.60
52	23.64	24.27	24.90	25.53	26.17	26.81	27.45	28.09	28.73	29.38	30.02	30.67	31.32	31.98	32.63	33.29
53	24.11	24.76	25.40	26.05	26.70	27.35	28.00	28.66	29.32	29.98	30.64	31.30	31.97	32.63	33.30	33.97
54	24.59	25.25	25.91	26.57	27.23	27.90	28.56	29.23	29.91	30.58	31.25	31.93	32.61	33.29	33.98	34.66
55	25.07	25.74	26.41	27.09	27.77	28.44	29.13	29.81	30.50	31.18	31.87	32.56	33.26	33.95	34.65	35.35
56	25.55	26.23	26.92	27.61	28.30	28.99	29.69	30.39	31.09	31.79	32.49	33.20	33.91	34.62	35.33	36.04
57	26.03	26.73	27.43	28.13	28.84	29.54	30.25	30.97	31.68	32.39	33.11	33.83	34.56	35.28	36.01	36.74
58	26.51	27.23	27.94	28.66	29.37	30.10	30.82	31.55	32.27	33.00	33.74	34.47	35.21	35.95	36.69	37.43
59	27.00	27.72	28.45	29.18	29.91	30.65	31.39	32.13	32.87	33.61	34.36	35.11	35.86	36.62	37.37	38.13
60	27.48	28.22	28.96	29.71	30.45	31.20	31.96	32.71	33.47	34.23	34.99	35.75	36.52	37.29	38.06	38.83

Note: For a more detailed set of tables from 2% to 21.75%, see the reference tables in the *Business Math Handbook*.

To look up $28.94 in Table 14.1, we go down the left side of the table until we come to 60 payments (the advertisement states 60 months). Then, moving to the right, we look for $28.94 or the two numbers closest to it. The number $28.94 is between $28.22 and $28.96. So we look at the column headings and see a rate between 10.25% and 10.5%. The Truth in Lending Act requires that when creditors state the APR, it must be accurate to the nearest $\frac{1}{4}$ of 1%.[1]

[1] If we wanted an exact reading of APR when the number is not exactly in the table, we would use the process of interpolating. We do not cover this method in this course.

TABLE 14.1 (concluded)

NUMBER OF PAYMENTS	14.00%	14.25%	14.50%	14.75%	15.00%	15.25%	15.50%	15.75%	16.00%	16.25%	16.50%	16.75%	17.00%	17.25%	17.50%	17.75%
	ANNUAL PERCENTAGE RATE (FINANCE CHARGE PER $100 OF AMOUNT FINANCED)															
1	1.17	1.19	1.21	1.23	1.25	1.27	1.29	1.31	1.33	1.35	1.37	1.40	1.42	1.44	1.46	1.48
2	1.75	1.78	1.82	1.85	1.88	1.91	1.94	1.97	2.00	2.04	2.07	2.10	2.13	2.16	2.19	2.22
3	2.34	2.38	2.43	2.47	2.51	2.55	2.59	2.64	2.68	2.72	2.76	2.80	2.85	2.89	2.93	2.97
4	2.93	2.99	3.04	3.09	3.14	3.20	3.25	3.30	3.36	3.41	3.46	3.51	3.57	3.62	3.67	3.73
5	3.53	3.59	3.65	3.72	3.78	3.84	3.91	3.97	4.04	4.10	4.16	4.23	4.29	4.35	4.42	4.48
6	4.12	4.20	4.27	4.35	4.42	4.49	4.57	4.64	4.72	4.79	4.87	4.94	5.02	5.09	5.17	5.24
7	4.72	4.81	4.89	4.98	5.06	5.15	5.23	5.32	5.40	5.49	5.58	5.66	5.75	5.83	5.92	6.00
8	5.32	5.42	5.51	5.61	5.71	5.80	5.90	6.00	6.09	6.19	6.29	6.38	6.48	6.58	6.67	6.77
9	5.92	6.03	6.14	6.25	6.35	6.46	6.57	6.68	6.78	6.89	7.00	7.11	7.22	7.32	7.43	7.54
10	6.53	6.65	6.77	6.88	7.00	7.12	7.24	7.36	7.48	7.60	7.72	7.84	7.96	8.08	8.19	8.31
11	7.14	7.27	7.40	7.53	7.66	7.79	7.92	8.05	8.18	8.31	8.44	8.57	8.70	8.83	8.96	9.09
12	7.74	7.89	8.03	8.17	8.31	8.45	8.59	8.74	8.88	9.02	9.16	9.30	9.45	9.59	9.73	9.87
13	8.36	8.51	8.66	8.81	8.97	9.12	9.27	9.43	9.58	9.73	9.89	10.04	10.20	10.35	10.50	10.66
14	8.97	9.13	9.30	9.46	9.63	9.79	9.96	10.12	10.29	10.45	10.62	10.78	10.95	11.11	11.28	11.45
15	9.59	9.76	9.94	10.11	10.29	10.47	10.64	10.82	11.00	11.17	11.35	11.53	11.71	11.88	12.06	12.24
16	10.20	10.39	10.58	10.77	10.95	11.14	11.33	11.52	11.71	11.90	12.09	12.28	12.46	12.65	12.84	13.03
17	10.82	11.02	11.22	11.42	11.62	11.82	12.02	12.22	12.42	12.62	12.83	13.03	13.23	13.43	13.63	13.83
18	11.45	11.66	11.87	12.08	12.29	12.50	12.72	12.93	13.14	13.35	13.57	13.78	13.99	14.21	14.42	14.64
19	12.07	12.30	12.52	12.74	12.97	13.19	13.41	13.64	13.86	14.09	14.31	14.54	14.76	14.99	15.22	15.44
20	12.70	12.93	13.17	13.41	13.64	13.88	14.11	14.35	14.59	14.82	15.06	15.30	15.54	15.77	16.01	16.25
21	13.33	13.58	13.82	14.07	14.32	14.57	14.82	15.06	15.31	15.56	15.81	16.06	16.31	16.56	16.81	17.07
22	13.96	14.22	14.48	14.74	15.00	15.26	15.52	15.78	16.04	16.30	16.57	16.83	17.09	17.36	17.62	17.88
23	14.59	14.87	15.14	15.41	15.68	15.96	16.23	16.50	16.78	17.05	17.32	17.60	17.88	18.15	18.43	18.70
24	15.23	15.51	15.80	16.08	16.37	16.65	16.94	17.22	17.51	17.80	18.09	18.37	18.66	18.95	19.24	19.53
25	15.87	16.17	16.46	16.76	17.06	17.35	17.65	17.95	18.25	18.55	18.85	19.15	19.45	19.75	20.05	20.36
26	16.51	16.82	17.13	17.44	17.75	18.06	18.37	18.68	18.99	19.30	19.62	19.93	20.24	20.56	20.87	21.19
27	17.15	17.47	17.80	18.12	18.44	18.76	19.09	19.41	19.74	20.06	20.39	20.71	21.04	21.37	21.69	22.02
28	17.80	18.13	18.47	18.80	19.14	19.47	19.81	20.15	20.48	20.82	21.16	21.50	21.84	22.18	22.52	22.86
29	18.45	18.79	19.14	19.49	19.83	20.18	20.53	20.88	21.23	21.58	21.94	22.29	22.64	22.99	23.35	23.70
30	19.10	19.45	19.81	20.17	20.54	20.90	21.26	21.62	21.99	22.35	22.72	23.08	23.45	23.81	24.18	24.55
31	19.75	20.12	20.49	20.87	21.24	21.61	21.99	22.37	22.74	23.12	23.50	23.88	24.26	24.64	25.02	25.40
32	20.40	20.79	21.17	21.56	21.95	22.33	22.72	23.11	23.50	23.89	24.28	24.68	25.07	25.46	25.86	26.25
33	21.06	21.46	21.85	22.25	22.65	23.06	23.46	23.86	24.26	24.67	25.07	25.48	25.88	26.29	26.70	27.11
34	21.72	22.13	22.54	22.95	23.37	23.78	24.19	24.61	25.03	25.44	25.86	26.28	26.70	27.12	27.54	27.97
35	22.38	22.80	23.23	23.65	24.08	24.51	24.94	25.36	25.79	26.23	26.66	27.09	27.52	27.96	28.39	28.83
36	23.04	23.48	23.92	24.35	24.80	25.24	25.68	26.12	26.57	27.01	27.46	27.90	28.35	28.80	29.25	29.70
37	23.70	24.16	24.61	25.06	25.51	25.97	26.42	26.88	27.34	27.80	28.26	28.72	29.18	29.64	30.10	30.57
38	24.37	24.84	25.30	25.77	26.24	26.70	27.17	27.64	28.11	28.59	29.06	29.53	30.01	30.49	30.96	31.44
39	25.04	25.52	26.00	26.48	26.96	27.44	27.92	28.41	28.89	29.38	29.87	30.36	30.85	31.34	31.83	32.32
40	25.71	26.20	26.70	27.19	27.69	28.18	28.68	29.18	29.68	30.18	30.68	31.18	31.68	32.19	32.69	33.20
41	26.39	26.89	27.40	27.91	28.41	28.92	29.44	29.95	30.46	30.97	31.49	32.01	32.52	33.04	33.56	34.08
42	27.06	27.58	28.10	28.62	29.15	29.67	30.19	30.72	31.25	31.78	32.31	32.84	33.37	33.90	34.44	34.97
43	27.74	28.27	28.81	29.34	29.88	30.42	30.96	31.50	32.04	32.58	33.13	33.67	34.22	34.76	35.31	35.86
44	28.42	28.97	29.52	30.07	30.62	31.17	31.72	32.28	32.83	33.39	33.95	34.51	35.07	35.63	36.19	36.76
45	29.11	29.67	30.23	30.79	31.36	31.92	32.49	33.06	33.63	34.20	34.77	35.35	35.92	36.50	37.08	37.66
46	29.79	30.36	30.94	31.52	32.10	32.68	33.26	33.84	34.43	35.01	35.60	36.19	36.78	37.37	37.96	38.56
47	30.48	31.07	31.66	32.25	32.84	33.44	34.03	34.63	35.23	35.83	36.43	37.04	37.64	38.25	38.86	39.46
48	31.17	31.77	32.37	32.98	33.59	34.20	34.81	35.42	36.03	36.65	37.27	37.88	38.50	39.13	39.75	40.37
49	31.86	32.48	33.09	33.71	34.34	34.96	35.59	36.21	36.84	37.47	38.10	38.74	39.37	40.01	40.65	41.29
50	32.55	33.18	33.82	34.45	35.09	35.73	36.37	37.01	37.65	38.30	38.94	39.59	40.24	40.89	41.55	42.20
51	33.25	33.89	34.54	35.19	35.84	36.49	37.15	37.81	38.46	39.12	39.79	40.45	41.11	41.78	42.45	43.12
52	33.95	34.61	35.27	35.93	36.60	37.27	37.94	38.61	39.28	39.96	40.63	41.31	41.99	42.67	43.36	44.04
53	34.65	35.32	36.00	36.68	37.36	38.04	38.72	39.41	40.10	40.79	41.48	42.17	42.87	43.57	44.27	44.97
54	35.35	36.04	36.73	37.42	38.12	38.82	39.52	40.22	40.92	41.63	42.33	43.04	43.75	44.47	45.18	45.90
55	36.05	36.76	37.46	38.17	38.88	39.60	40.31	41.03	41.74	42.47	43.19	43.91	44.64	45.37	46.10	46.83
56	36.76	37.48	38.20	38.92	39.65	40.38	41.11	41.84	42.57	43.31	44.05	44.79	45.53	46.27	47.02	47.77
57	37.47	38.20	38.94	39.68	40.42	41.16	41.91	42.65	43.40	44.15	44.91	45.66	46.42	47.18	47.94	48.71
58	38.18	38.93	39.68	40.43	41.19	41.95	42.71	43.47	44.23	45.00	45.77	46.54	47.32	48.09	48.87	49.65
59	38.89	39.66	40.42	41.19	41.96	42.74	43.51	44.29	45.07	45.85	46.64	47.42	48.21	49.01	49.80	50.60
60	39.61	40.39	41.17	41.95	42.74	43.53	44.32	45.11	45.91	46.71	47.51	48.31	49.12	49.92	50.73	51.55

LO 3

Calculating the Monthly Payment by Formula and Table 14.2 (p. 344)

The pickup truck advertisement showed a $194.38 monthly payment. We can check this by formula and by table lookup.

By Formula

$$\frac{\text{Finance charge} + \text{Amount financed}}{\text{Number of payments of loan}} = \frac{\$2{,}617.80 + \$9{,}045}{60} = \$194.38$$

TABLE 14.2 Loan amortization table (monthly payment per $1,000 to pay principal and interest on installment loan)

Terms in months	7.50%	8%	8.50%	9%	10.00%	10.50%	11.00%	11.50%	12.00%
6	$170.34	$170.58	$170.83	$171.20	$171.56	$171.81	$172.05	$172.30	$172.55
12	86.76	86.99	87.22	87.46	87.92	88.15	88.38	88.62	88.85
18	58.92	59.15	59.37	59.60	60.06	60.29	60.52	60.75	60.98
24	45.00	45.23	45.46	45.69	46.14	46.38	46.61	46.84	47.07
30	36.66	36.89	37.12	37.35	37.81	38.04	38.28	38.51	38.75
36	31.11	31.34	31.57	31.80	32.27	32.50	32.74	32.98	33.21
42	27.15	27.38	27.62	27.85	28.32	28.55	28.79	29.03	29.28
48	24.18	24.42	24.65	24.77	25.36	25.60	25.85	26.09	26.33
54	21.88	22.12	22.36	22.59	23.07	23.32	23.56	23.81	24.06
60	20.04	20.28	20.52	20.76	21.25	21.49	21.74	21.99	22.24

By Table 14.2 The **loan amortization table** (many variations of this table are available) in Table 14.2 can be used to calculate the monthly payment for the pickup truck. To calculate a monthly payment with a table, use the following steps:

CALCULATING MONTHLY PAYMENT BY TABLE LOOKUP

Step 1. Divide the loan amount by $1,000 (since Table 14.2 is per $1,000):

$$\frac{\$9{,}045}{\$1{,}000} = 9.045$$

Step 2. Look up the rate (10.5%) and number of months (60). At the intersection is the table factor showing the monthly payment per $1,000.

Step 3. Multiply quotient in Step 1 by the table factor in Step 2:

$9.045 \times \$21.49 = \$194.38$.

MONEY TIPS

Use a credit card company that provides you with a detailed annual statement. This is an EXCELLENT tool for tax time.

Remember that this $194.38 fixed payment includes interest and the reduction of the balance of the loan. As the number of payments increases, interest payments get smaller and the reduction of the principal gets larger.[2]

Now let's check your progress with the Practice Quiz.

LU 14–1 PRACTICE QUIZ

Complete this **Practice Quiz** to see how you are doing.

From the partial advertisement at the right calculate the following:

1. a. Amount financed.
   b. Finance charge.
   c. Deferred payment price.
   d. APR by Table 14.1.
   e. Monthly payment by formula.

$288 per month	
Sale price	$14,150
Down payment	$ 1,450
Term/Number of payments	60 months

2. Jay Miller bought a New Brunswick boat for $7,500. Jay put down $1,000 and financed the balance at 10% for 60 months. What is his monthly payment? Use Table 14.2.

Courtesy Brunswick Corporation

[2]In Chapter 15 we give an amortization schedule for home mortgages that shows how much of each fixed payment goes to interest and how much reduces the principal. This repayment schedule also gives a running balance of the loan.

TABLE 14.2 (concluded)

Terms in months	12.50%	13.00%	13.50%	14.00%	14.50%	15.00%	15.50%	16.00%
6	$172.80	$173.04	$173.29	$173.54	$173.79	$174.03	$174.28	$174.53
12	89.08	89.32	89.55	89.79	90.02	90.26	90.49	90.73
18	61.21	61.45	61.68	61.92	62.15	62.38	62.62	62.86
24	47.31	47.54	47.78	48.01	48.25	48.49	48.72	48.96
30	38.98	39.22	39.46	39.70	39.94	40.18	40.42	40.66
36	33.45	33.69	33.94	34.18	34.42	34.67	34.91	35.16
42	29.52	29.76	30.01	30.25	30.50	30.75	31.00	31.25
48	26.58	26.83	27.08	27.33	27.58	27.83	28.08	28.34
54	24.31	24.56	24.81	25.06	25.32	25.58	25.84	26.10
60	22.50	22.75	23.01	23.27	23.53	23.79	24.05	24.32

DVD *Solutions with Step-by-Step Help on DVD*

✓ Solutions

1. **a.** $14,150 − $1,450 = **$12,700**

   b. $17,280 ($288 × 60) − $12,700 = **$4,580**

   c. $17,280 ($288 × 60) + $1,450 = **$18,730**

   d. $\frac{\$4,580}{\$12,700} \times \$100 = \$36.06$; between **12.75%** and **13%**

   e. $\frac{\$4,580 + \$12,700}{60} = $ **$288**

2. $\frac{\$6,500}{\$1,000} = 6.5 \times \$21.25 = \$138.13$ (10%, 60 months)

LU 14–1a EXTRA PRACTICE QUIZ WITH WORKED-OUT SOLUTIONS

Need more practice? Try this **Extra Practice Quiz** (check figures in Chapter Organizer, p. 353). Worked-out Solutions can be found in Appendix B at end of text.

From the partial advertisement at the right calculate the following:

1. **a.** Amount financed.
   b. Finance charge.
   c. Deferred payment price.
   d. APR by Table 14.1.
   e. Monthly payment by formula.

2. Jay Miller bought a New Brunswick boat for $8,000. Jay puts down $1,000 and financed the balance at 8% for 60 months. What is his monthly payment? Use Table 14.2.

$295 per month

Sale price: $13,999
Down payment: $1,480
Term/Number of payments: 60 months

Learning Unit 14–2: Paying Off Installment Loans before Due Date

LO 1

In Learning Unit 10–3 (p. 262), you learned about the U.S. Rule. This rule applies partial payments to the interest *first,* and then the remainder of the payment reduces the principal. Many states and the federal government use this rule.

Some states use another method for prepaying a loan called the **Rule of 78.** It is a variation of the U.S. Rule. The Rule of 78 got its name because it bases the finance charge rebate and the payoff on a 12-month loan. (Any number of months can be used.) The Rule of 78 is used less today. However, GMAC says that about 50% of its auto loans still use the Rule of 78. For loans of 61 months or longer, the Rule of 78 is not allowed (some states have even shorter requirements).

TABLE 14.3

Rebate fraction table based on Rule of 78

Months to go	Sum of digits	Months to go	Sum of digits	
1	1	31	496	
2	3	32	528	
3	6	33	561	→ 33 months to go
4	10	34	595	
5	15	35	630	
6	21	36	666	
7	28	37	703	
8	36	38	741	
9	45	39	780	
10	55	40	820	
11	66	41	861	
12	78	42	903	
13	91	43	946	
14	105	44	990	
15	120	45	1,035	
16	136	46	1,081	
17	153	47	1,128	
18	171	48	1,176	
19	190	49	1,225	
20	210	50	1,275	
21	231	51	1,326	
22	253	52	1,378	
23	276	53	1,431	
24	300	54	1,485	
25	325	55	1,540	
26	351	56	1,596	
27	378	57	1,653	
28	406	58	1,711	
29	435	59	1,770	
30	465	60	1,830	→ 60 months = 1,830

With the Rule of 78, the finance charge earned the first month is $\frac{12}{78}$. The 78 comes from summing the digits of 12 months. The finance charge for the second month would be $\frac{11}{78}$, and so on. Table 14.3 simplifies these calculations.

When the installment loan is made, a larger portion of the interest is charged to the earlier payments. As a result, when a loan is paid off early, the borrower is entitled to a **rebate,** which is calculated as follows:

CALCULATING REBATE AND PAYOFF FOR RULE OF 78

Step 1. Find the balance of the loan outstanding.

Step 2. Calculate the total finance charge.

Step 3. Find the number of payments remaining.

Step 4. Set up the rebate fraction from Table 14.3.

Step 5. Calculate the rebate amount of the finance charge.

Step 6. Calculate the payoff.

Let's see what the rebate of the finance charge and payoff would be if the pickup truck loan were paid off after 27 months (instead of 60).

To find the finance charge rebate and the final payoff, we follow six specific steps listed below. Let's begin.

Step 1. Find the balance of the loan outstanding:

Total of monthly payments (60 × \$194.38)	\$11,662.80
Payments to date: 27 × \$194.38	− 5,248.26
Balance of loan outstanding	\$ 6,414.54

Step 2. Calculate the total finance charge:

\$11,662.80	Total of all payments (60 × \$194.38)
− 9,045.00	Amount financed (\$9,345 − \$300)
\$ 2,617.80	Total finance charge

Step 3. Find the number of payments remaining:

60 − 27 = 33

Step 4. Set up the **rebate fraction** from Table 14.3.[3]

$$\frac{\text{Sum of digits based on number of months to go}}{\text{Sum of digits based on total number of months of loan}} = \frac{561}{1{,}830}$$

561 ← 33 months to go
1,830 ← 60 months in loan

Note: If this loan were for 12 months, the denominator would be 78.

Step 5. Calculate the rebate amount of the finance charge:

Rebate fraction × Total finance charge = Rebate amount

$\frac{561}{1{,}830}$ (Step 4) × \$2,617.80 (Step 2) = \$802.51

Step 6. Calculate the payoff:

Balance of loan outstanding − Rebate = Payoff

\$6,414.54 (Step 1) − \$802.51 (Step 5) = \$5,612.03

$ MONEY TIPS

Memorize your credit card number, expiration date, and security code. You may be surprised how often this comes in handy.

LU 14–2 PRACTICE QUIZ

Complete this **Practice Quiz** to see how you are doing.

Calculate the finance charge rebate and payoff (calculate all six steps):

Loan	Months of loan	End-of-month loan is repaid	Monthly payment	Finance charge rebate	Final payoff
\$5,500	12	7	\$510		

Solutions with Step-by-Step Help on DVD

✓ Solutions

Step 1.

12 × \$510 =	\$6,120
7 × \$510 =	− 3,570
	\$2,550
	(balance outstanding)

Step 2.

12 × \$510 =	\$6,120
	− 5,500
	\$ 620
	(total finance charge)

(continued on next page)

[3]If no table is available, the following formula is available:

$$\frac{\frac{N(N+1)}{2}}{\frac{T(T+1)}{2}} = \frac{\frac{33(33+1)}{2}}{\frac{60(60+1)}{2}} = \frac{561}{1{,}830}$$

In the numerator, N stands for number of months to go, and in the denominator, T is total months of the loan.

Step 3. $12 - 7 = 5$

Step 4. $\frac{15}{78}$ (by Table 14.3)

Step 5. $\frac{15}{78} \times \$620 =$ **$119.23 rebate**
(Step 4) (Step 2)

Step 6. **Step 1 − Step 5**
$2,550 − $119.23
= **$2,430.77 payoff**

LU 14–2a EXTRA PRACTICE QUIZ WITH WORKED-OUT SOLUTIONS

Need more practice? Try this **Extra Practice Quiz** (check figures in Chapter Organizer, p. 353). Worked-out Solutions can be found in Appendix B at end of text.

Calculate the finance charge rebate and payoff (calculate steps):

Loan	Months of loan	End-of-month loan is repaid	Monthly payment	Finance charge rebate	Final payoff
$6,900	12	5	$690		

Learning Unit 14–3: Revolving Charge Credit Cards

Do you owe a balance on your credit card? Let's look at how long it will take to pay off your credit card balance payments with the minimum amount. Study the following clipping "Pay Just the Minimum, and Get Nowhere Fast."

Pay Just the Minimum, and Get Nowhere Fast

THE COST—IN YEARS AND DOLLARS—OF PAYING THE MINIMUM 2% OF BALANCES ON CREDIT CARDS CHARGING 17% ANNUAL INTEREST

Balance	Total Cost	Total Time
$1,000	$2,590.35	17 years, 3 months
$2,500	$7,733.49	30 years, 3 months
$5,000	$16,305.34	40 years, 2 months

SOURCE: WWW.BANKRATE.COM

The clipping assumes that the minimum rate on the balance of a credit card is 2%. Note that if the annual interest cost is 17%, it will take 17 years, 3 months to pay off a balance of $1,000, and the total cost will be $2,590.35. If the balance on your revolving charge credit card is more than $1,000, you can see how fast the total cost rises. If you cannot afford the total cost of paying only the minimum, it is time for you to reconsider how you use your revolving credit card. This is why when you have financial difficulties, experts often advise you first to work on getting rid of your revolving credit card debt.

Do you know why revolving credit cards are so popular? Businesses encourage customers to use credit cards because consumers tend to buy more when they can use a credit card for their purchases. Consumers find credit cards convenient to use and valuable in establishing credit. The problem is that when consumers do not pay their balance in full each month, they do not realize how expensive it is to pay only the minimum of their balance.

To protect consumers, Congress passed the **Fair Credit and Charge Card Disclosure Act of 1988.**[4] This act requires that for direct-mail application or solicitation, credit card companies must provide specific details involving all fees, grace period, calculation of finance charges, and so on. Effective July 2010, new regulations regarding credit card interest rates will go into effect.

We begin the unit by seeing how Moe's Furniture Store calculates the finance charge on Abby Jordan's previous month's credit card balance. Then we learn how to calculate the average daily balance on the partial bill of Joan Ring.

[4]An update to this act was made in 1997.

TABLE 14.4 Schedule of payments

Monthly payment number	Outstanding balance due	$1\frac{1}{2}$% interest payment	Amount of monthly payment	Reduction in balance due	Outstanding balance due
1	$8,000.00	$120.00	$500.00	$380.00	$7,620.00
		(.015 × $8,000.00)		($500.00 − $120.00)	($8,000.00 − $380.00)
2	$7,620.00	$114.30	$500.00	$385.70	$7,234.30
		(.015 × $7,620.00)		($500.00 − $114.30)	($7,620.00 − $385.70)
3	$7,234.30	$108.51	$500.00	$391.49	$6,842.81
		(.015 × $7,234.30)		($500.00 − $108.51)	($7,234.30 − $391.49)

Calculating Finance Charge on Previous Month's Balance

Abby Jordan bought a dining room set for $8,000 on credit. She has a **revolving charge account** at Moe's Furniture Store. A revolving charge account gives a buyer **open-end credit.** Abby can make as many purchases on credit as she wants until she reaches her maximum $10,000 credit limit.

LO 1

Often customers do not completely pay their revolving charge accounts at the end of a billing period. When this occurs, stores add interest charges to the customers' bills. Moe's furniture store calculates its interest using the *unpaid balance method.* It charges $1\frac{1}{2}$% on the *previous month's balance,* or 18% per year. Moe's has no minimum monthly payment (many stores require $10 or $15, or a percent of the outstanding balance).

Abby has no other charges on her revolving charge account. She plans to pay $500 per month until she completely pays off her dining room set. Abby realizes that when she makes a payment, Moe's Furniture Store first applies the money toward the interest and then reduces the **outstanding balance** due. (This is the U.S. Rule we discussed in Chapter 10.) For her own information, Abby worked out the first 3-month schedule of payments, shown in Table 14.4. Note how the interest payment is the rate times the outstanding balance.

Today, most companies with credit card accounts calculate the finance charge, or interest, as a percentage of the average daily balance. Interest on credit cards can be very expensive for consumers; however, interest is a source of income for credit card companies. The following is a letter I received from my credit card company when I questioned how my finance charge was calculated.

How City Bank Calculates My Finance Charge

Thank you for your recent inquiry regarding your Citi® / AAdvantage® MasterCard® account and how finance charges are calculated.

Finance charges for purchases, balance transfers, and cash advances will begin to accrue from the date the transaction is added to your balance. They will continue to accrue until payment in full is credited to your account. This means that when you make your final payment on these balances, you will be billed finance charges for the time between the date your last statement prints and the date your payment is received.

Paying your purchase balance in full each billing period by the payment due date saves you money because it allows you to take advantage of your grace period on purchases, which is not less than 20 days. You can avoid periodic finance charges on purchases (excluding balance transfers) that appear on your current billing statement if you paid the New Balance on the last statement by the payment due date on that statement and you pay your New Balance by the payment due date on your current statement. If you made a balance transfer, you may be unable to avoid periodic finance charges on new purchases, as described in the balance transfer offer.

Calculating Average Daily Balance

Let's look at the following steps for calculating the **average daily balance.** Remember that a **cash advance** is a cash loan from a credit card company.

CALCULATING AVERAGE DAILY BALANCE AND FINANCE CHARGE

Step 1. Calculate the daily balance or amount owed at the end of each day during the billing cycle:

$$\text{Daily balance} = \text{Previous balance} + \text{Cash advances} + \text{Purchases} - \text{Payments}$$

Step 2. When the daily balance is the same for more than one day, multiply it by the number of days the daily balance remained the same, or the number of days of the current balance. This gives a cumulative daily balance.

Step 3. Add the cumulative daily balances.

Step 4. Divide the sum of the cumulative daily balances by the number of days in the billing cycle.

Step 5. Finance charge = Rate per month × Average daily balance.

Following is the partial bill of Joan Ring and an explanation of how Joan's average daily balance and finance charge was calculated. Note how we calculated each **daily balance** and then multiplied each daily balance by the number of days the balance remained the same. Take a moment to study how we arrived at 8 days. The total of the cumulative daily balances was $16,390. To get the average daily balance, we divided by the number of days in the billing cycle—30. Joan's finance charge is $1\frac{1}{2}$% per month on the average daily balance.

30-day billing cycle

6/20	Billing date	Previous balance		$450
6/27	Payment		$ 50 cr.	
6/30	Charge: JCPenney		200	
7/9	Payment		40 cr.	
7/12	Cash advance		60	

7 days had a balance of $450

30-day cycle − 22 (7 + 3 + 9 + 3) equals 8 days left with a balance of $620.

	No. of days of current balance	Current daily balance	Extension	
Step 1 →	7	$450	$ 3,150	← Step 2
	3	400 ($450 − $50)	1,200	
	9	600 ($400 + $200)	5,400	
	3	560 ($600 − $40)	1,680	
	8	620 ($560 + $60)	4,960	
	30		$16,390	← Step 3

$$\text{Average daily balance} = \frac{\$16,390}{30} = \$546.33 \quad \leftarrow \text{Step 4}$$

Step 5 → Finance charge = $546.33 × .015 = $8.19

MONEY TIPS

Record credit card purchases in your checkbook register. When the credit card bill comes, you should already have the money available to pay your bill in full, saving on interest expense while reducing your debt to equity ratio.

Now try the following Practice Quiz to check your understanding of this unit.

LU 14–3 PRACTICE QUIZ

Complete this **Practice Quiz** to see how you are doing.

1. Calculate the balance outstanding at the end of month 2 lowing: purchased $600 desk; pay back $40 per montl unpaid balance.
2. Calculate the average daily balance and finance charge fr

31-day billing cycle				
8/20	Billing date	Previous balance		$210
8/27	Payment		$50 cr.	
8/31	Charge: Staples		30	
9/5	Payment		10 cr.	
9/10	Cash advance		60	

Rate = 2% per month on average daily balance.

Solutions with Step-by-Step Help on DVD

✓ Solutions

1.

Month	Balance due	Interest	Monthly payment	Reduction in balance	Balance outstanding
1	$600	$15.00 (.025 × $600)	$40	$25.00 ($40 − $15)	$575.00
2	$575	$14.38 (.025 × $575)	$40	$25.62	$549.38

2. Average daily balance calculated as follows:

No. of days of current balance	Current balance	Extension
7	$210	$1,470
4	160 ($210 − $50)	640
5	190 ($160 + $30)	950
5	180 ($190 − $10)	900
10	240 ($180 + $60)	2,400
31		$6,360

31 − 21 (7 + 4 + 5 + 5) → 10

$$\text{Average daily balance} = \frac{\$6{,}360}{31} = \$205.16$$

Finance charge = $4.10 ($205.16 × .02)

LU 14–3a EXTRA PRACTICE QUIZ WITH WORKED-OUT SOLUTIONS

Need more practice? Try this **Extra Practice Quiz** (check figures in Chapter Organizer, p. 353). Worked-out Solutions can be found in Appendix B at end of text.

1. Calculate the balance outstanding at the end of month 2 (use U.S. Rule) given the following: purchased $300 desk; pay back $20 per month; and charge of $1\frac{1}{4}$% interest on unpaid balance.
2. Calculate the average daily balance and finance charge from the following information:

31-day billing cycle

8/21	Billing date	Previous balance		$400
8/24	Payment		100 cr.	
8/31	Charge: Staples		60	
9/5	Payment		20 cr.	
9/10	Cash Advance		200	

Finance charge is 2% on average daily balance.

CHAPTER ORGANIZER AND REFERENCE GUIDE

Topic	Key point, procedure, formula	Example(s) to illustrate situation
Amount financed, p. 340	$\text{Amount financed} = \text{Cash price} - \text{Down payment}$	60 payments at $125.67 per month; cash price $5,295 with a $95 down payment Cash price $5,295 − Down payment − 95 = Amount financed **$5,200**
Total finance charge (interest), p. 340	$\text{Total finance charge} = \text{Total of all monthly payments} - \text{Amount financed}$	*(continued from above)* $125.67 per month × 60 months = $7,540.20 − Amount financed − 5,200.00 = Finance charge **$2,340.20**
Deferred payment price, p. 341	$\text{Deferred payment price} = \text{Total of all monthly payments} + \text{Down payment}$	*(continued from above)* $7,540.20 + $95 = $7,635.20
Calculating APR by Table 14.1, p. 341	$\dfrac{\text{Finance charge}}{\text{Amount financed}} \times \$100 = \text{Table 14.1 lookup number}$	*(continued from above)* $\dfrac{\$2,340.20}{\$5,200.00} \times \$100 = \$45.004$ Search in Table 14.1 between **15.50%** and **15.75%** for 60 payments.
Monthly payment, pp. 343–344	*By formula:* $\dfrac{\text{Finance charge} + \text{Amount financed}}{\text{Number of payments of loan}}$ *By table:* $\dfrac{\text{Loan}}{\$1,000} \times \text{Table factor (rate, months)}$	*(continued from above)* $\dfrac{\$2,340.20 + \$5,200.00}{60} = \mathbf{\$125.67}$ Given: 15.5% 60 months $5,200 loan $\dfrac{\$5,200}{\$1,000} = 5.2 \times \$24.05 = \mathbf{\$125.06^*}$ *Off due to rounding of rate.
Paying off installment loan before due date, p. 346	**1.** Find balance of loan outstanding (Total of monthly payments − Payments to date). **2.** Calculate total finance charge. **3.** Find number of payments remaining. **4.** Set up rebate fraction from Table 14.3. **5.** Calculate rebate amount of finance charge. **6.** Calculate payoff.	*Example:* Loan, $8,000; 20 monthly payments of $420; end of month repaid 7. 1. $8,400 (20 × $420) − 2,940 (7 × $420) **$5,460** (balance of loan outstanding) 2. $8,400 (total payments) − 8,000 (amount financed) **$ 400** (total finance charge) 3. 20 − 7 = **13** 4 and 5. $\dfrac{91}{210} \times \$400 = \mathbf{\$173.33}$ 6. $5,460.00 (Step 1) − 173.33 rebate (Step 5) **$5,286.67** payoff
Open-end credit, p. 349	Monthly payment applied to interest first before reducing balance outstanding.	$4,000 purchase $250 a month payment $2\frac{1}{2}$% interest on unpaid balance $4,000 × .025 = $100 interest $250 − $100 = $150 to lower balance $4,000 − $150 = **$3,850** Balance outstanding after month 1.

(continues)

CHAPTER ORGANIZER AND REFERENCE GUIDE

Topic	Key point, procedure, formula	Example(s) to illustrate situation
Average daily balance and finance charge, p. 350	$\text{Daily balance} = \text{Previous balance} + \text{Cash advances} + \text{Purchases} - \text{Payments}$ $\text{Average daily balance} = \dfrac{\text{Sum of cumulative daily balances}}{\text{Number of days in billing cycle}}$ 30-day billing cycle less the 8 and 14. ← $\text{Finance charge} = \text{Monthly rate} \times \text{Average daily balance}$	*30-day billing cycle;* $1\frac{1}{2}\%$ per month *Example:* 8/21 Balance $100 8/29 Payment $10 9/12 Charge 50 *Average daily balance equals:* 8 days × $100 = $ 800 14 days × 90 = 1,260 8 days × 140 = 1,120 $3,180 ÷ 30 Average daily balance = $106 Finance charge = $106 × .015 = $1.59

KEY TERMS

Amortization, *p. 340*	Deferred payment price, *p. 341*	Open-end credit, *p. 349*
Amount financed, *p. 340*	Down payment, *p. 340*	Outstanding balance, *p. 349*
Annual percentage rate (APR), *p. 341*	Fair Credit and Charge Card Disclosure Act of 1988, *p. 348*	Rebate, *p. 346*
Average daily balance, *p. 350*	Finance charge, *p. 340*	Rebate fraction, *p. 347*
Cash advance, *p. 350*	Installment loan, *p. 340*	Revolving charge account, *p. 349*
Daily balance, *p. 350*	Loan amortization table, *p. 344*	Rule of 78, *p. 345*
		Truth in Lending Act, *p. 341*

CHECK FIGURES FOR EXTRA PRACTICE QUIZZES WITH PAGE REFERENCES. (WORKED-OUT SOLUTIONS IN APPENDIX B.)	LU 14–1a (p. 345)	LU 14–2a (p. 348)	LU 14–3a (p. 351)
	1. a. $12,519 b. $5,181 c. $19,180 d. Bet. 14.50%–14.75% e. $295 **2.** $162.24	$4,334.62 payoff; $495.38 rebate	**1.** $267.30 end of month 2 **2.** $410.97 $8.22

Critical Thinking Discussion Questions

1. Explain how to calculate the amount financed, finance charge, and APR by table lookup. Do you think the Truth in Lending Act should regulate interest charges?
2. Explain how to use the loan amortization table. Check with a person who owns a home and find out what part of each payment goes to pay interest versus the amount that reduces the loan principal.
3. What are the six steps used to calculate the rebate and payoff for the Rule of 78? Do you think it is right for the Rule of 78 to charge a larger portion of the finance charges to the earlier payments?
4. What steps are used to calculate the average daily balance? Many credit card companies charge 18% annual interest. Do you think this is a justifiable rate? Defend your answer.

Classroom Notes

END-OF-CHAPTER PROBLEMS

connect plus+ www.mhhe.com/slater10e

Check figures for odd-numbered problems in Appendix C.

Name ______________________ Date ________

DRILL PROBLEMS

Complete the following table:

	Purchase price of product	Down payment	Amount financed	Number of monthly payments	Amount of monthly payments	Total of monthly payments	Total finance charge
14–1.	Acura MDX $35,000	$10,000		72	$380		
14–2.	Apple iPhone $299	$100		12	$20.50		

Calculate **(a)** the amount financed, **(b)** the total finance charge, and **(c)** APR by table lookup.

	Purchase price of a used car	Down payment	Number of monthly payments	Amount financed	Total of monthly payments	Total finance charge	APR
14–3.	$5,673	$1,223	48		$5,729.76		
14–4.	$4,195	$95	60		$5,944.00		

Calculate the monthly payment for Problems 14–3 and 14–4 by table lookup and formula. (Answers will not be exact due to rounding of percents in table lookup.)

14–5. **(14–3)** (Use 13% for table lookup.)

14–6. **(14–4)** (Use 15.5% for table lookup.)

Calculate the finance charge rebate and payoff:

	Loan	Months of loan	End-of-month loan is repaid	Monthly payment	Finance charge rebate	Final payoff
14–7.	$7,000	36	10	$210		

Step 1. **Step 2.**

Step 3. | Step 4.

Step 5. | Step 6.

	Loan	Months of loan	End-of-month loan is repaid	Monthly payment	Finance charge rebate	Final payoff
14–8.	$9,000	24	9	$440		

Step 1. | Step 2.

Step 3. | Step 4.

Step 5. | Step 6.

14–9. Calculate the average daily balance and finance charge

30-day billing cycle				
9/16	Billing date	Previous balance		$2,000
9/19	Payment		$ 60	
9/30	Charge: Home Depot		1,500	
10/3	Payment		60	
10/7	Cash advance		70	
Finance charge is $1\frac{1}{2}$% on average daily balance				

WORD PROBLEMS

14–10. The *Boston Globe* reported on August 21, 2009, credit card companies cut limits on 58 million cardholders spanning from May 2008 to April 2009. This affected about one-third of American consumers. Surprisingly, many of these consumers had good credit scores. Dionne McGrady had planned on using a 0% interest for a year transfer credit card offer to make $8,500 worth of home improvements before her credit limit was cut. Because of this cut, she had to take out a loan to finance the project. She was offered an 11%, 10% down, 12-month loan. What is her monthly payment to the nearest cent (use loan amortization table)? What will the reduction in credit limit cost her?

14–11. To help consumers in this tough economic climate, Pikes Peak Harley-Davidson offered to finance a new motorcycle for qualifying customers at 15% down, 7.5% interest for 48 months during July 2009. Rich Martinez was interested in calculating what his monthly payment would be if he bought a $29,386 bike. Use the loan amortization table to calculate his monthly payment to the nearest cent.

14–12. Ramon Hernandez saw the following advertisement for a used Volkswagen Bug and decided to work out the numbers to be sure the ad had no errors. Please help Ramon by calculating **(a)** the amount financed, **(b)** the finance charge, **(c)** APR by table lookup, **(d)** the monthly payment by formula, and **(e)** the monthly payment by table lookup (will be off slightly).

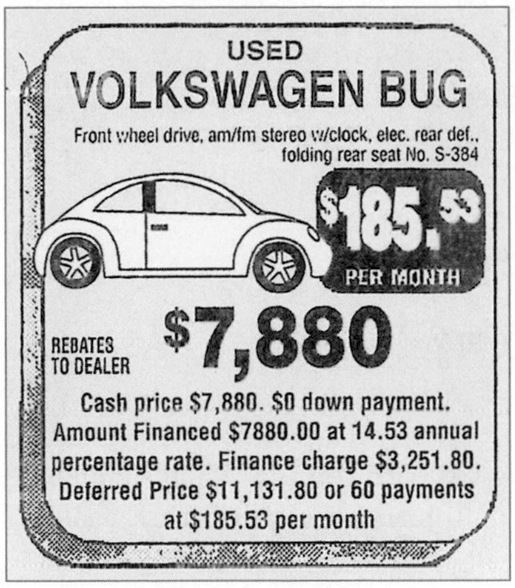

a. Amount financed:

b. Finance charge:

c. APR by table lookup:

d. Monthly payment by formula:

e. Monthly payment by table lookup (use 14.50%):

14–13. From this partial advertisement calculate:

> **$95.10 per month**
> #43892 Used car. Cash price $4,100. Down payment $50. For 60 months.

a. Amount financed.

b. Finance charge.

c. Deferred payment price.

d. APR by Table 14.1.

e. Check monthly payment (by formula).

14–14. Paula Westing borrowed $6,200 to travel to Sweden to see her son Arthur. Her loan was to be paid in 48 monthly installments of $170. At the end of 9 months, Paula's daughter Irene convinced her that she should pay off the loan early. What are Paula's rebate and her payoff amount?

Step 1.

Step 2.

Step 3.

Step 4.

Step 5.

Step 6.

14–15. Shirley Stewart is planning to buy a Toyota hybrid for $18,999 with $2,000 down and plans to finance the car. Citizens' Financial Bank quoted a finance charge at 8% for 48 months; Charter One bank quoted her a finance charge at 7.50% for 60 months. **(a)** What would be her monthly payment to Citizens' Financial Bank to the nearest cent? **(b)** What would be her monthly payment to Charter One Bank to the nearest cent? Use the loan amortization table. **(c)** How much more would her monthly payment be on the 48-month loan?

14–16. Joanne Flynn bought a new boat for \$14,500. She put a \$2,500 down payment on it. The bank's loan was for 48 months. Finance charges totaled \$4,400.16. Assume Joanne decided to pay off the loan at the end of the 28th month. What rebate would she be entitled to and what would be the actual payoff amount?

Step 1.

Step 2.

Step 3.

Step 4.

Step 5.

Step 6.

14–17. First America Bank's monthly payment charge on a 48-month \$20,000 loan is \$488.26. The U.S. Bank's monthly payment fee is \$497.70 for the same loan amount. What would be the APR for an auto loan for each of these banks? (Use the *Business Math Handbook.*)

14–18. From the following facts, Molly Roe has requested you to calculate the average daily balance. The customer believes the average daily balance should be \$877.67. Respond to the customer's concern.

28-day billing cycle				
3/18	Billing date	Previous balance		\$800
3/24	Payment		\$ 60	
3/29	Charge: Sears		250	
4/5	Payment		20	
4/9	Charge: Macy's		200	

14–19. Jill bought a \$500 rocking chair. The terms of her revolving charge are $1\frac{1}{2}\%$ on the unpaid balance from the previous month. If she pays \$100 per month, complete a schedule for the first 3 months like Table 14.4. Be sure to use the U.S. Rule.

Monthly payment number	Outstanding balance due	$1\frac{1}{2}\%$ interest payment	Amount of monthly payment	Reduction in balance due	Outstanding balance due

CHALLENGE PROBLEMS

14–20. Todd Miller just received a promotion including a $300 per month raise. He is interested in upgrading his 2001 Subaru Impreza to a 2008 Subaru Impreza WRX and wants to explore options of either selling his current car or trading it in. He went to the Kelly Blue Book online site at www.kbb.com and found that his 2001 Subaru Impreza has a trade-in value of $3,400 with a private party value of $4,700. The 2008 Subaru Impreza WRX is priced at $17,925 through a private party. His bank is offering him no down payment with 5 years at 7%. A comparable car is at the dealership in his town selling for $21,500 with terms of nothing down, 4 years at 6%. Both cars have clean titles through www.carfax.com. He has a buyer for his car if he chooses to sell the car privately. Do you recommend he trade in his car at the dealership and buy the $21,500 car or sell his car privately and purchase the private-party car for $17,925?

14–21. You have a $1,100 balance on your 15% credit card. You have lost your job and been unemployed for 6 months. You have been unable to make any payments on your balance. However, you received a tax refund and want to pay off the credit card. How much will you owe on the credit card, and how much interest will have accrued? What will be the effective rate of interest after the 6 months (to the nearest hundredth percent)?

DVD SUMMARY PRACTICE TEST

1. Walter Lantz buys a Volvo SUV for $42,500. Walter made a down payment of $16,000 and paid $510 monthly for 60 months. What are the total amount financed and the total finance charge that Walter paid at the end of the 60 months? *(p. 340)*

2. Joyce Mesnic bought an HP laptop computer at Staples for $699. Laura made a $100 down payment and financed the balance at 10% for 12 months. What is her monthly payment? (Use the loan amortization table.) *(p. 344)*

3. Lee Remick read the following partial advertisement: price, \$22,500; down payment, \$1,000 cash or trade; and \$399.99 per month for 60 months. Calculate **(a)** the total finance charge and **(b)** the APR by Table 14.1 (use the tables in *Business Math Handbook*) to the nearest hundredth percent. *(p. 343)*

4. Nancy Billows bought a \$7,000 desk at Furniture.com. Based on her income, Nancy could only afford to pay back \$700 per month. The charge on the unpaid balance is 3%. The U.S. Rule is used in the calculation. Calculate the balance outstanding at the end of month 2. *(p. 348)*

Month	Balance due	Interest	Monthly payment	Reduction in balance	Balance outstanding

5. Joan Hart borrowed \$9,800 to travel to France to see her son Dick. Joan's loan was to be paid in 50 monthly installments of \$250. At the end of 7 months, Joan's daughter Abby convinced her that she should pay off the loan early. What are Joan's rebate and payoff amount? *(p. 346)*

Step 1.

Step 2.

Step 3.

Step 4.

Step 5.

Step 6.

6. Calculate the average daily balance and finance charge on the statement below. *(p. 350)*

30-day billing cycle		
7/3	Balance	\$400
7/18	Payment	100
7/27	Charge Wal-Mart	250

Assume 2% finance charge on average daily balance.

Personal Finance

A KIPLINGER APPROACH

TOP-YIELDING MONEY-MARKET ACCOUNTS

TAXABLE FUNDS	30-day yield as of May 25	Minimum investment	Phone number
1. **USAA Money Market** (USAXX)	1.19%	$3,000	800-531-8448
2. **Ivy Money Market** (WRAXX)	1.04	500	800-777-6472
3. **W & R Advisors Cash Mgmt** (UNCXX)	0.93	500	888-923-3355
4. **Touchstone** (TMMXX)	0.82	1,000	800-543-0407
NATIONAL AVERAGE	**0.18%**		

TAX-FREE FUNDS	30-day yield as of May 26	Tax. eq. yield 25%/35% bracket	Minimum investment	Phone number
1. **Alpine Municipal** (AMUXX)	1.17%	1.6%/1.8%	$2,500	888-785-5578
2. **Marshall Tax Free*** (MTFXX)	1.05	1.4/1.6	1,000	800-236-3863
3. **USAA Tax Exempt** (USEXX)	1.04	1.4/1.6	3,000	800-531-8448
4. **Dreyfus AMT-Free** (DLRXX)	0.89	1.2/1.4	10,000	800-782-6620
NATIONAL AVERAGE	**0.30%**	**0.4%/0.5%**		

DEPOSIT ACCOUNTS	Annual yield as of May 27	Minimum amount	Web site (www.)
1. **Tenn. Commerce Bank** (Tenn.)	2.30%	$250	tncommercebank.com
2. **Ally Bank** (Utah)†	2.25	none	ally.com
3. **Corus Bank** (Ill.)	2.15	100‡	corusbank.com
4. **iGObanking.com** (N.Y.)†	2.12	none	igobanking.com
NATIONAL AVERAGE	**0.37%**		

*Fund is waiving all or a portion of its expenses. †Internet only. ‡Must maintain a $10,000 minimum balance to avoid fees. SOURCES: Bankrate.com; *Money Fund Report*, iMoneyNet Inc., One Research Dr., Westborough, MA 01581 (508-616-6600; www.imoneynet.com).

TOP-YIELDING CERTIFICATES OF DEPOSIT

1-YEAR	Annual yield as of June 10	Minimum amount	Web site (www.)
1. **Ally Bank** (Utah)†	2.49%	none	ally.com
2. **Corus Bank** (Ill.)	2.35	$10,000	corusbank.com
3. **Stonebridge Bank** (Pa.)	2.35	500	stonebridgebank.com
4. **Ascencia** (Ky.)†	2.34	500	ascenciabank.com
NATIONAL AVERAGE	**2.10%**		

5-YEAR	Annual yield as of June 10	Minimum amount	Web site (www.)
1. **Tenn. Commerce Bank** (Tenn.)	3.65%	$2,500	tncommercebank.com
2. **Intervest Natl Bank** (N.Y.)	3.62	2,500	intervestnatbank.com
3. **Lone Star Bank** (Tex.)	3.55	1,000	lonestarbank.com
4. **Ally Bank** (Utah)†	3.50	none	ally.com
NATIONAL AVERAGE	**3.10%**		

†Internet only. SOURCE: © 2009 Bankrate.com, a publication of Bankrate Inc., 11760 US Highway 1, N. Palm Beach, FL 33408; 800-327-7717, ext. 11410; www.bankrate.com/kip.

LOW-RATE CREDIT CARDS

Issuer	Rate as of May 27*	Annual fee	Late/ Over limit	800 number
Farm Bureau Bank MasterCard (P)	5.24%	none	$39†/$39†	308-6008
Pulaski Bank Visa	6.50	$35	35†/35	980-2265
Simmons First Visa (P)	7.25	none	29/29	636-5151

CASH-REBATE CREDIT CARDS

Issuer	Rate as of May 29*	Annual fee	Rebate terms Category/Other	800 number
American Express Blue Cash	11.24%	none	up to 5%/up to 1.5%	223-2670
Chase Freedom	12.24	none	1%‡	641-1774
Pentagon Fed. Visa Rewards (P)	13.99	none	up to 5%/1.25%	247-5626

Rates are adjustable. *If you do not qualify for this interest rate, the issuer will offer a higher-rate card. (P) Platinum card. †Depending on balance. ‡3% quarterly cash bonus. SOURCE: Bankrate.com. Banks may offer lower introductory rates.

FEWER TRAPS FOR CARDHOLDERS

Arbitrary penalties are history, but watch for higher fees. BY JOAN GOLDWASSER

OPPONENTS OF THE RECENTLY passed Credit CARD Act of 2009 have predicted dire consequences for borrowers. But if you pay your bills on time and have good credit, you should still qualify for a card. You may have to pay an annual fee to get a rewards card, however. Banks are already getting stingy with their rewards programs, cutting back on cash rebates and making it more difficult to earn free plane tickets.

Among the key provisions in the law, which goes into effect in February 2010:

Two egregious practices—**universal default** and **double-cycle billing**—are banned. If you are having trouble, say, paying your mortgage, your credit-card issuer can't raise your rate if you're making your card payments on time. And you won't be charged interest on a balance you have already paid.

Card issuers **may not raise your rate arbitrarily**, and your interest rate **will not increase for a year** after you open a new account. (Introductory teaser rates must last at least six months.) Plus, your issuer must provide **45 days' notice** if it is raising fees or interest rates, instead of the current 15-day standard.

Issuers may not **slap you with a penalty interest rate** unless your payment is at least 60 days overdue.

Kiplinger.com

RATE UPDATES

For the latest savings yields and loan rates, visit kiplinger.com/finances/yields.

Issuers must **apply your payment to your highest-rate balance**. That means that if you have a balance-transfer rate of 0% and a purchase rate of 11.99%, your payment will go toward the balance with the fee.

If you are under 21, you'll need a parent or someone over 21 to **cosign your credit-card application**, or you'll have to provide proof that you have income to obtain a credit card. ■

YIELD BENCHMARKS	Yield	Month-ago	Year-ago
U.S. series EE savings bonds*	0.70%	0.70%	1.40%
U.S. series I savings bonds	0.00	0.00	4.84
Six-month Treasury bills	0.28	0.30	1.93
Five-year Treasury notes	2.35	2.11	3.41
Ten-year Treasury notes	3.46	3.26	4.08

As of May 29. *EE savings bonds purchased after May 1, 2005, have a fixed rate of interest.

• Bonds purchased before May 1, 1995, earn a minimum of 4% or a market-based rate.

• Bonds bought between May 1, 1995, and May 1, 2005, earn a market-based rate from date of purchase.

SOURCES FOR TREASURIES: Bloomberg.com, U.S. Treasury.

From *Kiplinger's Personal Finance*, August 2009, p. 59.

BUSINESS MATH ISSUE

The Credit Card Act of 2009 will result in higher fees to cardholders.

1. List the key points of the article and information to support your position.
2. Write a group defense of your position using math calculations to support your view.

PROJECT A

List the key points you agree with in this article. List some key points you think are not helpful.

Slater's Business Math Scrapbook

Applying Your Skills

Avoiding College's Plastic Hangover

By AnnaMaria Andriotis
SmartMoney

THE IMMEDIATE gratification of using plastic to buy an iMac, tickets to a Coldplay concert and nights of bar hopping has a way of coming back to haunt college students after graduation.

Despite their lack of a credit history and sizable student loans, most college students can get their hands on credit cards with as much ease as a swipe. And they're often lured into doing so with awards like free T-shirts. Along with the freebies, however, come some not-so-pleasant surprises: high interest rates and a range of fees and penalties.

One reckless night of spending or one late payment can leave students with overwhelming debt and a damaged credit score—which could hurt their chances of landing a job or an apartment after college.

Many graduates know this all too well. More than three-quarters of undergraduates hold credit cards, according to student-loan provider Nellie Mae. Their average debt load: $2,169. That amount is nothing compared to the 10% of students who graduate with more than $10,000 in credit-card debt, according to a 2008 survey commissioned by credit bureau TransUnion's credit-management Web site TrueCredit.com and conducted by market-research company Zogby International.

College students "don't realize that anything they do now will stay on their credit report for the next seven to 10 years," says Thomas Fox, community outreach director at Cambridge Credit Counseling Corporation, a debt-management agency.

To graduate with honors in credit-card management, here's what students need to know:

Big Cards on Campus

Here's a sampling of some of the better deals currently available to students.

Credit card	APR	Additional features
Citi Platinum Select Visa Card for College Students	0% for six months on purchases, cash advances and balance transfers. Regular APR on purchases: 12.99%.	No minimum income required. Free online account management.
Citi Dividend Platinum Select Visa Card for College Students	0% for six months on purchases, cash advances and balance transfers. Regular APR on purchases: 13.99%.	Earn 5% cash back on purchases at supermarkets, gas stations, drugstores and utilities for six months, 2% thereafter. Earn 1% cash back on all other purchases. No minimum income required. Free online account management.
Discover Student	0% on purchases for six months. Regular APR on purchases: 14.99%.	Full 5% cash back bonus in categories like gas, groceries and restaurants. Up to 1% cash back bonus on all other purchases automatically.

Note: APRs subject to change. None of these cards have annual fees.

Sources: CreditCards.com; company Web sites

■ Don't be lured in by free T-shirts.

TrueCredit.com's survey found that four out of 10 consumers sign up for a credit card to receive a free gift or special offer, such as a T-shirt or baseball cap featuring the school's logo. That's a huge mistake, as these credit cards may not serve a student's best interest. Some universities even receive money from credit-card companies for allowing them to pitch their cards on campus, says Daniel Ray, editor-in-chief of CreditCards.com.

Make sure to compare a credit card's terms to other offers by going to Web sites like CreditCards.com and LowerMyBills.com.

■ Piggyback on a parent's card. Another option is to accept (yet another) helping hand from Mom and Dad. Signing onto a parent's credit card allows a student to take advantage of the more-established credit history (assuming they have good credit)—and lower rates, says Mr. Ray. This is especially helpful to students who have a hard time controlling their finances.

Once a student signs onto their parents' account, the parents are held responsible for their purchases and payments, and will also be able to monitor their spending habits, hopefully preventing them from racking up sizable debt, says Martha Doran, associate professor of accounting at San Diego State University.

■ Know your (credit) limits. With rare exceptions, all credit cards have limits. And because students lack established credit histories, they often receive fairly low ones—typically no more than $3,000, says Tom Dailey, a credit-card industry consultant and former senior vice president at Discover. (Limits are often as low as $500 or $1,000 per credit card, says Mr. Ray.)

It goes without saying that exceeding a card's limit can carry dire consequences, but there's also a way to make those limits work in one's favor.

By carrying a balance of, say, less than half of the available credit, a student can maintain a solid credit score, says Steven Katz, director of consumer education at TrueCredit.com.

■ Remember, promotional rates are temporary.

That 0% introductory rate is about as tempting as they come, but that temptation won't last.

Introductory annual percentage rates, or APRs, expire, and when they do they give way to high rates—especially for college students.

So make sure to find out how long the introductory rate lasts and what the APR will be afterward. (For most college students, the average APR is 15%, says Mr. Ray.)

Internet Projects: See text Web site (www.mhhe.com/slater10e) and The Business Math Internet Resource Guide.

Video Case

Honda and Green Product Design

Green product considerations are a growing concern for many individuals and businesses. Honda Corporation is demonstrating its concern for the environment by spending research and development dollars in alternative fuel vehicle design. One of its success stories is the Civic GS. The Civic GS has the same exceptional safety ratings, proven performance and Honda durability the Civic historically has had, but the Civic GS is powered by clean natural gas. It is nearly free of harmful emissions and yet has the same look and drive performance as the gasoline-powered Civic.

One of the challenges faced by alternative fuel vehicles in the growing green market is the lack of infrastructure available for refueling. Because of this challenge, engineers have created a home garage–designed refueling unit called Phill. This station permits the natural gas already coming into the home to be pumped into the Civic GS. A car can be filled overnight taking a half hour to fill one equivalent gallon of gasoline using Phill.

The Honda Civic GS is the greenest vehicle available to the public. It has received the title of the "most environmentally friendly vehicle" for the past five years. Because of this distinction, an array of government-backed incentives have been introduced through the federal government encouraging individuals to purchase the car despite the challenge of refueling. To help mitigate this challenge, the Civic GS averages 30 miles per gallon while producing virtually no emissions. Green shoppers find the value of no emissions outweigh the negatives of refueling challenges.

Honda has demonstrated a commitment to taking alternative fuel vehicles mainstream, thereby helping to protect the environment for future generations with the Civic GS. Honda engineers have also created a hydrogen-powered fuel cell vehicle—the FCX Clarity. This is the first fuel cell vehicle to be certified by the U.S. Environmental Protection Agency (EPA) for regular commercial use. The green movement has only just begun and the engineering of the Civic GS and FCX Clarity show that Honda Corporation is taking the movement seriously.

PROBLEM 1

The video discusses how the infrastructure for compressed natural gas has not been developed, thereby creating a challenge for refueling the Civic GS on the road. Phill, the compressed natural gas refueling appliance, is a personal garage unit engineered to refill the tank at one gallon every half hour. If 150 miles are driven in a day and the Civic GS gets 30 miles to the gallon, how long will it take to refuel the car using Phill?

PROBLEM 2

If the Civic GS has a fuel tank that will travel 330 miles before refueling, how many gallons does the tank hold? How long does it take to refill the tank using Phill?

PROBLEM 3

The 2009 Civic GS is recognized by the U.S. EPA as the cleanest internal combustion vehicle on earth, as noted in the video. Honda shows the Civic GS has a MSRP of $25,190. On August 31, 2009, *U.S. News and World Report* ranked the 2009 Honda Civic 2 out of 35 for affordable small cars. A 2009 Civic Coupe has a MSRP of $20,905. How much more does the 2009 Civic GS cost than the 2009 Civic Coupe? What percent is this? Round to the nearest percent.

PROBLEM 4

The video mentions that 1,000 Honda Civic GSs are currently produced. If production goes up to 2,750, what percent increase is this?

PROBLEM 5

Tameron Honda in Birmingham, Alabama, is offering 2009 summer financing specials. A 2009 Civic Coupe can be purchased with 2.9% financing for 24 to 36 months and 3.9% APR for 37 to 60 months for well-qualified buyers. If a well-qualified buyer purchased a 2009 Civic Coupe for $20,905, what would be the monthly payment for 36-month financing? How about 60-month financing?

PROBLEM 6

Honda lists the Civic GS with MPG of 24 city and 36 highway. The 2009 Civic has a listed MPG of 22 city and 31 highway. How much more average mileage does the 2009 Civic GS get than the 2009 Civic? Round to the nearest gallon. What percent is this? Round to the nearest percent.

PROBLEM 7

If you purchased a Civic GS from Westbrook Honda in Westbrook, Connecticut, for $25,190 with 48 monthly payments of $650.74 and no down payment, what is the APR on your loan?

chapter

15 THE COST OF HOME OWNERSHIP

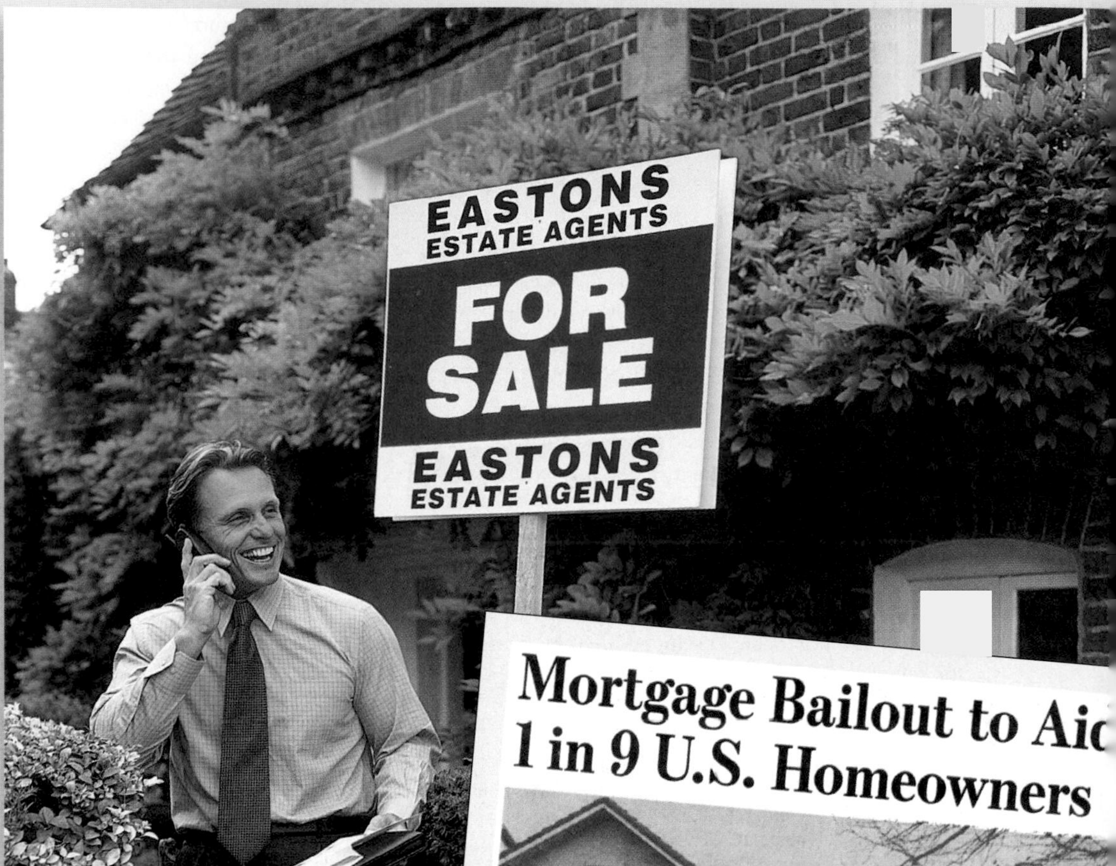

Digital Vision/Getty Images

Cartoon Features Syndicate © 2007

Wall Street Journal © 2009

LEARNING UNIT OBJECTIVES

LU 15–1: Types of Mortgages and the Monthly Mortgage Payment

1. List the types of mortgages available *(pp. 365–366)*.
2. Utilize an amortization chart to compute monthly mortgage payments *(p. 366)*.
3. Calculate the total cost of interest over the life of a mortgage *(p. •••)*.

LU 15–2: Amortization Schedule—Breaking Down the Monthly Payment

1. Calculate and identify the interest and principal portion of each monthly payment *(p. 369)*.
2. Prepare an amortization schedule *(p. 370)*.

VOCABULARY PREVIEW

Here are key terms in this chapter. After completing the chapter, if you know the term, place a checkmark in the parenthesis. If you don't know the term, look it up and put the page number where it can be found.

Adjustable rate mortgage, (ARM) . ( ) Amortization schedule . ( ) Amortization table . ( ) Biweekly mortgage . ( ) Closing costs . ( ) Escrow account . ( ) Fixed rate mortgage . ( ) Graduated-payment mortgages (GPM) . ( ) Home equity loan . ( ) Interest-only mortgage . ( ) Mortgage accelerator . ( ) Monthly payment . ( ) Mortgages . ( ) Points . ( ) Reverse mortgage . ( ) Subprime loans . ( )

FIGURE 15.1 Types of mortgages available

Loan types	Advantages	Disadvantages
30-year fixed rate mortgage	A predictable monthly payment.	If interest rates fall, you are locked in to higher rate unless you refinance. (Application and appraisal fees along with other closing costs will result.)
15-year fixed rate mortgage	Interest rate lower than 30-year fixed (usually $\frac{1}{4}$ to $\frac{1}{2}$ of a percent). Your equity builds up faster while interest costs are cut by more than one-half.	A larger down payment is needed. Monthly payment will be higher.
Graduated-payment mortgage (GPM)	Easier to qualify for than 30- or 15-year fixed rate. Monthly payments start low and increase over time.	May have higher APR than fixed or variable rates.
Biweekly mortgage*	Shortens term loan; saves substantial amount of interest; 26 biweekly payments per year. Builds equity twice as fast.	Not good for those not seeking an early loan payoff. Extra payment per year
Adjustable rate mortgage (ARM)	Lower rate than fixed. If rates fall, could be adjusted down without refinancing. Caps available that limit how high rate could go for each adjustment period over term of loan.	Monthly payment could rise if interest rates rise. Riskier than fixed rate mortgage in which monthly payment is stable.
Home equity loan	Cheap and reliable accessible lines of credit backed by equity in your home. Tax-deductible. Rates can be locked in. Reverse mortgages may be available to those 62 or older.	Could lose home if not paid. No annual or interest caps.
Interest-only mortgages	Borrowers pay interest but no principal in the early years (5 to 15) of the loan.	Early years build up no equity.

*A different type of mortgage loan, called a **mortgage accelerator** loan, has come to the United States. It uses home equity borrowing and the borrower's paycheck to shorten the time until a mortgage is paid off, saving tens of thousands in interest expense. The biweekly mortgage loan shortens a mortgage by paying an extra mortgage payment once a year, the mortgage accelerator loan program is based on an approach common in Australia and the United Kingdom, where borrowers deposit their paychecks into an account that, every month, applies every unspent dime against the mortgage loan balance.

The Financial Crises in Real Estate

The following *Wall Street Journal* clip, "Houses of Pain," (p. 366) shows how home prices have fallen and bankruptcies are way up. Why have there been so many foreclosures? Figure 15.1 lists various loan types. A type of adjustable rate mortgage called **subprime loan**

Houses of Pain

- Number of foreclosures expected over next four years: **8.1 million**
- Number of underwater home mortgages: **7.5 million**
- Number of homeowners Congress hoped to help with latest program*: **400,000**
- Number of homeowners that have applied so far: **357**

*Named 'Hope for Homeowners' and run by HUD

Sources: Credit Suisse, First American CoreLogic, HUD

"How high can the adjustable interest rate go? Well, now, we don't want to get bogged down in a lot of technicalities, do we?"

was at the root of so many foreclosures. This type of home loan allowed buyers to have a very low interest rate—sometimes even a zero rate. This helped customers qualify for expensive homes that they would not otherwise have qualified for. Lenders offering subprimes assumed prices of homes would rise and most buyers would convert to a fixed rate before the rate was substantially adjusted upward. As we now know, prices of homes have fallen. The clip "Houses of Pain" shows why banks and customers have been financially hurt.

Purchasing a home usually involves paying a large amount of interest. Note how your author was able to save $70,121.40.

Over the life of a 30-year **fixed rate mortgage** (Figure 15.1, p. 365) of $100,000, the interest would have cost $207,235. Monthly payments would have been $849.99. This would not include taxes, insurance, and so on.

Your author chose a **biweekly mortgage** (Figure 15.1, p. 365). This meant that every two weeks (26 times a year) the bank would receive $425. By paying every two weeks instead of once a month, the mortgage would be paid off in 23 years instead of 30—a $70,121.40 *savings* on interest. Why? When a payment is made every two weeks, the principal is reduced more quickly, which substantially reduces the interest cost.

Learning Unit 15–1: Types of Mortgages and the Monthly Mortgage Payment

LO 1

Thirty-Year Mortgage Hits a Low of 4.85%

By Amy Hoak

The average rate on 30-year fixed-rate home mortgages hit a record low this week, after the Federal Reserve announced it would purchase Treasury securities over the next six months, Freddie Mac's chief economist said on Thursday.

The 30-year mortgage averaged 4.85% in the week ended March 26, the lowest point since Freddie Mac's weekly survey began in 1971. Last week, the mortgage averaged 4.98%; the mortgage averaged 5.85% a year ago.

Fifteen-year fixed-rate mortgages and five-year adjustable-rate mortgages also hit record lows. The 15-year fixed-rate mortgage averaged 4.58% and hasn't been lower since 1991, when the survey began tracking the mortgage. The 15-year mortgage averaged 4.61% last week and 5.34% a year ago.

Five-year Treasury-indexed hybrid adjustable-rate mortgages averaged 4.96%, the lowest since the survey began tracking the ARM in 2005. The ARM averaged 4.98% last week and 5.67% a year ago.

One-year Treasury-indexed ARMs averaged 4.85%, down from 4.91% last week and 5.24% a year ago.

"The Federal Reserve's announcement that it intends to purchase Treasury securities over the next six months caused bond yields to drop and mortgage rates followed," said Frank Nothaft, Freddie Mac chief economist, in a statement. "Rates for 30-year fixed-rate mortgages peaked last year at 6.63% on July 24. With most recent average 30-year fixed-rate mortgage, the interest-rate difference is almost two percentage points, which amounts to a savings of about $225 in monthly mortgage payments for a $200,000 loan."

To obtain the rates, the fixed-rate mortgages as well as the five-year ARM required payment of an average 0.7 point. The one-year ARM required payment of an average 0.6 point. A point is 1% of the mortgage amount, charged as prepaid interest.

Potential home buyers are taking notice of the low rates, Mr. Nothaft said.

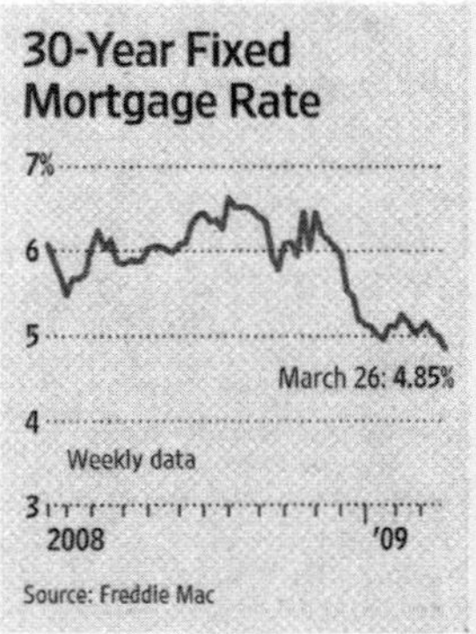

As a response to the financial mortgage crises, the government has produced a bailout package for the real estate industry. The *Wall Street Journal* article, "Thirty-Year Mortgage Hits a Low of 4.85%," shows how mortgage rates are falling. The question facing prospective buyers concerns which type of mortgage will be best for them. Figure 15.1 (p. 365) lists the type of mortgages available to home buyers. Depending on how interest rates are moving when you purchase a home, you may find one type of **mortgage** to be the most advantageous for you.

Have you heard that elderly people who are house-rich and cash-poor can use their home to get cash or monthly income? The Federal Housing Administration makes it possible for older homeowners to take out a **reverse mortgage** on their homes. Under reverse mortgages, senior homeowners borrow against the equity in their property, often getting fixed monthly checks. The debt is repaid only when the homeowners or their estate sells the home.

Now let's learn how to calculate a monthly mortgage payment and the total cost of loan interest over the life of a mortgage. We will use the following example in our discussion.

EXAMPLE Gary bought a home for $200,000. He made a 20% down payment. The 9% mortgage is for 30 years (30 × 12 = 360 payments). What are Gary's monthly payment and total cost of interest?

LO 2

Computing the Monthly Payment for Principal and Interest

You can calculate the principal and interest of Gary's **monthly payment** using the **amortization table** shown in Table 15.1 (p. 368) and the following steps. (Remember that this is the same type of amortization table used in Chapter 14 for installment loans.)

COMPUTING MONTHLY PAYMENT BY USING AN AMORTIZATION TABLE

Step 1. Divide the amount of the mortgage by $1,000.

Step 2. Look up the rate and term in the amortization table. At the intersection is the table factor.

Step 3. Multiply Step 1 by Step 2.

For Gary, we calculate the following:

$$\frac{\$160{,}000 \text{ (amount of mortgage)}}{\$1{,}000} = 160 \times \$8.05 \text{ (table rate)} = \$1{,}288$$

So $160,000 is the amount of the mortgage ($200,000 less 20%). The $8.05 is the table factor of 9% for 30 years per $1,000. Since Gary is mortgaging 160 units of $1,000, the factor of $8.05 is multiplied by 160. Remember that the $1,288 payment does not include taxes, insurance, and so on.

LO 3

What Is the Total Cost of Interest?

We can use the following formula to calculate Gary's total interest cost over the life of the mortgage:

$$\text{Total cost of interest} = \text{Total of all monthly payments} - \text{Amount of mortage}$$

$$\$303{,}680 = \underset{(\$1{,}288 \times 360)}{\$463{,}680} - \$160{,}000$$

Effects of Interest Rates on Monthly Payment and Total Interest Cost

Table 15.2 (p. 368) shows the effect that an increase in interest rates would have on Gary's monthly payment and his total cost of interest. Note that if Gary's interest rate rises to 11%, the 2% increase will result in Gary paying an additional $85,248 in total interest.

MONEY TIPS

When buying a house, if you do not have 20% in cash to put as a down payment lenders will require you to purchase PMI (Private Mortgage Insurance). This can be very expensive and only benefits the lender. It is important to know that as soon as 20% equity is reached in the home (determined by an appraisal), the borrower must petition to have the PMI removed. The mortgage lender will not be tracking this and you may continue to pay PMI after it is no longer required.

Realty Check | *June Fletcher*

Closing Time

For a typical mortgage*, closing costs for loan origination, title insurance and other settlement fees are $2,736 nationwide, according to a new study by Bankrate.com. But in some states, local customs and regulations push costs higher. Below are the five priciest:

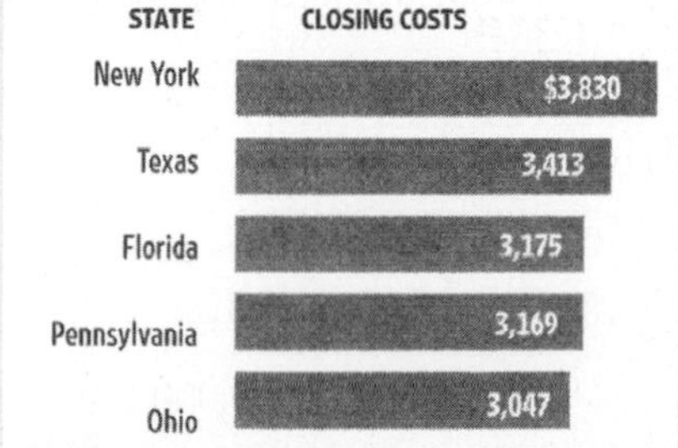

*Assuming a $200,000 mortgage, 20% down and good credit; does not include taxes and prepaid items like prorated interest, homeowners insurance and association fees.

Wall Street Journal © 2007

For most people, purchasing a home is a major lifetime decision. Many factors must be considered before this decision is made. One of these factors is how to pay for the home. The purpose of this unit is to tell you that being informed about the types of available mortgages can save you thousands of dollars.

In addition to the mortgage payment, buying a home can include the following costs:

- *Closing costs:* When property passes from seller to buyer, **closing costs** may include fees for credit reports, recording costs, lawyer's fees, points, title search, and so on. A **point** is a one-time charge that is a percent of the mortgage. Two points means 2% of the mortgage. The following *Wall Street Journal* clip, "Closing Time," shows the closing costs in various states.

TABLE 15.1 Amortization table (mortgage principal and interest per $1,000)

	INTEREST												
Term in years	5%	$5\frac{1}{2}$%	6%	$6\frac{1}{2}$%	7%	$7\frac{1}{2}$%	8%	$8\frac{1}{2}$%	9%	$9\frac{1}{2}$%	10%	$10\frac{1}{2}$%	11%
10	10.61	10.86	11.11	11.36	11.62	11.88	12.14	12.40	12.67	12.94	13.22	13.50	13.78
12	9.25	9.51	9.76	10.02	10.29	10.56	10.83	11.11	11.39	11.67	11.96	12.25	12.54
15	7.91	8.18	8.44	8.72	8.99	9.28	9.56	9.85	10.15	10.45	10.75	11.06	11.37
17	7.29	7.56	7.84	8.12	8.40	8.69	8.99	9.29	9.59	9.90	10.22	10.54	10.86
20	6.60	6.88	7.17	7.46	7.76	8.06	8.37	8.68	9.00	9.33	9.66	9.99	10.33
22	6.20	6.51	6.82	7.13	7.44	7.75	8.07	8.39	8.72	9.05	9.39	9.73	10.08
25	5.85	6.15	6.45	6.76	7.07	7.39	7.72	8.06	8.40	8.74	9.09	9.45	9.81
30	5.37	5.68	6.00	6.33	6.66	7.00	7.34	7.69	8.05	8.41	8.78	9.15	9.53
35	5.05	5.38	5.71	6.05	6.39	6.75	7.11	7.47	7.84	8.22	8.60	8.99	9.37

TABLE 15.2 Effect of interest rates on monthly payments

	9%	11%	Difference
Monthly payment	$1,288 (160 × $8.05)	$1,524.80 (160 × $9.53)	$236.80 per month
Total cost of interest	$303,680 ($1,288 × 360) − $160,000	$388,928 ($1,524.80 × 360) − $160,000	$85,248 ($236.80 × 360)

- *Escrow amount:* Usually, the lending institution, for its protection, requires that each month 1/12 of the insurance cost and 1/12 of the real estate taxes be kept in a special account called the **escrow account.** The monthly balance in this account will change depending on the cost of the insurance and taxes. Interest is paid on escrow accounts.
- *Repairs and maintenance:* This includes paint, wallpaper, landscaping, plumbing, electrical expenses, and so on.

As you can see, the cost of owning a home can be expensive. But remember that all interest costs of your monthly payment and your real estate taxes are deductible. For many, owning a home can have advantages over renting.

Before you study Learning Unit 15–2, let's check your understanding of Learning Unit 15–1.

LU 15–1 PRACTICE QUIZ

Complete this **Practice Quiz** to see how you are doing.

Given: Price of home, $225,000; 20% down payment; 9% interest rate; 25-year mortgage. Solve for:

1. Monthly payment and total cost of interest over 25 years.
2. If rate fell to 8%, what would be the total decrease in interest cost over the life of the mortgage?

Solutions with Step-by-Step Help on DVD

✓ Solutions

1. $225,000 − $45,000 = $180,000

$$\frac{\$180{,}000}{\$1{,}000} = 180 \times \$8.40 = \$1{,}512$$

$$\$273{,}600 = \underbrace{\$453{,}600}_{(\$1{,}512 \times 300)} - \$180{,}000$$

300 = 25 years × 12 payments per year

TABLE 15.1 (concluded)

Term in years	INTEREST $11\frac{1}{2}\%$	$11\frac{3}{4}\%$	12%	$12\frac{1}{2}\%$	$12\frac{3}{4}\%$	13%	$13\frac{1}{2}\%$	$13\frac{3}{4}\%$	14%	$14\frac{1}{2}\%$	$14\frac{3}{4}\%$	15%	$15\frac{1}{2}\%$
10	14.06	14.21	14.35	14.64	14.79	14.94	15.23	15.38	15.53	15.83	15.99	16.14	16.45
12	12.84	12.99	13.14	13.44	13.60	13.75	14.06	14.22	14.38	14.69	14.85	15.01	15.34
15	11.69	11.85	12.01	12.33	12.49	12.66	12.99	13.15	13.32	13.66	13.83	14.00	14.34
17	11.19	11.35	11.52	11.85	12.02	12.19	12.53	12.71	12.88	13.23	13.41	13.58	13.94
20	10.67	10.84	11.02	11.37	11.54	11.72	12.08	12.26	12.44	12.80	12.99	13.17	13.54
22	10.43	10.61	10.78	11.14	11.33	11.51	11.87	12.06	12.24	12.62	12.81	12.99	13.37
25	10.17	10.35	10.54	10.91	11.10	11.28	11.66	11.85	12.04	12.43	12.62	12.81	13.20
30	9.91	10.10	10.29	10.68	10.87	11.07	11.46	11.66	11.85	12.25	12.45	12.65	13.05
35	9.77	9.96	10.16	10.56	10.76	10.96	11.36	11.56	11.76	12.17	12.37	12.57	12.98

2. 8% = \$1,389.60 monthly payment
(180 × \$7.72)

Total interest cost \$236,880 = (\$1,389.60 × 300) − \$180,000

Savings **\$36,720** = (\$273,600 − \$236,880)

LU 15–1a EXTRA PRACTICE QUIZ WITH WORKED-OUT SOLUTIONS

Need more practice? Try this **Extra Practice Quiz** (check figures in Chapter Organizer, p. 372). Worked-out Solutions can be found in Appendix B at end of text.

Given: Price of home, \$180,000; 30% down payment; 7% interest rate; 30-year mortgage. Solve for:

1. Monthly payment and total cost of interest over 30 years.
2. If rate fell to 5%, what would be the total decrease in interest cost over the life of the mortgage?

Learning Unit 15–2: Amortization Schedule—Breaking Down the Monthly Payment

LO 1

In Learning Unit 15–1, we saw that over the life of Gary's \$160,000 loan, he would pay \$303,680 in interest. Now let's use the following steps to determine what portion of Gary's first monthly payment reduces the principal and what portion is interest.

CALCULATING INTEREST, PRINCIPAL, AND NEW BALANCE OF MONTHLY PAYMENT

Step 1. Calculate the interest for a month (use current principal):
Interest = Principal × Rate × Time.

Step 2. Calculate the amount used to reduce the principal:
Principal reduction = Monthly payment − Interest (Step 1).

Step 3. Calculate the new principal:
Current principal − Reduction of principal (Step 2) = New principal.

Step 1. Interest (I) = Principal (P) × Rate (R) × Time (T)

$$\$1{,}200 = \$160{,}000 \times .09 \times \frac{1}{12}$$

Step 2. The reduction of the $160,000 principal each month is equal to the payment less interest. So we can calculate Gary's new principal balance at the end of month 1 as follows:

Monthly payment at 9% (from Table 15.1)	$1,288 (160 × $8.05)
− Interest for first month	− 1,200
= Principal reduction	$ 88

Step 3. As the years go by, the interest portion of the payment decreases and the principal portion increases.

Principal balance	$160,000
Principal reduction	− 88
Balance of principal	$159,912

Let's do month 2:

Step 1. Interest = Principal × Rate × Time

$$= \$159{,}912 \times .09 \times \frac{1}{12}$$

$$= \$1{,}199.34$$

Step 2.

$1,288.00	monthly payment
− 1,199.34	interest for month 2
$ 88.66	principal reduction

Step 3.

$159,912.00	principal balance
− 88.66	principal reduction
$159,823.34	balance of principal

LO 2

MONEY TIPS

When refinancing a mortgage, make certain to include a clause that allows biweekly payments. Paying two times per month reduces interest cost over time yet costs the borrower no extra money.

Note that in month 2, interest costs drop 66 cents ($1,200.00 − $1,199.34). So in 2 months, Gary has reduced his mortgage balance by $176.66 ($88.00 + $88.66). After 2 months, Gary has paid a total interest of $2,399.34 ($1,200.00 + $1,199.34).

Example of an Amortization Schedule

The partial **amortization schedule** given in Table 15.3 shows the breakdown of Gary's monthly payment. Note the amount that goes toward reducing the principal and toward payment of actual interest. Also note how the outstanding balance of the loan is reduced. After 7 months, Gary still owes $159,369.97. Often when you take out a mortgage loan, you will receive an amortization schedule from the company that holds your mortgage.

TABLE 15.3 Partial amortization schedule

Payment number	Principal (current)	MONTHLY PAYMENT, $1,288: Interest	Principal reduction	Balance of principal
1	$160,000.00 $\left(\$160{,}000 \times .09 \times \frac{1}{12}\right)$	$1,200.00 ($1,288 − $1,200)	$88.00 ($160,000 − $88)	$159,912.00
2	$159,912.00 $\left(\$159{,}912 \times .09 \times \frac{1}{12}\right)$	$1,199.34 ($1,288 − $1,199.34)	$88.66 ($159,912 − $88.66)	$159,823.34
3	$159,823.34	$1,198.68	$89.32	$159,734.02
4	$159,734.02	$1,198.01	$89.99	$159,644.03
5	$159,644.03	$1,197.33	$90.67	$159,553.36
6	$159,553.36	$1,196.65	$91.35	$159,462.01
7	$159,462.01	$1,195.97*	$92.04	$159,369.97

*Off 1 cent due to rounding.

Mortgage Refinancings Seen Rising

By James R. Hagerty

The recent drop in interest rates will prompt about 18% of all U.S. households with mortgages to refinance this year, Jay Brinkmann, chief economist of the Mortgage Bankers Association, said in an interview.

Mr. Brinkmann said Tuesday that rates on 30-year fixed-rate mortgages for borrowers with strong credit records are likely to be in a range of roughly 4.6% to 4.75% at least through the summer. In recent days, those rates have hovered between about 4.75% and 5%, down from 6% in mid-November, just before the Federal Reserve embarked on a plan to drive mortgage rates lower. Mortgage rates for much of this year have been the lowest since the 1950s.

For a person with a $230,000 mortgage, refinancing to a 4.75% rate from 6% would yield savings of about $180 a month, Mr. Brinkmann said. But the best rates aren't available to all borrowers; higher costs apply to those with credit scores that are average or below, and those with high debts in relation to home values.

Mr. Brinkmann estimated that 9.5 million households will refinance their mortgages this year. The total number of households with mortgages is about 52 million.

As a result of that refinancing surge, new U.S. first-lien home-mortgage loans granted this year will surge to $2.78 trillion, up 72% from 2008's depressed level, the Mortgage Bankers Association said in a statement. The expected 2009 total includes refinancings of $1.96 trillion and home-purchase loans of $821 billion.

The Federal Reserve last week promised to spend as much as $1.25 trillion to buy mortgage securities in 2009. The Fed also is buying long-term Treasury bonds to push down rates on those securities, whose pricing affects mortgage rates.

The Fed's purchases of mortgage securities provide funds for banks to lend to homeowners. But Mr. Brinkmann said the reaction of other investors in such securities will be important in determining how far mortgage rates drop and how long they stay low.

With interest rates falling, the *Wall Street Journal* clip, "Mortgage Refinancings Seen Rising," may help you decide if refinancing is in your future.

It's time to test your knowledge of Learning Unit 15–2 with a Practice Quiz.

LU 15–2 PRACTICE QUIZ

Complete this **Practice Quiz** to see how you are doing.

Prepare an amortization schedule for first three periods for the following: mortgage, $100,000; 11%; 30 years.

DVD *Solutions with Step-by-Step Help on DVD*

✓ Solutions

$100,000 mortgage; monthly payment, $953 (100 × $9.53)

		PORTION TO—		
Payment number	**Principal (current)**	**Interest**	**Principal reduction**	**Balance of principal**
1	$100,000	$916.67 ($\left(\$100{,}000 \times .11 \times \frac{1}{12}\right)$)	$36.33 ($953.00 − $916.67)	$99,963.67 ($100,000 − $36.33)
2	$99,963.67	$916.33 ($\left(\$99{,}963.67 \times .11 \times \frac{1}{12}\right)$)	$36.67 ($953.00 − $916.33)	$99,927.00 ($99,963.67 − $36.67)
3	$99,927	$916.00 ($\left(\$99{,}927 \times .11 \times \frac{1}{12}\right)$)	$37.00 ($953.00 − $916.00)	$99,890.00 ($99,927.00 − $37.00)

LU 15–2a EXTRA PRACTICE QUIZ WITH WORKED-OUT SOLUTIONS

Need more practice? Try this **Extra Practice Quiz** (check figures in Chapter Organizer, p. 372). Worked-out Solutions can be found in Appendix B at end of text.

Prepare an amortization schedule for the first two periods for the following: mortgage, $70,000; 7%; 30 years.

CHAPTER ORGANIZER AND REFERENCE GUIDE

Topic	Key point, procedure, formula	Example(s) to illustrate situation
Computing monthly mortgage payment, p. 366	Based on per \$1,000 Table 15.1: $\frac{\text{Amount of mortgage}}{\$1{,}000} \times \text{Table rate}$	Use Table 15.1: 12% on \$60,000 mortgage for 30 years. $\frac{\$60{,}000}{\$1{,}000} = 60 \times \$10.29$ $= \$617.40$
Calculating total interest cost, p. 367	Total of all monthly payments − Amount of mortgage	Using example above: 30 years = 360 (payments) × \$617.40 \$222,264 − 60,000 \$162,264 (mortgage interest over life of mortgage)
Amortization schedule, p. 370	$I = P \times R \times T$ $\left(I \text{ for month} = P \times R \times \frac{1}{12}\right)$ Principal reduction = Monthly payment − Interest New principal = Current principal − Reduction of principal	Using same example: (Portion to— Interest, Principal reduction) Payment number 1: Interest \$600 $\left(\$60{,}000 \times .12 \times \frac{1}{12}\right)$; Principal reduction \$17.40 $\left(\begin{array}{r}\$617.40\\ -\$600.00\end{array}\right)$; Balance of principal \$59,982.60 $\left(\begin{array}{r}\$60{,}000.00\\ -\$17.40\end{array}\right)$ Payment number 2: Interest \$599.83 $\left(\$59{,}982.60 \times .12 \times \frac{1}{12}\right)$; Principal reduction \$17.57 $\left(\begin{array}{r}\$617.40\\ -\$599.83\end{array}\right)$; Balance of principal \$59,965.03 $\left(\begin{array}{r}\$59{,}982.60\\ -\$17.57\end{array}\right)$
KEY TERMS	Adjustable rate mortgage, (ARM), *p. 365* Amortization schedule, *p. 370* Amortization table, *p. 367* Biweekly mortgage, *p. 365* Closing costs, *p. 367* Escrow account, *p. 368* Fixed rate mortgage, *p. 366* Graduated-payment mortgages (GPM), *p. 365* Home equity loan, *p. 365* Interest-only mortgage, *p. 365*	Mortgage accelerator, *p. 365* Monthly payment, *p. 367* Mortgages, *p. 366* Points, *p. 367* Reverse mortgage, *p. 366* Subprime loans, *p. 365*
CHECK FIGURES FOR EXTRA PRACTICE QUIZZES WITH PAGE REFERENCES. (WORKED-OUT SOLUTIONS IN APPENDIX B.)	LU 15–1a (p. 369) 1. \$839.16 \$176,097.60 2. \$117,583.20 \$58,514.40	LU 15–2a (p. 371) \$408.33 \$57.87 \$69,942.13 \$408.00 \$58.20 \$69,833.93

Critical Thinking Discussion Questions

1. Explain the advantages and disadvantages of the following loan types: 30-year fixed rate, 15-year fixed rate, graduated-payment mortgage, biweekly mortgage, adjustable rate mortgage, and home equity loan. Why might a bank require a home buyer to establish an escrow account?
2. How is an amortization schedule calculated? Is there a best time to refinance a mortgage?
3. What is a point? Is paying points worth the cost?
4. Would you ever consider a jumbo mortgage?
5. Explain subprime loans and how foreclosures resulted.

END-OF-CHAPTER PROBLEMS

connect (plus+) www.mhhe.com/slater10e

Check figures for odd-numbered problems in Appendix C.

Name ______________________ Date ________

DRILL PROBLEMS

Complete the following amortization chart by using Table 15.1.

	Selling price of home	Down payment	Principal (loan)	Rate of interest	Years	Payment per $1,000	Monthly mortgage payment
15–1.	$120,000	$10,000		5%	25		
15–2.	$90,000	$5,000		$5\frac{1}{2}\%$	30		
15–3.	$190,000	$50,000		7%	35		

15–4. What is the total cost of interest in Problem 15–2?

15–5. If the interest rate rises to 7% in Problem 15–2, what is the total cost of interest?

Complete the following:

	Selling price	Down payment	Amount mortgage	Rate	Years	Monthly payment	First Payment Broken Down Into— Interest	First Payment Broken Down Into— Principal	Balance at end of month
15–6.	$125,000	$5,000		7%	30				
15–7.	$199,000	$40,000		$12\frac{1}{2}\%$	35				

15–8. Bob Jones bought a new log cabin for $70,000 at 11% interest for 30 years. Prepare an amortization schedule for the first 3 periods.

Payment number	Portion to— Interest	Portion to— Principal	Balance of loan outstanding

WORD PROBLEMS

15–9. In the summer of 2009, a man woke to an early morning fire causing $150,000 damage to his home in Avon, Ohio, the *Cleveland Plain Dealer* noted. The man decided to purchase a second home to live in during his home's reconstruction. When the repairs were done, he would turn one of the homes into a rental property. He purchased his second home for $215,000 at 5% for 30 years and put down 20% to avoid paying private mortgage insurance. Calculate his monthly payment.

15–10. Oprah Winfrey has closed on a 42-acre estate near Santa Barbara, California, for $50,000,000. If Oprah puts 20% down and finances at 7% for 30 years, what would her monthly payment be?

15–11. Joe Levi bought a home in Arlington, Texas, for $140,000. He put down 20% and obtained a mortgage for 30 years at $5\frac{1}{2}$%.

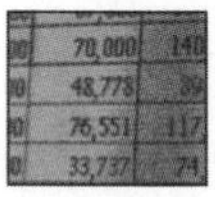

What is Joe's monthly payment? What is the total interest cost of the loan?

15–12. If in Problem 15–11 the rate of interest is $7\frac{1}{2}$%, what is the difference in interest cost?

15–13. Mike Jones bought a new split-level home for $150,000 with 20% down. He decided to use Victory Bank for his mortgage. They were offering $13\frac{3}{4}$% for 25-year mortgages. Provide Mike with an amortization schedule for the first three periods.

	Portion to—		
Payment number	**Interest**	**Principal**	**Balance of loan outstanding**

15–14. Harriet Marcus is concerned about the financing of a home. She saw a small cottage that sells for $50,000. If she puts 20% down, what will her monthly payment be at **(a)** 25 years, $11\frac{1}{2}$%; **(b)** 25 years, $12\frac{1}{2}$%; **(c)** 25 years, $13\frac{1}{2}$%; **(d)** 25 years, 15%? What is the total cost of interest over the cost of the loan for each assumption? **(e)** What is the savings in interest cost between $11\frac{1}{2}$% and 15%? **(f)** If Harriet uses 30 years instead of 25 for both $11\frac{1}{2}$% and 15%, what is the difference in interest?

15–15. The *Chicago Sun Times* reported on August 21, 2009, that nearly 14% of home mortgages in Illinois were in foreclosure or behind on payments. This is up from 9% a year earlier. Illinois ranks 17th in the nation for foreclosures started. This dismal news presented an opportunity for Norton Frank, who purchases repossessed homes. Currently he is looking at purchasing a home for $192,000 with a market value of $211,000. The terms are 5.5% for 15 years with 20% down. What will the monthly payment be on this property?

15–16. Daniel and Jan agreed to pay $560,000 for a four-bedroom colonial home in Waltham, Mass., with $60,000 down payment. They have a 30-year mortgage at a fixed rate of 6.00%. **(a)** How much is their monthly payment? **(b)** After the first payment, what would be the balance of the principal?

CHALLENGE PROBLEMS

15–17. Tony Saulino recently refinanced his $265,000 home from a 7.5%, 30-year mortgage to a 5%, 15-year mortgage. Calculate the monthly payment for both mortgages. Then calculate an estimate of how much interest he is saving with the 15-year mortgage.

15–18. Sharon Fox decided to buy a home in Marblehead, Massachusetts, for $275,000. Her bank requires a 30% down payment. Sue Willis, an attorney, has notified Sharon that besides the 30% down payment there will be the following additional costs:

Recording of the deed	$ 30.00
A credit and appraisal report	155.00
Preparation of appropriate documents	48.00

A transfer tax of 1.8% of the purchase price and a loan origination fee of 2.5% of the mortgage amount

Assume a 30-year mortgage at a rate of 10%.

a. What is the initial amount of cash Sharon will need?

b. What is her monthly payment?

c. What is the total cost of interest over the life of the mortgage?

SUMMARY PRACTICE TEST

1. Pat Lavoie bought a home for $180,000 with a down payment of $10,000. Her rate of interest is 6% for 30 years. Calculate her **(a)** monthly payment; **(b)** first payment, broken down into interest and principal; and **(c)** balance of mortgage at the end of the month. *(pp. 366, 370)*

2. Jen Logan bought a home in Iowa for $110,000. She put down 20% and obtained a mortgage for 30 years at $5\frac{1}{2}\%$. What are Jen's monthly payment and total interest cost of the loan? *(p. 367)*

3. Christina Sanders is concerned about the financing of a home. She saw a small Cape Cod–style house that sells for $90,000. If she puts 10% down, what will her monthly payment be at **(a)** 30 years, 5%; **(b)** 30 years, $5\frac{1}{2}\%$ **(c)** 30 years, 6%; and **(d)** 30 years, $6\frac{1}{2}\%$. What is the total cost of interest over the cost of the loan for each assumption? *(p. 367)*

4. Loretta Scholten bought a home for $210,000 with a down payment of $30,000. Her rate of interest is 6% for 35 years. Calculate Loretta's payment per $1,000 and her monthly mortgage payment. *(p. 366)*

5. Using Problem 4, calculate the total cost of interest for Loretta Scholten. *(p. 367)*

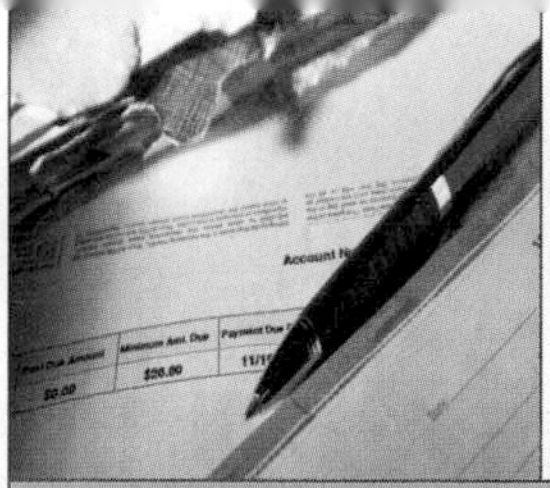

Personal Finance

A KIPLINGER APPROACH

REFINANCE, IF YOU CAN

Rates are tantalizingly low, but qualifying is a lot harder than it used to be. BY PAT MERTZ ESSWEIN

REFINANCE YOUR MORTGAGE now and you may capture the lowest interest rate of your life. But unlike a couple of years ago, when it seemed all you needed was a pay stub (if that) and an eager mortgage broker, today's process can be tedious. Demand is up, and the number of people processing mortgages is down. Plus, standards are stricter. Here's what you should know before you refinance.

What's the outlook for rates? Expect the 30-year fixed rate to hover near 5% for the rest of this year or, if the economy improves a tad, to creep up to 5.25%, says Keith Gumbinger, of financial publisher HSH Associates. HSH's survey of lenders pegged the national average 30-year fixed rate at 4.97% in early May. The average 15-year fixed rate was 4.60%, and the average 5/1 adjustable-rate mortgage (which has a rate that's fixed for five years, then changes every year thereafter) was 4.91%.

Given that rates are at historically low levels and the spread is so narrow between 30-year fixed-rate loans and 5/1 ARMs, it makes no sense to take out an ARM now.

Who qualifies for the best rates? You'll generally get the lowest rate if your loan is backed by Fannie Mae or Freddie Mac (which together guarantee about two-thirds of all mortgages) and if you're taking out a conforming loan—meaning that the mortgage falls within certain limits (see details below). You should also have a credit score of at least 720 and equity in your home of 20% or more. Other factors that will help: The property you're refinancing is the single-family home you live in, you're not taking out cash when you refinance, and you're not taking out a home-equity loan or line of credit. It's also possible to reduce your rate by paying discount points at closing. Each of these is equivalent to 1% of your loan amount. Paying one point usually lowers your interest rate by 0.25 percentage point.

What documents will I need? To get the most accurate estimate of the rate for which you'll qualify, provide a prospective lender with your FICO score (Equifax charges just $8 when you order a free credit report from the credit bureau at www.annualcreditreport.com) and an estimate of your home's market value. You can get this from a real estate agent or from Zillow.com and Trulia.com, which show recent comparable sales in your area.

When you apply to refinance your mortgage, you must provide pay stubs from a recent month, bank and other financial statements for two months, and W-2 statements for two years; plus, if you're self-employed, you'll need two years of tax returns showing self-sustaining income. The requirement for all these documents contrasts with the "no-doc" or "liar" loans available during the real estate boom, which allowed borrowers to state their income without providing proof.

You can take additional measures to speed up the process. Tracy Tolleson, a mortgage broker in Phoenix, urges his clients to fill out an application and pay for an appraisal (about $350) ahead of time. That can be particularly helpful if you're delaying your application in order to lock in a lower rate. There is a brief lag in applications between the time rates drop and the point at which lenders become swamped with new customers. Beat the rush by having your papers ready.

If you have a home-equity loan or line of credit, your current lender will have to document its willingness to *resubordinate* to your new first mortgage—that is, stand behind the first lender for compensation if you default.

Where should I apply? Guy Cecala, publisher of the newsletter *Inside Mortgage Finance*, recommends calling several lenders, including credit unions, branch offices of national and regional banks, and local banks in your area. Cecala says that at some banks, a division that would typically serve only the bank's more affluent customers (say, those with $100,000 or more in deposits) now offers good deals to nondepositors.

Also, check with a mortgage broker. Mortgage

From *Kiplinger's Personal Finance*, July 2009, p. 61.

BUSINESS MATH ISSUE

With low interest rates it makes more sense to take an ARM than to refinance.

1. List the key points of the article and information to support your position.
2. Write a group defense of your position using math calculations to support your view.

Slater's Business Math Scrapbook

Applying Your Skills

PROJECT A

Go to the Web and find out more about a hybrid ARM.

Low Rates Put Some Borrowers In a Quandary

Holders of 'Hybrid' ARMs Ponder: Rely on Resetting Lower, or Refinance Now?

BY NICK TIMIRAOS

Many homeowners are taking advantage of near-record-low mortgage rates to refinance their loans. But for one group of borrowers the low market rates can create a dilemma.

PROJECT B

Do you agree with the bailout package?

Who Would Qualify

Loan modification

For homeowners who are having trouble making mortgage payments because their interest rate has risen or their income has shrunk*

QUALIFY	Have payments of more than 31% of pretax monthly income and can prove hardship	Occupy a single-family home	Can prove the home is primary residence	Have an unpaid principal balance of $729,750 or less†	Have a mortgage originated on or before Jan. 1, 2009	Make all modified payments over a trial period of three months or more
DON'T QUALIFY	Aren't about to default	Are an investor with a home that isn't owner-occupied	Have a home that is vacant or condemned	Have an unpaid principal balance of more than $729,750†	Have a mortgage packaged into securities whose rules explicitly forbid modification	Have loan servicers who can't be reached or are unwilling to consider modification

Loan refinancing

For borrowers who aren't able to refinance, perhaps due to a decrease in the value of their home

QUALIFY	Have loans owned or guaranteed by Fannie Mae or Freddie Mac	Are current on mortgage payments	Can prove the ability to afford the new mortgage debt	Mortgage balance of no more than 105% of current estimated home value
DON'T QUALIFY	Have loans owned or guaranteed by a company other than Fannie or Freddie	Have been more than 30 days late on a payment in the past 12 months	Can't afford the new mortgage debt	Home price has fallen so that the loan is more than 105% of the market price

*Missed payments or current bankruptcy proceedings may not disqualify a borrower

†On a first lien on a one-unit home

Source: Treasury Department

Mortgage Bailout to Aid One in Nine U.S. Homeowners

Internet Projects: See text Web site (www.mhhe.com/slater10e) and The Business Math Internet Resource Guide.

Classroom Notes

chapter 16

HOW TO READ, ANALYZE, AND INTERPRET FINANCIAL REPORTS

Shift to Cheaper Chocolate Helps Boost Hershey

Bloomberg News

Despite a 20% rise in first-quarter profit, Hershey executives adopted a cautious tone on the outlook for consumer spending for the rest of the year.

BY ANJALI CORDEIRO

Hershey Co.'s first-quarter profit rose 20%, helped by higher prices, improved advertising and consumer shifts to cheaper chocolate.

Still, on a conference call with investors, the candy maker's executives struck a cautious tone about the outlook for consumer spending for the rest of the year. "Due to continued economic uncertainty and fluctuating consumer sentiment, we expect a challenging business environment for the remainder of the year," said Chief Financial Officer Humberto Alfonso.

Hershey's brands—which range from its namesake Kisses chocolate to Twizzlers—have held up reasonable well during the recession as consumers have turned away from premium brands to more moderately priced chocolates. More recently the company has also benefited from lower dairy prices.

The company, based in Hershey, Pa., reported a "solid" Easter season this year and said its results in convenience stores have been strong. As gas prices have fallen, several consumer-products brands have reported seeing improvements in their convenience-store businesses.

Hershey's net income rose to $75.9 million, or 33 cents a share, from $63.2 million, or 28 cents a share, a year earlier. Excluding charges Hershey earned 38 cents a share.

Sales rose to $1.24 billion from $1.16 billion a year earlier. Hershey said it continues to expect full-year net sales growth of 2% to 3%.

Carolyn Kaster/AP Photo

LEARNING UNIT OBJECTIVES

LU 16–1: Balance Sheet—Report as of a Particular Date

1. Explain the purpose and the key items on the balance sheet *(pp. 382–384).*
2. Explain and complete vertical and horizontal analysis *(pp. 385–386).*

LU 16–2: Income Statement—Report for a Specific Period of Time

1. Explain the purpose and the key items on the income statement *(pp. 388–390).*
2. Explain and complete vertical and horizontal analysis *(pp. 391–392).*

LU 16–3: Trend and Ratio Analysis

1. Explain and complete a trend analysis *(p. 393).*
2. List, explain, and calculate key financial ratios *(p. 396).*

VOCABULARY PREVIEW

Here are key terms in this chapter. After completing the chapter, if you know the term, place a checkmark in the parenthesis. If you don't know the term, look it up and put the page number where it can be found.

Accounts payable . ( ) Accounts receivable . ( ) Acid test . ( ) Assets . ( ) Asset turnover . ( ) Balance sheet . ( ) Capital . ( ) Common stock . ( ) Comparative statement . ( ) Corporation . ( ) Cost of merchandise (goods) sold . ( ) Current assets . ( ) Current liabilities . ( ) Current ratio . ( ) Expenses . ( ) Gross profit from sales . ( ) Gross sales . ( ) Horizontal analysis . ( ) Income statement . ( ) Liabilities . ( ) Long-term liabilities . ( ) Merchandise inventory . ( ) Mortgage note payable . ( ) Net income . ( ) Net purchases . ( ) Net sales . ( ) Operating expenses . ( ) Owner's equity . ( ) Partnership . ( ) Plant and equipment . ( ) Prepaid expenses . ( ) Purchase discounts . ( ) Purchase returns and allowances . ( ) Purchases . ( ) Quick assets . ( ) Quick ratio . ( ) Ratio analysis . ( ) Retained earnings . ( ) Return on equity . ( ) Revenues . ( ) Salaries payable . ( ) Sales (not trade) discounts . ( ) Sales returns and allowances . ( ) Sole proprietorship . ( ) Stockholders' equity . ( ) Trend analysis . ( ) Vertical analysis . ( )

"It might have been helpful if at least some of us had a fear of failure."

The Sarbanes-Oxley Act (2002) was passed to ensure public companies are accurately reporting their financial statements. The *Wall Street Journal* article, "Sarbanes-Oxley Costs for Compliance Decline," (p. 382) shows the cost of complying for companies has fallen. When this act was passed, one of the biggest issues raised by companies was the increased cost related to complying with the act. As you will see in this chapter, an understatement of expenses overstates the reported earnings or net income of a company. This overstatement presents a false picture of the company's financial position.

Sarbanes-Oxley Costs For Compliance Decline

BY JUDITH BURNS

A survey of financial executives offers signs of hope for containing the costs of complying with the Sarbanes-Oxley Act, even as overall audit expenses rose last year.

The Financial Executives International survey of 185 companies, conducted in late March and early April, found that larger firms spent an average of $3.6 million on total audit fees last year, up nearly 2% from 2006. But overall, there was a decline of 5.4% in the cost of auditors' reviewing the effectiveness of corporate management's internal controls over financial reports, as required by the Sarbanes-Oxley law.

Higher hourly rates for auditors likely explains why total costs are rising even as internal-control review costs fell, the FEI said. Larger companies paid an average of $210 an hour to auditors last year, up 5% from 2006, while smaller companies saw similar increases.

Larger firms, which accounted for more than 90% of those surveyed, spent about $846,000 on average for auditors' internal-controls reviews last year, nearly 24% of total audit fees, according to the survey.

For smaller companies, total audit fees averaged $500,000 last year, up 5.4% from the prior year, according to the survey. However, just 9% of those fees were devoted to the internal-controls reviews, reflecting that smaller firms aren't yet required to undergo such reviews.

Congress enacted the Sarbanes-Oxley corporate-governance regulations in 2002 in the wake of financial scandals to focus greater attention on internal financial-reporting controls. The law calls for companies to make an annual assessment of such controls, subject to review by the firm's outside auditor. For larger firms, those with at least $75 million in market capitalization, last year marked the fourth for the annual internal-controls reviews.

Compliance costs, once a political flash point, have come down, and the vast majority of those questioned said auditors took a more integrated approach to the task last year than in 2006. The amount of hours spent internally on assessing internal controls fell about 8.6% last year, while time spent by outsiders fell nearly 14%, according to the survey.

This chapter explains how to analyze two key financial reports: the *balance sheet* (shows a company's financial condition at a particular date) and the *income statement* (shows a company's profitability over a time period).[1] Business owners must understand their financial statements to avoid financial difficulties. This includes knowing how to read, analyze, and interpret financial reports.

Learning Unit 16–1: Balance Sheet—Report As of a Particular Date

LO 1

The **balance sheet** gives a financial picture of what a company is worth as of a particular date, usually at the end of a month or year. This report lists (1) how much the company owns (assets), (2) how much the company owes (liabilities), and (3) how much the owner (owner's equity) is worth.

Note that assets and liabilities are divided into two groups: current (*short term,* usually less than one year); and *long term,* usually more than one year. The basic formula for a balance sheet is as follows:

$$\text{Assets} - \text{Liabilities} = \text{Owner's equity}$$

Like all formulas, the items on both sides of the equal sign must balance.

By reversing the above formula, we have the following common balance sheet layout:

$$\text{Assets} = \text{Liabilities} + \text{Owner's equity}$$

To introduce you to the balance sheet, let's assume that you collect baseball cards and decide to open a baseball card shop. As the owner of The Card Shop, your investment, or owner's equity, is called **capital.** Since your business is small, your balance sheet is short. After the first year of operation, The Card Shop balance sheet looks like on page 383. The heading gives the name of the company, title of the report, and date of the report. Note how the totals of both sides of the balance sheet are the same. This is true of all balance sheets.

[1]The third key financial report is the statement of cash flows. We do not discuss this statement. For more information on the statement of cash flows, check your accounting text.

THE CARD SHOP Balance Sheet December 31, 2011			
Assets		**Liabilities**	
Cash	$ 3,000	Accounts payable	$ 2,500
Merchandise inventory (baseball cards)	4,000	**Owner's Equity**	
Equipment	3,000	E. Slott, capital	7,500
Total assets	$10,000	Total liabilities and owner's equity	$10,000

Report as of a particular date

Capital does not mean cash. It is the owner's investment in the company.

We can take figures from the balance sheet of The Card Shop and use our first formula to determine how much the business is worth:

Assets − Liabilities = Owner's equity (capital)

$10,000 − $2,500 = $7,500

David Young Wolff/PhotoEdit

Since you are the single owner of The Card Shop, your business is a **sole proprietorship.** If a business has two or more owners, it is a **partnership.** A **corporation** has many owners or stockholders, and the equity of these owners is called **stockholders' equity.** Now let's study the balance sheet elements of a corporation.

Elements of the Balance Sheet

The format and contents of all corporation balance sheets are similar. Figure 16.1 shows the balance sheet of Mool Company. As you can see, the formula Assets = Liabilities + Stockholders' equity (we have a corporation in this example) is also the framework of this balance sheet.

To help you understand the three main balance sheet groups (assets, liabilities, and stockholders' equity) and their elements, we have labeled them in Figure 16.1. An explanation of these groups and their elements follows on page 384. Do not try to memorize

FIGURE 16.1 Balance sheet

Assets broken down into current assets and plant and equipment

Put in heading who, what, when

Liabilities broken down into current and long-term

MOOL COMPANY Balance Sheet December 31, 2011									
		Assets					**Liabilities**		
1.	a.	Current assets:			2.	a.	Current liabilities:		
	b.	Cash	$ 7,000			b.	Accounts payable	$80,000	
	c.	Accounts receivable	9,000			c.	Salaries payable	12,000	
	d.	Merchandise inventory	30,000			d.	Total current liabilities		$ 92,000
	e.	Prepaid expenses	15,000			e.	Long-term liabilities:		
	f.	Total current assets		$ 61,000		f.	Mortgage note payable		58,000
	g.	Plant and equipment:				g.	Total liabilities		$150,000
	h.	Building (net)	$60,000				**Stockholders' Equity**		
	i.	Land	84,000		3.	a.	Common stock	$20,000	
	j.	Total plant and equipment		144,000		b.	Retained earnings	35,000	
						c.	Total stockholders' equity		55,000
	k.	Total assets		$205,000		d.	Total liabilities and stockholders' equity		$205,000

Total of current assets and plant and equipment

Total is double-ruled

Total of all liabilities and stockholders' equity

the elements. Just try to understand their meaning. Think of Figure 16.1 (p. 383) as a reference aid. You will find that the more you work with balance sheets, the easier it is for you to understand them.

1. **Assets:** Things of value *owned* by a company (economic resources of the company) that can be measured and expressed in monetary terms.
   a. **Current assets:** Assets that companies consume or convert to cash *within 1 year* or a normal operating cycle.
   b. **Cash:** Total cash in checking accounts, savings accounts, and on hand.
   c. **Accounts receivable:** Money *owed* to a company by customers from sales on account (buy now, pay later).
   d. **Merchandise inventory:** Cost of goods in stock for resale to customers.
   e. **Prepaid expenses:** The purchases of a company are assets until they expire (insurance or rent) or are consumed (supplies).
   f. **Total current assets:** Total of all assets that the company will consume or convert to cash within 1 year.
   g. **Plant and equipment:** Assets that will last longer than 1 year. These assets are used in the operation of the company.
   h. **Building (net):** The cost of the building minus the depreciation that has accumulated. Usually, balance sheets show this as "Building less accumulated depreciation." In Chapter 17 we discuss accumulated depreciation in greater detail.
   i. **Land:** An asset that does not depreciate, but it can increase or decrease in value.
   j. **Total plant and equipment:** Total of building and land, including machinery and equipment.
   k. **Total assets:** Total of current assets and plant and equipment.
2. **Liabilities:** Debts or obligations of the company.
   a. **Current liabilities:** Debts or obligations of the company that are *due within 1 year.*
   b. **Accounts payable:** A current liability that shows the amount the company owes to creditors for services or items purchased.
   c. **Salaries payable:** Obligations that the company must pay within 1 year for salaries earned but unpaid.
   d. **Total current liabilities:** Total obligations that the company must pay within 1 year.
   e. **Long-term liabilities:** Debts or obligations that the company does not have to pay within 1 year.
   f. **Mortgage note payable:** Debt owed on a building that is a long-term liability; often the building is the collateral.
   g. **Total liabilities:** Total of current and long-term liabilities.
3. **Stockholders' equity (owner's equity):** The rights or interest of the stockholders to assets of a corporation. If the company is not a corporation, the term *owner's equity* is used. The word *capital* follows the owner's name under the title *Owner's Equity.*

"An annual report is like a painting—you have to know what to leave out."

a. **Common stock:** Amount of the initial and additional investment of corporation owners by the purchase of stock.
b. **Retained earnings:** The amount of corporation earnings that the company retains, not necessarily in cash form.
c. **Total stockholders' equity:** Total of stock plus retained earnings.
d. **Total liabilities and stockholders' equity:** Total current liabilities, long-term liabilities, stock, and retained earnings. This total represents all the claims on assets—prior and present claims of creditors, owners' residual claims, and any other claims.

Now that you are familiar with the common balance sheet items, you are ready to analyze a balance sheet.

LO 2

Vertical Analysis and the Balance Sheet

Often financial statement readers want to analyze reports that contain data for two or more successive accounting periods. To make this possible, companies present a statement showing the data from these periods side by side. As you might expect, this statement is called a **comparative statement.**

Comparative reports help illustrate changes in data. Financial statement readers should compare the percents in the reports to industry percents and the percents of competitors.

Figure 16.2 shows the comparative balance sheet of Roger Company. Note that the statement analyzes each asset as a percent of total assets for a single period. The statement then

FIGURE 16.2

Comparative balance sheet: Vertical analysis

We divide each item by the total of assets.

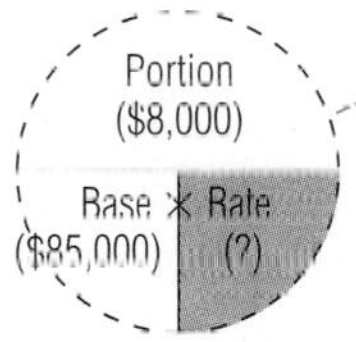

We divide each item by the total of liabilities and stockholders' equity.

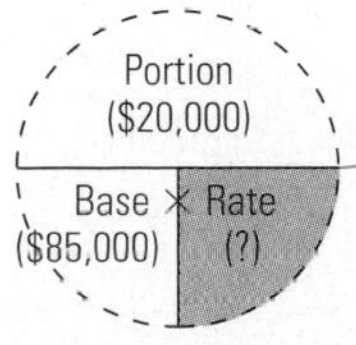

ROGER COMPANY
Comparative Balance Sheet
December 31, 2010 and 2011

	2011		2010	
	Amount	Percent	Amount	Percent
Assets				
Current assets:				
Cash	$22,000	25.88	$18,000	22.22
Accounts receivable	8,000	9.41	9,000	11.11
Merchandise inventory	9,000	10.59	7,000	8.64
Prepaid rent	4,000	4.71	5,000	6.17
Total current assets	$43,000	50.59	$39,000	48.15*
Plant and equipment:				
Building (net)	$18,000	21.18	$18,000	22.22
Land	24,000	28.24	24,000	29.63
Total plant and equipment	$42,000	49.41*	$42,000	51.85
Total assets	$85,000	100.00	$81,000	100.00
Liabilities				
Current liabilities:				
Accounts payable	$14,000	16.47	$8,000	9.88
Salaries payable	18,000	21.18	17,000	20.99
Total current liabilities	$32,000	37.65	$25,000	30.86*
Long-term liabilities:				
Mortgage note payable	12,000	14.12	20,000	24.69
Total liabilities	$44,000	51.76*	$45,000	55.56*
Stockholders' Equity				
Common stock	$20,000	23.53	$20,000	24.69
Retained earnings	21,000	24.71	16,000	19.75
Total stockholders' equity	$41,000	48.24	$36,000	44.44
Total liabilities and stockholders' equity	$85,000	100.00	$81,000	100.00

Note: All percents are rounded to the nearest hundredth percent.
*Due to rounding.

analyzes each liability and equity as a percent of total liabilities and stockholders' equity. We call this type of analysis **vertical analysis.**

The following steps use the portion formula to prepare a vertical analysis of a balance sheet.

PREPARING A VERTICAL ANALYSIS OF A BALANCE SHEET

Step 1. Divide each asset (the portion) as a percent of total assets (the base). Round as indicated.

Step 2. Round each liability and stockholders' equity (the portions) as a percent of total liabilities and stockholders' equity (the base). Round as indicated.

We can also analyze balance sheets for two or more periods by using **horizontal analysis.** Horizontal analysis compares each item in one year by amount, percent, or both with the same item of the previous year. Note the Abby Ellen Company horizontal analysis shown in Figure 16.3. To make a horizontal analysis, we use the portion formula and the steps that follow on page 387.

FIGURE 16.3

Comparative balance sheet: Horizontal analysis

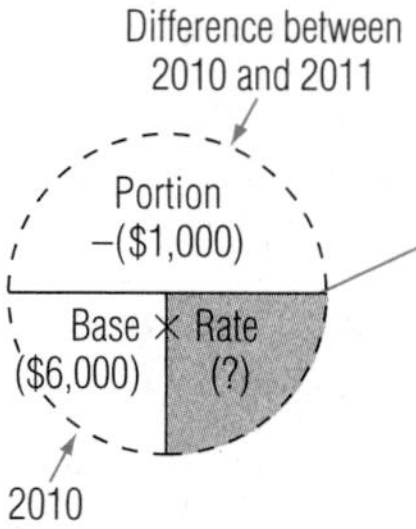

ABBY ELLEN COMPANY
Comparative Balance Sheet
December 31, 2010 and 2011

			Increase (decrease)	
	2011	**2010**	**Amount**	**Percent**
Assets				
Current assets:				
Cash	$ 6,000	$ 4,000	$2,000	50.00*
Accounts receivable	5,000	6,000	(1,000)	− 16.67
Merchandise inventory	9,000	4,000	5,000	125.00
Prepaid rent	5,000	7,000	(2,000)	− 28.57
Total current assets	$25,000	$21,000	$4,000	19.05
Plant and equipment:				
Building (net)	$12,000	$12,000	–0–	–0–
Land	18,000	18,000	–0–	–0–
Total plant and equipment	$30,000	$30,000	–0–	–0–
Total assets	$55,000	$51,000	$4,000	7.84
Liabilities				
Current liabilities:				
Accounts payable	$ 3,200	$ 1,800	$1,400	77.78
Salaries payable	2,900	3,200	(300)	− 9.38
Total current liabilities	$ 6,100	$ 5,000	$1,100	22.00
Long-term liabilities:				
Mortgage note payable	17,000	15,000	2,000	13.33
Total liabilities	$23,100	$20,000	$3,100	15.50
Owner's Equity				
Abby Ellen, capital	$31,900	$31,000	$ 900	2.90
Total liabilities and owner's equity	$55,000	$51,000	$4,000	7.84

*The percents are not summed vertically in horizontal analysis.

$ MONEY TIPS

A personal balance sheet provides you with the information needed to calculate your net worth—an important determinant of your financial standing. Net worth is a great tool to help measure your financial progress from year to year.

PREPARING A HORIZONTAL ANALYSIS OF A COMPARATIVE BALANCE SHEET

Step 1. Calculate the increase or decrease (portion) in each item from the base year.

Step 2. Divide the increase or decrease in Step 1 by the old or base year.

Step 3. Round as indicated.

You can see the difference between vertical analysis and horizontal analysis by looking at the example of vertical analysis in Figure 16.2 (p. 385). The percent calculations in Figure 16.2 are for each item of a particular year as a percent of that year's total assets or total liabilities and stockholders' equity.

Horizontal analysis needs comparative columns because we take the difference *between* periods. In Figure 16.3, for example, the accounts receivable decreased $1,000 from 2010 to 2011. Thus, by dividing $1,000 (amount of change) by $6,000 (base year), we see that Abby's receivables decreased 16.67%.

Let's now try the following Practice Quiz.

LU 16–1 PRACTICE QUIZ

Complete this **Practice Quiz** to see how you are doing.

1. Complete this partial comparative balance sheet by vertical analysis. Round percents to the nearest hundredth.

	2011		2010	
	Amount	Percent	Amount	Percent
Assets				
Current assets:				
a. Cash	$ 42,000		$ 40,000	
b. Accounts receivable	18,000		17,000	
c. Merchandise inventory	15,000		12,000	
d. Prepaid expenses	17,000		14,000	
.	.		.	
.	.		.	
.	.		.	
Total current assets	$160,000		$150,000	

2. What is the amount of change in merchandise inventory and the percent increase?

Solutions with Step-by-Step Help on DVD

✓ Solutions

		2011	2010
1. a.	Cash	$\frac{\$42,000}{\$160,000} = 26.25\%$	$\frac{\$40,000}{\$150,000} = 26.67\%$
b.	Accounts receivable	$\frac{\$18,000}{\$160,000} = 11.25\%$	$\frac{\$17,000}{\$150,000} = 11.33\%$
c.	Merchandise inventory	$\frac{\$15,000}{\$160,000} = 9.38\%$	$\frac{\$12,000}{\$150,000} = 8.00\%$
d.	Prepaid expenses	$\frac{\$17,000}{\$160,000} = 10.63\%$	$\frac{\$14,000}{\$150,000} = 9.33\%$

2.

$$\begin{array}{r} \$15,000 \\ -\ 12,000 \\ \hline \text{Amount} = \$\ 3,000 \end{array} \qquad \text{Percent} = \frac{\$3,000}{\$12,000} = 25\%$$

LU 16–1a EXTRA PRACTICE QUIZ WITH WORKED-OUT SOLUTIONS

Need more practice? Try this **Extra Practice Quiz** (check figures in Chapter Organizer, p. 398). Worked-out Solutions can be found in Appendix B at end of text.

1. Complete this partial comparative balance sheet by vertical analysis. Round percents to the nearest hundredth.

	2011		2010	
	Amount	Percent	Amount	Percent
Assets				
Current assets:				
a. Cash	$ 38,000		$ 35,000	
b. Accounts receivable	$ 19,000		$ 18,000	
c. Merchandise inventory	$ 16,000		$ 11,000	
d. Prepaid expenses	$ 20,000		$ 16,000	
.	.		.	
.	.		.	
.	.		.	
Total current assets	$180,000		$140,000	

2. What is the amount of change in merchandise inventory and the percent increase?

Learning Unit 16–2: Income Statement—Report for a Specific Period of Time

LO 1

One of the most important departments in a company is its accounting department. The job of the accounting department is to determine the financial results of the company's operations. Is the company making money or losing money? You can see in the *Wall Street Journal* clip, "Kraft Reformulates Oreo, Scores in China," that Kraft's annual sales are $37.2 billion. However, to increase Oreo sales in China, Kraft had to reinvent the Oreo to suit China's taste. Having reached such a big market, Kraft can now "taste" the increase in its profits.

GLOBAL

Imagine China/AP Photo

Kraft Reformulates Oreo, Scores in China

By Julie Jargon

Unlike its iconic American counterpart, the Oreo sold in China is frequently long, thin, four-layered and coated in chocolate. But both kinds of cookies have one important thing in common: They are now best sellers.

The Oreo has long been the top-selling cookie in the U.S. market. But **Kraft Foods** Inc. had to reinvent the Oreo to make it sell well in the world's most populous nation. While Chinese Oreo sales represent a tiny fraction of Kraft's $37.2 billion in annual revenue, the cookie's journey in China exemplifies the kind of entrepreneurial transformation that Chief Executive Irene Rosenfeld is trying to spread throughout the food giant.

Kraft, the world's second largest food company by revenue, reported a 13% drop in first-quarter net income Wednesday because of high commodity costs and increased spending on product research and marketing. Its international business, which now represents 40% of Kraft's revenue thanks to the company's recent acquisition of Groupe Danone's biscuits business, was a bright spot in the quarter, aided by the weak dollar. Kraft's profit in the European Union rose 48%, excluding special charges, and its profit in developing markets rose 57%.

To try to increase growth at the company, Ms. Rosenfeld has been putting more power in the hands of Kraft's various business units around the globe, telling employees that decisions about Kraft products at the Northfield, Ill., headquarters.

In this learning unit we look at the **income statement**—a financial report that tells how well a company is performing (its profitability or net profit) during a specific period of time (month, year, etc.). In general, the income statement reveals the inward flow of revenues (sales) against the outward or potential outward flow of costs and expenses.

The form of income statements varies depending on the company's type of business. However, the basic formula of the income is the same:

$$\text{Revenues} - \text{Operating expenses} = \text{Net income}$$

In a merchandising business like The Card Shop, we can enlarge on this formula:

Revenues (sales) ← After any returns, allowances, or discounts
− Cost of merchandise or goods ← Baseball cards
= Gross profit from sales
− Operating expenses
= Net income (profit)

THE CARD SHOP Income Statement For Month Ended December 31, 2011	
Revenues (sales)	$8,000
Cost of merchandise (goods) sold	3,000
Gross profit from sales	$5,000
Operating expenses	750
Net income	$4,250

Now let's look at The Card Shop's income statement to see how much profit The Card Shop made during its first year of operation. For simplicity, we assume The Card Shop sold all the cards it bought during the year. For its first year of business, The Card Shop made a profit of $4,250.

We can now go more deeply into the income statement elements as we study the income statement of a corporation.

Elements of the Corporation Income Statement

Figure 16.4 (p. 390) gives the format and content of the Mool Company income statement—a corporation. The five main items of an income statement are revenues, cost of merchandise (goods) sold, gross profit on sales, operating expenses, and net income. We will follow the same pattern we used in explaining the balance sheet and define the main items and the letter-coded subitems.

1. **Revenues:** Total earned sales (cash or credit) less any sales returns and allowances or sales discounts.
   a. **Gross sales:** Total earned sales before sales returns and allowances or sales discounts.
   b. **Sales returns and allowances:** Reductions in price or reductions in revenue due to goods returned because of product defects, errors, and so on. When the buyer keeps the damaged goods, an allowance results.
   c. **Sales (not trade) discounts:** Reductions in the selling price of goods due to early customer payment. For example, a store may give a 2% discount to a customer who pays a bill within 10 days.
   d. **Net sales:** Gross sales less sales returns and allowances less sales discounts.
2. **Cost of merchandise (goods) sold:** All the costs of getting the merchandise that the company sold. The cost of all unsold merchandise (goods) will be subtracted from this item (ending inventory).
   a. **Merchandise inventory, December 1, 2011:** Cost of inventory in the store that was for sale to customers at the beginning of the month.
   b. **Purchases:** Cost of additional merchandise brought into the store for resale to customers.
   c. **Purchase returns and allowances:** Cost of merchandise returned to the store due to damage, defects, errors, and so on. Damaged goods kept by the buyer result in a cost reduction called an *allowance*.
   d. **Purchase discounts:** Savings received by the buyer for paying for merchandise before a certain date. These discounts can result in a substantial savings to a company.

FIGURE 16.4 Income statement

MOOL COMPANY
Income Statement
For Month Ended December 31, 2011

		Revenues:				
1.	a.	Gross sales			$22,080	
	b.	Less: Sales returns and allowances		$ 1,082		
	c.	Sales discounts		432	1,514	
	d.	Net sales				$20,566
		Cost of merchandise (goods) sold:				
2.	a.	Merchandise inventory December 1, 2011			$1,248	
	b.	Purchases		$10,512		
	c.	Less: Purchase returns and allowances	$336			
	d.	Less: Purchase discounts	204	540		
	e.	Cost of net purchases			9,972	
	f.	Cost of merchandise (goods available for sale)			$11,220	
	g.	Less: Merchandise inventory, December 31, 2011			1,600	
	h.	Cost of merchandise (goods) sold				9,620
3.		Gross profit from sales				$10,946
		Operating expenses:				
4.	a.	Salary		$ 2,200		
	b.	Insurance		1,300		
	c.	Utilities		400		
	d.	Plumbing		120		
	e.	Rent		410		
	f.	Depreciation		200		
	g.	Total operating expenses				4,630
5.		Net income				$ 6,316

Report for a specific period

Put in heading who, what, when

Actual sales after discounts and returns

Inventory not yet sold

Net sales − Cost of merchandise (goods) sold

Gross profit − Operating expenses

Note: Numbers are subtotaled from left to right.

Tin cans make up about 20%, 15% and 8%, respectively, of the cost of goods sold for **Campbell Soup** Co., **Del Monte Foods** Co. and **General Mills** Inc., maker of Progresso-brand soups and Green Giant canned vegetables.

Wall Street Journal © 2009

e. **Cost of net purchases:** Cost of purchases less purchase returns and allowances less purchase discounts.

f. **Cost of merchandise (goods available for sale):** Sum of beginning inventory plus cost of net purchases.

g. **Merchandise inventory, December 31, 2011:** Cost of inventory remaining in the store to be sold.

h. **Cost of merchandise (goods) sold:** Beginning inventory plus net purchases less ending inventory. Note in the accompanying *Wall Street Journal* clipping that the cost of tin cans makes up 20% of the cost of goods sold for Campbell Soup Co.

3. **Gross profit from sales:** Net sales less cost of merchandise (goods) sold.
4. **Operating expenses:** Additional costs of operating the business beyond the actual cost of inventory sold.
   a.–f. **Expenses:** Individual expenses broken down.
   g. **Total operating expenses:** Total of all the individual expenses.
5. **Net income:** Gross profit less operating expenses.

You can read in the *Wall Street Journal* clip, "World's Biggest Food Companies" (p. 391) that although Nestle's sales were the highest among the companies listed, Nestle's also had the lowest operating profit margin.

In the next section you will learn some formulas that companies use to calculate various items on the income statement.

Calculating Net Sales, Cost of Merchandise (Goods) Sold, Gross Profit, and Net Income of an Income Statement

It is time to look closely at Figure 16.4 (p. 390) and see how each section is built. Use the previous vocabulary as a reference. We will study Figure 16.4 step by step.

Step 1. Calculate the net sales—what Mool earned:

Net sales = Gross sales − Sales returns and allowances − Sales discounts

$20,566 = $22,080 − $1,082 − $432

Step 2. Calculate the cost of merchandise (goods) sold:

Cost of merchandise (goods) sold = Beginning inventory + Net purchases (purchases less returns and discounts) − Ending inventory

$9,620 = $1,248 + $9,972 − $1,600

Step 3. Calculate the gross profit from sales—profit before operating expenses:

Gross profit from sales = Net sales − Cost of merchandise (goods) sold

$10,946 − $20,566 − $9,620

Step 4. Calculate the net income—profit after operating expenses:

Net income = Gross profit − Operating expenses

$6,316 = $10,946 − $4,630

LO 2

Analyzing Comparative Income Statements

We can apply the same procedures of vertical and horizontal analysis to the income statement that we used in analyzing the balance sheet. Let's first look at the vertical analysis for Royal Company, Figure 16.5 (p. 392). Then we will look at the horizontal analysis of Flint Company's 2010 and 2011 income statements shown in Figure 16.6 (p. 392). Note in the margin how numbers are calculated.

The following Practice Quiz will test your understanding of this *unit*.

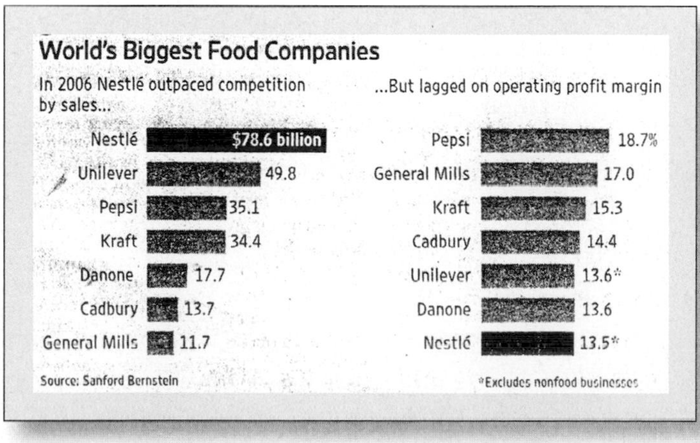

Wall Street Journal © 2007

Justin Sullivan/Getty Images

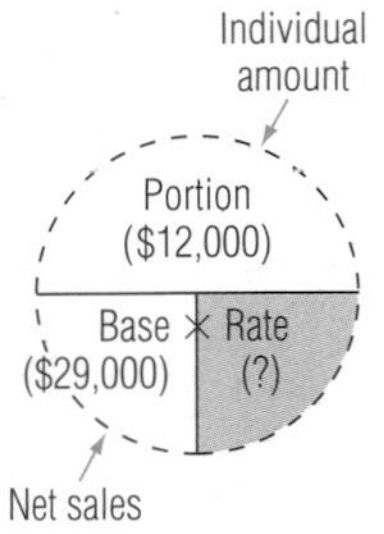

ROYAL COMPANY Comparative Income Statement For Years Ended December 31, 2010 and 2011	2011	Percent of net	2010	Percent of net
Net sales	$45,000	100.00	$29,000	100.00*
Cost of merchandise sold	19,000	42.22	12,000	41.38
Gross profit from sales	$26,000	57.78	$17,000	58.62
Operating expenses:				
Depreciation	$ 1,000	2.22	$ 500	1.72
Selling and advertising	4,200	9.33	1,600	5.52
Research	2,900	6.44	2,000	6.90
Miscellaneous	500	1.11	200	.69
Total operating expenses	$ 8,600	19.11†	$ 4,300	14.83
Income before interest and taxes	$17,400	38.67	$12,700	43.79
Interest expense	6,000	13.33	3,000	10.34
Income before taxes	$11,400	25.33†	$ 9,700	33.45
Provision for taxes	5,500	12.22	3,000	10.34
Net income	$ 5,900	13.11	$ 6,700	23.10†

*Net sales = 100%
†Off due to rounding.

FIGURE 16.6

Horizontal analysis

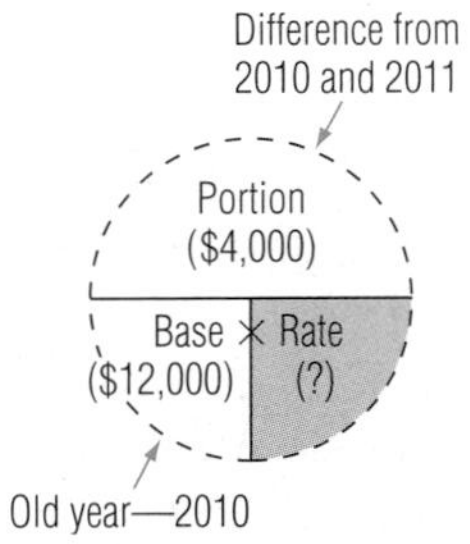

FLINT COMPANY Comparative Income Statement For Years Ended December 31, 2010 and 2011	2011	2010	INCREASE (DECREASE) Amount	Percent
Sales	$90,000	$80,000	$10,000	
Sales returns and allowances	2,000	2,000	-0-	
Net sales	$88,000	$78,000	$10,000	+ 12.82
Cost of merchandise (goods) sold	45,000	40,000	5,000	+ 12.50
Gross profit from sales	$43,000	$38,000	$ 5,000	+ 13.16
Operating expenses:				
Depreciation	$ 6,000	$ 5,000	$ 1,000	+ 20.00
Selling and administrative	16,000	12,000	4,000	+ 33.33
Research	600	1,000	(400)	− 40.00
Miscellaneous	1,200	500	700	+ 140.00
Total operating expenses	$23,800	$18,500	$ 5,300	+ 28.65
Income before interest and taxes	$19,200	$19,500	$ (300)	− 1.54
Interest expense	4,000	4,000	-0-	
Income before taxes	$15,200	$15,500	$ (300)	− 1.94
Provision for taxes	3,800	4,000	(200)	− 5.00
Net income	$11,400	$11,500	$ (100)	− .87

MONEY TIPS

The income statement allows you to see where your money comes from and where it goes. It is a tool that can be used to help you see the big picture of sources of money, costs, and expenses to allow you to make changes in your spending habits if necessary.

LU 16–2 PRACTICE QUIZ

Complete this **Practice Quiz** to see how you are doing.

From the following information, calculate:

a. Net sales.
b. Cost of merchandise (goods) sold.
c. Gross profit from sales.
d. Net income.

Given Gross sales, $35,000; sales returns and allowances, $3,000; beginning inventory, $6,000; net purchases, $7,000; ending inventory, $5,500; operating expenses, $7,900.

DVD *Solutions with Step-by-Step Help on DVD*

✓ Solutions

a. $35,000 − $3,000 = $32,000 (Gross sales − Sales returns and allowances)
b. $6,000 + $7,000 − $5,500 = $7,500 (Beginning inventory + Net purchases − Ending inventory)
c. $32,000 − $7,500 = $24,500 (Net sales − Cost of merchandise sold)
d. $24,500 − $7,900 = $16,600 (Gross profit from sales − Operating expenses)

LU 16–2a EXTRA PRACTICE QUIZ WITH WORKED-OUT SOLUTIONS

Need more practice? Try this **Extra Practice Quiz** (check figures in Chapter Organizer, p. 398). Worked-out Solutions can be found in Appendix B at end of text.

From the following information, calculate:

a. Net sales
b. Cost of merchandise (goods) sold
c. Gross profit from sales
d. Net income

Given: Gross sales, $36,000; sales returns and allowances, $2,800; beginning inventory, $5,900; net purchases, $6,800; ending inventory, $5,200; operating expenses, $8,100.

Learning Unit 16–3: Trend and Ratio Analysis

LO 1

Now that you understand the purpose of balance sheets and income statements, you are ready to study how experts look for various trends as they analyze the financial reports of companies. This learning unit discusses trend analysis and ratio analysis. The study of these trends is valuable to businesses, financial institutions, and consumers.

Trend Analysis

Many tools are available to analyze financial reports. When data cover several years, we can analyze changes that occur by expressing each number as a percent of the base year. The base year is a past period of time that we use to compare sales, profits, and so on, with other years. We call this **trend analysis.**

Using the following example of Rose Company, we complete a trend analysis with the following steps:

COMPLETING A TREND ANALYSIS

Step 1. Select the base year (100%).

Step 2. Express each amount as a percent of the base year amount (rounded to the nearest whole percent).

	GIVEN (BASE YEAR 2009)			
	2012	2011	2010	2009
Sales	$621,000	$460,000	$340,000	$420,000
Gross profit	182,000	141,000	112,000	124,000
Net income	48,000	41,000	22,000	38,000

	TREND ANALYSIS			
	2012	2011	2010	2009
Sales	148%	110%	81%	100%
Gross profit	147	114	90	100
Net income	126	108	58	100

How to Calculate Trend Analysis

Sales for 2010

$$\frac{\text{Each item}}{\text{Base amount}} = \frac{\$340{,}000}{\$420{,}000} = 80.95\% = 81\%$$

Sales for 2009

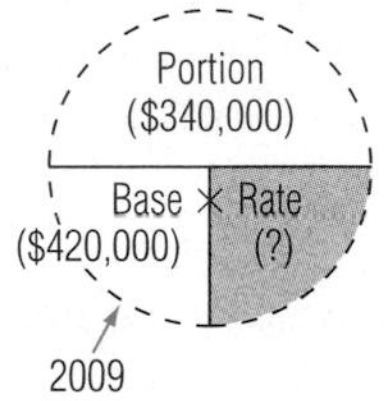

What Trend Analysis Means Sales of 2010 were 81% of the sales of 2009. Note that you would follow the same process no matter which of the three areas you were analyzing. All categories are compared to the base year—sales, gross profit, or net income.

We now will examine **ratio analysis**—another tool companies use to analyze performance.

Ratio Analysis

LO 2

A *ratio* is the relationship of one number to another. Many companies compare their ratios with those of previous years and with ratios of other companies in the industry. Companies can get ratios of the performance of other companies from their bankers, accountants, local small business center, libraries, and newspaper articles. For example, ratios at McDonald's will be different than at Toys "R" Us. McDonald's sells more perishable products.

Percentage ratios are used by companies to determine the following:

1. How well the company manages its assets—*asset management ratios.*
2. The company's debt situation—*debt management ratios.*
3. The company's profitability picture—*profitability ratios.*

Each company must decide the true meaning of what the three types of ratios (asset management, debt management, and profitability) are saying. Table 16.1 (p. 396) gives a summary of the key ratios, their calculations (rounded to the nearest hundredth), and what they mean. All calculations are from Figures 16.1 (p. 383) and 16.4 (p. 386). For some perspective on the time it takes companies to collect money owed by customers, see the accompanying *Wall Street Journal* clip, "The Check Is in the Mail."

$ MONEY TIPS

Financial ratios can be used as a road map to personal financial health. Three of the most important ratios are savings to income, debt to income, and savings rate (amount of pretax income saved each year) to income. The desired ratios change based on age and income.

Now you can check your knowledge with the Practice Quiz that follows on page 395.

LU 16–3 PRACTICE QUIZ

Complete this **Practice Quiz** to see how you are doing.

1. Prepare a trend analysis from the following sales, assuming a base year of 2009. Round to the nearest whole percent.

	2012	2011	2010	2009
Sales	$29,000	$44,000	$48,000	$60,000

2. **Given** Total current assets (CA), $15,000; accounts receivable (AR), $6,000; total current liabilities (CL), $10,000; inventory (Inv), $4,000; net sales, $36,000; total assets, $30,000; net income (NI), $7,500.

Calculate

a. Current ratio.

b. Acid test.

c. Average day's collection.

d. Profit margin on sales (round to the nearest hundredth percent).

Solutions with Step-by-Step Help on DVD

✓ Solutions

		2012	2011	2010	2009
1.	Sales	48%	73%	80%	100%
		$\left(\frac{\$29{,}000}{\$60{,}000}\right)$	$\left(\frac{\$44{,}000}{\$60{,}000}\right)$	$\left(\frac{\$48{,}000}{\$60{,}000}\right)$	

2. **a.** $\frac{CA}{CL} = \frac{\$15{,}000}{\$10{,}000} = 1.5$

b. $\frac{CA - Inv}{CL} = \frac{\$15{,}000 - \$4{,}000}{\$10{,}000} = 1.1$

c. $\frac{AR}{\frac{\text{Net sales}}{360}} = \frac{\$6{,}000}{\frac{\$36{,}000}{360}} = 60 \text{ days}$

d. $\frac{NI}{\text{Net sales}} = \frac{\$7{,}500}{\$36{,}000} = 20.83\%$

LU 16–3a EXTRA PRACTICE QUIZ WITH WORKED-OUT SOLUTIONS

Need more practice? Try this **Extra Practice Quiz** (check figures in Chapter Organizer, p. 398). Worked-out Solutions can be found in Appendix B at end of text.

1. Prepare a trend analysis from the following sales, assuming a base year of 2009. Round to the nearest whole percent.

	2012	2011	2010	2009
Sales	$25,000	$60,000	$50,000	$70,000

2. **Given:** Total current assets (CA), $14,000; accounts receivable (AR), $5,500; total current liabilities (CL), $9,000; inventory (Inv), $3,900; net sales, $36,500; total assets, $32,000; net income (NI), $8,000. Calculate:

a. Current ratio.

b. Acid test.

c. Average day's collection.

d. Profit margin on sales (round to the nearest hundredth percent).

TABLE 16.1 Summary of key ratios: A reference guide*

Ratio	Formula	Actual calculations	What it says	Questions that could be raised
1. Current ratio†	$\frac{\text{Current assets}}{\text{Current liabilities}}$ (Current assets include cash, accounts receivable, and marketable securities.)	$\frac{\$61{,}000}{\$92{,}000} = .66{:}1$ Industry average, 2 to 1	Business has 66¢ of current assets to meet each $1 of current debt.	Not enough current assets to pay off current liabilities. Industry standard is $2 for each $1 of current debt.
2. Acid test (quick ratio) Top of fraction often → referred to as *quick assets*	$\frac{\text{Current assets} - \text{Inventory} - \text{Prepaid expenses}}{\text{Current liabilities}}$ (Inventory and prepaid expenses are excluded because it may not be easy to convert these to cash.)	$\frac{\$61{,}000 - \$30{,}000 - \$15{,}000}{\$92{,}000} = .17{:}1$ Industry average, 1 to 1	Business has only 17¢ to cover each $1 of current debt. This calculation excludes inventory and prepaid expenses.	Same as above but more severe.
3. Average day's collection	$\frac{\text{Accounts receivable}}{\frac{\text{Net sales}}{360}}$	$\frac{\$9{,}000}{\frac{\$20{,}566}{360}} = 158\text{ days}$ Industry average, 90–120 days	On the average, it takes 158 days to collect accounts receivable.	Could we speed up collection since industry average is 90–120 days?
4. Total debt to total assets	$\frac{\text{Total liabilities}}{\text{Total assets}}$	$\frac{\$150{,}000}{\$205{,}000} = 73.17\%$ Industry average, 50%–70%	For each $1 of assets, the company owes 73¢ in current and long-term debt.	73% is slightly higher than industry average.
5. Return on equity	$\frac{\text{Net income}}{\text{Stockholders' equity}}$	$\frac{\$6{,}316}{\$55{,}000} = 11.48\%$ Industry average, 15%–20%	For each $1 invested by the owner, a return of 11¢ results.	Could we get a higher return on money somewhere else?
6. Asset turnover	$\frac{\text{Net sales}}{\text{Total assets}}$	$\frac{\$20{,}566}{\$205{,}000} = 10¢$ Industry average, 3¢ to 8¢	For each $1 invested in assets, it returns 10¢ in sales.	Are assets being utilized efficiently?
7. Profit margin on net sales	$\frac{\text{Net income}}{\text{Net sales}}$	$\frac{\$6{,}316}{\$20{,}566} = 30.71\%$ Industry average, 25%–40%	For each $1 of sales, company produces 31¢ in profit.	Compared to competitors, are we showing enough profits versus our increased sales?

*Inventory turnover is discussed in Chapter 18.
†For example, Wal-Mart Stores, Inc., has a current ratio of 1.51.

CHAPTER ORGANIZER AND REFERENCE GUIDE

Topic	Key point, procedure, formula	Example(s) to illustrate situation
Balance sheet		
Vertical analysis, p. 385	Process of relating each figure on a financial report (down the column) to a total figure.	Current assets $ 520 52% Plant and equipment 480 48 Total assets $1,000 100%
Horizontal analysis, p. 386	Analyzing comparative financial reports shows rate and amount of change across columns item by item.	**2011** | **2010** | **Change** | % Cash, $5,000 | $4,000 | $1,000 | 25% ← $\left(\frac{\$1{,}000}{\$4{,}000}\right)$

(continues)

CHAPTER ORGANIZER AND REFERENCE GUIDE

Topic	Key point, procedure, formula	Example(s) to illustrate situation
Income statement formulas, p. 391	(Horizontal and vertical analysis can also be done for income statements.)	
Net sales, p. 391	Gross sales − Sales returns and allowances − Sales discounts	$200 gross sales − 10 sales returns and allowances − 2 sales discounts **$188** net sales
Cost of merchandise (goods) sold, p. 391	Beginning inventory + Net purchases − Ending inventory	$50 + $100 − $20 = **$130** Beginning inventory + Net purchases − Ending inventory = Cost of merchandise (goods) sold
Gross profit from sales, p. 391	Net sales − Cost of merchandise (goods) sold	$188 − $130 = **$58** gross profit from sales Net sales − Cost of merchandise (goods) sold = Gross profit from sales
Net income, p. 391	Gross profit − Operating expenses	$58 − $28 = **$30** Gross profit from sales − Operating expenses = Net income
Trend analysis, p. 393	Each number expressed as a percent of the base year. $\frac{\text{Each item}}{\text{Base amount}}$	Sales: **2012** $200, **2011** $300, **2010** $400 ← Base year **50%** $\left(\frac{\$200}{\$400}\right)$ **75%** $\left(\frac{\$300}{\$400}\right)$ 100%
Ratios, p. 394	Tools to interpret items on financial reports.	Use this example for calculating the following ratios: current assets, $30,000; accounts receivable, $12,000; total current liabilities, $20,000; inventory, $6,000; prepaid expenses, $2,000; net sales, $72,000; total assets, $60,000; net income, $15,000; total liabilities, $30,000.
Current ratio, p. 396	$\frac{\text{Current assets}}{\text{Current liabilities}}$	$\frac{\$30{,}000}{\$20{,}000} = $ **1.5**
Acid test (quick ratio), p. 396	$\frac{\text{Current assets} - \text{Inventory} - \text{Prepaid expenses}}{\text{Current liabilities}}$ (numerator: Called quick assets)	$\frac{\$30{,}000 - \$6{,}000 - \$2{,}000}{\$20{,}000} = $ **1.1**
Average day's collection, p. 396	$\frac{\text{Accounts receivable}}{\frac{\text{Net sales}}{360}}$	$\frac{\$12{,}000}{\frac{\$72{,}000}{360}} = $ **60 days**
Total debt to total assets, p. 396	$\frac{\text{Total liabilities}}{\text{Total assets}}$	$\frac{\$30{,}000}{\$60{,}000} = $ **50%**
Return on equity, p. 396	$\frac{\text{Net income}}{\text{Stockholders' equity (A − L)}}$	$\frac{\$15{,}000}{\$30{,}000} = $ **50%**
Asset turnover, p. 396	$\frac{\text{Net sales}}{\text{Total assets}}$	$\frac{\$72{,}000}{\$60{,}000} = $ **1.2**
Profit margin on net sales, p. 396	$\frac{\text{Net income}}{\text{Net sales}}$	$\frac{\$15{,}000}{\$72{,}000} = .2083 = $ **20.83%**

(continues)

CHAPTER ORGANIZER AND REFERENCE GUIDE

Topic	Key point, procedure, formula		Example(s) to illustrate situation
KEY TERMS	Accounts payable, *p. 384* Accounts receivable, *p. 384* Acid test, *p. 396* Assets, *p. 384* Asset turnover, *p. 396* Balance sheet, *p. 382* Capital, *p. 382* Common stock, *p. 385* Comparative statement, *p. 385* Corporation, *p. 383* Cost of merchandise (goods) sold, *p. 389* Current assets, *p. 384* Current liabilities, *p. 384* Current ratio, *p. 396* Expenses, *p. 390* Gross profit from sales, *p. 390*	Gross sales, *p. 389* Horizontal analysis, *p. 386* Income statement, *p. 389* Liabilities, *p. 384* Long-term liabilities, *p. 384* Merchandise inventory, *p. 384* Mortgage note payable, *p. 384* Net income, *p. 390* Net purchases, *p. 390* Net sales, *p. 389* Operating expenses, *p. 390* Owner's equity, *p. 384* Partnership, *p. 383* Plant and equipment, *p. 384* Prepaid expenses, *p. 384* Purchase discounts, *p. 389* Purchase returns and allowances, *p. 389*	Purchases, *p. 389* Quick assets, *p. 396* Quick ratio, *p. 396* Ratio analysis, *p. 394* Retained earnings, *p. 385* Return on equity, *p. 396* Revenues, *p. 384* Salaries payable, *p. 384* Sales (not trade) discounts, *p. 389* Sales returns and allowances, *p. 389* Sole proprietorship, *p. 383* Stockholders' equity, *pp. 383, 384* Trend analysis, *p. 393* Vertical analysis, *p. 386*
CHECK FIGURES FOR EXTRA PRACTICE QUIZZES WITH PAGE REFERENCES. (WORKED-OUT SOLUTIONS IN APPENDIX B.)	LU 16–1a (p. 388) **1.** a. 21.11%; 25% b. 10.56%; 12.86% c. 8.89%; 7.86% d. 11.11%; 11.43% **2.** 45.45%	LU 16–2a (p. 393) **1.** a. $33,200 b. $7,500 c. $25,700 d. $17,600	LU 16–3a (p. 395) **1.** 36%; 86%; 71%; 100% **2.** a. 1.6 b. 1.12 c. 54.2 d. 21.92%

Critical Thinking Discussion Questions

1. What is the difference between current assets and plant and equipment? Do you think land should be allowed to depreciate?
2. What items make up stockholders' equity? Why might a person form a sole proprietorship instead of a corporation?
3. Explain the steps to complete a vertical or horizontal analysis relating to balance sheets. Why are the percents not summed vertically in horizontal analysis?
4. How do you calculate net sales, cost of merchandise (goods) sold, gross profit, and net income? Why do we need two separate figures for inventory in the cost of merchandise (goods) sold section?
5. Explain how to calculate the following: current ratios, acid test, average day's collection, total debt to assets, return on equity, asset turnover, and profit margin on net sales. How often do you think ratios should be calculated?
6. What is trend analysis? Explain how the portion formula assists in preparing a trend analysis.
7. In light of the economic crises of 2009, explain how companies such as GE are trying to gain market share and increase profit margins.

END-OF-CHAPTER PROBLEMS

connect plus+ www.mhhe.com/slater10e

Check figures for odd-numbered problems in Appendix C. Name ____________ Date ______

DRILL PROBLEMS

16–1. As the accountant for a local Petco store, prepare a December 31, 2012, balance sheet like that for The Card Shop (LU 16–1) from the following: cash, $30,000; accounts payable, $18,000; merchandise inventory, $14,000; Vic Sullivan, capital, $46,000; and equipment, $20,000.

16–2. From the following, prepare a classified balance sheet for Ranger Company as of December 31, 2012. Ending merchandise inventory was $4,000 for the year.

Cash	$6,000	Accounts payable	$1,800
Prepaid rent	1,600	Salaries payable	1,600
Prepaid insurance	4,000	Note payable (long term)	8,000
Office equipment (net)	5,000	J. Lowell, capital*	9,200

*What the owner supplies to the business. Replaces common stock and retained earnings section.

16–3. Complete a horizontal analysis for Brown Company (round percents to the nearest hundredth):

BROWN COMPANY Comparative Balance Sheet December 31, 2011 and 2012			INCREASE (DECREASE)	
	2012	2011	Amount	Percent
Assets				
Current assets:				
Cash	$ 15,750	$ 10,500		
Accounts receivable	18,000	13,500		
Merchandise inventory	18,750	22,500		
Prepaid advertising	54,000	45,000		
Total current assets	$106,500	$ 91,500		
Plant and equipment:				
Building (net)	$120,000	$126,000		
Land	90,000	90,000		
Total plant and equipment	$210,000	$216,000		
Total assets	$316,500	$307,500		
Liabilities				
Current liabilities:				
Accounts payable	$132,000	$120,000		
Salaries payable	22,500	18,000		
Total current liabilities	$154,500	$138,000		
Long-term liabilities:				
Mortgage note payable	99,000	87,000		
Total liabilities	$253,500	$225,000		
Owner's Equity				
J. Brown, capital	63,000	82,500		
Total liabilities and owner's equity	$316,500	$307,500		

16–4. Prepare an income statement for Munroe Sauce for the year ended December 31, 2012. Beginning inventory was $1,248. Ending inventory was $1,600.

Sales	$34,900
Sales returns and allowances	1,092
Sales discount	1,152
Purchases	10,512
Purchase discounts	540
Depreciation expense	115
Salary expense	5,200
Insurance expense	2,600
Utilities expense	210
Plumbing expense	250
Rent expense	180

16–5. Assume this is a partial list of financial highlights from a Motorola annual report:

	2010	2009
	(dollars in millions)	
Net sales	$37,580	$33,075
Earnings before taxes	2,231	1,283
Net earnings	1,318	891

Complete a horizontal and vertical analysis from the above information. Round to the nearest hundredth percent.

16–6. From the Lowell Instrument Corporation second-quarter report ended 2012, do a vertical analysis for the second quarter of 2012.

LOWELL INSTRUMENT CORPORATION AND SUBSIDIARIES Consolidated Statements of Operation (Unaudited) (In thousands of dollars, except share data)			
	SECOND QUARTER		
	2012	2011	Percent of net
Net sales	$6,698	$6,951	
Cost of sales	4,089	4,462	
Gross margin	2,609	2,489	
Expenses:			
Selling, general and administrative	1,045	1,703	
Product development	175	165	
Interest expense	98	123	
Other (income), net	(172)	(99)	
Total expenses	1,946	1,972	
Income before income taxes	663	517	
Provision for income taxes	265	209	
Net income	$398	$308	
Net income per common share*	$.05	$.03	
Weighted average number of common shares and equivalents	6,673,673	6,624,184	

*Income per common share reflects the deduction of the preferred stock dividend from net income.
†Off due to rounding.

16–7. Complete the comparative income statement and balance sheet for Logic Company (round percents to the nearest hundredth):

LOGIC COMPANY
Comparative Income Statement
For Years Ended December 31, 2012 and 2013

			INCREASE (DECREASE)	
	2013	2012	Amount	Percent
Gross sales	$19,000	$15,000		
Sales returns and allowances	1,000	100		
Net sales	$18,000	$14,900		
Cost of merchandise (goods) sold	12,000	9,000		
Gross profit	$ 6,000	$ 5,900		
Operating expenses:				
Depreciation	$ 700	$ 600		
Selling and administrative	2,200	2,000		
Research	550	500		
Miscellaneous	360	300		
Total operating expenses	$ 3,810	$ 3,400		
Income before interest and taxes	$ 2,190	$ 2,500		
Interest expense	560	500		
Income before taxes	$ 1,630	$ 2,000		
Provision for taxes	640	800		
Net income	$ 990	$ 1,200		

LOGIC COMPANY
Comparative Balance Sheet
December 31, 2012 and 2013

	2013		2012	
	Amount	Percent	Amount	Percent
Assets				
Current assets:				
Cash	$12,000		$ 9,000	
Accounts receivable	16,500		12,500	
Merchandise inventory	8,500		14,000	
Prepaid expenses	24,000		10,000	
Total current assets	$61,000		$45,500	
Plant and equipment:				
Building (net)	$14,500		$11,000	
Land	13,500		9,000	
Total plant and equipment	$28,000		$20,000	
Total assets	$89,000		$65,500	
Liabilities				
Current liabilities:				
Accounts payable	$13,000		$ 7,000	
Salaries payable	7,000		5,000	
Total current liabilities	$20,000		$12,000	
Long-term liabilities:				
Mortgage note payable	22,000		20,500	
Total liabilities	$42,000		$32,500	
Stockholders' Equity				
Common stock	$21,000		$21,000	
Retained earnings	26,000		12,000	
Total stockholders' equity	$47,000		$33,000	
Total liabilities and stockholders' equity	$89,000		$65,500	

*Due to rounding.

From Problem 16–7, your supervisor has requested that you calculate the following ratios (round to the nearest hundredth):

	2013	2012
16–8. Current ratio.		
16–9. Acid test.		
16–10. Average day's collection.		
16–11. Asset turnover.		
16–12. Total debt to total assets.		
16–13. Net income (after tax) to the net sales.		
16–14. Return on equity (after tax).		

16–8.

16–9.

16–10.

16–11.

16–12.

16–13.

16–14.

WORD PROBLEMS

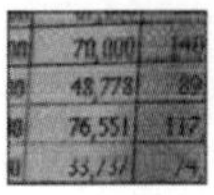

16–15. The March 2009 edition of *Kiplinger's Personal Finance* reported on what to do if you were victimized by Bernard Madoff's alleged Ponzi scheme. Recommendations include: ensure there is a third-party custodian, beware of group connections, and investigate who audits your advisor. Holocaust survivor Elie Wiesel's Foundation for Humanity lost $15.2 million of his charity's (stockholders equity) money. If he had been promised a 10% return on equity, what was the anticipated return?

16–16. The acai berry is a fruit that grows in the Amazon rain forest making up over 40% of the diet of the healthy people in that region. Marketers of this berry purport it to be significantly high in antioxidants, vitamin A, vitamin B, vitamin C, iron, and calcium, as well as other types of minerals and acids that benefit the body. According to "Weight-loss Berry Claiming Oprah Endorsement Makes Wallets Slim and Consumers Angry Warns BBB," an article by the Better Business Bureau from January 5, 2009, acai products approached sales of $15 million last year, up from $500,000 in previous years. If the profit margin for acai product sales is 23%, what is the net income if net sales is $12.5 million?

16–17. Find the following ratios for Motorola Credit Corporation's annual report: **(a)** total debt to total assets, **(b)** return on equity, **(c)** asset turnover (to nearest cent), and **(d)** profit margin on net sales. Round to the nearest hundredth percent.

	(dollars in millions)
Net revenue (sales)	$ 265
Net earnings	147
Total assets	2,015
Total liabilities	1,768
Total stockholders' equity	427

16–18. Assume figures were presented for the past 5 years on merchandise sold at Chicago department and discount stores ($ million) Sales in 2009 were $3,154; in 2008, $3,414; in 2007, $3,208; in 2006, $3,152; and in 2005, $3,216. Using 2005 as the base year, complete a trend analysis. Round each percent to the nearest whole percent.

16–19. Don Williams received a memo requesting that he complete a trend analysis of the following numbers using 2010 as the base year and rounding each percent to the nearest whole percent. Could you help Don with the request?

	2013	2012	2011	2010
Sales	$340,000	$400,000	$420,000	$500,000
Gross profit	180,000	240,000	340,000	400,000
Net income	70,000	90,000	40,000	50,000

CHALLENGE PROBLEMS

16–20. PepsiCo reported 2008 revenue of $43,251 million, net income of $5,142 million, total assets of $35,994 million, and EPS of $3.21. Common shareholders had $12,203 million in equity. In 2007 they reported revenue of $39,474 million, net income of $5,658 million, total assets of $34,628 million, and EPS of $3.41. Common shareholders had $17,325 million in equity. **(a)** What is the return on equity for each year? Round to the nearest hundredth percent. **(b)** What is the profit margin on net sales for each year? Round to the nearest hundredth percent as needed. **(c)** What is the asset turnover for each year? Round to the nearest hundredth percent. Analyze each ratio and mark which year had a better outcome.

16–21. As the accountant for Tootsie Roll, you are asked to calculate the current ratio and the quick ratio for the following partial financial statement. Round to the nearest tenth.

Assets		Liabilities	
Current assets:		Current liabilities:	
Cash and cash equivalents (Note 1)	$ 4,224,190	Notes payable to banks	$ 672,221
Investments (Note 1)	32,533,769	Accounts payable	7,004,075
Accounts receivable, less allowances of $748,000 and $744,000	16,206,648	Dividends payable	576,607
		Accrued liabilities (Note 5)	9,826,534
Inventories (Note 1):		Income taxes payable	4,471,429
Finished goods and work in progress	12,650,955		
Raw materials and supplies	10,275,858		
Prepaid expenses	2,037,710		

DVD SUMMARY PRACTICE TEST

1. Given: Gross sales, $170,000; sales returns and allowances, $9,000; beginning inventory, $8,000; net purchases, $18,000; ending inventory, $5,000; and operating expenses, $56,000. Calculate **(a)** net sales, **(b)** cost of merchandise (goods) sold, **(c)** gross profit from sales, and **(d)** net income. *(p. 391)*

2. Complete the following partial comparative balance sheet by filling in the total current assets and percent column; assume no plant and equipment (round to the nearest hundredth percent as needed). *(p. 385)*

	Amount	Percent	Amount	Percent
Assets				
Current assets:				
Cash	$ 9,000		$ 8,000	
Accounts receivable	5,000		7,500	
Merchandise inventory	12,000		6,900	
Prepaid expenses	7,000		8,000	
Total current assets				

*Due to rounding.

3. Calculate the amount of increase or decrease and the percent change of each item (round to the nearest hundredth percent as needed). *(p. 385)*

	2011	2010	Amount	Percent
Cash	$19,000	$ 8,000		
Land	70,000	30,000		
Accounts payable	21,000	10,000		

4. Complete a trend analysis for sales (round to the nearest whole percent and use 2010 as the base year). *(p. 393)*

2013 74%

	2013	2012	2011	2010
Sales	$140,000	$350,000	$210,000	$190,000
	.74	1.84	1.11	

5. From the following, prepare a balance sheet for True Corporation as of December 31, 2011. *(p. 385)*

Building	$40,000	Mortgage note payable	$70,000
Merchandise inventory	12,000	Common stock	10,000
Cash	15,000	Retained earnings	37,000
Land	90,000	Accounts receivable	9,000
Accounts payable	50,000	Salaries payable	8,000
Prepaid rent	9,000		

6. Solve from the following facts (round to the nearest hundredth). *(p. 396)*

Current assets	$14,000	Net sales	$40,000
Accounts receivable	5,000	Total assets	$38,000
Current liabilities	20,000	Net income	$10,100
Inventory	4,000		

a. Current ratio

b. Acid test

c. Average day's collection

d. Asset turnover

e. Profit margin on sales

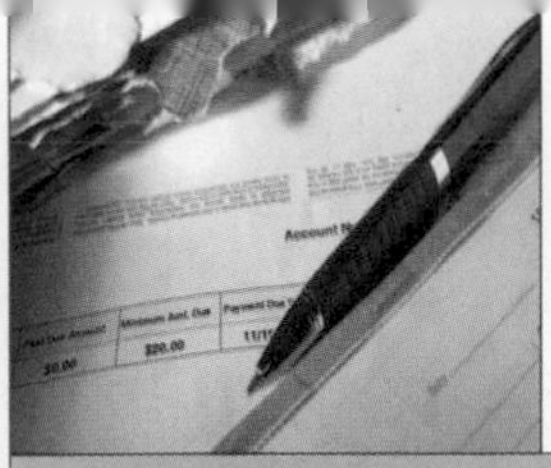

Personal Finance

A KIPLINGER APPROACH

Inflation Isn't a Problem—Yet. Take These Steps Just In Case

A weaker dollar, increased demand for commodities or a Fed fumble could cause prices to spike.

BY ROBERT FRICK

FIRST THINGS FIRST

WITH THE ECONOMY AT DEATH'S door last fall, the federal government prescribed the strongest medicines in its pharmacy. The bursting credit bubble bled the economy of money, so the Federal Reserve and U.S. Treasury started pumping in cash. The Fed is buying more than $1 trillion worth of mortgage-backed securities and debt of various government agencies, and it will buy hundreds of billions in Treasury bonds.

That's not all. The Fed effectively cut short-term interest rates to zero, a move that also boosts the money supply. Meanwhile, the economic-stimulus program enacted in February will feed almost $800 billion into the economy over the next two years through lower payroll taxes, higher jobless benefits and spending on such things as health care, education and energy projects.

Economics 101 tells you that a flood of money can result in dramatic price increases. And the resulting high inflation is detrimental to the health of the economy, to say the least. It erodes the value of money—particularly bad for people on fixed incomes—and makes the economy run in fits and starts. Eventually, the government takes steps to rein in inflation by slowing the economy, a move that often causes recessions and havoc in the financial markets. As Robert Samuelson says in *The Great Inflation and Its Aftermath*, which analyzes the 20 years of tenacious inflation that began in the 1960s: "The inflationary episode was a deeply disturbing and disillusioning experience that eroded Americans' confidence in their future and their leaders."

WHAT'S KEEPING PRICES DOWN

INFLATION IS NOT A PROBLEM now because of the weak economy. "One thing recessions are really good at is keeping inflation low," says Standard & Poor's chief economist David Wyss. The most obvious impact of a recession is a drop in retail spending, which takes pressure off prices. Retail spending in April was down $38 billion from the same month a year earlier. Although measures of consumer confidence increased dramatically in the spring, the figures are still well below historical averages.

Unemployment is one reason that spending is weak and confidence is low. As of May, 14.5 million Americans, or 9.4% of the workforce, were jobless. The number could rise to 15.5 million if the unemployment rate hits 10%, as many economists predict it will. Even the employed tend to cut back on spending when they fear that they, too, may lose their jobs.

Declining wealth—the result of falling home prices and the stock-market crash—also suppresses the urge to splurge. "We've lost a lot of wealth as the value of our houses has decreased and the value of investments in the stock market has plummeted," says Ann Owen, a former economist at the Fed and now a professor at Hamilton College, in Clinton, N.Y. In addition, the decline in the availability of consumer credit dampens spending, as does the increase in the savings rate. Owen says that the rise in the supply of money hasn't "caused inflation yet because people haven't started spending it yet."

Even if the economy starts to grow in the fourth quarter, as *Kiplinger's* forecasts it will, unemployment will probably continue to rise for a while, keeping a lid on prices in 2010. In addition, productivity, another anti-inflationary force, tends to improve at the beginning of a recovery. Says economist Ed Yardeni, of Yardeni Research: "You almost never have inflation for the first year of a recovery. You usually have big unemployment and get a big pop in productivity. And that productivity bump actually brings down labor costs." For all those reasons, most economists agree with Yardeni that inflation won't be a problem for at least another year.

From *Kiplinger's Personal Finance*, August 2009, p. 34

BUSINESS MATH ISSUE

In the long run the government stimulus package will hurt profits of corporations.

1. List the key points of the article and information to support your position.
2. Write a group defense of your position using math calculations to support your view.

PROJECT A

The Madoff case means the end to fraudulent financial statements. Agree or disagree?

Slater's Business Math Scrapbook

Applying Your Skills

Accountant Arrested for Sham Audits

By Amir Efrati

Federal prosecutors brought fraud charges on Wednesday against the auditor of Bernard Madoff's firm on allegations he helped Mr. Madoff deceive investors by signing off on fraudulent financial statements.

The arrest of David Friehling marks the first time someone aside from Mr. Madoff has been charged in connection with the decades-long Ponzi scheme that came to an end in December.

THE MADOFF FRAUD

Lev Dassin, acting U.S. attorney for the Southern District of New York, said in a statement that Mr. Friehling was "not charged with knowledge of the Madoff Ponzi scheme." Instead, Mr. Dassin said, Mr. Friehling conducted sham audits that allowed Mr. Madoff to perpetuate the fraud. Mr. Dassin said that, by falsely certifying that he audited financial statements for **Bernard L. Madoff Investment Securities** LLC, Mr. Friehling "helped foster the illusion that Mr. Madoff legitimately invested his clients' money."

Madoff auditor David Friehling, accused of signing off on fraudulent financial statements, leaves Manhattan federal courthouse Wednesday.

Reuters

Andrew Lankler, a lawyer for Mr. Friehling, declined to comment. If convicted of the charges, which include securities fraud, aiding and abetting investment adviser fraud and filing false audit reports to the Securities and Exchange Commission, Mr. Friehling faces a maximum of 105 years in prison, though he likely would serve many fewer if sentences run concurrently as is common, legal experts say. He was released Wednesday afternoon on a $2.5 million bail bond.

The charges came nearly a week after Mr. Madoff pleaded guilty to masterminding a scheme that caused losses of tens of billions of dollars for individuals, charities and institutional investors.

The prosecution of Mr. Friehling suggests the government may target individuals, including employees of the Madoff firm, who didn't know about the fraud scheme but may have lied to investors about performing an adequate review of Mr. Madoff's operation, says Cynthia Monaco, a former federal prosecutor uncon-

PROJECT B

It will be many years before Disney can come back as the leader in its field. Agree or disagree?

Disney Net Sinks as All Units Lose Steam

By Peter Sanders

Walt Disney Co.'s net income fell 32% in the fiscal first quarter, a sign that even one of the world's most diversified media and entertainment companies is struggling amid the sharp drop in consumer spending.

For the quarter ended Dec. 27, operating income fell from a year earlier at all of Disney's units, as the company's broad range of businesses—one of its bedrock strengths—failed to shield it from the dismal economic climate.

But President and Chief Executive Robert Iger said Disney's challenges extend beyond the economy. Several of its units are grappling with emerging weaknesses in their business models.

DVD sales, for example, dropped precipitously during the holiday period, putting pressure on what had been one of the main sources of revenue for the company's movie studio. In addition, its broadcast networks, which include ABC, have been hurt by declining viewership and dwindling revenues from once-reliable advertisers, such as auto makers and consumer-electronics companies.

"I don't think the changes we are seeing in consumers' behavior are all due to the economy," Mr. Iger said Tuesday on a conference call with analysts.

Operating income fell 64% from a year earlier at Disney's movie studio and dropped 29% at its media networks.

Mr. Iger said the company's theme parks and consumer-products divisions, while down for the quarter, are in a better position to rebound with the economy. But he didn't identify any quick fixes for Disney's TV networks or DVD business.

In the short term, Disney officials said they would continue to look for cost-cutting opportunities. The company has already shed jobs at its television operations and theme parks. Citing "the weakest economy in our lifetime," Mr. Iger said further cuts may be necessary.

Disney reported net income of $845 million, or 45 cents a share, for the quarter, down from $1.25 billion, or 63 cents a share, a year earlier. Revenue dropped 8.2% to $9.59 billion from $10.45 billion. Analysts had expected the Burbank, Calif., giant to earn 52 cents a share on revenue of $10.1 billion.

Associated Press

CEO Robert Iger, shown with Mickey Mouse at an event in April, says several Disney units are grappling with emerging problems in their business models.

Internet Projects: See text Web site (www.mhhe.com/slater10e) and The Business Math Internet Resource Guide.

Video Case

Buycostumes.com

As a child, Jalem Getz, the CEO of Buycostumes.com put little thought into his Halloween costumes. Now he thinks about costumes all year long.

Jalem Getz founded online business Buycostumes in a warehouse in the Milwaukee suburbs in 1999 taking advantage of Wisconsin's central U.S. location and cheap rent. Getz used to dislike the lack of seasons in his native California. Now, he uses the extreme seasonality of the Halloween business to turn a big profit.

The company got its start as brick-and-mortar retail business owned by Getz and partner Jon Majdoch. While still in their early 20s, the two began operating a chain of seasonal Halloween Express franchise stores, and then branched out into a couple of lamp and home accessory shops.

In 2001, the company changed its name to Buyseasons, Inc. to reflect its new broader focus. "Rather than just focus on one season, we target consumers in different seasons," said Jalem Getz. The Buycostumes name is still in broad use.

Being an e-tailer means not having to open a retail space for just two months of the year, or stock other items. Money saved on storefronts goes to maintaining a stock of 10,000 Halloween items – 100 times what most retailers carry for the season.

"Our selection sets us apart," Getz said. "A lot of customers are looking for something unique, by having that large selection we immediately build that additional goodwill."

The key to Buyseasons' success limiting the choice of merchandise to items that can't readily be found in neighborhood stores. That means less price competition and higher margins for Byseasons, which has been maintaining a 47.5 percent gross margin rate on the buycostumes.com site.

In July 2006, Liberty Media announced plans to acquire Buycostumes.com Inc. 500 company, for an undisclosed sum. Getz will stay on as CEO.

Buycostumes.com is the biggest online seller of costumes. It was ranked on October 2005 in Inc. magazine as the 75th –fastest growing U.S. private firm, with revenue of $17.6 million last year and three-year growth of 1,046 percent. Sales this year are expected to hit $25 million to $28 million, according to Getz.

Other online Halloween firms also predicted double-digit growth in 2005 – according to a forecast by the National Retail Federation the entire industry would have a 5% gain, leading to a record $3.3 billion in sales for the entire industry.

BuySeasons' sales reached nearly $30 million in 2005, Getz said, up from $17.6 million in 2004. The company's sales are expected to post 50% annual growth over the next three year. The company bills itself as the world's largest Internet retailer of Halloween costumes and accessories.

Problem 1

The video stated the shipment of packages will increase from a normal 500 packages per day to as many as 30,000 packages per day. Phone calls would increase from 1,600 per week to 30,000 a week. **(a)** What is the percent of increase in packages per day? Round to the nearest hundredth percent. **(b)** What is the percent of increase in phone calls per week?

Problem 2

The video advertises the "Mrs. Franklin Adult" costume with a retail value of $149.99 and Buycostumes.com price of $99.99. The "American Revolutionary Adult" costume with a retail value $314.99 and Buycostumes.com price of $239.99. **(a)** What is the dollar amount of savings achieved by purchasing on-line for each costume? **(b)** What is the percent savings by purchasing on-line for each costume? Round to the nearest hundredth percent.

Problem 3

On March 26, 2006, the *Milwaukee Journal Sentinel* reported BuySeasons, which now leases 81,000 square feet in a business park, wanted to move to a 200,000-square-foot building. The May 3, 2006 issue reported the Zoning, Neighborhoods & Development Committee voted 3-1 to recommend the sale of 9.2 acres in Menomonee Valley Industrial Center to house a new headquarters for BuySeasons, operative of Buycostumes.com., at a price of $110,000 per acre. **(a)** What would be the percent increase in space for BuySeasons? Round to the nearest hundredth percent. **(b)** What would be the total price for the land?

Problem 4

In 2007, the company expects to have just over 600 seasonal employees. The number of seasonal employees is expected to exceed 800 in 2008 and 900 in 2009. In 2007, the company would employ 90 full employees, 126 in 2008, and 161 in 2009. **(a)** Complete a trend analysis of seasonal employees for the three years. **(b)** Complete a trend analysis of full time employees for the three years using 2007 as the base year. Round to the nearest whole percent.

Problem 5

On October 30, 2006, *USA Today* reported on the booming number of young adults who treat themselves to Halloween fun. The 18- to 24-year old group is spending an average of $30.38 on costumes this year, a 38% increase over 2005, according to the National Federation and BIGresearch. Those 25 to 34 will spend an average of $31.33 up 17%. National Costumers Association President Debbie Lyn Owens says college students suiting up for parties are fueling much of the costume growth. **(a)** What was the average amount spent on costumes for the 18- to 24-year old group in 2004? **(b)** What was the average amount spent on costumes for the 26–34 group in 2004? Round your answer to the nearest cent.

PROBLEM 6

The company's seasonal employees earn between \$9.00 to \$16.00 per hour, the company is required to pay time and one half for overtime. A seasonal worker works 43 hours the first week of his employment. He is married and has no children. His hourly pay is \$14.50 per hour. **(a)** What is his gross pay for the week? **(b)** How much is deducted for Social Security? **(c)** How much is deducted for Medicare? **(d)** How much is withheld for Federal Income Tax? Round your answers to the nearest cents. (Note: See Chapter 9 on Payroll or Math Handbook)

PROBLEM 7

Buycostumes.com had annual sales in 2005 of \$30 million, mostly in the months before Halloween. The company had a 31% share of the online Halloween market. According to Hitwise, an Internet tracking company, the company is expected to hit \$50 million in sales in 2006. **(a)** with 31% of the market, what would be the total dollar amount spent for costumes? Round to the nearest million dollars. **(b)** What is the anticipated percent increase next year for Buycostumers? Round to the nearest hundredth percent.

PROBLEM 8

Sales reached nearly \$30 million in 2005, said the company CEO up from \$17.6 millions in 2004. What was the percent increase? Round to the nearest hundredth percent.

PROBLEM 9

The National Retail Federation predicted a 5 percent gain to a record \$3.3 billion for 2005. **(a)** What would have been the sales for 2004? The Halloween firms predicted at least a 10 percent gain for 2005. **(b)** What is the amount the Halloween firms predicted for 2005? **(c)** How much of an increase would this be? Round your answers to the nearest hundredth.

PROBLEM 10

In 2001 Buycostumes.com had sales of approximately \$4 million with 11 full-time employees. In 2005 sales grew nearly \$30 million and in 2009 full-time employees are expected to grow to 161. **(a)** What was the percent growth in sales? **(b)** What is the expected percent growth of full-time employees? Round to the nearest percent.

chapter

17 DEPRECIATION

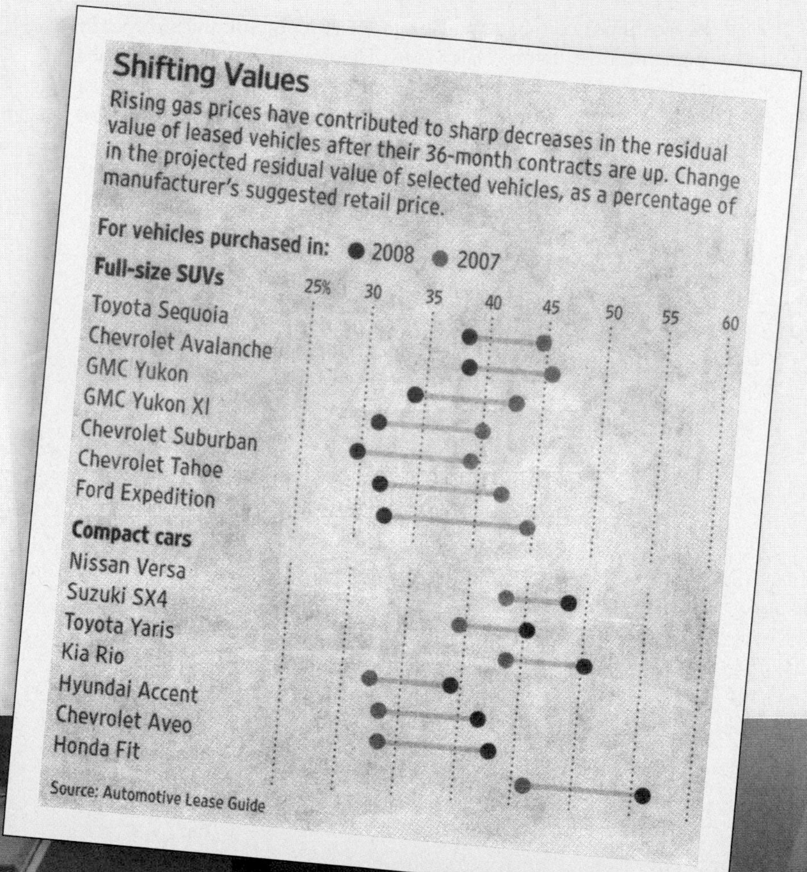

Wall Street Journal © 2008

China Photos/Getty Images

LEARNING UNIT OBJECTIVES

LU 17–1: Concept of Depreciation and the Straight-Line Method

1. Explain the concept and causes of depreciation *(pp. 413–414)*.
2. Prepare a depreciation schedule and calculate partial-year depreciation *(pp. 414–415)*.

LU 17–2: Units-of-Production Method

1. Explain how use affects the units-of-production method *(p. 416)*.
2. Prepare a depreciation schedule *(p. 417)*.

LU 17–3: Declining-Balance Method

1. Explain the importance of residual value in the depreciation schedule *(pp. 417–418)*.
2. Prepare a depreciation schedule *(p. 418)*.

LU 17–4: Modified Accelerated Cost Recovery System (MACRS) with Introduction to ACRS

1. Explain the goals of ACRS and MACRS and their limitations *(p. 419)*.
2. Calculate depreciation using the MACRS guidelines *(p. 419)*.

VOCABULARY PREVIEW

Here are key terms in this chapter. After completing the chapter, if you know the term, place a checkmark in the parenthesis. If you don't know the term, look it up and put the page number where it can be found.

Accelerated Cost Recovery System (ACRS) . ( ) Accelerated depreciation . ( ) Accumulated depreciation . ( ) Asset cost . ( ) Book value . ( ) Declining-balance method . ( ) Depreciation . ( ) Depreciation expense . ( ) Depreciation schedule . ( ) Estimated useful life . ( ) Modified Accelerated Cost Recovery System (MACRS) . ( ) Omnibus Budget Reconciliation Act of 1989 . ( ) Residual value . ( ) Salvage value . ( ) Straight-line method . ( ) Straight-line rate . ( ) Trade-in value . ( ) Units-of-production method . ( )

This chapter concentrates on depreciation—a business operating expense. In Learning Units 17–1 to 17–3, we discuss methods of calculating depreciation for financial reporting. In Learning Unit 17–4, we look at how tax laws force companies to report depreciation for tax purposes. Financial reporting methods and the tax-reporting methods are both legal.

Learning Unit 17–1: Concept of Depreciation and the Straight-Line Method

LO 1

Companies frequently buy assets such as equipment or buildings that will last longer than 1 year. Macy's would be an example of this. As time passes, these assets depreciate, or lose some of their market value. The total cost of these assets cannot be shown in *1 year* as an expense of running the business. In a systematic and logical way, companies must estimate the asset cost they show as an expense of a particular period. This process is called **depreciation.**

Remember that depreciation *does not* measure the amount of deterioration or decline in the market value of the asset. Depreciation is simply a means of recognizing that these

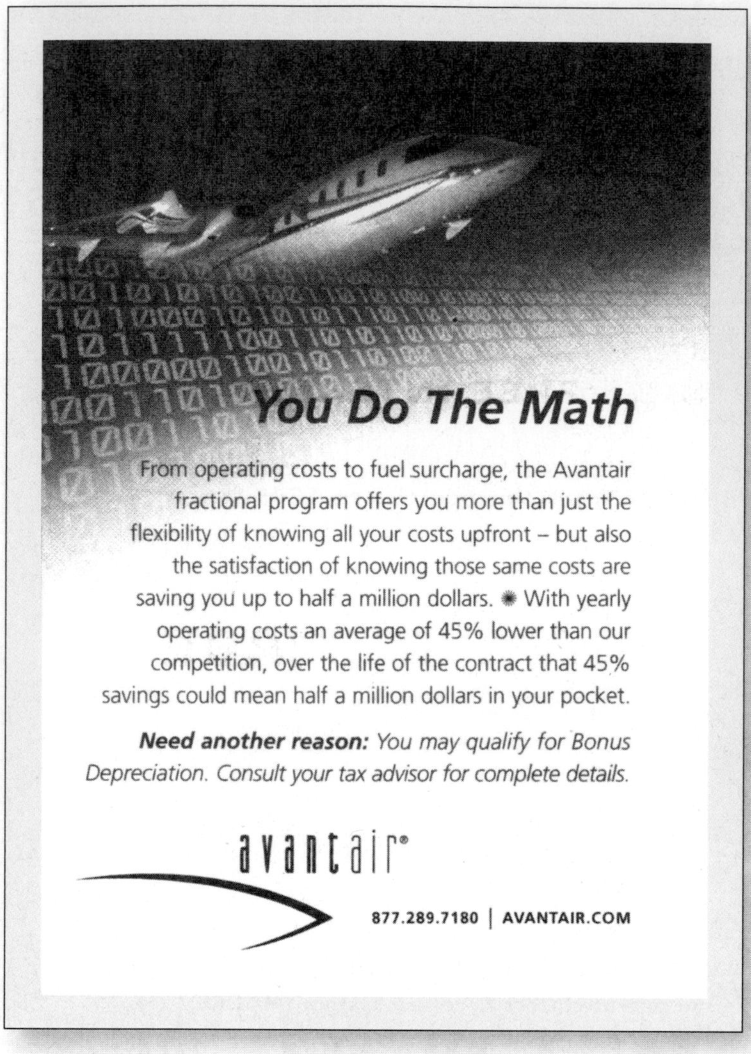

Wall Street Journal © 2008

assets are depreciating. For example, the Avantair ad "You Do the Math" shows that by using fractional ownership, airplanes with Avantair could result in bonus depreciation.

The depreciation process results in **depreciation expense** that involves three key factors: (1) **asset cost**—amount the company paid for the asset including freight and charges relating to the asset; (2) **estimated useful life**—number of years or time periods for which the company can use the asset; and (3) **residual value (salvage** or **trade-in value)**—expected cash value at the end of the asset's useful life. For example, the useful life of Macy's buildings is estimated at 50 years.

Depreciation expense is listed on the income statement. The **accumulated depreciation** title on the balance sheet gives the amount of the asset's depreciation taken to date. Asset cost less accumulated depreciation is the asset's book value. The **book value** shows the unused amount of the asset cost that the company may depreciate in future accounting periods. At the end of the asset's life, the asset's book value is the same as its residual value—book value cannot be less than residual value.

Depending on the amount and timetable of an asset's depreciation, a company can increase or decrease its profit. If a company shows greater depreciation in earlier years, the company will have a lower reported profit and pay less in taxes. Thus, depreciation can be an indirect tax savings for the company.

Later in the chapter we will discuss the different methods of computing depreciation that spread the cost of an asset over specified periods of time. However, first let's look at some of the major causes of depreciation.

Causes of Depreciation

As assets, all machines have an estimated amount of usefulness simply because as companies use the assets, the assets gradually wear out. The cause of this depreciation is *physical deterioration.*

The growth of a company can also cause depreciation. Many companies begin on a small scale. As the companies grow, they often find their equipment and buildings inadequate. The use of depreciation enables these businesses to "write off" their old, inadequate equipment and buildings. Companies cannot depreciate land. For example, a garbage dump can be depreciated but not the land.

Harry Cabluck/AP Photo

Another cause of depreciation is the result of advances in technology. The computers that companies bought a few years ago may be in perfect working condition but outdated. Companies may find it necessary to replace these old computers with more sophisticated, faster, and possibly more economical machines. Thus, *product obsolescence* is a key factor contributing to depreciation.

Now we are ready to begin our study of depreciation methods. The first method we will study is straight-line depreciation. It is also the most common of the three depreciation methods (straight line, units of production, and declining balance). In a survey of 600 corporations, 81% responded that they used straight-line depreciation.

Straight-Line Method

The **straight-line method** of depreciation is used more than any other method. It tries to distribute the same amount of expense to each period of time. Most large companies, such as Gillette Corporation, Southwest Airlines, Campbell's Soup, and General Mills use the straight-line method. *Today, more than 90% of U.S. companies depreciate by straight line.* For example, let's assume Ajax Company bought equipment for $2,500. The company estimates that the equipment's period of "usefulness"—or *useful life*—will be 5 years. After 5 years the equipment will have a residual value (salvage value) of $500. The company decides to calculate its depreciation with the straight-line method and uses the following formula:

$$\text{Depreciation expense each year} = \frac{\text{Cost} - \text{Residual value}}{\text{Estimated useful life in years}}$$

$$\frac{\$2{,}500 - \$500}{5 \text{ years}} = \$400 \text{ depreciation expense taken each year}$$

Table 17.1 gives a summary of the equipment depreciation that Ajax Company will take over the next 5 years. Companies call this summary a **depreciation schedule.** A corporation like Southwest Airlines depreciates its flight equipment 20 to 25 years.

TABLE 17.1

Depreciation schedule for straight-line method

$$\frac{100\%}{\text{Number of years}} = \frac{100\%}{5} = 20\%$$

Thus, the company is depreciating the equipment at a 20% rate each year.

End of year	Cost of equipment	Depreciation expense for year	Accumulated depreciation at end of year	Book value at end of year (Cost − Accumulated depreciation)
1	$2,500	$400	$ 400	$2,100 ($2,500 − $400)
2	2,500	400	800	1,700
3	2,500	400	1,200	1,300
4	2,500	400	1,600	900
5	2,500	400	2,000	500
	↑ Cost stays the same.	↑ Depreciation expense is same each year.	↑ Accumulated depreciation increases by $400 each year.	↑ Book value is lowered by $400 until residual value of $500 is reached.

LO 2

MONEY TIPS

Even personal assets depreciate. It is important to take into account the value of one's assets when determining whether or not to fix an item. It may cost you less to simply purchase new.

Depreciation for Partial Years

If a company buys an asset before the 15th of the month, the company calculates the asset's depreciation for a full month. Companies do not take the full month's depreciation for assets bought after the 15th of the month. For example, assume Ajax Company (Table 17.1) bought the equipment on May 6. The company would calculate the depreciation for the first year as follows:

$$\frac{\$2{,}500 - \$500}{5 \text{ years}} = \$400 \times \frac{8}{12} = \$266.67$$

Now let's check your progress with the Practice Quiz before we look at the next depreciation method.

LU 17–1 PRACTICE QUIZ

Complete this **Practice Quiz** to see how you are doing.

1. Prepare a depreciation schedule using straight-line depreciation for the following:

Cost of truck	$16,000
Residual value	$ 1,000
Life	5 years

2. If the truck were bought on February 3, what would the depreciation expense be in the first year?

Solutions with Step-by-Step Help on DVD

✓ **Solutions**

1.

End of year	Cost of truck	Depreciation expense for year	Accumulated depreciation at end of year	Book value at end of year (Cost − Accumulated depreciation)
1	$16,000	$3,000	$ 3,000	$13,000 ($16,000 − $3,000)
2	16,000	3,000	6,000	10,000
3	16,000	3,000	9,000	7,000
4	16,000	3,000	12,000	4,000
5	16,000	3,000	15,000	1,000 ← Note that we are down to residual value

2. $\frac{\$16{,}000 - \$1{,}000}{5} = \$3{,}000 \times \frac{11}{12} = \$2{,}750$

LU 17–1a EXTRA PRACTICE QUIZ WITH WORKED-OUT SOLUTIONS

Need more practice? Try this **Extra Practice Quiz** (check figures in Chapter Organizer, p. 422). Worked-out Solutions can be found in Appendix B at end of text.

1. Prepare a depreciation schedule using straight-line depreciation for the following:

Cost of truck	$20,000
Residual value	$ 2,000
Life	3 years

2. If the truck were bought on February 3, what would the depreciation expense be in the first year?

Learning Unit 17–2: Units-of-Production Method

LO 1

MONEY TIPS

Adult children living at home can create financial challenges. Set up a system of unit costs for food, utilities, rent, insurance, cable, phone, maintenance, etc. and put these in writing before the move-in to reduce any tension of the financial unknown.

Unlike in the straight-line depreciation method, in the **units-of-production method** the passage of time is not used to determine an asset's depreciation amount. Instead, the company determines the asset's depreciation according to how much the company uses the asset. This use could be miles driven, tons hauled, or units that a machine produces. For example, when a company such as Ajax Company (in Learning Unit 17–1) buys equipment, the company estimates how many units the equipment can produce. Let's assume the equipment has a useful life of 4,000 units. The following formulas are used to calculate the equipment's depreciation for the units-of-production method.

$$\text{Depreciation per unit} = \frac{\text{Cost} - \text{Residual value}}{\text{Total estimated units produced}} = \frac{\$2{,}500 - \$500}{4{,}000 \text{ units}} = \$.50 \text{ per unit}$$

$$\text{Depreciation amount} = \text{Unit depreciation} \times \text{Units produced} = \$.50 \text{ times actual number of units}$$

Now we can complete Table 17.2 (p. 417). Note that the table gives the units produced each year.

Let's check your understanding of this unit with the Practice Quiz.

LU 17–2 PRACTICE QUIZ

Complete this **Practice Quiz** to see how you are doing.

From the following facts prepare a depreciation schedule:

Machine cost	$20,000
Residual value	$ 4,000

Expected to produce 16,000 units over its expected life

	2008	2009	2010	2011	2012
Units produced:	2,000	8,000	3,000	1,800	1,600

$\frac{\$20{,}000 - \$4{,}000}{16{,}000} = \$1$

TABLE 17.2 Depreciation schedule for units-of-production method

End of year	Cost of equipment	Units produced	Depreciation expense for year	Accumulated depreciation at end of year	Book value at end of year (Cost − Accumulated depreciation)
1	$2,500	300	$ 150 (300 × $.50)	$ 150	$2,350 ($2,500 − $150)
2	2,500	400	200	350	2,150
3	2,500	600	300	650	1,850
4	2,500	2,000	1,000	1,650	850
5	2,500	700	350	2,000	500

Units produced (↑): At the end of 5 years, the equipment produced 4,000 units. If in year 5 the equipment produced 1,500 units, only 700 could be used in the calculation, or it will go below the equipment's residual value.

Depreciation expense for year (↑): Units produced per year times $.50 equals depreciation expense.

Book value (↑): Residual value of $500 is reached. (Be sure depreciation is not taken below the residual value.)

LO 2

Solutions with Step-by-Step Help on DVD

✓ Solutions

End of year	Cost of machine	Units produced	Depreciation expense for year	Accumulated depreciation at end of year	Book value at end of year (Cost − Accumulated depreciation)
1	$20,000	2,000	$2,000 (2,000 × $1)	$ 2,000	$18,000
2	20,000	8,000	8,000	10,000	10,000
3	20,000	3,000	3,000	13,000	7,000
4	20,000	1,800	1,800	14,800	5,200
5	20,000	1,600	1,200*	16,000	4,000

*Note that we only can depreciate 1,200 units since we cannot go below the residual value of $4,000.

LU 17–2a EXTRA PRACTICE QUIZ WITH WORKED-OUT SOLUTIONS

Need more practice? Try this **Extra Practice Quiz** (check figures in Chapter Organizer, p. 422). Worked-out Solutions can be found in Appendix B at end of text.

From the following facts prepare a depreciation expense:

Machine cost	$30,000
Residual value	$ 2,000

Expected to produce 56,000 units over its expected life

	2008	**2009**	**2010**	**2011**	**2012**
Units produced	1,000	6,000	4,000	2,000	2,500

Learning Unit 17–3: Declining-Balance Method

In the declining-balance method, we cannot depreciate below the residual value.

LO 1

The **declining-balance method** is another type of **accelerated depreciation** that takes larger amounts of depreciation expense in the earlier years of the asset. The straight-line method, you recall, estimates the life of the asset and distributes the same amount of depreciation expense to each period. To take larger amounts of depreciation expense in the asset's earlier years, the declining-balance method uses up to *twice* the **straight-line rate** in the first year of depreciation. A key point to remember is that the declining-balance method does

LO 2

$ MONEY TIPS

The law of depreciation, defined as the reduction in value of an asset due to usage and time passage, affects many personal purchases. The simple act of driving your newly purchased, brand-new vehicle off the sales lot results in up to a 20% reduction in value depending on the make and model. Make certain to research how well your chosen vehicle holds value before signing on the bottom line.

not deduct the residual value in calculating the depreciation expense. Today, the declining-balance method is the basis of current tax depreciation.

For all problems, we will use double the straight-line rate unless we indicate otherwise. Today, the rate is often 1.5 or 1.25 times the straight-line rate. Again we use our $2,500 equipment with its estimated useful life of 5 years. As we build the depreciation schedule in Table 17.3, note the following steps:

Step 1. Rate is equal to $\frac{100\%}{5 \text{ years}} \times 2 = 40\%$.

Or another way to look at it is that the straight-line rate is $\frac{1}{5} \times 2 = \frac{2}{5} = 40\%$.

Step 2. $\text{Depreciation expense each year} = \text{Book value of equipment at beginning of year} \times \text{Depreciation rate}$

Step 3. We cannot depreciate the equipment below its residual value ($500). The straight-line method automatically reduced the asset's book value to the residual value. This is not true with the declining-balance method. So you must be careful when you prepare the depreciation schedule.

TABLE 17.3 Depreciation schedule for declining-balance method

End of year	Cost of equipment	Accumulated depreciation at beginning of year	Book value at beginning of year (Cost − Accumulated depreciation)	Depreciation (Book value at beginning of year × Rate)	Accumulated depreciation at end of year	Book value at end of year (Cost − Accumulated depreciation)
1	$2,500	—	$2,500	$1,000 ($2,500 × .40)	$1,000	$1,500 ($2,500 − $1,000)
2	2,500	$1,000	1,500	600 ($1,500 × .40)	1,600	900
3	2,500	1,600	900	360 ($900 × .40)	1,960	540
4	2,500	1,960	540	40	2,000	500
5	2,500	2,000	500		2,000	500
	↑ Original cost of $2,500 does not change. Residual value was not subtracted.	↑ Ending accumulated depreciation of 1 year becomes next year's beginning.	↑ Cost less accumulated depreciation	↑ *Note:* In year 4, only $40 is taken since we cannot depreciate below residual value of $500. In year 5, no depreciation is taken.	↑ Accumulated depreciation balance plus depreciation expense this year.	↑ Book value now equals residual value.

Now let's check your progress again with another Practice Quiz.

LU 17–3 PRACTICE QUIZ

Complete this **Practice Quiz** to see how you are doing.

Prepare a depreciation schedule from the following:

Cost of machine: $16,000 | Estimated life: 5 years
Rate: 40% (this is twice the straight-line rate) | Residual value: $1,000

Solutions with Step-by-Step Help on DVD

✓ **Solutions**

End of year	Cost of machine	Accumulated depreciation at beginning of year	Book value at beginning of year (Cost − Accumulated depreciation)	Depreciation (Book value at beginning of year × Rate)	Accumulated depreciation at end of year	Book value at end of year (Cost − Accumulated depreciation)
1	$16,000	$ -0-	$16,000.00	$6,400.00	$ 6,400.00	$9,600.00
2	16,000	6,400.00	9,600.00	3,840.00	10,240.00	5,760.00
3	16,000	10,240.00	5,760.00	2,304.00	12,544.00	3,456.00
4	16,000	12,544.00	3,456.00	1,382.40	13,926.40	2,073.60
5	16,000	13,926.40	2,073.60	829.44*	14,755.84	1,244.16

*Since we do not reach the residual value of $1,000, another $244.16 could have been taken as depreciation expense to bring it to the estimated residual value of $1,000.

LU 17–3a EXTRA PRACTICE QUIZ WITH WORKED-OUT SOLUTIONS

Need more practice? Try this **Extra Practice Quiz** (check figures in Chapter Organizer, p. 422). Worked-out Solutions can be found in Appendix B at end of text.

Prepare a depreciation schedule for three years for the following:

Cost of machine: $31,000 Estimated life: 5 years
Rate: 40% (this is twice the straight-line rate) Residual value: $1,000

Learning Unit 17–4: Modified Accelerated Cost Recovery System (MACRS) with Introduction to ACRS

© Royalty-Free/Corbis

In Learning Units 17–1 to 17–3, we discussed the depreciation methods used for financial reporting. Since 1981, federal tax laws have been passed that state how depreciation must be taken for income tax purposes. Assets put in service from 1981 through 1986 fell under the federal **Accelerated Cost Recovery System (ACRS)** tax law enacted in 1981. The Tax Reform Act of 1986 established the **Modified Accelerated Cost Recovery System (MACRS)** for all property placed into service after December 31, 1986. Both these federal laws provide users with tables giving the useful lives of various assets and the depreciation rates. We look first at the MACRS and then at a 1989 update.

Depreciation for Tax Purposes Based on the Tax Reform Act of 1986 (MACRS)

LO 1

Tables 17.4 and 17.5 (p. 420) give the classes of recovery and annual depreciation percentages that MACRS established in 1986. The key points of MACRS are:

1. It calculates depreciation for tax purposes.
2. It ignores residual value.

TABLE 17.4

Modified Accelerated Cost Recovery System (MACRS) for assets placed in service after December 31, 1986

Class recovery period (life)	Asset types
3-year*	Racehorses more than 2 years old or any horse other than a racehorse that is more than 12 years old at the time placed into service; special tools of certain industries.
5-year*	Automobiles (not luxury); taxis; light general-purpose trucks; semiconductor manufacturing equipment; computer-based telephone central-office switching equipment; qualified technological equipment; property used in connection with research and experimentation.
7-year*	Railroad track; single-purpose agricultural (pigpens) or horticultural structures; fixtures; equipment; furniture.
10-year*	New law doesn't add any specific property under this class.
15-year†	Municipal wastewater treatment plants; telephone distribution plants and comparable equipment used for two-way exchange of voice and data communications.
20-year†	Municipal sewers.
27.5-year‡	Only residential rental property.
31.5-year‡	Only nonresidential real property.

*These classes use a 200% declining-balance method switching to the straight-line method.
†These classes use a 150% declining-balance method switching to the straight-line method.
‡These classes use a straight-line method.

TABLE 17.5 Annual recovery for MACRS

Recovery year	3-year class (200% D.B.)	5-year class (200% D.B.)	7-year class (200% D.B.)	10-year class (200% D.B.)	15-year class (150% D.B.)	20-year class (150% D.B.)
1	33.00	20.00	14.28	10.00	5.00	3.75
2	45.00	32.00	24.49	18.00	9.50	7.22
3	15.00*	19.20	17.49	14.40	8.55	6.68
4	7.00	11.52*	12.49	11.52	7.69	6.18
5		11.52	8.93*	9.22	6.93	5.71
6		5.76	8.93	7.37	6.23	5.28
7			8.93	6.55*	5.90*	4.89
8			4.46	6.55	5.90	4.52
9				6.55	5.90	4.46*
10				6.55	5.90	4.46
11				3.29	5.90	4.46
12					5.90	4.46
13					5.90	4.46
14					5.90	4.46
15					5.90	4.46
16					3.00	4.46

*Identifies when switch is made to straight line.

LO 2

3. Depreciation in the first year (for personal property) is based on the assumption that the asset was purchased halfway through the year. (A new law adds a midquarter convention for all personal property if more than 40% is placed in service during the last 3 months of the taxable year.)
4. Classes 3, 5, 7, and 10 use a 200% declining-balance method for a period of years before switching to straight-line depreciation. You do not have to determine the year in which to switch since Table 17.5 builds this into the calculation.
5. Classes 15 and 20 use a 150% declining-balance method before switching to straight-line depreciation.
6. Classes 27.5 and 31.5 use straight-line depreciation.

EXAMPLE Using the same equipment cost of $2,500 for Ajax, prepare a depreciation schedule under MACRS assuming the equipment is a 5-year class and not part of the tax bill of 1989. Use Table 17.5. Note that percent figures from Table 17.5 have been converted to decimals.

End of year	Cost	Depreciation expense	Accumulated depreciation	Book value at end of year
1	$2,500	$500 (.20 × $2,500)	$ 500	$2,000
2	2,500	800 (.32 × $2,500)	1,300	1,200
3	2,500	480 (.1920 × $2,500)	1,780	720
4	2,500	288 (.1152 × $2,500)	2,068	432
5	2,500	288 (.1152 × $2,500)	2,356	144
6	2,500	144 (.0576 × $2,500)	2,500	-0-

MONEY TIPS

Changes in tax laws can help you understand what the government's goal is for the economy. For example, if business spending is getting tax breaks, the government is trying to encourage market expansion. You can gauge personal spending by watching what the government is encouraging so you are not surprised by market fluctuations.

Update on MACRS: The 1989 Tax Bill

Before the 1989 tax bill (**Omnibus Budget Reconciliation Act of 1989**), cellular phones and similar equipment were depreciated under MACRS. Since cellular phones are subject to personal use, the 1989 act now treats them as "listed" property. This means that unless business use is greater than 50%, the straight-line method of depreciation is required.

Let's try another Practice Quiz.

LU 17–4 PRACTICE QUIZ

Complete this **Practice Quiz** to see how you are doing.

1. In 1991, Rancho Corporation bought semiconductor equipment for $80,000. Using MACRS, what is the depreciation expense in year 3?
2. What would depreciation be the first year for a wastewater treatment plant that cost $800,000?

Solutions with Step-by-Step Help on DVD

✓ Solutions

1. $\$80{,}000 \times .1920 = \boxed{\$15{,}360}$
2. $\$800{,}000 \times .05 = \boxed{\$40{,}000}$

LU 17–4a EXTRA PRACTICE QUIZ WITH WORKED-OUT SOLUTIONS

Need more practice? Try this **Extra Practice Quiz** (check figures in Chapter Organizer, p. 422). Worked-out Solutions can be found in Appendix B at end of text.

1. In 1991, Rancho Corporation bought semiconductor equipment for $90,000. Using MACRS, what is the depreciation expense in year 3?
2. What would depreciation be the first year for a wastewater treatment plan that cost $900,000?

CHAPTER ORGANIZER AND REFERENCE GUIDE

Topic	Key point, procedure, formula	Example(s) to illustrate situation
Straight-line method, p. 413	$\text{Depreciation expense each year} = \dfrac{\text{Cost} - \text{Residual value}}{\text{Estimated useful life in years}}$ For partial years if purchased before 15th of month depreciation is taken.	Truck, $25,000; $5,000 residual value, 4-year life. $\text{Depreciation expense} = \dfrac{\$25{,}000 - \$5{,}000}{4}$ $= \boxed{\$5{,}000}$ per year
Units-of-production method, p. 416	$\text{Depreciation per unit} = \dfrac{\text{Cost} - \text{Residual value}}{\text{Total estimated units produced}}$ Do not depreciate below residual value even if actual units are greater than estimate.	Machine, $5,000; estimated life in units, 900; residual value, $500. Assume first year produced 175 units. $\text{Depreciation expense} = \dfrac{\$5{,}000 - \$500}{900}$ $= \dfrac{\$4{,}500}{900}$ $= \$5$ depreciation per unit $175 \text{ units} \times \$5 = \boxed{\$875}$ depreciation expense

(continues)

CHAPTER ORGANIZER AND REFERENCE GUIDE

Topic	Key point, procedure, formula	Example(s) to illustrate situation
Declining-balance method, p. 417	An accelerated method. Residual value not subtracted from cost in depreciation schedule. Do not depreciate below residual value. Depreciation expense each year = Book value of equipment at beginning of year × Depreciation rate	Truck, $50,000; estimated life, 5 years; residual value, $10,000. $\frac{1}{5}$ = 20% × 2 = 40% (assume double the straight-line rate) **Year** / **Cost** / **Depreciation expense** / **Book value at end of year** 1 / $50,000 / $20,000 ($50,000 × .40) / $30,000 ($50,000 − $20,000) 2 / $50,000 / $12,000 ($30,000 × .40) / $18,000 ($50,000 − $32,000)
MACRS/Tax Bill of 1989, p. 419	After December 31, 1986, depreciation calculation is modified. Tax Act of 1989 modifies way to depreciate cellular phones and similar equipment.	Auto: $8,000, 5 years. First year, .20 × $8,000 = $1,600 depreciation expense

KEY TERMS

Accelerated Cost Recovery System (ACRS), *p. 419*	Depreciation expense, *p. 414*	Salvage value, *p. 414*
Accelerated depreciation, *p. 417*	Depreciation schedule, *p. 415*	Straight-line method, *p. 415*
Accumulated depreciation, *p. 414*	Estimated useful life, *p. 414*	Straight-line rate, *p. 417*
Asset cost, *p. 414*	Modified Accelerated Cost Recovery System (MACRS), *p. 419*	Trade-in value, *p. 414*
Book value, *p. 414*	Omnibus Budget Reconciliation Act of 1989, *p. 421*	Units-of-production method, *p. 416*
Declining-balance method, *p. 417*	Residual value, *p. 414*	
Depreciation, *p. 413*		

CHECK FIGURES FOR EXTRA PRACTICE QUIZZES WITH PAGE REFERENCES. (WORKED-OUT SOLUTIONS IN APPENDIX B.)

LU 17–1a (p. 416)	LU 17–2a (p. 417)	LU 17–3a (p. 419)	LU 17–4a (p. 421)
1. Book value EOY 3 $2,000 **2.** $5,500	$.50; Book value EOY 5 $22,250	*Depreciation expense year* **1.** $12,400 **2.** $7,440 **3.** 4,464	**1.** $17,280 **2.** $45,000

Critical Thinking Discussion Questions

1. What is the difference between depreciation expense and accumulated depreciation? Why does the book value of an asset never go below the residual value?

2. Compare the straight-line method to the units-of-production method. Should both methods be based on the passage of time?

3. Why is it possible in the declining-balance method for a person to depreciate below the residual value by mistake?

4. Explain the Modified Accelerated Cost Recovery System. Do you think this system will be eliminated in the future?

END-OF-CHAPTER PROBLEMS

connect plus+ www.mhhe.com/slater10e

Check figures for odd-numbered problems in Appendix C

Name ______________________ Date ________

DRILL PROBLEMS

From the following facts, complete a depreciation schedule using the straight-line method:

Given Cost of Toyota Hybrid Highlander $30,000
Residual value $ 6,000
Estimated life 8 years

	End of year	Cost of Highlander	Depreciation expense for year	Accumulated depreciation at end of year	Book value at end of year
17–1.					
17–2.					
17–3.					
17–4.					
17–5.					
17–6.					
17–7.					
17–8.					

Given Volvo truck $25,000
Residual value $ 5,000
Estimated life 5 years

Prepare a depreciation using the declining-balance (twice the straight-line rate)

	End of year	Cost of truck	Accumulated depreciation at beginning of year	Book value at beginning of year	Depreciation expense for year	Accumulated depreciation at end of year	Book value at end of year
17–9.							
17–10.							
17–11.							
17–12.							

For the first 2 years, calculate the depreciation expense for a $7,000 car under MACRS. This is a nonluxury car.

		MACRS			MACRS
17–13.	Year 1		**17–14.**	Year 2	

Complete the following table given this information:

Cost of machine	$94,000	Estimated units machine will produce	100,000
Residual value	$ 4,000	Actual production:	**Year 1** **Year 2**
Useful life	5 years		60,000 15,000

	Method	Depreciation Expense Year 1	Depreciation Expense Year 2
17–15.	Straight line		
17–16.	Units of production		
17–17.	Declining balance		
17–18.	MACRS (5-year class)		

WORD PROBLEMS

17–19. In an article on *www.edmunds.com* called "Strategies for Smart Car Buying," Philip Reed highlights the need to focus on resale value. After 5 years, some cars are worth 60% of their original value, some only 20%. Edmunds lists the 2008 Mini Cooper Clubman as the car most likely to depreciate the least. Trish Eberhart decided to purchase a Mini Cooper Clubman. She found a 2008 model for $22,220. During the first year using MACRS, how much will the car depreciate (assume a 5-year life class)? What is the value of the car after the first year?

17–20. Lena Horn bought a Toyota Tundra for $30,000 with an estimated life of 5 years. The residual value of the truck is $5,000. Assume a straight-line method of depreciation. **(a)** What will be the book value of the truck at the end of year 4? **(b)** If the Chevy truck was bought the first year on April 12, how much depreciation would be taken the first year?

17–21. Jim Company bought a machine for $36,000 with an estimated life of 5 years. The residual value of the machine is $6,000. Calculate **(a)** the annual depreciation and **(b)** the book value at the end of year 3. Assume straight-line depreciation.

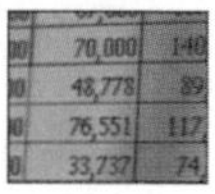

17–22. Using Problem 17–21, calculate the first 2 years' depreciation, assuming the units-of-production method. This machine is expected to produce 120,000 units. In year 1, it produced 19,000 units, and in year 2, 38,000 units.

17–23. Jim Clinnin purchased a used RV with 19,000 miles for $46,900. Originally the RV sold for $70,000 with a residual value of $20,000. After subtracting the residual value, depreciation allowance per mile was $.86. How much was Jim's purchase price over or below the book value?

17–24. The Ministry of Finance published the FY2009 Tax Reform (Main Points) on December 19, 2008. Included in the Reform is the introduction of a 2-year measure allowing immediate depreciation for investment in energy-saving facilities and appliances. If this measure doubles the MACRS allowable depreciation for the first year, what depreciation expense would a new energy-efficient HVAC system costing $138,500 be for the first year (assume a 15-year life class)?

17–25. Perry Wiseman of Truckers Accounting Service in Omaha, Nebraska, likes to use the straight-line method and take a little bit extra the first year, so there are three good years of depreciation. The cost of his truck was $108,000, with a useful life of 3 years and a residual value of $35,000. What would be the book value of the truck after the first year? Round your answers to the nearest dollar.

CHALLENGE PROBLEMS

17–26. Dave Ramsey, a three-time *New York Times* best-selling author, explains, "When you lease a car, you pay for the devaluation of the car. When you turn the car back in, the leasing company doesn't lose money on you." They are simply charging you for the depreciation cost of the vehicle plus any miles over the allotment. If anything goes wrong with the car, the leasing contract specifies you will pay for it. Assume you lease a $45,000 BMW. Using straight-line method with a 3-year useful life and a $16,675 residual value, what is the book value of the BMW after the first year? Round your answers to the nearest dollar.

17–27. Assume a piece of equipment was purchased July 26, 2012, at a cost of $72,000. The estimated residual value is $5,400 with a useful life of 5 years. Assume a production life of 60,000 units. Compute the depreciation for years 2012 and 2013 using **(a)** straight-line and **(b)** units-of-production (in 2012, 5,000 units produced and in 2013, 18,000 units produced).

DVD SUMMARY PRACTICE TEST

1. Leo Lucky, owner of a Pizza Hut franchise, bought a delivery truck for $30,000. The truck has an estimated life of 5 years with a residual value of $10,000. Leo wants to know which depreciation method will be the best for his truck. He asks you to prepare a depreciation schedule using the declining-balance method at twice the straight-line rate. *(p. 417)*

2. Using MACRS, what is the depreciation for the first year on furniture costing $12,000? *(p. 419)*

3. Abby Matthew bought a new Jeep Commander for $30,000. The Jeep Commander has a life expectancy of 5 years with a residual value of $10,000. Prepare a depreciation schedule for the straight-line-method. *(p. 415)*

4. Car.com bought a Toyota for $28,000. The Toyota has a life expectancy of 10 years with a residual value of $3,000. After 3 years, the Toyota was sold for $19,000. What was the difference between the book value and the amount received from selling the car if Car.com used the straight-line method of depreciation? *(p. 415)*

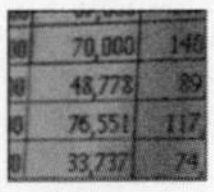

5. A machine cost $70,200; it had an estimated residual value of $6,000 and an expected life of 300,000 units. What would be the depreciation in year 3 if 60,000 units were produced?
(Round to nearest cent.) *(p. 417)*

Personal Finance

A KIPLINGER APPROACH

DRIVE TIME
JESSICA ANDERSON

Keep Your Clunker

With incentives on new cars at all-time highs and dealers desperate to move inventory, it is an excellent time to buy a new car. But what if you could eke out another 50,000 miles on your old car and save a lot of cash? // James, a reader from Easton, Md., recently wrote to us with just such a conundrum. He was considering trading in his 2003 Chevrolet Silverado pickup, which had 94,000 miles on the odometer, for a new, loaded Dodge Ram, even though the Chevy was paid off and in good condition. He acknowledged that he didn't really need a new truck but worried that the deals wouldn't be nearly as attractive if he waited.

Dollars and sense. How do the financials stack up? We asked Vincentric, an automotive research firm, to compare the cost of several new vehicles with their five-year-old counterparts. We assumed that the used vehicles were paid off and the new vehicles were paid for with a five-year, 6.6% loan and 15% down. Based on total ownership costs over five years—including insurance, fuel, repairs and depreciation—the results are firmly in favor of hanging on to your old car.

For example, a new Chevrolet Malibu will cost $33,064 over five years, or $7,343 more than the $25,721 it would cost you to maintain a 2004 model that's paid off. Likewise, a new Honda CR-V has a five-year ownership cost of $33,520, versus $24,597 for the five-year-old model. That's a savings of $8,923 if you keep the old vehicle.

James was tempted by Dodge's employee-pricing promotion, plus $3,000 in rebates and a $1,000 dealer coupon, all together knocking $11,000 off the sticker price. A generous trade-in value on the Silverado and 0% financing over four years (plus assurances that the feds would back the warranty) clinched the deal, and he's now the pleased owner of a new Dodge Ram pickup. But Vincentric's numbers aren't encouraging.

The biggest new-vehicle expense is depreciation (in James's case, the Dodge Ram will lose $25,000 in value over five years). Maintenance and repairs are the biggest hits for older vehicles: Repair costs are typically twice as much, and maintenance can cost as much as three times more for five-year-old models.

Factor it all in. Spooked by worries over the economy and unemployment, more people are taking the value route—keeping their cars longer and paying for repairs. The average length of vehicle ownership increased to four and a half years in 2008, up from four years in 2002, reports R.L. Polk, an automotive-information firm. And according to Sageworks, a private-company data provider, auto-repair shops' sales rose 2% in 2008.

"Based on ownership costs over five years, the results are firmly in favor of hanging on to your car."

What's more, a car-loan payment is a set amount, whereas holding on to your old car "provides an element of flexibility," says Philip Reed, of Edmunds.com. "Fixing up your clunker is a variable cost per month, and some repairs will be elective." The maintenance section of Edmunds.com has estimates for all service visits, so you can get an idea of typical expenses. One deal-breaker for your old car, says Reed, is a failed transmission—which can cost up to $3,000 to rebuild or replace. Other tipping points: The vehicle has been unreliable from the get-go or it looks as if you'll be making multiple repairs every month.

Uncle Sam's incentives might also help persuade you to junk the clunker. You can write off state and local sales taxes and excise taxes on new cars, light trucks, motor homes and motorcycles bought from February 17 through the end of 2009. You claim the deduction on your 2009 tax return regardless of whether you itemize or claim the standard deduction. And as we went to press, Congress was weighing the latest version of the "cash for clunkers" bill, which would give vouchers worth up to $4,500 to buyers who trade in their old cars for new, more fuel-efficient vehicles. ■

ASK JESSICA A QUESTION AT JANDERSON@KIPLINGER.COM, OR WRITE TO HER AT 1729 H STREET, N.W., WASHINGTON, DC 20006.

From Kiplinger's Personal Finance, July 2009, p. 78.

BUSINESS MATH ISSUE

Depreciation should never be a factor in buying or selling a car.

1. List the key points of the article and information to support your position.
2. Write a group defense of your position using math calculations to support your view.

PROJECT A

Depreciation has no effect on the selling of factories by Dell. Do you agree? Defend your position.

Slater's Business Math Scrapbook

Applying Your Skills

Dell Plans To Sell Factories In Effort To Cut Costs

By Justin Scheck

Dell Inc. is trying to sell its computer factories around the world, a move to sharply overhaul a production model that was long a hallmark of the PC giant's strategy but is no longer competitive.

In recent months, according to people familiar with the matter, Dell has approached contract computer manufacturers with offers to sell the plants. One person briefed on the plan said he expects the company to sell most—and possibly all—of its factories "within the next 18 months." Other factories could close, this person said. Dell would enter into agreements with the contract manufacturers to produce its PCs.

Dell in Talks to Sell Factories in Effort to Cut Costs

Continued from Page One

sign manufacturing partnerships and manufacturing outsourcing relationships."

Dell could face several obstacles to selling its plants. Contract manufacturers may be hesitant to buy factories in places with high labor costs, like the U.S., said one person with knowledge of the talks. And some facilities could be encumbered by agreements with local governments. Dell's North Carolina plant, for example, received several million dollars of state and local tax incentives that are contingent on the factory meeting certain employment and local-investment goals by 2015.

Michael Dell, the company's founder, drove an innovative strategy of selling computers directly to customers, only building them after they were ordered. After a customer places an order through the Web or over the phone, the company's factories assemble the needed components, load PCs with software and ship them in a matter of hours.

The system eliminated idle inventory and maximized Dell's cash flow. The company owns factories in Texas, Tennessee, North Carolina, Florida, Ireland, India, China, Brazil, Malaysia and Lodz, Poland, where it opened a plant early last year.

Dell's plants are still regarded as efficient at churning out desktop PCs. But within the industry, company-owned factories aren't considered the least expensive way to produce laptops, which have been the main driver of growth lately and are complex and labor-intensive to assemble. Rivals such as Hewlett-Packard Co. years ago shifted to contract manufacturers—companies that provide production services to others—to build their portable computers. H-P builds "less than half" of its PCs in facilities it owns, wrote Tony Prophet, H-P's senior vice president for PC supply chain, in an e-mail.

Contract manufacturers can generally produce computers more cheaply because their entire operations are narrowly focused on finding efficiencies in manufacturing, as opposed to large firms like Dell, which must also balance marketing and other considerations.

For many Dell notebooks, a contract manufacturer already partially builds each system in a plant in Asia. The half-built computers are then shipped to one of Dell's own plants where assembly is completed. Because each computer goes to two factories, Dell refers to the system as "two touch."

Dell began efforts to cut manufacturing costs last year. It has farmed out an increasing number of products to contract manufacturers such as Taiwan's Foxconn Group to eliminate two-touch production of some notebooks, and earlier this year closed down one of its own plants in Texas.

Selling factories could be a culmination of a plan Dell started last year to increase its reliance on contract manufacturers, something competitors did first. "A lot of companies are already on that model," said Mike Cannon, Dell's production chief, in an interview earlier this year. "We're playing catch-up there."

H-P, for example, transferred a leased PC plant in Australia to Foxconn in 2005. Apple Inc. has many of its PCs shipped directly from Asian manufacturers' plants to customers.

Series of Steps

Reducing costs for manufacturing and other operations is one of a series of steps Dell hopes will restore momentum after a slide that saw the company lose its position as the world's biggest PC maker by sales to H-P. Mr. Dell returned as chief executive in January 2007, and said he would revive the company through a combination of investments and strategy changes—including the introduction of sales through retail stores—and moves to cost cuts.

Since then, Dell has unveiled a series of more stylish products and laid off about 8,500 workers. The company sold 53% more consumer PCs in its fiscal quarter ended Aug. 1 than it did a year earlier, sending its world-wide consumer market share to 9.1%, up from 7.5% at the same time last year, the company said.

But Dell reported a 17% drop in quarterly income compared with last year. Profit margins fell, the consumer business lost money, and the company said costs remained too high to compensate for the growing investment in new markets, which included aggressive cuts to PC prices to help drive sales, especially in Europe.

Part of Dell's problem is the long-term shift by consumers to buy laptops, which many consumers prefer to buy in retail stores.

Where Dell Has Factories

- Austin, Texas
- Winston-Salem, N.C.
- Lebanon, Tenn.
- Limerick, Ireland
- Penang, Malaysia
- Xiamen, China
- Hortolândia, Brazil
- Chennai, India
- Lodz, Poland
- Miami
- Athlone, Ireland

Source: The company

Internet Projects: See text Web site (www.mhhe.com/slater10e) and The Business Math Internet Resource Guide.

Classroom Notes

chapter

18 INVENTORY AND OVERHEAD

Sears to Test New Outlet Featuring Drive-Through

By Karen Talley

Sears Holdings Corp. is turning to drive-throughs.

The retailer plans to create warehouse-like outlets, called MyGofer, where customers can pick up items they bought online without getting out of their cars.

Sears has received approval for a drive-through permit as part of plans to convert its 85,000-square-foot Kmart in Joliet, Ill.

The MyGofer will have a variety of products and brands and will open as soon as next month, Sears said in a statement. A Sears spokeswoman declined to elaborate.

The drive-through for the Joliet MyGofer will go where the Kmart's garden center now is, according to minutes of the City Council meeting where Sears executives discussed the plan in mid-December.

Sears sees the outlets as a "marriage between online shopping and bricks-and-mortar," city council members were told.

About 80% of the store will be devoted to storage. The other 20% is planned as a showroom and sales area, reminiscent of Service Merchandise Co. outlets in the 1970s and 1980s, where stock was kept in a warehouse and shoppers ordered on-site or picked up purchases.

MyGofer's layout is meant to reverse the general 80/20 percentage split between selling area and storage space.

Teri Stratford

LEARNING UNIT OBJECTIVES

LU 18–1: Assigning Costs to Ending Inventory—Specific Identification; Weighted Average; FIFO; LIFO

1. List the key assumptions of each inventory method *(pp. 432–436)*.
2. Calculate the cost of ending inventory and cost of goods sold for each inventory method *(pp. 432–436)*.

LU 18–2: Retail Method; Gross Profit Method; Inventory Turnover; Distribution of Overhead

1. Calculate the cost ratio and ending inventory at cost for the retail method *(p. 438)*.
2. Calculate the estimated inventory using the gross profit method *(p. 438)*.
3. Explain and calculate inventory turnover *(p. 439)*.
4. Explain overhead; allocate overhead according to floor space and sales *(p. 440)*.

VOCABULARY PREVIEW

Here are key terms in this chapter. After completing the chapter, if you know the term, place a checkmark in the parenthesis. If you don't know the term, look it up and put the page number where it can be found.

Average inventory . ( ) Distribution of overhead . ( ) First-in, first-out (FIFO) method . ( ) Gross profit method . ( ) Inventory turnover . ( ) Just-in-time (JIT) inventory system . ( ) Last-in, first-out (LIFO) method . ( ) Overhead expenses . ( ) Periodic inventory system . ( ) Perpetual inventory system . ( ) Retail method . ( ) Specific identification method . ( ) Weighted-average method . ( )

Firms Race To Regain Control Over Inventories

BY TIMOTHY AEPPEL

The economic downturn is hitting companies so hard and so fast that even those that have made huge strides implementing inventory-control systems haven't been able to react quickly enough to avoid a costly buildup.

After falling sharply for a year, U.S. inventories shot up by $6.2 billion unexpectedly in the fourth quarter of 2008, according to the latest U.S. Commerce Department figures. The surge underscores the rapid demand decline that is hitting large and small manufacturers.

Wall Street Journal © 2009

Have you ever wondered how a company keeps track of its inventory? The following *Wall Street Journal* article, "Firms Race to Regain Control over Inventories," shows the importance of keeping down inventory in today's economic crises. The two methods that a company can use to monitor its inventory are the *perpetual* method and the *periodic* method.

The perpetual inventory system should be familiar to most consumers. Today, it is common for cashiers to run scanners across the product code of each item sold. These scanners read pertinent information into a computer terminal, such as the item's number, department, and price. The computer then uses the **perpetual inventory system** as it subtracts outgoing merchandise from inventory and adds incoming merchandise to inventory. However, as you probably know, the computer cannot be completely relied on to maintain an accurate count of merchandise in stock. Since some products may be stolen or lost, periodically a physical count is necessary to verity the computer count.

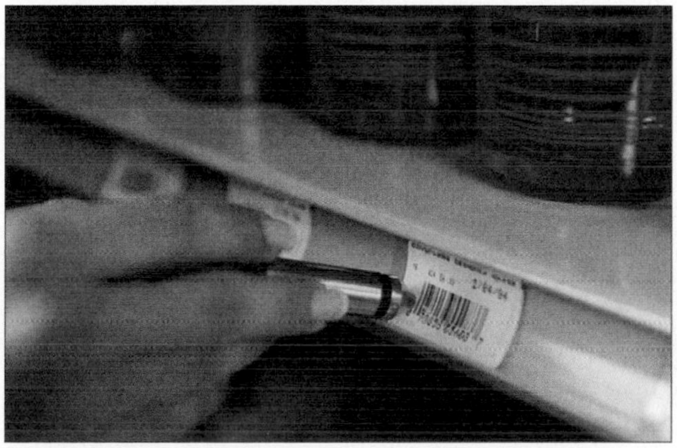

PhotoLink/Getty Images

ASK TERI

Fashion reporter Teri Agins answers readers' questions

Q: ***Before the weather even got warm this spring, a lot of department stores were already putting spring clothes on sale for 40% off. I just went to the mall and saw signs for prefall sales. Summer clothes just went on sale. What is going on? —M.J., Evanston, Ill.***

A: Retailers today work to turn over their inventory as often as possible. Long gone is the era when stores received only a couple of big seasonal deliveries. Now, most stores get fresh merchandise monthly—or as often as weekly at some fast-fashion chains. Frequent deliveries keep the stores looking fresh and inspire shoppers—led by the trendiest—to get into the habit of shopping early and often for the latest novelties.

Compounding the seasonal confusion, high-end designers now aggressively market "pre-collections," such as the fall items that are now in stores, well in advance of each season. In addition, stores may offer "special purchase" and "special value" items that are depicted as deals but were never really marked down.

Retailers typically start marking down goods after nine weeks on the sales floor—or sooner when retail traffic is sluggish or when they have very unpopular

With the increased use of computers, many companies are changing to a perpetual inventory system of maintaining inventory records. Some small stores, however, still use the **periodic inventory system.** This system usually does not keep a running account of its inventory but relies only on a physical inventory count taken at least once a year. The store then uses various accounting methods to value the cost of its merchandise. In this chapter we discuss the periodic method of inventory.

You may wonder why a company should know the status of its inventory. In Chapter 16 we introduced you to the balance sheet and the income statement. Companies cannot accurately prepare these statements unless they have placed the correct value on their inventory. To do this, a company must know (1) the cost of its ending inventory (found on the balance sheet) and (2) the cost of the goods (merchandise) sold (found on the income statement).

For example, retailers want to turn over their inventories as soon as possible. The *Wall Street Journal* clip "Ask Teri" explains how the flow of inventory has changed from previous years. No longer do retailers get a few seasonal deliveries; they now receive new items often, maybe even weekly, to keep their store looking fresh. Frequently, the same type of merchandise flows into a company at different costs. The value assumptions a company makes about the merchandise it sells affects the cost assigned to its ending inventory. Remember that different costs result in different levels of profit on a firm's financial reports.

This chapter begins by using the Blue Company to discuss four common methods (specific identification, weighted average, FIFO, and LIFO) that companies use to calculate costs of ending inventory and the cost of goods sold. In these methods, the flow of costs does not always match the flow of goods. The chapter continues with a discussion of two methods of estimating ending inventory (retail and gross profit methods), inventory turnover, and the distribution of overhead.

Learning Unit 18–1: Assigning Costs to Ending Inventory—Specific Identification; Weighted Average; FIFO; LIFO

LO 1, 2

Blue Company is a small artist supply store. Its beginning inventory is 40 tubes of art paint that cost $320 (at $8 a tube) to bring into the store. As shown in Figure 18.1, Blue made additional purchases in April, May, October, and December. Note that because of inflation and other competitive factors, the cost of the paint rose from $8 to $13 per tube. At the end of December, Blue had 48 unsold paint tubes. During the year, Blue had 120 paint tubes to sell. Blue wants to calculate (1) the cost of ending inventory (not sold) and (2) the cost of goods sold.

Specific Identification Method

Companies that sell high-cost items such as autos, jewelry, antiques, and so on, usually use the specific identification method.

Companies use the **specific identification method** when they can identify the original purchase cost of an item with the item. For example, Blue Company color codes its paint tubes as they come into the store. Blue can then attach a specific invoice price to each paint tube.

FIGURE 18.1

Blue Company—a case study

	Number of units purchased	Cost per unit	Total cost
Beginning inventory	40	$ 8	$ 320
First purchase (April 1)	20	9	180
Second purchase (May 1)	20	10	200
Third purchase (October 1)	20	12	240
Fourth purchase (December 1)	20	13	260
Goods (merchandise) available for sale	120		$1,200 ← Step 1
Units sold	72		
Units in ending inventory	48		

This makes the flow of goods and flow of costs the same. Then, when Blue computes its ending inventory and cost of goods sold, it can associate the actual invoice cost with each item sold and in inventory.

To help Blue calculate its inventory with the specific identification method, use the steps that follow.

CALCULATING THE SPECIFIC IDENTIFICATION METHOD
Step 1. Calculate the cost of goods (merchandise available for sale).
Step 2. Calculate the cost of the ending inventory.
Step 3. Calculate the cost of goods sold (Step 1 – Step 2).

First, Blue must actually count the tubes of paint on hand. Since Blue coded these paint tubes, it can identify the tubes with their purchase cost and multiply them by this cost to arrive at a total cost of ending inventory. Let's do this now.

	Cost per unit	Total cost	
20 units from April 1	$ 9	$180	
20 units from October 1	12	240	
8 units from December 1	13	104	
Cost of ending inventory		$524	← **Step 2**

Blue uses the following cost of goods sold formula to determine its cost of goods sold:

Cost of goods available for sale	−	Cost of ending inventory	=	Cost of goods sold	← **Step 3**
↑		↑		↑	
$1,200 (Figure 18.1)	−	$524	=	$676	

Note that the $1,200 for cost of goods available for sale comes from Figure 18.1 (p. 432). Remember, we are focusing our attention on Blue's *purchase costs*. Blue's actual *selling price* does not concern us.

Now let's look at how Blue would use the weighted-average method.

Weighted-Average Method[1]

The **weighted-average method** prices the ending inventory by using an average unit cost. Let's replay Blue Company and use the weighted-average method to find the average unit cost of its ending inventory and its cost of goods sold. Blue would use the steps that follow.

CALCULATING THE WEIGHTED-AVERAGE METHOD
Step 1. Calculate the average unit cost.
Step 2. Calculate the cost of the ending inventory.
Step 3. Calculate the cost of goods sold.

[1]Virtually all countries permit the use of the weighted-average method.

In the table that follows, Blue makes the calculation.

	Number of units purchased	Cost per unit	Total cost
Beginning inventory	40	$ 8	$ 320
First purchase (April 1)	20	9	180
Second purchase (May 1)	20	10	200
Third purchase (October 1)	20	12	240
Fourth purchase (December 1)	20	13	260
Goods (merchandise) available for sale	120		$1,200
Units sold	72		
Units in ending inventory	48		

$$\text{Weighted average unit cost} = \frac{\text{Total cost of goods available for sale}}{\text{Total number of units available for sale}} = \frac{\$1{,}200}{120 \text{ units}} = \$10 \text{ average unit cost} \leftarrow \textbf{Step 1}$$

Average cost of ending inventory: 48 units at $10 = $480 ← **Step 2**

Cost of goods available for sale − Cost of ending inventory = Cost of goods sold

$1,200 − $480 = $720 ← **Step 3**

Remember that some of the costs we used to determine the average unit cost were higher and others were lower. The weighted-average method, then, calculates an *average unit price* for goods. Companies with similar units of goods, such as rolls of wallpaper, often use the weighted-average method. Also, companies with homogeneous products such as fuels and grains may use the weighted-average method.

Now let's see how Blue Company would value its inventory with the FIFO method.

FIFO—First-In, First-Out Method[2]

The **first-in, first-out (FIFO)** inventory valuation method assumes that the first goods (paint tubes for Blue) brought into the store are the first goods sold. Thus, FIFO assumes that each sale is from the oldest goods in inventory. FIFO also assumes that the inventory remaining in the store at the end of the period is the most recently acquired goods. This cost flow assumption may or may not hold in the actual physical flow of the goods. An example of a corporation using the FIFO method is Gillette Corporation.

Use the following steps to calculate inventory with the FIFO method.

CALCULATING THE FIFO INVENTORY

Step 1. List the units to be included in the ending inventory and their costs.

Step 2. Calculate the cost of the ending inventory.

Step 3. Calculate the cost of goods sold.

[2]Virtually all countries permit the use of the FIFO method.

In the table that follows, we show how to calculate FIFO for Blue using the above steps.

FIFO (bottom up)	Number of units purchased	Cost per unit	Total cost
Beginning inventory	40	$ 8	$ 320
First purchase (April 1)	20	9	180
Second purchase (May 1)	20	10	200
Third purchase (October 1)	20	12	240
Fourth purchase (December 1)	20	13	260
Goods (merchandise) available for sale	120		$1,200
Units sold	72		
Units in ending inventory	48		

20 units from December 1 purchased at $13		$260	
20 units from October 1 purchased at $12	← Step 1 →	240	
8 units from May 1 purchased at $10		80	
48 units result in an ending inventory cost of		$580	← Step 2

Cost of goods available for sale − Cost of ending inventory = Cost of goods sold

$1,200 − $580 = $620 ← Step 3

In FIFO, the cost flow of goods tends to follow the physical flow. For example, a fish market could use FIFO because it wants to sell its old inventory first. Note that during inflation, FIFO produces a higher income than other methods. So companies using FIFO during this time must pay more taxes.

We conclude this unit by using the LIFO method to value Blue Company's inventory.

LIFO—Last-In, First-Out Method[3]

If Blue Company chooses the **last-in, first-out (LIFO)** method of inventory valuation, then the goods sold by Blue will be the last goods brought into the store. The ending inventory would consist of the old goods that Blue bought earlier.

You can calculate inventory with the LIFO method by using the steps that follow.

CALCULATING THE LIFO INVENTORY

Step 1. List the units to be included in the ending inventory and their costs.

Step 2. Calculate the cost of the ending inventory.

Step 3. Calculate the cost of goods sold.

Now we use the above steps to calculate LIFO for Blue.

[3]Many countries, such as Australia, Hong Kong, South Africa, and the United Kingdom, do not permit the use of LIFO.

LIFO (top down)	Number of units purchased	Cost per unit	Total cost
Beginning inventory	40	$ 8	$ 320
First purchase (April 1)	20	9	180
Second purchase (May 1)	20	10	200
Third purchase (October 1)	20	12	240
Fourth purchase (December 1)	20	13	260
Goods (merchandise) available for sale	120		$1,200
Units sold	72		
Units in ending inventory	48		

40 units of beginning inventory at $8 — $320

8 units from April at $9 ← Step 1 → 72

48 units result in an ending inventory cost of $392 ← Step 2

Cost of goods available for sale − Cost of ending inventory = Cost of goods sold

$1,200 − $392 = $808 ← Step 3

Although LIFO doesn't always match the physical flow of goods, companies do still use it to calculate the flow of costs for products such as DVDs and computers, which have declining replacement costs. Also, during inflation, LIFO produces less income than other methods. This results in lower taxes for companies using LIFO.

Before concluding this unit, we will make a summary for the cost of ending inventory and cost of goods sold under the weighted-average, FIFO, and LIFO methods. From this summary, you can see that in times of rising prices, LIFO gives the highest cost of goods sold ($808). This results in a tax savings for Blue. The weighted-average method tends to smooth out the fluctuations between LIFO and FIFO and falls in the middle.

The key to this discussion of inventory valuation is that different costing methods produce different results. So management, investors, and potential investors should understand the different inventory costing methods and should know which method a particular company uses. For example, Fruit of the Loom, Inc., changed its inventories from LIFO to FIFO due to cost reductions.

Let's check your understanding of this unit with a Practice Quiz.

MONEY TIPS

Don't throw good money after bad. When making financial decisions, avoid looking at what you already put into an item—your sunk costs. Instead, project what that item might still cost you in the future and do a cost/benefit analysis to determine if more money should be spent.

Inventory method	Cost of goods available for sale	Cost of ending inventory	Cost of goods sold
Weighted average	$1,200	$480 **Step 1:** Total goods, $1,200 Total units, 120 $\frac{\$1,200}{120} = \$10$ **Step 2:** $10 × 48 = $480	$1,200 − $480 = $720
FIFO	$1,200	Bottom up to inventory level (48) 20 × $13 = $260 20 × $12 = 240 8 × $10 = 80 $580	$1,200 − $580 = $620
LIFO	$1,200	Top down to inventory level (48) 40 × $8 = $320 8 × $9 = 72 $392	$1,200 − $392 = $808

LU 18–1 PRACTICE QUIZ

Complete this **Practice Quiz** to see how you are doing.

From the following, calculate **(a)** the cost of ending inventory and **(b)** the cost of goods sold under the assumption of (1) weighted-average method, (2) FIFO, and (3) LIFO (ending inventory shows 72 units):

	Number of books purchased for resale	Cost per unit	Total
January 1 inventory	30	$3	$ 90
March 1	50	2	100
April 1	20	4	80
November 1	60	6	360

Solutions with Step-by-Step Help on DVD

✓ Solutions

1. **a.** 72 units of ending inventory × $3.94 = $283.68 cost of ending inventory
($630 ÷ 160)

b. Cost of goods available for sale − Cost of ending inventory = Cost of goods sold
↓ ↓ ↓
$630 − $283.68 = **$346.32**

2. **a.** 60 units from November 1 purchased at $6 — $360
12 units from April 1 purchased at $4 — 48
72 units — Cost of ending inventory — $408

b. Cost of goods available for sale − Cost of ending inventory = Cost of goods sold
↓ ↓ ↓
$630 − $408 − **$222**

3. **a.** 30 units from January 1 purchased at $3 — $ 90
42 units from March 1 purchased at $2 — 84
72 — Cost of ending inventory — $174

b. Cost of goods available for sale − Cost of ending inventory = Cost of goods sold
↓ ↓ ↓
$630 − $174 = **$456**

LU 18–1a EXTRA PRACTICE QUIZ WITH WORKED-OUT SOLUTIONS

Need more practice? Try this **Extra Practice Quiz** (check figures in Chapter Organizer, p. 445). Worked-out Solutions can be found in Appendix B at end of text.

From the following, calculate **(a)** the cost of ending inventory and **(b)** the cost of goods sold under the assumption of (1) weighted-average, (2) FIFO, and LIFO (ending inventory shows 58 units):

	Number of books purchased for resale	Cost per unit	Total
January 1 inventory	20	$4	$ 80
March 1	60	3	180
April 1	40	5	200
November 1	50	7	350

Learning Unit 18–2: Retail Method; Gross Profit Method; Inventory Turnover; Distribution of Overhead

Customers want stores to have products available for sale as soon as possible. This has led to outsourced warehouses offshore where tens of thousands of products can be stored ready to be quickly shipped to various stores.

When retailers receive their products, they go into one of their most important assets—their inventory. When the product is sold, it must be removed from inventory so

Digital Vision/PunchStock

it can be replaced or discontinued. Often these transactions occur electronically at the registers that customers use to pay for products. How is inventory controlled when the register of the store cannot perform the task of adding and subtracting products from inventory?

Convenience stores often try to control their inventory by taking physical inventories. This can be time-consuming and expensive. Some stores draw up monthly financial reports but do not want to spend the time or money to take a monthly physical inventory.

Many stores estimate the amount of inventory on hand. Stores may also have to estimate their inventories when they have a loss of goods due to fire, theft, flood, and the like. This unit begins with two methods of estimating the value of ending inventory—the *retail method* and the *gross profit method.*

Retail Method

Many companies use the **retail method** to estimate their inventory. As shown in Figure 18.2, this method does not require that a company calculate an inventory cost for each item. To calculate the $3,500 ending inventory in Figure 18.2, Green Company used the steps that follow.

LO 1

CALCULATING THE RETAIL METHOD

Step 1. Calculate the cost of goods available for sale at cost and retail: $6,300; $9,000.

Step 2. Calculate a cost ratio using the following formula:

$$\frac{\text{Cost of goods available for sale at cost}}{\text{Cost of goods available for sale at retail}} = \frac{\$6{,}300}{\$9{,}000} = .70$$

Step 3. Deduct net sales from cost of goods available for sale at retail: $9,000 − $4,000.

Step 4. Multiply the cost ratio by the ending inventory at retail: .70 × $5,000.

FIGURE 18.2

Estimating inventory with the retail method

	Cost	Retail	
Beginning inventory	$4,000	$6,000	
Net purchases during month	2,300	3,000	
Cost of goods available for sale **(Step 1)**	$6,300	$9,000	
Less net sales for month		4,000	**(Step 3)**
Ending inventory at retail		$5,000	
Cost ratio ($6,300 ÷ $9,000) **(Step 2)**		70%	
Ending inventory at cost (.70 × $5,000) **(Step 4)**		$3,500	

Now let's look at the gross profit method.

Gross Profit Method

To use the **gross profit method** to estimate inventory, the company must keep track of (1) average gross profit rate, (2) net sales at retail, (3) beginning inventory, and (4) net purchases. You can use the following steps to calculate the gross profit method:

LO 2

CALCULATING THE GROSS PROFIT METHOD

Step 1. Calculate the cost of goods available for sale (Beginning inventory + Net purchases).

Step 2. Multiply the net sales at retail by the complement of the gross profit rate. This is the estimated cost of goods sold.

Step 3. Calculate the cost of estimated ending inventory (Step 1 − Step 2).

EXAMPLE Assume Radar Company has the following information in its records:

Gross profit on sales	30%
Beginning inventory, January 1, 2011	$20,000
Net purchases	$ 8,000
Net sales at retail for January	$12,000

If you use the gross profit method, what is the company's estimated inventory?

The gross profit method calculates Radar's estimated cost of ending inventory at the end of January as follows:

Goods available for sale				
Beginning inventory, January 1, 2011			$20,000	
Net purchases			8,000	
Cost of goods available for sale			$28,000	← Step 1
Less estimated cost of goods sold:				
Net sales at retail		$12,000		
Cost percentage (100% − 30%)	Step 2 →	.70		
Estimated cost of goods sold			8,400	
Estimated ending inventory, January 31, 2011			$19,600	← Step 3

Note that the cost of goods available for sale less the estimated cost of goods sold gives the estimated cost of ending inventory.

Since this chapter has looked at inventory flow, let's discuss inventory turnover—a key business ratio.

LO 3

Inventory Turnover

Inventory turnover is the number of times the company replaces inventory during a specific time. Companies use the following two formulas to calculate inventory turnover:

$$\text{Inventory turnover at retail} = \frac{\text{Net sales}}{\text{Average inventory at retail}}$$

$$\text{Inventory turnover at cost} = \frac{\text{Cost of goods sold}}{\text{Average inventory at cost}}$$

You should note that inventory turnover at retail is usually lower than inventory turnover at cost. This is due to theft, markdowns, spoilage, and so on. Also, retail outlets and grocery stores usually have a higher turnover, but jewelry and appliance stores have a low turnover.

Now let's use an example to calculate the inventory turnover at retail and at cost.

EXAMPLE The following facts are for Abby Company, a local sporting goods store (rounded to the nearest hundredth):

Net sales	$32,000	Cost of goods sold	$22,000
Beginning inventory at retail	$11,000	Beginning inventory at cost	$ 7,500
Ending inventory at retail	$ 8,900	Ending inventory at cost	$ 5,600

With these facts, we can make the following calculations:

$$\textbf{Average inventory} = \frac{\text{Beginning inventory} + \text{Ending inventory}}{2}$$

$$\text{At retail: } \frac{\$32{,}000}{\frac{\$11{,}000 + \$8{,}900}{2}} = \frac{\$32{,}000}{\$9{,}950} = 3.22$$

$$\text{At cost: } \frac{\$22{,}000}{\frac{\$7{,}500 + \$5{,}600}{2}} = \frac{\$22{,}000}{\$6{,}550} = 3.36$$

What Turnover Means

Inventory is often a company's most expensive asset. The turnover of inventory can have important implications. Too much inventory results in the use of needed space, extra insurance coverage, and so on. A low inventory turnover could indicate customer dissatisfaction, too much tied-up capital, and possible product obsolescence. A high inventory turnover might mean insufficient amounts of inventory causing stockouts that may lead to future lost sales. If inventory is moving out quickly, perhaps the company's selling price is too low compared to that of its competitors.

In recent years the **just-in-time (JIT) inventory system** from Japan has been introduced in the United States. Under ideal conditions, manufacturers must have suppliers that will provide materials daily as the manufacturing company needs them, thus eliminating inventories. The companies that are using this system, however, have often not been able to completely eliminate the need to maintain some inventory.

LO 4

Distribution of Overhead

In Chapter 16 we studied the cost of goods sold and operating expenses shown on the income statement. The operating expenses included **overhead expenses**—expenses that are *not* directly associated with a specific department or product but that contribute indirectly to the running of the business. Examples of such overhead expenses are rent, taxes, and insurance. The *Wall Street Journal* clip "Warner Bros." indicates that the Warner Bros. studio is slashing its overhead in order to streamline costs.

China Foto Press/Getty Images

Warner Bros.

Move Is Part of Bid To Slash Overhead, Trim Film Output

BY PETER SANDERS AND MERISSA MARR

IN THE LATEST SIGN that Hollywood studios are gun shy about the art-house movie market they once coveted, Warner Bros. said it is shutting down its two specialty film labels as part of a broader effort to streamline costs.

Warner Bros.' move to close the two boutique labels, Picturehouse and Warner Independent Pictures, comes just a few weeks after the company absorbed a third specialty label, New Line Cinema, into the main Warner studio operation. While both of Warner's ministudios have produced Oscar-winning films—including a Best Actress win this year for French actress Marion Cotillard in Picturehouse's "La Vie en Rose"—the studio saw a way to reduce the overall number of films on its calendar and slash overhead.

In recent years, the major studios rushed to set up small specialty labels as a way to tap the market for so-called independent films: small, high-quality movies often pitched toward niche audiences that are inexpensive to produce and can become very profitable if they break out commercially. The specialty units also give

Wall Street Journal © 2008

Companies must allocate their overhead expenses to the various departments in the company. The two common methods of calculating the **distribution of overhead** are by (1) floor space (square feet) or (2) sales volume.

Calculations by Floor Space

To calculate the distribution of overhead by floor space, use the steps that follow.

CALCULATING THE DISTRIBUTION OF OVERHEAD BY FLOOR SPACE

Step 1. Calculate the total square feet in all departments.

Step 2. Calculate the ratio for each department based on floor space.

Step 3. Multiply each department's floor space ratio by the total overhead.

EXAMPLE Roy Company has three departments with the following floor space:

Department A	6,000 square feet
Department B	3,000 square feet
Department C	1,000 square feet

The accountant's job is to allocate $90,000 of overhead expenses to the three departments. To allocate this overhead by floor space:

	Floor space in square feet	Ratio	
Department A	6,000	$\frac{6,000}{10,000} = 60\%$	← Steps 1 and 2
Department B	3,000	$\frac{3,000}{10,000} = 30\%$	
Department C	$\frac{1,000}{10,000}$ total square feet	$\frac{1,000}{10,000} = 10\%$	

Department A	.60 × $90,000 =	$54,000	← Step 3
Department B	.30 × $90,000 =	27,000	
Department C	.10 × $90,000 =	9,000	
		$90,000	

Calculations by Sales

To calculate the distribution of overhead by sales, use the steps that follow.

MONEY TIPS

If sharing a home with others, distributing the overhead costs of utilities, rent, and the like can be a challenge. Consider distributing these costs based on awake hours per person in the home. That way the roommate with endless guests will pay a fair share.

CALCULATING THE DISTRIBUTION OF OVERHEAD BY SALES

Step 1. Calculate the total sales in all departments.

Step 2. Calculate the ratio for each department based on sales.

Step 3. Multiply each department's sales ratio by the total overhead.

EXAMPLE Morse Company distributes its overhead expenses based on the sales of its departments. For example, last year Morse's overhead expenses were $60,000. Sales of its two departments were as follows, along with its ratio calculation.

Since Department A makes 80% of the sales, it is allocated 80% of the overhead expenses.

	Sales	Ratio	
Department A	$ 80,000	$\frac{\$80,000}{\$100,000} = .80$	← Steps 1 and 2
Department B	20,000	$\frac{\$20,000}{\$100,000} = .20$	
Total sales	$100,000		

These ratios are then multiplied by the overhead expense to be allocated.

Department A	.80 × $60,000 =	$48,000	← Step 3
Department B	.20 × $60,000 =	12,000	
		$60,000	

It's time to try another Practice Quiz.

LU 18–2 PRACTICE QUIZ

Complete this **Practice Quiz** to see how you are doing.

1. From the following facts, calculate the cost of ending inventory using the retail method (round the cost ratio to the nearest tenth percent):

January 1—inventory at cost	$ 18,000
January 1—inventory at retail	$ 58,000
Net purchases at cost	$220,000
Net purchases at retail	$376,000
Net sales at retail	$364,000

2. Given the following, calculate the estimated cost of ending inventory using the gross profit method:

Gross profit on sales	40%
Beginning inventory, January 1, 2011	$27,000
Net purchases	$ 7,500
Net sales at retail for January	$15,000

3. Calculate the inventory turnover at cost and at retail from the following (round the turnover to the nearest hundredth):

Average inventory at cost	Average inventory at retail	Net sales	Cost of goods sold
$10,590	$19,180	$109,890	$60,990

4. From the following, calculate the distribution of overhead to Departments A and B based on floor space.

Amount of overhead expense to be allocated	Square footage
$70,000	10,000 Department A
	30,000 Department B

Solutions with Step-by-Step Help on DVD

✓ Solutions

1.

	Cost	Retail
Beginning inventory	$ 18,000	$ 58,000
Net purchases during the month	220,000	376,000
Cost of goods available for sale	$238,000	$434,000
Less net sales for the month		364,000
Ending inventory at retail		$ 70,000
Cost ratio ($238,000 ÷ $434,000)		54.8%
Ending inventory at cost (.548 × $70,000)		$ 38,360

2.

Goods available for sale		
Beginning inventory, January 1, 2011		$ 27,000
Net purchases		7,500
Cost of goods available for sale		$ 34,500
Less estimated cost of goods sold:		
Net sales at retail	$ 15,000	
Cost percentage (100% − 40%)	.60	
Estimated cost of goods sold		9,000
Estimated ending inventory, January 31, 2011		$ 25,500

3. $$\text{Inventory turnover at cost} = \frac{\text{Cost of goods sold}}{\text{Average inventory at cost}} = \frac{\$60,900}{\$10,590} = 5.75$$

$$\text{Inventory turnover at retail} = \frac{\text{Net sales}}{\text{Average inventory at retail}} = \frac{\$109,890}{\$19,180} = 5.73$$

4.

		Ratio
Department A	10,000	$\frac{10,000}{40,000} = .25 \times \$70,000 = \$17,500$
Department B	30,000	$\frac{30,000}{40,000} = .75 \times \$70,000 = 52,500$
		$ 70,000

LU 18–2a EXTRA PRACTICE QUIZ WITH WORKED-OUT SOLUTIONS

Need more practice? Try this **Extra Practice Quiz** (check figures in Chapter Organizer, p. 445). Worked-out Solutions can be found in Appendix B at end of text.

1. From the following, calculate the cost of ending inventory using the retail method (round the cost ratio to the nearest tenth percent):

January 1—inventory at cost	$19,000
January 1—inventory at retail	$60,000
Net purchases at cost	$265,000
Net purchases at retail	$392,000
Net sales at retail	$375,000

2. Given the following, calculate the estimated cost of ending inventory using the gross profit method:

Gross profit on sales	30%
Beginning inventory, January 1, 2011	$30,000
Net purchases	$8,000
Net sales at retail for January	$16,000

3. Calculate the inventory turnover at cost and at retail from the following (round the turnover to the nearest hundredth):

Average inventory at cost	**Average inventory at retail**	**Net sales**	**Cost of goods sold**
$11,200	$21,800	$129,500	$76,500

4. From the following, calculate the distribution of overhead to Departments A and B based on floor space.

Amount of overhead expense to be allocated	**Square footage**
$60,000	10,000 Department A
	50,000 Department B

CHAPTER ORGANIZER AND REFERENCE GUIDE

Topic	Key point, procedure, formula	Example(s) to illustrate situation
Specific identification method, p. 432	Identification could be by serial number, physical description, or coding. The flow of goods and flow of costs are the same.	**Cost per unit** **Total cost** April 1, 3 units at $7 $21 May 5, 4 units at 8 32 $53 If 1 unit from each group is left, ending inventory is: 1 × $7 = $ 7 + 1 × 8 = 8 $15 Cost of goods available for sale − Cost of ending inventory = Cost of goods sold $53 − $15 = **$38**

(continues)

CHAPTER ORGANIZER AND REFERENCE GUIDE

Topic	Key point, procedure, formula	Example(s) to illustrate situation
Weighted-average method, p. 433	$\text{Weighted average unit cost} = \dfrac{\text{Total cost of goods available for sale}}{\text{Total number of units available for sale}}$	Cost per unit / Total cost 1/XX, 4 units at $4 — $16 5/XX, 2 units at 5 — 10 8/XX, 3 units at 6 — 18 $44 $\text{Unit cost} = \dfrac{\$44}{9} = \$4.89$ If 5 units left, cost of ending inventory is 5 units × $4.89 = $24.45
FIFO—first-in, first-out method, p. 434	Sell old inventory first. Ending inventory is made up of last merchandise brought into store.	Using example above: 5 units left: (Last into store) 3 units at $6 — $18 2 units at $5 — 10 Cost of ending inventory — $28
LIFO—last-in, first-out method, p. 435	Sell last inventory brought into store first. Ending inventory is made up of oldest merchandise in store.	Using weighted-average example: 5 units left: (First into store) 4 units at $4 — $16 1 unit at $5 — 5 Cost of ending inventory — $21
Retail method, p. 438	Ending inventory at cost equals: $\dfrac{\text{Cost of goods available at cost}}{\text{Cost of goods available at retail}} \times \text{Ending inventory at retail}$ (This is cost ratio.)	Cost / Retail Beginning inventory — $52,000 — $ 83,000 Net purchases — 28,000 — 37,000 Cost of goods available for sale — $80,000 — $120,000 Less net sales for month — 80,000 Ending inventory at retail — $ 40,000 $\text{Cost ratio} = \dfrac{\$80,000}{\$120,000} = .67 = 67\%$ Rounded to nearest percent. Ending inventory at cost, $26,800 (.67 × $40,000)
Gross profit method, p. 438	Beg. inv. + Net purchases − Estimated cost of goods sold = Estimated ending inventory	**Goods available for sale** Beginning inventory — $30,000 Net purchases — 3,000 Cost of goods available for sale — $33,000 Less: Estimated cost of goods sold: Net sales at retail — $18,000 Cost percentage (100% − 30%) — .70 Estimated cost of goods sold — 12,600 Estimated ending inventory — $20,400

(continues)

CHAPTER ORGANIZER AND REFERENCE GUIDE

Topic	Key point, procedure, formula	Example(s) to illustrate situation
Inventory turnover at retail and at cost, p. 439	$\frac{\text{Net sales}}{\text{Average inventory at retail}}$ or $\frac{\text{Cost of goods sold}}{\text{Average inventory at cost}}$	Inventory, January 1 at cost $20,000 Inventory, December 31 at cost 48,000 Cost of goods sold 62,000 At cost: $\frac{\$62,000}{\frac{\$20,000 + \$48,000}{2}} = 1.82$ (inventory turnover at cost)
Distribution of overhead, p. 440	Based on floor space or sales volume, calculate: 1. Ratios of department floor space or sales to the total. 2. Multiply ratios by total amount of overhead to be distributed.	Total overhead to be distributed, $10,000 **Floor space** Department A 6,000 sq. ft. Department B 2,000 sq. ft. 8,000 sq. ft. $\text{Ratio A} = \frac{6,000}{8,000} = .75$ $\text{Ratio B} = \frac{2,000}{8,000} = .25$ Dept. A = .75 × $10,000 = $7,500 Dept. B = .25 × $10,000 = $2,500
KEY TERMS	Average inventory, *p. 439* Distribution of overhead, *p. 440* First-in, first-out (FIFO) method, *p. 434* Gross profit method, *p. 438* Inventory turnover, *p. 439* Just-in-time (JIT) inventory system, *p. 440* Last-in, first-out (LIFO) method, *p. 435* Overhead expenses, *p. 440* Periodic inventory system, *p. 432*	Perpetual inventory system, *p. 431* Retail method, *p. 438* Specific identification method, *p. 432* Weighted-average method, *p. 433*
CHECK FIGURES FOR EXTRA PRACTICE QUIZZES WITH PAGE REFERENCES. (WORKED-OUT SOLUTIONS IN APPENDIX B.)	LU 18–1a (p. 437) 1. a. $276.08; b. $533.92 2. a. $390; b. $420 3. a. $194; b. $616	LU 18–2a (p. 443) 1. $48,356 2. $26,800 3. 6.83; 5.94 4. $10,200; $42,000

Critical Thinking Discussion Questions

1. Explain how you would calculate the cost of ending inventory and cost of goods sold for specific identification, FIFO, LIFO, and weighted-average methods. Explain why during inflation, LIFO results in a tax savings for a business.
2. Explain the cost ratio in the retail method of calculating inventory. What effect will the increased use of computers have on the retail method?
3. What is inventory turnover? Explain the effect of a high inventory turnover during the Christmas shopping season.
4. How is the distribution of overhead calculated by floor space or sales? Give an example of why a store in your area cut back one department to expand another. Did it work?
5. What have you seen of levels of inventory affected by the economic crises at your local mall?

Classroom Notes

END-OF-CHAPTER PROBLEMS

connect plus+ www.mhhe.com/slater10e

Check figures for odd-numbered problems in Appendix C. Name ______________________ Date ________

DRILL PROBLEMS

18–1. Using the specific identification method, calculate **(a)** the ending inventory and **(b)** the cost of goods sold given the following:

Date	Units purchased	Cost per iPod	Ending inventory
June 1	12 Blackberrys	$ 99	7 Blackberrys from June 1
October 1	30 Blackberrys	109	9 Blackberrys from Oct. 1
December 1	37 Blackberrys	125	10 Blackberrys from Dec. 1

From the following, **(a)** calculate the cost of ending inventory (round the average unit cost to the nearest cent) and **(b)** cost of goods sold using the weighted-average method, FIFO, and LIFO (ending inventory shows 61 units).

	Number purchased	Cost per unit	Total
January 1 inventory	40	$4	$160
April 1	60	7	420
June 1	50	8	400
November 1	55	9	495

18–2. Weighted average:

18–3. FIFO:

18–4. LIFO:

From the following, (18–5 to 18–12) calculate the cost of ending inventory and cost of goods sold for LIFO (18–13), FIFO (18–14), and the weighted-average (18–15) methods (make sure to first find total cost to complete the table); ending inventory is 49 units:

	Beginning inventory and purchases	Units	Unit cost	Total dollar cost
18–5.	Beginning inventory, January 1	5	$2.00	
18–6.	April 10	10	2.50	
18–7.	May 15	12	3.00	
18–8.	July 22	15	3.25	
18–9.	August 19	18	4.00	
18–10.	September 30	20	4.20	
18–11.	November 10	32	4.40	
18–12.	December 15	16	4.80	

18–13. LIFO:

Cost of ending inventory	**Cost of goods sold**

18–14. FIFO:

Cost of ending inventory	**Cost of goods sold**

18–15. Weighted average:

Cost of ending inventory	**Cost of goods sold**

18–16. From the following, calculate the cost ratio (round to the nearest hundredth percent) and the cost of ending inventory to the nearest cent under the retail method.

Net sales at retail for year	$40,000	Purchases—cost	$14,000
Beginning inventory—cost	$27,000	Purchases—retail	$19,000
Beginning inventory—retail	$49,000		

18–17. Complete the following (round answers to the nearest hundredth):

a. Average inventory at cost	**b.** Average inventory at retail	**c.** Net sales	**d.** Cost of goods sold	**e.** Inventory turnover at cost	**f.** Inventory turnover at retail
$14,000	$21,540	$70,000	$49,800		

Complete the following (assume $90,000 of overhead to be distributed):

	Square feet	**Ratio**	**Amount of overhead allocated**
18–18. Department A	10,000		
18–19. Department B	30,000		

18–20. Given the following, calculate the estimated cost of ending inventory using the gross profit method.

Gross profit on sales	55%	Net purchases	$ 3,900
Beginning inventory	$29,000	Net sales at retail	$17,000

WORD PROBLEMS

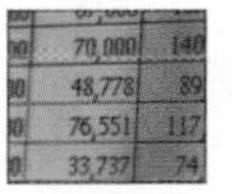

18–21. Lee Corp. purchased 10 keychains on January 1, 2010, for $9.00 each and 5 keychains were purchased on December 1, 2010, at $10.00. Seven keychains were sold. **(a)** What would be the inventory amount using LIFO? **(b)** What would be the inventory amount using FIFO?

18–22. Marvin Company has a beginning inventory of 12 sets of paints at a cost of $1.50 each. During the year, the store purchased 4 sets at $1.60, 6 sets at $2.20, 6 sets at $2.50, and 10 sets at $3.00. By the end of the year, 25 sets were sold. Calculate **(a)** the number of paint sets in stock and **(b)** the cost of ending inventory under LIFO, FIFO, and the weighted-average methods. Round to nearest cent for the weighted average.

18–23. On January 30, 2009, Seneca Foods, from Marion, NY, announced the effect of LIFO on their inventory valuation method. Kraig H. Kayser, president and CEO, included a statement regarding inventory valuation. He stated: "Bottom-line performance has also been strong, notwithstanding the over doubling of the company's LIFO provision from $20.1 million to $41.9 million. The LIFO provision is a noncash adjustment to cost of goods that removes the inflationary impact on inventory costs." Assume Seneca purchased 25 units for $10.50 on January 1, 2008. On March 15, 2008, Seneca purchased an additional 15 units at $14.35. Finally, on November 30, 2008, 30 units were purchased at $15.75. Fifty units were sold. **(a)** What is the cost of ending inventory using LIFO? **(b)** What is the cost of merchandise sold using LIFO?

18–24. Joe Ponzio, a financial advisor who bases his investing strategies on the teachings of Warren Buffett, explains why inventory turnover rates matter to managers, owners, and investors on his August 7, 2009, blog post. He states: "The company doing five turns a year is often in better shape." Jerry Waite is interested in calculating his inventory turnover at retail for his flower and tree nursery. Net sales last year were $57,250, beginning inventory at retail was $23,750, and ending inventory at retail was $5,050. What is his inventory turnover at retail? Round to the nearest hundredth.

18–25. May's Dress Shop's inventory at cost on January 1 was $39,000. Its retail value was $59,000. During the year, May purchased additional merchandise at a cost of $195,000 with a retail value of $395,000. The net sales at retail for the year were $348,000. Could you calculate May's inventory at cost by the retail method? Round the cost ratio to the nearest whole percent.

18–26. A sneaker outlet has made the following wholesale purchases of new running shoes: 12 pairs at $45, 18 pairs at $40, and 20 pairs at $50. An inventory taken last week indicates that 23 pairs are still in stock. Calculate the cost of this inventory by FIFO.

18–27. Over the past 3 years, the gross profit rate for Jini Company was 35%. Last week a fire destroyed all Jini's inventory. Using the gross profit method, estimate the cost of inventory destroyed in the fire, given the following facts that were recorded in a fireproof safe:

Beginning inventory	$ 6,000
Net purchases	$64,000
Net sales at retail	$49,000

CHALLENGE PROBLEMS

18–28. The concept of inventory valuation is common to business but does not get discussed much for personal use. Yet the idea of inventory valuation is important to personal financial health as well. In her 2008 book *The Road to Wealth,* Suze Orman discusses a variety of typical business practices applied to personal use. She discusses the importance of valuing what you own. Joanne Greenwood runs a small business out of her home and had never considered calculating what she had available for sale before reading about the need to take inventory. She calculated the cost of goods she had available for sale at the beginning of the month to be $3,100. She sold $525 during the month. The retail value of this merchandise is $4,960. Using the retail method, calculate the value of her ending inventory to the nearest cent.

18–29. Logan Company uses a perpetual inventory system on a FIFO basis. Assuming inventory on January 1 was 800 units at $8 each, what is the cost of ending inventory at the end of October 5?

Received			Sold	
Date	**Quantity**	**Cost per unit**	**Date**	**Quantity**
Apr. 15	220	$5	Mar. 8	500
Nov. 12	1,900	9	Oct. 5	200

SUMMARY PRACTICE TEST

1. Writing.com has a beginning inventory of 16 sets of pens at a cost of $2.12 each. During the year, Writing.com purchased 8 sets at $2.15, 9 sets at $2.25, 14 sets at $3.05, and 13 sets at $3.20. By the end of the year, 29 sets were sold. Calculate **(a)** the number of pen sets in stock and **(b)** the cost of ending inventory under LIFO, FIFO, and weighted-average methods. *(pp. 431–436)*

2. Lee Company allocates overhead expenses to all departments on the basis of floor space (square feet) occupied by each department. The total overhead expenses for a recent year were $200,000. Department A occupied 8,000 square feet; Department B, 20,000 square feet; and Department C, 7,000 square feet. What is the overhead allocated to Department C? In your calculations, round to the nearest whole percent. *(p. 440)*

3. A local college bookstore has a beginning inventory costing $80,000 and an ending inventory costing $84,000. Sales for the year were $300,000. Assume the bookstore markup rate on selling price is 70%. Based on the selling price, what is the inventory turnover at cost? Round to the nearest hundredth. *(p. 439)*

4. Dollar Dress Shop's inventory at cost on January 1 was $82,800. Its retail value was $87,500. During the year, Dollar purchased additional merchandise at a cost of $300,000 with a retail value of $325,000. The net sales at retail for the year were $295,000. Calculate Dollar's inventory at cost by the retail method. Round the cost ratio to the nearest whole percent. *(p. 438)*

5. On January 1, Randy Company had an inventory costing $95,000. During January, Randy had net purchases of $118,900. Over recent years, Randy's gross profit in January has averaged 45% on sales. The company's net sales in January were $210,800. Calculate the estimated cost of ending inventory using the gross profit method. *(p. 438)*

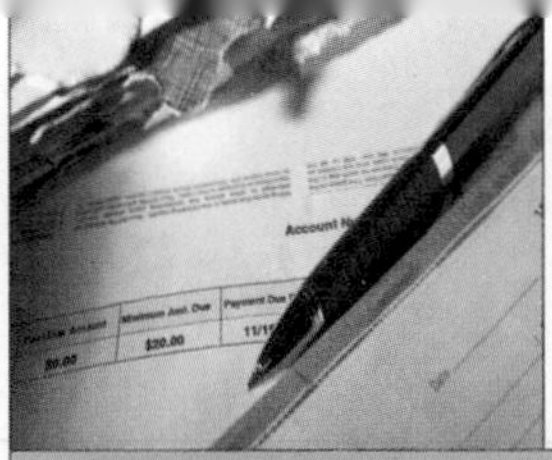

Personal Finance

A KIPLINGER APPROACH

ASK KIM
KIMBERLY LANKFORD

Should You Buy a GM?

I'm in the market for a new car. General Motors filed for Chapter 11 bankruptcy in June, and now I'm wondering whether this is a particularly good or bad time to buy a GM vehicle.

J.S., VIA E-MAIL

As GM restructures into a leaner company by shedding brands and dealerships, you can get some great deals. Expect to find the best bargains through the fall at dealerships that are closing, says Jesse Toprak, an analyst at Edmunds.com (the site has a list of GM dealers that are going out of business). The deals may get better as the closing dates get nearer, but you will also have fewer choices and may have to compromise on color and options. By late fall, dealers will work through excess inventory and prices are likely to rise.

To target a fair price, research incentives. For example, in June GM was offering $1,000 cash back on both the 2009 Cadillac CTS and the Chevrolet Malibu. As for how much dealers are charging, price differences are wider than normal. And prices may vary by thousands of dollars even at the same dealer for the same model, Toprak says.

General Motors hopes to keep core brands, such as Buick, Cadillac, Chevrolet and GMC, and shed less-profitable brands. It already has buyers for Hummer and Saturn, and Saab is also on the block. GM will completely eliminate the Pontiac brand in the next few months. That means resale value will vary a lot depending on the brand you buy. Toprak expects Pontiac models to experience the biggest drop in resale value. Cars remaining in the GM lineup will take a resale hit over the short term, he says, but don't expect a big drop over, say, five years.

General Motors will continue to honor its warranties. And the U.S. Treasury Department has offered to back warranties for any GM vehicles bought during the restructuring period. So if the company doesn't ultimately emerge from bankruptcy, the government will pay for service.

From Kiplinger's Personal Finance, August 2009, p. 57.

BUSINESS MATH ISSUE

Large auto inventories always mean increased rebates.

1. List the key points of the article and information to support your position.
2. Write a group defense of your position using math calculations to support your view.

PROJECT A

Do you agree with Chrysler's position. Defend your answer.

Slater's Business Math Scrapbook

Applying Your Skills

Chrysler Tightens Terms on Dealers

Auto Maker to Begin Charging New Fees for Unsold Vehicles; Move Could Trigger New Outlet Closings

By Alex P. Kellogg And Neal E. Boudette

Dealers selling new **Chrysler** LLC vehicles are about to come under additional financial pressures that could trigger the closing of more sales outlets in 2009.

Starting Jan. 1, the struggling auto maker's financing arm will impose large fees on dealers holding new cars and trucks that are unsold after more than 360 days, and will require the payment of all remaining balances on any used vehicles unsold after more than six months.

Some dealerships could incur charges totaling hundreds of thousands of dollars over the course of 2009 at a time when many are already losing money and battling to stay in business, according to dealers familiar with the plans.

Boston Globe / Landov

Chrysler is set to assess new charges on its dealers for vehicles that languish in showrooms and on sales lots.

Chrysler Financial acknowledged it has changed the terms on aging inventory. It said it is working with dealers "to ensure we minimize the impact."

Further financial troubles for dealers would complicate Chrysler's struggle to stay afloat. On Wednesday, it said it would halt production for at least a month to reduce inventory and conserve cash. The sudden loss of dealers could hurt the auto maker's sales and increase consumer worries about the company's future.

Chrysler, along with **General Motors** Corp., has asked the U.S. government for billions of dollars in emergency loans. Chrysler Chief Executive Robert Nardelli recently told Congress the company needs $7 billion by the end of this month or it may not be able to stay in business.

The new fees for aging inventory come amid other signs of dealer strain.

Chrysler's financing arm recently has warned dealers it may have to temporarily stop providing loans for dealers to stock vehicles on their lots because of a wave of withdrawals from a fund used to pay off those loans.

In a letter dated Dec. 12, Chrysler Financial Chief Executive Tom Gilman said dealers have been withdrawing up to $60 million a day from the fund. A copy of the letter was reviewed by The Wall Street Journal.

Dealers put their own money into the fund and use it to pay off loans that they take out to stock their lots with new vehicles. But since July, dealers have pulled $1.5 billion from the account on worries that Chrysler could go bankrupt.

In the letter, Mr. Gilman said continued withdrawals "could potentially force us to temporarily suspend" new-inventory loans, known in the industry as floor planning.

The new charges for aging inventory represent a bigger problem.

Starting in January, dealers will have to pay 10% a month of the amount they owe on new 2008 cars that are over 360 days old, and 50% of the amount on any new 2009 models that are over 360 days old. Chrysler Financial also will levy monthly charges: $10 for every new car that is unsold after six months, $15 for cars after 270 days, and $25 for each vehicle over 360 days.

At Freedom Dodge Chrysler Jeep in Lexington, Ky., owner Paul Cleaver said he has about 18 vehicles that have been on the lot for more than a year, and estimates the annual charges will add up to tens of thousands of dollars.

"Do I like it? Absolutely not," Mr. Cleaver said. He is rushing to clear out the old models as quickly as he can before the end of the year.

He said he blames tight credit markets for the problem, not Chrysler, and said some dealers may not be able to bear the additional costs. "If you can't pay," he said, "you're out of business."

David Kelleher, who owns two Chrysler dealerships in metro Philadelphia, said he has 56 vehicles that are currently more than 360 days old. Mr. Kelleher said he knows of many dealers in worse shape, some with hundreds of vehicles nearly a year old or older.

He is cutting deals to sell his aged inventory before he gets the first bill from Chrysler on Jan. 1. "I'm taking, in some cases, a loss to get rid of cars before I face curtailment," Mr. Kelleher said.

Like GM and **Ford Motor** Co., Chrysler is trying to reduce the number of dealers it has, and several hundred Detroit-brand dealers have thrown in the towel already this year, according to the National Automobile Dealers Association.

Paul Melville, an expert in dealer restructuring at consulting firm Grant Thornton LLP, said the new charges are "the last thing that dealers can stand at the moment." For some Chrysler dealers, the costs of aging inventory will be "the final straw," he said.

PROJECT B

Do you agree with Toyota's strategy? Defend your position.

Toyota Sticks by 'Just in Time' Strategy After Qua

By Amy Chozick

TOKYO—**Toyota Motor** Corp. President Katsuaki Watanabe reiterated his belief in the auto maker's vaunted "just in time" production system, even as he apologized for vehicle-delivery delays stemming from an earthquake disruption at a parts supplier.

"We've been implementing this strategy for decades...and we'll keep on with it," Mr. Watanabe said, discussing the auto maker's purposefully lean parts inventories.

Last week, Toyota said it would said the interruption would delay the delivery of 55,000 vehicles.

Mr. Watanabe said the company will examine its risk management and risk control and look for ways to become less dependent on single suppliers. He stressed the auto maker won't change its *kanban*, or just-in-time, strategy of keeping as little inventory as possible on hand, which reduces warehouse costs and ensures quality. "Quality is the most vital aspect of our organization," Mr. Watanabe said.

Despite the production setbacks, Mr. Watanabe said he is leaving the

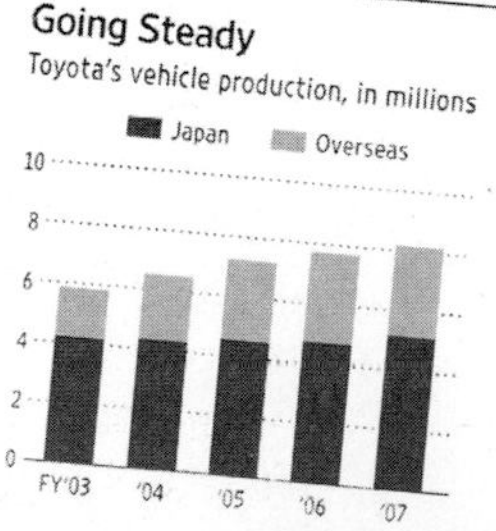

Riken's closure last week nearly 70% of Japan's auto tion to temporarily shut down **Motor** Co. closed a plant th duces the popular Civic and F els. **Nissan Motor** Co., **Mitsubi tors** Corp., **Mazda Motor** Co **zuki Motors** Corp. and **Fuji He dustries** Ltd., the latter of makes the Subaru brand of v also stopped or slowed pro last week. Most major auto said they will resume operat day or tomorrow.

Toyota plans to make up the l duction of vehicles, at least

Internet Projects: See text Web site (www.mhhe.com/slater10e) and The Business Math Internet Resource Guide.

Classroom Notes

chapter

19 SALES, EXCISE, AND PROPERTY TAXES

© Comstock/PunchStock

Ask Personal Journal.

Q: *Can you tell me the qualifications for deducting doctor bills on my tax return?*
—S.K., Aurora, Colo.

A: Sure, but first get ready for some unpleasant news: Most taxpayers can't deduct any of their doctors' bills because of what's known as the 7.5% rule. You're allowed to deduct unreimbursed medical expenses on Schedule A if you itemize your deductions and only to the extent they exceed 7.5% of your adjusted gross income. For example, suppose your adjusted gross income for this year comes to $50,000. To exceed 7.5% of your income, your medical bills would have to be more than $3,750. If your medical bills come to $4,000, you typically would be allowed to deduct only $250 of that amount. For more details, such as what expenses are deductible, see IRS Publications 17 and 502. See if you're eligible for a flexible spending account to use pretax dollars to pay for health-care and dependent-care expenses. *—Tom Herman*

LEARNING UNIT OBJECTIVES

LU 19–1: Sales and Excise Taxes

1. Compute sales tax on goods sold involving trade and cash discounts and shipping charges *(pp. 457–458)*.
2. Explain and calculate excise tax *(p. 459)*.

LU 19–2: Property Tax

1. Calculate the tax rate in decimal *(p. 459)*.
2. Convert tax rate in decimal to percent, per $100 of assessed value, per $1,000 of assessed value, and in mills *(p. 460)*.
3. Compute property tax due *(p. 460)*.

VOCABULARY PREVIEW

Here are key terms in this chapter. After completing the chapter, if you know the term, place a checkmark in the parenthesis. If you don't know the term, look it up and put the page number where it can be found.

Assessed value . ( ) Excise tax . ( ) Mill . ( ) Personal property . ( ) Property tax . ( ) Real property . ( ) Sales tax . ( ) Tax rate . ( )

P&G's Pringles Exempt From Tax

LONDON—Britain's High Court ruled that Pringles aren't a potato snack, and thus aren't subject to value-added tax.

Friday's ruling by Justice Nicholas Warren is expected to save millions of dollars for the manufacturer, **Procter & Gamble** Co. Justice Warren overruled a VAT Tribunal decision that Pringles should be subject to the 17.5% tax because it met the definition of "potato crisps, potato sticks, potato puffs and similar products made from the potato, or from potato flour, or from potato starch."

The judge found that Pringles were only 42% potato, and thus exempt.

Did you know if you buy Pringles in London they will not be subject to the value-added tax on potatoes? The *Wall Street Journal* clip "P&G's Pringles Exempt from Tax" reports that because only 42% of Pringles ingredients comprise potato, the snack is exempt from the tax.

As you know, in the United States sales tax rates vary from state to state. Four state capitals (Concord, New Hampshire; Dover, Delaware; Helena, Montana; and Salem, Oregon) do not impose a sales tax. However, if you live in California, Florida, Texas, or Washington, your combined state and local tax rate reaches 7% or more.

In Learning Unit 19–1 you will learn how sales taxes are calculated. This learning unit also discusses the excise tax that is collected in addition to the sales tax. Learning Unit 19–2 explains the use of property tax.

Learning Unit 19–1: Sales and Excise Taxes

Today, many states have been raising their sales tax and excise tax.

LO 1

Sales Tax

In many cities, counties, and states, the sellers of certain goods and services collect **sales tax** and forward it to the appropriate government agency. Forty-five states have a sales tax. Of the 45 states, 28 states and the District of Columbia exempt food; 44 states and the District of Columbia exempt prescription drugs.

Sales taxes are usually computed electronically by the new cash register systems and scanners. However, it is important to know how sellers calculate sales tax manually. The following example of a car battery will show you how to manually calculate sales tax.

EXAMPLE

Selling price of a Sears battery	$32.00	Shipping charge	$3.50
Trade discount to local garage	$10.50	Sales tax	5%

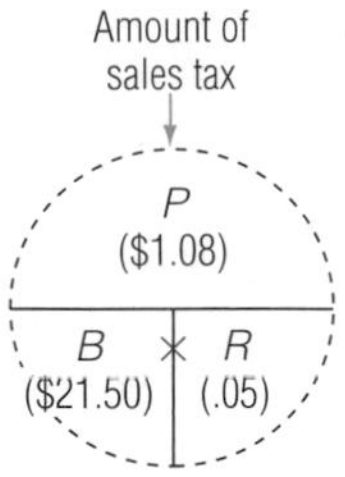

$21.50 + $1.08 = $22.58
(sale) (tax amount)

Manual calculation

$32.00 − $10.50 = $21.50 taxable
× .05
$ 1.08 tax
+ 21.50 taxable
+ 3.50 shipping
$26.08 total price with tax and shipping

Check

100% is base + 5% is tax = 105%
1.05 × $21.50 = $22.58
+ 3.50 shipping
$26.08

In this example, note how the trade discount is subtracted from the selling price before any cash discounts are taken. If the buyer is entitled to a 6% cash discount, it is calculated as follows:

.06 × $21.50 = $1.29

Also, remember that we do not take cash discounts on the sales tax or shipping charges.

Calculating Actual Sales

Managers often use the cash register to get a summary of their total sales for the day. The total sales figure includes the sales tax. So the sales tax must be deducted from the total sales. To illustrate this, let's assume the total sales for the day were $40,000, which included a 7% sales tax. What were the actual sales?

Hint: $40,000 is 107% of actual sales

$$\text{Actual sales} = \frac{\text{Total sales}}{1 + \text{Tax rate}}$$

Total sales

$$\text{Actual sales} = \frac{\$40{,}000}{1.07} = \$37{,}383.18$$

100% sales
+ 7% tax
107% → 1.07

Thus, the store's actual sales were $37,383.18. The actual sales plus the tax equal $40,000.

Check

$37,383.18 × .07 = $ 2,616.82 sales tax
+ 37,383.18 actual sales
$40,000.00 total sales including sales tax

LO 2

Excise Tax

Governments (local, federal, and state) levy **excise tax** on particular products and services. This can be a sizable source of revenue for these governments.

Consumers pay the excise tax in addition to the sales tax. The excise tax is based on a percent of the *retail* price of a product or service. This tax, which varies in different states, is imposed on luxury items or nonessentials. Examples of products or services subject to the excise tax include airline travel, telephone service, alcoholic beverages, jewelry, furs, fishing rods, tobacco products, and motor vehicles. Although excise tax is often calculated as a percent of the selling price, the tax can be stated as a fixed amount per item sold. The following example calculates excise tax as a percent of the selling price.[1]

MONEY TIPS

If making a large purchase, consider traveling to a city or state with no sales tax on the item being purchased. You could end up saving much more than the cost of the trip.

EXAMPLE On June 1, Angel Rowe bought a fur coat for a retail price of $5,000. Sales tax is 7% with an excise tax of 8%. Her total cost is as follows:

$5,000
+ 350 sales tax (.07 × $5,000)
+ 400 excise tax (.08 × $5,000)
$5,750

Let's check your progress with a Practice Quiz.

[1] If excise tax were a stated fixed amount per item, it would have to be added to the cost of goods or services before any sales tax were taken. For example, a $100 truck tire with a $4 excise tax would be $104 before the sales tax was calculated.

LU 19–1 PRACTICE QUIZ

Complete this **Practice Quiz** to see how you are doing.

From the following shopping list, calculate the total sales tax (food items are excluded from sales tax, which is 8%):

Chicken	$6.10	Orange juice	$1.29	Shampoo	$4.10
Lettuce	$ .75	Laundry detergent	$3.65		

Solutions with Step-by-Step Help on DVD

✓ Solutions

Shampoo	$4.10
Laundry detergent	+ 3.65
	$7.75 × .08 = **$.62**

LU 19–1a EXTRA PRACTICE QUIZ WITH WORKED-OUT SOLUTIONS

Need more practice? Try this **Extra Practice Quiz** (check figures in Chapter Organizer, p. 462). Worked-out Solutions can be found in Appendix B at end of text.

From the following shopping list, calculate the total sales tax (food items are excluded from sales tax, which is 7%):

Chicken	$7.90	Orange juice	$1.50	Shampoo	$5.90
Lettuce	$ .85	Laundry detergent	$4.10		

Learning Unit 19–2: Property Tax

When you own property, you must pay property tax. In this unit we listen in on a conversation between a property owner and a tax assessor.

Defining Assessed Value

Bill Adams was concerned when he read in the local paper that the property tax rate had been increased. Bill knows that the revenue the town receives from the tax helps pay for fire and police protection, schools, and other public services. However, Bill wants to know how the town set the new rate and the amount of the new property tax.

Bill went to the town assessor's office to get specific details. The assessor is a local official who estimates the fair market value of a house. Before you read the summary of Bill's discussion, note the following formula:

Property Can Have Two Meanings

Both subject to property tax:
1. **Real property**—land, buildings, etc.
2. **Personal property**—possessions like jewelry, autos, furniture, etc.

$$\text{Assessed value} = \text{Assessment rate} \times \text{Market value}$$

Bill: What does **assessed value** mean?

Assessor: *Assessed value* is the value of the property for purposes of computing property taxes. We estimated the market value of your home at $210,000. In our town, we assess property at 30% of the market value. Thus, your home has an assessed value of $63,000 ($210,000 × .30). Usually, assessed value is rounded to the nearest dollar.

Bill: I know that the **tax rate** multiplied by my assessed value ($63,000) determines the amount of my property tax. What I would like to know is how did you set the new tax rate?

Determining the Tax Rate

LO 1

Assessor: In our town first we estimate the total amount of revenue needed to meet our budget. Then we divide the total of all assessed property into this figure to get the *tax rate*. The formula looks like this:

$$\text{Tax rate} = \frac{\text{Budget needed}}{\text{Total assessed value}^{2}}$$

Our town budget is $125,000, and we have a total assessed property value of $1,930,000. Using the formula, we have the following:

$$\frac{\$125{,}000}{\$1{,}930{,}000} = \$.0647668 = \boxed{.0648} \text{ tax rate per dollar}$$

[2]Remember that exemptions include land and buildings used for educational and religious purposes and the like.

Note that the rate should be rounded up to the indicated digit, *even if the digit is less than 5.* Here we rounded to the nearest ten thousandth.

How the Tax Rate Is Expressed

LO 2

Assessor: We can express the .0648 tax rate per dollar in the following forms:

By percent	Per $100 of assessed value	Per $1,000 of assessed value	In mills
6.48%	$6.48	$64.80	64.80
(Move decimal two places to right.)	(.0648 × 100)	(.0648 × 1,000)	$\left(\frac{.0648}{.001}\right)$

A **mill** is $\frac{1}{10}$ of a cent or $\frac{1}{1,000}$ of a dollar (.001). To represent the number of mills as a tax rate per dollar, we divide the tax rate in decimal by .001. Rounding practices vary from state to state. Colorado tax bills are now rounded to the thousandth mill. An alternative to finding the rate in mills is to multiply the rate per dollar by 1,000, since a dollar has 1,000 mills. In the problems in this text, we round the mills per dollar to nearest hundredth.

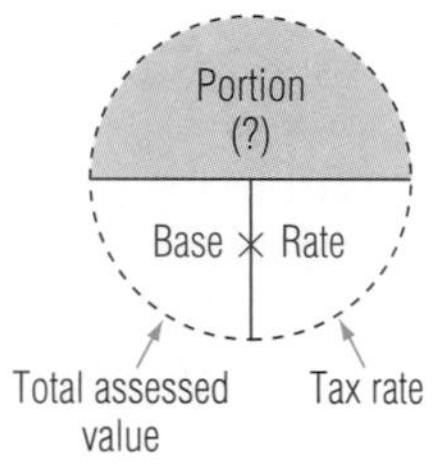

How to Calculate Property Tax Due[3]

LO 3

Assessor: The following formula will show you how we arrive at your **property tax:**

Total property tax due (Portion) = Tax rate (Rate) × Total assessed value (Base)

$4,082.40 = .0648 × $63,000

$ MONEY TIPS

If you are in the market for real estate, considering those properties that are in foreclosure due to a tax lien may provide a cost-effective way to purchase property.

We can use the other forms of the decimal tax rate to show you how the property tax will not change even when expressed in various forms:

By percent	Per $100	Per $1,000	Mills
6.48% × $63,000	$\frac{\$63,000}{\$100} = 630$	$\frac{\$63,000}{\$1,000} = 63$	Property tax due
= $4,082.40	630 × $6.48	63 × $64.80	= Mills × .001 × Assessed value
	= $4,082.40	= $4,082.40	= 64.80 × .001 × $63,000
			= $4,082.40

Now it's time to try the Practice Quiz.

LU 19–2 PRACTICE QUIZ

Complete this **Practice Quiz** to see how you are doing.

From the following facts: (1) calculate assessed value of Bill's home; (2) calculate the tax rate for the community in decimal (to nearest ten thousandths); (3) convert the decimal to **(a)** %, **(b)** per $100 of assessed value, **(c)** per $1,000 of assessed value, and **(d)** in mills (to nearest hundredth); and (4) calculate the property tax due on Bill's home in decimal, per $100, per $1,000, and in mills.

Given

Assessed market value	40%	Total budget needed	$ 176,000
Market value of Bill's home	$210,000	Total assessed value	$1,910,000

Solutions with Step-by-Step Help on DVD

✓ Solutions

1. .40 × $210,000 = $84,000

2. $\frac{\$176,000}{\$1,910,000}$ = .0922 per dollar

[3]Some states have credits available to reduce what the homeowner actually pays. For example, 42 out of 50 states give tax breaks to people over age 65. In Alaska, the state's homestead exemption reduces the property tax of a $168,000 house from $1,512 to $253.

3. a. .0922 = 9.22% b. .0922 × 100 = $9.22

c. .0922 × 1,000 = $92.20 d. $\frac{.0922}{.001}$ = 92.2 mills (or .0922 × 1,000)

4. .0922 × $84,000 = $7,744.80

$9.22 × 840 = $7,744.80

$92.20 × 84 = $7,744.80

92.20 × .001 × $84,000 = $7,744.80

LU 19–2a EXTRA PRACTICE QUIZ WITH WORKED-OUT SOLUTIONS

Need more practice? Try this **Extra Practice Quiz** (check figures in Chapter Organizer, p. 462). Worked-out Solutions can be found in Appendix B at end of text.

From the following facts: (1) calculate assessed value of Bill's home; (2) calculate the tax rate for the community in decimal (to nearest ten thousandths); (3) convert the decimal to **(a)** %, **(b)** per $100 of assessed value, **(c)** per $1,000 of assessed value, and **(d)** in mills (to nearest hundredth); and (4) calculate the property tax due on Bill's home in decimal, per $100, per $1,000, and in mills.

Given

Assessed market value	40%	Total budget needed	$ 159,000
Market value of Bill's home	$150,000	Total assessed value	$1,680,000

CHAPTER ORGANIZER AND REFERENCE GUIDE

Topic	Key point, procedure, formula	Example(s) to illustrate situation
Sales tax, p. 457	Sales tax is not calculated on trade discounts. Shipping charges, etc., also are not subject to sales tax. Actual sales = $\frac{\text{Total sales}}{1 + \text{Tax rate}}$ Cash discounts are calculated on sale price before sales tax is added on.	Calculate sales tax: Purchased 12 bags of mulch at $59.40; 10% trade discount; 5% sales tax. $59.40 − $5.94 = $53.46 $53.46 × .05 $2.67 sales tax Any cash discount would be calculated on $53.46.
Excise tax, p. 459	Excise tax is calculated separately from sales tax and is an additional tax. It is based as a percent of the selling price. It could be stated as a fixed amount per item sold. In that case, the excise tax would be added to the cost of the item before any sales tax calculations. Rates for excise tax will vary.	Jewelry $4,000 retail price Sales tax 7% Excise tax 10% $4,000 + 280 sales tax + 400 excise tax $4,680
Assessed value, p. 459	Assessment rate × Market value	$100,000 house; rate, 30%; $30,000 assessed value.
Tax rate, p. 460	$\frac{\text{Budget needed}}{\text{Total assessed value}}$ = Tax rate (Round rate up to indicated digit even if less than 5.)	$\frac{\$800{,}000}{\$9{,}200{,}000}$ = .08695 = .0870 tax rate per $1
Expressing tax rate in other forms, p. 460	1. Percent: Move decimal two places to right. Add % sign. 2. Per $100: Multiply by 100. 3. Per $1,000: Multiply by 1,000. 4. Mills: Divide by .001.	1. .0870 = 8.7% 2. .0870 × 100 = $8.70 3. .0870 × 1,000 = $87 4. $\frac{.0870}{.001}$ = 87 mills

(continues)

CHAPTER ORGANIZER AND REFERENCE GUIDE

Topic	Key point, procedure, formula	Example(s) to illustrate situation
Calculating property tax, p. 460	Total property tax due = Tax rate × Total assessed value Various forms: **1.** Percent × Assessed value **2.** Per \$100: $\frac{\text{Assessed value}}{\$100}$ × Rate **3.** Per \$1,000: $\frac{\text{Assessed value}}{\$1{,}000}$ × Rate **4.** Mills: Mills × .001 × Assessed value	*Example:* Rate, .0870 per \$1; \$30,000 assessed value **1.** (.087)8.7% × \$30,000 = **\$2,610** **2.** $\frac{\$30{,}000}{\$100}$ = 300 × \$8.70 = **\$2,610** **3.** $\frac{\$30{,}000}{\$1{,}000}$ = 30 × \$87 = **\$2,610** **4.** $\frac{.0870}{.001}$ = 87 mills 87 mills × .001 × \$30,000 = **\$2,610**
KEY TERMS	Assessed value, *p. 459* Excise tax, *p. 458* Mill, *p. 460* Personal property, *p. 459* Property tax, *p. 460* Real property, *p. 459*	Sales tax, *p. 457* Tax rate, *p. 459*
CHECK FIGURES FOR EXTRA PRACTICE QUIZZES WITH PAGE REFERENCES. (WORKED-OUT SOLUTIONS IN APPENDIX B.)	LU 19–1a (p. 459) \$.70	LU 19–2a (p. 461) **1.** \$60,000 **2.** \$.0946 **3.** a. 9.46% b. \$9.46; c. 94.60; d. 94.6 mills **4.** \$5,676

Critical Thinking Discussion Questions

1. Explain sales and excise taxes. Should all states have the same tax rate for sales tax?

2. Explain how to calculate actual sales when the sales tax was included in the sales figure. Is a sales tax necessary?

3. How is assessed value calculated? If you think your value is unfair, what could you do?

4. What is a mill? When we calculate property tax in mills, why do we use .001 in the calculation?

END-OF-CHAPTER PROBLEMS

Check figures for odd-numbered problems in Appendix C.

Name ____________________ Date ________

DRILL PROBLEMS

Calculate the following:

	Retail selling price	Sales tax (5%)	Excise tax (9%)	Total price including taxes
19–1.	$800			
19–2.	$1,500			

Calculate the actual sales since the sales and sales tax were rung up together; assume a 6% sales tax (round your answer to the nearest cent):

19–3. $88,000

19–4. $26,000

Calculate the assessed value of the following pieces of property:

	Assessment rate	Market value	Assessed value
19–5.	30%	$130,000	
19–6.	80%	$210,000	

Calculate the tax rate in decimal form to the nearest ten thousandth:

	Required budget	Total assessed value	Tax rate per dollar
19–7.	$920,000	$39,500,000	

Complete the following:

	Tax rate per dollar	In percent	Per $100	Per $1,000	Mills
19–8.	.0956				
19–9.	.0699				

Complete the amount of property tax due to the nearest cent for each situation:

	Tax rate	Assessed value	Amount of property tax due
19–10.	40 mills	$ 65,000	
19–11.	$42.50 per $1,000	105,000	
19–12.	$8.75 per $100	125,000	
19–13.	$94.10 per $1,000	180,500	

WORD PROBLEMS

19–14. Lenore Right went to Firestone Tires and bought 4 tires for $800; they are subject to 5% sales tax and 6% excise tax. What is the total amount Lenore paid?

19–15. Don Chather bought a new Dell computer for $1,995. This included a 6% sales tax. What is the amount of sales tax and the selling price before the tax?

19–16. According to *The Ledger* on July 29, 2009, Lake Hamilton, FL, town councilman Gary White was the sole dissenting vote against a 17% property tax increase. His argument against the hike was based on declining property values and a poor economy. Without a tax hike, the town's budget of $499,094 will not be met. If the town has $7,129,914 in total assessed value, what tax rate per $1,000 is needed to meet the $499,094 budget? If the tax rate stays at $60.00 per thousand, what will the budget shortfall be?

19–17. In the town of Marblehead, the market value of a home is $280,000. The assessment rate is 40%. What is the assessed value?

19–18. In the June 22, 2009, edition of *The Los Angeles Times,* Scott Wilson reports on how "the five-county Los Angeles area is in the process of cutting property taxes on more than half a million homes because of plunging home values." This decline-in-value reduction amounts to a significant reduction for many homeowners. If a property is currently assessed at $425,000 and there is a 25% reduction in assessed value, what is the current and proposed property tax at $21.50 per $1,000 of assessed value?

19–19. Lois Clark bought a ring for $6,000. She must still pay a 5% sales tax and a 10% excise tax. The jeweler is shipping the ring, so Lois must also pay a $40 shipping charge. What is the total purchase price of Lois's ring?

19–20. Blunt County needs $700,000 from property tax to meet its budget. The total value of assessed property in Blunt is $110,000,000. What is the tax rate of Blunt? Round to the nearest ten thousandth. Express the rate in mills.

19–21. Bill Shass pays a property tax of $3,200. In his community, the tax rate is 50 mills. What is Bill's assessed value?

19–22. The home of Bill Burton is assessed at $80,000. The tax rate is 18.50 mills. What is the tax on Bill's home?

19–23. Jesse Garza has a home assessed at $285,000. The tax rate is 7.9 mills. What is the tax on Jesse's home?

19–24. Bill Blake pays a property tax of $2,500. In his community, the tax rate is 55 mills. What is Bill's assessed value? Round to the nearest dollar.

19–25. The property tax rate for Minneapolis is $8.73 per square foot, and the Denver rate is $2.14 a square foot. If 3,500 square feet is occupied at each location, what is the difference paid in property taxes?

CHALLENGE PROBLEMS

19–26. On March 17, 2009, Philadelphia's Mayor Michael Nutter confirmed a temporary 19% increase in property taxes to help cover the city's budget. If current property rates are 8.2% of the assessed value and they increase to 9.75%, what is the increase in property taxes for a $180,000 home with a 33% assessed market value?

19–27. Art Neuner, an investor in real estate, bought an office condominium. The market value of the condo was $250,000 with a 70% assessment rate. Art feels that his return should be 12% per month on his investment after all expenses. The tax rate is $31.50 per $1,000. Art estimates it will cost $275 per month to cover general repairs, insurance, and so on. He pays a $140 condo fee per month. All utilities and heat are the responsibility of the tenant. Calculate the monthly rent for Art. Round your answer to the nearest dollar (at intermediate stages).

DVD SUMMARY PRACTICE TEST

1. Carol Shan bought a new Apple iPod at Best Buy for $299. The price included a 5% sales tax. What are the sales tax and the selling price before the tax? *(p. 458)*

2. Jeff Jones bought a ring for $4,000 from Zales. He must pay a 7% sales tax and 10% excise tax. Since the jeweler is shipping the ring, Jeff must also pay a $30 shipping charge. What is the total purchase price of Jeff's ring? *(p. 459)*

3. The market value of a home in Boston, Massachusetts, is $365,000. The assessment rate is 40%. What is the assessed value? *(p. 459)*

4. Jan County needs $910,000 from its property tax to meet the budget. The total value of assessed property in Jan is $180,000,000. What is Jan's tax rate? Round to the nearest ten-thousandth. Express the rate in mills (to the nearest tenth). *(p. 460)*

5. The home of Nancy Billows is assessed at $250,000. The tax rate is 4.95 mills. What is the tax on Nancy's home? *(p. 460)*

6. V's Warehouse has a market value of $880,000. The property in V's area is assessed at 35% of the market value. The tax rate is $58.90 per $1,000 of assessed value. What is V's property tax? *(p. 460)*

Personal Finance

A KIPLINGER APPROACH

LOWDOWN

What You Need to Know About Paying Your Taxes

If you don't pay up you'll be penalized—unlike some high-ranking public officials.

BY MARY BETH FRANKLIN

1. EVEN THE PROS MAKE MISTAKES. Just ask Treasury Secretary Timothy Geithner, who admits he failed to pay more than $34,000 in self-employment taxes between 2001 and 2004. Or Rep. Charles Rangel (D-N.Y.), chairman of the House tax-writing committee, who neglected to report $75,000 worth of rental income from his Caribbean beach house. Geithner paid the back taxes and interest, but the IRS (which he now oversees) graciously waived the penalties. Rangel simply wrote a check for more than $10,000 in back taxes, and he hasn't had to pay any penalties, either.

2. IGNORANCE IS NO EXCUSE. Geithner used tax software (but admitted the error was his fault). Rangel attributed his unreported foreign-earned income to a "language barrier." But it doesn't matter. When you sign a tax return, whether you prepare it yourself or leave the number-crunching to a professional, you are responsible for the accuracy of your return and the consequences if you make a mistake.

3. YOU WON'T GET OFF SO EASY. Most taxpayers who fail to file or pay their taxes on time face stiff penalties and interest charges. Say you owe the IRS but you don't have the cash to pay. If you file your return by April 15—or you file for an extension to push your tax-filing deadline (but not your tax payment) back to October 15—you'll incur interest charges and a penalty of 0.5% a month on the unpaid balance, up to 25%, until the taxes are paid. Still, if you owe taxes, it's better to file on time and delay paying your bill than not file at all. That's because the penalty for not filing is ten times higher. For instance, if you file for an extension and pay your $5,000 tax bill three months late, you'll owe a $75 penalty plus interest. But if you don't file your tax return on time and pay your tax bill three months late, you'll owe a $750 penalty plus interest. At that rate, it may be cheaper to pay your taxes on time with a credit card—or borrow money from your local loan shark.

4. YOU COULD LOSE YOUR HOUSE. If you don't pay up, you're in for a fight that you probably won't win. The number of levies issued by the IRS—including seizures of wages, pensions, tax refunds, bank accounts and property—increased by 1,600% in recent years, from 220,000 in 2000 to 3.75 million in 2007. Although the IRS seldom seizes a house, it can place a lien that prevents you from selling it or refinancing your mortgage until your tax debt is paid in full. And even filing for bankruptcy may not protect you; the IRS can force you to sell your home or raid your retirement accounts—assets that are explicitly excluded from certain types of bankruptcy liquidations—to settle a tax debt.

5. BUT YOU PROBABLY WON'T GET CAUGHT. Americans profess to abhor tax cheating (in the latest survey of taxpayer attitudes, 89% described it as unacceptable). But unless IRS computers spot a discrepancy—such as a shortfall between the salary you report and what your W-2 says you were paid—the chances of getting caught are minuscule. Maybe that's why there's a $350-billion annual gap between what Americans owe and what they pay. Possible solution: Appoint everyone to cabinet positions so they have to 'fess up. That would be one way to help finance the economic-stimulus package. ■

From *Kiplinger's Personal Finance*, May 2009, p. 87.

BUSINESS MATH ISSUE

Unemployment rates have no effect on taxes.

1. List the key points of the article and information to support your position.
2. Write a group defense of your position using math calculations to support your view.

Slater's Business Math Scrapbook

Applying Your Skills

PROJECT A

Taxes on car sharing should be eliminated. Agree or disagree?

If Your Zipcar Is Costing More, The Taxman May Be to Blame

BY SARAH NASSAUER

IN CITIES around the country, fans of **Zipcar** Inc. and other car-sharing companies are seeing prices rise for those jaunts to the grocery store. For that, they can blame the taxman.

As car-sharing companies have enjoyed skyrocketing growth in recent years, several state and city governments have ruled that car-sharing companies need to charge their members car-rental tax. The laws are affecting customers in places such as Seattle, Pittsburgh and Chicago—and are likely to spread to other areas soon.

Rental-car taxes are already paid by the big players like Enterprise Rent-A-Car and **Hertz Global Holdings** Inc.'s Hertz Corp. But since customers often use car-sharing services for just a few hours, those extra charges can end up making members' bills a lot higher. In Pittsburgh, a two-hour errand run now costs about \$22 instead of \$18 with Zipcar, not including sales tax. In Seattle, two hours of Zipcar use is now about \$21 instead of \$19, without sales tax. The issue is creating a lobbying headache for the small, up-and-coming car-share industry and putting it at loggerheads with traditional car-rental companies.

The concept of car sharing started in the U.S. as small, local, mostly non-profit ventures with explicitly green ambitions, but as national for-profit players Flexcar and Zipcar started to grow, city and state governments started to take note. Then Cambridge, Mass.-based Zipcar bought Flexcar last October, making it the largest and only national game in town, raising the question—is "car sharing" the same as "car rental" and should services' members be paying rental-car tax?

Getty Images

"This is a policy issue that is not going away," says Scott Griffith, chairman and chief executive of Zipcar. Mr. Griffith says that in a place like Pittsburgh, where the tax adds a significant percentage to prices, "I don't have hopes of growth until we get this resolved." He says membership peaked in the city at the end of February and is now falling. A revision to the car-rental-tax law—which led to higher prices for many Zipcar customers—went into effect in Allegheny County, Pa., which encompasses Pittsburgh, in January.

The new taxes on car sharing are enraging some customers. "We are kind of being punished for being more aware of our carbon foot print," says Jean-Michel Brejard, a 51-year-old retail manager in Seattle. "It's the

Please turn to page D4

Internet Projects: See text Web site (www.mhhe.com/slater10e) and The Business Math Internet Resource Guide.

chapter

20 LIFE, FIRE, AND AUTO INSURANCE

Cutting Back on Car Insurance

By Jonathan Welsh

More drivers are saving money by keeping and maintaining their cars instead of buying new ones. Now, the economic downturn has them looking to save more by tuning up their aging cars' insurance.

"It's a conversation we are having more and more," says Ron Brunell, an agent with B & B Coverage, an insurance broker in Valley Stream, N.Y. People are shopping around for price quotes and looking for other ways to save on car insurance, he says.

Insurers including **Travelers Cos.**, based in St. Paul, Minn., and **State Farm Insurance**, based in Bloomington, Ill., say they have recently noticed that customers are keeping cars longer. State Farm says more drivers are choosing higher deductibles as a way to cut their premium costs.

Modern cars have the potential to last longer than the autos of decades past, so keeping them for several years makes sense.

Additionally, drivers who finance a vehicle may not realize that once they finish paying for it, they can reduce the amount of collision and comprehensive coverage from the high levels that lenders typically require. Collision covers damage resulting from a road accident, and comprehensive covers theft and damage not caused by another car.

When an older car's value falls to just a few thousand dollars, the owner should consider dropping collision and comprehensive coverage altogether. After a point, it makes more sense for the owner to simply pay out of pocket for damages. By contrast, they should resist the temptation to reduce liability coverage—which covers damage to other people or property—to the minimum required level, says Robert Hartwig of the Insurance Information Institute in New York.

"Your 10-year-old car is no less likely to kill someone than a 2009 model," he says.

Another reason to carry plenty of liability insurance is to make sure you are covered after a collision with an uninsured motorist. About one in seven U.S. drivers was uninsured in 2007, according to an Insurance Research Council report. The group says it expects the figure to reach one in six in 2010.

Drivers can track their vehicle's value online at Web sites such as www.edmunds.com and www.nadaguides.com. Your insurer can tell you how much it will pay if the covered vehicle is "totaled" after an accident. Insurers advise drivers to speak regularly with their agents to make sure their coverage matches the car's value.

LEARNING UNIT OBJECTIVES

LU 20–1: Life Insurance

1. Explain the types of life insurance; calculate life insurance premiums *(pp. 470–472)*.
2. Explain and calculate cash value and other nonforfeiture options *(pp. 473–474)*.

LU 20–2: Fire Insurance

1. Explain and calculate premiums for fire insurance of buildings and their contents *(pp. 475–476)*.
2. Calculate refunds when the insured and the insurance company cancel fire insurance *(p. 476)*.
3. Explain and calculate insurance loss when coinsurance is not met *(p. 476)*.

LU 20–3: Auto Insurance

1. Explain and calculate the cost of auto insurance *(pp. 477–482)*.

VOCABULARY PREVIEW

Here are key terms in this chapter. After completing the chapter, if you know the term, place a checkmark in the parenthesis. If you don't know the term, look it up and put the page number where it can be found.

Beneficiary . ( ) Bodily injury . ( ) Cash value . ( ) Coinsurance . ( ) Collision . ( ) Comprehensive insurance . ( ) Compulsory insurance . ( ) Deductibles . ( ) Extended term insurance . ( ) Face amount . ( ) Fire insurance . ( ) Indemnity . ( ) Insured . ( ) Insurer . ( ) Level premium term . ( ) Liability insurance . ( ) No-fault insurance . ( ) Nonforfeiture values . ( ) Paid-up insurance . ( ) Policyholder . ( ) Premium . ( ) Property damage . ( ) Reduced paid-up insurance . ( ) Short-rate table . ( ) Statisticians . ( ) Straight life insurance . ( ) Term insurance . ( ) 20-payment life . ( ) 20-year endowment . ( ) Universal life . ( ) Whole life . ( )

Kid-Friendly Auto Insurance

A sampling of youth-driver programs some insurers are offering.

Insurer	Comment
Safeco Corp.	Up to a 15% discount for **"Teensurance"** program participants who pay $14.99 per month for a Safety Beacon GPS tracking service, roadside assistance, Web tutorial and tools. Available in 44 states.
Nationwide Mutual Insurance Co.	**"SmartRide"** program in Ohio, West Virginia, Maryland, Virginia, Delaware and Washington, D.C., available by March 31 for drivers ages 16 to 24, offers a discount of up to 5% for customers who complete an online safety tutorial and receive a certificate.
American Family Mutual Insurance Co.	**"Teen Safe Driver Program"** supplies an in-vehicle video and audio surveillance camera for no fee. Available in 18 mostly Midwestern and Western states. In February, the company added 10% discount on liability insurance and some other coverages for customers in Colorado and Minnesota.
Fireman's Fund Insurance Co.	In its **"Youthful Driver"** program, independent young adult drivers up to age 27 can qualify for their parents' multiline, multicar and long-time customer discounts, reducing premiums from 35% to 50%. Available in most states by the end of the year.
State Farm Mutual Automobile Insurance Co.	Up to a 15% discount in most states for drivers under 25 who complete the **"Steer Clear"** driver safety program, which requires completing a driver's log.

Sources: the companies

How can young drivers save money on their auto insurance? The accompanying *Wall Street Journal* clip, "Kid-Friendly Auto Insurance," gives a sampling of discounts for young drivers from insurance companies. Check it out.

Regardless of the type of insurance you buy—Auto, nursing home, property, life, or fire—be sure to read and understand the policy before you buy the insurance. It has been reported that half of the people in the United States who have property insurance have not read their policy and 60% do not understand their policy. If you do not understand your life, fire, or auto insurance policies, this chapter should answer many of your questions. We begin by studying life insurance.

Learning Unit 20–1: Life Insurance

Bob Brady owns Bob's Deli. He is 40 years of age, married, and has three children. Bob wants to know what type of life insurance protection will best meet his needs. Following is a discussion between an insurance agent, Rick Jones, and Bob.

Bob: I would like to buy a life insurance policy that will pay my wife $200,000 in the event of my death. My problem is that I do not have much cash. You know, bills, bills, bills. Can you explain some types of life insurance and their costs?

Rick: Let's begin by explaining some life insurance terminology. The **insured** is you—the **policyholder** receiving coverage. The **insurer** is the company selling the insurance policy. Your wife is the **beneficiary.** As the beneficiary, she is the person named in the policy to receive the insurance proceeds at the death of the insured (that's you, Bob). The amount stated in the policy, say, $200,000, is the **face amount** of the policy. The **premium** (determined by **statisticians** called *actuaries*) is the periodic payments you agree to make for the cost of the insurance policy. You can pay premiums annually, semiannually, quarterly, or monthly. The more frequent the payment, the higher the total cost due to increased paperwork, billing, and so on. Now we look at the different types of insurance.

Types of Insurance

In this section Rick explains term insurance, straight life (ordinary life), 20-payment life, 20-year endowment, and universal life insurance.

LO 1

Term Insurance

Rick: The cheapest type of life insurance is **term insurance,** but it only provides *temporary* protection. Term insurance pays the face amount to your wife (beneficiary) only if you die within the period of the insurance (1, 5, 10 years, and so on).

For example, let's say you take out a 5-year term policy. The insurance company automatically allows you to renew the policy at increased rates until age 70. A new policy called **level premium term** may be less expensive than an annual term policy since each year for, say, 50 years, the premium will be fixed.

The policy of my company lets you convert to other insurance types without a medical examination. To determine your rates under 5-year term insurance, check this table (Table 20.1, p. 471). The annual premium at 40 years per $1,000 of insurance is $3.52. We use the following steps to calculate the total yearly premium.

CALCULATING ANNUAL LIFE INSURANCE PREMIUMS

Step 1. Look up the age of the insured and the type of insurance in Table 20.1 (for females, subtract 3 years). This gives the premium cost per $1,000.

Step 2. Divide the amount of coverage by $1,000 and multiply the answer by the premium cost per $1,000.

$$\frac{\$200{,}000\text{ (coverage)}}{\$1{,}000} = 200 \times \$3.52 = \$704$$

Number of thousands (200); Cost per $1,000 for age 40 ($3.52); Annual premium ($704)

Airport flight insurance is a type of term insurance.

From this formula you can see that for $704 per year for the next 5 years, we, your insurance company, offer to pay your wife $200,000 in the event of your death. At the end of the 5th year, you are not entitled to any cash from your paid premiums. If you do not renew your policy (at a higher rate) and die in the 6th year, we will not pay your wife anything. Term insurance provides protection for only a specific period of time.

Bob: Are you telling me that my premium does not build up any cash savings that you call **cash value**?

Rick: The term insurance policy does not build up cash savings. Let me show you a policy that does build up cash value. This policy is straight life.

TABLE 20.1

Life insurance rates for males (for females, subtract 3 years from the age)*

Age	Five-year term	Age	Straight life	Age	Twenty-payment life	Age	Twenty-year endowment
20	1.85	20	5.90	20	8.28	20	13.85
21	1.85	21	6.13	21	8.61	21	14.35
22	1.85	22	6.35	22	8.91	22	14.92
23	1.85	23	6.60	23	9.23	23	15.54
24	1.85	24	6.85	24	9.56	24	16.05
25	1.85	25	7.13	25	9.91	25	17.55
26	1.85	26	7.43	26	10.29	26	17.66
27	1.86	27	7.75	27	10.70	27	18.33
28	1.86	28	8.08	28	11.12	28	19.12
29	1.87	29	8.46	29	11.58	29	20.00
30	1.87	30	8.85	30	12.05	30	20.90
31	1.87	31	9.27	31	12.57	31	21.88
32	1.88	32	9.71	32	13.10	32	22.89
33	1.95	33	10.20	33	13.67	33	23.98
34	2.08	34	10.71	34	14.28	34	25.13
35	2.23	35	11.26	35	14.92	35	26.35
36	2.44	36	11.84	36	15.60	36	27.64
37	2.67	37	12.46	37	16.30	37	28.97
38	2.95	38	13.12	38	17.04	38	30.38
39	3.24	39	13.81	39	17.81	39	31.84
40	3.52	40	14.54	40	18.61	40	33.36
41	3.79	41	15.30	41	19.44	41	34.94
42	4.04	42	16.11	42	20.31	42	36.59
43	4.26	43	16.96	43	21.21	43	38.29
44	4.50	44	17.86	44	22.15	44	40.09

*Note that these tables are a sampling of age groups, premium costs, and insurance coverage that are available under 45 years of age.

Straight Life (Ordinary Life)

Rick: Straight life insurance provides *permanent* protection rather than the temporary protection provided by term insurance. The insured pays the same premium each year or until death.[1] The premium for straight life is higher than that for term insurance because straight life provides both protection and a built-in cash savings feature. According to our table (Table 20.1), your annual premium, Bob, would be:

Face value is usually the amount paid to the beneficiary at the time of insured's death.

$$\frac{\$200{,}000}{\$1{,}000} = 200 \times \$14.54 = \boxed{\$2{,}908} \text{ annual premium}$$

Bob: Compared to term, straight life is quite expensive.

Rick: Remember that term insurance has no cash value accumulating, as straight life does. Let me show you another type of insurance—20-payment life—that builds up cash value.

Twenty-Payment Life

Rick: A **20-payment life** policy is similar to straight life in that 20-payment life provides permanent protection and cash value, but you (the insured) pay premiums for only the first 20 years. After 20 years you own **paid-up insurance.** According to my table (Table 20.1), your annual premium would be:

$$\frac{\$200{,}000}{\$1{,}000} = 200 \times \$18.61 = \boxed{\$3{,}722} \text{ annual premium}$$

[1] In the following section on nonforfeiture values, we show how a policyholder in later years can stop making payments and still be covered by using the accumulated cash value built up.

Bob: The 20-payment life policy is more expensive than straight life.

Rick: This is because you are only paying for 20 years. The shorter period of time does result in increased yearly costs. Remember that in straight life you pay premiums over your entire life. Let me show you another alternative that we call 20-year endowment.

Twenty-Year Endowment

Rick: The **20-year endowment** insurance policy is the most expensive. It is a combination of term insurance and cash value. For example, from age 40 to 60, you receive term insurance protection in that your wife would receive $200,000 should you die. At age 60, your protection *ends* and you receive the face value of the policy that equals the $200,000 cash value. Let's use my table again (Table 20.1) to see how expensive the 20-year endowment is:

$$\frac{\$200{,}000}{\$1{,}000} = 200 \times \$33.36 = \$6{,}672 \text{ annual premium}$$

In summary, Bob, following is a review of the costs for the various types of insurance we have talked about:

	5-year term	Straight life	20-payment life	20-year endowment
Premium cost per year	$704	$2,908	$3,722	$6,672

Before we proceed, I have another policy that may interest you—universal life.

LO 2

Universal Life Insurance

Rick: **Universal life** is basically a **whole-life** insurance plan with flexible premium schedules and death benefits. Under whole life, the premiums and death benefits are fixed. Universal has limited guarantees with greater risk on the holder of the policy. For example, if interest rates fall, the policyholder must pay higher premiums, increase the number of payments, or switch to smaller death benefits in the future.

Bob: That policy is not for me—too much risk. I'd prefer fixed premiums and death benefits.

Rick: OK, let's look at how straight life, 20-payment life, and 20-year endowment can build up cash value and provide an opportunity for insurance coverage without requiring additional premiums. We call these options **nonforfeiture values.**

Nonforfeiture Values

Rick: Except for term insurance, the other types of life insurance build up cash value as you pay premiums. These policies provide three options should you, the policyholder, ever want to cancel your policy, stop paying premiums, or collect the cash value. My company lists these options here (Figure 20.1).

FIGURE 20.1

Nonforfeiture options

Option 1: Cash value (cash surrender value)
a. Receive cash value of policy.
b. Policy is terminated.
The longer the policy has been in effect, the higher the cash value because more premiums have been paid in.
Option 2: Reduced paid-up insurance
a. Cash value buys protection without paying new premiums.
b. Face amount of policy is related to cash value buildup and age of insured. The **face amount is less than original policy.**
c. Policy continues for life (at a reduced face amount).
Option 3: Extended term insurance
a. Original face amount of policy continues for a certain period of time.
b. Length of policy depends on cash value built up and on insured's age.
c. This option results automatically if policyholder doesn't pay premiums and fails to elect another option.

TABLE 20.2 Nonforfeiture options based on $1,000 face value

	STRAIGHT LIFE				20-PAYMENT LIFE				20-YEAR ENDOWMENT			
			EXTENDED TERM				EXTENDED TERM				EXTENDED TERM	
Years insurance policy in force	Cash value	Amount of paid-up insurance	Years	Day	Cash value	Amount of paid-up insurance	Years	Day	Cash value	Amount of paid-up insurance	Years	Day
5	29	86	9	91	71	220	19	190	92	229	23	140
10	96	259	18	76	186	521	28	195	319	520	30	160
15	148	371	20	165	317	781	32	176	610	790	35	300
20	265	550	21	300	475	1,000		Life	1,000	1,000		Life

Option 1: Cash value
$\frac{\$200{,}000}{\$1{,}000} = 200 \times \$148 = \$29{,}600$

Option 2: Reduced paid-up insurance
$\frac{\$200{,}000}{\$1{,}000} = 200 \times \$371 = \$74{,}200$

Option 3: Extended term insurance
Bob could continue this $200,000 policy for 20 years and 165 days.

$ MONEY TIPS

Burial insurance is important for everyone to have. Having this insurance reduces the stress on loved ones who are already in a difficult emotional time due to the loss. In addition, providing burial instructions reduces the likelihood that loved ones will be talked into spending more than the deceased desired on their burial.

Alternate:
Increase your deductibles on your policies to save money on the cost of your premiums. Keep the deductible amounts in an interest earning account for easy access if and when they are needed.

For example, Bob, let's assume that at age 40 we sell you a $200,000 straight-life policy. Assume that at age 55, after the policy has been in force for 15 years, you want to stop paying premiums. From this table (Table 20.2), I can show you the options that are available.

Insight into Health and Business Insurance Often people who interview for a new job are more concerned with the salary offered than the whole health care package such as eye care, dental care, hospital and doctor care, and so on. Be sure you know exactly what the new job offers in health insurance. For employees, company health insurance and life insurance benefits can be an important job consideration.

Some of the key types of business insurance that you may need as a business owner include fire insurance, business interruption insurance (business loss until physical damages are fixed), casualty insurance (insurance against a customer's suing your business due to an accident on company property), workers' compensation (insurance against injuries or sickness from being on the job), and group insurance (life, health, and accident).

Although group health insurance costs have soared today, many companies still pay the major portion of the cost. Some companies also provide health insurance benefits for retirees. As health costs continue to rise, we can expect to see some changes in this employee benefit.

Companies vary in the type of life insurance benefits they provide to their employees. This insurance can be a percent of the employee's salary with the employee naming the beneficiary; or in the case of key employees, the company can be the beneficiary.

If as an employer you need any of the types of insurance mentioned in this section, be sure to shop around for the best price. If you are in the job market, consider the benefits offered by a company as part of your salary and make your decisions accordingly.

In the next unit, we look specifically at fire insurance. Now let's check your understanding of this unit with a Practice Quiz.

LU 20–1 PRACTICE QUIZ

Complete this **Practice Quiz** to see how you are doing.

1. Bill Boot, age 39, purchased a $60,000, 5-year term life insurance policy. Calculate his annual premium from Table 20.1. After 4 years, what is his cash value?
2. Ginny Katz, age 32, purchased a $78,000, straight life policy. Calculate her annual premium. If after 10 years she wants to surrender her policy, what options and what amounts are available to her?

Solutions with Step-by-Step Help on DVD

✓ Solutions

1. $\frac{\$60{,}000}{\$1{,}000} = 60 \times \$3.24 = \$194.40$ No cash value in term insurance.
2. $\frac{\$78{,}000}{\$1{,}000} = 78 \times \$8.46^* = \$659.88$

Option 1: Cash value 78 × $96 = $7,488

Option 2: Paid up 78 × $259 = $20,202

Option 3: Extended term 18 years 76 days

*For females we subtract 3 years.

LU 20–1a EXTRA PRACTICE QUIZ WITH WORKED-OUT SOLUTIONS

Need more practice? Try this **Extra Practice Quiz** (check figures in Chapter Organizer, p. 484). Worked-out Solutions can be found in Appendix B at end of text.

1. Bill Boot, age 37, purchased a $70,000, 5-year term life insurance policy. Calculate his annual premium from Table 20.1. After 3 years, what is his cash value?
2. Ginny Katz, age 30, purchased a $95,000, straight-life policy. Calculate her annual premium. If after 5 years she wants to surrender her policy, what options and what amounts are available to her?

Learning Unit 20–2: Fire Insurance

LO 1

Periodically, some areas of the United States, especially California, have experienced drought followed by devastating fires. These fires spread quickly and destroy wooded areas and homes. When the fires occur, the first thought of the owners is the adequacy of their **fire insurance.** Homeowners are made more aware of the importance of fire insurance that provides for the replacement value of their home. Out-of-date fire insurance policies can result in great financial loss.

This unit looks at Alice Swan and the discussion with her insurance agent about her fire insurance needs for her new dress shop at 4 Park Plaza. (Alice owns the building.)

Alice: What is *extended coverage?*

Bob: Your basic fire insurance policy provides financial protection if fire or lightning damages your property. However, the extended coverage protects you from smoke, chemicals, water, or other damages that firefighters may cause to control the fire. We have many options available.

© J. D. Griggs/U.S. Geological Survey

Alice: What is the cost of a fire insurance policy?

Bob: Years ago, if you bought a policy for 2, 3, 5, or more years, reduced rates were available. Today, with rising costs of reimbursing losses from fires, most insurance companies write policies for 1 to 3 years. The cost of a 3-year policy premium is 3 times the annual premium. Because of rising insurance premiums, your total costs are cheaper if you buy one 3-year policy than three 1-year policies.

Alice: For my purpose, I will need coverage for 1 year. Before you give me the premium rates, what factors affect the cost of my premium?

Bob: In your case, you have several factors in your favor that will result in a lower premium. For example, (1) your building is brick, (2) the roof is fire-resistant, (3) the building is located next to a fire hydrant, (4) the building is in a good location (not next to a gas station) with easy access for the fire department, and (5) the goods within your store are not as flammable as, say, those of a paint store. I have a table here (Table 20.3) that gives an example of typical fire insurance rates for buildings and contents (furniture, fixtures, etc.).

TABLE 20.3

Fire insurance rates per $100 of coverage for buildings and contents

	CLASSIFICATION OF BUILDING			
	CLASS A		CLASS B	
Rating of area	Building	Contents	Building	Contents
1	.28	.35	.41	.54
2	.33	.47	.50	.60
3	.41	.50	.61	.65

Fire insurance premium equals premium for building and premium for contents.

Let's assume your building has an insured value of $190,000 and is rated Class B, Area No. 2, and we insure your contents for $80,000. Then we calculate your total annual premium for building and contents as follows:

$$\text{Premium} = \frac{\text{Insured value}}{\$100} \times \text{Rate}$$

Building

$$\frac{\$190{,}000}{\$100} = 1{,}900 \times \$.50 = \$950$$

Contents

$$\frac{\$80{,}000}{\$100} = 800 \times \$.60 = \$480$$

Total premium = $950 + $480 = $1,430

For our purpose, we round all premiums to the nearest cent. In practice, the premium is rounded to the nearest dollar.

LO 2

Canceling Fire Insurance

Alice: What if my business fails in 7 months? Do I get back any portion of my premium when I cancel?

Bob: If the insured—that's you, Alice—cancels or wants a policy for less than 1 year, we use this **short-rate table** (Table 20.4). The rates in the short-rate table will cost you more. For example, if you cancel at the end of 7 months, the premium cost is 67% of the annual premium. These rates are higher because it is more expensive to process a policy for a short time. We would calculate your refund as follows:

Short-rate premium = Annual premium × Short rate

$958.10 = $1,430 × .67

Refund = Annual premium − Short-rate premium

$471.90 = $1,430 − $958.10

Alice: Let's say that I don't pay my premium or follow the fire codes. What happens if your insurance company cancels me?

Bob: If the insurance company cancels you, the company is *not* allowed to use the short-rate table. To calculate what part of the premium the company may keep,[2] you can prorate

TABLE 20.4

Fire insurance short-rate and cancellation table

Time policy is in force		Percent of annual rate to be charged	Time policy is in force		Percent of annual rate to be charged
Days:	5	8%	Months:	5	52%
	10	10		6	61
	20	15		7	67
	25	17		8	74
Months:	1	19		9	81
	2	27		10	87
	3	35		11	96
	4	44		12	100%

[2]Many companies use $\frac{\text{Days}}{365}$

the premium based on the actual days that have elapsed. We can illustrate the amount of your refund by assuming you are canceled after 7 months:

Note that when the insurance company cancels the policy, the refund ($595.83) is greater than if the insured cancels ($471.90).

For insurance company: Charge $= \$1{,}430 \text{ annual premium} \times \frac{7 \text{ months elapsed}}{12}$

Charge = $834.17

For insured: Refund = $1,430 annual premium − $834.17 charge

Refund = $595.83

LO 3

Coinsurance

Alice: My friend tells me that I should meet the coinsurance clause. What is coinsurance?

Bob: Usually, fire does not destroy the entire property. **Coinsurance** means that you and the insurance company *share* the risk. The reason for this coinsurance clause[3] is to encourage property owners to purchase adequate coverage.

Alice: What is adequate coverage?

Bob: In the fire insurance industry, the usual rate for coinsurance is 80% of the current replacement cost. This cost equals the value to replace what was destroyed. If your insurance coverage is 80% of the current value, the insurance company will pay all damages up to the face value of the policy.

Alice: Hold it Bob! Will you please show me how this coinsurance is figured?

Bob: Yes, Alice, I'll be happy to show you how we figure coinsurance. Let's begin by looking at the following steps so you can see what amount of the insurance the company will pay.

$ MONEY TIPS

Keep a memory card with photos of both the inside and outside of all structures and property you own in a safety deposit box. Photographing serial numbers is a wise idea as well. This will help with the claim process in the event of a loss.

CALCULATING WHAT INSURANCE COMPANY PAYS WITH COINSURANCE CLAUSE

Step 1. Set up a fraction. The numerator is the actual amount of the insurance carried on the property. The denominator is the amount of insurance you should be carrying on the property to meet coinsurance (80% times the replacement value).

Step 2. Multiply the fraction by the amount of loss (up to the face value of the policy).

Let's assume for this example that you carry $60,000 fire insurance on property that will cost $100,000 to replace. If the coinsurance clause in your policy is 80% and you suffer a loss of $20,000, your insurance company will pay the following:

Although there are many types of property and homeowner's insurance policies, they usually include fire protection.

Insurance coverage → numerator; What you should have carried ($100,000 × .80) → denominator; Loss → $20,000

Step 1 → $\frac{\$60{,}000}{\$80{,}000} \times \$20{,}000 = \$15{,}000$[4] ← **Step 2**

If you had had actual insurance coverage of $80,000, then the insurance company would have paid $20,000. Remember that if the coinsurance clause is met, the most an insurance company will pay is the face value of the policy.

You are now ready for the following Practice Quiz.

LU 20–2 PRACTICE QUIZ

Complete this **Practice Quiz** to see how you are doing.

1. Calculate the total annual premium of a warehouse that has an area rating of 2 with a building classification of B. The value of the warehouse is $90,000 with contents valued at $30,000.
2. If insured cancels in problem 1 at the end of month 9, what are the cost of the premium and the refund?

[3] In some states (including Wisconsin), the clause is not in effect for losses under $1,000.

[4] This kind of limited insurance payment for a loss is often called an **indemnity.**

3. Jones insures a building for \$120,000 with an 80% coinsurance clause. The replacement value is \$200,000. Assume a loss of \$60,000 from fire. What will the insurance company pay? If the loss was \$160,000 and coinsurance *was* met, what will the insurance company pay?

Solutions with Step-by-Step Help on DVD

✓ **Solutions**

1. $\frac{\$90{,}000}{\$100} = 900 \times \$.50 = \$450$

   $\frac{\$30{,}000}{\$100} = 300 \times \$.60 = \underline{\ \ 180}$

   \$630 ← total premium

2. $\$630 \times .81 = \$510.30$ $\$630 - \$510.30 = \$119.70$

3. $\frac{\$120{,}000}{\$160{,}000} = \frac{3}{4} \times \$60{,}000 = \$45{,}000$

   ↑

   (.80 × \$200,000) \$160,000 never more than face value

LU 20–2a EXTRA PRACTICE QUIZ WITH WORKED-OUT SOLUTIONS

Need more practice? Try this **Extra Practice Quiz** (check figures in Chapter Organizer, p. 484). Worked-out Solutions can be found in Appendix B at end of text.

1. Calculate the total annual fire insurance premium of a warehouse that has an area rating of 3 with a building classification of A. The value of the warehouse is \$80,000 with contents valued at \$20,000.
2. If the insured from problem 1 cancels at the end of month 8, what are the costs of the premium and the refund?
3. Jones insures a building for \$140,000 with an 80% coinsurance clause. The replacement value is \$250,000. Assume a loss of \$50,000 from fire. What will the insurance company pay? If the loss was \$170,000 and coinsurance was met, what will the insurance company pay?

Learning Unit 20–3: Auto Insurance

If you own an auto, you have had some experience purchasing auto insurance. Often first-time auto owners do not realize that auto insurance can be a substantial expense. The chapter opener talked about discounts for young drivers. The next *Wall Street Journal* clip, "Insurers Offer Low-Mileage Discounts," indicates that a change in driving habits could result in a lower auto premium for a driver.

Insurers Offer Low-Mileage Discounts

BY M.P. MCQUEEN

Car owners who are changing their driving habits because of soaring gas prices may be able to save a few dollars on auto insurance.

Major car insurers including **State Farm Mutual Insurance** Cos., **Travelers** Cos. and Farmers Insurance Group say that drivers who log less than about 7,500 miles a year may be eligible for "low mileage" programs that reduce premiums an average of about 10% to 12%. State Farm's program earns drivers discounts ranging from 12% to 18%, says spokesman Dick Luedke.

Car owners who drive more than that but less than they used to—perhaps because they have started using public transportation or walking to work—may also save on premiums, according to a mainly on their driving history and miles driven, so driving more or fewer miles significantly affects the premium drivers there pay. Consumers should inform their agents of any big changes in their driving habits, says Mr. Hunter. Hutchinson, usage-based insurance general manager.

Insurance rates often increase when a driver is involved in an accident. Some insurance companies give reduced rates to accident-free drivers—a practice that has encouraged drivers to be more safety conscious. For example, State Farm Insurance offers a discount to drivers who maintain a safety record. An important factor in safe driving is the use of a seat belt. Make it a habit to always put on your seat belt.

In this unit we follow Shirley as she learns about auto insurance. Shirley, who just bought a new auto, has never purchased auto insurance. So she called her insurance agent, Bob Long, who agreed to meet her for lunch. We will listen in on their conversation.

Shirley: Bob, where do I start?

Liability insurance includes
1. **Bodily injury**—injury or death to people in passenger car or other cars, etc.
2. **Property damage**—injury to other people's autos, trees, buildings, hydrants, etc.

Bob: Our state has two kinds of **liability insurance,** or **compulsory insurance,** that by law you must buy (regulations and requirements vary among states). Liability insurance covers any physical damages that you inflict on others or their property. You must buy liability insurance for the following:

1. **Bodily injury** to others: 10/20. This means that the insurance company will pay damages to people injured or killed by your auto up to $10,000 for injury to one person per accident or a total of $20,000 for injuries to two or more people per accident.
2. **Property damage** to someone else's property: 5. The insurance company will pay up to $5,000 for damages that you have caused to the property of others.

Now we leave Shirley and Bob for a few moments as we calculate Shirley's premium for compulsory insurance.

Calculating Premium for Compulsory Insurance[5]

Insurance companies base auto insurance rates on the territory you live in, the class of driver (class 10 is experienced driver with driver training), whether the auto is for business use, how much you drive the car, the age of the car, and the make of the car (symbol). Shirley lives in Territory 5 (suburbia). She is classified as 17 because she is an inexperienced operator licensed for less than 6 years. Her car is age 3 and symbol 4 (make of car). We use Table 20.5 to calculate Shirley's compulsory insurance. Note that the table rates in this unit are not representative of all areas of the country. In case of lawsuits, the minimum coverage may not be adequate. Some states add surcharges to the premium if the person has a poor driving record. The tables are designed to show how rates are calculated. From Table 20.5, we have the following:

The tables we use in this unit are for Territory 5. Other tables are available for different territories.

Bodily	$ 98
+ Property	160
	$258

Remember that the $258 premium represents minimum coverage. Assume Shirley hits two people and the courts award them $13,000 and $5,000, respectively. Shirley would be

TABLE 20.5

Compulsory insurance (based on class of driver)

BODILY INJURY TO OTHERS		DAMAGE TO SOMEONE ELSE'S PROPERTY	
Class	10/20	Class	5M*
10	$ 55	10	$129
17	98	17	160
18	80	18	160
20	116	20	186

Explanation of 10/20 and 5

10	20	5
Maximum paid to one person per accident for bodily injury	Maximum paid for total bodily injury per accident	Maximum paid for property damage per accident

*M means thousands.

[5]Some states may offer medical payment insurance (a supplement to policyholders' health and accident insurance) as well as personal injury protection against uninsured or underinsured motorists.

responsible for $3,000 because the insurance company would pay only up to $10,000 per person and a total of $20,000 per accident.

Although total damages of $18,000 are less than $20,000, the insurance company pays only $15,000.

	(1)		(2)	
	$13,000	+	$5,000 =	$18,000
Paid by insurance company ⟶	− 10,000	−	5,000 =	− 15,000
Paid by Shirley ⟶	$ 3,000	+	$ 0 =	$ 3,000

We return to Shirley and Bob. Bob now shows Shirley how to calculate her optional insurance coverage. Remember that optional insurance coverages (Tables 20.6 to 20.10) are added to the costs in Table 20.5 (p. 478).

Calculating Optional Insurance Coverage

Bob: In our state, you can add optional bodily injury to the compulsory amount. If you finance your car, the lender may require specific amounts of optional insurance to protect its investment. I have two tables (Tables 20.6 and 20.7) here that we use to calculate the option of 250/500/50. This means that in an accident the insurance company will pay $250,000 per person, up to $500,000 per accident, and up to $50,000 for property damage.

Bob then explains the tables to Shirley. By studying the tables, you can see how insurance companies figure bodily injury and damage to someone else's property. Shirley is Class 17:

Bodily

250/500 = $228

Property

50M = + 168

$396 premium for optional bodily injury and property damage

Note: These are additional amounts to compulsory.

Collision and comprehensive are optional insurance types that pay only the insured. Note that Tables 20.8 and 20.9 are based on territory, age, and car symbol. The higher the symbol, the more expensive the car.

Shirley: Is that all I need?

Bob: No, I would recommend two more types of optional coverage: **collision** and **comprehensive.** Collision provides protection against damages to your car caused by a moving vehicle. It covers the cost of repairs less **deductibles** (amount of repair you cover first before the insurance company pays the rest) and depreciation.[6] In collision, insurance companies pay the resale or book value. So as the car gets older, after 5 or more years, it might make sense to drop the collision. The decision depends on how much risk you are willing

TABLE 20.6

Bodily injury

Class	15/30	20/40	20/50	25/50	25/60	50/100	100/300	250/500	500/1,000
10	27	37	40	44	47	69	94	144	187
17	37	52	58	63	69	104	146	228	298
18	33	46	50	55	60	89	124	193	251
20	41	59	65	72	78	119	168	263	344

TABLE 20.7

Damage to someone else's property

Class	10M	25M	50M	100M
10	132	134	135	136
17	164	166	168	169
18	164	166	168	169
20	191	193	195	197

[6] In some states, repair to glass has no deductible and many insurance companies now use a $500 deductible instead of $300.

TABLE 20.8 Collision

Classes	Age group	Symbols 1–3 $300 ded.	Symbol 4 $300 ded.	Symbol 5 $300 ded.	Symbol 6 $300 ded.	Symbol 7 $300 ded.	Symbol 8 $300 ded.	Symbol 10 $300 ded.
10–20	1	180	180	187	194	214	264	279
	2	160	160	166	172	190	233	246
	3	148	148	154	166	183	221	233
	4	136	136	142	160	176	208	221
	5	124	124	130	154	169	196	208

These classes would use all this information.

To find the premium, use the age and symbol only.

Additional cost to reduce deductible

Class	From $300 to $200	From $300 to $100
10	13	27
17	20	43
18	16	33
20	26	55

TABLE 20.9 Comprehensive

Classes	Age group	Symbols 1–3 $300 ded.	Symbol 4 $300 ded.	Symbol 5 $300 ded.	Symbol 6 $300 ded.	Symbol 7 $300 ded.	Symbol 8 $300 ded.	Symbol 10 $300 ded.
10–25	1	61	61	65	85	123	157	211
	2	55	55	58	75	108	138	185
	3	52	52	55	73	104	131	178
	4	49	49	52	70	99	124	170
	5	47	47	49	67	94	116	163

Additional cost to reduce deductible: From $300 to $200 add $4

to assume. Comprehensive covers damages resulting from theft, fire, falling objects, and so on. Now let's calculate the cost of these two types of coverage—assuming a $100 deductible for collision and a $200 deductible for comprehensive—with some more of my tables (Tables 20.8 and 20.9).

	Class	Age	Symbol	Premium
Collision	17	3	4	$191 ($148 + $43)
Comprehensive	17	3	4	+ 56 ($52 + $4)
				$247

Cost to reduce deductibles

Total premium for collision and comprehensive

Shirley: Anything else?

Bob: I would also recommend that you buy towing and substitute transportation coverage. The insurance company will pay up to $25 for each tow. Under substitute transportation, the insurance company will pay you $12 a day for renting a car, up to $300 total. Again, from

TABLE 20.10

Transportation and towing

Substitute transportation	$16
Towing and labor	4

TABLE 20.11

Worksheet for calculating Shirley's auto premium

Compulsory insurance	Limits	Deductible	Premium
Bodily injury to others	$10,000 per person $20,000 per accident	None	$ 98 (Table 20.5)
Damage to someone else's property	$5,000 per accident	None	$160 (Table 20.5)
Options			
Optional bodily injury to others	$250,000 per person $500,000 per accident	None	$228 (Table 20.6)
Optional property damage	$50,000 per accident	None	$168 (Table 20.7)
Collision	Actual cash value	$100	$191 (Table 20.8) ($148 + $43)
Comprehensive	Actual cash value	$200	$ 56 (Table 20.9) ($52 + $4)
Substitute transportation	Up to $12 per day or $300 total	None	$ 16 (Table 20.10)
Towing and labor	$25 per tow	None	$ 4 (Table 20.10)
			$ 921 Total premium

$ MONEY TIPS

When making an auto insurance claim: 1. Never say you are sorry at the scene of a crime to an insurance agent or police officer; 2. State only what you know, not what you think. Your thoughts may not be accurate during a loss. Stick to the facts and say, "I'm not sure" for anything else; 3. Do not use the term whiplash. Instead wait until your doctor makes a diagnosis and share that with your insurance company.

another table (Table 20.10), we find the additional premium for towing and substitute transportation is $20 ($16 + $4).

We leave Shirley and Bob now as we make a summary of Shirley's total auto premium in Table 20.11.

Premiums for collision, property damage, and comprehensive are not reduced by no fault.

No-Fault Insurance Some states have **no-fault insurance,** a type of auto insurance that was intended to reduce premium costs on bodily injury. With no fault, one forfeits the right to sue for *small* claims involving medical expense, loss of wages, and so on. Each person collects the bodily injury from his or her insurance company no matter who is at fault. In reality, no-fault insurance has not reduced premium costs, due to large lawsuits, fraud, and operating costs of insurance companies. Many states that were once considering no fault are no longer pursuing its adoption. Note that states with no-fault insurance require the purchase of *personal-injury protection (PIP).* The most successful no-fault law seems to be in Michigan, since it has tough restrictions on the right to sue along with unlimited medical and rehabilitation benefits.

It's time to take your final Practice Quiz in this chapter.

LU 20–3 PRACTICE QUIZ

Complete this **Practice Quiz** to see how you are doing.

Calculate the annual auto premium for Mel Jones who lives in Territory 5, is a driver classified 18, and has a car with age 4 and symbol 7. His state has compulsory insurance, and Mel wants to add the following options:

1. Bodily injury, 100/300.
2. Damage to someone else's property, 10M.
3. Collision, $200 deductible.
4. Comprehensive, $200 deductible.
5. Towing.

(solutions on page 482)

Solutions with Step-by-Step Help on DVD

✓ Solutions

Compulsory			
Bodily	$ 80		(Table 20.5)
Property	160		(Table 20.5)
Options			
Bodily	124		(Table 20.6)
Property	164		(Table 20.7)
Collision	192	($176 + $16)	(Table 20.8)
Comprehensive	103	($99 + $4)	(Table 20.9)
Towing	4		(Table 20.10)
Total annual premium	$827		

LU 20–3a EXTRA PRACTICE QUIZ WITH WORKED-OUT SOLUTIONS

Need more practice? Try this **Extra Practice Quiz** (check figures in Chapter Organizer, p. 484). Worked-out Solutions can be found in Appendix B at end of text.

Calculate the annual auto premium for Mel Jones who lives in Territory 5, is a driver classified 17, and has a car with age 5 and symbol 6. His state has compulsory insurance, and Mel wants to add the following options:

1. Bodily injury, 100/300.
2. Damage to someone else's property, 10M.
3. Collision, $200 deductible.
4. Comprehensive, $200 deductible.
5. Towing.

CHAPTER ORGANIZER AND REFERENCE GUIDE

Topic	Key point, procedure, formula	Example(s) to illustrate situation
Life insurance, p. 470	Using Table 20.1, per $1,000: $\frac{\text{Coverage desired}}{\$1,000} \times \text{Rate}$ For females, subtract 3 years.	**Given** $80,000 of insurance desired; age 34; male. **1.** Five-year term: $\frac{\$80,000}{\$1,000} = 80 \times \$2.08 = \$166.40$ **2.** Straight life: $\frac{\$80,000}{\$1,000} = 80 \times \$10.71 = \$856.80$ **3.** Twenty-payment life: $\frac{\$80,000}{\$1,000} = 80 \times \$14.28 = \$1,142.40$ **4.** Twenty-year endowment: $\frac{\$80,000}{\$1,000} = 80 \times \$25.13 = \$2,010.40$
Nonforfeiture values, p. 472	**By Table 20.2** Option 1: Cash surrender value. Option 2: Reduced paid-up insurance policy continues for life at reduced face amount. Option 3: Extended term—original face policy continued for a certain period of time.	A $50,000 straight-life policy was issued to Jim Rose at age 28. At age 48 Jim wants to stop paying premiums. What are his nonforfeiture options? Option 1: $\frac{\$50,000}{\$1,000} = 50 \times \$265 = \$13,250$ Option 2: $50 \times \$550 = \$27,500$ Option 3: 21 years 300 days

(continues)

CHAPTER ORGANIZER AND REFERENCE GUIDE

Topic	Key point, procedure, formula	Example(s) to illustrate situation
Fire insurance, p. 475	Per $100 Premium $= \frac{\text{Insurance value}}{\$100} \times$ Rate Rate can be for buildings or contents.	**Given** Area 3; Class B; building insured for $90,000; contents, $30,000. Building: $\frac{\$90,000}{\$100} = 900 \times \$.61$ $= \$549$ Contents: $\frac{\$30,000}{\$100} = 300 \times \$.65$ $= \$195$ Total: $549 + $195 = **$744**
Canceling fire insurance—short-rate Table 20.4 (canceling by policyholder), p. 475	$\text{Short-rate premium} = \text{Annual premium} \times \text{Short rate}$ $\text{Refund} = \text{Annual premium} - \text{Short-rate premium}$ If insurance company cancels, do not use Table 20.4.	Annual premium is $400. Short rate is .35 (cancel end of 3 months). $400 × .35 = $140 Refund = $400 − $140 = **$260**
Canceling by insurance company, p. 475	Annual premium $\times \frac{\text{Months elapsed}}{12}$ (Refund is higher since company cancels.)	Using example above but if insurance company cancels at end of 3 months. $\$400 \times \frac{1}{4} = \$100$ Refund = $400 − $100 = **$300**
Coinsurance, p. 476	Amount insurance company pays: $\frac{\text{Insurance carried (Face value)}}{\text{Insurance required to meet coinsurance (Rate} \times \text{Replacement value)}} \times \text{Loss}$ (Numerator: Actual insurance → Insurance carried; Denominator: What coverage should have been → to meet coinsurance) Insurance company never pays more than the face value.	**Given** Face value, $30,000; replacement value, $50,000; coinsurance rate, 80%; loss, $10,000; insurance to meet required coinsurance, $40,000. $\frac{\$30,000}{\$40,000} \times \$10,000 = \$7,500$ paid by insurance company ($40,000 ← ($50,000 × .80))
Auto insurance, p. 477	**Compulsory** Required insurance. **Optional** Added to cost of compulsory. Bodily injury—pays for injury to person caused by insured. Property damage—pays for property damage (not for insured auto). Collision—pays for damages to insured auto. Comprehensive—pays for damage to insured auto for fire, theft, etc. Towing. Substitute transportation.	Calculate the annual premium. Driver class 10; compulsory 10/20/5. **Optional** Bodily—100/300 Property—10M Collision—age 3, symbol 10, $100 deductible Comprehensive—$300 deductible 10/20/5 $184 (\$55 + \$129) Table 20.5 Bodily 94 Table 20.6 Property 132 Table 20.7 Collision 260 (\$233 + \$27) Table 20.8 Comprehensive 178 Table 20.9 Total premium **$848**

(continues)

CHAPTER ORGANIZER AND REFERENCE GUIDE

Topic	Key point, procedure, formula		Example(s) to illustrate situation
KEY TERMS	Beneficiary, *p. 470* Bodily injury, *p. 478* Cash value, *pp. 470, 472* Coinsurance, *p. 476* Collision, *p. 479* Comprehensive insurance, *p. 479* Compulsory insurance, *p. 478* Deductibles, *p. 479* Extended term insurance, *p. 472* Face amount, *p. 470*	Fire insurance, *p. 474* Indemnity, *p. 476* Insured, *p. 470* Insurer, *p. 470* Level premium term, *p. 470* Liability insurance, *p. 478* No-fault insurance, *p. 481* Nonforfeiture values, *p. 472* Paid-up insurance, *p. 471* Policyholder, *p. 470* Premium, *p. 470*	Property damage, *p. 478* Reduced paid-up insurance, *p. 472* Short-rate table, *p. 475* Statisticians, *p. 470* Straight life insurance, *p. 471* Term insurance, *p. 470* 20-payment life, *p. 471* 20-year endowment, *p. 472* Universal life, *p. 472* Whole life, *p. 472*
CHECK FIGURES FOR EXTRA PRACTICE QUIZZES WITH PAGE REFERENCES. (WORKED-OUT SOLUTIONS IN APPENDIX B.)	LU 20–1a (p. 474) **1.** $186.90; no cash value **2.** $736.25 Opt. **1.** $2,755 **2.** $8,170 **3.** 9 years 91 days	LU 20–2a (p. 477) **1.** $428 **2.** $111.28; $316.72 **3.** $35,000 Never more than $170,000	LU 20–3a (p. 482) $817

Critical Thinking Discussion Questions

1. Compare and contrast term insurance versus whole-life insurance. At what age do you think people should take out life insurance?
2. What is meant by *nonforfeiture values?* If you take the cash value option, should it be paid in a lump sum or over a number of years?
3. How do you use a short-rate table? Explain why an insurance company gets less in premiums if it cancels a policy than if the insured cancels.
4. What is coinsurance? Do you feel that an insurance company should pay more than the face value of a policy in the event of a catastrophe?
5. Explain compulsory auto insurance, collision, and comprehensive. If your car is stolen, explain the steps you might take with your insurance company.
6. "Health insurance is not that important. It would not be worth the premiums." Please take a stand.

END-OF-CHAPTER PROBLEMS

Check figures for odd-numbered problems in Appendix C.

Name ______________________ Date __________

DRILL PROBLEMS

Calculate the annual premium for the following policies using Table 20.1 (for females subtract 3 years from the table).

	Amount of coverage (face value of policy)	Age and sex of insured	Type of insurance policy	Annual premium
20–1.	$70,000	35 F	Straight life	
20–2.	$120,000	42 M	20-payment life	
20–3.	$150,000	29 F	5-year term	
20–4.	$50,000	27 F	20-year endowment	

Calculate the following nonforfeiture options for Lee Chin, age 42, who purchased a $200,000 straight-life policy. At the end of year 20, Lee stopped paying premiums.

20–5. Option 1: Cash surrender value

20–6. Option 2: Reduced paid-up insurance

20–7. Option 3: Extended term insurance

Calculate the total cost of a fire insurance premium for a building and contents given the following (round to nearest cent):

	Rating of area	Class	Building	Contents	Total premium cost
20–8.	3	B	$90,000	$40,000	

Calculate the short-rate premium and refund of the following:

	Annual premium	Canceled after	Short-rate premium	Refund
20–9.	$700	8 months by insured		
20–10.	$360	4 months by insurance company		

Complete the following:

	Replacement value of property	Amount of insurance	Kind of policy	Actual fire loss	Amount insurance company will pay
20–11.	$100,000	$60,000	80% coinsurance	$22,000	
20–12.	$60,000	$40,000	80% coinsurance	$42,000	

Calculate the annual auto insurance premium for the following:

20–13. Britney Sper, Territory 5
Class 17 operator
Compulsory, 10/20/5 ______

Optional

a. Bodily injury, 500/1,000 ______

b. Property damage, 25M ______

c. Collision, $100 deductible ______
Age of car is 2; symbol of car is 7

d. Comprehensive, $200 deductible ______

Total annual premium ______

WORD PROBLEMS

20–14. "Texans still pay the highest insurance rates for homeowners' policies," quotes *The Dallas Morning News* on March 3, 2009. "The average annual premium in Texas for the most common homeowner policy was $1,409 a year, considerably more than the nationwide average of $804. Florida was second at $1,386—after a jump of 28 percent in one year—and Louisiana was third at $1,257." This is due mostly to mold claims and unpredictable weather including hurricanes, hailstorms, and tornadoes. Lisa and Marvin Davis pay $1,547 per year for their homeowner's insurance. They are selling their home and canceling their policy after 3 months. What is the amount of their refund?

20–15. Mike Reno, age 44, saw an Insurance Solutions Direct advertisement stating that its $500,000 term policy costs $395 per year. Compare this to Table 20.1 in the text. How much would he save by going with Insurance Solutions Direct?

20–16. Margie Rale, age 38, a well-known actress, decided to take out a limited-payment life policy. She chose this since she

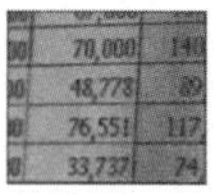

expects her income to decline in future years. Margie decided to take out a 20-year payment life policy with a coverage amount of $90,000. Could you advise Margie about what her annual premium will be? If she decides to stop paying premiums after 15 years, what will be her cash value?

20–17. Janette Raffa has two young children and wants to take out an additional $300,000 of 5-year term insurance. Janette is 40 years old. What will be her additional annual premium? In 3 years, what cash value will have been built up?

20–18. Roger's office building has a $320,000 value, a 2 rating, and a B building classification. The contents in the building are valued at $105,000. Could you help Roger calculate his total annual premium?

20–19. Abby Ellen's toy store is worth $400,000 and is insured for $200,000. Assume an 80% coinsurance clause and that a fire caused $190,000 damage. What is the liability of the insurance company?

20–20. The May 13, 2009, *Times-Picayune* in New Orleans, LA, reported "homeowners holding policies with the state-run insurer of last resort would see their premiums increased less or possibly decreased under" a unanimously approved bill. *Fortune* magazine noted State Farm, which has 32% of the homeowner's market in the state, says the average premium on a $100,000 wood construction New Orleans home has risen 30% since Hurricane Katrina to $2,162 a year. If Bill Hopkins owns a $325,000 building with contents valued at $110,000 in New Orleans rated as Class A for building and Class B for contents Area No. 2, what is his premium after a 30% rate hike? (Round to nearest cent.)

20–21. As given via the Internet, auto insurance quotes gathered online could vary from $947 to $1,558. A class 18 operator carries compulsory 10/20/5 insurance. He has the following optional coverage: bodily injury, 500/1,000; property damage, 50M; and collision, $200 deductible. His car is 1 year old, and the symbol of the car is 8. He has comprehensive insurance with a $200 deductible. Using your text, what is the total annual premium?

20–22. Dan Miller insured his pizza shop for $100,000 for fire insurance at an annual rate per $100 of $.66. At the end of 11 months, Earl canceled the policy since his pizza shop went out of business. What was the cost of Earl's premium and his refund?

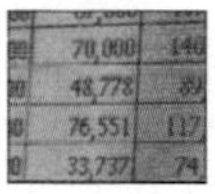

20–23. Warren Ford insured his real estate office with a fire insurance policy for $95,000 at a cost of $.59 per $100. Eight months later the insurance company canceled his policy because of a failure to correct a fire hazard. What did Warren have to pay for the 8 months of coverage? Round to the nearest cent.

20–24. Drivers in Gilroy, California, saw an 11% increase in automobile insurance, whereas San Jose drivers saw a 6% decrease. Marvin Braun lives in Gilroy and is comparing the cost of collision insurance. He is also thinking about relocating to San Jose. Based on Class 18, age 4, symbol 5, **(a)** what is his present premium for collision? **(b)** What will his premium be if he stays in Gilroy? **(c)** What will his premium be if he moves to San Jose?

20–25. Tina Grey bought a new Honda Civic and insured it with only 10/20/5 compulsory insurance. Driving up to her ski chalet one snowy evening, Tina hit a parked van and injured the couple inside. Tina's car had damage of $4,200, and the van she struck had damage of $5,500. After a lengthy court suit, the injured persons were awarded personal injury judgments of $16,000 and $7,900, respectively. What will the insurance company pay for this accident, and what is Tina's responsibility?

20–26. Rusty Reft, who lives in Territory 5, carries 10/20/5 compulsory liability insurance along with optional collision that has a $300 deductible. Rusty was at fault in an accident that caused $3,600 damage to the other auto and $900 damage to his own. Also, the courts awarded $15,000 and $7,000, respectively, to the two passengers in the other car for personal injuries. How much will the insurance company pay, and what is Rusty's share of the responsibility?

20–27. Marika Katz bought a new Blazer and insured it with only compulsory insurance 10/20/5. Driving up to her summer home one evening, Marika hit a parked car and injured the couple inside. Marika's car had damage of $7,500, and the car she struck had damage of $5,800. After a lengthy court suit, the couple struck were awarded personal injury judgments of $18,000 and $9,000, respectively. What will the insurance company pay for this accident, and what is Marika's responsibility?

CHALLENGE PROBLEMS

20–28. Money.cnn.com states, "The single most important reason to own life insurance is to provide support for your dependents." Insurance4usa.com states, "Professionals suggest you have 8 to 12 times your income in life insurance." Pat and Bonnie Marsh are calculating how much life insurance they need. They have two young children with no college fund set up. Bonnie is a 35-year-old stay-at-home mom. Pat, 39, earns $68,000 per year. How much life insurance do you recommend each person have? (Note that a spouse who stays at home to raise the family generates the equivalent of a salary that needs to be taken into account. Assume Bonnie's salary is $25,000.) What will be the cost of straight-life insurance for both policies if the lowest recommended amount is used? What is the monthly premium owed?

20–29. Bill, who understands the types of insurance that are available, is planning his life insurance needs. At this stage of his life (age 35), he has budgeted $200 a year for life insurance premiums. Could you calculate for Bill the amount of coverage that is available under straight life and for a 5-year term? Could you also show Bill that if he were to die at age 40, how much more his beneficiary would receive if he'd been covered under the 5-year term? Round to the nearest thousand.

DVD SUMMARY PRACTICE TEST

1. Howard Slater, age 44, an actor, expects his income to decline in future years. He decided to take out a 20-year payment life policy with a $90,000 coverage. What will be Howard's annual premium? If he decides to stop paying premiums after 15 years, what will be his cash value? *(p. 472)*

2. J.C. Monahan, age 40, bought a straight-life insurance policy for $210,000. Calculate her annual premium. If after 20 years J.C. no longer pays her premiums, what nonforfeiture options will be available to her? *(p. 472)*

3. The property of Pote's Garage is worth $900,000. Pote has a $375,000 fire insurance policy that contains an 80% coinsurance clause. What will the insurance company pay on a fire that causes $450,000 damage? If Pote meets the coinsurance, how much will the insurance company pay? *(p. 476)*

4. Lee Collins insured her pizza shop with an $90,000 fire insurance policy at a $1.10 annual rate per $100. At the end of 7 months, Lee's pizza shop went out of business so she canceled the policy. What is the cost of Lee's premium and her refund? *(p. 475)*

5. Charles Prose insured his real estate office with a $300,000 fire insurance policy at $.78 annual rate per $100. Nine months later the insurance company canceled his policy because Charles failed to correct a fire hazard. What was Charles's cost for the 9-month coverage? Round to the nearest cent. *(p. 476)*

6. Roger Laut, who lives in Territory 5, carries 10/20/5 compulsory liability insurance along with optional collision that has a $1,000 deductible. Roger was at fault in an accident that caused $4,800 damage to the other car and $8,800 damage to his own car. Also, the courts awarded $19,000 and $9,000, respectively, to the two passengers in the other car for personal injuries. How much does the insurance company pay, and what is Roger's share of the responsibility? *(pp. 477–482)*

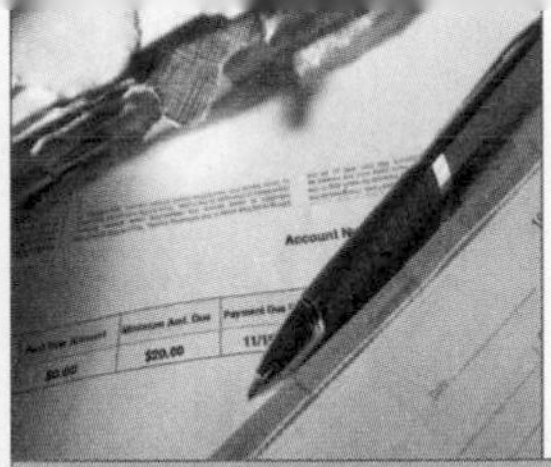

Personal Finance

A KIPLINGER APPROACH

LOWDOWN

What You Need to Know About Leasing a Car Now

Automakers flooded with off-lease gas guzzlers shut off the tap. BY MARK SOLHEIM

1. THE COST OF LEASING IS GOING UP. Leasing is a pretty good deal. After all, you get to drive a new vehicle every two to three years with little or no down payment and pay only for the time you "rent" it. And until recently, carmakers were subsidizing leases using low interest rates or high residuals—the anticipated cost of the vehicle at the end of the lease—to prop up sales. Now, residuals are lower and payments are higher. That's especially true of the Detroit Big Three, but foreign automakers are sharing the pain. BMW, which led the industry in leases, is cutting back and raising vehicle prices. Toyota, too, is smarting from big lease-related losses.

2. AND THE DEALS ARE GETTING SCARCE. Chrysler's financing arm is no longer writing leases, and GM and Ford have put the brakes on SUV and pickup-truck leases. The reason? Buyers are shunning SUVs and trucks because of high gas prices. That's driven down prices, so gas guzzlers coming off lease are worth a lot less than the leasing companies thought they'd be when they wrote the leases two or three years ago. If you *do* have to turn to a bank instead of a carmaker's financing arm, you'll forgo the incentives and will likely need stellar credit to qualify.

3. BUYING COULD BE A BETTER DEAL. Carmakers are redirecting incentives from leases to low-rate financing and rebates (note Chrysler's recent $2,500 rebate or 0% financing for 36 months on its Town & Country minivan and Pacifica SUV). BMW was recently offering 0.9% 60-month loans on most models. Plus, carmakers are offering incentives on used models—so-called certified preowned cars, which are inspected by factory technicians and sold with an extended warranty.

4. BREAKING UP IS HARD TO DO. If you love the vehicle you're leasing and want to buy it, you may be able to negotiate a lower price than the one written into the lease—especially if the dealer can make more money from you than it could at auction. Or ask for, say, a six-month extension at the same payment, says Tarry Shebesta, president of LeaseCompare.com. By then, he says, the market may settle down and more sources of financing will have returned. Another option is to lease a used vehicle. For as little as $615 a month, you could lease a 2006 Lexus IS 250 worth $31,000 for three years—about the same payments as if you purchased the car with a 60-month, 7.3% loan, according to LeaseCompare.com. Caveat leaser: Don't jump at an offer to waive your last few payments in exchange for leasing another vehicle longer term. It may make more sense to buy your next vehicle and take the cash rebate or low-rate financing.

5. DON'T SWEAT THE SMALL STUFF. If you're turning in a leased car, remember that only three things really matter: dents, tears in the upholstery, and mismatched or bald tires. If the leasing company doesn't offer a pre-lease-end inspection, ask for one. Then you can fix the problems yourself rather than risk a pricier penalty.

6. AND HEAVE A SIGH OF RELIEF. If the vehicle you turn back in is a big ol' SUV or pickup, you don't have to worry about its low resale value. The leasing company, not you, shoulders the risk of a price miscall—one reason leasing can still be a good strategy. ■

Taken from *Kiplinger's Personal Finance*, October 2009, p. 90.

BUSINESS MATH ISSUE

Leasing always is better than buying.

1. List the key points of the article and information to support your position.
2. Write a group defense of your position using math calculations to support your view.

Slater's Business Math Scrapbook

Applying Your Skills

PROJECT A

Based on your age, income, and marital status what is your reaction to the article on whole life.

Fusty Insurance Lures Buyers Seeking Safety

Whole-Life Policies Offer Steady Ride, but Figuring Actual Returns Can Be Tricky

BY M.P. MCQUEEN

As the economy sinks, a growing number of Americans are turning to a stodgy financial product favored by their parents and grandparents: whole-life insurance.

These policies' steady, tax-deferred returns, many now in the 4% to 5.5% range or more over 20 years, look enticing after the 40%-plus declines in the stock market over the past year and a half. Indeed, investor angst is helping insurance agents sell whole-life insurance.

Whole-life policies are "permanent" policies that include a guaranteed savings component, as well as a death benefit. They differ from less-expensive term-life insurance, which provides only a death benefit in return for premiums paid over a specific period and offers no cash buildup.

But potential buyers of whole-life insurance should be aware of its downsides. Because it isn't a transparent product, it's difficult to assess what its actual returns are. Part of the policy's returns may also include a partial return of premiums paid. In other words, you may be getting some of your own money back.

What Price Whole Life?

Sales of whole-life insurance, which offers buyers a guaranteed return, are rising as the economy falters.

- The policies have a low market risk, but give holders exposure to an insurer's potential troubles
- Returns can be distorted by the complex structure of these policies.
- Whole is not suitable for short-term use.

Though many risk-averse consumers are attracted to whole life, the insurance presents its own set of risks. A whole-life policy can bind the owner to the fate of a single company for decades, with steep costs to get out early. Some insurers now struggling looked very strong as recently as two years ago.

For all these reasons, many financial advisers recommend against purchasing whole-life insurance primarily as an investment vehicle.

PROJECT B

All states should mandate auto coverage. No driver should be allowed to be on the road with out coverage. Defend or reject this statement.

Road Risks Rise As More Drivers Drop Insurance

Higher Premiums, Joblessness Contribute to Alarming Trend; What to Do When You're Hit

BY M.P. MCQUEEN

More drivers are letting their car insurance lapse because of the sour economy, putting themselves and others at risk.

Several hundred thousand drivers dropped their insurance in the past year as the jobless rate climbed, estimates a study to be released next month by the Insurance Research Council, an industry-funded group. Online agency Insurance.com says it also is seeing evidence recently of more uninsured motorists. It says that as many as 40% of callers following up on online applications had let their previous policies lapse, up from less than 10% a couple years ago.

"I am seeing a lot more canceled policies than ever, especially in the last couple of months, usually due to job loss," said Christine Williams, a licensed agent at Insurance.com's call center outside Cleveland.

The trend is bad news for everybody on the road. If you're hit by an uninsured motorist, you may have to sue to recover costs, and many uninsured motorists have few assets. You can protect yourself by carrying uninsured-motorist coverage—almost half of states require the added coverage—but this may boost your premium.

Without a Net

A slumping economy is putting more uninsured drivers on the road. Here's how to protect yourself:

- Make sure you have **extra coverage** that compensates you if you're hit by an uninsured motorist.
- Set your own **liability insurance** amount commensurate with your assets. This amount also helps determine the limit of your uninsured motorist coverage.

Even in good times, many Americans drive without insurance. The Insurance Research Council's previous study, released in 2006, found that nearly 15% of drivers nationally were uninsured in 2004, up from about 13% in 1999. In some states, including Mississippi, California and Arizona, roughly a quarter of drivers weren't insured.

Internet Projects: See text Web site (www.mhhe.com/slater10e) and The Business Math Internet Resource Guide.

chapter

21 STOCKS, BONDS, AND MUTUAL FUNDS

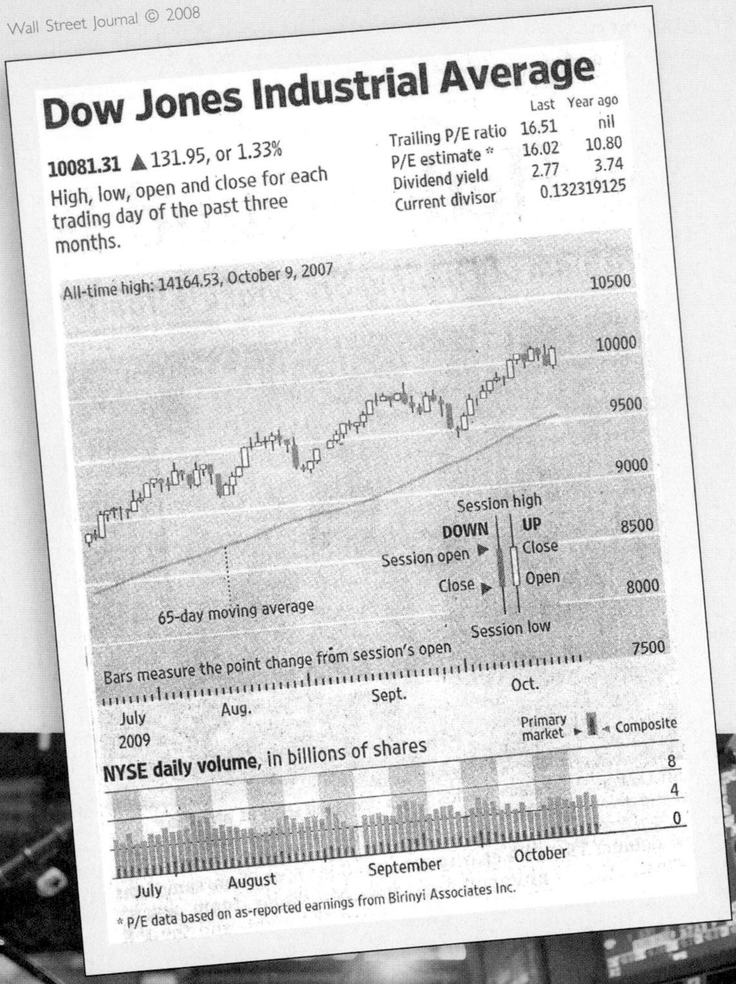

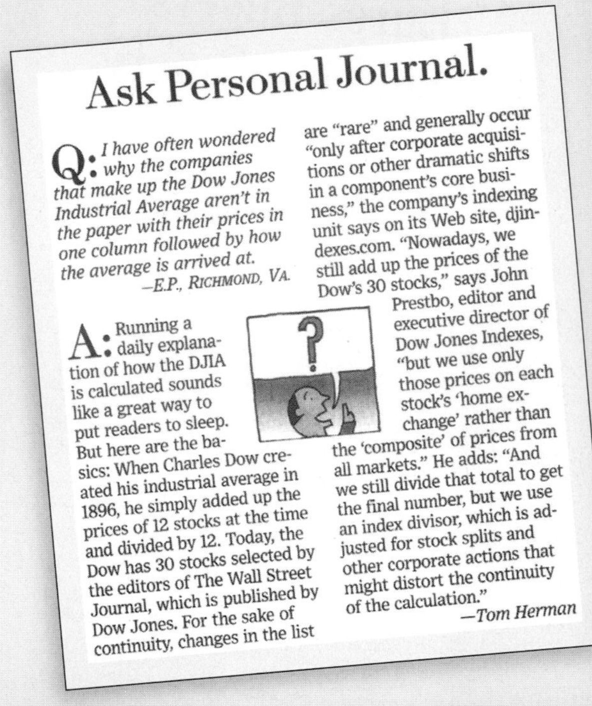

Ask Personal Journal.

Q: *I have often wondered why the companies that make up the Dow Jones Industrial Average aren't in the paper with their prices in one column followed by how the average is arrived at.*

—E.P., Richmond, Va.

A: Running a daily explanation of how the DJIA is calculated sounds like a great way to put readers to sleep. But here are the basics: When Charles Dow created his industrial average in 1896, he simply added up the prices of 12 stocks at the time and divided by 12. Today, the Dow has 30 stocks selected by the editors of The Wall Street Journal, which is published by Dow Jones. For the sake of continuity, changes in the list are "rare" and generally occur "only after corporate acquisitions or other dramatic shifts in a component's core business," the company's indexing unit says on its Web site, djindexes.com. "Nowadays, we still add up the prices of the Dow's 30 stocks," says John Prestbo, editor and executive director of Dow Jones Indexes, "but we use only those prices on each stock's 'home exchange' rather than the 'composite' of prices from all markets." He adds: "And we still divide that total to get the final number, but we use an index divisor, which is adjusted for stock splits and other corporate actions that might distort the continuity of the calculation."

—Tom Herman

LEARNING UNIT OBJECTIVES

LU 21–1: Stocks

1. Read and explain stock quotations *(p. 495)*.
2. Calculate dividends of preferred and common stocks; calculate return on investment *(p. 496)*.

LU 21–2: Bonds

1. Read and explain bond quotations *(p. 498)*.
2. Compare bond yields to bond premiums and discounts *(pp. 499–500)*.

LU 21–3: Mutual Funds

1. Explain and calculate net asset value and mutual fund commissions *(p. 500)*.
2. Read and explain mutual fund quotations *(p. 501)*.

VOCABULARY PREVIEW

Here are key terms in this chapter. After completing the chapter, if you know the term, place a checkmark in the parenthesis. If you don't know the term, look it up and put the page number where it can be found.

Bonds . ( ) Bond yield . ( ) Cash dividend . ( ) Common stocks . ( ) Cumulative preferred stock . ( ) Discount . ( ) Dividends . ( ) Dividends in arrears . ( ) Earnings per share (EPS) . ( ) Mutual fund . ( ) Net asset value (NAV) . ( ) PE ratio . ( ) Preferred stock . ( ) Premium . ( ) Price-earnings ratio . ( ) Stockbrokers . ( ) Stock certificate . ( ) Stockholders . ( ) Stocks . ( ) Stock yield . ( )

Claiborne Loss Widens As Revenue Falls 22%

BY KAREN TALLEY

Liz Claiborne Inc.'s fourth-quarter net loss widened sharply as the retailer took $693 million in write-downs and its revenue fell 22%.

Chief Executive William McComb called the quarter "the most challenging environment the company has experienced in decades."

The fashion company posted a net loss of $828.9 million, or $8.85 a share, compared with a loss of $435.7 million, or $4.55 a share, a year earlier, when results also included write-downs. Excluding those and other items, Liz Claiborne would have posted a loss of four cents a share, compared with earnings of 20 cents a share a year earlier.

Revenue declined to $911.2 million, falling short of Wall Street expectations.

Liz Claiborne shares fell 11%, or 32 cents, to $2.50 in 4 p.m. New York Stock Exchange composite trading Wednesday.

The company has gone through wrenching changes in the past couple of years, and is trying to refocus its apparel brands amid the downturn.

The rollout of a new Isaac Mizrahi-designed line is seen as a key to restoring the company's fortunes and reputation. During a conference call with analysts, Mr. McComb said the early response has been positive.

Like many other retailers, Liz Claiborne said it wouldn't provide an earnings outlook for the full year because of economic uncertainties.

The company warned that it expects to post a "meaningful" first-quarter loss. The loss is forecast to narrow each quarter afterward. Analysts expect a nine-cent loss for the first quarter. The company projects same-store sales declines of 15% to 25% through the third quarter for all of its brands.

The company ended the fourth quarter with $25 million in cash, down from $205 million a year ago. Debt totaled $744 million, below the range it projected in November. Inventory was reduced 14% compared with a year earlier. Capital-raising avenues include sales of real estate and sale-leasebacks of certain properties, company executives said.

More than half of the $683 million noncash write-down stems from the company's market capitalization falling below its book value during the quarter. The rest relates to declining performance of business segments, cash flows and a trademark-impairment charge.

The company plans to open just 12 stores this year, compared with 139 in 2008, part of a "ruthless" cost-management drive this year, Mr. McComb said.

Liz Claiborne is also tinkering with its brands. Kate Spade is further expanding its jewelry. The Lucky brand—known for jeans—is increasing tops as a percentage of total assortment.

Newscom

Lucky, one of Liz Claiborne's core brands, is tweaking its product mix by increasing the numbers of tops it offers.

Have you ever bought Liz Claiborne clothes? Brands include Kate Spade, Lucky Brand, and Mexx. The following *Wall Street Journal* clip shows that in 2008 Liz Claiborne sales and earnings were lower. The company's stock is traded on the New York Stock Exchange. Before we explain the concept of stock, consider the following general investor principles: (1) know your risk tolerance and the risk of the investments you are considering—determine whether you are a low-risk conservative investor or a high-risk speculative investor; (2) know your time frame—how soon you need your money; (3) know the liquidity of the investments you are considering—how easy it is to get your money; (4) know the return you can expect on your money—how much your money should earn; and (5) do not put "all your eggs in one basket"—diversify with a mixture of stocks, bonds, and cash equivalents. It is most important that before you seek financial advice from others, you go to the library and/or the Internet for information. When you do your own research first, you can judge the advice you receive from others.

This chapter introduces you to the major types of investments—stocks, bonds, and mutual funds. These investments indicate the performance of the companies they represent and the economy of the country at home and abroad.

Learning Unit 21–1: Stocks

We begin this unit with an introduction to the basic stock terms. Then we explain the reason why people buy stocks, newspaper stock quotations, dividends on preferred and common stocks, and return on investment.

Introduction to Basic Stock Terms

Companies sell shares of ownership in their company to raise money to finance operations, plan expansion, and so on. These ownership shares are called **stocks.** The buyers of the stock (**stockholders**) receive **stock certificates** verifying the number of shares of stock they own.

If you own 50 shares of common stock, you are entitled to 50 votes in company elections. Preferred stockholders do not have this right.

The two basic types of stock are **common stock** and **preferred stock.** Common stockholders have voting rights. Preferred stockholders do not have voting rights, but they receive preference over common stockholders in **dividends** (payments from profit) and in the company's assets if the company goes bankrupt. **Cumulative preferred stock** entitles its owners to a specific amount of dividends in 1 year. Should the company fail to pay these dividends, the **dividends in arrears** accumulate. The company pays no dividends to common stockholders until the company brings the preferred dividend payments up to date.

Why Buy Stocks?

Some investors own stock because they think the stock will become more valuable, for example, if the company makes more profit, new discoveries, and the like. Other investors own stock to share in the profit distributed by the company in dividends (cash or stock).

For various reasons, investors at different times want to sell their stock or buy more stock. Strikes, inflation, or technological changes may cause some investors to think their stock will decline in value. These investors may decide to sell. Then the law of supply and demand takes over. As more people want to sell, the stock price goes down. Should more people want to buy, the stock price would go up.

How Are Stocks Traded?

Stock exchanges provide an orderly trading place for stock. You can think of these exchanges as an auction place. Only **stockbrokers** and their representatives are allowed to

FIGURE 21.1

New York Stock Exchange

Stockholders
↓
elect
↓
board of directors
↓
elect
↓
officers of corporation

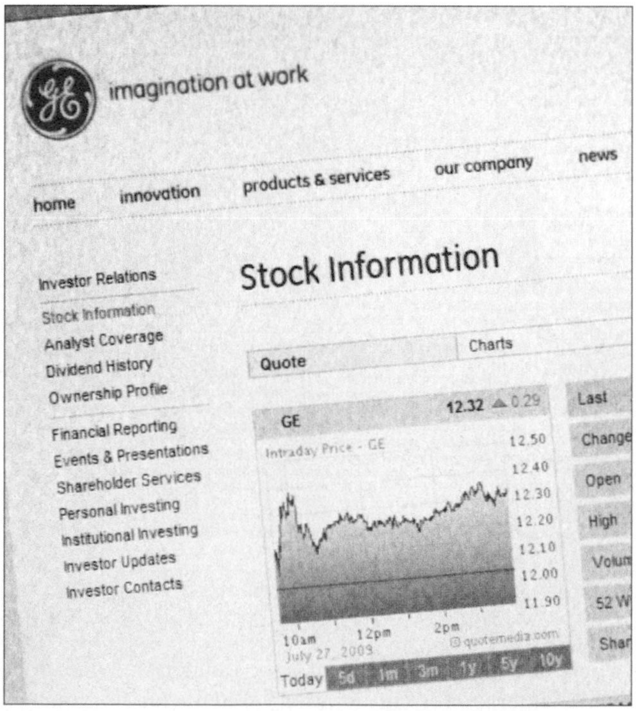

Teri Stratford

trade on the floor of the exchange. Stockbrokers charge commissions for stock trading—buying and selling stock for investors. As you might expect, in this age of the Internet, stock trades can also be made on the Internet.

LO 1

How to Read Stock Quotations in the Newspaper's Financial Section*

We will use General Electric stock (see Figure 21.1 on page 494) to learn how to read the stock quotations found in your newspaper. Note the following newspaper listing of General Electric stock:

52 WEEKS				YLD		VOL		NET
HI	LO	STOCK (SYM)	DIV	%	PE	100's	CLOSE	CHG
40.49	17.27	General Electric (GE)	1.24	6.8	8.73	75,537	18.34	1.59

The highest price at which General Electric stock traded during the past 52 weeks was \$40.49 per share. This means that during the year someone was willing to pay \$40.49 for a share of stock.

The lowest price at which GE stock traded during the year was \$17.27 per share.

The newspaper lists the company name. The symbol that General Electric uses for trading is GE. General Electric paid a dividend of \$1.24 per share to stock owners last year. So if you owned 100 shares, you receive a **cash dividend** of \$124 (100 shares $\times$ \$1.24).

The **stock yield** percent tells stockholders that the dividend per share is returning a rate of 6.8% to investors. This 6.8% is based on the closing price. The calculation is:

$$\text{Stock yield} = \frac{\text{Annual dividend per share}}{\text{Today's closing price per share}} = \frac{\$1.24}{\$18.34} = \text{6.8\% (rounded to nearest tenth percent)}$$

The 6.8% return may seem low to people who could earn a better return on their money elsewhere. Remember that if the stock price rises and you sell, your investment may result in a high rate of return.

The GE stock is selling at \$18.34; it is selling at 8.73 times its **earning per share (EPS).** Earnings per share are not listed on the stock quote.

$$\text{Earnings per share} = \text{Closing price} \div \text{Price earning ratio}$$

The **price-earnings ratio,** or **PE ratio,** measures the relationship between the closing price per share of stock and the annual earnings per share. For GE we calculate the following price-earnings ratio. (Assume GE earns \$2.10 per share. This is not listed in the newspaper.)

Round PE to the nearest whole number.

$$\text{PE ratio} = \frac{\text{Closing price per share of stock}}{\text{Annual earnings per share}} = \frac{\$18.34}{\$2.10} = 8.73$$

If the PE ratio column shows ". . . ," this means the company has no earnings. The PE ratio will often vary depending on quality of stock, future expectations, economic conditions, and so on.

In the newspaper stock quotations for GE, the number in the volume column is in the 100s. Thus, to 75,537, you add two zeros to get 7,553,700. This indicates that 7,553,700 shares were traded on this day. Remember that shares of stock need a buyer and a seller to trade.

The last trade of the day, called the closing price, was at \$18.34 per share.

On the *previous day,* the closing price was \$19.93 (not given). The *new* close is \$18.34. The result is that the closing price is down \$1.59 from the *previous day.*

*For centuries, stocks were traded and reported in fraction form as shown in the chapter opening photo. In 2001 the New York Stock Exchange and NASDAQ began the conversion to decimals, which is how it is reported today.

LO 2

Dividends on Preferred and Common Stocks

If you own stock in a company, the company may pay out dividends. (Not all companies pay dividends.) The amount of the dividend is determined by the net earnings of the company listed in its financial report. The following clip from Barron's shows some companies and their quarterly dividends. Note GE's dividend is $.31 per quarter or $1.24 per year.

QUARTERLY DIVIDENDS: DOW JONES INDUSTRIAL AVERAGE

This table lists the dividends of the Dow Jones Industrial Averages component stocks based on the record date and adjusted by the Dow Divisor in effect at the end of the quarter.

Company	2008 June	2008 Mar.	2007 Dec.	2007 Sept.	2007 June
AIG (AIG)	.22	.20	.20	.20	.165
Alcoa (AA)	.17	.17	.17	.17	.17
Altria Group (MO)	a	a	.75	.75	.69
Am Exp (AXP)	.18	.18	.15	.15	.15
AT&T (T)	.40	.40	.355	.355	.355
Bank of Amer (BAC)	.64	.64	a	a	a
Boeing (BA)	.40	.40	.35	.35	.35
Caterpillar (CAT)	.36	.36	.36	.36	.30
Chevron Corp (CVX)	.65	.58	a	a	a
Citigroup (C)	.32	.32	.54	.54	.54
Coca-Cola (KO)	.38	.38	.34	.34	.34
Disney, Walt (DIS)	Nil	Nil	.35	Nil	Nil
du Pont (DD)	.41	.41	.41	.37	.37
ExxonMob (XOM)	.40	.35	.35	.35	.35
Gen Elec (GE)	.31	.31	.31	.28	.28
Gen Motors (GM)	.25	.25	.25	.25	.25
Hewl-Pack (HPQ)	.08	.08	.08	.08	.08
Home Depot (HD)	.225	.225	.225	.225	.225
Honeywell (HON)	a	a	.25	.25	.25
IBM (IBM)	.50	.40	.40	.40	.40
Intel (INTC)	.14	.1275	.1125	.1125	.1125
JohnsonJ (JNJ)	.46	.415	.415	.415	.415
JP MorgCh (JPM)	.38	.38	.38	.38	.34
McDonalds (MCD)	br.375	br.375	1.50	Nil	Nil
Merck (MRK)	.38	.38	.38	.38	.38
Microsoft (MSFT)	.11	.11	.11	.10	.10
Pfizer (PFE)	.32	.32	.29	.29	.29
Proc Gamble (PG)	.40	.35	.35	.35	.35
3M Co. (MMM)	.50	.50	.48	.48	.48
Untd Tech (UTX)	.32	.32	.32	.32	.265
Verizon (VZ)	.43	.43	.43	.405	.405
Wal-Mart (WMT)	.2375	.2375	.22	.22	.22
Total Dividends	9.9275	r9.60	10.8275	8.8725	8.6225
DJIA Divisor	0.122834016	0.122834016	0.123017848	0.123017848	0.123017848
DJIA Average	11350.01	12262.89	13264.82	13895.63	13408.62
DJIA Qtr. Divs	80.83	r78.15	88.02	72.12	70.09
DJIA 4-Qtr. Divs	319.12	r308.38	298.99	287.57	280.58
DJIA Div Yield, %	2.81	2.51	2.25	2.07	2.09

a-Bank of America and Chevron replaced Altria and Honeywell. b-Changed to quarterly payer. r-Revised.

Wall Street Journal © 2008

Earlier we stated that cumulative preferred stockholders must be paid all past and present dividends before common stockholders can receive any dividends. Following is an example to illustrate the calculation of dividends on preferred and common stocks for 2011 and 2012.

EXAMPLE The stock records of Jason Corporation show the following:

Preferred stock issued: 20,000 shares.

Preferred stock cumulative at $.80 per share.

Common stock issued: 400,000 shares.

In 2011, Jason paid no dividends.

In 2012, Jason paid $512,000 in dividends.

Remember that common stockholders do not have the cumulative feature as preferred do.

Since Jason declared no dividends in 2011, the company has $16,000 (20,000 shares × $.80 = $16,000) dividends in arrears to preferred stockholders. The dividend of $512,000 in 2012 is divided between preferred and common stocks as follows:

	2011	2012	
Dividends paid	0	$512,000	
Preferred stockholders*	Paid: 0	Paid for 2011 (20,000 shares × $.80)	$ 16,000
	Owe: Preferred, $16,000 (20,000 shares × $.80)	Paid for 2010	16,000
			$ 32,000
Common stockholders	0	Total dividend	$512,000
		Paid preferred for 2011 and 2012	− 32,000
		To common	$480,000
		$\frac{\$480,000}{400,000 \text{ shares}} = \$1.20$ per share	

*For a discussion of par value (arbitrary value placed on stock for accounting purposes) and cash and stock dividend distribution, check your accounting text.

Calculating Return on Investment

Now let's learn how to calculate a return on your investment of General Electric stock, assuming the following:

Bought 200 shares at $18.34.

Sold at end of 1 year 200 shares at $22.10.

1% commission rate on buying and selling stock.

Current $1.24 dividend per share in effect.

MONEY TIPS

Go with a discount broker or trade for free online (offered by some companies if a minimum balance is maintained) to save on investing costs.

Bought		**Sold**	
200 shares at $18.34	$3,668.00	200 shares at $22.10	$4,420.00
+ Broker's commission (.01 × $3,668)	+ 36.68	− Broker's commission (.01 × $4,420)	− 44.20
Total cost	$3,704.68	Total receipt	$4,375.80

Note: A commission is charged on both the buying and selling of stock.

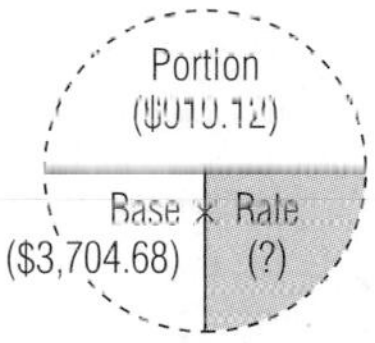

Total receipt	$4,375.80	
Total cost	− 3,704.68	
Net gain	$ 671.12	
Dividends	+ 248.00	(200 shares × $1.24)
Total gain	$ 919.12	

Portion ↗ $\frac{\$919.12}{\$3,704.68} = 24.81\%$ rate of return (to nearest hundredth percent)

↑ Base

It's time for another Practice Quiz.

LU 21–1 PRACTICE QUIZ

Complete this **Practice Quiz** to see how you are doing.

1. From the following Texaco stock quotation **(a)** explain the letters, **(b)** estimate the company's earnings per share, and **(c)** show how "YLD %" was calculated.

52 WEEKS HI	LO	STOCK (SYM)	DIV	YLD %	PE	VOL 100's	CLOSE	NET CHG
73.90	48.25	Texaco TX	1.80	2.5	14	13020	72.25	+0.46
(A)	(B)	(C)	(D)	(E)	(F)	(G)	(H)	(I)

2. **Given:** 30,000 shares of preferred cumulative stock at $.70 per share; 200,000 shares of common; 2010, no dividend; 2011, $109,000. How much is paid to each class of stock in 2010?

Solutions with Step-by-Step Help on DVD

✓ Solutions

1. a. (A) Highest price traded in last 52 weeks.
(B) Lowest price traded in past 52 weeks.
(C) Name of corporation is Texaco (symbol TX).
(D) Dividend per share per year is \$1.80.
(E) Yield for year is 2.5%.
(F) Texaco stock sells at 14 times its earnings.
(G) Sales volume for the day is 1,302,000 shares.
(H) The last price (closing price for the day) is \$72.25.
(I) Stock is up \$.46 from closing price yesterday.

b. EPS $= \frac{\$72.25}{14} = \$5.16$ per share

c. $\frac{\$1.80}{\$72.25} = 2.5\%$

2. **Preferred:** 30,000 × \$.70 = \$21,000 Arrears 2010
+ 21,000 2011
\$42,000

Common: **\$67,000** (\$109,000 − \$42,000)

LU 21–1a EXTRA PRACTICE QUIZ WITH WORKED-OUT SOLUTIONS

Need more practice? Try this **Extra Practice Quiz** (check figures in Chapter Organizer, p. 503). Worked-out Solutions can be found in Appendix B at end of text.

1. From the following Goodyear stock quotation **(a)** explain the letters, **(b)** estimate the company's earnings per share, and **(c)** show how YLD % was calculated.

52 WEEKS HI	52 WEEKS LO	STOCK (SYM)	DIV	YLD %	PE	VOL 100'S	CLOSE	NET CHG
23.14	3.17	Goodyear GT	.07	5.4	16	30800	13.08	+.11
(A)	(B)	(C)	(D)	(E)	(F)	(G)	(H)	(I)

2. **Given:** 40,000 shares of preferred cumulative stock at a \$.60 per share; 300,000 shares of common; 2010, no dividend; 2011, \$210,000. How much is paid to each class of stock in 2011?

Learning Unit 21–2: Bonds

LO 1

Have you heard of the Rule of 115? This rule is used as a rough measure to show how quickly an investment will triple in value. To use the rule, divide 115 by the rate of return your money earns. For example, if a bond earns 5% interest, divide 115 by 5. This measure estimates that your money in the bond will triple in 23 years.

This unit begins by explaining the difference between bonds and stocks. Then you will learn how to read bond quotations and calculate bond yields.

Reading Bond Quotations

Sometimes companies raise money by selling bonds instead of stock. When you buy stock, you become a part owner in the company. To raise money, companies may not want to sell more stock and thus dilute the ownership of their current stock owners, so they sell bonds. **Bonds** represent a promise from the company to pay the face amount to the bond owner at a future date, along with interest payments at a stated rate.

Bond quotes are stated in percents of the face value of the bond and not in dollars as stock is. Interest is paid semiannually.

Once a company issues bonds, they are traded as stock is. If a company goes bankrupt, bondholders have the first claim to the assets of the corporation—before stockholders. As with stock, changes in bond prices vary according to supply and demand. Brokers also charge commissions on bond trading. These commissions vary.

LO 2

How to Read the Bond Section of the Newspaper

The bond section of the newspaper shows the bonds that are traded that day. The information given on bonds differs from the information given on stocks. The newspaper states bond prices in *percents of face amount, not in dollar amounts* as stock prices are stated. Also, bonds are usually in denominations of \$1,000 (the face amount).

When a bond sells at a price below its face value, the bond is sold at a discount. Why? The interest that the bond pays may not be as high as the current market rate. When this happens, the bond is not as attractive to investors, and it sells for a **discount.** The opposite could, of course, also occur. The bond may sell at a **premium,** which means that the bond sells for more than its face value or the bond interest is higher than the current market rate.

Let's look at this newspaper information given for Coke bonds:

Bonds	Current yield	Vol.	Close	Net change
Coke 5.65 14	5.7%	6	99.59	−1

Note: Bond prices are stated as a percent of face amount.

The name of the company is Coke. It produces a wide range of consumer drinks. The interest on the bond is 5.65%. The company pays the interest semiannually. The bond matures (comes due) in 2014. The total interest for the year is \$56.50 (.0565 × \$1,000). Remember that the face value of the bond is \$1,000. Now let's show this with the following formula:

Yearly interest = Face value of bond × Stated yearly interest rate

\$56.50 = \$1,000 × .0565

We calculate the 5.7% yield by dividing the total annual interest of the bond by the total cost of the bond. (For our purposes, we will omit the commission cost.) All bond yields are rounded to the nearest tenth percent.

Note this bond is selling for more than \$1,000 since its interest is very attractive compared to other new offerings.

$$\frac{\text{Yearly interest}}{\text{Cost of bond at closing}} = \frac{\$56.50\ (.0565 \times \$1{,}000)}{\$995.90\ (.9959 \times \$1{,}000)} = 5.69\% = 5.7\%$$

This is same as 99.59%.

Six \$1,000 bonds were traded. Note that we do *not* add two zeros as we did to the sales volume of stock.

The last bond traded on this day was 99.59% of face value, or in dollars, \$.9959.

The last trade of the day was down 1% of the face value from the last trade of yesterday. In dollars this is 1% = \$10.

1% = .01 × \$1,000 = \$10

Thus, the closing price on this day, 99.59% + 1%, equals yesterday's close of 100.59% (\$1,005,90). Note that *yesterday's close is not listed in today's quotations.*

Calculating Bond Yields

The Coke bond (selling at a discount) pays 5.65% interest when it is yielding investors 5%.

$$\text{Bond yield} = \frac{\text{Total annual interest of bond}}{\text{Total current cost of bond at closing*}}$$

*We assume this to be the buyer's purchase price.

$ MONEY TIPS

In a tough economic environment and/or if you are close to retirement, bonds may be the best investment option. Treasury bonds have almost no credit risk and municipal bonds (munis) are tax-free. Check the issuer's credit rating and stick with triple A's when buying.

The following example will show us how to calculate **bond yields.**

EXAMPLE Jim Smith bought 5 bonds of Coke at the closing price of 99.59 (remember that in dollars 99.59% is \$995.90). Jim's total cost excluding commission is:

5 × \$995.90 = \$4,979.50

What is Jim's interest?

No matter what Jim pays for the bonds, he will still receive interest of \$56.50 per bond (.5650 × \$1,000). Jim bought the bonds at \$995.90 each, resulting in a bond yield of 5.7%. Let's calculate Jim's yield to the nearest tenth percent:

(5 bonds × \$56.50 interest per bond per year)

$$\frac{\$282.50}{\$4{,}979.50} = 5.7\%$$

Now let's try another Practice Quiz.

LU 21–2 PRACTICE QUIZ

Complete this **Practice Quiz** to see how you are doing.

Bonds	Yield	Sales	Close	Net change
Aetna 6.375% 13	6.4	20	100.375	.875

From the above bond quotation, **(1)** calculate the cost of 5 bonds at closing (disregard commissions) and **(2)** check the current yield of 6.4%.

DVD *Solutions with Step-by-Step Help on DVD*

✓ Solutions

1. $100.375\% = 1.00375 \times \$1{,}000 = \$1{,}003.75 \times 5 = \boxed{\$5{,}018.75}$
2. $6.375\% = .06375 \times \$1{,}000 = \$63.75$ annual interest

$$\frac{\$63.75}{\$1{,}003.75} = 6.35\% = \boxed{6.4\%}$$

LU 21–2a EXTRA PRACTICE QUIZ WITH WORKED-OUT SOLUTIONS

Need more practice? Try this **Extra Practice Quiz** (check figures in Chapter Organizer, p. 503). Worked-out Solutions can be found in Appendix B at end of text.

Bonds	Yield	Sales	Close	Net change
Aetna 7.5 14	7.5%	20	100.25	+.75

From the above bond quotation, **(1)** calculate the cost of 5 bonds at closing (disregard commissions) and **(2)** check the current yield of 7.5%.

Learning Unit 21–3: Mutual Funds

Steve Senne/AP Photo

In recent years, mutual funds have increased dramatically and people in the United States have invested billions in mutual funds. Investors can choose from several fund types—stock funds, bond funds, international funds, balanced (stocks and bonds) funds, and so on. This learning unit tells you why investors choose mutual funds and discusses the net asset value of mutual funds, mutual fund commissions, and how to read a mutual fund quotation.

Why Investors Choose Mutual Funds

The main reasons investors choose mutual funds are the following:

LO 1

1. **Diversification.** When you invest in a mutual fund, you own a small portion of many different companies. This protects you against the poor performance of a single company but not against a sell-off in the market (stock and bond exchanges) or fluctuations in the interest rate.
2. **Professional management.** You are hiring a professional manager to look after your money when you own shares in mutual funds. The success of a particular fund is often due to the person(s) managing the fund.
3. **Liquidity.** Most funds will buy back your fund shares whenever you decide to sell.
4. **Low fund expenses.** Competition forces funds to keep their expenses low to maximize their performance. Because stocks and bonds in a mutual fund represent thousands of shareholders, funds can trade in large blocks, reducing transaction costs.
5. **Access to foreign markets.** Through mutual funds, investors can conveniently and inexpensively invest in foreign markets.

Net Asset Value

Investing in a **mutual fund** means that you buy shares in the fund's portfolio (group of stocks and/or bonds). The value of your mutual fund share is expressed in the share's **net asset value (NAV),** which is the dollar value of one mutual fund share. You calculate the NAV by subtracting the fund's current liabilities from the current market value of the fund's investments and dividing this by the number of shares outstanding.

$$\text{NAV} = \frac{\text{Current market value of fund's investments} - \text{Current liabilities}}{\text{Number of shares outstanding}}$$

The NAV helps investors track the value of their fund investment. After the market closes on each business day, the fund uses the closing prices of the investments it owns to find the dollar value of one fund share, or NAV. This is the price investors receive if they sell fund shares on that day or pay if they buy fund shares on that day.

Commissions When Buying Mutual Funds

The following table is a quick reference for the cost of buying mutual fund shares. Commissions vary from 0% to $8\frac{1}{2}$% depending on how the mutual fund is classified.

MONEY TIPS

Save money by sticking with no-load mutual funds. There is a good chance you can find one with similar attributes to the load fund you were interested in.

Classification	Commission charge*	Offer price to buy
No-load (NL) fund	No sales charge	NAV (buy directly from investment company)
Low-load (LL) fund	3% or less	NAV + commission % (buy directly from investment company or from a broker)
Load fund	$8\frac{1}{2}$% or less	NAV + commission % (buy from a broker)

*On a front-end load, you pay commission a when you purchase the fund shares, while on a back-end load, you pay when you redeem or sell. In general, if you hold the shares for more than 5 years, you pay no commission charge.

The offer price to buy a share for a low-load or load fund is the NAV plus the commission. Now let's look at how to read a mutual fund quotation.

LO 2

How to Read a Mutual Fund Quotation

SpecInc	10.74	0.05	6.3
Value	16.37	0.42	8.1
Putnam Funds Class A			
GrIn p	9.72	0.24	4.1

STU

Wall Street Journal © 2008

We will be studying the Putnam Mutual Funds. Cindy Joelson has invested in the Growth and Income Fund with the hope that over the years this will provide her with financial security when she retires. On May 27, Cindy turns to the *Wall Street Journal* and looks up the Putnam Growth Income Fund quotation.

The name of the fund is Growth and Income, which has the investment objective of growth and income securities as set forth in the fund's prospectus (document giving information about the fund). Note that this is only one fund in the Putnam family of funds.

- The $9.72 figure is the NAV plus the sales commission.
- The fund has increased $.24 from the NAV quotation of the previous day.
- The fund has a 4.1% return this year (January through December 7). This assumes reinvestments of all distributions. Sales charges are not reflected.

Now let's check your understanding of this unit with a Practice Quiz.

LU 21–3 PRACTICE QUIZ

Complete this **Practice Quiz** to see how you are doing.

From the mutual fund quotation of the Fidelity Investment Growth Fund shown below, complete the following:

1. NAV ________
2. NAV change ________
3. Total return, YTD ________

Fidelity Invest			
100Index	6.61	0.15	−0.5
AilSectEq	9.77	0.22	7.2
AMgr50%	11.87	0.16	10.1
Balanc	13.97	0.20	7.2
BluCh	29.06	0.82	10.5
CapAp	17.13	0.43	8.9
CpInc r	6.52	0.03	23.8
Contra	47.19	1.08	4.3
DisEq	17.42	0.42	0.1
DivGth	18.30	0.55	15.9
DivIntl	23.34	0.33	8.5
Eq Inc	31.83	0.89	4.0
EQII	13.41	0.38	1.5
Fidel	23.90	0.61	5.6
GNMA	11.31	−0.01	3.4
GovtInc	10.71	−0.03	−0.9
GroCo	53.88	1.55	10.0
GroInc	13.19	0.34	0.4
HighInc r	7.05	0.01	20.5
IntlDisc	24.98	0.39	5.7
InvGB	6.55	−0.01	5.2
InvGrBd	10.79	−0.03	2.5
LgCpVal	9.74	0.25	−4.4

Wall Street Journal © 2009

Solutions with Step-by-Step Help on DVD

✓ Solutions

1. 13.19
2. +.34
3. +.4

LU 21–3a EXTRA PRACTICE QUIZ WITH WORKED-OUT SOLUTIONS

Need more practice? Try this **Extra Practice Quiz** (check figures in Chapter Organizer, p. 503). Worked-out Solutions can be found in Appendix B at end of text.

From the mutual fund quotation of the Franklin/Temp Income Fund shown below, complete the following:

1. NAV ________
2. NAV change ________
3. Total return, YTD ________

Fidelity Spartan			
500IdxInv r	63.33	1.62	2.0
EqIdxInv	32.30	0.83	2.0
TotMktIdxInv	25.71	0.71	3.0
Fidelity Spartan Adv			
500Ad r	63.34	1.62	2.0
EqIdxAd	32.30	0.82	2.0
First Eagle Funds			
GlbA	34.68	0.32	5.1
FrankTemp/Franklin A			
CA TF A p	6.71	-0.01	9.7
Fed TF A p	11.44	-0.01	10.1
FoundFAIA p	8.25	0.10	5.4
HY TF A p	9.27	-0.01	15.9
IncomeA p	1.73	0.01	7.8
NY TF A p	11.42	-0.02	8.4
US Gov A p	6.66	...	2.5

Wall Street Journal © 2009

CHAPTER ORGANIZER AND REFERENCE GUIDE

Topic	Key point, procedure, formula	Example(s) to illustrate situation
Stock yield, p. 495	$\frac{\text{Annual dividend per share}}{\text{Today's closing price per share}}$ (Round yield to nearest tenth percent.)	Annual dividend, \$.72 Today's closing price, \$42.375 $\frac{\$.72}{\$42.375} = \boxed{1.7\%}$
Price-earnings ratio, p. 495	$PE = \frac{\text{Closing price per share of stock}}{\text{Annual earnings per share}}$ (Round answer to nearest whole number.)	From previous example: Closing price, \$42.375 Annual earnings per share, \$4.24 $\frac{\$42.375}{\$4.24} = 9.99 = \boxed{10}$
Dividends with cumulative preferred stock, p. 496	Cumulative preferred stock is entitled to all dividends in arrears before common stock receives dividend.	2009 dividend omitted; in 2010, \$400,000 in dividends paid out. Preferred is cumulative at \$.90 per share; 20,000 shares of preferred issued and 100,000 shares of common issued. To preferred: 20,000 shares × \$.90 = \$18,000 In arrears 2009: 20,000 shares × .90 = 18,000 Dividend to preferred **\$36,000** To common: \$364,000 (\$400,000 − \$36,000) $\frac{\$364{,}000}{100{,}000 \text{ shares}}$ = \$3.64 dividend to common per share
Cost of a bond, p. 498	Bond prices are stated as a percent of the face value. Bonds selling for less than face value result in bond discounts. Bonds selling for more than face value result in bond premiums.	Bill purchases 5 \$1,000, 12% bonds at closing price of $103\frac{1}{4}$. What is his cost (omitting commissions)? $103\frac{1}{4}\%$ = 103.25% = 1.0325 in decimal 1.0325 × \$1,000 bond = **\$1,032.50 per bond** 5 bonds × \$1,032.50 = **\$5,162.50**
Bond yield, p. 499	$\frac{\text{Total annual interest of bond}}{\text{Total current cost of bond at closing}}$ (Round to nearest tenth percent.)	Calculate bond yield from last example on one bond. (\$1,000 × .12) $\frac{\$120}{\$1{,}032.50} = \boxed{11.6\%}$

(continues)

CHAPTER ORGANIZER AND REFERENCE GUIDE

Topic	Key point, procedure, formula	Example(s) to illustrate situation
Mutual fund, p. 500	$\text{NAV} = \dfrac{\text{Current market value of fund's investment} - \text{Current liabilities}}{\text{Number of shares outstanding}}$	The NAV of the Scudder Income Bond Fund was $12.84. The NAV change was 0.01. What was the NAV yesterday? $12.83

KEY TERMS			
	Bonds, *p. 498* Bond yield, *p. 499* Cash dividend, *p. 495* Common stocks, *p. 494* Cumulative preferred stock, *p. 494* Discount, *p. 499*	Dividends, *p. 494* Dividends in arrears, *p. 494* Earnings per share (EPS), *p. 495* Mutual fund, *p. 500* Net asset value (NAV), *p. 500* PE ratio, *p. 495* Preferred stock, *p. 494*	Premium, *p. 499* Price-earnings ratio, *p. 495* Stockbrokers, *p. 494* Stock certificate, *p. 494* Stockholders, *p. 494* Stocks, *p. 494* Stock yield, *p. 495*

CHECK FIGURES FOR EXTRA PRACTICE QUIZZES WITH PAGE REFERENCES. (WORKED-OUT SOLUTIONS IN APPENDIX B.)	LU 21–1a (p. 498)	LU 21–2a (p. 500)	LU 21–3a (p. 502)
	1. b. $.73 per share c. .4% **2.** Pref. $48,000 Com. $168,000	**1.** $5,012.50 **2.** $\dfrac{\$75}{\$1{,}002.50} = 7.48\%$	**1.** 13.25 **2.** −.09 **3.** −5.2%

Critical Thinking Discussion Questions

1. Explain how to read a stock quotation. What are some of the red flags of buying stock?
2. What is the difference between odd and round lots? Explain why the commission on odd lots could be quite expensive.
3. Explain how to read a bond quote. What could be a drawback of investing in bonds?
4. Compare and contrast stock yields and bond yields. As a conservative investor, which option might be better? Defend your answer.
5. Explain what NAV means. What is the difference between a load and a no-load fund? How safe are mutual funds?

Classroom Notes

END-OF-CHAPTER PROBLEMS

connect (plus+) www.mhhe.com/slater10e

Check figures for odd-numbered problems in Appendix C.

Name ______________________ Date ________

DRILL PROBLEMS

Calculate the cost (omit commission) of buying the following shares of stock:

21–1. 300 shares of Google at $382.99

21–2. 1,200 shares of Apple at $77.90

Calculate the yield of each of the following stocks (round to the nearest tenth percent):

	Company	Yearly dividend	Closing price per share	Yield
21–3.	Boeing	$.68	$64.63	____
21–4.	Best Buy	$.07	$9.56	____

Calculate the earnings per share, price-earnings ratio (to nearest whole number), or stock price as needed:

	Company	Earnings per share	Closing price per share	Price-earnings ratio
21–5.	BellSouth	$3.15	$40.13	___
21–6.	American Express	$3.85	______	26

21–7. Calculate the total cost of buying 400 shares of CVS at $59.38. Assume a 2% commission.

21–8. If in Problem 21–1 the 300 shares of Google stock were sold at $360.00, what would be the loss? Commission is omitted.

21–9. Given: 20,000 shares cumulative preferred stock ($2.25 dividend per share): 40,000 shares common stock. Dividends paid: 2010, $8,000; 2011, 0; and 2012, $160,000. How much will preferred and common receive each year?

For each of these bonds, calculate the total dollar amount you would pay at the quoted price (disregard commission or any interest that may have accrued):

	Company	Bond price	Number of bonds purchased	Dollar amount of purchase price
21–10.	Petro	87.75	3	________
21–11.	Wang	114	2	________

For the following bonds, calculate the total annual interest, total cost, and current yield (to the nearest tenth percent):

	Bond	Number of bonds purchased	Selling price	Total annual interest	Total cost	Current yield
21–12.	Sharn $11\frac{3}{4}$ 12	2	115	______	______	______
21–13.	Wang $6\frac{1}{2}$ 14	4	68.125	______	______	______

21–14. From the following calculate the net asset values. Round to the nearest cent.

	Current market value of fund investment	Current liabilities	Number of shares outstanding	NAV
a.	\$5,550,000	\$770,000	600,000	_____
b.	\$13,560,000	\$780,000	840,000	_____

21–15. From the following mutual fund quotation, complete the blanks:

				TOTAL RETURN		
	Inv. obj.	NAV	NAV chg.	YTD	4 wks.	1 yr.
EuGr	ITL	12.04	−0.06	+8.2	+0.9	+9.6

NAV ________ NAV change ________

Total return, 1 year ________

WORD PROBLEMS

21–16. Ryan Neal bought 1,200 shares of Ford at \$1.98 per share. Assume a commission of 2% of the purchase price. What is the total cost to Ryan?

21–17. Assume in Problem 21–16 that Ryan sells the stock for \$2.25 with the same 2% commission rate. What is the bottom line for Ryan?

21–18. Jim Corporation pays its cumulative preferred stockholders \$1.60 per share. Jim has 30,000 shares of preferred and 75,000 shares of common. In 2010, 2011, and 2012, due to slowdowns in the economy, Jim paid no dividends. Now in 2013, the board of directors decided to pay out \$500,000 in dividends. How much of the \$500,000 does each class of stock receive as dividends?

21–19. Maytag Company earns $4.80 per share. Today the stock is trading at $59.25. The company pays an annual dividend of $1.40. Calculate **(a)** the price-earnings ratio (round to the nearest whole number) and **(b)** the yield on the stock (to the nearest tenth percent).

21–20. The August 2009 issue of *Redbook* lists some easy ways to invest in bonds as mentioned in "Are Bonds a Safe Way to Invest?" by David Bach. He recommends purchasing savings bonds directly from the U.S. Treasury at savingsbonds.gov. Bond funds, as part of an IRA or employer's retirement plan, is another easy way. DeeDee Backstrom purchased a bond for 101 at 5% interest. How much did she pay for this bond? What is the current yield of this bond? Round to the nearest hundredth percent.

21–21. The following bond was quoted in the *Wall Street Journal:*

Bonds	Curr. yld.	Vol.	Close	Net chg.
NY Tel $7\frac{1}{4}$ 11	7.2	10	100.875	$+1\frac{1}{8}$

Five bonds were purchased yesterday, and 5 bonds were purchased today. How much more did the 5 bonds cost today (in dollars)?

21–22. Chris Luna is researching the DuPont Corporation. The following is the current stock listing: Price is $48.75, and the 52 week range $39–$49. Average earnings per share is $3.20 and the dividend is $1.47 **(a)** What is the P/E ratio to the nearest whole number? **(b)** What is the yield to the nearest hundredth?

21–23. Ron bought a bond of Bee Company for 79.25. The original bond was $5\frac{3}{4}$ 12. Ron wants to know the current yield (to the nearest tenth percent). Please help Ron with the calculation.

21–24. Abby Sane decided to buy corporate bonds instead of stock. She desired to have the fixed-interest payments. She purchased 5 bonds of Meg Corporation $11\frac{3}{4}$ 09 at 88.25. As the stockbroker for Abby (assume you charge her a $5 commission per bond), please provide her with the following: **(a)** the total cost of the purchase, **(b)** total annual interest to be received, and **(c)** current yield (to nearest tenth percent).

21–25. Mary Blake is considering whether to buy stocks or bonds. She has a good understanding of the pros and cons of both. The stock she is looking at is trading at $59.25, with an annual dividend of $3.99. Meanwhile, the bond is trading at 96.25, with an annual interest rate of $11\frac{1}{2}\%$. Calculate for Mary her yield (to the nearest tenth percent) for the stock and the bond.

21–26. The March 2009 edition of *Forbes* magazine listed Warren Buffett, largest shareholder and CEO of Berkshire Hathaway, as the second most wealthy billionaire in the world this year. This is down from his first-place ranking from last year after losing $25 billion in 12 months. Berkshire Hathaway (BRK-A) has a 52-week stock trading high of $147,000 and a low of $70,050. If you purchased 2 shares of BRK-A at $137,875 with a 3% commission, what is the commission paid on this transaction? What is the total price of the stock purchase?

21–27. Louis Hall read in the paper that Fidelity Growth Fund has a NAV of $16.02. He called Fidelity and asked them how the NAV was calculated. Fidelity gave him the following information:

Current market value of fund investment	$8,550,000
Current liabilities	$ 860,000
Number of shares outstanding	480,000

Did Fidelity provide Louis with the correct information?

21–28. Lee Ray bought 130 shares of a mutual fund with a NAV of $13.10. This fund also has a load charge of $8\frac{1}{2}\%$. **(a)** What is the offer price and **(b)** what did Lee pay for his investment?

21–29. Ron and Madeleine Couple received their 2010 Form 1099-DIV (dividends received) in the amount of $1,585. Ron and Madeleine are in the 28% bracket. What would be their tax liability on the dividends received?

CHALLENGE PROBLEMS

21–30. Mutual funds with a sales charge are called load funds. Those without a sales charge are called no-load funds. According to the mutual fund analyzer, www.morningstar.com, "No-load funds actually have a superior record to load funds over the last 3-year and 5-year periods. . . . Funds that impose no cost to purchase have outperformed those that brokers pay themselves to find for their clients." Vanguard Wellington (VWELX) has a NAV of $27.47 with no load. Jane Roche buys 150 shares. What is her total purchase price? What would her sales charge have been if this was a load fund with a sales charge of 5%? Round to the nearest cent.

21–31. On September 6, Irene Westing purchased one bond of Mick Corporation at 98.50. The bond pays $8\frac{3}{4}$ interest on June 1 and December 1. The stockbroker told Irene that she would have to pay the accrued interest and the market price of the bond and a \$6 brokerage fee. What was the total purchase price for Irene? Assume a 360-day year (each month is 30 days) in calculating the accrued interest. (*Hint:* Final cost = Cost of bond + Accrued interest + Brokerage fee. Calculate time for accrued interest.)

DVD SUMMARY PRACTICE TEST

1. Russell Slater bought 700 shares of Disney stock at \$24.90 per share. Assume a commission of 4% of the purchase price. What is the total cost to Russell? *(p. 495)*

2. Avis Company earns \$2.50 per share. Today, the stock is trading at \$18.99. The company pays an annual dividend of \$.25. Calculate **(a)** the price-earnings ratio (to the nearest whole number) and **(b)** the yield on the stock (to the nearest tenth percent). *(p. 495)*

3. The stock of Aware is trading at \$4.90. The price-earnings ratio is 4 times earnings. Calculate the earnings per share (to the nearest cent) for Aware. *(p. 495)*

4. Tom Fox bought 8 bonds of UXY Company $3\frac{1}{2}$ 09 at 84 and 4 bonds of Foot Company $4\frac{1}{8}$ 10 at 93. Assume the commission on the bonds is \$3 per bond. What was the total cost of all the purchases? *(p. 499)*

5. Leah Long bought one bond of Vick Company for 147. The original bond was 8.25 10. Leah wants to know the current yield to the nearest tenth percent. Help Leah with the calculation. *(p. 499)*

6. Cumulative preferred stockholders of Rale Company receive \$.80 per share. The company has 70,000 shares outstanding. For the last 9 years, Rale paid no dividends. This year, Rale paid \$400,000 in dividends. What is the amount of dividends in arrears that is still owed to preferred stockholders? *(p. 494)*

7. Bill Roundy bought 800 shares of a mutual fund with a NAV of \$14.10. This fund has a load charge of 3%. **(a)** What is the offer price and **(b)** what did Bill pay for the investment? *(p. 500)*

Personal Finance

A KIPLINGER APPROACH

ANATOMY OF A BOND

Everything you need to know before you buy an individual bond. BY ELIZABETH ODY

WHO'S THE ISSUER?
Coca-Cola Enterprises is the largest bottler and distributor of Coke products. Not to be confused with the Coca-Cola Co., which develops beverages and sells syrups to bottlers, Coca-Cola Enterprises generated sales of $22 billion in the four quarters that ended last September.

WHAT'S THE INTEREST?
This issue pays 7.125% on a face value of $1,000, or $71.25 a year per bond, in semiannual payments.

WHAT DOES IT COST?
Think of the quoted price—111.707—as a percentage of the bond's $1,000 face value. Each bond sells for $1,117—at a premium—because the 7.125% interest coupon is better than the going rate on similar bonds. Brokerage commissions are usually built into the price of a bond. But Fidelity, on whose Web site we found this IOU, tacks a $1-per-bond commission on top of the quoted price.

WHEN DOES IT MATURE?
As long as Coca-Cola Enterprises doesn't go bust, it will repay bondholders on August 1, 2017.

WHAT DOES IT EARN?
The yield to maturity, which is 5.40%, sums up the total return you'll earn on your investment of $1,117 per bond if you hold until maturity. This figure takes into account all the cash payments you'll receive over the life of the bond and the loss of the $117-per-bond premium when you receive the bond's $1,000 face value at maturity.

WHAT'S THE QUALITY?
A single-A credit rating is solid but not bulletproof. It signals that the company should be able to repay its debts under current business conditions, but it could run into problems if the economy or its industry weakens. The firm's $9.4 billion in total debt works out to a debt-to-capital ratio of 0.5, which is reasonable for its industry. Keep in mind that bond raters are not infallible.

		Description	Coupon	Maturity Date ▽	Rating Moody's	Rating S&P	Price Bid Ask	Yield Bid Ask	Quantity Bid(min) Ask(min)	Yield Type	❸❹ utes
☐ 218	Trade	*COCA COLA ENTERPRI❶S INC 7.12500% 08/01/2017 DEB	7.125	08/01/2017	A3	A	-- 111.707	-- 5.400	-❷-) 20 (10)	M	IE CP PO RO SFP

❶ DEB : This bond is a debenture, which means it is not backed by collateral, such as buildings or equipment.

❷ 20 (10): There are 20 bonds available for purchase, and the minimum investment quantity is 10 bonds, or $11,171, at this price.

❸ IE: *Issuer Event* signals some relatively recent news about the company that affects its bonds—in this case, a Moody's downgrade.

❹ CP: *Call Protection* means the issuer isn't allowed to pay back bondholders early (see box on facing page).

YOU CAN FIND INFORMATION ON OTHER ABBREVIATIONS—*PO* FOR PRICE OUTLIER; *RO* FOR RISK OUTLIER; AND *SFP* FOR SINKING FUND PROTECTION—ON YOUR BROKER'S WEB SITE.

From *Kiplinger's Personal Finance,* March 2009, p. 27.

BUSINESS MATH ISSUE

Bonds are always a better investment than stocks.

1. List the key points of the article and information to support your position.
2. Write a group defense of your position using math calculations to support your view.

Slater's Business Math Scrapbook

Applying Your Skills

PROJECT A

With the economy the way it is, Macy's will continue to struggle. Do you agree with this statement. Defend your position.

Macy's to Shed 7,000 Jobs, Cut Payout by 62%

By Rachel Dodes

Macy's Inc. said it is eliminating 7,000 jobs, or 4% of its work force, and taking other steps to cut costs, in the latest sign that slumping consumer spending is forcing retailers to change the way they do business.

The Cincinnati-based operator of 840 department stores also said it is cutting its dividend by 62%, ending merit pay increases for executives and slashing its 2009 capital-spending budget by another \$100 million to \$150 million to around \$450 million. The original budget was \$1 billion.

"This is a time where nothing should be considered a sacred cow," said Macy's Chief Executive Terry Lundgren in a conference call with analysts Monday.

The moves are expected to save the company \$250 million this year and \$400 million a year thereafter.

Separately, Macy's said it is launching a tender offer to buy back \$950 million in debt maturing in 2009, using cash on hand. The offer will expire at 5:00 p.m. EST next Tuesday. Chief Financial Officer Karen Hoguet described the decision not to refinance the maturing debt as part of a "deleveraging strategy."

Macy's shares were down 00 cents, or 4%, at \$8.59 Monday in 4 p.m. composite trading on the New York Stock Exchange.

The job cuts are part of a broad reorganization that will merge four different buying and planning offices into one centralized unit. Macy's said it will also roll out nationwide an experimental program called "My Macy's," in which 15% of a store's merchandise is tailored to local tastes. Launched in 20 markets in the spring of 2008, the program will be extended to 49 more "districts" in the second quarter.

Mr. Lundgren said the program has shown early signs of success: 13 of Macy's top 15 performing geographic markets in December were in "My Macy's" pilot regions. "That has given us the confidence we can expand 'My Macy's' across the country," he said.

The company, which had revenue of \$25.5 billion in the 12 months ended Nov. 1, offered a gloomy outlook for the rest of the fiscal year ending this month, predicting sales at stores open at least a year would be down 6% to 8% from a year earlier. It forecast earnings in the range of 40 cents to 55 cents a share, well below consensus estimates of 87 cents a share, according to Thomson Reuters.

Moody's Investor Service said it put Macy's credit ratings under review for a possible downgrade, citing the lower forecasts. Thursday, Macy's plans to announce sales figures for January, which analysts expect to be down 6.3%.

As part of the reorganization, two top members of Mr. Lundgren's team said they will retire when their contracts expire. Susan Kronick, 57 years old, who oversaw Macy's four divisions and will now work on the transition to one, will retire in early 2010. Janet Grove, 58, who had been chairman and chief executive of Macy's Merchandising Group, will oversee international store development initiatives until she retires 2011. Another senior executive, Tom Cody, 67, will retire in 2010.

Mr. Lundgren said in an interview that all three executives had been planning to retire, but "none of them wanted to leave at a time when the company was going through these changes."

Bloomberg News/Landov

Macy's is slashing spending. Above, the New York flagship store on Monday.

Internet Projects: See text Web site (www.mhhe.com/slater10e) and The Business Math Internet Resource Guide.

Video Case

Federal Signal Corporation

Federal Signal Corporation began its operations in 1901. The company is a manufacturer and worldwide supplier of safety, signaling, and communications equipment; hazardous area lighting; fire rescue vehicles; vehicle-mounted aerial access platforms; and street sweeping and vacuum loader vehicles. The four major operating groups are Safety Products, Tool, Environmental Products, and Fire Rescue.

U.S. fire departments buy 3,000 to 4,000 fire trucks every year, priced from $110,000 for a small pumper to more than $600,000 for an elaborate aerial ladder. Federal Signal, a publicly held corporation, is one of the largest national players with an estimated 20% of the U.S. market, but its share of the crowded international market is still only about 20%.

While the economic downshift has hurt most manufacturers of trucks and heavy equipment, it appears to have helped Federal Signal by making available the raw materials the company needs. Four years ago, Federal Signal was struggling to get enough chassis to manufacture a growing backlog of fire truck orders at its three North American fire truck plants. The chassis shortage pulled down profits for the company's Fire Rescue Group. Federal Signal began turning the corner on the chassis shortage, primarily because of its suppliers' bad fortune.

Now the market for big trucks is oversaturated. That's bad news for truck manufacturers but good news for Federal Signal, which is whittling down some of its backorders for fire trucks and, as a result, picking up its bottom line and stock price.

One factor that protects Federal Signal during economic downturns is municipal budgeting. Generally, municipalities have longer lead time for spending on bigger capital equipment. Since Federal Signal is not dependent on private industry for business, the future does look as bright as Federal's warning lights.

PROBLEM 1

The Fire Rescue Group is Federal Signal's biggest sales generator with revenue of $310 million, followed by the Safety Products Group with $262 million and the Environment Products Group with $247 million. What percent are the sales of the Fire Rescue Group to the total sales? Round to the nearest hundredth percent.

PROBLEM 2

With Federal Signal stock selling at $23.22, there were 58,200 shares traded in one day on the New York Stock Exchange. What was the total value of the stock traded?

PROBLEM 3

Federal Signal's current assets were as follows:

Cash and cash equivalents	$ 15,336
Trade accounts receivable	162,878
Inventories	176,892
Prepaid expenses	10,745

Current liabilities totaled $362,457. What is Federal Signal's current ratio? Round to the nearest hundredth.

PROBLEM 4

With a share price of $23.22 for Federal Signal stock: **(a)** What would be the price of 300 shares with a 2% commission? **(b)** Earnings per share (EPS) are $1.23; what would be the price-earnings (PE) ratio? Round to the nearest whole number.

PROBLEM 5

With a $23.22 closing price and an annual dividend of $.78, what would be Federal Signal's dividend yield? Round to the nearest hundredth percent.

PROBLEM 6

Federal Signal has a quarterly EPS of $.26. The company expects the quarterly EPS to grow by 14%. What is the expected dollar amount for the quarterly EPS? Round to the nearest cent.

PROBLEM 7

Federal Signal's interest expense increased to $7.8 million from $7.0 million, largely as a result of increased financial services assets. What was the percent increase in interest expense? Round to the nearest hundredth percent.

PROBLEM 8

Net cash provided by operations for the first quarter was $21.9 million, up 30% from last year. What was last year's cash flow?

Classroom Notes

chapter

22 BUSINESS STATISTICS

SpongeBob is the most most watched show on Nickelodeon.

Dawn Villella/AP Photo

Debit-Card Use Overtakes Credit

Visa's Results Show Tilt Toward Paying It Now; What Does It Mean?

By Robin Sidel

Brad Sagara uses a debit card to buy everything from groceries to climbing gear to bottled water. He barely uses his two credit cards anymore, and is trying to pay off a combined balance of $4,000.

"The painful realization is that I need to be an adult, and this is a time to save," said Mr. Sagara, a 26-year-old consulting-firm analyst who lives in Tucson, Ariz.

Wall Street Journal © 2009

LEARNING UNIT OBJECTIVES

LU 22–1: Mean, Median, and Mode

1. Define and calculate the mean *(p. 516)*.
2. Explain and calculate a weighted mean *(p. 516)*.
3. Define and calculate the median *(p. 518)*.
4. Define and identify the mode *(p. 518)*.

LU 22–2: Frequency Distributions and Graphs

1. Prepare a frequency distribution *(pp. 519–520)*.
2. Prepare bar, line, and circle graphs *(pp. 520–522)*.
3. Calculate price relatives and cost comparisons *(p. 523)*.

LU 22–3: Measures of Dispersion (Optional)

1. Explain and calculate the range *(p. 524)*.
2. Define and calculate the standard deviation *(p. 524)*.
3. Estimate percentage of data by using standard deviations *(p. 525)*.

VOCABULARY PREVIEW

Here are key terms in this chapter. After completing the chapter, if you know the term, place a checkmark in the parenthesis. If you don't know the term, look it up and put the page number where it can be found.

Bar graph . ( ) Circle graph . ( ) Frequency distribution . ( ) Index numbers . ( ) Line graph . ( ) Mean . ( ) Measure of dispersion . ( ) Median . ( ) Mode . ( ) Normal distribution . ( ) Price relative . ( ) Range . ( ) Standard deviation . ( ) Weighted mean . ( )

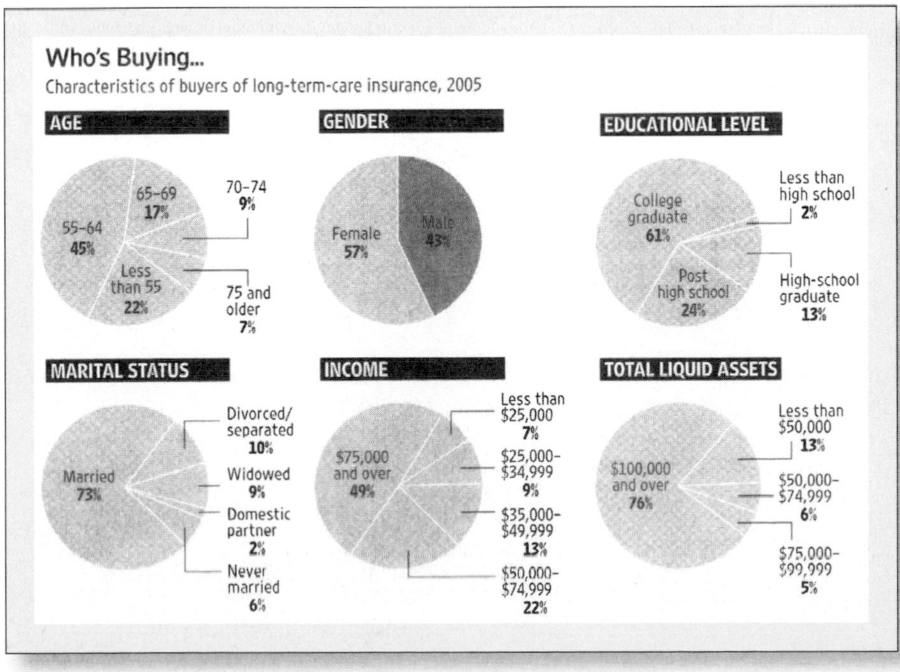

Buying long-term health insurance is not cheap. Premiums could range from $1,500 to $5,000 per year. Note in the *Wall Street Journal* clip the characteristics of those buying long-term health care.

In this chapter we look at various techniques that analyze and graphically represent business statistics. Learning Unit 22–1 discusses the mean, median, and mode. Learning Unit 22–2 explains how to gather data by using frequency distributions and to express these data visually in graphs. Emphasis is placed on whether graphs are indeed giving accurate information. The chapter concludes with an introduction to index numbers—an application of statistics—and an optional learning unit on measures of dispersion.

Learning Unit 22–1: Mean, Median, and Mode

Companies frequently use averages and measurements to guide their business decisions. The mean and median are the two most common averages used to indicate a single value that represents an entire group of numbers. The mode can also be used to describe a set of data.

Mean

The accountant of Bill's Sport Shop told Bill, the owner, that the average daily sales for the week were $150.14. The accountant stressed that $150.14 was an average and did not represent specific daily sales. Bill wanted to know how the accountant arrived at $150.14.

LO 1

The accountant went on to explain that he used an arithmetic average, or **mean** (a measurement), to arrive at $150.14 (rounded to the nearest hundredth). He showed Bill the following formula:

$$\text{Mean} = \frac{\text{Sum of all values}}{\text{Number of values}}$$

The accountant used the following data:

	Sun.	Mon.	Tues.	Wed.	Thur.	Fri.	Sat.
Sport Shop sales	$400	$100	$68	$115	$120	$68	$180

To compute the mean, the accountant used these data:

$$\text{Mean} = \frac{\$400 + \$100 + \$68 + \$115 + \$120 + \$68 + \$180}{7} = \$150.14$$

When values appear more than once, businesses often look for a **weighted mean.** The format for the weighted mean is slightly different from that for the mean. The concept, however, is the same except that you weight each value by how often it occurs (its frequency). Thus, considering the frequency of the occurrence of each value allows a weighting of each day's sales in proper importance. To calculate the weighted mean, use the following formula:

$$\text{Weighted mean} = \frac{\text{Sum of products}}{\text{Sum of frequencies}}$$

LO 2

Let's change the sales data for Bill's Sport Shop and see how to calculate a weighted mean:

	Sun.	Mon.	Tues.	Wed.	Thur.	Fri.	Sat.
Sport Shop sales	$400	$100	$100	$80	$80	$100	$400

Value	Frequency	Product
$400	2	$ 800
100	3	300
80	2	160
		$1,260

The weighted mean is $\frac{\$1,260}{7} = \$180$

Note how we multiply each value by its frequency of occurrence to arrive at the product. Then we divide the sum of the products by the sum of the frequencies.

When you calculate your grade point average (GPA), you are using a weighted average. The following formula is used to calculate GPA:

$$\text{GPA} = \frac{\text{Total points}}{\text{Total credits}}$$

Now let's show how Jill Rivers calculated her GPA to the nearest tenth.

Given A = 4; B = 3; C = 2; D = 1; F = 0

Courses	Credits attempted	Grade received	Points (Credits × Grade)	
Introduction to Computers	4	A	16 (4 × 4)	
Psychology	3	B	9 (3 × 3)	
English Composition	3	B	9 (3 × 3)	
Business Law	3	C	6 (2 × 3)	
Business Math	3	B	9 (3 × 3)	
	16		49	$\frac{49}{16}$ = 3.1

When high or low numbers do not significantly affect a list of numbers, the mean is a good indicator of the center of the data. If high or low numbers do have an effect, the median may be a better indicator to use.

LO 3

Median

The **median** is another measurement that indicates the center of the data. An average that has one or more extreme values is not distorted by the median. As you can see from the *Wall Street Journal* clipping, "A Heavier Burden," medians for property taxes are shown for various states. For example, let's look at the following yearly salaries of the employees of Rusty's Clothing Shop.

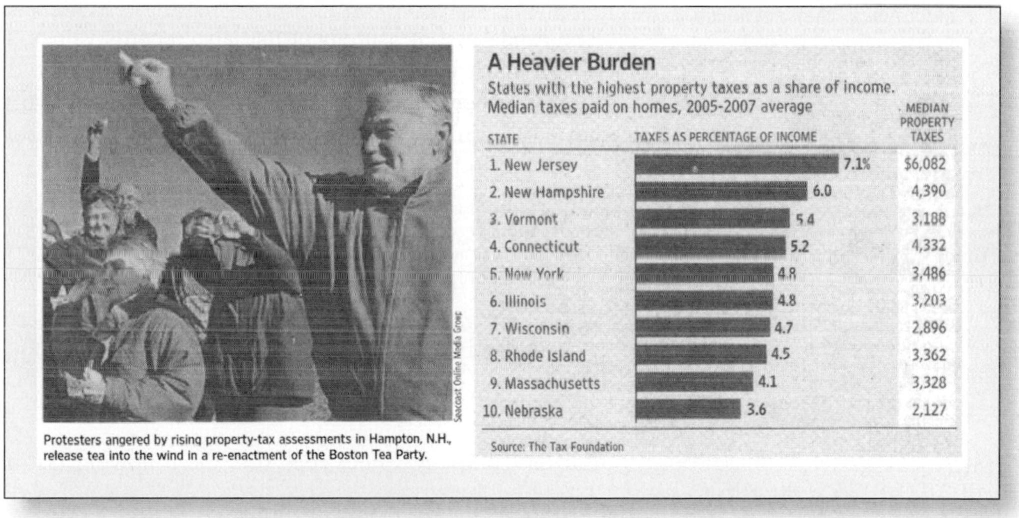

Alice Knight	$95,000	Jane Wang	$67,000
Jane Hess	27,000	Bill Joy	40,000
Joel Floyd	32,000		

Note how Alice's salary of $95,000 will distort an average calculated by the mean.

$$\frac{\$95{,}000 + \$27{,}000 + \$32{,}000 + \$67{,}000 + \$40{,}000}{5} = \$52{,}200$$

The $52,200 average salary is considerably more than the salary of three of the employees. So it is not a good representation of the store's average salary. Let's use the following steps to find the median.

FINDING THE MEDIAN OF A GROUP OF VALUES

Step 1. Orderly arrange values from the smallest to the largest.

Step 2. Find the middle value.

- **a.** *Odd number of values:* Median is the middle value. You find this by first dividing the total number of numbers by 2. The next-higher number is the median.
- **b.** *Even number of values:* Median is the average of the two middle values.

For Rusty's Clothing Shop, we find the median as follows:

1. Arrange values from smallest to largest:
   $27,000; $32,000; $40,000; $67,000; $95,000
2. Since the middle value is an odd number, $40,000 is the median. Note that half of the salaries fall below the median and half fall above ($5 \div 2 = 2\frac{1}{2}$—next number is the median).

If Jane Hess ($27,000) were not on the payroll, we would find the median as follows:

1. Arrange values from smallest to largest:
   $32,000; $40,000; $67,000; $95,000
2. Average the two middle values:

$$\frac{\$40{,}000 + \$67{,}000}{2} = \$53{,}500$$

Note that the median results in two salaries below and two salaries above the average.

Now we'll look at another measurement tool—the mode.

$ MONEY TIPS

Reduce the mean utility bill in your household by installing a smart thermometer, buying compact fluorescent light bulbs, replacing pre-1994 inefficient shower heads, caulking and weather-stripping doors and windows, hooking up power strips to easily turn off electronics when not in use, and flushing your toilet frugally.

LO 4

Mode

The **mode** is a measurement that also records values. In a series of numbers, the value that occurs most often is the mode. If all the values are different, there is no mode. If two or more numbers appear most often, you may have two or more modes. Note that we do not have to arrange the numbers in the lowest-to-highest order, although this could make it easier to find the mode.

EXAMPLE 3, 4, 5, 6, 3, 8, 9, 3, 5, 3

3 is the mode since it is listed 4 times.

Now let's check your progress with a Practice Quiz.

LU 22–1 PRACTICE QUIZ

Complete this **Practice Quiz** to see how you are doing.

Barton Company's sales reps sold the following last month:

Sales rep	Sales volume	Sales rep	Sales volume
A	$16,500	C	$12,000
B	15,000	D	48,900

Calculate the mean and the median. Which is the better indicator of the center of the data? Is there a mode?

Solutions with Step-by-Step Help on DVD

✓ Solutions

$$\text{Mean} = \frac{\$16{,}500 + \$15{,}000 + \$12{,}000 + \$48{,}900}{4} = \$23{,}100$$

$$\text{Median} = \frac{\$15{,}000 + \$16{,}500}{2} = \$15{,}750$$

$12,000, $15,000, $16,500, $48,900. Note how we arrange numbers from smallest to highest to calculate median.

Median is the better indicator since in calculating the mean, the $48,900 puts the average of $23,100 much too high. There is no mode.

LU 22–1a EXTRA PRACTICE QUIZ WITH WORKED-OUT SOLUTIONS

Need more practice? Try this **Extra Practice Quiz** (check figures in Chapter Organizer, p. 528). Worked-out Solutions can be found in Appendix B at end of text.

Barton's Company sales reps sold the following last month:

Sales rep	Sales volume	Sales rep	Sales volume
A	$17,000	C	$11,000
B	14,000	D	51,000

Calculate the mean and median. Which is the better indicator of the center of the data? Is there a mode?

Learning Unit 22–2: Frequency Distributions and Graphs

In this unit you will learn how to gather data and illustrate these data. Today, computer software programs can make beautiful color graphics. But how accurate are these graphics? This *Wall Street Journal* clipping gives an example of graphics that did not agree with the numbers beneath them. The clipping reminds all readers to check the numbers illustrated by the graphics.

What's Wrong With this Picture? Utility's Glasses Are Never Empty

By Kathleen Deveny
Staff Reporter of The Wall Street Journal

When Les Waas, an investor in Philadelphia Suburban Corp., paged through the company's 1994 annual report, he was impressed by what he saw.

The water utility had used a series of charts to represent its revenues, net income and book value per share, among other results. Each figure was represented by the level of water in a glass. Each chart showed strong growth.

Then Mr. Waas looked a little more carefully. The bars in the chart seemed to indicate far more impressive growth than the numbers beneath them. A chart showing the growth in the number of Philadelphia Suburban's water customers, for example, seemed to indicate the company's customer base had more than tripled since 1990. But the numbers actually increased only 6.4%.

The reason for the disparity: The charts don't begin at zero. Even an empty glass in the accompanying chart would represent a customer base of 230,000.

Wall Street Journal © 1995

LO 1

Collecting raw data and organizing the data is a prerequisite to presenting statistics graphically. Let's illustrate this by looking at the following example.

A computer industry consultant wants to know how much college freshmen are willing to spend to set up a computer in their dormitory rooms. After visiting a local college dorm, the consultant gathered the following data on the amount of money 20 students spent on computers:

$1,000	$7,000	$4,000	$1,000	$ 5,000	$1,000	$3,000
5,000	2,000	3,000	3,000	3,000	8,000	9,000
3,000	6,000	6,000	1,000	10,000	1,000	

Note that these raw data are not arranged in any order. To make the data more meaningful, the consultant made the **frequency distribution** table. Think of this distribution table as a way to organize a list of numbers to show the patterns that may exist.

Price of computer	Tally	Frequency
$ 1,000	𝍸	5
2,000	I	1
3,000	𝍸	5
4,000	I	1
5,000	II	2
6,000	II	2
7,000	I	1
8,000	I	1
9,000	I	1
10,000	I	1

As you can see, 25% ($\frac{5}{20} = \frac{1}{4} = 25\%$) of the students spent $1,000 and another 25% spent $3,000. Only four students spent $7,000 or more.

Now let's see how we can use bar graphs.

Bar Graphs

Bar graphs help readers see the changes that have occurred over a period of time. This is especially true when the same type of data is repeatedly studied. Note the following example of the use of bar graphs.

The following *Wall Street Journal* clippings, "Moving Target" and "Gas Engines Rev Up," use bar graphs to show the amount of mobile advertising spending and the projected sales of cars and trucks.

LO 2

Wall Street Journal © 2008

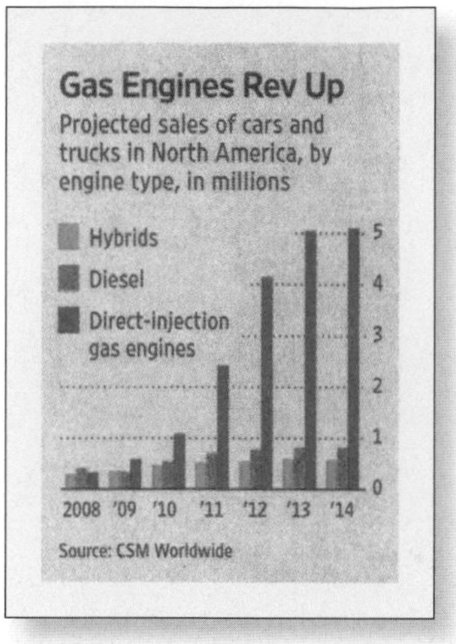

Wall Street Journal © 2009

Let's return to our computer consultant example and make a bar graph of the computer purchases data collected by the consultant. Note that the height of the bar represents the frequency of each purchase. Bar graphs can be vertical or horizontal.

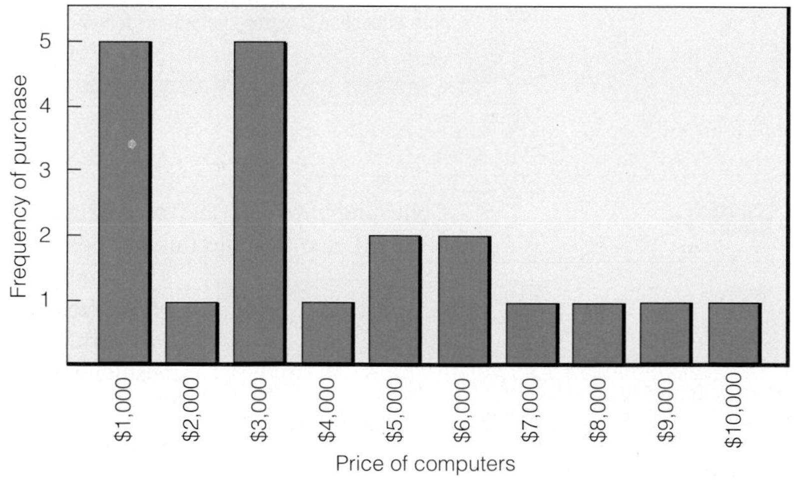

We can simplify this bar graph by grouping the prices of the computers. The grouping, or *intervals,* should be of equal sizes.

A bar graph for the grouped data follows.

Class	Frequency
$1,000–$3,000.99	11
3,001– 5,000.99	3
5,001– 7,000.99	3
7,001– 9,000.99	2
9,001–11,000.99	1

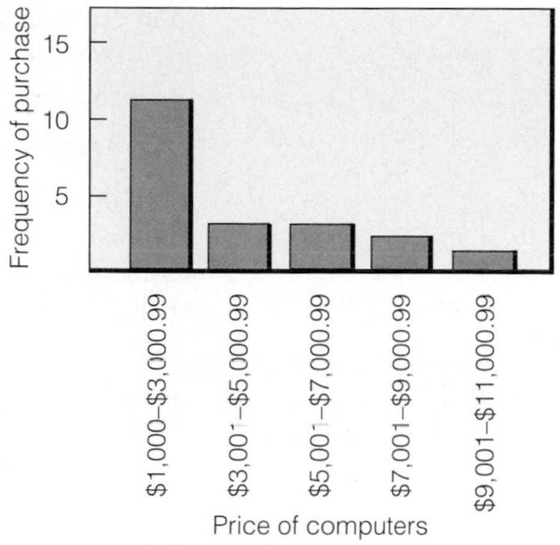

Next, let's see how we can use line graphs.

Line Graphs

A **line graph** shows trends over a period of time. Often separate lines are drawn to show the comparison between two or more trends.

Note the trend in higher emissions of carbon dioxide, which is contributing to global warming.

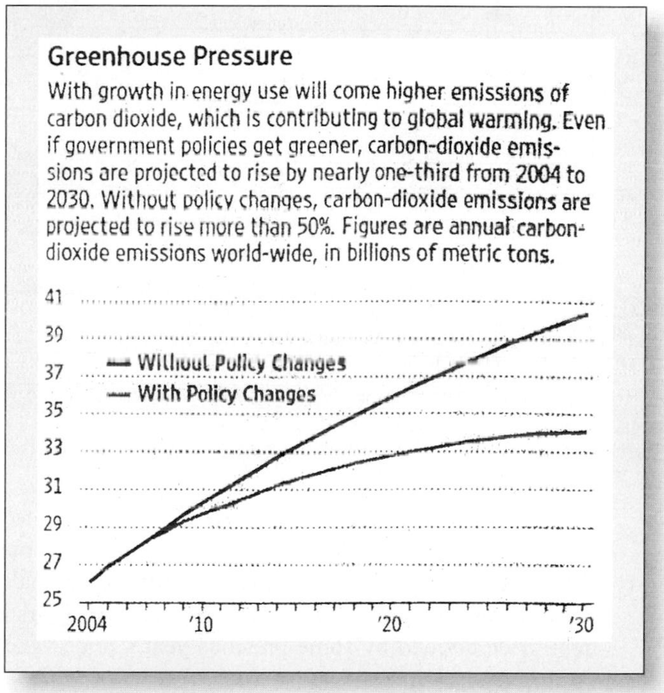

National E. © 2005 *Higher Education Advocate*.

We conclude our discussion of graphics with the use of the circle graph.

Circle Graphs

.15 × 360° = 54.0
.11 × 360° = 39.6
.36 × 360° = 129.6
.38 × 360° = 136.8
360.0

Circle graphs, often called *pie charts,* are especially helpful for showing the relationship of parts to a whole. The entire circle represents 100%, or 360°; the pie-shaped pieces represent the subcategories. Note at the middle of the following page (p. 522) how the circle graph in the *Wall Street Journal* clipping "An Enduring Challenge," uses pie charts to show the world energy outlook by 2030.

To draw a circle graph (or pie chart), begin by drawing a circle. Then take the percentages and convert each percentage to a decimal. Next multiply each decimal by 360° to get the degrees represented by the percentage. Circle graphs must total 360°.

We conclude this unit with a brief discussion of index numbers.

An Application of Statistics: Index Numbers

The financial section of a newspaper often gives different index numbers describing the changes in business. These **index numbers** express the relative changes in a variable compared with some base, which is taken as 100. The changes may be measured from time to time or from place to place. Index numbers function as percents and are calculated like percents.

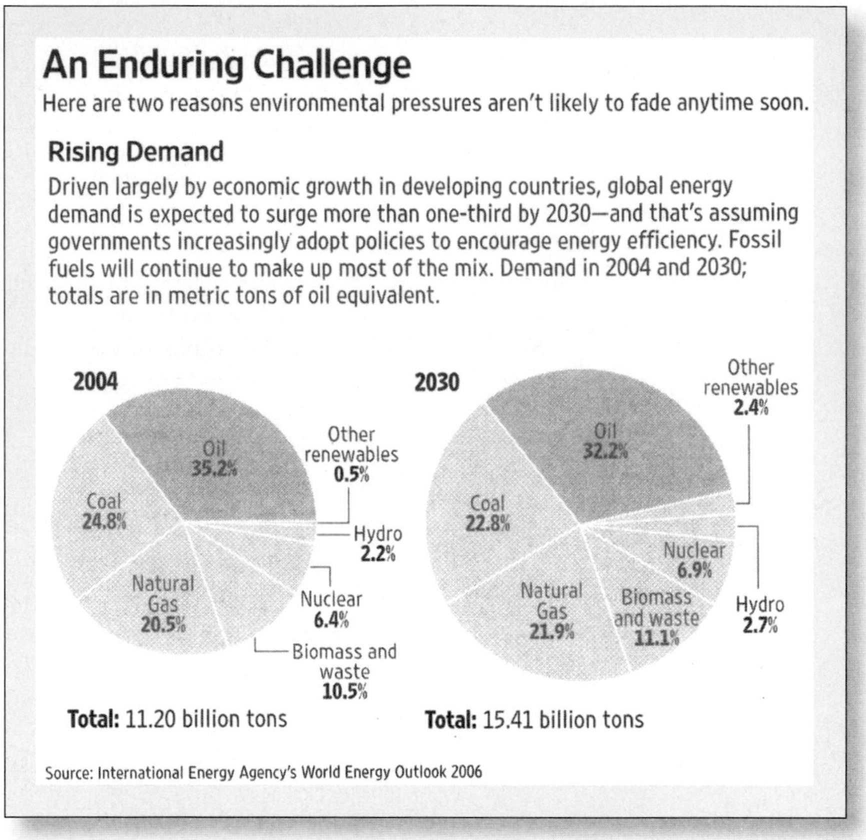

Wall Street Journal © 2007

LO 3

MONEY TIPS

Check out the many free money-management online sites. Do an Internet search for the one that fits your needs. You can track your accounts, create pie charts, bar charts, and other graphics depicting your spending habits. Graphing your common expenditures such as money you spend on entertainment by month may assist you in seeing a spending trend you may want to alter.

Frequently, a business will use index numbers to make comparisons of a current price relative to a given year. For example, a calculator may cost \$9 today relative to a cost of \$75 some 30 years ago. The **price relative** of the calculator is $\frac{\$9}{\$75} \times 100 = 12\%$. The calculator now costs 12% of what it cost some 30 years ago. A price relative, then, is the current price divided by some previous year's price—the base year—multiplied by 100.

$$\text{Price relative} = \frac{\text{Current price}}{\text{Base year's price}} \times 100$$

Index numbers can also be used to estimate current prices at various geographic locations. The frequently quoted Consumer Price Index (CPI), calculated and published monthly by the U.S. Bureau of Labor Statistics, records the price relative percentage cost of many goods and services nationwide compared to a base period. Table 22.1 (p. 523) gives a portion of the CPI that uses 1982–84 as its base period. Note that the table shows, for example, that the price relative for housing in Los Angeles is 139.3% of what it cost in 1982–84. Thus, Los Angeles housing costs amounting to \$100.00 in 1982–84 now cost \$139.30. So if you built a \$90,000 house in 1982–84, it is worth \$125,370 today. (Convert 139.3% to the decimal 1.393; multiply \$90,000 by 1.393 = \$125,370.)

Once again, we complete the unit with a Practice Quiz.

TABLE 22.1

Consumer Price Index (in percent)

Expense	Atlanta	Chicago	New York	Los Angeles
Food	131.9	130.3	139.6	130.9
Housing	128.8	131.4	139.3	139.3
Clothing	133.8	124.3	121.8	126.4
Medical care	177.6	163.0	172.4	163.3

LU 22–2 PRACTICE QUIZ

Complete this **Practice Quiz** to see how you are doing.

1. The following is the number of sales made by 20 salespeople on a given day. Prepare a frequency distribution and a bar graph. Do not use intervals for this example.

5	8	9	1	4	4	0	3	2	8
8	9	5	1	9	6	7	5	9	10

2. Assuming the following market shares for diapers 5 years ago, prepare a circle graph:

Pampers	32%	Huggies	24%
Luvs	20%	Others	24%

3. Today a new Explorer costs \$30,000. In 1991 the Explorer cost \$19,000. What is the price relative? Round to the nearest tenth percent.

Solutions with Step-by-Step Help on DVD

✓ Solutions

1.

Number of sales	Tally	Frequency
0	I	1
1	II	2
2	I	1
3	I	1
4	II	2
5	III	3
6	I	1
7	I	1
8	III	3
9	IIII	4
10	I	1

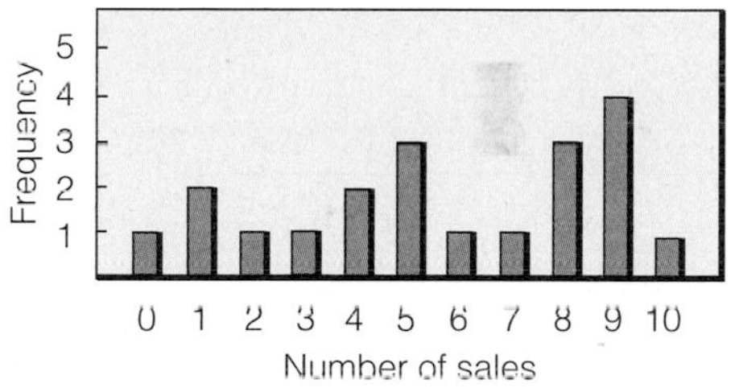

2.

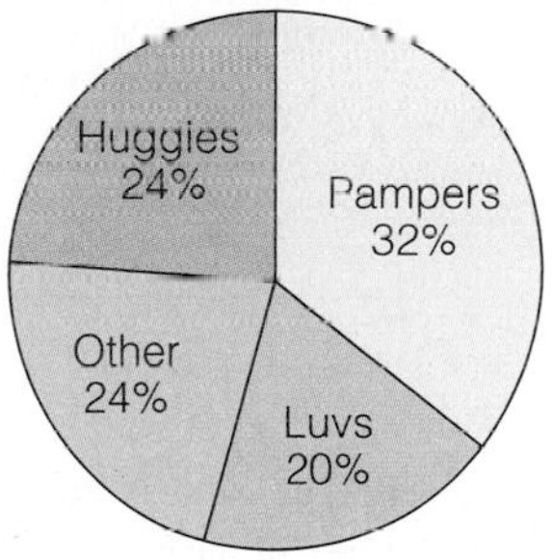

$.32 \times 360° = 115.20°$

$.20 \times 360° = 72.00°$

$.24 \times 360° = 86.40°$

$.24 \times 360° = 86.40°$

3. $\dfrac{\$30{,}000}{\$19{,}000} \times 100 = 157.9$

LU 22–2a EXTRA PRACTICE QUIZ WITH WORKED-OUT SOLUTIONS

Need more practice? Try this **Extra Practice Quiz** (check figures in Chapter Organizer, p. 528). Worked-out Solutions can be found in Appendix B at end of text.

1. The following is the number of sales made by 20 salespeople on a given day. Prepare a frequency distribution and a bar graph. Do not use intervals for this example.

0	8	9	1	4	4	0	3	2	8
8	9	0	1	9	6	7	0	9	10

2. Assuming the following market shares for diapers 5 years ago, prepare a circle graph.

Pampers	40%	Huggies	25%
Luvs	20%	Others	15%

3. Today a new Explorer costs \$35,000. In 1991, the Explorer cost \$19,000. What is the price relative? Round to the nearest tenth percent.

Learning Unit 22–3: Measures of Dispersion (Optional)

In Learning Unit 22–1 you learned how companies use the mean, median, and mode to indicate a single value, or number, that represents an entire group of numbers, or data. Often it is valuable to know how the information is scattered (spread or dispersed) within a data set. A **measure of dispersion** is a number that describes how the numbers of a set of data are spread out or dispersed.

This learning unit discusses three measures of dispersion—range, standard deviation, and normal distribution. We begin with the range—the simplest measure of dispersion.

Range

LO 1

The **range** is the difference between the two extreme values (highest and lowest) in a group of values or a set of data. For example, often the actual extreme values of hourly temperature readings during the past 24 hours are given but not the range or difference between the high and low readings. To find the range in a group of data, subtract the lowest value from the highest value.

Range = Highest value − Lowest value

Thus, if the high temperature reading during the past 24 hours was 90° and the low temperature reading was 60° the range is 90° − 60°, or 30°.

The range is difficult to use since it depends only on the values of the extremes and not on other values in the data set. Also, the range depends on the *number* of values on which it is based; that is, the larger the number of values, the larger the range is apt to be. The range gives only a general idea of the spread of values in a data set.

EXAMPLE Find the range of the following values: 83.6, 77.3, 69.2, 93.1, 85.4, 71.6.

Range = 93.1 − 69.2 = 23.9

Standard Deviation

Since the **standard deviation** is intended to measure the spread of data around the mean, you must first determine the mean of a set of data. The following diagram shows two sets of data—A and B. In the diagram, the means of A and B are equal. Now look at how the data in these two sets are spread or dispersed.

LO 2

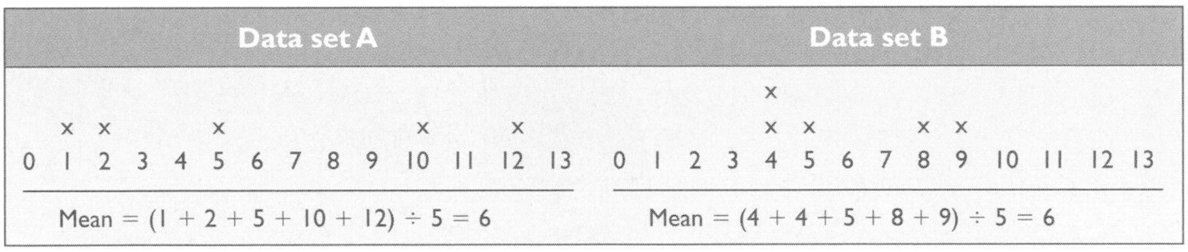

Note that although the means of data sets A and B are equal, A is more widely dispersed, which means B will have a smaller standard deviation than A.

To find the standard deviation of an ungrouped set of data, use the following steps:

FINDING THE STANDARD DEVIATION

Step 1. Find the mean of the set of data.

Step 2. Subtract the mean from each piece of data to find each deviation.

Step 3. Square each deviation (multiply the deviation by itself).

Step 4. Sum all squared deviations.

Step 5. Divide the sum of the squared deviations by $n - 1$, where n equals the number of pieces of data.

Step 6. Find the square root ($\sqrt{\ }$) of the number obtained in Step 5 (use a calculator). This is the standard deviation. (The square root is a number that when multiplied by itself equals the amount shown inside the square root symbol.)

Two additional points should be made. First, Step 2 sometimes results in negative numbers. Since the sum of the deviations obtained in Step 2 should always be zero, we would not be able to find the average deviation. This is why we square each deviation—to generate positive quantities only. Second, the standard deviation we refer to is used with *sample* sets of data, that is, a collection of data from a population. The population is the *entire* collection of data. When the standard deviation for a population is calculated, the sum of the squared deviations is divided by n instead of by $n - 1$. In all problems that follow, sample sets of data are being examined.

EXAMPLE Calculate the standard deviations for the sample data sets A and B given in the diagram on p. 524. Round the final answer to the nearest tenth. Note that Step 1—find the mean—is given in the diagram.

Standard deviation of data sets A and B: The table on the left uses Steps 2 through 6 to find the standard deviation of data set A, and the table on the right uses Steps 2 through 6 to find the standard deviation of data set B.

Data	Step 2 Data − Mean	Step 3 (Data − Mean)^2
1	1 − 6 = −5	25
2	2 − 6 = −4	16
5	5 − 6 = −1	1
10	10 − 6 = 4	16
12	12 − 6 = 6	36
	Total 0	94 **(Step 4)**

Step 5: Divide by $n - 1$: $\frac{94}{5-1} = \frac{94}{4} = 23.5$

Step 6: The square root of $\sqrt{23.5}$ is 4.8 (rounded).

The standard deviation of data set A is 4.8.

Data	Step 2 Data − Mean	Step 3 (Data − Mean)^2
4	4 − 6 = −2	4
4	4 − 6 = −2	4
5	5 − 6 = −1	1
8	8 − 6 = 2	4
9	9 − 6 = 3	9
	Total 0	22 **(Step 4)**

Step 5: Divide by $n - 1$: $\frac{22}{5-1} = \frac{22}{4} = 5.5$

Step 6: The square root of $\sqrt{5.5}$ is 2.3.

The standard deviation of data set B is 2.3.

As suspected, the standard deviation of data set B is less than that of set A. The standard deviation value reinforces what we see in the diagram.

LO 3

Normal Distribution

One of the most important distributions of data is the **normal distribution.** In a normal distribution, data are spread *symmetrically* about the mean. A graph of such a distribution looks like the bell-shaped curve in Figure 22.1. Many data sets are normally distributed. Examples are the life span of automobile engines, women's heights, and intelligence quotients.

FIGURE 22.1

Standard deviation and the normal distribution

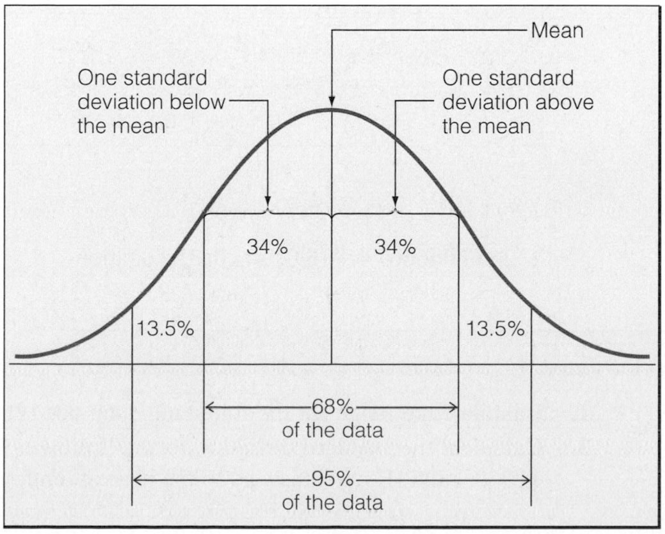

In a normal distribution, the data are spread out symmetrically—50% of the data lie above the mean, and 50% of the data lie below the mean. Additionally, if the data are normally distributed, 68% of the data should be found within one standard deviation above and below the mean. About 95% of the data should be found within two standard deviations above and below the mean. Figure 22.1 illustrates these facts.

MONEY TIPS

Save money on gas. Quit aggressive driving, get rid of unneeded weight stored in your vehicle, keep it tuned, tires inflated, and air filters replaced regularly saving up to 35% on fuel consumption and reducing the dispersion of your gas mileage.

EXAMPLE Assume that the mean useful life of a particular lightbulb is 2,000 hours and is normally distributed with a standard deviation of 300 hours. Calculate the useful life of the lightbulb with **(a)** one standard deviation of the mean and **(b)** two standard deviations of the mean; also **(c)** calculate the percent of lightbulbs that will last 2,300 hours or longer.

a. The useful life of the lightbulb one standard deviation from the mean is one standard deviation above *and* below the mean.

$2{,}000 \pm 300 = 1{,}700$ and $2{,}300$ hours

The useful life is somewhere between 1,700 and 2,300 hours.

b. The useful life of the lightbulb within two standard deviations of the mean is within two standard deviations above *and* below the mean.

$2{,}000 \pm 2(300) = 1{,}400$ and $2{,}600$ hours

c. Since 50% of the data in a normal distribution lie below the mean and 34% represent the amount of data one standard deviation above the mean, we must calculate the percent of data that lies beyond one standard deviation above the mean.

$100\% - (50\% + 34\%) = 16\%$

So 16% of the bulbs should last 2,300 hours or longer.

It's time for another Practice Quiz.

LU 22–3 PRACTICE QUIZ

Complete this **Practice Quiz** to see how you are doing.

1. Calculate the range for the following data: 58, 13, 17, 26, 5, 41.
2. Calculate the standard deviation for the following sample set of data: 113, 92, 77, 125, 110, 93, 111. Round answers to the nearest tenth.

Solutions with Step-by-Step Help on DVD

✓ Solutions

1. $58 - 5 = 53$ range
2.

Data	Data − Mean	(Data − Mean)^2
113	113 − 103 = 10	100
92	92 − 103 = −11	121
77	77 − 103 = −26	676
125	125 − 103 = 22	484
110	110 − 103 = 7	49
93	93 − 103 = −10	100
111	111 − 103 = 8	64
		Total 1,594

$1{,}594 \div (7 - 1) = 265.6666667$

$\sqrt{265.6666667} = 16.3$ standard deviation

LU 22–3a EXTRA PRACTICE QUIZ WITH WORKED-OUT SOLUTIONS

Need more practice? Try this **Extra Practice Quiz** (check figures in Chapter Organizer, p. 528). Worked-out Solutions can be found in Appendix B at end of text.

1. Calculate the range for the following data: 60, 13, 17, 26, 5, 41.
2. Calculate the standard deviation for the following sample set of data: 120, 88, 77, 125, 110, 93, 111. Round answers to the nearest tenth.

CHAPTER ORGANIZER AND REFERENCE GUIDE

Topic	Key point, procedure, formula	Example(s) to illustrate situation
Mean, p. 516	$\frac{\text{Sum of all values}}{\text{Number of values}}$	Age of basketball team: 22, 28, 31, 19, 15 $\text{Mean} = \frac{22 + 28 + 31 + 19 + 15}{5}$ $= 23$
Weighted mean, p. 516	$\frac{\text{Sum of products}}{\text{Sum of frequencies}}$	**S. M. T. W. Th. F. S.** Sales $90 $75 $80 $75 $80 $90 $90 **Value / Frequency / Product** $90 / 3 / $270 75 / 2 / 150 80 / 2 / 160 7 / $580 $\text{Mean} = \frac{\$580}{7} = \$82.86$
Median, p. 518	**1.** Arrange values from smallest to largest. **2.** Find the middle value. **a. Odd number of values:** median is middle value. $\left(\frac{\text{Total number of numbers}}{2}\right)$ Next-higher number is median. **b. Even number of values:** average of two middle values.	12, 15, 8, 6, 3 **1.** 3 6 8 12 15 **2.** $\frac{5}{2} = 2.5$ Median is third number, 8.
Frequency distribution, p. 519	Method of listing numbers or amounts not arranged in any particular way by columns for numbers (amounts), tally, and frequency	Number of sodas consumed in one day: 1, 5, 4, 3, 4, 2, 2, 3, 2, 0 **Number of sodas / Tally / Frequency** 0 / | / 1 1 / | / 1 2 / ||| / 3 3 / || / 2 4 / || / 2 5 / | / 1
Bar graphs, p. 520	Height of bar represents frequency. Bar graph used for grouped data. Bar graphs can be vertical or horizontal.	From soda example above: 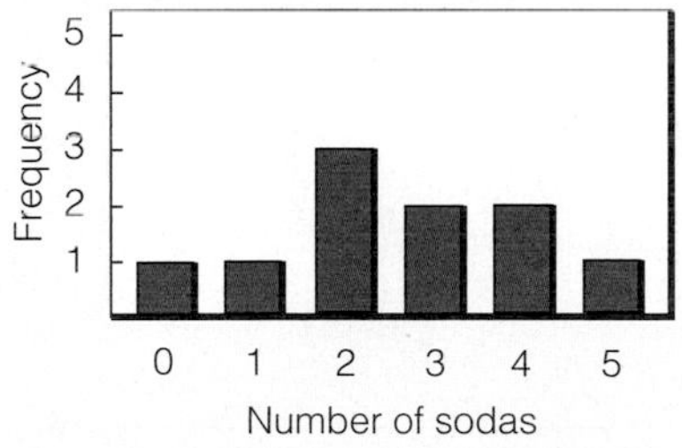
Line graphs, p. 521	Shows trend. Helps to put numbers in order.	**Sales** 2005 $1,000 2006 2,000 2007 3,000 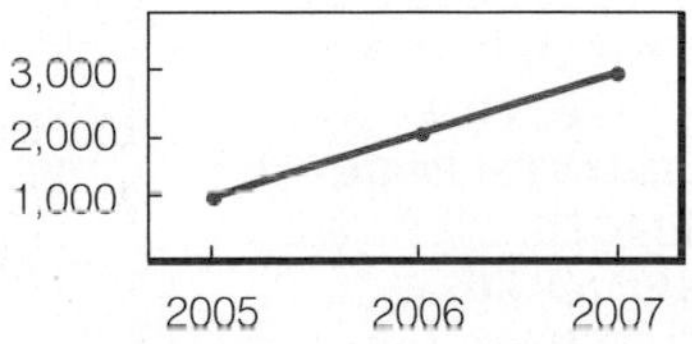

(continues)

CHAPTER ORGANIZER AND REFERENCE GUIDE

Topic	Key point, procedure, formula	Example(s) to illustrate situation
Circle graphs, p. 521	Circle = 360° % × 360° = Degrees of pie to represent percent Total should = 360°	60% favor diet soda 40% favor sugared soda 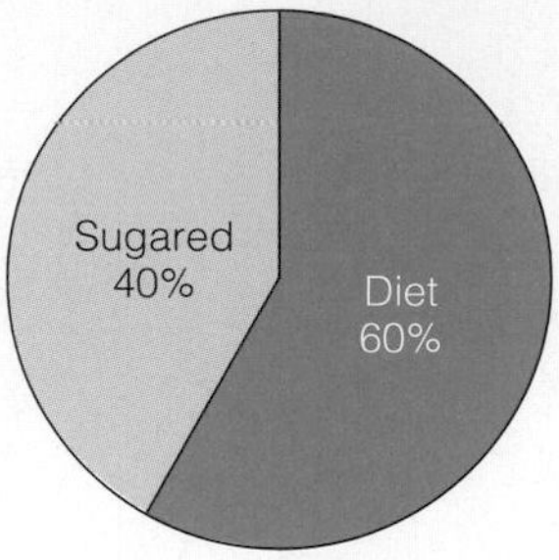 $.60 \times 360° = 216°$ $.40 \times 360° = \underline{144°}$ **360°**
Mode, p. 518	Value that occurs most often in a set of numbers	66856 6 with mode
Price relative, p. 522	$\text{Price relative} = \frac{\text{Current price}}{\text{Base year's price}} \times 100$	A station wagon's sticker price was $8,799 in 1982. Today it is $14,900. $\text{Price relative} = \frac{\$14,900}{\$8,799} \times 100 = $ **169.3** (rounded to nearest tenth percent)
Range (optional), p. 524	Range = Highest value − Lowest value	Calculate range of the data set consisting of 5, 9, 13, 2, 8 Range = 13 − 2 = 11
Standard deviation (optional), p. 524	**1.** Calculate mean. **2.** Subtract mean from each piece of data. **3.** Square each deviation. **4.** Sum squares. **5.** Divide sum of squares by $n - 1$, where n = number of pieces of data. **6.** Take square root of number obtained in Step 5, to find the standard deviation.	Calculate the standard deviation of this set of data: 7, 2, 5, 3, 3. **1.** $\text{Mean} = \frac{20}{5} = 4$ **2.** $7 - 4 = 3$ $2 - 4 = -2$ $5 - 4 = 1$ $3 - 4 = -1$ $3 - 4 = -1$ **3.** $(3)^2 = 9$ $(-2)^2 = 4$ $(1)^2 = 1$ $(-1)^2 = 1$ $\underline{(-1)^2 = 1}$ **4.** 16 **5.** $16 \div 4 = 4$ **6.** Standard deviation = **2**

KEY TERMS			
	Bar graph, p. 520 *Circle graph, p. 521* *Frequency distribution, p. 519* *Index numbers, p. 522* *Line graph, p. 521*	*Mean, p. 516* *Measure of dispersion, p. 524* *Median, p. 517* *Mode, p. 518* *Normal distribution, p. 525*	*Price relative, p. 522* *Range, p. 524* *Standard deviation, p. 524* *Weighted mean, p. 516*

CHECK FIGURES FOR EXTRA PRACTICE QUIZZES WITH PAGE REFERENCES. (WORKED-OUT SOLUTIONS IN APPENDIX B.)	LU 22–1a (p. 519)	LU 22–2a (p. 523)	LU 22–3a (p. 526)
	Mean $23,250 Median $15,500	**1.** 9 IIII 4 **2.** Pampers 40% 144° **3.** 184.2%	**1.** 55 Standard deviation

Critical Thinking Discussion Questions

1. Explain the mean, median, and mode. Give an example that shows you must be careful when you read statistics in an article.
2. Explain frequency distributions and the types of graphs. Locate a company annual report and explain how the company shows graphs to highlight its performance. Does the company need more or fewer of these visuals? Could price relatives be used?
3. Explain the statement that standard deviations are not accurate.

Classroom Notes

END-OF-CHAPTER PROBLEMS

Name ________________________ Date ________

DRILL PROBLEMS (*Note:* Problems for optional Learning Unit 22–3 follow the Challenge Problem 22–24, page 537.)

Calculate the mean (to the nearest hundredth):

22–1. 12, 9, 8, 3

22–2. 8, 11, 19, 17, 15

22–3. \$55.83, \$66.92, \$108.93

22–4. \$1,001, \$68.50, \$33.82, \$581.95

22–5. Calculate the grade-point average: A = 4, B = 3, C = 2, D = 1, F = 0 (to nearest tenth).

Courses	Credits	Grade
Computer Principles	3	B
Business Law	3	C
Logic	3	D
Biology	4	A
Marketing	3	B

22–6. Find the weighted mean (to the nearest tenth):

Value	Frequency	Product
4	7	
8	3	
2	9	
4	2	

Find the median:

22–7. 55, 10, 19, 38, 100, 25

22–8. 95, 103, 98, 62, 31, 15, 82

Find the mode:

22–9. 8, 9, 3, 4, 12, 8, 8, 9

22–10. 22, 19, 15, 16, 18, 18, 5, 18

22–11. Given:

Truck cost	2012	\$30,000
Truck cost	2008	\$21,000

Calculate the price relative (round to the nearest tenth percent).

22–12. Given the following sales of Lowe Corporation, prepare a line graph (run sales from \$5,000 to \$20,000).

2009	\$ 8,000
2010	11,000
2011	13,000
2012	18,000

22–13. Prepare a frequency distribution from the following weekly salaries of teachers at Moore Community College. Use the following intervals:

$200–$299.99
300– 399.99
400– 499.99
500– 599.99

$210	$505	$310	$380	$275
290	480	550	490	200
286	410	305	444	368

22–14. Prepare a bar graph from the frequency distribution in Problem 22–13.

22–15. How many degrees on a pie chart would each be given from the following?

Wear digital watch	42%
Wear traditional watch	51%
Wear no watch	7%

WORD PROBLEMS

22–16. Baby boomers are discussed frequently with regard to their potential drain on the Social Security system. A baby boomer dies every 39 seconds. Less than 10% of baby boomers have already died (8.98%) with 77,694,487 left to go. The U.S. Census Bureau estimates that there will be 57.8 million baby boomers still living in 2030 with 54.9% of them female. The following are estimates of deaths each day for a week: 2,880 3,050 2,880 3,100 2,789 3,074 2,932
Calculate the mean, median, and mode. Round to the nearest whole number.

22–17. The American Kennel Club posted a list of the most popular purebred dogs in the United States on January 21, 2009. Labrador Retrievers hold the number-one spot again for the 18th consecutive year. Twice as many Labs were registered last year than any other breed. Angela Newman's dog club has the following dogs as members: 35 Labrador Retrievers, 15 Yorkshire Terriers, 12 German Shepherds, 10 Golden Retrievers, 8 Beagles, and 6 Boxers. Create a pie chart showing these statistics.

22–18. In the August 21, 2009, *Dallas Morning News,* the tax-free weekend made headlines. This is Texas' 11th annual sales tax holiday, in which the state waives state and local taxes on many clothing and school supply items purchased up to $100, providing consumers with an automatic 8% savings. Cindy Halseth spent the following on tax-exempt items: $98.50 $46.87 $74.89 $33.61 $53.25 $89.78. Calculate her tax savings to the nearest cent and then prepare a bar chart of her individual savings.

22–19. Bill Small, a travel agent, provided Alice Hall with the following information regarding the cost of her upcoming vacation:

Transportation	35%
Hotel	28%
Food and entertainment	20%
Miscellaneous	17%

Construct a circle graph for Alice.

22–20. Jim Smith, a marketing student, observed how much each customer spent in a local convenience store. Based on the following results, prepare **(a)** a frequency distribution and **(b)** a bar graph. Use intervals of $0–$5.99, $6.00–$11.99, $12.00–$17.99, and $18.00–$23.99.

$18.50	$18.24	$ 6.88	$9.95
16.10	3.55	14.10	6.80
12.11	3.82	2.10	
15.88	3.95	5.50	

22–21. Angie's Bakery bakes bagels. Find the weighted mean (to the nearest whole bagel) given the following daily production for June:

200	150	200	150	200
150	190	360	360	150
190	190	190	200	150
360	400	400	150	200
400	360	150	400	360
400	400	200	150	150

22–22. Melvin Company reported sales in 2011 of $300,000. This compared to sales of $150,000 in 2010 and $100,000 in 2009. Construct a line graph for Melvin Company.

CHALLENGE PROBLEMS

22–23. Mortgage rates have fluctuated greatly over the past 20 years. Prepare a frequency distribution of the following 30-year fixed-rate mortgage rates from Freddie Mac. Calculate the mean, median, mode, range, and standard deviation. Round to the nearest hundredth. Is this a normal distribution?

Year	Rate	Year	Rate	Year	Rate	Year	Rate
1990	10.13	1995	7.93	2000	8.05	2005	5.87
1991	9.25	1996	7.81	2001	6.97	2006	6.41
1992	8.39	1997	7.60	2002	6.54	2007	6.34
1993	7.31	1998	6.94	2003	5.83	2008	6.03
1994	8.38	1999	7.44	2004	5.84	2009	5.07 est.

Use the following intervals for the frequency distribution:

5.00–6.0
6.01–7.0
7.01–8.0
8.01–9.0
9.01–10.0
10.01–11.0

22–24. The following circle graph is a suggested budget for Ron Rye and his family for a month:

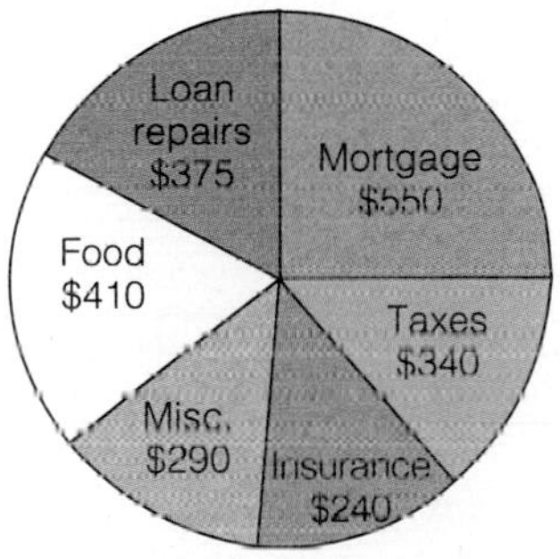

Ron would like you to calculate the percent (to the hundredth) for each part of the circle graph along with the appropriate number of degrees.

Classroom Notes

LEARNING UNIT 22–3 OPTIONAL ASSIGNMENTS

connect plus+
www.mhhe.com/slater10e

Name ______________________ Date ________

DRILL PROBLEMS

1. Calculate the range for the following set of data: 117, 98, 133, 52, 114, 35.

Calculate the standard deviation for the following sample sets of data. Round the final answers to the nearest tenth.

2. 83.6, 92.3, 56.5, 43.8, 77.1, 66.7

3. 7, 3, 12, 17, 5, 8, 9, 9, 13, 15, 6, 6, 4, 5

4. 41, 41, 38, 27, 53, 56, 28, 45, 47, 49, 55, 60

WORD PROBLEMS

5. The mean useful life of car batteries is 48 months. They have a standard deviation of 3. If the useful life of batteries is normally distributed, calculate (**a**) the percent of batteries with a useful life of less than 45 months and (**b**) the percent of batteries that will last longer than 54 months.

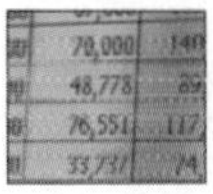

6. The average weight of a particular box of crackers is 24.5 ounces with a standard deviation of 0.8 ounce. The weights of the boxes are normally distributed. What percent of the boxes (**a**) weighs more than 22.9 ounces and (**b**) weighs less than 23.7 ounces?

7. An examination is normally distributed with a mean score of 77 and a standard deviation of 6. Find the percent of individuals scoring as indicated below.

a. Between 71 and 83
b. Between 83 and 65
c. Above 89
d. Less than 65
e. Between 77 and 65

8. Listed below are the sales figures in thousands of dollars for a group of insurance salespeople. Calculate the mean sales figure and the standard deviation.

$117	$350	$400	$245	$420
223	275	516	265	135
486	320	285	374	190

9. The time in seconds it takes for 20 individual sewing machines to stitch a border onto a particular garment is listed below. Calculate the mean stitching time and the standard deviation to the nearest hundredth.

67	69	64	71	73
58	71	64	62	67
62	57	67	60	65
60	63	72	56	64

DVD SUMMARY PRACTICE TEST

1. In July, Lee Realty sold 10 homes at the following prices: $140,000; $166,000; $80,000; $98,000; $185,000; $150,000; $108,000; $114,000; $142,000; and $250,000. Calculate the mean and median. *(pp. 516, 517)*

2. Lowes counted the number of customers entering the store for a week. The results were 1,100; 950; 1,100; 1,700; 880; 920; and 1,100. What is the mode? *(p. 518)*

3. This semester Hung Lee took four 3-credit courses at Riverside Community College. She received an A in accounting and C's in history, psychology, and algebra. What is her cumulative grade point average (assume A = 4 and B = 3) to the nearest hundredth? *(p. 517)*

4. Pete's Variety Shop reported the following sales for the first 20 days of May. *(p. 519)*

$100	$400	$600	$400	$600
100	600	300	500	700
200	600	700	500	200
100	600	100	700	700

Prepare a frequency distribution for Pete.

5. Leeds Company produced the following number of maps during the first 5 weeks of last year. Prepare a bar graph. *(p. 520)*

Week	**Maps**
1	800
2	600
3	400
4	700
5	300

6. Laser Corporation reported record profits of 30%. It stated in the report that the cost of sales was 40% with expenses of 30%. Prepare a circle graph for Laser. *(p. 520)*

7. Today a new Explorer costs $39,900. In 1990, Explorers cost $24,000. What is the price relative to the nearest tenth percent? *(p. 523)*

***8.** Calculate the standard deviation for the following set of data: 7, 2, 5, 3, 3, 10. Round final answer to nearest tenth. *(p. 526)*

*Optional problem.

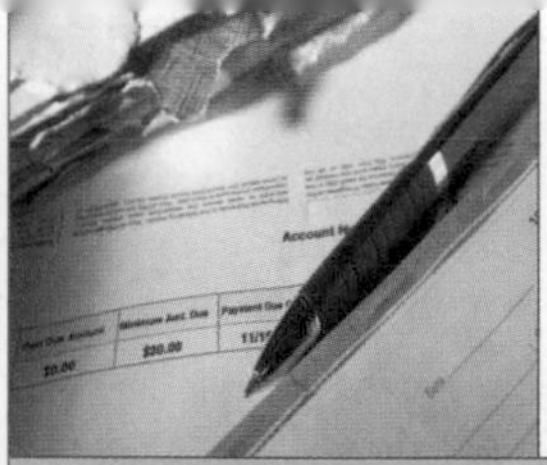

Personal Finance

A KIPLINGER APPROACH

When Will I Get My Money Back?

It all depends on your rate of return and how much you contribute to your investments. For a customized return calculation, go to kiplinger.com/links/recover. BY MARY BETH FRANKLIN

YOU HAD A 30% LOSS IN YOUR PORTFOLIO

If you add nothing to your account, you'll need a longer time frame or higher return to recover.

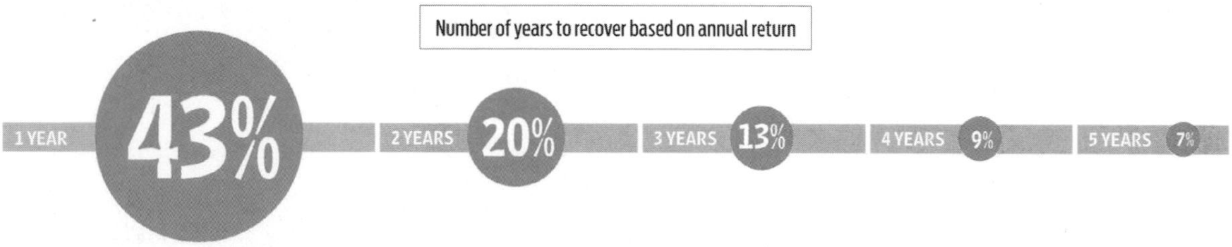

If you add to your account, what you'll need to recover in 3 YEARS

YOU STARTED WITH $100,000 | YOU STARTED WITH $300,000 | YOU STARTED WITH $500,000

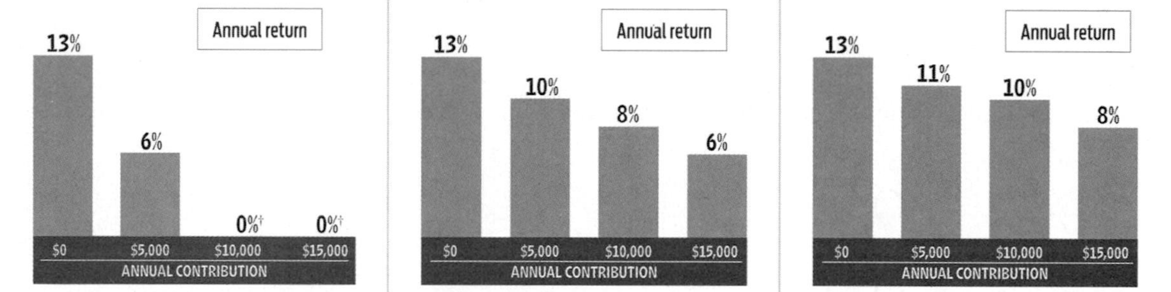

If you add to your account, what you'll need to recover in 5 YEARS

YOU STARTED WITH $100,000 | YOU STARTED WITH $300,000 | YOU STARTED WITH $500,000

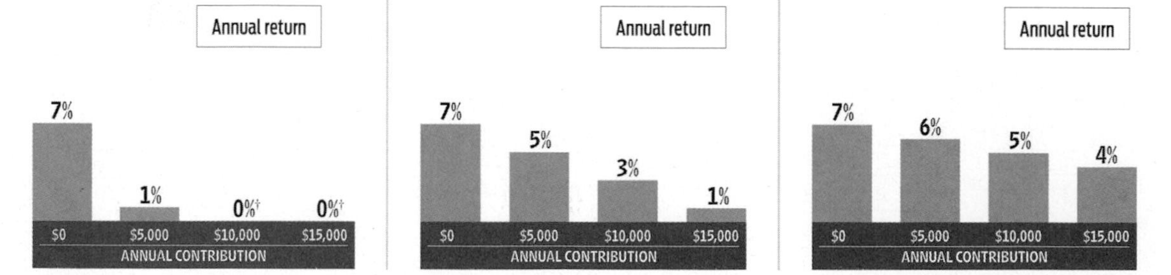

†Contributions alone will likely restore account balance. SOURCE: T. Rowe Price

From Kiplinger's Personal Finance, July 2009, p. 33.

BUSINESS MATH ISSUE

These statistics are misleading.

1. List the key points of the article and information to support your position.
2. Write a group defense of your position using math calculations to support your view.

PROJECT A

Do you agree that going green is really needed. Defend your position.

Slater's Business Math Scrapbook

Applying Your Skills

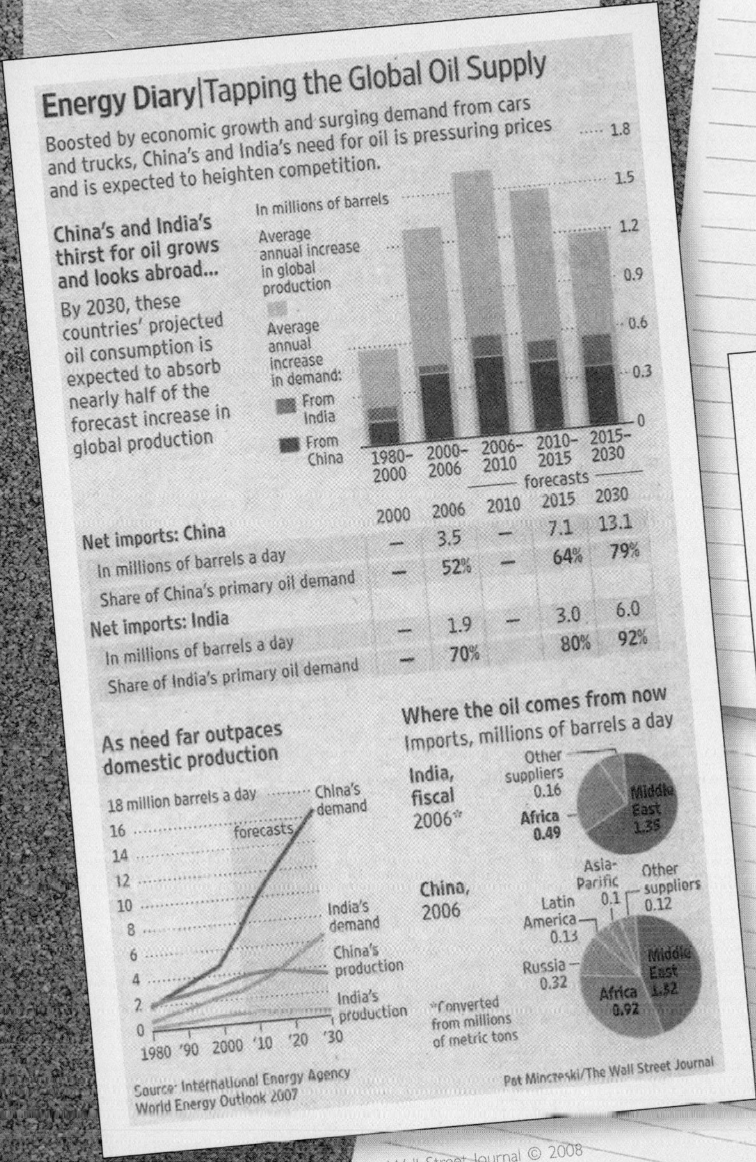

	2000	2006	2010	2015	2030
Net imports: China					
In millions of barrels a day	–	3.5	–	7.1	13.1
Share of China's primary oil demand	–	52%	–	64%	79%
Net imports: India					
In millions of barrels a day	–	1.9	–	3.0	6.0
Share of India's primary oil demand	–	70%		80%	92%

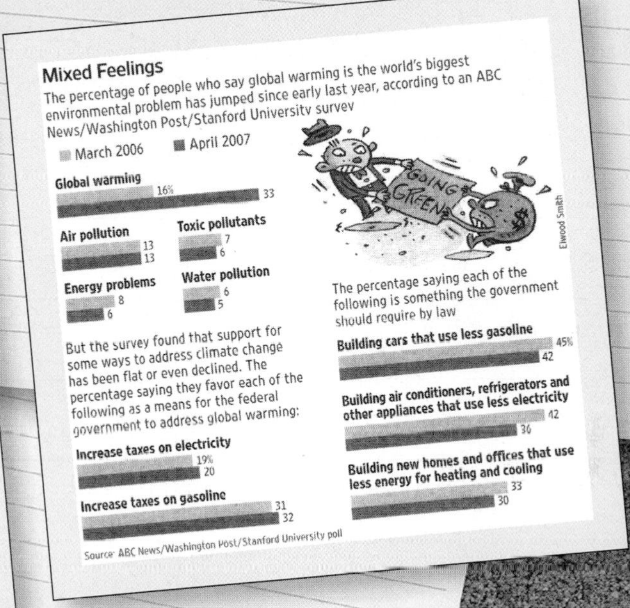

PROJECT B

There should be quotas set for oil consumption since it is a global problem. Do you agree or not. Defend your position.

Toyota Truck Sales to Falter in U.S.

Auto Outlook Solid For North America; Easing Production

By Norihiko Shirouzu

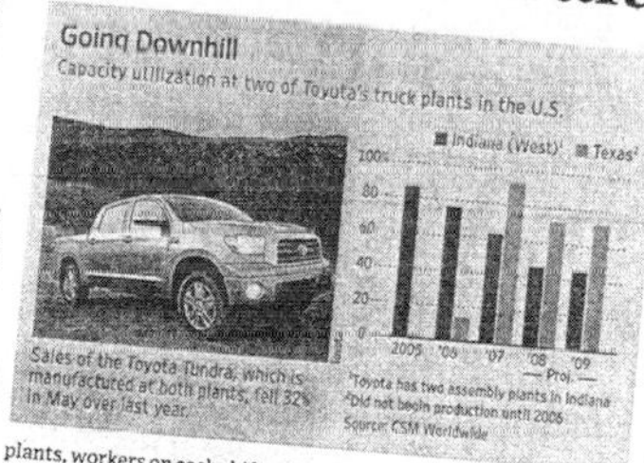

Sales of the Toyota Tundra, which is manufactured at both plants, fell 32% in May over last year.

[1]Toyota has two assembly plants in Indiana
[2]Did not begin production until 2006
Source: CSM Worldwide

Toyota Motor Corp. is likely to struggle to make money at its two truck plants in the U.S. this year, a consulting firm said, underscoring the toll slumping sales of trucks and sport-utility vehicles are taking on auto makers of all stripes.

The company is still likely to generate substantial profits in North America, thanks to booming sales of cars such as the Camry sedan and the Prius hybrid. But until recently Toyota had hoped an expansion into trucks would boost its bottom line in the U.S.

Wednesday, Toyota said it is slowing production at two of its truck plants in North America, in San Antonio, Texas, and Princeton, Ind., in a second such move to adjust the pace of work. In addition to slowing the assembly-line speed, San Antonio's truck line, which makes the Tundra pickup, will be shut down for 14 days between now and the end of October. The Princeton plant is taking out six days or more of production between now and the end of August. At both plants, workers on each shift will work seven hours instead of eight assembling cars and will spend one hour in training. The seven-hour shift will start in July. It wasn't clear how long the new work arrangement will last.

Toyota had slowed production at the plants previously this year. According to a study by CSM Worldwide, a market-research firm in Michigan, the San Antonio plant is projected to operate at 72% of its capacity this year, and the Princeton plant at 45%. CSM's projections already reflect the most-recent production cutbacks Toyota announced, the firm said.

Both expected capacity-utilization levels mark big drops from the near-100% utilization rates Toyota usually has maintained.

At those rates, Toyota most likely no longer can expect to make a profit producing trucks in the U.S., which in the past have offered fat profit margins. "Typically you need to be at 75% to 80% of the capacity to be profitable," said Mike Jackson, a senior analyst at CSM.

"Clearly we are not in good shape [at those two truck plants], but we're doing everything we can to be flexible and keep the plants open," Toyota spokesman Mike Goss said. He declined to discuss the profitability of the plants.

The anticipated drop in utilization raises a "cause for concern," said Mr. Jackson. Since the late 1980s when Toyota began producing cars independently in North America, the auto maker has operated those factories as a whole at higher than 95% and sometimes above 100%.

According to CSM, the San Antonio plant has the capacity to make 200,000 trucks a year, but CSM expects it to produce about 144,000 this year, bringing its capacity-utilization rate down to 72%. CSM expects the plant's capacity utilization to rise to about 73% in 2009. The utilization rate was 92% in 2007.

Toyota's plant in Princeton is also capable of producing 200,000 trucks a year but CSM projects it will make around 91,000, dropping its capacity usage to about 45% from 62.5% in 2007 and 76% in 2006. The plant produces the Tundra pickup truck and the Sequoia SUV. CSM expects the rate to stay at 45% in 2009. (In Princeton, Toyota also produces Sienna minivans at a separate plant on the same site.)

CSM's Mr. Jackson believes Toyota is paying for having succeeded in transforming itself from a small-car producer into a company with a full line of vehicles from subcompacts to big trucks. The full-line strategy spurred dramatic sales and profit growth in North America, but skyrocketing gasoline prices and the weak U.S. economy are damping demand for trucks.

Internet Projects: See text Web site (www.mhhe.com/slater10e) and The Business Math Internet Resource Guide.

Classroom Notes

Additional Homework by Learning Unit

APPENDIX A

Name ____________________ Date ____________

Learning Unit 1–1 : Reading, Writing, and Rounding Whole Numbers

DRILL PROBLEMS

1. Express the following numbers in verbal form:
   a. 6,448 ____________________
   b. 160,501 ____________________
   c. 2,098,767 ____________________
   d. 58,003 ____________________
   e. 50,025,212,015 ____________________

2. Write in numeric form:
   a. Seventy thousand, two hundred eighty-one ________
   b. Fifty-eight thousand, three ________
   c. Two hundred eighty thousand, five ________
   d. Three million, ten ________
   e. Sixty-seven thousand, seven hundred sixty ________

3. Round the following numbers:
   a. To the nearest ten:
      64 _____ 379 _____ 855 _____ 5,981 _____ 206 _____
   b. To the nearest hundred:
      9,664 _____ 2,074 _____ 888 _____ 271 _____ 75 _____
   c. To the nearest thousand:
      21,486 _____ 621 _____ 3,504 _____ 9,735 _____

4. Round off each number to the nearest ten, nearest hundred, nearest thousand, and round all the way. (Remember that you are rounding the original number each time.)

		Nearest ten	Nearest hundred	Nearest thousand	Round all the way
a.	4,752	_____	_____	_____	_____
b.	70,351	_____	_____	_____	_____
c.	9,386	_____	_____	_____	_____
d.	4,983	_____	_____	_____	_____
e.	408,119	_____	_____	_____	_____
f.	30,051	_____	_____	_____	_____

5. Name the place position (place value) of the underlined digit.
   a. 8,348 ____________________
   b. 9,734 ____________________
   c. 347,107 ____________________
   d. 723 ____________________

e. 28,200,000,121 ______________________________

f. 706,359,005 ______________________________

g. 27,563,530 ______________________________

WORD PROBLEMS

6. Gim Smith was shopping for an Apple computer. He went to three different Web sites and found the computer he wanted at three different prices. At Web site A the price was $2,018, at Web site B the price was $1,985, and at Web site C the price was $2,030. What is the approximate price Gim will have to pay for the computer? Round to the nearest thousand. (Just one price.)

7. Amy Parker had to write a check at the bookstore when she purchased her books for the new semester. The total cost of the books was $384. How will she write this amount in verbal form on her check?

8. Matt Schaeffer was listening to the news and heard that steel production last week was one million, five hundred eighty-seven thousand tons. Express this amount in numeric form.

9. Jackie Martin is the city clerk and must go to the aldermen's meetings and take notes on what is discussed. At last night's meeting, they were discussing repairs for the public library, which will cost three hundred seventy-five thousand, nine hundred eighty-five dollars. Write this in numeric form as Jackie would.

10. A government survey revealed that 25,963,400 people are employed as office workers. To show the approximate number of office workers, round the number all the way.

11. Bob Donaldson wished to present his top student with a certificate of achievement at the end of the school year in 2004. To make it appear more official, he wanted to write the year in verbal form. How did he write the year?

12. Nancy Morrissey has a problem reading large numbers and determining place value. She asked her brother to name the place value of the 4 in the number 13,542,966. Can you tell Nancy the place value of the 4? What is the place value of the 3?

The 4 is in the ______________ place.

The 3 is in the ______________ place.

Learning Unit 1–2 : Adding and Subtracting Whole Numbers

DRILL PROBLEMS

1. Add by totaling each separate column:

a.	b.	c.	d.	e.	f.	g.	h.
668	43	493	36	716	535	751	75,730
338	58	826	76	458	107	378	48,531
	96		43	397	778	135	15,797
			24	139	215	747	
				478	391	368	

2. Estimate by rounding all the way, then add the actual numbers:

a.	b.	c.
580	1,470	475
971	7,631	837
548	4,383	213
430		775
506		432

d. 442 609 766 410 128	**e.** 2,571 3,625 4,091 928	**f.** 10,928 9,321 12,654 15,492

3. Estimate by rounding all the way, then subtract the actual numbers:

a. 90 − 38	**b.** 91 − 33	**c.** 68 − 59
d. 981 − 283	**e.** 622 − 328	**f.** 1,125 − 913

4. Subtract and check:

a. 4,947 − 4,362	**b.** 3,724 − 2,138	**c.** 474,820 − 85,847
d. 50,000 − 21,762	**e.** 65,003 − 24,987	**f.** 15,715 − 3,503

5. In the following sales report, total the rows and the columns, then check that the grand total is the same both horizontally and vertically.

Salesperson	Region 1	Region 2	Region 3	Total
a. Becker	$ 5,692	$ 7,403	$ 3,591	
b. Edwards	7,652	7,590	3,021	
c. Graff	6,545	6,738	4,545	
d. Jackson	6,937	6,950	4,913	
e. Total				

WORD PROBLEMS

6. Meg Harris owes $7,700 on her car loan, plus interest of $510. How much will it cost her to pay off this loan?

7. Sales at Rich's Convenience Store were $3,587 on Monday, $3,944 on Tuesday, $4,007 on Wednesday, $3,890 on Thursday, and $4,545 on Friday. What were the total sales for the week?

8. Poor's Variety Store sold $5,000 worth of lottery tickets in the first week of August; it sold $289 less in the second week. How much were the lottery ticket sales in the second week of August?

9. A truck weighed 9,550 pounds when it was empty. After being filled with rubbish, it was driven to the dump where it weighed in at 22,347 pounds. How much did the rubbish weigh?

10. Lynn Jackson had $549 in her checking account when she went to the bookstore. Lynn purchased an accounting book for $62, the working papers for $28, a study guide for $25, and a mechanical pencil for $5. After Lynn writes a check for the entire purchase, how much money will remain in her checking account?

11. A new hard-body truck is advertised with a base price of $6,986 delivered. However, the window sticker on the truck reads as follows: tinted glass, $210; automatic transmission, $650; power steering, $210; power brakes, $215; safety locks, $95; air conditioning, $1,056. Estimate the total price, including the accessories, by rounding all the way and *then* calculating the exact price.

12. Four different stores are offering the same make and model of a Panasonic plasma television:

Store A	Store B	Store C	Store D
$1,285	$1,380	$1,440	$1,355

Find the difference between the highest price and the lowest price. Check your answer.

13. A Xerox XC830 copy machine has a suggested retail price of $1,395. The net price is $649. How much is the discount on the copy machine?

Learning Unit 1–3: Multiplying and Dividing Whole Numbers

DRILL PROBLEMS

1. In the following problems, first estimate by rounding all the way, then work the actual problems and check:

	Actual	Estimate	Check
a.	160 × 15		
b.	4,216 × 45		
c.	52,376 × 309		
d.	3,106 × 28		

2. Multiply (use the shortcut when applicable):

a. 4,072 × 100

b. 5,100 × 40

c. 76,000 × 1,200

d. 93 × 100,000

3. Divide by rounding all the way; then do the actual calculation and check showing the remainder as a whole number.

Actual	Estimate	Check
a. $8\overline{)7{,}709}$		
b. $26\overline{)5{,}910}$		
c. $151\overline{)3{,}783}$		
d. $46\overline{)19{,}550}$		

4. Divide by the shortcut method:

a. $200\overline{)5{,}400}$

b. $50\overline{)5{,}650}$

c. $1{,}200\overline{)43{,}200}$

d. $17{,}000\overline{)510{,}000}$

WORD PROBLEMS

5. Matty Slater sells state lottery tickets in his variety store. If Matty's Variety Store sells 550 lottery tickets per day, how many tickets will be sold in a 7-day period?

6. Arlex Oil Company employs 100 people who are eligible for profit sharing. The financial manager has announced that the profits to be shared amount to $64,000. How much will each employee receive?

7. John Duncan's employer withheld $4,056 in federal taxes from his pay for the year. If equal deductions are made each week, what is John's weekly deduction?

8. Anne Domingoes drives a Volvo that gets 32 miles per gallon of gasoline. How many miles can she travel on 25 gallons of gas?

9. How many 8-inch pieces of yellow ribbon can be cut from a spool of ribbon that contains 6 yards (1 yard = 36 inches)?

10. The number of commercials aired per day on a local television station is 672. How many commercials are aired in 1 year?

11. The computer department at City College purchased 18 computers at a cost of $2,400 each. What was the total price for the computer purchase?

12. Net income for Goodwin's Partnership was $64,500. The five partners share profits and losses equally. What was each partner's share?

13. Ben Krenshaw's supervisor at the construction site told Ben to divide a load of 1,423 bricks into stacks containing 35 bricks each. How many stacks will there be when Ben has finished the job? How many "extra" bricks will there be?

Name ______________________ Date ______________

Learning Unit 2–1 : Types of Fractions and Conversion Procedures

DRILL PROBLEMS

1. Identify the type of fraction—proper, improper, or mixed number:

a. $8\frac{1}{8}$ b. $\frac{31}{29}$ c. $\frac{29}{27}$

d. $9\frac{3}{11}$ e. $\frac{18}{5}$ f. $\frac{30}{37}$

2. Convert to a mixed number:

a. $\frac{29}{4}$ b. $\frac{137}{8}$ c. $\frac{27}{5}$

d. $\frac{29}{9}$ e. $\frac{71}{8}$ f. $\frac{43}{6}$

3. Convert the mixed number to an improper fraction:

a. $8\frac{1}{5}$ b. $12\frac{3}{11}$ c. $4\frac{3}{7}$

d. $20\frac{4}{9}$ e. $10\frac{11}{12}$ f. $17\frac{2}{3}$

4. Tell whether the fractions in each pair are equivalent or not:

a. $\frac{3}{4}$ $\frac{9}{12}$ ______ b. $\frac{2}{3}$ $\frac{12}{18}$ ______ c. $\frac{7}{8}$ $\frac{15}{16}$ ______

d. $\frac{4}{5}$ $\frac{12}{15}$ ______ e. $\frac{3}{2}$ $\frac{9}{4}$ ______ f. $\frac{5}{8}$ $\frac{7}{11}$ ______

g. $\frac{7}{12}$ $\frac{7}{24}$ ______ h. $\frac{5}{4}$ $\frac{30}{24}$ ______ i. $\frac{10}{26}$ $\frac{12}{26}$ ______

5. Find the greatest common divisor by the step approach and reduce to lowest terms:

a. $\frac{36}{42}$

b. $\frac{30}{75}$

c. $\frac{74}{148}$

d. $\frac{15}{600}$

e. $\frac{96}{132}$

f. $\frac{84}{154}$

6. Convert to higher terms:

a. $\frac{8}{10} = \frac{\quad}{70}$

b. $\frac{2}{15} = \frac{\quad}{30}$

c. $\frac{6}{11} = \frac{\quad}{132}$

d. $\frac{4}{9} = \frac{\quad}{36}$

e. $\frac{7}{20} = \frac{\quad}{100}$

f. $\frac{7}{8} = \frac{\quad}{560}$

WORD PROBLEMS

7. Ken drove to college in $3\frac{1}{4}$ hours. How many quarter-hours is that? Show your answer as an improper fraction.

8. Mary looked in the refrigerator for a dozen eggs. When she found the box, only 5 eggs were left. What fractional part of the box of eggs was left?

9. At a recent meeting of a local Boosters Club, 17 of the 25 members attending were men. What fraction of those in attendance were men?

10. By weight, water is two parts out of three parts of the human body. What fraction of the body is water?

11. Three out of 5 students who begin college will continue until they receive their degree. Show in fractional form how many out of 100 beginning students will graduate.

12. Tina and her friends came in late to a party and found only $\frac{3}{4}$ of a pizza remaining. In order for everyone to get some pizza, she wanted to divide it into smaller pieces. If she divides the pizza into twelfths, how many pieces will she have? Show your answer in fractional form.

13. Sharon and Spunky noted that it took them 35 minutes to do their exercise routine. What fractional part of an hour is that? Show your answer in lowest terms.

14. Norman and his friend ordered several pizzas, which were all cut into eighths. The group ate 43 pieces of pizza. How many pizzas did they eat? Show your answer as a mixed number.

Learning Unit 2–2 : Adding and Subtracting Fractions

DRILL PROBLEMS

1. Find the least common denominator (LCD) for each of the following groups of denominators using the prime numbers:

a. 8, 16, 32

b. 9, 15, 20

c. 12, 15, 32

d. 7, 9, 14, 28

2. Add and reduce to lowest terms or change to a mixed number if needed:

a. $\frac{1}{8} + \frac{4}{8}$

b. $\frac{5}{12} + \frac{8}{15}$

c. $\frac{7}{8} + \frac{5}{12}$

d. $7\frac{2}{3} + 5\frac{1}{4}$

e. $\frac{2}{3} + \frac{4}{9} + \frac{1}{4}$

3. Subtract and reduce to lowest terms:

a. $\frac{5}{9} - \frac{2}{9}$

b. $\frac{14}{15} - \frac{4}{15}$

c. $\frac{8}{9} - \frac{5}{6}$

d. $\frac{7}{12} - \frac{9}{16}$

e. $33\frac{5}{8} - 27\frac{1}{2}$

f. $9 - 2\frac{3}{7}$

g. $15\frac{1}{3} - 9\frac{7}{12}$

h. $92\frac{3}{10} - 35\frac{7}{15}$

i. $93 - 57\frac{5}{12}$

j. $22\frac{5}{8} - 17\frac{1}{4}$

WORD PROBLEMS

4. Dan Lund took a cross-country trip. He drove $5\frac{3}{8}$ hours on Monday, $6\frac{1}{2}$ hours on Tuesday, $9\frac{3}{4}$ hours on Wednesday, $6\frac{3}{8}$ hours on Thursday, and $10\frac{1}{4}$ hours on Friday. Find the total number of hours Dan drove in the first 5 days of his trip.

5. Sharon Parker bought 20 yards of material to make curtains. She used $4\frac{1}{2}$ yards for one bedroom window, $8\frac{3}{5}$ yards for another bedroom window, and $3\frac{7}{8}$ yards for a hall window. How much material did she have left?

6. Molly Ring visited a local gym and lost $2\frac{1}{4}$ pounds the first weekend and $6\frac{1}{8}$ pounds in week 2. What is Molly's total weight loss?

7. Bill Williams had to drive $46\frac{1}{4}$ miles to work. After driving $28\frac{5}{6}$ miles he noticed he was low on gas and had to decide whether he should stop to fill the gas tank. How many more miles does Bill have to drive to get to work?

8. Albert's Lumber Yard purchased $52\frac{1}{2}$ cords of lumber on Monday and $48\frac{3}{4}$ cords on Tuesday. It sold $21\frac{3}{8}$ cords on Friday. How many cords of lumber remain at Albert's Lumber Yard?

9. At Arlen Oil Company, where Dave Bursett is the service manager, it took $42\frac{1}{3}$ hours to clean five boilers. After a new cleaning tool was purchased, the time for cleaning five boilers was reduced to $37\frac{4}{9}$ hours. How much time was saved?

Learning Unit 2–3 : Multiplying and Dividing Fractions

DRILL PROBLEMS

1. Multiply (use cancellation technique):

a. $\frac{6}{13} \times \frac{26}{12}$

b. $\frac{3}{8} \times \frac{2}{3}$

c. $\frac{5}{7} \times \frac{9}{10}$

d. $\frac{3}{4} \times \frac{9}{13} \times \frac{26}{27}$

e. $6\frac{2}{5} \times 3\frac{1}{8}$

f. $2\frac{2}{3} \times 2\frac{7}{10}$

g. $45 \times \frac{7}{9}$

h. $3\frac{1}{9} \times 1\frac{2}{7} \times \frac{3}{4}$

i. $\frac{3}{4} \times \frac{7}{9} \times 3\frac{1}{3}$

j. $\frac{1}{8} \times 6\frac{2}{3} \times \frac{1}{10}$

2. Multiply (do not use canceling; reduce by finding the greatest common divisor):

a. $\frac{3}{4} \times \frac{8}{9}$

b. $\frac{7}{16} \times \frac{8}{13}$

3. Multiply or divide as indicated:

a. $\frac{25}{36} \div \frac{5}{9}$

b. $\frac{18}{8} \div \frac{12}{16}$

c. $2\frac{6}{7} \div 2\frac{2}{5}$

d. $3\frac{1}{4} \div 16$

e. $24 \div 1\frac{1}{3}$

f. $6 \times \frac{3}{2}$

g. $3\frac{1}{5} \times 7\frac{1}{2}$

h. $\frac{3}{8} \div \frac{7}{4}$

i. $9 \div 3\frac{3}{4}$

j. $\frac{11}{24} \times \frac{24}{33}$

k. $\frac{12}{14} \div 27$

l. $\frac{3}{5} \times \frac{2}{7} \div \frac{3}{10}$

WORD PROBLEMS

4. Mary Smith plans to make 12 meatloafs to store in her freezer. Each meatloaf requires $2\frac{1}{4}$ pounds of ground beef. How much ground beef does Mary need?

5. Judy Carter purchased a real estate lot for $24,000. She sold it 2 years later for $1\frac{5}{8}$ times as much as she had paid for it. What was the selling price?

6. Lynn Clarkson saw an ad for a camcorder that cost $980. She knew of a discount store that would sell it to her for a markdown of $\frac{3}{20}$ off the advertised price. How much is the discount she can get?

7. To raise money for their club, the members of the Marketing Club purchased 68 bushels of popcorn to resell. They plan to repackage the popcorn in bags that hold $\frac{2}{21}$ of a bushel each. How many bags of popcorn will they be able to fill?

8. Richard Tracy paid a total of $375 for lumber costing $\$9\frac{3}{8}$ per foot. How many feet did he purchase?

9. While training for a marathon, Kristin Woods jogged $7\frac{3}{4}$ miles per hour for $2\frac{2}{3}$ hours. How many miles did Kristin jog?

10. On a map, 1 inch represents 240 miles. How many miles are represented by $\frac{3}{8}$ of an inch?

11. In Massachusetts, the governor wants to allot $\frac{1}{6}$ of the total sales tax collections to public education. The total sales tax collected is $2,472,000; how much will go to education?

Name ______________________________ Date ______________

Learning Unit 3–1: Rounding Decimals; Fraction and Decimal Conversions

DRILL PROBLEMS

1. Write in decimal:

a. Forty-one hundredths ________

b. Six tenths ________

c. Nine hundred fifty-three thousandths ________

d. Four hundred one thousandths ________

e. Six hundredths ________

2. Round each decimal to the place indicated:

a. .4326 to the nearest thousandth ________

b. .051 to the nearest tenth ________

c. 8.207 to the nearest hundredth ________

d. 2.094 to the nearest hundredth ________

e. .511172 to the nearest ten thousandth ________

3. Name the place position of the underlined digit:

a. .8<u>2</u>6 ________________

b. .91<u>4</u> ________________

c. 3.<u>1</u>169 ________________

d. 53.17<u>5</u> ________________

e. 1.017<u>4</u> ________________

4. Convert to fractions (do not reduce):

a. .83 ________ **b.** .426 ________ **c.** 2.516 ________

d. $.62\frac{1}{2}$ ________ **e.** 13.007 ________ **f.** $5.03\frac{1}{4}$ ________

5. Convert to fractions and reduce to lowest terms:

a. .4 **b.** .44 **c.** .53

d. .336 **e.** .096 **f.** .125

g. .3125 **h.** .008 **i.** 2.625

j. 5.75 **k.** 3.375 **l.** 9.04

6. Convert the following fractions to decimals and round your answer to the nearest hundredth:

a. $\frac{1}{8}$ **b.** $\frac{7}{16}$

c. $\frac{2}{3}$ **d.** $\frac{3}{4}$

e. $\frac{9}{16}$

f. $\frac{5}{6}$

g. $\frac{7}{9}$

h. $\frac{38}{79}$

i. $2\frac{3}{8}$

j. $9\frac{1}{3}$

k. $11\frac{19}{50}$

l. $6\frac{21}{32}$

m. $4\frac{83}{97}$

n. $1\frac{2}{5}$

o. $2\frac{2}{11}$

p. $13\frac{30}{42}$

WORD PROBLEMS

7. Alan Angel got 2 hits in his first 7 times at bat. What is his average to the nearest thousandths place?

8. Bill Breen earned $1,555, and his employer calculated that Bill's total FICA deduction should be $118.9575. Round this deduction to the nearest cent.

9. At the local college, .566 of the students are men. Convert to a fraction. Do not reduce.

10. The average television set is watched 2,400 hours a year. If there are 8,760 hours in a year, what fractional part of the year is spent watching television? Reduce to lowest terms.

11. On Saturday, the employees at the Empire Fish Company work only $\frac{1}{3}$ of a day. How could this be expressed as a decimal to nearest thousandths?

12. The North Shore Cinema has 610 seats. At a recent film screening there were 55 vacant seats. Show as a fraction the number of filled seats. Reduce as needed.

13. Michael Sullivan was planning his marketing strategy for a new product his company had produced. He was fascinated to discover that Rhode Island, the smallest state in the United States, was only twenty thousand, five hundred seven ten millionths the size of the largest state, Alaska. Write this number in decimal.

14. Bull Moose Company purchased a new manufacturing plant, located on an acre of land, for a total price of $2,250,000. The accountant determined that $\frac{3}{7}$ of the total price should be allocated as the price of the building. What decimal portion is the price of the building? Round to the nearest thousandth.

Learning Unit 3–2 : Adding, Subtracting, Multiplying, and Dividing Decimals

DRILL PROBLEMS

1. Rearrange vertically and add:

a. 7.57 + 6.2 + 13.008 + 4.83 **b.** 1.0625 + 4.0881 + .0775

c. .903 + .078 + .17 + .1 + .96 **d.** 3.38 + .175 + .0186 + .2

2. Rearrange and subtract:

a. .86 − .43 **b.** .885 − .069

c. 11.67 − .935 **d.** 261.2 − 8.08

3. Multiply and round to the nearest tenth:

a. 13.6 × .02 **b.** 1.73 × .069

c. 400 × 3.7 **d.** 0.025 × 5.6

4. Divide and round to the nearest hundredth:

a. 13.869 ÷ .6 **b.** 1.0088 ÷ .14 **c.** 18.7 ÷ 2.16 **d.** 15.64 ÷ .34

5. Complete by the shortcut method:

a. 6.87 × 1,000	**b.** 927,530 ÷ 100	**c.** 27.2 ÷ 1,000
d. .21 × 1,000	**e.** 347 × 100	**f.** 347 ÷ 100
g. .0021 ÷ 10	**h.** 85.44 × 10,000	**i.** 83.298 × 100
j. 23.0109 ÷ 100		

WORD PROBLEMS (Use *Business Math Handbook* Tables as Needed.)

6. Andy Hay noted his Hummer H3 cruiser odometer reading of 18,969.4 at the beginning of his vacation. At the end of his vacation the reading was 21,510.4. How many miles did he drive during his vacation?

7. Jeanne Allyn purchased 12.25 yards of ribbon for a craft project. The ribbon cost 37¢ per yard. What was the total cost of the ribbon?

8. Leo Green wanted to find out the gas mileage for his company truck. When he filled the gas tank, he wrote down the odometer reading of 9,650.7. The next time he filled the gas tank the odometer reading was 10,112.2. He looked at the gas pump and saw that he had taken 18.5 gallons of gas. Find the gas mileage per gallon for Leo's truck. Round to the nearest tenth.

9. At Halley's Rent-a-Car, the cost per day to rent a medium-size car is $35.25 plus 37¢ a mile. What would be the charge to rent this car for 1 day if you drove 205.4 miles?

10. A trip to Mexico costs 6,000 pesos. What is this in U.S. dollars? Check your answer.

11. If a commemorative gold coin weighs 7.842 grams, find the number of coins that can be produced from 116 grams of gold. Round to the nearest whole number.

Name ______________________________ Date ______________

Learning Unit 4–1 : The Checking Account

DRILL PROBLEMS

1. The following is a deposit slip made out by Fred Young of the F. W. Young Company.

a. How much cash did Young deposit? __________

b. How many checks did Young deposit? __________

c. What was the total amount deposited? __________

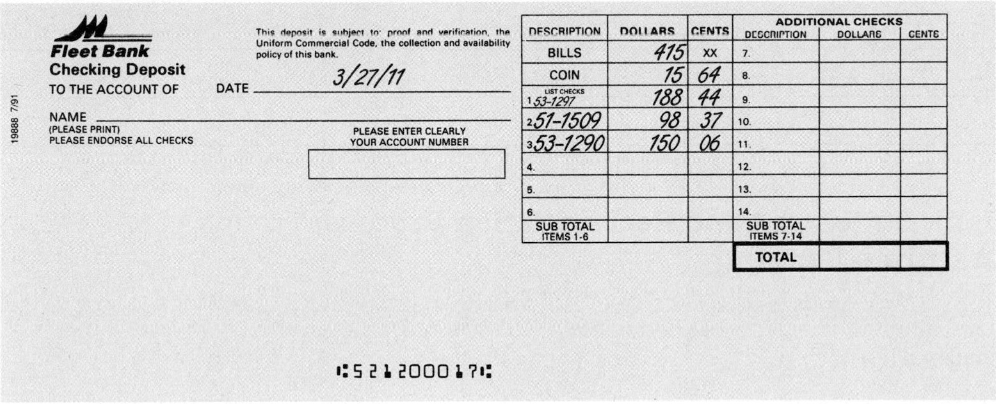
Fleet Bank
Checking Deposit
TO THE ACCOUNT OF DATE 3/27/11
NAME (PLEASE PRINT)
PLEASE ENDORSE ALL CHECKS
This deposit is subject to proof and verification, the Uniform Commercial Code, the collection and availability policy of this bank.
PLEASE ENTER CLEARLY YOUR ACCOUNT NUMBER
19888 7/91

DESCRIPTION	DOLLARS	CENTS	ADDITIONAL CHECKS DESCRIPTION	DOLLARS	CENTS
BILLS	415	XX	7.		
COIN	15	64	8.		
LIST CHECKS 1 53-1297	188	44	9.		
2 51-1509	98	37	10.		
3 53-1290	150	06	11.		
4.			12.		
5.			13.		
6.			14.		
SUB TOTAL ITEMS 1-6			SUB TOTAL ITEMS 7-14		
			TOTAL		

⑆5212000171⑆

2. Blackstone Company had a balance of $2,173.18 in its checking account. Henry James, Blackstone's accountant, made a deposit that consisted of 2 fifty-dollar bills, 120 ten-dollar bills, 6 five-dollar bills, 14 one-dollar bills, $9.54 in change, plus two checks they had accepted, one for $16.38 and the other for $102.50. Find the amount of the deposit and the new balance in Blackstone's checking account.

3. Answer the following questions using the illustration:

No. 113 $ 750 00/100
October 4 20 XX
To Neuner Realty
For real estate

	DOLLARS	CENTS
BALANCE	1,020	93
AMT. DEPOSITED	2,756	80
TOTAL	3,777	73
AMT. THIS CHECK	750	00
BALANCE FORWARD	3,027	73

Jones Company
22 Aster Road
Salem, MA 01970

No. 113

October 4 20 XX 5-13/110

PAY TO THE ORDER OF Neuner Realty Company $ 750 00/100

Seven Hundred Fifty and 00/100 DOLLARS

Fleet Bank FLEET BANK OF MASSACHUSETTS, NATIONAL ASSOCIATION BOSTON, MASSACHUSETTS

Kevin Jones

MEMO real estate

⑆0110001381⑆ 14 0380 113

a. Who is the payee? ______________________________

b. Who is the drawer? ______________________________

c. Who is the drawee? ______________________________

d. What is the bank's identification number ______________________________

e. What is Jones Company's account number? ______

f. What was the balance in the account on September 30? ______

g. For how much did Jones write Check No. 113? ______

h. How much was deposited on October 1? ______

i. How much was left after Check No. 113 was written? ______

4. Write each of the following amounts in verbal form as you would on a check:

a. $25 ______

b. $245.75 ______

c. $3.98 ______

d. $1,205.05 ______

e. $3,013 ______

f. $510.10 ______

Learning Unit 4–2 : Bank Statement and Reconciliation Process; Trends in Online Banking

WORD PROBLEMS

1. Find the bank balance on January 31.

Date	Checks and payments			Deposits	Balance
January 1					401.17
January 2	108.64				______
January 5	116.50			432.16	______
January 6	14.92	150.00	10.00		______
January 11	12.29			633.89	______
January 18	108.64	18.60			______
January 25	43.91	23.77		657.22	______
January 26	75.00				______
January 31	6.75 sc				______

2. Joe Madruga, of Madruga's Taxi Service, received a bank statement for the month of May showing a balance of $932.36. His records show that the bank had not yet recorded two of his deposits, one for $521.50 and the other for $98.46. There are outstanding checks in the amounts of $41.67, $135.18, and $25.30. The statement also shows a service charge of $3.38. The balance in the check register is $1,353.55. Prepare a bank reconciliation for Madruga's as of May 31.

3. In reconciling the checking account for Nasser Enterprises, Beth Accomando found that the bank had collected a $3,000 promissory note on the company's behalf and had charged a $15 collection fee. There was also a service charge of $7.25. What amount should be added/subtracted from the checkbook balance to bring it up to date?

Add: ________ Deduct: ________

4. In reconciling the checking account for Colonial Cleaners, Steve Papa found that a check for $34.50 had been recorded in the check register as $43.50. The bank returned an NSF check in the amount of $62.55. Interest income of $8.25 was earned and a service charge of $10.32 was assessed. What amount should be added/subtracted from the checkbook balance to bring it up to date?

Add: ________ Deduct: ________

5. Matthew Stokes was completing the bank reconciliation for Parker's Tool and Die Company. The check register balance was $1,503.67. Matthew found that a $76.00 check had been recorded in the check register as $67.00; that a note for $1,500 had been collected by the bank for Parker's and the collection fee was $12.00; that $15.60 interest was earned on the account; and that an $8.35 service charge had been assessed. What should the check register balance be after Matthew updates it with the bank reconciliation information?

6. Consumers, community activists, and politicians are decrying the new line of accounts because several include a $3 service charge for some customers who use bank tellers for transactions that can be done through an automated teller machine. Bill Wade banks at a local bank that charges this fee. He was having difficulty balancing his checkbook because he did not notice this fee on his bank statement. His bank statement showed a balance of $822.18. Bill's checkbook had a balance of $206.48. Check No. 406 for $116.08 and Check No. 407 for $12.50 were outstanding. A $521 deposit was not on the statement. Bill has his payroll check electronically deposited to his checking account—the payroll check was for $1,015.12 (Bill's payroll checks vary each month). There are also a $1 service fee and a teller fee of $6. Complete Bill's bank reconciliation.

7. At First National Bank in San Diego, some customers have to pay $25 each year as an ATM card fee. John Levi banks at First National Bank and just received his bank statement showing a balance of $829.25; his checkbook balance is $467.40. The bank statement shows an ATM card fee of $25.00, teller fee of $9.00, interest of $1.80, and John's $880 IRS refund check, which was processed by the IRS and deposited to his account. John has two checks that have not cleared—No. 112 for $620.10 and No. 113 for $206.05. There is also a deposit in transit for $1,312.10. Prepare John's bank reconciliation.

Classroom Notes

Name ______________________________ Date ______________

Learning Unit 5–1: Solving Equations for the Unknown

DRILL PROBLEMS

1. Write equations for the following situations. Use N for the unknown number. Do not solve the equations.

a. Four times a number is 120.

b. A number increased by 13 equals 25.

c. Seven less than a number is 5.

d. Fifty-seven decreased by 3 times a number is 21.

e. Fourteen added to one-third of a number is 18.

f. Twice the sum of a number and 4 is 32.

g. Three-fourths of a number is 9.

h. Two times a number plus 3 times the same number plus 8 is 68.

2. Solve for the unknown number:

a. $B + 10 = 45$ **b.** $29 + M = 44$ **c.** $D - 77 = 98$

d. $7N = 63$ **e.** $\frac{X}{12} = 11$ **f.** $3Q + 4Q + 2Q = 108$

g. $H + 5H + 3 = 57$ **h.** $2(N - 3) = 62$ **i.** $\frac{3R}{4} = 27$

j. $E - 32 = 41$ **k.** $5(2T - 2) = 120$ **l.** $12W - 5W = 98$

m. $49 - X = 37$ **n.** $12(V + 2) = 84$ **o.** $7D + 4 = 5D + 14$

p. $7(T - 2) = 2T - 9$

Learning Unit 5–2 : Solving Word Problems for the Unknown

WORD PROBLEMS

1. A blue denim shirt at the Old Navy was marked down $20. The sale price was $40. What was the original price?

Unknown(s)	Variables(s)	Relationship

2. Goodwin's Corporation found that $\frac{2}{3}$ of its employees were vested in their retirement plan. If 124 employees are vested, what is the total number of employees at Goodwin's?

Unknown(s)	Variables(s)	Relationship

3. Eileen Haskin's utility and telephone bills for the month totaled $180. The utility bill was 3 times as much as the telephone bill. How much was each bill?

Unknown(s)	Variables(s)	Relationship

4. Ryan and his friends went to the golf course to hunt for golf balls. Ryan found 15 more than $\frac{1}{3}$ of the total number of golf balls that were found. How many golf balls were found if Ryan found 75 golf balls?

Unknown(s)	Variables(s)	Relationship

5. Linda Mills and Sherry Somers sold 459 tickets for the Advertising Club's raffle. If Linda sold 8 times as many tickets as Sherry, how many tickets did each one sell?

Unknown(s)	Variables(s)	Relationship

6. Jason Mazzola wanted to buy a suit at Giblee's. Jason did not have enough money with him, so Mr. Giblee told him he would hold the suit if Jason gave him a deposit of $\frac{1}{5}$ of the cost of the suit. Jason agreed and gave Mr. Giblee $79. What was the price of the suit?

Unknown(s)	Variables(s)	Relationship

7. Peter sold watches ($7) and necklaces ($4) at a flea market. Total sales were $300. People bought 3 times as many watches as necklaces. How many of each did Peter sell? What were the total dollar sales of each?

Unknown(s)	Variables(s)	Price	Relationship

8. Peter sold watches ($7) and necklaces ($4) at a flea market. Total sales for 48 watches and necklaces were $300. How many of each did Peter sell? What were the total dollar sales of each?

Unknown(s)	Variables(s)	Price	Relationship

9. A 3,000 piece of direct mailing cost $1,435. Printing cost is $550, about $3\frac{1}{2}$ times the cost of typesetting. How much did the typesetting cost? Round to the nearest cent.

Unknown(s)	Variables(s)	Relationship

10. In 2012, Tony Rigato, owner of MRM, saw an increase in sales to $13.5 million. Rigato states that since 2009, sales have more than tripled. What were his sales in 2009?

Unknown(s)	Variables(s)	Relationship

Classroom Notes

Name ______________________________ Date ______________

Learning Unit 6–1 : Conversions

DRILL PROBLEMS

1. Convert the following to percents (round to the nearest tenth of a percent if needed):

a. .03 ________ % **b.** .729 ________ % **c.** .009 ________ %

d. 8.3 ________ % **e.** 5.26 ________ % **f.** 6 ________ %

g. .0105 ________ % **h.** .1180 ________ % **i.** 5.0375 ________ %

j. .862 ________ % **k.** .2615 ________ % **l.** .8 ________ %

m. .025 ________ % **n.** .06 ________ %

2. Convert the following to decimals (do not round):

a. 33% ________ **b.** .09% ________

c. 4.7% ________ **d.** 9.67% ________

e. .2% ________ **f.** $\frac{1}{4}$% ________

g. .76% ________ **h.** 110% ________

i. $12\frac{1}{2}$% ________ **j.** 5% ________

k. .004% ________ **l.** $7\frac{5}{10}$% ________

m. $\frac{3}{4}$% ________ **n.** 1% ________

3. Convert the following to percents (round to the nearest tenth of a percent if needed):

a. $\frac{4}{10}$ ________ % **b.** $\frac{1}{5}$ ________ %

c. $1\frac{5}{8}$ ________ % **d.** $\frac{2}{7}$ ________ %

e. 2 ________ % **f.** $\frac{14}{100}$ ________ %

g. $\frac{1}{6}$ ________ % **h.** $\frac{1}{2}$ ________ %

i. $\frac{3}{5}$ ________ % **j.** $\frac{3}{25}$ ________ %

k. $\frac{5}{16}$ ________ % **l.** $\frac{11}{50}$ ________ %

m. $4\frac{3}{4}$ ________ % **n.** $\frac{3}{200}$ ________ %

4. Convert the following to fractions in simplest form:

a. 40% ________ **b.** 15% ________

c. 50% ________ **d.** 75% ________

e. 35% ________ **f.** 85% ________

g. $12\frac{1}{2}$% ________ **h.** $37\frac{1}{2}$% ________

i. $33\frac{1}{3}$% ________ **j.** 3% ________

k. 8.5% ________ **l.** $5\frac{3}{4}$% ________

m. 100% ________ **n.** 10% ________

5. Complete the following table by finding the missing fraction, decimal, or percent equivalent:

	Fraction	Decimal	Percent		Fraction	Decimal	Percent
a.	______	.25	25%	**h.**	$\frac{1}{6}$	$.16\overline{6}$	______
b.	$\frac{3}{8}$	______	$37\frac{1}{2}\%$	**i.**	______	$.083\overline{3}$	$8\frac{1}{3}\%$
c.	$\frac{1}{2}$	.5	______	**j.**	$\frac{1}{9}$	______	$11\frac{1}{9}\%$
d.	$\frac{2}{3}$	______	$66\frac{2}{3}\%$	**k.**	______	.3125	$31\frac{1}{4}\%$
e.	______	.4	40%	**l.**	$\frac{3}{40}$	.075	______
f.	$\frac{3}{5}$	.6	______	**m.**	$\frac{1}{5}$	______	20%
g.	$\frac{7}{10}$	______	70%	**n.**	______	1.125	$112\frac{1}{2}\%$

WORD PROBLEMS

6. If in 2011, Mutual of New York reported that 60% of its new sales came from existing clients. What fractional part of its new sales came from existing clients? Reduce to simplest form.

7. Six hundred ninety corporations and design firms competed for the Industrial Design Excellence Award (IDEA). Twenty were selected as the year's best and received gold awards. Show the gold award winners as a fraction; then show what percent of the entrants received gold awards. Round to the nearest tenth of a percent.

8. If in the first half of 2010, stock prices in the Standard & Poor's 500-stock index rose 3.2%. Show the increase as a decimal.

9. In the recent banking crisis, many banks were unable to cover their bad loans. Citicorp, the nation's largest real estate lender, was reported as having only enough reserves to cover 39% of its bad loans. What fractional part of its loan losses was covered?

10. Dave Mattera spent his vacation in Las Vegas. He ordered breakfast in his room, and when he went downstairs to the coffee shop, he discovered that the same breakfast was much less expensive. He had paid 1.884 times as much for the breakfast in his room. What was the percent of increase for the breakfast in his room?

11. Putnam Management Company of Boston recently increased its management fee by .09%. What is the increase as a decimal? What is the same increase as a fraction?

12. Joel Black and Karen Whyte formed a partnership and drew up a partnership agreement, with profits and losses to be divided equally after each partner receives a $7\frac{1}{2}\%$ return on his or her capital contribution. Show their return on investment as a decimal and as a fraction. Reduce.

Learning Unit 6–2: Application of Percents—Portion Formula

DRILL PROBLEMS

1. Fill in the amount of the base, rate, and portion in each of the following statements:

a. The Logans spend \$3,000 a month on food, which is 20% of their monthly income of \$15,000.
Base ____________ Rate ____________ Portion ____________

b. Rocky Norman got a \$15 discount when he purchased a new camera. This was 20% off the sticker price of \$75.
Base ____________ Rate ____________ Portion ____________

c. Mary Burns got a 12% senior citizens discount when she bought a \$7.00 movie ticket. She saved \$0.84.
Base ____________ Rate ____________ Portion ____________

d. Arthur Bogey received a commission of \$13,500 when he sold the Brown's house for \$225,000. His commission rate is 6%.
Base ____________ Rate ____________ Portion ____________

e. Leo Davis deposited \$5,000 in a certificate of deposit (CD). A year later he received an interest payment of \$450, which was a yield of 9%.
Base ____________ Rate ____________ Portion ____________

f. Grace Tremblay is on a diet that allows her to eat 1,600 calories per day. For breakfast she had 600 calories, which is $37\frac{1}{2}$% of her allowance.
Base ____________ Rate ____________ Portion ____________

2. Find the portion; round to the nearest hundredth if necessary:

a. 7% of 74 ____________ **b.** 12% of 205 ____________ **c.** 16% of 630 ____________

d. 7.5% of 920 ____________ **e.** 25% of 1,004 ____________ **f.** 10% of 79 ____________

g. 103% of 44 ____________ **h.** 30% of 78 ____________ **i.** .2% of 50 ____________

j. 1% of 5,622 ____________ **k.** $6\frac{1}{4}$% of 480 ____________ **l.** 150% of 10 ____________

m. 100% of 34 ____________ **n.** $\frac{1}{2}$% of 27 ____________

3. Find the rate; round to the nearest tenth of a percent as needed:

a. 30 is what percent of 90? ____________ **b.** 6 is what percent of 200? ____________

c. 275 is what percent of 1,000? ____________ **d.** .8 is what percent of 44? ____________

e. 67 is what percent of 2,010? ____________ **f.** 550 is what percent of 250? ____________

g. 13 is what percent of 650? ____________ **h.** \$15 is what percent of \$455? ____________

i. .05 is what percent of 100? ____________ **j.** \$6.25 is what percent of \$10? ____________

4. Find the base; round to the nearest tenth as needed:

a. 63 is 30% of ____________ **b.** 60 is 33% of ____________ **c.** 150 is 25% of ____________

d. 47 is 1% of ____________ **e.** \$21 is 120% of ____________ **f.** 2.26 is 40% of ____________

g. 75 is $12\frac{1}{2}$% of ____________ **h.** 18 is 22.2% of ____________ **i.** \$37.50 is 50% of ____________

j. 250 is 100% of ____________

5. Find the percent of increase or decrease. Round to nearest tenth percent as needed:

	Last year	This year	Amount of change	Percent of change
a.	5,962	4,378	____________	____________
b.	\$10,995	\$12,250	____________	____________
c.	120,000	140,000	____________	____________
d.	120,000	100,000	____________	____________

WORD PROBLEMS

6. A machine that originally cost $5,000 was sold for $500 at the end of 5 years. What percent of the original cost is the selling price?

7. Joanne Byrne invested $75,000 in a candy shop and is making 12% per year on her investment. How much money per year is she making on her investment?

8. There was a fire in Bill Porper's store that caused 2,780 inventory items to be destroyed. Before the fire, 9,565 inventory items were in the store. What percent of inventory was destroyed? Round to nearest tenth percent.

9. Elyse's Dress Shoppe makes 25% of its sales for cash. If the cash receipts on January 21 were $799, what were the total sales for the day?

10. The YMCA is holding a fund-raiser to collect money for a new gym floor. So far it has collected $7,875, which is 63% of the goal. What is the amount of the goal? How much more money must the YMCA collect?

11. Leslie Tracey purchased her home for $51,500. She sold it last year for $221,200. What percent profit did she make on the sale? Round to nearest tenth percent.

12. Maplewood Park Tool & Die had an annual production of 375,165 units this year. This is 140% of the annual production last year. What was last year's annual production?

Name ______________________________ Date ______________

Learning Unit 7–1: Trade Discounts—Single and Chain*

DRILL PROBLEMS

1. Calculate the trade discount amount for each of the following items:

Item	List price	Trade discount	Trade discount amount
a. BlackBerry	$ 250	30%	________
b. Flat-screen TV	$1,200	30%	________
c. Suit	$ 500	10%	________
d. Bicycle	$ 800	$12\frac{1}{2}$	________
e. David Yurman bracelet	$ 950	40%	________

2. Calculate the net price for each of the following items:

Item	List price	Trade discount amount	Net price
a. Home Depot table	$600	$250	________
b. Bookcase	$525	$129	________
c. Rocking chair	$480	$ 95	________

3. Fill in the missing amount for each of the following items:

Item	List price	Trade discount amount	Net price
a. Sears electric saw	________	$19	$56.00
b. Electric drill	$90	________	$68.50
c. Ladder	$56	$15.25	________

4. For each of the following, find the percent paid (complement of trade discount) and the net price:

List price	Trade discount	Percent paid	Net price
a. $45	15%	________	________
b. $195	12.2%	________	________
c. $325	50%	________	________
d. $120	18%	________	________

5. In each of the following examples, find the net price equivalent rate and the single equivalent discount rate:

Chain discount	Net price equivalent rate	Single equivalent discount rate
a. 25/5	________	________
b. 15/15	________	________
c. 15/10/5	________	________
d. 12/12/6	________	________

*Freight problems to be shown in LU 7–2 material.

6. In each of the following examples, find the net price and the trade discount:

	List price	Chain discount	Net price	Trade discount
a.	$5,000	10/10/5	________	________
b.	$7,500	9/6/3	________	________
c.	$898	20/7/2	________	________
d.	$1,500	25/10	________	________

7. The list price of a handheld calculator is $19.50, and the trade discount is 18%. Find the trade discount amount.

8. The list price of a silver picture frame is $29.95, and the trade discount is 15%. Find the trade discount amount and the net price.

9. The net price of a set of pots and pans is $65, and the trade discount is 20%. What is the list price?

10. Jennie's Variety Store has the opportunity to purchase candy from three different wholesalers; each of the wholesalers offers a different chain discount. Company A offers 25/5/5, Company B offers 20/10/5, and Company C offers 15/20. Which company should Jennie deal with? *Hint:* Choose the company with the highest single equivalent discount rate.

11. The list price of a television set is $625. Find the net price after a series discount of 30/20/10.

12. Mandy's Accessories Shop purchased 12 purses with a total list price of $726. What was the net price of each purse if the wholesaler offered a chain discount of 25/20?

13. Kransberg Furniture Store purchased a bedroom set for $1,097.25 from Furniture Wholesalers. The list price of the set was $1,995. What trade discount rate did Kransberg receive?

14. Susan Monk teaches second grade and receives a discount at the local art supply store. Recently she paid $47.25 for art supplies after receiving a chain discount of 30/10. What was the regular price of the art supplies?

Learning Unit 7–2 : Cash Discounts, Credit Terms, and Partial Payments

DRILL PROBLEMS

1. Complete the following table:

	Date of invoice	Date goods received	Terms	Last day of discount period	End of credit period
a.	February 8		2/10, n/30	______	______
b.	August 26		2/10, n/30	______	______
c.	October 17		3/10, n/60	______	______
d.	March 11	May 10	3/10, n/30, ROG	______	______
e.	September 14		2/10, EOM	______	______
f.	May 31		2/10, EOM	______	______

2. Calculate the cash discount and the net amount paid.

	Invoice amount	Cash discount rate	Discount amount	Net amount paid
a.	$75	3%	______	______
b.	$1,559	2%	______	______
c.	$546.25	2%	______	______
d.	$9,788.75	1%	______	______

3. Use the complement of the cash discount to calculate the net amount paid. Assume all invoices are paid within the discount period.

	Terms of invoice	Amount of invoice	Complement	Net amount paid
a.	2/10, n/30	$1,125	______	______
b.	3/10, n/30 ROG	$4,500	______	______
c.	2/10, EOM	$375.50	______	______
d.	1/15, n/45	$3,998	______	______

4. Calculate the amount of cash discount and the net amount paid.

	Date of invoice	Terms of invoice	Amount of invoice	Date paid	Cash discount	Amount paid
a.	January 12	2/10, n/30	$5,320	January 22	______	______
b.	May 28	2/10, n/30	$975	June 7	______	______
c.	August 15	2/10, n/30	$7,700	August 26	______	______
d.	March 8	2/10, EOM	$480	April 10	______	______
e.	January 24	3/10, n/60	$1,225	February 3	______	______

5. Complete the following table:

	Total invoice	Freight charges included in invoice total	Date of invoice	Terms of invoice	Date of payment	Cash discount	Amount paid
a.	$852	$12.50	3/19	2/10, n/30	3/29	______	______
b.	$669.57	$15.63	7/28	3/10, EOM	9/10	______	______
c.	$500	$11.50	4/25	2/10, n/60	6/5	______	______
d.	$188	$9.70	1/12	2/10, EOM	2/10	______	______

6. In the following table, assume that all the partial payments were made within the discount period.

	Amount of invoice	Terms of invoice	Partial payment	Amount to be credited	Balance outstanding
a.	$481.90	2/10, n/30	$90.00	________	________
b.	$1,000	2/10, EOM	$500.00	________	________
c.	$782.88	3/10, n/30, ROG	$275.00	________	________
d.	$318.80	2/15, n/60	$200.00	________	________

WORD PROBLEMS

7. Lynch Chemical Company received an invoice for $14,800, dated March 14, with terms of 2/10, n/30. If the invoice was paid March 22, what was the amount due?

8. On May 27, Trotter Hardware Store received an invoice for trash barrels purchased for $13,650 with terms of 3/10, EOM; the freight charge, which is included in the price, is $412. What are **(a)** the last day of the discount period and **(b)** the amount of the payment due on this date?

9. The Glass Sailboat received an invoice for $930.50 with terms 2/10, n/30 on April 19. On April 29, it sent a payment of $430.50. **(a)** How much credit will be given on the total due? **(b)** What is the new balance due?

10. Dallas Ductworks offers cash discounts of 2/10, 1/15, n/30 on all purchases. If an invoice for $544 dated July 18 is paid on August 2, what is the amount due?

11. The list price of a DVD player is $299.90 with trade discounts of 10/20 and terms of 3/10, n/30. If a retailer pays the invoice within the discount period, what amount must the retailer pay?

12. The invoice of a sneakers supplier totaled $2,488.50, was dated February 7, and offered terms 2/10, ROG. The shipment of sneakers was received on March 7. What are **(a)** the last date of the discount period and **(b)** the amount of the discount that will be lost if the invoice is paid after that date?

13. Starburst Toy Company receives an invoice amounting to $1,152.30 with terms of 2/10, EOM and dated November 6. If a partial payment of $750 is made on December 8, what are **(a)** the credit given for the partial payment and **(b)** the balance due on the invoice?

14. Todd's Sporting Goods received an invoice for soccer equipment dated July 26 with terms 3/10, 1/15, n/30 in the amount of $3,225.83, which included shipping charges of $375.50. If this bill is paid on August 5, what amount must be paid?

Name ______ Date ______

Learning Unit 8–1: Markups Based on Cost (100%)

DRILL PROBLEMS

1. Fill in the missing numbers:

	Cost	Dollar markup	Selling price
a.	$12.10	$3.25	______
b.	$8.32	______	$11.04
c.	$25.27	______	$29.62
d.	______	$75.00	$165.00
e.	$86.54	$29.77	______

2. Calculate the markup based on cost (round to the nearest cent).

	Cost	Markup (percent of cost)	Dollar markup
a.	$425.00	30%	______
b.	$1.52	20%	______
c.	$9.90	$12\frac{1}{2}$	______
d.	$298.10	50%	______
e.	$74.25	38%	______
f.	$552.25	100%	______

3. Calculate the dollar markup and rate of the markup as a percent of cost (round percents to nearest tenth percent). Verify your result, which may be slightly off due to rounding.

	Cost	Selling price	Dollar markup	Markup (percent of cost)	Verify
a.	$2.50	$4.50	______	______	______
b.	$12.50	$19.00	______	______	______
c.	$0.97	$1.25	______	______	______
d.	$132.25	$175.00	______	______	______
e.	$65.00	$89.99	______	______	______

4. Calculate the dollar markup and the selling price.

	Cost	Markup (percent of cost)	Dollar markup	Selling price
a.	$2.20	40%	______	______
b.	$2.80	16%	______	______
c.	$840.00	$12\frac{1}{2}\%$	______	______
d.	$24.36	30%	______	______

5. Calculate the cost (round to the nearest cent).

	Selling price	Rate of markup based on cost	Cost
a.	$1.98	30%	________
b.	$360.00	60%	________
c.	$447.50	20%	________
d.	$1,250.00	100%	________

6. Find the missing numbers. Round money to the nearest cent and percents to the nearest tenth percent.

	Cost	Dollar markup	Percent markup on cost	Selling price
a.	$72.00	________	40%	________
b.	________	$7.00	________	$35.00
c.	$8.80	$1.10	________	________
d.	________	________	28%	$19.84
e.	$175.00	________	________	$236.25

WORD PROBLEMS

7. The cost of an recliner chair is $399 and the markup rate is 35% of the cost. What are **(a)** the dollar markup and **(b)** the selling price?

8. If Barry's Furniture Store purchased a floor lamp for $120 and plans to add a markup of $90, **(a)** what will the selling price be and **(b)** what is the markup as a percent of cost?

9. If Lesjardin's Jewelry Store is selling a gold bracelet for $349, which includes a markup of 35% on cost, what are **(a)** Lesjardin's cost and **(b)** the amount of the dollar markup?

10. Toll's Variety Store sells an alarm clock for $14.75. The alarm clock cost Toll's $9.90. What is the markup amount as a percent of cost? Round to the nearest whole percent.

11. Swanson's Audio Supply marks up its merchandise by 40% on cost. If the markup on a cassette player is $85, what are **(a)** the cost of the cassette player and **(b)** the selling price?

12. Brown's Department Store is selling a shirt for $55. If the markup is 70% on cost, what is Brown's cost (to the nearest cent)?

13. Ward's Greenhouse purchased tomato flats for $5.75 each. Ward's has decided to use a markup of 42% on cost. Find the selling price.

Learning Unit 8–2: Markups Based on Selling Price (100%)

DRILL PROBLEMS

1. Calculate the markup based on the selling price.

	Selling price	Markup (percent of selling price)	Dollar markup
a.	$18.00	30%	______
b.	$230.00	25%	______
c.	$81.00	42.5%	______
d.	$72.88	$37\frac{1}{2}\%$	______
e.	$1.98	$7\frac{1}{2}\%$	______

2. Calculate the dollar markup and the markup as a percent of selling price (to the nearest tenth percent). Verify your answer, which may be slightly off due to rounding.

	Cost	Selling price	Dollar markup	Markup (percent of selling price)	Verify
a.	$2.50	$4.25	______	______	______
b.	$16.00	$24.00	______	______	______
c.	$45.25	$85.00	______	______	______
d.	$0.19	$0.25	______	______	______
e.	$5.50	$8.98	______	______	______

3. Given the *cost* and the markup as a percent of *selling price*, calculate the selling price.

	Cost	Markup (percent of selling price)	Selling price
a.	$5.90	15%	______
b.	$600	32%	______
c.	$15	50%	______
d.	$120	30%	______
e.	$0.29	20%	______

4. Given the selling price and the percent markup on selling price, calculate the cost.

	Cost	Markup (percent of selling price)	Selling price
a.	______	40%	$6.25
b.	______	20%	$16.25
c.	______	19%	$63.89
d.	______	$62\frac{1}{2}\%$	$44.00

5. Calculate the equivalent rate of markup (round to the nearest hundredth percent).

	Markup on cost	Markup on selling price		Markup on cost	Markup on selling price
a.	40%	_______	b.	50%	_______
c.	_______	50%	d.	_______	35%
e.	_______	40%			

WORD PROBLEMS

6. Fisher Equipment is selling a Wet/Dry Shop Vac for $49.97. If Fisher's markup is 40% of the selling price, what is the cost of the Shop Vac?

7. Gove Lumber Company purchased a 10-inch table saw for $225 and will mark up the price 35% on the selling price. What will the selling price be?

8. To realize a sufficient gross margin, City Paint and Supply Company marks up its paint 27% on the selling price. If a gallon of Latex Semi-Gloss Enamel has a markup of $4.02, find **(a)** the selling price and **(b)** the cost.

9. A Magnavox 20-inch color TV cost $180 and sells for $297. What is the markup based on the selling price? Round to the nearest hundredth percent.

10. Bargain Furniture sells a five-piece country maple bedroom set for $1,299. The cost of this set is $700. What are **(a)** the markup on the bedroom set, **(b)** the markup percent on cost, and **(c)** the markup percent on the selling price? Round to the nearest hundredth percent.

11. Robert's Department Store marks up its sundries by 28% on the selling price. If a 6.4-ounce tube of toothpaste costs $1.65, what will the selling price be?

12. To be competitive, Tinker Toys must sell the Nintendo Control Deck for $89.99. To meet expenses and make a sufficient profit, Tinker Toys must add a markup on the selling price of 23%. What is the maximum amount that Tinker Toys can afford to pay a wholesaler for Nintendo?

13. Nicole's Restaurant charges $7.50 for a linguini dinner that costs $2.75 for the ingredients. What rate of markup is earned on the selling price? Round to the nearest hundredth percent.

Learning Unit 8–3 : Markdowns and Perishables

DRILL PROBLEMS

1. Find the dollar markdown and the sale price.

	Original selling price	Markdown percent	Dollar markdown	Sale price
a.	$100	30%	______	________
b.	$2,099.98	25%	______	________
c.	$729	30%	______	________

2. Find the dollar markdown and the markdown percent on original selling price.

	Original selling price	Sale price	Dollar markdown	Markdown percent
a.	$19.50	$9.75	_______	______
b.	$250	$175	_______	______
c.	$39.95	$29.96	_______	______

3. Find the original selling price.

	Sale price	Markdown percent	Original selling price
a.	$328	20%	_______
b.	$15.85	15%	_______

4. Calculate the final selling price.

	Original selling price	First markdown	Second markdown	Final markup	Final selling price
a.	$4.96	25%	8%	5%	_______
b.	$130	30%	10%	20%	_______

5. Find the missing amounts.

	Number of units	Unit cost	Total cost	Estimated* spoilage	Desired markup (percent of cost)	Total selling price	Selling price per unit
a.	72	$3	______	12%	50%	______	______
b.	50	$0.90	______	16%	42%	______	______

*Round to the nearest whole unit as needed.

WORD PROBLEMS

6. Speedy King is having a 30%-off sale on their box springs and mattresses. A queen-size, back-supporter mattress is priced at $325. What is the sale price of the mattress?

7. Murray and Sons sell a personal fax machine for $602.27. It is having a sale, and the fax machine is marked down to $499.88. What is the percent of the markdown?

8. Coleman's is having a clearance sale. A lamp with an original selling price of $249 is now selling for $198. Find the percent of the markdown. Round to the nearest hundredth percent.

9. Johnny's Sports Shop has advertised markdowns on certain items of 22%. A soccer ball is marked with a sale price of $16.50. What was the original price of the soccer ball?

10. Sam Grillo sells seasonal furnishings. Near the end of the summer a five-piece patio set that was priced $349.99 had not been sold, so he marked it down by 12%. As Labor Day approached, he still had not sold the patio set, so he marked it down an additional 18%. What was the final selling price of the patio set?

11. Calsey's Department Store sells their down comforters for a regular price of $325. During its white sale the comforters were marked down 22%. Then, at the end of the sale, Calsey's held a special promotion and gave a second markdown of 10%. When the sale was over, the remaining comforters were marked up 20%. What was the final selling price of the remaining comforters?

12. The New Howard Bakery wants to make a 60% profit on the cost of its pies. To calculate the price of the pies, it estimated that the usual amount of spoilage is 5 pies. Calculate the selling price for each pie if the number of pies baked each day is 24 and the cost of the ingredients for each pie is $1.80.

13. Sunshine Bakery bakes 660 loaves of bread each day and estimates that 10% of the bread will go stale before it is sold and will have to be discarded. The owner of the bakery wishes to realize a 55% markup on cost on the bread. If the cost to make a loaf of bread is $0.46, what should the owner sell each loaf for?

Learning Unit 8–4 : Breakeven Analysis

DRILL PROBLEMS

1. Calculate the contribution margin.

	Selling Price per unit	Variable cost per unit	Contribution margin
a.	$12.00	$5.00	
b.	$15.99	$4.88	
c.	$18.99	$4.99	
d.	$251.86	$110.00	
e.	$510.99	$310.00	
f.	$1,000.10	$410.00	

2. Calculate the selling price per unit.

	Selling price per unit	Variable cost per unit	Contribution margin
a.		$12.18	$ 4.10
b.		$19.19	$ 5.18
c.		$21.00	$13.00
d.		$41.00	$14.88
e.		$128.10	$79.50
f.		$99.99	$60.00

3. Calculate the breakeven point (round to nearest whole unit)

	Break even point	Fixed cost	Selling price per unit	Variable cost per unit
a.		$50,000	$4.00	$1.00
b.		$30,000	$6.00	$2.00
c.		$20,000	$9.00	$3.00
d.		$100,000	$12.00	$4.00
e.		$120,000	$14.00	$5.00
f.		$90,000	$26.00	$8.00

WORD PROBLEMS

4. Jones Co. produces bars of candy. Each bar sells for 3.99. The variable cost per unit is $2.85. What is the contribution margin for Jones Co.?

5. Logan Co. produces stuffed animals. They have $40,000 in fixed costs. Logan sells each animal for $19.99 with a $12.10 cost per unit. What is the breakeven point for Logan? Round to the nearest whole number.

6. Ranyo Company produces lawn mowers. It has a breakeven point 6,000 lawn mowers. If its contribution margin is $150. What is Ranyo's fixed cost?

7. Moore company has $100,000 in fixed costs. Its contribution margin is $4.50. Calculate the breakeven point for Moore to the nearest whole number.

Classroom Notes

Name ______________________ Date ______________

Learning Unit 9–1: Calculating Various Types of Employees' Gross Pay

DRILL PROBLEMS

1. Fill in the missing amounts for each of the following employees. Do not round the overtime rate in your calculations and round your final answers to the nearest cent.

	Employee	Total hours	Rate per hour	Regular pay	Overtime pay	Gross pay
a.	Ed Slope	40	$9.20	______	______	______
b.	Casey Guitare	43	$9.00	______	______	______
c.	Norma Harris	37	$7.50	______	______	______
d.	Ed Jackson	45	$12.25	______	______	______

2. Calculate each employee's gross from the following data. Do not round the overtime rate in your calculation but round your final answers to the nearest cent.

	Employee	S	M	Tu	W	Th	F	S	Total hours	Rate per hour	Regular pay	Overtime pay	Gross pay
a.	L. Adams	0	8	8	8	8	8	0	____	$8.10	______	______	______
b.	M. Card	0	9	8	9	8	8	4	____	$11.35	______	______	______
c.	P. Kline	2	$7\frac{1}{2}$	$8\frac{1}{4}$	8	$10\frac{3}{4}$	9	2	____	$10.60	______	______	______
d.	J. Mack	0	$9\frac{1}{2}$	$9\frac{3}{4}$	$9\frac{1}{2}$	10	10	4	____	$9.95	______	______	______

3. Calculate the gross wages of the following production workers.

	Employee	Rate per unit	No. of units produced	Gross pay
a.	A. Bossie	$0.67	655	______
b.	J. Carson	$0.87\frac{1}{2}$	703	______

4. Using the given differential scale, calculate the gross wages of the following production workers.

Units produced	Amount per unit
From 1–50	$.55
From 51–100	.65
From 101–200	.72
More than 200	.95

	Employee	Units produced	Gross pay
a.	F. Burns	190	______
b.	B. English	210	______
c.	E. Jackson	200	______

5. Calculate the following salespersons' gross wages.

a. Straight commission:

Employee	Net sales	Commission	Gross pay
M. Salley	$40,000	13%	______

b. Straight commission with draw:

Employee	Net sales	Commission	Draw	Commission minus draw
G. Gorsbeck	$38,000	12%	$600	________

c. Variable commission scale:

Up to $25,000	8%
Excess of $25,000 to $40,000	10%
More than $40,000	12%

Employee	Net sales	Gross pay
H. Lloyd	$42,000	________

d. Salary plus commission:

Employee	Salary	Commission	Quota	Net sales	Gross pay
P. Floyd	$2,500	3%	$400,000	$475,000	________

WORD PROBLEMS

For all problems with overtime, be sure to round only the final answer.

6. In the first week of December, Dana Robinson worked 52 hours. His regular rate of pay is $11.25 per hour. What was Dana's gross pay for the week?

7. Davis Fisheries pays its workers for each box of fish they pack. Sunny Melanson receives $.30 per box. During the third week of July, Sunny packed 2,410 boxes of fish. What is Sunny's gross pay?

8. Maye George is a real estate broker who receives a straight commission of 6%. What would her commission be for a house that sold for $197,500?

9. Devon Company pays Eileen Haskins a straight commission of $12\frac{1}{2}$% on net sales. In January, Devon gave Eileen a draw of $600. She had net sales that month of $35,570. What was Eileen's commission minus draw?

10. Parker and Company pays Selma Stokes on a variable commission scale. In a month when Selma had net sales of $155,000, what was her gross pay based on the following schedule?

Net sales	Commission rate
Up to $40,000	5%
Excess of $40,000 to $75,000	5.5%
Excess of $75,000 to $100,000	6%
More than $100,000	7%

11. Marsh Furniture Company pays Joshua Charles a monthly salary of $1,900 plus a commission of $2\frac{1}{2}$% on sales over $12,500. Last month, Joshua had net sales of $17,799. What was Joshua's gross pay for the month?

12. Amy McWha works at Lamplighter Bookstore where she earns $7.75 per hour plus a commission of 2% on her weekly sales in excess of $1,500. Last week, Amy worked 39 hours and had total sales of $2,250. What was Amy's gross pay for the week?

Learning Unit 9–2: Computing Payroll Deductions for Employees' Pay; Employers' Responsibilities

DRILL PROBLEMS

Use tables in the *Business Math Handbook* (assume FICA rates in text).

	Employee	Allowances and marital status	Cumulative earnings	Salary per week	Taxable earnings S.S.	Taxable earnings Medicare
1.	Pete Small	M—3	$106,300	$2,300	**a.** ______	**b.** ______
2.	Alice Hall	M—1	$90,000	$1,100	**c.** ______	**d.** ______
3.	Jean Rose	M—2	$100,000	$2,000	**e.** ______	**f.** ______

4. What is the tax for Social Security and Medicare for Pete in Problem 1?

5. Calculate Pete's FIT by the percentage method.

6. What would employer's contribute for this week's payroll for SUTA and FUTA?

WORD PROBLEMS

7. Cynthia Pratt has earned $105,300 thus far this year. This week she earned $3,500. Find her total FICA tax deduction (Social Security and Medicare).

8. If Cynthia (Problem 7) earns $1,050 the following week, what will be her new total FICA tax deduction?

9. Roger Alley, a service dispatcher, has weekly earnings of $750. He claimed four allowances on his W-4 form and is married. Besides his FIT and FICA deductions, he has deductions of $35.16 for medical insurance and $17.25 for union dues. Calculate his net earnings for the third week in February. Use the percentage method.

10. Nicole Mariotte is unmarried and claimed one withholding allowance on her W-4 form. In the second week of February, she earned $707.35. Deductions from her pay included federal withholding, Social Security, Medicare, health insurance for $47.75, and $30.00 for the company meal plan. What is Nicole's net pay for the week? Use the percentage method.

11. Gerald Knowlton had total gross earnings of $106,500 in the last week of November. His earnings for the first week in December were $804.70. His employer uses the percentage method to calculate federal withholding. If Gerald is married, claims two allowances, and has medical insurance of $52.25 deducted each week from his pay, what is his net pay for the week?

Name ______________________________ Date ______________

Learning Unit 10–1: Calculation of Simple Interest and Maturity Value

DRILL PROBLEMS

1. Find the simple interest for each of the following loans:

	Principal	Rate	Time	Interest
a.	$9,000	3%	1 year	______
b.	$3,000	12%	3 years	______
c.	$18,000	$8\frac{1}{2}\%$	10 months	______

2. Find the simple interest for each of the following loans; use the exact interest method. Use the days-in-a-year calendar in the text when needed.

	Principal	Rate	Time	Interest
a.	$900	4%	30 days	______
b.	$4,290	8%	250 days	______
c.	$1,500	8%	Made March 11 Due July 11	______

3. Find the simple interest for each of the following loans using the ordinary interest method (Banker's Rule).

	Principal	Rate	Time	Interest
a.	$5,250	$7\frac{1}{2}\%$	120 days	______
b.	$700	3%	70 days	______
c.	$2,600	11%	Made on June 15 Due October 17	______

WORD PROBLEMS

4. On October 17, Gill Iowa borrowed $6,000 at a rate of 4%. She promised to repay the loan in 7 months. What are **(a)** the amount of the simple interest and **(b)** the total amount owed upon maturity?

5. Marjorie Folsom borrowed $5,500 to purchase a computer. The loan was for 9 months at an annual interest rate of $12\frac{1}{2}\%$. What are **(a)** the amount of interest Marjorie must pay and **(b)** the maturity value of the loan?

6. Eric has a loan for $1,200 at an ordinary interest rate of 9.5% for 80 days. Julie has a loan for $1,200 at an exact interest rate of 9.5% for 80 days. Calculate **(a)** the total amount due on Eric's loan and **(b)** the total amount due on Julie's loan.

7. Roger Lee borrowed \$5,280 at $13\frac{1}{2}\%$ on May 24 and agreed to repay the loan on August 24. The lender calculates interest using the exact interest method. How much will Roger be required to pay on August 24?

8. On March 8, Jack Faltin borrowed \$10,225 at $9\frac{3}{4}\%$. He signed a note agreeing to repay the loan and interest on November 8. If the lender calculates interest using the ordinary interest method, what will Jack's repayment be?

9. Dianne Smith's real estate taxes of \$641.49 were due on November 1, 2009. Due to financial difficulties, Dianne was unable to pay her tax bill until January 15, 2010. The penalty for late payment is $13\frac{3}{8}\%$ ordinary interest. What is the penalty Dianne will have to pay, and what is Dianne's total payment on January 15?

10. On August 8, Rex Eason had a credit card balance of \$550, but he was unable to pay his bill. The credit card company charges interest of $18\frac{1}{2}\%$ annually on late payments. What amount will Rex have to pay if he pays his bill 1 month late?

11. An issue of *Your Money* discussed average consumers who carry a balance of \$2,000 on one credit card. If the yearly rate of interest is 18%, how much are consumers paying in interest per year?

12. AFBA Industrial Bank of Colorado Springs, Colorado, charges a credit card interest rate of 11% per year. If you had a credit card debt of \$1,500, what would your interest amount be after 3 months?

Learning Unit 10–2 : Finding Unknown in Simple Interest Formula

DRILL PROBLEMS

1. Find the principal in each of the following. Round to the nearest cent. Assume 360 days. *Calculator hint:* Do denominator calculation first, do not round; when answer is displayed, save it in memory by pressing [M+]. Now key in the numerator (interest amount), [÷], [MR], [=] for the answer. Be sure to clear memory after each problem by pressing [MR] again so that the M is no longer in the display.

	Rate	Time	Interest	Principal
a.	8%	70 days	\$68	________
b.	11%	90 days	\$125	________
c.	9%	120 days	\$103	________
d.	$8\frac{1}{2}\%$	60 days	\$150	________

2. Find the rate in each of the following. Round to the nearest tenth of a percent. Assume 360 days.

	Principal	Time	Interest	Rate
a.	$7,500	120 days	$350	________
b.	$975	60 days	$25	________
c.	$20,800	220 days	$910	________
d.	$150	30 days	$2.10	________

3. Find the time (to the nearest day) in each of the following. Assuming ordinary interest, use 360 days.

	Principal	Rate	Interest	Time (days)	Time (years) (Round to nearest hundredth)
a.	$400	11%	$7.33	________	________
b.	$7,000	12.5%	$292	________	________
c.	$1,550	9.2%	$106.95	________	________
d.	$157,000	10.75%	$6,797.88	________	________

4. Complete the following. Assume 360 days for all examples.

	Principal	Rate (nearest tenth percent)	Time (nearest day)	Simple interest
a.	$345	________	150 days	$14.38
b.	________	12.5%	90 days	$46.88
c.	$750	12.2%	________	$19.06
d.	$20,260	16.7%	110 days	________

WORD PROBLEMS

Use 360 days.

5. In June, Becky opened a $10,000 bank CD paying 2% interest, but she had to withdraw the money in a few days to cover one child's college tuition. The bank charged her $500 in penalties for the withdrawal. What percent of the $10,000 was she charged?

6. Dr. Vaccarro invested his money at $12\frac{1}{2}$% for 175 days and earned interest of $760. How much money did Dr. Vaccarro invest?

7. If you invested $10,000 at 5% interest in a 6-month CD compounding interest daily, you would earn $252.43 in interest. How much would the same $10,000 invested in a bank paying simple interest earn?

8. Thomas Kyrouz opened a savings account and deposited $750 in a bank that was paying 7.2% simple interest. How much were his savings worth in 200 days?

9. Mary Millitello paid the bank $53.90 in interest on a 66-day loan at 9.8%. How much money did Mary borrow? Round to the nearest dollar.

10. If Anthony Lucido deposits $2,400 for 66 days and makes $60.72 in interest, what interest rate is he receiving?

11. Find how long in days David Wong must invest $23,500 of his company's cash at 8.4% in order to earn $652.50 in interest.

Learning Unit 10–3: U.S. Rule—Making Partial Note Payments before Due Date

DRILL PROBLEMS

1. A merchant borrowed $3,000 for 320 days at 11% (assume a 360-day year). Use the U.S. Rule to complete the following table:

Payment number	Payment day	Amount paid	Interest to date	Principal payment	Adjusted balance
					$3,000
1	75	$500	________	________	________
2	160	$750	________	________	________
3	220	$1,000	________	________	________
4	320	________	________	________	________

2. Use the U.S. Rule to solve for total interest costs, balances, and final payments (use ordinary interest).

Given

Principal, $6,000, 5%, 100 days
Partial payments on 30th day, $2,000
on 70th day, $1,000

WORD PROBLEMS

3. John Joseph borrowed $10,800 for 1 year at 14%. After 60 days, he paid $2,500 on the note. On the 200th day, he paid an additional $5,000. Use the U.S. Rule and ordinary interest to find the final balance due.

4. Doris Davis borrowed $8,200 on March 5 for 90 days at $8\frac{3}{4}$%. After 32 days, Doris made a payment on the loan of $2,700. On the 65th day, she made another payment of $2,500. What is her final payment if you use the U.S. Rule with ordinary interest?

5. David Ring borrowed $6,000 on a 13%, 60-day note. After 10 days, David paid $500 on the note. On day 40, David paid $900 on the note. What are the total interest and ending balance due by the U.S. Rule? Use ordinary interest.

Name ______________________________ Date ______________

Learning Unit 11–1 : Structure of Promissory Notes; the Simple Discount Note

DRILL PROBLEMS

1. Identify each of the following characteristics of promissory notes with an **I** for simple interest note, a **D** for simple discount note, or a **B** if it is true for both.
   ___ Interest is computed on face value, or what is actually borrowed.
   ___ A promissory note for a loan usually less than 1 year.
   ___ Borrower receives proceeds = Face value − Bank discount.
   ___ Maturity value = Face value + Interest.
   ___ Maturity value = Face value.
   ___ Borrower receives the face value.
   ___ Paid back by one payment at maturity.
   ___ Interest computed on maturity value, or what will be repaid, and not on actual amount borrowed.

2. Find the bank discount and the proceeds for the following (assume 360 days):

	Maturity value	Discount rate	Time (days)	Bank discount	Proceeds
a.	$7,000	2%	90	________	________
b.	$4,550	8.1%	110	________	________
c.	$19,350	12.7%	55	________	________
d.	$63,400	10%	90	________	________
e.	$13,490	7.9%	200	________	________
f.	$780	$12\frac{1}{2}\%$	65	________	________

3. Find the effective rate of interest for each of the loans in Problem 2. Use the answers you calculated in Problem 2 to solve these problems (round to the nearest tenth percent).

	Maturity value	Discount rate	Time (days)	Effective rate
a.	$7,000	2%	90	________
b.	$4,550	8.1%	110	________
c.	$19,350	12.7%	55	________
d.	$63,400	10%	90	________

e. $13,490	7.9%	200	______
f. $780	$12\frac{1}{2}\%$	65	______

WORD PROBLEMS

Assume 360 days.

4. Mary Smith signed a $9,000 note for 135 days at a discount rate of 4%. Find the discount and the proceeds Mary received.

5. The Salem Cooperative Bank charges an $8\frac{3}{4}\%$ discount rate. What are the discount and the proceeds for a $16,200 note for 60 days?

6. Bill Jackson is planning to buy a used car. He went to City Credit Union to take out a loan for $6,400 for 300 days. If the credit union charges a discount rate of $11\frac{1}{2}\%$, what will the proceeds of this loan be?

7. Mike Drislane goes to the bank and signs a note for $9,700. The bank charges a 15% discount rate. Find the discount and the proceeds if the loan is for 210 days.

8. Flora Foley plans to have a deck built on the back of her house. She decides to take out a loan at the bank for $14,300. She signs a note promising to pay back the loan in 280 days. If the note was discounted at 9.2%, how much money will Flora receive from the bank?

9. At the end of 280 days, Flora (Problem 8) must pay back the loan. What is the maturity value of the loan?

10. Dave Cassidy signed a $7,855 note at a bank that charges a 14.2% discount rate. If the loan is for 190 days, find **(a)** the proceeds and **(b)** the effective rate charged by the bank (to the nearest tenth percent).

11. How much money must Dave (Problem 10) pay back to the bank?

Learning Unit 11–2 : Discounting an Interest-Bearing Note before Maturity

DRILL PROBLEMS

1. Calculate the maturity value for each of the following promissory notes (use 360 days):

	Date of note	Principal of note	Length of note (days)	Interest rate	Maturity value
a.	April 12	$4,000	160	4%	________
b.	August 23	$15,990	85	13%	________
c.	December 10	$985	30	11.5%	________

2. Find the maturity date and the discount period for the following; assume no leap years. *Hint:* See Exact Days-in-a-Year Calendar, Chapter 7.

	Date of note	Length of note (days)	Date of discount	Maturity date	Discount period
a.	March 11	200	June 28	________	________
b.	January 22	60	March 2	________	________
c.	April 19	85	June 6	________	________
d.	November 17	120	February 15	________	________

3. Find the bank discount for each of the following (use 360 days):

	Date of note	Principal of note	Length of note	Interest rate	Bank discount rate	Date of discount	Bank discount
a.	October 5	$2,475	88 days	11%	9.5%	December 10	________
b.	June 13	$9,055	112 days	15%	16%	August 11	________
c.	March 20	$1,065	75 days	12%	11.5%	May 24	________

4. Find the proceeds for each of the discounted notes in Problem 3.

a. __________

b. __________

c. __________

WORD PROBLEMS

5. Connors Company received a $4,000, 90-day, 10% note dated April 6 from one of its customers. Connors Company held the note until May 16, when the company discounted it at a bank at a discount rate of 12%. What were the proceeds that Connors Company received?

6. Souza & Sons accepted a 9%, $22,000, 120-day note from one of its customers on July 22. On October 2, the company discounted the note at Cooperative Bank. The discount rate was 12%. What were **(a)** the bank discount and **(b)** the proceeds?

7. The Fargate Store accepted an $8,250, 75-day, 9% note from one of its customers on March 18. Fargate discounted the note at Parkside National Bank at $9\frac{1}{2}$% on March 29. What proceeds did Fargate receive?

8. On November 1, Marjorie's Clothing Store accepted a $5,200, $8\frac{1}{2}$%, 90-day note from Mary Rose in granting her a time extension on her bill. On January 13, Marjorie discounted the note at Seawater Bank, which charged a 10% discount rate. What were the proceeds that Majorie received?

9. On December 3, Duncan's Company accepted a $5,000, 90-day, 12% note from Al Finney in exchange for a $5,000 bill that was past due. On January 29, Duncan discounted the note at The Sidwell Bank at 13.1%. What were the proceeds from the note?

10. On February 26, Sullivan Company accepted a 60-day, 10% note in exchange for a $1,500 past-due bill from Tabot Company. On March 28, Sullivan Company discounted at National Bank the note received from Tabot Company. The bank discount rate was 12%. What are **(a)** the bank discount and **(b)** the proceeds?

11. On June 4, Johnson Company received from Marty Russo a 30-day, 11% note for $720 to settle Russo's debt. On June 17, Johnson discounted the note at Eastern Bank whose discount rate was 15%. What proceeds did Johnson receive?

12. On December 15, Lawlers Company went to the bank and discounted a 10%, 90-day, $14,000 note dated October 21. The bank charged a discount rate of 12%. What were the proceeds of the note?

Name ______________________________ Date ______________

Learning Unit 12–1: Compound Interest (Future Value)—The Big Picture

DRILL PROBLEMS

1. In the following examples, calculate manually the amount at year-end for each of the deposits, assuming that interest is compounded annually. Round to the nearest cent each year.

	Principal	Rate	Number of years	Year 1	Year 2	Year 3	Year 4
a.	$530	4%	2	______	______		
b.	$1,980	12%	4	______	______	______	______

2. In the following examples, calculate the simple interest, the compound interest, and the difference between the two. Round to the nearest cent; do not use tables.

	Principal	Rate	Number of years	Simple interest	Compound interest	Difference
a.	$4,600	10%	2	______	______	______
b.	$18,400	9%	4	______	______	______
c.	$855	$7\frac{1}{5}\%$	3	______	______	______

3. Find the future value and the compound interest using the Future Value of $1 at Compound Interest table or the Compound Daily table. Round to the nearest cent.

	Principal	Investment terms	Future value	Compound interest
a.	$10,000	6 years at 8% compounded annually	______	______
b.	$10,000	6 years at 8% compounded quarterly	______	______
c.	$8,400	7 years at 12% compounded semiannually	______	______
d.	$2,500	15 years at 10% compounded daily	______	______
e.	$9,600	5 years at 6% compounded quarterly	______	______
f.	$20,000	2 years at 6% compounded monthly	______	______

4. Calculate the effective rate (APY) of interest using the Future Value of $1 at Compound Interest table.

	Investment terms	**Effective rate (annual percentage yield)**
a.	12% compounded quarterly	_______
b.	12% compounded semiannually	_______
c.	6% compounded quarterly	_______

WORD PROBLEMS

5. John Mackey deposited $5,000 in his savings account at Salem Savings Bank. If the bank pays 6% interest compounded quarterly, what will be the balance of his account at the end of 3 years?

6. Pine Valley Savings Bank offers a certificate of deposit at 12% interest compounded quarterly. What is the effective rate (APY) of interest?

7. Jack Billings loaned $6,000 to his brother-in-law Dan, who was opening a new business. Dan promised to repay the loan at the end of 5 years, with interest of 8% compounded semiannually. How much will Dan pay Jack at the end of 5 years?

8. Eileen Hogarty deposits $5,630 in City Bank, which pays 12% interest compounded quarterly. How much money will Eileen have in her account at the end of 7 years?

9. If Kevin Bassage deposits $3,500 in Scarsdale Savings Bank, which pays 8% interest compounded quarterly, what will be in his account at the end of 6 years? How much interest will he have earned at that time?

10. Arlington Trust pays 6% compounded semiannually. How much interest would be earned on $7,200 for 1 year?

11. Paladium Savings Bank pays 9% compounded quarterly. Find the amount and the interest on $3,000 after three quarters. Do not use a table.

12. David Siderski bought a $7,500 bank certificate paying 16% compounded semiannually. How much money did he obtain upon cashing in the certificate 3 years later?

13. An issue of *Your Money* showed that the more frequently the bank compounds your money, the better. Just how much better is a function of time. A $10,000 investment for 6% in a 5-year certificate of deposit at three different banks can result in different interest being earned.

a. Bank A (simple interest, no compounding)
b. Bank B (quarterly compounding)
c. Bank C (daily compounding)
What would be the interest for each bank?

Learning Unit 12–2 : Present Value—The Big Picture

DRILL PROBLEMS

1. Use the *Business Math Handbook* to find the table factor for each of the following:

	Future value	Rate	Number of years	Compounded	Table value
a.	$1.00	10%	5	Annually	______
b.	$1.00	12%	8	Semiannually	______
c.	$1.00	6%	10	Quarterly	______
d.	$1.00	12%	2	Monthly	______
e.	$1.00	8%	15	Semiannually	______

2. Use the *Business Math Handbook* to find the table factor and the present value for each of the following:

	Future value	Rate	Number of years	Compounded	Table value	Present value
a.	$1,000	14%	6	Semiannually	______	______
b.	$1,000	16%	7	Quarterly	______	______
c.	$1,000	8%	7	Quarterly	______	______
d.	$1,000	8%	7	Semiannually	______	______
e.	$1,000	8%	7	Annually	______	______

3. Find the present value and the interest earned for the following:

	Future value	Number of years	Rate	Compounded	Present value	Interest earned
a.	$2,500	6	8%	Annually	______	______
b.	$4,600	10	6%	Semiannually	______	______
c.	$12,800	8	10%	Semiannually	______	______
d.	$28,400	7	8%	Quarterly	______	______
e.	$53,050	1	12%	Monthly	______	______

4. Find the missing amount (present value or future value) for each of the following:

	Present value	Investment terms	Future value
a.	$3,500	5 years at 8% compounded annually	______
b.	______	6 years at 12% compounded semiannually	$9,000
c.	$4,700	9 years at 14% compounded semiannually	______

WORD PROBLEMS

Solve for future value or present value.

5. Paul Palumbo assumes that he will need to have a new roof put on his house in 4 years. He estimates that the roof will cost him $18,000 at that time. What amount of money should Paul invest today at 8%, compounded semiannually, to be able to pay for the roof?

6. Tilton, a pharmacist, rents his store and has signed a lease that will expire in 3 years. When the lease expires, Tilton wants to buy his own store. He wants to have a down payment of $35,000 at that time. How much money should Tilton invest today at 6%, compounded quarterly, to yield $35,000?

7. Brad Morrissey loans $8,200 to his brother-in-law. He will be repaid at the end of 5 years, with interest at 10% compounded semiannually. Find out how much he will be repaid.

8. The owner of Waverly Sheet Metal Company plans to buy some new machinery in 6 years. He estimates that the machines he wishes to purchase will cost $39,700 at that time. What must he invest today at 8%, compounded semiannually, to have sufficient money to purchase the new machines?

9. Paul Stevens's grandparents want to buy him a car when he graduates from college in 4 years. They feel that they should have $27,000 in the bank at that time. How much should they invest at 12%, compounded quarterly, to reach their goal?

10. Gilda Nardi deposits $5,325 in a bank that pays 12% interest compounded quarterly. Find the amount she will have at the end of 7 years.

11. Mary Wilson wants to buy a new set of golf clubs in 2 years. They will cost $775. How much money should she invest today at 9%, compounded annually, so that she will have enough money to buy the new clubs?

12. Jack Beggs plans to invest $30,000 at 10%, compounded semiannually, for 5 years. What is the future value of the investment?

13. Ron Thrift has a 2000 Honda that he expects will last 3 more years. Ron does not like to finance his purchases. He went to First National Bank to find out how much money he should put in the bank to purchase a $20,300 car in 3 years. The bank's 3-year CD is compounded quarterly with a 4% rate. How much should Ron invest in the CD?

14. The Downers Grove YMCA had a fund-raising campaign to build a swimming pool in 6 years. Members raised $825,000; the pool is estimated to cost $1,230,000. The money will be placed in Downers Grove Bank, which pays daily interest at 6%. Will the YMCA have enough money to pay for the pool in 6 years?

Name ______________________ Date ____________

Learning Unit 13–1 : Annuities: Ordinary Annuity and Annuity Due (Find Future Value)

DRILL PROBLEMS

1. Find the value of the following ordinary annuities (calculate manually):

	Amount of each annual deposit	Interest rate	Value at end of year 1	Value at end of year 2	Value at end of year 3
a.	$1,000	8%	______	______	______
b.	$2,500	12%	______	______	______
c.	$7,200	10%	______	______	______

2. Use the Ordinary Annuity Table: Compound Sum of an Annuity of $1 to find the value of the following ordinary annuities:

	Annuity payment	Payment period	Term of annuity	Interest rate	Value of annuity
a.	$650	Semiannually	5 years	6%	______
b.	$3,790	Annually	13 years	12%	______
c.	$500	Quarterly	1 year	8%	______

3. Find the annuity due (deposits are made at beginning of period) for each of the following using the Ordinary Annuity Table:

	Amount of payment	Payment period	Interest rate	Time (years)	Amount of annuity
a.	$900	Annually	7%	6	______
b.	$1,200	Annually	11%	4	______
c.	$550	Semiannually	10%	9	______

4. Find the amount of each annuity:

	Amount of payment	Payment period	Interest rate	Time (years)	Type of annuity	Amount of annuity
a.	$600	Semiannually	12%	8	Ordinary	______
b.	$600	Semiannually	12%	8	Due	______
c.	$1,100	Annually	9%	7	Ordinary	______

WORD PROBLEMS

5. At the end of each year for the next 9 years, D'Aldo Company will deposit $25,000 in an ordinary annuity account paying 9% interest compounded annually. Find the value of the annuity at the end of the 9 years.

6. David McCarthy is a professional baseball player who expects to play in the major leagues for 10 years. To save for the future, he will deposit $50,000 at the beginning of each year into an account that pays 11% interest compounded annually. How much will he have in this account at the end of 10 years?

7. Tom and Sue plan to get married soon. Because they hope to have a large wedding, they are going to deposit $1,000 at the end of each month into an account that pays 24% compounded monthly. How much will they have in this account at the end of 1 year?

8. Chris Dennen deposits $15,000 at the end of each year for 13 years into an account paying 7% interest compounded annually. What is the value of her annuity at the end of 13 years? How much interest will she have earned?

9. Amanda Blinn is 52 years old today and has just opened an IRA. She plans to deposit $500 at the end of each quarter into her account. If Amanda retires on her 62nd birthday, what amount will she have in her account if the account pays 8% interest compounded quarterly?

10. Jerry Davis won the citywide sweepstakes and will receive a check for $2,000 at the beginning of each 6 months for the next 5 years. If Jerry deposits each check in an account that pays 8% compounded semiannually, how much will he have at the end of 5 years?

11. Mary Hynes purchased an ordinary annuity from an investment broker at 8% interest compounded semiannually. If her semiannual deposit is $600, what will be the value of the annuity at the end of 15 years?

Learning Unit 13–2 : Present Value of an Ordinary Annuity (Find Present Value)

DRILL PROBLEMS

1. Use the Present Value of an Annuity of $1 table to find the amount to be invested today to receive a stream of payments for a given number of years in the future. Show the manual check of your answer. (Check may be a few pennies off due to rounding.)

	Amount of expected payments	Payment period	Interest rate	Term of annuity	Present value of annuity
a.	$1,500	Yearly	9%	2 years	________
b.	$2,700	Yearly	13%	3 years	________
c.	$2,700	Yearly	6%	3 years	________

2. Find the present value of the following annuities. Use the Present Value of an Annuity of $1 table.

	Amount of each payment	Payment period	Interest rate	Time (years)	Compounded	Present value of annuity
a.	$2,000	Year	7%	25	Annually	________
b.	$7,000	Year	11%	12	Annually	________
c.	$850	6 months	12%	5	Semiannually	________
d.	$1,950	6 months	14%	9	Semiannually	________
e.	$500	Quarter	12%	10	Quarterly	________

WORD PROBLEMS

3. Tom Hanson would like to receive $200 each quarter for the 4 years he is in college. If his bank account pays 8% compounded quarterly, how much must he have in his account when he begins college?

4. Jean Reith has just retired and will receive a $12,500 retirement check every 6 months for the next 20 years. If her employer can invest money at 12% compounded semiannually, what amount must be invested today to make the semiannual payments to Jean?

5. Tom Herrick will pay $4,500 at the end of each year for the next 7 years to pay the balance of his college loans. If Tom can invest his money at 7% compounded annually, how much must he invest today to make the annual payments?

6. Helen Grahan is planning an extended sabbatical for the next 3 years. She would like to invest a lump sum of money at 10% interest so that she can withdraw $6,000 every 6 months while on sabbatical. What is the amount of the lump sum that Helen must invest?

7. Linda Rudd has signed a rental contract for office equipment, agreeing to pay $3,200 at the end of each quarter for the next 5 years. If Linda can invest money at 12% compounded quarterly, find the lump sum she can deposit today to make the payments for the length of the contract.

8. Sam Adams is considering lending his brother John $6,000. John said that he would repay Sam $775 every 6 months for 4 years. If money can be invested at 8%, calculate the equivalent cash value of the offer today. Should Sam go ahead with the loan?

9. The State Lotto Game offers a grand prize of $1,000,000 paid in 20 yearly payments of $50,000. If the state treasurer can invest money at 9% compounded annually, how much must she invest today to make the payments to the grand prize winner?

10. Thomas Martin's uncle has promised him upon graduation a gift of $20,000 in cash or $2,000 every quarter for the next 3 years. If money can be invested at 8%, which offer will Thomas accept? (Thomas is a business major.)

11. Paul Sasso is selling a piece of land. He has received two solid offers. Jason Smith has offered a $60,000 down payment and $50,000 a year for the next 5 years. Kevin Bassage offered $35,000 down and $55,000 a year for the next 5 years. If money can be invested at 7% compounded annually, which offer should Paul accept? (To make the comparison, find the equivalent cash price of each offer.)

12. Abe Hoster decided to retire to Spain in 10 years. What amount should Abe invest today so that he will be able to withdraw $30,000 at the end of each year for 20 years after he retires? Assume he can invest money at 8% interest compounded annually.

Learning Unit 13–3 : Sinking Funds (Find Periodic Payments)

DRILL PROBLEMS

1. Given the number of years and the interest rate, use the Sinking Fund Table based on $1 to calculate the amount of the periodic payment.

Frequency of payment	Length of time	Interest rate	Future amount	Sinking fund payment
a. Annually	19 years	5%	$125,000	__________
b. Annually	7 years	10%	$205,000	__________
c. Semiannually	10 years	6%	$37,500	__________
d. Quarterly	9 years	12%	$12,750	__________
e. Quarterly	6 years	8%	$25,600	__________

2. Find the amount of each payment into the sinking fund and the amount of interest earned.

Maturity value	Interest rate	Term (years)	Frequency of payment	Sinking fund payment	Interest earned
a. $45,500	5%	13	Annually	__________	__________
b. $8,500	10%	20	Semiannually	__________	__________
c. $11,000	8%	5	Quarterly	__________	__________
d. $66,600	12%	$7\frac{1}{2}$	Semiannually	__________	__________

WORD PROBLEMS

3. To finance a new police station, the town of Pine Valley issued bonds totaling $600,000. The town treasurer set up a sinking fund at 8% compounded quarterly in order to redeem the bonds in 7 years. What is the quarterly payment that must be deposited into the fund?

4. Arlex Oil Corporation plans to build a new garage in 6 years. To finance the project, the financial manager established a $250,000 sinking fund at 6% compounded semianually. Find the semiannual payment required for the fund.

5. The City Fisheries Corporation sold $300,000 worth of bonds that must be redeemed in 9 years. The corporation agreed to set up a sinking fund to accumulate the $300,000. Find the amount of the periodic payments made into the fund if payments are made annually and the fund earns 8% compounded annually.

6. Gregory Mines Corporation wishes to purchase a new piece of equipment in 4 years. The estimated price of the equipment is $100,000. If the corporation makes periodic payments into a sinking fund with 12% interest compounded quarterly, find the amount of the periodic payments.

7. The Best Corporation must buy a new piece of machinery in $4\frac{1}{2}$ years that will cost $350,000. If the firm sets up a sinking fund to finance this new machine, what will the quarterly deposits be assuming the fund earns 8% interest compounded quarterly?

8. The Lowest-Price-in-Town Company needs $75,500 in 6 years to pay off a debt. The company makes a decision to set up a sinking fund and make semiannual deposits. What will their payments be if the fund pays 10% interest compounded semiannually?

9. The WIR Company plans to renovate their offices in 5 years. They estimate that the cost will be $235,000. If they set up a sinking fund that pays 12% quarterly, what will their quarterly payments be?

Name ______________________ Date ______________

Learning Unit 14–1 : Cost of Installment Buying

DRILL PROBLEMS

1. For the following installment problems, find the amount financed and the finance charge.

	Sale price	Down payment	Number of monthly payments	Monthly payment	Amount financed	Finance charge
a.	$1,500	$300	24	$58	______	______
b.	$12,000	$3,000	30	$340	______	______
c.	$62,500	$4,700	48	$1,500	______	______
d.	$4,975	$620	18	$272	______	______
e.	$825	$82.50	12	$67.45	______	______

2. For each of the above purchases, find the deferred payment price.

	Sale price	Down payment	Number of monthly payments	Monthly payment	Deferred payment price
a.	$1,500	$300	24	$58	______
b.	$12,000	$3,000	30	$340	______
c.	$62,500	$4,700	48	$1,500	______
d.	$4,975	$620	18	$272	______
e.	$825	$82.50	12	$67.45	______

3. Use the Annual Percentage Rate Table per $100 to calculate the estimated APR for each of the previous purchases.

	Sale price	Down payment	Number of monthly payments	Monthly payment	Annual percentage rate
a.	$1,500	$300	24	$58	______
b.	$12,000	$3,000	30	$340	______
c.	$62,500	$4,700	48	$1,500	______
d.	$4,975	$620	18	$272	______
e.	$825	$82.50	12	$67.45	______

4. Given the following information, calculate the monthly payment by the loan amortization table.

	Amount financed	Interest rate	Number of months of loan	Monthly payment
a.	$12,000	10%	18	______
b.	$18,000	11%	36	______
c.	$25,500	13.50%	54	______

WORD PROBLEMS

5. Jill Walsh purchases a bedroom set for a cash price of $3,920. The down payment is $392, and the monthly installment payment is $176 for 24 months. Find **(a)** the amount financed, **(b)** the finance charge, and **(c)** the deferred payment price.

6. An automaker promotion loan on a $20,000 automobile and a down payment of 20% are being financed for 48 months. The monthly payments will be $367.74. What will be the APR for this auto loan? Use the table in the *Business Math Handbook*.

7. David Nason purchased a recreational vehicle for $25,000. David went to City Bank to finance the purchase. The bank required that David make a 10% down payment and monthly payments of $571.50 for 4 years. Find **(a)** the amount financed, **(b)** the finance charge, and **(c)** the deferred payment that David paid.

8. Calculate the estimated APR that David (Problem 7) was charged per $100 using the Annual Percentage Rate Table.

9. Young's Motors advertised a new car for $16,720. They offered an installment plan of 5% down and 42 monthly payments of $470. What are **(a)** the deferred payment price and **(b)** the estimated APR for this car (use the table)?

10. Angie French bought a used car for $9,000. Angie put down $2,000 and financed the balance at 11.50% for 36 months. What is her monthly payment? Use the loan amortization table.

Learning Unit 14–2 : Paying Off Installment Loans before Due Date

DRILL PROBLEMS

1. Find the balance of each loan outstanding and the total finance charge.

	Amount financed	Monthly payment	Number of payments	Payments to date	Balance of loan outstanding	Finance charge
a.	$1,500	$125	15	10	______	______
b.	$21,090	$600	40	24	______	______
c.	$895	$60	18	10	______	______
d.	$4,850	$150	42	30	______	______

2. For the loans in Problem 1, find the number of payments remaining and calculate the rebate amount of the finance charge (use Rebate Fraction Table Based on Rule of 78).

	Amount financed	Monthly payment	Number of payments	Payments to date	Number of payments remaining	Finance charge rebate
a.	$1,500	$125	15	10	____	______
b.	$21,090	$600	40	24	____	______
c.	$895	$60	18	10	____	______
d.	$4,850	$150	42	30	____	______

3. For the loans in Problems 1 and 2, show the remaining balance of the loan and calculate the payoff amount to retire the loan at this time.

	Amount financed	Monthly payment	Number of payments	Payments to date	Balance of loan outstanding	Final payoff
a.	$1,500	$125	15	10	______	______
b.	$21,090	$600	40	24	______	______
c.	$895	$60	18	10	______	______
d.	$4,850	$150	42	30	______	______

4. Complete the following; show all the steps.

	Loan	Months of loan	Monthly payment	End of month loan is repaid	Final payoff
a.	$6,200	36	$219	24	______
b.	$960	12	$99	8	______

WORD PROBLEMS

5. Maryjane Hannon took out a loan for $5,600 to have a swimming pool installed in her backyard. The note she signed required 21 monthly payments of $293. At the end of 15 months, Maryjane wants to know the balance of her loan outstanding and her total finance charge.

6. After calculating the above data (Problem 5), Maryjane is considering paying off the rest of the loan. To make her decision, Maryjane wants to know the finance charge rebate she will receive and the final payoff amount.

7. Ben Casey decided to buy a used car for $7,200. He agreed to make monthly payments of $225 for 36 months. What is Ben's total finance charge?

8. After making 20 payments, Ben (Problem 7) wants to pay off the rest of the loan. What will be the amount of Ben's final payoff?

9. Jeremy Vagos took out a loan to buy a new boat that cost $12,440. He agreed to pay $350 a month for 48 months. After 24 monthly payments, he calculates that he has paid $8,400 on his loan and has 24 payments remaining. Jeremy's friend Luke tells Jeremy that he will pay off the rest of the loan (in a single payment) if he can be half-owner of the boat. What is the amount that Luke will have to pay?

Learning Unit 14–3 : Revolving Charge Credit Cards

DRILL PROBLEMS

1. Use the U.S. Rule to calculate the outstanding balance due for each of the following independent situations:

	Monthly payment number	Outstanding balance due	$1\frac{1}{2}\%$ interest payment	Amount of monthly payment	Reduction in balance due	Outstanding balance due
a.	1	$9,000.00	______	$600	______	______
b.	5	$5,625.00	______	$1,000	______	______
c.	4	$926.50	______	$250	______	______
d.	12	$62,391.28	______	$1,200	______	______
e.	8	$3,255.19	______	$325	______	______

2. Complete the missing data for a $6,500 purchase made on credit. The annual interest charge on this revolving charge account is 18%, or $1\frac{1}{2}\%$ interest on previous month's balance. Use the U.S. Rule.

Monthly payment number	Outstanding balance due	$1\frac{1}{2}\%$ interest payment	Amount of monthly payment	Reduction in balance due	Outstanding balance due
1	$6,500	______	$700	______	______
2	______	______	$700	______	______
3	______	______	$700	______	______

3. Calculate the average billing daily balance for each of the monthly statements for the following revolving credit accounts (assume a 30-day billing cycle):

	Billing date	Previous balance	Payment date	Payment amount	Charge date(s)	Charge amount(s)	Average daily balance
a.	4/10	$329	4/25	$35	4/29	$56	______
b.	6/15	$573	6/25	$60	6/26 6/30	$25 $72	______
c.	9/15	$335.50	9/20	$33.55	9/25 9/26	$12.50 $108	______

4. Find the finance charge for each monthly statement (Problem 3) if the annual percentage rate is 15%.

a. ______ b. ______ c. ______

WORD PROBLEMS

5. Niki Marshall is going to buy a new bedroom set at Scottie's Furniture Store, where she has a revolving charge account. The cost of the bedroom set is $5,500. Niki does not plan to charge anything else to her account until she has completely paid for the bedroom set. Scottie's Furniture Store charges an annual percentage rate of 18%, or $1\frac{1}{2}$% per month. Niki plans to pay $1,000 per month until she has paid for the bedroom set. Set up a schedule for Niki to show her outstanding balance at the end of each month after her $1,000 payment and also the amount of her final payment. Use the U.S. Rule.

6. Frances Dollof received her monthly statement from Brown's Department Store. The following is part of the information contained on that statement. Finance charge is calculated on the average daily balance.

Date	Reference	Department	Description	Amount
Dec. 15	5921	359	Petite sportswear	84.98
Dec. 15	9612	432	Footwear	55.99
Dec. 15	2600	126	Women's fragrance	35.18
Dec. 23	6247	61	Ralph Lauren towels	20.99
Dec. 24	0129	998	Payment received—thank you	100.00CR

Previous balance		Annual percentage rate	Billing date
719.04	12/13	18%	JAN 13

Brown's Charge Account Terms

Payment is required in monthly installments upon receipt of monthly statement in accordance with Brown's payment terms.

When my new balance is:	My minimum required payment is:	When my new balance is:	My minimum required payment is:
Up to $20.00	New Balance	$350.01 to $400.00	$40.00
$ 20.01 to $200.00	$20.00	$400.01 to $450.00	$45.00
$200.01 to $250.00	$25.00	$450.01 to $500.00	$50.00
$250.01 to $300.00	$30.00	More than $500.00	$50.00 plus $10.00 for each $50.00 (or fraction thereof) of New Balance over $500.00
$300.01 to $350.00	$35.00		

a. Calculate the average daily balance for the month.

b. What is Ms. Dollof's finance charge?

c. What is the new balance for Ms. Dollof's account?

d. What is the minimum payment Frances is required to pay according to Brown's payment terms?

7. What is the finance charge for a Brown's customer who has an average daily balance of $3,422.67?

8. What is the minimum payment for a Brown's customer with a new balance of $522.00?

9. What is the minimum payment for a Brown's customer with a new balance of $325.01?

10. What is the new balance for a Brown's customer with a previous balance of $309.35 whose purchases totaled $213.00, given that the customer made a payment of $75.00 and the finance charge was $4.65?

RECAP OF WORD PROBLEMS IN LU 14–1

11. A home equity loan on a $20,000 automobile with a down payment of 20% is being financed for 48 months. The interest is tax deductible. The monthly payments will be $401.97. What is the APR on this loan? Use the table in the *Business Math Handbook*. If the person is in the 28% income tax bracket, what will be the tax savings with this type of a loan?

12. An automobile with a total transaction price of $20,000 with a down payment of 20% is being financed for 48 months. Banks and credit unions require a monthly payment of $400.36. What is the APR for this auto loan? Use the table in the *Business Math Handbook*.

13. Assume you received a $2,000 rebate that brought the price of a car down to $20,000; the financing rate was for 48 months, and your total interest was $3,279. Using the table in the *Business Math Handbook*, what was your APR?

Classroom Notes

Name ______________________ Date ______________

Learning Unit 15–1: Types of Mortgages and the Monthly Mortgage Payment

DRILL PROBLEMS

1. Use the table in the *Business Math Handbook* to calculate the monthly payment for principal and interest for the following mortgages:

	Price of home	Down payment	Interest rate	Term in years	Monthly payment
a.	$200,000	15%	6%	25	________
b.	$200,000	15%	$5\frac{1}{2}\%$	30	________
c.	$450,000	10%	$11\frac{3}{4}\%$	30	________
d.	$450,000	10%	11%	30	________

2. For each of the mortgages, calculate the amount of interest that will be paid over the life of the loan.

	Price of home	Down payment	Interest rate	Term in years	Total interest paid
a.	$200,000	15%	$6\frac{1}{2}\%$	25	________
b.	$200,000	15%	$10\frac{1}{2}\%$	30	________
c.	$450,000	10%	$11\frac{3}{4}\%$	30	________
d.	$450,000	10%	11%	30	________

3. Calculate the increase in the monthly mortgage payments for each of the rate increases in the following mortgages. Also calculate what percent of change the increase represents (round to the tenth percent).

	Mortgage amount	Term in years	Interest rate	Increase in interest rate	Increase in monthly payment	Percent change
a.	$175,000	22	9%	1%	________	______
b.	$300,000	30	$11\frac{3}{4}\%$	$\frac{3}{4}\%$	________	______

4. Calculate the increase in total interest paid for the increase in interest rates in Problem 3.

	Mortgage amount	Term in years	Interest rate	Increase in interest rate	Increase in total interest paid
a.	$175,000	22	9%	1%	________
b.	$300,000	30	$11\frac{3}{4}\%$	$\frac{3}{4}\%$	________

WORD PROBLEMS

5. The Counties are planning to purchase a new home that costs $150,000. The bank is charging them 6% interest and requires a 20% down payment. The Counties are planning to take a 25-year mortgage. How much will their monthly payment be for principal and interest?

6. The MacEacherns wish to buy a new house that costs $299,000. The bank requires a 15% down payment and charges $11\frac{1}{2}\%$ interest. If the MacEacherns take out a 15-year mortgage, what will their monthly payment for principal and interest be?

7. Because the monthly payments are so high, the MacEacherns (Problem 6) want to know what the monthly payments would be for **(a)** a 25-year mortgage and **(b)** a 30-year mortgage. Calculate these two payments.

8. If the MacEacherns choose a 30-year mortgage instead of a 15-year mortgage, **(a)** how much money will they "save" monthly and **(b)** how much more interest will they pay over the life of the loan?

9. If the MacEacherns choose the 25-year mortgage instead of the 30-year mortgage, **(a)** how much more will they pay monthly and **(b)** how much less interest will they pay over the life of the loan?

10. Larry and Doris Davis plan to purchase a new home that costs $415,000. The bank that they are dealing with requires a 20% down payment and charges $12\frac{3}{4}$%. The Davises are planning to take a 25-year mortgage. What will the monthly payment be?

11. How much interest will the Davises (Problem 10) pay over the life of the loan?

Learning Unit 15–2: Amortization Schedule—Breaking Down the Monthly Payment

DRILL PROBLEMS

1. In the following, calculate the monthly payment for each mortgage, the portion of the first monthly payment that goes to interest, and the portion of the payment that goes toward the principal.

	Amount of mortgage	Interest rate	Term in years	Monthly payment	Portion to interest	Portion to principal
a.	$170,000	8%	22	________	________	________
b.	$222,000	$11\frac{3}{4}$%	30	________	________	________
c.	$167,000	$10\frac{1}{2}$%	25	________	________	________
d.	$307,000	13%	15	________	________	________
e.	$409,500	$12\frac{1}{2}$%	20	________	________	________

2. Prepare an amortization schedule for the first 3 months of a 25-year, 12% mortgage on $265,000.

Payment number	Monthly payment	Portion to interest	Portion to principal	Balance of loan outstanding
1	________	________	________	________
2	________	________	________	________
3	________	________	________	________

3. Prepare an amortization schedule for the first 4 months of a 30-year, $10\frac{1}{2}$% mortgage on $195,500.

Payment number	Monthly payment	Portion to interest	Portion to principal	Balance of loan outstanding
1	________	________	________	________
2	________	________	________	________
3	________	________	________	________
4	________	________	________	________

WORD PROBLEMS

4. Jim and Janice Hurst are buying a new home for $235,000. The bank that is financing the home requires a 20% down payment and charges a $13\frac{1}{2}$% interest rate. Janice wants to know **(a)** what the monthly payment for the principal and interest will be if they take out a 30-year mortgage and **(b)** how much of the first payment will be for interest on the loan.

5. The Hursts (Problem 4) thought that a lot of their money was going to interest. They asked the banker just how much they would be paying for interest over the life of the loan. Calculate the total amount of interest that the Hursts will pay.

6. The banker told the Hursts (Problem 4) that they could, of course, save on the interest payments if they took out a loan for a shorter period of time. Jim and Janice decided to see if they could afford a 15-year mortgage. Calculate how much more the Hursts would have to pay each month for principal and interest if they took a 15-year mortgage for their loan.

7. The Hursts (Problem 4) thought that they might be able to afford this, but first wanted to see **(a)** how much of the first payment would go to the principal and **(b)** how much total interest they would be paying with a 15-year mortgage.

8.

	1980	**2011**
Cost of median-priced new home	\$44,200	\$136,600
10% down payment	\$4,420	
Fixed-rate, 30-year mortgage		
Interest rate	8.9%	$7\frac{1}{2}$%
Total monthly principal and interest	\$316	

Complete the 2011 year.

9. You can't count on your home mortgage lender to keep you from getting in debt over your head. The old standards of allowing 28% of your income for mortgage debt (including taxes and insurance) usually still apply. If your total monthly payment is \$1,033, what should be your annual income to buy a home?

10. Assume that a 30-year fixed-rate mortgage for \$100,000 was 9% at one date as opposed to 7% the previous year. What is the difference in monthly payments for these 2 years?

11. If you had a \$100,000 mortgage with $7\frac{1}{2}$% interest for 25 years and wanted a $7\frac{1}{2}$% loan for 35 years, what would be the change in monthly payments? How much more would you pay in interest?

Classroom Notes

Name ______________________________ Date ______________

Learning Unit 16–1 : Balance Sheet—Report as of a Particular Date

DRILL PROBLEMS

1. Complete the balance sheet for David Harrison, Attorney, and show that

Assets = Liabilities + Owner's equity

Account totals are as follows: accounts receivable, \$4,800; office supplies, \$375; building (net), \$130,000; accounts payable, \$1,200; notes payable, \$137,200; cash, \$2,250; prepaid insurance, \$1,050; office equipment (net), \$11,250; land, \$75,000; capital, \$85,900; and salaries payable, \$425.

DAVID HARRISON, ATTORNEY Balance Sheet December 31, 2011			
Assets			
Current assets:			
Cash	______		
Accounts receivable	______		
Prepaid insurance	______		
Office supplies	______		
Total current assets		______	
Plant and equipment:			
Office equipment (net)	______		
Building (net)	______		
Land	______		
Total plant and equipment		______	
Total assets			______
Liabilities			
Current liabilities:			
Accounts payable	______		
Salaries payable	______		
Total current liabilities			
Long-term liabilities:			
Notes payable		______	
Total liabilities			______
Owner's Equity			
David Harrison, capital, December 31, 2009			______
Total liabilities and owner's equity			______

2. Given the amounts in each of the accounts of Fisher-George Electric Corporation, fill in these amounts on the balance sheet to show that

Assets = Liabilities + Stockholders' equity

Account totals are as follows: cash, \$2,500; merchandise inventory, \$1,325; automobiles (net), \$9,250; common stock, \$10,000; accounts payable, \$275; office equipment (net), \$5,065; accounts receivable, \$300; retained earnings, \$6,895; prepaid insurance, \$1,075; salaries payable, \$175; and mortgage payable, \$2,170.

FISHER-GEORGE ELECTRIC CORPORATION Balance Sheet December 31, 2011			
Assets			
Current assets:			
Cash			
Accounts receivable			
Merchandise inventory			
Prepaid insurance			
Total current assets			
Plant and equipment:			
Office equipment (net)			
Automobiles (net)			
Total plant and equipment			
Total assets			
Liabilities			
Current liabilities:			
Accounts payable			
Salaries payable			
Total current liabilities			
Long-term liabilities:			
Mortgage payable			
Total liabilities			
Stockholders' Equity			
Common stock			
Retained earnings			
Total stockholders' equity			
Total liabilities and stockholders' equity			

3. Complete a vertical analysis of the following partial balance sheet (round all percents to the nearest hundredth percent).

THREEMAX, INC. Comparative Balance Sheet Vertical Analysis At December 31, 2010 and 2011	2010		2011	
	Amount	Percent	Amount	Percent
Assets				
Cash	$ 8,500		$ 10,200	
Accounts receivable (net)	11,750		15,300	
Merchandise inventory	55,430		54,370	
Store supplies	700		532	
Office supplies	650		640	
Prepaid insurance	2,450		2,675	
Office equipment (net)	12,000		14,300	
Store equipment (net)	32,000		31,000	
Building (net)	75,400		80,500	
Land	200,000		150,000	
Total assets	$398,880		$359,517	

4. Complete a horizontal analysis of the following partial balance sheet (round all percents to the nearest hundredth percent).

THREEMAX, INC.
Comparative Balance Sheet Horizontal Analysis
At December 31, 2010 and 2011

	2011	2010	Change	Percent
Assets				
Cash	$ 8,500	$ 10,200	______	______
Accounts receivable (net)	11,750	15,300	______	______
Merchandise inventory	55,430	54,370	______	______
Store supplies	700	532	______	______
Office supplies	650	640	______	______
Prepaid insurance	2,450	2,675	______	______
Office equipment (net)	12,000	14,300	______	______
Store equipment (net)	32,000	31,000	______	______
Building (net)	75,400	80,500	______	______
Land	200,000	150,000	______	______
Total assets	$398,880	$359,517		

Learning Unit 16–2 : Income Statement—Report for a Specific Period of Time

DRILL PROBLEMS

1. Complete the income statement for the year ended December 31, 2011, for Foley Realty, doing all the necessary addition. Account totals are as follows: office salaries expense, $15,255; advertising expense, $2,400; rent expense, $18,000; telephone expense, $650; insurance expense, $1,550; office supplies, $980; depreciation expense, office equipment, $990; depreciation expense, automobile, $2,100; sales commissions earned, $98,400; and management fees earned, $1,260.

FOLEY REALTY
Income Statement
For the Year Ended December 31, 2011

Revenues:		
Sales commissions earned	______	
Management fees earned	______	
Total revenues		
Operating expenses:		
Office salaries expense	______	
Advertising expense	______	
Rent expense	______	
Telephone expense	______	
Insurance expense	______	
Office supplies expense	______	
Depreciation expense, office equipment	______	
Depreciation expense, automobile	______	
Total operating expenses		______
Net income		______

2. Complete the income statement for Toll's, Inc., a merchandising concern, doing all the necessary addition and subtraction. Sales were $250,000; sales returns and allowances were $1,400; sales discounts were $2,100; merchandise inventory, December 31, 2010, was $42,000; purchases were $156,000; purchases returns and allowances were $1,100; purchases discounts were $3,000; merchandise inventory, December 31, 2011, was $47,000; selling expenses were $37,000; and general and administrative expenses were $29,000.

TOLL'S, INC. Income Statement For the Year Ended December 31, 2011				
Revenues:				
Sales				______
Less: Sales return and allowances			______	
Sales discounts			______	______
Net sales				______
Cost of goods sold:				
Merchandise inventory, December 31, 2010			______	
Purchases		______		
Less: Purchases returns and allowances	______			
Purchase discounts	______	______		
Cost of net purchases			______	
Goods available for sale			______	
Merchandise inventory, December 31, 2011			______	
Total cost of goods sold				______
Gross profit from sales				______
Operating expenses:				
Selling expenses			______	
General and administrative expenses			______	
Total operating expenses				______
Net income				______

3. Complete a vertical analysis of the following partial income statement (round all percents to the nearest hundredth percent). Note net sales are 100%.

THREEMAX, INC. Comparative Income Statement Vertical Analysis For Years Ended December 31, 2010 and 2011	2011		2010	
	Amount	Percent	Amount	Percent
Sales	$795,450		$665,532	
Sales returns and allowances	−6,250		−5,340	
Sales discounts	−6,470	------	−5,125	------
Net sales	$782,730	------	$655,067	------
Cost of goods sold:				
Beginning inventory	$ 75,394		$ 81,083	
Purchases	575,980		467,920	
Purchases discounts	−4,976	------	−2,290	------
Goods available for sale	$646,398		$546,713	
Less ending inventory	−66,254	------	−65,712	------
Total costs of goods sold	$580,144	------	$481,001	------
Gross profit	$202,586		$174,066	

4. Complete a horizontal analysis of the following partial income statement (round all percents to the nearest hundredth percent).

THREEMAX, INC.
Comparative Income Statement Horizontal Analysis
For Years Ended December 31, 2011 and 2010

	2011	2010	Change	Percent
Sales	$795,450	$665,532		
Sales returns and allowances	−6,250	−5,340		
Sales discounts	−6,470	−5,125		
Net sales	$782,730	$655,067		
Cost of goods sold:				
Beginning inventory	$ 75,394	$ 81,083		
Purchases	575,980	467,920		
Purchases discounts	−4,976	−2,290		
Goods available for sale	$646,398	$546,713		
Less ending inventory	−66,254	−65,712		
Total cost of goods sold	$580,144	$481,001		
Gross profit	$202,586	$174,066		

Learning Unit 16–3 : Trend and Ratio Analysis

DRILL PROBLEMS

1. Express each amount as a percent of the base-year (2009) amount. Round to the nearest tenth percent.

	2012	2011	2010	2009
Sales	$562,791	$560,776	$588,096	$601,982
Percent				
Gross profit	$168,837	$196,271	$235,238	$270,891
Percent				
Net income	$67,934	$65,927	$56,737	$62,762
Percent				

2. If current assets = $42,500 and current liabilities = $56,400, what is the current ratio (to the nearest hundredth)?

3. In Problem 2, if inventory = $20,500 and prepaid expenses = $9,750, what is the quick ratio, or acid test (to the nearest hundredth)?

4. If accounts receivable = $36,720 and net sales = $249,700, what is the average day's collection (to the nearest whole day)?

5. If total liabilities = $243,000 and total assets = $409,870, what is the ratio of total debt to total assets (to the nearest hundredth percent)?

6. If net income = $55,970 and total stockholders' equity = $440,780, what is the return on equity (to the nearest hundredth percent)?

7. If net sales = $900,000 and total assets = $1,090,000, what is the asset turnover (to the nearest hundredth)?

8. In Problem 7, if the net income is $36,600, what is the profit margin on net sales (to the nearest hundredth percent)?

WORD PROBLEMS

9. Calculate trend percentages for the following items using 2009 as the base year. Round to the nearest hundredth percent.

	2012	2011	2010	2009
Sales	$298,000	$280,000	$264,000	$249,250
Cost of goods sold	187,085	175,227	164,687	156,785
Accounts receivable	29,820	28,850	27,300	26,250

10. According to the balance sheet for Ralph's Market, current assets = $165,500 and current liabilities = $70,500. Find the current ratio (to the nearest hundredth).

11. On the balance sheet for Ralph's Market (Problem 10), merchandise inventory = $102,000. Find the quick ratio (acid test).

12. The balance sheet of Moses Contractors shows cash of $5,500, accounts receivable of $64,500, an inventory of $42,500, and current liabilities of $57,500. Find Moses' current ratio and acid test ratio (both to the nearest hundredth).

13. Moses' income statement shows gross sales of $413,000, sales returns of $8,600, and net income of $22,300. Find the profit margin on net sales (to the nearest hundredth percent).

14. **Given:**

Cash	$ 39,000	Retained earnings	$194,000
Accounts receivable	109,000	Net sales	825,000
Inventory	150,000	Cost of goods sold	528,000
Prepaid expenses	48,000	Operating expenses	209,300
Plant and equipment (net)	487,000	Interest expense	13,500
Accounts payable	46,000	Income taxes	32,400
Other current liabilities	43,000	Net income	41,800
Long-term liabilities	225,000		
Common stock	325,000		

Calculate (to nearest hundredth or hundredth percent as needed):

a. Current ratio. **b.** Quick ratio. **c.** Average day's collection.

d. Total debt to total assets. **e.** Return on equity. **f.** Asset turnover.

g. Profit margin on net sales.

15. The Vale Group lost $18.4 million in profits for the year 2010 as sales dropped to $401 million. Sales in 2009 were $450.6 million. What percent is the decrease in Vale's sales? Round to the nearest hundredth percent.

Name ______________________ Date ______________

Learning Unit 17–1 : Concept of Depreciation and the Straight-Line Method

DRILL PROBLEMS

1. Find the annual straight-line rate of depreciation, given the following estimated lives.

Life	Annual rate	Life	Annual rate
a. 25 years	______	**b.** 4 years	______
c. 10 years	______	**d.** 5 years	______
e. 8 years	______	**f.** 30 years	______

2. Find the annual depreciation using the straight-line depreciation method (round to the nearest whole dollar).

Cost of asset	Residual value	Useful life	Annual depreciation
a. $2,460	$400	4 years	______
b. $24,300	$2,000	6 years	______
c. $350,000	$42,500	12 years	______
d. $17,325	$5,000	5 years	______
e. $2,550,000	$75,000	30 years	______

3. Find the annual depreciation and ending book value for the first year using the straight-line depreciation method. Round to the nearest dollar.

Cost	Residual value	Useful life	Annual depreciation	Ending book value
a. $6,700	$600	3 years	______	______
b. $11,600	$500	6 years	______	______
c. $9,980	–0–	5 years	______	______
d. $36,950	$2,500	12 years	______	______
e. $101,690	$3,600	27 years	______	______

4. Find the first-year depreciation to the nearest dollar for the following assets, which were only owned for part of a year. Round to the nearest whole dollar the annual depreciation for in-between calculations.

Date of purchase	Cost of asset	Residual value	Useful life	First year depreciation
a. April 8	$10,500	$1,200	4 years	______
b. July 12	$23,900	$3,200	6 years	______
c. June 19	$8,880	$800	3 years	______
d. November 2	$125,675	$6,000	17 years	______
e. May 25	$44,050	–0–	9 years	______

WORD PROBLEMS

5. North Shore Grinding purchased a lathe for $37,500. This machine has a residual value of $3,000 and an expected useful life of 4 years. Prepare a depreciation schedule for the lathe using the straight-line depreciation method.

6. Colby Wayne paid $7,750 for a photocopy machine with an estimated life of 6 years and a residual value of $900. Prepare a depreciation schedule using the straight-line depreciation method. Round to the nearest whole dollar. (Last year's depreciation may have to be adjusted due to rounding.)

7. The Leo Brothers purchased a machine for $8,400 that has an estimated life of 3 years. At the end of 3 years the machine will have no value. Prepare a depreciation schedule using the straight-line depreciation method for this machine.

8. Fox Realty bought a computer table for $1,700. The estimated useful life of the table is 7 years. The residual value at the end of 7 years is $370. Find **(a)** the annual rate of depreciation to the nearest hundredth percent, **(b)** the annual amount of depreciation, and **(c)** the book value of the table at the end of the *third* year using the straight-line depreciation method.

9. Cashman, Inc., purchased an overhead projector for $560. It has an estimated useful life of 6 years, at which time it will have no remaining value. Find the book value at the end of 5 years using the straight-line depreciation method. Round the annual depreciation to the nearest whole dollar.

10. Shelley Corporation purchased a new machine for $15,000. The estimated life of the machine is 12 years with a residual value of $2,400. Find **(a)** the annual rate of depreciation by the straight-line method to the nearest hundredth percent, **(b)** the annual amount of depreciation, **(c)** the accumulated depreciation at the end of 7 years, and **(d)** the book value at the end of 9 years.

11. Wolfe Ltd. purchased a supercomputer for $75,000 on July 7, 2009. The computer has an estimated life of 5 years and will have a residual value of $15,000. Find **(a)** the annual depreciation amount by the straight-line method, **(b)** the depreciation amount for 2009, **(c)** the accumulated depreciation at the end of 2010, and **(d)** the book value at the end of 2011.

Learning Unit 17–2 : Units-of-Production Method

DRILL PROBLEMS

1. Find the depreciation per unit for each of the following assets. Round to three decimal places.

	Cost of asset	Residual value	Estimated production	Depreciation per unit
a.	$3,500	$800	9,000 units	______
b.	$309,560	$22,000	1,500,000 units	______
c.	$54,890	$6,500	275,000 units	______

2. Find the annual depreciation expense for each of the assets in Problem 1.

	Cost of asset	Residual value	Estimated production	Depreciation per unit	Units produced	Amount of depreciation
a.	$3,500	$800	9,000 units	______	3,000	______
b.	$309,560	$22,000	1,500,000 units	______	45,500	______
c.	$54,890	$6,500	275,000 units	______	4,788	______

3. Find the book value at the end of the first year for each of the assets in Problems 1 and 2.

	Cost of asset	Residual value	Estimated production	Depreciation per unit	Units produced	Book value
a.	$3,500	$800	9,000 units	______	3,000	________
b.	$309,560	$22,000	1,500,000 units	______	45,500	________
c.	$54,890	$6,500	275,000 units	______	4,788	________

4. Calculate the accumulated depreciation at the end of year 2 for each of the following machines. Carry out the unit depreciation to three decimal places.

	Cost of machine	Residual value	Estimated life	Hours used during year 1	Hours used during year 2	Accumulated depreciation
a.	$67,900	$4,300	19,000 hours	5,430	4,856	__________
b.	$3,810	$600	33,000 hours	10,500	9,330	__________
c.	$25,000	$4,900	80,000 hours	7,000	12,600	__________

WORD PROBLEMS

5. Prepare a depreciation schedule for the following machine: The machine cost $63,400; it has an estimated residual value of $5,300 and expected life of 290,500 units. The units produced were:

Year 1	95,000 units
Year 2	80,000 units
Year 3	50,000 units
Year 4	35,500 units
Year 5	30,000 units

6. Forsmann & Smythe purchased a new machine that cost $46,030. The machine has a residual value of $2,200 and estimated output of 430,000 hours. Prepare a units-of-production depreciation schedule for this machine (round the unit depreciation to three decimal places). The hours of use were:

Year 1	90,000 hours
Year 2	150,000 hours
Year 3	105,000 hours
Year 4	90,000 hours

7. Young Electrical Company depreciates its vans using the units-of-production method. The cost of its new van was $24,600, the useful life is 125,000 miles, and the trade-in value is $5,250. What are **(a)** the depreciation expense per mile (to three decimal places) and **(b)** the book value at the end of the first year if it is driven 29,667 miles?

8. Tremblay Manufacturing Company purchased a new machine for $52,000. The machine has an estimated useful life of 185,000 hours and a residual value of $10,000. The machine was used for 51,200 hours the first year. Find **(a)** the depreciation rate per hour (round to three decimal places), **(b)** the depreciation expense for the first year, and **(c)** the book value of the machine at the end of the first year.

Learning Unit 17–3 : Declining-Balance Method

DRILL PROBLEMS

1. Find the declining-balance rate of depreciation, given the following estimated lives.

Life	Declining rate
a. 25 years	________
b. 10 years	________
c. 8 years	________

2. Find the first year depreciation amount for the following assets using the declining-balance depreciation method. Round to the nearest whole dollar.

Cost of asset	Residual value	Useful life	First year depreciation
a. $2,460	$400	4 years	________
b. $24,300	$2,000	6 years	________
c. $350,000	$42,500	12 years	________
d. $17,325	$5,000	5 years	________
e. $2,550,000	$75,000	30 years	________

3. Find the depreciation expense and ending book value for the first year, using the declining-balance depreciation method. Round to the nearest dollar.

Cost	Residual value	Useful life	First year depreciation	Ending book value
a. $6,700	$600	3 years	______	______
b. $11,600	$500	6 years	______	______
c. $9,980	–0–	5 years	______	______
d. $36,950	$2,500	12 years	______	______
e. $101,690	$3,600	27 years	______	______

WORD PROBLEMS

4. North Shore Grinding purchased a lathe for $37,500. This machine has a residual value of $3,000 and an expected useful life of 4 years. Prepare a depreciation schedule for the lathe using the declining-balance depreciation method. Round to the nearest whole dollar.

5. Colby Wayne paid $7,750 for a photocopy machine with an estimated life of 6 years and a residual value of $900. Prepare a depreciation schedule using the declining-balance depreciation method. Round to the nearest whole dollar.

6. The Leo Brothers purchased a machine for $8,400 that has an estimated life of 3 years. At the end of 3 years, the machine will have no value. Prepare a depreciation schedule for this machine. Round to the nearest whole dollar.

7. Fox Realty bought a computer table for $1,700. The estimated useful life of the table is 7 years. The residual value at the end of 7 years is $370. Find **(a)** the declining depreciation rate to the nearest hundredth percent, **(b)** the amount of depreciation at the end of the *third* year, and **(c)** the book value of the table at the end of the *third* year using the declining-balance depreciation method. Round to the nearest whole dollar.

8. Cashman, Inc., purchased an overhead projector for $560. It has an estimated useful life of 6 years, at which time it will have no remaining value. Find the book value at the end of 5 years using the declining-balance depreciation method. Round to the nearest whole dollar.

9. Shelley Corporation purchased a new machine for $15,000. The estimated life of the machine is 12 years with a residual value of $2,400. Find **(a)** the declining-balance depreciation rate as a fraction and as a percent (hundredth percent), **(b)** the amount of depreciation at the end of the first year, **(c)** the accumulated depreciation at the end of 7 years, and **(d)** the book value at the end of 9 years. Round to the nearest dollar.

Learning Unit 17–4: Modified Accelerated Cost Recovery System (MACRS) with Introduction to ACRS

DRILL PROBLEMS

1. Using the MACRS method of depreciation, find the recovery rate, first-year depreciation expense, and book value of the asset at the end of the first year. Round to the nearest whole dollar.

	Cost of asset	Recovery period	Recovery rate	Depreciation expense	End-of-year book value
a.	$2,500	3 years	____	______	______
b.	$52,980	3 years	____	______	______
c.	$4,250	5 years	____	______	______
d.	$128,950	10 years	____	______	______
e.	$13,775	5 years	____	______	______

2. Find the accumulated depreciation at the end of the second year for each of the following assets. Round to the nearest whole dollar.

	Cost of asset	Recovery period	Accumulated depreciation at end of 2nd year using MACRS	Book value at end of 2nd year using MACRS
a.	$2,500	3 years	______	______
b.	$52,980	3 years	______	______
c.	$4,250	5 years	______	______
d.	$128,950	10 years	______	______
e.	$13,775	5 years	______	______

WORD PROBLEMS

3. Colby Wayne paid $7,750 for a photocopy machine that is classified as equipment and has a residual value of $900. Prepare a depreciation schedule using the MACRS depreciation method. Round all calculations to the nearest whole dollar.

4. Fox Realty bought a computer table for $1,700. The table is classified as furniture. The residual value at the end of the table's useful life is $370. Using the MACRS depreciation method, find **(a)** the amount of depreciation at the end of the *third* year, **(b)** the total accumulated depreciation at the end of year 3, and **(c)** the book value of the table at the end of the *third* year. Round all calculations to the nearest dollar.

5. Cashman, Inc., purchased an overhead projector for $560. It is classified as office equipment and will have no residual value. Find the book value at the end of 5 years using the MACRS depreciation method. Round to the nearest whole dollar.

6. Shelley Corporation purchased a new machine for $15,000. The machine is comparable to equipment used for two-way exchange of voice and data with a residual value of $2,400. Find **(a)** the amount of depreciation at the end of the first year, **(b)** the accumulated depreciation at the end of 7 years, and **(c)** the book value at the end of 9 years. Round to the nearest dollar.

7.* Wolfe Ltd. purchased a supercomputer for $75,000 at the beginning of 1996. The computer is classified as a 5-year asset and will have a residual value of $15,000. Using MACRS, find **(a)** the depreciation amount for 1996, **(b)** the accumulated depreciation at the end of 1997, **(c)** the book value at the end of 1998, and **(d)** the last year that the asset will be depreciated.

8.* Cummins Engine Company uses a straight-line depreciation method to calculate the cost of an asset of $1,200,000 with a $200,000 residual value and a life expectancy of 15 years. How much would Cummins have for depreciation expense for each of the first 2 years? Round to the nearest dollar for each year.

9. An article in an issue of *Management Accounting* stated that Cummins Engine Company changed its depreciation. The cost of its asset was $1,200,000 with a $200,000 residual value (with a life expectancy of 15 years) and an estimated productive capacity of 864,000 products. Cummins produced 59,000 products this year. What would it write off for depreciation using the units-of-production method?

*These problems are placed here for a quick review.

Classroom Notes

Name ______________________ Date ______________

Learning Unit 18–1: Assigning Costs to Ending Inventory—Specific Identification; Weighted Average; FIFO; LIFO

DRILL PROBLEMS

1. Given the value of the beginning inventory, purchases for the year, and ending inventory, find the cost of goods available for sale and the cost of goods sold.

	Beginning inventory	Purchases	Ending inventory	Cost of goods available for sale	Cost of goods sold
a.	$1,000	$4,120	$2,100	________	________
b.	$52,400	$270,846	$49,700	________	________
c.	$205	$48,445	$376	________	________
d.	$78,470	$2,788,560	$100,600	________	________
e.	$965	$53,799	$2,876	________	________

2. Find the missing amounts; then calculate the number of units available for sale and the cost of the goods available for sale.

Date	Category	Quantity	Unit cost	Total cost
January 1	Beginning inventory	1,207	$45	________
February 7	Purchase	850	$46	________
April 19	Purchase	700	$47	________
July 5	Purchase	1,050	$49	________
November 2	Purchase	450	$52	________
Goods available for sale		______		________

3. Using the *specific identification* method, find the ending inventory and cost of goods sold for the merchandising concern in Problem 2.

Remaining inventory	Unit cost	Total cost
20 units from beginning inventory	____	________
35 units from February 7	____	________
257 units from July 5	____	________
400 units from November 2	____	________
Cost of ending inventory		________
Cost of goods sold		________

4. Using the *weighted-average* method, find the average cost per unit (to the nearest cent) and the cost of ending inventory.

	Units available for sale	Cost of goods available for sale	Units in ending inventory	Weighted-average unit cost	Cost of ending inventory
a.	2,350	$120,320	1,265	______	________
b.	7,090	$151,017	1,876	______	________
c.	855	$12,790	989	______	________
d.	12,964	$125,970	9,542	______	________
e.	235,780	$507,398	239,013	______	________

5. Use the *FIFO* method of inventory valuation to determine the value of ending inventory, which consists of 40 units, and the cost of goods sold.

Date	Category	Quantity	Unit cost	Total cost
January 1	Beginning inventory	37	$219.00	________
March 5	Purchases	18	230.60	________
June 17	Purchases	22	255.70	________
October 18	Purchases	34	264.00	________
Goods available for sale		___		________

Ending inventory = ________ Cost of goods sold = ________

6. Use the *LIFO* method of inventory valuation to determine the value of the ending inventory, which consists of 40 units, and the cost of goods sold.

Date	Category	Quantity	Unit cost	Total cost
January 1	Beginning inventory	37	$219.00	________
March 5	Purchases	18	230.60	________
June 17	Purchases	22	255.70	________
October 18	Purchases	34	264.00	________
Goods available for sale		___		________

Ending inventory = ________ Cost of goods sold = ________

WORD PROBLEMS

7. At the beginning of September, Green's of Gloucester had 13 yellow raincoats in stock. These raincoats cost $36.80 each. During the month, Green's purchased 14 raincoats for $37.50 each and 16 raincoats for $38.40 each, and they sold 26 raincoats. Calculate **(a)** the average unit cost (round to the nearest cent) and **(b)** the ending inventory value using the weighted-average method.

8. If Green's of Gloucester (Problem 7) used the FIFO method, what would the value of the ending inventory be?

9. If Green's of Gloucester (Problem 7) used the LIFO method, what would the value of the ending inventory be?

10. Hobby Caterers purchased recycled-paper sketch pads during the year as follows:

January	350 pads for $.27 each
March	400 pads for $.31 each
July	200 pads for $.36 each
October	850 pads for $.26 each
November	400 pads for $.31 each

At the end of the year, the company had 775 of these sketch pads in stock. Find the ending inventory value using **(a)** the weighted-average method (round to the nearest cent), **(b)** the FIFO method, and **(c)** the LIFO method.

11. On March 1, Sandler's Shoe Store had the following sports shoes in stock:

13 pairs running shoes for $33 a pair
22 pairs walking shoes for $29 a pair
35 pairs aerobic shoes for $26 a pair
21 pairs cross-trainers for $52 a pair

During the month Sandler's sold 10 pairs of running shoes, 15 pairs of walking shoes, 28 pairs of aerobic shoes, and 12 pairs of cross-trainers. Use the specific identification method to find **(a)** the cost of the goods available for sale, **(b)** the value of the ending inventory, and **(c)** the cost of goods sold.

Learning Unit 18–2: Retail Method; Gross Profit Method; Inventory Turnover; Distribution of Overhead

DRILL PROBLEMS

1. Given the following information, calculate **(a)** the goods available for sale at cost and retail, **(b)** the cost ratio (to the nearest thousandth), **(c)** the ending inventory at retail, and **(d)** the cost of the March 31 inventory (to the nearest dollar) by the retail inventory method.

	Cost	Retail
Beginning inventory, March 1	$57,300	$95,500
Purchases during March	$28,400	$48,000
Sales during March		$79,000

2. Given the following information, use the gross profit method to calculate **(a)** the cost of goods available for sale, **(b)** the cost percentage, **(c)** the estimated cost of goods sold, and **(d)** the estimated cost of the inventory as of April 30.

Beginning inventory, April 1	$30,000
Net purchases during April	81,800
Sales during April	98,000
Average gross profit on sales	40%

3. Given the following information, find the average inventory.

Merchandise inventory, January 1, 200A	$82,000
Merchandise inventory, December 31, 200A	$88,000

4. Given the following information, find the inventory turnover for the company in Problem 3 to the nearest hundredth.

Cost of goods sold (12/31/0A)	$625,000

5. Given the following information, calculate the **(a)** average inventory at retail, **(b)** average inventory at cost, **(c)** inventory turnover at retail, and **(d)** inventory turnover at cost. Round to the nearest hundredth.

	Cost	Retail
Merchandise inventory, January 1	$ 250,000	$ 355,000
Merchandise inventory, December 31	$ 235,000	$ 329,000
Cost of goods sold	$1,525,000	
Sales		$2,001,000

6. Given the floor space for the following departments, find the entire floor space and the percent each department represents.

		Percent of floor space
Department A	15,000 square feet	_____
Department B	25,000 square feet	_____
Department C	10,000 square feet	_____
Total floor space	50,000 square feet	_____

7. If the total overhead for all the departments (Problem 6) is $200,000, how much of the overhead expense should be allocated to each department?

	Overhead/department
Department A	
Department B	________
Department C	________

WORD PROBLEMS

8. During the accounting period, Ward's Greenery sold $290,000 of merchandise at marked retail prices. At the end of the period, the following information was available from Ward's records:

	Cost	Retail
Beginning inventory	$ 53,000	$ 79,000
Net purchases	$204,000	$280,000

Use the retail method to estimate Ward's ending inventory at cost. Round the cost ratio to the nearest thousandth.

9. On January 1, Benny's Retail Mart had a $49,000 inventory at cost. During the first quarter of the year, Benny's made net purchases of $199,900. Benny's records show that during the past several years, the store's gross profit on sales has averaged 35%. If Benny's records show $275,000 in sales for the quarter, estimate the ending inventory for the first quarter, using the gross profit method.

10. On April 4, there was a big fire and the entire inventory of R. W. Wilson Company was destroyed. The company records were salvaged. They showed the following information:

Sales (January 1 through April 4)	$127,000
Merchandise inventory, January 1	16,000
Net purchases	71,250

On January 1, the inventory was priced to sell for $38,000 and additional items bought during the period were priced to sell for $102,000. Calculate the cost of the inventory that was destroyed by the fire using the retail method. Round the cost ratio to the nearest thousandth.

11. During the past 4 years, the average gross margin on sales for R. W. Wilson Company was 36% of net sales. Using the data in Problem 10, calculate the cost of the ending inventory destroyed by fire using the gross profit method.

12. Chase Bank has to make a decision on whether to grant a loan to Sally's Furniture store. The lending officer is interested in how often Sally's inventory is turned over. Using selected information from Sally's income statement, calculate the inventory turnover for Sally's Furniture Store (to the nearest hundredth).

Merchandise inventory, January 1, 200A	$ 43,000
Merchandise inventory, December 31, 200A	55,000
Cost of goods sold	128,000

13. Wanting to know more about a business he was considering buying, Jake Paige studied the business's books. He found that beginning inventory for the previous year was $51,000 at cost and $91,800 at retail, ending inventory was $44,000 at cost and $72,600 at retail, sales were $251,000, and cost of goods sold was $154,000. Using this information, calculate for Jake the inventory turnover at cost and the inventory turnover at retail.

14. Ralph's Retail Outlet has calculated its expenses for the year. Total overhead expenses are $147,000. Ralph's accountant must allocate this overhead to four different departments. Given the following information regarding the floor space occupied by each department, calculate how much overhead expense should be allocated to each department.

Department W	12,000 square feet
Department X	9,000 square feet
Department Y	14,000 square feet
Department Z	7,000 square feet

15. How much overhead would be allocated to each department of Ralph's Retail Outlet (Problem 14) if the basis of allocation were the sales of each department? Sales for each of the departments were:

Department W	$110,000
Department X	$120,000
Department Y	$170,000
Department Z	$100,000

Name ______________________________ Date ______________

Learning Unit 19–1 : Sales and Excise Taxes

DRILL PROBLEMS

1. Calculate the sales tax and the total amount due for each of the following:

	Total sales	Sales tax rate	Sales tax	Total amount due
a.	\$536	5%	______	______
b.	\$11,980	6%	______	______
c.	\$3,090	$8\frac{1}{4}\%$	______	______
d.	\$17.65	$5\frac{1}{2}\%$	______	______
e.	\$294	7.42%	______	______

2. Find the amount of actual sales and amount of sales tax on the following total receipts:

	Total receipts	Sales tax rate	Actual sales	Sales tax
a.	\$27,932.15	5.5%	______	______
b.	\$35,911.53	7%	______	______
c.	\$115,677.06	$6\frac{1}{2}\%$	______	______
d.	\$142.96	$5\frac{1}{4}\%$	______	______
e.	\$5,799.24	4.75%	______	______

3. Find the sales tax, excise tax, and total cost for each of the following items:

	Retail price	Sales tax, 5.2%	Excise tax, 11%	Total cost
a.	\$399	______	______	______
b.	\$22,684	______	______	______
c.	\$7,703	______	______	______

4. Calculate the amount, subtotal, sales tax, and total amount due of the following:

Quantity	Description	Unit price	Amount
3	Taxable item	\$4.30	______
2	Taxable item	\$5.23	______
4	Taxable item	\$1.20	______
		Subtotal	______
		5% sales tax	______
		Total	______

5. Given the sales tax rate and the amount of the sales tax, calculate the price of the following purchases (before tax was added):

	Tax rate	Tax amount	Price of purchase
a.	7%	\$71.61	______
b.	$5\frac{1}{2}\%$	\$3.22	______

6. Given the sales tax rate and the total price (including tax), calculate the price of the following purchases (before the tax was added):

	Tax rate	Total price	Price of purchase
a.	5%	\$340.20	______
b.	6%	\$1,224.30	______

WORD PROBLEMS

7. In a state with a 4.75% sales tax, what will be the sales tax and the total price of a video game marked $110?

8. Browning's invoice included a sales tax of $38.15. If the sales tax rate is 6%, what was the total cost of the taxable goods on the invoice?

9. David Bowan paid a total of $2,763 for a new computer. If this includes a sales tax of 5.3%, what was the marked price of the computer?

10. After a 5% sales tax and a 12% excise tax, the total cost of a leather jacket was $972. What was the selling price of the jacket?

11. A customer at the RDM Discount Store purchased four tubes of toothpaste priced at $1.88 each, six toothbrushes for $1.69 each, and three bottles of shampoo for $2.39 each. What did the customer have to pay if the sales tax is $5\frac{1}{2}$%?

12. Bill Harrington purchased a mountain bike for $875. Bill had to pay a sales tax of 6% and an excise tax of 11%. What was the total amount Bill had to pay for his mountain bike?

13. Donna DeCoff received a bill for $754 for a new chair she had purchased. The bill included a 6.2% sales tax and a delivery charge of $26. What was the selling price of the chair?

Learning Unit 19–2 : Property Tax

DRILL PROBLEMS

1. Find the assessed value of the following properties (round to the nearest whole dollar):

	Market value	Assessment rate	Assessed value
a.	$195,000	35%	________
b.	$1,550,900	50%	________
c.	$75,000	75%	________
d.	$2,585,400	65%	________
e.	$349,500	85%	________

2. Find the tax rate for each of the following municipalities (round to the nearest tenth of a percent):

	Budget needed	Total assessed value	Tax rate
a.	$2,594,000	$44,392,000	______
b.	$17,989,000	$221,900,000	______
c.	$6,750,000	$47,635,000	______
d.	$13,540,000	$143,555,500	______
e.	$1,099,000	$12,687,000	______

3. Express each of the following tax rates in all the indicated forms:

	By percent	Per $100 of assessed value	Per $1,000 of assessed value	In mills
a.	7.45%	______	______	______
b.	______	$14.24	______	______
c.	______	______	______	90.8
d.	______	______	$62.00	______

4. Calculate the property tax due for each of the following:

	Total assessed value	Tax rate	Total property tax due
a.	$12,900	$6.60 per $100	________
b.	$175,400	43 mills	________
c.	$320,500	2.7%	________
d.	$2,480,000	$17.85 per $1,000	________
e.	$78,900	59 mills	________
f.	$225,550	$11.39 per $1,000	________
g.	$198,750	$2.63 per $100	________

WORD PROBLEMS

5. The county of Chelsea approved a budget of $3,450,000, which had to be raised through property taxation. If the total assessed value of properties in the county of Chelsea was $37,923,854, what will the tax rate be? The tax rate is stated per $100 of assessed valuation.

6. Linda Tawse lives in Camden and her home has a market value of $235,000. Property in Camden is assessed at 55% of its market value, and the tax rate for the current year is $64.75 per $1,000. What is the assessed valuation of Linda's home?

7. Using the information in Problem 6, find the amount of property tax that Linda will have to pay.

8. Mary Faye Souza has property with a fair market value of $219,500. Property in Mary Faye's city is assessed at 65% of its market value and the tax rate is $3.64 per $100. How much is Mary Faye's property tax due?

9. Cagney's Greenhouse has a fair market value of $1,880,000. Property is assessed at 35% by the city. The tax rate is 6.4%. What is the property tax due for Cagney's Greenhouse?

10. In Chester County, property is assessed at 40% of its market value, the residential tax rate is $12.30 per $1,000, and the commercial tax rate is $13.85 per $1,000. What is the property tax due on a home that has a market value of $205,000?

11. Using the information in Problem 10, find the property tax due on a grocery store with a market value of $5,875,000.

12. Bob Rose's home is assessed at $195,900. Last year the tax rate was 11.8 mills, and this year the rate was raised to 13.2 mills. How much more will Bob have to pay in taxes this year?

Classroom Notes

Name ______________________________ Date ______________

Learning Unit 20–1 : Life Insurance

DRILL PROBLEMS

1. Use the table in the *Business Math Handbook* to find the annual premium per $1,000 of life insurance and calculate the annual premiums for each policy listed. Assume the insureds are males.

	Face value of policy	Type of insurance	Age at issue	Annual premium per $1,000	Number of $1,000s in face value	Annual premium
a.	$25,000	Straight life	31	______	______	______
b.	$40,500	20-year endowment	40	______	______	______
c.	$200,000	Straight life	44	______	______	______
d.	$62,500	20-payment life	25	______	______	______
e.	$12,250	5-year term	35	______	______	______
f.	$42,500	20-year endowment	42	______	______	______

2. Use Table 20.1 to find the annual premium for each of the following life insurance policies. Assume the insured is a 30-year-old male.

	Face value of policy	Five-year term policy	Straight life policy	Twenty-payment life policy	Twenty-year endowment
a.	$50,000	______	______	______	______
b.	$1,000,000	______	______	______	______
c.	$250,000	______	______	______	______
d.	$72,500	______	______	______	______

3. Use the table in the *Business Math Handbook* to find the annual premium for each of the following life insurance policies. Assume the insured is a 30-year-old female.

	Face value of policy	Five-year term policy	Straight life policy	Twenty-payment life policy	Twenty-year endowment
a.	$50,000	______	______	______	______
b.	$1,000,000	______	______	______	______
c.	$250,000	______	______	______	______
d.	$72,500	______	______	______	______

4. Use the table in the *Business Math Handbook* to find the nonforfeiture options for the following policies:

	Years policy in force	Type of policy	Face value	Cash value	Amount of paid-up insurance	Extended term
a.	10	Straight life	$25,000	______	______	______
b.	20	20-year endowment	$500,000	______	______	______
c.	5	20-payment life	$2,000,000	______	______	______
d.	15	Straight life	$750,000	______	______	______
e.	5	20-year endowment	$93,500	______	______	______

WORD PROBLEMS

5. If Mr. Davis, aged 39, buys a $90,000 straight life policy, what is the amount of his annual premium?

6. If Miss Jennie McDonald, age 27, takes out a $65,000 20-year endowment policy, what premium amount will she pay each year?

7. If Gary Thomas decides to cash in his $45,000 20-payment life insurance policy after 15 years, what cash surrender value will he receive?

8. Mary Allyn purchased a $70,000 20-year endowment policy when she was 26 years old. Ten years later, she decided that she could no longer afford the premiums. If Mary decides to convert her policy to paid-up insurance, what amount of paid-up insurance coverage will she have?

9. Peter and Jane Rizzo are both 28 years old and are both planning to take out $50,000 straight life insurance policies. What is the difference in the annual premiums they will have to pay?

10. Paul Nasser purchased a $125,000 straight life policy when he was 30 years old. He is now 50 years old. Two months ago, he slipped in the bathtub and injured his back; he will not be able to return to his regular job for several months. Due to a lack of income, he feels that he can no longer continue to pay the premiums on his life insurance policy. If Paul decides to surrender his policy for cash, how much cash will he receive?

11. If Paul Nasser (Problem 10) chooses to convert his policy to paid-up insurance, what will the face value of his new policy be?

Learning Unit 20–2 : Fire Insurance

DRILL PROBLEMS

1. Use the tables in the *Business Math Handbook* to find the premium for each of the following:

	Rating of area	Building class	Building value	Value of contents	Total annual premium
a.	3	A	$80,000	$32,000	________
b.	2	B	$340,000	$202,000	________
c.	2	A	$221,700	$190,000	________
d.	1	B	$96,400	$23,400	________
e.	3	B	$65,780	$62,000	________

2. Use the tables in the *Business Math Handbook* to find the short-term premium and the amount of refund due if the insured cancels.

	Annual premium	Months of coverage	Short-term premium	Refund due
a.	$1,860	3	________	________
b.	$650	7	________	________
c.	$1,200	10	________	________
d.	$341	12	________	________
e.	$1,051	4	________	________

3. Find the amount to be paid for each of the following losses:

	Property value	Coinsurance clause	Insurance required	Insurance carried	Amount of loss	Insurance company pays (indemnity)
a.	$85,000	80%	________	$70,000	$60,000	________
b.	$52,000	80%	________	$45,000	$50,000	________
c.	$44,000	80%	________	$33,000	$33,000	________
d.	$182,000	80%	________	$127,400	$61,000	________

WORD PROBLEMS

4. Mary Rose wants to purchase fire insurance for her building, which is rated as Class B; the rating of the area is 2. If her building is worth $225,000 and the contents are worth $70,000, what will her annual premium be?

5. Janet Ambrose owns a Class A building valued at $180,000. The contents of the building are valued at $145,000. The territory rating is 3. What is her annual fire insurance premium?

6. Jack Altshuler owns a building worth $355,500. The contents are worth $120,000. The classification of the building is B, and the rating of the area is 1. What annual premium must Jack pay for his fire insurance?

7. Jay Viola owns a store valued at $460,000. His fire insurance policy (which has an 80% coinsurance clause) has a face value of $345,000. A recent fire resulted in a loss of $125,000. How much will the insurance company pay?

8. The building that is owned by Tally's Garage is valued at $275,000 and is insured for $225,000. The policy has an 80% coinsurance clause. If there is a fire in the building and the damages amount to $220,000, how much of the loss will be paid for by the insurance company?

9. Michael Dannon owns a building worth $420,000. He has a fire insurance policy with a face value of $336,000 (there is an 80% coinsurance clause). There was recently a fire that resulted in a $400,000 loss. How much money will he receive from the insurance company?

10. Rice's Rent-A-Center business is worth $375,000. He has purchased a $250,000 fire insurance policy. The policy has an 80% coinsurance clause. What will Rice's reimbursement be **(a)** after a $150,000 fire and **(b)** after a $330,000 fire?

11. If Maria's Pizza Shop is valued at $210,000 and is insured for $147,000 with a policy that contains an 80% coinsurance clause, what settlement is due after a fire that causes **(a)** $150,000 in damages and **(b)** $175,000 in damages?

Learning Unit 20–3: Auto Insurance

DRILL PROBLEMS

1. Calculate the annual premium for compulsory coverage for each of the following.

Driver classification	Bodily	Property	Total premium
a. 17	_____	_____	_____
b. 20	_____	_____	_____
c. 10	_____	_____	_____

2. Calculate the amount of money the insurance company and the driver should pay for each of the following accidents, assuming the driver carries compulsory insurance only.

Accident and court award	Insurance company pays	Driver pays
a. Driver hit one person and court awarded $15,000.	_____	_____
b. Driver hit one person and court awarded $12,000 for personal injury.	_____	_____
c. Driver hit two people; court awarded first person $9,000 and the second person $12,000.	_____	_____

3. Calculate the additional premium payment for each of the following options.

Optional insurance coverage	Addition to premium
a. Bodily injury 50/100/25, driver class 20	_____
b. Bodily injury 25/60/10, driver class 17	_____
c. Collision insurance, driver class 10, age group 3, symbol 5, deductible $100	_____
d. Comprehensive insurance, driver class 10, age group 3, symbol 5, deductible $200	_____
e. Substitute transportation, towing, and labor; driver class 10, age group 3, symbol 5	_____

4. Compute the annual premium for compulsory insurance with optional liability coverage for bodily injury and damage to someone else's property.

	Driver classification	Bodily coverage	Premium
a.	17	50/100/25	______
b.	20	100/300/10	______
c.	10	25/60/25	______
d.	18	250/500/50	______
e.	20	25/50/10	______

5. Calculate the annual premium for each of the following drivers with the indicated options. All drivers must carry compulsory insurance.

	Driver classification	Car age	Car symbol	Bodily injury	Collision	Comprehensive	Transportation and towing	Annual premium
a.	10	2	4	50/100/10	$100 deductible	$300 deductible	Yes	______
b.	18	3	2	25/60/25	$200 deductible	$200 deductible	Yes	______

WORD PROBLEMS

6. Ann Centerino's driver classification is 10. She carries only compulsory insurance coverage. What annual insurance premium must she pay?

7. Gary Hines is a class 18 driver. He wants to add optional bodily injury and property damage of 250/500/50 to his compulsory insurance coverage. What will be Gary's total annual premium?

8. Sara Goldberg wants optional bodily injury coverage of 50/100/25 and collision coverage with a deductible of $300 in addition to the compulsory coverage her state requires. Sara is a class 17 driver and has a symbol 4 car that is 2 years old. What annual premium must Sara pay?

9. Karen Babson has just purchased a new car with a symbol of 8. She wants bodily injury and property liability of 500/1,000/100, comprehensive and collision insurance with a $200 deductible, and transportation and towing coverage. If Karen is a class 10 driver, what will be her annual insurance premium? There is no compulsory insurance requirement in her state. Assume age group 1.

10. Craig Haberland is a class 18 driver. He has a 5-year-old car with a symbol of 4. His state requires compulsory insurance coverage. In addition, he wishes to purchase collision and comprehensive coverage with the maximum deductible. He also wants towing insurance. What will Craig's annual insurance premium be?

11. Nancy Poland has an insurance policy with limits of 10/20. If Nancy injures a pedestrian and the judge awards damages of $18,000, **(a)** how much will the insurance company pay and **(b)** how much will Nancy pay?

12. Peter Bell carries insurance with bodily injury limits of 25/60. Peter is in an accident and is charged with injuring four people. The judge awards damages of $10,000 to each of the injured parties. How much will the insurance company pay? How much will Peter pay?

13. Jerry Greeley carries an insurance policy with bodily injury limits of 25/60. Jerry is in an accident and is charged with injuring four people. If the judge awards damages of $20,000 to each of the injured parties, **(a)** how much will the insurance company pay and **(b)** how much will Jerry pay?

14. An issue of *Your Money* reported that the Illinois Department of Insurance gave a typical premium for a brick house in Chicago built in 1950, assuming no policy discounts and a replacement cost estimated at $100,000. With a $100 deductible, the annual premium will be $653. Using the rate in your textbook, with a rating area 3 and class B, what would be the annual premium? (This problem reviews fire insurance.)

15. An issue of *Money* ran a story on cutting car insurance premiums. Raising the car insurance deductible to $500 will cut the collision premium 15%. Theresa Mendex insures her car; her age group is 5 and symbol is 5. What would be her reduction if she changed her policy to a $500 deductible? What would the collision insurance now cost?

16. Robert Stuono lost his life insurance when he was downsized from an investment banking company early this year. So Stuono, age 44, enlisted the help of an independent agent who works with several insurance companies. His goal is $350,000 in term coverage with a level premium for 5 years. What will Robert's annual premium be for term insurance? (This problem reviews life insurance.)

Classroom Notes

Name ______________________________ Date ______________

Learning Unit 21–1 : Stocks

DRILL PROBLEMS

52 weeks Hi	Lo	Stocks	SYM	Div	Yld %	PE	Vol 100s	High	Low	Close	Net chg
43.88	25.51	Disney	DIS	.21	.8	49	49633	27.69	26.50	27.69	+0.63

1. From the listed information for Disney, complete the following:

a. __________ was the highest price at which Disney stock traded during the year.
b. __________ was the lowest price at which Disney stock traded during the year.
c. __________ was the amount of the dividend Disney paid to shareholders last year.
d. __________ is the dividend amount a shareholder with 100 shares would receive.
e. __________ is the rate of return the stock yielded to its stockholders.
f. __________ is how many times the earnings per share the stock is selling for.
g. __________ is the number of shares traded on the day of this stock quote.
h. __________ is the highest price paid for Disney stock on this day.
i. __________ is the lowest price paid for Disney stock on this day.
j. __________ is the change in price from yesterday's closing price.

2. Use the Disney information to show how the yield percent was calculated.

3. What was the price of the last trade of Disney stock yesterday?

WORD PROBLEMS

4. Assume a stockbroker's commission of 2%. What will it cost to purchase 200 shares of Saplent Corporation at $10.75?

5. In Problem 4, the stockbroker's commission for selling stock is the same as that for buying stock. If the customer who purchased 200 shares at $10.75 sells the 200 shares of stock at the end of the year at $18.12, what will be the gain on investment?

6. Holtz Corporation's records show 80,000 shares of preferred stock issued. The preferred dividend is $2 per share, which is cumulative. The records show 750,000 shares of common stock issued. In 2009, no dividends were paid. In 2010, the board of directors declared a dividend of $582,500. What are **(a)** the total amount of dividends paid to preferred stockholders, **(b)** the total amount of dividends paid to common stockholders, and **(c)** the amount of the common dividend per share?

7. Melissa Tucker bought 300 shares of Delta Air Lines stock listed at $61.22 per share. What is the total amount she paid if the stockbroker's commission is 2.5%?

8. A year later, Melissa (Problem 7) sold the stock she had purchased. The market price of the stock at this time was $72.43. Delta Air Lines had paid its shareholders a dividend of $1.20 per share. If the stockbroker's commission to sell stock is 2.5%, what gain did Melissa realize?

9. The board of directors of Parker Electronics, Inc., declared a $539,000 dividend. If the corporation has 70,000 shares of common stock outstanding, what is the dividend per share?

Learning Unit 21–2 : Bonds

DRILL PROBLEMS

Bond	Current yield	Sales	Close	Net change
IBM $10\frac{1}{4}$ 11	10.0	11	102.5	+.125

1. From the bond listing above complete the following:

a. ________ is the name of the company.

b. ________ is the percent of interest paid on the bond.

c. ________ is the year in which the bond matures.

d. ________ is the total interest for the year.

e. ________ was yesterday's close on the IBM bond.

2. Show how to calculate the current yield of 10.0% for IBM. (Trade commissions have been omitted.)

3. Use the information for the IBM bonds to calculate **(a)** the amount the last bond traded for on this day and **(b)** the amount the last bond traded for yesterday.

4. What will be the annual interest payment **(a)** to the bondholder assuming he paid $101\frac{3}{4}$ and **(b)** to the bondholder who purchased the bond for $102\frac{1}{2}$?

5. If Terry Gambol purchased three IBM bonds at this day's closing price, **(a)** what will be her total cost excluding commission and **(b)** how much interest will she receive for the year?

6. Calculate the bond yield (to the nearest tenth percent) for each of the following:

	Bond interest rate	Purchase price	Bond yield
a.	7%	97	______
b.	$9\frac{1}{2}$%	101.625	______
c.	$13\frac{1}{4}$%	104.25	______

7. For each of the following, state whether the bond sold at a premium or a discount and give the amount of the premium or discount.

	Bond interest rate	Purchase price	Premium or discount
a.	7%	97	____________
b.	$9\frac{1}{2}$%	101.625	____________
c.	$13\frac{1}{4}$%	104.25	____________

WORD PROBLEMS

8. Rob Morrisey purchased a $1,000 bond that was quoted at 102.25 and paying $8\frac{7}{8}$% interest. **(a)** How much did Rob pay for the bond? **(b)** What was the premium or discount? **(c)** How much annual interest will he receive?

9. Jackie Anderson purchased a bond that was quoted at 62.50 and paying interest of $10\frac{1}{2}$%. **(a)** How much did Jackie pay for the bond? **(b)** What was the premium or discount? **(c)** What interest will Jackie receive annually? **(d)** What is the bond's current annual yield (to the nearest tenth percent)?

10. Swartz Company issued bonds totaling $2,000,000 in order to purchase updated equipment. If the bonds pay interest of 11%, what is the total amount of interest the Swartz Company must pay semiannually?

11. The RJR and ACyan companies have both issued bonds that are paying $7\frac{3}{8}$% interest. The quoted price of the RJR bond is 94.125, and the quoted price of the ACyan bond is $102\frac{7}{8}$. Find the current annual yield on each (to the nearest tenth percent).

12. Mary Rowe purchased 25 of Chrysler Corporation $8\frac{3}{8}$% bonds of 2009. The bonds closed at 93.25. Find **(a)** the total purchase price and **(b)** the amount of the first semiannual interest payment Mary will receive.

13. What is the annual yield (to the nearest hundredth percent) of the bonds Mary Rowe purchased?

14. Mary Rowe purchased a $1,000 bond listed as ARch $10\frac{7}{8}$ 09 for 122.75. What is the annual yield of this bond (to the nearest tenth percent)?

Learning Unit 21–3 : Mutual Funds

DRILL PROBLEMS

From the following, calculate the NAV. Round to the nearest cent.

	Current market value of fund investments	Current liabilities	Number of shares outstanding	NAV
1.	$6,800,000	$850,000	500,000	______
2.	$11,425,000	$690,000	810,000	______
3.	$22,580,000	$1,300,000	1,400,000	______

Complete the following using this information:

NAV	Net change	Fund name	Inv. obj.	YTD %Ret	Total return 1 Yr R
$23.48	+.14	EuroA	Eu	+37.3	+7.6 E

4. NAV ________

5. NAV change ________

6. Total return year to date ________

7. Return for the last 12 months ________

8. What does an E rating mean? ________

Calculate the commission (load) charge and the offer to buy.

	NAV	% commission (load) charge	Dollar amount of commission (load) charge	Offer price
9.	$17.00	$8\frac{1}{2}$%	______	______
10.	$21.55	6%	______	______
11.	$14.10	4%	______	______

WORD PROBLEMS

12. Paul wanted to know how his Fidelity mutual fund $14.33 NAV in the newspaper was calculated. He called Fidelity, and he received the following information:

Current market value of fund investment	$7,500,000
Current liabilities	$910,000
Number of shares outstanding	460,000

Please calculate the NAV for Paul. Was the NAV in the newspaper correct?

13. Jeff Jones bought 150 shares of Putnam Vista Fund. The NAV of the fund was $9.88. The offer price was $10.49. What did Jeff pay for these 150 shares?

14. Pam Long purchased 300 shares of the no-load Scudder's European Growth Company Fund. The NAV is $12.61. What did Pam pay for the 300 shares?

15. Assume in Problem 14 that 8 years later Pam sells her 300 shares. The NAV at the time of sale was $12.20. What is the amount of her profit or loss on the sale?

16. Financial planner J. Michael Martin recommended that Jim Kelly choose a long-term bond because it gives high income while Kelly waits for better stock market opportunities down the road. The bond Martin recommended matures in 2012 and was originally issued at $8\frac{1}{2}$% interest and the current yield is 7.9%. What would be the current selling price for this bond and how would that price appear in the bond quotations?

17.

Bonds	Vol.	Close	Net chg.
Comp USA $9\frac{1}{2}$ 09	70	102.375	−.125
GMA 7 10	5	101.625	−1.25

From the above information, compare the two bonds for:

a. When the bonds expire.
b. The yield of each bond.
c. The current selling price.
d. Whether the bond is selling at a discount or premium.
e. Yesterday's bond close.

Name ______________________________ Date ______________

Learning Unit 22–1 : Mean, Median, and Mode

Note: Optional problems for LU 22–3 are found on page 537.

DRILL PROBLEMS

1. Find the mean for the following lists of numbers. Round to the nearest hundredth.

a. 12, 16, 20, 25, 29 Mean _____

b. 80, 91, 98, 82, 68, 82, 79, 90 Mean _____

c. 9.5, 12.3, 10.5, 7.5, 10.1, 18.4, 9.8, 6.2, 11.1, 4.8, 10.6 Mean _____

2. Find the weighted mean for the following. Round to the nearest hundredth.

a. 4, 4, 6, 8, 8, 13, 4, 6, 8 Weighted mean _____

b. 82, 85, 87, 82, 82, 90, 87, 63, 100, 85, 87 Weighted mean _____

3. Find the median for the following:

a. 56, 89, 47, 36, 90, 63, 55, 82, 46, 81 Median _____

b. 59, 22, 39, 47, 33, 98, 50, 73, 54, 46, 99 Median _____

4. Find the mode for the following:
24, 35, 49, 35, 52, 35, 52 Mode _____

5. Find the mean, median, and mode for each of the following:

a. 72, 48, 62, 54, 73, 62, 75, 57, 62, 58, 78
Mean _______ Median _______ Mode _______

b. $0.50, $1.19, $0.58, $1.19, $2.83, $1.71, $2.21, $0.58, $1.29, $0.58
Mean _______ Median _______ Mode _______

c. $92, $113, $99, $117, $99, $105, $119, $112, $95, $116, $102, $120
Mean _______ Median _______ Mode _______

d. 88, 105, 120, 119, 105, 128, 160, 151, 90, 153, 107, 119, 105
Mean _______ Median _______ Mode _______

WORD PROBLEMS

6. The sales for the year at the 8 Bed and Linen Stores were $1,442,897, $1,556,793, $1,703,767, $1,093,320, $1,443,984, $1,665,308, $1,197,692, and $1,880,443. Find the mean earnings for a Bed and Linen Store for the year.

7. To avoid having an extreme number affect the average, the manager of Bed and Linen Stores (Problem 6) would like you to find the median earnings for the 8 stores.

8. The Bed and Linen Store in Salem sells many different towels. Following are the prices of all the towels that were sold on Wednesday: $7.98, $9.98, $9.98, $11.49, $11.98, $7.98, $12.49, $12.49, $11.49, $9.98, $9.98, $16.00, and $7.98. Find the mean price of a towel.

9. Looking at the towel prices, the Salem manager (Problem 8) decided that he should have calculated a weighted mean. Find the weighted mean price of a towel.

10. The manager of the Salem Bed and Linen Store above would like to find another measure of the central tendency called the *median*. Find the median price for the towels sold.

11. The manager at the Salem Bed and Linen Store would like to know the most popular towel among the group of towels sold on Wednesday. Find the mode for the towel prices for Wednesday.

Learning Unit 22–2 : Frequency Distributions and Graphs

DRILL PROBLEMS

1. A local dairy distributor wants to know how many containers of yogurt health club members consume in a month. The distributor gathered the following data:

17	17	22	14	26	23	23	15	18	16
18	15	23	18	29	20	24	17	12	15
18	19	18	20	28	21	25	21	26	14
16	18	15	19	27	15	22	19	19	13
20	17	13	24	28	18	28	20	17	16

Construct a frequency distribution table to organize this data.

2. Construct a bar graph for the Problem 1 data. The height of each bar should represent the frequency of each amount consumed.

3. To simplify the amount of data concerning yogurt consumption, construct a relative frequency distribution table. The range will be from 1 to 30 with five class intervals: 1–6, 7–12, 13–18, 19–24, and 25–30.

4. Construct a bar graph for the grouped data.

5. Prepare a pie chart to represent the above data.

WORD PROBLEMS

6. The women's department of a local department store lists its total sales for the year: January, $39,800; February, $22,400; March, $32,500; April, $33,000; May, $30,000; June, $29,200; July, $26,400; August, $24,800; September, $34,000; October, $34,200; November, $38,400; December, $41,100. Draw a line graph to represent the monthly sales of the women's department for the year. The vertical axis should represent the dollar amount of the sales.

7. The following list shows the number of television sets sold in a year by the sales associates at Souza's TV and Appliance Store.

115	125	139	127	142	153	169	126	141
130	137	150	169	157	146	173	168	156
140	146	134	123	142	129	141	122	141

Construct a relative frequency distribution table to represent the data. The range will be from 115 to 174 with intervals of 10.

8. Use the data in the distribution table for Problem 7 to construct a bar graph for the grouped data.

9. Expenses for Flora Foley Real Estate Agency for the month of June were as follows: salaries expense, $2,790; utilities expense, $280; rent expense, $2,000; commissions expense, $4,800; and other expenses, $340. Present this data in a circle graph. (First calculate the percent relationship between each item and the total, then determine the number of degrees that represents each item.)

10. Today a new Jeep costs $25,000. In 1970, the Jeep cost $4,500. What is the price relative? (Round to the nearest tenth percent.)

APPENDIX B Worked-Out Solutions to Extra Practice Quizzes

Chapter 1

LU 1-1A

1. a. Eight thousand, six hundred eighty-two
   b. Fifty-six thousand, two hundred ninety-five
   c. Seven hundred thirty-two billion, three hundred ten million, four hundred forty-four thousand, eight hundred eighty-eight

2. a. 43 = 40   b. 654 = 700   c. 7,328 = 7,000   d. 5,980 = 6,000

3. Kellogg's sales and profit:

The facts	Solving for?	Steps to take	Key points
Sales: Three million, two hundred ninety-one thousand dollars. *Profit:* Four hundred five thousand dollars.	Sales and profit rounded all the way.	Express each verbal form in numeric form. Identify leftmost digit in each number.	Rounding all the way means only the leftmost digit will remain. All other digits become zeros.

Steps to solving problem

1. Convert verbal to numeric.
   Three million, two hundred ninety-one thousand ——→ $3,291,000
   Four hundred five thousand ——→ $ 405,000
2. Identify leftmost digit of each number.
   $3,291,000 ↓ $3,000,000
   $405,000 ↓ $400,000

LU 1-2A

1.
10
18
19
24
26,090

2.
Estimate	Actual
3,000	3,482
7,000	6,981
+ 5,000	5,490
15,000	15,953

3.
8 17 7 17
9,787
−5,968
3,819

Check
3,819
+ 5,968
9,787

4. Jackson Manufacturing Company over- or underestimated sales:

The facts	Solving for?	Steps to take	Key points
Projected 2011 sales: $878,000 *Major clients:* $492,900 *Other clients:* $342,000	How much were sales over- or underestimated?	Total projected sales − Total actual sales = Over- or underestimated sales.	Projected sales (minuend) − Actual sales (subtrahend) = Difference.

Steps to solving problem

1. Calculate total actual sales.
   $492,900
   + 342,000
   $834,900
2. Calculate over- or underestimated sales.
   $878,000
   − 834,900
   $ 43,100 (overestimated)

LU 1-3A

1. **Estimate** 5,000 × 20 = 100,000

   Actual
   ```
     4,938
   ×    19
     44442
     4938
    93,822
   ```

   Check
   9 × 4,938 = 44,442
   10 × 4,938 = +49,380
   93,822

2. 86 × 19 = 1,634 + 5 zeros = 163,400,000

3. 86 + 4 zeros = 860,000

4. **Rounding**
   ```
       200
   30)6,000
      6 0
   ```

   Actual
   ```
        245  R24
   26)6,394
      52
      119
      104
       154
       130
        24
   ```

   Check
   25 × 255 = 6,375
   + 19
   6,394

5. Drop 3 zeros = 3)99 = 33

6. General Motors' total cost per year:

The facts	Solving for?	Steps to take	Key points
Cars produced each workday: 850 *Workweek:* 5 days *Cost per car:* $7,000	Total cost per year.	Cars produced per week × 52 = Total cars produced per year. Total cars produced per year × Total cost per car = Total cost per year.	Whenever possible, use multiplication and division shortcuts with zeros. Multiplication can be checked by division.

Steps to solving problem

1. Calculate total cars produced per week. 5 × 850 = 4,250 cars produced per week
2. Calculate total cars produced per year. 4,250 cars × 52 weeks = 221,000 total cars produced per year
3. Calculate total cost per year. 221,000 cars × $7,000 = $1,547,000,000 (multiply 221 × 7 and add zeros)

Check $1,547,000,000 ÷ 221,000 = $7,000 (drop 3 zeros before dividing)

Chapter 2

LU 2-1A

1. **a.** Proper
   b. Improper
   c. Mixed
   d. Improper

2.
   ```
      22 1/7
   7)155
     14
      15
      14
       1
   ```

3. $\frac{(9 \times 8) + 7}{9} = \frac{79}{9}$

4. **a.**
   ```
       1          1          2
   42)70  →  28)42  →  14)28
      42         28         28
      28         14          0
   ```
   14 is greatest common divisor

   $\frac{42 \div 14}{70 \div 14} = \frac{3}{5}$

3–21. $\frac{125}{10,000}$
3–23. $\frac{825}{1,000}$
3–25. $\frac{7,065}{10,000}$
3–27. $28\frac{48}{100}$
3–29. .004
3–31. .0085
3–33. 818.1279
3–35. 3.4
3–37. 2.32
3–39. 1.2; 1.26791
3–41. 4; 4.0425
3–43. 24,526.67
3–45. 161.29
3–47. 6,824.15
3–49. .04
3–51. .63
3–53. 2.585
3–55. .0086
3–57. 486
3–59. 3.950
3–61. 7,913.2
3–63. .583
3–65. \$19.57
3–67. \$1.40
3–69. \$119.47
3–71. \$29.00
3–73. \$116 savings
3–75. \$423.16
3–77. \$105.08
3–79. \$255.88
3–81. \$73.52
3–83. \$1.58; \$3,713
3–85. \$6,465.60
3–86. Flying: \$1193.65; Driving drive: \$659
3–87. \$560.45

Summary Practice Test

1. 767.849
2. .7
3. .07
4. .007
5. $\frac{9}{10}$
6. $6\frac{97}{100}$
7. $\frac{685}{1,000}$
8. .29
9. .13
10. 4.57
11. .08
12. 390.2702
13. 9.2
14. 118.67
15. 34,684.01
16. 62,940
17. 832,224,982.1
18. \$24.56
19. \$936.30
20. \$385.40
21. A \$.12
22. \$449.05
23. \$28.10

Cumulative Review 1, 2, 3

1. \$405
2. \$200,000
3. \$50,560,000
4. \$10.00
5. \$225,000
6. \$750
7. \$369.56
8. \$130,000,000
9. \$63.64

Chapter 4

End-of-Chapter Problems

4–1. \$4,720.33
4–3. \$4,705.33
4–5. \$753
4–7. \$540.82
4–9. \$577.95
4–11. \$998.86
4–12. \$11,109
4–13. \$3,061.67

Summary Practice Test

1. End Bal. \$15,649.12
2. \$8,730
3. \$1,282.70
4. \$10,968.50

Chapter 5

End-of-Chapter Problems

5–1. $E = 130$
5–3. $Q = 300$
5–5. $Y = 15$
5–7. $Y = 12$
5–9. $P = 25$
5–11. Jeanne 24; Kathy 36
5–13. Hugh 50; Joe 250
5–15. 50 shorts; 200 T-shirts
5–17. $B = 70$
5–19. $N = 63$
5–21. $Y = 7$
5–23. $P = \$610.99$
5–25. Pete = 90; Bill = 450
5–27. 48 boxes pens; 240 batteries
5–29. $A = 135$
5–31. $M = 60$
5–33. $X = 3; 5X = 15$
5–35. $W = 129$
5–37. Shift 1: 3,360; shift 2: 2,240
5–39. 22 cartons of hammers
18 cartons of wrenches
5–40. 180 ice cream cones; \$135; \$90
5–41. $B = 10; 6B = 30$

Summary Practice Test

1. \$541.90
2. \$84,000
3. Sears, 70; Buy 560
4. Abby 200; Jill 1,000
5. 13 dishes; 78 pots
6. Pasta 300; 1,300 pizzas

Chapter 6

End-of-Chapter Problems

6–1. 66%
6–3. 80%
6–5. 356.1%
6–7. .09
6–9. .643
6–11. 1.19
6–13. 8.3%
6–15. 87.5%
6–17. $\frac{1}{25}$
6–19. $\frac{19}{60}$
6–21. $\frac{27}{400}$
6–23. 10.5
6–25. 102.5
6–27. 156.6
6–29. 114.88
6–31. 16.2
6–33. 141.67
6–35. 10,000
6–37. 17,777.78
6–39. 108.2%
6–41. 110%
6–43. 400%
6–45. 59.40
6–47. 1,100
6–49. 40%
6–51. +20%
6–53. 80%
6–55. \$10,000
6–57. \$160
6–59. 677.78%
6–61. 6%
6–63. \$30,000
6–65. \$15,480 yes
6–67. 900
6–69. \$742,500
6–71. \$220,000
6–73. 33.3%
6–75. 480
6–77. \$39,063.83
6–79. \$138.89
6–81. \$1,900
6–83. \$102.50
6–85. 3.7%

6–87. $2,571
6–89. $41,176
6–91. 40%
6–93. 585,000
6–94. $316
6–95. $55,429

Summary Practice Test

1. 92.1%
2. 40%
3. 1,588%
4. 800%
5. .42
6. .0798
7. 4.0
8. .0025
9. 16.7%
10. 33.3%
11. $\frac{31}{160}$
12. $\frac{31}{500}$
13. $540,000
14. $2,330,000
15. 75%
16. 2.67%
17. $382.61
18. $639
19. $150,000

Chapter 7

End-of-Chapter Problems

7–1. .9504; .0496; $14.83; $284.17
7–3. .893079; .106921; $28.76; $240.24
7–5. $369.70; $80.30
7–7. $1,392.59; $457.41
7–9. June 28; July 18
7–11. June 15; July 5
7–13. July 10; July 30
7–15. $138; $6,862
7–17. $2; $198
7–19. $408.16; $291.84
7–21. $195; $455
7–23. .648; .352; $54.36; $100.44
7–25. $576.06; $48.94
7–27. $5,100; $5,250
7–29. $5,850
7–31. $8,571.43
7–33. $8,173.20
7–35. $8,333.33; $11,666.67
7–37. $99.99
7–39. $489.90; $711.10
7–41. $4,658.97
7–43. $1,083.46; $116.54
7–45. $5,008.45
7–47. $363.38; $382.50
7–48. August 15; September 4; $206.86
7–49. $4,794.99

Summary Practice Test

1. $332.50
2. $211.11
3. $819.89; $79.11
4. **a.** Nov. 14; Dec. 4
b. March 20; April 9
c. June 10; June 30
d. Jan. 10; Jan. 30
5. $15; $285
6. $7,120
7. B: 20.95%
8. $1,938.78; $6,061.22
9. $7,076.35

Chapter 8

End-of-Chapter Problems

8–1. $210; $910
8–3. $4,285.71
8–5. $6.90; 45.70%
8–7. $450; $550
8–9. $110.83
8–11. $34.20; 69.8%
8–13. 11%
8–15. $3,830.40; $1,169.60; 23.39%
8–17. 16,250; $4.00
8–19. $3,000; 25%
8–21. $14.29
8–23. $600; $262.50
8–25. $84
8–27. 42.86%
8–29. $3.56
8–31. 20,000
8–33. $558.60
8–35. $195
8–37. $129.99
8–39. $2.31
8–41. 12,000
8–42. $14; $10; $20
8–43. $94.98; $20.36; loss

Summary Practice Test

1. $126
2. 30.26%
3. $482.76; $217.24
4. $79; 37.97%
5. $133.33
6. $292.50
7. 27.27%
8. $160
9. 25.9%
10. $1.15
11. 11,500

Cumulative Review 6, 7, 8

1. 650,000
2. $296.35
3. $133
4. $2,562.14
5. $48.75
6. $259.26
7. $1.96; $1.89

Chapter 9

End-of-Chapter Problems

9–1. 38; $280.82
9–3. $12.00; $452
9–5. $1,680
9–7. $60
9–9. $13,000
9–11. $4,500
9–13. $11,900; $6,900; $138; $388
9–15. $465; $116
9–17. $150.49; $86.80; $20.30; $1,142.41
9–19. $752.60; $113.60
9–21. $1,284.80
9–23. $297
9–25. $825
9–27. $1,083.66
9–29. $357; $56
9–31. $233.38; $195.70; $37.68
9–32. Net pay $1,653.60

Summary Practice Test

1. 49; $428
2. $794
3. $24,700
4. $465; $290
5. $280.96
6. $798 SUTA; $112 FUTA; no tax in quarter 2

Chapter 10

End-of-Chapter Problems

10–1. $1,215; $19,215
10–3. $978.75; $18,978.75
10–5. $28.23; $613.23
10–7. $20.38; $1,020.38
10–9. $73.78; $1,273.78
10–11. $1,904.76
10–13. $4,390.61
10–15. $618.75; $15,618.75
10–17. $2,377.70; Save $1.08
10–19. 4.7 years
10–21. $21,596.11
10–23. $714.87; $44.87
10–25. $3,569.27; $3,540.10
10–27. $2,608.65
10–29. $18,720.12
10–31. 12.37%
10–33. 72 days
10–35. 5.6%
10–36. $12,500; $4,500
10–37. $7.82; $275.33

Summary Practice Test

1. $27.23; $2,038.11
2. $86,400
3. $14,901.25
4. $14,888.90
5. $32,516
6. $191.09; $10,191.09

Chapter 11

End-of-Chapter Problems

11-1. $408.33; $13,591.67
11-3. 25 days
11-5. $51,451.39; 57; $733.18; $50,718.21
11-7. 4.04%
11-9. $7,566.67; 6.9%
11-11. $8,937
11-13. 5.06%
11-15. $5,133.33; 56; $71.87; $5,061.46
11-17. $4,836.44
11-18. $31,739.66
11-19. $2,127.66; 9.57%

Summary Practice Test

1. $160,000
2. $302.22; $16,697.98; $17,000; 4.1%
3. $61,132.87
4. $71,264.84
5. $57,462.50; 7.6%
6. 5.58%

Chapter 12

End-of-Chapter Problems

12-1. 4; 3%; $1,800.81; $200.81
12-3. $10,404; $404
12-5. 12.55%
12-7. 16; $1\frac{1}{2}$%; .7880; $4,728
12-9. 28; 3%; .4371; $7,692.96
12-11. 2.2879 × $7,692.96
12-13. $64,188
12-15. Mystic $4,775
12-17. $25,734.40
12-19. $3,807
12-21. 5.06%
12-23. $37,644
12-25. Yes, $17,908 (compounding) or $8,376 (p. v.)
12-27. $3,739.20
12-29. $13,883.30
12-31. $514,904.36 Linda surpassed goal
12-32. $689,125; $34,125 Bank B

Summary Practice Test

1. $48,760
2. $31,160
3. $133,123.12
4. No, $26,898 (compounding) or $22,308 (p. v.)
5. 6.14%
6. $46,137
7. $187,470
8. $28,916.10

Chapter 13

End-of-Chapter Problems

13-1. $610,321.50
13-3. $619,476
13-5. $3,118.59
13-7. End of first year $2,405.71
13-9. $1,410
13-11. $3,397.20
13-13. $59,077.80
13-15. $1,245
13-17. $900,655
13-19. $33,444
13-21. $13,838.25
13-23. Annuity $12,219.11 or $12,219.93
13-25. $3,625.60
13-27. $111,013.29
13-29. $404,313.97
13-30. $488.32
13-31. $120,747.09

Summary Practice Test

1. $100,952.82
2. $33,914.88 or $33,913.57
3. $108,722.40
4. $2,120
5. $2,054
6. $264,915.20
7. $83,304.59
8. $237,501.36
9. $473,811.99
10. $713,776.37

Cumulative Review 10, 11, 12, 13

1. Annuity $2,058.62 or $2,058.59
2. $5,118.70
3. $116,963.02
4. $3,113.92
5. $5,797.92
6. $18,465.20
7. $29,632.35
8. $55,251

Chapter 14

End-of-Chapter Problems

14-1. Finance charge $2,360
14-3. Finance charge $1,279.76; 12.75%–13%
14-5. $119.39; $119.37
14-7. $295.14; $5,164.86
14-9. $2,741; $41.12
14-11. $604.07
14-13. a. $4,050 b. $1,656 c. $5,756 d. 14.25% to 14.50% e. $95.10
14-15. $415.12; $340.66; $74.46
14-17. 8.00% to 8.25%; 8.75% to 9%
14-19. $218.31 outstanding balance
14-20. $17,853.75; $22,444 private party
14-21. 15.48%

Summary Practice Test

1. $26,500; $4,100
2. $52.66
3. 4.25% to 4.5%
4. $6,005.30
5. $2,003.29; $8,746.71
6. $400; $8

Chapter 15

End-of-Chapter Problems

15-1. $643.50
15-3. $894.60
15-5. $118,796
15-7. $1,679.04; $1,656.25; $22.79; $158,977.21
15-9. $923.64
15-11. $636.16; $117,017.60
15-13. Payment 3, $119,857.38
15-15. $1,256.45
15-17. $290,493
15-18. $1,690.15; $415,954

Summary Practice Test

1. $1,020; $850; $169,830
2. $499.84; $91,942.40
3. a. $434.97; $75,589.20
   b. $460.08; $84,628.80
   c. $486; $93,960
   d. $512.73; $103,582.80
4. $5.71; $1,027.80
5. $251,676

Chapter 16

End-of-Chapter Problems

16-1. Total assets $64,000
16-3. Inventory −16.67%; mortgage note +13.79%
16-5. Net sales 13.62%; Net earnings 2010 47.92%
16-7. Depreciation $100; + 16.67%
16-9. 1.43; 1.79
16-11. .20; .23
16-13. .06; .08
16-15. $1.52 million
16-17. 87.74%; 34.43%; .13; 55.47%
16-19. 2013 68% sales
16-20.

	2008	2007
a.	42.14%	32.66%
b.	11.89%	14.33%
c.	1.20	1.14

16-21. 3.5; 2.3

Summary Practice Test

1. a. $161,000
   b. $21,000
   c. $140,000
   d. $84,000
2. Acc. rec. 15.15%; 24.67%
3. Cash $11,000; 137.50%
4. 2,013; 74%

5. Total assets $175,000

6. **a.** .70 **b.** .50 **c.** 45 days
d. 1.05 **e.** .25

Chapter 17

00
00
0

1. **a.** 31 **b.** $66.87; $93.30; $80.29
2. $40,000
3. 1.10
4. $109,275
5. $97,960

Chapter 19

End-of-Chapter Problems

19–1. $912
19–3. $83,018.87
19–5. $39,000
19–7. $.0233
19–9. 6.99%; $6.99; $69.90; 69.90
19–11. $4,462.50
19–13. $16,985.05
19–15. $112.92
19–17. $112,000
19–19. $6,940
19–21. $64,000
19–23. $2,251.50
19–25. $23,065 more in Minn.
19–26. $920.70
19–27. $979

Summary Practice Test

1. $284.76; $14.24
2. $4,710
3. $146,000
4. 5.1 mills
5. $1,237.50
6. $18,141.20

Chapter 20

End-of-Chapter Problems

20–1. $679.70
20–3. $277.50
20–5. $53,000
20–7. 21 years, 300 days
0–9. $518; $182
–11. $16,500
–13. $1,067
15. $1,855 cheaper
20–17. $801
20–19. $118,750
20–21. $1,100
20–23. $373.67
20–25. $22,900; $10,700
20–27. $24,000; $16,300
20–28. $7,512.64; $1,942.00; $787.89
20–29. $72,000

Summary Practice Test

1. $1,993.50; $28,530
2. $2,616.60; $55,650; $115,500; 21 years 300 days
3. $234,375; $450,000
4. $990; $326.70
5. $1,755
6. Insurance company pays $31,600; Roger pays $10,000

Chapter 21

End-of-Chapter Problems

21–1. $114,897
21–3. 1.1%
21–5. 13
21–7. $24,227.04
21–9. 2010 preferred $8,000
2011 0
2012 preferred $127,000
common $33,000
21–11. $2,280
21–13. $260; $2,725; 9.5%
21–15. $12.04; $−.06; 9.6%
21–17. Gain $222.48
21–19. 12; 2.4%
21–21. $5,043.75; $56.25
21–23. 7.3%
21–25. Stock 6.7%; bond 11.9%
21–27. Yes, $16.02
21–29. $443.80
21–30. $4,120.50; $206.03
21–31. $1,014.33

Summary Practice Test

1. $18,127.26
2. 8; 1.3%
3. $1.23
4. $10,476
5. 5.6%
6. $160,000
7. $14.52; $11,616

Chapter 22

End-of-Chapter Problems

22–1. 8.00
22–3. $77.23
22–5. 2.7
22–7. 31.5
22–9. 8
22–11. 142.9
22–13. $200–$299.99 𝍸
22–15. Traditional watch 183.6°
22–17. $\frac{35}{86} = 147.6°$
$\frac{15}{86} = 61.2°$
$\frac{12}{86} = 50.4°$
22–19. Transportation 126°
Hotel 100.8°
Food 72°
Miscellaneous 61.2°

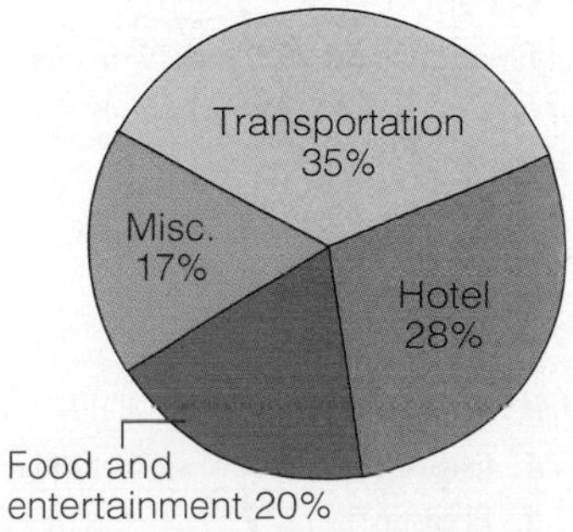

22–21. 250
22–23. Range 5.06 not normal distribution
St. Dev. 1.27
22–24. 24.94%

Optional Assignment

1. 98
3. 4.3
5. 16%; 2.5%
7. 68%; 81.5%; 2.5%; 2.5%; 47.5%
9. 5.02

Summary Practice Test

1. $143,300; $141,000
2. 1,100
3. 2.50
4. 100; ||||; 4
5. Bar 1 on horizontal axis goes up to 800 on vertical axis
6. Profits 108°
   Cost of sales 144°
   Expense 108°
7. 166.3%
8. 3.0 standard deviation

Check Figures (Odds) to Additional Assignments by Learning Unit from Appendix A

LU 1–1

1. **a.** Six thousand, four hundred forty-eight
   d. Fifty-eight thousand, three
3. **a.** 60; 380; 860; 5,980; 210
   c. 21,000; 1,000; 4,000; 10,000
5. **a.** Hundreds place
   c. Ten thousands place
   e. Billions place
7. Three hundred eighty-four
9. $375,985
11. Two thousand, four

LU 1–2

1. **a.** 1,006
   c. 1,319
   d. 179
3. **a.** Estimated 50; 52
   c. Estimated 10; 9
5. $71,577
7. $19,973
9. 12,797 lbs
11. Estimated $9,400; $9,422
13. $746 discount

LU 1–3

1. **a.** Estimated 4,000; actual 2,400
   c. Estimated 15,000,000; actual 16,184,184
3. **a.** Estimated 1,000; actual 963 R5
   c. Estimated 20; actual 25 R8
5. 3,850
7. $78
9. 27
11. $43,200
13. 40 stacks and 23 "extra" bricks

LU 2–1

1. **a.** Mixed
   b. Improper
   c. Improper
   d. Mixed number
   e. Improper
   f. Proper
3. **a.** $\frac{41}{5}$ **c.** $\frac{31}{7}$ **f.** $\frac{53}{3}$
5. **a.** $6;\frac{6}{7}$ **b.** $15;\frac{2}{5}$ **e.** $12;\frac{8}{11}$
7. $\frac{13}{4}$
9. $\frac{17}{25}$
11. $\frac{60}{100}$
13. $\frac{7}{12}$

LU 2–2

1. **a.** 32 **b.** 180 **c.** 480 **d.** 252
3. **a.** $\frac{1}{3}$ **b.** $\frac{2}{3}$ **e.** $6\frac{1}{8}$ **h.** $56\frac{5}{6}$
5. $3\frac{1}{40}$ yards
7. $17\frac{5}{12}$ miles
9. $4\frac{8}{9}$ hours

LU 2–3

1. **a.** $\frac{\overset{1}{\cancel{6}}}{\underset{1}{\cancel{13}}} \times \frac{\overset{1}{\cancel{\overset{2}{\cancel{26}}}}}{\underset{1}{\cancel{\underset{2}{\cancel{12}}}}} = 1$
3. **a.** $1\frac{1}{4}$ **b.** 3 **g.** 24 **l.** $\frac{4}{7}$
5. $39,000
7. 714
9. $20\frac{2}{3}$ miles
11. $412,000

LU 3–1

1. **a.** .41 **b.** .6 **c.** .953
   d. .401 **e.** .06
3. **a.** Hundredths place
   d. Thousandths place
5. **a.** $\frac{2}{5}$ **b.** $\frac{11}{25}$
   g. $\frac{5}{16}$ **l.** $9\frac{1}{25}$
7. .286
9. $\frac{566}{1,000}$
11. .333
13. .0020507

LU 3–2

1. **a.** 31.608 **b.** 5.2281 **d.** 3.7736
3. **a.** .3 **b.** .1 **c.** 1,480.0 **d.** .1
5. **a.** 6,870 **c.** .0272
   e. 34,700 **i.** 8,329.8
7. $4.53
9. $111.25
11. 15

LU 4–1

1. **a.** $430.64 **b.** 3 **c.** $867.51
3. **a.** Neuner Realty Co.
   b. Kevin Jones
   h. $2,756.80

LU 4–2

1. $1,435.42
3. Add $3,000; deduct $22.25
5. $2,989.92
7. $1,315.20

LU 5–1

1. **a.** $4N = 120$ **e.** $14 + \frac{N}{3} = 18$
   h. $2N + 3N + 8 = 68$

LU 5–2

1. $60
3. $45 telephone; $135 utility
5. 51 tickets—Sherry; 408 tickets—Linda
7. 12 necklaces ($48); 36 watches ($252)
9. $157.14

LU 6–1

1. **a.** 3% **b.** 72.9% **i.** 503.8% **l.** 80%
3. **a.** 40% **c.** 162.5%
   h. 50% **n.** 1.5%
5. **a.** $\frac{1}{4}$ **b.** .375 **c.** 50%
   d. $.66\bar{6}$ **n.** $1\frac{1}{8}$
7. 2.9%
9. $\frac{39}{100}$
11. $\frac{9}{10,000}$

LU 6–2

1. a. $15,000; 20%; $3,000
   c. $7.00; 12%; $.84
3. a. 33.3% b. 3% c. 27.5%
5. a. −1,584; −26.6%
   d. −20,000; −16.7%
7. $9,000
9. $3,196
11. 329.5%

LU 7–1

1. a. $75 b. $360 c. $50
   d. $100 e. $380
3. a. $75 b. $21.50; $40.75
5. a. .7125; .2875 b. .7225; .2775
7. $3.51
9. $81.25
11. $315
13. 45%

LU 7–2

1. a. February 18; March 10
   d. May 20; June 9
   e. October 10; October 30
3. a. .98; $1,102.50
   c. .98; $367.99
5. a. $16.79; $835.21
7. $14,504
9. a. $439.29 b. $491.21
11. $209.45
13. a. $765.31 b. $386.99

LU 8–1

1. a. $15.35 b. $2.72
   c. $4.35 d. $90 e. $116.31
3. a. $2; 80% b. $6.50; 52%
   c. $.28; 28.9%
5. a. $1.52 b. $225
   c. $372.92 d. $625
7. a. $139.65 b. $538.65
9. a. $258.52 b. $90.48
11. a. $212.50 b. $297.50
13. $8.17

LU 8–2

1. a. $5.40 b. $57.50
   c. $34.43 d. $27.33 e. $.15
3. a. $6.94 b. $882.35 c. $30
   d. $171.43
5. a. 28.57% b. 33.33% d. 53.85%
7. $346.15
9. 39.39%
11. $2.29
13. 63.33%

LU 8–3

1. a. $30.00; $70
   b. $525; $1,574.98
3. a. $410 b. $18.65
5. a. $216; $324; $5.14
   b. $45; $63.90; $1.52
7. 17%
9. $21.15
11. $273.78
13. $.79

LU 8–4

1. a. $7.00 b. $11.11
3. a. 16,667 b. 7,500
5. 5,070
7. 22,222

LU 9–1

1. a. $368; 0; $368
   b. $360; $40.50; $400.50
3. a. $438.85 b. $615.13
5. a. $5,200 b. $3,960
   c. $3,740 d. $4,750
7. $723.00
9. $3,846.25
11. $2,032.48

LU 9–2

1. a. $500; $2,300
3. $2,000; $2,000
5. $338.41
7. $143.75
9. $608.27
11. $660.98

LU 10–1

1. a. $270 b. $1,080 c. $1,275
3. a. $131.25 b. $4.08 c. $98.51
5. a. $515.63 b. $6,015.63
7. a. $5,459.66
9. $659.36
11. $360

LU 10–2

1. a. $4,371.44 b. $4,545.45
   c. $3,433.33
3. a. 60; .17 b. 120; .33
   c. 270; .75 d. 145; .40
5. 5%
7. $250
9. $3,000
11. 119 days

LU 10–3

1. a. $2,568.75; $1,885.47; $920.04
3. $4,267.59
5. $4,715.30; $115.30

LU 11–1

1. I; B; D; I; D; I; B; D
3. a. 2%
   c. 13%
5. $15,963.75
7. $848.75; $8,851.25
9. $14,300
11. $7,855

LU 11–2

1. a. $4,071.11
   b. $16,480.80
   c. $994.44
3. a. $14.76
   b. $223.25
   c. $3.49
5. $4,031.67
7. $8,262.74
9. $5,088.16
11. $721.45

LU 12–1

1. a. $573.25 year 2
   b. $3,115.57 year 4
3. a. $15,869; $5,869
   b. $16,084; $6,084
5. $5,980
7. $8,881.20
9. $2,129.40
11. $3,207.09; $207.09
13. $3,000; $3,469; $3,498

LU 12–2

1. a. .6209 b. .3936 c. .5513
3. a. $1,575.50; $924.50
   b. $2,547.02; $2,052.98
5. $13,152.60
7. $13,356.98
9. $16,826.40
11. $652.32
13. $18,014.22

LU 13–1

1. a. $1,000; $2,080; $3,246.40
3. a. $6,888.60 b. $6,273.36
5. $325,525
7. $13,412
9. $30,200.85
11. $33,650.94

LU 13–2

1. a. $2,638.65 b. $6,375.24; $7,217.10
3. $2,715.54
5. $24,251.85
7. $47,608
9. $456,425
11. Accept Jason $265,010

LU 13–3

1. a. $4,087.50
3. $16,200
5. $24,030
7. $16,345
9. $8,742

LU 14–1

1. a. $1,200; $192
   b. $9,000; $1,200
3. a. 14.75% b. 10%
   c. 11.25%
5. a. $3,528 b. $696
   c. $4,616
7. a. $22,500 b. $4,932
   c. $29,932
9. a. $20,576 b. 12.75%

LU 14–2

1. a. $625; $375 b. $9,600; $2,910
3. a. $625; $578.12
5. $1,758; $553
7. $900
9. $7,287.76

LU 14–3

1. a. $465; $8,535
   b. $915.62; $4,709.38
3. a. $332.03 b. $584.83
   c. $384.28
5. Final payment $784.39
7. $51.34
9. $35
11. $922.49
13. 7.50% to 7.75%

LU 15–1

1. a. $1,096.50 b. $965.60; $4,090.50; $3,859.65
3. a. $117.25, 7.7%
   b. $174, 5.7%
5. $774
7. $2,584.71; $2,518.63
9. a. $66.08 b. $131,293.80
11. $773,560

LU 15–2

1. a. $1,371.90; $1,133.33; $238.57
3. #4 balance outstanding $195,183.05
5. $587,612.80
7. $327.12; $251,581.60
9. $44,271.43
11. $61,800

LU 16–1

1. Total assets $224,725
3. Merch. inventory 13.90%; 15.12%

LU 16–2

1. Net income $57,765
3. Purchases 73.59%; 71.43%

LU 16–3

1. Sales 2012, 93.5%; 2011, 93.2%
3. .22
5. 59.29%
7. .83
9. COGS 119.33%; 111.76%; 105.04%
11. .90
13. 5.51%
15. 11.01%

LU 17–1

1. a. 4% b. 25% c. 10%
   d. 20%
3. a. $2,033; $4,667
   b. $1,850; $9,750
5. $8,625 depreciation per year
7. $2,800 depreciation per year
9. $95
11. a. $12,000 b. $6,000
    c. $18,000 d. $45,000

LU 17–2

1. a. $.300 b. $.192 c. $.176
3. a. $.300, $2,600
   b. $.192, $300,824
5. $5,300 book value end of year 5
7. a. $.155 b. $20,001.61

LU 17–3

1. a. 8% b. 20% c. 25%
3. a. $4,467; $2,233
   b. $3,867; $7,733
5. $121, year 6
7. a. 28.57% b. $248 c. $619
9. a. 16.67% b. $2,500
   c. $10,814 d. $2,907

LU 17–4

1. a. 33%; $825; $1,675
3. Depreciation year 8, $346
5. $125
7. a. $15,000 b. $39,000
   c. $21,600 d. 2001
9. $68,440

LU 18–1

1. a. $5,120; $3,020
   b. $323,246; $273,546
3. $35,903; $165,262
5. $10,510.20; $16,345
7. $37.62; $639.54
9. $628.40
11. $3,069; $952; $2,117

LU 18–2

1. a. $85,700; $143,500; .597; $64,500; $38,507
3. $85,000
5. $342,000; $242,500; 5.85; 6.29
7. $60,000; $100,000; $40,000
9. $70,150
11. $5,970
13. 3.24; 3.05
15. $32,340; $35,280; $49,980; $29,400

LU 19–1

1. a. $26.80; $562.80
   b. $718.80; $12,698.80
3. a. $20.75; $43.89; $463.64
5. Total is **(a)** $1,023; **(b)** $58.55
7. $5.23; $115.23
9. $2,623.93
11. $26.20
13. $685.50

LU 19–2

1. a. $68,250 b. $775,450
3. a. $7.45; $74.50; 74.50
5. $9.10
7. $8,368.94
9. $42,112
11. $32,547.50

LU 20–1

1. a. $9.27; 25; $231.75
3. a. $93.00; $387.50; $535.00; $916.50
5. $1,242.90
7. $14,265
9. $47.50 more
11. $68,750

LU 20–2

1. a. $488 b. $2,912
3. a. $68,000; $60,000
   b. $41,600; $45,000
5. $1,463
7. $117,187.50
9. $336,000
11. a. $131,250 b. $147,000

LU 20–3

1. a. $98; $160; $258
3. a. $312 b. $233 c. $181
   d. $59; $20
5. a. $647 b. $706
7. $601
9. $781
11. $10,000; $8,000
13. $60,000; $20,000
15. $19.50; $110.50

LU 21–1

1. a. $43.88 f. 49
3. $27.06
5. $1,358.52 gain
7. $18,825.15
9. $7.70

LU 21–2

1. **a.** IBM **b.** $10\frac{1}{4}$ **c.** 2011
d. $102.50 **e.** 102.375
3. **a.** $1,025
b. $1,023.75
5. **a.** $3,075
b. $307.50
7. **a.** $30 discount
b. $16.25 premium
c. $42.50 premium
9. **a.** $625 **b.** $375 discount
c. $105 **d.** 16.8%
11. 7.8%; 7.2%
13. 8.98%

LU 21–3

1. $11.90
3. $15.20
5. +$.14
7. 7.6%
9. $1.45; $18.45
11. $.56; $14.66
13. $1,573.50
15. $123.00 loss
17. **a.** 2009; 2010
b. 9.3% Comp USA 6.9% GMA
c. $1,023.75 Comp USA
$1,016.25 GMA
d. Both at premium
e. $1,025 Comp USA $1,028.75 GMA

LU 22–1

1. **a.** 20.4 **b.** 83.75 **c.** 10.07
3. **a.** 59.5 **b.** 50
5. **a.** 63.7; 62; 62
7. $1,500,388.50
9. $10.75
11. $9.98

LU 22–2

1. 18: ~~||||~~ || 7
3. 25–30: ~~||||~~ ||| 8
5. 7.2°
7. 145–154: |||| 4
9. 98.4°; 9.9°; 70.5°; 169.2°; 11.9°

Classroom Notes

Classroom Notes

Classroom Notes

Classroom Notes

Classroom Notes

Classroom Notes

APPENDIX D

Glossary

The Glossary contains a comprehensive list of the key terms used in the text. In many cases, examples are also included in the definitions. Recall that key terms and their page references are listed in the Chapter Organizer and Study Guide for each chapter.

Accelerated Cost Recovery System (ACRS) (p. 419) Tax law enacted in 1981 for assets put in service from 1981 through 1986.

Accelerated depreciation (p. 417) Computes more depreciation expense in the early years of the asset's life than in the later years.

Accounts payable (p. 384) Amounts owed to creditors for services or items purchased.

Accounts receivable (p. 384) Amount owed by customers to a business from previous sales.

Accumulated depreciation (p. 414) Amount of depreciation that has accumulated on plant and equipment assets.

Acid test (p. 396) Current assets less inventory less prepaid expenses divided by current liabilities.

Addends (p. 10) Numbers that are combined in the addition process. *Example:* $8 + 9 = 17$, of which 8 and 9 are the addends.

Adjustable rate mortgage (ARM) (p. 365) Rate of mortgage is lower than a fixed rate mortgage. Rates adjusted without refinancing. Caps available to limit how high rate can go for each adjustment period over term of loan.

Adjusted bank balance (p. 95) Current balance of checkbook after reconciliation process.

Amortization (p. 340) Process of paying back a loan (principal plus interest) by equal periodic payments (see **amortization schedule**).

Amortization schedule (p. 370) Shows monthly payment to pay back loan at maturity. Payment also includes interest. Note payment is fixed at same amount each month.

Amount financed (p. 340) Cash price less down payment.

Annual percentage rate (APR) (p. 341) True or effective annual interest rate charged by sellers. Required to be stated by Truth in Lending Act.

Annual percentage rate (APR) table (p. 341) Effective annual rate of interest on a loan or installment purchase as shown by table lookup.

Annual percentage yield (APY) (p. 298) Truth in savings law forced banks to report actual interest in form of APY. Interest yield must be calculated on actual number of days bank has the money.

Annuities certain (p. 317) Annuities that have stated beginning and ending dates.

Annuity (p. 316) Stream of equal payments made at periodic times.

Annuity due (p. 317) Annuity that is paid (or received) at the beginning of the time period.

Assessed value (p. 459) Value of a property that an assessor sets (usually a percent of property's market value) that is used in calculating property taxes.

Asset cost (p. 414) Amount company paid for the asset.

Assets (p. 384) Things of value owned by a business.

Asset turnover (p. 396) Net sales divided by total assets.

ATM (p. 89) Automatic teller machine that allows customers of a bank to transfer funds and make deposits or withdrawals.

Average daily balance (p. 350) Sum of daily balances divided by number of days in billing cycle.

Average inventory (p. 439) Total of all inventories divided by number of times inventory taken.

Balance sheet (p. 382) Financial report that lists assets, liabilities, and equity. Report reflects the financial position of the company as of a particular date.

Bank discount (pp. 278, 281) The amount of interest charged by a bank on a note. (Maturity value × Bank discount rate × Number of days bank holds note) ÷ 360.

Bank discount rate (p. 278) Percent of interest.

Banker's Rule (p. 259) Time is exact days/360 in calculating simple interest.

Bank reconciliation (p. 95) Process of comparing the bank balance to the checkbook balance so adjustments can be made regarding checks outstanding, deposits in transit, and the like.

Bank statement (p. 94) Report sent by the bank to the owner of the checking account indicating checks processed, deposits made, and so on, along with beginning and ending balances.

Bar graph (p. 520) Visual representation using horizontal or vertical bars to make comparison or to show relationship on items of similar makeup.

Base (p. 143) Number that represents the whole 100%. It is the whole to which something is being compared. Usually follows word *of*.

Beneficiary (p. 470) Person(s) designated to receive the face value of the life insurance when insured dies.

Biweekly (p. 236) Every 2 weeks (26 times in a year).

Biweekly mortgage (p. 365) Mortgage payments made every 2 weeks rather than monthly. This payment method takes years off the life of the mortgage and substantially reduces the cost of interest.

Blank endorsement (p. 91) Current owner of check signs name on back. Whoever presents checks for payment receives the money.

Bodily injury (p. 478) Auto insurance that pays damages to people injured or killed by your auto.

Bond discount (p. 499) Bond selling for less than the face value.

Bond premium (p. 499) Bond selling for more than the face value.

Bonds (p. 498) Written promise by a company that borrows money usually with fixed-interest payment until maturity (repayment time).

Bond yield (p. 498) Total annual interest divided by total cost.

Book value (p. 414) Cost less accumulated depreciation.

Breakeven point (p. 219) Point at which seller has covered all expenses and costs and has made no profit or suffered a loss.

Cancellation (p. 48) Reducing process that is used to simplify the multiplication and division of fractions. *Example:*

$$\frac{\overset{1}{\cancel{4}}}{8} \times \frac{1}{\underset{1}{\cancel{4}}}$$

Capital (p. 382) Owners' investment in the business.

Cash advance (p. 350) Money borrowed by holder of credit card. It is recorded as another purchase and is used in the calculation of the average daily balance.

Cash discount (p. 172) Savings that result from early payment by taking advantage of discounts offered by the seller; discount is not taken on freight or taxes.

Cash dividend (p. 495) Cash distribution of company's profit to owners of stock.

Cash value (pp. 470, 472) Except for term insurance, this indicates the value of the policy when terminated. Options fall under the heading of nonforfeiture values.

Centi- (Appendix E) Prefix indicating .01 of a basic metric unit.

Chain discount (p. 176) Two or more trade discounts that are applied to the balance remaining after the previous discount is taken. Often called a **series discount.**

Check register (p. 91) Record-keeping device that records checks paid and deposits made by companies using a checking account.

Checks (p. 90) Written documents signed by appropriate person that directs the bank to pay a specific amount of money to a particular person or company.

Check stub (p. 91) Provides a record of checks written. It is attached to the check.

Circle graph (p. 521) A visual representation of the parts to the whole.

Closing costs (p. 367) Costs incurred when property passes from seller to buyer such as for credit reports, recording costs, points, and so on.

CM (p. 97) Abbreviation for **credit memorandum.** The bank is adding to your account. The CM is found on the bank statement. *Example:* Bank collects a note for you.

Coinsurance (p. 476) Type of fire insurance in which the insurer and insured share the risk. Usually there is an 80% coinsurance clause.

Collision (p. 479) Optional auto insurance that pays for the repairs to your auto from an accident after deductible is met. Insurance company will only pay for repairs up to the value of the auto (less deductible).

Commissions (p. 238) Payments based on established performance criteria.

Common denominator (p. 41) To add two or more fractions, denominators must be the same.

Common stocks (pp. 385, 494) Units of ownership called shares.

Comparative statement (p. 385) Statement showing data from two or more periods side by side.

Complement (p. 175) 100% less the stated percent. *Example:* 18% → 82% is the complement (100% − 18%).

Compounded daily (pp. 294, 299) Interest calculated on balance each day.

Compounding (p. 293) Calculating the interest periodically over the life of the loan and adding it to the principal.

Compound interest (p. 293) The interest that is calculated periodically and then added to the principal. The next period the interest is calculated on the adjusted principal (old principal plus interest).

Comprehensive insurance (p. 479) Optional auto insurance that pays for damages to the auto caused by factors other than from collision (fire, vandalism, theft, and the like).

Compulsory insurance (p. 478) Insurance required by law—standard coverage.

Constants (p. 115) Numbers that have a fixed value such as 3 or −7. Placed on right side of equation; also called *knowns.*

Contingent annuities (p. 317) Beginning and ending dates of the annuity are uncertain (not fixed).

Contingent liability (p. 281) Potential liability that may or may not result from discounting a note.

Contribution margin (p. 219) Difference between selling price and variable cost.

Conversion periods (p. 298) How often (a period of time) the interest is calculated in the compounding process. *Example:* Daily—each day; monthly—12 times a year; quarterly—every 3 months; semiannually—every 6 months.

Corporation (p. 383) Company with many owners or stockholders. Equity of these owners is called *stockholders' equity.*

Cost (p. 203) Price retailers pay to manufacturer or supplier to bring merchandise into store.

Cost of merchandise (goods) sold (p. 389) Beginning inventory + Net purchases − Ending inventory.

Credit card (p. 348) A piece of plastic that allows you to buy on credit.

Credit memo (CM) (p. 97) Bank transactions that increase customer's account.

Credit period (p. 180) Credit days are counted from date of invoice. Has no relationship to the discount period.

Cumulative preferred stock (p. 494) Holders of preferred stock must receive current year and any dividends in arrears before any dividends are paid out to the holders of common stock.

Current assets (p. 384) Assets that are used up or converted into cash within 1 year or operating cycle.

Current liabilities (p. 384) Obligations of a company due within 1 year.

Current ratio (p. 396) Current assets divided by current liabilities.

Daily balance (p. 350) Calculated to determine customer's finance charge: Previous balance + Any cash advances + Purchases − Payments.

Debit card (p. 89) Transactions result in money being immediately deducted from customer's checking account.

Debit memo (DM) (p. 97) A debit transaction bank does for customers.

Deca- (Appendix E) Prefix indicating 10 times basic metric unit.

Deci- (Appendix E) Prefix indicating .1 of basic metric unit.

Decimal equivalent (p. 68) Decimal represents the same value as the fraction. *Example:*

$$.05 = \frac{5}{100}$$

Decimal fraction (p. 68) Decimal representing a fraction; the denominator has a power of 10.

Decimal point (pp. 4, 66) Center of the decimal system—located between units and tenths. Numbers to left are *whole numbers;* to the right are *decimal numbers.*

Decimal system (p. 4) The U.S. base 10 numbering system that uses the 10 single-digit numbers shown on a calculator.

Decimals (p. 66) Numbers written to the right of a decimal point. *Example:* 5.3, 18.22.

Declining-balance method (p. 417) Accelerated method of depreciation. The depreciation each year is calculated by book value beginning each year times the rate.

Deductibles (p. 479) Amount insured pays before insurance company pays. Usually the higher the deductible, the lower the premium will be.

Deductions (p. 237) Amounts deducted from gross earnings to arrive at net pay.

Deferred payment price (p. 341) Total of all monthly payments plus down payment.

Denominator (p. 36) The number of a common fraction below the division line (bar). *Example:*

$\frac{8}{9}$, of which 9 is the denominator

Deposit slip (p. 90) Document that shows date, name, account number, and items making up a deposit.

Deposits in transit (p. 97) Deposits not received or processed by bank at the time the bank statement is prepared.

Depreciation (p. 413) Process of allocating the cost of an asset (less residual value) over the asset's estimated life.

Depreciation causes (p. 413) Normal use, product obsolescence, aging, and so on.

Depreciation expense (p. 414) Process involving asset cost, estimated useful life, and residual value (salvage or trade-in value).

Depreciation schedule (p. 415) Table showing amount of depreciation expense, accumulated depreciation, and book value for each period of time for a plant asset.

Difference (p. 16) The resulting answer from a subtraction problem. *Example:* Minuend less subtrahend equals difference.

215 − 15 = 200

Differential pay schedule (p. 238) Pay rate is based on a schedule of units completed.

Digit (p. 4) Our decimal number system of 10 characters from 0 to 9.

Discounting a note (p. 281) Receiving cash from selling a note to a bank before the due date of a note. Steps to discount include: (1) calculate maturity value, (2) calculate number of days bank waits for money, (3) calculate bank discount, and (4) calculate proceeds.

Discount period (pp. 180, 281) Amount of time to take advantage of a cash discount.

Distribution of overhead (p. 440) Companies distribute overhead by floor space or sales volume.

Dividend (p. 16) Number in the division process that is being divided by another. *Example:* $5\overline{)15}$, in which 15 is the dividend.

Dividends (p. 494) Distribution of company's profit in cash or stock to owners of stock.

Dividends in arrears (p. 494) Dividends that accumulate when a company fails to pay dividends to cumulative preferred stockholders.

Divisor (p. 16) Number in the division process that is dividing into another. *Example:* $5\overline{)15}$, in which 5 is the divisor.

DM (p. 97) Abbreviation for **debit memorandum.** The bank is charging your account. The DM is found on the bank statement. *Example:* NSF.

Dollar markdown (p. 216) Original selling price less the reduction to price. Markdown may be stated as a percent of the original selling price. *Example:*

$$\frac{\text{Dollar markdown}}{\text{Original selling price}}$$

Dollar markup (p. 204) Selling price less cost. Difference is the amount of the markup. Markup is also expressed in percent.

Down payment (p. 340) Amount of initial cash payment made when item is purchased.

Drafts (p. 90) Written orders like checks instructing a bank, credit union, or savings and loan institution to pay your money to a person or organization.

Draw (p. 238) The receiving of advance wages to cover business or personal expenses. Once wages are earned, drawing amount reduces actual amount received.

Drawee (p. 91) One ordered to pay the check.

Drawer (p. 91) One who writes the check.

Due date (p. 180) Maturity date, or when the note will be repaid.

Earnings per share (EPS) (p. 495) Annual earnings ÷ Total number of shares outstanding.

Effective rate (pp. 280, 298) True rate of interest. The more frequent the compounding, the higher the effective rate.

Electronic deposits (p. 93) Credit card run through terminal which approves (or disapproves) the amount and adds it to company's bank balance.

Electronic funds transfer (EFT) (p. 94) A computerized operation that electronically transfers funds among parties without the use of paper checks.

Employee's Withholding Allowance Certificate (W-4) (p. 240) Completed by employee to indicate allowance claimed to determine amount of FIT that is deducted.

End of credit period (p. 180) Last day from date of invoice when customer can take cash discount.

End of month (EOM) (also **proximo**) **(p. 185)** Cash discount period begins at the end of the month invoice is dated. After the 25th discount period, one additional month results.

Endorse (p. 91) Signing the back of the check; thus ownership is transferred to another party.

Endowment life (p. 472) Form of insurance that pays at maturity a fixed amount of money to insured or to the beneficiary. Insurance coverage would terminate when paid—similar to term life.

Equation (p. 114) Math statement that shows equality for expressions or numbers, or both.

Equivalent (fractional) (p. 39) Two or more fractions equivalent in value.

Escrow account (p. 368) Lending institution requires that each month $\frac{1}{12}$ of the insurance cost and real estate taxes be kept in a special account.

Exact interest (p. 259) Calculating simple interest using 365 days per year in time.

Excise tax (p. 458) Tax that government levies on particular products and services. Tax on specific luxury items or nonessentials.

Expression (p. 114) A meaningful combination of numbers and letters called *terms*.

Extended term insurance (p. 472) Resulting from nonforfeiture, it keeps the policy for the full face value going without further premium payments for a specific period of time.

Face amount (p. 470) Dollar amount stated in policy.

Face value (p. 278) Amount of insurance that is stated on the policy. It is usually the maximum amount for which the insurance company is liable.

Fair Credit and Charge Card Disclosure Act of 1988 (p. 348) Act that tightens controls on credit card companies soliciting new business.

Fair Labor Standards Act (p. 236) Federal law has minimum wage standards and the requirement of overtime pay. There are many exemptions for administrative personnel and for others.

Federal income tax (FIT) withholding (p. 241) Federal tax withheld from paycheck.

Federal Insurance Contribution Act (FICA) (p. 241) Percent of base amount of each employee's salary. FICA taxes used to fund retirement, disabled workers, Medicare, and so on. FICA is now broken down into Social Security and Medicare.

Federal Unemployment Tax Act (FUTA) (p. 243) Tax paid by employer. Current rate is .8% on first $7,000 of earnings.

Federal withholding tax (p. 241) See **Income tax.**

Finance charge (p. 340) Total payments − Actual loan cost.

Fire insurance (p. 474) Stipulated percent (normally 80%) of value that is required for insurance company to pay to reimburse one's losses.

First-in, first-out (FIFO) method (p. 434) This method assumes the first inventory brought into the store will be the first sold. Ending inventory is made up of goods most recently purchased.

Fixed cost (p. 218) Costs that do not change with increase or decrease in sales.

Fixed rate mortgage (p. 366) Monthly payment fixed over number of years, usually 30 years.

FOB destination (p. 174) Seller pays cost of freight in getting goods to buyer's location.

FOB shipping point (p. 174) Buyer pays cost of freight in getting goods to his location.

Formula (p. 115) Equation that expresses in symbols a general fact, rule, or principle.

Fraction (p. 36) Expresses a part of a whole number. *Example:*

$\frac{5}{6}$ expresses 5 parts out of 6

Freight terms (p. 173) Determine how freight will be paid. Most common freight terms are **FOB shipping point** and **FOB destination.**

Frequency distribution (p. 519) Shows by table the number of times event(s) occurs.

Full endorsement (p. 91) This endorsement identifies the next person or company to whom the check is to be transferred.

Future value (FV) (p. 293) Final amount of the loan or investment at the end of the last period. Also called *compound amount*.

Future value of annuity (p. 316) Future dollar amount of a series of payments plus interest.

Graduated-payment mortgage (GPM) (p. 365) Borrower pays less at beginning of mortgage. As years go on, the payments increase.

Graduated plans (p. 365) In beginning years, mortgage payment is less. As years go on, monthly payments rise.

Gram (Appendix E) Basic unit of weight in metric system. An ounce equals about 28 grams.

Greatest common divisor (p. 38) The largest possible number that will divide evenly into both the numerator and denominator.

Gross pay (p. 237) Wages before deductions.

Gross profit (p. 203) Difference between cost of bringing goods into the store and selling price of the goods.

Gross profit from sales (p. 390) Net sales − Cost of goods sold.

Gross profit method (p. 438) Used to estimate value of inventory.

Gross sales (p. 389) Total earned sales before sales returns and allowances or sales discounts.

Hecto- (Appendix E) Prefix indicating 100 times basic metric unit.

Higher terms (p. 39) Expressing a fraction with a new numerator and denominator that is equivalent to the original. *Example:*

$\frac{2}{9} \rightarrow \frac{6}{27}$

Home equity loan (p. 365) Cheap and readily accessible lines of credit backed by equity in your home; tax-deductible; rates can be locked in.

Horizontal analysis (p. 386) Method of analyzing financial reports where each total this period is compared by amount of percent to the same total last period.

Improper fraction (p. 37) Fraction that has a value equal to or greater than 1; numerator is equal to or greater than the denominator. *Example:*

$$\frac{6}{6}, \frac{14}{9}$$

Income statement (p. 389) Financial report that lists the revenues and expenses for a specific period of time. It reflects how well the company is performing.

Income tax or FIT (p. 241) Tax that depends on allowances claimed, marital status, and wages earned.

Indemnity (p. 476) Insurance company's payment to insured for loss.

Index numbers (p. 522) Express the relative changes in a variable compared with some base, which is taken as 100.

Individual retirement account (IRA) (p. 325) An account established for retirement planning.

Installment cost (p. 348) Down payment + (Number of payments × Monthly payment). Also called deferred payment.

Installment loan (p. 340) Loan paid off with a series of equal periodic payments.

Installment purchases (p. 348) Purchase of an item(s) that requires periodic payments for a specific period of time with usually a high rate of interest.

Insured (p. 470) Customer or policyholder.

Insurer (p. 470) The insurance company that issues the policy.

Interest (p. 258) Principal × Rate × Time.

Interest-bearing note (p. 278) Maturity value of note is greater than amount borrowed since interest is added on.

Interest-only mortgage (p. 365) Type of mortgage where in early years only interest payment is required.

Inventory turnover (p. 439) Ratio that indicates how quickly inventory turns:

$$\frac{\text{Cost of goods sold}}{\text{Average inventory at cost}}$$

Invoice (p. 172) Document recording purchase and sales transactions.

Just-in-time (JIT) inventory system (p. 440) System that eliminates inventories. Suppliers provide materials daily as manufacturing company needs them.

Kilo- (Appendix E) Prefix indicating 1,000 times basic metric unit.

Last-in, first-out (LIFO) method (p. 435) This method assumes the last inventory brought into the store will be the first sold. Ending inventory is made up of the oldest goods purchased.

Least common denominator (LCD) (p. 41) Smallest nonzero whole number into which all denominators will divide evenly. *Example:*

$$\frac{2}{3} \textit{ and } \frac{1}{4} \quad \text{LCD} = 12$$

Level premium term (p. 470) Insurance premium that is fixed, say, for 50 years.

Liabilities (p. 384) Amount business owes to creditors.

Liability insurance (p. 478) Insurance for bodily injury to others and damage to someone else's property.

Like fractions (p. 41) Proper fractions with the same denominators.

Like terms (p. 114) Terms that are made up with the same variable:

$$A + 2A + 3A = 6A$$

Limited payment life (20-payment life) (p. 471) Premiums are for 20 years (a fixed period) and provide paid-up insurance for the full face value of the policy.

Line graphs (p. 521) Graphical presentation that involves a time element. Shows trends, failures, backlogs, and the like.

Line of credit (p. 241) Provides immediate financing up to an approved limit.

Liquid assets (p. 396) Cash or other assets that can be converted quickly into cash.

List price (p. 172) Suggested retail price paid by customers.

Liter (Appendix E) Basic unit of measure in metric, for volume.

Loan amortization table (p. 344) Table used to calculate monthly payments.

Long-term liabilities (p. 384) Debts or obligations that company does not have to pay within 1 year.

Lowest terms (p. 38) Expressing a fraction when no number divides evenly into the numerator and denominator except the number 1. *Example:*

$$\frac{5}{10} \rightarrow \frac{1}{2}$$

Maker (p. 278) One who writes the note.

Margin (p. 203) Difference between cost of bringing goods into store and selling price of goods.

Markdowns (p. 216) Reductions from original selling price caused by seasonal changes, special promotions, and so on.

Markup (p. 203) Amount retailers add to cost of goods to cover operating expenses and make a profit.

Markup percent calculation (p. 213) Markup percent on cost × Cost = Dollar markup; or Markup percent on selling price × Selling price = Dollar markup.

Maturity date (p. 281) Date the principal and interest are due.

Maturity value (MV) (pp. 258, 278) Principal plus interest (if interest is charged). Represents amount due on the due date.

Maturity value of note (p. 278) Amount of cash paid on the due date. If interest-bearing maturity, value is greater than amount borrowed.

Mean (p. 516) Statistical term that is found by:

$$\frac{\text{Sum of all figures}}{\text{Number of figures}}$$

Measure of dispersion (p. 524) Number that describes how the numbers of a set of data are spread out or dispersed.

Median (p. 517) Statistical term that represents the central point or midpoint of a series of numbers.

Merchandise inventory (p. 384) Cost of goods for resale.

Meter (Appendix E) Basic unit of length in metric system. A meter is a little longer than a yard.

Metric system (Appendix E) A decimal system of weights and measures. The basic units are meters, grams, and liters.

Mill (p. 460) $\frac{1}{10}$ of a cent or $\frac{1}{1{,}000}$ of a dollar. In decimal, it is .001. *In application:*

$$\text{Property tax due} = \text{Mills} \times .001 \times \text{Assessed valuation}$$

Milli- (Appendix E) Prefix indicating .001 of basic metric unit.

Minuend (p. 11) In a subtraction problem, the larger number from which another is subtracted. *Example:*

$$50 - 40 = 10$$

Mixed decimal (p. 69) Combination of a whole number and decimal, such as 59.8, 810.85.

Mixed number (p. 37) Sum of a whole number greater than zero and a proper fraction:

$$2\frac{1}{4}, 3\frac{3}{9}$$

Mode (p. 518) Value that occurs most often in a series of numbers.

Modified Accelerated Cost Recovery System (MACRS) (p. 419) Part of Tax Reform Act of 1986 that revised depreciation schedules of ACRS. Tax Bill of 1989 updates MACRS.

Monthly (p. 236) Some employers pay employees monthly.

Mortgage (p. 366) Cost of home less down payment.

Mortgage note payable (p. 384) Debt owed on a building that is a long-term liability; often the building is the collateral.

Multiplicand (p. 14) The first or top number being multiplied in a multiplication problem. *Example:*

Product = Multiplicand × Multiplier
40 = 20 × 2

Multiplier (p. 14) The second or bottom number doing the multiplication in a problem. *Example:*

Product = Multiplicand × Multiplier
40 = 20 × 2

Mutual fund (p. 500) Investors buy shares in the fund's portfolio (group of stocks and/or bonds).

Net asset value (NAV) (p. 500) The dollar value of one mutual fund share; calculated by subtracting current liabilities from current market value of fund's investments and dividing this by number of shares outstanding.

Net income (p. 390) Gross profit less operating expenses.

Net pay (p. 243) See **Net wages.**

Net price (p. 173) List price less amount of trade discount. The net price is before any cash discount.

Net price equivalent rate (p. 177) When multiplied times the list price, this rate or factor produces the actual cost to the buyer. Rate is found by taking the complement of each term in the discount and multiplying them together (do not round off).

Net proceeds (p. 280) Maturity value less bank discount.

Net profit (net income) (p. 204) Gross profit − Operating expenses.

Net purchases (p. 390) Purchases − Purchase discounts − Purchase returns and allowances.

Net sales (p. 389) Gross sales − Sales discounts − Sales returns and allowances.

Net wages (p. 243) Gross pay less deductions.

Net worth (p. 382) Assets less liabilities.

No-fault insurance (p. 481) Involves bodily injury. Damage (before a certain level) that is paid by an insurance company no matter who is to blame.

Nominal rate (p. 298) Stated rate.

Nonforfeiture values (p. 472) When a life insurance policy is terminated (except term), it represents (1) the available cash value, (2) additional extended term, or (3) additional paid-up insurance.

Noninterest-bearing note (p. 278) Note where the maturity value will be equal to the amount of money borrowed since no additional interest is charged.

Nonsufficient funds (NSF) (p. 97) Drawer's account lacked sufficient funds to pay written amount of check.

Normal distribution (p. 525) Data is spread symmetrically about the mean.

Numerator (p. 36) Number of a common fraction above the division line (bar). *Example:*

$\frac{8}{9}$, in which 8 is the numerator

Omnibus Budget Reconciliation Act of 1989 (p. 421) An update of MACRS. Unless business use of equipment is greater than 50%, straight-line depreciation is required.

Open-end credit (p. 349) Set payment period. Also, additional credit amounts can be added up to a set limit. It is a revolving charge account.

Operating expenses (overhead) (pp. 204, 390) Regular expenses of doing business. These are not costs.

Ordinary annuity (p. 317) Annuity that is paid (or received) at end of the time period.

Ordinary dating (p. 181) Cash discount is available within the discount period. Full amount due by end of credit period if discount is missed.

Ordinary interest (p. 259) Calculating simple interest using 360 days per year in time.

Ordinary life insurance (p. 471) See **Straight life insurance.**

Outstanding balance (p. 349) Amount left to be paid on a loan.

Outstanding checks (p. 97) Checks written but not yet processed by the bank before bank statement preparation.

Overdraft (p. 95) Occurs when company or person wrote a check without enough money in the bank to pay for it (NSF check).

Overhead expenses (p. 440) Operating expenses *not* directly associated with a specific department or product.

Override (p. 239) Commission that managers receive due to sales by people that they supervise.

Overtime (p. 237) Time-and-a-half pay for more than 40 hours of work.

Owner's equity (p. 384) See **Capital.**

Paid-up insurance (p. 471) A certain level of insurance can continue, although the premiums are terminated. This results from the nonforfeiture value (except term). Result is a reduced paid up policy until death.

Partial products (p. 14) Numbers between multiplier and product.

Partial quotient (p. 16) Occurs when divisor doesn't divide evenly into the dividend.

Partnership (p. 383) Business with two or more owners.

Payee (pp. 91, 278) One who is named to receive the amount of the check.

Payroll register (p. 240) Multicolumn form to record payroll data.

Percent (p. 138) Stands for hundredths. *Example:*

4% is 4 parts of one hundred, or $\frac{4}{100}$

Percentage method (p. 241) A method to calculate withholdings. Opposite of wage bracket method.

Percent decrease (p. 148) Calculated by decrease in price over original amount.

Percent increase (p. 148) Calculated by increase in price over original amount.

Percent markup on cost (p. 205) Dollar markup divided by the cost; thus, markup is a percent of the cost.

Percent markup on selling price (p. 209) Dollar markup divided by the selling price; thus, markup is a percent of the selling price.

Periodic inventory system (p. 432) Physical count of inventory taken at end of a time period. Inventory records are not continually updated.

Periods (p. 298) Number of years times the number of times compounded per year (see **Conversion period**).

Perishables (p. 216) Goods or services with a limited life.

Perpetual inventory system (p. 431) Inventory records are continually updated; opposite of periodic inventory system.

Personal property (p. 459) Items of possession, like cars, home, furnishings, jewelry, and so on. These are taxed by the property tax (don't forget real property is also taxed).

Piecework (p. 238) Compensation based on the number of items produced or completed.

Place value (p. 4) The digit value that results from its position in a number.

Plant and equipment (p. 384) Assets that will last longer than 1 year.

Point of sale (p. 95) Terminal that accepts cards (like those used at ATMs) to purchase items at retail outlets. No cash is physically exchanged.

Points (p. 367) Percentage(s) of mortgage that represents an additional cost of borrowing. It is a one-time payment made at closing.

Policy (p. 470) Written insurance contract.

Policyholder (p. 470) The insured.

Portion (p. 143) Amount, part, or portion that results from multiplying the base times the rate. Not expressed as a percent; it is expressed as a number.

Preferred stock (p. 494) Type of stock that has a preference regarding a corporation's profits and assets.

Premium (p. 470) Periodic payments that one makes for various kinds of insurance protection.

Prepaid expenses (p. 384) Items a company buys that have not been used are shown as assets.

Prepaid rent (p. 384) Rent paid in advance.

Present value (PV) (p. 294) How much money will have to be deposited today (or at some date) to reach a specific amount of maturity (in the future).

Present value of an ordinary annuity (p. 322) Amount of money needed today to receive a specified stream (annuity) of money in the future.

Price-earnings (PE) ratio (p. 495) Closing price per share of stock divided by earnings per share.

Price relative (p. 522) The quotient of the current price divided by some previous year's price—the base year—multiplied by 100.

Prime number (p. 42) Whole number greater than 1 that is only divisible by itself and 1. *Examples:* 2, 3, 5.

Principal (p. 258) Amount of money that is originally borrowed, loaned, or deposited.

Proceeds (pp. 279, 281) Maturity value less the bank charge.

Product (p. 14) Answer of a multiplication process, such as:

Product = Multiplicand × Multiplier
50 = 5 × 10

Promissory note (p. 278) Written unconditional promise to pay a certain sum (with or without interest) at a fixed time in the future.

Proper fractions (p. 37) Fractions with a value less than 1; numerator is smaller than denominator, such as $\frac{5}{9}$.

Property damage (p. 478) Auto insurance covering damages that are caused to the property of others.

Property tax (p. 460) Tax that raises revenue for school districts, cities, counties, and the like.

Property tax due (p. 459) Tax rate × Assessed valuation

Proximo (prox) (p. 185) Same as end of month.

Purchase discounts (p. 389) Savings received by buyer for paying for merchandise before a certain date.

Purchase returns and allowances (p. 389) Cost of merchandise returned to store due to damage, defects, and so on. An *allowance* is a cost reduction that results when buyer keeps or buys damaged goods.

Pure decimal (p. 69) Has no whole number(s) to the left of the decimal point, such as .45.

Quick assets (p. 396) Current assets − Inventory − Prepaid expenses.

Quick ratio (p. 396) (Current assets − Inventory − Prepaid expenses) ÷ Current liabilities.

Quotient (p. 16) The answer of a division problem.

Range (p. 524) Difference between the highest and lowest values in a group of values or set of data.

Rate (p. 143) Percent that is multiplied times the base that indicates what part of the base we are trying to compare to. Rate is not a whole number.

Rate of interest (p. 294) Percent of interest that is used to compute the interest charge on a loan for a specific time.

Ratio analysis (p. 394) Relationship of one number to another.

Real property (p. 459) Land, buildings, and so on, which are taxed by the property tax.

Rebate (p. 346) Finance charge that a customer receives for paying off a loan early.

Rebate fraction (p. 347) Sum of digits based on number of months to go divided by sum of digits based on total number of months of loan.

Receipt of goods (ROG) (p. 184) Used in calculating the cash discount period; begins the day that the goods are received.

Reciprocal of a fraction (p. 49) The interchanging of the numerator and the denominator. Inverted number is the reciprocal. *Example:*

$\frac{6}{7} \rightarrow \frac{7}{6}$

Reduced paid-up insurance (p. 472) Insurance that uses cash value to buy protection, face amount is less than original policy, and policy continues for life.

Remainder (p. 16) Leftover amount in division.

Repeating decimals (p. 67) Decimal numbers that repeat themselves continuously and thus do not end.

Residual value (p. 414) Estimated value of a plant asset after depreciation is taken (or end of useful life).

Restrictive endorsement (p. 91) Check must be deposited to the payee's account. This restricts one from cashing it.

Retail method (p. 438) Method to estimate cost of ending inventory. The cost ratio times ending inventory at retail equals the ending cost of inventory.

Retained earnings (p. 385) Amount of earnings that is kept in the business.

Return on equity (p. 396) Net income divided by stockholders' equity.

Revenues (p. 389) Total earned sales (cash or credit) less any sales discounts, returns, or allowances.

Reverse mortgage (p. 366) Federal Housing Administration makes it possible for older homeowners to live in their homes and get cash or monthly income.

Revolving charge account (p. 349) Charges for a customer are allowed up to a specified maximum, a minimum monthly payment is required, and interest is charged on balance outstanding.

ROG (p. 184) Receipt of goods; cash discount period begins when goods are received, not ordered.

Rounding decimals (p. 67) Reducing the number of decimals to an indicated position, such as 59.59 → 59.6 to the nearest tenth.

Rounding all the way (p. 7) Process to estimate actual answer. When rounding all the way, only one nonzero digit is left. Rounding all the way gives the least degree of accuracy. *Example:* 1,251 to 1,000; 2,995 to 3,000.

Rule of 78 (p. 345) Method to compute rebates on consumer finance loans. How much of finance charge are you entitled to? Formula or table lookup may be used.

Salaries payable (p. 384) Obligations that a company must pay within 1 year for salaries earned but unpaid.

Sales (not trade) discounts (p. 389) Reductions in selling price of goods due to early customer payment.

Sales returns and allowances (p. 389) Reductions in price or reductions in revenue due to goods returned because of product defects, errors, and so on. When the buyer keeps the damaged goods, an allowance results.

Sales tax (p. 457) Tax levied on consumers for certain sales of merchandise or services by states, counties, or various local governments.

Salvage value (p. 414) Cost less accumulated depreciation.

Selling price (pp. 203, 218) Cost plus markup equals selling price.

Semiannually (p. 241) Twice a year.

Semimonthly (p. 241) Some employees are paid twice a month.

Series discount (p. 176) See **chain discount.**

Short-rate table (p. 475) Fire insurance rate table used when insured cancels the policy.

Short-term policy (p. 475) Fire insurance policy for less than 1 year.

Signature card (p. 90) Information card signed by person opening a checking account.

Simple discount note (p. 278) A note in which bank deducts interest in advance.

Simple interest (p. 258) Interest is only calculated on the principal. In $I = P \times R \times T$, the interest plus original principal equals the maturity value of an interest-bearing note.

Simple interest formula (p. 258)

Interest = Principal × Rate × Time

$$\text{Principal} = \frac{\text{Interest}}{\text{Rate} \times \text{Time}}$$

$$\text{Rate} = \frac{\text{Interest}}{\text{Principal} \times \text{Time}}$$

$$\text{Time} = \frac{\text{Interest}}{\text{Principal} \times \text{Rate}}$$

Single equivalent discount rate (p. 178) Rate or factor as a single discount that calculates the amount of the trade discount by multiplying the rate times the list price. This single equivalent discount replaces a series of chain discounts. The single equivalent rate is (1 − Net price equivalent rate).

Single trade discount (p. 175) Company gives only one trade discount.

Sinking fund (p. 325) An annuity in which the stream of deposits with appropriate interest will equal a specified amount in the future.

Sliding scale commissions (p. 238) Different commission. Rates depend on different levels of sales.

Sole proprietorship (p. 383) A business owned by one person.

Specific identification method (p. 432) This method calculates the cost of ending inventory by identifying each item remaining to invoice price.

Standard deviation (p. 524) Measures the spread of data around the mean.

State Unemployment Tax Act (SUTA) (p. 243) Tax paid by employer. Rate varies depending on amount of unemployment the company experiences.

Stockbrokers (p. 494) People who with their representatives do the trading on the floor of the stock exchange.

Stockholder (p. 494) One who owns stock in a company.

Stockholders' equity (pp. 383, 384) Assets less liabilities.

Stocks (p. 494) Ownership shares in the company sold to buyers, who receive stock certificates.

Stock yield (p. 495) Dividend per share divided by the closing price per share.

Straight commission (p. 238) Wages calculated as a percent of the value of goods sold.

Straight life insurance (p. 471) Protection (full value of policy) results from continual payment of premiums by insured. Until death or retirement, nonforfeiture values exist for straight life.

Straight-line method (p. 415) Method of depreciation that spreads an equal amount of depreciation each year over the life of the assets.

Straight-line rate (rate of depreciation) (p. 417) One divided by number of years of expected life.

Subtrahend (p. 11) In a subtraction problem smaller number that is being subtracted from another. *Example:* 30 in

150 − 30 = 120

Sum (p. 10) Total in the adding process.

Tax rate (p. 459) $\dfrac{\text{Budget needed}}{\text{Total assessed value}}$

Term insurance (p. 470) Inexpensive life insurance that provides protection for a specific period of time. No nonforfeiture values exist for term.

Term policy (p. 471) Period of time that the policy is in effect.

Terms of the sale (p. 180) Criteria on invoice showing when cash discounts are available, such as rate and time period.

Time (p. 259) Expressed as years or fractional years, used to calculate the simple interest.

Trade discount (p. 172) Reduction off original selling price (list price) not related to early payment.

Trade discount amount (p. 172) List price less net price.

Trade discount rate (p. 173) Trade discount amount given in percent.

Trade-in value (p. 414) Estimated value of a plant asset after depreciation is taken (or end of useful life).

Treasury bill (p. 280) Loan to the federal government for 91 days (13 weeks), 182 days (26 weeks), or 1 year.

Trend analysis (p. 393) Analyzing each number as a percentage of a base year.

Truth in Lending Act (p. 341) Federal law that requires sellers to inform buyers, in writing, of (1) the finance charge and (2) the annual percentage rate. The law doesn't dictate what can be charged.

20-payment life (p. 471) Provides permanent protection and cash value, but insured pays premiums for first 20 years.

20-year endowment (p. 472) Most expensive life insurance policy. It is a combination of term insurance and cash value.

Unemployment tax (p. 243) Tax paid by the employer that is used to aid unemployed persons.

Units-of-production method (p. 416) Depreciation method that estimates amount of depreciation based on usage.

Universal life (p. 472) Whole life insurance plan with flexible premium and death benefits. This life plan has limited guarantees.

Unknown (p. 115) The variable we are solving for.

Unlike fractions (p. 41) Proper fractions with different denominators.

Useful life (p. 414) Estimated number of years the plant asset is used.

U.S. Rule (p. 262) Method that allows the borrower to receive proper interest credits when paying off a loan in more than one payment before the maturity date.

U.S. Treasury bill (p. 280) A note issued by federal government to investors.

Value of an annuity (p. 316) Sum of series of payments and interest (think of this as the maturity value of compounding).

Variable commission scale (p. 238) Company pays different commission rates for different levels of net sales.

Variable cost (p. 218) Costs that do change in response to change in volume of sales.

Variable rate (p. 365) Home mortgage rate is not fixed over its lifetime.

Variables (p. 115) Letters or symbols that represent unknowns.

Vertical analysis (p. 386) Method of analyzing financial reports where each total is compared to one total. *Example:* Cash is a percent of total assets.

W-4 (p. 240) See **Employee's Withholding Allowance Certificate.**

Wage bracket method (In Handbook) Tables used in Circular E to compute FIT withholdings.

Weekly (p. 236) Some employers pay employees weekly.

Weighted-average method (p. 433) Calculates the cost of ending inventory by applying an average unit cost to items remaining in inventory for that period of time.

Weighted mean (p. 516) Used to find an average when values appear more than once.

Whole life (p. 472) See **Straight life insurance.**

Whole number (p. 4) Number that is 0 or larger and doesn't contain a decimal or fraction, such as 10, 55, 92.

Withholding (p. 240) Amount of deduction from one's paycheck.

Workers' compensation (p. 243) Business insurance covering sickness or accidental injuries to employees that result from on-the job activities.

E

APPENDIX

Metric System

John Sullivan: Angie, I drove into the gas station last night to fill the tank up. Did I get upset! The pumps were not in gallons but in liters. This country (U.S.) going to metric is sure making it confusing.

Angie Smith: Don't get upset. Let me first explain the key units of measure in metric, and then I'll show you a convenient table I keep in my purse to convert metric to U.S. (also called customary system), and U.S. to metric. Let's go on.

The metric system is really a decimal system in which each unit of measure is exactly 10 times as large as the previous unit. In a moment, we will see how this aids in conversions. First, look at the middle column (Units) of this to see the basic units of measure:

U.S.	Thousands	Hundreds	Tens	Units	Tenths	Hundredths	Thousandths
Metric	Kilo-	Hecto-	Deka-	Gram	Deci-	Centi-	Milli-
	1,000	100	10	Meter	.1	.01	.001
				Liter			
				1			

- Weight: Gram (think of it as $\frac{1}{30}$ of an ounce).
- Length: Meter (think of it for now as a little more than a yard).
- Volume: Liter (a little more than a quart).

To aid you in looking at this, think of a decimeter, a centimeter, or a millimeter as being "shorter" (smaller) than a meter, whereas a dekameter, hectometer, and kilometer are "larger" than a meter. For example:

1 centimeter = $\frac{1}{100}$ of a meter; or 100 centimeters equals 1 meter.

1 millimeter = $\frac{1}{1{,}000}$ meter; or 1,000 millimeters equals 1 meter.

1 hectometer = 100 meters.

1 kilometer = 1,000 meters.

Remember we could have used the same setup for grams or liters. Note the summary here.

Length	Volume	Mass
1 meter:	1 liter:	1 gram:
= 10 decimeters	= 10 deciliters	= 10 decigrams
= 100 centimeters	= 100 centiliters	= 100 centigrams
= 1,000 millimeters	= 1,000 milliliters	= 1,000 milligrams
= .1 dekameter	= .1 dekaliter	= .1 dekagram
= .01 hectometer	= .01 hectoliter	= .01 hectogram
= .001 kilometer	= .001 kiloliter	= .001 kilogram

Practice these conversions and check solutions.

1 PRACTICE QUIZ

Convert the following:

1. 7.2 meters to centimeters
2. .89 meter to millimeters
3. 64 centimeters to meters
4. 350 grams to kilograms
5. 7.4 liters to centiliters
6. 2,500 milligrams to grams

DVD *Solutions with Step-by-Step Help on DVD*

✓ Solutions

1. 7.2 meters = 7.2 × 100 = 720 centimeters (remember, 1 meter = 100 centimeters)
2. .89 meters = .89 × 1,000 = 890 millimeters (remember, 1 meter = 1,000 millimeters)
3. 64 centimeters = 64/100 = .64 meters (remember, 1 meter = 100 centimeters)
4. 350 grams = $\frac{350}{1{,}000}$ = .35 kilograms (remember 1 kilogram = 1,000 grams)
5. 7.4 liters = 7.4 × 100 = 740 centiliters (remember, 1 liter = 100 centiliters)
6. 2,500 milligrams = $\frac{2{,}500}{1{,}000}$ = 2.5 grams (remember, 1 gram = 1,000 milligrams

Angie: Look at the table of conversions and I'll show you how easy it is. Note how we can convert liters to gallons. Using the conversion from meters to U.S. (liters to gallons), we see that you multiply numbers of liters by .26, or 37.95 × .26 = 9.84 gallons.

Common conversion factors for English/metric					
A. To convert from U.S. to	**Metric**	**Multiply by**	**B. To convert from metric to**	**U.S.**	**Multiply by**
Length:			*Length:*		
Inches (in)	Meters (m)	.025	Meters (m)	Inches (in)	39.37
Feet (ft)	Meters (m)	.31	Meters (m)	Feet (ft)	3.28
Yards (yd)	Meters (m)	.91	Meters (m)	Yards (yd)	1.1
Miles	Kilometers (km)	1.6	Kilometers (km)	Miles	.62
Weight:			*Weight:*		
Ounces (oz)	Grams (g)	28	Grams (g)	Ounces (oz)	.035
Pounds (lb)	Grams (g)	454	Grams (g)	Pounds (lb)	.0022
Pounds (lb)	Kilograms (kg)	.45	Kilograms (kg)	Pounds (lb)	2.2
Volume or capacity:			*Volume or capacity:*		
Pints	Liters (L)	.47	Liters (L)	Pints	2.1
Quarts	Liters (L)	.95	Liters (L)	Quarts	1.06
Gallons (gal)	Liters (L)	3.8	Liters (L)	Gallons	.26

John: How would I convert 6 miles to kilometers?

Angie: Take the number of miles times 1.6, thus 6 miles × 1.6 = 9.6 kilometers.

John: If I weigh 120 pounds, what is my weight in kilograms?

Angie: 120 times .45 (use the conversion table) equals 54 kilograms.

John: OK. Last night, when I bought 16.6 liters of gas, I really bought 4.3 gallons (16.6 liters times .26).

2 PRACTICE QUIZ

Convert the following:

1. 10 meters to yards
2. 110 quarts to liters
3. 78 kilometers to miles
4. 52 yards to meters
5. 82 meters to inches
6. 292 miles to kilometers

DVD *Solutions with Step-by-Step Help on DVD*

✓ Solutions

1. 10 meters × 1.1 = 11 yards
2. 110 quarts × .95 = 104.5 liters
3. 78 kilometers × .62 = 48.36 miles
4. 52 yards × .91 = 47.32 meters
5. 82 meters × 39.37 = 3,228.34 inches
6. 292 miles × 1.6 = 467.20 kilometers

Name ______________________ Date ______________

Appendix E: Problems

DRILL PROBLEMS

Convert:

1. 65 centimeters to meters
2. 7.85 meters to centimeters
3. 44 centiliters to liters
4. 1,500 grams to kilograms
5. 842 millimeters to meters
6. 9.4 kilograms to grams
7. .854 kilograms to grams
8. 5.9 meters to millimeters
9. 8.91 kilograms to grams
10. 2.3 meters to millimeters

Convert (round off to nearest tenth):

11. 50.9 kilograms to pounds
12. 8.9 pounds to grams
13. 395 kilometers to miles
14. 33 yards to meters
15. 13.9 pounds to grams
16. 594 miles to kilometers
17. 4.9 feet to meters
18. 9.9 feet to meters
19. 100 yards to meters
20. 40.9 kilograms to pounds
21. 895 miles to kilometers
22. 1,000 grams to pounds
23. 79.1 meters to yards
24. 12 liters to quarts
25. 2.92 meters to feet
26. 5 liters to gallons
27. 8.7 meters to feet
28. 8 gallons to liters
29. 1,600 grams to pounds
30. 310 meters to yards

WORD PROBLEM

31. **Given:** A metric ton is 39.4 bushels of corn. Calculate number of bushels purchased from metric tons to bushels of corn.
Problem: The Russians bought 450,000 metric tons of U.S. corn, valued at $58 million, for delivery after September 30.

Index

Student DVD-ROM

This student DVD-ROM contains the following assets designed to help you succeed in the business math course:

- **Videos** bring the author to you, where Jeff Slater carefully walks you through a review of each of the Learning Unit Practice Quizzes, with brief real applications to introduce each chapter segment.
- **Video Cases** applying business math concepts to real companies tied to information and assignments in the text.
- **Excel Spreadsheet Templates** to assist in solving end-of-chapter exercises that are indicated by an Excel logo.
- **PowerPoint** lecture slides walk you through the chapter concepts.
- **Practice Quizzes** covering key concepts in each chapter and giving you quick feedback on your responses.
- **Internet Resource Guide** providing information on using the Internet and useful Web sites for use with each chapter.
- **Web Link** to the Practical Business Math Procedures text Web site, which contains additional material to help you.